RGINIA

MASSAWOMECKS

QVI

SCHONI SOYT ALY PENSE

CKS

lyough R

Potomac R

(Washington)

MOR

T A N

Bolus (Patapsco) R

(Annapolis)
1709

(Baltimore)
1723

Kent P.t
1611

Barnes
Pt.

B A L

SASQUESÁ-

Sasquesahanough R

HANOUGH

Smyth's Falls

(Havre de Grace)
Gunter's H'b.

TOCK

WOUGHS

Peregrin's Mt.

Vincere Siquere

ques

D1199112

This map is a simplification of
the Smith map of 1612 and later
editions. Modern names are in
(parentheses).

5   10   15

ques

overed by Cpt. J. Smith

30°   41°   Raisz

THE COLONIAL EXPERIENCE

THE

Books by David Hawke

IN THE MIDST OF A REVOLUTION *(1961)*

AMERICAN COLLOQUY *(edited, with Leonard Lief, 1963)*

A TRANSACTION OF FREE MEN *(1964)*

THE COLONIAL EXPERIENCE *(1966)*

U.S. COLONIAL HISTORY: READINGS AND DOCUMENTS *(1966)*

David Hawke

COLONIAL

EXPERIENCE

The Bobbs-Merrill Company, Inc.

INDIANAPOLIS

The Bobbs-Merrill Company, Inc.
4300 W. 62nd Street
Indianapolis, Indiana 46268

First Edition
Tenth Printing—1976
Designed by Stefan Salter Associates
Library of Congress Catalogue Card Number: 66–14829
ISBN 0-672-60688-7

ACKNOWLEDGMENTS

Maps (All maps were drawn especially for this book by Erwin Raisz, except 1, 2, 9, 14, and 21.)

Pages 10–11. The Vinland Map, from *The Vinland Map and the Tartar Relation,* by R. A. Skelton, Thomas E. Marston, and George D. Painter (New Haven and London: Yale University Press). Copyright © 1965 by Yale University.

Page 15. The Behaim Globe, from E. Raisz, *Principles of Cartography* (New York: McGraw-Hill, 1962).

Page 76. Emigration from England to America, 1620–1642, from E. Raisz, *Principles of Cartography* (New York: McGraw-Hill, 1962).

Page 159. A Map of New England, by John Foster, from *Narrative of Troubles with the Indians,* by William Hubbard, courtesy of The New York Public Library, Rare Book Division.

Page 224. Land Patterns of Colonial New York, from David Ellis, *et al., A Short History of New York State* (Ithaca: Cornell University Press, 1957). © 1957 by Cornell University. Used by permission of Cornell University Press.

Illustrations

Opposite page 1. Queen Elizabeth I, courtesy of His Grace the Duke of Bedford, Woburn Abbey, England.

Page 42. Reformation Leaders, courtesy of The Bettmann Archive.

Page 84. John Smith, courtesy of The New York Public Library, Rare Book Division.

Page 122. Richard Mather, courtesy of The Massachusetts Historical Society.

Page 166. John Winthrop, courtesy of the Massachusetts Art Commission, photograph by Gilbert Friedberg; Charles II, courtesy of The National Portrait Gallery, London, England.

Page 206. William Penn, courtesy of The Historical Society of Pennsylvania.

Page 242. Title page from *Strange News from Virginia,* courtesy of The New York Public Library, Rare Book Division.

Page 276. The Mason Children, courtesy of Nathaniel Hamlen, photograph by Gilbert Friedberg.

Page 314. William III and Mary II, courtesy of The National Portrait Gallery, London, England.

Page 360. "The Trustees of Georgia," courtesy of The Henry Francis du Pont Winterthur Museum.

Page 416. "Watson and the Shark," courtesy of The Museum of Fine Arts, Boston. (Gift of Mrs. George Von Lengerke Meyer.)

Page 468. "The Plantation," courtesy of The Metropolitan Museum of Art, New York. (Gift of Edgar William and Bernice Chrysler Garbisch, 1963.)

Page 516. George III, courtesy of The National Portrait Gallery, London, England.

Page 556. "Congress Voting Independence," courtesy of The Historical Society of Pennsylvania.

Page 598. "Surrender of Lord Cornwallis at Yorktown," courtesy of The Yale University Art Gallery.

Page 642. "Map of Philadelphia, etc.," courtesy of The John Carter Brown Library, Brown University.

Illustrations

Frontispiece: *Queen Elizabeth*. Discourtesy of His Grace the Duke of Bedford, Woburn Abbey, England.

TO LEONARD AND RUTH ANN LIEF

Author's Note

Because an effort has been made to interest the layman and the student in the American colonial experience, it has seemed wise to remove an obstacle—the archaic orthography especially of the seventeenth and to a limited degree of the eighteenth centuries. The language of the past whenever quoted has been respected; no modern words have been substituted. But spelling, capitalization, and punctuation have been brought up to date.

The bibliographies, which appear at the end of each chapter, will help to remind the reader that *The Colonial Experience* has been shaped mainly to serve as a beginning, not an end, and to arouse him to dig deeper into the colonial story, in the hope that he may emerge from his burrowings with generalizations of his own, perhaps even to contradict those offered in this volume.

Here, before the reader sweeps into the colonial story, let me give thanks to several who had a hand in this volume. I must thank first Pace College, which in ways large and small did much to make this work possible. I wish also to thank Alexander Baltzly, who gave encouragement in a dark moment; the publisher, who chose the book's cartographer and its designer and went on to do all he could to make it distinctive in both content and appearance; to Freeman Keith, whose assiduous reading of galleys and page proofs, at a time when he was hard pressed by other duties, purged out a great many errors; I want finally to give special thanks to Robert Friedberg, who, more than anyone I have worked with in publishing, taught me what a distinguished editor can contribute to the making of a book.

November 1965   David Hawke

Contents

1. The Age of Discovery   I

     AN OLD WORLD BECOMES NEW   I
     The Medieval World, Widening Horizons, The New Era

     A NEW WORLD IS FOUND   7
     Portugal, Columbus, "Terra Incognita" Becomes America

     STAKING-OUT THE CLAIMS   20
     The Spanish Heritage; The Intruders; Gilbert, Raleigh,
     and the Hakluyts

2. Background for Settlement   43

     THE REFORMATION   43
     Luther, Anabaptism, Calvinism, The Church of England,
     Puritanism

     ENGLAND ON THE EVE OF COLONIZATION   56
     The People, The Government, The Economy

     A GREAT MIGRATION BEGINS   68
     Who Came and Why, How They Came and Where They
     Went, What They Found

3. The Chesapeake Colonies   85

     FIRST STONES   85
     The Charter of 1606, Sagadahoc, Jamestown

     VIRGINIA   94
     Life Without Liberty, Under New Management, Virginia
     on Its Own: 1623–1640

     MARYLAND   107
     Gentlemen Adventurers, The Charter of 1632, The Early
     Years

     CHESAPEAKE SOCIETY   114
     The Great Bay of Chesapeake, The Farm, Government
     and Religion

4. The New England Way   123

     BEGINNINGS   123
     The Pilgrims, The Puritan Charter of 1629, "A City upon
     a Hill"

MASSACHUSETTS BAY 134
The Church, The State, Archbishop Laud

HIVINGS-OUT 142
Roger Williams, Anne Hutchinson, Plantations of the Otherwise Minded, Connecticut and New Haven

NEW ENGLAND SOCIETY 151
The Town, Economic Life, Indians and the Pequot War, The Puritan Heritage

5. Puritans and Cavaliers: 1640–1676 167

NEW ENGLAND 168
The Confederation of New England; A Mercantile Economy; Politics, Government, and Religion

THE CHESAPEAKE COLONIES 179
Trade, Religion, Indians, Politics

A NEW IMPERIALISM: 1650–1676 186
The Commonwealth, The Restoration

THE RESTORATION IN THE COLONIES: 1660–1676 195
New England, The Chesapeake Colonies

6. The Proprietaries 207

CAROLINA 208
The Charter of 1663, First Failures, The Fundamental Constitutions of 1669, Success

NEW YORK 216
New Netherland, The Dutch Heritage, English Rule: 1664–1689

NEW JERSEY 225
East Jersey, West Jersey

PENNSYLVANIA 229
William Penn, The Charter of 1681, Plans for Settlement, Settlement

7. Wars and Insurrections: 1675–1690 243

THE FIRST ROUND OF OUTBURSTS 243
Bacon's Rebellion, Maryland and Carolina, King Philip's War

THE DOMINION OF NEW ENGLAND 255
Edward Randolph, The Crown Takes Over, Sir Edmund Andros

THE GLORIOUS REVOLUTION IN AMERICA 265
New England, The Middle Colonies, The South

8. America at the End of the Seventeenth Century 277

THE WAY THEY LIVED 278
Enemies, Town and Country, The Arts

SOCIETY 288
Labor, The Elite, Education

THE WAY THEY THOUGHT 298
Science, Religion, Language and Literature

9. The Empire Takes Shape: 1689–1713 315

IMPERIAL WARS 315
The French Menace, King William's War, Period of Unrest, Queen Anne's War

THE DEVELOPMENT OF IMPERIAL CONTROL 333
The Crown and the Colonies, The Board of Trade, Imperial Machinery

GOVERNMENT IN THE COLONIES 343
The Governor and Council, The Assembly, The Judiciary

10. A Half Century of Expansion: 1713–1763 361

NEW BLOOD AND A NEW COLONY 362
Who Came and Where They Went, What They Found, Failure in Georgia

THE FRENCH EXPELLED 376
War Resumed, The French and Indian War, The Effect of the War on America

IMPERIAL RELATIONS: 1713–1763 398
Parliament and Colonies, Crown and Colonies, Ominous Straws in the Wind: 1759–1763

11. The American Mind in the Eighteenth Century 417

THE GREAT AWAKENING 418
First Waves, Floodtide, Aftermath

THE AMERICAN ENLIGHTENMENT 430
Natural Philosophy, Enlightened Americans, Town and Country

DAWN OF A NEW ERA 442
Education, Science, Language and Literature, The Arts

12. Life in Eighteenth-Century America 469

THE NORTH 470
New England, The Hudson Valley, The Delaware Valley

THE SOUTH 486
Chesapeake Country, Carolina Country

THE BACKCOUNTRY 496
Settlement, Customs and Manners, Relations with the East

13. Imperial Reorganization: 1763–1770   517

   THE NEW WEST   519
   The Proclamation of 1763, The Indian Uprising of 1763,
   The Aftermath

   THE GRENVILLE-ROCKINGHAM MINISTRY: 1763–1766   531
   The Revenue Act of 1764, The Stamp Act, The Repeal

   THE ROAD TO AN UNEASY TRUCE: 1766–1770   542
   The Townshend Acts, Reception in America, A Compro-
   mise Accepted

14. The Road to Independence: 1770–1776   557

   IRRITATIONS MOUNT: 1770–1774   558
   Committees of Correspondence, Trouble over Tea, The
   Intolerable Acts

   REBELLION: 1774–1775   568
   The First Congress, Lexington and Concord, Problems of
   Defense

   INDEPENDENCE: 1775–1776   582
   A House Divided, Congress Acts, The Declaration

15. War and Peace: 1776–1783   599

   TRYING TIMES: 1775–1777   600
   Boston and Canada, Long Island to New Jersey, The
   Home Front

   THE TURNING POINT: 1777–1778   612
   Saratoga and Philadelphia, The Diplomatic Front, From
   Valley Forge to a Deadlock

   VICTORY: 1778–1783   626
   The South's Time of Troubles, The Path to Yorktown,
   Peace

16. An Age of Experiments: 1775–1788   643

   PROBLEMS OF REVOLUTION   644
   "Governments of Our Own," The Articles of Confeder-
   ation, Was It a Real Revolution?

   PROBLEMS OF PEACE   656
   The West, The Economy, Political Power

   THE CONSTITUTION   668
   The Convention, Ratification, A New Beginning?

Appendix: Chief Magistrates of the Colonies and States   686

Index   699

Maps

1. The Vinland Map, from *The Vinland Map and the*
   Tartar Relation   10–11
2. The Behaim Globe   15
3. The Discovery   19
4. Spanish Exploration in the Sixteenth Century   22
5. Exploration of the Atlantic Seabord Before 1600   28–29
6. Passage to the Orient   32
7. Religions in Europe About 1560   48
8. Land the Settlers Found, Early Seventeenth Century   74–75
9. Emigration from England to America, 1620–1642   76
10. Land Grants of 1606, 1609, 1620   90
11. Simplification of the Smith Map of 1612   98
12. The Plymouth Plantation, 1620–1650   128
13. Massachusetts Bay Colony   139
14. A Map of New England, by John Foster, from
    Narrative of the Troubles with the Indians   159
15. Settlement by 1660   172–173
16. English Colonial Trade, Seventeenth Century   175
17. Middle America   188
18. Early Grants, 1600–1663   196
19. Proprietary Grants   210
20. Dutch Settlements on the Lower Hudson River, 1624–1664   218
21. Land Patterns of Colonial New York, from
    A Short History of New York State   224
22. King Philip's War, 1675–1676   252
23. English Colonies and Their Enemies,
    Late Seventeenth Century   280–281
24. French Exploration Before 1740   318
25. King William's War, 1680–1697   322–323
26. Queen Anne's War, 1702–1713   330–331
27. Settlement in Early Eighteenth Century   366–367
28. King George's War, 1743–1748   380–381
29. Braddock's Defeat, July 9, 1755   389
30. French and Indian War, 1755–1760   392–393
31. The Montreal-Albany Corridor   395
32. Southeastern Pennsylvania in the Eighteenth Century   483

33. The Great Wagon Road   498
34. Claims of European Powers in North America   520–521
35. Proclamation Line of 1763   524
36. Indian Uprising of 1763   527
37. The Quebec Act of 1774   567
38. "The Shot Heard Round the World"   575
39. The New York–Philadelphia Campaign, 1776–1778   604
40. The Revolutionary War, 1775–1781   614–615
41. Cessions of Western Lands   652
42. The Seven Ranges of Townships Northwest of the Ohio River,
        1785, and the Division of Townships into Sections   658
43. Settlement, 1790   676–677

Illustrations

Elizabeth I, "The Armada Portrait," attributed to
  Marcus Gheeraerts, the Younger   *Opposite Page* 1
Reformation Leaders, from "Epitaph des Bürgermeisters
  Myenburg" ("Burgomaster Myenburg's Funeral Oration"),
  by Lucas Cranach, the Younger   42
John Smith, from *The General History of Virginia*   84
Richard Mather, from a wood engraving by John Foster   122
John Winthrop and Charles II   166
William Penn, by Francis Place   206
Title page from *Strange News from Virginia*   242
The Mason Children, "Young Puritans"   276
William III and Mary II   314
"The Trustees of Georgia," by William Verelst   360
"Watson and the Shark," by John Singleton Copley   416
"The Plantation"   468
George III, from the Studio of Sir William Beechey   516
"Congress Voting Independence," by Robert Pine and
  Edward Savage   556
"Surrender of Lord Cornwallis at Yorktown," by John Trumbull   598
"Map of Philadelphia and Parts Adjacent, with a Perspective
  View of the State House," drawn by N. Scull and G. Heap   642

THE COLONIAL EXPERIENCE

Elizabeth I, "The Armada Portrait," attributed to
Marcus Gheeraerts, the Younger

1. The Age of Discovery

AN OLD WORLD BECOMES NEW
    The Medieval World
    Widening Horizons
    The New Era

A NEW WORLD IS FOUND
    Portugal
    Columbus
    "Terra Incognita" Becomes America

STAKING-OUT THE CLAIMS
    The Spanish Heritage
    Intruders
    Gilbert, Raleigh, and the Hakluyts

AN OLD WORLD BECOMES NEW

The age that discovered America discovered more than sailors saw from ships or explorers from a forest trail. About the time that Columbus glimpsed a new world through the shore mists of the western Atlantic, another equally new world had begun to take shape in the minds of Europeans. By 1492, qualities that had long characterized the life of Europe had eroded, and in their place had come new ones that led to a shift of "values in the consciousness of men," a shift that helped impel Columbus across the sea and that eventually would shape a wilderness of strange beasts and redskinned men into a new nation, or, as some would have it, into a new civilization. The shift in values did not extinguish the past. Much of the medieval world successfully traveled the ocean, and some of it survived the trip well enough to become an intrinsic part of the United States of America.

The Medieval World

Outwardly, life in Europe in 1300 had changed little in more than a thousand years, and to the medieval mind that was as it should be. The universe, for medieval man, was regulated from top to bottom and organized in a firm hierarchical order, a "great chain of being," that ran from the smallest stone up through man to the angels and God. All things had their place, and any man who promoted change, who sought to disturb the order, risked the wrath of God. All institutions of the age—feudalism, the manorial system, the towns, and the church—were designed to maintain the stability that characterized the medieval world.

This stability owed much to feudalism, which has been defined as "a means of carrying on some kind of government on a local basis where no organized state existed." There was more to it than that. The web of vows, contracts, and customs that comprised feudalism wove man into society. No man could be an island isolated from his neighbors. Each, even a king or a pope, played a fixed but complicated role that carried with it a multitude of obligations. Any man who tried to alter his role was, for the good of the community, forced back into line. A vassal remiss in his duties was subdued by the king; a king who trampled on the rights of his vassal risked, and often met, rebellion. The individual free to do as he wished, unfettered by responsibilities, did not exist in feudal society.

The feudal system ordered the lives mainly of the upper classes, while the manorial system imposed stability on the lives of the peasants and on the agrarian economy. Mutual obligations similar to those that permeated feudalism carried into the manorial system. The lord exacted from the peasant certain duties and a specific amount of work on the manor lands. The lord could not deprive the peasant of the strips of land he tilled nor change the tenure under which those strips were held without what might today be called due process of law. The lord owed his peasants protection of life and property; they owed him service and allegiance. Neither was free of duties.

The towns lay outside the feudal and manorial systems, for their needs differed from those of the agrarian community; yet they did not disrupt the medieval world. The guilds, which dominated town life, preserved all the qualities of that world. A graduated apprentice system held craftsmen in a hierarchical order. Guilds controlled the quality and quantity of a town's products. They protected the public from shoddy merchandise; the public accepted guild merchandise at the "fair price" offered. No one competed against a guild product or price, for competition threatened the stability of a town's life. Unrestrained freedom flourished no more within the towns than on the manor.

The church, the fourth institution that steadied the medieval world, thrived nicely with the others; indeed, with at least a third of the land of Germany and France owned by the church and with many of its bishops powerful feudal lords, it was inextricably entwined with them. The doctrines of the church fitted perfectly with the medieval situation. The church's refusal to judge poverty as a sign of evil or weakness in men went well with an agricultural civilization that lived close to a subsistence level. Its definition of a "fair price" as one that let a man "have the necessaries of life suitable for his station" helped keep order in society without discriminating against the lower classes. It condemned usury because most medieval men borrowed only when famine, flood, fire, or some other disaster struck; the church made it a sin to inflict interest rates on men in trouble. The Christian concept of man's responsibility to man squared with concepts implicit in feudalism and helped to inhibit the acquisitive instinct of townsmen. The church's hierarchical organization reflected the facts of medieval existence.

Stability characterized one half of medieval life, unity the other half. Feudal and manorial practices, for all their basic similarities, differed in detail from area to area, and towns, too, varied considerably, but the church unified all into a Christian commonwealth. When a pope called for a crusade, he drew from all Europe men who reacted first as Christians and only later as Normans, Germans, or Englishmen. The church was the moral force that welded medieval Europe into a single block. The church dominated the age and conditioned all men's values and habits. All life, Johan Huizinga has remarked, was so saturated with religion that people were "in constant danger of losing sight of the distinction between things spiritual and things temporal." When distinction emerged, the medieval world had begun to fade, taking with it the stability and unity that had characterized it.

That world might fade; it would never vanish. The medieval belief that privileges carry with them responsibilities would become an integral part of colonial American thought. The medieval world restrained the individual, but it also protected him from unrestrained abuse. When the Middle Ages transformed customs into rights, according to one historian, the foundations were laid for eighteenth-century political theory. Howard Mumford Jones finds the medieval insistence on "the primary values of life" as theological of great influence on American development. Clearly, whatever the heritage, the medieval world cannot lightly be divorced from the story of American settlement.

Widening Horizons

"The settlement of America," Lewis Mumford has said, "had its origins in the unsettlement of Europe." That unsettlement began long before the medieval world crumbled. Its seed sprang from medieval soil, in large part from the empirical side of the medieval temper. The Middle Ages either invented or adapted to its use the mechanical clock, gunpowder, the compass, the horse collar, the horseshoe, an improved plow, the three-field system, and the water mill. All helped to widen the horizon of medieval man beyond the rim of his manor. "The efficient harnessing and shoeing of horses, for example, was significant not only for agriculture," says William Carroll Bark, "but also for locomotion, hence for communications and transport, hence for construction of all kinds, for conveying food and other produce to towns, for the growth of population, eventually for the expansion of commerce."

Inventions aided commerce, and commerce, in turn, further broadened the horizons of medieval man. Luxuries from the East—dyes, rich cloths, precious stones, spices like pepper for flavoring gamy food and "notmege" for ale—began to flow into Europe before the First Crusade in 1099. A wall of ignorance obscured the origin of these goods. Europe only knew that after months en route and after passing through many hands, each of which pushed the price up a bit further, such goods arrived in Cairo, Antioch, Acre, or Constantinople, and that from these "leaks" in the wall they trickled into Europe.

For a time it seemed this stream would dry up. By the mid-thirteenth century, the Mongols—or Tartars, as Europe called them, after "Tartarus," the hell of Greek mythology—were "erupting as it were from the confines of Hell" and had pushed westward to the Danube. Their advance ended there, and Europe relaxed. Emissaries were sent out to learn more about these wild men from the East and also to trace down Prester (Priest) John, a Christian priest-king who supposedly ruled somewhere in Asia. Once contact had been made with him, his kingdom could be used as a base from which to Christianize all Asia. (Columbus, among others, would be on the lookout for him.) Friar William of Rubruck traveled eastward in 1253. He did not find Prester John, but he got close enough to China to hear tales of incredible wealth. "Whoever wanteth gold," he reported, "diggeth till he hath found some quantity." About 1260 two Venetian jewel merchants, Maffeo and Nicolo Polo, sufficiently spurred by such tales to defy the "terrible trumpet of dire forewarning," ventured into Asia. Tribesmen passed them along until eventually the two reached China and the great Kublai, khan of all the Mongols.

The Grand Khan treated them well and urged them to return to him with "a hundred men learned in the Christian religion, well versed in the seven arts, and able to demonstrate the superiority of their own beliefs." In 1271, having arrived home and passed along the khan's request, the Polo brothers started eastward again with only two of the promised hundred missionaries (and those two soon dropped by the way) and also with Nicolo's son Marco, who was still in his teens. It took them four years to reach Cambuluc (Peking). They stayed there for seventeen years. The khan allowed young Polo to travel so widely throughout the empire that Marco would later claim, rightfully, that no man "has known or explored so many of the various parts of the world." The splendors of the cities, the abundance of riches overwhelmed him wherever he went. He saw that only a fraction of the gold and spices and precious stones trickled westward to Europe. Into the port of Zaiton alone came a hundred times the pepper exported to all Christendom. Eventually the Polos wearied of this magnificence and yearned for home. The khan reluctantly allowed them to depart, and in 1295, nearly a quarter of a century after they had begun their journey, they arrived back in Venice.

Presently, while in prison, following a fight between Genoa and Venice, Marco wrote—rather, dictated to a popular romance-writer of the day—an account of his years in the East. Scholars ever since have been impressed by the accuracy of his observations; he stumbled only when reporting what others had told him, as that Cipangu (Japan) lies "some fifteen hundred miles from the mainland." Polo's remarks about Cipangu were among those that excited contemporaries. Unlike earlier writers, he said that the eastern border of Asia was edged not by great marshes, as had once been thought, but by an ocean. That meant the East could be reached by seagoing ships. If ships managed the trip, they would be welcomed, Polo assured, not only by the Grand Khan but by Prester John, whom Polo never met but "knew" to be living in Asia. Europeans would find on arrival that all they paid dearly for came cheaply at the source. Eighty pounds of fresh ginger could be had for a Venetian groat; "an asper of silver" for only three pheasants.

All this and much more in *The Travels of Marco Polo*—or *Description of the World,* to use his title—fascinated Europe. England paid little attention to it, but everywhere else a variety of manuscript versions circulated and in 1477, when it was first printed, it became something of a best seller. Few books have so shaped and driven men's imagination. Polo's vivid descriptions drove along explorers in the employ of Portugal as they inched their way down the coast of Africa; they drove Columbus westward; after him, John Cabot; and then a host of others. Marco Polo "discovered China in the thirteenth century, when he was alive," Eileen Power has said, "and in the fifteenth century, when he was dead, he discovered America!"

Nearly two centuries slipped past before Europeans reached Cathay by sea. Europe in Polo's day lacked the ships, the maps, the navigational skills to travel the water route. It lacked the power, too, for such an expedition required more money and organization than Europe could yet focus on such a project. Nor was the mind of Europe prepared to make the trip. A shift in values had first to take place.

The New Era

The changes most obviously fatal to the medieval world occurred in religion. From the fourteenth century onward the church endured insults from all quarters. England and France began to tax its property. The French sacked the Vatican in 1303 and soon after forced the pope to live at Avignon under French influence. The humiliation of the so-called Babylonian captivity (1305–1378) was followed by the Great Schism (1378–1415), when two popes, one in France and another in Rome, competed for Europe's respect. The monastic orders of poverty, once so respected, came to be ridiculed, for as material wealth flowed through Europe, poverty ceased to be considered a virtue. John Wycliffe in England and later John Huss in Bohemia attacked the vast possessions of church and clergy and preached against the papacy. Huss was burned at the stake in 1415, but even in death both he and Wycliffe continued to prepare the ground for the Reformation of the sixteenth century, and the national states that began to take form toward the end of the Middle Ages challenged the church in secular affairs.

The rise of the political state did not in itself diminish the church's moral authority. The church continued to serve as arbiter of international quarrels; it still judged and imposed its judgment by excommunication or interdict on moral issues. All lost respect might have been recouped if a new adversary had not appeared: With the middle of the fifteenth century, a group came to the thrones of Europe—Henry VII in England, Louis XI in France, Ferdinand and Isabella in Spain—who flouted the church's moral authority and imposed law and order in their own names, without reference to the church, except as it suited their own ends. These "new monarchs" sought to be in the secular world what the pope was in the spiritual. They rejected the restraints of customary law of the medieval world and drew on Roman law, wherein the ruler, it has been said, incorporated the will and welfare of the people in his own person, and he could *make* law, enact it by his own authority, regardless of previous custom or authority. Men, strictly speaking, no longer had rights. The monarch was "sovereign"; he alone judged the right and wrong of his acts.

Flaws within itself produced the first cracks in the church's once formidable moral force. The new monarchs did even more to undermine that authority. And the new merchant, shunning medieval restraints, proved equally subversive. He operated outside the towns and the guilds. He purchased his raw material, say, wool, in the countryside at the lowest possible price, "put it out" to peasant weavers who worked in their homes at the wage he offered, then sold the finished product at the highest price obtainable. The techniques of this "entrepreneur" or "capitalist" shattered much that was left of the medieval framework. He believed in competition, worried little about the welfare of peasant or craftsman, and considered a fair price the lowest he could get for raw materials, the highest for finished goods. The state allied itself with the new merchant and drew on his power and wealth to increase its own strength. Landed lords, particularly in England, found ways to consolidate peasants' strips into enclosed fields suitable for pasturing sheep, and the peasant often became a wandering vagabond, picking up work where he could. The church that had once protected him could do little now, and the state, as in England, passed "poor laws" that made vagrancy a crime and unemployment a man's own fault.

By the middle of the fourteenth century, medieval conceptions had waned to the point where a new era was taking shape. Men still gave spiritual allegiance to the church, but in worldly affairs the amoral state, for which Machiavelli would write the rule book, claimed their loyalty. And worldly affairs now occupied much of men's thoughts. Life had become secularized in the sense that not all things nor all values were related to religion. Men did not cease to wonder and worry about the afterworld, but they did become more interested in living to the fullest in this world. This shift of "values in the consciousness of men," so long in arriving, at last put Europe in the mood to explore beyond that narrow strip of seas that had hemmed in the medieval mind as well as medieval man.

This shift of values destroyed the soul of the medieval world, yet much of the form lived on. Religion ceased to dominate but not to influence men's thoughts. The crusading spirit, for instance, still thrived. Backed now by the increasing power of the new states, the new mercantile spirit, and the intensified interest in practical matters, this spirit would launch Europe on an age of exploration. Prince Henry of Portugal and after him Columbus blended the old and new spirit perfectly. "In the East many cities were lost through idolatry and belief in hellish sects," Columbus told Ferdinand and Isabella. Therefore, it was "determined to send me, Christopher Columbus, to the countries of India, so that I might see what they were like, the lands and the people, and might seek out and know the nature of everything that is there."

A NEW WORLD IS FOUND

Historical events seldom occur in the neat way historians would prefer. No sudden burst of exploration took place once the medieval world began to collapse and men's minds shifted to worldly concerns. Pilots had begun to push past Gibraltar into the gloomy unknown long before adequate ships and navigational tools were available, long before sailors had settled their fears of sea monsters that might lurk over the horizon, and long before any intense desire to reach the East by a cheap all-water route existed. Many of the tools that aided exploration developed out of the explorations themselves, and superstitious fears of the unknown lingered in sailors' heads long after America had been found. Nor did the Ottoman Turks' control of all Levantine ports by 1453 create a pressing urge for a new route to the East, for the Turks continued to permit trade to flow much as before.

Portugal

The voyages of discovery began from Portugal because that tiny nation, of all the nations then taking shape in Europe, was best prepared to launch them. Nationalism flourished stronger there than elsewhere in Europe, for a mountain chain hemmed in Portugal's million and a quarter population; and the people within that slim area spoke one language, a linguistic unity absent elsewhere in Europe. Portugal faced the Atlantic, a position that deprived her of the cream of Mediterranean trade; she possessed a long ocean seaboard, a large seafaring population, and, for the times, a strong commercial class. The medieval crusading spirit persisted still, particularly against the recently ejected Moslems. Above all, the tiny nation possessed the Infante Dom Henrique, or, as he has been nicknamed, Prince Henry the Navigator. In the face of abuse and ridicule, he forced Portugal to blaze the way to India.

Curiously, a water route to India intrigued Prince Henry little. He hoped by sailing down the coast of Africa to come upon Prester John and join with him to subdue the Moslems. He hoped, too, to turn up the source of Moslem gold and ivory trade. He was also simply curious to discover "things which were hidden from other men, and secret." He returned from a crusade against the Moslems in 1418 and retired to Sagres, the sacred promontory, on the rocky tip of southwest Portugal. Here he created an informal university of the sea, welcoming anyone—sailor, map maker, mathematician, instrument maker, or shipbuilder—who could help unravel the mystery of the unknown. Hitherto, discovery had been a haphazard affair. Prince Henry was the first, as Boies Penrose notes, to make "a systematic and continuous campaign of exploration," to convert it into an art and science tied to national interest.

Prince Henry sent out his first ships in 1420 and continued sending them out for the next forty years. His men rediscovered and conquered the Canary, Madeira, and Azore Islands, but thereafter progress was unbearably slow and to outsiders fruitless. All the while Prince Henry endured "what every barking tongue could allege against a service so unserviceable and needless," he and his men were learning much. For one thing, they revolutionized ship designs. As pilots returned from their trips with complaints about the broad-bottomed, single masted, square-rigged vessel they had been using, the shipwrights at Sagres produced a series of modifications that eventually resulted in the caravel, which would become the favorite of explorers throughout the fifteenth and sixteenth centuries. The caravel was borrowed with variations from the Moslem world. Its hull was long and narrow, and in an early version it carried two large lateen sails—that is, triangular sails with one edge laced to a long yard. A later version, the *caravela redonda*—the *Niña* and *Pinta* of Columbus' first voyage were of this type—carried a square sail on the foremast and lateen rigs on the main- and mizzenmasts and was so swift that few sailing ships since have bettered it for speed.

The experts at Sagres also did much to improve the tools of navigation and techniques of map making. By now the works of the Alexandrian geographer called Ptolemy had been recovered. Ptolemy systematized the mapping of the earth, laying down principles and methods—he oriented maps to the north, for instance—that map makers then and since have followed. Three concepts were involved in Ptolemaic cartography: the earth is round; distance on it can be measured in degrees; and, by taking "fixes" on known celestial bodies, a man can precisely determine his location north or south of the equator (latitude) and east or west of an arbitrary line (longitude). The experts at Sagres simplified the principles and techniques of Ptolemy so that they could be used by sailors. In place of the fairly precise but awkward astrolabe used by Ptolemy to make celestial observations, Henry's men were taught to use the simpler quadrant, which was more easily handled at sea. Later in the fifteenth century the cross-staff and still later the back-staff were designed to help sailors make more accurate observations from the deck of a bobbing vessel. Taking a celestial fix requires several mathematical calculations, and, here, to aid the sailor, an ephemerides, an early version of the modern nautical almanac with calculated tables of planet elevations and time differences, was devised independently by Johann Müller, a German, and by Abraham Zacuto, a Spanish Jew. Sailors still lacked a reliable instrument for measuring a ship's speed and thus the distance the vessel covered, and longitude would remain difficult to determine until an accurate chronometer became available in 1735. Even so, with the skills and tools available toward the end of the fifteenth century, it was possible for an intelligent sailor to determine his direction and to locate his latitude with some precision.

Map 1. The Vinland Map, the earliest map of the New World.

While ship designs and navigation techniques improved, sailors' old fears about the unknown persisted. They called the water below Cape Bojador the Sea of Darkness, and, said the chronicler Azurara, "although many set out—and they were men who had won fair renown by their exploits in the trade of arms—none dared go beyond this cape." Not until 1434, after fourteen years of prodding by Henry, was the cape rounded. It was Gil Eannes who took the risk and found the sea below like that above. After that, exploration moved along swiftly. Seven years later, a pilot brought back a load of slaves and gold dust from the coast of Guinea. "Gold," says the chronicler, "made a recantation of former murmurings, and now Prince Henry was extolled."

Success balked rather than helped Henry; eagerness for gold killed interest in exploration. A trading post, or "factory," was erected to expedite trade, and pilots refused to push past Guinea, preferring to return home laden with cargo rather than information. Henry continued to prod, and eventually his ships once again began to push deeper into the unknown. When he died in 1460, his pilots had sailed past the site of modern Dakar.

Exploration lagged for nearly a decade after Henry's death. When the notion arose that with the new ships and skills sailors might be able to reach India by water, Portugal's crown took up where Henry had left off. Under its urging, navigators soon rounded the great western bulge of Africa. By 1472 the end of the bulge had been reached, but sailors saw with dismay that there was more land, which trended south again. A pause ensued while Portugal and Spain warred over the throne of Castile. Portugal lost the war but gained a route to India. The Treaty of Alcaçovas (1479) gave her the right to all African lands discovered and to all known islands in the Atlantic except the Canaries. The treaty in time proved a boon to Columbus, for the closing of Africa put Spain in a favorable mood to any suggestion about a new water route to India.

In 1481, the able, unscrupulous John II came to the throne of Portugal determined to push ahead to India. The six-foot stone pillars he ordered erected to mark the farthest reach of each expedition soon stretched down the African coast. In 1487 Bartholomew Diaz left Lisbon, and soon after he had passed the pillar placed on shore the previous year by Diogo Cão a gale swept him out to sea. Fourteen days later, when the winds had subsided, he turned eastward, then, having failed to raise the coast, north. Land, when it came, rose in the west and trended to the northeast. Diaz knew he had reached the Indian Ocean. He pushed on four hundred miles more and would have continued to India, but the crew forced him back. On the return trip he saw the tip of Africa, the Tempestuous Cape, as he would have named it, the Cape of Good Hope as King John preferred to call it. But before Portugal could realize the hope of a half-century's work, a man from Genoa who had caught the spirit of exploration in Lisbon would insist that he had found a shorter route to the East.

Columbus

Columbus was born in Genoa around 1451 and named—appropriately, it turned out—for Saint Christopher, protector of all travelers. He went to sea early, traveling throughout the Mediterranean, but eventually venturing with masters who searched for trade in lands that fronted the Atlantic. A vessel on which he shipped in 1476 was wrecked in a sea battle off the coast of Portugal. After drifting ashore, Columbus journeyed to Lisbon, where he joined his brother in a chart-making office. A few months later, perhaps bored with a landlubber's life, he returned to sea on a ship that traveled between Lisbon, the Azores, and Ireland. Two years later, now twenty-seven, he captained a ship that ran between Madeira and Genoa. By his early thirties, he had married into one of the better families of Portugal and was a master mariner, who had learned all the practical navigation that could be picked up from experience. The prospect of a prosperous, dull middle age loomed ahead. That prospect vanished in the 1480's when Columbus became obsessed with the idea of reaching the East by sailing westward.

It matters little where Columbus got the idea; he could hardly have escaped from it. Perhaps on trips into the northern Atlantic he had picked up tales preserved in the Icelandic sagas of Leif Ericson's landfall to the west, where the Vikings had traded with natives they called skraellings (dwarfs). (Historians have argued not only the veracity of these sagas, but, assuming they are true, where the Vikings actually landed. The latest account has it that they made a landing some five hundred years before Columbus on the northern tip of Newfoundland Island, where archaeologists believe that they have recently uncovered Viking artifacts.) If the Icelandic sagas escaped notice, Columbus may have acquired the notion from listening to northern fishermen who often traveled far westward in search of better catches. (No evidence has ever been found that fishermen visited the New World before Columbus, but, as Bernard De Voto remarks, "many a historian has had to suppress the twitch of a nerve that comes from certain inexplicable data, of which the most galling one is this: that as early as there are accounts of visits to these shores there are also Indians offering to trade furs for manufactured goods.") Columbus' son Ferdinand cites several "natural reasons" why his father traveled westward with confidence. For one: "the world was round." Another: "the testimony of sailors" who, far out to sea, had picked up oddly carved pieces of wood and the corpses of men of a strange race (Eskimos most likely).

And still another: "the authority of writers," among them Marco Polo and Pierre d'Ailly.

Cardinal d'Ailly's *Imago Mundi,* an erudite geography of the world written about 1410, was among the books that Columbus studied with care. D'Ailly insisted with an authority backed by quotations from Greek, Latin, and Moslem sources that the ocean—there was only one then—was "of no great width," and he followed this thought with a sentence that Columbus underlined heavily: *"For it is evident that this sea is navigable in a very few days if the wind be fair."* This sentence especially appealed to Columbus because it contradicted the revered Ptolemy at a crucial point. Ptolemy's estimate of the stretch of ocean between eastern Asia and Spain was so huge that, if accurate, it obviated the possibility of a direct sea voyage westward. Ptolemy's immense authority long blocked acceptance of Columbus' plan to sail westward.

Columbus tried first to interest John II in his project. This was in the early 1480's when Portugal still found Africa's coast heading southward and it looked as though the immense block of land could not be rounded. King John found him "to be a big talker and boastful . . . and full of fancy and imagination with his Isle of Cipangu," but he gave Columbus a fair hearing, ultimately rejecting the plan because of the expense involved. Columbus turned to Spain in 1485. A wealthy merchant agreed to back him, but Queen Isabella refused to permit a private venture in which the crown might not benefit, and the crown at the moment was too busy strengthening its power and warring against the Moslems to undertake another project. She created a commission to study Columbus' plan. While the commission pondered, Columbus again approached John II, now more receptive after enduring a half year without word from Bartholomew Diaz. While the king and Columbus dickered, Diaz returned to say he had rounded Africa; that ended interest in Columbus' scheme. Next, Henry VII of England was approached, then Charles VIII of France. Both these "new monarchs," like their colleagues in Spain, were too busy with internal problems and too short of money to take on anything more.

In 1490 the queen's commission rejected Columbus' project on the ground that the "ocean" was too large for a nonstop trip to Asia. Columbus lingered in Spain on a hint of hope from the queen, who was fond of him, and toward the end of 1491 another commission recommended that his plan be accepted. Columbus had originally asked the crown only to underwrite his trip. He now upped his demands. The crown rejected them; he packed his bags and, in the best of melodramatic tradition, was on the road to France when Isabella was persuaded that to accept his demands would cost no more than a week's entertainment for a visiting dignitary. The contract soon signed authorized Columbus to "discover and

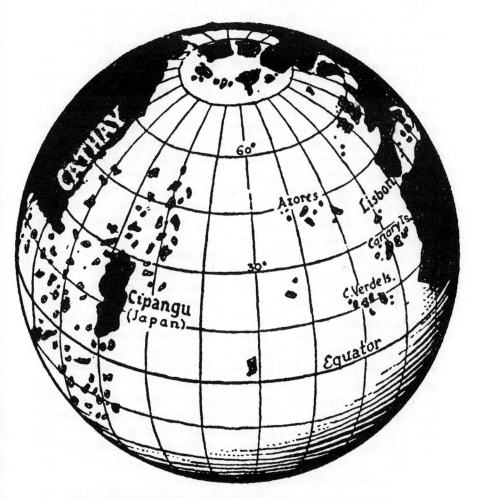

Map 2. The Behaim Globe of 1492 came close to the ideas of Columbus.

acquire certain islands and mainland in the ocean"; to take for himself a tenth of all precious metals found (one of his demands); and to be "Admiral of the said islands and mainland, and Admiral and Viceroy and Governor therein" (another of them).

Three months later, on August 3, 1492, the tiny *Niña, Pinta,* and *Santa Maria,* with a total crew of about ninety, set out. The first leg of the trip, something of a shakedown cruise, ended at the Canary Islands less than a week later. The ships were restocked with supplies, minor repairs were made, and the rigging of one of the vessels was altered to make full use of the westward-blowing trade winds. From the Canaries the group headed dead west, and during the first ten days steady winds swept them a thousand miles into the unknown. But the winds soon died, and the days at sea dragged into weeks. Mutterings arose among the crew. The strange swings of the compass terrified the men, for this "variation" still remained a puzzling phenomenon. They wondered whether the trade winds that carried them westward would permit their return. As they pushed through the Sargasso Sea—a thick mat of seaweed-like algae that covers parts of the Atlantic—they felt certain that the ships were edging into the impenetrable swamp of legend.

The fourth week found even Columbus uneasy. No ship had ever before traveled out of sight of land longer than three weeks. The expedition had gone more than two thousand four hundred miles—it had passed north of Puerto Rico without knowing it—and should have hit Cipangu (Japan) long ago. On the thirty-first day out of sight of land mutiny flared up. Columbus "cheered them as best he could, holding out good hope of the advantages they might gain." He also made clear "it was useless to complain, since he had come to go to the Indies, and so had to continue until he found them, with our Lord's help."

On October 11, seventy days out from Spain, a lookout on the *Pinta* shouted *"Tierra! Tierra!"* and the following morning everyone traveled ashore to a tiny island in the Bahamas, and there on the beach they "rendered thanks to Our Lord, kneeling on the ground, embracing it with tears of joy for the immeasurable mercy of having reached it." Columbus named the island San Salvador (Holy Saviour).

Columbus cruised through the islands of the West Indies for two and a half months searching for gold and spices and great cities. He discovered Haiti, which he named Hispaniola (Spanish Isle), and Cuba, which he took to be the mainland of Asia; and he came upon enough gold to preserve the delusion that he had arrived in the East. At Hispaniola he lost the *Santa Maria.* The ship's crew of thirty-nine was left behind to explore further, and Columbus headed for home. He had seen the first Indian corn (maize), the first hammocks woven from native cloth, the first yams (sweet potatoes). He had seen natives carrying firebrands they called "tobacos" and from which they "drink the smoke thereof." Gold and spices in quantity, great cities, and the Grand Khan had all eluded him, but he gathered up cinnamon and coconuts, which had been mentioned by Marco Polo, kidnapped several natives, and headed for Spain, certain he had reached the Indies.

"Terra Incognita" Becomes America

Columbus while sailing homeward wrote a report to Ferdinand and Isabella in the form of a letter, and the printing press, one of the inventions of the new era, swiftly spread it over the Continent. The explorer turned propagandist took care to relate in his letter only what he wished known. He made the lands discovered seem like Polo's Cathay and Cipangu. The Indians were generous, innocent humans "of a very keen intelligence"; the land was "fat for planting and sowing, and for livestock of every sort, and for building towns and cities"; the harbors were "such as you could not believe in without seeing them"; and most of the many and great rivers held gold. The land offered more than gold—spices and cotton, aloe woods, slaves "as many as they shall order," rhubarb and cinnamon, and "a thousand other things of value, which the people whom I have left there will have discovered."

All Europe except John II assumed India had been reached. King John believed that Columbus' account failed to jibe with those of other travelers and that he had turned up only a few worthless islands in mid-ocean. Still, he did not like the idea of Spanish ships wandering about the Atlantic, hitherto a Portuguese preserve. He claimed the islands for Portugal under the provisions of the Treaty of Alcaçovas, arguing that they lay close enough to the Azores to be considered part of that group. Spain turned to the pope (Alexander VI), who happened to be a Spaniard, to settle the dispute. The pope issued a series of bulls, which were in effect charters similar to those the kings of England and France would later give their own explorers and colonizers. The first papal bull confirmed the discoveries as Spanish possessions; the second, of June 1493, established a north-south line one hundred leagues (a league roughly equals three miles) west of the Azores, with the area beyond that line to be a Spanish sphere of exploration. John II accepted the bull in principle: it obviated a war over a few islands, and it preserved the Portuguese sphere of operations. He asked only that the line be placed halfway between the Azores and the newly discovered islands, or some 370 leagues west of the Azores. Spain saw no reason to object, not knowing that South America, yet to be discovered, bulged out to the east and that Brazil, as it would be called, lay to the east of this new line and would thus belong to Portugal.

The Treaty of Tordesillas, incorporating this change, was signed in 1494.

Columbus had in the same year departed at the head of a fleet of seventeen ships carrying twelve hundred settlers. This time he discovered and named the Lesser Antilles (apparently a pluralization of "Antilla," the name of a mythical island long assumed to exist in the Atlantic), striking first at Dominica, then Guadeloupe, and soon after St. Croix, largest of the Virgin Islands and the first future United States territory he touched. From the Virgin Islands he moved on to what one of his crew, Ponce de León, would later name Puerto Rico; he discovered Jamaica on his way to reinspect Cuba, which still seemed to him the mainland of Asia. When he arrived at Hispaniola, he learned that Indians had murdered all the men he had left behind. Columbus landed the settlers, founded the town of Isabela, and returned to Spain in 1496, leaving his brothers Bartholomew and Diego behind. Back in Spain he found that the early enthusiasm over his discovery had waned. But Spain had committed too many men and too much money to abandon further effort, especially when it learned Portugal was about to fit out an expedition led by Vasco da Gama and that Henry VII of England had given John Cabot permission to sail westward to "the island of Cipangu." Moreover, the notion had occurred to some that Columbus had stumbled upon a new continent. Europe was balanced by Africa to the south; surely Asia had its own antipode, the fourth part of the world. If so, Spain must stake out a claim to it.

Columbus departed on his third voyage (1498–1500) with a fleet of six vessels and about 350 passengers. Soon after raising Trinidad, Columbus noticed a deluge of fresh water mingling with the ocean. He reasoned that such an outpouring could only come from an enormous river that drained a huge body of land. "I believe," he said, "that this is a very great continent, until hitherto unknown," meaning that he had come upon the antipode of Asia. Columbus headed for Hispaniola with the news only to find that his brothers had abandoned Isabela for higher, healthier ground (now Santo Domingo, capital of the Dominican Republic) and dissension raged among the settlers. An investigator sent out from Spain arrived and tried to solve all troubles by shipping Columbus and his brothers home in chains.

The crown dallied six weeks after Columbus' return before ordering the chains removed, then followed the first affront with another. It left him the titles of Viceroy and Admiral but denied the promised percentage of wealth that had now begun to trickle in, and it began to grant lands that according to the original agreement were his alone to grant. Worse news greeted him. Da Gama had returned in 1499 having found "large cities and great populations." And in the months Columbus had been cruising off South America, Alvarez Cabral, sailing for Portugal, had been

Map 3. The Discovery

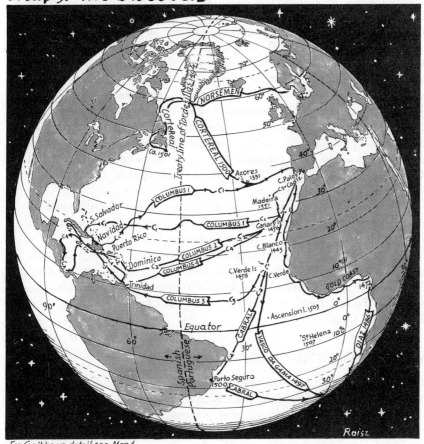

For Caribbean detail see Map 4

"blown off his track" by a great storm and in the process discovered Brazil, which Portugal promptly claimed.

By now Spain had received a variety of reports from others—among them Amerigo Vespucci—coasting along the edge of the world Columbus had revealed that made it clear this was a New World and also a world of wealth. Spain decided to commit itself fully in 1502. Nicholas de Ovando sailed with thirty-two ships and twenty-five hundred settlers, and with his departure the Spanish Empire began to take shape. Columbus at the same time received permission to make another and, as it turned out, final voyage (1502–1504). He searched almost frantically for the passage to India. He came upon natives wearing "delicately wrought" jewelry who told of finding gold "among the roots of trees, along the banks and amongst the rock and stones left by torrents"; he spent a full year marooned on Jamaica; and he returned to Spain to find no one interested in him or his tales. He remained to the end convinced he had reached Asia, and the more people doubted him the more arrogant he became. Ferdinand offered a reasonable compromise to the claim against the crown, but Columbus, as always, refused to compromise. He died in 1506, penniless. Few turned out for his funeral.

Even death did not end his humiliation. Amerigo Vespucci had remarked after his trip along the coast of South America that this "may be called a New World, since our ancestors had no knowledge of it." Martin Waldseemüller said in his *Introduction to Cosmography* (1507) this was the "fourth part of the world," and he labeled it "America" on his map. He removed the label from the map in a 1513 edition of the book, substituting "Terra Incognita" (unknown land), but by then the name was fixed for all time.

STAKING-OUT THE CLAIMS

Spain came first and had the New World to herself for nearly a century. She faced an unprecedented situation. Rich lands far from home were hers to exploit if they could be organized to prevent rebellion from within and intrusion from without. She solved the problem so swiftly and effectively that the large native population within her empire remained docile and outsiders were held at bay for centuries. Sea dogs snapped at her heels, occasionally catching a treasure ship or two but rarely inflicting serious wounds. France, rebuffed in Florida, retreated to Canada, and England dared venture no closer to Spanish settlements than Virginia. Still, both intruders edged close enough to learn much that in time would shape the development of their own New World colonies.

The Spanish Heritage

A lull in exploration came with Columbus' final voyage in 1504. It lasted until 1509, when young Spanish adventurers, as if refreshed, spurted out from Hispaniola in several directions. One group strengthened Spanish control in the Antilles. Ponce de León conquered the eastern part of Haiti and moved on to Puerto Rico. In 1513 he explored the Bahamas and then the shore of the land he came upon in the Easter season, *pascua florida,* and called Florida. Others, meanwhile, charted much of eastern South America's coast in an attempt to find a way through or around the great barrier. A third group focused on Central America. In late 1513 Vasco Núñez de Balboa set out over the Isthmus of Panama. He found, fought, and defeated Indians who blocked his way. He came upon cities rich in gold and from a mountain pass saw an ocean he called the South Sea because it supposedly lay south of Asia. Cortez burned his ships behind him in 1519, and two years later Mexico City and the riches of the Aztecs fell to him. A decade later Francisco Pizarro found the land of the Incas in Peru even richer.

Conquests were consolidated in the south, while explorations continued in the north. After Spain heard in 1522 that the Portuguese, Ferdinand Magellan, had rounded South America without finding a short cut to Asia, search for a passage through the land block centered in the north. In 1524–1525 Estevan Gómez surveyed the coast from the Grand Banks to Florida, hunting for a passage "leading to the Kingdom of him whom we commonly call the Grand Khan." He found no passage, and his report of the climate produced no enthusiasm for settlement. "It is toward the south, not toward the frozen north," wrote Peter Martyr, chronicler of the Spanish story, "that those who seek fortune should bend their way; for everything at the equator is rich." (By "rich" he meant more than abundant. The sixteenth century believed the sun's heat determined the amount of gold in the earth; the closer one came to the equator, the hotter the sun and thus more gold.)

By the 1540's Spaniards had explored North America westward to the Pacific and northward to Oregon. Within little more than a generation Spain had discovered, conquered, and colonized the most extensive empire in Europe's history. She now had to devise ways of developing and controlling her great wealth. The first step was to hamstring the conquistador. Columbus had been financed by Isabella, but from his time on expeditions of discovery and colonization were promoted by private enterprise. The conquistador—explorer, soldier, administrator rolled into one—bore the expense and reaped the bulk of the wealth. The crown in the beginning

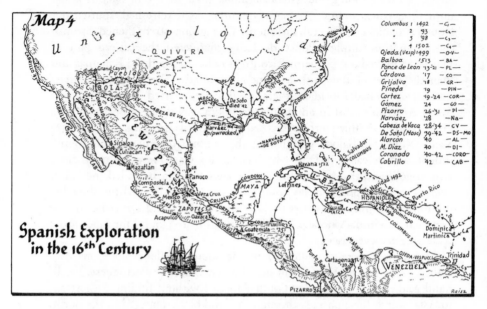

Map 4

Spanish Exploration
in the 16ᵗʰ Century

Columbus 1	1492	— C₁ —
" 2	'93	— C₂ —
" 3	'98	— C₃ —
" 4	1502	— C₄ —
Ojeda (Vesp.)	1499	— OV —
Balboa	1513	— BA —
Ponce de León	'13-21	— PL —
Córdova	'17	— CO —
Grijalva	'18	— GR —
Pineda	'19	— PIN —
Cortez	'19-24	— COR —
Gómez	'24	— GO —
Pizarro	'26-'31	— PI —
Narváez	'28	— Na —
Cabeza de Vaca	'28-'34	— CV —
De Soto (Mosc.)	'39-'42	— DS — Mo
Alarcón	'40	— AL —
M. Díaz	'40	— DI —
Coronado	'40-'42	— CORO —
Cabrillo	'42	— CAB —

allowed him to govern with a free hand territory he had subdued, demanding only an oath of loyalty and a fifth of the mineral wealth. The crown soon saw that it had relinquished too much power, and it replaced the conquistadors with royal governors directly under its control. By the middle of the sixteenth century Spain had developed a clear theory of empire and an organization for governing it that lasted well into the eighteenth century with only modifications in detail.

This was the theory: the Indies, as they were called, were considered a direct possession of the crown, not of the Spanish state. They were not technically colonies but kingdoms separate but equal to those that comprised the Spanish homeland. The king was sole proprietor and every privilege and position in the Indies came directly from him.

This was the organization: two great viceroyalties were created—New Spain in 1535 and Peru in 1544—each with its crown-appointed viceroy. These huge territories were subdivided into provinces, or *audiencias,* each with its own appointed governor and an administrative-judicial tribunal. The laws of Spain were to be the laws of the Indies, wherever they could be applied without destroying local traditions. Spanish justice was to prevail. The state-supported church would work with the government to spread Christianity. An elaborate bureaucracy responsible to crown officials checked local initiative. All important decisions were made in Spain, and any action taken in the Indies could be reversed, or, as the English would phrase it, "disallowed." The heart of this organization lay in Spain, where the Council of the Indies handled political administration and the *Casa de contratación,* or House of Trade, kept tight control over commerce. The completeness of this royal control prevailed more on paper than in fact. Laws that flouted the facts of a local situation often went ignored. *Obesez-caso, pero no se cumpla,* went a saying among officials in the Indies: "I obey but do not execute."

Several features distinguished Spain's empire from those England and France would erect to the north. The quantity of gold and silver Spain found failed to turn up in North America. The large native population Spain had to exploit and to control was absent in the north. Various consequences stemmed from all this. The Spanish settlers had almost at once a leisure it took colonists to the north nearly a century to achieve. Leisure and wealth combined to foster a vigorous cultural life. By the time England began to settle the New World, the Spanish Indies had their own universities—the University of Peru antedated by nearly a century Harvard's founding in 1636—their own press, theater, and a flourishing literature. The large number of natives, together with the Negro slaves soon imported in great numbers, limited the need for immigrants, and those coming from Spain averaged no more than fifteen to twenty-five hundred settlers annually. Spain, unlike England later, had little trouble dominating the native population. The Indians were accustomed to a highly organized society tightly controlled from above, and the conquistadors quickly learned that by decapitating the head of Indian society, literally, and substituting themselves at the top, they could dominate the population with ease.

For all this, the Spanish Empire in some ways resembled the one England would create. Both were frontier outposts far from home. Both solved a labor problem with Negro slavery. Both were agricultural empires. (The exploits of the conquistadors and the abundance of gold and silver have obscured the fact that the raising of cattle, sugar, and tobacco occupied the majority of settlers in the Indies.) How much England used Spain as a model for her own imperial government eludes a firm judgment. The techniques of control and organization were similar, but whether that similarity stemmed from the limitation of choice, from a common European inheritance, or from the Spanish model cannot be determined. Suffice to say that the Spanish model was there for England to study.

Some English borrowings are nonetheless clear. Spain mapped and described much of the New World, and England leaned heavily on these findings, assimilating error mixed with fact into her own conceptions of America. The charters of Virginia, Massachusetts, Connecticut, and the Carolinas extended from sea to sea, grants that seem absurd today but sensible then because Spanish reports read by the English pictured the Pacific much nearer than facts warranted. In the process of shaping England's image of the New World, Spain conditioned England's taste. The Spaniard introduced Indian corn, potatoes, and tomatoes to Europe and popularized sugar, tobacco, and cocoa. England by the time of Virginia's settlement had been prepared for a century by Spain to accept what the New World produced.

Spain became a reluctant mentor in other ways. By the time the English arrived, Spanish farmers had developed sugar planting, cattle ranching, and sheep raising into profitable ventures. They had experimented with olive oil, indigo, and rice and had planted mulberry trees for raising silk worms. They had developed tobacco from the harsh Indian product they had found into a sweet-tasting smoke. They had showed, in short, the variety of ways men could prosper in the New World. "If your men will follow their steps," an Englishman of the day advised, "I doubt but in due time they shall reap no less comity and benefit." The English took the cue. When hope of quick wealth collapsed, they watched and surreptitiously copied the Spanish. The first tobacco in Virginia came from purloined Spanish seed. South Carolina's staple crop of rice emerged from Spanish experiments. Mulberry trees were planted to create a silk industry similar to that in the Indies. The Negroes that came into the South through the seventeenth century often came from the Spanish Indies bearing Spanish names that are still found in the South today.

Economic ties between the American colonies and the Spanish islands increased through the seventeenth and eighteenth centuries. American ships slipped into island ports with Virginia horses, New England fish, Pennsylvania flour and returned northward with sugar, slaves, and Spanish currency. The United States could adopt a decimal system of currency with relative ease in 1776 because as British pounds, shillings, and pence drained back to the mother country through the colonial period the Spanish pieces of eight, equal to a dollar, became the money most frequently handled by Americans. The man today who says "gimme two bits" uses a phrase familiar in colonial times, when "two bits" equaled a quarter of a piece of eight.

Half the territory of the continental United States once belonged to Spain, and the names on the land show it. Four states—Florida, Colorado, Nevada, and California—together with rivers and mountains, cities and towns throughout all but the northern part of the country bear Spanish names. The oldest surviving building in the land is the Spanish fort at

Saint Augustine, Florida. In the Southwest, the Indians speak Spanish, the architecture is Spanish or pseudo-Spanish, and the Catholic Church predominates because of Spanish influence. The cowboy inherited his horse, his outfit, his methods, everything but his six-shooter and saloon, from his Spanish counterpart.

Spain entrenched herself so firmly in those parts of the New World she desired that she forced others to stake out claims elsewhere. She lost little she wanted to keep. When intruders came, they settled where Spain let them settle. Because the land north of Saint Augustine seemed worthless, she "gave" it to them. This, perhaps, was her greatest heritage to the United States.

The Intruders

France challenged first but only after John Cabot had staked out a claim for England. Cabot came from Italy to England sometime in the late 1480's, settling in the west-country port of Bristol, from where, even before Columbus had set out, ships had sailed westward "in search of the island of Brazil and the Seven Cities." Henry VII backed Cabot's plan to sail for Cipangu by heading due west from England, and in early May 1497, shortly after Columbus' second voyage, Cabot pushed out from Bristol in a ship so small its crew numbered only eighteen. In late June he anchored off the coast of "the territory of the Grand Khan," or, as we know it, the western end of Newfoundland. He lingered briefly and was back in England by early August. The crown gave a grant of ten pounds "to him that found the new isle." Henry VII turned his mind to other affairs, and England ceased to intrude officially in the New World for three-fourths of a century.

The consequences of a voyage at first lightly dismissed enlarged with time. Thousands of emigrants would travel the route Cabot had blazed west through the stormy northern latitudes, for it gave a swift if rough trip far from lanes traveled by the Spanish. Cabot's reports of a sea that teemed with fish pricked the interest of Bristol fishermen, and in the early 1500's ships by the score sailed regularly to the "new found land," as it came to be called. As the first recorded discoverer of North America, he had laid the basis for all English claims to the continent. And Henry's support of the voyage put England on record as opposed to the pope's division of the world between Spain and Portugal. When the Spanish ambassador protested after Cabot's trip that the new continent belonged to Spain, Henry VII suggested that effective occupation alone should determine claims in the New World. His suggestion in time came to be the rule.

On a second voyage in 1498, Cabot appears to have drifted down the

American coast perhaps as far as Virginia, but no record of the trip exists. The first recorded trip along the coast was made in 1524 by Giovanni da Verrazano, an Italian sailing for Francis I of France. He came upon natives "the color of russet" and coastlands that "yield most sweet savours far from shore." He sailed into the harbor of New York, along Long Island, poked about Narragansett Bay, and continued up the coast of Maine. But what excited Europe was his supposed view of the South Sea across a stretch of the coastland. (Historians argue whether he saw Chesapeake or Delaware Bay or, more likely, Pamlico Sound across the sandspits of the Carolina coast.) A map drawn by Verrazano's brother pinched America in at the center, and for centuries thereafter every Englishman who ventured into the wilderness hoped to come upon this "isthmus" that would carry men to the Sea of Verrazano.

Francis I was too involved in Continental affairs to send Verrazano back for a second look. A decade passed before the king felt free to subsidize a further reconnaissance. Jacques Cartier sailed out in 1534. He pushed past Labrador—"the land God gave Cain"—and far enough up the St. Lawrence River to be convinced that *he* was on the road to China. Francis I willingly put up the money for a second voyage in 1535, and Cartier traveled about a thousand miles up the St. Lawrence, past the site of Quebec, to the Indian village of Hochelaga. From a nearby summit— "Mont Real" Cartier called it—the river could be seen twisting inland "large, wide, and broad." Indians said "one could navigate along the river for more than three moons," which meant it was not a quick route to the South Sea. They also told, as their brethren to the south had told Columbus, that cities of gold lay over the horizon, and when Francis I heard this tale from the lips of a native who had traveled back to France with Cartier, he decided on a full-scale expedition to Canada, as Indians called the land. The Spanish ambassador protested. Francis I answered much as Henry VII had: "the popes hold spiritual jurisdiction, but it does not lie with them to distribute lands among kings." Spain considered sending a task force against the expedition, then decided to let the French fritter away energy and money in frigid Canada, a place where they could hardly do less damage.

Cartier set out after the elusive cities of gold in 1541 with a formidable force. At the same time he pushed inland from the north, Francisco Coronado was moving through New Mexico and Arizona on a similar errand. Both men ended their quests disillusioned about the cities of gold. By 1543 Cartier's colony had diminished to nothing. French support for New World enterprise dimmed when the "gold" Cartier sent back turned out to be rubbish (Fool's Gold, or pyrite); official support vanished as France became embroiled in a series of religious wars that lasted out the century.

Up to now gold and the elusive northwest passage had drawn France to the New World. A decade after Cartier's return Gaspard de Coligny, a Huguenot of great political influence, convinced the king that the Americas offered a way to weaken France's enemies in Europe. Self-sufficient colonies there would serve as outposts for privateers to pick off treasure ships and, he added privately, as refuges for oppressed Huguenots. The plan was initiated in 1555 with a settlement of Huguenots on an island off the coast of Brazil. The settlers had little idea how to manage an enterprise far from home, and when the Portuguese had a free moment they demolished the settlement with ease in 1558. But Coligny held to his plan. In 1562 Jean Ribaut, a Huguenot captain, built a garrison at Port Royal, South Carolina. Indians again told of cities of gold only twenty days distant and this, rather than the dull job of settlement, occupied the thoughts of all. Ribaut returned to France for men and supplies, and in his absence the garrison quarreled among itself, murdered its leader, and headed for home in a jerry-built boat. Two years later the persistent Coligny promoted a third effort. This time René de Laudonnière taunted the Spanish by building a garrison, Fort Caroline, further south, on the St. Johns River in Florida. It was perfectly located to tap the treasure of Spain as it moved slowly up the Florida coast on its way home. As before, gold obsessed the settlers, and when Sir John Hawkins stopped by in 1565 to replenish his water supply, he found the settlement falling apart. He gave Laudonnière a spare ship to travel home in, but before it could be put to use, Ribault arrived with reinforcements. Pedro Menéndez de Avilés arrived about the same time with an army from Spain. Months earlier Menéndez had been preparing to settle Florida at his own expense when word arrived that French heretics had occupied the coast at a spot potentially disastrous to Spanish shipping. King Philip increased Menéndez' force and gave him power to establish outposts all along the North American coast. Menéndez landed fifty miles south of the French, laid the foundations of Saint Augustine, then marched overland to take Fort Caroline by surprise. At the end of the slaughter, 142 bodies lay heaped on the river bank. An attempt soon after by Ribaut to take Saint Augustine failed, and he with all his men who admitted being Huguenots were slain. The massacre shocked France, which was then at peace with Spain. France protested the insult but did little more, for Fort Caroline had been a Huguenot enterprise. France forgot the affair in the bloodier slaughter of St. Bartholomew's Day Massacre, and she forgot the New World for the rest of the century.

Huguenot efforts left no mark on the New World but they did upon the English. All the great names involved in British efforts overseas— Gilbert, Raleigh, Hakluyt, Hawkins, Drake—had close ties with French Protestants. The talk of Huguenot friends about America aroused the

Map 5. Exploration of the Atlantic Seaboard

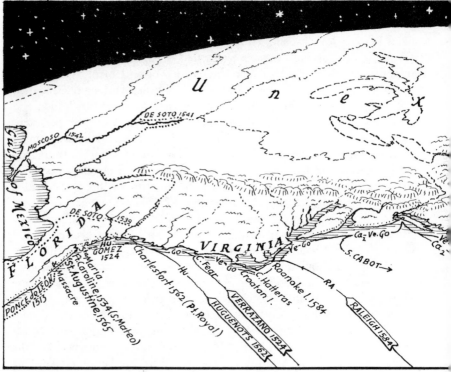

interest of a scholarly young man named Richard Eden, who in 1555 translated Peter Martyr's chronicle of Spanish achievements, *De Orbe Novo,* into English under the title *Decades of the New World.* It is hard to exaggerate the general ignorance in England of the New World prior to Eden's translation. The book exposed his countrymen for the first time to a vivid, accurate account of Spanish achievements and the abundance of wealth they had found. Eden's rendering stirred the imagination, and by reminding his readers that "there yet remaineth another portion of that main land," he did as much as any writer can do to goad a nation to activity.

Elizabeth's government took care to restrain that activity. England

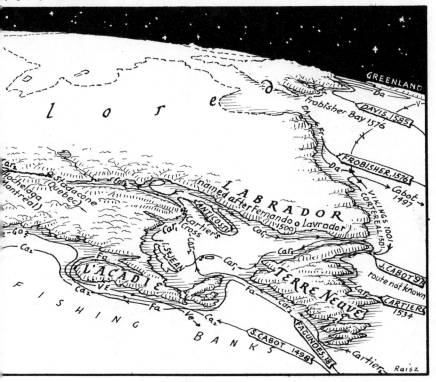

fore 1600

still lacked the strength to challenge Spain. For that reason attention centered first in areas where Spain showed no interest. The Newfoundland fisheries offered a safe way of increasing English power quietly. The old habit of fast days was revived to strengthen the fishing industry. Fishing led to furs. The fishermen dried their catches on wooden "stages" or frames on shore, which brought them into contact with the natives. Indians, eager for a European hammer, an iron pot, a shiny trinket, brought furs into the seaside camps, and by the 1540's this trade had developed into a lucrative business.

The profits from fishing and furs seemed minute compared to the wealth of the Far East. England, a century after Spain and Portugal, began to dream of a route to the Grand Khan. It had to be, of course, a route that did not cross the path of the Spanish or Portuguese. The obvious spot to search was toward the northeast and in 1553 a group of London merchants sent Hugh Willoughby and Richard Chancellor to search out a passage beyond the Gulf of Archangel, in the Barents Sea. A storm carried Willoughby to his death. But Chancellor survived, and out of an eventual meeting with Ivan IV (Ivan the Terrible) came the Muscovy Company and the opening of trade between Russia and England. In 1558 Anthony Jenkinson, an agent of the Muscovy Company, found his way across Russia, down to the Caspian Sea, and into Persia. His reports of the riches there attracted others. William Harborne reached Constantinople in 1579 and got permission from the sultan for English merchants to trade throughout the Near East. Two years later Elizabeth granted a charter to the Levant Company, and through the rest of her reign luxuries of the East entered England by a route she had blazed.

England had remained on reasonably good terms with Spain through the early part of this period. She depended on Spain for vegetable oil used as a base for dyes; without them her cloth industry would have been in trouble. And she profited from trade with the Canary Islands, which Spain still kept open to British ships. The risk of losing what she had and the hope that Spain might grant even more concessions kept England in a well-mannered mood.

The main concession hoped for was permission to trade in the West Indies, which Spain kept closed to all outsiders. When Sir John Hawkins brought over his first load of Negroes in 1562 and exchanged them for sugar and hides, he comported himself well, paid the required license fees and customs duties, and went on his way convinced he had cracked open a long-closed door. But by the time of his next trip, in 1565, word had come out from Spain to turn him away. He slipped in anyway, sold his cargo, then blithely sailed up the Florida coast to call on the French at Fort Caroline. Spain complained and Elizabeth forbade further trips. She relented two years later on the assumption that Spanish tempers had calmed down. They had not. Hawkins was attacked at San Juan de Ulua, Mexico, in 1568, and of his five ships only two, his own and that captained by his cousin Francis Drake, escaped.

Hawkins' defeat marked the start of deteriorating relations between England and Spain that culminated twenty years later in the destruction of the Spanish Armada. During this period the Catholic Counter-Reformation reached an intensity that strained relations between all Protestant and Catholic countries. Spain increased that strain in England by promoting Mary of Scotland for the British throne. Elizabeth countered these threats by unleashing her sea dogs, and English pirates began to loot around the world. It is hard to judge how much they hobbled Spain's might, but a newsletter of 1585 to the great Fugger banking house reported that "the sea remains so blockaded and shut off, commerce is quite at a standstill."

While pirates like Drake and Hawkins roamed the seas for England, men at home like Gilbert, Raleigh, and the Hakluyts—all with close ties among Huguenot colonizers—promoted the idea of colonization. Gaspard de Coligny had argued that a sure way to weaken one's enemy in Europe was to attack him from self-sufficient colonial bases in the New World. From the transplanted seed of that belief would grow England's first colony in North America—Roanoke.

Gilbert, Raleigh, and the Hakluyts

Sir Humphrey Gilbert—"one of the giants of the age" a recent historian calls him—gave drive and direction to the Elizabethan movement against Spain in the New World. He took care, though, to direct the drive away from lands settled by Spain and to promote it under the guise of a search for the northwest passage. Gilbert's *Discourse of a Discovery for a New Passage to Catia,* written in 1566 but not published till a decade later, popularized the possibility of a northwest passage to India. He argued that America was really the mythical Atlantis, "ever known to be an island," and that around its northern tip lay a clear path to Cathay. He adjusted the argument to the times by urging that in the search for the passage, overseas outposts should be established that would permit ships on the long voyage to Asia to pause for refreshment.

Sir Martin Frobisher went out in 1576 to test Gilbert's theory. He brought back an "Asiatic" Eskimo as proof he had touched China and a shipload of trash he thought gold. Philip II of Spain prodded his ambassador to get a chart of the trip, though he found it "difficult to believe that in so cold a region there can be any richness of metal." Gold fever temporarily killed interest in a passage to China, and on further voyages in 1577 and 1578 Frobisher—"whom God forgive," said his wife—spent his family's fortune hauling back further loads of rubbish to England.

While others through the remainder of the sixteenth and most of the seventeenth centuries took up the search Gilbert had popularized, Gilbert himself became obsessed with the idea of erecting a colony in America. In 1577, about the time Drake slipped out from England to sap the strength of Spain by lifting her treasure, Gilbert was arguing at court that colonization would achieve the same end more effectively and with greater gains for England. The next year, 1578, the queen gave Sir Humphrey a charter that allowed him six years to build a colony in the New World. The charter gave Gilbert something close to the rights of a medieval baron over

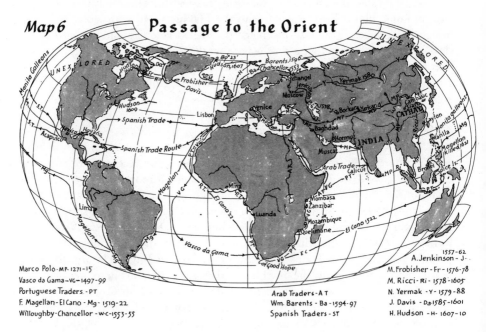

Map 6   **Passage to the Orient**

Marco Polo · MP· 1271-15
Vasco da Gama · VG · 1497-99
Portuguese Traders · PT
F. Magellan-ElCano · Mg · 1519-22
Willoughby-Chancellor · WC-1553-55

Arab Traders · A T
Wm. Barents · Ba · 1594-97
Spanish Traders · ST

1557-62
A. Jenkinson · J-
M. Frobisher · Fr · 1576-78
M. Ricci · Ri · 1578-1605
N. Yermak · Y · 1579-88
J. Davis · Da·1585-1601
H. Hudson · H· 1607-10

all the lands he staked out and settled. Here at the beginning a pattern was being set for English colonization: land and power were offered as bait to entice men into venturing their lives and their fortunes in settling the New World.

French friends, made when he had fought alongside Huguenot forces in Normandy, had no doubt first pricked Gilbert's interest in colonization. Experiences gained in Ireland had furthered that interest: Gilbert had attempted with several other gentlemen—all these early ventures were backed mainly by land-hungry gentlemen with influence at court—to make a planting, or "plantation," as it was called, on crown lands in Ireland a decade before he received his American charter. Ireland at the time somewhat resembled America: both were wild and uncivilized and offered boundless land to develop; both were peopled with belligerent natives. Gilbert planned to, and others actually did, transplant to America colonizing techniques learned or first tried in Ireland.

A third source that shaped Gilbert's ideas on colonization was a collection of "Notes" written by Richard Hakluyt, the elder, which advised him where to settle and how to go about it. There were two Richard

Hakluyts: the elder, a lawyer who advised Gilbert and Raleigh and, later, commercial companies on the practical aspects of colonization and who laid down a program for settlement of America that men held to throughout the seventeenth century; the younger, a cousin, clergyman, scholar, and publicist who through his writings did more to keep the subject of colonization before the public than anyone of his day. Though neither man ever came to America, no contemporary knew as much about the continent as the Hakluyts.

Sir Humphrey and his half-brother Walter Raleigh set out in 1578 with seven ships and nearly four hundred men, England's first great effort to settle the New World. The size of the all-male expedition shows that the goal was to erect somewhere in America a self-sufficient armed outpost for use as a base against Spain. Only after this planting had taken root would the time come for a true colony, peopled with families. Storms killed these plans for the moment, forcing the ships to turn back without even sighting America. Five years elapsed before Gilbert ventured out again. Lack of money, not interest, caused the delay. Hakluyt, the younger, helped drum up interest by publishing in 1582 *Divers Voyages Touching the Discovery of America and the Islands Adjacent.* The slim volume contained most of the little that Englishmen then knew about North America, and much of the book—Verrazano's trip of 1524, Ribaut's colony in Florida—had been translated from the French by Hakluyt. The elder Hakluyt's "Notes" were included to explain what was to be gained from colonization.

Gilbert sailed again in June 1583 with five ships and over two hundred and fifty men. He had pledged nearly all the family fortune to the project. A few gentlemen, lured by the huge land grants Gilbert dispensed with kingly aplomb, had helped to a limited extent, but the crown and merchants had contributed nothing. He headed first for Newfoundland and there, amid fleets of fishing boats from several lands, took formal possession of the land. He now planned to drift down the coast until he came upon a suitable spot for setting up an outpost from whose seed he saw growing a great landed proprietary colony by which he would recoup his fortune. Storms once again shattered his dreams. The flagship of the task force sank in the first one, and Gilbert's ship vanished in the second; he was shouting to his crew as a wave swept them from sight, "We are as near Heaven by sea as by land." The line was a paraphrase from Sir Thomas More's *Utopia,* "The way to heaven out of all places is of like length and distance."

Gilbert failed in all his practical projects, but he failed on a grand scale. His vision of a great proprietary colony soon captured the imagination of England's land-hungry aristocracy. Maryland, the Carolinas, New

York, and Pennsylvania all sprang from dreams similar to the one Gilbert first spread forth. Out of that dream, too, emerged Raleigh's Roanoke, the first seed of the British Empire in North America.

The charter Raleigh got from Queen Elizabeth in 1584 essentially duplicated Gilbert's six-year grant. He put it to use at once. Despite the mass of Spanish and French accounts that Hakluyt, the younger, was accumulating, England still knew little firsthand about America. To repair that failing, Raleigh, in April 1584, dispatched a reconnaissance—"two barks well furnished with men and victuals" under the command of Philip Amadas and Arthur Barlow and piloted by the Portuguese Simon Fernandez, "a great rogue" who knew more about the American coast than any Englishman. The barks followed Columbus' longer but less stormy course down to the Canaries, then cut west to the Indies and north. They smelled a "strong and sweet smell" as they neared the Carolina shore. They coasted northward until they found a break in the ridge of islands and sandbars, then sailed in, landing first on Hatteras Island. Later they took possession of an island, which the Indians called Roanoke, near the opening of Albemarle Sound. They made a hasty survey and hurried back to England with two natives to report the climate pleasant, the soil rich, the Indians friendly, and signs of mineral wealth everywhere. Raleigh flattered his "Virgin Queen" by asking to name the discovery Virginia. She accepted the compliment as a woman and also as a monarch who wished to tell the world the crown of England favored this intrusion into lands Spain claimed. England had handed Spain no stronger insult.

The queen's acceptance of Raleigh's name for the land encouraged him to believe the crown might help finance what up to now he alone had subsidized. Hakluyt, the younger, who had "served for a very good trumpet" for Gilbert and who in 1583 had gone to France in search "of such things as may yield any light unto our western discovery," had at Raleigh's request written *A Discourse of Western Planting,* which was now presented to the queen. It was an impressive "collection of certain reasons to induce her Majesty and the state to take in hand the western voyage and the planting there." Hakluyt raised in this paper nearly every argument advanced for colonies in the next two centuries. They would, he said, promote trade, strengthen the navy, provide raw materials for English industry, offer an outlet for "the fry of wandering beggars of England," advance the Protestant religion, and, above all, undercut the power of Spain.

Hakluyt argued well, but Elizabeth rejected the plan. Virginia offered no immediate profits and long-range gains did not interest the queen when war with Spain lay just ahead. Raleigh, like Gilbert, hoped to build an armed outpost on the American shores to harbor and provision privateers. This appealed to Elizabeth, but the treasury could not bear the expense of such an undertaking. Private enterprise must carry the load, she said, reaffirming a decision Spain had made a century earlier and still held to. The crown would sanction exploitation of the New World. It would do no more.

That, slight as it was, was something, and Raleigh set about raising money for a second expedition. Hakluyt, the elder, advised sending over a battery of experts to study the land with care before making a fuller commitment—men skillful "in all mineral causes," "in all kinds of drugs," husbandmen, vineyard men, "makers of oars," and the like. The expedition of 1585, headed by Richard Grenville, carried, among its complement of some one hundred men, John White, a "skillful painter" who would serve the role photographers do on modern expeditions; Thomas Hariot, mathematician, expert on navigation, and historian for the party; and with these, sixteenth-century versions of mineralogists, agronomists, and herbalists.

The expedition paused en route at the West Indies, as Hakluyt suggested, to take on "such cattle and beasts as are fit and necessary for manuring the country" and also a variety of "fruits and plants" to try out in Virginia. Grenville landed the party on Roanoke in June with Ralph Lane in charge. The men had arrived too late to plant; the Indians soon became less than friendly; and storms that slammed against the exposed island made the winter a rough one. Still, much was accomplished. The party survived a year in the wilderness, though near the end the men were reduced to eating dogs steeped in sassafras leaves. The land was reconnoitered as far north as Chesapeake Bay, and it was agreed that that area should be the site of the next settlement.

In June 1586 Sir Francis Drake dropped anchor off Roanoke. He had spent the previous months ravaging the West Indies and decided that before returning home he would do what he could to help the Virginia enterprise along. He leveled Saint Augustine, both the wooden fort and the village, and with that threat gone pushed on up the coast to Roanoke. He offered supplies and reinforcements to carry the settlement through another year. Lane accepted the offer, and the transfer of men and stores was nearly completed when a great storm spread havoc. Lane, disheartened by the debris around him, decided to return home.

Thus far, Raleigh had moved with caution and intelligence toward America. Now, with the experience gained from two exploratory trips, the time had come to attempt a real planting. Increased tension with Spain, to some degree the result of Drake's most recent voyage, made the need for a fortified American base the more apparent. Thomas Hariot's *Brief and True Report of the New Found Land of Virginia,* illustrated with engravings of John White's watercolors, advertised the glories of Virginia. With the help of such propaganda, plus the promise of large land grants to settlers—two lures that would be used throughout America's early history—Raleigh found 117 persons, among them 17 women, 2 of them pregnant, and 9 children, willing to adventure their lives and fortunes in Virginia. The problem of governing an outpost of Englishmen far from home was solved by drawing on the English borough pattern. Governor John White—apparently the artist of the previous voyage—and twelve others were incorporated by charter as "the Governor and Assistants of the City of Raleigh in Virginia." The band of adventurers would now enjoy the rights of self-government under their own leaders. Agents in England would see to it that the corporation was kept well supplied from the mother country until the outpost could take care of its own needs.

Despite firm orders to settle somewhere on Chesapeake Bay, the landing was made in July 1587 at Roanoke, apparently because the pilot, again that "great rogue" Simon Fernandez, refused to push on up the coast. A month after landing, White returned to England for additional supplies, leaving the colony without a head. He left behind his daughter and son-in-law and their baby Virginia Dare, the first white child born in English America. Back home, White found no one concerned about Roanoke; the nation was in the midst of preparations to combat the great Spanish Armada. When White finally managed to return in 1591, the colony had vanished. He found scattered about the site "many of my things spoiled and broken and my books torn from the covers, the frames of some of my pictures and maps rotten and spoiled with rain, and my armor almost eaten through with rust." But he was not disheartened, for he had left for England knowing the colony "intended to remove fifty miles farther up into the mainland presently." White found the letters "CRO" carved on a tree and the word "CROATOAN" on a doorpost to the palisade. Since neither carving carried a cross, which had been agreed upon as a distress signal, White assumed the colony had moved to the vicinity of the friendly Croatans. An uneasy crew anxious to clear away before bad weather set in refused to let White linger in the area to search for the "lost" colony. Though historians still puzzle over the mystery of what happened to the Roanoke colonists, no one has improved on the judgment of Robert Beverley in 1705: "it is supposed that the Indians seeing them forsaken by their country, and unfurnished of their expected supplies, cut them off. For to this day they were never more heard of."

England's imperial dream lay dormant for twelve years. The war with Spain lasted until 1604, and this absorbed much of her energies.

But it was clear that England needed more than energy to build a base in the New World. Raleigh had poured energy along with fortune into Virginia. In 1589, before he learned the Roanoke colony had disappeared, he gave the right to colonize Virginia to a group of nineteen men, mostly London merchants, who had the money to invest in a risky enterprise. Raleigh was attempting, without abandoning his own legal title to settle America, to make certain that others would continue what he had begun and might not be able to complete. By this time he realized what other Englishmen would take longer to learn—that colonization of the New World would be a long, slow process. The land Spain had left open to England, rich as it was, offered slight chance for quick wealth. Virginia presented difficulties Spain had never had to face. New techniques would have to be developed before England could reap profit from the colony. Raleigh remarked on this in his *History of the World,* driving home the point with an adage of the day: "No man makes haste to the market, where there is nothing to be bought but blows." The years that followed proved this saying rooted at best in a half-truth. Virginia for years offered little but blows, and yet men continued to make haste to it.

BIBLIOGRAPHICAL NOTE

There are several guides that any reader interested in expanding his knowledge of the material covered in this book must at sometime or other turn to. First and most important is the *Harvard Guide to American History* (1954), an indispensable work for any student of the colonial period. This book contains full, though unannotated, listings of all important books and articles up to the date of its publication. A more recent volume, designed mainly for the layman and graduate student, is *The American Historical Association's Guide to Historical Literature* (1961). Coverage of the American story is limited, compared to the *Harvard Guide,* but a virtue of the volume is that most books mentioned are accompanied by editorial comment; a defect is that articles are excluded. A third work, which also excludes articles, is the Library of Congress's *A Guide to the Study of the United States of America* (1960). The annotations here are full, reliable, and perceptive. Finally, there is *America: History and Life,* the first of whose regularly appearing volumes was published in mid-1964. This guide to articles on American history covers five hundred American and Canadian journals and about a thousand foreign publications.

The purpose of the bibliographies that follow is both to point up those books and articles that have been published since the *Harvard Guide* came out, more than a decade ago, and also to comment on those books that seem to excel in illuminating the colonial period. The comments on the works mentioned, it should be understood, are personal and not to be taken as gospel. A book or an article that strikes one historian as especially perceptive may impress another as wrong-headed or dull.

BIBLIOGRAPHY

An Old World Becomes New

Any competent text will fill out the background of this period. Robert R. Palmer and Joel Cotton, *A History of the Modern World* (3rd ed., 1965), is especially recommended. Edward P. Cheyney's *Dawn of a New Era, 1250–1453* (1936; now in paperback [hereafter abbreviated pb.]) covers the period in detail. Accounts that specifically relate the European background to America are Cheyney's *European Background of American History, 1300–1600* (1904; pb.) ; Howard Mumford Jones, "The European Background," *Literary History of the United States,* Vol. I (3 vols., 1948), whose theme has recently been elaborated in his magnificent *O Strange New World* (1964) ; and Lewis Mumford's first chapter in *Golden Day* (1926; pb.), an impressionistic, original interpretation of the break-up of the medieval world and its relation to America.

From the mountain of excellent material on the medieval world the student should glance especially at Johan Huizinga, *The Waning of the Middle Ages* (1924; pb.) ; Will Durant's *Age of Faith* (1950) ; and Sidney Painter's brief *Medieval Life* (1953)—all of which catch the tone of the era. Eileen Power has a succinct, well-written chapter on Marco Polo in *Medieval People* (1924; pb.). Economic changes of the age are well handled by the great Belgian historian Henri Pirenne in *History of Europe* (2 vols., pb. original) and his *Economic and Social History of Medieval Europe* (1937; pb.). William Carroll Bark, *Origins of the Medieval World* (1958; pb.), challenges several of Pirenne's views and in the process presents his own stimulating picture of the medieval world.

Three volumes on the Renaissance are Wallace K. Ferguson's brief but excellent *The Renaissance* (1940) ; H. S. Lucas' fuller *The Renaissance and Reformation* (1934) ; and V. H. H. Green, *Renaissance and Reformation* (1952).

A New World Is Found

J. H. Parry describes the development of new tools succinctly in *Europe and the Wider World: The Establishment of the European Hegemony, 1415–1715* (1949; pb.) and fully in his more recent *The Age of Reconnaissance* (1963; pb.). A glance at C. R. Beazley's *Dawn of Modern Geography* (3 vols., 1897–1906) makes it clear why it has been called definitive, indispensable, and "the greatest work on medieval geography." Lloyd A. Brown, *The Story of Maps* (1950), presents a more general but nonetheless authoritative account of the subject, as do G. R. Crone, *Maps and Map Makers* (1953), and E. G. R. Taylor, *The Haven-Finding Art: A History of Navigation from Odysseus to Captain Cook* (1956). The most detailed word on developments in technology appears in Charles Singer, *et al.,* eds., *A History of Technology,* Vol. II of *The Mediterranean and the Middle Ages,* c. 700 B.C. *to* c. A.D. 1500 (5 vols., 1954–1958).

Parry presents excellent brief accounts of the age of exploration. For fuller discussions, all equally reliable and distinguished, see J. N. L. Baker, *History of Geographical Discovery and Exploration* (1931) ; J. B. Brebner, *The Explorers of North America, 1492–1806* (1933; pb.) ; J. E. Gillespie, *A History of Geographical Discovery, 1400–1800* (1933) ; A. P. Newton, ed., *The Great Age of Discovery* (1932) ; and Boies Penrose, *Travel and Discovery in the Renaissance* (1955; pb.).

The Portuguese story is told in H. V. Livermore, *A History of Portugal* (1953), and in Edgar Prestage, *The Portuguese Pioneers* (1933). Elaine Sanceau's *Henry the Navigator* (1945) is the best of recent biographies, but no one should miss Garrett Mattingly's essay "Navigator to the Modern Age," *Horizon*, 3 (Nov., 1960), 78–83. Samuel Eliot Morison, *Admiral of the Ocean Sea* (2 vols. with notes, 1 vol. without; 1942), has written the most authoritative modern biography of Columbus, and, as usual, with great style. More recently he has produced a briefer *Christopher Columbus, Mariner* (1955; pb.). Morison has also recently translated and edited *Journals and Other Documents on the Life and Voyages of Christopher Columbus* (1964).

Staking-Out the Claims

There are several competent surveys for the student to consult, among them, John E. Fagg, *Latin America: A General History* (1963) ; Vera Brown Holmes, *A History of the Americas* (1950) ; C. H. Haring, *The Spanish Empire in America* (1952) ; Bailey W. Diffie, *Latin American Civilization: Colonial Period* (1945) ; and J. Fred Rippy, *Latin America: A Modern History* (1960). Silvio Zavala's *The Colonial Period in the History of the New World*, translated and abridged by Max Savelle (1962), opens a new trail by comparing the development of colonial institutions throughout the New World.

Accounts that deal specifically with Spanish settlements and explorations in the United States are H. E. Bolton, *Rim of Christendom* (1936) ; E. G. Bourne, *Spain in America, 1450–1580* (1905) ; Woodbury Lowery, *The Spanish Settlements Within the Present Limits of the United States, 1513–1848* (1901) ; and Herbert I. Priestley, *The Coming of the White Man, 1492–1848* (1929). Accounts that cover the story on both sides of the ocean are R. T. Davies, *The Golden Century of Spain, 1501–1621* (1937; rev. ed., 1957) ; E. D. Salmon, *Imperial Spain* (1931) ; and J. H. Parry, *The Spanish Theory of Empire in the Sixteenth Century* (1940). The best single source of the Spanish story is Peter Martyr's *De Orbe Novo;* Richard Eden's translation of 1555, which reveals more of the English mind than the Spanish story, has been reprinted by Edward Arber in *The First Three English Books on America* (1885) ; a modern and more accurate version was edited by F. A. MacNutt in 1912.

James A. Williamson, "England and the Opening of the Atlantic," in J. H. Rose, *et al.*, eds., *Cambridge History of the British Empire* (7 vols., 1929–1930) ; Vol. I, Ch. 2, offers an introduction to the English story hard to surpass. (Incidentally, this volume of the *Cambridge History,* though in some respects dated, is probably still the best single collection of essays on the American story available. All students of the colonial period should become acquainted with its contents.) Williamson's excellent *Voyages of the Cabots and English Discovery of North America* (1929) has recently been augmented by his *The Cabot Voyages and Bristol Discovery Under Henry VII* (1962), but material discussed so thoroughly is likely to interest only the specialized student.

Vols. I and II of Francis Parkman's *France and England in North America* (8 vols., 1874–1896) still offer the liveliest report of early French efforts. G. M. Wrong presents a later view in his excellent *Rise and Fall of New France* (2 vols., 1928). Brebner gives a brief but perceptive account of the same material in *Explorers of North America.*

Two able studies of how the English appropriated ideas and information to clarify their picture of the New World and improve their seafaring skills are Franklin T. McCann, *English Discovery of America to 1585* (1952), and D. W. Water, *The Art of Navigation in England in Elizabethan and Early Stuart Times* (1958). Three additional works of Williamson's to be recommended are *The Age of Drake* (1938; pb.), *The Ocean in English History* (1941), and *Sir Francis Drake* (1951; pb.). A good introduction to the work of Hakluyt, the younger, is W. Nelson Francis' essay, "Hakluyt's *Voyages:* An Epic of Discovery," *William and Mary Quarterly (WMQ),* 12 (1955), 447–455. (The *WMQ* is the best of the professional magazines for authoritative articles about specialized aspects of colonial America. An excellent cumulative index makes its mass of material easily available. Unless otherwise noted, it will be assumed that all volume references are to the third series, which inaugurated the journal's concentrated interest in the colonial period.) Samuel Eliot Morison's essay in *Builders of the Bay Colony* (1930; pb.) has the usual charm of his writing. George B. Parks has written of both Hakluyts in his *Richard Hakluyt and the English Voyages* (1928). David Beers Quinn covers *Raleigh and the British Empire* (1947; pb.) with extraordinary fullness in a brief compass; his introduction to *The Roanoke Voyages, 1584–1590* (2 vols., 1955) makes these volumes more than a collection of sources. Two recent biographies of Raleigh are Margaret Irwin's *That Great Lucifer* (1960) and Willard M. Wallace's more scholarly *Sir Walter Raleigh* (1959). The early chapters of A. L. Rowse, *The Elizabethans and America* (1959; pb.), give an adequate summary of the period; see also his *Expansion of Elizabethan England* (1955; pb.).

The large number of secondary accounts of the English story, for all their excellence, are no substitute for the younger Hakluyt's collection of firsthand reports in *The Principal Navigations, Voyages, and Discoveries of the English Nation* (1589 and 1599). These are available in the inexpensive Everyman's Library under the title of *Hakluyt's Voyages* (8 vols., 1962). Hakluyt's work is being continued under today's severer editorial standards by the Hakluyt Society. Among the society's volumes relevant to this early period are Quinn's edition of *The Voyages and Colonising Enterprises of Sir*

Humphrey Gilbert (2 vols,, 1940) and *The Roanoke Voyages* (1962). John White's drawings are most easily found in Stefan Lorant's *The New World* (1947), but their splendid coloring can be appreciated only in Paul Hulton's and David Beers Quinn's recent edition of *The American Drawings of John White, 1577–1590* (2 vols., 1964).

For further references see the *Harvard Guide,* Sections 71, "European Background and Approach to American Discovery"; 72, "Christopher Columbus and His Discoveries"; 73, "Cabots and Corte-Reals"; 74, "The Spanish Colonial Empire"; 75, "Spanish Explorations and Settlements in the United States to 1600"; 76, "French Explorations of the Americas to 1608"; 77, "Causes and Background of English Expansion"; and 78, "English Voyages and Settlements, 1527–1606."

Reformation Leaders, from "Epitaph des Bürgermeisters Myenburg"
("Burgomaster Myenburg's Funeral Oration"), by Lucas Cranach, the Younger
Courtesy of The Bettmann Archive

2. Background for Settlement

THE REFORMATION
    Luther
    Anabaptism
    Calvinism
    The Church of England
    Puritanism

ENGLAND ON THE EVE OF COLONIZATION
    The People
    The Government
    The Economy

A GREAT MIGRATION BEGINS
    Who Came and Why
    How They Came and Where They Went
    What They Found

THE REFORMATION

The Protestant Reformation completed the unsettlement of Europe. It exploded on an age already distracted by the economic consequences of Columbus' discoveries and added an inflammatory ingredient to the competition for New World wealth. The eagerness of Gilbert, the Hakluyts, and Raleigh to promote American settlement stemmed as much from their Protestant aversion for Catholic Spain and France as from economic motives. Time nourished this feeling. Protestants who followed —and nearly all who came to English North America were Protestants— found their settlements endangered throughout the colonial period by Spain's presence on the south and France's on the north and west. Also,

43

many who came viewed America, it has been remarked, as "an experiment in constructive Protestantism," a land where they might cease to protest against the established religion at home and begin to build as they wished. Luther, upon whom Columbus' discoveries made little impress, wrought more than he knew. The United States became something it might never have been if he had not lived.

Luther

Martin Luther sought no more than Erasmus and other reformers had sought for a half century—to purify the Church of corrupt practices and to recover the spirit of primitive Christianity. Reform, not revolution, was his goal. But Luther was a violent and obstinate as well as a devout man: he soon passed from urging reforms to favoring the overthrow of doctrines that had guided men for more than a millennium.

Luther had trained for the law but became a monk in 1505, the year before Columbus died. He wore the habit for nineteen years, obsessed through nearly all of them with doubts about his salvation. His private turmoil about the future world turned on the question of how God could permit the salvation of a man as corrupt as he. Nothing the church offered—confession, the Mass, prayer, pilgrimages to shrines in Rome—relieved his distress about salvation. In the midst of his misery, St. Paul's remark that "the just shall live by faith" sparked the thought that God gave His grace to those who had faith in Him. All the church's "machinery for mediation" between man and God—the ritual, the priesthood, the sacraments—were needless for the man with faith. They might help to induce faith; they were not necessary for salvation.

Luther suppressed the radical side of his views in his first attack on the church, which was provoked by the sale of indulgences. An indulgence was a grant by the church from credits accumulated in heaven by the righteous to those eager to reduce their time in purgatory. Normally, only the faithful received indulgences, but their dispensation in Germany became so abusive that in 1517 they were being retailed to the tune of a jingle:

> As soon as the coin in the coffer rings
> The soul from purgatory springs.

Luther, at the time nearly thirty-four years old, drew up ninety-five theses, or arguments, against indulgences and tacked them up on the Wittenberg church door, inviting a public debate on the matter. He objected to them as a German (part of the money collected would be used to rebuild St. Peter's in Rome), went on to attack Pope Leo X (if he had power over purgatory, "why does he not empty the place out of most holy love?"), then moved on to question the concept of stored-up credits (man's nature is so perverted, he said, that even the cup of saints never overflows with goodness) and the belief that by good works a man might ease his way into heaven.

The church's vigorous rebuttal led Luther from reform to revolt. He next questioned all bases of the church's authority—the pope, church councils, even canon law. God was a law unto Himself, and no man dared to presume to know His will except as He had revealed Himself in the Bible. "Unless I am convinced by Scripture and plain reason . . . my conscience is captive to the Word of God," Luther told papal legates. "I will not recant anything, for to go against conscience is neither right nor safe." (The famous concluding sentence—"Here I stand; I cannot do otherwise"—appears to be apocryphal.)

Soon after Luther formed his own church. He abolished fast days, monasteries, a celibate clergy, and the cult of saints, because, he said, nothing in the Bible justified them. He attacked the sacraments, those visible signs of God's grace, on the same ground, reducing seven (baptism, marriage, penance, extreme unction, ordination, confirmation, and the Mass) to the two (baptism and communion) justified by the Scriptures for Christians alone. (Luther's use of the Scriptures differed from later Protestant leaders like Huldreich Zwingli and John Calvin. He wanted nothing in his church contrary to the word of God, but he assumed that whatever the Bible did not explicitly prohibit was allowable, and for that reason he saw no need to eliminate vestments, private confession, stained-glass windows, and similar "corruptions" that were to disturb others.) Luther cast out marriage because it existed among heathens. He eliminated ordination, the rite that makes a plain man a priest, because "we are all consecrated as priests by baptism." The man who leads a community's religious life only *administers* God's teachings; what the minister does any man can do, although those trained for the work can do it better. Luther carved out the core of the Mass when he denied the doctrine of transubstantiation—that is, when the priest says "this is my body," the bread and wine substantially and exclusively become the body and blood of Christ—because the act implied a miracle by ordinary men. Luther transformed this sacrament into a rite of communion between God and Christ and the congregation, an act of thanksgiving rather than sacrifice. This rite would be called the Lord's Supper, the Mass as such being nowhere mentioned in the Bible.

Luther undermined the church's authority, then revised the ritual. He translated the Bible into German and for the first time made it available to the congregation. The sermon, also in the vernacular, assumed a new though still limited importance in the service. Luther took song away from the choir and gave it to the congregation, and then composed hymns to promote the innovation. He had said the clergy could marry, and led the way here, too, by taking a wife. These mild innovations— mild judged by what was to come—satisfied Luther's desire to purify the church. He died convinced he had only reformed the old, not founded a new church.

Luther expected his reformation of the church to spread swiftly across Europe. The hope was soon dashed, for Lutheranism, like some wines, did not travel well, even when entrusted to apostles. Huldreich Zwingli, a contemporary of Luther's and one of the most eminent of his early allies, imported the Reformation into German Switzerland, where it was further reformed. Zwingli stripped away more of the Catholic color than Luther had dared or desired, for Zwingli held that the church could accept only what the Bible explicitly sanctioned. For that reason, hymns were rejected and a metrical version of the Psalms substituted. Ornaments vanished from the church; ministers dressed as laymen; and communion was removed from the altar to a table placed before the congregation. The service centered around the sermon, which became an exposition of the word of God. The act of communion became for Zwingli only a way to commemorate Christ's sacrifice and a sign of the covenant between God and man. He regarded baptism simply as an initiation into society. He, unlike Luther, neither considered the sacraments as a means of grace nor required faith from those who participated in them.

Luther broke the mold of Europe's religious thought; and though his church never bulked large in colonial America, the reforms he introduced shaped the life and thought of nearly every settler. His view that faith alone would save men and that the church was composed of a priesthood of all believers were doctrines on which every Protestant sect was founded. Most of his innovations—the use of sermons and hymns, the substitution of the vernacular for Latin in the service, the abbreviated version of the sacraments, the allowing the clergy to marry, and the ending of monastical orders—found their way in one form or another into all of Protestantism. Zwingli added his own touches to the new religious mold Luther created. Calvin, and later the Puritans, would adopt and modify Zwinglianism to their own needs. But before Calvin arrived on the scene, the Anabaptists gave a radical twist to Zwingli's ideas that left Luther aghast at the horrors his revolt had unleashed.

Anabaptism

While Luther and Zwingli debated the sacraments, long-suppressed political and social bitterness broke forth in a revolt of the German peasants in 1524. But the conservative Luther repudiated the uprising, called the peasants filthy swine, and encouraged the princes to subdue them. Fifty thousand people died in the repression. The unrest that still boiled beneath the surface now manifested itself in religion. A variety of sects distinct from and opposed to Lutheranism emerged—among them Mennonites, Amish, Familists, Dunkers, and Schwenkfelders, all of whom established churches in eighteenth-century America. They held that God as a spirit must be worshiped in spirit, and from this they deduced that all religious images, all church music, all the glories of the medieval cathedral obstructed rather than aided worship. They, like Zwingli, sought something closer to the primitive church of the early Christians than Luther's conception.

These new sects diverged over details but agreed on a central doctrine that earned them the opprobrious label Anabaptists or rebaptizers. They held with Luther that faith, not works, determines a man's holiness and that the sacrament of baptism is a sign of God's grace reserved for those who had faith. But they argued—as Luther, anxious for his church to embrace the whole community, had not dared to—that infants were incapable of being truly baptized. A child cannot know God through a religious experience and thus can have no faith.

The implications buried within this seemingly innocuous doctrine caused Anabaptism to be despised everywhere. If only adults and only those adults who had faith could be baptized, then the church must include something less than the whole community. It would consist only of the devout, those whose faith in God was founded on a deep religious experience. From this proceeded a belief intolerable to the sixteenth century: the separation of church and state. The state was created to restrain sinners; it concerns itself with the entire community. The church harbors only the saved, and to maintain its purity must remain apart from the state.

The Anabaptists' desire to return to the primitive church of true believers led them to interpret the Bible literally. They refused to take oaths, for Christ had said "swear not at all." They were equalitarians, and their plain clothes, their refusal to accept all forms of social respect were their way of practicing the Christian concept that all men were created equal in the sight of God. Their desire to avoid the evils of the world made them more monastic than monks. They were pacifists. They refused to hold any civil office, for this associated them with the sins of the state. Their beliefs, in short, entailed the dissolution of society as the sixteenth century knew it.

The Anabaptists obviously were not an easy people to endure. Luther, belatedly horrified that his religious views had been used to foment social revolution, sought to redefine his position. The individualism of Lutheran-

Map 7. Religions in Europe About 1560

Religions were mixed at many places, and proportions changed rapidly

† Roman Catholics   c Calvinists   н Huguenots   z Zwinglists
A Anglicans   Anabaptists, Mennonites, Amish
L Lutherans   M Moravians   ‡ Eastern Rites

Raisz

ism was internal, purely spiritual, and concerned only with man's relation to God. In affairs of this world, he said, the good Christian must obey established authority. The church would support the state in secular matters, expecting in return full backing from the state on things spiritual.

Luther died in 1546. The religious wars then sweeping Europe continued for nearly a decade more. The Peace of Augsburg (1555) settled the boundaries of Lutheranism on the principle of *cuius regio eius religio,* "whose the region, his the religion." Princes determined the religion of their people, and religious freedom existed no more than it had in the medieval world. The church still embraced the community, church and state worked together as always, and nowhere were Anabaptists welcomed. Lutheranism's antipathy to Anabaptism indirectly shaped American development. For the Anabaptists persisted. They survived in Holland, Switzerland, and in the Rhineland states of Germany. When the Quakers, who shared many of their beliefs, opened Pennsylvania in the 1680's as an asylum to the oppressed, they would emigrate there in droves.

Calvinism

It is appropriate, someone has remarked, that a President of the United States, a dour one at that, was named Calvin Coolidge, for Calvinism in one form or another supplied the theology and shaped the attitudes of a majority of the people who came to America in the colonial period.

John Calvin was born in 1509, nearly a generation after Luther. This French lawyer with a cool, precise mind became embroiled in the religious controversies of the day only after the lines had been drawn between Catholics and Protestants. His *Institutes of the Christian Religion,* published in 1536, sharpened the division by stating with clarity and force much that Luther had put vaguely. Both men agreed on essentials that Luther had first enunciated—justification by faith, man's corrupt nature, close ties between church and state, a church founded on the Scriptures—and neither tolerated any divergence from these essentials. Calvin, however, tended to emphasize points Luther touched lightly, and in so doing he transformed Protestantism into something distinctly different.

Luther was preoccupied with salvation, a problem Calvin paid little attention to, except to agree that it was achieved by faith alone. Calvin believed that the chief end of man was not to save himself but to glorify and honor God. No one knows nor can know what God requires for salvation; His ideas of right and wrong are not necessarily man's. Therefore, said Calvin, cease worrying about salvation and work only to glorify Him. Calvin's emphasis tended to free men from concern about their chances in the afterworld and let them devote their energies to earthly tasks that would add to the glory of God. It also dignified, indeed, gave a *religious* dignity, to all men's work. A man who fulfilled the obligations of his "calling," regardless of how menial it was, pleased God and added to His glory.

Calvin's downgrading of the question of salvation allowed him to face the issue of predestination. Now that a man's fate mattered less than his obligation to glorify God, he could endure knowledge of his ultimate end. Luther had accepted the idea of predestination but had wondered how to tell the elect from the damned. Calvin proposed three tests: profession of faith, an upright life, and participation in the sacraments. The person who passed these trials became one of the "elect," a "saint." (Calvin ignored personal experience or revelation as a sign of election; this would enter later as a part of Puritan belief.) The tests were so modest that nearly any devout man could feel fairly certain the road to heaven lay clear to him.

Having found a way of sifting the tares from the wheat, Calvin proposed to build his church around the saints. Both Calvin and the Anabaptists equated their church with the elect of the community, with the kingdom of God on earth. But where the Anabaptists were exclusive, Calvin maintained the medieval tradition of an inclusive, community-wide church by making sure the elect and the community were one and the same, that only those who qualified for his church lived within the community. He had all the intolerance of the medieval church for competing creeds.

Calvin's view of the role of the state assured a community of saints. Unlike the Anabaptists, his elect would not cut themselves off from the world. They must participate in daily affairs; they must, in fact, control the state. Calvin believed with Luther that church and state operated in separate spheres, each with its own work cut out for it; but he insisted that each had the same end—to glorify God—and each must help the other impose a righteous life on the community. Calvin tested his ideas in Geneva, making it a city of saints—all heretics were banished—where magistrates and ministers alike served the holy commonwealth. Calvin and his followers, like leaders within the medieval church, refused to venerate the state. They sought to impose the moral restraints of religious life on public life. The new monarchs found little that appealed to them in Calvinism.

Calvin retained so much of the medieval tradition—an inclusive church that maintained religious unity within the community and allied itself with and morally controlled the state—that his breaks with the past come as a surprise. He extended Luther's concept of a priesthood of all believers to its logical end by rejecting the medieval idea that authority flowed from God downward through a hierarchy of kings and nobles, popes and bishops. Authority, he said, rose upward from the people. (He was, of course, too much a man of his times to condone democracy. His "people" were the saints, the aristocrats of the community. But because all in this holy community were saints, a democratic element appears in Calvinistic thinking.) The church was governed by presbyteries, that is, bodies composed of ministers and laymen elected by the congregations. Lay control entered religious affairs for the first time.

Word of Calvin's experiment in Geneva brought men from all Europe to see the holy commonwealth in action. Calvinism soon spread, into Germany, Poland, Hungary, and Bohemia, always without the help of the state and usually in the face of official resistance. (Calvin wrote in Latin, the language of all Europe, which helped to speed the dispersion of his ideas; Luther had written in German for Germans.) The Huguenots in France were Calvinist, as were the Dutch Reformed in Holland. John Knox carried Calvinism to Scotland in the 1550's, where it eventually became the established, that is, state-supported, religion—Presbyterianism. About the same time, it penetrated England, where the government was then trying to work out its own accommodation to the religious turmoil of the day.

The Church of England

The Reformation seeped slowly into England. Luther's ideas drifted across the Channel only to meet a blunt denunciation in *Defense of the Seven Sacraments,* written by none other than Henry VIII. Pope Clement VII in gratitude gave Henry the title of "Defender of the Faith"; the gratitude, it turned out, had limits. Henry wanted to remarry, hoping that a new, young wife would provide the male heir he yearned for. In 1527 he asked the pope to void his marriage to Catherine of Aragon. Catherine's blood ties to Charles V, who had shortly before sacked and occupied Rome, forced the pope to temporize, then finally to reject the request. Henry thereafter snapped the link with Rome. But he broke with Rome, not with Catholicism. He coerced the clergy into recognizing him as head of the English Church, seized the monasteries, and introduced the English Bible into church services. He did not abolish the episcopal hierarchy, however, or in any way change Catholic doctrine. He remained in essence defender of the faith.

It proved hard for Henry to hold this position as Lutheran and Calvinistic doctrines spread through England. Schism veered toward heresy after 1547, when Henry died and was succeeded by his young son Edward VI. England for the next five years swung between Lutheranism and Calvinism, with overtones of both appearing in the two editions of prayer books issued during the period. Indecision ended briefly under Catholic Mary I. Some three hundred dissenters were burned at the stake, and hundreds of others left the country. The Marian Exiles, as they were called, absorbed Continental Protestantism in Geneva and in the Rhineland states during Mary's five-year reign. They returned to England with the accession of Elizabeth I in 1558, bringing with them ideas and practices picked up on the Continent and expecting their program for reform to be welcomed by the new young queen and her advisers.

Elizabeth, the consummate politician, knew that the drastic reform desired by the so-called Puritans would increase rather than alleviate tension within England. Elizabeth's settlement of the religious problem blended Continental reforms with the English experience to produce a mild and eclectic Protestantism that took ideas from Luther, Zwingli, and also Calvin. The Church of England resembled that of the Lutherans in that it was a state church; its doctrines determined and its leaders selected by the crown. It embraced the whole community. Much from the past— the episcopal hierarchy, holy days, vestments for the clergy, choral music, stained-glass windows—was retained. The church kept its episcopal courts, which controlled marriages and wills; the tithes continued to come to it; and the old parish structure remained. The Thirty-Nine Articles of 1571, drawn up by the bishops and approved by the queen, gave the church a creed "marked by moderation and studied ambiguity" but definitely Protestant and broad enough to satisfy all but the most scrupulous. They reduced the sacraments to two (baptism and the Lord's Supper), denied transubstantiation, recognized predestination as "full of sweet, pleasant, and unspeakable comfort to godly persons," allowed communion to the congregation, replaced Latin with English in the liturgy, prohibited the cult of saints, and permitted the clergy to marry. "The Queen did fish for men's souls," it was said, "and had so sweet a bait that no one could escape her network."

But many ignored the queen's bait and escaped her network. Elizabeth for a long while tolerated those who insisted the church had not been sufficiently purified of the taint of Rome, hoping that when the old generation died out uniformity would come. She failed to listen when they found the prayer book "culled and picked out of that popish dunghill, the mass-book, full of abominations," or when they referred to an Anglican minister as "a common gamester and pot-companion" and said of another he "cometh very seldom to his church, and is a whore-master."

Eventually the noise grew too loud to ignore. The Puritans and their "fruitless jars and janglings" resounded over England. In 1585 the Puritans sought to take control of Parliament, hoping from this vantage point to force their will on the queen. She crushed them as a political force, but when she died in 1603 Puritanism still flourished mightily in England. The accession of James I, a Stuart who had been reared in Presbyterian Scotland, raised hope among Puritans that the "winter of their discontent" had ended. In January 1604 James scheduled a debate between Anglican and Puritan ministers at Hampton Court, and the dissenters were certain their views would prevail. Little debating occurred at the meeting. James dominated it and by his own judgment "peppered the Puritans soundly." At the end of the second day of discussion the king rose from his chair and said of the Puritans: "I shall make them conform themselves, or I will harry them out of this land, or else do worse." The promise made that day was a promise James I kept.

Puritanism

Puritanism was a way of life that has since vanished. It was an historical movement that emerged in Elizabeth I's reign, reached a peak between 1640 and 1660, then began to disintegrate, until by the end of the seventeenth century it had dissolved into other movements.

Puritans were Elizabethan Englishmen who, strange as it seems, lived with gusto and joined fully in the spirit of their great age. They loved England and had no desire to abandon English allegiance. They shared the accepted belief that the state must help the church maintain a Christian society, that government had every right to interfere in men's social and economic affairs, that one church alone should serve the community, and that society should be ordered along hierarchical lines. Neither Puritans nor Anglicans argued for separation of church and state, for religious tolerance, or for the unfettered individual who traveled through life disregarding the welfare of society as a whole. Puritans acknowledged no great doctrinal differences with their Anglican brethren, believing that they differed only over matters of form and discipline. They held a warm hate for Catholic Spain and France. They saw salvation mainly as a matter between the individual and God.

Puritanism resists easy definition. It lacked a single leader to impress form and order on the movement, and, above all, it significantly changed in time. The early Puritans held moderate views compared to those who would follow. They, like the Anglicans, believed that the church should embrace the whole community, that attendance should be enforced by the state, and that church and state should be bound together. They agreed with Bishop Hall that it was "better to swallow a ceremony than to rend a church" and asked only to replace the Episcopal organization with the Presbyterian model. They wanted all church affairs to be coordinated and settled by lay-clerical groups.

Two major variations arose out of this early moderate brand of what might be called Presbyterian Puritanism. From the seed of one variation, Nonseparating Congregationalism, flowered American Puritanism. The Nonseparatists thought of the church as "a city, compact within itself, without subordination under or dependence upon any other but Jesus Christ." They rejected any form of control that came from outside the congregation. They demanded a free hand in spiritual affairs but at the same time expected the state to impose orthodoxy on the community and to see to it that the "unchurched" tithed, attended service, and were otherwise kept in order. Exactly who should be cast among the unchurched proved a nettlesome question. The Nonseparatists seem to have settled the issue, at least for the early decades of the seventeenth century, by expelling only the "visibly wicked" from the church.

The Nonseparating Congregationalists wished to work their reforms from within the Church of England. A minority of extreme Puritans called Separatists considered the church hopelessly corrupt and held they must sever all ties with it if they hoped to be saved. They also held that only the elect, God's visible saints, whom He had predestined for heaven, could be members of the church. Separatist congregations numbered few in England, and their radicalism made them among the first to be harried from the land.

Separatists and Nonseparatists alike agreed that Anglicanism only re-created the Catholic Church within an English pattern. Both sought to restore the primitive apostolic church "pure and unspotted" and held that all taints of popery must go. They agreed, too, that the pure church must be constructed on a scriptural basis. "All ecclesiastical actions invented and devised by man," they said, "are utterly to be excluded out of the exercise of religion." Nonseparatists in time accepted the idea of an exclusive church composed only of saints, and they, with the Separatists, came eventually to insist that "we must have Christ as it were born in us" to qualify as one of the elect. This rebirth was no casual affair. When God's spirit rushed in, it often left a man "bruised" or "smoking," and it always left him unsettled.

This regenerating experience, which by the mid-1630's had become central to American Puritanism particularly, contributed to the Puritan's zeal for reform. Once God had revealed truth to him he must make war against sin wherever he found it. Reform, like conversion, began with the individual, which helps explain the Puritan's steady and often indiscreet interest in his neighbor's affairs. Since to the seventeenth century no man was an island cut off from the community, the Puritan reformer was impelled to remake all society. Puritanism thereby became far more than a religious movement; it was a way of life that had vast social and political implications.

The Puritan's spiritual rebirth conditioned his way of life and so, too, did the covenant theology. It held that those who had been regenerated had in effect covenanted with God, much as God had covenanted with Adam and later with Abraham. ("And when Abram was ninety years old and nine, the Lord appeared and said unto him, 'I am the Almighty God; walk before me, and be thou perfect. And I will make my covenant between me and thee, and will multiply thee exceedingly.' ") The Puritans did not conceive of the covenant as a contract. No *quid pro quo* was involved. They believed that man wrings nothing from God. God plants His spirit in a man for reasons known only to Himself, not because the individual has fulfilled some sort of bargain.

The covenant had been of peripheral importance to Calvin. The Puritans here turned to the Rhineland reformers, such as Zwingli, whose use of the covenant had created a God of less awesome wrath than Calvin's. A God who offered such an agreement became understandable in human terms. But the Puritans took care not to make God too soft and reasonable. "You must not think to go to heaven on a feather-bed," one warned; "if you will be Christ's disciple, you must take up His cross, and it will make you sweat."

By 1603 the doctrines and geographical boundaries of Protestantism had been formed. The stability and unity of medieval Christendom had crumbled into a variety of religious sects, and yet within those sects prevailed a unity that in time would help hold together thirteen diverse American colonies. All Protestants rejected papal authority, the use of Latin for their services, the sacerdotal character of priests, and the virtues of monastic life. The creeds of all reduced the sacraments to two, at most three; denied transubstantiation, purgatory, and the cult of saints; omitted obligatory confession; and accepted the authority only of the Bible.

The effect of the Reformation on traditions that developed in colonial America resists easy generalization. Characteristics long associated with America—religious liberty, democracy, separation of church and state, individualism—were not direct results of the Reformation. The American belief that the state is more than a power bloc, that it must always be checked by morality, may owe something to Calvinism, but Calvin did not introduce this idea so much as revive and reinvigorate a heritage from the medieval era.

Scholars have debated for more than a half century the influence of Protestantism on capitalism. It has been held that Calvin's emphasis on a man's calling made the working class content in its misery and cleansed the aggressive capitalist of guilt feelings as he pursued riches. Protestantism did exalt work; it did appeal to the rising middle class in all countries.

But long before Luther nailed his theses to the church door, the spirit of capitalism was undermining the medieval world. Possibly Protestantism helped to promote the capitalistic impulse in Europe and America by casting a mantle of righteousness over it, and certainly Calvinistic disapproval of men's enjoying the fruits of their gains helped to inhibit conspicuous consumption in America for a long while.

Protestantism reveals its greatest influence on American traditions in the area of domestic life. Luther exalted marriage when he abolished monasticism and clerical celibacy. He took the focus off the cathedral and centered life in the home. Here the family prayed and worked together; here children's characters were shaped, with the father serving as both priest and magistrate. Calvin, in turn, introduced the idea that marriage is, as one scholar puts it, "a partnership based on a common faith and a common commitment." This ban on mixed marriages raised one more barrier against Catholicism. The partnership could be dissolved by divorce if the faith of one lapsed or became other than that of his partner.

Only when it is remembered that the Reformation was, above all, a revival of religion, does its most pervasive and enduring influence become obvious. The discovery of America sprang from explorations carried on during the Renaissance; the settlement of America occurred after the Reformation and when, especially in England, religious fervor waxed strong. The medieval world and the Renaissance both gave much to English America, but the Reformation gave more. Protestantism, regardless of the brand, permeated the social, political, and economic ideas of virtually every man who came from England to the colonies. The United States would have been a nation quite different but for the religious upheaval begun by a man called Luther.

ENGLAND ON THE EVE OF COLONIZATION

When Elizabeth I came to the throne, England was an outpost on the edge of Europe, powerful enough to be considered in the decisions of Continental monarchs but little to be feared. Elizabeth's long rule changed that, and much of the change, as much as can be attributed to an individual, was due to the queen. "She is a great woman; and were she only Catholic she would be without her match," Pope Sixtus V had said. "Just look how well she governs; she is only a woman, only mistress of half an island, and yet she makes herself feared by Spain, by France, by the Emperor, by all." This "great land-lady of England," as Thomas Dekker called her, was summoned in early 1603 "to appear in the star-chamber of heaven." She had nurtured her nation's strength well and left behind an England ready at last to embark on a full-scale attempt to colonize the New World.

The People

Some seven million people lived in the British Isles around the turn of the century. They spoke twelve languages, and their customs and interests varied as much as the landscape that lay within the realm's seven thousand miles of seacoast. For centuries men had grubbed an existence from the soil and earned for their toil a crude, hard life barely touched by the amenities of civilization. Vast changes occurred in Elizabeth's reign. The shacks and mud huts of old made way for brick and stone cottages, lighted by glass windows; crockery replaced the wooden trencher; the bench gave way to chairs; the ladder, to stairs; and knives and forks, once luxuries, became standard dining equipment. These only hinted at deeper changes that had swept through England, changes exemplified as well as led by London.

London, a city of a quarter of a million people at the start of the seventeenth century, ten times the size of any other English city, dominated all sides of the nation's life. Here centered the government whose arm by the time of Elizabeth's death reached into every town, village, and lonely farmhouse. London printing presses served the kingdom and shaped its intellectual life. London merchants financed iron mines in the hinterlands, colonial ventures in Ireland; they drew coal from Newcastle and sent back manufactured goods. Furs from Russia, silks from China, spices from the East Indies, tobacco from the West Indies—all were displayed in London shops.

London was the nation's largest seaport, handling seven-eighths of the seaborne trade. A visitor judged that on a typical day some twenty thousand boats, varying from heavy barges and scuttling river ferries to the towering floating fortresses of the East India Company, crowned the Thames. The shroud of smoke that hung overhead reminded visitors that London was also a city of industry. Coal had now replaced wood as fuel; it fired glass furnaces and brick kilns, ran breweries, soap factories, and sugar refineries, and made London Europe's leading industrial city.

London was bigger, noisier, dirtier, richer, and busier than any spot in England. It set the tone and shaped the direction of English society. But London was not England. There were the towns—Gloucester, a center of the wool trade; Bristol and Plymouth, which sent fishing fleets to the New World; York, England's second capital, with an archbishop of its own and the seat of the king's government for the north—each with its own character and customs. And there were the villages, still largely self-contained, where men spent their lives rarely wandering beyond sight of the church spire. All the changes London had worked on the kingdom had disturbed but not destroyed the order of English society as it had existed since medieval days.

English society still remained hierarchic. "God Almighty in His most holy and wise providence," said John Winthrop, "hath so disposed of the condition of mankind as in all times some must be rich, some poor; some high and eminent in power and dignity, others mean and in subjection." Society, as well as the universe, was structured in a "great chain of being," created by God and not to be altered by man.

All society deferred first to the king then to the nobility. The nobility's former monopoly on power had waned by the seventeenth century, partly because money now carried more weight than prestige. A peer remarked in 1628 that the House of Commons, home of the gentry, could buy the House of Lords three times over. A noble now found maintaining a town and country house and the two hundred servants necessary to his position a difficult feat in an inflationary age. He fumed when the Stuarts debased the class by opening it up to those willing and able to pay a stiff entrance fee, but he quickly sensed that the newcomers' wealth actually strengthened the whole of nobility. He married off his children to the newcomers, took their advice on sound investments, and whatever else they had to give that might ease his economic distress.

The nobles led society, it has been said, and the gentry led the nation. Gentlemen, according to a cynic of the day, are "all those who can live idly, and without manual labor, and will bear up the port, charge and countenance of a gentleman." By custom the clergy, university students, lawyers, and army commanders could sign themselves "gent.," but generally land and gentility went together. And the gentry ran the countryside. In a time when England lacked a police force and a standing army, they alone were allowed the right to bear arms. They were, in Sir Walter Raleigh's words, literally "the garrisons of good order throughout the realm." The bulk of the House of Commons and the majority of the nation's justices of the peace came from this class.

Few gentlemen came to America—John Winthrop was an exception—but many of their younger sons, deprived of an inheritance by the rules of primogeniture and entail (by which all land went in bulk to the eldest son), uninterested in a career in the army or clergy, or too unlucky to catch a rich girl for a wife, did come, bringing the traditions of the gentry with them. The country squire of England became the squire of New England; the manor of England became the plantation of the South. The strong sense of public duty that marked the elite of eighteenth-century America stemmed from the English gentry. Perhaps even the belief that a gentleman should be able to "bear up the port" is rooted in the gentry's traditions.

The more prosperous farmers who had not quite managed to become gentlemen were called yeomen. They usually owned their land outright;

they could vote, and though they invariably chose gentlemen to fill the more important positions, they occasionally found themselves elected to minor posts. They farmed for money and prospered, but they were often more than farmers. The less prosperous pieced out their incomes as weavers, tanners, blacksmiths, carpenters, and painters. The American jack-of-all-trades might trace himself back to the yeoman.

Below the yeomen spread the great mass of "laboring poor"—the "day-laborers, poor husbandmen, and some retailers (which have no free land), copyholders, and all artificers, as tailors, shoemakers, carpenters, brickmakers, masons, etc."—who, William Harrison continues, "have neither voice nor authority in the commonwealth but are to be ruled and not to rule others." The poor of England lacked all rights. They were conscripted to work in mines, whisked off to Ireland or America regardless of their wishes, whipped and jailed simply for being unemployed. Their wages were fixed low by law and made lower still by the steady rise of prices, which reduced their purchasing power by two-thirds. The prosperity that swept through England affected them only adversely.

A duplicate of this social hierarchy existed within the Anglican Church, beginning with the curate or vicar at the bottom, moving upward through the clergy, bishop, to the archbishop. The English clergyman was not supported by his congregation but appointed to a "living," a church with an income attached to it. He could not be removed from his church except for grave cause, but he could be promoted to a better living. His income in the early seventeenth century came from various sources. Glebe lands—lands attached to the church—could be leased or worked by the clergyman himself. Tithes, or tenths, might come in from the farmers in the form of food or from villagers in the form of money. All this together produced a slim income for a minister, which helps to explain why the church failed through the seventeenth century to attract a talented clergy. The church admitted privately in 1603 that nearly 60 per cent of its benefices were held by incompetent persons, a fact that did much to strengthen the Puritan movement.

The social hierarchy remained clearly defined in the early seventeenth century, but the barriers between classes were not insurmountable. A talented lad like Adam Winthrop, grandfather of John, could travel up to London, progress from lowly clothier to rich merchant, then return to the country and buy his way into the gentry. But the movement up—and down—the social ladder did not erase differences between the classes. A bow, a curtsey, the removal of the hat kept distinctions alive; servants were addressed as "thee," gentlemen as "you." A gentleman's coach made way for a nobleman's; a yeoman played at ninepins but only a gentleman at bowls.

Regardless of a man's class, the core of his life was the family, a word that in the seventeenth century included all who lived beneath one roof, whether blood relation or not. The male head of the family ruled absolutely in law, relatively in fact. English women enjoyed more freedom than their Continental counterparts: no laws prevented them marrying whom they wished, and tradition argued that the wife should share in all major decisions. "If the pilot would both hold the stern, and hoist up the sail, and be upon the hatches, and labor at the pump, and do all himself, it must needs go ill with the ship," went a Puritan injunction, which applied equally well to all English husbands.

A child learned manners and morals at home. He was reared to be superstitious. He believed fervently in witches, put little faith in physicians and much in the remedies and tales of the village's old wives. He was taught, usually by his mother, to read. If he seemed slow or little interested in books, he was apprenticed out when he reached puberty. This meant only trading one family for another. A bonded servant became part of the family of the master, whose role was legally that of a father; he was responsible for the apprentice's spiritual, moral, and physical well-being. A bright lad was allowed to continue his education in the village grammar school, a private institution often endowed by a former local citizen who had made his fortune in London. The boy studied Latin and Greek—both practical subjects in that day, necessary for anyone who wished to become a doctor, lawyer, or minister—and if he did well, he might go on to Oxford or Cambridge.

Only a thin line existed between family and community. Both assumed responsibility for and kept a watchful eye on a child's deportment. A youth in his teens had English habits and traditions so well fixed in his mind and had been so thoroughly taught to cherish them that it would take several generations in America to wash them away.

The seventeenth-century child, whether of a Puritan or Anglican family, matured in a world that centered on religion. The Old Testament received particular emphasis. An Italian visitor was stunned to find that Englishmen of all creeds gave "their sons Hebrew names and called their daughters after the virtues and have quite abandoned those in use among Christians." The visitor might have been equally astonished to learn how Old Testament judgments on the family were used to justify the Stuart view of government. James I emphasized in a manual on the duties of a king that the relationship between monarch and people was that of an Old Testament patriarch to his children. A king's authority, said James, was founded, like that of a father, on God's unalterable decrees. No misconduct on the part of the father frees the offspring from obedience to the fifth commandment and no misgovernment on the part of a king can release his subjects from their allegiance. So said James I, and few in the early seventeenth century took issue with him.

The Government

A glance at England at the beginning and America at the end of the seventeenth century suggests to the unwary that the New World alone worked the multitude of changes that eventually produced the American culture. It should be remembered, however, that at the turn of the century English culture was by no means fixed. Government, for instance, was undergoing changes that touched all sides of an Englishman's life just when American settlement was getting underway. The changes continued through the seventeenth century, and many of them were passed in time across the water.

The king at the turn of the century reigned in theory absolutely. He ordered the coming and going of Parliament, commissioned all officials, exercised all justice, issued all charters, and protected all rights. He ruled by "divine right" and was considered "above the law by his absolute power." But theory and fact failed to jibe by the time James I came to the throne. The problem centered on money. The king was expected to "live of his own," paying for his private as well as the nation's need out of income from crown lands, feudal dues, and custom duties, turning to the nation for money only in emergencies. In an inflationary age when administrative costs doubled and every war created a financial catastrophe, even thrifty Elizabeth had failed to manage on her "allowance." The situation worsened with James I. His income from crown lands dropped 25 per cent during the first two decades of his reign. The crown obviously needed some form of regular taxation if it were to maintain its power, but the gentlemen of Commons, though prosperous and ridiculously under-taxed, refused to grant it, aware that to do so would deprive them of their single weapon against the crown. The king devised stopgap remedies. Customs duties were raised, monopolies were dispensed for a price to merchants, the rank of baronet was created in order to sell it. These only sufficed to delay rather than settle the issue with Parliament, only to increase rather than alleviate the tension between gentry and crown.

The king's fight to preserve his power was abetted by the Privy Council, an advisory body responsible only to the crown. By Charles I's time it numbered some forty members. It met almost daily, and the problems it took up touched the life of all England. Both Elizabeth I and James I used it to oversee the colonization of Ireland, a precedent that led to its eventual involvement in American affairs. It advised the king on foreign affairs, on trading-company charters, on the quality of a candidate for a justice of the peaceship in a remote county. It worried about the amount of bullion

in the country, the timber available for ships, the low freight-rates of
Dutch shippers. It could and did limit the number of alehouses in a town,
the quality of meat sold, the strength of beer. It maneuvered the king's
legislation through Parliament. It worked always to promote the welfare
of the nation in light of what the king judged that welfare to be.

The House of Commons often saw that welfare in another light.
(Parliament's upper chamber, the House of Lords, was made up of great
churchmen and opulent lay-magnates, few of whom had any serious
quarrel with the crown.) Commons was composed of two knights or
gentlemen from each county, one or two burgesses from each of nearly
three hundred boroughs. (By Elizabeth I's time, boroughs commonly went
outside town limits to find able gentlemen to represent their interests.)
There was no attempt to make Commons' system of representation equal
or democratic. Members from the counties were elected by those who held
a "forty-shilling freehold," that is, those who owned or rented land for that
amount, a large sum in those days. Voting qualifications in the towns were
equally restrictive. Commons represented only the propertied classes; and
when members spoke of "rights," they meant only the rights of propertied
people.

The great migration to America spanned those years of the early
seventeenth century when the House of Commons sought to impose its
will on the king. Commons had previously won many privileges, among
them freedom of elections, freedom from arrest during sessions, freedom
of speech during debate, and freedom from libel for anything said on the
floor of Parliament. But the crown still managed to manipulate debate
through the Privy Councillors, the king's agents on the floor, and through
the speaker, a royal appointee. Commons retaliated by developing the use
of committees, which allowed decisions to be shaped informally off the
floor, and by inventing the device of the "committee of the whole House,"
whereby Commons resolved itself into an informal committee that permitted it to replace the king's speaker with one of its own choosing. By
1642 Commons had sufficiently "won the initiative" that when Charles
I called to arrest five members the speaker refused to act "but as the House
is pleased to direct me, whose servant I am." Those who came to America
carried with them the memory of Commons' battle against the king, the
outcome of which left an enduring imprint on the development of colonial
legislatures during the seventeenth century.

The real source of the English government's strength lay with neither
king nor Commons, but in the shire, or county. In times past, the key
official therein had been the sheriff, or *schir-reeve,* as Chaucer called him.
The king had appointed him, and he served to link the central government with local affairs. He watched over the crown's private domains,
transmitted the king's proclamations to the people, and called the county

court into monthly session. Gentlemen accepted the post as a duty, but reluctantly: it involved great expense—the sheriff had to entertain all royal visitors to the county—and great risk, for all royal debts in his jurisdiction were his to collect and his to pay if they went uncollected. By Elizabeth I's day, the sheriff's authority had waned; the focus of power had shifted to the justice of the peace.

The justice of the peace, also a royal appointee, invariably came from the gentry, for "no poor man ought to be in authority," said a gentleman of the day, adding that the poor man "will so bribe you and extort you that the sweet scent of riches and gain taketh away and confoundeth the true taste of justice and equity." The office could be an exasperating burden but was one few gentlemen refused. It was an honor to receive and also a training ground and stepping stone for those eager to serve in Parliament.

A justice carried heavy administrative duties. He fixed wages, licensed alehouses and checked that they observed hours, apprenticed boys to trades, saw to the care of the poor and infirm, disciplined the obstreperous, inspected roads and bridges, and punished infractions of the Poor Law. He kept the king's ministers informed and served as the main administrative link between London and the local scene. All aspects of county life intrigued the central government, and most of the queries and orders that came down from above arrived on the justice's desk.

The justice, too, served as a key link in the nation's legal system. Since he was rarely versed in law, he guided himself through the legal jungle by common sense and whatever he could pick up from any of several "how-to" books available in the bookstalls. For the most part he alone dispensed justice in his village. In serious cases he let the accused stand free on bail—jails were few, and men could not be kept long from their land—until he met with colleagues from other parts of the county in Quarter Sessions Court, which could try all crimes except treason and offenses by servants of the crown. Decisions could be appealed in the common-law courts of the realm—King's Bench, which handled cases between the crown and subjects; Court of Common Pleas, which dealt with actions between subject and subject. The English of the day were a litigious people; they warmed to a good trial. ("Every ploughman with us . . . can talk of essoins, vouchers, withernams, and recaptions," said a lawyer in 1602.) They held a low opinion of the law, calling it the "babblative art"; they knew that judges could be bribed, that decisions tended to favor gentlemen, and that only the "meaner sort" received physical punishment. They also knew that for all this the legal system worked. Hearings were open, which helped to minimize flagrant unfairness; juries were only occasionally pressured into outright dishonest decisions.

The crown's legal and administrative system for the kingdom focused on the county. Government for the average Englishman centered on the village. The justice of the peace was a village squire, who tempered his decisions to people he knew well. The man who executed the justice's orders, the constable—or petty constable as he was often called to distinguish him from the sheriff, or high constable, a county official—was usually a neighboring yeoman, born and reared in the village and well acquainted with its idiosyncrasies. The constable apprehended thieves, chased vagrants, collected fines, and in general served as the village police force. He worked closely with the churchwarden, who, though he bore an ecclesiastical title and was chosen by an exclusive group within the church that eventually came to be known as the vestry, concerned himself principally with village affairs. The break with Rome had deposited much of the property and many of the duties of the monasteries in the lap of the local parish, which, in effect, meant the village, for they were one and the same. The warden, collaborating with the justice of the peace and the constable, supervised the care of the poor, the infirm, and the aged and the rearing of an illegitimate child; he rented church property and gathered tithes, both duties leading in some instances to the job of tax collecting.

The English government's authority filtered out and down from London, and its strength pushed upward from the village. It was a vigorous government, accustomed to interfering in all sides of men's lives. It was inefficient, thick with inept and corrupt officials, and gave justice only to those with a stake in society. The elite of the countryside ran it, but with their roots deep in village life they invariably responded to community pressures. What was said in 1602 of English laws could be applied to English government: it was "rather popular than peremptory, rather accepted than exacted." The king in theory remained absolute, but in fact his success rested on the consent of the governed, the governed in this case meaning only those with property.

The Economy

Between the time Gilbert conceived a colony and Jamestown was settled, England acquired the power and techniques to invade the New World in force. To work the change required an economic upheaval that involved the collapse of a once stable price structure, a revolution in agriculture and industry, the rise to power of the merchant, and the creation of a new economic attitude on the part of government and business alike.

The first of these forces to hit England took the form of inflation. The flood of goods first from the East, then from the New World shoved prices up slowly. They spurted ahead in the mid-sixteenth century when Spain uncovered a rich deposit of silver in Peru and about the same time perfected techniques for extracting silver from the ore. A half million pounds of silver and over ten thousand pounds of gold flowed annually into Europe, depressing the value of bullion and skyrocketing the cost of goods. By 1650 prices had risen some 250 per cent over the past century and a half, while the workingman's "real" wages dropped nearly 50 per cent. The merchant gained most. His wealth was in goods whose cash value constantly rose while the labor costs to produce the goods steadily dropped. "Never in the annals of the modern world," Lord Keynes once remarked, "has there existed so prolonged and so rich an opportunity for the businessman, the speculator, and the profiteer."

The crown, accustomed to a fixed income, suffered with the wage earner. Elizabeth adopted a variety of expedients to dodge bankruptcy. She devalued the currency, raised customs duties, demanded and got stiff cash payment for town charters; but ultimately she was forced to ask Parliament for new taxes, which were granted only after she had made concessions. The Stuarts, of course, fared even worse. Parliament's eventual triumph over royal absolutism owed much to the price revolution.

Inflation forced changes on the English countryside. The peasant, his dues fixed by custom, gained at first. He got more for his crops, yet owed the same rent to the landlord. The lords recouped somewhat when Henry VIII dispersed the great monastery lands and still more when they broke through the old feudal restraints, combined the peasants' strip holdings into great, enclosed fields, and pastured them with sheep. The gentleman as sheep owner became more of a merchant than a farmer. The evicted tenant joined an army of vagabonds roaming England in search of work. "Sheep," wrote Sir Thomas More in *Utopia,* "that were wont to be so meek and tame, and so small eaters, now, as I hear say, be become so great devourers, and so wild, that they eat up and swallow down the very men themselves."

An industrial revolution intensified the chaos of English life in these years. "Correct your maps; Newcastle is Peru," John Cleveland said, meaning that coal served England as silver did Spain. Coal production shot from two hundred thousand tons in 1600 to one and a half million tons in 1640, by which time England was mining three times as much as the rest of Europe put together. In a land where timber had all but vanished, coal became "the one principal commodity of this realm." Some three hundred ships were engaged solely in hauling coals from Newcastle to London. The abundance of cheap fuel helped to account for the 500 to 1,000 per cent increase in the production of salt, iron and steel, lead, ships, and glass in the century after the Reformation. Such new industries as cannon founding, sugar refining, and papermaking were all called into being by the availability of coal.

Both Elizabeth and the Stuarts did their best to impose order and direction on the confusion of the times. Their regulatory attitudes, like so much English thought, arose out of the medieval past. The basis of wealth and power, it was held, lay in trade, and the amount of trade in the world was fixed. One acquired trade by usurping a competitor's and protecting against his incursions. Towns erected elaborate barriers to protect their economic activity from outsiders. As the medieval pattern disintegrated, the state adopted protectionist policies that were only those of the towns writ large. Richard II said merchants should export only in British ships. Edward IV sought to prohibit the importation of foreign cloth. Elizabeth I deprived foreign merchants of the right to maintain trade depots inside the realm. She regulated wages and working conditions in part to keep English industry competitive with outsiders, and the Stuarts continued her policies.

The flow of gold and silver from the New World had called for an elaboration of protectionism. A nation prospered to the degree it held a favorable balance of trade, and bullion, a tangible sign of wealth, determined the favorableness of one's trade. "If we send out more commodities in value than we bring home, the overplus cometh in in coin," said a man of the day, who might have added that coin paid for ships and soldiers. Money in the kingdom came to be a yardstick of power, and bullionism blended with protectionism to shape the nation's economic activity.

Out of these two "isms" developed a third—mercantilism. Scholars have grumbled that the word has "become a positive nuisance," one "confused with autarky, with nationalism, with protectionism. . . ." Adam Smith coined the word in the late eighteenth century to describe a clear-cut policy that strove to strengthen the state by a highly regulated, largely self-sufficing economy. He failed to realize that he depicted a policy that had required over a century and a half to evolve. It is wrong to read a conscious mercantilist philosophy back into the reigns of Elizabeth and the early Stuarts. Elizabeth granted monopolies as much to fatten her income as to protect infant industries. The Stuarts concerned themselves with trade only to the degree that it produced them revenue. The Hakluyts argued that colonies would benefit the nation by producing staples imported from elsewhere and taking products England produced, and Captain John Smith saw Virginia as "a nurse for soldiers, a practice for mariners, a trade for merchants"; but the government paid little heed to these mercantilist notions. Mercantilism foisted itself on the crown only after the merchants had quietly pushed themselves into the center of English life.

The techniques merchants first used to handle overseas trading sprang from medieval soil. They adapted the guild system into a "regulated company." Members of the company were controlled from without by a royal charter that bestowed a monopoly in the area where the company operated and from within by a "governor" and "assistants" of their own choosing, who administered guild-like regulations. The length of a man's membership determined the amount of goods he could ship; quality was checked; competition was controlled by specifying the days and hours sales could be made. Members shared company expenses, the company warehouse and offices, and whatever privileges that had been gained from the nation where the company operated. This marked the limit of joint effort. Members did not pool capital or share profits. They traded individually with their own goods and purchased singly with their own money.

As trade lines lengthened from the Baltic to Russia, from the Near East to the Far East, a merchant's costs and risks climbed. To tie up a ship and crew and cargo for a voyage that might last two, three, even four years involved an outlay of cash few men could spare. By the mid-sixteenth century, merchants began to favor the "joint-stock company." (Drake's forays against the Spanish were backed by joint-stock financing. His voyage around the world netted stockholders, among them Queen Elizabeth, between 6,000 and 11,000 per cent return on their investment, depending on the authority read.) Members of a joint-stock company pooled their resources in a common fund. Each member took a certain number of shares, and all buying and selling was handled by company officials. The organization differed from a modern corporation in that each venture or voyage involved a separate investment and the "adventurers," or shareholders, might change with every venture. The joint-stock company operated under a charter essentially like that of the regulated company, with the same privileges and responsibilities.

The greatest of all the joint-stock enterprises was the East India Company, established on the last day of the sixteenth century. The charter gave it the world to trade in. Members had the right to assemble and to make all reasonable laws for their government not in opposition to the laws of England, and they could punish all offenders against these laws. Customs duties were suspended until the company was on its feet. The officers consisted of a governor, deputy governor, and twenty-four assistants—all annually elected by the "general court," or assembly, of company members. All officers took an oath of allegiance to the crown. In the beginning each company venture was a separate investment by the stockholders. In 1609 and 1612 the charter was revised, and thereafter profits and losses from all ventures were pooled. With this revision the transition from the medieval guild to the modern corporation neared completion.

The London Company, which would settle Jamestown, drew heavily on the charter and experience of the East India Company. Membership in the two overlapped considerably, for mainly London merchants financed both. The vigor and intelligence of Sir Thomas Smith, the greatest merchant of his day, dominated both companies. Sir Thomas exemplified the quality and character of mercantile leadership at the turn of the century. He was a devout man, convinced that God had his eye on the destinies of both Smith and England. Profits pleased him, but boldness, confidence, and a strong feeling for England made him willing to take huge immediate losses in the hope of future gains for both nation and company.

Smith had seven years' experience with the East India Company when he faced the problems of settling Jamestown. Much of that experience would ease the London Company's early years in Virginia; much of it would mislead Smith into awkward errors. It took time to learn that Virginia was not India, that once a small piece of territory had been seized and fortified no huge native population would arrive with goods to trade. No precedents in English, Spanish, or Portuguese experience existed to guide Smith. No one dreamed in 1607 that when the London Company embarked on the colonization of Virginia, the first great folk migration in modern history was about to begin.

A GREAT MIGRATION BEGINS

The start of the "great migration," as historians call the early seventeenth-century flood of emigrants to America, has been variously placed at 1630, when the stream of Puritans into Massachusetts Bay began; at 1618, when the Thirty Years' War opened; or at 1609, when the London Company dispatched a "great fleet" of six hundred settlers for Virginia. Regardless of when the great migration started, by 1641 eighty thousand men, women, and children had endured the voyage across the ocean to the West Indies, Bermuda, and the mainland of America. The outbreak of the English civil war cut the flow to a trickle, but the stream never dried up. Nor did the fundamental characteristics of the migration ever change. Those who came, the way they came, and the reasons they came remained essentially the same well into the nineteenth century.

Who Came and Why

To hear the seventeenth century tell it, only the dregs of England came this way—"unruly gallants packed thither by their friends to escape ill destinies." In Massinger's *City Madam*, a play of the day, there is a shocked response when someone suggests that a character's sister-in-law and her daughters be shipped off to America:

Lady Frugal: How! Virginia!
High Heaven forbid! Remember, sir, I beseech you, what creatures are shipped thither.
Anne: Condemned wretches, forfeited to the law.
Mary: Strumpets and bawds, for the abomination of life spewed out of their country.

Many did come against their will—vagrants, orphaned children, paupers, those judged "lewd and dangerous," thieves, and probably a good number of "strumpets and bawds." (Early Virginia's reputation as a land of death led some criminals, according to John Smith, to "choose to be hanged ere they would go thither.") Scots taken at the Battle of Worcester in the English civil war were deported to America in 1651, and two years later a hundred Irish Tories were sent to Virginia. For all that, the bulk of emigrants came voluntarily. They were not the shiftless, lewd, dangerous, or pauperized but, more likely, as Alfred North Whitehead said, the most "vivid people" of seventeenth-century England.

The migration drew on all parts of England and on all classes. The few gentlemen who came usually found life on the edge of a forest too rude and soon returned home, but many of their younger sons, who could expect little in the way of inheritance or preferment at home, came and stayed. They generally arrived with enough money to purchase cleared land and enough prestige to step into positions of power. Few of the laboring poor came. The names of farmers dominate extant lists of emigrants from London and Bristol, followed by artisans—plowrights, carpenters, sawyers, and joiners, some fishermen from western England, an occasional miller or cooper. Most paid their way over. Servants in the early years of the migration generally traveled as members of a family. The number of "indentured" servants increased in time until they comprised at least half the incoming flood. In exchange for passage, a servant, indentured, or bonded, himself for four or five years servitude. His rights were protected by a contract signed before departing England. The indenture system, a variation of the medieval apprenticeship pattern, was viewed in the seventeenth century as a reasonable way of settling the colonies with people who had the will and energy to come but lacked the money.

Why people came to America, aside from those who had no choice, eludes a quick answer. Surely discontent, political discontent in particular, put some Englishmen in the mood to migrate. The Stuarts, in their efforts to keep crown and government solvent, had resorted to forced loans from the gentry that raised complaints on all sides. Martial law, the Star Chamber, and the billeting of troops gave added cause for growling. Charles I dissolved Parliament in 1629 and for eleven years gave the gentry no legal outlet for grievances.

Economic unrest also increased in the early years of the seventeenth century. The Thirty Years' War deprived England of continental markets for her wool cloth, and the ensuing depression in textiles affected the whole country. The number of roving bands of unemployed mounted; towns complained of "the burden of their poor"; and John Winthrop, among others, watched his own income diminish. "This land grows weary of her inhabitants," he said. "Why then should we stand striving here for places of habitation, . . . and in the meantime suffer a whole continent as fruitful and convenient for the use of man to lie waste without any improvement?" Idle men "willing to labor" found no labor, John White noted, adding that skilled artisans such as "shoemakers, tailors, nay masons, carpenters, and the like, . . . live in such a low condition as is little better than beggary."

The country seethed with religious discontent. "God is packing up His gospel because nobody will buy His wares, nor come to His price," the Puritan preacher Thomas Hooker said. Dissatisfaction with the Church of England, especially among Londoners and people in the eastern and southern counties, increased during Charles I's reign when those Anglicans known as Arminians—they emphasized free will and an elaborate ritual— came to dominate the church. Charles I's orthodoxy, coupled with affection for his wife Henrietta, a Catholic, led to a tightening of restrictions against Puritans and an easing of them toward Catholics. "Instead of purging out Popery, a farther compliance was sought," said Edward Johnson, who migrated because, among other things, he found the first Reformation "very imperfect" and without much chance of improvement in England.

Discontent prepared men's minds for adventures they might never have contemplated in quieter times; a flood of propaganda, which first spewed forth as the "great fleet" embarked for Virginia, inspired them. One brand of appeal urged the well-to-do to back colonization in order to rid the nation of jailbirds and the swarming poor. The mayor of London spoke in 1609 of the need "to ease the City and suburbs of a swarm of unnecessary inmates, as a continual cause of dearth and famine, and the very original cause of all the plagues that happen in this kingdom." The London Company told Parliament in 1624 it sought to remove "the surcharge of necessitous people, the matter or fuel of dangerous insurrections, and thereby leaving the greater plenty to sustain those remaining within the land." John Donne's congregation heard that Virginia would "redeem many a wretch from the jaws of death [and] the hands of the executioner, . . . shall sweep your streets, and wash your doors from idle persons and the children of idle persons, and employ them." Colonization, Donne added, "is not only a spleen to drain ill humors from the body, but a liver to breed good blood."

Publicity aimed at the mass of people made different points. Captain Smith eulogized Virginia in *A True Relation* and in a later pamphlet called New England "the paradise of these parts." Englishmen hungered after land, for land in seventeenth-century Europe meant wealth; and Smith, along with every propagandist from Columbus on, made the most of its abundance and richness in the New World. A couplet of 1647 made the point effectively:

> In Virginia land free and labor scarce;
> In England land scarce and labor plenty.

All this still fails to explain why so many endured political oppression, religious restraints, and economic distress; why so few came to America— why so many resisted, and only a relative few succumbed to the propaganda of the day. "Human behavior is conditioned by economic and social factors in the sense that these establish the problems to be solved," Henry Bamford Parkes says, "but it is not determined by them: how particular individuals choose to act in a given situation depends upon deeper, more intangible, and more mysterious forces." The process of emigration, then, was not a mass movement, but one in which each individual made his own private and personal decision.

"Intentions are secret," John White wrote in *Planter's Plea;* "who can discover them?" The end of a love affair apparently sent Caleb Heathcote, a young aristocrat, across the ocean. Another man sought "the pure and full dispensations of the gospel." Roger Williams came, so he said, because "Bishop Laud pursued me out of the land"; Richard Mather, because the New World gave him the chance "to censure those that ought to be censured. . . ." Thomas Shephard's reasons were "mixt": friends were going, and "I did think I should feel many miseries if I stayed behind"; besides, "my dear wife did much long to see me settled there in peace, and so put me on to it." Some came for adventure. "As it happened some ages before to be the fashion to saunter to the Holy Land," William Byrd said, "and go upon other Quixote adventures, so it was now grown the humor to make a trip to America." Many went "for merchandise and gain's sake" or, as Raleigh put it, "To seek new worlds for gold, for praise, for glory." Some sought escape. "The world's in a heap of troubles and confusion," said George Alsop, bound for Maryland, "and while they are in the midst of their changes and amazes, the best way to give them the bag, is to go out of the world and leave them." A distraught character in a Ben Jonson play shouts at one point: "I'll go to Virginia, like some cheating bankrupt, and leave my creditor in the suds." Robert Evelyn departed England in 1661 on "a long and dangerous voyage" to America "to make me to be able to pay my debts and to restore my decayed estate again." Lady Finche's son, on the other hand, had no choice, for this was the boy "whom she sent to Virginia to be tamed."

How They Came and Where They Went

Getting there was not half the fun in the seventeenth century. Departures lacked the gaiety of modern sailings; "breast-breaking sobs" swept the crowds at all leave-takings. Cheerful thoughts came hard when it was known that after "two, three, or four months spent with daily expectation of swallowing waves and cruel pirates, you are to be landed among barbarous Indians, famous for nothing but cruelty, where you are like to spend your days in a famishing condition for a long space."

Of the two main routes to America that of Columbus, with its pleasant stopovers in the Canaries and West Indies, its steady trade winds, and its calm seas, was favored for a century and a half. Early seventeenth-century English mariners preferred the more direct northern passage, despite the imposition of a longer unbroken time at sea in a region often wracked by violent storms. The duration of a voyage, depending on luck, varied from three to five months by the southern route, from six to eight weeks by the northern route in summer, twelve to fourteen weeks over a cold, rough, "surly ocean" in winter.

Ships and navigation had changed little since Columbus' day. Pilots still leaned mainly on dead reckoning and would continue to do so well into the eighteenth century, even after the development of an accurate chronometer and, in 1731, of Hadley's quadrant, which made ascertaining longitude at sea much simpler. Sanitary conditions aboard ship remained as crude as the navigational techniques. This, with overcrowding, kept the death rate for most trips high. William Bradford tells of a Virginia-bound vessel that lost 100 of its 138 passengers. The *Mayflower* lost only one passenger, but the rigors of the trip left the people so weakened that over half succumbed to the first winter ashore.

The daily diet at sea consisted of bread, ship's biscuits, meat, peas, cheese—and fish for passengers lucky enough to catch them. (Winthrop reports that at one point in the crossing the Puritans "took in less than two hours, with a few hooks, sixty-seven codfish, most of them very large greatfish, some yard and a half long, and a yard in compass," but Samuel Eliot Morison wonders if he consulted "his conscience as well as his yardstick before he handed down that yarn to posterity.") When storms delayed a crossing, provisions often dipped dangerously low. "Women and children made dismal cries and grievous complaints," goes one diary entry. "The infinite number of rats that all the voyage had been our plague, we now were glad to make out prey to feed on; and as they were ensnared and taken, a well grown rat was sold for sixteen shillings as a market rate. Nay, before the voyage did end, a woman great with child offered twenty shillings for a rat, which the proprietor refused; the woman died."

Food and accommodations made the best trip an ordeal. That "surly ocean" made it terrifying. "The wind blew mightily, the sea roared and the waves tossed us horridly," Francis Higginson wrote; "besides, it was fearful dark and the mariners made us afraid with their running here and there and loud crying one to another to pull at this and that rope." Even ships' crews could be unnerved by a severe storm. One murdered an old woman they suspected as a witch and tossed her body into the sea; they were surprised to find the winds did not "remit their violence, or the raging sea its threatenings."

Seasickness was a minor trial of the trip, though doubtless at the time it seemed major to those who endured it. After the *Arbella's* first storm, the crew stretched a line on deck and those "who lay groaning in the cabins" were hauled out, as Winthrop tells it, and forced to "sway it up and down till they were warm, and by this means they soon grew well and merry." The cure, if it worked, probably did little to revive those who had drunk their way to peace. Heavy drinking was common on every emigrant ship. It surprised no one that Sunday-morning prayers aboard the *London* had to be postponed, the "parson being indisposed by drinking too much grog the night before." Even Winthrop admits that the Puritans occasionally fended off gloom by imbibing "hot waters very immoderately."

A brush with pirates or privateers occasionally spiced a dull day. The *Arbella* at one point suspected sails on the horizon to be those of Spanish warships. "Our captain caused the gunroom and gundeck to be cleared, all the hammocks were taken down, our ordnance loaded and our powder-chests and fireworks made ready for our people quartered with the seamen and twenty-five of them appointed for muskets." The alarm proved false for the *Arbella* but not for others coming later.

Allusions to ships and the sea weave through the speech and writings of colonists long after the crossing should have faded from memory. Roger Williams, who endured six crossings, opens his most famous passage with the sentence, "There goes many a ship to sea." When a gust of wind upset a Miss Kitty Fleming of Annapolis, it "carried away all her top rigging,"

Map 8. Land the Settlers Found

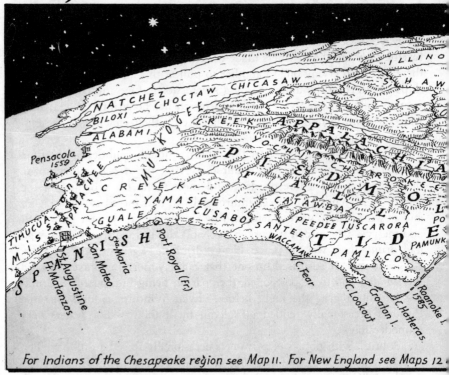

For Indians of the Chesapeake region see Map 11. For New England see Maps 12

TAWATOMI L. des Hurons CHIPPEWA HUDSON BAY
L. des Eries HURON NEUTRALS ALGON CREE
ERIE L. Ontario St. Lawrence Q U I N St. Charles
M T S IROQUOIS SENECA CAYUGA ONONDAGA ONEIDA MOHAWK L. Champlain Montreal Quebec
SUSQUEHANNA E N D MOHICAN PENNACOOK ABNAKI PENOBSCOT
ANT COOK Christina 38 Orange Hartford Cagadahoc Ft. Loyal, 32 Ft. Castine Penobscot, 26
Delaware Bay New Amsterdam 26 New Haven Ft. Loyal, 32 Pemaquid
ake Bay Zwanendael 31 Windsor Saybrook Piscataqua, 1623 Ft. Castine
  New Haven Prov. 36 Naumkeag (Salem) 1630
  Newport, 39 Boston, 1630
  Plymouth, 1620
  C. Cod Fishing Banks
  Nantucket 1659

Indians of New England see Map 22

Raisz

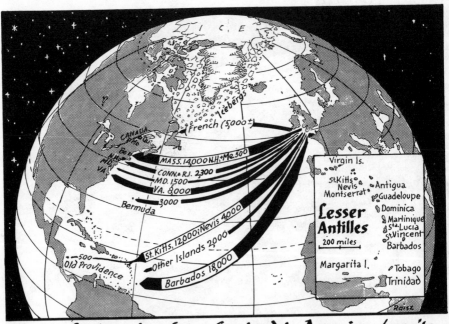

Map 9. Emigration from England to America, 1620-'42

The following labels appear on the map:

French (5000±)
CANADA
MASS. 14000 N.H.+Me.500
CONN.+R.I. 2300
MD. 1500
VA. 8000
Bermuda
3000
St.Kitts 12000; Nevis 4000
Other Islands 2000
500 Old Providence
Barbados 18000

Lesser Antilles inset:
Virgin Is.
St.Kitts
Nevis
Montserrat
Antigua
Guadeloupe
Dominica
Martinique
Sta.Lucia
St.Vincent
Barbados
Margarita I.
Tobago
Trinidad
Lesser Antilles
200 miles

Raisz

according to the observer. "Sometimes we hear you are sailing into port with a prosperous gale," William Byrd, II, wrote to a friend wooing a widow, "just ready to let go your anchor. Soon after, we are told, the wind took you short and had spitefully blown you out to sea again." Those who reached the New World rarely managed to wash the sea from their minds.

What They Found

They smelled the land before they saw it, and that "sweet perfume" so many diaries record, especially sweet compared to the smoky atmosphere of a London left behind, cheered them after the ordeal by sea. The land itself buoyed them up even more, though disappointment soon set in when reality was stacked beside the propaganda accounts. They had brought all the seventeenth-century England that their trunks and minds would hold only to find much of it irrelevant in a wilderness of deep forests, strange animals, and barbaric natives.

They had expected, since most early eulogies centered on Virginia, all America to be warm and lush. They soon found it different. The climate went from cold-temperate in the north to subtropical in the south; the land varied from the thin, rock-filled glacial soil of the north to the rich loam of the south. Regardless of where a settler put down roots, he believed his region surpassed other parts of America. An outsider visiting Virginia found the climate "fevers the blood and sets all the animal spirits in an uproar," while a Virginian in New England said that "except for fishing there is not much in that land."

All colonists shared two topographical features. First, thick forests blanketed nearly all the land. Farms had to be hacked out of a wilderness of trees, a back-breaking job none of the publicity in England had talked much about. Second, all shared the Appalachian Mountain system, a relatively low but broad, rugged wall that cut on a bias from north to south, easing inland as it worked southward. It blocked the westward path of settlers some fifty miles inland in New England, about one hundred and fifty miles in Pennsylvania, and around three hundred miles in South Carolina. Occasional traders and trappers trickled through gaps in the chain, but for most the mountains were an effective barrier. Settlers throughout the seventeenth century kept their backs to the continent and hugged the coast. They remained as they had in England oriented toward the sea, and this made them easier to control by the mother country.

Settlers who did push inland found the country varied from east to west much as it did from north to south. The land between the coast and mountains splits into two regions. The lowlands that begin in New Jersey and gradually spread inland to one hundred and fifty miles at South

Carolina are known as the tidelands, or tidewater country. The belt of rolling country that varies in width from one hundred miles in Pennsylvania to two hundred miles in South Carolina is the piedmont region. The spot where streams from the higher land drop down to the coastal plain marks the fall line, where the piedmont and tidelands divide. The backcountry begins at the fall line. Here, the farthest point for inland navigation, trading towns would materialize as way stations and depots between the two regions.

Nearly a century would elapse before the colonists cut far into the backcountry. By then, time had accustomed them to much of the strangeness and wildness of the new world's flora and fauna. They had made themselves at home by Anglicizing much that was new. A strange tree that "yields a kind of sap or juice, which by boiling is made into sugar" became the "sugar-tree" and eventually the sugar maple. Frogs of "an incredible bigness" were, "from the roaring they make," called bullfrogs. Two venomous vipers were dubbed the rattlesnake and the "copper-bellied snake," or the copperhead. "A sort of flat bug, which lurks in the bedsteads and bedding, and disturbs peoples' rest a-nights," became, naturally, the bedbug. A bird whose wings buzzed in flight became the "humbird." Occasionally the colonists borrowed names. A troublesome "sort of vermin" became, after the Spanish name, "muskeeto." (Those who cannot "endure the biting of a muskeeto," said William Bradford, should "keep at home till at least they be muskeeto proof.") Indian nomenclature was resisted, as if to take from barbarians demeaned Englishmen. Maize always remained "Indian corn" or simply "corn," though "Indian plum" did eventually succumb to "persimmon," and only reluctantly did the colonists accept other Indian names like "skunk" and "squash."

The abundance and size of American flora and fauna fascinated settlers as much as the strangeness. Persimmons grew like ropes of onions and "the branches very often break down by the mighty weight of the fruit." Strawberries "as delicious as any in the world" sprouted "almost everywhere in the woods and fields." In the spring "herrings come up in such abundance into their brooks and fords to spawn that it is almost impossible to ride through without treading on them." Turkeys of "incredible bigness" ran in flocks of four to five hundred. Migrating ducks blackened the water until it resembled "a mass of filth or turf," and when they took flight there was a "rushing and vibration of the air like a great storm coming through the trees or like the rumbling of distant thunder." Everything was outsize in America, giving the tall tale natural ground in which to flourish.

An occasional visitor carried a sour view of the country back to England. Virginia acquired a bad reputation from sailors who "go sweltering about in their thick clothes all the summer," and "greedily devour all the green fruit and unripe trash they can meet with, and so fall into fluxes, fevers, and the belly-ache, and then, to spare their own indiscretion, they in their tarpaulin language, cry, God D—— the country." A lady visiting New England found the air "sharp, the rocks many, the trees innumerable, the grass little, the winter cold, the summer hot, the gnats in summer biting, the wolves at midnight howling," but even she admitted that for all its faults the country deserved to be well regarded, for "it hath the means of grace, and, if you please, you may call it Canaan."

But Canaan was blemished. The presence of the Indian flawed the Englishman's paradise. Though North American Indians numbered less than two hundred thousand east of the Mississippi, as opposed to some thirty million spread throughout South America, they would give English intruders an incredible amount of trouble compared to what the Spanish had received. The Spanish dealt with tightly organized, highly developed cultures that tended to be submissive to authority. More important, the Spanish alone overran South America, except for Brazil; the eastern part of North America was about to be invaded by Spanish, Dutch, French, and English. Each intruder competed with the others for land and sought Indian aid to promote his interests.

Indians, like white men, varied in size and color but shared several characteristics. They had slight beards, straight black hair, high cheekbones, broad faces, and slightly slanted eyes. Language differences set them apart. The Algonquins, the largest language group east of the Mississippi, controlled most of Canada and the Ohio Valley, all of New England, and were scattered southward through eastern Pennsylvania, New Jersey, Maryland, and Virginia. They greeted the English at Jamestown, Plymouth, and Boston, and the French wherever they went in Canada. They were semi-nomadic, lived in bark-covered huts, and were noted for their enterprise and for the birchbark canoe, which they invented.

The Iroquois, the second language group, had long ago pushed up from the south, cutting the Algonquin country in two. They centered in New York, northern Ohio, and western Pennsylvania. Sometime in the fifteenth century the five Iroquois tribes living in New York—Seneca, Cayuga, Onondaga, Oneida, and Mohawk—joined in a league that early settlers called the Five Nations. Widely separated from the main group were the Cherokee in the southern Appalachians and the Tuscarora in eastern Carolina. (The Tuscarora moved north after their defeat by whites in 1713 and joined with their brethren in New York to form the Six Nations.) The Iroquois were aggressive and as intruders themselves usually had a war on their hands. They could field armies of five hundred to one thousand warriors, a feat only white men could duplicate. They loathed the Algonquins. Wars between the two groups invariably involved competing white powers—the French backing the Algonquins, the English behind the Iroquois.

The third language group, the Muskogean, centered in the deep south. From Georgia their influence radiated into northern Florida, Tennessee, Alabama, and Mississippi. The Chickasaw, Choctaw, Creek, and Seminole tribes belonged to the Muskogean group. All would be courted, by the French along the Mississippi, the Spanish in Florida, and the English along the coast. A fourth language group, the Sioux, roamed mainly west of the Mississippi, except for the Catawba, who flourished in the piedmont region of the Carolinas.

The white man's coming devastated the Indian's way of life. He had previously lived in a world devoid of beasts of burden and of all but the most primitive tools, his stage of civilization roughly that of the Mediterranean basin about 6000 B.C. Almost literally overnight the white man swept him into the modern world. He gave the Indian a knife, a cotton shirt, a steel needle, an iron pot, a gun, and alcohol; and with these gifts he made the red man a "cultural prisoner." "The wonder is that the Indians resisted decadence as well as they did, preserved as much as they did, and fought the whites off so obstinately and so long," Bernard De Voto remarks.

The French regarded the Indian with genuine respect and sought to accept him on his own terms. A few English colonists—notably John Eliot, Roger Williams, and Robert Beverley—treated the Indian honorably, but most were patronizing and obtuse in their attitude. The prevailing colonial view held the Indian to be a barbaric innocent who must adapt to superior white ways, become Christian, live in houses, work hard. The English never dreamed that the Indian would, once offered it, reject civilization. By 1619 at least fifty missionaries had been sent over to spread the gospel among the red men. When a good number of these clerics were a few years later slaughtered, the English, after recovering from the shock, gave up the attempt to civilize and set out to crush the Indian.

While the American settler tossed aside his old image of the Indian, the Englishman at home continued to picture him as a noble savage, innocent and dignified, pure and strong, needing only Christianity to make him a perfect man. The colonist's view puzzled and distressed the Englishman at home. And as he failed to see how the American experience had changed the settler's image of the Indian, he failed also to see other changes the New World was working on ideas and habits carried across the sea. The shell of old forms remained in America, and so it was assumed the substance, too, had come through unchanged. The land and the Indians and the distance from England had conspired slowly to dilute and alter what the settlers brought with them. Within a generation, a society had arisen around the shores of Chesapeake Bay and Massachusetts Bay that was something considerably different from a little bit of England overseas.

BIBLIOGRAPHY

The Reformation

In addition to accounts of the Renaissance and Reformation previously mentioned, there are these reliable volumes: G. L. Mosse, *The Reformation* (1952); Harold J. Grimm, *The Reformation Era, 1500–1650* (1954); E. H. Harbison, *The Age of Reformation* (1955; pb.); Roland H. Bainton, *The Reformation of the Sixteenth Century* (1952; pb.); Preserved Smith, *Reformation in Europe* (2 vols., 1920; pb.); and Owen Chadwick, *The Reformation* (1964; pb. original). Bainton's *Here I Stand* (1950; pb.) is the most readable of the authoritative biographies of Luther. Studies of Calvin are numerous, among the best being those by W. Walker (1906), Georgia Harkness (1931), and James MacKinnon (1936). John T. McNeill, *The History and Character of Calvinism* (1954), is excellent; but perhaps of more interest to the colonial student is François Wendal, *Calvin—Origins and Development of His Religious Thought* (1963). Every student should be acquainted with R. H. Tawney, *Religion and the Rise of Capitalism* (1926; pb.), still provocative and highly readable. Three fine volumes that deal with the English story are H. M. Smith's *Henry VIII and the Reformation* (1948), Sir Maurice Powicke's brief *The Reformation in England* (1941; pb.), and, most recently, C. H. and Katherine George's *The Protestant Mind of the English Reformation* (1961). The background of Puritanism is best read in William Haller's *Rise of Puritanism* (1938; pb.) and M. M. Knappen, *Tudor Puritanism* (1939). The core of the late Perry Miller's view of the covenant theology is summarized in "The Marrow of Puritan Divinity," *Errand into the Wilderness* (1956; pb.); Miller concerns himself with the precise design of Puritan thought. Alan Simpson, in a style at once graceful and succinct, deals with the emotional side as well in *Puritanism in Old and New England* (1955; pb.). The first chapter of John Dykstra Eusden's *Puritans, Lawyers, and Politics in Early Seventeenth-Century England* (1958) presents a summary of Puritanism that emphasizes the Calvinistic content. An able summary of Puritanism in both old and New England is found in the first hundred pages of George Lee Haskins' *Law and Authority in Early Massachusetts* (1960), which all students are urged to read. Two notable articles are those by L. J. Trinterud, who discusses the European sources of Puritan ideas in "Origins of Puritanism," *Church History*, 20 (1951), 37–57, and by Jerald C. Brauer's "Reflections on the Nature of English Puritanism," *ibid.*, 23 (1954), 99–108.

England on the Eve of Colonization

Two general accounts are the latter half of Edward P. Cheyney's *European Background of American History* and Wallace Notestein's *England on the Eve of Colonization, 1603–1630* (1954; pb.), which is especially sound on the political and legal institutions of the age. George Kitson Clark gives an impressionistic survey in *The English Inheritance* (1950). C. V. Wedgwood's *The King's Peace, 1637–1641* (1955) gives in its early chapters a brilliantly evocative picture of England in the reign of Charles I, but Miss Wedgwood's account should be balanced by Christopher Hill's *The Century of Revolution, 1603–1714* (1961), perhaps the best single volume on the English scene.

For social and economic conditions in England at this time the student should begin with Tawney, again his *Religion and the Rise of Capitalism*, plus *The Agrarian Problem in the Sixteenth Century* (1912) and especially "The Rise of the Gentry, 1558–1640," *Economic History Review (EHR)*, 11 (1941), 1–38. Tawney's article initiated a still-flourishing argument among historians about the gentry—were they rising or actually falling in power during the sixteenth century?—that has been summed up and continued by J. H. Hexter's "Storm over the Gentry," in his collection of essays, *Reappraisals in History* (1961; pb.). Mildred Campbell's *The English Yeoman Under Elizabeth and the Early Stuarts* (1942) is an elaborate and careful study that is highly recommended. Wallace T. MacCaffey's *Exeter, 1540–1640: The Growth of an English Country Town* (1958) is a specialized work that points up the persistence of the medieval world in town life.

A brief, broad, and competent introduction to the economic side of this period is found in Lawrence B. Packard, *The Commercial Revolution, 1501–1650* (1927). John U. Nef's *Industry and Government in France and England, 1540–1640* (1940) is an imaginative pioneering study. Ephraim Lipson, *Economic History of England* (1931), presents a sound general account. Among many specialized works recommended are David Hannary, *The Great Chartered Companies* (1926) ; S. Kramer, *The English Craft Gilds: Studies in Their Progress and Decline* (1927) ; George Unwin, *Gilds and Companies of London* (1909; rev. ed., 1925) ; and Louis B. Wright, *Religion and Empire: The Alliance Between Piety and Commerce in English Expansion, 1558–1625* (1943). *The Encyclopedia of the Social Sciences*, edited by E. R. A. Seligman (15 vols., 1930–1934), a reference work every student should become acquainted with, has an excellent article on mercantilism. (The *Encyclopedia*, incidentally, is now being revised and expanded.) J. W. Horrocks, *A Short History of Mercantilism* (1925), and P. Buck, *The Politics of Mercantilism* (1942), are fuller studies, and fuller still is Eli Hecksher's authoritative *Mercantilism* (2 vols., 1935). The brief account in Herbert Heaton, *Economic History of Europe* (1948), is notably good.

A Great Migration Begins

A brief general account of the great migration is Raymond E. Stearns, "Great Migration," *Dictionary of American History*, Vol. II (7 vols., 1940–1963). The story told more fully from the English viewpoint is found in Arthur P. Newton's, "The Great Migration, 1618–1648," *Cambridge History of the British Empire*, Vol. I (8 vols., 1929–1963). For opposing sides of the story see Wesley F. Craven's *Southern Colonies in the Seventeenth Century* (1949) and J. T. Adams' *Founding of New England* (1921; pb.), especially Ch. 6.

Who came and why has been ably discussed by Campbell in "Social Origins of Some Early Americans," in James Morton Smith, ed., *Seventeenth-Century America: Essays in Colonial History* (1959). An excellent brief account appears in Marcus Lee Hansen, *The Atlantic Migration 1607–1860* (1940; pb.). Arthur Pierce Middleton, *Tobacco Coast: A Maritime History of Chesapeake Bay in the Colonial Era* (1953), has a fine opening chapter on the crossing. Henry Bamford Parkes's discussion of the conditions for the migration is found in *The American Experience* (1947; pb.).

Albert P. Brigham's *Geographic Influences in American History* (1903) and Ellen Semple Churchill's *American History and Its Geographic Conditions* (rev. ed., 1933) adequately describe the land the settlers found, but Ralph H. Brown's superb *Historical Geography of the United States* (1948) goes further and details how they settled it. The maps and charts in Brown are especially good. Peter Matthiesen gives a marvelous account of *Wildlife in America* (1959; pb.), the first five chapters of which are relevant to the colonial story.

The amount of material on the Indian is enormous. Clark Wissler's *American Indian* (1922) and *Indians of the United States: Four Centuries of Their History and Culture* (1940) are standard. The early chapters of Roy H. Pearce's *The Savages of America* (1953) deal with the colonial attitude toward the Indian. Ruth M. Underhill's *Red Man's America* (1953) is excellent. Bernard De Voto's remarks on the Indian scattered through *Course of Empire* (1952; pb.) are always worth attention. Two recent and satisfactory popular accounts, accompanied by a mass of illustrations, are Oliver Lafarge, *A Pictorial History of the American Indian* (1956), and the *American Heritage Book of Indians* (1961). To counterbalance these light reports, see two provocative articles in James Morton Smith, ed., *Seventeenth-Century America:* Wilcomb E. Washburn, "The Moral and Legal Justification for Dispossessing the Indians" and Nancy O. Lurie, "Indian Cultural Adjustment to European Civilization."

For further references there are two recent bibliographical articles available: Roland H. Bainton, "Interpretations of the Reformation," *American Historical Review (AHR),* 66 (1960), 74–84; and Perez Zagorin, "English History, 1558–1640: A Bibliographical Survey," *ibid.,* 68 (1963), 364–384. There is also an elaborate bibliography in Notestein's *England on the Eve of Colonization.* And, finally, there is the *Harvard Guide,* Sections 67, "Physiography and Geography of North America"; 68, "North American Archaeology"; 69, "North American Indians"; 77, "Causes and Background of English Expansion"; and 83, "English Puritanism and Background of Puritan Migration."

THE PORTRAICTUER OF CAPTAYNE IOHN SMITH ADMIRALL OF NEW ENGLAND.

Ætia 37
Aº 1616

These are the Lines that shew thy Face; but those
That shew thy Grace and Glory, brighter bee:
Thy Faire-Discoueries and Fowle-Overthrowes
Of Salvages, much Civillizd by thee
Best shew thy Spirit; and to it Glory Wyn;
So, thou art Braße without, but Golde within.

John Smith, from *The General History of Virginia*

3. The Chesapeake Colonies

FIRST STONES
The Charter of 1606
Sagadahoc
Jamestown

VIRGINIA
Life Without Liberty
Under New Management
Virginia on Its Own: 1623–1640

MARYLAND
Gentlemen Adventurers
The Charter of 1632
The Early Years

CHESAPEAKE SOCIETY
The Great Bay of Chesapeake
The Farm
Government and Religion

FIRST STONES

The seventeenth century opened with Spain forced to face competitors who flouted the pope's division of the New World. England wrenched an agreement from Spain in 1604 that settled the long war between these two nations in Europe but sidestepped their disputes across the seas. Force alone would resolve those claims. All nations would continue to talk loudly about their "rights of discovery" and how such "rights" determined boundaries in the New World, but all assumed there would be "no peace

beyond the line [of demarcation]," a policy that would make the seventeenth and eighteenth centuries bloody ones for European settlers in
North America.

France began to pursue this policy while England and Spain still
warred. Peace within the realm had released the energy to resume imperial
ambitions; Samuel de Champlain provided the genius to direct those
energies. He had spent two years in the West Indies studying Spanish
techniques of colonization. In 1603 he picked up where Cartier had left
off in the exploration of the St. Lawrence area. He founded Quebec in
1609, developed the fur trade, and trained men who steadily pushed
French power into the heart of the continent. The momentum from
Champlain's initial drive eventually carried French influence westward to
the Rockies and southward down the Mississippi to the Gulf of Mexico,
where Spain waited in trepidation.

The Dutch moved in 1609, hiring the Englishman Henry Hudson to
find the Northwest Passage. He failed in his mission but claimed for his
employers the river named after him. Adriaen Block, on a similar mission
in 1614, sailed fifty miles up the Connecticut River. While the Dutch
built posts at the mouth of both rivers and exploited the rich hinterlands,
the English had committed themselves to a bolder, costlier, but in the
long run more profitable project than either the French or Dutch had
dared to undertake.

The Charter of 1606

America roused the interests of two groups of well-to-do Englishmen. One
centered in London. London money had explored the route to Russia and
now controlled the Muscovy Company; it ran the lucrative Levant Company that operated out of Constantinople; and it had created the gigantic
East India Company. Raleigh, nearly bankrupted by Roanoke, had turned
over the rights to his charter to nineteen London merchants, and out of
that nucleus had developed in the city an ever-widening interest in southern Virginia. (Virginia then stretched from South Carolina to Maine, with
southern Virginia ending somewhere around the mouth of the Hudson
River.)

The second group clustered in the West Country port towns where
feeling waxed strong against "the engrossing and restraint of trade by the
rich merchants of London." The outports had sent fishermen to the
Newfoundland area for over a century. They began in 1600 to dispatch a
series of exploratory voyages off the coast south of Newfoundland. Each
of the commanders—Bartholomew Gosnold, Martin Pring, George Weymouth—added details to the picture of New England, as it would be
called. The region abounded in furs, timber, and fish. The merchants of

Bristol, Devonshire, Dorsetshire, Plymouth, and other West Country towns began to talk of financing a colony to tap this wealth.

Sir John Popham, a West Country man, devised a scheme that satisfied these divergent interests and harnessed them to the national interest in a way that cost the government nothing. Sir John had represented Bristol in Parliament and had been speaker of Commons before becoming lord chief justice. As chief justice he had ordered the jury to find Raleigh guilty of treason; they did. As a private citizen he soon involved himself in America, where Raleigh, convicted, had lost his rights. He was "a huge, heavy, ugly man," with such a drive for work he "could endure to sit at it day and night," and with a wry outlook on the affairs of men. (Once, when the queen asked at the end of a session what had passed in Commons, he answered, "If it please your Majesty, seven weeks.") Popham saw to it that the charter issued by the crown in 1606 to certain "firm and hearty lovers" of colonization protected West Country interests as well as the crown's.

The charter split America between the Plymouth and London Companies; it allowed the London Company to settle anywhere between Cape Fear in North Carolina and the current site of New York City, and the Plymouth Company anywhere between the Potomac River and a spot slightly north of present day Bangor, Maine. The assigned areas overlapped, but neither company could put men within one hundred miles of the other. Once a "first seat," or settlement had been made, the company got a grant of land that extended a hundred miles along the coast and the same distance inland and out to sea.

Popham's desire to blend public and private interests produced an awkward form of government for the proposed colonies. A royal council, its members chosen by the crown, controlled "all matters that shall or may concern the government." The royal council chose and instructed subsidiary councils to rule directly over each of the two settlements. Company members, or adventurers, furnished the capital, the settlers, and had charge of trade and profits, if any. On paper, the crown governed the colonies and held all political power; in practice, the royal council was composed mainly of company leaders, and thus in effect the companies ran their own shows, only in the crown's name.

Supreme authority overseas rested with the subsidiary council, composed of thirteen men, all of whom had an equal voice in decisions. The council represented the company in economic matters and the crown in government affairs. Their regulations had the force of law, but the charter guaranteed Englishmen overseas all "liberties, franchises, and immunities" held at home.

The flaws that time would reveal in this first charter obscured its virtues. Its provisions represented the best thought available in England. "That many of them proved unworkable is no reflection on their authors," A. P. Newton has said. "The whole adventure was an experiment in a yet untrodden field, and we should rather remark the soundness and liberality of the principles than criticise the impracticability of many of the details."

Sagadahoc

The Plymouth Company failed first in the transition from commerce to colony. Sir Ferdinando Gorges, governor of the company, started cautiously by drawing on the pattern laid down by Raleigh in the Roanoke project. He dispatched an exploratory party—no women or children were included—to New England in the summer of 1607. Once they had established a base a larger contingent would be sent over. The party settled on a rocky spit of the Maine coast at the mouth of the Kennebec River— the Sagadahoc, to the Indians. Fort St. George was built and forty-four men left behind to hold it through the winter, under the nominal leadership of George Popham, a relative of Sir John.

George Popham, "a discreet, careful man" but also "timorously fearful to offend," was not the man to carve a plantation out of the wilderness. Natives told him that in this land grew nutmegs, mace, and cinnamon, and he believed it. Winter soon disabused him of the climate's tropical quality, and a fire that destroyed much of the fort's stores dampened his spirits further. Popham was too "fearful to offend or contest with others that will or do oppose him," but even if he had been other than he was he lacked the power as president of the council to impose his will on the settlement. The pattern of government laid out in the charter bred the "childish factions" that riddled the settlement, for it dispersed authority among all council members.

Popham died before the winter was out. Raleigh Gilbert, the twenty-four-year-old son of Sir Humphrey, might have imposed order on the group, for he was "desirous of supremacy and rule" and had the boldness to ignore the unworkable government required by the charter. But with the spring thaw came word that Gilbert had inherited the family estates, and he prepared to return home. The further news that Sir John Popham, the colony's most influential backer, had died proved "such a corrosive to all as struck them with despair of future remedy." By the following autumn only the rotting timbers of Fort St. George commemorated the Plymouth Company's effort. One try in America sufficed to disillusion West Country merchants. The Plymouth Company vegetated for several years but made no further attempt to colonize. Original investors were invited by Londoners in 1609 to join in the Virginia enterprise and many of them accepted the offer. In 1620 Sir Ferdinando Gorges, Sir Francis Popham, and Raleigh Gilbert secured another charter from the crown that created the Council for New England, and in this new guise the old company kept a toehold in land the Puritans later assumed God gave them alone.

Jamestown

The London Company, like the Plymouth Company, sought in its first effort only to establish a beachhead. The effort, however, was better conceived and financed. (Hakluyt, the younger, went so far as to ask a Spanish official for information on the way his country governed its colonies.) Company officers decided that the first contingent would set up a base and report back what the pattern of settlement should be. The company would build up the base by feeding in new batches of settlers and supplies slowly.

Three ships—the *Susan Constant, Godspeed,* and *Discovery*—sailed from England in late 1606 with 144 colonists—among them several "gentlemen," a surgeon, blacksmith, carpenter, barber, minister, and a number of bricklayers and soldiers. Captain Christopher Newport, one of the ablest mariners of the day, was in command until "they shall fortune to land upon the said coast of Virginia," at which time he would open a locked steel box entrusted to him, and the royal council's instructions for governing the colony would be read aloud.

The ships departed in December and arrived off the Virginia coast in April. During the four months at sea thirty-nine died, and despite a refreshing pause in the West Indies, tempers toward the end mounted; one set-to led to Captain John Smith, military officer for the settlement, being charged with mutinous talk and put below decks in irons. When it came time for Captain Newport to break open the steel box, it was found that a council of seven was directed to take charge of the colony. Listed among the seven was John Smith. Royal instructions said the council could depose any member by a majority vote. President Edward Wingfield promptly asked for and got permission to expel the unironed Smith. On that note, search for a suitable site began.

The company's own "instructions given by way of advice" urged avoiding mistakes made at Roanoke. Locate, they suggested, on easily defended ground on a large river that gives access to the backcountry and can thus tap a wide area for native trade. Settle sufficiently inland to avoid a surprise attack from the sea and shun marshy ground. After a month's search the council opted for a spit of land jutting into the James River, as they named it, some thirty miles in from the sea. The site was low and swampy but otherwise exactly what the instructions had advised.

The company further advised the council to divide the settlers into

Map 10. Land Grants of 1606, '09, '20

0 100 200
Miles

NEW FRANCE

St. Lawrence R.

Quebec

Montreal

45°

L. Ontario

Ft St George

44

48°

Council for New England, 1620

NEW ENGLAND

London Co. 1609 (revoked 1611)

Hudson R.

Plymouth

Plymouth Co. 1606

Open to both
Companies

40°

40°

Potomac R.

38°

London Co. 1609

London Co. 1606

Jamestown

Old Point
Comfort

James R.

VIRGINIA

36°

34° including Bermuda

C. Fear 34°

72°

68° Raisz

76°

three groups: one to build a fort and housing within it; another to clear the ground for planting and to erect a warning outpost on the seacoast; and a third to explore the river for a possible passage to the East. Company planners had modified the old factory-fort concept to make the settlement self-sustaining for long periods of time. When Captain Newport in late June headed back to England with a load of Virginia clapboard, the settlers knew that their first "supply" would not arrive for at least a half year.

Despite painstaking planning, Jamestown's chances for surviving the first winter looked no better than Sagadahoc's. The colonists had eaten deeply into their provisions on the lengthy sea voyage, and the sailors cut into them further as the ships lingered on into the summer. The settlers had hurried to plant orange trees, cotton, potatoes, and melons—all experimental crops—but lagged in sowing grain; their tardiness precluded an early crop, which would relieve short supplies. The summer turned hot and malaria swept through the mosquito-infested fort. The Indians, led by the able and observant Powhatan, swung from friendly to hostile, and food once given willingly was now withheld. By mid-September forty-six settlers had died, most from "mere famine," according to one account.

Winter inaugurated a string of troubles similar to those Fort St. George was enduring. Jamestown, like Sagadahoc, suffered most from lack of leadership. Quarrels wracked the council and their bitterness increased with that of the winter. The colony suffered from "too many chiefs, not enough Indians," to use the phrase of a later day. One-third to one-half the settlers were gentlemen accustomed to taking orders from no one, "ten times more fit to spoil a commonwealth than . . . to maintain one." Each did as he liked and gave little thought to the settlement's best interests.

Captain Newport arrived with the first supply in early January 1608, bringing 120 more settlers and finding only 38 of the original ones still alive. Five days after he docked, a fire "consumed all the buildings of the fort and storehouse of ammunition and provisions," leaving only three habitable houses at the coldest season of the year. The colonists survived the winter but continued with the spring "to give themselves as much perplexity by their own distraction," said an early historian, "as the Indians did by their watchfulness and resentments." Jamestown seemed headed for the fate that lay dead ahead for Sagadahoc and doubtless would have met it but for the presence of Captain John Smith—perhaps a liar, certainly a braggart, but, for all that, still Jamestown's saviour.

Smith, who was twenty-seven, had been hired by the company on the basis of military exploits in the Balkans and Turkey. His expulsion from the council temporarily left him free of responsibilities and in the summer of 1608 he set out in an open boat to explore Chesapeake Bay; he mapped the area so accurately that his work remained unsurpassed for over a century. He returned from the trip to find Jamestown bitten by gold fever. "No talk, no hope, nor work," he wrote, "but dig gold, wash gold, refine gold, load gold." No one had bothered to provide food for the months ahead, for council members were as obsessed as settlers with the search for gold. Smith set out on a foraging expedition and returned early in September with a boatload of provisions. Three days later the council made him president. When Newport arrived a short while later with the second supply and seventy more settlers, among them eight Polish and German experts in the manufacture of glass, pitch, tar, and soap ashes, he found Smith had brought a strong hand to bear on the colony. Buildings were repaired, seed had been sown, and the settlers were raising livestock, chickens, and swine. Slackers, threatened with banishment to the wilderness, worked with a will. Smith visited the Indians during the winter and returned with food. A well was dug; some twenty new houses were built; and some pitch, tar, "sope ashes," and glass were produced. Less than a dozen settlers out of some two hundred died that winter, and by the summer of 1609 Jamestown seemed to have a chance to survive.

The London Company determined to back up Smith's achievements. Its officers in England settled on a broad, three-part program. A nationwide appeal would be launched for settlers and money to build up the colony swiftly, rather than by slow steps, as had been the plan up to now. A new charter had to be obtained from the crown to strengthen the company's hand. And the government of the colony had to be revamped.

The campaign to attract men and money made Virginia's fate a national affair. "The eyes of all Europe are looking upon our endeavors to spread the gospel among the heathen people of Virginia," one circular read, "to plant an English nation there, and to settle a trade in those parts, which may be peculiar to our nation, to the end we may thereby be secured from being eaten out of all profits of trade by our more industrious neighbors." Robert Johnson's *Nova Britannia* talked more practically of how settlers could improve their status and material well-being. Hakluyt did his part by publishing an account of Hernando De Soto's travels under the title of *Virginia richly valued by the description of the main land of Florida, her next neighbor.*

The new effort would pool men and money. Those who lacked money but "go in their persons, to be planters," would share in the profits with those who "go not, but advance their monies. . . ." The company announced that the average planter going to the colony would receive one share whose market value was £12 10s. All the stock of both planters and adventurers would go into a common pool for seven years. During that time all land held and trading done would be by the company. Settlers would give their time and labor to the common effort and draw on the company storehouse or magazine for their supplies. The communal plan as well as this particular joint-stock venture would end in 1616. At that time all accumulated profits would be divided among shareholders, and the land that had been cleared would be divided, with settlers receiving a minimum of one hundred acres.

The effort to attract wide support succeeded. If members of the 56 city companies of tradesmen are counted with the 650 individuals who contributed, well over 1,000 persons had a personal financial stake in the project, and over 600 others who had agreed to travel to Virginia had an even greater stake in it. The success of the appeal astonished and worried the Spanish ambassador, who saw in it the first serious threat to his nation's own holdings in the New World.

The crown in 1609 gave out a new charter tailored to please company officials. Boundaries were extended two hundred miles north and south of Old Point Comfort and "from sea to sea, west and northwest." The royal council of the first charter now became a semi-autonomous company council. It still drew its authority from the crown, but none of its actions had to be ratified by the company. The council had "full power and authority" to decide all business of the colony, governmental as well as economic. However, emphasis in the charter on the role of the company treasurer made certain that the man who held that post virtually ran the company. The autocratic rule that James I sought to impose on England was duplicated in the company's new organization.

The newly selected treasurer was Sir Thomas Smith, now fifty-one and at the peak of his vigor. Smith promptly persuaded the council to revise Virginia's government along autocratic lines like that of the home office. The ineffective local council and its president were swept aside to make room for a governor, as he was to be called, with "full power and authority" to direct the affairs of the colony. He was to have authority for life and to control military as well as civil affairs. He might choose a council of the substantial men of the colony to advise him, but he need not take their advice. The revision was prompted by the sad experiences with dispersed authority at Sagadahoc and Jamestown thus far, by John Smith's example of what a single man with authority could achieve, by a desire to duplicate the company's London organization as much as possible in the New World, and, finally, by Stuart resistance to Parliamentary or popular control.

The company's appeals for funds and settlers had been taking effect while the charter and organizational changes were in the making, and in the spring of 1609 some six hundred men, women, and children were set to leave for Virginia. Lord De La Warr, a member of the royal council

who had been chosen by his colleagues to be the first governor of the
colony, could not make the sailing; but on May 15, six ships, with Thomas
Gates aboard as deputy governor, George Somers in command of the
fleet, and Captain Newport as vice admiral, drifted down the Thames.
They were joined by three more vessels, also loaded with settlers, at
Plymouth. The greatest folk movement in history was underway.

VIRGINIA

Virginia's early years receive and deserve extraordinary attention. The
first success in any enterprise fascinates more than those that follow. England was attempting something new in the field of colonization; doubt
that she would learn in time the techniques needed to plant a colony in
the wilderness and that faith, energy, and money would last long enough
to carry the settlement through its time of troubles give the melodramatic
quality of a cliff-hanger movie to the venture. The story has an added interest. Maryland's birth came easier for the pains Virginia endured. Later,
as Virginians migrated along the coast and into the backcountry, they took
with them customs and habits acquired on the rivers and inlets around
Chesapeake Bay. Virginia, like Massachusetts to the north, would become
something of a mother for other colonies and, still later, for states throughout the land.

Life Without Liberty

The "great fleet" left in June 1609. Toward the end of the trip it hit "the
tail of the West Indian horacano." One ship went down, and one, with
the expedition's three leaders aboard—Gates, Newport, and Somers—was
wrecked on Bermuda, an island the English now "discovered," though it
had long been known to the Spanish. The remaining seven vessels limped
into Jamestown, where the four hundred arrivals found little after nine
weeks at sea to cheer about. Less than a hundred of the old settlers were
alive to greet them; no housing had been prepared; no food planted for
the newcomers. John Smith lacked authority under the new charter and
could impose no order on the new immigrants. Their own leaders were
gone, and "no man would acknowledge a superior nor could from this
headless and unbridled multitude be anything expected but disorder and
riot." Smith, suffering from a gunpowder wound and unable to defend
himself adequately, was ousted from the council and shipped home, and
thus, said an admirer,

we lost him that, in all his proceedings, made justice his first guide, and
experience his second; ever hating baseness, sloth, pride, and indignity more
than any dangers; that never allowed more for himself than his soldiers with

him; that upon no danger, would send them where he would not lead them himself; that would never see us want what he either had or could by any means get us; that would rather want than borrow, or starve than not pay; that loved actions more than words, and hated falsehood and cousenage [deceit] worse than death; whose adventures were our lives, and whose loss our deaths.

Virginia's "unbridled multitude" now entered the "starving time." Through the summer and autumn settlers still weak from their trip and not yet immune to the miasmic vapors of Jamestown died by the score. "Though there be fish in the sea, fowls in the air, and beasts in the woods," Smith remarked before he left, "their bounds are so large, they so wild, and we so weak and ignorant, we cannot much trouble them." The Indians, sensing weakness, penned the settlers inside the palisades and slaughtered the livestock that roamed the forests, "as fast killing without as the famine and pestilence within." Winter brought unrelieved horror. "So lamentable was our scarcity," goes one recollection,

that we were constrained to eat dogs, cats, rats, snakes, toadstools, horsehides, and what not; one man out of the misery endured, killing his wife powdered her up to eat her, for which he was burned. Many besides fed on the corpses of dead men, and one who had gotten unsatiable, out of custom to that food, could not be restrained until such time as he was executed for it; and indeed so miserable was our estate that the happiest day that ever some of them hoped to see, was when the Indians had killed a mare they wishing whilst she was boiling that Sir Thomas Smith was upon her back in the kettle.

Gates and the survivors of the Bermuda wreck—some 175 more mouths to feed—arrived in two jerry-built ships in May 1610. They found alive out of nearly five hundred from the previous June some sixty weak and quarreling settlers living like animals within the rotting fort. It took little debate to decide to abandon Jamestown. The settlers wanted to burn what remained of the settlement, leaving nothing for the Indians, but Gates said: "let the town stand, we know not but that as homeless men as ourselves may come and inhabit here." Gates had his way. The survivors packed, boarded the ships, and were drifting downstream when "suddenly we espied a boat make toward us." It was the advance guard of Lord De La Warr's relief fleet "who was come . . . with many gentlemen of quality and three hundred, besides great store of victuals, munitions and other provisions."

De La Warr took firm hold at once. He sent a ship to Bermuda, where hogs ran wild over the island, to secure a cargo of pork. Gates and Newport, with a note from De La Warr saying colonists of better quality were needed to be "the carpenters and workers in this so glorious a building," went back to England to discuss matters with company officers. De

La Warr meanwhile inaugurated a new technique for settlement by drawing on the absolute powers given him under the 1609 charter and on British experience in Ireland. He shaped Virginia along the lines of a military beachhead established in enemy country. Most of the council members bore military titles. Settlers were organized under captains in groups of fifteen and ruled by martial law. English liberties for the time being were allowed to slip by the board.

De La Warr's regime ended the starving time but not Virginia's troubles. Settlers continued to die, and De La Warr himself, struck first by "a hot and violent ague," then the flux, cramps, and finally by scurvy, fled for home in March 1611. Fortunately, by that time Sir Thomas Smith had seen that Virginia deserved at least one more effort and had agreed to raise another £30,000 for two further relief expeditions. The first of these, three ships and three hundred settlers, sailed under Thomas Dale the month De La Warr headed back. The second followed in May under Gates, with six ships, three hundred men, and a great supply of cattle, swine, and poultry.

While the company strove to round up money and settlers, it also had pressed for a new charter, which it got in 1612. The charter relieved the company's financial problems by allowing it to run national lotteries to raise money. The company was handed a seven-year exemption on all customs duties in England. Virginia's boundary was extended from one hundred to three hundred leagues out to sea, thus taking in Bermuda. (The two settlements were treated as a single part of company holdings until 1615, when Bermuda—then called Somers Island—got its own charter. Since the same men managed both, the Bermuda Company remained essentially a subsidiary of the London Company. Bermuda had several attractions that allowed it to flourish while Virginia was enduring its roughest days: the encircling coral reef made it fairly safe from enemy attack; the absence of forests simplified the job of planting crops; there was a long growing season; and there were no Indians to plague the settlers.)

Grumblings from the adventurers in England brought about the charter's most striking change. The crown abandoned the attempt to maintain some form of control over Virginia and resurrected the trading-company charter of precolonization days, where company members managed their own affairs. Power was now shifted from a council responsible only to the crown to a "Court and Assembly"; from, so to speak, the board of directors to the stockholders. The charter authorized four great courts to be held annually and to include all members of the company to determine matters of policy. Lesser matters were handled by an "ordinary court" that met weekly and at which only a quorum of twenty members and the presence of the treasurer were required. While the charter of 1612 gave adventurers in England control over company affairs, it made no changes in the management of the government in Virginia. An absolute governor would still dominate the settlement's business.

Gates, as Lord De La Warr's official replacement, arrived in the colony in August 1611 with two hundred men and twenty women, among them his wife and daughters. He governed for two years and a half before returning "home," as England was still considered, but it is Thomas Dale's name that dominates this period, to some degree unjustly. Dale, with his relief party, had arrived three months before Gates to find the people "at their daily and usual work bowling in the streets." He picked up at once where Lord De La Warr had left off, clamping down a tight control, expanding the laws De La Warr had ruled under, and applying them so strictly they have ever since been misnamed Dale's Laws. William Strachey, an historian of Virginia's early years, entitled them *Laws Divine, Moral and Martial* when he published them in London in 1612, with an eye to showing investors at home that the lawlessness said to thrive in Virginia had been stamped out. Strachey's code combined civil with martial law, for it was now assumed that the colonist played the dual role of farmer and soldier. The severity of punishments for seemingly minor infractions emphasized that Virginia was regarded as a military outpost and not, at the moment, as a home way from home. Gates enforced these laws to the letter. When several colonists sought in 1612 to escape from Virginia in stolen boats, he ordered them shot, hanged, and broken on the wheel, according to their part in the plot. The severity apparently worked. If these "laws had not been so strictly executed," writes Ralph Hamor, another historian of the early years, "I see not how the utter subversion of the colony should have been prevented." And for all their harshness, they did give the settlers a government of laws; they were not "as slaves after the will and lust of any superior."

The colony expanded under Gates and Dale, who both preceded and followed Gates as governor. Dale with a band of settler-soldiers in 1611 traveled forty miles up the James River, and near the fall line founded the town of Henrico on high healthy ground. He enclosed seven acres of ground with a stockade and built within a storehouse, a church, and three rows of houses. Bricks made on the spot went into the houses. Enough land was cleared to raise grain for the entire colony. By 1616 six similar settlements were spread along the river. Though Jamestown continued as the seat of government, over half the colony's population of 381 was scattered in stockades above the town and slightly less than half in two settlements near the mouth of the river, leaving Jamestown nearly a deserted village.

All these plantations were cooperative projects, for both Gates and Dale continued the communal management of the colony's life that had begun in 1609 and was to continue for seven years, at the end of which the hoped-for profits would be divided among planters and adventurers. Both men knew that circumstances required joint effort at this stage of the enterprise, and both saw, too, that joint effort deadened a planter's incentive. They hoped severe enforcement of the laws divine, moral, and martial would compel the drones to share the load. The method worked for a while, but in time the sluggards found ways to slip from their duties and slumber while others labored, "presuming that howsoever the harvest prospered, the general store must maintain them."

Dale, a flexible man, knew when to ease up. In 1613–1614 he modified the communal plan by giving old settlers three acres of clear ground, in return for which they devoted one month's service to the colony and two and a half barrels of grain to the company storehouse, or magazine. The incentive of free land came as it appeared Virginia soil might provide settlers with more than food. John Rolfe had, a short while earlier, produced his first crop of tobacco. Others saw with him that though the land had failed to produce gold or silver, tobacco might provide a path to prosperity.

Dale returned home in 1616, accompanied by John Rolfe, his wife Pocahontas, and her retinue of Indians. The public gaped at the quiet, dignified Indian princesses who had been converted to Christianity; the company praised Dale, who had "reclaimed almost miraculously those idle and disordered people, and reduced them to labor and an honest fashion of life." But enthusiasm for Virginia had waned. Thousands of pounds and hundreds of lives had been lost to create a flimsy colony of 351 people—"a small number to advance so great a work," said John Rolfe. The seven-year period of joint stock was about to end; the company had no dividends to offer but land and lacked even the money to administer the division of land among planters and adventurers. Planters had found a cash crop, but the tobacco they sent home tasted harsh and bitter and offered little competition to the mild Spanish product, still preferred by most Englishman.

Virginia settlers, for their own reasons, shared the dismal view of the colony's future. Trading was monopolized by a London-controlled group, the Society of Particular Adventurers for Traffique with Virginia, which dumped over-priced, often useless products—it sent luxuries when farm tools were needed—on the colonists and offered ridiculously little for the tobacco crop. They grumbled, too, about their governor, Captain Samuel Argall. They had liked George Yeardley, Dale's replacement, who had given them a year of relaxed rule, allowing them to do as they wished. Argall, a relative of Sir Thomas Smith, sailed onto the scene in 1617 to find Jamestown once again rotting away, the settlers tending to little but the growing of tobacco. Argall at once set to "repairing and making straight what he found decayed and crooked." He revived the laws divine, moral, and martial and reprimanded the company at home for policies that "wholly discouraged" the colonists, thus making enemies on both sides of the ocean.

While Argall sought to impose order on the colony, plans progressed in England once again to reinvigorate the enterprise. Bermuda, with far less effort and investment, had turned into a prospering, profitable affair. Its success convinced many that in time Virginia, too, would pay off. Argall's arbitrary rule served as a handy justification for the reform movement that was about to occur.

Under New Management

A reform faction among the adventurers formed about the time of Dale's return to demand an overhauling of company policy toward Virginia. It agitated for change, not abandonment, of the colony. Something had to be done about local government, for settlements were appearing up and down the James River, and more could be expected as the colony expanded. The company's own lands had to be developed to protect the adventurers' investment but in a way that involved a minimum of expense. (The company debt in 1616 stood at over £8,000.) New ways had to be found to entice individual settlers and also associated groups of settlers—the Pilgrims were such a group—who would finance themselves across to Virginia to erect private plantations within the colony. The reformers sought, in short, to "reduce the people and affairs in Virginia into a regular course" and by so doing to make the colony a more attractive place to live.

After a year of meandering and sometimes violent discussion, company members in 1618 dealt with all these matters in the instructions drawn up for Sir George Yeardley, who, as he was about to return to govern the colony, had been knighted "to grace him more." When Yeardley arrived at Jamestown, he announced that the role of absolute governor had been abandoned, that the laws Gates, Dale, and Argall had ruled under were abrogated, and that the settlers "are now governed by those free laws which his Majesty's subjects live under in England." As he revealed more of his instructions from the company, the colonists saw a new order opening up for Virginia. They quickly came to call these instructions of 1618 "the great charter."

A good part of the instructions dealt with the distribution of land, which was now to be used as bait to draw settlers across the ocean. The company promised a minimum of a hundred acres to all adventurers and to all "ancient"—that is, pre-1616—planters. Those carried over at company expense would work company land, or the "public estate" as it was called, at half-rent for seven years and be free at the end of that time to set out on their own. Those who went at their own expense would receive a "headright" of at least fifty acres and additional grants for every person they brought with them. The headright system became fixed in Virginia tradition, and, in one form or another, was adopted by all colonies in time.

The instructions' remarks about the public estate made clear the company did not intend to pull out of Virginia. Four boroughs were to be created—James City, Charles City, Henrico, and Kecoughtan—and within each, tenants would till the company's three thousand acres of land while the rest remained in private hands. The income from these lands would be used "to ease all the inhabitants of Virginia forever of all taxes and public burdens as much as may be" and also to pay dividends to the adventurers back home.

The private plantations had presented a tricky problem to the company. They often represented the investment of influential men, the sort the company wanted to attract to Virginia but also the sort who would bridle at interference in their affairs. And yet to allow these private "corporations" a free hand would create a chaotic diversity in the colony. The issue was resolved by binding it up with the question of local government. The company instructed Yeardley to create "a laudable form of government . . . like as we have already done for the well ordering of our courts here," a way of saying the company pattern of managing its affairs in London was to be duplicated in Virginia. Once each year—more often in case of emergency—two members from each corporation and borough would be chosen on the local level to assemble in Jamestown, there to meet as a House of Burgesses. The creation of a colonial assembly similar to the company assembly in London completed the equality between the Virginia planter and the London adventurer. The instructions further promised that once Virginia's government operated effectively "no orders of our court afterward shall bind [the] colony unless they be ratified in like manner in their general Assembly." And through the assembly the company hoped to balance diverse local interests against the colony's interests. Private plantations and boroughs remained free to run their economic and local political affairs without interference. The assembly would represent diverse interests of the colony, not necessarily the people. The laws of the assembly would be the laws of the colony.

The first assembly met in the Jamestown church on July 30, 1619. The governor and his council sat in the choir, the twenty-two burgesses in the body of the church, and the speaker, John Pory, between the two groups. The session lasted only six days, for the weather was stifling and several members were down with malaria. In that time the body approved, and thus made law, several company instructions regarding the Indians, the morals and religion of the settlers, the encouragement of agricultural experiments, contracts with tenants and servants, and the maintenance of the company storehouse. They provided for their own salaries by levying a tax of one pound of tobacco on every man over sixteen. They agreed that the company could disallow their laws but asked for a reciprocal right on company ordinances.

The great charter, with its harnessing of local interests to those of the province and its gift of representative government to the colony, had been produced while Sir Thomas Smith still led the company, but while prodded by the imaginative and mercurial Sir Edwin Sandys, a widely traveled Oxonian who tolerated Puritanism and fought hard in Parliament against extension of the king's prerogatives. Sandys and Smith, whose tempers and talents nicely complemented one another, had worked together for over a decade nurturing Virginia. In 1619 Sandys became the company's treasurer. It is not clear whether he manipulated Smith from power or the aging Sir Thomas gracefully stepped aside. Regardless, the two men did not differ over policy—Smith had backed Sandys' reforms— but over how that policy should be administered. Sandys was convinced that a bold and vigorous management of the enterprise could make Virginia as profitable as Bermuda, that talisman hanging in the background to bolster faith in Virginia's future.

Sandys came to power with Virginia's hardest years behind. The military-outpost approach had been abandoned; a staple in the form of tobacco had been found; and a hardy nucleus of ancient planters had arisen. Sandys' immediate troubles centered at home. Debt plagued the company. Its seven-year exemption from customs duties ended in 1619, and the government indicated that the flood of tobacco beginning to pour in would be hit with a heavy tax. These troubles momentarily drifted into the background as Sandys applied all his energies to building up the colony. Well over half the 1,261 emigrants during his first year in office went at company expense to company lands, financed by the national lottery, which was now promoted with such zeal that some called it a national nuisance. He promoted Virginia's beauties so effectively throughout England that after 1620 most emigrants came at their own expense or were sent by private groups.

Sandys popularized the use of private plantations to settle Virginia. By 1622 the patents handed out to subsidiary companies numbered over fifty—among them, one to John Pierce for a group of settlers later known as the Pilgrims. The practice of settling Virginia in semi-independent groups stemmed in large part from the English pattern of village life, where men acted as one of the whole and rarely independently. As the village pattern died out in Virginia, reliance on subsidiary companies for settlement died, too.

Behind Sandy's skillful promotion lay a plan. Virginia had concentrated so heavily on tobacco as a cash crop that a single crop failure could ruin the entire colony. Sandys wanted to diversify along the lines that the elder Hakluyt had suggested to Gilbert nearly a half century earlier. Since individual settlers and subsidiary companies would resist any sort of experimentation that might increase the risk of failure, Sandys knew that the company must lead the way. Under his prodding the company sent out at its own expense a variety of experts—some 150 men to develop an iron industry, Germans to erect and operate a sawmill, Italian glass-blowers, shipbuilders, a Frenchman skilled in making salt from sea water. The company's public estate became something like a modern day experimental farm where colonists came to observe, then, if impressed, returned home to carry on what they had seen. Company tenants experimented with cotton brought from the West Indies, with sugar cane, oranges, lemons, pineapples, and potatoes from Bermuda, with silkworms from Italy.

The perceptive in England saw Sandys' goal and backed his efforts. John Donne told disgruntled investors, "though you see not your men, though a flood, a flood of blood have broken in upon them, . . . great creatures lie long in the womb." The birth would come without Edwin Sandys as midwife. The boldness of his management shook the faith of many adventurers who preferred the caution and proved acumen of Sir Thomas Smith. Sandys' prickly personality helped him little nor did the running battle he carried on with several of his powerful supporters. His gravest error was to attempt too much too quickly. He pushed over thirty-five hundred unseasoned settlers into a land where neither adequate food nor housing awaited them and in less than three years 75 per cent of them were dead. In light of this figure, the government's edict in 1621 forbidding further use of the lottery to raise money can be viewed as a disguised blessing. Sandys might still have carried his project to success but for the disaster of the next year, that "flood of blood"—the massacre of 1622—John Donne spoke of.

The Indians had nearly managed to wipe the white man out of Virginia during the starving time. When he survived that ordeal, they settled back to wait the death of the colony; and an uneasy truce between native and interloper came into being. Captain Newport's capture in 1613 of Pocahontas, daughter of Powhatan, chief of a confederacy of Virginia Indians, changed the situation. He carried her to Jamestown, where William Strachey later remembered her as "well-featured but wanton." John Rolfe, a widower of twenty-nine at the moment deep in his experiments with tobacco, fell in love with her and wrote Governor Dale that he wished to marry this girl "to whom my hearty and best thoughts are, and have a long time been, so entangled and enthralled in so intricate a labyrinth that I was even awearied to unwind myself thereout." Rolfe's desire raised a storm. Some said a white man should not marry a savage, others that a commoner should not marry one of royal blood, though that blood be savage. Governor Dale backed Rolfe; permission soon came from England; and the marriage was performed in 1614, bringing with it a softening of Powhatan's bitterness toward the English. Pocahontas' grace, dignity, and her conversion to Christianity convinced many who met her in England that a greater effort should be made to civilize, that is, Anglicize, the Indians. Pocahontas' death in 1617, as she and Rolfe were about to return to Virginia, set afoot a national project for a college both to convert and educate Virginia's Indians. The company donated ten thousand acres near Henrico.

The well-meaning plan was doomed by the steady encroachment of the English into Indian lands. Powhatan's death in 1618 brought his "brother" Opechancanough—he may have been only a fellow chief rather than blood brother—to power. Opechancanough held the English in deep contempt, but he continued Powhatan's policy of coexistence for four years, by which time he was convinced that force alone would preserve his tribes from the advancing white man. He persuaded fellow chiefs through the confederacy to his view, then began to plan an attack designed to wipe out every Englishman in Virginia.

The blow came on March 22, 1622. Throughout the previous week the Indians had been unusually friendly: "they came unarmed into our houses with deer, turkies, fish, fruits, and other provision to sell us; yea, in some places sat down at breakfast with our people. . . ." The morning of the massacre Indians had dispersed themselves through the settlements along the James River and on signal "they slew most barbarously, not sparing either age or sex, man, woman or child." Within a few hours, 347 settlers died, among them John Rolfe.

The massacre disrupted Virginia's life. Colonists had to withdraw into stockades for safety, and there, amid cramped quarters made worse by the unexpected arrival of 340 new settlers, some five hundred more persons died within the year. Plans for the college died in the massacre and with them went all effort to Christianize the Indians. The settlers carried out wholesale reprisals; at one point 250 Indians seeking peace were lured to death by drinking a toast in poisoned wine. Attempts to understand or to deal fairly with the Indian expired. Hands that had been tied "with gentleness and fair usage, are now set at liberty," a contemporary said with a touch of hypocrisy. The English, he added, "may now by a right of war and the law of nations invade the country and destroy them who sought to destroy us." After 1622 Virginians dismissed forever the European image of the Indian as a noble savage, a shift in attitude that would occur in every other American colony before the seventeenth century ended.

Virginia on Its Own: 1623–1640

The massacre annihilated Sandys' grand plans for Virginia. The approach of bankruptcy fed a growing opposition within the company. Any thought of expansion and experimentation had to wait until the company recouped strength, and tobacco alone—that "deceivable weed," Sandys called it—seemed to offer the only hope of salvation. It seemed unwise to build a colony on a weed that King James detested on moral grounds and might at any time outlaw and that, as Sandys thought, "served neither for necessity, for ornament to the life of a man, but was founded only on humor [that is, fashion] which might soon vanish into smoke and come to nothing." Worst of all, Virginia tobacco, though improved in quality since the planters had learned to cure it by hanging the leaves on poles to dry, now had to compete with the still superior Spanish product in price, for in 1619 the company's seven-year exemption from import duties had ended.

Circumstances forced Sandys to overlook the folly of a tobacco-based economy, and in the weeks after he had heard of the massacre he negotiated a contract with the government—the so-called tobacco contract—in which the company received a monopoly to handle all tobacco brought into England and the king in return got a fixed revenue on every pound imported, plus a cut of the company's overall profits. This seemingly sensible arrangement led to disaster rather than salvation. Rumblings against Sandys' leadership now exploded into the open. There were complaints that those who administered the contract were overpaid and, worse, were all Sandys' men. Those who controlled private plantations in Bermuda and Virginia resented having to market their crop through the company when they might do better on the open market. The bickering became so intense that in April 1623 the government declared the tobacco contract void. Soon afterward the Privy Council took over the management of company affairs in London while a five-man commission traveled to Virginia to investigate matters there.

The commission received a cool welcome in Virginia. The assembly refused to sign documents attacking the company or to open its records to the commissioners, and to underline its independence it ordered that a clerk who had been bribed to talk be placed in the pillory and his ears sliced off. For all that, the commission learned that the company's American affairs were in a hopeless state. The crown, meanwhile, had suggested a compromise in the form of a new charter patterned after the one of 1606, which would give the government some control over company affairs. The company refused the offer flatly, and in October 1623 the government issued a writ of quo warranto—an order forcing a person or organization to justify in court its claims to a privilege or liberty. The disastrous-state of company affairs emerged in the trial held in mid-1624, and it came as no surprise when the court ordered the London Company to be divested of its privileges under the charter of 1612.

The company failed mainly because it went bankrupt. Factional quarrels only hastened what was inevitable after the loss of the lottery and the massacre of 1622. Few saw at the time that the money, lives, and energy poured into the effort of building a colony had not been wasted. The company had created in the wilderness a colony that still lived after seventeen years. The settlers had learned how to sustain themselves and were producing a crop that gave them a cash income. The company had bestowed on the colony "a laudable form of government" whose liberality astonished men who compared Virginia's institutions with those being established in the Irish plantations during the same period. The London Company failed financially; by all other standards it succeeded.

Promptly after the company had been divested of its powers, the Privy Council dispatched Francis Wyatt as governor. The absence in Wyatt's instructions of reference to the assembly made it seem that the crown planned to revive the absolute governor of Virginia's early years. Wyatt soon found that a stranger to America could rule intelligently only with advice from those who knew the country's special conditions, and he soon began to depend on local eminents for help. Out of these informal sessions came the governor's council with a form and functions that would persist through the colonial period. In 1625 a situation arose where Wyatt wanted the advice and backing of all interests in the colony. Since he lacked authority to convene the assembly he called a "convention" composed of former assembly delegates. The extralegal gathering indicated how Americans throughout the colonial period would create new political machinery to deal with extraordinary conditions that demanded prompt attention.

While the Virginia convention deliberated, Charles I, who had only recently come to the throne, announced that "the government of the colony of Virginia shall immediately depend upon ourself, and not be committed to any company or corporation, to whom it may trust matters of trade and commerce, but cannot be fit or safe to communicate the ordering of state affairs, be they of never so mean consequence." That proclamation settled the company's future for the time being but did little to clarify the position of the government of Virginia or who would foot the burden of administering it. Charles side-stepped a positive stand. In 1627 he ordered Wyatt to convene the assembly in order to resolve a specific problem about tobacco and nothing else. The colonists each year gathered together on their own to discuss their affairs and to petition the king to grant them the rights of assembly they had held under the company. He neither denied nor agreed to the repeated requests. As governors came and went—Sir George Yeardley in 1626, Sir John Harvey in 1630, Sir Francis Wyatt again in 1639, Sir William Berkeley in 1642— their instructions remained essentially the instructions the company had written for its own governors.

Throughout this period of indecision the governor's council became the most effective foil against arbitrary authority. In 1634 it rebuked Governor Harvey—"a proper man, though perhaps somewhat choleric and impatient"—for exceeding his power. Harvey answered that the council "were to give their attendance as assistants only to advise with him," then proceeded to knock out the teeth of one member and threaten the others with hanging. The following year the council arrested Harvey, packed him off to London, and elected one of their own, John West, in his place. The king forced Harvey back upon the Virginians, but once the point had been made that a crown representative could not be maltreated, Harvey was recalled and Governor Wyatt reappointed to his old post, bringing with him news that annual assemblies might once again begin.

Gradually throughout this fifteen-year period the pattern of colonial royal government took shape—a shape largely determined by practices established by the London Company. The government, as Charles I had insisted, would "depend on ourself" in that the crown would appoint the governor and council, but the settlers would have a large measure of control over their affairs through an annually chosen representative assembly. The company had given the pattern to Virginia, but Virginians themselves brought the crown around to perpetuating that pattern.

MARYLAND

Gilbert had dreamed of reproducing in the New World the England he knew, a land of great estates where nobles reigned over tenants and freeholders and were, so to speak, kings of the countryside. The crown shaped Gilbert's charter to fit this dream, handing him a grant of lordship by feudal tenure to all the land he settled. He financed his voyages by handing out for a fee, huge parcels of the grant to those who shared his vision. Raleigh cherished the same dream, received the same understanding treatment from the crown, and paid for his voyages to Roanoke in a similar way. Merchants backed both men's ventures, for commerce and colonization could never be completely separated; but where the gentleman adventurer desired not only the profit but the power and prestige that came with the land, the merchant was for the most part satisfied with the profit.

Gentlemen Adventurers

The impetus for settling Virginia came mainly from merchants, a fluke not to be repeated in the seventeenth century. And even in that enterprise the old dream of Gilbert and Raleigh played a part. In the early years of the colony every Virginia-bound ship carried a complement of second- and third-son gentlemen who hoped to make their mark in the New World. Once the London Company had collapsed, the disenchanted merchant searched elsewhere for profit; but the gentlemen adventurers still held to the dream of a great American estate, and with backing from the crown they sought throughout the seventeenth century to realize it. Nova Scotia, Maryland, New York, New Jersey, the Carolinas, Pennsylvania, Maine, and New Hampshire all represent great proprietary grants in the tradition of Gilbert's. These grants came in two waves in the seventeenth century, one each side of the English civil war. The first wave, from 1621 to 1640, began with the grant of Nova Scotia to Sir William Alexander and closed with the grant of Maine to Sir Ferdinando Gorges in 1639.

The Stuarts encouraged gentlemen to colonize. Both James I and Charles I distrusted merchants, who gave them a hard time in Parliament and seemed always eager to peck away at royal prerogatives. If colonies were to arise in America, it seemed best to have them in friendly hands. Moreover, land still determined social status in England; and the abundant tracts in America, if judiciously handed out, might make it possible to raise up a new nobility to strengthen the crown against its opponents. The New World itself further encouraged the gentlemen: Virginia proved America could be settled and Bermuda that it could be profitable. The hazards of settlement remained, but they had been so greatly reduced that one man, sufficiently well off, might now undertake what earlier had required the resources of a company.

Sir Ferdinando Gorges had been among the first to be lured by the vision of a great feudal barony in America. He had governed the Plymouth Company and had been deeply involved in the Sagadahoc disaster. His dream refused to die with the failure of the Plymouth Company. He helped to revive the company in 1620 under the new name of Council for New England. The council received from the crown the right to settle and control all the land of America from the fortieth to forty-eighth parallel (roughly, from the southern boundary of present-day Pennsylvania to just beyond the northern tip of Maine) and from sea to sea. While Gorges and his associates pondered how to exploit this gift and fumed at court over the intrusion of the Puritans into their territory, George Calvert, a member of the council who had helped extract the grant from the crown, proceeded to colonize his own equally magnificent tract of New World land.

Calvert, "a forward and knowing person," came of a well-connected but not especially distinguished family. At Oxford, where he took a Master of Arts degree in 1605, he met Robert Cecil, later Earl of Salisbury. Soon afterward, he became Cecil's secretary; then, in 1608, clerk to the Privy Council. The king made him a secretary of state in 1619. He held the post for six years, during which he became a member of the Council for New England, received a large grant under an extraordinarily generous charter on the Avalon Peninsula of Newfoundland, ordered the dissolution of the London Company for the crown, and, finally, turned Catholic. Aware that his conversion limited his political usefulness, he resigned from the government, an abdication from power eased by his elevation to the peerage and also by his hope of acquiring even more power in America. Calvert had begun to develop plans for a colony in Newfoundland before his departure from government. A summer visit to America did nothing to belie the encouraging reports he had received about the land and weather. He ordered storehouses and a baronial home built for himself and in 1628 came over with his family and forty settlers. Troubles struck at once. "I came to build, and settle and sow; and I am fallen to fighting Frenchmen," he said, referring to privateers who had invaded the main harbor of his peninsula. Winter revealed the nature of the land and broke his optimism. "I am determined to commit this place to fishermen," he told the king as he headed for Virginia, where he hoped "your Majesty will please to grant me a precinct of land."

Governor Harvey, who could spot a court favorite when he saw one, welcomed George Calvert, now Lord Baltimore, warmly. Since Harvey's likes generally became his council's hates, this did little to endear Baltimore to Virginians. His Catholicism made him the more suspect. He was asked to take an oath of allegiance to the king, which he did gladly, and an oath of supremacy, which referred to the king as the head of the church. This, Baltimore refused, possibly on the ground that the king himself had excused him from it. Virginians made it clear they did not wish the visiting Lord to became a permanent resident. Baltimore, whom the French ambassador had once called an honorable, sensible, courteous, and well-intentioned man, managed to allay ill feeling. He left his family in Jamestown and returned to England to ask for a grant south of Virginia.

He failed to get what he asked for. Robert Heath, who as attorney-general had managed the dissolution of the London Company, had been given a great tract to the south a few months earlier. A grant between Heath's and Jamestown would have satisfied Baltimore, but the crown preferred to put him further up Chesapeake Bay, partly to pacify Virginians, who complained loudly that their colony was being sliced up to please a Catholic, and partly perhaps in the hope that Baltimore's settlement to the north might check the spread of Dutch settlements beginning to sprout along the Hudson and Delaware Rivers. The perceptive in government saw that not Spain but the aggressive Dutch trader, who was already cutting in on the Virginia tobacco trade, was the future rival England must contend with in America.

Whatever Baltimore's thought about the land to the north, he knew that the sun warmed it more than Newfoundland. The king, Charles I, named Heath's grant Carolina, after himself; he called Baltimore's after his Catholic wife Queen Henrietta Maria, "Terra Mariae," which "Englished," as they said then, into "Mary Land." If Baltimore held hurt feelings about the location of his tract they were assuaged by the charter the king handed him in 1632.

The Charter of 1632

The boundaries for Maryland fixed by the charter unexpectedly proved less generous than the king planned for his friend. The northern boundary originally ran westward from Delaware Bay along the fortieth parallel, taking in all of what is today called the Delmarva Peninsula. Virginia immediately demanded the tip of the peninsula, for some of her people had already settled there. Also, she wished to have both sides of the bay's mouth in her control. The crown acceded to the request but supposedly retrieved Baltimore's loss there by extending his tract to the south bank of the Potomac River, then westward to the river's "first fountain." No one realized then that the river trended sharply northwest and as a result hemmed Maryland in so tightly that she would become among the smallest of the colonies. The compromises and vagaries involved in the boundaries created troubles throughout the colonial period. William Penn later claimed and got part of the Delmarva Peninsula for Delaware; later still, Maryland lost a slice off her northern boundary to Pennsylvania. The placing of both sides of the mouth of Chesapeake Bay in Virginia's hands and all the Potomac River in Maryland's raised questions of navigation rights and responsibilities that remained unsolved until the Constitution of 1787.

Lord Baltimore ended up with about ten million acres of land, but what his grant lacked in size he retrieved in power. The charter made him absolute lord and proprietor of Maryland, and all this authority could be passed on to his heirs. He owned all the land, and it was held in his, not the king's, name. He controlled all branches of the government. He could appoint all officers and delegate power as he saw fit. He had the right to establish courts, appoint judges, and try all cases, civil and criminal. He could erect towns, boroughs, and cities. He could bestow titles. The people were entitled to give their advice and consent to laws, but the proprietor alone could initiate legislation. The king relinquished the right to pardon criminals, to tax, to disallow any laws except those that clearly contravened the laws of England. The crown reserved only the right to control war and trade and its usual one-fifth "of all gold and silver" found within the province.

Lord Baltimore theoretically held more power in Maryland than the king in England, for the charter gave him all the authority "as any bishop of Durham" ever had, which was a great deal more than Charles

I held in 1632. The county of Durham had been created in the fourteenth century when marauding Scots terrorized northern England, and the preoccupied king lacked the strength to subdue them. Durham's lord, a bishop as well as a magnate, was given the authority to act as if he were king. The saying arose about Durham that "what the king was without, the bishop was within." Lord Baltimore asked for all the bishop's ancient power, though his autonomy had long since been cut back. Possibly experiences in Ireland, where the lands that came with Baltimore's peerage were located, had taught him a man needed absolute power to erect a plantation in a wilderness; or perhaps Virginia's early travails suggested the need to him. Regardless, it was only natural for Baltimore, as a landed aristocrat who lived surrounded by fragments of the medieval world, to draw on a medieval precedent for that power. Moreover, the massacre of 1622 may have reminded him that conditions in America differed little from those in northern England three centuries earlier. The crown thought well enough of Baltimore's suggestion to include a Bishop of Durham clause not only in his charters for Newfoundland and Maryland, but also in the ones issued to Sir Edmund Plowden, who planned but failed to settle a tract north of Maryland, and to the later proprietors of Carolina. It seemed as logical to give such authority to individual colonizers as it had been to dispense it through a trading-company charter to the London Company.

The realities of seventeenth-century life withheld from Baltimore the absolute powers bestowed upon him by the charter. He was restrained, on one side, by colonists who were accustomed to the liberties of England and who saw those liberties prevailing in neighboring Virginia, by the "advice and consent" clause of the charter, and by the distance from home and the strange conditions that forced settlers to act first and inform later; and, on the other side, by himself and the traditions of his class. Lord Baltimore was a tolerant man. He was also a gentleman who believed that authority carried with it responsibility for the welfare of those under his power.

The Maryland charter still lacked the king's seal when Lord Baltimore died, leaving "his lands, plans, obligations, and hopes" to his eldest son Cecilius Calvert, then twenty-six years old. Fortunately, the son inherited his father's qualities as well as his title and lands. Lord Baltimore's death did little to deter the settlement of Maryland or, it would seem, to alter the shape of its history.

The Early Years

Young Lord Baltimore blended tolerance with common sense. He hoped to create a refuge for oppressed English Catholics but knew no colony could thrive on Catholics alone. The appeal for settlers was directed to all Englishmen, regardless of religion. Aboard the *Ark* and the *Dove,* the first two ships sent out, were two Jesuits, seventeen gentlemen and their families, and some two hundred craftsmen, servants, and farm laborers. The leaders were Catholics, but the majority of settlers were Protestants, and at no time in Maryland's history were Catholics in a majority. Leonard Calvert, the second Lord Baltimore's brother and commander of the enterprise, was told that he should "suffer no scandal nor offense to be given to any of the Protestants" and that the Catholics should remain mute "upon all occasions of discourse concerning matters of religion."

Departure had been set for the summer of 1634, but anti-Catholic rumors—among them that Baltimore "intended to carry nuns over into Spain and soldiers to serve that king"—delayed the leaving until November. Cecilius Calvert had drawn heavily on Virginia's experience to ease the birth of his colony. He had used land to attract settlers, offering special inducement to firstcomers—a hundred acres each for a settler, his wife, and every servant, plus fifty acres for every child under sixteen; two thousand acres for every settler who brought five others with him, with the right to erect a manor "with all such royalties and privileges as are usually belonging to manors in England." He published lists of things a colonist would need in America to ease the early months there. The quitrent was fixed at the Virginia rate of two shillings per hundred acres. He sought to avoid Jamestown's starving time by ordering "provisions of victual" planted before other projects were undertaken. When Marylanders became too tobacco-conscious, a law modeled on the Virginia Two Acres Act of 1624 ordered "every person planting tobacco shall plant and tend two acres of corn."

The effort to avoid Virginia's mistakes surely contributed to Maryland's immediate prosperity. After a four month voyage, the *Ark* and the *Dove* touched first at Virginia, where Governor Harvey gave them a decent welcome and offer of help if needed; the governor's council said "that they would rather knock their cattle on the heads than sell them to Maryland." After some time searching for a suitable site, land was purchased from the local Indians and a stockade erected and gardens planted on the present site of St. Mary's, Maryland. A haze now drops over the story, for many of the records of these early years have since been lost. Two themes appear to dominate the first decade in the Maryland wilderness—one centering on a principle, the other on a man.

The principle concerned Lord Baltimore's charter-given right to initiate all legislation for the colony, a right he showed no desire to relinquish. The settlers first met in general assembly at the proprietor's direction in 1635, and though records for that and several succeeding sessions have vanished, much about these early gatherings can be surmised.

Writs had been issued singly to individual gentlemen and in general to all freemen ordering them to attend in person or by proxy. (The proxy system remained a Maryland peculiarity for many years.) Clergymen were present but denied a vote. Governor Calvert, along with being "Lieutenant-General, Admiral, Chief, Captain, and Commander, as well by sea as land," presided with his governor's council in attendance. The assembly modeled itself as much as possible on Parliament in procedure —members rose to speak, addressed the chair for recognition, and referred to a colleague as "the gentleman who spoke last"—and in privileges sought, such as freedom from arrest during session and, most insistently, the right to initiate legislation. In 1638, the first year of adequate extant records, the settlers openly balked at taking laws handed down from above by rejecting a body of statutes sent over from England. The opposition was led by a gentleman on the governor's council, Thomas Cornwallis, who seems to have been behind the suggestion that the assembly "might do well to agree upon some laws till we could hear from England again." Governor Calvert denied "any such power to be in the house," but sensing the mood of the assembly played for time by favoring the creation of committees to prepare drafts of statutes. In August, Lord Baltimore sent over word that the assembly might in a limited way draw up legislation; and though he still held to the principle involved, the first great battle in Maryland's history had ended.

While this struggle had been going on, the first phase of another one involving William Claiborne had also ended. Claiborne, for all the vituperation since heaped upon him, seems within his particular frame of reference to have been an honorable man. He had arrived in Virginia in 1621 and quickly became the colony's secretary of state, holding the post under several governors. Between 1627 and 1629 he explored the upper parts of Chesapeake Bay for Virginia. The colony soon after sent him to England to oppose the grant to Baltimore. While there he received permission from the king to trade for furs on Chesapeake Bay. He returned in 1631 with a hundred settlers to establish a trading post on Kent Island, "unplanted. by any man," as he later remarked. This was before the Maryland charter had passed the seals (that is, had safely negotiated the elaborate red tape of the day and received the king's seal of approval); and because Baltimore was granted only land "hitherto uncultivated," Claiborne believed he had a solid legal claim to the island. His staunch rebuff to Baltimore's authority muddied Maryland affairs for years.

Claiborne's post tapped the rich fur country up the Susquehanna River that Lord Baltimore had planned to exploit, and in his dealings with Indians Claiborne propagated an anti-Catholic, anti-Maryland attitude. Worst of all, he increased the strain between Maryland and Virginia. The unpopular Governor Harvey sided with Baltimore and that, of course, instantly placed the anti-Harvey council with Claiborne and against Maryland. The ensuing bitterness between the two colonies may have prompted Lord Baltimore's eagerness, shortly after Harvey's ouster, to take over the governorship of Virginia. He told the king that he would improve the income from Virginia without raising taxes. While the king pondered this offer—ultimately to reject it—Leonard Calvert in 1637 took advantage of Claiborne's absence in England to invade Kent Island. It fell with little trouble. The following year the Maryland assembly passed a bill of attainder against Claiborne that deprived him of all his property within the colony. The crown compensated him for losses by making him treasurer of Virginia for life. Within a few years Claiborne would find a way to compensate himself still further at Maryland's expense.

CHESAPEAKE SOCIETY

For all the feeling engendered by Claiborne's quarrel among the people of Maryland and Virginia, the two colonies remained officially on speaking terms, offering one another what the king had demanded—"such lawful assistance as may conduce to both your safeties and the advancement of the plantation of those countries." Virginia might put an anti-Catholic measure on the books, Maryland might undermine the tobacco market by exporting the "trash of that commodity," but the colonies had too much in common to oppose one another constantly. "I shall be talking about Virginia," Robert Beverley wrote in 1705, "though you may consider at the same time that there cannot be much difference between this and Maryland, they being contiguous one to the other, lying in the same Bay, producing the same sort of commodities, and being fallen into the same unhappy form of settlements, altogether upon country seats, without towns." By 1640 a Chesapeake society had come into being that separate boundaries and different governments had little to do with.

The Great Bay of Chesapeake

Chesapeake Bay stretched nearly two hundred miles in length and from three to twenty-two miles in width. Some 150 rivers, creeks, and branches fed into it, most of them navigable streams; ships could travel up several of them for nearly a hundred miles. The total shoreline has recently been calculated at fifty-six hundred miles, almost a thousand miles more than the entire coastal outline of the continental United States. Nearly two thousand miles of that shoreline was open to seagoing seventeenth-century vessels.

The bay's extraordinary shoreline helps explain why the area took so readily to tobacco, a weed that by the end of the colonial period was being successfully grown as far north as Massachusetts. The availability of water transportation, not the soil alone, encouraged its growth in the Chesapeake area. A hogshead of tobacco weighed nearly a half ton; to roll or haul it over miles of rough countryside was costly, wearying, and injurious to the leaf. In the "well-watered" Chesapeake country "none of the plantation houses, even the most remote," a visiting Frenchman noted, "is more than one hundred or one hundred fifty feet from a 'crik,' and the people are thus enabled not only to pay their visits in their canoes, but to do all their freight carrying by the same means."

The bay's shoreline also helps explain why no sizable towns developed in the area. The towns that eventually did arise were located at or near the fall line—Baltimore on the Patapsco, for example, or Fredericksburg on the Appomattox—which marked the upper limit of navigation. Elsewhere the tobacco trader sailed up to the planter's backdoor.

Every planter desired an outlet on a navigable stream. As the choice sites were taken up in Jamestown or St. Mary's, new arrivals searched elsewhere for well-watered land. Within a few years the desire for lots that abutted on water had shattered the village pattern of life. Occasionally, in a time of Indian troubles, the settlers might huddle together temporarily, but the farm soon replaced the village throughout the Chesapeake area. And to the degree that the bay killed the village, it also forced changes in the settlers' religious habits and in the forms of both local and central government. By 1640 a pattern of life alien to the English experience had taken shape. Authorities found the change difficult to accept. "For how is it possible to govern a people so dispersed; especially such [rabble] as for the most part are sent over?" George Sandys mourned to his brother, Sir Edwin.

How can they repair to divine service except every plantation have a minister? How can we raise soldiers to go upon the enemy or workmen for public employments, without weakening them too much, or undoing them by drawing them from their labors? Whereas if we had planted together we could have borne out one another's labors and given both strength and beauty to the colony.

The Farm

The Chesapeake wilderness demanded certain immediate but supposedly temporary alterations in English habits. Settlers lived behind palisades and, in Virginia at least, worked the land in common and drew supplies from the company storehouse. The government regulated every side of daily life and forced the farmer to be both soldier and farmer at once. But the settler still lived in a home much like the home he had left; he still traveled out to the fields in the morning and back to his house at night as he had done in his village; and he attended church even more regularly than he had in England—thirteen times a week during Governor Dale's regime. The old pattern disintegrated slowly after the headright system—a gift of land, usually fifty acres, to every new settler—came in, in 1618 and swiftly after reprisals for the 1622 massacre appeared to end the Indian menace. Settlers moved out from the stockade and built homes on their plots of land, coming into the "village" only occasionally for supplies, for gossip, and possibly for church. The American farmer, as opposed to the English yeoman, had come into being.

The farm, as it took shape in the Chesapeake area, was a self-sustaining unit. Tobacco was the crop raised to pay taxes and debts and buy an occasional saucepan or bolt of cloth for the wife, but much of the farmer's time and energy went into producing food for his table. In the spring, after the tobacco seedlings were in, the rest of the land went to wheat and corn, except for a truck patch near the house. The orchard provided fresh fruit for the table, the ingredients for hard cider and peach brandy, and, now that the village cemetery was a thing of the past, a suitable setting for the family burial ground. Horses were rare on the seventeenth-century Chesapeake farm, but cattle, hogs, and sheep were common. Crops were fenced in—a well-built rail fence had to be "pig-tight, horse-high, and bull-strong," as a later age put it—and the stock was turned out. The settler soon abandoned his English dishes. Pork formed the basis of most meals. And by the 1640's, American game and fish were found on most tables when in season; such Indian dishes as succotash, roasted ears of corn, hominy and corn pone, and ash-baked potatoes were common.

These early farms, however, were not plantations. A man might hold title to two thousand acres but rarely planted over a hundred of them, if that. The land itself checked him. Clearing the ground was a major task. The new settler picked up the Indian habit of deadening the trees by "girdling," or chopping away a strip of bark, then planting his first crop beneath their withering branches. In time the dead trees would be chopped down and burned, their roots yanked or burned out. Every cleared acre bespoke months of effort, most of it by the farmer himself and one or two servants. The labor shortage as much as the land limited the size of the farm. Nearly all the labor was white through most of the seventeenth century. Negroes remained few. Estimates put the number in Virginia around three hundred in 1640 and thirty years later around two thousand out of a population of some forty thousand. Most of the Negroes came from the Spanish Indies or directly from Africa and were of small use to a farmer with little time to spare in directing an untrained man who spoke a strange tongue.

No plantation mansions or lovely belles dressed in crinoline skirts graced this land in the early seventeenth century. It was a hard, lonely life. The farmer's family, which included his servants as well as his kin, lived mainly unto itself. The land imposed an equality of sorts on all, master and servant alike. "Some distinction, indeed, is made between them in their clothes and food," Robert Beverley remarked, "but the work of both is no other than what the overseers, the freemen, and the planters themselves do."

Government and Religion

Leaders in both Chesapeake colonies stoutly resisted the idea that in America all men were equal. Emigrants with any rank and influence at home slipped naturally into positions of power, usually as members of the governor's council. Prior to the 1640's the indentured servant, even with his service completed, rarely rose to a position of authority. The colonial governments tried, as in England, to dominate all sides of men's lives. Among other things, they parceled out the land, decided the pay for clergymen, determined the rules of servitude, and tried to legislate the settlers' economic affairs.

The governments of Maryland and Virginia differed in detail. The Maryland governor held more power and reported only to the proprietor, while his Virginia counterpart drew authority from the king and was considerably restrained by his council, which was far more than the advisory body of Maryland. These details aside, the two colonies developed along strikingly similar lines, with Maryland drawing heavily on her neighbor's precedents for guidance. The governor and council of both colonies administered all affairs, and they sat with the assembly when the governor called that body into session. Opposition against control from above came early in both colonies and from the council, not the assembly as might be suspected. The assembly in 1640 had little power in either colony. With Parliament as a model and the council as an ally, it would soon turn on both governor and council, demanding first to sit apart and choose its own speaker, then later using its tentative power to legislate taxes to expand its authority in other directions.

Provincial government assumed a durable form early, but only the outline of local government had materialized by 1640. In the beginning, when town and colony were one, the English borough had sufficed as a model for Chesapeake government. As Jamestown settlers fanned out to choice spots along the river and bay, the borough plan became awkward. In 1624 two monthly courts were erected for settlers above and below Jamestown. These courts were supposed to travel about their districts, much as the monthly courts in England. By 1632 five such courts were in operation, and it was apparent that the English county would be the pattern for local government in Virginia. The obvious became official in 1634 when the assembly divided Virginia into eight counties, each with its own monthly court. The governor and council controlled local affairs to a large degree by their power to appoint the court commissioners, or justices of the peace as they would be called, as well as sheriffs, constables, clerks, and coroners. The duties of all these officials conformed to the English pattern.

The county pattern was superimposed on the old borough pattern, and it was some time before the old one completely died away. The assembly at the time it created the county also substituted the office of sheriff for provost marshal, a hangover from the days when the colony had been regarded as a military outpost. The county became the unit for determining assembly representation, but the right of a borough to send a burgess survived for many years.

Maryland for the most part reproduced the Virginia pattern. Lord Baltimore tried to promote the development of great baronies, where the local lord erected and controlled his own courts, but the effort died before it was born. As St. Mary's settlers moved out, the old English hundred was resurrected as the key local unit, only quickly to be supplanted by the county. Both colonies consciously took English forms and changed them to fit new needs. The Chesapeake sheriff resembled the English sheriff but even more the English petty constable. The county court seemed modeled on its English predecessor, yet in time its powers and duties would vary considerably. The settlers took the broad form of the English pattern—central authority tied to local authority in a way that left a great deal of freedom on the local level—and adapted it to their particular requirements.

The religious life of the colonists during the early decades of the Great Bay's settlement drew heavily on Puritanism. Reverend Alexander Whitaker wondered in *Good News from Virginia* (1613) why "few of our English ministers that were so hot against the surplice and subscription [enforced assent to church doctrine] come hither, where neither are spoken of." His Jamestown church was organized along Presbyterian lines, with "church affairs" being "consulted on by the minister and four of the most religious men," the first hint of the dominant role the vestry would later play in the American version of the Anglican Church. George Keith, a Scotsman who followed Whitaker in 1617, continued the pattern. "Ceremonies are in no request, nor the Book of Common Prayer; I use it not at all," he said. "I have, by the help of God, begun a church government by ministers and elders. I made bold to choose four elders publicly by the lifting up of hands and calling upon God." A band of Puritans who settled south of the James River during Keith's tenure apparently disturbed no one's religious scruples. Early Virginia and New England diverged in religion over details rather than principles.

What, then, was the special quality of the way of life taking shape in the South? Wesley Frank Craven perhaps provides the best answer. "The most noticeable feature of the Chesapeake settlements is the absence of a common purpose and goal except such as was dictated principally by the requirements of individual interests," he writes. "Here, in short, was the first typically American frontier community, its development planless in any larger sense and its end the service of individual wants." The settlers of New England, who drew on the same general traditions as the colonists of Chesapeake Bay but adapted them differently, would find the Southerners' lack of common purpose and emphasis on the individual sharply at odds with their own views. The differences between the two groups will trace throughout the colonial story.

BIBLIOGRAPHY

First Stones

Louise Phelps Kellogg, "The American Colonial Charter," *American Historical Association, Annual Report for 1903,* Vol. I (2 vols., 1904), is still the best general study of the subject. The fullest account of Sagadahoc is in Charles M. Andrews, *Colonial Period of American History* (4 vols., 1936-1938; pb.), Vol. I, pp. 78–97. (Andrews' great work deals mainly with the institutional roots of the American story, and in this area he remains unsurpassed.) Henry Adams' diatribe against John Smith is most conveniently found in *The Henry Adams Reader* (pb. original), edited by Elizabeth Stevenson. Bradford Smith's *Captain John Smith* (1953) refurbishes Smith's reputation. Philip L. Barbour depicts the time as well as the man in his scholarly account of *The Three Worlds of Captain John Smith* (1964). The best accounts of Jamestown are in Wesley Frank Craven, *The Southern Colonies in the Seventeenth Century* (1949) ; Richard L. Morton, *Colonial Virginia* (2 vols., 1960) ; and David B. Quinn's *Raleigh and the British Empire* (1949). In the *Jamestown 350th Anniversary Historical Booklets* (1957), under the general editorship of E. G. Swem, Wesley Frank Craven's *The Virginia Company of London, 1606–1624* is relevant here. (Nearly all the pamphlets in the series are excellent and deserve the attention of students interested in the early history of Virginia.)

Two of the most useful collections of source material for this part and the remainder of the chapter are Alexander Brown's *Genesis of the United States* (2 vols., 1890) and Peter Force's *Tracts and Other Papers Relating Principally to the Origin, Settlement, and Progress of the Colonies in North America* (4 vols., 1836–1846). The most convenient collection on early Virginia is that edited by L. G. Tyler, *Narratives of Early Virginia, 1606–1626* (1907). John Smith's *Works*, edited by Edward Arber (1889; 2-vol. ed., 1910), and William Strachey's *The History of Travel into Virginia Britania,* edited by Louis B. Wright and Virginia Freund (1953), are the main authorities for the early days of Jamestown.

Virginia

Nearly all the above works are relevant here. Decidedly the ablest work on the subject is Craven's *Southern Colonies,* which is both perceptive and gracefully written. Because Craven occasionally presumes the reader's knowledge, the beginning student might ease into the subject through Andrews' account in *Colonial Period,* Vol. I or, better yet, Morton's *Colonial Virginia,* the first volume of which covers the period 1607 through 1710. Craven's detailed *Dissolution of the Virginia Company* (1932) should fascinate those attracted to the subject. For a good account of the 1622 massacre see Thomas J. Wertenbaker's *Virginia Under the Stuarts* (1914). (It should be noted here for those who might wish to follow up the Virginia story that what Craven, Morton, and other authorities, call the Virginia Company is in these pages referred to as the London Company. Both are informal names for what was officially known as The Treasurer and Company of Adventurers and Planters of the City of London for the First Colony in Virginia. London Company was preferred here to distinguish it from the West Country Group that settled Sagadahoc and also to emphasize the source of strength behind the Virginia settlement.)

Maryland

Craven's *Southern Colonies* and the second volume of Andrews' *Colonial Period* again offer the best introductions. Matthew Page Andrews, *Founding of Maryland* (1933) and *History of Maryland: Province and State* (1929), are full and more popular accounts. Newton D. Mereness, *Maryland as a Proprietary Province* (1901), gives a great deal of documentary material. The ablest detailed account is Elizabeth Baer's *Seventeenth-Century Maryland* (1949). Three older, but still useful, specialized studies worth consulting are Bernard C. Steiner, *Beginnings of Maryland, 1631–1639* (1903); Gaillard T. Lapsley, *The County Palatine of Durham: A Study in Constitutional History* (1900); and J. H. Latané, *Early Relations Between Maryland and Virginia* (1895). The most available volume of source material is C. C. Hall's edition of *Narratives of Early Maryland, 1633–1684* (1910).

Chesapeake Society

Craven, *Southern Colonies,* gives an especially good introductory account here, which incorporates much of the original work on the role of the seventeenth-century Virginia farmer first presented by Thomas J. Wertenbaker in *Patrician and Plebeian in Virginia* (1910), and more elaborately in *Planters of Colonial Virginia* (1922). Miss Baer's volume gives the Maryland story, and Latané's should be consulted for the relations between the two colonies. Other accounts that touch the subject peripherally are Richard B. Morris, *Studies in the History of American Law, with Special Reference to the Seventeenth and Eighteenth Centuries* (1946); Abbot E. Smith, *Colonists in Bondage: White Servitude and Convict Labor in America, 1607–1776* (1947); Edgar A. J. Johnson, *American Economic Thought in the Seventeenth Century* (1932);

and Marcus W. Jernegan, *Laboring and Dependent Classes in Colonial America, 1607–1783* (1931; pb.).

For further references see Craven's bibliography, especially full on the original sources available in print; and also the *Harvard Guide,* Sections 81, "Virginia Company and Virginia, 1606–1624," and 87, "Maryland in the Seventeenth Century."

Richard Mather, from a wood engraving by John Foster

4. The New England Way

BEGINNINGS
>   The Pilgrims
>   The Puritan Charter of 1629
>   "A City upon a Hill"

MASSACHUSETTS BAY
>   The Church
>   The State
>   Archbishop Laud

HIVINGS-OUT
>   Roger Williams
>   Anne Hutchinson
>   Plantations of the Otherwise Minded
>   Connecticut and New Haven

NEW ENGLAND SOCIETY
>   The Town
>   Economic Life
>   Indians and the Pequot War
>   The Puritan Heritage

BEGINNINGS

Captain John Smith did much to spark the planting of New England. This time he colonized with his pen. Smith had passed the years 1608 to 1614 in England, uselessly by his lights, when two London merchants hired him to hunt whales off the American coast. He found no whales but returned with a shipload of fish that paid for the voyage and a mind full of impressions about the northern coast of America. In 1616 he published *A Description of New England*. The pamphlet and the map that accompanied it became something of a best seller, and Smith's name for the area quickly replaced the earlier ones of Norumbega and North Virginia. His enthusiasm for "the Paradise of these parts," as he called it, did much to raise the interest of the Puritans and Pilgrims—those "great grim earnest men," Emerson spoke of, "who solemnized the heyday of their strength by planting New England."

The Pilgrims

In the southern part of Yorkshire lay "the mean townlet of Scrooby," and in the townlet was "a great manor-place, standing within a moat" where William Brewster lived. Brewster, a well-to-do member of the gentry who had been exposed to Puritanism at Cambridge, had exiled himself to Scrooby after a tour of duty in Queen Elizabeth's diplomatic service. His distaste for Anglicanism led him to separate from the church completely, and soon neighboring farmers and the sons of farmers like William Bradford were gathering at Brewster's manor to worship under the leadership of another Cambridge man, the Reverend John Robinson, whom even a despiser of separatism could call "a man of excellent parts, and the most learned, polished and modest spirit that ever separated from the Church of England."

Robinson's flock did not seek to reform England. It asked only to be let alone. The English Church and government respected its wishes, but the people of Scrooby did not. They harassed so steadily that in 1607 the congregation decided to move to Holland, which tolerated all shades of Protestantism. Brewster sold his property to finance the trip, and after two false starts about 125 of the group finally "gat over." They paused a year in Amsterdam, joining a group of London Separatists there, then moved on to Leyden.

They worshiped as they wished in this strange land but remained uneasy. City life disconcerted them, for, as Bradford put it, they were "used to a plain country life and the innocent trade of husbandry." The Dutch view of Sunday as a day of pleasure disturbed these solemn Englishmen, as did the effect of Holland on their children, who were learning the language and customs of the country and marrying Dutch youngsters— some joined the army; some took to sea; and "some worse courses." The Scrooby separatists had not left England to become something other than English. Strong emotional ties remained—and would remain forever, as the place names of New England testify. Worst of all, they saw the end of tolerance in Holland as Spain prepared, after a twelve-year truce, to reassert its control over the country, which would leave the Separatists "entrapped or surrounded by their enemies, so as they should neither be able to fight nor to fly." After long consultations among themselves, they "thought it better to dislodge betimes to some place of better advantage and less danger, if any could be found."

Brewster knew Sir Edwin Sandys, then in the midst of his drive to build up Virginia. Two of the Scrooby group went to London to talk with Sandys, who welcomed their expressed desire to emigrate. But would the king permit Separatists to populate Virginia? Robinson, in the artfully worded Leyden Agreement, pictured his congregation as loyal and orthodox. The king responded with a promise not to molest the Separatists "provided they carried themselves peaceably." The London Company thereupon issued them a patent on February 2, 1620, for a town-plantation in the name of John Pierce, one of their London friends.

The problem of financing the second exodus now arose. The London Company offered £300, but this was hardly a beginning. Thomas Weston, a hardware dealer with a shady reputation, said that he and several fellow merchants would underwrite the trip. Everything about the arrangement presaged trouble. His terms were those offered to the first Jamestown settlers and ignored everything that had been learned about colonization since 1607. A terminable joint-stock company would be formed. At the end of seven years all property and profits, held in common up to then, would be divided among adventurers and planters. Management of the plantation's affairs, as in early Virginia, would be split between London and America. Virginia's troubles with this arrangement would be compounded, for now a business group concerned only with profit would deal with a religious group eager to pursue a pure and simple existence. Nonetheless, the Separatists preferred a bad bargain to none; they accepted Thomas Weston's offer.

About fifty, or less than half the congregation, made the trip from Holland to England, and of those only thirty-five went on to America. By sailing time two-thirds of the party were "strangers," as the non-Puritans were called, among them a cooper named John Alden and Miles Standish, the party's military officer. The Pilgrims had assimilated enough from the Virginia experience to realize that at the start their plantation would be a military outpost. They declined John Smith's services "to save charges," as Smith put it, "saying my books and maps were much better cheap to teach them, than myself," and the stubby, explosive Standish was taken on instead.

The April departure date, timed to allow the planting of a crop for fall harvest, slipped past, and not until August did the Pilgrims set out in two ships, the *Speedwell* and the *Mayflower*. The *Speedwell* quickly belied her name; and after twice turning back because of leaks, the Pilgrims sold her for a loss, crammed those still willing to go—a number backed out at this point—aboard the *Mayflower,* and in early September 102 saints and strangers let England drop behind forever. They had only the dimmest chance to survive the next twelve months. They were setting out at the worst time of year, when storms blanketed the Atlantic and winter approached. Weston was determined to exploit rather than help them. They brought no cattle or livestock of any kind; they had, said Bradford, no "butter, or oil, not a sole to mend a shoe, not every man a sword to his side, wanting many muskets, much armor, etc." They were truly Pilgrims, poor and innocent of what lay ahead, and could only "trust to the good providence of God."

It took sixty-six days to cross. One passenger died and one child was born. They sighted the tip of Cape Cod in early November. Winter lay too close to head for the Hudson River, where they had apparently planned to settle. It would have been best to turn toward the French post at Port Royal, Nova Scotia, but the thought of a winter among Catholics probably horrified the Pilgrims. Instead, they reconnoitered the cape; then on the advice of two of the *Mayflower's* mates who had visited the area on earlier trips, they chose to settle at Plymouth.

By then the saints had disposed of their first political crisis. On the last day at sea some of the strangers aboard had remarked that since they were beyond the bounds of southern Virginia "none had power to command them," and once ashore they would go off on their own. Someone among the saints proposed drawing up a compact similar to a church covenant but this time for a secular purpose. The Mayflower Compact opened with an acknowledgment of loyalty to "our dread sovereign Lord, King James," went on to propose that the settlers form a civil body to frame laws and appoint officers, and closed with the signatures of forty-one Pilgrims who promised "due submission and obedience" to the officers elected and the laws passed. All signers, even those who were servants, automatically became freemen with the right to share in the government that was to be formed.

The compact was not a constitution, nor did it have legal validity, because the Pilgrims were settling where they had no right to be. It was a temporary expedient designed to give the saints control over mutinous strangers. It provided a basis for order and authority at a time when the Pilgrims had been thrust, so to speak, into a state of nature. It was designed to serve only until the settlement obtained a patent from the Council for New England, in whose territory the colonists had landed, or better yet, a royal charter. Under the authority of the compact the self-created freemen, with the saints a majority of one, elected John Carver their governor. He was forty-four, the wealthiest of the passengers, who had used his own fortune to pay for what Weston had refused to advance.

The Pilgrims landed at Plymouth on December 21, and "all things stared upon them with a weather-beaten face." Death instantly swept through the exhausted party, and by spring nearly half the passengers were gone, among them Governor Carver, whose post was assumed by William Bradford. The survivors endured a starving time that differed from Jamestown's only in the absence of marauding Indians, most of whom had been wiped out by a smallpox epidemic shortly before the Pilgrims arrived. A few "came skulking about," but none attacked, and one, Squanto, befriended them, teaching them how to plant corn, showing them the best streams for fishing, and acting as emissary with tribes in the area.

The Pilgrims gathered sometime in October 1621 to give thanks to God for their first harvest. They had little else to cheer them. No relief ships came from England to help them over the rough spots. In November Weston sent over thirty-five recruits who "brought not so much as a biscuit-cake or any other victuals with them." The *Mayflower,* whose master had stuck by the destitute settlers, departed with Plymouth's first cargo —"good clapboard, as full as she could stow, and beaver and otter skins," worth all told £500—only to be picked up by a French warship, which erased the first effort to reduce the debt to Weston and his associates. And so it went. Weston continued to exploit the Pilgrims, sending over fishing crews for them to feed and house free of charge and offering nothing in return but complaints for the slim cargoes being shipped back to England. He railed when Bradford, like Dale, abandoned the communal plan ahead of schedule and gave each family its own plot of ground, which made "all hands very industrious." And when the Pilgrims bought out the London investors in 1627, they saddled themselves with a debt of £2,400 that took seventeen years to pay off, mainly because Weston and those who handled the plantation's affairs in England cheated Plymouth from dawn to dusk through the years.

The Pilgrims had their political problems, too. A patent from the Council for New England in 1621 legalized their plantation, but this failed to satisfy Bradford, who throughout his long governorship worked hard to get a royal charter, which would make the colony responsible to the crown alone. Plymouth, to promote its cause at court, always behaved correctly toward the crown. It conducted official business in the king's name, gave juries an oath to uphold the king's justice, registered wills in the "year of the reign of our Sovereign Lord Charles" or whoever was on the throne. For all that, Plymouth never got her charter, largely because she refused to bribe officials at court who might have expedited

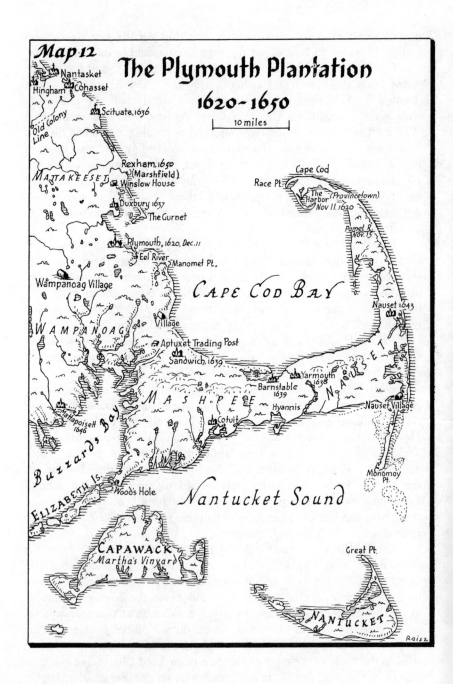

Map 12
The Plymouth Plantation
1620-1650

10 miles

Nantasket
Hingham   Cohasset
Old Colony Line
Scituate, 1636
MATTAKEESET
Rexham, 1650
(Marshfield)
Winslow House
Duxbury 1637
The Gurnet
Plymouth, 1620, Dec.11
Eel River
Manomet Pt.
Wampanoag Village
WAMPANOAG
Village
Aptuxet Trading Post
Sandwich, 1639
MASHPEE
Barnstable 1639
Hyannis
Cotuit
Mattapoisett 1646
Buzzards Bay
Elizabeth Is.
Wood's Hole

CAPAWACK
Martha's Vinyard

Cape Cod
Race Pt.
The Harbor (Provincetown)
Nov.11.1620
Pamet R. Nov.15

CAPE COD BAY

Nauset 1643
NAUSET
Yarmouth 1638
Nauset Village
Monomoy Pt.

Nantucket Sound

Great Pt.
NANTUCKET

Raisz

the matter. The lack of a charter to protect her rights made inevitable Plymouth's eventual absorption by Massachusetts Bay.

The issue of who should share in Plymouth's government was settled on an *ad hoc* basis. The Mayflower Compact disposed only temporarily of the traditional English voting requirement of a "forty shilling freehold." By 1671 a man needed to own £20 of property to qualify as a freeman. The liberality of the early years swiftly vanished. Democratic notions at no time took root. Even the English habit of choosing leaders from the elite remained strong. Elections occurred annually but rarely produced a change in leadership. Governor Bradford remained in office most of the time from 1620 until his death in 1657.

By Bradford's death Plymouth and the cluster of villages she had spawned had become backwater settlements. Once Boston arose, ships from England by-passed Plymouth's small harbor. This did not distress the Pilgrims, to judge by remarks in Bradford's great history *Of Plymouth Plantation*. They were content as long as they could worship as they pleased. They had left England with no sense of mission, with no desire to build a holy commonwealth in the wilderness. They lacked everything—money, supplies, supporters, even a charter—and yet they survived. They were as Reinhold Niebuhr has said, "in the true apostolic succession," humble people uninterested in wealth or in building empires. Their goals were modest, and if they claimed any honor it was, said Bradford, that they had "been instruments to break the ice for others who come after with less difficulty."

The Puritan Charter of 1629

The Indians had had New England largely to themselves until the Pilgrims broke "the ice for others." By 1622 clumps of fish-drying and fur-buying depots dotted the coast, and their number increased yearly. One of the liveliest was that of Thomas Morton and his wild band, who, with Indian women for consorts, welcomed spring by "dancing and frisking together like so many fairies or furies," according to the sedate Bradford. The Pilgrims fumed about these neighbors but did nothing until they learned Morton was selling firearms to Indians. They dispatched Miles Standish—"Captain Shrimp, a quondam drummer," Morton called him— to the scene, and peace soon reigned at Merry Mount.

Another group, appropriately more sober since the roots of the Massachusetts Bay Company trace back to it, had settled at Cape Ann. In 1623 several West Country merchants inspired by Reverend John White had organized themselves into the Dorchester Company and taken out a patent from the Council for New England to found a fishing settlement in America. The plan was to send over settlers who would grow food for the fishing crews and double as fishermen in season. Puritan ministers would care for both the settlers' and fishermen's religious needs and also "save" the Indians from French Catholics. It took only a season at Cape Ann to learn that fishing and planting refused to mix, for, said John White, "rarely any fisherman will work at land, neither are husbandmen fit for fishermen but with long use and experience."

The Dorchester Company collapsed in 1626, but several of the fishermen-planters led by Roger Conant remained in New England. John White, "being grieved in his spirit that so good a work should be suffered to fall to the ground by the Adventurers thus abruptly breaking off, did write to Master Conant not so to desert the business." Conant led his men to a spot soon to be named Salem but which the Indians called Naumkeag. (John White thought the name indicated "some commerce with the Jews in past times," because *Nahum Keike* in Hebrew means "the bosom of consolation." The belief that American Indians had descended from the lost tribes of Israel persisted in America thought well into the nineteenth century; Joseph Smith incorporated it into Mormonism.)

While Conant held his men at Salem through the winter and talked them out of dispersing to Virginia, John White worked to strengthen the foundation stone of what he hoped would become a mighty colony. It was largely through his efforts that in early 1628 a new group of Puritan merchants took out a patent from the Council for New England that conveyed to them the land roughly between the Merrimac and Charles Rivers—it was assumed they ran parallel to each other—and from sea to sea. The New England Company, as it was called, bought the defunct Dorchester Company's equipment and outfitted a shipload of some forty settlers. They departed for Salem in June 1628 under the leadership of John Endecott with orders to prepare the way for others soon to follow.

While Endecott built up Salem, Puritan leaders at home converted their patent into a royal charter and the New England Company into the incorporated Massachusetts Bay Company. The charter confirmed the original land grant and in addition gave the company all rights of government over any colony it created. (How the Puritans managed this remains a mystery, for the grant occurred not long after Charles I had announced he would no longer tolerate the right of government for trading companies. No doubt men of influence like the Earl of Warwick and Lord Say and Seal, both Puritans, did much to effect the coup.) The charter, modeled after Virginia's of 1612, formed twenty-six investors into a corporation that controlled all company property and the right to administer its affairs. Members would meet quarterly in a General Court to decide important business. The court could pass any laws and ordinances it deemed necessary, as long as "such laws and ordinances be not contrary or repugnant to the laws and statutes . . . of England." The "generality"—a vague term later to cause trouble—would choose the company governor, deputy governor, and eighteen "assistants." Through accident or design there was no provision that the charter and company headquarters must remain in England. It was assumed both would; there was no precedent for anything else, nor, it seems, was there any plan afoot in the beginning to break with the past. The original plan was to have the company remain in England and to avoid the London Company's early mistakes by letting settlers work out things with little interference from home.

The charter passed the seals on March 4, 1629, and a month later a contingent of nearly four hundred settlers set out for Salem. This vanguard was a well-provisioned, disciplined, and carefully planned expedition. It had behind it as much wealth as had backed the London Company's ventures, plus a half century of colonizing experience to draw on. The fleet's purpose differed from that of the "great fleet" of 1609. Then, the goal had been to build a settlement that would promote trade. The hope for profit had not been discarded from the new enterprise, but it had been subordinated to another goal—the creation of a refuge for beleaguered Puritans.

In the months since John Endecott had rubbed out the cold of his first New England winter by a fireside, much had happened at home. Charles I had dissolved Parliament two weeks before the Bay Company got its charter, leaving him and his favorite bishop, William Laud, free to harass Puritans without restraint. By the summer of 1629 events had convinced many company members that if they were to worship as they wished, they must emigrate to America. Not only would they go themselves, but they would take the company with them and merge it in New England with the colonial government. It disturbed them that the charter had created an open corporation, making it possible for persons unfriendly to Puritanism to buy into control of the company and from a London base to destroy the settlement overseas. John Winthrop, a Puritan gentleman from East Anglia who had recently joined the company, agreed with fellow members that they must "transfer the government of the plantation to those that shall inhabit there, and not . . . continue the same in subordination to the company here, as now it is." (The plan to blend company management and colonial government may have emerged out of the Virginia experience. Governor Wyatt only three years earlier had said that the "slow proceeding of the growth of the plantation" owed something to the split in authority between England and America. No doubt, too, the recent annulment of Virginia's charter on a slight pretext made clear the advantage of having the charter three thousand miles from home.) On August 29 an arrangement (since known as the Cambridge Agreement) was worked out, whereby all company members who did not wish to emigrate sold out to those who did; and the company charter was turned over to them to carry to America, "so [long] as it may be done legally." A subordinate government "for financial affairs only" was maintained in London and worked so well as a blind that the crown apparently remained unaware of the charter's location until 1634, when Laud set out to get it annulled. John Winthrop was chosen to head the new venture, and plans went ahead for the greatest of the great fleets to set out for America.

"A City upon a Hill"

In March 1630 a fleet of eleven ships—seven with some seven hundred passengers aboard, the rest loaded with livestock and supplies—slipped out of Cowes bound for New England. The great fleet in many respects resembled earlier ones dispatched by the London Company. Men of influence and education led the expedition. John Winthrop of Groton Manor, educated at Cambridge, trained to the law at Gray's Inn, a man "not sparing, but always as the burning torch spending his health and wealth for the good of others," shared many of the qualities and most of the views of Sir Thomas Dale. The Bay Company was backed by men of wealth who would make sure the enterprise would not fail for lack of support from home. Much thought had gone into every detail of the voyage—from the March departure date, which allowed for an early planting on arrival, to the inclusion of lime juice to avoid scurvy.

Only an expert eye could spot essential differences between this and earlier fleets sent out by the London Company. Religion gave a unity of purpose and strength to the Puritan venture absent in the Virginia enterprise. The machinery for controlling company-colony affairs was the same, except that now all that machinery would reside in America. Boston would become both company and colony headquarters. The third distinction emerged clearly only after England had slipped below the horizon. Those who went to Virginia, even those who traveled to Plymouth, did so mainly for private reasons; the Puritans bound for Massachusetts Bay went with a larger purpose in mind, though this had been carefully obscured up to now. Governor Endecott had been warned not to "render yourself or us distasteful to the state here, to which (as we ought) we must and will have an obsequious eye." Shortly before departure an open letter to "Brethren in and of the *Church of* ENGLAND" sought to correct any "misreport of our intention." But once at sea John Winthrop made those intentions clear. "We shall be as a city upon a hill," he said in a Sunday sermon to the passengers of the *Arbella,* "the eyes of all people are upon us. . . ."

This sense of mission, so central to the American tradition, had a special quality about it. These people were bent upon building a holy commonwealth out of a trading company, of making, as men of the day might have put it, a silk purse out of a sow's ear. The attempt alone, especially as it was being made by hard-headed, practical people, makes the story of Massachusetts Bay's early years among the most fascinating in the colonial past. These people were embarked on an enterprise that lifted them out of themselves, and they knew it. " 'Tis a great thing to be a foundation stone in such a spiritual building," an early Puritan said. They not only knew what they were doing, they knew they were right. "We doubt not but God will be with us," said one, "and if God be with us, who can be against us."

The fleet arrived in June, after an easy crossing, and John Endecott met them at Salem with housing prepared and fresh food on hand. Within a few weeks it had been agreed that the hub of the holy commonwealth should center on the great bay a few miles south of Salem, and here in the summer of 1630 began the building of Boston and the clumps of villages around it. All went so well it appeared that the Puritans would escape trials others had endured. Then came their first New England winter. Some two hundred died. A relief ship in February slowed the death toll, but the ship's departure reduced the colony by some eighty settlers who had had enough and were returning home. Another shipload of returnees left in the spring, and Puritans in England urged Winthrop to move the colony farther south to avoid the severe winters. He refused, sensing correctly that the colony's worst times were behind. The absence of Indians and the presence of Pilgrims, who sold cattle and food and gave advice when asked, helped to carry the colony over rough spots. The home-bound exodus slowed to a trickle; and by the end of the summer in 1631, some two thousand Puritans had arrived in Massachusetts Bay. An influx of such proportions, which nearly destroyed Virginia, actually sustained the economy while the colony searched for a source of income. Those coming in brought window glass, kettles, guns, cloth, saws, and a variety of other needed articles; and with these they bartered for food, lumber, and livestock. Winthrop avoided the communal plan tried in Virginia and Plymouth, preferring words to laws, to promote a community effort. "For the work we have in hand, . . . we must be knit together as one man," he had told the congregation aboard the *Arbella,* adding "that if we shall deal falsely with our

God in this work we have undertaken, and so cause Him to withdraw His present help from us, we shall be made a story and a by-word through the world." On that injunction the holy commonwealth began.

MASSACHUSETTS BAY

It has been said that "where Virginia was an extrapolation of normal Elizabethan society, Massachusetts was dominantly an extrapolation of the opposition." The remark, for all its truth, hides distinctions that emerged between Puritanism in England and in America. The New England Way, as it came to be called, took shape in a remarkably short time, for the founding fathers faced fewer obstacles than Puritans at home. They could create new institutions in the wilderness without having first to tear down old ones, and if the new failed to satisfy some, it required only a short trip further into the wilderness to re-create once again. The New England Way came forth in variant patterns as each of the strong-minded founders sought to practice what he had only preached in England. Each variant, however, began always with the church, for "it is better," said John Cotton, "that the commonwealth be fashioned to the setting forth of God's house, which is His church, than to accommodate the church in the civil state."

The Church

The Scriptures said, "Gather my saints together unto me; those that have made a covenant with me by sacrifice" (Psalms 50: 5), and on that injunction thirty of some two hundred settlers at Salem joined together, as had the Pilgrims nearly a decade earlier, to announce: "We covenant with the Lord and with one another and do bind ourselves in the presence of God to walk together in all His ways according as He is pleased to reveal Himself unto us in His blessed word of truth." With these words the saints of Salem put behind them several centuries of Christian tradition. Hitherto God's grace had been passed from Christ to the apostles, then down through the vast hierarchy of first the Church of Rome and later the Church of England. Now God's elect covenanted directly with Him. They challenged the past boldly and with confidence.

A year after Salem's church had been erected, a half dozen covenanted communities dotted the Massachusetts coast; and a decade later nearly thirty others were scattered through the Bay Colony, New Haven, Connecticut, and Plymouth. The church within each town had "complete liberty to stand alone," or as John Cotton put it, "to walk on her own legs." The entire community made up the congregation, but the church consisted solely of saints. Professor Edmund Morgan has recently argued with conviction that this exclusiveness of the American Puritans' churches disturbed their nonseparating brethren at home, who apparently had not yet developed the idea of a church composed solely of the saved. He holds, too, that another innovation, New England's definition of "saint," shocked the stay-at-homes even more. Hitherto a "saint" had been defined as one who professed faith and repentance and lived free from gross or open scandal. New England Puritans held that they must now show that they had been reborn, "that they have been wounded in their hearts for their original sin and actual transgressions." The remarks of a contemporary suggest that John Cotton had much to do with the innovation. The early churches "walked something in an untrodden path"; but such was Mr. Cotton's authority that after his arrival in 1633, "the administration of all ecclesiastical matters was tied up more strictly than before to the rules of that which is since owned for the Congregational Way. . . ."

Once the saints had created the church visible within the community, they chose a pastor, whose "special work is to attend exhortation, and therein to administer a word of wisdom." They chose also a teacher, whose duty was "to attend to doctrine and therein to administer a word of knowledge." The elders, as in Calvin's day, were chosen by members of the meeting, or church, to serve as disciplinary officials. They admonished and punished sinners and in general sought to "prevent and heal such offenses in life or in doctrine as might corrupt the Church." Finally, a deacon was selected "to receive the offerings of the Church, gifts given to the Church, and to keep the treasury of the Church. . . ." On the local level the organization of the congregation differed hardly at all from the one created by Calvin a century earlier in Geneva. Some wished to carry out the rest of Calvin's organizational structure, with its presbyteries, synods, and assemblies, but those who held that each individual congregation should be sufficient unto itself and subject to no higher authority ruled the day. They held that the regenerate, having been imbued with God's spirit, would think and act in like-minded ways, thus obviating the need for organization. Puritans back in England thought congregationalism smacked too much of separatism—after all, had not the Pilgrims organized their churches in this manner?—and the New England Way aroused their suspicions from the start. It took much persuasion on the part of John Cotton and other divines to allay these fears.

The clergy's power in colonial New England emerged in part from the authority of their office but even more from the quality of the men who occupied that office. Never before had a people been led into the wilderness by men of such intellectual and moral stature. Among those divines who might be "accounted great even by the heroic standards of the seventeenth century" were John Cotton, "a walking library" according to his grandson Cotton Mather and of whom Roger Williams said that some Puritans "could hardly believe that God would suffer Mr. Cotton to err"; Thomas Hooker, who told his congregations that "the spawn of all abomination hath overspread man" but who blended bluntness with such eloquence that he could "put a king into his pocket"; Nathaniel Ward, lawyer as well as minister, who wrote *A Simple Cobbler of Agawam,* a wrathful, witty book filled with bigotry, sarcasm, and clean, sharp prose; Thomas Shepard, pale and weak, a preacher's preacher, who believed with Hooker that "every natural man and woman is born full of sin, as full as a toad of poison."

These great, grim men blinked none of the harshness of life and none of the evil in man. The purified church they led bleached out "all ec-clesiastical actions invented and devised by man." It demanded much of the people. But when the people faltered, the ministers turned for support to other equally great, grim men—the civil rulers. The church knit to-gether the saints and set the tone of society; the state enforced this tone. Ministers could exhort and advise, but laymen alone held power in the holy commonwealth.

The State

The Puritans' major problem was to transmute a trading company into a colonial government without letting power slip from the hands of the saints and without doing such violence to their charter that they would lose it. The Bible's vagueness about civil institutions left them uncommitted to any particular form of government, but the charter appeared to impose certain limitations. It placed power with the freemen or shareholders of the company, who were to assemble four times a year as a General Court to elect all officers and pass all ordinances and laws.

Only a handful of the company's original hundred-odd freemen, all of them saints, emigrated with Winthrop. When the first General Court met in America in October 1630, eight qualified freemen attended. They voted to transfer the right to select all company officers and to make all laws to the governor's Court of Assistants, consisting of the same eight men. The assistants, or "magistrates" as they would hereafter be called, had kept to the form but warped the intent of the charter by concentrat-ing all power—executive, legislative, and judicial—in their and the gov-ernor's hands.

They used their new powers at once and to the fullest. They granted lands to incoming bands of settlers and erected town boundaries. They voted taxes, appointed officers, and banished from the colony those they deemed unfit. Sitting as judges, they passed on such matters as drunkenness, manslaughter, breach of contract, and the use of tobacco, dice, and cards.

Once Winthrop and his colleagues had the colony on its feet, they called a second meeting of the General Court in May 1631, at which time, perhaps to silence any grumblings against rule by an oligarchy, 118 settlers were admitted as freemen. These new freemen, probably all covenanted saints, now proceeded, acting as the General Court, to further distort the charter by stating that "no man shall be admitted to the freedom of this body politic, but such as are members of some of the churches within the limits of the same." It was further agreed that all settlers, freemen and nonfreemen alike, must take an oath of loyalty to the Massachusetts government. The oath made no mention of allegiance to the crown, which made it clear that the state, like the church, was in fact, if not theory, separating from English ties.

Winthrop, whom even a scholar with little affection for Puritans judged a cultivated gentleman with a tender and sympathetic nature for all his "sodden Toryism," kept tight control of Massachusetts political affairs for four years. The first noticeable complaint came in 1632, when the assistants levied a colony-wide tax. The minister at Watertown warned his flock that it was wrong to pay taxes that they had not consented to. Winthrop quieted the town's fears, but the ruckus cracked the door to representative government. The General Court soon after said that in the next election two men from every town should be appointed "to advise with the governor and assistants about the raising of a public stock, so what they should agree upon should bind all, etc." The court agreed at the same meeting, either from public pressure or because Winthrop saw no reason to fear the innovation, that the election of the governor should be transferred from the assistants to the freemen of the colony.

Two years later a group of deputies to the General Court led by Thomas Dudley, who thought Winthrop too lenient and wished to oust him from power, called on the governor and asked to see the charter. From it they learned that the General Court should make all laws and that it should consist of *all* freemen. Dudley's contingent, convinced the freemen would impose a stricter rule than Winthrop's, demanded that the charter be followed to the letter. Winthrop managed a compromise that called for each town to send two deputies to the General Court. The court now became a representative legislative assembly consisting of some twenty deputies, the governor, the deputy-governor, and the assistants, all sitting together. The evolution of a trading company charter into a colony constitution had been completed.

But a government by law had yet to come. Winthrop wanted laws to arise out of judicial decisions rather than legislative acts, which he suspected would draw too much on English experience. He said that laws should take into account "the condition of the country and other circumstances" and that "such laws would be fittest for us, which should arise pro re nata [for an unexpected contingency] upon occasions." Laws would impose a rigidity on the Bay Colony at a time when he felt room for experiment was needed. Winthrop fought a losing battle—one lost, strangely enough, because the clergy refused to support the governor. "Let all the world learn," John Cotton said, "to give mortal men no greater power than they are content they shall use—for use it they will." Heeding that injunction, the General Court in 1641 approved the Body of Liberties, drawn up by Nathaniel Ward, which codified a number of offenses and punishments for citizens of the colony.

The Puritans suspected power and whoever held it. They leashed their church and their government into specific spheres of action and tolerated no overstepping the bounds. The magistrates were expected to protect but "not to give the horns to the church," because it was "necessary for magistrates to keep their power in their own hands, and not to take things *ipso facto* from the church." The clergy wielded authority in secular affairs in that they advised and warned the people and the leaders of God's will, but real power rested with the laymen. Puritans talked much about the separation between church and state, and in a sense they spoke accurately. The church had no power in government—ministers were forbidden to hold public office—and the government refused to allow the actions of any congregation to affect civil or political rights.

Puritans checked their state by law and the Scriptures. They restrained their church, in part, by the congregational form of organization, for "when it comes to power, that one church shall have power over the rest, then look for a beast," John Cotton remarked. "Amplitude of dominion was never a note of the Church of Christ since the world began." The "beast" was further checked by the rule of the covenant, the Scriptures, and the dispersion of power within the church among the ministers, elders, and the brethren.

Church and state regarded themselves, in John Davenport's words, as "coordinate states, in the same place reaching forth to help mutually each other, for the welfare of both according to God." The state backed up the church's spiritual decrees, and the church the state's civil laws. The state saw to it that the church was supported by local taxation; it passed laws to protect ministers against insults; and it enforced compulsory attendance at worship. The church condemned political radicals; it denied the people the right of revolution on the ground that this flouted one of God's institutions. State and church cooperated to excommunicate and banish here-

Map 13. Massachusetts Bay Colony

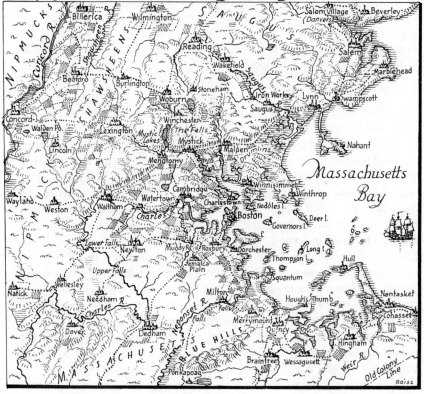

tics, political and religious. The relationship was a partnership between equals in which members of the elect dominated in both. The leaders in both spheres regarded themselves and their colleagues with a wary eye. Whatever power a man receives, "he hath a corrupt nature that will improve it in one thing or other," John Cotton reminded the Puritans, adding that it was

most wholesome for magistrates and officers in church and commonwealth never to affect more liberty and authority than will do them good, and the people good: for whatever transcendent power is given will certainly overrun those that give it and those that receive it. There is a strain in a man's heart that will sometime or other run out to excess, unless the Lord restrain it; but it is not good to venture it. It is necessary, therefore, that all power that is on earth be limited, church-power or other.

Archbishop Laud

There is, it has been said, witty justness in the phrase that dubs William Laud "the father of New England." Laud became Charles I's Archbishop of Canterbury in 1633, a year Puritans marked by the emigration of seven hundred persons to New England, double the total for the two previous years. This opinionated, high-strung, short-tempered, "little, low, red-faced man" brought to his position a zeal for reform that matched the Puritans' and for that reason infuriated them all the more. Laud's Arminianism—a term coined from the name of Jacobus Arminius, a sixteenth-century Dutch divine who believed that a man's earthly efforts could condition God's mind about his fate—distressed those fervent believers of predestination. Worse still, Laud believed that the Church of England in concept, doctrine, and organization was perfect and needed only to be purged of its heretical—that is, Puritanical—or inadequate clergy. He was convinced that the English Church perpetuated the true Catholic faith and that once Rome had been purified, the old union would return. He sought, in a sense, to do for Catholicism what Puritans wished to do for Anglicanism—reform without separating.

The intense feeling Laud engendered among Puritans stemmed from the effectiveness of his reform movement, which he pushed with such vigor and thoroughness that it blocked the Puritans' own reform efforts at every point. His attempts to improve the church's economic position and the quality of its clergy especially hurt. Henry VIII had undermined the church's economic foundations by parceling out much of its landed wealth to the nobility. By the seventeenth century the church's inability to support its clergy had led to pluralism—the holding of several "livings" by one minister, who required their combined income to piece out a livelihood—which in turn led to numerous parishes being occupied by absentee ministers. (Aggrandizing bishops complicated the problem further by taking the best livings for themselves.) The church's difficulty in providing for its own made it hard to attract able, well-trained men into the nation's nearly ten thousand pulpits. Nearly 60 per cent of the pulpits in Laud's day were held by men lacking a university degree, often so inadequately trained they embarrassed the church.

Puritanism had thrived on the church's economic troubles. Wealthy Puritans often offered to endow a local pulpit if they could choose the minister and the offer was invariably accepted. If that plot failed, a lectureship was sometimes established. A lecturer, always chosen by the local congregations, gave sermons when the regular service had ended. These ministers were paid by the people, and thus, said Laud, they become "the people's creatures and blow the bellows of their sedition."

Laud strove mightily to correct these abuses. He spread about the good livings, encouraged able young men to enter the church, searched hard for ways to increase church income, and, above all, he removed Puritans from the pulpits wherever he found them. When they tried to argue with him, as young Thomas Shepard did, the archbishop shook with fury and looked, as Shepard put it, "as though blood would have gushed out of his face." Shepard, taking his congregation with him, eventually fled to New England, where John Cotton, Thomas Hooker, and Roger Williams, to name only three other divines Laud had harried from the land, had already preceded him.

Laud did not relax once the prey had flown. He determined to stamp them out in America, too. The tales he heard about the holy commonwealth there made him tremble all the more with rage. Sir Ferdinando Gorges handed Laud an excuse to start proceedings against the colony, for Gorges swore that the company's original land grant had been obtained from the Council for New England by subterfuge. In 1634 Charles I created the Commission for Regulating Plantations, composed of Privy Councillors and headed by Laud, with the purpose of retrieving the Bay Colony's charter.

In Massachusetts the General Court reacted to the threat in a Puritan way. It drew up plans for an army to resist any attempted invasion, and at the same time set out to remove those sins that had apparently provoked God's wrath. All ostentatious clothing such as lace, girdles, and beaver hats were judged "prejudicial to the general good" and forbidden to be worn. The use of tobacco was prohibited in public, though it might still be taken medicinally. A day of fasting and prayer was ordered, during which the commonwealth would ask for God's forgiveness.

By 1635 Laud had learned of the charter's trip across the ocean. His commission directed the attorney-general to open suit for its repeal. Two years later the courts declared it revoked. Charles thereupon claimed the colony for the crown and appointed Sir Ferdinando the royal governor. Charles was too occupied with unruly Puritans at home to enforce the decree; and Gorges refused to make the trip to New England, for at seventy he had "grown a little doubtful of the state of my own body" and "not able to endure the sea any long time." Perhaps, too, he suspected the reception he would have met in Massachusetts. Winthrop had made clear instantly on hearing of the revocation that he would not relinquish the charter. The clergy had agreed that if a new governor were sent out "we ought not to accept him, but defend our lawful possession." The new flood of immigrants increased the colony's confidence. Some three thousand settlers arrived in the summer of 1638 alone. By then a crown overwhelmed with troubles at home provided no threat at all to the Bay Colony. But the victory over Laud came too easy, for as Richard Dunn has pointed out, "it encouraged Massachusetts to adopt a studied insolence toward the outside world which was hardly appropriate to her real feebleness."

HIVINGS-OUT

In its early years the Bay Colony knew no rest. Its leaders argued among themselves who should hold power within the government, then joined together to scorn the crown and at the same time deal with an Indian war that threatened to wipe the commonwealth from the map. In the midst of these disturbances occurred the expulsion of Roger Williams and Anne Hutchinson along with their followers, the secession of Thomas Hooker's congregation, and the refusal of a group led by John Davenport to settle within the Bay Colony. Each of these splinter groups chipped away at the unity of the holy commonwealth. All of these "hivings-out" distressed Winthrop, but those of Separatist tendencies pained him most, for they raised the spectre of revolution.

The Separatist was an idealist who, said a man of the day, "lives by the air, and there he builds castles and churches; none on earth will please him." His demand to worship God as he pleased made him a rebel against authority and the established religion. His threat to the state made him as intolerable to Anglican Virginia as to Puritan Massachusetts. For all that, no one in the Puritan colony made a career out of pursuing these religious radicals. No one was assigned to root out heresy. The government stepped into a religious dispute only when it became notorious. Even then the state made every effort to persuade the lost soul back to the fold. It saddened no one in all Massachusetts Bay more than John

Winthrop to pronounce that "sweet and amiable man" Roger Williams a heretic and a danger to the holy commonwealth.

Roger Williams

Roger Williams was born in 1603, the year of Queen Elizabeth's death. As a youngster, he attracted the attention of Sir Edward Coke and became the great chief justice's secretary. No doubt Coke impelled him to Cambridge. There, in the 1620's, he was exposed to Puritan ideas; and soon after he became the family chaplain for Sir William Masham, a friend of Oliver Cromwell and an acquaintance of neighboring John Winthrop and such Puritan preachers as Thomas Hooker, John Eliot, Hugh Peter, and John Cotton. In 1629 the close ties were cut between Williams and his mentor Coke, a devout Anglican; and a year later Williams left for Massachusetts, saying that "Bishop Laud pursued me out of the land."

The Bay Colony complimented him on arrival with the offer of a post in the Boston church. Williams rejected it because he "durst not officiate to an unseparated people." John Winthrop urged his young friend —Williams was then twenty-seven—to be less noisy but did nothing more. Williams moved on to Salem, raised a storm there, then traveled to Plymouth, a truly separated community. Here the church pleased him, but he was soon asked to leave because of his "strange opinions." Williams had mustered a friendship with Indians around Plymouth and out of his acquaintance he began to noise about the idea that Plymouth's patent and Massachusetts Bay's charter were worthless, for the king had no right to give away land that belonged to others. He challenged the validity of the charter just as the crown was developing plans to recall it and send over a royal governor. Williams pushed his charge to the point of writing King Charles about "the evil of that part of the patent which respects the donation of land, etc.," and Puritans when they heard this complained he had "provoked our king against us, and put a sword into his hand to destroy us." Still, though many railed against him, no one tormented Williams from the land.

Not until April 1635 did the General Court take notice of the maverick, and only then because Williams had said that "a magistrate ought not to tender an oath to an unregenerate man," a remark that challenged the entire foundation of the holy commonwealth. He had, in effect, said that oaths were sacred and magistrates must keep hands off all sacred things. They could punish civil offenses, but those against God—the first four of the ten commandments—must be punished by the church alone. Church and state, he was saying, must be kept separate.

Williams, a man of the seventeenth century, approached this view by a route far removed from the one Thomas Jefferson took in the eighteenth century. Williams believed the link between the two corrupted the church; where Jefferson thought it poisoned the state. Government, said Williams, is man-made and designed to order the lives of all, regenerate and unregenerate alike. To tie this institution to the church, pure and unspotted, defiled the church. Church and state are completely different societies, and the gulf between them can never be closed. God gave his saints no commission to rule the world—"Abstract yourself with a holy violence from the dung heap of this earth," he told Winthrop—for that is the business of those trained for it.

Williams went further. He challenged the certainty of the saints that God had revealed Himself only to them. The devout of all religions must be respected, for who is to judge the mysterious ways in which God reveals Himself. Williams detested Quakers as warmly as any Puritan, believing their doctrine would lead "to the very absolute cutting down and overturning relations and civil government among men," but he refused to persecute them. A ship at sea, he said, with a complement of Papists, Protestants, Jews, and Turks, offered "a true picture of a commonwealth." None of this company should be forced to attend church services or be disturbed in its own "particular prayers or worship"; but in directing the ship's course and preserving good order, the captain might properly enforce obedience upon all aboard.

Williams had no argument with most Puritan doctrines. He believed in predestination and the absolute authority of the Bible. No democratic notions poisoned *his* thoughts. He broke with his brethren on the bond between church and state; on the issue of forced worship, which he said "stinks in God's nostrils"; and on the question of religious liberty, which he felt was needed to bring peace in the world. These divergences challenged the authority of the holy commonwealth; and after repeated efforts to persuade him either to change his mind or keep silent, the magistrates in October 1635 ordered his banishment. They based their action on a provision in the charter that said the settlers might "expulse" anyone who attempted any "detriment, or annoyance to the said plantation or inhabitants." Soon after sentence had been passed, friends in England commended John Winthrop "for disclaiming Mr. Williams' opinions" and stated that by banishing him the Bay Colony "took off much prejudice from you with us, and hath stopt the mouths of some."

The magistrates planned to ship Williams back to England; but when the time came to retrieve him, he had slipped away into the wilderness. John Winthrop had joined in convicting his friend; he lacked the heart to do more. By a secret letter he urged "me to steer my course to Narragansett Bay and Indians," Williams long afterward revealed, "for many high and heavenly public ends, encouraging me, from the freeness of the place from English claims or patents. I took his prudent notion as a hint and voice from God, and waving all other thoughts and motions, I steered my course from Salem (though in winter snow which I feel yet) unto these parts. . . ."

Anne Hutchinson

Another tempest, this one centering on a woman, roiled the waters as the storm over Williams subsided. Anne Hutchinson arrived in Boston with her husband in 1634. She came as a devout admirer of John Cotton and with no intention of disrupting the commonwealth. She soon was holding Thursday evening prayer meetings in her home, during which she interpreted the previous Sunday sermon for women who had been unable to attend the service. Distaste for the dull Boston pastor, John Wilson, and affection for John Cotton caused her in time to do more than interpret. She suggested that although a man "acted sanctified," lived an outwardly devout life, as Wilson did, it by no means meant he was saved. His inner life must change, she said, echoing Cotton's views and reviving a sentiment held so strongly by the earlier English Puritans. Her attacks on the importance of regular church attendance, moral uprightness, modest dress, and the like, weakened a weapon the church used to discipline the people. Mrs. Hutchinson went further by suggesting that the "Holy Spirit illumines the heart of every true believer," and every saved individual can commune directly with God. This struck at the orthodox Puritan view that God had spoken to man once and for all time in the Scriptures and that these alone were the source for inspiration and instruction. Mrs. Hutchinson's doctrine that God could and did reveal Himself directly to a devout believer endangered the Biblical basis of the holy commonwealth, substituting the revelations of individuals for the firm law of the Scriptures. To the leaders of the Bay Colony the logical extension of her views would lead to a lawless society.

Mrs. Hutchinson's influence soon fanned outward from the Thursday evening meeting until by 1636 all Boston was divided into two camps, and the split was spreading throughout the colony. Those who followed Mrs. Hutchinson came to be called Antinomians (from *anti,* "against," and *nomos,* "law"). Factors other than her charm and intelligence, both of which she had in abundance, determined the strength of her following. Many favored her simply because they had political complaints against the government that opposed her. The merchants of the colony, among them Mrs. Hutchinson's husband, were bridling against the government's economic restrictions; they sided almost to a man with her. Many of the young people, such as the recently arrived Henry Vane, a gifted twenty-six-year-old, preferred her views over those of their more rigid elders. Some, who felt the spirit had waned from Puritanism, joined her ranks. The discontented of the colony flocked to her banner. John Cotton's sermons kept alive what was turning out to be a religious revival.

The revival soon spilled over into politics. Antinomian strength proved great enough in 1636 to elect Henry Vane governor over John Winthrop. The orthodox regrouped during the ensuing months. They managed the following year, by clever maneuvering in an election so tense that voters came close to violence, to slip Winthrop back into office. The governor now set about to avert the dismemberment of his beloved commonwealth. First, it had to be made clear to all exactly where Mrs. Hutchinson and her followers had gone wrong. Winthrop had a hidden hand in calling in the late summer of 1637 a synod of twenty-five ministers to define heresy. The hope was that the great John Cotton and such lesser lights among the clergy as John Wheelwright could be won away from Antinomianism. A long list of doctrinal errors, "some blasphemous, others erroneous and all unsafe" were placed on record and condemned "to the devil of hell, from whence they came." Cotton recanted one opinion and modified others but refused to sign the record.

The synod rebuked Mrs. Hutchinson implicitly and ordered the Reverend Wheelwright to recant. Wheelwright refused. He was banished by Winthrop in November, as were many of those who had signed a petition in his favor. He and his followers went northward to found the town of Exeter, New Hampshire.

Wheelwright proved easier to deal with than Mrs. Hutchinson. Winthrop found that she had "a nimble wit and active spirit and a very voluble tongue" that gave him many uncomfortable moments during her two-day trial. Despite Mrs. Hutchinson's skillful and, to detached observers, successful defense, the court, with Winthrop presiding, found her guilty of sedition and contempt and ordered her banished for "being a woman not fit for our society." She received a reprieve while Cotton set about persuading her to recant. She did write out a confession, but it failed to satisfy the clergy; and after the Boston church in March 1638 had excommunicated her, the sentence was carried out. She headed with her family and a few followers for the wilds of Aquidneck, as the Indians called it, where Roger Williams had already established a plantation.

Plantations of the Otherwise Minded

Rhode Island was not a planned child nor, after birth, an especially welcomed one. It began and long remained, a home for the otherwise minded. Roger Williams had trudged southward from Salem through winter snows with the lonely thought that "I had the whole country before me."

He had asked no one "to come with me into these parts," and the four Salem acquaintances who traveled along were uninvited companions. He wintered with Indians. In the spring he purchased land from them, and having "a sense of God's merciful providence unto me in my distress [I] called the place Providence."

Dissension arose almost at once within the plantation. Williams regarded himself as the proprietor, much as Lord Baltimore did of Maryland. He had bought the land, and he granted it out as he saw fit, not with absolute rights of ownership but more as fiefs in the medieval sense. Democratic government held no appeal for him. He accepted all comers to his plantation but tried to keep as much political power as possible in his own hands. William Harris, one of the Salem traveling companions, opposed him from the start. Harris, an irritating, contentious person whose experience as an attorney's clerk increased his natural bent, held the modern view that the conveyance of a piece of property conferred absolute rights of ownership upon the new owner, allowing him to dispose of it as he wished and to whom he wished. He fought Williams' medieval concept throughout Providence's early history.

While Harris and Williams quarreled over land rights, another center of contention came into being in 1638 when the village of Portsmouth, Rhode Island, was founded by the Hutchinsons and their followers, among them a merchant named William Coddington. Coddington was shrewd, able, and well-educated and, like so many Englishmen of the day, he had dreams of building a great feudal manor in the wilderness. He soon quarreled with Mrs. Hutchinson and with Samuel Gorton, who had left Boston of his own accord and had been expelled from Plymouth before coming to Portsmouth. (Gorton was described by a contemporary as "a proud and pestilent seducer, and deeply leavened with blasphemous and familistical opinions.") Coddington hived off on his own in 1639 to establish the village of Newport, Rhode Island. The next year by force and suasion he united Newport and Portsmouth, hoping to use them as a base for his feudal barony. The luckless Gorton was expelled once again, this time heading for Providence, where he got along no better than elsewhere. He soon after founded his own settlement, Warwick, Rhode Island, some twelve miles from Williams' plantation but close enough so that it could be said he "madded poor Providence" for forty years.

These four villages—Providence, Portsmouth, Newport, and Warwick —were absolutely independent of each other. Nothing like a colony had come into being, and the continual dissension among themselves suggested none ever would. Nothing united them except their distaste for Massachusetts Bay and Plymouth and their fear that either or both those colonies might soon take their lands by force. Coddington hoped he might be the saviour of the settlements. He went so far as to design a seal with the motto "love conquers all," which must have evoked a smile from even the most humorless among the otherwise minded. In the end, it was Williams who saved the settlements from being swallowed by their neighbors.

Connecticut and New Haven

The Dutch came first to the Connecticut Valley, building a trading post near the site of Hartford. The Pilgrims infiltrated in 1633; "and though the Dutch threatened them hard, yet they shot not," and the Pilgrims sailed past and on up the Connecticut River to erect a post at Windsor. Meanwhile, other plans for the area were afoot in England, where several influential Puritans, headed by Lord Say and Seal and Lord Brooke, had in early 1632 obtained from the Earl of Warwick, president of the Council for New England, a vaguely worded patent for a tract of land that stretched 120 miles along the coast and westward from "sea to sea." John Winthrop, Jr., founded Saybrook near the mouth of the Connecticut River in 1635, shortly before the migrations from Massachusetts Bay began.

The emigration from the Bay Colony to Rhode Island resembled that from England to Massachusetts in that both were undertaken by minorities mainly for religious reasons. But those who emigrated to Connecticut did not consider themselves an oppressed minority, and religion had little or nothing to do with their hiving-out. Reports of the rich bottom land along the river, of the profitable fur trade, and of a smallpox epidemic that had apparently rendered once dangerous Indians harmless made Connecticut seem especially attractive at a time when all was not well within Massachusetts.

Much of the dissatisfaction in Massachusetts centered on the arbitrary rule that Winthrop and the magistrates continued to maintain. Thomas Hooker led the agitation for a government of laws rather than men. Hooker, among the most eminent Puritan divines in England, had settled with his flock in Newtown (Cambridge today) in 1633. He found his former authority in religious matters overshadowed by John Cotton, and this may have contributed to his uneasiness in the Bay Colony. (Edward Eggleston has remarked that all Cotton's formidable rivals—Williams, Hooker, Davenport, and Hugh Peter—eventually settled outside Massachusetts. "There cannot be two queen bees in one hive, nor can there well be more than one master mind in the ecclesiastical order of a petty theocratic state.") Hooker may have privately differed with Cotton's conception of the church, for a friend quoted him as saying before leaving England that "although I know all must not be admitted, yet this may do much hurt"; but publicly he preferred to make an issue over the authoritarian control of the Bay Colony's political affairs. Winthrop, backed by Cotton, defended the *status quo* by saying: "The best part is always the least, and of that best part the wiser part is always the lesser." Hooker answered that "in matters that concern the common good, a general council, chosen by all, to transact business which concerns all, I conceive most suitable to rule and most safe for the relief of the whole people."

These complaints were not aired in Newtown's petition of 1634 to the General Court, which stressed the "insufficient lands" for cattle and the danger that the fruitful Connecticut Valley might be "possessed by others." The petition was rejected. Winthrop argued that to move outside the boundaries of Massachusetts would break the charter and the political covenant, for all the towns were "knit in one body and bound by oath to seek the welfare of this commonwealth." Moreover, "the departure of Mr. Hooker would not only draw from us, but also divert other friends that would come to us." The General Court tried to appease the petitioners by granting Newtown more land.

During the winter other towns—Dorchester, Roxbury, and Watertown—complained that they were "much straitened by their own nearness to one another." By mid-July 1635 the Pilgrims at Windsor found "the Massachusetts men are coming almost daily, some by water and some by land." The people from Roxbury settled up the Connecticut River at Springfield, inside the Massachusetts boundary; those from Watertown at Wethersfield, Connecticut; and those from Dorchester on land (now called Windsor) in Connecticut the Pilgrims had purchased from the Indians and "entered with much difficulty and danger." In May 1636 Hooker, with "about an hundred persons in the first company, some of [whom] had lived in splendor and delicacy in England," trekked 120 miles overland to found the town of Hartford. By the end of the year, over eight hundred persons had spread themselves along the river in three towns—Windsor, Hartford, and Wethersfield—that would become the nucleus of Connecticut.

Massachusetts had permitted these settlers to move "whither they pleased, so [long] as they continue still under this government." As the river towns took shape, it was agreed that the General Court would appoint commissioners to oversee them for one year. That agreement ended in May 1637, about the time the supposedly feckless Indians began the Pequot War. A General Court from the river towns, consisting of six magistrates and six deputies, convened at Hartford to deal with the emergency and also with the general governmental problems that the three towns faced. This *ad hoc* government, patterned largely after that of Massachusetts, lasted two years.

Guided by this experience and Hooker's belief that government should be based on "the free consent of the people," who alone "set the bounds and limitations of the power," the three river-towns adopted the Fundamental Orders of Connecticut in January 1639. These orders were not, strictly speaking, a constitution, for they could be revoked or altered by a simple majority of the freemen. They sought to form a commonwealth as holy as the one just left; and the pattern, with its governor, assistants, and General Court, drew heavily on Massachusetts. Freemen alone could vote; and while no requirement restricted freemanship to church members, this became the fact in practice. Church and state remained partners working for the welfare of the community. Still, great changes had been worked within the old form. Authority came directly from the people, not from the king, who went unmentioned, nor even from God. Power centered in the General Court. The governor could not veto the court's laws; he could vote only in case of a tie; and he could not serve two terms in succession. The governor alone of all the officials had to be "always a member of some approved congregation," and he had to have served a term as an assistant. He and the assistants were elected by the "admitted freemen," and the deputies to the General Court by the "admitted inhabitants" of the towns, a distinction never quite clear, though obviously it included a larger part of the population.

While the river towns shaped themselves into the colony of Connecticut, the plantation of New Haven materialized under the leadership of John Davenport, who had arrived in Boston in 1637 at the head of a group of London Puritans. Davenport had ministered to the congregation of St. Stephens in London until Laud harried him over to Holland, which he found, like the Pilgrims before him, much too tolerant a place for a Puritan. He slipped back to London and urged Theophilus Eaton, an Oxonian friend and merchant, who had become one of his richest parishioners, to find a way to carry St. Stephens' worshipers to America. The suggestion appealed to Eaton, a devout Puritan and also an able businessman eager to exploit the trading possibilities of New England. It appealed to other well-to-do merchants, like Eaton's son-in-law Edward Hopkins, Richard Malbon, and David Yale. The group Davenport led across the ocean was the wealthiest yet to arrive in Boston.

The St. Stephens congregation wintered in Boston, long enough to reveal that as far as they were concerned Winthrop ran a lax colony. (The Antinomian furor was at its peak when they arrived.) A short while later, they founded their "New Haven" at the mouth of the Quinnipiac River in southern Connecticut. Here they had a harbor spacious enough to accommodate a fleet. The location seemed perfect for trade, convenient to both New Amsterdam and Massachusetts Bay and to the fur region of the Connecticut Valley, and yet sufficiently isolated to raise up a commonwealth holier than the one just left. New Haven's Fundamental Articles of 1639 agreed that "the word of God shall be the only rule to be attended unto in ordering the affairs of government in this plantation." Only church members could vote. When English traditions—trial by jury, for example—conflicted with the Bible, it was the Bible that set the pattern.

New Haven soon spawned other towns—Milford and Guilford in 1639, Stamford in 1640, then Fairfield, Greenwich, and Branford. In 1643 they joined together as the colony of New Haven, forming a government like that of Massachusetts but imbued with a stricter spirit. The river towns of Connecticut and New Haven existed in a state of suppressed hostility. A united Connecticut seemed a dream with little chance of becoming a reality.

New Haven for the moment completed the hivings-out. Massachusetts tried through the coming decades to control these out-settlements but with little success except in New Hampshire. The Council for New England had granted the land north of the Merrimac River to Sir Ferdinando Gorges and John Mason. These two agreed in 1629 to split the territory between them, Maine going to Gorges, New Hampshire to Mason. The arrangement meant little, for by the 1640's Massachusetts had extended its domination over all settlements within both grants. New Hampshire remained a fief of the Bay Colony until 1677, when it became a separate colony; and Maine's separation was delayed until 1820, when it became the twenty-third state in the union.

NEW ENGLAND SOCIETY

By 1640, division seemed ready to rip New England apart. Massachusetts and Connecticut looked with contempt upon the plantations of the otherwise minded. The river towns disliked New Haven and New Haven viewed all its neighbors as morally lax. Settlements in New Hampshire and Maine waited uneasily to be swallowed by the Bay Colony. But these differences, so clear at close view, vanish at a distance; and when the colonies in the North are compared to those on Chesapeake Bay, it is clear that a homogeneous New England society had come into being.

The Town

Geography helped to shape the society. New England settlements, like those to the South, hugged the water and showed little interest in the wilderness at their backs. But where the Chesapeake colonists scattered along the vast bay's shoreline and lived unto themselves, New Englanders settled in clumps along the Connecticut River or around the multitude of harbors and inlets that dotted the northern coast. English traditions, intensified by a passion to worship in a particular way, might have led them to group together regardless of the land, but where in the South land and shoreline encouraged dispersal they helped in the north to preserve and strengthen habits brought from England. The town, or township, as it is known formally, rather than the county became the key political unit.

Few of the twenty thousand Englishmen who migrated to New England in the 1630's wished to abandon the village and farm life they had known at home. The paucity of rich land—much of New England soil was salted with rocks and gravel—helped to preserve English habits. Puritanism, too, with its emphasis on the godly community that existed for the good of all, kept alive old habits. The covenant knit men together, they formed a congregation of visible saints and out of the congregation grew the church, and out of the church grew the town. When townsmen agreed to disagree and decided to move elsewhere, they did so as a group; and after they had moved, they first formed a new church and then erected their new town. The meetinghouse was usually the first public building put up.

Village life centered around the meetinghouse, so called said Cotton Mather because there was "no just ground in Scripture to apply such a trope as *church* to a place of assembly." Since religion permeated all sides of life, no one held this building more sacred than any other. It was the place of assembly for all, "built by our own vote, framed by our own hammers and saw, and by our own hands set in the convenientest place for all." It was a plain building, partly because the settlers lacked the skills and tools for something more elaborate, partly because Puritanism, the perfect religion to bring to the wilderness, favored plainness in all things.

"Where to set" the meetinghouse provided the village with its first quarrel, often shaking the congregation, as one diarist put it, "with violence before it was well set and the parts firmly knit." If a congregation could not settle its differences, the General Court stepped in to "stick the stake." The house faced south "to be square with the sun at noon." Windows of plain glass let in God's light pure and unadorned. An interior bare of adornment prevented distraction from the sermon, though when the doors were left open on a warm morning dogs wandered in and were "often the occasion of great disorder and disturbance by their quarreling and fighting." A spire to the early Puritans smacked of popery; a turret instead surmounted the building and atop the turret a weathercock replaced the cross to remind villagers of Peter's fall from grace as well as to inform them of the wind and weather.

The General Court determined the shape and size of the town. A congregation in from England received from the court a block of land that averaged out to about five miles by five miles. The town thereafter went its own way, though the strength of English habits gave a certain uniformity to its development. The layout drew on both the English village and, as in Jamestown, though to a lesser degree, on the Ulster plantation pattern. Every town created in the first decade of settlement centered around a tight nucleus of dwellings having a fort or a fortified dwelling, "garrison house," where settlers could escape to in troubled times. Some of the villages were split by a single street with the meetinghouse at one end and long, narrow home lots stretching away from the street on either side. These strips were ample enough for a house and barn, an orchard, vegetable garden, and fields for raising Indian corn and English wheat. The lack of tools made it difficult to farm more than these strips for some time; the Pilgrims had no plow for twelve years, and in 1636 there were only thirty-six plows in the whole of the Bay Colony.

Distributing the village strips, all so similar, raised few problems for community leaders, but lots located elsewhere in the town did. Lot sizes and locations were to a degree determined by "the rule of persons and estates," that is, by a man's wealth, social position, and the size of his family. Little thought went to village expansion or to future settlement elsewhere in the town. Roads stretched out from the village haphazardly, with an eye only to getting the citizen to his outlying lands and with no thought of communication with neighboring towns.

Few ties bound towns to the central government. "Particular towns have many things which concern only themselves," the General Court said in 1635, adding that they could dispose of their lands as they wished, levy local taxes, choose "their own particular officers, as constables, surveyors and the like." No state-appointed justices of the peace or centrally controlled courts, as in Virginia and Maryland, strengthened the government's hand over local affairs. The state restricted the vote for provincial officers to church members; but towns established their own qualifications, which were usually more liberal, for choosing local officers. All citizens gathered once a year at the meetinghouse for "town meeting," and here all business was conducted and officials for the coming year were elected. Town selectmen ran affairs between these meetings, always with a knowledge their conduct would be scrutinized at the year's end.

Everything encouraged a tightly knit village life and at the same time little communication with the world beyond town boundaries. Everyone was expected to "watch over his neighbor's soul as his own," in order to ease the way to heaven by alerting him to his weaknesses. Since all were engaged in erecting a holy community, the "unsanctified" must be "warned out," which not only kept the town pure but, as in England, reduced the chance of becoming burdened with any wandering poor. Once a town had acquired a blacksmith to make and repair necessary tools, a sawmill and a gristmill, it became as self-sufficient as a medieval manor. Improved communications and the need for labor would soon break down the isolation of the early towns, but by that time the town pattern was well-fixed.

Economic Life

The Pilgrims came first and the ways they discovered to sustain their colony did much to shape the economic pattern of those who came after. They wasted little time searching for a profitable staple crop, for the land around Plymouth was too poor for commercial farming. The fur trade offered the best possibilities. A backwater location precluded the trade coming to Plymouth. The Pilgrims overcame this disadvantage by building trading posts up and down the coast; and by the time the Puritans arrived they had "engrossed all the chief places of trade," as Winthrop put it, and built a prosperous business.

The fur business did not long support the Pilgrims. The coastal lands were soon trapped out and competitors began to cut in on the remaining supply. Boston moved into the Kennebec region of Maine; the French under D'Aulnay seized Penobscot, Maine; and the Puritans of Dorchester shoved into Windsor, Connecticut. But by this time the Pilgrims had turned to another business—cattle raising. Incoming Puritans with money to pay offered a steady and profitable market through the 1630's. Plymouth prospered until 1641, when the flood of immigrants fell off. "The mighty Cow her crown hath lost" goes a line from an early almanac, and with her fall Plymouth's economy slumped. Plymouth and the villages she had spawned settled back to become communities of farmers and fishermen; and from this time on, they remained economic satellites of Massachusetts Bay.

The Bay Colony in 1641 fared only slightly better than Plymouth. In her search for a staple crop the possibilities of hemp, of sassafras, then considered a cure for syphilis, and of grapes for wine had been explored. These experiments soon collapsed. The holy commonwealth sustained itself by supplying new arrivals with necessities. The newcomers traded what they brought for fresh food, lumber, corn, and cattle. Often they bought homes and land from earlier arrivals who had decided to strike out for less settled places. (Hooker's congregation at Newtown sold its land and dwellings to the newly arrived congregation of Thomas Shepard.) The end of this great migration hit Massachusetts with devastating force, and the colony began the new decade aware it must find a way out of its economic troubles if it was to survive.

The boom of the 1630's and the depression of the early 1640's passed by
the rest of New England, where settlements were small and isolated and
did little trading with the outside world. Neither their economy nor their
economic ideas were exposed to the severe drubbing that Massachusetts
endured.

Bay Colony leaders' economic ideas were summed up in Winthrop's
remark that "the care of the public must over-sway all private respects."
The government must see to it that buyers and sellers charged only a "just
price," that interest rates were reasonable, that wages were controlled, that
dishonest dealings were publicly punished. The American experience
quickly subjected these ideas to great pressures. Within a year wages shot
up in the face of a shortage of labor, especially of skilled persons like
blacksmiths, carpenters, and shipwrights. The inflow of manufactured
goods failed to meet needs, and the price of an iron pot or a yard of cloth
soon exceeded the reach of most settlers. A disillusioned General Court
abandoned the attempt to control prices and wages and turned the problem over to the towns. In its next effort to control the economy the Court
limited the right to trade with incoming ships to a few men. This attempt
to transplant the old merchant guild system to America failed before the
ink dried on the statute.

The reality of America wrecked the Old World's sense of order.
Carpenters and masons soon had the income of their social superiors.
Gentlemen could no longer maintain a staff of servants to care for them.
Winthrop knew a man who,

being forced to sell a pair of his oxen to pay his servant his wages, told his
servant he could keep him no longer, not knowing how to pay him the next
year. The servant answered, he would serve him for more of his cattle. "But
how shall I do," saith the master, "when all my cattle are gone?" The servant
replied, "You shall then serve me, and so you may have your cattle again."

Winthrop and the other leaders, all landed gentlemen in England,
found it hardest to adjust to the merchant in their midst. The merchant-
tradesman who immigrated to Boston had been reared in the competitive
society of London, where he lived and prospered by his wits. He was brash
and aggressive and gave little thought to the welfare of the community.
The restraints the government tried to impose on his activities outraged
him; and when the church, too, censured him, he was deeply hurt. He
lived an exemplary life, never "idle, lazy, or dronish"; and yet he was
attacked from all sides, blamed for soaring wages, for unjust prices, for
the shortage of necessities. "To be both a pious Puritan and a successful
merchant," Bernard Bailyn has remarked, "meant to live under what
would seem to have been insupportable pressures." When Anne Hutchin-

son came under fire, the merchants tended to make her cause theirs, mainly because she was being attacked by those who attacked them. Her defeat was a defeat for them, and many merchants left the Bay Colony when she was banished. Only in the 1640's would they come into power; even then the church would continue to oppose them so vehemently that they would turn to the crown as an ally.

Indians and the Pequot War

New England began with few enemies to fear. The Spanish were far to the south; the French had yet to build up strength in Canada; and the Indians had apparently been decimated by smallpox. This last proved false.

The Puritans came expecting to make the Indians over in their own image. When the Indians resisted this educational program, the Puritans adopted a get-tough policy that lasted throughout the colonial period. Roger Williams was numbered among the few who took the natives on their own terms. He lodged "with them in their filthy, smoky holes to gain their tongue"; he traded with them, preached to them, and in all his dealings treated them as equals. He became deeply fond of individual Indians but never sentimentalized the race. "Their treacheries exceed Machiavelli's," he once said.

Williams' fairness toward the Indian was rare. Within a few years Puritans had developed a logic for usurping Indian lands that calmed uneasy consciences. Upon moving into Connecticut, they announced that the land was "the Lord's waste"; and though natives already inhabited it, they had not "minded the employment thereof to the right ends for which land was created." The unbridled expansion of white men into the Connecticut Valley at last convinced the up-to-now pacific Pequots—"a stout and warlike people," Bradford called them—the time had come to fight back.

A dissolute, wandering Virginia trader named Captain Stone was killed by the Pequots in 1633. The following year they murdered John Oldham, something of a thorn himself. Massachusetts sent John Endecott down with about a hundred men to exact retribution. The rash and tempestuous Endecott plundered the Indians and intensified rather than settled the tensions between the whites and natives in the Connecticut Valley. "You come hither to raise these wasps about my ears," a Saybrook settler remarked to Endecott, "and then you will take wings and flee away." Once the blundering Endecott had departed, the Pequots made peace with their enemies, the Narragansetts, and then sacked Saybrook and Wethersfield in 1635–1636. On a plea from Massachusetts, Roger Williams set out "all alone in a poor canoe," cutting "through a stormy wind with great seas, every minute in hazard of life," to break up the

Narragansetts' alliance with the Pequots. He succeeded after three days of palavering, but the Pequots continued on their own to ravage the Connecticut countryside.

In May 1637 the river towns sent ninety men led by John Mason and John Underhill to crush the Indians in their fort on the Pequot River. After a clever ruse, they surprised the Indians at night in their fort and set fire to it. Underhill was told "that there were about four hundred souls in this fort and not above five of them escaped out of our hands." Those who tried to flee the fire were "entertained with the point of the sword." "Should not Christians have more mercy and compassion?" Underhill later asked, and answered: "We had sufficient light from the word of God for our proceedings."

Soon after, reinforcements were sent out from Massachusetts. The remaining Pequots were tracked down and either killed, enslaved, or sold to the West Indies. (The Pequots were not exterminated, however, as was once thought. Ezra Stiles of Connecticut reported in 1765 that some three hundred members of the once powerful tribe still lived.) In September 1638 Roger Williams was called in again, and at a council with the Mohegans and Narragansetts—the virtual extermination of the Pequots accounted for their absence—he worked out a peace settlement. The Indians gave expanding New England no further serious trouble until the outbreak of King Philip's War in 1675.

The Puritan Heritage

The holy commonwealth envisioned by Winthrop began to fade within a decade of its founding. The Puritans' resistance to the Anglican Church had led in America to a religious pattern more rigid than that Elizabeth had imposed on England. The saints soon faced rebellions from among their own kind. The most obstreperous rebels were shunted from the holy land into the wilderness. Some departed without urging and some—the merchants, for example—remained to undermine the experiment from within. The history of the New England Way both within the Bay Colony and in its deviate forms elsewhere is that of an ideal briefly realized, which soon after eroded under a variety of pressures. Yet in their failure, the founding fathers of the New England Way left an indelible mark on the American experience.

Exactly what that mark was is not easy to determine, for the Puritans have often been made to bear the weight of all the seventeenth century's weaknesses. They have been called inhuman, intolerant, and acquisitive, as if these qualities were not shared by others of their age. Still, a New England Way did evolve out of the Puritan settlements, and several of its characteristics are not pleasing. These people rarely reveal a sense of humor, and the few times it breaks through in their writings it is didactic and heavy-handed. The Puritans were great people, as Emerson said, and also grim. They seldom enjoyed life for itself but only as it pointed a moral. Their urge to discipline all passions but love of God produced a Winthrop and a Williams, and also the killjoy. Their desire to be knit together as one all too often degenerated into the tale-bearing busybody, into "blue laws" and other sumptuary legislation that interfered with men's private lives.

Much that was peculiar to the New England Way never entered into the mainstream of the American experience. The Congregational Church as the Puritans first conceived it soon died, and even in a later version it, along with the town meeting, remained mainly in New England. The county rather than the town became the typical form of local government throughout America. The Puritan bequeathed few institutions, but he contributed attitudes that shaped American institutions. Take politics, for example. The average Puritan distrusted arbitrary power. He migrated at a time when the great battle between crown and Parliament was at its peak, and for the most part he favored the Parliamentary view. He did not hold the state in awe, for he believed God alone deserved worship. While others who came to America showed similar distaste for arbitrary power and an omnipotent state, the Puritans through their voluminous writings did much to clarify and perpetuate this view.

Belief in a limited state did not, of course, imply complete freedom. The Puritan viewed man as corrupt and in constant need of discipline. The discipline must come first from within the individual; then, if that failed, from the congregation or local community; and, only as a last resort, from the state. It has been suggested that "the acquisitive energy of the nineteenth century would have created far more havoc than it did" if the Puritan strain had been absent from the American experience.

Perhaps the Puritans' greatest achievement was, as Alan Simpson says, "to give an intellectual structure to their religion without depleting it of emotion." Puritan discipline infected both the mind and the heart. The evangelical side would burst forth in the eighteenth century's Great Awakening and again in the revival meetings of the nineteenth century; but these eruptions lacked an old ingredient—Puritanism's respect for knowledge. The Puritans have been praised for their village schools and the early founding of Harvard College, but these achievements were the product of English rather than Puritan habits. Their contribution was to meld the evangelical spirit with the inquiring mind. They believed that knowledge of God's word would only further reveal His glory. They might warp knowledge to fit their scheme of the universe, but they at least had the ability to face new findings when they came along, such as

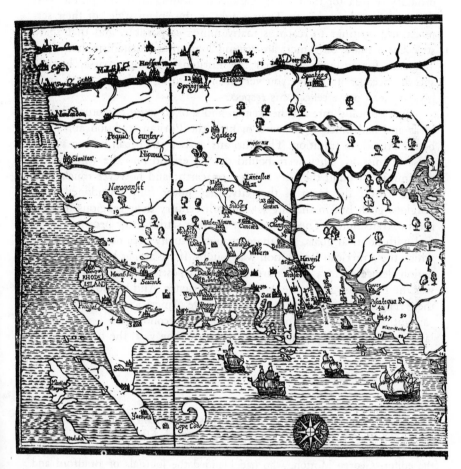

New England by John Foster, 1677

Map. 14. The legend which appeared on the original map reads: "A Map of New England, being the first that was ever here cut, and done by the best pattern that could be had, which, being in some places defective, it made the other less exact; yet doth it sufficiently show the situation of the country and conveniently well the distance of places. The figures that are joined with the names of places are to distinguish such as have been assaulted by the Indians and others."

Copernicus' theory that the earth revolved around the sun, and to deal with them as honestly as possible. More than that, they showed an extraordinary respect for their congregations by dealing from the pulpit with the most complex subjects. They sought in the "plain style" of their sermons and writings to reach as many minds as possible, and that spare style left a mark on American writing long after Puritanism had died. Thoreau, for instance, admired the Puritans' "strong, coarse, homely speech" because it "brings you very near the thing itself described," and his own lean prose reflects his respect.

The Puritans' care for the written and spoken word perpetuated their ideas and had much to do with making the Puritan tradition appear to be the American tradition. The Puritans crossed the ocean with a strong sense of mission. They were bound on "an errand into the wilderness," determined to build the City of God on earth; and however much they diverged over the form of that city, they never fully abandoned their religious goal. But in the late seventeenth century their religious mission became transmuted. The purposes of the first settlers now became identified with political goals, and these goals eventually became the rights for which the American Revolution was fought. If we are, as has been said, a nation dedicated to a high purpose, that purpose, that sense of mission, was the Puritans' gift to the American experience. And to the degree that their religious spirit survives, they also gave America, as Emerson said, "an antidote to the spirit of commerce and of economy . . .—always enlarging, firing man, prompting the pursuit of the vast, the beautiful, the unattainable."

BIBLIOGRAPHY

Beginnings

The book to begin the story of the Pilgrims is William Bradford's *Of Plymouth Plantation,* which is best read in Samuel Eliot Morison's edition (1952). *Mourt's Relation*—so called because the printer twisted the name of the editor, George Morton, who had blended the journals of Bradford and Edward Winslow and published them in 1622—gives the fullest account of the Pilgrims' early days in New England; Alexander Young has reprinted it in *Chronicles of the Pilgrim Fathers of the Colony of Plymouth from 1602 to 1625* (1841); and Dwight B. Heath has re-edited it under the title of *A Journal of the Pilgrims at Plymouth* (pb. original). Thomas Morton writes with wit against the Pilgrims in *New English Canaan* (1637, 1883).

G. F. Willison's *Saints and Strangers* (1945; pb.) is a reliable popular account of the Pilgrim saga. Charles M. Andrews gives a more scholarly approach in the first volume of his *The Colonial Period of American History* (4 vols., 1936–1938). Bradford Smith's *Bradford of Plymouth* (1951), though uneven, is the best biography available. Some useful articles on Plymouth are Samuel Eliot Morison's "The Pilgrim Fathers' Significance in History," *By Land and by Sea* (1953); his "New Light Wanted on the Old Colony," *WMQ*, 15 (1958), 359–364; Darrett B. Rutman, "The Pilgrims and Their Harbor," *WMQ*, 17 (1960), 164–182, wherein it is argued that the Pilgrims had no foreknowledge of Plymouth harbor until they reached it; and Thomas W. Perry, "New Plymouth and Old England: A Suggestion," *WMQ*, 18 (1961), 251–265, which emphasizes the Pilgrims' loyalty to England and the crown. Two excellent, but specialized, slim volumes are Sydney V. James, Jr., ed., *Three Visitors to Early Plymouth: Letters About the Pilgrim Settlement in New England During Its First Seven Years by John Pory, Emmanuel Altham, and Isaack de Rasières* (1963); and Ruth A. McIntyre, *Debts Hopeful and Desperate: Financing the Plymouth Colony* (1963). At least one expert of Plymouth history considers Miss McIntyre's book "one of the most valuable introductions to Pilgrim history." The best work on the Pilgrim legend and its influence in American history is Wesley Frank Craven, *The Legend of the Founding Fathers* (1956; pb.).

In addition to the works on Puritans mentioned in Chapter 2, consult Perry Miller's *Orthodoxy in Massachusetts* (1935; pb.) and *The New England Mind: The Seventeenth Century* (1939; pb.), both difficult works that at times are impenetrable. Thomas Hutchinson's account of Massachusetts' early years, *History of the Colony and Province of Massachusetts Bay* (3 vols., 1936), written in the eighteenth century but first published in 1828, is reliable, comprehensive, and readable; the best edition is that edited by Lawrence S. Mayo (3 vols., 1936). Andrews' version of the early years in *Colonial Period* may be fleshed out by Thomas J. Wertenbaker's *The Puritan Oligarchy* (1947; pb.) and James Truslow Adams' *The Founding of New England* (1921; pb.), whose grudge against the Puritans is counterbalanced by Morison's sympathetic sketches in *Builders of the Bay Colony* (1930; pb.).

The published source material on the Puritan experiment is massive. John Winthrop's *Journal* is basic to any study of the holy commonwealth's early years; James Savage's edition (2 vols., 1853) is the best, J. K. Hosmer's (2 vols., 1908) is modernized and expurgated. Young's *Chronicles of the First Planters of the Colony of Massachusetts Bay from 1623 to 1636* (1846) offers a number of diaries and other records of the early years.

Massachusetts Bay

Much of the material mentioned above is, of course, applicable here. For those who want to hear the Puritans tell their own story, the best single collection of their writings is Perry Miller and Thomas H. Johnson, eds., *The Puritans* (2 vols., 1938; pb.). An abbreviated version with new material added and all in modern dress has been edited by Miller alone, *The American Puritans* (pb. original). Anything Clifford K. Shipton has written on the Puritans bears reading. An article of his that helped to renew respect for their achievements is "A Plea for Puritanism," *AHR*, 40 (1935), 460–467, which offers as good a starting place as any for the beginning student. Daniel Boorstin's provocative essay on the Puritans is found in *The Americans: The*

Colonial Experience (1958; pb.). George Lee Haskins' *Law and Authority in Early Massachusetts* (1960), mentioned earlier, is again pertinent. Two useful biographies are Mayo's *John Endecott* (1936) and Larzer Ziff's *The Career of John Cotton: Puritanism and the American Experience* (1962). Ziff's excellent work gives the best available account of Cotton's views on the relations between church and state. Edmund S. Morgan's *The Puritan Dilemma: The Story of John Winthrop* (1958; pb.) can be supplemented by V. L. Parrington's sketch of Winthrop in the first volume of *Main Currents in American Thought* (1927; pb.), which contains accounts of several other early, eminent Puritans; and by Richard S. Dunn's chapter on Winthrop in *Puritans and Yankees—The Winthrop Dynasty of New England, 1630–1717* (1962). Anyone planning research in the Puritan story should first read Morgan's brief "New England Puritanism: Another Approach," *WMQ*, 18 (1961), 236–242, as well as his recent *The Visible Saints: The History of a Puritan Idea* (1963; pb.), and also Darrett B. Rutman, "God's Bridge Falling Down: 'Another Approach' to New England Puritanism Assayed," *WMQ*, 19 (1962), 408–421. More recently Rutman has published a detailed account of *Winthrop's Boston: Portrait of a Puritan Town, 1630–1649* (1965).

Hivings-Out

A good, if prejudiced, place to begin a study of the turmoil in the early years of the Bay Colony is Charles Francis Adams' *Three Episodes of Massachusetts History* (2 vols., 1892), the second volume of which presents basic documents in the Antinomian controversy. Ola Elizabeth Winslow's *Master Roger Williams* (1957) is the best and most balanced of many works on Williams. S. H. Brockunier's *The Irrepressible Democrat: Roger Williams* (1940) is thorough and scholarly but the point of view must be balanced by Alan Simpson's "How Democratic Was Roger Williams?" *WMQ*, 13 (1956), 53–67. The prolix and discursive *The Complete Writings of Roger Williams* (6 vols., 1866–1874) have recently been reprinted with a seventh volume, edited by Perry Miller, that includes material missed in the original collection. Miller has also condensed, edited, and put into modern English the core of Williams' writing in *Roger Williams: His Contribution to the American Tradition* (1953; pb.). A still useful article is Henry Bamford Parkes, "John Cotton and Roger Williams Debate Toleration, 1644–1652," *New England Quarterly (NEQ)*, 4 (1931), 735–756.

A revived interest in the Antinomian controversy has produced two biographies on the key figures. Ziff's on Cotton gives a sympathetic and convincing account of that divine's role in the affair. Emery Battis' *Saints and Sectaries: Anne Hutchinson and the Antinomian Controversy in the Massachusetts Bay Colony* (1962) draws heavily on the lingo of sociology and psychology to explain Mrs. Hutchinson's actions and the warm support her views attracted. Mrs. Hutchinson's trial transcript is given in the appendix of the second volume of Hutchinson's *History of the Colony and Province of Massachusetts Bay.*

The Tercentenary Commission of Connecticut between 1933 and 1936 published sixty historical pamphlets of excellent quality on Connecticut history. Among those that deal with the early settlement are Warren S. Archibald, *Thomas Hooker* (No. 4) ; Dorothy Deming, *The Settlement of the Connecticut Towns* (No. 6) ; Charles M. Andrews, *The Beginnings of Connecticut* (No. 32) ; and Andrews' *The Rise and Fall of the New Haven Colony* (No. 48). Andrews is *the* authority on the colony's early years and his last of a great number of words on it are in the second volume of *Colonial Period*.

New England Society

Roy A. Akagi, *The Town Proprietors of the New England Colonies: A Study of Their Development, Organization, Activities, and Controversies, 1620–1670* (1924), is a distinguished work. John F. Sly treats in full another aspect of the subject in *Town Government in Massachusetts* (1930). Ola Elizabeth Winslow handles with her usual charm and perception what might otherwise be a dull subject in *Meetinghouse Hill, 1630–1783* (1952), always treating the Puritans with respect but missing no chance for humor. Sumner Chilton Powell's study of Sudbury in *Puritan Village: The Formation of a New England Town* (1963; pb.) seeks to explain the origins of the New England town. As a case study it is superb, but that its generalizations hold for all New England is doubtful. Two articles that deal with franchise requirements might be mentioned here, though they cover a period beyond the scope of this chapter: Richard C. Simmons, "Freemanship in Early Massachusetts: Some Suggestions and a Case Study," *WMQ*, 19 (1962), 422–428; and B. Katherine Brown, "Puritan Democracy: A Case Study," *Mississippi Valley Historical Review (MVHR)*, 50 (1964), 377–396. An introductory essay on all aspects of the town is Carl Bridenbaugh's "The New England Town: A Way of Life," *American Antiquarian Society Proceedings*, 56 (1946), 15–18.

The most recent and original work on the early economy of New England is Bernard Bailyn, *The New England Merchants in the Seventeenth Century* (1955; pb.), a basic book for all interested in the subject. An old but still important survey is William B. Weeden, *Economic and Social History of New England, 1620–1789* (2 vols., 1891). Joseph Dorfman's *The Economic Mind in American Civilization* (5 vols., 1946–1959) has an excellent chapter on the Puritans in the first volume. Another sound account is E. A. J. Johnson, *American Economic Thought in the Seventeenth Century* (1932). A recent specialized study is Rutman's "Governor Winthrop's Garden Crop: The Significance of Agriculture in the Early Commerce of Massachusetts Bay," *WMQ*, 20 (1963), 396–415.

On the Pequot War, see Howard Bradstreet, *The Story of the Pequot War Retold* (1953). The latest word on "Pequots and Puritans: The Causes of the War of 1637" has been related by Alden T. Vaughan in *WMQ*, 21 (1964), 256–269. Bradford writes of the war in *Of Plymouth Plantation;* Winthrop comments on it throughout his *Journal;* and both Captains Mason and Underhill published their firsthand accounts of the fight at Mystic. Wesley Frank Craven develops the influence of the Puritan tradition with imagination and wit in *The Legend of the Founding Fathers* (1956; pb.), and Alan

Simpson comments on it in the final pages of his *Puritanism in Old and New England* (1955; pb.). A full treatment of the Puritan literary heritage is found in Kenneth Murdock's *Literature and Theology in Colonial New England* (1949; pb.) and is scattered throughout Moses Coit Tyler's *History of American Literature* (2 vols., 1878; pb.).

For further references see the *Harvard Guide,* Sections 83, "English Puritanism and Background of Puritan Migration"; 84, "New England Settlements to 1630"; 85, "Massachusetts Bay Colony, 1630–1660"; 88, "Southern New England Colonies to 1663"; and 90, "New England in the Seventeenth Century: Social, Economic, Institutional."

John Winthrop and Charles II

5. Puritans and Cavaliers: 1640–1676

NEW ENGLAND
 The Confederation of New England
 A Mercantile Economy
 Politics, Government, and Religion

THE CHESAPEAKE COLONIES
 Trade
 Religion
 Indians
 Politics

A NEW IMPERIALISM: 1650–1676
 The Commonwealth
 The Restoration

THE RESTORATION IN THE COLONIES: 1660–1676
 New England
 The Chesapeake Colonies

By 1640 approximately twelve thousand Englishmen were scratching a living from Chesapeake soil; and some twenty thousand others, three-fifths of them within the Bay Colony, were attempting the same in twelve independent settlements scattered through New England. The population of St. Kitts at that time exceeded Massachusetts Bay's and that of Barbados, no more than a spot in the ocean, equaled Virginia's. English authorities valued these and other possessions in the West Indies more than the mainland colonies and gave the Indies most of what little care they had to spare for overseas possessions.

Even the slight thought spent on the mainland colonies vanished in 1640. Eleven years of Charles I's arbitrary rule ended that year when the Puritan-dominated Long Parliament met and soon after accumulated enough strength to force the king to abandon London. For three years Puritans and Cavaliers at home battled for power while their neglected counterparts across the ocean, involved with their own troubles, looked on with something close to disinterest. After Cromwell's victories at Marston Moor (1644) and Naseby (1645), four more years passed while the king's fate was debated; then, with his execution in 1649, England was exposed to a decade of Puritan rule. Charles II retrieved the crown in 1660. He returned eager to invigorate the new imperial system begun by Cromwell but soon found that Puritans and Cavaliers, divided at home, could unite in America when an effort was made after two decades of neglect to supervise their lives.

NEW ENGLAND

English Puritans worked throughout the Civil War to woo New England to their cause, only to be rebuffed as bluntly as Laud had been. Parliament exempted the plantations from import and export duties, permitted the soliciting of funds in London to pay shipping costs for bonded servants, and even offered to consider whatever legislation Massachusetts required to promote the well-being of the holy experiment. John Winthrop refused all offers of aid, "lest in . . . after times . . . hostile forces might be in control, and meantime a precedent would have been established." Bay Colony merchants backed his refusal, insisting that self-interest, their own and New England's, demanded a neutral stand on affairs at home; and throughout the civil war they traded with Puritans and Cavaliers alike. All the while New England traveled an independent road, her life was being reshaped into a pattern that, much as it distressed Winthrop and his associates, would remain substantially unchanged until the American Revolution.

The Confederation of New England

The depression that had set in with the end of the great migration worsened through the 1640's. "Merchants would sell no wares but for ready money," Winthrop wrote; "men could not pay their debts though they had enough, prices of land and cattle fell soon to the one-half, yea, to a third, and after one-fourth part." The depression "put many into an unsettled frame of spirit" and prompted further hivings-out, only now orthodox Puritans led the way. This "removing for outward advantage" by the orthodox saddened Winthrop. "If one may go, another may," he said, "and so the greater part, and so church and commonwealth may be left destitute in a wilderness, exposed to misery and reproach and all for thy ease and pleasure."

A few of the emigrants headed back to England to carry on the holy work there, but that stream never amounted to more than a trickle. Several shiploads went to the West Indies to erect further Puritan experiments in softer climes. A good number slipped into territory nominally held by the Dutch. First came "diverse servants whose time had expired," according to a Dutch observer, "afterwards families, and finally, whole colonies, having been forced to quit that place in order to enjoy freedom of conscience, and escape from the insupportable government of New England." Anne Hutchinson, her husband now dead, left Rhode Island and settled northeast of New Amsterdam along the river that now bears her name. She and her family were murdered by Indians in the fall of 1643. Settlers from Lynn, Massachusetts, went to Southampton, on the eastern tip of Long Island. Reverend Francis Doughty, banished from Cohasset, Massachusetts, received thirteen thousand acres from the Dutch in 1642, and with his congregation founded Newtown, New York. John Throgmorton came the same year with thirty-five families to settle on the East River at Throg's Neck. Soon after Robert Fordham founded Hempstead, Lady Deborah Moody—"a nice and anciently religious woman," as Winthrop put it—founded Gravesend, and others such villages as Huntington, Setauket, and Brookhaven—all on Long Island.

Winthrop grieved less when he realized that these dispersions strengthened rather than vitiated the New England Way. The unity of the holy experiment might still be maintained if these and other towns scattered about New England could be welded together under a single government. As a step in this direction, Massachusetts in 1641 took over settlements to the north along the Piscataqua River, a move that presaged the eventual absorption of all settlements in New Hampshire and Maine by the Bay Colony. Heretical Rhode Island alone now flawed New England unity, and in 1642 Winthrop moved southward to erase that blemish. He might have managed, amid the distractions of the civil war in England, to usurp the Narragansett settlements except for the forehanded action of Roger Williams. Soon after Gorton's outpost north of Providence had been annexed by the Bay Colony in 1643, Williams sailed from New Amsterdam for England—Massachusetts had threatened him with arrest if he entered Boston—to obtain a charter for the plantations of the otherwise minded. He whiled away the time on shipboard writing *A Key into the Language of America,* a combined lexicon and essay on the Indian language, wherein he reported his experiences among the natives. He reached London as the civil war approached its crisis, hardly an auspicious time to plead for a charter and made even less so by the presence of Massachusetts Bay agents on hand to fight his claim. Yet less than ten months after he had left the "dreadful Atlantic Ocean" behind, Williams had his charter. Powerful friends among the Puritans who were sympathetic to his views on religious toleration had helped him; his influence had been further increased by *A Key,* which had been published soon after his arrival. The book made clear that he had been the first "to break the ice" with the natives by purchasing Providence from them. This enhanced Williams' reputation in England—where the old image of the Indian as a "noble savage" still prevailed—and at the same time weakened Massachusetts' claim for the same territory.

The charter gave full power and authority to Providence Plantations —they were, however, to be "henceforth called the ile of Rods, or Rhod-Island"—to rule themselves by such a form of civil government as they should find most suitable to their estate and condition, provided only that such government "be conformable to the laws of England, so far as the nature and constitution of the place will admit." The grant shocked New England, for Cromwell had in effect handed a license to the devil's own kind. Since Rhode Island could not now be absorbed, she must be ignored. The Islanders, as Winthrop called them, were pointedly snubbed in 1643 when the Confederation of New England was formed, because "we have no conversing with them, nor desire to have, further than necessity or humanity may require."

During Williams' absence in England, the confederation came into being, a product of Puritan fears—of the French ringing New England from the northeast to the northwest, of the Dutch on the southeast and west, and of the Indians in their midst—and of orthodoxy's desire to solidify its control over New England affairs. William Bradford gives the "plottings of the Narragansetts" as the sole reason for the confederation, but the danger from foreign enemies bulked larger than he would admit. The Dutch opposed New England advances at several points—at Albany on the west; at Hartford, where their trading post still stood; on the Delaware, where New Haven had tried to erect a trading post; on Long Island; and along the southern border of Connecticut, where Puritan settlements lay within forty miles of Manhattan.

The Dutch were a clear and present danger; the French were a potential but nonetheless positive danger. Acadia (Nova Scotia) and Quebec had fallen into British hands shortly before New England's settlement, but Charles I returned them to France in 1632. Jesuit missionaries once again pushed inland, exploring as they went, closing off Indian trade that might have drifted to the coast and into Puritan hands, and, worst of all, converting Indians to the Catholic faith. The Iroquois further complicated matters in 1643 by warring on Indians allied to the French. This inevitably disturbed New England's relations with its own Indians.

Massachusetts had first proposed a union of New England settlements in 1637 during the Pequot War. The river towns had rejected the offer, fearing that they would be dominated by the Bay Colony. Five years later, with marauding Indians again at their backs, the river towns themselves advanced the idea, insisting only that each colony have an equal vote in all proceedings. Massachusetts accepted this unrealistic condition; and in May 1643 she, with the river towns of Connecticut, Plymouth, and New Haven, signed the constitution for "the Confederation of the United Colonies of New England." The settlements in Maine were not admitted, ostensibly because "they ran a different course from us both in their ministry and civil administration," but more likely because the Bay Colony hoped to, and soon would, absorb them. Rhode Island's later request for admission was answered with an "utter refusal."

The constitution on the whole reflected intelligent thought, considering that nothing like it had been attempted before. The colonies joined together "into a firm and perpetual League of Friendship and Amity for offense and defense, mutual advice and succour upon all just occasions, both for preserving and propagating the truth and liberties of the Gospel and for their own mutual safety and welfare." Each colony retained its "peculiar jurisdiction." Any six of the eight commissioners—two from each colony—had the power to act for the confederation. The commissioners, all required to be church members, had considerable power. They could determine the affairs of war and peace, the division of spoils, the reception of new confederates. They were to "endeavor to frame and establish agreements and orders in general cases of a civil nature wherein all the plantations are interested." They would manage Indian affairs and see to it that any escaped servant "shall be delivered to his master, or any other that pursues. . . ." (This last might be construed as the forerunner of the fugitive-slave law of a later time.)

It is difficult to judge the effectiveness of this first American experiment in federalism. The commissioners worked hard to manage Indian affairs in a way that avoided war. They kept a close watch over religious affairs, advising the colonies to tax all who refused to support Puritan ministers and to banish Quakers, and warning all congregations to take care whom they admitted to membership. They promoted missionary work among the Indians, mainly by disbursing funds from an English society for Propagating the Gospel in New England and by setting up a program for educating young Indians at Harvard. Negotiations with the Dutch produced in 1650 the Treaty of Hartford, which sought "to dispose of pending conflicts between New England and New Netherland

Map 15. Settlement b

La Pointe

L. des Hurons

U n e x p l o r e

SUSQUEHANNA

MARYLAND

DELAWA

VIRGINIA

POWHATAN

Calvert Town

Providence 1649

Ft. Christi

Kent I.

Ft. Casimir

St. Mary's

Mattapony

Zwaanendael, 163.

TUSCARORA

PAMUNKEY

Williamsburg

Jamestown

SECOTAN

Hampton

Norfolk

PAMLICO

Edenton 1658

C. Hatteras

For detail on Virginia see Map 11. For New A

Unexplored

Hudson Bay

French route

ALGONQUIN

Ontario

IROQUOIS

CATSKILL MTS.

Lachine

Trois Rivières

Quebec

Montreal

Ft. Richelieu

L. Champlain

Schenectady

Ft. Orange

Esopus

Corakie

Springfield

Windsor

Hartford

Saybrook

New London

Southampton

Setauket

Yonkers

Nieuw Amsterdam

PENNACOOK

ABNAKI

Exeter

Providence

Bristol

Newport

Nantucket

Piscataqua (Portsmouth)

Saco

Casco

Pemaquid

Salisbury

Salem

Boston

Plymouth

C. Cod

area see Map 20

Raisz

and to locate a definite boundary between the two." (Holland accepted this treaty; but England refused to, thus pointing out that the Dutch had no rights in America and reminding the confederation that it had no business dealing with foreign nations.)

The flaw that inhibited lasting achievements stemmed from the constitution's making Massachusetts one among equals. As a result, the Bay Colony consistently ignored decisions that violated its interests. When an argument arose whether the river towns could tax Springfield, which Massachusetts claimed as its own, the majority favored such a tax. Massachusetts answered that rebuff by imposing taxes on all products that entered Boston from Plymouth, New Haven, and the river towns. When the commissioners voted to war on the Dutch during the second Anglo-Dutch War (1652–1654), the Bay Colony balked; and the Confederation found it could do nothing. When Massachusetts took foreign affairs into its own hands and aided a friendly Frenchman's efforts to take over Acadia, the confederation could only look on in anger. It would take nearly a century and a half of political experience before Americans would learn that for a federal system to work well, power in the central government must be proportional to power on the local level.

A Mercantile Economy

Puritan leaders, drawing on the medieval past, worked hard to alleviate distress from the depression of the 1640's, arguing that in time of disaster the welfare of all must be protected from the greedy few. Laws were passed restraining the seizure of property for debts and permitting the paying of debts in "corn, cattle, fish, or other commodities, at such rates as this Court shall set down from time to time." These and other efforts of the General Court were mildly effective in limiting the depression but of no help in carrying Massachusetts or other parts of New England out of the economic slough. The fur trade had collapsed in the first decade of settlement, eliminating an important means of paying for English manufactured goods. The search for a profitable staple crop had failed. Winthrop and his colleagues decided New England could survive only by cutting its economic dependence on the mother country and becoming sufficient unto itself.

First, an iron industry of its own was needed. With a push from the Massachusetts General Court in the form of bounties, prospectors soon turned up iron deposits around Saugus and Braintree. New England had the craftsmen to fashion iron into pots, guns, plow irons, kettles, and the like, but the lack of an iron works forced the importation of all such goods in their expensive manufactured form. John Winthrop, Jr., traveled to London and in 1643 returned with financial backing and a shipload

Map 16. English Colonial Trade, 17ᵗʰ cent.

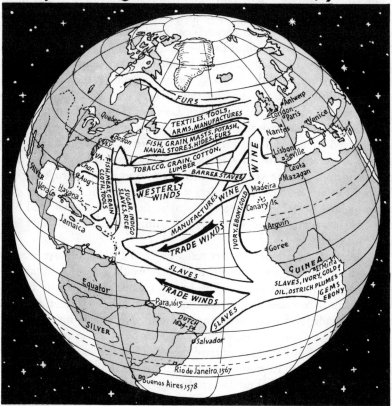

of skilled ironworkers. Five years later a furnace and refinery at Saugus were producing a ton of iron a day. Production rose steadily, but the lack of profits opened a rift between the English investors and Massachusetts authorities. The General Court, concerned only with the colony's welfare, banned exports and permitted sales by barter; the investors wanted to sell in the open market for cash only, and when the Court refused to lift its restrictions they balked at further investments in the struggling enterprise. The company declared bankruptcy in 1652, underwent a reorganization only to slip again into debt. It collapsed for good in 1676.

Meanwhile, the merchants sought to solve New England's economic problems by another route. They ventured into the fishing business. Men from the out-ports of England monopolized the fishing industry in Amer-

ican waters until the civil war, when their ships were turned into privateers or pressed into the navy. New Englanders swept into the nearly
vacant grounds off their coast. More than three hundred thousand cod
alone entered Massachusetts ports in 1641. Hauls of this size had in the
past been disposed of through the once well-organized but now defunct
Bristol market. The inexperienced New England merchants were forced
to market the fish locally until London merchants offered to assume functions previously borne by Bristol. London shipped out manufactured
goods, picked up the fish, and sold them in Spain or the Wine Islands
(Madeira, the Azores, and the Canaries), where subtropical products were
loaded aboard, to be eventually sold in London. New England merchants
appreciated the beauty of this cycle but found it marred by the slight role
they played in it. As their experience in foreign trade increased, they
sought to overcome this flaw by becoming partners with London merchants or by launching voyages of their own to southern European ports.
With these wedges New Englanders soon enlarged their role in the cycle
to the point where, by the Restoration, with fleets of their own and business contacts that relieved them of depending on Londoners, they controlled it completely.

Success in the fishing industry reshaped New England's former agrarian economy into a mercantile pattern that would remain substantially
unchanged until the American Revolution. Contacts with Spain and the
Wine Islands revealed that barrel staves and hoops were needed for
the wine trade, and soon New England ships were carrying these over.
A vessel out of Boston in 1643 picked up a cargo of slaves in Africa and
dropped them in Barbados, carried home a profitable load of sugar,
and that led to New England's involvement in the slave trade and later in
the entire trade of the West Indies. By the Restoration English colonies
in the Indies had shifted from diversified farming to growing sugar alone.
New England supplied the islands with food and horses and carried home
sugar, much of which eventually ended up in rum.

These trade ties with southern Europe and the West Indies did not
break the links with England. The failure to develop manufacturing
forced New England to depend on the home country for all supplies.
"Thus," says Bernard Bailyn, "despite their physical removal from the
home country, and despite their advances into continental American trade
routes, into the West Indies, and into Spanish markets, the New England
merchants from the start conducted their trade mainly within the confines
of the British commercial system."

Whether orthodox Puritans liked it or not the merchant controlled
New England's economy by the 1650's. His influences permeated all parts
of the region, partly because the shortage of money forced him to barter
and thus become involved in all sides of the economy and partly because

he wanted to control the resources—timber, horses, sheep, and the like—
of his trade. To cut costs, he built ships and went into the sawmill and
rum-making business. Land in particular absorbed his interest and much
of his money. Land was useful for speculative purposes, a source of trade
commodities—the Boston merchant John Hull bought timber lands and
sawmills in New Hampshire to assure a continuous flow of lumber products for his ships bound to the Wine Islands—a safe form of investment
in a country that lacked a sufficient quantity of reliable money, and, finally, the basis of social status, for the values of rural Englishmen still
dominated New England.

The merchant might be and often was a Puritan in good standing
with his congregation, but business interests and Puritanism could conflict. Puritanism thrived best isolated from Old World ills, whereas the
merchant prospered on tight ties with Europe. Orthodox Puritans welcomed trade only to the degree it nourished the holy experiment; they
detested the baubles of life—the raucous sailors, the gaudy gowns for their
womenfolk—that trade brought to their shores. At heart they detested the
merchant, too, whose interests and attitudes conflicted with the holy commonwealth as Winthrop and other early leaders conceived it. The merchants might dominate economic affairs, but orthodox Puritans were
determined that all other sides of New England life must remain in their
hands.

Politics, Government, and Religion

An early sign that the elite among the saints were losing control came
when they yielded to pressure for a rule of law as opposed to a rule of
discretion. The magistrates wanted a free hand, but the freemen, backed
by a firm Parliamentary tradition, wanted rule by law. Winthrop resisted
their demands until 1641, when he reluctantly allowed the Body of Liberties to become the law of the land. The code, more a general bill of rights
than a body of laws, was shaped as if it came from or was authorized by
the Bible, when in fact it stemmed for the most part from English common-law experience. Though the Body of Liberties granted such rights
as trial by jury and provided specific punishments for a number of offenses, its scope was sufficiently limited that government by judicial fiat
was only slightly restricted. Winthrop opposed rule by law, that is, restraints on the magistrates' authority, because God had made specific
penalties only in certain cases and as "judges are Gods upon earth" their
power should not be limited more than His. He believed further that the
uniqueness of the American experience could best be dealt with by
judges rather than by a rigid body of laws from the English past. But
Winthrop was not to have his way, for the public forced through a new,
more detailed code in 1648 that sharply limited the magistrates' power.

The Laws and Liberties, the Western World's first modern code of laws, stemmed from nearly two decades of American experience and "was no mere collection of English laws and customs," according to George Haskins. "Many of its provisions were notable improvements on the law of contemporary England in the sense that judicial procedure was simplified, criminal penalties mitigated, primogeniture abolished, debtors accorded humane treatment, and rules of the judicial process instituted to safeguard men's lives from the arbitrary exercise of governmental power."

The fight for a government of laws raged against the background of an even noisier battle over the magistrates' unbridled power within the General Court. A trivial incident—a disagreement over the ownership of a sow—brought the issue into the open. Both Robert Keayne, a rich and disliked merchant, and Mrs. Sherman, a widow who ran a boarding-house, claimed the pig. The case eventually reached the General Court. The deputies favored the widow, at whose house many of them boarded, but the magistrates, or assistants, who held veto power over all decisions by the deputies, sided with Keayne. The question of who owned the pig no longer mattered. The deputies railed against the right of a few magistrates to thwart the will of the people's representatives. Winthrop answered that if the magistrates were not allowed to veto the actions of the deputies the colony would be a democracy and that "there was no such government in Israel." The issue was resolved by an act in 1644, whereby deputies and assistants would thereafter sit separately; and the concurrence of both bodies was required for the adoption of any measure. Thus did a bicameral legislature begin in the Bay Colony.

The two previous attacks on orthodoxy's rule had assailed the form but not the essence of the holy experiment. Soon after the magistrates and deputies came to sit apart, the merchants in the Bay Colony began to batter at the commonwealth's foundations. They petitioned the General Court to suspend all laws that persecuted Anabaptists and Antinomians. The merchants were, in effect, asking for religious toleration, arguing, from ground less lofty than Roger Williams', that persecution harmed business and "makes us stink everywhere." Old-timers like Edward Johnson said merchants had become so greedy for profit "they would willingly have had the Commonwealth tolerate diverse kinds of sinful opinions." The trouble was that about this time the Cromwellian Puritans at home also favored toleration of dissenting Protestant sects, a shift of view that left the orthodox of New England close to speechless. They had exiled Roger Williams for such notions, the insanity of which was revealed by the anarchical state of Rhode Island's affairs.

The merchants would not be silenced. Several of them, led by a bright young scientist named Dr. Robert Child, backed a "Remonstrance and Petition" to the General Court in 1646, which demanded that church membership be broadened and that "civil liberty and freedom be forth-with granted to all truly English." The court rejected the petition as scandalous, fined the petitioners, and imprisoned two of them. But the issue refused to die. Soon after, on request from a group of church elders, the court sent out a call for a synod to consider, among other things, the question of "more liberty and latitude" in the matter of church member-ship. Delays followed—at least three churches boycotted the gathering—but in 1648 the Cambridge Platform of Church Discipline emerged from the synod. The platform explicitly granted the state's power to enforce obedience "in matters of godliness." With heretical congregations, those that "shall walk incorrigibly or obstinately in any corrupt way of their own," the synod said "the Magistrate is to put forth his coercive power, as the matter shall require." Nothing was said about broadening church membership. It continued for years as a qualification to vote for provin-cial officers, but by 1652 men in the colony who had taken an oath of loyalty to the Bay Colony could at least vote for local officials.

The Cambridge Platform spoke the sentiments of an older passing generation. Thomas Hooker died in 1647, the year the synod began its work; Winthrop in 1649; and John Cotton three years later. Not until 1651 could sufficient votes be mustered in the General Court to accept the synod's work, and even then fourteen deputies opposed it. The old saints even from the grave still controlled New England's religious and political affairs, but the end of their tenure lay only a few years ahead.

Throughout the Interregnum of 1649–1660, New England continued to go its own way, paying little more attention to the Puritan leaders controlling English affairs than it had to the crown. Through the con-federation New England conducted its own foreign affairs. It refused to grant suffrage and freedom of religious worship to all it considered heret-ical, despite pressure from within and without. Massachusetts over-came the shortage of coin by boldly setting up its own mint in 1651 and turning out the Pine Tree shilling. The Bay Colony interpreted the charter in a way that allowed it to annex settlements in Maine and New Hampshire. Massachusetts opened its harbors to all nations. All this it did not to flout English power but to promote New England's best in-terests. Distance and new conditions demanded swift action if the New England Way was to flourish. A milder version of the same trend was occurring in the Chesapeake colonies.

THE CHESAPEAKE COLONIES

The colonies to the south looked with less enthusiasm than New Eng-land upon the confusing events in England that began when the Long

Parliament ended Charles I's eleven years of personal rule. Natural sympathies aside, they favored the king because they had much at stake in his success. Maryland, less than six years old and owned by a proprietor bound to the king's cause, risked losing its charter through the slightest indiscretion. The stability of Virginia's royal government depended in fact and theory on the crown. Virginians liked William Berkeley, a thirty-four–year–old Oxonian whom the king had sent out as governor in 1642, and they had no desire to face the uncertainties a Puritan victory would bring into their lives. These ties with England forced the Chesapeake colonies to deal with the problems of the period in ways often quite different from those of New England. At the same time three thousand miles of ocean between them and England led to decisions during the civil war and the Interregnum of 1649–1660 every bit as bold and strikingly American as those carried out to the north.

Trade

While New Englanders sought to make themselves self-sufficient, the Chesapeake colonies at first worked only to improve their main source of income, tobacco. Laws placed on the books after 1640 show that Maryland and Virginia strove no less assiduously than New England to direct the economic affairs of their people. Statutes against "engrossing"—the purchase of a "necessary commodity" at low cost to sell at a "dearer rate" —and against fixing the prices of even tavern drinks suggest the tight control attempted. Most attention, especially in Virginia, went to reducing the quantity and improving the quality of tobacco marketed. The House of Burgesses in 1640 ordered colonists to reduce their plantings in the hope a smaller crop would raise prices. Success depended on cooperation from Maryland, and the lack of it soon doomed the experiment.

After the civil war broke, an even more difficult problem faced tobacco growers of both colonies. Most were royalist in sympathy, but economic self-interest called for a neutral stand, especially since a majority of the London merchants who marketed the Chesapeake crop leaned toward Parliament and the Puritans. Trade moved in accustomed channels until around 1643. Ships from Bristol and New England showed up, eager for the business and willing to assume more of the shipping risks than London merchants. The omnipresent and efficient Dutch also appeared, offering exceedingly good prices. But the tobacco trade involved more than good prices. The problem of supply was of equal importance. London had funneled new settlers into the Chesapeake area, and it had provided on good credit terms exactly the manufactured goods colonists wanted and were accustomed to. New England and Bristol merchants offered little more than fish, and while the Dutch did better, their ladings tended to run heavy in liquor. None brought in new settlers.

The isolation arising out of the civil war helped to direct energies along lines similar to those in New England. Interest in making the Chesapeake area self-sufficient revived the program Sandys had pushed so hard in 1619. Acts promoting the crafts were shoved through the Virginia assembly; shipbuilding was encouraged to cut down carrying charges. Governor Berkeley experimented with rice, sugar, indigo, ginger, and cotton on his estate in a manner the Hakluyts would have approved of. Plans to mint a local coin in 1645 were accompanied by legislation fixing the rate of exchange for Spanish pieces of eight in the hope that this would attract foreign money through the Dutch trade.

None of these efforts to develop a self-sufficient economy succeeded much more than they had in New England. Tobacco trade and its ties with the English markets remained paramount. Parliament in 1650 threatened to boycott that trade unless the Chesapeake colonies surrendered to the Commonwealth. The threat, backed by an armed force, helped persuade Virginia, after token resistance, and Maryland at once to capitulate.

Religion

Virginia and Maryland, each with its own problems, diverged over religious matters in this period. Virginia, much like Massachusetts, tended to demand more conformity. The assembly in 1643 passed laws strengthening the Anglican Church's role in Virginia life. Ministers were required to conform to the "orders and constitutions" of the Church of England, and "all nonconformists" were to "be compelled to depart the colony with all convenience." The laws were put on the books partly because church and state were so intertwined that to allow attacks on the church theoretically weakened the state and partly because the laws might help ward off a religious controversy that appeared to be brewing. A band of Puritans from Boston seemed to the assembly in 1648 to be raising a "schismatical party, of whose intentions our native country of England hath had and yet hath too sad experience." Sufficient pressure soon eased them out of Virginia and into Maryland. Even more pressure was put on the scattering of Quakers—"an unreasonable and turbulent sort of people," according to assembly in 1660—who had filtered into Virginia, and by the time of the Restoration the colony could boast that outwardly at least the established church met with less competition in Virginia than it did in England.

Lord Baltimore carried Maryland down a different road, out of personal inclination and political necessity. Between 1644 and 1647 Protestants and Catholics in Maryland steadily ripped away at each other. Governor Leonard Calvert was forced to flee from the Protestants and regained his government later only with the help of Berkeley. Throughout all this

Lord Baltimore steered a neutral course. Powerful friends among the Puritans, like the Earl of Warwick, aided him in the fight to keep his charter and colony. He furthered his cause by appointing William Stone, a Protestant, as governor in 1648 and then telling Stone to welcome the several hundred Puritans being ejected from Virginia. Soon after this he sent over an "Act concerning Religion."

The act as passed appears to blend two statutes from different hands. The second, more tolerant, part was probably written by Baltimore in England. It notes that heretofore "the enforcing of conscience in matters of religion" has led to "dangerous consequences"; hereafter no person who admits belief in Jesus Christ shall be troubled or molested for his religious beliefs. This part of the act is a generous statement of the belief that men of different Christian faiths can live together, and as such it embodies what would come to be one of the basic principles in the American way of life. The first part of the act most likely was written by the Maryland legislature. It enumerates a series of religious offenses and the drastic penalties that accompany them. (Anyone cursing God shall be punished by death; anyone calling another a heretic, Puritan, Antinomian, or other such offensive name shall be fined and imprisoned.) All these offenses were to be punished by the state, thus making clear that toleration did not include such radical doctrine as separation between church and state. By this very limitation, Wesley Frank Craven remarks, the act "cut to the heart of the problem that was to be peculiarly America's. That problem has been to live together in peace, and only slowly and by an uneven course did men come to a general acceptance of the separation of church and state as a necessary means to that end."

Indians

The Indians rose again in 1644 against the Virginians, and again Opechancanough, now old and enfeebled, led them into battle. He had heard England was embroiled in a civil war and decided, according to a contemporary, "that now was his time or never, to root out all the English" while they could get no help from "their own country." Virginians had relaxed their vigil since the previous massacre, to the point where the assembly signed a treaty of "peace and friendship" with the Indians in 1642.

Opechancanough and the chiefs of the Chesapeake tribes he persuaded to join him in the venture knew from the experience of 1622 that failure meant merciless reprisals on the part of the white man. Their deep hatred provoked them to take the all-out gamble. Opechancanough, "his sinews slackened and his eyelids . . . so heavy that he could not see but as they were lifted by his servants," directed the opening attack from a litter that had been carried to the battle scene. The Indians slaughtered as many white men as they had in the earlier massacre, but the effect on the expanded settlements was slighter and on the Indians disastrous. Opechancanough was captured. Governor Berkeley saw that he was "treated with all the respect and tenderness imaginable," Robert Beverley reports, but one of his guards "basely shot him through the back, . . . of which wound he died."

Virginia answered the massacre with all the ferocity the Indians had expected, and more. They begged for peace in 1646. By the treaty they signed, they became subjects of England and ceded all the land between the York and James Rivers from the fall line to the ocean. No Indian was allowed to enter this area except with the governor's permission. In an attempt at fairness, the treaty forbade white settlers to enter what was in effect the Indians' reservation beyond the fall line.

This well-meant effort to give the Indians land reserved exclusively for themselves failed before it went into effect, for it was devised in the midst of a population explosion. Virginia's population doubled in the 1640's—from eight to sixteen thousand—and shot to forty thousand in the following decade. Berkeley did his best to respect the treaty terms, but white settlers eager for land pressed on past the falls. The assembly complained in 1648 of "the great and clamorous necessities of divers of the inhabitants occasioned and brought upon them through the mean produce of their labors upon barren and overwrought grounds and the apparent decay of their cattle and hogs for want of sufficient range." The next year settlers were allowed to move into the Indian preserves, and within three years three new counties had been carved out of the reservation. The Indians fought back but the "injuries" and "insolencies" they inflicted did little to stem the invasion.

Once the assembly realized segregation had failed, it searched for a new solution to the Indian problem. It decided in 1653 to try to civilize him. The headright system, which had worked so well for the white settler, was extended to the red man. White families were encouraged to accept Indian children for rearing. To help the Indian farmer get started, he was given a cow for every eight wolf heads brought in. Less than a decade after the experiment began, the assembly admitted defeat. The Indian refused to be converted to the white man's way of life. Those who did adapt became dependent rather than independent settlers, and those who resisted, hovering on the edge of occupied land, were a constant source of trouble. It was a hopeless situation bound to bring great misery to both sides in the years that followed.

Politics

Virginia and Maryland, as has been seen, went their own ways with little interference until Parliament threatened both colonies in 1650 with a trade boycott unless they accepted the Puritan regime in England. Parliament backed the threat with action the following year. An expedition was dispatched with orders to obtain Virginia's surrender to the Commonwealth. Governor Berkeley, with only a weak force to support him, resisted enough to get his views on record in the event royalty ever returned to power in England. He relinquished the government to the Commonwealth's commissioners on March 12, 1652, under terms few could complain about. The articles of surrender obliged Virginians to acknowledge the authority of the Commonwealth, but otherwise they had the privileges of free-born Englishmen. They retained the right to govern themselves, and no one was to suffer for his former support of the king's cause. The generous settlement persuaded Sir William Berkeley to remain in Virginia throughout the Commonwealth years. (In England, Virginia became known as "the only city of refuge left in his majesty's dominions in those times for distressed Cavaliers." Seven shiploads of royalist sympathizers left for Virginia in 1649 and two years later 1,610 royalist prisoners were allowed to emigrate. Many of the colony's most distinguished families—among them, the Lees, Carters, Randolphs, Masons, and Pages—were established during this period.) The assembly chose in Berkeley's stead as governor, Richard Bennett, who had earlier been driven out of Virginia by his predecessor, and as secretary for the colony, William Claiborne. Both men had been assigned to the commission created by Parliament.

The commissioners' instructions regarding Maryland were vague, but Claiborne, with old grievances to settle, fretted little about ambiguities. Maryland's political affairs had been confused throughout the civil war. Shortly after fighting broke out in England, a complex dispute erupted in Maryland between Catholics and Protestants and also between those for and those against the proprietor. It began in 1644 when the governor, a Catholic, arrested Richard Ingle, a Protestant, for treasonable remarks. A small-scale civil war resulted, which led to the expulsion of Calvert and the seizure of Kent Island by Claiborne. Order had settled in when Claiborne returned in March 1652. He forced the recently appointed Governor Stone and his council from power and put in his own men. English authorities repudiated this high-handed action, reinstated Stone, and devised a compromise that permitted writs to be issued in the name of the Commonwealth but allowed officials to consider their oaths to the proprietor as binding. The compromise increased rather than resolved confusion, for when Lord Baltimore soon after ordered that settlers take an oath of loyalty to him, that writs be issued in his name, and that failure to accept all this meant loss of land, civil war broke forth again in Maryland. Puritans who had settled on invitation at Providence (near the Annapolis of today) after their ejection from Virginia led the opposition. Governor Stone, defeated in a battle on the Severn River (1655), was imprisoned; and William Fuller, a Puritan, was installed as governor. A Puritan-dominated assembly repudiated the proprietor and his authority, repealed his statute of religious toleration, and deprived Catholics of all legal protection. Puritans ran the colony for three years. Lord Baltimore did not recoup power until 1658 and only then with the help of Puritan friends in England.

The turmoil in Maryland would pass in time, leaving behind little of lasting effect. Meanwhile, less noticeable events were permanently altering the political affairs of both Maryland and Virginia. The steady dispersion of Chesapeake people gave increasing importance to local units of government. In 1640 there were ten counties in Virginia; in 1664 there were nineteen. A similar increase occurred in Maryland. As the distance between settlers and provincial capitals increased, more and more of the decisions and work once handled by the governor and his council descended to the commissioners of the county court.

The county court hardly resembled a court in the modern sense. Its duties embraced the entire field of local government, a field that constantly expanded in the Chesapeake area. Wills, once probated at Jamestown or St. Mary's, were now filed with the county clerk. Tavern keepers who once received their licenses from the governor now received them from the county commissioners. Land titles, births, deaths, burials, and the like were recorded at the county seat rather than the provincial capital, as in the past. The commissioners enforced, or at least had the authority to enforce, all regulations concerning the quantity and quality of Chesapeake tobacco. Even marriages came within their purview. The English custom of publishing banns three times to warn all interested parties had sufficed for small, tightly knit communities. It hardly worked in the large Chesapeake parishes. The marriage license was devised as a substitute to alert the wide-spread community of the intended event. The governor issued the licenses at first until distance between county and capital made it reasonable to put the duty on the county court. The court's involvement with marital affairs, Craven says, "marks a significant break with the principles of English law and reveals the developing importance of the county court in molding the basic assumptions of an American law and an American society."

The sheriff became the ranking police and financial officer of the county. He served warrants and made arrests. He collected taxes, the minister's dues, the king's or proprietor's quitrents, and fees owed the governor, secretary, or clerk of the court. He got 10 per cent of all he took in. (All accounts, public and private, were settled in the fall when the tobacco fleet arrived to gather the annual harvest. Those who failed to collect then—be he merchant, minister, clerk of the court, or tavern keeper— waited until the next autumn.) At first the sheriff was chosen from a list of three men submitted by the county court to the governor, but with the Restoration he was picked from among the eight members of the county court, with the post rotating annually to a new member. The job became a financial reward for the overworked commissioners, who otherwise went unpaid.

The provincial government, like the county court and the office of sheriff, assumed a fixed form during these years. The legislatures of Maryland and Virginia, like that of Massachusetts, became bicameral during the Interregnum of 1649–1660. The vague records of Maryland note passage of an act in 1650 that called for separation between council and deputies, but it is not until nine years later that the records of the "upper house" appear. The assembly at that time claimed to be "a lawful assembly without dependence on any other power in the province," a claim the governor refused to countenance. Virginia had better luck, to a large extent because the surrender terms in 1652 stipulated "that the authority now exercised by the governor, secretary, and council depended upon a grant from the assembly." Throughout the Commonwealth period this agreement served as the basis of Virginia's government, and the burgesses retained the substance of power in their hands. They selected both the governor and his councillors, and this led them gradually to assume the position of a separate house, an assumption that had become fixed in Virginia traditions by the Restoration.

It should be emphasized that the centering of power in the House of Burgesses, as it now came officially to be called, did not produce a revolutionary upheaval in leadership. The composition of the governor's council, the assembly, and of the county courts remained substantially the same from the early 1640's to 1660. A man might prefer the Puritan cause to that of the Cavaliers in England; he might like peach brandy more than hard cider. His views in neither instance were considered of great importance. Provincial affairs and local judgments of his character and abilities determined his role in Virginia's political life.

A NEW IMPERIALISM: 1650–1676

The Elizabethans developed their colonies with no help and a minimum of interference from the state. Neither they nor the crown gave thought to the problems of running an empire. Spain had required a half century before it began to weld its colonies into a unified empire; and England, too, fumbled along for about the same length of time. When the London Company failed, the crown wondered what to do with the Jamestown settlements; when Massachusetts talked back, it was puzzled how to cope with the effrontery; and when settlements sprouted in Connecticut and Rhode Island without royal permission, the king dealt with the situation by ignoring it.

With Cromwell, England hesitantly began to deal with the problems of empire according to certain general concepts. French practices initiated by Jean Colbert helped to clarify thinking. Scores of English pamphlets, the most famous and effective being Thomas Mun's *England's Treasure by Foreign Trade,* written in 1630 but not published until 1663, discussed the issue with warmth and thoroughness throughout the remainder of the seventeenth century. Neither Mun nor his colleagues quarreled with Sir Walter Raleigh's remark that: "Whosoever commands the sea commands the trade; whosoever commands the trade of the world commands the riches of the world, and consequently the world itself." They argued, however, that the problem of acquiring a favorable balance of trade had become more complicated since Elizabeth's days. The Dutch, long an English ally, had replaced Spain as the nation's outstanding competitor for world trade. England had now acquired an empire of some fifty settlements scattered about the world; these had to be knit together if the mother country was to benefit from them. The state, which had previously played a passive role in colonization, had to assume responsibilities it had hitherto shunned. Mun and other mercantilists of his day accepted the core of Elizabethan imperialism—the purpose of colonies was to promote trade, which in turn nourished the mother country—but they so refined and elaborated that central thought that they ended up by creating a new brand of imperialism, rooted in the past but shaped to fit a changed world.

The Commonwealth

The year 1650 marked a turning point in England's attitude toward its colonies. Parliament had tried during the civil war to entice the colonies to its side by granting trading privileges and either reducing or eliminating tariffs. The colonies responded—Virginia in 1643, Maryland in 1649, and Massachusetts in 1645—by throwing open their ports to all ships. Once the king had been beheaded and the Puritans had prevailed, those, like Lords Warwick and Say and Seal, who had encouraged a tolerant attitude toward the colonies were eased from power; and "citizens and inferior persons," as a Cavalier put it, meaning merchants, moved in to tighten

Map 17. Middle America

Ft. St. Joseph
Cahokia
Kaskaskia
Mississippi
Ft. Prudhomme
Ft. Arkansas
Ft. St. Louis

Boston
Newport
New York
Philadelphia
VIRGINIA
Norfolk
CAROLINA
Charleston

St. Augustine

Bermuda

Matamoros
Gulf of Mexico
Pánuco
México
Vera Cruz
Campeche
Belize
Acapulco
Tehuantepec
Guatemala
S. Salvador
Grenada

Truxillo
MOSQUITO COAST
S. Juan
Old Providence
Porto Bello
Panama
Darien

BAHAMA IS.

Havana
Cayman I.
Santiago
JAMAICA

British settlements
are underlined

HISPANIOLA
Sto. Domingo

Caribbean Sea

Puerto Rico
Virgin Is.
Barbuda
Antigua
St. Kitts
Nevis
Montserrat
GuadeLupe
Dominica
Martinique
Sta. Lucia
S. Vicente
Barbados
Grenada
Tobago
Trinidad

Sta. Marta
Cartagena
Maracaibo
Curaçao
Caracas
Margarita

Bogotá

0   500   1000
Miles

Raisz

control over England's wayward dependents. They struck at the colonies through the Dutch.

Holland by the mid-seventeenth century dominated world trade. Colbert estimated that of the twenty thousand ships engaged in European commerce, the Dutch owned sixteen thousand of them. Each year they sent some five hundred ships to Norway and Denmark, two thousand to Spain, seven hundred into the Baltic, and not less than one thousand fishing smacks into the North Sea. Holdings in Java, Sumatra, Formosa, Malacca, and Ceylon gave the Dutch East India Company a near monopoly of the spice trade. The Dutch West India Company had captured over five hundred Spanish vessels in the Caribbean, occupied large parts of the coast of Brazil, and established settlements along the Delaware, Hudson, and Connecticut Rivers in America. Amsterdam and not London had become the entrepôt of Europe.

Holland specialized in commerce, not colonies. Its settlements in America never became more than trading stations and supply depots, mainly because the Dutch saw no reason to trade their pleasant life at home for a rude existence in the wilderness. "Obviously," Dixon Ryan Fox has said, "a generation that conquered the markets of the world, that fought itself free from the most powerful state in Europe, that produced Rembrandt, Leeuwenhoek, and Grotius, could have developed a great colony of population if it had really wanted to."

No one in the seventeenth century surpassed them as traders. Their ships were designed and built to carry a large cargo safely with the fewest possible seamen. Fore-and-aft rigging gave them a maneuverability lacking in other vessels of the day, winches speeded loading and unloading, and sheathing protected the hulls from marine borers. They stowed cargoes with such care that English merchants often surreptitiously shipped their own cargoes with them. Colonial merchants remarked that the Dutch stocked their vessels with a great variety of merchandise, paid higher prices for goods, gave longer credit, and were content with a smaller profit than Londoners.

The Dutch advantage in America increased with England's civil war. The war disrupted industry at home, forcing up production costs and thus the price of manufactured goods. A divided England preyed upon its own commerce: Puritans and Cavaliers alike turned to privateering; and goods shipped from America in English vessels ran the risk of being captured by one side or the other. "The Dutch found and relieved us," Sir William Berkeley remarked in 1651. New Englanders welcomed their ships and their money, which had become an accepted medium of exchange by the time the civil war had ended in England.

Once the fighting ceased, Puritan merchants in Parliament demanded something be done to cut Holland's inroads into colonial trade. Cromwell and his followers preferred to deal gently with the Dutch, good Protestants all and long England's staunchest friends on the Continent. Cromwell, an Elizabethan at heart, regarded Catholic Spain as England's greatest enemy. Parliament faced the issue obliquely in 1650 by passing a hastily concocted measure designed ostensibly to force the submission of rebellious colonies to the Puritan government but also to undercut Dutch trade with those colonies. The act subjected Virginia, Barbados, Bermuda, and Antigua to the laws of Parliament and forbade all ships to trade with those colonies; if and when the trade ban was lifted, all who wished to deal with the colonies had still to obtain trading licenses from either Parliament or Cromwell's Council of State. Obviously, any Dutch applications would be turned down.

A year later Parliament passed another bill, generally known as England's first Navigation Act. The act of 1651 sought to block Holland from *all* trade with England or her colonies. It was Parliament's first attempt to shift the commercial center of Europe from Amsterdam to London. It provided that no goods from America, Asia, and Africa could enter England, Ireland, or the colonies save in English vessels ("English" included Irish and colonial ships); that coastal trading, whether between English or colonial ports, had to be in English ships; and that goods from Europe had to be imported in English ships or in ships of the country producing the goods or commodities. This exception that permitted countries to bring their own products in their own ships did not lessen the blow to the Dutch. Holland had few manufactures, except woolens, of her own. The clause pleased France and Spain, with whom England had important trade.

The effectiveness of the act is hard to judge. The lack of enforcement machinery made it easy to evade. Colonial traffic in and out of New Amsterdam continued heavy. Years later, when John Winthrop, Jr., of Connecticut searched for a copy of the act, he could find none in New England; and the governor of Massachusetts told him "they have refused the execution of it here and would so do still, it too much entrenching upon us." Governor Stuyvesant of New Netherland asked if the act was an "interdiction to prevent our people from freely trading in your colonies just as New Englanders may trade here," and Winthrop replied that so far as he was concerned it was not.

Soon after the act passed, the first Anglo-Dutch War (1652–1654) came about. Cromwell had deplored the idea of war with Protestant Holland. England drifted into it against his will; he pursued it with little enthusiasm and pulled the nation out at the first honorable opportunity. The peace in 1654 settled none of the contended issues between the two countries, but it left Cromwell free to push what he had long been forced to suppress—his "Western Design" against Spain in the New World. The Spanish had seized the English island of Tortuga in 1635 and the Puritan colony on Providence Island, off the coast of Nicaragua, in 1641; and Cromwell yearned to revenge these humiliations. He desired to spread the Puritan brand of Protestantism throughout the Indies before they become irreparably Catholicized. His government needed money, and he hoped Spanish wealth would solve that problem.

Thomas Gage's *Travels in the New World,* published in 1648, gave Cromwell a further reason to invade the Spanish Empire. Gage, the first Englishman in a century and a half to slip within the supposedly tightly guarded empire, had returned after extensive travels through it to report that Mexico City, Havana, and other supposed strongholds were defenseless, for "the Spaniards live so secure from enemies that there is neither gate, wall, bulwark, platform, tower, armory, ammunition, or ordnance to secure and defend the city from a domestic or foreign army." Caribbean islands already held by the English "have not only advanced our journey the better part of the way, but so inured our people to the clime of the Indies as they are the more enabled thereby to undertake any enterprise upon the firm land with greater facility."

The book, and further talks with Gage, did much to convince Cromwell of what he was already inclined to do. In 1654 he dispatched a fleet under Robert Venable and William Penn, the elder, with instructions to occupy Puerto Rico, Hispaniola, or Cartagena, on the mainland. "The design in general," he wrote, "is to gain an interest in that part of the West Indies in possession of the Spaniard, for the effecting whereof we shall not tie you up to a method by any particular instructions." After a pause for refreshment and reinforcements at Barbados, a force that totaled eight thousand headed for Hispaniola, the largest island in the Antilles. Disease, mismanagement, underestimation of Spanish strength, and exaggeration of God's concern for the Puritan cause led to a humiliating defeat. The force moved on to Jamaica, a mountainous island over a hundred miles in length, slightly populated, and perfectly located to "gall [the Spaniards] on every side." The English occupied the island with little trouble, but it took four years of guerrilla warfare to conquer it.

Cromwell regarded the entire expedition as a disaster and took little cheer from the conquest of Jamaica. He died unaware that its seizure, the first major loss since Spain had created her empire over a century and a half earlier, would inaugurate an epoch in English commerce. It would become the center of trade with Spanish colonies, replacing the once prosperous Dutch base at Curaçao. It would serve throughout the colonial period as the chief distributing point for Negro slaves to other English

islands in the Indies and to colonies on the American mainland. While
the project failed in Cromwell's eyes, it had lasting effect on American
history in that, as Christopher Hill remarks, "the Western Design for the
first time made the Caribbean the theater of European power politics
which it was to remain for 150 years."

The Restoration

With the Restoration, control of colonial affairs shifted from Parliamentary
committees back to the hands of royal officers. Otherwise little change occurred. Charles II arrived back in England eager, according to the Earl of
Clarendon, his chief adviser, "to improve the general traffic and trade of
the kingdom"; and in the year of his return, Parliament, as if to emphasize the continuity of the Commonwealth colonial policy, passed the Navigation Act of 1660.

Presumably the act of 1651 would have been revised soon; such
measures rarely work out the first time around. The Restoration speeded
revision, for the crown ruled invalid all legislation passed under the
Interregnum of 1649–1660. One object of the 1660 act was to tighten up
loopholes in the previous navigation statute through which Dutch traders
continued to sail. An English ship, previously defined as one in which
half the sailors were English, now required the master and three-fourths
of the crew to be English. Colonial governors were now ordered to take
an oath to enforce the act and to keep records of all vessels trading with
their particular plantations.

An innovation in the revised act—the famous enumeration clause—
also struck at the Dutch. All enumerated, or listed, products must hereafter be shipped only to England or to another English colony. To enforce
this clause all ship captains were required to post a bond at their departure port, which they could recover at their port of arrival only after
giving proof that they had complied with the law. Enumerated items
would in time include virtually all colonial products, but the 1660 act
ticked off only tobacco, sugar, cotton, indigo, ginger, and dyewoods. Except for tobacco, all these were West Indian products that could not be
produced in England. The clause favored New England, whose products
—mainly fish and lumber—were not enumerated because they competed
with English products or could not be imported into England at a profit.
New England merchants could buy and sell where they wished as long
as they shipped in English vessels, and a colonial-built and -manned ship
was considered English.

The principle of enumeration marked a new step in the attempt to
control colonial trade, one designed to hurt the Dutch and benefit the
crown, merchants, and English industry. Enumerated products paid cus-

toms duties, which meant a healthy increase in royal revenues. Continental trade in enumerated items was closed off to the colonies, thus giving English merchants a lucrative monopoly in goods the Dutch had prospered on. The sugar that would now flow into England had to be refined or distilled into molasses; the tobacco sorted, cut, and rolled; the cotton spun, woven, and dyed. All this meant thousands of new jobs for English workmen and additional income to merchants who shipped manufactured items back to the colonies. It mattered little to the act's authors— among them Sir George Downing, an early Harvard graduate and nephew of John Winthrop, who had returned to England during the civil war and then switched to Charles's side as the Restoration approached— that the average colonial would now pay considerably more for his manufactured goods. If England and merchants on both sides of the water prospered then the statute justified itself.

The act of 1660 became the cornerstone of the English trade and navigation system throughout the rest of the colonial period, and most legislation passed afterward repaired flaws that practice had revealed. The question arose almost immediately about English merchants owning foreign ships, which were now prohibited from trade within the empire. To repair this flaw an act of 1662 said that ships not of English construction should be considered foreign if they were not registered in England; this statute initiated the registration of ships.

The following year the crown and Parliament passed another law that, technically at least, completed the colonies' economic dependence upon England. The Staple Act of 1663 dealt with colonial imports. It laid down the rule that all goods from Europe to the colonies had to pass through England. Every ship that now entered the colonies had to prove that the goods it landed had been loaded in England. A few items much in demand in America were excepted—salt for the fisheries of New England might be brought directly from, say, the Cape Verde Islands; wine from the Portuguese islands in the Azores; servants, horses, and provisions from Ireland and Scotland, which was still not legally part of England. The Staple Act imposed a national monopoly shared by all English merchants on all colonial imports. It encouraged English manufacturers, too. Foreign goods passing through England could be taxed, thereby upping their prices and allowing English goods to undersell them overseas.

England rounded out its legislative efforts to dominate colonial trade by provoking a war with Holland. The second Anglo-Dutch War (1664– 1667) initiated a calculated effort on England's part to eliminate Dutch holdings on the American continent. England sought, and succeeded with hardly a shot being fired, to remove New Amsterdam as a center for illicit trade. The Treaty of Breda, which closed the war in 1667, drove home what the Navigation Acts had first revealed to colonial Americans —their lives hereafter were to a large extent to be conditioned by decisions agreed to in Europe. The diplomats at Breda ceded New Netherland and Dutch slave-trading stations in Africa to England. From England, France received Nova Scotia, thus depriving New England of one of the lucrative centers of her commerce, in return for ceding the islands of Antigua, Montserrat, and the conquered half of St. Kitts.

England warred with the Dutch again from 1672 to 1674. The Dutch recaptured New Amsterdam in 1673, but the peace treaty of the following year restored it again to England. The treaty marked the end of Holland in America. From this time on she confined her commerce to Europe, Africa, the Far East, and the Caribbean.

During the third Anglo-Dutch War, England plugged one more loophole that time had revealed in its trade system. The act of 1660 had permitted coastwise trade between the colonies even of enumerated articles to be carried on duty free. Colonial merchants used this privilege to clear their home ports with goods ostensibly bound for another colonial port but actually destined for a European market. New England shippers were the greatest offenders and found the loophole hard to resist when prices in England on sugar and tobacco were dropping. American goods on the Continent brought prices equal to or better than those in England, with no cut going to an English middleman; and French goods smuggled home sold for 20 per cent less than their English equivalents. The Plantations Duty Act of 1673 was designed to block this subterfuge. It levied a duty at the point of departure on all enumerated articles bound to another colonial port. While the act in effect imposed the English customs duty at the start rather than the end of a voyage, its purpose was solely to regulate trade. The law also provided for the appointment of customs agents to enforce all Navigation Laws in the colonies and to collect the duties. While no one in America relished the act, Parliament's right to impose a duty on intercolonial trade went unchallenged. The act, Andrews has said, "did more to systematize the commercial activities of the colonists than did any other regulation of the navigation acts except the enumeration, of which it was an integral part."

The principles embodied in the statutes of 1660, 1663, and 1673 governed the economic structure of the English Empire for over a century. The effect of the navigation system on England seems to have been immediate and impressive. Merchant shipping doubled between 1660 and 1688, and the Dutch lost their uncontested lead in world commerce. Christopher Hill has pointed out that colonial goods imported and then reexported accounted for 5 per cent of England's trade in 1640, well over

25 per cent by the end of the century. Tobacco, sugar, and calico, rarely reexported before the Navigation Acts, comprised two-thirds of English reexports to Europe at the end of the century. A variety of refining and finishing industries sprouted while the protective navigation system kept cheaper foreign goods at bay.

For all that, the immediate effect of the acts in America was negligible, mainly because the trade system of New England and the Chesapeake colonies had for the most part conformed to the navigation system before the system had been enacted. New Englanders preferred English manufactured goods and the Chesapeake settlers were accustomed to market their tobacco with London merchants. And even when the laws irritated, the lack of enforcement machinery made them easy to avoid. Only near the end of the century, when American trade branched into new channels and the crown developed machinery to enforce the navigation system, would the colonies complain bitterly about the new imperialism.

THE RESTORATION IN THE COLONIES: 1660–1676

The New England and Chesapeake colonies, all of whom had done much as they had wished before 1660, found themselves dividing their attention about equally between local and imperial affairs after that year. All strove to retain the autonomy acquired during the Interregnum without antagonizing authorities at home. The restored and reinvigorated crown had much to offer the colonies—generous charters to those that lived in a legal no-man's-land, war contracts (Massachusetts had provisioned the fleets that took Jamaica and fought in the Dutch wars), and positions of power to those sympathetic to the king's interests. The strengthened English navy and merchant marine offered protection against pirates, against the Dutch in time of war, against the growing strength of the French to the north. Much, too, could be lost defying the crown. The threat of revoking a charter was no longer the empty threat it had once been. A wayward attitude could now prompt an investigatory commission backed by an armed fleet to impress order on a recalcitrant colony. The new imperialism imposed a period of adjustment that varied in length of time and degree of severity with each colony. All found it difficult, but those of New England found it nerve-racking.

New England

Massachusetts' time of troubles arrived slowly, but Connecticut's and Rhode Island's, both of whom lacked royal charters, descended the moment Charles II retrieved the throne. Connecticut dispatched its governor,

Map 18. Early Grants, 1600-1663

NEW FRANCE

Claimed by New Engl'd
Council, 1620, to Lat. 48°

ACADIA
French

MAINE
to Mass. 1651

Massachusetts Charter 1621
from sea to sea

GORGES
GRANT
1639

MASS.
1629

Connecticut Charter 1662
from sea to sea

NEW NETHERLAND
1626-1664

CONN.
1662

R.I.
1644

Charterline 1632

MARYLAND
1632

NEW SWEDEN
1638-1655

VIRGINIA
Royal Province
1624, from sea to sea

CAROLINA
Grant 1639

FLORIDA
Spanish

45

41°

37°

36°

33°

31°

29°

0   100   200
Miles

79°   75°   71°

Raisz

John Winthrop, Jr., to London in 1661 to obtain royal approval of her existence as a colony. Winthrop, a man more pliant and popular than his father but as skilled in politics, a doctor who treated half the people of Connecticut and New Haven during his active years, a scientist well regarded even in England, was the single man of ability and learning living in the farming communities of the Connecticut Valley. The river towns elected him governor in 1657 and changed the restrictive clause in the Fundamental Orders—"no person [shall] be chosen governor above once in two years"—to permit him to hold the office until his death in 1676.

Three months after arrival in London, Winthrop became the first colonial admitted to the newly formed Royal Society, an honor which, combined with £500 in bribes—or "tips," to use a gentler word—helped to ease the charter he sought through the seals. It was an extraordinary document. It extended Connecticut's boundaries to include New Haven, part of Rhode Island, and from sea to sea. In an era of tightening controls it made Connecticut an entirely self-governing colony. There was no provision for a royal governor nor for any other officials of the crown to direct affairs. The king disclaimed the right to control legislation or to administer justice, and required of provincial officers only an oath of supremacy. The franchise, as Winthrop had desired, was limited to freemen, where "admitted inhabitants" had previously been allowed to vote for deputies. (Earlier, as Connecticut churches relaxed requirements for church membership, the General Court had sought to limit the electorate by imposing a qualification of £30 on all freemen; the further restrictions Winthrop managed to slip into the charter of 1662 pleased rather than distressed authorities at home.)

Rhode Island's negotiations for a charter, carried on simultaneously with Connecticut's, fared well, too—though only after John Clarke, who represented the colony's interests in London, had fought off Winthrop's efforts to usurp a large part of its territory. (Winthrop made it clear that Connecticut wanted only part of Rhode Island, not all of it; he dreaded the thought of union, "for Rhode Island is—pardon necessity's word of truth—a *rod* to those that love to live in order—a road, refuge, asylum to evil livers.") Once Winthrop had Connecticut's charter in his pocket, he did an about-face; and Rhode Island's was granted in 1663 largely, according to crown authorities, on the strength of "the good opinion and confidence we had in the said Mr. Winthrop." The provisions for self-government virtually duplicated Connecticut's, except for the notable clause that said no person in the colony should ever be "molested, punished, disquieted, or called in question, for any differences in opinion in matters of religion," any law enacted in England notwithstanding. The charter remained the constitution of colony and state until 1843.

No one knows why the crown allowed two such generous charters at a moment when it endeavored to retrieve, not relinquish, control over the colonies. One explanation might be that since neither colony had given the crown trouble in the past, there was no need for strict supervision. Besides, both were agrarian territories that produced little of value for England. Perhaps, too, it was reasoned that loose controls might encourage settlement and thus build up two barriers against the aggressive plans of Massachusetts, the one New England colony that the crown was eager to bring to heel.

Something of the Bay Colony's old assertiveness toward England had died in 1649 with John Winthrop, whose passing symbolized the waning power of first generation settlers. Political power was now drifting into the hands of those who set the economic and social tone of the colony—the merchants. Ministers, rankling at the changes, railed about the decay of piety and talked endlessly about "God's controversy with New England." Their words had little effect. "The merchants represented the spirit of a new age—not social stability, order, and the discipline of the senses, but mobility, growth, and the enjoyment of life," Bernard Bailyn has said. "They took the pattern of conduct not from the Bible but from Restoration England."

As the saints lost authority, the church, too, was nudged aside. Many merchants, though they continued to attend services, no longer considered church membership important, and some dared openly to admit they preferred the still repudiated Church of England to the severer Congregational form of worship. A clergy distressed by the dwindling church membership gathered in 1657 to devise a way in which they could once again encompass wandering sheep within the fold. The upshot of their synod was the Half-Way Covenant, a device that allowed the children of saints who held to the "forms of godliness"—that is, lived upright lives —but had failed to receive God's grace, to become church members simply by professing their faith. These half-way members were deprived only of the right to share in the Lord's Supper and of a vote in church affairs.

The Half-Way Covenant sufficed to keep within the fold many of the prosperous of New England whose parents had been among the founding fathers. It was *not,* Edmund Morgan has emphasized, a symptom of decline in piety, but an honest attempt to perpetuate the pure church of the early saints. In effect, however, it marked the end of the holy experiment as Winthrop, Cotton, and their associates had conceived it some twenty-five years earlier. It opened the way to altering the character of the church from one of visible saints to those "not scandalous in life," and eventually to a church that embraced virtually the whole community. The adoption of the covenant was optional with every church, and though it provoked lively resistance from the orthodox, it spread rapidly through New England. Distinctions between full and half-way members vanished in many communities and the Congregational Church in time acquired a sedateness that made it indistinguishable from other forms of Protestantism.

Even so, many of the well-to-do merchants in Massachusetts shunned this easy entry into the church. They had come by now to judge the church and those who supported its central role in the Bay Colony's life as obdurate enemies to the mercantile view of the world. Puritanism had become unfashionable in Restoration England, and the merchants' awareness of this made them hope that together they and the crown might oust the orthodox from power. Petitions, complaints, and accusations began to flow across the water from the disaffected in Massachusetts. Their number mounted to the point where the king took notice. A royal commission was created in 1664 with the double purpose of directing the capture of New Netherland from the Dutch and investigating conditions in New England. Once the Dutch had been subdued, the commission was "to remove all jealousies and misunderstandings" in New England, draw the colonies closer under English rule, and insist that all English liberties, secular and religious, be maintained. The commission was told to check on colonial obedience to the Navigation Act of 1660, to sit as a royal court of appeal, and to hear and determine grievances. It was warned not to sit in judgment on any matter within the jurisdiction of the colonies "except those proceedings be expressly contrary to the rules prescribed in some grant under our Great Seal of England." Richard Nicolls, newly appointed deputy governor of New York (though it still belonged to the Dutch), headed the group, which was rounded out by Sir Robert Carr, Colonel George Cartwright, and Samuel Maverick of Massachusetts, a bitter complainer of Bay authorities and a prime instigator in the creation of the commission.

Once New Netherland had been invested by English troops, the commission visited Connecticut. Winthrop handled it adroitly. The commission deprived the colony of her claim to Long Island but revoked the Duke of York's claim eastward to the Connecticut River; it put the New York–Connecticut boundary at a spot west of the Dutch-English boundary of 1650, exactly where Winthrop wanted it and where it has remained since. Rhode Island came next, then Plymouth, which put on its best manners in the hope the commission would recommend a royal charter to protect it against the aggressions of Massachusetts. The commissioners praised both colonies for their loyalty to the crown and suggested only slight changes in the way they conducted their affairs.

The group tarried until 1665 before reaching the Bay Colony, and by then rumors had raced ahead that the commissioners planned to establish the Church of England, impose a stiff land tax, and in other ways inhibit the Bay Colony's way of life. The General Court blocked the commission at every point, refusing to allow it to meet within the boundaries of the colony. The commissioners moved on to New Hampshire but again achieved little, for Massachusetts controlled the settlements there and obstructed all investigatory efforts. Maine, unhappy under Massachusetts' domination, greeted the commission warmly. It ordered Maine to be made a temporary province of the crown, appointing justices of the peace and "leaving the final determination to his majesty."

The commission's report to the king suggested that Massachusetts' charter be revoked and the colony be made a royal ward. The recommendation died on paper, for by the time the crown received it other troubles had come to the fore. A series of disasters—the plague of 1665, the great fire of 1666 ("which consumed what the plague could not touch," as Defoe later put it), a second Dutch war, and the fall of Clarendon from power—left the crown with little energy to spare for the affairs of Massachusetts. Once again events in England had allowed the Bay Colony to escape a deserved chastisement. God, it appeared, sided with the righteous. The Bay Colony resumed the government of Maine and rebuffed further attempts by the merchants to gain power. For a few years longer the assertive tone of John Winthrop's day remained in style.

The Chesapeake Colonies

Sir William Berkeley, upon the urgings of local leaders, stepped in as unofficial acting governor of Virginia in 1658. With the Restoration, the assembly commissioned him to represent Virginia's interests to Charles II. He departed in 1661 with instructions to request trained ministers for the church, to urge the founding of a college, and to promote the revival of subsidized experimental projects.

While Berkeley tended to Virginia's interests at court, the assembly settled down to revise and codify the multitude of laws that had accumulated during the half century of the colony's existence. The work was carried out by men reared and trained in America, for the colony had by now acquired a home-grown governing class. Local rather than provincial government received most of their attention. (". . . It is easy to forget," Wesley Frank Craven has remarked, "that in colonial America the demand for self-government often emphasized a local rather than a provincial right.") The county courts retained most of their expanded jurisdiction and in addition were awarded the lucrative sheriff's office. The county commissioners now came officially to be called justices of the peace. The Anglican Church was reestablished, and the vestry within each parish was made a self-perpetuating body, thus fixing control in the hands of those in power at the moment. Appointment of the governor and his council had returned to the crown's control with the Restoration, but the loss mattered little. The dispersal of power in Virginia's government made it difficult for either the governor or council to act arbitrarily.

Berkeley had been warmly welcomed by Charles II, who reappointed him governor of what the king affectionately called "my old dominion." The governor returned to Virginia in 1664 and ran the government with a firm hand for the next quarter of a century. What, from a distance, strikes many historians as Berkeley's autocratic manner apparently satisfied Virginians of the day. He was a leading planter himself and spoke effectively for planter interests, deriding the Navigation Acts whenever they conflicted with Virginia interests and promoting the welfare of his colony on every occasion. He showed indifference to the assembly, but so did most of the colony's leaders. Local government's firm footing and the recent revision of laws left the assembly with little need to pass new legislation and thus little to do. The steady influx of immigrants added to the colony's prosperity and helped to ease the labor shortage in a period before slavery had taken a strong hold.

By the end of the 1660's the new settlers had disturbed the placidity of Virginia society. A law in 1670, similar to an earlier statute in Connecticut, tightened suffrage requirements. This was an obvious attempt to block the new blood's rise to political power. The immigrants' challenge would intensify in time and this, coupled with an increasingly stronger imperial policy, would do much to revitalize the assembly's role in Virginia's political life.

Maryland's experience with the Restoration, in contrast with Virginia's, raised serious problems of adjustment. A compromise had been worked out in 1657–1658 whereby Lord Baltimore retrieved his colony from the Puritans and installed his own man, Josias Fendall, as governor. Baltimore had successfully withstood one more attempt to steal his colony only instantly to face another attack, this time from Governor Fendall. Time and trouble had not softened Baltimore's belief that he held absolute authority to do as he wished in Maryland. Many who opposed the Puritans' rule showed a distaste for rule by the proprietor. Among such persons, apparently—the loss of relevant records makes a hesitant statement necessary—was Fendall. When in 1660 the assembly demanded it be recognized as the "highest court of judicature" and "without dependence on any other power in the Province," Fendall acceded to the demand. It seems clear he hoped to win from the king more self-government for Maryland than that granted by the bargain of 1657–1658, which restored full rights to the proprietor. (The so-called Fendall's Rebellion came at a time when the Virginia assembly had reasserted its rights and when

Connecticut and Rhode Island were gaining their generous charters from the crown.)

The king backed Lord Baltimore and within a few months the proprietor had sent his brother Philip to rule as governor. Baltimore refused still to concede his absolute powers in any way, mainly for economic rather than political reasons. Throughout these years Maryland grew steadily—five thousand settlers arrived in the 1660's—and the proprietor's tight control over the land meant that every newcomer was putting money in his pocket. Quitrents from land holdings brought him in at least £8,000 a year, and his share of the export duty on tobacco added to profits from other sources upped his annual income to a minimum of £10,000, which has been conservatively estimated at about $350,000 in modern terms.

Baltimore tied the substantial planters to his interests by a careful dispensing of political appointments and by maintaining a tight hold on the land office, which controlled the disbursement of land. A good part of Maryland's elite was tied to the proprietor's family either by marriage or blood ties. From this inbred group came the governor's council and a large proportion of the assembly's upper house. Maryland, it has been said, came closer than any other American colony to reproducing the English peerage and the House of Lords.

Despite this tight control from above, no outburst from below occurred for several years after the Restoration. Then in 1669 members of the assembly, the majority of whom were, like their Virginia counterparts, powerful in local affairs, submitted a list of grievances. The governor told them "not to conceive that their privileges run parallel to the Commons in the Parliament of England" and that whatever the proprietor "lawfully doth by power of his patent must not be styled a grievance unless you mean to quarrel with the king who granted it." The assembly's temper subsided, and nothing more was heard of their grievances, but their loud complaint in 1669 marked the beginning of a long struggle between the proprietor and his people. Tension would increase as incoming settlers rebuffed the authority of established local leaders. When this is added to the old split between Protestant and Catholic, it becomes apparent that the calm of the early years of the Restoration in Maryland, as elsewhere in colonial America, only held in suspended animation the ingredients for a first-class storm.

BIBLIOGRAPHY

New England

James T. Adams' thorough summary in *The Founding of New England* (1921; pb.) can be balanced by Charles M. Andrews' account in the first vol-

ume of *The Colonial Period of American History* (4 vols., 1936–1938; pb.).
Bernard Bailyn's *New England Merchants in the Seventeenth Century* (1955;
pb.) is indispensable here. Two of Samuel Eliot Morison's books—*Builders of
the Bay Colony* (1963; pb.) and *Harvard College in the Seventeenth Century*
(2 vols., 1936)—contain relevant material. John Winthrop's role in these
events is told fully from his point of view in the *Journal,* and with more detachment in the latter part of Edmund Morgan's *Puritan Dilemma* (1958;
pb.) and the first section of R. S. Dunn's *Puritans and Yankees* (1962).
George Lee Haskins' *Law and Authority in Early Massachusetts* (1960; pb.)
is *the* volume to consult on the Body of Liberties and Laws and Liberties. Also
still worth attention is W. B. Weeden's *Economic and Social History of New
England* (2 vols., 1890) especially the first volume. On the Confederation,
see the brief but excellent chapter by Constance McL. Green in Albert B. Hart,
ed., *The Commonwealth History of Massachusetts* (1927).

The Chesapeake Colonies

The best accounts are found in Wesley Frank Craven's *Southern Colonies in
the Seventeenth Century* (1949) and Richard L. Morton's *Colonial Virginia*
(2 vols., 1960). A reliable study on local government is Cyrus H. Karraker,
*The Seventeenth-Century Sheriff: A Comparative Study of the Sheriff in Eng-
land and the Chesapeake Colonies, 1607–1689* (1930). For fuller accounts of
Baltimore's colony see Bernard C. Steiner, *Maryland During the English Civil
Wars* (2 vols., 1906–1907), and his *Maryland Under the Commonwealth:
A Chronicle of the Years 1649–1658* (1911). Details on the Old Dominion
are found in Thomas J. Wertenbaker's *Virginia Under the Stuarts, 1607–1688*
(1914) and P. A. Bruce's *Economic History of Virginia in the Seventeenth
Century* (2 vols., 1896).

A New Imperialism: 1650–1676

An excellent start for any student is James A. Williamson, "Beginnings of an
Imperial Policy, 1649–1660" and Charles M. Andrews, "The Acts of Trade,"
Chs. 7 and 9 respectively in Vol. I, *The Cambridge History of the British
Empire* (8 vols., 1920–1963). The student who wishes more on the subject
should go on to Andrews' fourth volume in *Colonial Period,* which the author
considered his most important. George Edmundson gives a full account of
The Anglo-Dutch Rivalry During the First Half of the Seventeenth Century
(1931). Lawrence A. Harper's *The English Navigation Laws* (1939) is the
most elaborate recent discussion of the subject. Thomas Mun's *England's
Treasure by Foreign Trade* (1664) has been reprinted several times in the
twentieth century. In addition to the material on mercantilism mentioned
for Chapter 2, see the second volume of William Cunningham, *Growth of
English Industry and Commerce* (3 vols., 1921–1927) and Charles Wilson,
Profit and Power (1957). Wilson's "Mercantilism: Some Vicissitudes of an
Idea," *Economic History Review,* 10 (1957), 181–188 is an excellent general
account.

The Restoration in the Colonies: 1660–1676

Most of the volumes mentioned above are relevant here. George M. Trevelyan's *England Under the Stuarts* (12th ed., 1925) gives an adequate and lively account of the English story, but Christopher Hill's *England in the Seventeenth Century* (1961) is an abler and more profound work. Craven's *Southern Colonies,* Bailyn's *New England Merchants,* and Wertenbaker's *Virginia Under the Stuarts* fill out the American picture. Andrews' full account in the second volume of *Colonial Period* can be supplemented by that in Morton's *Colonial Virginia.* An essay of wider interest than its title indicates is Philip S. Haffenden, "The Anglican Church in Restoration Policy," in James Morton Smith, ed., *Seventeenth-Century America* (1959). Edmund Morgan's discussion of the Half-Way Covenant is found in *Visible Saints: The History of a Puritan Idea* (1963; pb).

For further references see the *Harvard Guide,* Sections 87, "Maryland in the Seventeenth Century"; 89, "The English Civil War and the Colonies, 1641–1660"; 90, "New England in the Seventeenth Century: Social, Economic, Institutional"; 91, "Chesapeake Colonies in the Seventeenth Century: Social, Economic, Institutional"; and 92, "The Restoration and English Colonial Policy."

William Penn, by Francis Place

6. The Proprietaries

CAROLINA
  The Charter of 1663
  First Failures
  The Fundamental Constitutions of 1669
  Success

NEW YORK
  New Netherland
  The Dutch Heritage
  English Rule: 1664–1689

NEW JERSEY
  East Jersey
  West Jersey

PENNSYLVANIA
  William Penn
  The Charter of 1681
  Plans for Settlement
  Settlement

England during the Restoration revived its oldest device for settling the New World—the proprietary colony. Charles II adopted the technique reluctantly. Since the proprietor received authority directly from the crown, it might be supposed the king resurrected the form as part of his design to tighten control over the empire. Actually, the proprietary colony counteracted the trend toward imperial centralization, for these aristocratic landlords guarded their chartered privileges and resisted restraints on their power with the tenacity of medieval barons. There were other drawbacks. Some grants, such as the one in 1673 that made most of Virginia a proprietary to Lords Arlington and Culpeper, only confused the governments of already stable colonies. Others roused the ire of Parliament, unhappy at seeing control over the colonies slip from its hands, and of powerful merchants who disliked courtiers and nobles moving into a field that had been theirs up to now. Two virtues of the proprietary grant could be set against these disadvantages. First, Spain might be bested in the race to occupy the vacant land south of Virginia; and the Dutch might be divested of continental holdings wedged between the English colonies by offering the territory to land-hungry nobles rather than to merchants, who at the moment preferred the risks of trade and industry to colonization. Second, the generous grants offered Charles II a cheap, easy way to pay off political debts and to appease friends who had stood by him in his time of troubles. The king let the virtues cancel the drawbacks, and in 1663 he launched England on its second and final wave of American colonization, this time dominated by proprietors rather than companies. When the wave died, the embryos of twelve of the thirteen colonies had come into being.

CAROLINA

Men had eyed the land south of Virginia from the time Roanoke had been abandoned. Explorers from Virginia wandered in and reported it "fruitful and pleasant" and the soil exceedingly fertile. They cut through the swamps and wilderness and established profitable fur-trading connections with local Indian tribes. But settlement lagged. The land lacked a good harbor in the north, and it lay exposed to the Spanish in the south. Nonetheless, Lord Baltimore decided that this was the spot for his Catholic refuge, only to find on returning to England that the crown had granted the "province of Carolana" (land of Charles) to Sir Robert Heath. Heath's plans to colonize came to nothing, nor did the Duke of Norfolk's, to whom Heath had assigned his rights a decade later. In time, an informal series of individual investments in the area began, especially after Edward Bland in 1650 had exaggerated the land into an Eden in a promotional tract entitled *The Discovery of New Britain*. Francis Yeardley spent £300 exploring and purchasing tracts from the Indians; he had found the land free from "nipping frosts" and hoped to produce silk, olives, and wine from the rich soil. By 1662 a number of Virginians had drifted into the area around Albemarle Sound in the north, and a short-lived colony of New Englanders had set up housekeeping at the mouth of the Cape Fear River in the south.

The Charter of 1663

Over the years enough news about the glories of Carolina had filtered back to England that when Sir John Colleton began to talk of establishing a full-scale colony there he had a primed audience. Sir John had immigrated to Barbados with the rise of Cromwell, and after an interlude as a West Indies planter had, with the Restoration, returned to England to become a member of the Privy Council and of the Committee for Foreign Plantations. He took more than an official interest in the empire; he promoted the virtues of Carolina and the chance for great profits it offered among his colleagues. Sir William Berkeley, in London on business for Virginia, joined forces with him, and Berkeley's brother Lord John Berkeley agreed to push the project among the most influential of the king's advisers.

John Berkeley did his job well. He persuaded five of the most influential men in the government—Sir Anthony Ashley Cooper, later Earl of Shaftesbury; George Monck, Duke of Albemarle; Sir George Carteret; William, Earl of Craven; and Edward Hyde, Earl of Clarendon—to join the two Berkeleys and Colleton in developing a colony in Carolina. For all his reluctance to antagonize Parliament or the merchants at the start of his reign, the king could not resist such a formidable group. All eight had worked for his restoration, and all were involved in either shaping or administering colonial policy.

The charter Charles granted in 1663 was the first of his regime and thus drew heavily on previous proprietary grants, notably Lord Baltimore's, rather than initiate new policies. The grant of land duplicated that to Heath in 1629, extending from modern Florida to Virginia and from sea to sea. (Two years later the boundaries were altered by half a degree to the north to include settlements on Albemarle Sound and two degrees to the south as a "thrust at Spanish Florida," but the original boundaries were eventually restored.) The grant contained a Bishop of Durham clause that conferred on the proprietors all the rights of jurisdiction Lord Baltimore had been given some thirty years earlier.

The charter had two novel provisions, both of which seem to have been requested by the proprietors. One sought to encourage settlement by granting exemptions from English customs duties on wines, silks, olives, and a variety of other subtropical products for seven years after experimental tests had ended. The other gave settlers the right to worship as they pleased, only requiring that they worship. The indulgence was made, the charter noted, despite "the unity and uniformity established in this nation." This must have been a hard concession for Clarendon, so firm an Anglican that the strict religious laws he administered for Charles II have

Map 19. Proprietary Grants

Map content labels:

NEW FRANCE

L. Huron

44°

L. Ontario

St. Lawrence R.

MAINE to Mass.

45°

NEW HAMP. 1679

Mass. Charter 1691, from sea to sea

Pa. line of 1681

NEW YORK 1664

MASS.

L. Erie

42°

Conn.-Mass. boundary

PENNSYLVANIA Charter 1681

CONN. 1662

R.I. 1663

Conn. Charter line 1662

EAST J.

41°

Pa. line 5° West of Delaware R.

Md. Charter line 1632

40°

N.J. 1664 divided 1676

Mass. charter was cancelled in 1684 DOM. OF N.ENGL'D 1689 New Charter in 1691

Ohio R.

MD.

Pa. line claimed

WEST JERSEY

DEL.

VIRGINIA

37°

Carolina Charter line 1665

36°34'

CAROLINA

Charter 1665, from sea to sea

33°

31° Carolina Charter line of 1663

FLORIDA Spanish

29° Carolina Charter line including Bahama Is.

0   100   200
Miles

73°

69° Ra132

29°

been called the "Clarendon Code," but he was enough of a realist to see that religious toleration had proved to be an effective way to entice people to the wilderness. In this same year Rhode Island received royal approval for its own experiment in toleration and probably for a similar reason.

First Failures

The proprietors sought what Gilbert and Raleigh had attempted three-quarters of a century earlier—to make money for themselves and at the same time promote the welfare of England. They planned to follow closely the prospectus the younger Hakluyt had drawn up for Roanoke, encouraging a variety of agricultural experiments that would lead to products England could not grow.

Their plans differed from Gilbert's and Raleigh's in that they did not propose to invest much in the enterprise. Changed conditions seemed to justify their penuriousness. It struck them as senseless to carry out costly colonization from England when the New World was already populated with hundreds of people in search of free land. The proprietors would, then, draw from those who had already made the debilitating ocean trip and gained some immunity to New World diseases, using the land to attract them from New England, Virginia, and Barbados. Their reasoning seemed so sound that it looked as though the proprietors might get something for nothing.

As part of the promotional campaign, the proprietors in 1663 issued "A Declaration and Proposals to All That Will Plant in Carolina," wherein they promised settlers as much if not more political freedom than they might get elsewhere in America. An assembly was authorized to make all laws, subject only to the consent of the governor and possible disallowance by the proprietors. In addition to religious freedom, generous land grants would be dispensed to all settlers, including servants at the end of their indenture. The only charge on the settlers would be a quit-rent of a half penny per acre to underwrite administrative costs.

The proprietors delegated responsibility for settlement of the northern section to their colleague Governor Berkeley. He would issue land patents, encourage newcomers arriving in Virginia to continue on to that part of Carolina that would eventually be organized as Albemarle County. Despite Berkeley's best efforts, settlement dragged, for the northern section had little to offer that Virginia could not grant on better terms. The lack of a harbor forced most supplies to enter and exports to leave through Virginia. Quitrents were less there (one shilling for fifty acres) and the land grants as generous. Albemarle settlers demanded at once the right to hold land "upon the same terms and conditions that the inhabitants of Virginia hold theirs"; the proprietors made the adjustment in 1668, then, as they saw profits dwindle, quickly rescinded it.

While Berkeley worked to promote the Albemarle settlements, the other proprietors gave thought to the southern part of the grant. William Hilton of Barbados had explored the Cape Fear region in 1663, and his report did much to stir up enthusiasm in Barbados among the small planters there who had been suffering economically. Barbados had once been an island of medium-sized farms and diversified crops—tobacco, cotton, indigo, and ginger—but after 1640 sugar had come to be the main export and large plantations manned by Negro slaves dominated the landscape. The small planter and the white servant completing his indenture found themselves at loose ends and ready to move. A group of these Barbadians settled the Cape Fear region in 1664. Two years later the plantations contained some eight hundred people and appeared to be thriving.

To encourage further settlement, the proprietors in 1665 amplified their earlier "Declaration and Proposals" with a long document entitled "Concessions and Agreements," which, in addition to detailing the settlers' privileges, divided Carolina into three counties—Albemarle in the north, Clarendon and Craven in the south—each with its own assembly, governor, and council. (Virtually the entire document was adopted six weeks later for New Jersey, where it played a greater part in the management of local affairs than in Carolina.) In the same year, a fleet of three ships left Barbados to establish a colony at Port Royal, the area in which the French had long ago erected their own ill-fated enterprise. The largest of the ships was wrecked and with it to the bottom went most of the settlers' supplies. The projected Port Royal colony came to nothing, and the supposedly successful Cape Fear settlement soon after collapsed, the colonists dispersing northward to Albemarle, Virginia, and New England, with some returning to Barbados.

The future of Carolina looked dismal. Settlers remained in the Albemarle region, but chances of creating a colony independent of Virginia seemed dim. All had failed even in the south, where the magnet of a good harbor had attracted a greater effort. The proprietors' hope of something for nothing—not nothing exactly, for each did invest £75 in the colony—had vanished, and they were set to abandon further attempts at settlement. Fortunately, Sir Ashley Cooper, soon to be the Earl of Shaftesbury, had the energy and interest to step in and revive the dying colony.

The Fundamental Constitutions of 1669

Shaftesbury saw at once that success required more than hope for investment. He persuaded his colleagues to pledge £500 each to launch a new effort and £200 more annually for four years. Three ships set out in the late summer of 1669 with settlers and supplies. They stopped at Barbados to pick up various seeds to try out in the Carolina climate and soil. Shaftesbury instructed the settlers first to provide "for the belly by planting stores of provisions," for these would be "the foundation of your plantations," and then, without worrying about a staple crop, to begin their agricultural experiments. To encourage the experiments and give the settlers a boost when they most needed it, he offered to purchase all crops grown at London prices, which meant a hefty subsidy on the part of the proprietors. "We aim not at the profit of merchants," he explained, "but the encouragement of landlords."

Meanwhile, Shaftesbury, with help from John Locke, his physician, friend, and confidential secretary, had drawn up the Fundamental Constitutions for Carolina in 1669. No document in the colonial story has provoked more ridicule from historians, who for the most part have seen it simply as an idiotic desire to re-create in America the vanishing feudal world of England. They forget that Shaftesbury, one of the ablest and most imaginative politicians of his day, treasured the past less than most men.

The constitutions sought essentially to fashion a pattern for the orderly settlement of Carolina, a hopeless goal as it turned out, but one Americans still pursued in 1785 when the Land Ordinance was enacted. The land was to be surveyed into giant squares of twelve thousand acres each. Forty of these squares (480,000 acres) comprised a county. In every county eight squares (96,000 acres) were "seigniories" of the proprietors, eight became "baronies" for an American-based hereditary nobility, and the remaining twenty-four (288,000 acres)—called "colonies," which were further divided into four "precincts" (72,000 acres)—would be settled by freeholders. Manors of the English type could be erected inside a "colony," but it was expected that most of the land would go to small planters. Of the nobility's eight squares, four (48,000 acres) went to "landgraves," and two (24,000 acres) each to two "caciques," a title taken from the Spanish word for Indian chief and pronounced as it was sometimes spelled, "cassocks." As settlement advanced, each new county would be laid out on this grid.

Shaftesbury sought to develop a pattern of settlement that would attract well-to-do gentlemen and at the same time give the small planter a voice in affairs. Every county was designated to put three-fifths of the land and thus the power in the hands of the ordinary settlers and two-fifths in the hands of the nobility. He wanted both society and government organized in a way "agreeable to the monarch under which we live" and that avoided "a numerous democracy." He believed with James Harrington, author of *The Commonwealth of Oceana* (1656), that society functioned best when the factions within it were checked and balanced, that power followed property, and that a nobility was "the very life and soul" of society; but when it ruled unrestrained, it became "the utter bane and destruction" of the state.

The form of government resembled that of early Virginia and Massachusetts. Only the names had been changed. Proprietors, nobles, and deputies of the freeholders sat together in a one-house "Parliament." The "Grand Council," comprised of the proprietors or their deputies, prepared all bills and Parliament merely approved or disapproved them, as had been the case in Maryland and would be in early Pennsylvania.

Several features of the constitutions were devised to fit American conditions. To avoid the disorderly and dispersed type of settlements of the Chesapeake area, which was blamed on the absence of towns, it offered trading privileges and certain exemptions to all towns erected within Carolina. As a further attempt at order, it provided for the registration of all births, marriages, and deaths, and land titles. It accepted what was already an American tradition, that deputies should live in the district they represented. It foresaw the shortage of labor on the large estates, and to overcome this the constitutions implicitly encouraged the development of Negro slavery. And it clearly understood the magnetic quality of free land by making it the basic attraction for all settlers. First settlers received between 100 and 150 acres as their headright, with the amount diminishing to 60 for late comers.

The Fundamental Constitutions was cumbersome, and after four revisions and thirty years of trial it dropped from sight. It failed mainly because it tried to impose orderly settlement on a people who preferred to move when and where they wished. But out of the failure much survived, especially in South Carolina. There government and society, stripped of their strange names, and the landed aristocracy, minus its hereditary nobility, bore a striking resemblance in the eighteenth century to that envisioned by Locke and Shaftesbury in the seventeenth.

Success

Shaftesbury's efforts cleared the way for a viable colony in lower Carolina. His small fleet arrived at Port Royal in April 1670 after a miserable eight-month trip. The ghosts of Frenchmen who had settled there long ago may have recalled the nearness of the Spanish at Saint Augustine; the colonists soon moved northward and built a fort on Albemarle Point, some twenty-five miles inland on the Ashley River (which, along with the Cooper River, was named after Lord Shaftesbury, Ashley Cooper), a spot safer from attack but still "in the very chops of the Spanish," as a settler put it. A Spanish task force tried to evict the intruders, but a storm swept away the ships before they could attack. Another piece of luck followed. A well-timed relief ship arrived to carry the settlement through the first winter without the usual starving time. Two hundred colonists had settled by 1672. A party of forty-five French Huguenots came in 1680, and more soon followed. The next year a band of Scots founded Stuart's Town, and though the Spanish soon wiped out the village the Scots stayed.

Few of Shaftesbury's plans lasted long in the wilderness. Neat ten-acre plots were laid out around the fort, giving settlers space to experiment with oranges, lemons, rice, cotton, and a variety of other crops, but soon people drifted inland. They followed the waterways, ignoring the grid plan for settlement and choosing sites that fronted on the Ashley and Cooper Rivers. Only Charles Town, founded in 1680 at the junction of these two rivers, remained to remind posterity of Shaftesbury's orderly dream. Proprietary instructions had called for the town's streets to be laid out in checkerboard fashion, and, for once, these orders had been adhered to. Charleston, as it eventually came to be called, followed a pattern begun by New Haven, continued by Philadelphia and by scores of other towns laid out in the wilderness during the eighteenth century. They survived as vestigial examples of the seventeenth century's attempt to impose order on chaos.

By the end of the century some three thousand persons had settled around Albemarle Sound in the northern part of Carolina and some five thousand had spread outward from Charleston in the south. The northern part remained dependent on Virginia. Settlers lived on small farms carved from the forest, growing tobacco for a cash crop and living largely isolated existences. They had their own governor and assembly, and the county was their basic unit of government. Little distinguished their lives from those who farmed in Virginia.

Life to the south focused on Charleston. Economic ties as well as the origin of many early settlers oriented Charleston toward the West Indies rather than toward other continental colonies. Farmers up the Ashley and Cooper floated their crops down to town, and from there the pork, corn, lumber, and cattle—and later rice, which seems to have been commercially successful sometime in the 1690's—were carried to Barbados. Charleston ships sold their cargoes at Barbados and reloaded with sugar and ginger, which was exchanged in England for manufactured articles that were sold back in Charleston. This triangular trade pattern seldom overlapped the trade lines of other American colonies.

Charleston prospered in part, a contemporary told Shaftesbury, because "the Apalataean Mountains—though like the prodigious wall that divides China from Tartary, they deny Virginia passage into the west continent—stoop to your lordship's dominions and lay open a prospect into unlimited empires." Only New York had equally easy access to the back-country, and as with New York that access would embroil southern Carolina with other intruders on the continent. A lucrative fur trade and a heavy traffic in Indian slaves flowed through Charleston from the inland entrepôt at Savannah Town, today Augusta. Carolinian traders pushed their frontier westward faster and farther than any other English settlers. They had by the end of the century turned the Spanish advance into a retreat, and they had reached the Mississippi, where they found the French trekking eastward. The Indian tribes—principally the Catawba, Cherokee, Creek, Chickasaw, and Choctaw—kept the backcountry in con-stant turmoil by dividing their allegiance among the white intruders. Carolina's Indian trade, with its consequent collision with French and Spanish traders, would involve the colony in every imperial war of the next generation.

The backcountry, for all the wealth it poured eastward, remained a social, commercial, and political appendage of Charleston. The dominance of Charleston forced a form of government on southern Carolina different from what had taken shape in the Chesapeake region. The county, so important in the north, remained largely confined to paper. Charleston delegated slight political authority to communities developing in the in-terior. This meant little in the seventeenth century, but later, as the back-country filled up, it would come to mean much.

NEW YORK

About the time Captain John Smith prepared to leave for Virginia a friend of Smith's named Henry Hudson also set out for America. Hud-son's expedition was underwritten by the Muscovy Company, which sought a shorter route to India. Hudson searched for the desired passage in 1607 and again in 1608, and when he returned from the second voyage without having found it, the company, its treasury nearly empty, let him go. The next year Hudson signed up with the Dutch East India Company and headed out in the *Half Moon* on the same mission. He paused at Newfoundland to catch "one hundred and eighteen great cods," plagued a band of Indians in the area of Penobscot Bay, then dropped down to Delaware Bay, and after discarding that as a route to India moved up the coast. He traveled up the broad Hudson River, as it was to be called, for eleven days. When the *Half Moon* passed the spot where Albany is now and could go no farther, he pushed ahead in a longboat until the stream petered out into a trickling creek, and it was clear this was no Northwest Passage. English merchants, on hearing of the trip, made disparaging remarks about Hudson's loyalty, but they hired him away from the Dutch. On another search for the passage in 1611, he vanished amid the icy mists of Hudson Bay.

The Dutch were too busy elsewhere in the world to give more than desultory attention to the claim Hudson had staked out for them. Adriaen Block toured Long Island in 1641, however, and ventured up the Connecticut River as far as Hartford; Cornelis May about the same time traveled up Delaware Bay. No one paid more than casual thought to the Delaware region until 1624, the year the Dutch West India Company got control of the coast of Brazil, an event that raised interest in other parts of the New World. Captain May settled a group of thirty Walloons at Albany, or Fort Orange, as they named the spot; and in 1625 three more ships arrived with more colonists and with horses, cattle, hogs, sheep, seeds, and plows. This new contingent camped near the mouth of the river on the tip of an island they called New Amsterdam. Peter Minuit, director-general, or governor, of the colony, purchased the island from the Manhates in 1626 for sixty guilders, or about $24, worth of trinkets, which was no extraordinary bargain, because the Manhates sold land they had no claim to.

New Netherland

Minuit—he seems to have pronounced his name as it was sometimes spelled, "Minnewit"—ruled the tiny settlement with a strong hand. He began to build a fort on the lower tip of Manhattan, erected a mill and several houses, and developed the fur trade of the river valley to the point where it yielded a small profit for the company. But New Amsterdam remained a sideline concession to the West India Company's more lucrative trading and privateering operations in the Caribbean area. Kiliaen Van Rensselaer, a wealthy jeweler and company stockholder, believed the American outpost could be more wisely exploited. He wanted to create an agricultural settlement that could serve as a supply and repair station for ships going to and from the West Indies. Company members who profited from refitting these ships in Holland opposed the plan, but the mounting costs of subsidizing the trading posts in New Netherland led to its eventual acceptance.

A virtue of the plan as it finally took shape was that it shifted the burden of colonization from the company's shoulders onto those of individuals, much as the London Company had done through its subsidiary or associated companies. The Charter of Freedoms and Exemptions issued in 1629 stated that any company member who in four years transported fifty families to America at his own expense would be entitled to an extensive tract of land to do with as he wished. The patroon, as he was

Map 20.

Dutch Settlements on the Lower Hudson River 1624-1664

called, would have, like Lord Baltimore, all the rights of a feudal lord. He held full title to his land, could levy rents on his tenants and organize and hold courts that had jurisdiction over the property and lives of all settlers. Members with inside information grabbed up the best sites at once. Staten Island went to Michael Pauw; Samuel Godyn and Samuel Blommaert got what would become the state of Delaware; Van Rensselaer took lands around Albany. Of all the patroonships only Van Rensselaer's succeeded.

While the patroonships struggled to come alive, Wouter van Twiller became director-general in 1633. He survives in one contemporary reference as a vain and intolerant man happy only "as long as there is any wine," and in Washington Irving's *Knickerbocker History* as Walter the Doubter, an appellation, says Edward Channing, that libels "the good name of an estimable man." Twiller more than held his own during trying times. New Netherland by then consisted of several trading posts scattered along three rivers—the Connecticut, Hudson, and Delaware—and all lying in disputed territory. Virginia, New Haven, and the Swedes challenged the Dutch on the Delaware, and New Englanders ignored them on the Connecticut. Authorities in England encouraged these aggressions, urging the colonists "to push forward their plantations and crowd on, crowding the Dutch out of those places where they have occupied, but without hostility or any act of violence."

New Netherland's holdings remained intact when Twiller was replaced by Willem Kieft in 1638. Kieft came at a bad time, and a violent temper coupled with a fondness for the bottle did little to relieve the situation. The influx of farmers, whose fields destroyed the supply of game, had created friction between settlers and Indians. Kieft determined to resolve the problem by force, and in 1643 he marched on the River Indians, who up to now had been friendly toward the Dutch. The war backfired, and within a year all New Netherland was beleaguered. "Our fields lie fallow and wasted, our dwellings and other buildings are burnt," settlers complained to the company. The directors, faced with a colony close to bankruptcy, looked around for someone with the talent to make it solvent. They came up with Peter Stuyvesant.

Stuyvesant, who had managed the company's West Indian holdings in Curaçao with apparent skill, losing his right leg during the tour of duty, faced an impossible task in the assignment handed him in 1647. He had to rule in the company's interests over a diversified community—Puritans on Long Island, infiltrating Swedes on the Delaware, and some four hundred people in New Amsterdam speaking eighteen different languages—where religious differences splintered the population into violent factions. He had to defend settlements dispersed along the Hudson (North) River, the Delaware (South) River, and the Connecticut River, and at the same time he was also responsible for Dutch holdings in the Caribbean area.

Whatever Stuyvesant did seemed wrong. Faced with an empty treasury, he levied a 30 per cent customs duty to pay administrative costs; ships from the Chesapeake area and New England began to avoid New Amsterdam, and a calm fell on commerce. Trade fed the town, and its decline exacerbated political unrest. Settlers complained to the company in 1649 about the lack of self-government, the lack of schools, the failure of trade; and they asked for a governor less covetous, less "strongly inclined to confiscating" than Stuyvesant. The first Anglo-Dutch War, which began in 1652, did little to ease the situation. A convention that met the next year to decide what to do in case of invasion was taken over by Puritans from Long Island, who demanded the right to govern themselves. Stuyvesant gave a blunt reply to the appeal: "We derive our authority from God and the West India Company, not from the pleasure of a few ignorant subjects."

Little came of these complaints, for the Dutch never granted self-government to overseas possessions. Religious toleration was another question. Lutherans in 1654 asked the governor to permit them a minister of their own persuasion. Stuyvesant refused, saying his oath forbade any form of worship but that of the established Dutch Reformed Church. If Lutherans were tolerated, then he must grant the same rights to the dreaded Anabaptists and Quakers. The company agreed, but urged Stuyvesant to use only "moderate exertions" to win over others from their errors. A few years later the company revised this tactful reprimand into a blunt order to allow freedom of worship, for the "consciences of men should be free and unshackled."

The directors at home traded reprimands for compliments when they learned of Stuyvesant's efficient dispatching of the Swedes on the Delaware. The Swedish West India Company had been formed in 1638, and a short while later some fifty colonists were settled not far from the Dutch outpost on the Delaware, led by the same Peter Minuit who had been director-general of New Netherland. They built their fort near modern Wilmington, and named it Christina, after their queen. More forts were built above and below the Dutch posts, and soon the Swedes were cutting deeply into the fur trade. Stuyvesant mounted an expedition against these intruders in 1655 that ended their competition for good.

By the time the second Anglo-Dutch War began in 1664, New Netherland numbered less than eight thousand settlers. Stuyvesant's seventeen years of rule had created neither a prosperous colony nor a peaceful one, but during those years a plantation had emerged that served the purposes of the West India Company more than adequately. New Amsterdam repaired and provisioned company ships. It served as an entrepôt for a continental trade sufficiently lucrative to help provoke passage of the Navigation Act of 1660. The taxes on trade together with income from furs more than paid administrative expenses. The colony failed to grow because it satisfied the company as it was.

Peace under the most blessed ruler could never have prevailed among the mixed people of New Netherland, but Peter Stuyvesant's often highhanded actions did much to make a bad situation worse. The citizens of New Amsterdam found the chance to express their feelings toward the director-general in the year 1664. Richard Nicolls, in charge of the Duke of York's expeditionary force, anchored his small fleet off Coney Island in August. Once troops from New England, with John Winthrop, Jr., among their leaders, had joined him, he sent a demand for surrender of the colony to Stuyvesant. The Dutch were assured of their property and the liberties, such as they were, that they had hitherto enjoyed. Though Stuyvesant was or pretended to be reluctant to give up without a fight (like Governor Berkeley upon the arrival of the Commissioners in Virginia), the people of the town forced him to.

The Articles of Capitulation were generous. They permitted the Dutch West India Company to use its property in the colony and to have six months in which to transport arms and ammunition out. The inhabitants had a year and a half to move out; those who chose to stay would be free inhabitants under English law, would have liberty of conscience, would not be pressed into service in time of war nor have soldiers billeted upon them, and could continue to enjoy their own customs concerning inheritances. Minor officials were to continue to hold their positions until the time for new elections, when those going out might choose their successors, as was customary in Dutch municipalities; but those coming in must take an oath of loyalty to the king. It was also agreed that Dutch ships would have free access to the port, but this provision, clearly against the Navigation Act of 1660, was later retracted.

Nicolls became New York's first governor, and life was so pleasant under his firm but fair rule that Stuyvesant remained in the colony until his death in 1672. Nicolls changed names on the land to remind the people who ran things. Fort Orange became Albany, after the Duke of York's second title; New Amsterdam became New York; Long Island became Yorkshire. The towns on Long Island lost their Dutch names: Midwout became Flatbush and Folestone became Oyster Bay, for example. Such titles as mayor, alderman, and sheriff replaced their Dutch equivalents; and soon, in spite of the Articles of Capitulation, Nicolls was supplanting Dutch officials with English ones. But the Dutch had been around too long for their imprint on the land to be easily erased.

The Dutch Heritage

The Dutch contributed nothing in literature and little in art or government. They left their strongest impress on social customs. Sleighing, coasting, and ice skating count among their innovations. "It is admirable," wrote a visiting Englishman in 1678, "to see men and women, as it were flying upon their skates from place to place with markets [baskets] on their heads and backs." They gave the Easter egg and Santa Claus to America. St. Nicholas was the patron saint of New Amsterdam, and the children set out their shoes on his birthday, December 6, to receive his gifts; gradually the custom shifted to Christmas Eve. The habit of paying calls on friends on New Year's Day began with the Dutch.

The Dutch gave to the city of New York its colors and seal and to the state some of its most distinguished names: the Van Rensselaers, Van Burens, and Roosevelts. And they gave to the nation several words from their language: "bowery" (farm), "brief" (letter), "spook" (ghost), "scow" (river boat), and "yacht." "Cruller" and "cooky" are Dutch words, as are "boss," "dope" (as in "give me the inside dope"), "lope," and "kill" (meaning creek, and common mainly in the Middle Atlantic states). The front "stoop" is a Dutch word and architectural innovation.

The Dutch heritage shaped New York's development in many unnoticed ways. The English found, whether they liked it or not, that they had to take over the alliance with the Iroquois established by the Dutch, and that alliance would have deep effect on eighteenth-century America's history. Albany (Fort Orange) continued as it had been, a Dutch village, with former Dutchmen controlling political and economic affairs and the Dutch language being spoken there well into the nineteenth century. (A Dutch translation of the Constitution eased opposition to its ratification in the Albany area in 1788, where Dutch-speaking residents could be found as late as 1897.) The Dutch pattern of granting enormous tracts of lands to individuals continued under the English, and a varied form of patroonship would influence New York's affairs into the nineteenth century, when the rent wars of the Jacksonian era exploded. The parochial school, which the Dutch devised to keep alive their language, traditions, and religion under English rule, was an innovation in education to be put to even greater use at another time by Catholics. Their effect on government was mainly negative. Local self-government had been retarded under Dutch rule and it continued to lag compared to developments elsewhere throughout the colonial period.

English Rule: 1664–1689

A good deal of Dutch tradition survived in part because the Duke of York sympathized with the authoritarian views fostered by the Dutch West India Company. The extraordinarily brief charter for New York, hastily written and slipped through the seals in a scant four days, possibly because the duke's brother, King Charles, hastened it along (the process took months for most charters), made the duke absolute proprietor of his province. He was not even required, as was Lord Baltimore, to obtain the advice and consent of the freemen for his laws. That obviated the need for a representative assembly, and the duke managed without one for nearly two decades.

The land grant in the charter resembled none previously given by the crown. It took in all the continent between the Connecticut and Delaware Rivers plus Long Island, Nantucket, Martha's Vineyard, and all of Maine east of the Kennebec River. Its vague boundaries involved the duke in litigation with neighboring colonies almost from the moment the Dutch struck their colors. The cost of administering lands that stretched from Maine to Maryland put the duke in the red at the start. Aware he had bitten off too much, he began to give away slices at once. To his friends Lord John Berkeley and Sir George Carteret, already deep in the Carolina project, he ceded the lands between the Hudson and Delaware as the "Province of Nova Caesaria or New Jersey." Later he relinquished the three lower counties, as Delaware was then called, to William Penn. The royal commission of 1664 gave Connecticut part of his land on the east, and over a century later a portion of Vermont, the fourteenth state, was carved out of New York's northern sector.

Fortunately for the duke, he had found in Richard Nicolls an able, tactful man to administer this oddly-fashioned territory. Nicolls' legal knowledge—he held the degree of doctor of civil law from Oxford—allowed him, only four months after taking over the colony, to publish a code known as the Duke's Laws. Nicolls based the code on Massachusetts and Connecticut laws, partly because he assumed that American law would be more pertinent to American needs than English law and partly because he designed the code mainly for the Puritan towns on Long Island. While seemingly administering to the needs of the people, he made certain the code did not impair the duke's authority. He sought to give the impression of local control over local affairs while preserving the actual power of government almost intact in the hands of those whom the duke appointed to administer the affairs of his province.

The code eliminated the town meeting and substituted locally elected officials—constables and overseers—who were held accountable to the governor. Justices of the peace were appointed by the governor and held office at his pleasure. They combined judicial and legislative functions, and regulations they adopted became, with the governor's consent, the laws of the towns and counties. The code provided for trial by jury. Punishments for crime were liberal compared to English practices. Religious toleration was authorized. Every town was required to build a church and to provide for its support. If a minority group within a town grew large enough to support a church, it, too, could form one and receive tax support. The code created not one established church but many. The Long Island Puritans disparaged this and other parts of the Duke's Laws because they were imposed on them from above, and called for taxation without their consent.

Francis Lovelace, another friend of Charles II and the Duke of York, replaced Nicolls as governor in 1668. Lovelace had the bad luck to be absent in Connecticut when, during the third Anglo-Dutch War, Holland recaptured New York City. The city remained in Dutch hands for fifteen months.

Lovelace, recalled and jailed for negligence of duty, was succeeded by Major Edmund Andros—apparently pronounced "Andrews" at the time— a professional soldier with sufficient connections at court to be made a landgrave in Carolina, an empty honor as it turned out, because he never profited from his forty-eight-thousand–acre grant. Andros seems to have been a man of ability, but he lacked the tact needed for governing a colony inhabited by a belligerent assortment of people. Under his administration

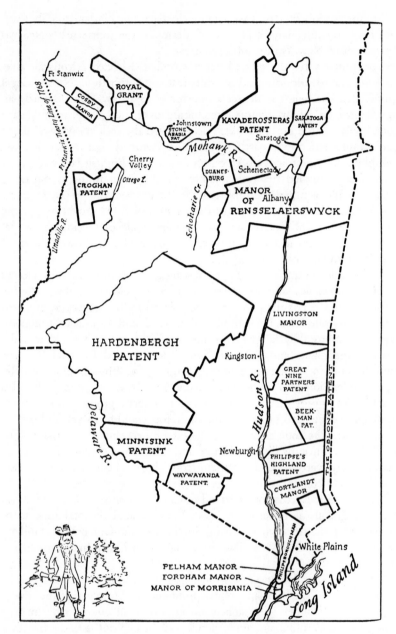

Map 21. Land Patterns of Colonial New York.

the duke inaugurated customs duties, modest in amount but enacted without the consent of the people. The Long Islanders promptly stepped up their demand for a representative assembly, asserting that they would refuse to pay taxes if it were not forthcoming. Andros favored their demand. The duke said it was common knowledge that such bodies "prove destructive to, or very oft disturb, the peace of the government wherein they are allowed," but, he added, if Andros still insisted, "I shall be ready to consider of any proposals you shall send to that purpose." Andros insisted and the duke, hoping taxes would become easier to collect, complied.

Thomas Dongan became governor in 1683, and though it might be expected that his Catholicism would raise Puritan hackles, his rule passed smoothly, largely because he had the luck to be instructed by the duke to call an assembly to consult "with yourself and the said council what laws are fit and necessary to be made and established for the good weal and government of the said colony. . . ." The first assembly, consisting of the governor, his council, and eighteen deputies, passed fifteen laws, among them a Charter of Liberties and Privileges, essentially a constitution for the colony that guaranteed the rights of property and the liberties of Englishmen and provided for a legislative assembly elected by freeholders and freemen and based on proportional representation. The duke approved the charter, only later, as James II, to rescind it in order to clear the ground for formation of the Dominion of New England in 1686.

New York's population nearly quadrupled during its first twenty-four years under English rule. New habits were grafted onto old during these transitional years as the province swung from a company outpost to a ducal proprietary and finally to a royal province, but much of the past lingered on. The town of New York remained Dutch in tone and appearance for all its polyglot population. A few closely knit wealthy families, usually of Dutch background, continued to dominate New York politics. Economic life focused on the fur trade. But changes were occurring. Newcomers to the colony were storing up a reservoir of discontent against the entrenched elite, which would burst forth in Leisler's Rebellion. The fur trade was complicating New York's relations with the Iroquois and with the French, who were tightening their control over the western sources of that trade. All signs pointed to nothing but troubles ahead for the colony.

NEW JERSEY

It has been said of New Jersey that it was blessed by natural boundaries but has not been otherwise well treated by man or nature. Few good harbors dented its long seacoast, and its sandy soil was not the best for agriculture. Contentions literally split the colony in half, and not until the American Revolution did a semblance of order and unity take place.

New Jersey's history was conditioned by the development of two large metropolitan regions on its borders—New York to the east, Philadelphia to the west—each seeking to pull the adjacent part of the colony within its orbit. Its history was also conditioned by having the land parceled out to two individuals. These occurrences led to a sharp east-west cleavage in New Jersey that persisted through the colonial period and down to the present.

East Jersey

Three and a half months after the Duke of York received his grant from the king, he sliced off the land between the Hudson and Delaware Rivers for his friends Lord John Berkeley and Sir George Carteret. The gift came only a year after they had become proprietors of Carolina. From that enterprise they lifted and published a slightly abbreviated version of the Concessions and Agreements, wherein settlers were promised freedom of worship, the rights of freemen upon taking an oath of allegiance to the king, a representative assembly with the power to levy all taxes, and a moratorium on quitrents until 1670. Such generosity was prompted solely by the desire to populate the colony with settlers already in the New World. The proprietors were once again attempting to acquire something for nothing.

Captain Philip Carteret, Sir George's twenty-six–year–old cousin, was chosen governor. He arrived on a confused scene. The sprinkling of Swedes and Dutch in the Delaware Valley presented no problems. The core of trouble, present and future, lay in the eastern sector, a region occupied by some 250 Dutch colonists spread along the Hudson and by a sprinkling of Puritan families from Long Island and from New Haven, whose displeasure at being forced to join with Connecticut under the recently issued charter had led them to accept an offer to occupy an area they would call Newark. These settlements had been promoted by Governor Nicolls of New York before he learned that what he regarded as the best part of the duke's province had been given away. One of Nicolls' grants, known as the Monmouth patent, embraced the settlements of Middletown, Shrewsbury, and Portland Point. It exempted settlers from taxation for seven years and allowed them to set up their own general assembly, creating, in effect, a colony within a colony. The people balked when Governor Carteret attempted to collect taxes and quitrents and demanded oaths of loyalty. As Puritans accustomed to governing themselves and owning their land outright, they found proprietary government something "we simple creatures never heard of before." The rebellion spread to other settlements. In 1672 a group of settlers met in an unauthorized assembly—the governor called it a gathering of the "disorderly assembled" —ostensibly to discuss "the safety of the country," actually to devise ways to resist proprietary authority. The Duke of York shortly afterward resolved the confusion by denying the validity of Nicolls' grants and insisting that only those who held their lands by proprietary grants and paid quitrents could be considered freeholders. Resistance, for the time being, subsided.

Lord Berkeley sensed only a calm before further storms. He eased his way out of New Jersey in 1674 by selling his share for £1,000 to two Quakers—John Fenwick and Edward Byllinge. The Quakers apparently bought the ill will along with the land, for a feud soon developed between Fenwick and Byllinge over their purchase. William Penn was called in to arbitrate the matter. Penn, with other Friends, had for over a decade contemplated a haven in America for their persecuted sect. George Fox had kept his eyes open for a likely site during a tour of the colonies. Thought had been given to a tract along the Susquehanna River, for claims covered virtually all habitable land on the coast, and what little remained would hardly be bestowed on the unpopular Quakers. The Fenwick-Byllinge acquisition, if it could be straightened out, offered what had been searched for. Penn persuaded Byllinge to convey his nine-tenths share of half of New Jersey to three trustees, of whom Penn was one. While negotiations continued with the refractory Fenwick, who owned the remaining one-tenth share, Penn worked out a further settlement in 1676, whereby a division line was drawn that split New Jersey into fairly equal sections. Carteret kept East Jersey; it was the most populous part and had the added virtue of adjoining the lands of his friend the duke. The Quakers took the western half.

West Jersey

Over a half century earlier the Dutch had erected Fort Nassau on Delaware Bay. They exploited the area for furs without competition from 1624 to 1638, when a group of Swedes led by Peter Minuit pushed in. The Dutch protested the intrusion only mildly, for the Swedes and they had been partners in the Thirty Years' War, just ending, and merchants of both countries were joint stockholders in this new venture. Three years later a company of New Haven Puritans arrived, bent on tapping the fur trade. The Dutch ousted this advance party, but the tenacious Puritans still infested the area in 1643 when Johan Printz, a "furious and passionate" man, became governor of the tiny Swedish settlements, perhaps a dozen in number by now. "Big Tub," as the Indians called Printz—he weighed over four hundred pounds—found the Puritans laying hard "upon my neck" and the Dutch opposing "us on every side."

A live-and-let-live policy developed between Swedes and English. The Swedes drew on the Puritans for credit; they bought cattle from and sold grain to Virginia. Dutch competition was something else again, for "they destroy our trade everywhere" and, worse still, "they strengthen the savages with guns, shot, and powder, publicly trading with these against the edict of all Christians." Governor Johan Rising, newly strengthened by an influx of settlers, decided to eliminate the Dutch from the valley and in 1654 took over their main fort. This audacity provoked Stuyvesant to his expedition of the following year, which subdued Rising's posts and ended Swedish pretensions in the Delaware Valley. Sweden tried to retrieve her holdings through diplomatic channels and to strengthen her hand by shipping over a boatload of Finns. The Finns and those Swedes already in the valley remained to farm the land, but title to the region stayed with the Dutch until Richard Nicolls showed up off New Amsterdam in 1664. Soon after Stuyvesant's capitulation Nicolls dispatched a force to take over Dutch holdings in the Delaware Valley. Few, except the farmers who lived there, gave further thought to the area until the Quakers' interest was aroused a decade later.

Penn's agreement with Carteret in 1676 did not evoke either from the Duke of York or the crown an acknowledgment of the Friends' proprietorship or of their right to govern West Jersey. They nonetheless went ahead with plans to settle the area. Penn in 1677 published a document entitled Laws, Concessions, and Agreements. It has been called the most sane and progressive colonial constitution issued up to that time. Settlers received full rights to their lands. All deeds were to be recorded to avoid confusion. Citizens would elect annually and by secret ballot ten men to serve as the colony's executive and others to serve as their deputies in a representative assembly. The assembly controlled itself. It, not the governor, decided when and where to meet, when to adjourn. Freedom of speech would prevail on the floor and members would be paid. All settlers were guaranteed freedom of religion. Criminal trials were to be conducted with juries and carried on in public, "that justice may not be done in a corner."

Settlement proceeded slowly. Fenwick proved troublesome and started to develop his one-tenth share as though it were an independent colony. Governor Andros compounded the confusion by insisting that because the Duke of York had not approved the transfer of proprietorship, the land remained part of New York. Since Andros plagued East Jersey, too—he arrested Philip Carteret when the East Jersey assembly in 1679 had balked at paying New York customs on cargoes unloaded at Jersey wharves—the crown was asked to resolve the question of authority for both provinces. The decision went against the Duke of York, who thereupon confirmed the titles of the proprietors of both sections and declared that Andros had acted without authority.

Carteret died in 1680. The following year twelve Quakers, Penn among them, purchased at auction the rights to East Jersey for £3,400, and a few months later they bought Fenwick's claims to the southwestern part of West Jersey. East and West Jersey now rested in the hands of a single group of proprietors, but this did little to diminish "the muddle of perplexity." The grant of Pennsylvania to Penn at this time weakened Quaker interest in Jersey. East Jersey fell into the control of men whose careless management created such chaos that the region was ravaged by litigation over land titles throughout the colonial period. Control of West Jersey drifted in 1683 into the hands of Dr. Daniel Coxe, "an honest gentleman and a very good doctor," who worked hard to build up the domain during the nine years he owned it. The two Jerseys were governed as one when the crown incorporated the territory into the Dominion of New England in 1686, but their separate characters were too well fixed for the unity to penetrate beneath the surface. With the dominion's end in 1689, each again went its individual, distracted way. Discord prevailed once more, as it had from the beginning.

PENNSYLVANIA

Pennsylvania, more than any other English colony in America, was the lengthened shadow of a single man. William Penn blended the ideal and the practical to a fine balance. He envisioned a haven for the oppressed and also a prosperous colony to fatten his fortune. He died a disillusioned old man, nearly bankrupt and with his colony riddled with dissension. Some say his dream for a holy commonwealth failed more swiftly and completely than John Winthrop's. Others insist the achievement verged closer to the dream than even Penn realized as he lay dying in England.

William Penn

William Penn was born on October 14, 1644, about the time his father decided to throw in his lot with Cromwell. Admiral William Penn, who became something of a national hero in his day, did good work for the Commonwealth in the first Dutch war; and whereas he accumulated less impressive successes against Spain in the Caribbean area, Cromwell nonetheless rewarded him with several Irish estates. For reasons still not clear, the admiral was thrown into the Tower toward the end of the Interregnum, only to be released after five weeks, apparently for lack of evidence against him. Once free, he took his family away from the intrigues of London to his estates in Ireland. By the time of the Restoration, William was off to Oxford and the admiral had joined forces with the royal brothers Charles II and the Duke of York. The friendship between them was close enough that Charles felt free to ask the admiral for a £16,000 loan, an enormous sum for those days. At the time of the Restoration, Admiral Penn was thirty-nine years old, essentially a self-made man, devoted to his son, and eager for the boy to add further glory to the name of Penn.

A contemporary of the admiral named George Fox seemed certain in the father's eyes to destroy these hopes. Sometime during the civil war, when England was a hotbed of religious as well as political radicalism, Fox began to preach the doctrine of the "Inner Light." His followers were called by such names as Professors of the Light or Children of the Light. A justice of the peace in the process of sentencing Fox to one of his periodic visits to prison was warned by the evangelist to "tremble at the word of the Lord." The magistrate laughed and called Fox and his companions Quakers. The name stuck.

The Society of Friends, as they called themselves, held notions contemporaries found strange and unsettling. They refused to take oaths because the Bible said "thou shalt not swear" and because oaths implied a double standard of veracity. They challenged the hierarchical order of society by insisting that all men were created equal in the eyes of God. They refused to uncover before any man because that implied superiority. They adopted the "plain language" of "thee" and "thou" because "you" in the seventeenth century was used only to address equals or superiors. They were pacifists. They were, in short, "bad citizens," and for that reason the strictest punishment was invariably meted out to them.

Much of Fox's teaching showed a clear debt to Puritanism and to the Continental sources that early Puritanism had drawn on. He sought to return to the primitive church of the Bible. The early Quakers' rejection of the arts and graces of life made them more puritanical than the Puritans, who seemed almost debauched in speech and dress by comparison. The religious experience had to permeate all sides of life. The church became the meetinghouse. Quakers dropped the pagan names for days of the week and substituted First Day (Sunday), Second Day, etc., to make clear that all days were alike in God's eyes and no particular one should be set aside for worship. Government was, as Penn put it, "a part of religion itself, a thing sacred in its institutions and end." Friends shared with Puritans the belief that a man's actions should always be shaped to the welfare of the community. They also shared the conviction that there was but one morality for the individual and for the state.

Cromwell, who sensed the bond between Puritan and Quaker, was impressed by George Fox and did much to ease persecution against his people while in power, but Puritans generally detested this "pernicious sect." Even Roger Williams, though he tolerated their presence in Rhode Island, railed against their doctrines to the end of his life. Their pacifism seemed senseless to him. Their belief that the Innner Light took precedence over God's word as revealed in the Bible struck him as blasphemous. He mocked their acceptance of free will and warned that their belief in equality would destroy all distinctions among men and endanger civil order.

Penn approached the Society of Friends by a circuitous route. His open disgust over the conformity Clarendon was attempting to enforce in religion led to expulsion from Oxford in 1662. His father sent him on a gentleman's tour of the Continent, from which he returned two years later outwardly cleansed of radicalism—modish in his dress and with "much of the vanity of the French garb, and affected manner of speech and gait." He studied law briefly after his return, primarily in order to manage his father's estates in Ireland, to which he went shortly after the great fire of 1666. He seems first to have met up with Quakers in Ireland. Conversion to their way of life came after only a brief exposure. It enraged his father to hear his son use plain language and admit that he would refuse to uncover even before the king. It distressed him when the young man was committed with other Friends to jail in 1668 and kept there nine months. The admiral, Lady Penn once remarked, "had intended to make William a great man, but the boy would not hearken." But estrangement between the two never led to a complete break. When William wrote *No Cross, No Crown* while confined to the Tower in 1669, it became apparent that the early excesses of his conversion had washed away, leaving behind a sedater form of Quakerism. Father and son were fully reconciled by the time of the admiral's death in 1670 at the age of forty-nine.

In the year of his father's death Penn, then twenty-six, was involved with a linen draper named William Mead in a trial that marked a milestone in English jurisprudence. The two men were called to court for holding an unlawful religious meeting, a deed of which they were obviously guilty. The jury, however, found them innocent. The judge refused to accept the verdict, but the jury, led by its foreman Edward Bushel, held fast. The judge satisfied his fury by remanding the twelve jurors as well as Penn and Mead to Newgate Prison. A writ of habeas corpus soon freed the jury, which promptly sued the judge for illegal imprisonment. The case went before Sir John Vaughan, the lord chief justice, who held that the jury's verdict must stand. Judges, the court said, "may try to open the eyes of the jurors, but not to lead them by the nose." Penn soon after published a pamphlet on the case, *The People's Ancient and Just Liberties Asserted* (1670).

Shortly after his release from the "common stinking jail" of Newgate, Penn married, and during the next few years a calm descended on his public and private life. George Fox during this period visited America, stopping first at Barbados and Jamaica, crossing to Virginia, then traveling northward to Maryland, New Jersey, and Long Island, "through bogs, rivers and creeks, and wild woods where it was said never man was known to ride," ending his stay with a marathon debate with the aged but still prolix and sharp Roger Williams. Fox brought back a detailed knowledge of the continent and of possible havens for his harassed followers.

Throughout these years Penn held both to his principles and to his friendships with Charles II and the Duke of York, which dated from the youths of all three men. Politically, Penn favored a strong Parliament and opposed Charles's attempts to increase royal power; religiously, he was exposed to constant persecution by the crown's officers. But Penn refused to renounce a personal relationship because he differed on public issues. His steadfastness undoubtedly helped to win his charter for Pennsylvania and at a later date to keep it in the face of strong opposition. But more than royal influence contributed to his success in political affairs. Few Englishmen were better informed about their times and about English politics than William Penn. Knowledge and skill in this arena as much as influence won the remarkable charter granted to him by Charles II.

The Charter of 1681

Penn, who by 1680 had determined to found a colony of his own, knew that the king would have to refuse such a conspicuous favor as a land grant to one of the odious Quakers. Such a gesture in trying times could cost the crown at least the goodwill and perhaps the support of the court party. Penn searched for a face-saving device for the king. He found it in the large sum of money the crown owed the admiral's estate for services and outright loans. It is hard to believe that Sir William had given to the crown with the idea of expecting repayment, or that Charles would have worried about paying such a debt. He had plenty of creditors about whom he did not worry. Penn's request that the debt be settled gave Charles public reason for the land grant; privately, he could tell the Privy Council that this arrangement offered an effective way to rid the realm of shiploads of disturbing citizens. William Penn many years later admitted that "the government at home was glad to be rid of us at so cheap a rate as a little parchment to be practiced in a desert three thousand

miles off. . . ." It has also been suggested that Charles hurried him on his
way to America to save Penn and his fellow worshipers from an impending royal purge of all dissidents. In 1681, less than nine months after
formally petitioning the king for a grant, Penn had received his charter.
No doubt the king himself and Lord Sunderland, a friend of Penn's
youth who was now secretary of state, did what they could to speed the
charter through the red tape.

The charter was skillfully devised to please those who might oppose
it. There was no mention of seeking a haven for the oppressed or conduct-
ing a holy experiment. The purposes, as stated in the preamble, were to
"enlarge our British empire," to increase British trade and commerce, and
to convert the Indians. Penn became absolute proprietor of an immense
tract of land, with full right to all the soil, except for the normal provisions on precious metals and two beaver skins payable at Windsor Castle
annually. There was no Bishop of Durham clause, but one was hardly
needed. Penn could initiate legislation and promulgate laws, though only
with the advice and consent of the freemen. The rent on all lands he
parceled out was reserved to him. He was granted the power to establish
judges and other legal officers, to pardon and abolish crimes—except
treason and murder—and to do whatever was necessary for the establishment of justice, provided it was not contrary to the laws of England.

Several limitations in the charter that had not existed in earlier proprietary grants indicated a maturing and tightening colonial policy. The
grant did not stretch from sea to sea but ended at five degrees (three
hundred miles) west of the eastern boundary. Pennsylvania was ordered
to pay strict obedience to the Navigation Acts. The proprietor had to
admit all royal officials to collect duties. The province was required to send
within five years transcripts of all laws for confirmation by the king. Penn
had to appoint an agent residing in London who would be available at all
times to represent the colony in any of the courts or before any royal or
Parliamentary commission. The proprietor was denied the power to wage
war, although he might create a militia for internal security and defense.
All this revealed a disposition on the part of Charles II and his advisers to
strengthen royal control over all parts of the empire, even the proprietaries.

Penn wanted to call his land New Wales because it was "pretty hilly
country," but a Welshman in authority refused to allow that. Penn then
proposed Sylvania (land of woods), "and they added Penn to it; and
though I much opposed it, and went to the king to have it struck out and
altered, he said it was past, and would not take it upon him; nor could
twenty guineas move the under secretary to vary the name. . . ." And so,
despite the attempted bribe and despite Penn's fear that "it should be
looked on as a vanity in men," the land came to be called Pennsylvania.

Plans for Settlement

Penn worked prodigiously to make sure his colony prospered from the start. While still in England, he arranged for land grants, laid plans for a city, searched the nation and Europe for settlers, and designed a framework to govern the people. He had a century of colonizing experience to draw on, and he made full use of it.

Agents in London, on the Continent, and in Wales, Ireland, and Scotland spread the word about Pennsylvania. Pamphlets written by Penn publicized the venture. Several of these were translated into French, Dutch, and German and helped make Pennsylvania the best-advertised colony in English history. Penn avoided rash claims for his province, a virtue uncommon in most promotion work of the time. Prospective settlers were told the journey would cost six pounds per head for masters and their wives, five pounds for each servant, and fifty shillings for each child under ten, suckling children traveling free. Each passenger could ship one chest free and additional freight at forty shillings per ton. Land was to be granted outright, except for a small quitrent "reserved for the security of the title."

Care was taken to encourage commerce. Friends already held the land of West Jersey that fronted on Delaware Bay. Fully to protect Pennsylvania's exit to the sea, Penn persuaded the Duke of York to turn over the territory along the bay's western edge in 1682, and these three lower counties, as Delaware was called throughout the colonial period, were hereafter considered part of Pennsylvania. That done, he gave thought to the location of the colony's main port, Philadelphia, a word meaning "brotherly love." He cautioned the surveyor to choose a site along the Delaware "where it is most navigable, high, dry, and healthy"; he then went on to say: "Be sure to settle the figure of the town so as that the streets hereafter may be uniform down to the water," and out of that demand grew the great checkerboard layout of Philadelphia. Streets parallel to the river were to be called, with Quaker simplicity, First, Second, etc., and those perpendicular to the river were named after trees— Pine, Spruce, Chestnut, etc. Recollections of congested London and of the disastrous great fire of his youth led him to add: "Let every house be placed . . . so there may be ground on each side for gardens or orchards or fields, that it may be a green country town, which will never be burnt and always be wholesome."

Towns need merchants to thrive, and Penn did his best to promote their coming. Every purchaser of five thousand acres received a lot in the "great town." The Free Society of Traders, a joint-stock company with £10,000 capital, was granted twenty thousand acres. The company planned among other things to erect "a glass house for [making] bottles, drinking glasses, and window glass, to plant and improve land and for cattle, to supply the Islands and continent of America, and we hope . . . it may come to be a famous company." (The society flourished only briefly, mainly because of bad management and local opposition to it as a monopoly.)

While these plans were afoot, Penn found time to map out a government for his colony. His first Frame of Government was issued in 1682 while he was still in England. The Frame he offered was not democratic but so designed "that the will of one man may not hinder the good of an whole country." The proprietor reserved the right for himself or the governor whom he chose to run the province to reject all legislation. A council elected by the freeholders—in other colonies the council was generally appointed by the governor—would be composed of seventy-two men "of most note for their wisdom, virtue, and ability." They would have exclusive right to initiate legislation, oversee all justice, appoint provincial officers, and through committees of their choice supervise the safety of the province, which meant keeping an eye on everything from trade to the manners and morals of the inhabitants. The elected assembly, to be limited to two hundred deputies, could impeach members, approve or reject bills submitted to it by the council, but do little more. Penn seems to have believed that the assembly had the right neither to amend nor debate legislation.

Penn assumed that the chief object of government was to terrify those who do evil and to cherish those who do good. He paid more attention to its moral character than to its form. "Governments, like clocks," goes the preamble to his Frame, "go from the motion men give them; and as governments are made and moved by men, so by them they are ruined too. Wherefore governments rather depend upon men, than men upon governments. Let men be good, and the government cannot be bad; if it be ill, they will cure it. . . ." He was a seventeenth-century constitutionalist, not an eighteenth-century philosopher. He contended for the rights of man from a historical and legal point of view, not from a rationalistic one. The rights he treasured—liberty of conscience, no taxation without the consent of the taxed, use of the ballot, protection of the individual from illegal arrest, trial by jury with verdicts binding on the judges, and the right of the assembly to make the laws—he saw as the historical rights of Englishmen.

Algernon Sidney, who had been consulted on the Frame, shared these views, as did James Harrington, whom Penn had read, and John Locke. Locke castigated Penn's Frame but only for its practical flaws and ambiguities. Where the Frame said that those who "spoke loosely and profanely" of God shall be punished, Locke wondered, "What is loosely and profanely?" The provision that the freemen should "meet in one place to choose their provincial council" Locke found "inconvenient." The discretionary power officials had to "take care of the peace and safety of the province" Locke objected to as "arbitrary power." He found the constitution as a whole "scarce contains a part of the materials" for a frame of government, and the people of Pennsylvania, much to Penn's sadness, were to agree. The "holy experiment" in Pennsylvania, as Locke might have predicted, suffered through more frames of government in its early years than any other colony.

Settlement

Penn soon discovered the hard way what every man who had engaged in colonization since Elizabeth's day had learned—it is one thing to plan a colony, another to settle it. Problems of planning kept Penn tied to England for a year; and not until October 1682, after a terrible voyage during which one-third the passengers died of smallpox, did he reach America. He landed first at New Castle, Delaware, where agents of the Duke of York in a fittingly feudal ceremony turned over the key to the fort and delivered "unto him one turf, with a twig upon it, a porringer with river water and soil." Penn moved on up Delaware Bay to disembark again at Upland (today Chester), Pennsylvania, where well-fed, prospering colonists met him. No one had endured a starving time, for settlers long in the area had supplied food until the first harvest. Some four thousand people, counting those there before the land became Penn's, inhabited the colony, and more "people were coming in fast."

After a hasty survey of what had been accomplished thus far, Penn traveled over to New York where Anthony Brockholls, the acting governor, inspected and improved his deed to the three lower counties, then returned to Upland, where the first assembly gathered on December 4. The delegates showed their familiarity with politics at home by adopting rules of order based on those used by Parliament. At this first three-day meeting an Act of Union was passed, bringing the lower counties to Pennsylvania under a common government; a petition to naturalize all Swedes, Finns, and Dutch in the area was approved; the body of forty laws in the Frame of Government was expanded to sixty-nine; and the vagaries of the Pennsylvania-Maryland boundary, which were to plague the colony for years to come, were discussed at length.

Both the assembly and the council left it up to Penn to deal with the Indians. He assured them of his friendship and promised to protect them. He took care to purchase their lands, but the vagueness of the Indian deeds—one conveyed all the land a man could cover on foot in a day and a half—left the door open for future misunderstandings. Penn's respect and fairness obviously contributed to early Pennsylvania's comfortable relations with the Indians, but it should be pointed out that the colony lacked a serious Indian problem at the time. The Delawares had been cowed for years by the Iroquois; they welcomed the white settlers as protectors against their ancient enemies.

Penn remained in the colony for two years. By the time he was ready to leave, some fifty ships had brought settlers from England, Wales, Ireland, Holland, and Germany. The Welsh had been enticed by a grant of thirty thousand acres, known as the Welsh Tract. The Germans came from the Rhineland district and were led by the learned Francis Daniel Pastorius, who staked out a claim north of Philadelphia that eventually became Germantown. (These early Germans were mostly Quakers and held little in common with most of the other German sects that flooded into the colony during the eighteenth century.) Pennsylvania's population had edged close to seven thousand, nearly a third of whom lived in Philadelphia. The city almost overnight challenged Boston's supremacy. Ships of the world came to her wharves. "There have been many horses sold of late to Barbados, and here is plenty of rum, sugar, ginger, and molasses," said a colonist, who went on to speak of other virtues offered: "Here are peaches in abundance of three sorts I have seen rot on the ground, and the hogs eat them; they make good spirits from them, also from corn and cherries, and a sort of wild plums and grapes, and most people have stills of copper for that use."

Little of the settlers' prosperity flowed into Penn's pockets. "Your friend and landlord," as Penn called himself in an address to the colonists, soon learned of the slim chance he had to make money out of Pennsylvania. Settlers grumbled at once at paying quitrents, slight as they were. "I hope," Penn wrote, "my half of my quitrents to supply me with bread will not be made a reason of rebellion by men in their wits that love their lives and estates." The colonists did not rebel, nor did they pay.

It is too bad that Penn could not be in two places at once. When physically at hand, he was able to preserve peace in Pennsylvania; he was much less able to provide the machinery to preserve peace in his absence. He left reluctantly for England in 1684, first to settle the Pennsylvania-Maryland boundary—he failed on this, and not until the crown ratified the Mason-Dixon Line in 1769 was the issue resolved—and second to aid Quakers still being harassed in England. He arrived home to find things "sour and stern," the king ruling without Parliament, and dissenters of all sects being persecuted worse than ever. Penn persuaded James II, with whom, for all his licentiousness, Penn still remained friendly, to release some thirteen hundred Quakers from jail in 1686.

Years passed, and while Penn watched from afar, dissension wracked his holy experiment. The assembly fought steadily to enlarge its powers. It wanted more than simply to approve or disapprove legislation handed down by the council. Over the council's objection it interpreted the word "advice" in the charter to mean the right to amend all bills "as it thought fit." The situation turned nasty in 1688 when the assembly met behind doors in secret session. The commissioners appointed by Penn to govern in his absence demanded prompt assent or dissent to the bills before it and nothing more. The assembly refused to accept a money bill drawn up by the council. Commons had recently won the right to initiate money bills and the assembly in Pennsylvania now sought the same privilege. "For the love of God, me, and the poor country," Penn wrote, "be not so governmentish; so noisy and open in your disaffection."

Penn pleaded that "virtue be cherished." He worried about "the number of drinking houses and looseness" in Philadelphia. Above all, he feared the loss of his charter. It appeared that he might quiet criticism at home and ease tension in the colony if he chose a non-Quaker as acting governor, and to that end he sent over Captain John Blackwell in 1688, "a grave, sober, wise man," Penn called him. He could have made no worse choice. The holy experiment seemed headed for disaster when the Glorious Revolution broke in America.

Not long after Penn had received his charter, the Lords of Trade and Plantations, a royal commission created in 1675 to oversee all colonies, announced: "We think it not convenient to constitute any new propriety in America nor to grant any further powers that may render the plantations less dependent on the crown." Authorities now saw that the proprietary colony worked against England and Englishmen and for only the proprietor's benefit. Colonists who lived in New York, the Jerseys, Carolina, and perhaps even Pennsylvania were deprived of rights enjoyed by their compatriots at home or in such colonies as Virginia, Connecticut, and Rhode Island. Also, the proprietary colony counteracted the crown's effort to impose the new imperialism uniformly on the empire. Officials in royal colonies could be made to enforce the trade laws much more effectively than administrators responsible only to their proprietors.

The Lords of Trade displayed its distaste for the proprietary colony almost immediately after its creation. New Hampshire was detached from Massachusetts and created a royal colony in 1679. Only pressure from the crown and Penn's willingness to accept restrictions that other proprietors had hitherto escaped won its reluctant approval of the Pennsylvania charter in 1681, the last such granted. Plans were formed to hedge the powers of all American proprietors, but over a decade passed before action was taken. A series of wars and insurrections on both sides of the Atlantic inhibited a reformation until 1696, and even then it was inaugurated quietly and with great caution.

BIBLIOGRAPHY

Carolina

General accounts are found in Charles M. Andrews, *The Colonial Period of American History*, Vol. III (4 vols., 1936–1938) ; and Wesley Frank Craven, *Southern Colonies in the Seventeenth Century* (1949). Edward McCrady's *The History of South Carolina Under the Proprietary Government, 1670– 1719* (1897) is, as Craven puts it so well, "a work which continues to serve as a principal reliance of all students of early Carolina history." David D. Wallace's *South Carolina: A Short History, 1520–1948* (1951) is a succinct version of the same author's more expansive *History of South Carolina* (3 vols., 1934).

Though no single volume details the seventeenth-century story of the northern part of the Carolina grant, a number of satisfactory works touch on it in varying degrees, among them: Samuel A. Ashe, *The History of North Carolina* (2 vols., 1908) ; R. D. Connor, *History of North Carolina: The Colonial and Revolutionary Periods* (1919) ; Hugh T. Lefler and A. Ray Newsome, *North Carolina: The History of a Southern State* (1954) ; and C. L. Raper, *North Carolina: A Study in English Colonial Government* (1904).

For the Carolina backcountry see Clarence W. Alvord and Lee Bidgood, *The First Explorations of the Trans-Allegheny Region by the Virginians, 1650–1674* (1912), which brought Abraham Wood into prominence for the first time; Verner W. Crane's *The Southern Frontier, 1670–1732* (1928; pb.), particularly the early chapters; and Robert L. Meriwether, *The Expansion of South Carolina, 1729–1765* (1940). Lefler's *North Carolina History Told by Contemporaries* (1934) can be supplemented by A. B. Salley, ed., *Narratives of Early Carolina, 1650–1708* (1911). The old *Colonial Records of North Carolina* (10 vols., 1886–1890) is being superseded by a new series, whose first volume, *North Carolina Charters and Constitutions, 1578–1698*, was issued in 1963.

New York

Edward Channing's relevant chapters in *The History of the United States*, Vols. I and II (6 vols., 1905–1925) and Andrews' in Vol. III, *Colonial Period*, offer authoritative introductory discussions. Wertenbaker's *The Founding of American Civilization: The Middle Colonies* (1938; pb.) gives a convenient summary of the Dutch in New York and elsewhere in America with emphasis on their contributions to the American heritage. The most entertaining brief account is Dixon Ryan Fox's *Yankees and Yorkers* (1940), though only the early chapters are relevant here. The standard work is A. C. Flick, ed., *History of the State of New York* (10 vols., 1933–1937), whose chapters are written by specialists on the social, intellectual, and political life of the colony. Flick's volumes have been supplemented but not replaced by the recent *A Short History of New York State* (1957) by David M. Ellis, *et al.*

Henry Kessler and Eugene Rachlis have most recently told the story of *Peter Stuyvesant and His New York* (1959) well and accurately. Other works worth consulting are Maud W. Goodwin, *Dutch and English on the Hudson* (1919); W. R. Shepherd, *The Story of New Amsterdam* (1926); and J. H. Innes, *New Amsterdam and Its People* (1902). Two specialized articles are Victor H. Paltsits, "The Founding of New Amsterdam in 1626," *American Antiquarian Society Proceedings*, 34 (1924), 39–65; and Albert E. McKinley, "The English and Dutch Towns of New Netherland," *AHR*, 6 (1900), 1–18. A full account of a little-investigated subject is Morton Pennypacker, *The Duke's Laws: Their Antecedents, Implications, and Importance* (1944). The laws themselves are found in *The Colonial Laws of New York*, Vol. I, pp. 5–100 (1894). David S. Lovejoy's "Equality and Empire: The New York Charter of Liberties, 1683," *WMQ*, 21 (1964), 493–515 finds New Yorkers seeking equality within the empire long before they rose up in the eighteenth century. J. F. Jameson offers a collection of readings in *Narratives of New Netherland* (1909). The fullest compilation of early records is found in Edward B. O'Callaghan and Berthold Fernow, eds., *Documents Relative to the Colonial History of the State of New York* (15 vols., 1856–1887).

New Jersey

The story of the Dutch and others in the Delaware Valley is well told in two volumes by Christopher Ward—*Dutch and Swedes on the Delaware, 1609–1664* (1930) and *New Sweden on the Delaware* (1938)—and more exhaustively in Amandus Johnson, *Swedish Settlements on the Delaware, 1638–1664* (2 vols., 1911). Albert C. Myers presents the story through contemporary documents in *Narratives of Early Pennsylvania, West New Jersey, and Delaware* (1912). A new and fuller volume of documents that concentrates on the Dutch story is C. A. Weslager and A. R. Dunlap, *Dutch Explorers, Traders, and Settlers in the Delaware Valley, 1609–1664* (1962). The two fullest accounts of the New Jersey story are both by John E. Pomfret— *The Province of West New Jersey, 1609–1702: A History of the Origins of an American Colony* (1956) and *The Province of East New Jersey 1609–1702: The Rebellious Proprietary* (1962). The narrative in Samuel Smith's *History of the Colony of Nova Caesaria, or New Jersey* (1765), is often wrong-headed and more often plain wrong, but the abundance of documents difficult to find elsewhere help to overcome this deficiency. Edwin P. Tanner, *The Province of New Jersey, 1664–1738* (1908), is a reliable work whose early chapters relate to this period. A monograph for those interested in the subject is Austin Scott, *Influence of the Proprietors in the Founding of New Jersey* (1885). The fullest collection of documentary material illuminating the early years for both East and West Jersey is found in the first volume of the *Archives of the State of New Jersey, 1631–1800* (30 vols., 1880–1906).

The New Jersey Tercentenary Commission is in the process of issuing a series of brief volumes written for popular consumption by authorities on the colonial period. Among those that are relevant here are Julian P. Boyd, *Fundamental Laws and Constitutions of New Jersey* (1964) ; Wesley Frank Craven, *New Jersey and the English Colonization of North America* (1964) ; Adrian C. Leiby, *The Early Dutch and Swedish Settlers of New Jersey* (1964) ; and John E. Pomfret, *The New Jersey Proprietors and Their Lands* (1964).

Pennsylvania

Again, both Channing's *History of the United States* and Andrews' *Colonial Period* present first-rate introductory statements of the material covered here. Among the satisfactory general histories of early Pennsylvania are W. F. Dunaway, *A History of Pennsylvania* (1948) ; Paul A. W. Wallace, *Pennsylvania: Seed of a Nation* (1962) ; two, more detailed, volumes by Sydney G. Fisher— *The Making of Pennsylvania* (1896) and *The Quaker Colonies* (1919)—and a volume by Rufus M. Jones, himself a Quaker, entitled *The Quakers in the American Colonies* (1911). Still more detailed but by far the best modern work on the early years is Edwin B. Bronner, *William Penn's "Holy Experiment": The Founding of Pennsylvania, 1681–1701* (1962). Frederick B. Tolles, *Meeting House and Counting House: Quaker Merchants of Colonial Philadelphia* (1948; pb.), deals ably but briefly with this part of the province's story. Tolles's *Quakers and the Atlantic Culture* (1960) is a collection of several excellent, sometimes eloquent, essays that should not be missed. The complexities of William Penn's character have thus far proved too much for his biographers. Four of the more adequate studies are those by William W. Comfort (1944), Bonamy Dobrée (1932), William I. Hull (1937), and Catherine Owens Peare (1957). The fourth number in Vol. 68 (1944), 339– 429 of the *Pennsylvania Magazine of History and Biography (PMHB),* is devoted entirely to articles on Penn. Myers' *Narratives* offers the best collection of readings on early Pennsylvania, and the well-edited anthology by Tolles and E. Gordon Alderfer, *The Witness of William Penn* (1957), is, for all its brevity, an excellent selection of Penn's writings. The elaborate index to the first seventy-five volumes of the *PMHB* and the indexes to individual volumes thereafter are crammed with hundreds of references to Penn and the early years of Pennsylvania.

For further references see the *Harvard Guide,* Sections 93, "New York"; 94, "The Carolinas"; and 95, "New Jersey, Pennsylvania, and Delaware."

STRANGE NEWS

FROM

VIRGINIA;

Being a full and true

ACCOUNT

OF THE

LIFE and DEATH

OF

Nathanael Bacon Esquire,

Who was the only Cause and Original of all the late
Troubles in that COUNTRY.

With a full Relation of all the Accidents which have
happened in the late War there between the
Christians and Indians.

LONDON,

Printed for *William Harris*, next door to the Turn-
Stile without *Moor-gate.* 1677.

Title page from *Strange News from Virginia*

7. Wars and Insurrections: 1675–1690

THE FIRST ROUND OF OUTBURSTS
Bacon's Rebellion
Maryland and Carolina
King Philip's War

THE DOMINION OF NEW ENGLAND
Edward Randolph
The Crown Takes Over
Sir Edmund Andros

THE GLORIOUS REVOLUTION IN AMERICA
New England
The Middle Colonies
The South

The year 1675 opened an era of anarchy in the American colonies that ended only with the century. Ostensibly, Indians caused the trouble; actually, the source lay deeper. The hivings-out from Massachusetts that began with Roger Williams' expulsion in 1635 and the thrusting-out of Governor Harvey from Virginia in the same year revealed a common discontent among settlers wherever they lived on the American continent. Authorities managed to contain but not to resolve the discontent during the next forty years. It finally burst forth with Bacon's Rebellion in Virginia, and dissension infested the colonies from then until a calm settled upon the land after the Glorious Revolution.

THE FIRST ROUND OF OUTBURSTS

The Indians intensified the settlers' difficulty in adjusting to their new surroundings. Any trouble with the red man, no matter how localized, unsettled a whole colony, for the Indian problem was inextricably entwined with all sides of American life. Though men of ability and compassion in every colony made sincere and to some degree effective efforts to deal fairly with the Indian, they failed, partly because the Indian resisted being made over in the white man's image and partly because any plan for humane treatment inevitably conflicted with some segment of colonial interests. Bacon's Rebellion in Virginia, upheavals in Maryland and Carolina, and King Philip's War in New England were united by a common failure to resolve the tensions between white and red men.

Bacon's Rebellion

Virginians had much to disturb them in 1675. There was, according to an historian of the day, "the extreme low price of tobacco, and the ill usage of the planters in the exchange of goods for it." The huge tax-exempt grants given to Lords Arlington and Culpeper in 1673 had deprived the colony of revenues and increased the tax burden on all settlers. The need for money to fight the Dutch, to build blockhouses against the Indians, to pay for agents in England, and to build courthouses had led to new and irritating boosts in the tax rate. Trade restraints created by the Navigation Acts, particularly the Plantation Duty Act of 1673, added to the economic grievances.

Political grievances had multiplied since the Restoration, when control of both local and provincial affairs flowed into the hands of Governor Berkeley and a clique of friends. The House of Burgesses presented slight challenge to this oligarchy. The complexion of the house had changed little in more than a decade, for the governor had sidestepped new elections by proroguing the house from session to session so that legally it sat steadily, as the Long Parliament had. It had become, in effect, a closed corporation, rather than a representative body. The house, on Berkeley's bidding, had in 1670 limited the vote in provincial elections to freeholders —those who owned at least a headright of land—depriving freemen and householders of their franchise on the ground that only those who had a fair-sized stake in society should share in government.

These political grievances should not be used to create an inaccurate picture of the rebellion of 1676. That uprising has often been reviewed as a conflict between the common people and an entrenched elite. Certainly the landless freeman, the ordinary planter, had much to complain about and hoped Bacon would settle his grievances; but a glance at the leaders of the rebellion, nearly all of them substantial planters, suggests that at the top level this was a conflict between two factions of the elite. Bacon may have attracted "the scum of the country," as an opponent said, but he also won over the elite—men like William Byrd, Sr.; William Drummond, "a sober Scotch gentleman of good repute"; and Richard Lawrence, an Oxonian, "nicely honest, affable and without blemish in his conversation and dealings."

An issue that divided the elite of both Maryland and Virginia was that of expansion into the backcountry. Berkeley had tried, after the massacre of 1644, to block expansion by erecting a line of forts to separate lands reserved for whites and those for Indians. His policy was an honest attempt to resolve a difficult problem, but because it favored those who had already carved their farms from the wilderness, newcomers railed against it. Berkeley, under pressure, opened new lands for settlement. But his policy of orderly, controlled expansion might have worked, except for factors beyond his control.

Berkeley in 1671 believed the Indians on Virginia's borders "absolutely subjected, so that there is no fear of them." He seemed unaware that any local Indian problem had continental associations. The outbreak that came in 1675 was part of a chain reaction begun in distant Canada by the French, who were usurping much of the western fur trade once controlled by the Senecas. The Senecas, in search of new fur sources, pushed southward into Susquehannock territory. Meanwhile, Maryland edged into lands the Susquehannocks held at the head of Chesapeake Bay. Pressed from two sides, the Susquehannocks fell back to the Potomac River, and into the territory of the Doeg Indians on Virginia's borders. A shortage of food in this crowded (by Indian terms) area, forced the Susquehannocks to forage across Berkeley's latest demarcation line into white territory. A clash of some sort had soon to occur.

One Sunday morning in July 1675, a family bound for church came upon the bleeding body of a planter's overseer. The man lived long enough to say that Indians had inflicted his wounds. Reprisals were exacted on a band of innocent Doegs, who now, in turn, sought revenge. By January every inhabitant of the fall-line country lived in terror. One cold morning marauding Indians killed the overseer of a young, wealthy farmer named Nathaniel Bacon. Soon after, Governor Berkeley ordered out the militia, then remanded the order on receiving word that the Indians wished to halt reprisals and talk of peace. But Berkeley had been misinformed. Assaults continued along the undefended frontier and by March, when the assembly convened, over three hundred Virginians had been slaughtered.

The assembly, intimidated by Berkeley, spoke softly. It decided that because Virginia faced "an enemy whose retirements are not easily discovered," a defensive war seemed the sanest policy. The militia would patrol the frontier from blockhouses, and would not be allowed to attack any Indians until they had been assaulted first. Berkeley forced this policy on the assembly in the hope that the colony could avoid a general war, which would add to the colony's already heavy tax burden and disrupt trade lines into the backcountry. The governor and many of his friends were heavily involved in the Indian trade, which led Bacon to remark that the province's leaders were willing to "buy and sell our blood" to protect their purses.

The forts did little good. The Indians found which "mouse traps were set," avoided them, and struck at unprotected spots. Settlers near the frontier pleaded for an expeditionary force, but Berkeley called those who urged attack "fools and loggerheads" and threatened with severe punishment any who undertook aggressive action. At this point planters along the frontier determined to take affairs in their own hands. Three hundred volunteers under the leadership of Nathaniel Bacon marched into the wilderness in April 1676.

A contemporary who disliked Bacon found him "young, bold, active, of an inviting aspect, and powerful elocution." He had graduated from Cambridge, toured the Continent, studied law at Gray's Inn—one of the Inns of Court, where barristers were educated—married well, and lost a fortune—all by his twenty-sixth birthday. His father agreed to stake him to a new start in Virginia, where his cousin Nathaniel Bacon, Sr., once a resident of an English debtors' prison, had already acquired prestige and power. The parental gift of £1,800 purchased a fine farm already cleared of forest, and family ties won the young man a seat at once on the governor's council. "Gentlemen of your quality come very rarely into this country," Berkeley had said, "and therefore when they do come are used by me with all respect." Less than two years later the mercurial young Bacon and the seventy-year-old governor were implacable enemies.

News of Bacon's defiance led Berkeley to oust him from the council and to declare him and the volunteers "rebels and mutineers." He sent three hundred men to halt the expedition, but Bacon eluded the pursuers and vanished into the forest. In his absence, Berkeley made a bid for support by calling for a new election of burgesses, the first general election to be held in fourteen years. He ignored the restrictions of the 1670 law and extended the franchise to all freemen. He also issued in May a Declaration and Remonstrance, wherein he called Bacon's expedition "a dishonor to the English nation." Bacon returned shortly before the election with news that his men had slain some 150 Indians. He learned about the election and also that the governor had removed him from the council. Bacon answered the rebuff by standing for the House of Burgesses. He won in a landslide.

In June Bacon left for Jamestown for the assembly's session. He traveled with a bodyguard of forty men, but they failed to prevent his capture by the governor's forces. "Now, I behold the greatest rebel that ever was in Virginia," Berkeley said when he confronted his rival. He could do little more than fume; he dared not hang this "darling of the people." Bacon feigned remorsefulness, as one report puts it, and a reconciliation was worked out. The governor pardoned Bacon, promised him a commission to go against the Indians, and restored him to the council. Privately, Berkeley admitted that he returned Bacon to the council to appease the people and at the same time to keep their hero out of the House of Burgesses, where he might have provoked more trouble.

The house convened on June 5. The governor told the burgesses "to meddle with nothing" until they had resolved the Indian problem, and they did as demanded. Bacon, still waiting in Jamestown for a commission to fight the Indians, soon became convinced that the governor was dallying until the opportune moment to murder him. Bacon thereupon left Jamestown surreptitiously and in the backcountry rounded up a band of one hundred armed men. On June 23 he returned to the capital, and with a small army at his back, once again confronted the governor. The old man reacted dramatically to the ploy. "Here! Shoot me," he shouted, "before God, fair mark, shoot!" and made as if to draw his sword. Bacon answered that he "came not, nor intend to hurt a hair of your honor's head," that he sought only a commission to go "against the heathen who daily inhumanely murder us and spill our brethren's blood." He ended shouting at Berkeley: "God damn my blood, I came for a commission, and a commission I will have before I go." The burgesses had watched the scene from nearby windows. One now said: "For God's sake hold your hands and forbear a little, and you shall have what you please." The next day, June 24, Bacon and his men marched away with a commission to deal with the Indians.

Bacon's boldness invigorated the burgesses, and during the last three days of their session (June 23–25), they became a reforming body that sought to settle grievances that had accumulated during the past decade. Most of their attention went to local government, which in recent years had atrophied under the governor's and his friends' aggrandizing rule. Among Bacon's Laws, as the assembly's reforming measures were called, one forbade a man to hold the job of sheriff two years in succession. Another outlawed pluralism on the local level; a man could now hold only one post at a time. County courts received the power to appoint their own clerks. Freemen were once again allowed to vote for burgesses. The vestry, which had long been a self-perpetuating, closed corporation, had to be elected once every three years. County courts, rather than the governor, could appoint collectors for local levies; justices of the court, together with an equal number of locally elected citizens, determined what the levies should be. Members of the governor's council were forbidden to sit with the county courts. The governor's signature was no longer required on probates. Finally, the assembly repealed the law that had exempted councillors from paying taxes. "Now," said a supporter of Berkeley, "tag, rag, and bobtail carry a high hand." More to the point, the assembly sought to break the governor's hold on local government.

Not long after the assembly had completed its three busy days, Bacon made ready to march against the Indians. He had collected an army of thirteen hundred men. All had taken an oath of allegiance to the king and were prepared to set off for the forests when word arrived that Berkeley for some still unaccountable reason had, the moment the assembly disbanded, again declared Bacon and his followers rebels against the king's authority. What up to now had been mainly a sectional dispute over how best to deal with the Indians swung into a real rebellion. Bacon's army turned back from the wilderness and in late July headed for Jamestown. The governor decamped across the bay to the eastern shore, and Bacon took charge of provincial affairs. Momentarily, Bacon appeared to lose control of himself. For he talked of independence—not only from Berkeley but from the crown, too. "Your followers," one of his lieutenants, John Goode, warned, "do not think themselves engaged against the king's authority, but merely against the Indians."

Bacon took the hint and headed out again after Indians. Berkeley used Bacon's absence to reoccupy Jamestown. Bacon, though near exhaustion, hurried out of the wilderness and marched toward Jamestown once more, "the people on the highways coming forth praying for his happiness and railing against the governor and his party." He took the town again, then burned it to prevent Berkeley from using it as a base. The civil war seemed near an end; Bacon's forces ruled the colony. At the moment of apparent victory, Bacon was struck with dysentery. He died on October 26, and the force of the rebellion died with him. By the end of 1676 Berkeley once again controlled all Virginia. ("Indeed," Wesley Frank Craven remarks, "one of the most impressive facts of the whole rebellion, which at times takes on a character close to that of a comic opera, is the fact that Sir William, for all his faults and the grievous complaints of the people, was able to reassert his authority without assistance from England.")

Meanwhile, Charles II had learned of Virginia's troubles and reacted by dispatching a fleet of eleven ships with a thousand troops to quell the rebellion. He also sent over a commission of three men—one of them to replace Berkeley as governor—with orders to deal tolerantly with the rebels and to investigate their grievances. Berkeley treated the commissioners with contempt. He refused to answer their questions, accept his replacement, or treat the rebels fairly. ("Mr. Drummond, you are welcome," he had remarked when William Drummond, one of Bacon's lieutenants, had been brought to him. "I am more glad to see you than any man in Virginia. Mr. Drummond, you shall be hanged in half an hour." Drummond had answered, "As your honor pleases," and died four hours later.) A new assembly under the governor's thumb revoked most of Bacon's Laws, passed acts inflicting severe punishment on all rebels, and confiscated property by bills of attainder. Having tidied up Virginia affairs to his satisfaction, Berkeley set out for England in May 1677 to defend his actions before the king. He died shortly after stepping ashore in London.

The rebellion left its mark on Virginia. The crown's swift reaction showed the colonists that the mother country would now back words with action. The new imperialism, hitherto expressed only in the Navigation Acts, was to be implemented by direct supervision of American affairs. The rebellion, too, settled once and for all Virginia's Indian problem. A new plan was adopted to deal with the natives, a modification of Berkeley's blockhouse system. Patrols of scouts would rove the frontier to keep the colony posted on all untoward movements. Defensive maneuvers were out; any hint of an uprising would be dealt with by direct and aggressive action. The scheme worked. Within a few decades the on-pressing settlers had pushed the natives across the mountains, and Indian wars had become something only old-timers reminisced about.

The rebellion left less of a mark on Virginia's government, mainly because the rebels had not sought to make basic changes. They desired principally to shift political power from the central government back to the counties, where it had been before Berkeley came to power. They wanted to reinvigorate local government and restrict the governor's power. Under Sir Henry Chicheley, who became governor in 1678, several of the Bacon Laws were reenacted. The benign "very old, sickly" Chicheley, however, soon left, to be replaced by the tyrannical Lord Culpeper. But even without Culpeper the governor would have continued to dominate Virginia affairs, for the crown was learning that the best way to impose its new imperialism upon the people was to shore up the governor's powers at the expense of local government.

And what about Nathaniel Bacon? What mark did he leave upon Virginia? Let Professor Craven's judgment serve as his epitaph.

If he did not succeed in destroying the special privilege of a governing class, he succeeded in underscoring for a group to which he himself belonged, the responsibility which properly goes with privilege. His very name, celebrated in verse and song down through the years, was destined to correct abuses in a system of government from which the nation, through Washington, Jefferson, Madison, and others would draw great advantage.

Maryland and Carolina

Virginia's assembly in April 1677 declared that "if Maryland and Carolina had been both subordinate to the king there had been little or no need of sending forces from England upon this late unhappy occasion." The assembly was right to the extent that settlers in both colonies encouraged and were encouraged by Bacon's successes, for they shared all Virginia's problems—taxes and quitrents they considered burdensome, the currently low price on tobacco, an oligarchy in control of political affairs, marauding Indians on their frontiers—plus one of their own, proprietary rule.

Lord Baltimore's insistence on absolute control of Maryland politics had not abated with time. His grant to the assembly of the right to initiate legislation only briefly appeased that body, for while giving with one hand he took with the other. He had followed Virginia's lead in 1670 and limited the right to vote to freeholders only, then tried to make the assembly more manageable by reducing each county's deputies from four to two.

Dissension occurred in Maryland, as in Virginia, between two wings of the elite, those in power against those out; but in Maryland, religion rather than Indians determined the lines of division. Baltimore's Catholicism still embroiled Maryland affairs, and in the 1670's, as reports of a Catholic conspiracy against the crown drifted in from England, all other dissatisfactions were buried in the religious issue. Protestants grumbled again about the predominance of Catholics in the government and especially on the powerful council. The Protestant majority in the lower house bickered steadily with the upper house, and every problem, whether taxes, Indians, or quitrents, eventually became entwined with the religious issue. The disputes spilled out from the assembly into the countryside. In September 1676, the month Bacon leveled Jamestown, William Davyes and John Pate led an ineffectual mob against the government. The affair amounted to little, but the news from Virginia caused Maryland authorities to react strongly. Both Davyes and Pate were hanged. Discontent simmered quietly until 1681, when Josias Fendall and John Coode—pronounced, as contemporaries often spelled it, "Code"—led another protest movement. Both men were arrested on the charge of sedition and accused of saying that the "papists and Indians were joined together" to crush Maryland Protestants. Both men were banished, but Coode returned to lead a more successful outbreak at the time of the Glorious Revolution.

Success came earlier and easier to the colonists in northern Carolina. There, in Albemarle County, settlers appeared to divide over the issue of proprietary rule. The faction led by George Durant, whose plantation

antedated the proprietors' charter, complained about quitrents, the plantation duty that the proprietors sought to enforce in order to please the
crown, and the general conduct of political affairs by those in power.
Bacon's Rebellion increased the general uneasiness; the Albemarle settlements lay mainly along the "backside of Virginia," and many of Bacon's
supporters, among them a planter named John Culpeper, fled to Carolina
when Berkeley retrieved power. The uneasiness developed into Culpeper's
Rebellion in 1677 with the reappearance in Albemarle of Thomas Miller—
who, after an earlier tilt with the dissidents, had fled to England, told his
story to the proprietors, and then headed back to the colony with the
appointment of customs collector in his pocket. The newly appointed
governor, Thomas Eastchurch, traveled along. While the charms of a lady
detained Eastchurch in the West Indies, Miller went on to Albemarle
with orders to serve as the governor's temporary stand-in. Miller quickly
stirred up a storm by arresting George Durant on a flimsy charge. Farmers
from all parts of the county flocked to Durant's aid, and within a few
weeks a revolutionary government had been inaugurated. Miller was
jailed, and John Culpeper assumed the post of customs collector.

Once in power, however, the Culpeper-Durant faction showed no
antipathy toward proprietary rule. In 1680 Culpeper confidently traveled
to England to justify the rebellion to the proprietors. He was tried for
treason, but the intervention of the proprietors, notably Shaftesbury, who
saw that order had returned to the colony, led to his acquittal. The dissidents were allowed to remain in power because they were obviously, as
Charles Andrews says, "the most representative group of the planters in
Albemarle and the only one that could be trusted with the colony's well
being."

King Philip's War

Governor Berkeley blamed Virginia's Indian troubles on New England.
He sensed that more than local conditions had stirred up the natives on
Virginia's borders, but to trace their restlessness back to New England
went too far. The outbreaks in 1675 in Virginia and New England were
connected by a common enemy, the Indian, and by a common cause, the
spread of colonists inland. Some fifty thousand settlers had flooded into
the northern colonies by 1675, sweeping the Indians from their path as
they pushed up the streams and valleys. But the effects of this expansion
did not spill beyond New England's borders. The Algonquins' retreat was
blocked on the west by the Appalachian Mountains and by the hostile
Iroquois. These barriers localized and intensified the Indians' smoldering
hatred, which, when it burst forth, came close to consuming all New
England.

Map 22. King Philip's War, 1675-76

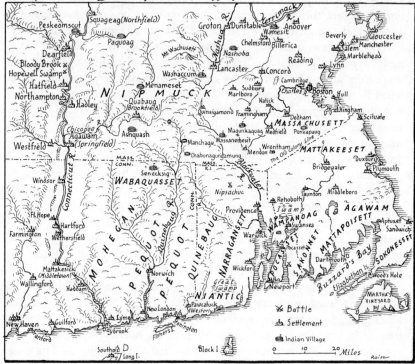

Tension between whites and natives had been contained for nearly forty years. Recollections of the Pequots' annihilation in 1637 helped restrain any fervor for war among the Indians. The missionary work of men like Roger Williams, Thomas Mayhew, and John Eliot also did something to alleviate the strain. Some four thousand converted, or "praying," Indians had come to live in the Puritan communities, adopting the white man's ways and all but severing their ties with the wilderness. The unconverted, who still roamed the forests, grumbled as settlers trampled through their game preserves; but they held their fire, for they, too, were tied to civilization. They bought blankets, kettles, trinkets, and "fire water" from traders, and the gun had replaced the bow as their means of livelihood.

These restraints might have forestalled an uprising if the Puritans had suppressed their contempt for Indians. Cotton Mather called them "pernicious creatures," and his views reflected those of most New Englanders. Indians were forced to obey Puritan laws and live by Puritan standards. They were punished if they hunted or fished on Sunday, jailed if they stole, fined if they became drunk on alcohol sold to them by white men. The laws were harsher than the men who enforced them, and they were balanced by other laws that protected Indian rights, but their very existence was bound to irritate and anger the proud redman.

Metacomet—King Philip to the Puritans—was such an Indian. He was the son of Massasoit, the great sachem who had befriended the Pilgrims. Philip lacked his father's dignity and character. He was weak, deceitful, and vain enough to have his clothes made by a Boston tailor, but he was also the sachem of the Wampanoags. Plymouth, which in 1621 had humbly sent a delegation to entreat with Massasoit, in 1671 sent soldiers to arrest Philip on charges of plotting against the colony. He was sentenced to pay a heavy fine, forced to admit that he and his people were subject to English law, and ordered to deposit his people's guns with the Plymouth court, which considered the weapons "justly forfeit" and divided them among the towns of the colony.

Philip no doubt at once began to think of ways to avenge this humiliation, but when war came in 1675, he found himself hurrying after his warriors in order that he might lead them. A group of Wampanoags had without Philip's permission murdered a family of settlers at Swansea, Massachusetts, in late June. Boston and Plymouth mustered five companies of men and marched after the Indians. All New England backed the repressive measures officially, though privately it was agreed that Plymouth's harshness toward Philip and his people had provoked the slaughter.

Philip's warriors enticed their pursuers into a swamp. The Puritans found "it is ill fighting with a wild beast in his own den," and the Indians slipped away with little trouble. Massachusetts troops had, meanwhile, traveled into Narragansett territory with orders to "make peace with a sword in their hand." The desire for unsettled land prompted this move; a Bostonian remarked a few days after this venture began that the territory "already gained is worth £10,000." This foray provoked the most powerful and, up to now, peaceful tribe in New England. Philip, who began the war unprepared and without allies, now had the Narragansetts on his side. Soon the Nipmucks joined in. A private grievance between Philip and Plymouth had become the cause of all New England's Indians.

The war spread swiftly from the Atlantic coast up the Connecticut Valley, and Puritan contempt for the Indian now bore bitter fruit. "We were too ready to think that we could easily suppress that flea," John Eliot said, "but now we find that all the craft is in catching them, and that in the meanwhile they give us many a sore nip." By the end of the summer the Connecticut-Massachusetts frontier was in flames, and all but five villages had been abandoned. The Indians outmaneuvered the colonists at every turn. They attacked during Sunday meeting. They feinted toward Hadley, and when the Springfield militia responded to the call for help, they slipped in and burned Springfield. And so it went through the summer and fall of 1675.

Massachusetts set out again after the Narragansetts in the early winter of 1675, promising her soldiers that if they "played the man" they would be rewarded with allotments of Narragansett land in addition to their pay. In the great swamp fight of mid-December, the Narragansetts lost between two and three hundred men, women, and children, but bickering among colonial leaders allowed the main body to escape. The Indians kept up their attacks through the winter until by April 1676 they had penetrated to the village of Sudbury, only seventeen miles from Boston, the heart of New England civilization. If the Indians at this point could have united under one leader, they might have pushed the Puritans into the sea. As it was, they came close.

The desperate situation led to a draft law that made every male inhabitant between sixteen and sixty liable to military service. Massachusetts fixed the death penalty for those who refused to serve, whereas Connecticut forbade emigration of the able-bodied. Men sought to evade service by "skulking from one town to another." Refugees streaming in from the frontier became another problem. They had been welcomed at first, but the greetings vanished as all inland New England sought to crowd into the coastal towns. The scarcity of food and housing led to profiteering. Towns began to fuss about who should bear responsibility for the welfare of those made widows and orphans by the war.

The clergy stepped up its exhortations as the war continued. Five years earlier God had punished New England for its sins with sickness, poor crops, and shipping losses. Now He had inflicted a terrible war upon the people. Days of public fasting and prayer were ordered. Men were told to cease swearing and women to shed ostentatious clothing and dress plainly. Ministers searched wide for the sins that had angered God, but only Peter Folger, a friend of the Indians, saw that "the sin of persecution" had provoked the enemy.

Time rather than prayers saved New England. While Boston's ships drew on other colonies for food and supplies, hunger, disease, battle losses, and divided councils were eroding Indian strength. The Indians had received no aid from the French, except on the Maine frontier, where they were supplied with ammunition and arms. The whites outnumbered the natives four to one, and this had begun to tell by the spring of 1676. But the main cause of defeat was the lack of food reserves. The Indians were facing starvation when the winter snows melted, and the necessity for food forced them to break off fighting. The death of Philip, shot by one of the "praying" Indians, whom Massachusetts had refused to make use of until affairs became desperate, brought the war officially to an end. Peace treaties were signed with the tribes of southern New England, but those to the north continued to raid the settlements of New Hampshire and Maine until 1678.

"In proportion to population, King Philip's War inflicted greater casualties upon the people than any other war in our history," Douglas Edward Leach has said. At least thirteen frontier villages were totally destroyed and six others partially burned. A tenth of Massachusetts' five thousand males of military age had been captured or killed. New England commerce had been disrupted for over a year. The colonies estimated the total cost around £100,000, a sum greater than the personal property of all New England's inhabitants. The war had cost the Indians heavily in lives, too, and peace did not bring much relief. Leaders were executed by the New Englanders, and warriors by the score were shipped as slaves to the West Indies. But no tribe had been annihilated in the war. Those natives that survived, their hate intact, would, under French encouragement, rise within the decade to lay waste again to New England's frontier villages.

The war killed, along with men, the long-dying Confederation of New England. The conquest of New Netherland in 1664 had removed one of the hostile neighbors who had made the union necessary. With the Restoration, the crown's resumption of control over foreign affairs had deprived the confederation of another reason for being. It had failed in every emergency to produce cooperation among the colonies, and by 1675 each colony fended for itself with little concern for its neighbor's welfare. Connecticut and Massachusetts had joined during King Philip's War, but they did little together except denounce Governor Andros of New York, who had refused their request to bring the Mohawks in against the New England Indians and whom they suspected of selling powder to the natives. After the war, Massachusetts still had the Maine Indians to contend with, but neither Plymouth nor Connecticut could or would lend a hand.

By 1676 New England had developed a distaste for any plan of union. That, blended with the leaders' dislike for Sir Edmund Andros, weakened any chance of success for an experiment in union that the crown was about to impose on New England.

THE DOMINION OF NEW ENGLAND

A special committee of the Privy Council, the Lords of Trade and Plantations, had been created in 1675 to enforce the acts of trade and unify the administration of the empire. One of its goals was to revise and

extend the pattern of royal government in America. The committee resisted the idea of proprietary grants and did its best to convince Charles
II that they weakened royal power. It failed, as has been seen, to prevent
the grant of Pennsylvania but succeeded in denying Penn some of the
extensive powers held by Lord Baltimore. A year later, in 1682, the Lords
of Trade refused to sanction the creation of a proprietary colony in the
Florida area because it was unwise "to constitute any new proprietaries
in America or to grant any further powers that may render the plantations less dependent on the crown," and the king accepted the decision.

The Lords of Trade studied all the colonies with an eye to strengthening royal control over their affairs, but those in New England received
particular attention. There, the board heard, smuggling had become a big
business. Such merchants as Phillippe L'Anglois, who came to Salem
around 1665 and changed his name to Philip English, were making fortunes out of an illicit trade with France. English merchants complained
about lost business and the commissioners of customs fumed about lost
revenues—as much as £60,000 annually in cloth imports alone, according
to one estimate. The Lords of Trade thought New England's subordination to the home country was not all it should be, and in 1676 an order
went out that Massachusetts must send an agent to England within six
months to answer charges. Meanwhile, the lords dispatched their own
man to make a firsthand report on the state of affairs in Massachusetts.
They chose Edward Randolph.

Edward Randolph

Historians and contemporaries agree that Edward Randolph was ambitious and intelligent. They agree on little else. Some view him as an able,
forthright, and honest public servant, others as a man whose lack of tact,
greed for money, and urge for power were excelled by none who visited
seventeenth-century America. Randolph provoked harsh remarks from
the gentle William Penn. "He is the scandal of the government . . . as
arbitrary a villain as lives," Penn wrote, adding: "His name and a lie
goes for the same thing a thousand miles upon the continent of America."
On the other hand, he has been called an "unswerving, tireless civil
servant" by his latest biographer, Michael Garibaldi Hall. "Randolph
generated from his own activities a new concept of what London's colonial
policy could be," Hall writes. "Between 1679 and 1684 he stood alone in
New England, challenged the Massachusetts republic and defeated it."

Randolph reached Massachusetts in the summer of 1676, as the colony
was recovering from King Philip's War. He received a cool reception.
When he asked Governor John Leverett to justify Massachusetts' control
over New Hampshire, he heard that the claims to the territory descend-

ing from the Council for New England's charter were based on "imperti-
nences, mistakes, and falsehoods." The governor said that he would take
under advisement the royal demand that an agent be sent to England.
Randolph, bristling after that greeting, looked about now with a jaundiced
eye. He found the leaders were "inconsiderable mechanics," the ministers "generally inclined to sedition, being proud, ignorant, and imperious." He saw ships arriving with the French flag flying and loaded to
the gunwales with wine, brandy, and other illegal items. His reports
flowing back to England in a steady stream denounced everything about
Massachusetts. New England laws suited only New Englanders' convenience and flouted English statutes. He found trials being conducted
"by word of God" and defendants put to death by Biblical injunctions.
Ministers were ordained by the people. Magistrates performed the marriage ceremony. Five-year possession of the land gave absolute title. There
were no oaths of allegiance to the king. Magistrates ignored royal orders.
Quakers were persecuted; the Church of England did not exist within the
colony's borders. The people coined their own money from melted Spanish
silver that arrived from the West Indies. Maine and New Hampshire had
been annexed to Massachusetts without authority and against the will of
the residents.

Randolph returned to England after a half year of investigation. He
handed the Lords of Trade a list of twenty-four "Assumed Powers" not
granted to Massachusetts in its charter. He thought that the king had a
great chance "to settle that country under his royal authority with little
charge" and that the people, "wearied out with the arbitrary proceedings
of those in the present government," would welcome royal rule, a judgment he had reached from talks with merchants in the colony who railed
against the still powerful oligarchy of orthodox Puritans. Finally, Randolph suggested that the troops sent to Virginia to quell Bacon's Rebellion
might be used "to reduce Massachusetts to obedience."

The Lords of Trade mulled over Randolph's reports, then proceeded
to act slowly. First, they demanded an explanation from Massachusetts.
The General Court answered boldly that the laws of England "are
bounded with the four seas, and do not reach America." The Court went
on to add an argument that would be used later by Massachusetts: "The
subjects of his majesty here being not represented in Parliament, so we
have not looked at ourselves to be impeded in our trade with them, nor
yet we abated in our relative allegiance to his majesty." The Lords of
Trade reflected on those and other words from the colony, then in 1679
they ordered Massachusetts to withdraw all officers from New Hampshire,
thereupon making that colony a royal dependent. In the same year
Randolph returned to the Bay Colony, this time as collector of customs.

During his first year Randolph seized ten ships for illegal entry. Juries found against the crown in every instance. Randolph lost factually airtight cases; nevertheless, all ten were legally weak. Massachusetts merchants pointed out that he "had no more power to seize and prosecute . . . than any other person," and they were right. The law allowed customs commissioners in America to enforce only the Plantation Duty Act of 1673. The duty to enforce the Navigation Acts of 1660 and 1663 belonged to colonial governors and naval officers. Some historians see Randolph as the progenitor of the "customs racketeer" that flourished in eighteenth-century America and hold that he only used "the real illegalities of trade as an excuse to fleece the merchants." A more generous judgment might be that he sought through illegal seizures to point up the inadequacy of his instructions. A customs commissioner permitted to enforce only the Plantation Duty Act, which required the collection of an export duty on enumerated goods alone, could do little to direct trade back to the straight path, for New England produced no enumerated goods. If this was Randolph's intent in seizing the ten ships he technically had no right to take, then he achieved quick success. The gap in his instructions was corrected in 1681 when the king gave him explicit authority to enforce all the Navigation Acts.

The hate that Randolph and Massachusetts felt for one another never overstepped certain bounds. Randolph lost all his cases but always by due process of law. No one tried to murder nor even to assault him. He seems to have been a man with great presence—forceful, haughty, and fearless, not the sort who invites a brawl in the streets. He was, after all— he believed it and made others believe it—the king's servant. He repeatedly and courageously faced down his waterfront opponents. The Puritan oligarchy detested him, but out of respect for government by law, it also protected him.

The Crown Takes Over

Massachusetts continued to talk back to Randolph, to the Lords of Trade, even to the king. Its leaders, desperately trying to keep alive John Winthrop's dream of a holy commonwealth, still considered themselves and the Bay Colony's inhabitants God's chosen people. They had created a new way of life for His pleasure, and it should not be tied to or influenced by any corrupt government or church such as that of England. Twice before their charter had been threatened and twice circumstances had saved them. Surely God would protect them from this third challenge. The oligarchy of orthodox Puritans that still controlled Massachusetts affairs sent agents to London to discuss matters with the Lords of Trade but with firm orders not to compromise on issues the colony re-

garded as its own business, such as suffrage and religious liberty. Shortly
thereafter the board recommended that proceedings be started to revoke
the Bay Colony's charter. The Court of Chancery in 1684 declared the
charter vacated, and Massachusetts thereupon became a royal colony.

Revocation of the charter completed the first phase of an administrative scheme for the American colonies taking shape in the minds of English authorities. Next, writs were filed against the charters of Connecticut
and Rhode Island. Once these colonies had been made royal dependents,
all New England would be united under a single royal governor. The
original plan had called for the creation of two, possibly three, administrative units for the eleven continental colonies, but the Lords of Trade soon
saw that this dream must wait. It would take time to revoke the charters
of the proprietaries, especially when the government faced such skilled and
powerful opponents as Penn and Baltimore. Meanwhile, New England
might serve as a testing ground for their conception. The need for strong
centralized control was greatest there, where the king's authority had
been most openly defied and where the menace of the encroaching French
was the most serious. Perhaps some sort of central control of defenses was
required if French incursions were to be thwarted.

Geography and economy, together with social and political customs
shared by all the people, bound New England into a natural unit and
gave the Lords of Trade an ideal laboratory for their experiment. The
growing French menace led them to expand their laboratory beyond its
natural boundaries, for Governor Dongan of New York convinced them
that his colony would be centrally involved in any trouble with the enemy
on the north. Plans were reshaped to include not only New York but
New Jersey, too, in the Dominion of New England, as it was to be
called. It would stretch from Nova Scotia to the Delaware River and
would embrace over half the settlers on the American continent.

The death of Charles II in 1685 delayed inception of the dominion
until his brother, the Duke of York, now James II, gave royal assent to
the plan. In the interim, the Lords of Trade arranged for a provisional
government that took in Massachusetts, Maine, New Hampshire, and the
Narragansett country. Joseph Dudley, then acting governor of Massachusetts, became president. Because no representative assembly was provided for, he ruled with a council of seventeen—all, with the exception of
Edward Randolph and George Mason, New Englanders by birth or long
residence. None were old-line theocrats; all were moderates who had
favored the crown's taking over the colony. With their coming to power
the government of Massachusetts had at last slipped from the control of
the orthodox Puritan oligarchy that had dominated the colony's political
life from the beginning.

President Dudley and his council took office on May 25, 1686. They first searched for "loyal" men to put in public posts. Randolph demanded a complete overhaul of personnel, but the council moved cautiously. Most of the old local officers were allowed to stay on, but new justices of the peace and military officers were sworn in. Randolph also insisted that the Church of England receive immediate and special favor from the government. The church was accustomed to state support, and Randolph wanted the council to provide a place of worship and pay the minister's salary. Dudley saw to it that Anglicans had a place to worship but did little more to promote the church. His moderation pleased the people and led Randolph to call him a "false president."

Trade and financial problems gave the provisional government its worst troubles. A huge debt from King Philip's War waited to be paid. The council had no authority to pass new revenue measures, and the General Court had repealed all the old ones on the books when the charter was revoked, hoping this would eventually force the crown to call it into session in order to vote new taxes. The closing of the mint on orders from England had created a severe currency shortage. French incursions into the Newfoundland fishing grounds were reducing Massachusetts' share of that once profitable trade.

The provisional government could do little during its seven months of existence to solve these problems. It avoided a general assessment on the people and depended for its income on the old import duties on wine and rum and on receipts from fees. The few hundred pounds from these two sources barely paid the administrative costs of the council. The omission of Connecticut and Rhode Island from the provisional government allowed them to become centers of smuggling. Dudley sought less to enforce than to appear to enforce the Navigation Laws. He confined imports to four ports and created at Boston a vice-admiralty court, which he headed. This was a prerogative court where the judge, not a jury, handed down decisions.

Randolph, a man who would have liked to remake the world in a day, judged the provisional government an unmitigated disaster. The Lords of Trade were more tolerant. They felt it had "unhinged the commonwealth" and paved the way for the coming of the royal governor. It had failed to stop the flow of illegal trade but through lack of power more than anything else.

During Dudley's tenure, England had devised a constitution for the dominion. It provided for freedom of worship but gave favor to the Church of England. James II, on looking over an early draft, had eliminated a provision for a representative assembly. His brother's troubles with popular government and his own respect for France's autocratic colonial system had reinforced a conviction that representative government only caused trouble and clogged the efficiency of government. The constitution included a further innovation to displease New England. All land henceforth granted would be held in the king's name and a quitrent of two shillings six pence (only slightly more than Virginians paid) would be levied on every hundred acres. This would tie the settler closer to the crown and also produce sufficient revenue to make the dominion's government self-supporting. The Lords of Trade did not consider the innovation oppressive. They sought only to make New England's land laws and customs conform to those in England and to obtain a constant and certain source of income for the government.

Sir Edmund Andros

On December 20, 1686, the roar of guns in Boston harbor announced the arrival of Sir Edmund Andros, governor of the Dominion of New England. He stepped from the gangplank of the *Kingfisher* into a mire of troubles. The territory he ruled exceeded that of England in size. He had a king's power but ruled as a stranger without the people's good wishes. He lacked an adequate bureaucracy. He had somehow to defend his sprawling domain, without forts and soldiers, from the French without and the Indians within. At the same time he had to reform a society whose customs and habits were fixed by a half century's experience in the New World. All this had to be done by an outsider, a member of the Church of England, a military man, and an aristocrat who had already enraged many New Englanders during King Philip's War when, as governor of New York, he had refused to come to their aid. He worsened his position at the start by bringing along "a crew of abject persons fetched from New York" to help run the dominion. Increase Mather spoke for many when he said: "The foxes were now made the administrators of justice to the poultry."

Andros instantly rubbed the orthodox of Massachusetts the wrong way. Three hours after arrival he demanded a hall in which to hold an Anglican service. A few days later he mocked the Puritans' refusal to celebrate Christmas—to do so smacked of popery, they said—by attending divine services twice on that day. The following spring he broke the Sabbath by celebrating the king's coronation with bonfires and fireworks. He soon followed that blasphemy by allowing a fencing event to occur "immediately after the [midweek] lecture," then four days later permitting a maypole to be erected in Charlestown, a sure sign to Mather that the devil had come to New England.

Andros' power to make laws, levy taxes, and administer justice was limited only by the consent of his council. Representation on the council was distributed more equitably than under the Confederation of New England. Massachusetts held seven votes, New Hampshire one, Maine two, Plymouth six, Narragansett one, Rhode Island seven, Connecticut two, New York eight, and New Jersey none. The council met quarterly in its legislative capacity, weekly in its administrative role. Since members were not paid, only those in and around Boston—or New York, when meetings were held there—attended regularly. Also, the obloquy that came to be attached to any who served the administration caused many to absent themselves. Those regularly present—Randolph, Dudley, William Stoughton, John Usher, and Francis Nicholson—came to be called Andros' "tools."

The government's first task was to produce a revenue measure. But the council turned out a bill that held little in common with former New England revenue laws. It put a heavy tax on imported rum, wine, and brandy. Those who sanctioned the measure were predominantly landowners eager to shift the tax burden from land to trade. Sir Edmund's aristocratic background persuaded him to their view, but a desire to be fair and equalize the burden also led him to push through a direct tax on landowners that could not be passed on to the consumer, as the merchants' imposts could. The land tax handed Andros his first test of power when it came due, for it provoked dissension in nearly every town. People complained that the law "did infringe their liberty as free-born English subjects." Andros hit swiftly. Several of the ringleaders—among them, Reverend John Wise—were brought to trial, jailed, and fined heavily. This prompt, vigorous action carried the government through its first crisis. People continued to grumble that they paid taxes levied without their consent, but gradually they saw that Massachusetts' rates were lower under Andros than they had been for many years—or were to be for years to come.

Another of Andros' jobs was to establish a judicial system that conformed to English practice and custom. He set rates on legal fees similar to those in other colonies where English customs prevailed, but because they exceeded the old rates, Puritans called them extortionate. He ordered all writs issued in the king's name. He introduced the English manner of taking oaths—a witness must kiss the Bible rather than simply place one hand on it and raise the other as New Englanders did—and those who resisted the change could not serve on juries. Justices of the peace, now appointed by the governor, received duties more in line with their English equivalents. Care of the poor, for instance, once handled by town meetings, now became the responsibility of the justices of the peace. All these innovations altered the form but left the essence of the judicial system untouched, mainly because Andros soon saw that New England law and procedure resembled English law and procedure more than it had seemed at first glance.

The merchants, who had opposed the rule of orthodox Puritans and had favored making Massachusetts a royal colony, viewed Andros with mixed feelings. His firm enforcement of the Navigation Acts stifled trade. His use of vice-admiralty rather than common-law courts to try violations of the acts filled them with fury. He tempered their anger by siding with them on the currency question. Andros realized that stopping the illegal trade with Spanish colonies had dried up New England merchants' main source of cash, for that trade had always provided a favorable balance of payments in metal coin. He recommended to the Lords of Trade that Massachusetts be permitted to reestablish its own mint. Permission was refused, however, and Andros gained one more black mark in the eyes of New England through no fault of his own.

The problem of aligning New England's land system—where land was not held in the king's name, as was the English and generally the colonial custom—with that of England's gave Andros particular trouble. Bay Colony leaders had allocated land to town leaders, who, in turn, handed out lots to individuals. And quitrents had not been required in Massachusetts, as in Virginia or the proprietary colonies, nor had oaths of allegiance to the king. Andros proceeded slowly to correct these discrepancies by demanding rents only when he granted titles to vacant lands, but by 1688 he was questioning the validity of all New England land titles. If landowners wanted secure titles, they had to obtain new patents from the king's men in the king's name at a uniform quitrent of 2s. 6d. per hundred acres. The innovation was resisted on all sides, and only about two hundred persons in the entire dominion filed for new titles.

Andros' land policy raised little noise in Connecticut and Plymouth, where greater care had been taken to grant lands according to recognized legal forms. Most of the commotion occurred in Massachusetts. Orthodox Puritans objected because the innovations limited their independence, taxed them without their consent, and required recognition of the crown as the ultimate power. Moderates, who otherwise enjoyed being part of the empire, complained that the scarcity of coin made the required cash payments of quitrents and of the heavy fees for validating titles impossible burdens. The new system seemed especially severe to these second generation New Englanders, who knew nothing of English land laws from personal experience. For them, land was secured either by purchase from fellow colonists or from Indians by "fair contract or just conquest." The feeling against Andros' system reached such a point that when Joseph Dudley agreed to have his lands repatented "for a good example to others," it was said of him: "Oh, the poison of the serpent is deadly."

The need for a strong, centrally controlled defense system against the French had been an important reason for creating the dominion and for choosing Andros, a military man, as its first governor. Andros' commission designated him captain-general of all military forces from the St. Croix to the Delaware Rivers. An early tour of the frontiers revealed the forlorn condition of New England's defenses. Andros worked well and hard to resurrect them. He built forts, imported English troops, organized militias, and developed a uniform policy toward the Indians. By late 1688 the dominion's defenses were sound. The overthrow of Andros in 1688, with the coming of the Glorious Revolution, destroyed all his military accomplishments; England lost the only effective system of defense she ever had in America; and New France, whom Andros might have checked, continued to harass the colonies for three-quarters of a century more.

The Dominion of New England lasted slightly over two years, from December 1686 to April 1689. Its purpose had been to reconstruct New England society quickly and radically. But the experiment failed, and England never revived it. And yet the experiment might have succeeded, given two or three years' more time, for Andros was an exceedingly able man who accomplished much that lasted beyond his brief tenure. He has been censured for loading his administration with New York cronies, when he might have won local support by handing lucrative appointments to New England magnates; for following his instructions too literally, when tact and patience might have accomplished more; for alienating the merchants, who, after a generation of opposing the orthodox rulers of Massachusetts, joined up with their enemies to help overthrow Andros. He ruled with a harsh, autocratic hand, but he acted under orders to effect changes swiftly. Once his innovations had been imposed on the people, it is likely, being a generally reasonable man, he would have been less severe. He requested that the mint be revived to ease Massachusetts' economic distress; a few years later he might also have asked that the representative assembly be once again allowed, for by then his innovations might have been accepted.

Andros had been handed an impossible assignment—a territory too large and responsibilities too many for one man to handle. His burdens became heavier with the death of his wife during their first winter in Boston. Yet by the end of his rule, he had done all the crown had asked him to do. The Navigation Acts were being enforced by the end of his second year in office. The vice-admiralty court was handing out convictions against offending merchants. Local government's power had been weakened; centralized government's power strengthened. Colonial militias had been brought under the unified control of a royal commander. Land taxes had been lowered. The costs of government administration came from current income. Andros might have added to these achievements given time. News of the Glorious Revolution in England handed New Englanders the excuse they wanted to cut short his experiment in reconstruction.

THE GLORIOUS REVOLUTION IN AMERICA

William of Orange landed in England in November 1688, and soon after, as William III, he and his wife Mary acceded to the throne in place of the deposed James II. Few of the gains that made the Glorious Revolution memorable in English history were passed on to the American colonies. In January William issued a circular letter that directed all colonial officers, except those who were Catholics, to continue in their posts. (Increase Mather, in London at the time as Massachusetts' agent, saw to it that this letter never reached Boston, where it might have prevented the ousting of Andros.) A few months later William had saddled the colonists with a war (King William's War) against France that unleashed the Indians upon New York and all New England. When the war ended, the king inaugurated an imperial administration so vigorous that the Stuarts' rule seemed lax and genial by comparison. The colonists retrieved only a single immediate benefit from the Glorious Revolution: they used it as an excuse to stage revolts of their own. "When the body is disturbed, the members need be affected," William Byrd, Sr., remarked, as if to justify the state of colonial affairs. "Therefore we here can expect no settled times till England is in peace."

New England

News of events in England did not drift into Boston until April, but by then the groundwork had been laid for the city to stage a glorious revolt of its own. In August 1688 Indians had raided the hamlet of Northfield in the Connecticut Valley. Another attack, which struck at settlements on Penobscot Bay, Maine, in November, provoked Andros to move out with troops. The militia that accompanied him resented being pressed into service and their resentment increased when they found several Catholics among their officers. Rumors planted about Boston soon had it that Andros was secretly a "papist"; that if James II were forced from the throne, the governor planned to turn New England over to the French; and that to expedite this maneuver, he had dispatched the militia to the frontier under popish officers.

When news of William and Mary's accession arrived, it required little to persuade the people that Andros must be imprisoned if his plans were to be thwarted. Andros was jailed—he escaped only to be recaptured, disguised in a woman's dress—as were Randolph and other dominion officials. "We have been quiet, hitherto, but now that the Lord has prospered the undertaking of the Prince of Orange, we think we should follow such an example," went the pious justification for the revolt. "We, therefore, seize the vile persons who oppressed us." The rebels blamed the loss of Massachusetts' charter on the "slanderous accusations" of Edward Randolph and heaped abuse on Andros, making it clear that they fought against the extension of British rule, rather than the policy of British kings, as one historian puts it. Andros and his colleagues remained in jail until February 1690, when authorities in England ordered that they be set free to return home.

The rebels established a Council of Safety with Simon Bradstreet, a former governor, as its president. On May 24, following the example of those in England, the council summoned a convention, which voted to reestablish the government as it had existed under the charter. Two days later, a ship arrived with orders for the proclamation of William and Mary as king and queen. This was done, but it little eased the troubles that were besetting the provisional government. The lack of a charter and of William's explicit approval of the new regime made it hard to acquire the respect of the people. The government needed money desperately—to fight the French and Indians on the frontiers, to carry on the campaign in England for a new charter, to pay the ordinary expenses of administration—but the people refused to pay taxes. Though barely a half year had elapsed since the last Indian raid, troops were pulled in from the frontiers in order to cut expenses. Though the French threatened by sea, a royal frigate in the harbor, whose captain had been jailed with Andros, was dismantled, leaving the city without this protection. The government's ineffectiveness led to a curious result. A stream of petitions began arriving in England from citizens of the Bay Colony pleading for the restoration of a royal government. The crown was not long in obliging.

The turmoil in Boston was not duplicated elsewhere in New England. Neither Connecticut nor Rhode Island had surrendered its charter when Andros had demanded them. With Andros' fall, both colonies proceeded to govern themselves as they had before the dominion.

The Middle Colonies

King William quietly returned New Jersey to the control of its proprietors, who had been dispossessed when James II made their colony part of the dominion. Pennsylvania accepted the change in England with little fuss. But in New York a rebellion broke forth that engendered bitter divisions that would mark the colony's affairs for nearly a century.

Andros was represented in New York by his lieutenant governor, Captain Francis Nicholson, who ruled both New York and New Jersey with the assistance of the local members of Andros' council. Nicholson was one of the small cadre of professional bureaucrats who served in America; by the end of the colonial period, he would have held a variety of government positions equaled by no other Englishman. He was an able man, but in 1689 he failed to show himself at his best. An informal report of William's accession arrived in March, but the lack of official orders caused Nicholson to hold off proclaiming the news to the province. Hesitancy proved his undoing.

Shortly after learning of William's assumption of power, Nicholson heard from Boston of the revolt against Andros. Nicholson proceeded to strengthen Fort James on Manhattan. He wanted to protect the town against a possible invasion from New England; the local elite wanted a refuge in case rebellion flared up in New York. In the past decade both colony and city had splintered into a number of factions, each with its own reasons for bitterness against those in control of affairs. New Englanders on Long Island had transferred their hate for Dutch rule to the royal government; they were quick to drive out royal officers stationed among them when they learned of their brethren's activity in Boston. Farmers along the Hudson smoldered over the monopoly of flour production granted to city merchants by the government. The city's prosperity, said a contemporary, was "chiefly upheld by the manufacture of flour and bread," but this did little to alleviate the anger of farmers who had to sell their wheat at prices controlled by town merchants. For a generation both city and provincial politics had rested in the hands of a few families—the Bayards, Livingstons, Schuylers, Van Rensselaers—who had used their power to protect their own interests to the detriment of those on the outside. All this ill feeling needed only a man and an event to focus it, and New York would have the equivalent of Bacon's Rebellion on its hands.

Nicholson's timidity provided the event. Rumors of a "popish plot" to turn the colony over to France, similar to those seeded in Boston and strengthened by the revolt there, had flourished for months in New York. Many of the English officials in New York—among them, the collector of revenue, the commander of Fort James, and several of his officers— were Catholics. Thomas Dongan, the former governor and also Catholic, still lived in the province. Nicholson himself, though an Anglican, occasionally attended Catholic services. When Nicholson tarried in proclaiming William and Mary king and queen, many citizens, among them Dutch supporters of William of Orange, assumed the rumors were facts. One person who proceeded as if the rumors were true was Jacob Leisler, a native of Frankfort, Germany, who came to New Amsterdam in 1660 as a soldier in the Dutch West India Company. Three years later he had married a rich widow; and though the leading Dutch families of the city refused to accept him, he had soon become one of the wealthiest merchants in the colony. He was a contentious man, often in court on trivial issues, always at odds with fellow members of the aristocracy. On May 31 Leisler, with about five hundred men, seized Fort James, acting on a rumor, entirely false as it turned out, that Nicholson planned to set fire to the city and allow the citizens to be "sold, betrayed, and murdered."

A short while after Leisler's seizure of the fort, Nicholson decamped for England, handing his authority to a council of three. Power, however, remained with Leisler, for he had strong support among the people. He called a convention of the freemen and delegates from seven counties appeared. The convention appointed him "captain of the fort and commander-in-chief of the province." One of Leisler's first acts under this authority was to proclaim William and Mary king and queen on June 12. Ten days later he set up a Committee of Public Safety, and the following month the legislature convened, though Suffolk, Ulster, and Albany Counties refused to send delegates. In December orders arrived from King William authorizing Nicholson or, in his absence, "such as for the time being take care for the preserving the peace and administering the laws" to rule the province. Nicholson's council claimed the dispatch, but Leisler seized it from those "popishly affected dogs and rogues," and continued to rule with the advice and consent of an elected legislature.

Albany alone held out against Leisler. Jacob Millborne, his lieutenant and also his son-in-law, traveled up to the village to convince "the common people . . . that it was in their power to free themselves from the yoke of arbitrary power . . . of the illegal King James." Robert Livingston convinced the people King William would soon be deposed, and with aid from Connecticut's conservative government and the Iroquois, the town withstood Millborne's efforts to take control. In February 1690, a band of French and Indians demolished the nearby village of Schenectady, murdering all the residents they could lay hands on. Soon after this, Albany had second thoughts about Leisler, who controlled the colony's military forces. Not long after Albany surrendered, Leisler held an intercolonial conference there, which was attended by delegates from three New England colonies. At this conference plans were worked out for the elaborate yet unsuccessful land-sea invasion of Canada, during King William's War.

Leisler ruled New York for over a year, drawing support from all parts of the population. Small landowners and town artisans were his principal backers, but several aristocratic families—the Lodwycks, De-Peysters, DeLanceys, and others—also supported him. Leisler ran the government efficiently. He set up courts, among them a vice-admiralty court, commissioned officers, fortified the city, and issued letters of marque and reprisal to privateers. His legislature redressed grievances—it abolished, for instance, the trade monopolies of the city merchants—but also faced the responsibility of levying a tax on real and personal property to raise money for King William's War against the French. A Bostonian could only compliment the Leislerian government: "being so like our pattern, we cannot but love our own brat."

Colonel Henry Sloughter, about whom little except his fondness for drinking is known, was chosen by William to become New York's new governor. Major Richard Ingoldesby, commanding two companies of troops, preceded the governor by two months. He allied himself with Leisler's enemies and demanded the surrender of Fort James. Leisler asked for Ingoldesby's authority, and because he had none, the fort did not change hands. When Sloughter arrived in March 1691, he, too, asked for surrender of the fort. Leisler submitted but only after temporizing long enough to allow the anti-Leislerites to brand him a traitor. Leisler and nine others were brought to trial for treason. All were acquitted or pardoned but Leisler and his son-in-law Millborne, who, in seventeenth-century fashion, were sentenced "to be hanged by the neck and, being alive, their bodies be cut down to the earth, that their bowels be taken out and, they being alive, burnt before their faces, that their heads shall be struck off and their bodies cut in four parts."

Leisler and Millborne, as one historian has said, died "not so much for the crimes they had committed as for the enemies they had made." Parliament reversed the convictions in 1695, but by then New York politics ran in two deeply dug channels—Leislerian and anti-Leislerian.

The South

Carolina absorbed news of the Glorious Revolution quietly. The proprietors' order to proclaim the new monarchs produced no demonstrations, even though politics in the southern section of the colony were at the moment far from placid. The colony's parliament objected to high quit-rents, to the inappropriateness of Carolina's Fundamental Constitutions, to the lack of the right to initiate legislation, and, above all, to Governor John Colleton's arbitrary rule. But the opposition lacked strength and a leader and failed to use the Glorious Revolution as an excuse to stage a revolt of its own. Carolina grumbled but endured its grievances, even when Governor Colleton dissolved parliament and ruled by executive decree.

News of the revolution found Virginia still agitated from earlier troubles. Thomas Lord Culpeper, who had, said a contemporary, "a singular dexterity in making use of all advantages of his own interest," had arrived as governor in the spring of 1680. Whatever good emerged during his tenure came about only when his interests and the colony's happened to coincide. When Culpeper left in 1684, he carried home a small fortune, most of it from quitrents collected from the large grants the king had leased to him, Lord Arlington, and others years earlier. (Soon after returning home, Culpeper bought out his coproprietors to the Northern Neck grant—between the Rappahannock and Potomac Rivers— and in 1688 acquired a perpetual charter to the region, a coup that would muddle Virginian affairs until after the American Revolution, when the Fairfax grant, as it was then called, finally passed to the state.) Culpeper was replaced by Lord Howard of Effingham, handpicked by the Lords of Trade to govern the colony with a firm hand. Lord Howard spent four years in Virginia, none of them peaceful. He was a Catholic, and when James II came to power in 1685 Lord Howard took it upon himself to replace with Catholics several local officials who had opposed him. He quarreled steadily with the assembly. He answered a request to see the records and accounts of provincial officials with a reprimand: members should not meddle "with that which did not belong to them." He withdrew the assembly's right to hear appeals from the General Court, which meant that since he appointed the court all justice now lay within the control of the executive. He denied the assembly the right to appoint its own clerk; to have granted it would have blocked his access to their proceedings. Effingham dissolved the assembly in May 1688 and ruled without it until February 1689.

Word of the revolution in England prompted some malcontents to duplicate in Virginia the anti-Catholic revolt underway in Maryland. The governor's council squashed the movement at once by a decisive denial of a Catholic plot to use Indians to overthrow the government, and talk of an uprising soon faded. Orders that came from England in April to celebrate the accession of William and Mary were carried out with "unfeigned joy and exultation." Soon afterward, Sir Francis Nicholson, having recovered from his humiliation in New York, arrived as lieutenant governor. He had been handed the assignment because the war with France made it wise to have a military man in the colony. Pirates and privateers hung off the coast waiting for unescorted ships; Indians still lurked about the frontiers; and the people expected an invasion by the French at any moment. Nicholson calmed the settlers' fears about invasion, toured the frontiers, and arranged with Maryland to work together on the Indian problem.

Virginia's economy foundered under the continued low price of tobacco during Nicholson's two-year tenure, but fair weather prevailed on the political front. Nicholson was a bachelor who liked to pass a convivial evening with members of his council or the assembly. The distance between executive and legislative lessened in the relaxed atmosphere, and much was achieved politically. Conferences he arranged between the House of Burgesses and council diminished tension between those two bodies. The assembly passed laws encouraging the production of such items as hemp and leather, placed a tax on imported liquor, and freed Indian trade of its old restrictions. One statute called for the establishment of a free school and college, and James Blair, the Bishop of London's representative, or commissary, to oversee church affairs in Virginia, was chosen by the assembly to obtain an endowment and charter in England for William and Mary, as it would be called. Nicholson's first administration—he would return for a less satisfactory one, 1698–1705—ended in 1692 with the arrival of his replacement, none other than Sir Edmund Andros.

Affairs progressed less smoothly in Maryland, where a Protestant electorate still rankled over the Catholic hue to government, quitrents had recently been doubled, the price of tobacco continued to fall, and trouble with Indians persisted on the frontiers. A widespread rumor in 1688 had it that the "popish administration, supported by papists" and leagued with the French and Indians, intended to massacre all Protestants in the colony. Governor William Joseph, a shortsighted man, arrested several of the gossipmongers, which only lent credence to the tales.

Early in 1689 word drifted in with ships from England that William and Mary had been enthroned, but nothing had been heard from Lord Baltimore ordering the colonists to honor their new sovereigns. (Baltimore had sent out the orders but had not been informed that the messenger carrying them had died before leaving England.) The delay reinforced another rumor that Baltimore did not intend to recognize the new sovereigns but planned to make Maryland a Catholic colony by force.

Opposition swiftly crystallized into the Protestant Association, whose professed purpose was to defend the Protestant religion and proclaim William and Mary rulers. The revolt that followed was led by, or at least takes its name from, John Coode, a former Anglican minister who had already clashed once with the government. He was joined by the collector of customs, his brother-in-law Nehemiah Blakiston; by Kenelm Cheseldyne, several times speaker of the assembly; and by Henry Jowles. Coode led some 250 men into St. Mary's in July 1689 and there forced Governor Joseph and his council to turn the government over to the association. The legislature convened the next month, announced its loyalty to the new monarchs, and begged the crown to assume control of the province. Blakiston was elected the colony's temporary president, as Maryland preferred to call its governor. In November the association published a *Declaration of the Reasons and Motives for the Present Appearing in Arms,* which detailed the people's grievances—maladministered customs service, conversion of the church to the "use of popish idolatry and superstition," unrepresentative government, excessive taxes and fees, unlawful arrest of Protestants, and "private and public outrages and murders committed by papists upon Protestants."

Despite the harsh tone of the declaration, Coode's administration proved moderate and fair. It ended in 1692 with the appointment of Sir Lionel Copley as Maryland's first royal governor. Though no legal proceedings had been instituted against Baltimore's charter, of which he was never formally deprived, he lost all right of direct control over his colony. The king left his revenue and land titles unimpaired but took the government into his own hands. The colony remained a royal province for nearly a quarter of a century. Benedict Calvert, the fourth Lord Baltimore, retrieved Maryland's government in 1715 with his conversion to Protestantism and his loyal support of George I. The colony remained family property until 1776.

The significance of the Glorious Revolution increased for Americans as the event itself receded into the past. Throughout the remainder of the colonial period settlers would look back to 1688 as the turning point in their history. The liberties John Dickinson would write about in 1766 in *Letters from a Farmer in Pennsylvania* were those he saw emerging out of this era. New Englanders would hereafter view their past in a new light. The Puritans would not have emigrated, Increase Mather said in 1689, "if their reward after all must be to be deprived of their English liberties," and New England historians would ever after see the Puritan migration as one that sought as much to preserve political as religious liberties.

The revolution also had a religious significance for the colonies. It greatly strengthened the established church in England, and the effect would be felt in America through the eighteenth century. Up to now the Anglican Church flourished on a colony-wide basis only in Virginia. After 1689 every royal governor would be instructed to promote and safeguard the English Church. The Society for the Propagation of the Gospel was organized in 1701 with an eye to strengthening the church in America. Much attention had been aroused by the recent conversion of George Keith, a Quaker preacher well-known throughout the colonies; and it was argued that if the opportunity were offered, considerable numbers of America's numerous sectarians would be induced to conform.

The revolution's political significance, from the English government's point of view, resists easy measurement. The shift of constitutional power in England from the crown to Parliament would take time to be felt and never be fully comprehended by the colonists. But a subtle change in the crown's attitude toward the colonies proved easier to observe: the arbitrary quality of royal administration faded; never again was there an attempt to rule without a colonial legislature; the experiment in centralization was never repeated. A new tightening-up did begin with William that Americans could see and feel but that they objected to less than they had to Stuart control, for the uniform system that William inaugurated always sought to make allowance for local habits and customs and generally observed a respect for the rights of individuals.

BIBLIOGRAPHY

The First Round of Outbursts

Richard L. Morton's *Colonial Virginia* (2 vols., 1960) presents the most recent and reliable account of Bacon's Rebellion. Also excellent is Thomas J. Wertenbaker's pamphlet *Bacon's Rebellion* (1957), in the Jamestown Booklets series. Wertenbaker's earlier *Torchbearer of the Revolution* (1940) offers a picture of "oppressed yeomen" versus "corrupt grandees" that should be counterbalanced by Wilcomb E. Washburn, *The Governor and the Rebel* (1957), which makes Berkeley the hero and Bacon something of the villain of the story. Wesley Frank Craven in *Southern Colonies in the Seventeenth Century* (1949) presents the rebellion as a "complex problem" for which there was no "simple answer." Bernard Bailyn sees it as a struggle for power by two elite groups in "Politics and Social Structure in Virginia," in James Morton Smith, ed., *Seventeenth-Century America: Essays on Colonial History* (1959).

An adequate brief account of King Philip's War can be found in James T. Adams, *The Founding of New England* (1921; pb.). D. E. Leach's *Flintlock and Tomahawk: New England in King Philip's War* (1958; pb.) gives the latest and fullest account of that event; Leach prefaces his elaborate bibliography with remarks on the varying reliability of firsthand accounts of the war. He has recently edited *A Rhode Islander Reports on King Philip's War* (1963). Still worth consulting is George W. Ellis and John E. Morris, *King Philip's War* (1906).

The most accessible collection of source material on Bacon's Rebellion is Charles M. Andrews, ed., *Narratives of the Insurrections, 1675–1690* (1915). Charles H. Lincoln's edition of *Narratives of the Indian Wars, 1675–1699* (1913) contains the most important contemporary accounts of King Philip's War.

The Dominion of New England

The bedrock book here is Viola F. Barnes, *The Dominion of New England* (1928). All other accounts build on Miss Barnes's solid study. Gertrude Ann

Jacobsen, *William Blathwayt: A Later Seventeenth-Century English Admin-istrator* (1932), presents a good introduction to the type of colonial adminis-trator coming into power about this time; but more directly relevant to the story here is Michael Garibaldi Hall's competent study of *Edward Randolph and the American Colonies, 1676–1703* (1960), which should be supple-mented by Robert N. Toppan and Alfred T. S. Goodrick, eds., *Edward Randolph: Including His Letters and Official Papers . . . 1676–1703* (7 vols., 1898–1909). Two studies of men who loomed large in events of the day are Everett Kimball's *The Public Life of Joseph Dudley* (1911) and Kenneth Murdock's *Increase Mather: Foremost American Puritan* (1925). There is no satisfactory biography of Governor Andros. Contemporary pro and con opin-ion of his administration is found in *The Andros Tracts* (3 vols., 1868–1874); several of these tracts are reprinted in Andrews' *Narratives of the Insurrections.* The student particularly interested in this subject should dig out the excellent articles by Winfred T. Root, "The Lords of Trade and Planta-tions, 1675–1696," *AHR,* 23 (1917), 20–41; and Philip Haffenden, "The Crown and the Colonial Charters, 1675–1688," *WMQ,* 15 (1958), 297–311, 452–466. John Gorham Palfrey, *History of New England* (5 vols., 1858–1890), and Thomas Hutchinson, *History of the Colony and Province of Massachusetts Bay* (3 vols., 1936), contain details of the story found nowhere else. Edward Channing offers an effective anti-Andros version of the events in the second volume of *The History of the United States* (6 vols., 1905–1925).

The Glorious Revolution in America

Much of the material cited above also illuminates this aspect of the story of New England. That of Leisler's Rebellion has most recently been told by Jerome R. Reich in *Jacob Leisler's Rebellion: A Study of Democracy in New York, 1664–1720* (1953); he pictures the small farmer-tradesman as rising up against the aristocrats. Lawrence H. Leder tells of the revolt from the viewpoint of one of the aristocrats in *Robert Livingston, 1654–1728, and the Politics of Colonial New York* (1961). Michael Garibaldi Hall, Lawrence H. Leder, and Michael G. Kammen have edited *The Glorious Revolution in America: Documents on the Colonial Crisis of 1689* (pb. original). Morton's *Colonial Virginia* relates the Virginia story fully and well. Craven's *Southern Colonies* is best on events in Maryland. Again, see Andrews' *Narratives* for contemporary accounts.

For the long-term effect of the Glorious Revolution on American ideas, see Craven's remarks in *The Legend of the Founding Fathers* (1956; pb.). Perry Miller is particularly good on its effect on the New England mind in *From Colony to Province* (1953; pb.). An essay that does much to clarify the influence of the Glorious Revolution on one who participated in a later upris-ing is H. Trevor Colbourn, "John Dickinson: Historical Revolutionary," *PMHB,* 83 (1959), 271–292.

For further references see the *Harvard Guide,* Section 96, "Wars, Insur-rections, and Other Disturbances, 1675–1692."

The Mason Children, "Young Puritans"

8. America at the End of the Seventeenth Century

THE WAY THEY LIVED
    Enemies
    Town and Country
    The Arts

SOCIETY
    Labor
    The Elite
    Education

THE WAY THEY THOUGHT
    Science
    Religion
    Language and Literature

The colonists belonged both to England and America in 1689. The land they occupied stretched some one thousand miles along the coast, but the settlers hugged the water, their backs to the continent and their eyes toward England, "that most comfortable and renowned island," as Nathaniel Ward put it. Most colonists, though Americans by birth, considered themselves Englishmen overseas. ("My desires are now to breathe my native air and enjoy the fruition of my native soil," said William Fitzhugh, Virginia planter who had been reared in England and still considered it "home.") They aped English fashions, read English books, drew on England for their supplies. Like the English, they still believed in witches, still lived, dressed, and talked much as they had at home. They had come, as Stephen Vincent Benét once phrased it, "resolved to be Englishmen." They had worked hard to keep the resolve, but by 1689 the embryo of a new man, the American, had begun to take form. The year 1689 marks the halfway point between the first settlements and the outbreak of the American Revolution. It was the turning point in their history. Soon after that date another "great migration" would begin, this time composed mainly of non-English stock. The backcountry would be opened up, changing the pattern of life in all colonies. And Newtonianism would help change people's thought. After 1689 a good deal of the old America would vanish in the new.

THE WAY THEY LIVED

The population of the twelve colonies numbered around a quarter of a million in 1689. Well over half the people had settled in the Chesapeake area and in New England. Nearly all were farmers, and less than twenty-five thousand lived in the major towns. Life for those outside the towns remained primitive. Men lived mainly unto themselves. Like the medieval serf who lived and died within sight of the manor, they seldom strayed beyond the spot where they had been born. Ruts in the land passed for roads, and when settlers traveled they generally went on foot, for horses, though slowly replacing oxen as draft animals, were still relatively few. There were no great fortunes in the colonies and no leisure class. Men's energies went into the struggle to survive. While England produced Donne, Milton, Newton, and Locke, Americans cleared the land. After three-quarters of a century, life for Americans continued rough and hard—dangerous, too, for enemies continued to harass the colonists from all sides.

Enemies

Undiluted good comes rarely to men. America offered the land-hungry immigrant an abundance of rich soil and also an abundance of enemies—pirates and privateers on the east, French on the north and west, Spanish on the south, and Indians within.

The colonists had mixed feelings about pirates and privateers. Those who infested American waters were welcomed by merchants for the coin they brought to purchase goods—"the condemned pirates," goes a 1690 diary entry of a visitor to Boston, "are now told they may be at liberty, paying £13 6s. 8d. a man [in] fees or be sold into Virginia"—and were reviled only when they hijacked cargoes bound for Europe. The Barbary pirates were another matter. In 1697 they robbed Virginia of thirteen ships, their greatest but far from only coup during the seventeenth century. No one knows how many colonial sailors ended up pulling an oar in a Barbary galley, but there were enough to cause Cotton Mather to direct A Pastoral Letter to the English Captives in Africa, wherein he sought to "comfort them under their terrible calamities and counsel them how to make such an use of their calamities as to prepare them for the salvation of God." These pirates "rob our trading ships of the stoutest and likeliest of their men and of all their provisions," Lord Bellomont, governor of New York, said, adding that while men-of-war could subdue the pirates with ease, "the Lords of Admiralty are pleased not to allow us a single ship." French and Dutch privateers added to the dangers of shipping.

While pirates and privateers worked the seas, the French hemmed the colonists from the rear. New England first felt their presence and suffered from it, but by 1689 men in every colony were concerned about French operations west of the Appalachians. The Carolina trader moved westward with pack trains, and the New Yorker glided by canoe over the Great Lakes only to find that Frenchmen had preceded them, building forts to protect their territory and trading posts to garner the Indian trade.

Spain's presence concerned mainly the southern colonies. In 1670 England and Spain had sought to settle their differences in the New World by a treaty that recognized England's claims as far south as Port Royal, South Carolina, and that, in effect, accepted the doctrine of effective occupation as a valid title to lands in the New World. This agreement, part of the Treaty of Madrid, which dealt mainly with European affairs, marked the first attempt to extend the peace of Europe "beyond the line" to America, reversing an attitude that had dominated European diplomacy since the pope's demarcation line of 1494. But the treaty did not fit the realities of American life, for Carolinians had already settled inside Spanish Florida on the Ashley River (now in South Carolina). Spain dealt with the situation in 1687, when she completed Castillo de San Marcos, an immense stone fortress that still stands at Saint Augustine. It blocked the southward drift of Americans for the rest of the colonial period and longer.

The Indians, aided by both the Spanish and French, blocked the American advancement inland by unremitting guerrilla warfare, and in 1689 they were still the greatest menace to the colonists' well-being. The Americans' patronizing attitude toward the natives prohibited any chance of coexistence. Rather than accept the Indian for what he was, as the French did, Americans judged and rejected him. New Englanders were relentless in their efforts to impose their way of life on the natives. "About this time," Cotton Mather wrote in 1705,

among other endeavors to be serviceable I considered that our Christianized Indians need[ed] a better acquaintance with the laws of the province against punishable wickedness. An abstract of the said laws turned into their language and printed for them, to have the same scattered among them, I was advised

Map 23. English Colonies and Their Enemies, Late 17ᵗʰ

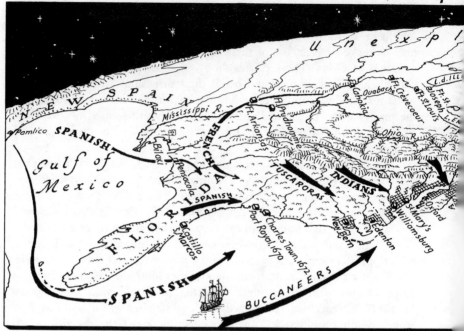

that would be greatly beneficial to them. I composed such an abstract and procured another to translate it that it might be accordingly published. I suited their genius with this title: HATCHETS TO HEW DOWN THE TREE OF SIN, WHICH BRINGS FORTH THE FRUIT OF DEATH.

The novelist David Garnett, in imagining what went through the mind of Pocahontas shortly after her capture by Captain Argall, has caught well the Indian attitude toward the white man's ways.

Such a life of unremitting toil, which is lived by every farmer's wife throughout the world, was completely new to her. She had seen Indians work hard for a few days while the fishing was good, or rounding up and driving deer; she had seen the English felling trees at Jamestown; but she had never met this compelling passion to build, to transform the face of nature and to impose as rapidly as possible something entirely alien, and never to be finished, in its place.

Toward the end of the seventeenth century it dawned on authorities in London that unless something were done, the French and Indians together might push the English off the continent. The attempt to remake the native in the Englishman's image began to fade as far as the authorities were concerned, and official English policy came to treat the Indian less as a barbarian who needed to be civilized and more as an instrument of trade and a useful ally. Missionaries were still encouraged to propa-

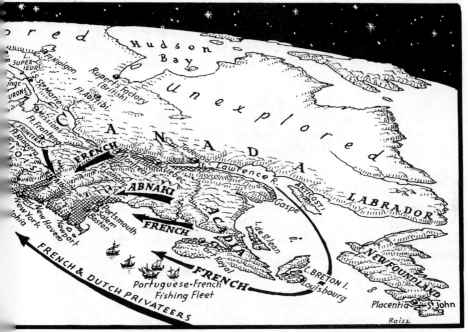

gate the gospel among them, but by the end of the century settlers were being ordered to stay off Indian lands and only licensed traders were permitted to deal with the natives.

The colonies' multitude of enemies affected all sides of American life. They dampened the interest of many who might have moved inland to stake out unsettled lands. They increased colonial dependence on England, for the colonies alone were too weak to fend off attacks. Many leaders, especially those within the proprietaries, urged the crown to take over their governments, hoping thereby they would receive aid against their enemies. Conversely, the rash of aggressors contributed to colonial self-reliance. An Indian raid, a foray of the French, an invasion by Spanish troops needed to be dealt with quickly. There was no time to wait for orders or aid from England. When England did come through, the offering was often inadequate, tardy, or at odds with what the colonists had done or wanted to do. America's enemies caused the relations between England and her colonies on the continent to swing constantly across the thin line that separates love from hate.

Town and Country

The first settlers surveyed the wilderness and filled their diaries with remarks on the beauties of nature. They talked of the "goodly groves of trees," of the "dainty, fine, round hillocks," and of the "sweet crystal fountains and clear running streams." It took only a short while to change their minds. John Smith returned from a trek through the Chesapeake wilderness and called it "uncouth." Michael Wigglesworth in 1662 called the forest a "Devil's den,"

> A waste and howling wilderness
> Where none inhabited
> But hellish fiends and brutish men
> That devils worshiped.

The forest became another, indeed, for many *the* enemy. Trees had to be hacked away to plant a crop. Out of the woods came wolves that killed cattle, Indians that murdered settlers. The wilderness, as Lewis Mumford has said, did not beckon these people. Nature had become an obstruction, an enemy huge and monstrous, and it would be a long time before a romantic picture of it again appeared in the writings of the colonists.

The wilderness did not beckon, but neither did the village. Every year weakened the village pattern brought over from England. New England spoke of the town, but there as elsewhere the relatively isolated farm dominated the way of life. "There was no longer any holding them together, but now they must of necessity go to their great lots," William Bradford said.

And no man now thought he could live except he had cattle and a great deal of ground to keep them, all striving to increase their stocks. By which means they were scattered all over the bay quickly and the town, in which they had lived compactly till now, was left very thin, and in a short time almost desolate.

The urge to disperse came quickly. Massachusetts' General Court tried to check it in 1635 by ordering all houses to be built within a half mile of the meetinghouse, but five years later the unworkable ruling had to be rescinded. In 1685 Increase Mather complained that "people are ready to run wild into the woods again and to be as heathenish as ever, if you do not prevent it." By the end of the century probably 80 per cent of the settlers in New England and the Middle Colonies lived outside the villages and port towns and had only intermittent contact with the sort of life they or their parents had known in England.

The situation was even more extreme in the Chesapeake country, where "the great number of rivers and the thinness of the inhabitants distract and disperse a trade, so that all ships in general gather each their loading up and down an hundred miles distant, and the best of trade that can be driven is only a sort of Scotch peddling." English officials did what they could to reverse this pattern, for settlers grouped around a village were easier to control. Education "flourishes only in such places," a southerner remarked, and they "highly advance religion," for "in towns congregations are never wanting." In 1662 Virginians were ordered to build a town on each river, and ships were instructed to unload only at specific points. Soon after these rulings were issued, the plague, then the great fire, hit London, "and the terror the people were in, lest the plague should be brought over with the goods from London, prevented them from residing at those ports." British authorities abandoned the experiment, and Chesapeake settlers were soon "at liberty again" to settle where they wished. The Virginia assembly made a new attempt in 1680 with the Cohabitation Act, whereby towns were to be erected in every county. The act, says Robert Beverley, "was kindly brought to nothing by the opposition of the merchants of London," an opinion that was at best a half-truth.

Boston, with some seven thousand inhabitants in 1689, stood forth as America's most important town. It had remained a farming village for over a decade after its founding, but with the outbreak of civil war in England it blossomed as a trading center. By 1650 it was extending control into the backcountry and developing something similar to a modern metropolitan economy. As the town grew, it continued outwardly to resemble an English borough: Slums developed along the waterfront; the inhabitants dumped rubbish in the streets, where it accumulated until the rains washed it away or the hogs that roamed through the town devoured it; farmers and craftsmen sold their produce and wares at the town market under the eye of officials who controlled the price and quality of goods and regulated weights and measures; the "watch" of old England called out the hours and protected the town at night; and municipal authorities tried to control labor by perpetuating the guild and apprentice system they had known at home.

By the end of the century many of the customs and habits imported from England had died. The shortage of labor had caused the rigid apprentice system to collapse almost at once, though in time a modified form of it would revive. Success at controlling wages and prices lasted longer, but by the end of the century supply and demand were regulating these more effectively than governmental control. The town meeting, which elected all municipal officials, had replaced the self-perpetuating council of English boroughs. Citizens steadily forced the town government to relinquish much of the power it had held over their lives in England. Yet when crime became more of a problem than it had been in Boston's earlier, holier days, when fire became a serious menace, when a shortage of workers caused wages to rise, when a drought forced up the price of food—they complained bitterly that the authorities did nothing to protect them. At the end of the century, Bostonians were searching desperately for a way to order municipal life without entrusting too much authority to the local government. To bridge the gap, the eighteenth century would devise the "voluntary association," an American innovation in the art of government that would long outlast the colonial period.

America's other important towns—New York, Philadelphia, Newport, and Charleston—experienced their own versions of Boston's growth pains. Each expected to perpetuate what it considered the best of English traditions and hoped to shed what it judged to be shoddy. Penn's dream of a "green country town" vanished quickly in the slums that arose along the Delaware; his attempts to enforce a "just price" and other forms of government control over the quality of goods and scale of wages met similar failure. For all the disillusionments these towns shared, each from the beginning developed a character of its own that would become more pronounced as the eighteenth century unrolled. Boston struck visitors who had touched elsewhere on the continent as staid. The finery many of its citizens wore and the mansions some of its wealthier merchants had built did little to relieve the town's high moral tone. Newport's mixture of Jews, Baptists, Catholics, Quakers, and Puritans, together with a large number of Negroes—Newport's merchant-shippers specialized in the slave trade—gave a cosmopolitan air to the town that belied its recent emergence from the village stage. New York lacked a town meeting to spice up local politics—it, like other towns, was governed by a board of self-perpetuating aldermen—but visitors rated it the liveliest town on the continent. The Sabbath there was a day reserved for pleasure, an inheritance perhaps from the Dutch habit of observing the Continental Sunday. In an age when men abominated water, every town spawned taverns; but none so many as dotted the streets of New York, which may explain why some surly visitors called it little more than a drowsy Dutch village. Philadelphia's variety of settlers gave it something of New York's and Newport's cosmopolitan air; the Quakers, who set the town's tone, contributed a staidness that resembled Boston's. Philadelphia and Charleston resembled one another in that both had been created after the great fire in London, and the proprietors had sought to avoid a similar disaster in their towns by creating a checkerboard layout for settlement. Charleston was still too young and small at the end of the century for more than a hint of the aristocratic quality of its society to show through. Its greatness, like that of Philadelphia and New York, lay in the eighteenth century.

The quality of American social life in 1689 in both town and country rated low by any standard. Not one newspaper existed on the continent, and whatever communications came from the outside world were brought by ship captains or found in journals imported from London. Books were few. Sophisticated diversions like the theater or concerts did not exist, for they required the patronage of a monied leisure class, which had not appeared by the end of the century. Every town highlighted the year with an annual fair, and in the less saintly spots, like New York, horseracing was a popular pastime. Men's lives centered in their work and in their homes. And whatever art they produced emerged from those two centers.

The Arts

The land imposed a rude existence on the earliest settlers. They knew nothing of log cabins and failed to free themselves enough from their past to invent them (the Swedes brought that structure to America). The first Englishmen pitched tents on the beaches or crept into hillside caves while they sought a toehold in the wilderness. Maryland's pioneers moved into shelters the Indians had abandoned. At Salem, John Endecott adapted the wigwam, adding a door at one end and a fireplace at the other. Here, in the first months, according to Edward Johnson, the Salem band "made [to] shift out the winter's cold by the fireside, . . . turning down many a drop of the bottle, and burning tobacco with all the ease they could, discoursing between one while and another, of the great progress they would make after the summer's sun had changed the earth's white furred gown into a green mantle."

The houses they eventually built duplicated to the best of their ability those they had known in England. They were not, Anthony Garvan has noted, haphazard or accidental responses to the demands of the forest but a product of English experience. Every English village sported numerous types of houses. All, from the manor house to the peasant's hut, were reproduced in varying degrees in the colonies, but the one built most often was that of the yeoman. The yeoman's house as it appeared in the English countryside had a large central chimney, flanked on one side by the kitchen, on the other by the living room and parlor; sometimes a fireplace appeared at each end of the building, a variation Virginia settlers were to prefer. A second floor, reached by a ladder or ladder-like stairway, held two rooms for sleeping. A lean-to for storing tools and farming equipment often jutted from the rear. Sometimes the house was constructed of brick. If built of wood, clapboard siding covered the outside walls. The roof sloped sharply. The second floor often extended out slightly over the first. Londoners had invented this overhang, as it was called, to increase the space of their upper floors. Country yeomen adopted it for much the same reasons their wives copied the dress of London women—to be fashionable—and also because it served as a practical way to protect the lower walls of the house from rain.

Colonists in seventeenth-century America adapted the English yeo-

man's house to America with only a few basic modifications. They kept
the overhang and the clapboard siding. Clapboards, however, came from
riven, or split, not sawed oak timber, for saws and sawmills were rare in
America. Splitting a log was a simple operation that required only a bit
and an ax, and when done by an expert produced a reasonably smooth
board that became smoother when weathered. New Englanders made
their clapboards of the same width, length, and thickness as barrel staves
and exported their surplus to the West Indies for barreling sugar. The
lack of suitable thatching grass forced the colonists to substitute wooden
shingles for roofing materials. Shingles were cut and placed to resemble
the slate roofing of an English manor house.

New England's meetinghouse, once thought to be a product of the
colonists' simple existence in the wilderness, came to America as an offshoot from the plain style of religious architecture that had been developing in Europe as an answer to the ornateness of Catholic architecture. All
the ingredients of both the Puritan and Quaker meetinghouses—stark
interior, clear windows, two-story façade, blunt tower (the steeple came
much later), movable communion table, box pew—had been evolving for
nearly a century among Protestant builders in England, Holland, Germany, and Huguenot France. American builders invented little in what
has since been called a characteristically American building.

The tools the colonial builders used throughout the seventeenth century were English in design and were usually made in England. The ax,
the primary tool for clearing the forest and building homes, remained
unchanged from the English ax throughout the seventeenth century. It
had a single bit, or cutting edge; a heavy poll, or dull end, some three to
five inches high; and a long straight handle. The curved-handled American ax did not evolve until the mid-eighteenth century and the double-
bitted ax did not come into use until the nineteenth century.

Changes occurred in American architecture as the seventeenth century aged, but again mainly because of developments in England. The
great fire of London caused English builders to shift to brick, and the
change was reflected in America. Builders in Carolina and Pennsylvania,
both post-Restoration colonies, imitated the brick buildings most recently
erected in London. New buildings in Boston, too, followed the English
pattern, especially after 1679, when the town endured a disastrous fire of
its own. Throughout the seventeenth century building styles in America
swung with the fashions in England, though it usually took from five to
ten years before the new fashion managed to travel the ocean.

The contents of American houses, as well as the houses themselves,
reflected changes in European tastes through the seventeenth century.
The heavy, ornate chests, bureaus, and chairs the early Puritans hauled

across the ocean exemplified the Renaissance-type furniture then popular in England. The early settlers ate from pewter ware as they had done at home. The first furniture made by the colonists was simple in design and construction mainly because of the limited skill of the craftsmen. The expense of pewter led many to replace worn out utensils with wooden versions. Village craftsmen used poplar and soft white basswood for "dish timber," turning out bowls, ladles, trenchers (plates), and noggins (drinking mugs), which were simple and graceful in design. Few then prized these homemade articles for their beauty. As the settlers grew prosperous toward the end of the century, they turned again to Europe to furnish their homes. When Virginia's well-to-do William Byrd, Sr., began to build a mansion in 1690, he sent to Rotterdam for bedsteads, curtains, looking glasses, tables, and upholstered chairs. In Byrd's house, as elsewhere in the colonies, china began to replace pewter on the dining table.

When Americans could not buy from Europe, they purchased imitations from local workshops. Boston had twenty-four silversmiths in 1680, but the work of all followed styles set across the ocean. Colonial craftsmen in the seventeenth century were ingenious and skilled but seldom original. Only when they worked alone without a backward glance toward Europe did they occasionally produce articles that combined beauty with practicality. Every village had its "native mechanical genius," one settler remarked, who with the few tools brought overseas "certainly performed wonders"—harrows with graceful wooden teeth, cedar ware whose alternate white and red stave "was then thought beautiful," puncheon floors that "were very neat, their joints close at the top, even and smooth."

The fine arts flourished only to the degree that they could be tied to some useful end. "The plowman that raiseth grain is more serviceable to mankind than the painter who draws only to please the eye," remarked an early New Englander. John Foster, who died in 1681 at the age of thirty-two, worked in the Cambridge, Massachusetts, printing shop where he taught himself wood engraving. His woodcut of Richard Mather served the practical purpose of illustrating a biography of that worthy, and Foster's excellent woodcut map of New England was used in William Hubbard's *Narrative of the Troubles with the Indians* (1677). The paintings of the seventeenth century (only a few survive) served the same useful end then that a photograph provides today. "Our early limner set a value on the unvarnished recording of hard-bitten men, of sturdy women," Oliver Larkin has said. "As he proceeded to paint those few colonial personalities who were important enough to have their likenesses made, he depicted not the accidents of light and shadow, but those elements which he knew to be permanent in the sitter." None of the few paintings that have survived from this period—the stark, forthright likenesses of Ann Pollard and Reverend Thomas Thacher, the self-portrait of a seamed old sailor named Thomas Smith, or the lively depiction of the three Gibbs children—can be called great art. These painters sought only to capture on canvas the character of their subjects; they lacked the skill or interest to be especially concerned with perspective, the subtleties of color, the elements of balance and contrast. But where they fail to delight the art critic, they please the historian; for as Larkin has said, "their work gives as clear a view as we can get of what the people of seventeenth-century America were like as they faced the job of carving a way of life out of the wilderness."

SOCIETY

The rigid sense of rank and order settlers brought from England disintegrated in America. Outward distinctions remained and were observed. Gentlemen in New England continued to be addressed as "master" and their wives as "mistress"; ordinary folk answered to "goodman" and "goodwife"; and servants and children were called by their first names. But these distinctions lacked the force they had had in England. Virginia gentlemen learned early that if they wanted land cleared, they, too, had to lift the ax; if they wanted food, they, too, had to join foraging expeditions or help plant the crop. It was not unusual for a New Englander to find that the enterprising young man he had brought over as a servant five years earlier now owned more land than his former master.

Labor

No one in the seventeenth century conceived of an individual as an independent, unattached unit in society. Men were tied inextricably to their family. The father ruled the family much like a patriarch out of the Old Testament: His decisions were not to be questioned; he represented the family in all its political, economic, and religious relations with the community. The family was held to be the nursery of the church and the commonwealth. "Ruin families, and you ruin all," went a maxim of the day.

America changed the concept of family and the roles of various members within it without reducing the importance of family in social and economic life. The limited opportunities for the young to branch out on their own made it difficult to establish independent households in England; sons were expected to bring their wives home to live. The abundance of land in America reversed that routine. The young could create their own homes early in life, and it was the parents who eventually came to live with their sons. In New England, family life blended with that of the village and of the church. In the South, life centered around the family. Funerals and christenings occurred in the home. The dead were buried in the family cemetery on the farm. Isolation forced the Southern farmer to depend almost completely on his family for companionship and amusement. The role of the woman within the family changed somewhat from what it had been in England. The demands of wilderness life forced her outside the accustomed role of housewife. She worked in the fields in harvest time and sometimes shouldered a gun in times of danger.

Servants and apprentices belonged within the family. Masters legally had the rights of a father to discipline those who worked for him and also the responsibility for their well-being. The English custom of a servant committing himself for life to the service of a family died quickly in the colonies. An ambitious man broke with his master and set out on his own as soon as he had accumulated a small stake, which did not take too long in a land where wages were three to four times what they were in England. Indentured servitude proved a more reliable method to procure servants. A man who lacked the funds to reach the New World signed a contract in England whereby he agreed to indenture himself for a particular length of time to whoever paid the cost of his transportation. All colonies by 1689 had a body of laws to protect the indentured servant—he could, for instance, sue in court against violations of his indenture or for maltreatment—and also to control him. A runaway servant could expect to face heavy punishment if caught, and most governments had laws that provided for extradition if the fugitive escaped beyond the boundaries of his home colony. The statutes dealing with indentured servants would need only slight modification to become slave codes at a later date.

The early Negroes were technically considered indentured servants, but the trend from the beginning was to treat them differently from white servants. His indenture usually lacked a terminal date, which made the Negro actually, if not legally, a slave from the start. The courts affirmed this prejudicial treatment. No general uneasiness about enslaving Negroes appeared in any of the colonies during the seventeenth century. A group of German Quakers in 1688 spoke out for "liberty of body" as well as liberty of conscience, but their plea died on the wind. Samuel Sewall at the end of the century condemned the institution in *The Selling of Joseph*. "Liberty is in real value next unto life," Sewall said. "None ought to part with it themselves, or deprive others of it but upon most mature consideration." But the Quakers and Sewall cried alone in the wilderness. Cotton Mather spoke for the multitude. "There is a fondness for freedom in many of you," Mather told Negroes attending one of his lectures, then went on to warn them to live patiently in their servitude, for that was "what God will have to be the thing appointed for you." (Not all colored people in America were slaves. A visitor to New York in 1679 came upon a colony of free West Indian Negroes on Manhattan Island; the colony eventually vanished, with its inhabitants apparently blending into the white population.)

Negro labor remained of slight importance throughout the seventeenth century. Virginia had received her first contingent of African slaves—14 in number—in 1619, but as late as 1641 not more than 250 Negroes were counted in the colony. Governor Berkeley estimated their number in 1670 at 2,000 out of a total population of 40,000. Slavery at the end of the century hovered as a cloud no bigger than a man's hand, but a cloud growing steadily larger, for conditions were right to promote its growth. Slave labor remained unimportant as long as only foreign-born Negroes were available and the small farm dominated the South, for the farmer had no time to supervise a man who spoke an unintelligible tongue and knew next to nothing about farming. By the 1680's, when the plantation began to supplant the farm, the Chesapeake country had a sizable stock of English-speaking Negroes on hand. William Fitzhugh said in 1686 that he owed twenty-nine slaves, most of them American born. He regarded these people much as he did his draft animals. They "increase," he told a friend, "being all young and a considerable parcel of breeders." A "dumb Negro" he had bought, who was "bad at work, worse at talking," was something to be rid of quickly.

Wealthy farmers like Fitzhugh who could afford to buy a number of slaves—Fitzhugh paid £23 10s. for the "dumb Negro" he complained of— were a rarity in seventeenth-century America, and indentured servitude remained throughout the century the standard form of labor. Once a servant had worked off his indenture, he was free to go where he wished. More often than not he headed toward the Middle Colonies, where there was still plenty of land available and society was more open than in the older colonies. "There is little or no encouragement for men of any tolerable parts to come hither," Governor Nicholson said of Virginia in 1701, though he might have been speaking of the Bay Colony, too.

Formerly there was good convenient land to be taken up, and there were widows [who] had pretty good fortunes, which were encouragements for men of parts to come. But now all or most of these good lands are taken up, and if there be any widows or maids of any fortune, the natives for the most parts get them; for they begin to have a sort of aversion to others, calling them strangers.

Opportunities for the laboring man in the older colonies were by the end of the century becoming limited. The word got around quickly, and not until the backcountry opened up would immigrants once again begin to stream toward these provinces.

The Elite

The path to power, be it social, political, or economic power, varied throughout the century and from colony to colony. However, two general patterns, both based on English models, appear to have emerged by 1689, one for the South and one for New England, with the Middle Colonies drawing on each.

The South's pattern, exemplified by developments in Virginia, did not take shape before the middle of the century. The sons of English gentlemen had originally settled Virginia and controlled its affairs, but this early governing elite soon faded away. Most either died or returned home. The void was filled from below by survivors of the colony's years of trial, men who lacked social status by English standards but who had shown the ability to endure in the wilderness. But they failed to pass their power on to their sons, for beginning in the 1640's and continuing for thirty years the younger sons of substantial English families once again came to Virginia. Names like Bacon, Byrd, Carter, Digges, Ludwell, and Mason—all prominent in England—now turned up in Virginia. More often than not these young men had sufficient backing to avoid the labor of hacking a farm from the forest; they usually purchased land that had been cleared. Governor Berkeley made room for Nathaniel Bacon on the council and slipped others into positions of power as swiftly as he could. Those he did not take care of were among the leaders of Bacon's Rebellion. By 1689 this new blood formed the basis of what would become the most celebrated oligarchy in American history.

The Virginia pattern of giving power to those who came from the elite in England was repeated in Maryland and Carolina and even New York. For example, soon after young Caleb Heathcote, who came from an eminent family, arrived in New York, the governor made room for him on the council. Political preferment helped promote Heathcote's activities as a merchant and land speculator, and within a few years he numbered among New York's richest and most influential gentlemen.

The routes to fortune and political power diverged until near the end of the century in New England. Orthodox Puritans, abetted by the still powerful ministers, maintained political control, whereas the merchants dominated economic affairs. Merchants had welcomed royal rule with the hope that it would bring them control of political affairs. They joined briefly with the orthodox to overthrow Andros but greeted the first royal governor under the new charter warmly. After 1689 merchants dominated New England politically as well as socially, their wealth rather than family ties in England having given them power. The clergy, however, continued as a strong voice in New England, especially beyond the rims of the port towns, where the merchants' grip on power was neither complete nor welcomed. In 1689, when a man named Nelson was proposed to lead an expedition against the French, he was rejected by the General Court because, said a diarist, "the country deputies said he was a merchant and not to be trusted, so it is offered to Sir William Phips. . . ."

The elite of America, like that of Bristol, York, or other outlying parts of England, was a provincial one that turned to London for cultural guidance. London shaped its tastes, set the fashion in dress, art, and architecture. Londoners wrote most of the books the elite read. But this colonial elite shared a quality that set it apart from English provincials. The abundance of land and an expanding economy created room at the top for more than one member of a family. Entail and primogeniture, encumbrances that the English attached to inheritances to preserve a family's power intact, faded away in the colonies. Economic, social, and political power, which had once passed down from eldest son to eldest son, tended now to spread throughout the family. Younger sons, if talented and ambitious, could win position and power that in England still went only to the eldest. This equality at the top created an elite in America that continued to puzzle the English throughout the colonial period.

Neither doctors nor lawyers by virtue of their profession alone were considered among the elite in America at the turn of the century, though those who practiced medicine (like Cotton Mather, usually members of the clergy) and those who handled legal matters (either merchants like Samuel Sewall or planters like William Fitzhugh) certainly numbered among the aristocracy, such as it was. Robert Beverley spoke for all when he said that Virginians "have the happiness to have very few doctors," adding that "there is not mystery enough" in the few diseases that plagued Virginians "to make a trade of physic there, as the learned do in other countries, to the great oppression of mankind." The antipathy toward lawyers in Virginia reached its peak in 1658 when they were totally ejected from the colony. New England had a like prejudice. John Hull viewed the "law to be very much like a lottery—great charge, little benefit." The Fundamental Constitutions of Carolina repeated this view, saying "it [was] a base and vile thing to plead for money or reward." Part of the objections were "the natural reaction of a frontier society to a profession identified with the complexities of civilization." These feelings were reinforced by the inferior quality of those who went into the profession, if it could be called that. At the end of the century, New York counted seven lawyers in its midst, two of whom were transported criminals, one a former dancing master, one a glover, and none who in England had risen to the status of attorney. The chief justice had been bred a soldier, and the attorney general had come over as a merchant. Andros had searched for able lawyers to fill judicial posts in the dominion and found so few that he had had to ask London to send over suitable candidates.

All who numbered themselves among the elite sought, publicly at least, to live up to the code laid down by Sir Thomas Smith in the sixteenth century and repeated in the seventeenth in Richard Braithwaite's *English Gentleman,* wherein it was said "that such whose very persons should be examples or patterns of vigilancy, providence, and industry must not sleep out their time under the fruitless shadow of security. Men in great place (saith one) are thrice servants—servants of the sovereign or state, servants of fame, and servants of business—so as they have no freedom neither in their persons, nor in their actions, nor in their times."

Education

Elementary education concerned the colonists little in the beginning. In England the family handled that duty, and settlers expected the pattern to continue in America. Early attention, therefore, went to creating colleges that would build on the educational base begun in the home. Virginia made the first attempt to establish a college, only to have its dream vanish in the massacre of 1622. Talk of a college continued through the seventeenth century, but nothing concrete had been achieved by the time of the Glorious Revolution. The founding of William and Mary was delayed until 1693, over a half century after the Puritans had created Harvard.

The need for a school to educate new ministers as the old ones died off prompted Massachusetts' General Court in 1636 to appropriate £400 for the founding of a college. A year later, after the Pequot Indians and Anne Hutchinson had been disposed of, a Board of Overseers consisting of six magistrates and six ministers was appointed; a house and an acre of land were purchased in Cambridge; a professor was hired; and the following summer the first class was admitted. John Harvard, who died in 1638, left his library of about four hundred volumes and half his estate (just over £700) to the college, which was then named for him.

Both Harvard and William and Mary planned to emulate Oxford and Cambridge, where the faculties controlled all university affairs. But Protestantism and the American environment combined to create something entirely different. Protestantism introduced the element of lay control into clerical affairs. It was not a drastic step from admitting men who were not clerics into church government to admitting men who were not teachers into college government. Americans of the seventeenth century saw this as an advance, for it broke up the priestly autonomy of education and brought it under the control of the community. But lay control might have developed in the American college without Protestantism. European colleges had evolved out of long-established communities of scholarship and teaching. Harvard and William and Mary had been created literally overnight by the community. They had to be nursed, and because the public would do the nursing—often through public benefactions—the public thought it should share in their management. Moreover, it would have been impossible for the faculties to govern, for there were no faculties until after the colleges had been founded.

The initial lack of a faculty led to another difference in the American college. The president became of key importance. At Oxford he served as little more than the faculty's voice. At William and Mary and Harvard he taught, he selected the faculty, he dealt with the trustees. The prestige and pride that elsewhere were vested in the faculties came to center in him, and there, with some modification, they have remained to this day. Strong presidents, like Harvard's Henry Dunster, could make strong colleges. Dunster replaced the college's ineffective first president in 1640, and he immediately sought to broaden the curriculum. In 1647 he asked for money to buy books, "especially in law, physics, philosophy, and mathematics" for the use of the scholars "whose various inclinations to all professions might thereby be encouraged and furthered." In 1650 the General Court, under Dunster's urging, gave a charter that created a separate corporation of the college, though the state still maintained a hand in controlling affairs. Neither Harvard nor William and Mary, with their dual boards of control, were characteristic of the future American college, which would be governed by unitary lay boards with absolute powers. (Yale, granted a charter by the Connecticut legislature in 1701, created a single board of trustees to govern the college, a decision, says Richard Hofstadter, that "marks a momentous break" with the past, but in all other ways Yale belongs to the seventeenth century rather than with those colleges that emerged out of the Great Awakening of the eighteenth century.)

By the end of the century the sharp distinction between the English and American college had been duplicated by an equally sharp break with old traditions on the elementary level. Studies of deeds and petitions reveal that about 40 per cent of the women and 90 per cent of the men in New England and around 25 per cent of the women and 55 per cent of the men in Virginia could write their names. The validity of these estimates in terms of literacy may be slight, because they exclude those people, indentured servants and the like, who had little chance to sign deeds and petitions and they misleadingly imply that anyone who can write his name is literate. But whatever the true literacy figures, education lagged in the South. To some degree this stemmed from the dispersion of the population, which made it difficult to establish schools. New England offered a friendlier environment to promote education. Communities were more compact, local government more vigorous, and it was a matter of importance to the holy commonwealth to educate ministers. The region's high concentration of university graduates—about one person out of every forty families in early Massachusetts was a graduate of Cambridge or Oxford—gave the community its educational ideals.

Despite the advantages of environment and motivation, the quality of education deteriorated through the century in New England, perhaps because there, as in Virginia, the family was failing to fulfill its educational duties. In England a child learned to read and write at home. If he appeared sufficiently bright, he was sent to grammar school—some five hundred of these privately and religiously endowed schools were scattered through England in the early seventeenth century—where he learned to use Latin with ease and received a start in Greek, both practical subjects in that day for anyone training to be a minister, public servant, architect, lawyer, or doctor. The ablest of the grammar-school graduates went on to either Cambridge or Oxford. In New England, however, the family's failure to do its part endangered the entire educational structure. Massachusetts decided to force parents to do what they had once done voluntarily. A law passed by the General Court in 1642 directed parents and masters of indentured servants to teach their children and servants "to read and understand the principles of religion and the capital laws of the country," and to see to it that they were kept constantly employed in some useful occupation. The desire to have all children able to read was not unique, but making it compulsory was.

The act of 1642 did not order the establishment of schools but merely demanded that parents fulfill their duty as educators. Meanwhile, some of the larger, more prosperous coastal towns had on their own set up grammar schools for children similar to those of England. Where the English schools were supported by private endowments, the New England towns, lacking that resource, turned to church-levied contributions or used income from public property to subsidize education. But progress was slow. Only eleven schools existed in 1647 throughout New England to educate a population of some twenty-five thousand. The poverty of the people made it difficult to support education on an informal basis. In 1647 the General Court passed an act designed, according to its preamble, to prevent "that old deluder, Satan" from keeping men "from the knowledge of the Scriptures." The act that followed that cliché introduction marked a sharp break with English educational traditions. It ordered all towns of fifty families or more to appoint someone to teach the children to read, which in effect meant that they must establish some form of public education. Parents were not obligated to send youngsters to school but only to see that they learned somehow to read. By 1671 all New England, except Rhode Island, had similar acts on the books. The quality of the schools varied, as always, with the quality of the schoolmasters. Ezekiel Cheever, who "held the rod for seventy years" in New England, taught at New Haven, Ipswich, Charlestown, and Boston; and wherever he went, the number of students from that town who went on to Harvard shot upward.

The view held by some historians that the state stepped into education in order to shore up "the weakening structure of family discipline" must be taken with care, for it is notable that a similar development was occurring simultaneously under the Commonwealth in England, where the state for the first time actively promoted and supported the establishment of schools. As a result, W. K. Jordan has pointed out, educational opportunities in England by 1660 "were more widespread and stronger than they had ever been before or were ever to be again until well into the nineteenth century." It is likely that here as elsewhere, New England took its cue from old England, where such reformers as Sir William Petty were arguing that no one should be excluded from education "by reason of the poverty and inability of their parents, for hereby it hath come to pass that many are now holding the plough that might have been made fit to steer the state."

The schools established in New England in the seventeenth century resembled the new Puritan, rather than the traditional, grammar schools of England. Some were free, some demanded tuition, but in all the poor entered free. None were church schools; the state, not private donors, had created them. The clergy's omnipresent role in education vanished in New England about the time it did in old England. The new schools on both sides of the ocean emphasized but did not concentrate solely on Latin and Greek; the empirical and the utilitarian were also given their day. (It should be noted that the Quakers of Pennsylvania shared with the Puritans—English and American—this educational reformation of the seventeenth century. "There is no positive evidence," says Frederick Tolles,

that Quaker leaders or schoolmasters were influenced by the treatises of John Durie, Sir William Petty, Samuel Hartlib, and the other [English] reformers, but there is abundant evidence that the Quaker theory of education was in harmony with their insistence upon "the importance of dealing sensibly with concrete and material things, of actually expending energy in the pursuit of truth . . . in contrast to the non-physical activity . . . of those who sought truth in books and the minds.")

The Restoration unleashed attacks in England on grammar schools. They endangered the monarchy and diverted "those whom nature or fortune had determined to the plough, the oar, or other handicrafts" out of their assigned niche in life, thereby disturbing the social hierarchy. Something of this spirit soon drifted to America. Governor Berkeley thanked God in 1671 that *"there are no free schools* nor *printing* in Virginia." He hoped none should appear for a century to come, "for *learning* has brought disobedience, and heresy, and sects into the world, and *printing* has divulged them, and libels against the best government. God keep us from both!" By the 1670's the vigor had vanished from New England's school system, to judge by the complaints of the ministers. "There is a great decay in inferior [elementary-secondary] schools," Thomas Shepard said in 1672, and the next year he told the people "that the schools languish, and are in a low condition in the country." The schools appear to have languished even more after King Philip's War, until by the end of the century only the poor were being educated at public expense, and the well-to-do were sending their children to private schools.

Public education made no headway elsewhere in America. Pennsylvania founded a school in the first year of its existence, but the tuition charged limited it to the children of the "better sort." The Dutch continued to educate their children in parochial schools, and elsewhere in New York only private academies existed. By the end of the century illiteracy was rising rapidly in all colonies. These second- and third-generation settlers may have been better adapted to the wilderness than the most accomplished of the first colonists, but they were clumsy writers, ill-read, and often illiterate.

The decline in literacy stemmed in part from the lack of something to read. In the seventeenth century no newspaper existed in the colonies. Boston's *Public Occurrences* produced a single issue in 1690; the paper was immediately suppressed and no other appeared until the *Boston News-Letter* in 1704, which was "published by authority." Printing fared a little better—in New England, at least. A press set up at Cambridge in 1639 produced in the first decade the "Bay Psalm Book," *The Body of Laws and Liberties,* and ten almanacs among its imprints. The General Court worried enough about its influence to appoint two men in 1662 to supervise its productions. These officers five years later stirred up a storm by consenting to Thomas a Kempis' *The Imitation of Christ.* Bay leaders found the book written "by a popish minister, wherein is contained some things that are less safe to be infused amongst the people of this place," and they directed it returned to the licensers for a "more full revisal." A second press established in Boston in 1675 under the eye of the General Court performed its job more discreetly.

The lack of a free press should not be blamed on the Puritan mentality. When Virginia acquired its first press in 1681, Lord Culpeper summoned the printer and ordered him to post a bond and to agree "not to print anything hereafter, until his Majesty's pleasure shall be known," the severest form of censorship possible, because the printer could never be sure what "his Majesty's pleasure" might be. Lord Howard of Effingham's instructions in 1683 ordered him "to allow no person to use a printing press on any occasion whatsoever," and from that day until 1729 Virginia lived without a printer.

The almanac remained through the seventeenth century the only popular medium for spreading ideas in the colonies. Most of the almanacs were issued from New England until near the end of the century, when Philadelphia and New York began to produce their own versions. All were rough imitations of European almanacs, filled with astrological prophecies about man and weather. Those printed at Cambridge, Massachusetts, did something toward spreading Copernicus' revolutionary conception of the universe, which might be marked as the first attempt at scientific popularization in American history.

THE WAY THEY THOUGHT

Americans of the seventeenth century sought to think as well as to live like Englishmen, but again, though they often took their cues from England, the lines they spoke differed in accent and content. Even when they consciously tried to reproduce the English pattern, something went wrong.

Science

The century that saw the settlement of the American colonies saw, too, the rise of modern science in Europe. Kepler produced his laws on the motions of planets and thereby contributed to the foundations of modern astronomy in the years between the founding of Jamestown and Plymouth. William Harvey published his discovery of the circulation of the blood in 1628, two years before Boston was established. The hivings-out of New England were underway the year Galileo was forced to "abjure, curse and detest the error and the heresy of the movement of the earth." Newton's *Principia Mathematica* and the Glorious Revolution jointly marked the end of this "century of genius," as Alfred North Whitehead has called it.

America here contributed little to the achievements of the age. Thomas Brattle, whose astronomical observations in 1680 were used by Newton in the *Principia,* gives one explanation for the poor showing. "I am here all alone by myself, without a meet help in my studies," adding at a later date, "I never had anybody to direct me, to assist me, or to encourage me." John Winthrop, Jr., had another explanation. When urged by the Royal Society to "make it a good part of your business to recommend this real experimental way of acquiring knowledge," he replied in 1668 that hope for achievements out of America was at the moment dim. Too many other matters needed tending to first.

Plantations in their beginnings have work enough and find difficulties sufficient to settle a comfortable way of subsistence, there being buildings, fencings, clearing and breaking up of ground, lands to be attended, orchards to be planted, highways and bridges and fortifications to be made, and all things to do, as in the beginning of the world.

To say that seventeenth-century America contributed little to the rise of science is not to say that the stream of new ideas coming out of Europe passed America by. The best minds in America absorbed the new findings almost as rapidly as they were accepted in England. (Which may not be saying much. English academics were no swifter than the Catholic Church in acknowledging Copernicus' conception of an earth that moved around the sun. Many among the learned still rejected Galileo's theory after he had made his humiliating retraction. Harvey's discovery was still being warmly debated among English intellectuals in the 1660's.) By 1659 Harvard was using a text that expounded the Copernican system, only three years after the book had come out in England. In 1660 the circulation of the blood was the subject of a master's thesis at Harvard. By the end of the century, two Americans—William Byrd, Sr., of Virginia and John Winthrop, Jr., of Connecticut—had been elected to the Royal Society in London, and a small band of others were sending in a stream of reports to the society about the "poison-wood-tree," the color of Indian children at birth, "the natural history of whales with a particular account of the ambergris," the opossum's sack for its young, and so forth, *ad infinitum*.

Much of the information sent across the water was either inaccurate or dead wrong. (Or so it seemed at the time). Winthrop did see a fifth satellite circling Jupiter—Galileo had found four and not until 1892 was the fifth finally confirmed—through the three-and-a-half–foot telescope he had brought back from England. Perhaps it was chagrin over his supposed error as much as generosity that soon after led him to give the telescope to Harvard. Cotton Mather dispatched a series of wild surmises to the Society. A flight of pigeons produced his idea that they belonged to some "undiscovered satellite accompanying the earth at a near distance." He wrote of rattlesnake venom so powerful that a drop on an ax blade discolored the steel and when used "the discolored part broke out, leaving a gap." The discovery of a mammoth's bones in New York led to talk about a lost race of giants, perhaps of the sort mentioned in Genesis. Credulity about the natural world was not, however, an American monopoly. It belonged to the age. The great English chemist, Robert Boyle, held that good and bad angels controlled men's destinies. Harvey believed that the heart's beat came from heat embedded in the spirit of the blood, a spirit "identical with the essence of the stars." Newton wasted his declining years exploring the art of alchemy. The trouble was, Richard Shryock has remarked, "no clear distinction between the natural and the supernatural had been devised." It comes as no surprise, then, to find Cotton Mather, perhaps the most informed American of his day on the new experimental science, sharing in the persecution of the Salem witches. "The seventeenth century by its own standards was an age of reason," Shryock has said, "yet from the present viewpoint it was still a credulous age."

Nothing reveals this credulity more clearly than the medical knowledge of the day. Except for Harvey's discovery, it advanced little in the seventeenth century in England and thus little in America. John Winthrop, Jr., whose first love was medicine, depended for the most part on a set of old wives' remedies plus a few new ones drawn from Indian lore. Among the books he and other "physicians" used were Johan Glauber's *Chemistry,* Galen's *Art of Physics* and *The Unlearned Chemist,* and Philip Barrough's *Method of Physic,* all of which held that nothing got well of itself and that there was a remedy to cure every illness if only men could find it. Bloodletting remained through the century the most popular cure-all for whatever might ail man. A "black powder" made of toads cured smallpox, for toads were considered poisonous and all poison drew poison unto itself. The rattlesnake exorcised a variety of ills. Its flesh was fed to the infirm in broths; its gall mixed with chalk was made into "snake balls" and given internally; its heart was dried and powdered and drunk in wine or beer to cure the venom of the snake, on the principle that like cures like. Its oil, according to Edward Eggleston, was used in Virginia for gout and in New England for frozen limbs.

Men of the seventeenth century held that God made all things with reference to man and his needs. "We have the Scriptures to back it that God created nothing in vain," said John Josselyn, who made at least two trips to New England to study the flora and fauna there with an eye to their medicinal value. Josselyn learned from his research that the rough surface of green pine cones served to remove wrinkles from the face. The kidney bean was, of course, "good to strengthen the kidneys." The eggs of the turkey buzzard restored "decayed nature exceedingly." The fangs of wolves strung about the neck saved children from fright. While settlers practiced these rites, they continued to ridicule the Indian and his dependence on the medicine man. The search by men like Josselyn for remedies among the new plants found in America had one virtue greater than the "remedies" uncovered: it created a strong interest in botany, the one field of science in which colonial Americans would make significant contributions.

The primitive conditions in seventeenth-century America inhibited the growth of science. Everything else favored its acceptance. The clergy were for it because they did not fear its revelations. They believed that studying the universe would reveal God's ways more clearly and perhaps clarify His scriptural pronouncements. Knowledge as well as faith could make men realize the glory of God and the wonders of His work. (The techniques of science had revealed a universe more immense than men had imagined possible. The microscope showed Cotton Mather "animals of which many hundreds would not equal a grain of sand," and the telescope revealed that "all this globe is but as a pin's point, if compared with the mighty universe.") The clergy continued to draw moral lessons from natural events. A brilliant comet in 1680 led to a sermon on "Heaven's Alarm to the World." An earthquake, a flood, or a famine continued to offer ministers a chance to wonder aloud what the people had done to offend God. But the clergy was also interested in science as a way to improve man's lot on earth. It was Cotton Mather, after all, over the objections of Boston doctors, who fought and won the battle for smallpox inoculation in the early eighteenth century. Mather, with his "curious way of backing into modernity," did as much as any colonist of the day to lay the basis for the scientific achievements of such men of the eighteenth century as Benjamin Franklin.

Religion

Religion in America during the seventeenth century underwent a change so great that, for all its gradualness, the break with past traditions equaled that perpetrated by Luther and Calvin. Settlement had not long been underway before colonial promoters were rejecting the idea of the state fostering a particular brand of religion. A single state-supported church would deter dissidents who as settlers might contribute to the colony's prosperity. By the end of the century the old belief that no state could endure without a tight union with the church was on the wane in every colony. The multiplicity of sects made it difficult to establish one church where many competed for attention. England's Act of Toleration in 1689, which allowed all Protestants to worship as they pleased, gave official sanction to an accomplished fact in over half the colonies, and prodded those still clinging to the past to adjust to the new climate. True religious liberty—the right to be free from religion as well as to worship as one wished—existed in America no more than it did in England, though William Byrd, Sr., found on a visit to New York in 1685 that few there cared "what religion their neighbor is of, or whether he hath any or none."

The habit of an established church tied to the state took longest to die in Virginia and Massachusetts. Early Virginians sought to duplicate the Church of England in America. Laws were passed that required tithes from all, gave glebe lands to ministers, and ordered parish churches built by local taxation. Dissenters—Puritans, Quakers, and Anabaptists—could be banished, fined, and imprisoned, and Catholics were forbidden to hold public office. For all the effort, Virginia's established church resembled, rather than duplicated, the Church of England. The lack of a resident bishop—the Bishop of London was responsible for Virginia's religious affairs—allowed control over church matters to drift into the hands of the assembly, the governor, and, most important, the parish vestry. The appointment of James Blair in 1689 as the bishop's local representative to guard church interests came too late, for by that time the Church of England in Virginia had been transmuted into something new. The vestry selected and disciplined the clergy, a duty performed by church authorities in England. A string of ineffectual ministers—"such as wore black coats, and could babble in a pulpit, roar in a tavern, . . . and rather, by their dissoluteness, destroy than feed their flocks"—led to a policy of "hiring" ministers by the year rather than making an appointment for life as in England. The number of sermons the minister had to preach and other aspects of his duties were determined by the assembly. The minister had no fixed "living" as in England but was paid in tobacco, whose price fluctuated sharply from year to year. Infractions could be tried by the General Court, consisting of the governor and the council. The size of the parish, often the same as the county, forced the minister to become a "circuit rider" to reach his people. The parlor often became the scene for Sunday service; the family burying ground replaced the consecrated ground of the church yard; and lay readers substituted in a minister's absence.

Religious differences between New England and Virginia had remained more superficial than deep from the first days of settlement. The early Virginia clergy, though officially Anglican, favored the non-separating hand of Puritanism. The assembly's directive in 1676 to set aside "days of public fasting and humiliation" in order to "humbly implore the divine assistance and blessing" upon the colony's "endeavors in this war" resembled a similar proclamation issued during King Philip's War by the Bay Colony's General Court. A Virginia statute that any person who "shall blaspheme the name of God, either drunk or sober, shall for every offense run the gauntlet, through one hundred men or thereabouts," and if he continues to blaspheme "shall be bored through the tongue with a hot iron" sounds more puritanical than the Puritans. Virginians disliked hierarchical control of their religious affairs as fully as New Englanders. Local citizens in both regions monopolized the management of religious matters—hired the minister, paid him, and dismissed him when they wished. What differences existed earlier in the century had diminished by the end, as the pronounced Calvinistic bent of the founding fathers of New England began to wane among the prosperous gentlemen of the third generation.

Throughout the seventeenth century in Massachusetts there had been a "weakening sense of sin," as Henry Bamford Parkes puts it, adding: "As the New Englanders advanced in material security and well-being, they were less inclined to regard themselves as creatures of complete depravity who could be saved only by supernatural grace." Displeasure against old-line Puritans simmered until 1699, when a group composed mostly of well-to-do inhabitants, among them several merchants, broke off from the Boston meeting and founded the Brattle Street Church. This dissident body favored the Half-Way Covenant, condemned public confessions, said baptism could not be refused "to *any* child," and left the selection of minister up to all in the congregation who shared in the maintenance of the church. Soon after, Increase Mather published *The Order of the Gospel,* which urged a return to the tenets of the founding fathers. A copy of Mather's volume turned up in Plymouth with some light-hearted lines scribbled within the cover, among which were these:

> The old strait gate is now out of date,
> The street it must be broad. . . .
>
> Relations are rattle with Brattle and Brattle;
> Lord brother mayn't command.
> But Mather and Mather had rather and rather
> The good old way should stand.

The decline in old-fashioned piety disturbed New England's ministers to the point where they became anxious about the collective soul of their people. They warned of a sign from God of His wrath, a sign they hoped would direct their parishioners back to orthodoxy. The sign turned up in 1692 in Salem village, a suburb some two miles distant from Salem proper. In over a half century of settlement, the village had barely escaped from the frontier. Wolves and bears still roamed the area. The horrors of King Philip's War remained a vivid memory, and within the past three years men from the village had been killed by Indians, those "children of Satan." Those who had come from England originally to settle the town had only recently died off. The new leaders for the most part had only a scanty education; several were unable to write. The supernatural impressed them, and Increase Mather's *Essay for the Recording of Illustrious Providences* (1684)—earthquakes, cyclones, witches, and anything that revealed God's power, but did not, like miracles, contradict the laws of nature, came under the heading of providences—reinforced their inclination toward the superstitious. Cotton Mather's *Memorable Providences, Relating to Witchcrafts and Possessions* (1689), the product of experiments conducted on children subject to fits, had come out in a second edition the year before the horrors of Salem village burst forth.

The times were right for a witchcraft craze, especially in Salem. The village was uneasy with its young and rigid minister; several teenage girls gathered regularly in the minister's kitchen to listen to tales of voodoo told by a West Indian Negress. Two of the girls began to behave oddly. A doctor called in to diagnose their illness said they were afflicted by "an evil hand," that is, a witch. The Bible said: "Thou shalt not suffer a witch to live." Two magistrates, both respected men, came out from Boston to conduct an examination. The girls in public screamed and shouted and pointed out their tormentors. Soon Salem wives accused husbands of being witches, and husbands wondered about their wives. As news of the examination spread through New England, the craze, too, spread to other villages—Reading, Gloucester, Beverly, Charlestown, Andover, and eventually even Boston.

The trials of the accused began in early June with seven experienced judges on hand to hear evidence and mete out sentences. First to be convicted and hanged was Bridget Bishop, an attractive young woman who ran a tavern in the village. A delay occurred before the next trial, for some of the judges wondered if spectral "evidence" ("evidence" given by the voices or apparitions to the witnesses) should be accepted in court to condemn a person. The judges turned to the clergy for advice. Samuel Willard and Increase Mather seemed to say spectral evidence was valid if used with caution. The trials continued. Five more "witches" were hanged in July, five in August, eight in September. Giles Corey was crushed to death by rocks. He had first accused his wife of being a witch, but when he himself was accused, he realized her innocence. He willed his property to the two sons-in-law who had stood by his wife, then "stood mute" in court. A man found guilty of a felony in common law lost his property to the state, unless he refused to plead. But to stand mute exposed a man to the terrible penalty of *peine forte et dure,* being pressed to death. If he endured that ordeal without confessing, then his heirs would inherit. Tradition has it that as the stones were piled on Corey he gasped "more weight," repeating the words until the last breath had been crushed from him.

By the end of September, 20 "witches" were dead and some 150 were in jail around the Bay Colony awaiting trial. Up to now the intellectuals of New England, most of whom privately condemned the events, had said nothing publicly. Their respect for law and fear of undermining the structure of society caused them, so they said, to hold their tongues. Several of the clergy had been the first to write Governor Phips and the council of the "need of a very critical and exquisite *caution,* lest by too much *credulity* for things received only on the Devil's authority, there be a door opened for a long train of miserable consequences," but their remarks were ignored. Early in October Increase Mather spoke out against the emphasis on spectral evidence, saying: "It is better that ten suspected witches should escape than one innocent person should be condemned." Thomas Brattle, who had been horrified by the hangings but had said nothing publicly, now wrote an open letter censuring the whole business. Governor Phips, his nerve stiffened by these opinions, plus an accusation against Lady Phips of witchcraft, ordered those accused of being witches to be freed from the jails. The General Court, which up to now had avoided a stand, called for a fast "and convocation of ministers that may be led in the right way as to witchcraft."

But the trials continued into 1693. Now, however, though the same judges presided, the atmosphere had changed, and nearly all the accused were acquitted. The delusion subsided, and the horror of what had been done took hold of those who had shared in the affair. Several of the young girls who had begun the craze admitted they had lied. One of the judges, Samuel Sewall, publicly confessed his errors. Reverend John Hale, the chief witness against Bridget Bishop, the first to die, allowed his confession to be published in 1697 as *A Modest Inquiry into the Nature of Witchcraft.* Cotton Mather kept silent in public but had private doubts "for my not appearing with *vigor* to stop the proceedings of the judges when the inexplicable storm from the invisible world assaulted the country." On that note of remorse, Mather, along with a good deal of New England, stepped into the eighteenth century.

Language and Literature

A language carried into a new environment, it has been said, brings with it preconceived notions that seldom harmonize with the new setting. Wherever possible the seventeenth-century colonist used old names to make the new seem familiar. "Bison" became "buffalo," which the English knew from Far Eastern travelers; "puma" became "lyon" in Virginia, "tyger" in South Carolina, "panther" in Pennsylvania, and "catamount," or "cat-of-the-mountain," in Maryland and elsewhere. A "red-breasted thrush" was called "robin," though it only resembled robin redbreast of England. When the colonist came upon birds or beasts that bore no likeness at all to what he had known, he gave them blunt descriptive names: "bluebird," "garter snake," "mockingbird," "bullfrog," "catbird," "mudhen," "muskrat," "razorback," "groundhog," "canvasback," and "flying squirrel." The head of an Indian "nation" became a "king" and his daughter a "princess," because the Englishman could think of nothing better. Only toward the end of the seventeenth century did the Indian's bark house cease to be called a "palace" and become the "wigwam" it was, and only then did such Indian titles as "werowance," "sachem," "sagamore," and "cockerouse" drift into the language. Englishmen overseas were reluctant to cease being Englishmen. Indian "maize" became "corn," the generic word for grain in England, and "maize" never entered the vernacular. Children continued to be reared on English proverbs ("Nothing succeeds like success") and English jingles ("Thirty days hath September, April, June, and November . . ."). Only occasionally did changed social conditions affect the language. A seventeenth-century settler preferred to be called a "hired servant" to distinguish him from a "bonded servant," and this in time was altered to "hired hand" or simply "hand."

Some new words more easily crept into the language. "Succotash" and "hominy" slipped in when those Indian dishes became part of the diet. "Squaw," "papoose," "moccasin," and "toboggan" were all part of the vernacular by the end of the century. The word "hickory" was carved out of "pawcohiccora" and "squash" from "askútasquash." "Wampumpeak," the Indian name for the white shell beads used for money, slipped in as "wampum" in New England and as "peak" or "peague" in the South. But the language the colonists spoke and wrote remained through the seventeenth century an English only occasionally salted with American words.

Fortunately, the colonies were settled when the English that Shakespeare wrote flourished, when the language was still forming, and, as Morison puts it, "new words were being coined by the score, and in the hands of their first users they had all the brightness and beauty of newly minted guineas." The writings of Captain John Smith, William Bradford, and John Winthrop, to name the best of the lot, lacked form, for they were done hurriedly, usually in moments snatched from the business of carving a life from the wilderness, but they had great power. All these settlers, be it a Smith out mainly for adventure or a Winthrop determined to build "a city upon a hill," were engaged in a great experiment, and they wished to communicate the sense and feeling of settling a wilderness. They "wrote the English language spontaneously, forcefully, like honest men," says Moses Coit Tyler (whose own magnificent *History of American Literature* has in it much of the force and beauty of these early writings he so admired). They "wrote books not because they cared to write books, but because by writing books they could accomplish certain other things which they did care for."

What has been said of the chronicles that caught the excitement of opening up America can be said, too, for the sermon, which in seventeenth-century America was to literature much what the novel is today. The sermon was also, as Daniel Boorstin has recently said, "the communal ceremony which brought a strong orthodoxy to bear on the minutiae of life," or as Tyler has phrased the thought, "the central and commanding incident" in the colonists' lives; "the one stately spectacle for all men and all women year after year; the grandest matter of anticipation or of memory; the theme for hot disputes on which all New England would take sides, and which would seem sometimes to shake the world to its center." A great preacher worked hard at his sermons. He aimed, said Increase Mather, "not over his people's heads, but into their hearts." If the discourse came forth in "a homely dress and course habit," said Thomas Hooker, that was because "plainness and perspicuity, both for matter and manner of expression, are the things that I have conscientiously endeavored in the whole debate," for writings "are not to dazzle but [to] direct the apprehension of the meanest, and . . . to make a hard point easy and familiar in explication." Today these sermons, for the most part, make dull reading, but through their dryness shines the effort to make the vernacular, the "language and dialect" of the people, part of literature.

The homely directness and sometimes earthy quality of the sermon continued through the century in Roger Williams' essays, in Nathaniel Ward's tale of a "simple cobbler"; and toward the end of the century, when educated people had swung to an ornate, pompous style imported from England, the plain style persisted in a new form of literature—the Indian narrative, which took two forms. There were the firsthand accounts of the Indian wars, like Benjamin Church's memoir of King Philip's War and William Hubbard's inaccurate but vivid *Narrative of the Troubles with the Indians in New England* (1677). Then there were the captive tales. Mary Rowlandson's account of her three months of captivity during King Philip's War, told in a plain, blunt style, might be called America's first best seller. Her narrative fixed the pattern for what in the eighteenth century would become a standardized and popular form of reading fare.

Almost no humor has come down from seventeenth-century America, partly because most of the writing that survives was produced by Puritans. But even in New England men of wit must have relieved the monotony of life with droll stories. Sarah Kemble Knight's account of a trip to Connecticut shows the people could laugh at themselves and those around

them, but almost none of this humor comes through in the formal writings of the time. Nathaniel Ward's *Simple Cobbler of Agawam* (1647)
is filled with wit and even a flash or two of humor, but these light touches
are lost in the foam of his wrath at the foibles of the times.

The earnest view of life pervaded what passed for poetry. The great
poem of the age, so far as popularity went, was Michael Wigglesworth's
Day of Doom (1662), which in singsong verses describes God's treatment
of saints and sinners on Judgment Day. "If it seems today a poetic failure," Kenneth Murdock has said, "it is worth remembering that it
probably also seemed so to Cotton Mather and to Wigglesworth himself.
They knew that the *Day of Doom* was not aimed at literary critics but
at simple folk who liked their 'Truths' and 'Meeter' plain." The poem
was, in effect, a doggerel version of Puritan theology, and its enormous
popular success calls to mind Morison's observation on the Puritans: "Very
seldom in history has an intellectual class succeeded so well in breaking
through to the common consciousness." (Two poets of distinction—Anne
Bradstreet and Edward Taylor—did emerge out of seventeenth-century
America. Their work survives purely for its literary merit rather than for
its value to the historian, and it is to the literary critic that the interested
student should turn for judgments of their poetry.)

The plain style dominated American literature through the first half
of the seventeenth century, but with the Restoration came a change directly related to events in the mother country. There, a mannered prose,
packed with puns and epigrams, pedantic conceits and smart phrases,
came into being. No sooner had the next style taken hold in England than
it swept across the water to America, where "a race of literary snobs," as
Tyler calls them, materialized—"writers who in their thin and timid
ideas, their nerveless diction, and their slavish simulation of the supposed
literary accent of the mother-country, make confession of the inborn weakness and beggarliness of literary provincials."

Cotton Mather, a man quick to sense new fashions, was among the
first to adopt the new literary style. Soon his writings were filled with
lumbering, florid sentences the length of a paragraph, spotted with clever
phrases and adorned with pompous allusions. Occasionally, however, he
forgot himself and wrote in the direct and forceful manner of his fore-
bears. Mather, for all his outward certainty, often seemed a man at loose
ends. In his thought, as in his style, he wavered between an age dying
and an age dawning. He saw that much that the original settlers had
brought with them early in the century had either been discarded or reshaped into an unrecognizable form. Old values had waned or vanished
and new ones for a new age had yet to take shape. A once simple society
was beginning to become complex, and men like Mather, accustomed to

old forms, were puzzled how to deal with the situation. "Damned if I don't sometimes think it's easier to pioneer a country than to settle down in it," a character in a twentieth-century drama remarks. Americans who watched the seventeenth century fade must have known something of that same bewildered feeling. The eighteenth century was going to be a difficult one to get through.

BIBLIOGRAPHY

The Way They Lived

The early chapters in Merle Curti's tightly written *Growth of American Thought* (1943) give a balanced survey of the scene. Fuller, less trustworthy, but lively reading is the first volume of Vernon L. Parrington's *Main Currents in American Thought* (1927; pb.). Daniel Boorstin's *The Americans: The Colonial Experience* (1958; pb.) is equally entertaining and equally provocative. Edward Eggleston's beautifully written social history, *The Transit of Civilization* (1900; pb.), though the first to cover the subject, gives a still unsurpassed picture of life in seventeenth-century America.

The material on Indians is vast, as can be seen in a glance at *American Indian and White Relations to 1830: Needs and Opportunities for Study* (1957), which consists of an essay by William N. Fenton and a bibliography by Lyman H. Butterfield. Roy H. Pearce, *The Savages of America: A Study of the Indian and the Idea of Civilization* (1953), discusses Indian relations with the early settlers. Two informative surveys are R. M. Underhill, *Red Man's America: A History of Indians in the United States* (1953), and C. T. Foreman, *Indians Abroad, 1493–1938* (1943). A recent collection of readings is Wilcomb E. Washburn, ed., *The Indian and the White Man* (pb. original).

Hugh Morrison's *Early American Architecture* (1952) is a comprehensive and excellent survey. It does not, however, completely outdate S. Fiske Kimball's *Domestic Architecture in the American Colonies* (1927). Anthony Garvan's *Architecture and Town Planning in Colonial Connecticut* (1951) covers more than its title indicates and should not be missed. Early Southern buildings have been well treated in Howard C. Forman, *The Architecture of the Old South* (1948). Edward W. Sinnot's *Meeting House and Church in Early New England* (1963) is profusely illustrated, as is Alan Gowans' *Images of American Living: Four Centuries of Architecture and Furniture as Cultural Experience* (1964), which gives considerable space to the colonial period.

Oliver W. Larkin covers both art and architecture in *Art and Life in America* (1949; rev. ed., 1960). Oskar Hagen, *Birth of the American Tradition in Art* (1940), and James Thomas Flexner, *American Painting: First Flowers of Our Wilderness* (1947), confine their remarks to painting. More specialized accounts are those of Louisa Dress, *Seventeenth-Century Painting in New England* (1935), and Alan Burroughs, *Limners and Likenesses*

(1936). A full bibliography is found in Waldron P. Belknap, Jr., *American Colonial Painting: Materials for a History* (1959). E. McClury Fleming writes on "Early American Decorative Arts as Social Documents," *MVHR*, 45 (1958), 276–284.

The way of life in the Southern colonies is covered in Lewis C. Gray, *History of Agriculture in the Southern United States to 1860* (2 vols., 1941) ; P. A. Bruce, *Institutional History of Virginia in the Seventeenth Century* (2 vols., 1910) ; the same author, *Economic History of Virginia in the Seventeenth Century* (2 vols., 1896) ; and Robert Beverley, who knew it firsthand and wrote about it brilliantly in *The History of Virginia* (1704; 2nd ed., 1722; reprinted with introduction by Louis Wright, 1947). What Bruce did for seventeenth-century Virginia, the early volumes of John G. Palfrey's *History of New England* (5 vols., 1858–1890) accomplish for this area. A broader, modern survey of the economic life is Percy W. Bidwell and John I. Falconer, *History of Agriculture in the Northern United States, 1620–1860* (1925). Details on daily existence are found in George F. Dow's *Everyday Life in the Massachusetts Bay Colony* (1935).

Society

Bernard Bailyn's *Education in the Forming of American Society* (1960; pb.) is as much about seventeenth-century American society as it is about education, and the bibliographical essay that comprises the second half of the book is a superb survey of the work done and needed to be done. A. W. Calhoun's *A Social History of the American Family* (3 vols., 1917–1919; pb.) presents more the raw material than the results of his research. Edmund S. Morgan writes with his usual skill on *The Puritan Family: Essays on Religion and Domestic Relations in Seventeenth-Century New England* (1944; pb.). Alice Mead Earle's *Child Life in Colonial Days* (1899) and *Home Life in Colonial Days* (1898) cover both the seventeenth and eighteenth centuries, as does E. A. Dexter's *Colonial Women* (1924). Richard B. Morris, *Government and Labor in Early America* (1946; pb.), gives a detailed, scholarly account of the subject, one aspect of which—the indentured servant—is treated more fully in Abbott Emerson Smith's *Colonists in Bondage: White Servitude and Convict Labor in America, 1607–1776* (1947). Edwin Miles Riley's new edition of *The Journal of John Harrower, An Indentured Servant in the Colony of Virginia, 1773–1776* (1963) is a marvelous firsthand account that serves as adequately for the seventeenth as for the eighteenth century in which it was written. Lawrence W. Towner discusses slaves and servants in seventeenth-century New England in two articles: "A Fondness for Freedom': Servant Protest in Puritan Society," *WMQ*, 19 (1962), 201–219; and "The Sewall-Saffin Dialogue on Slavery," *ibid.*, 21 (1964), 40–52. There is no general study on the elite of early America; although Edwin Cady makes some relevant remarks in his *Gentleman in America* (1949), the book is mainly a literary study.

In addition to Bailyn's *Education,* the student is urged to read Robert

Middlekauff's *Ancients and Axioms: Secondary Education in Eighteenth-Century New England* (1963), which, despite its title, ably fills out the seventeenth-century picture. Middlekauff builds on the brief treatment presented by Samuel Eliot Morison in *The Intellectual Life of the New England Colonies* (originally published as *The Puritan Pronaos* [1936]; rev. ed., 1956; pb.). Despite the title, Marcus L. Jernegan's *Laboring and Dependent Classes in Colonial America* (1931; pb.) is also mainly about education in seventeenth-century America. The best book available on college education is Richard Hofstadter's *Academic Freedom in the Age of the College* (1955; pb.), particularly in showing how American higher education came to differ from that in England. Morison's *Harvard College in the Seventeenth Century* (2 vols., 1936) is an exhaustive but not exhausting study.

The Way They Thought

A guide for exploring the history of science in early America is Whitfield J. Bell, Jr., *Early American Science: Needs and Opportunities for Study* (1955), which also gives a full bibliography of what has been done. The early chapters of Richard H. Shryock's *Medicine and Society in America, 1660–1860* (1960) are the best on the subject. Shryock and Otho T. Beall, Jr., have written *Cotton Mather: The First Significant Figure in American Medicine* (1954), and Beall alone has written on *"Aristotle's Master Piece* in America: A Landmark in the Folklore of Medicine," *WMQ*, 20 (1963), 207–222. Morison's first volume on *Harvard College* explores the quality of science there. The best survey is Theodore Hornberger, *Scientific Thought in the American Colleges, 1638–1800* (1945).

No single book completely explores religion in seventeenth-century America, but one of the most helpful for the student is Warren W. Sweet, *Religion in Colonial America* (1942). For religion in the South, see William H. Seiler, "The Church of England as the Established Church in Seventeenth-Century Virginia," *Journal of Southern History (JSH)*, 15 (1949), 478–508, and the same author's essay "The Anglican Parish in Virginia," in James Morton Smith, ed., *Seventeenth-Century America: Essays on Colonial History* (1959). Marion L. Starkey gives a lively, accurate account of the Salem witchcraft episode in *The Devil in Massachusetts* (1950; pb.). Miss Starkey's bibliography discusses the work previously done on the affair. Two general articles that put the story of colonial religion in perspective are Sidney E. Mead, "Religion in English America," and Kenneth Scott Latourette, "The Contribution of the Religion of the Colonial Period to the Ideals and Life of the United States," both in *The Americas*, 14 (1958), 340–355.

The literary material on seventeenth-century America has been surveyed by Marcus Cunliffe in *The Literature of the United States* (1954; pb.) and in the early essays in Robert Spiller, *et al.*, eds., *Literary History of the United States* (3 vols., 1948); but none of this work really supersedes the first volume of Moses Coit Tyler's marvelous *History of American Literature 1607–1763* (2 vols., 1878; reprinted as one vol., 1949; pb.). Howard Mumford Jones discusses colonial writings briefly in *Ideas in America* (1944). Strong cases are made for the excellence of New England's literary achievements by Morison's *The Intellectual Life of the New England Colonies,* by Thomas G. Wright's *Literary Culture in Early New England* (1920), and by Kenneth Murdock's *Literature and Theology in Colonial New England* (1949; pb.). The work done on the early development of the American language is for the most part specialized. The best essays for those with a layman's interest are in Eggleston's *Transit of Civilization* and Boorstin's *Americans.* The most accessible and fullest bibliography is found in Boorstin. Of the two biographies of Cotton Mather—one by Barrett Wendell (1891; pb.), the other by Louise Boas (1928)—Wendell's is better. A recent article on Mather, but only slightly relevant here, is Peter H. Smith's "Politics and Sainthood: Biography by Cotton Mather," *WMQ,* 20 (1963), 186–206.

For further references see the *Harvard Guide,* Sections 90, "New England in the Seventeenth Century: Social, Economic, Institutional"; and 91, "Chesapeake Colonies in the Seventeenth Century: Social, Economic, Institutional."

William III and Mary II

9. The Empire Takes Shape: 1689–1713

IMPERIAL WARS
The French Menace

King William's War

Period of Unrest

Queen Anne's War

THE DEVELOPMENT OF IMPERIAL CONTROL
The Crown and the Colonies

The Board of Trade

Imperial Machinery

GOVERNMENT IN THE COLONIES
The Governor and Council

The Assembly

The Judiciary

After 1689 much that had characterized seventeenth-century America waned under conditions and pressures largely new to the colonies. The crown steadily tightened its control, and a uniform administration of the colonies came to predominate. American society at the same time grew increasingly complex. The settlers welcomed imperial control when it protected them from their enemies but complained when it restrained their freedom of action. Relations between crown and colony, which had been confused up to now, took on a shape that would remain to the end of the colonial period. Imperial machinery and colonial government assumed forms that would last at least until 1763.

IMPERIAL WARS

All these changes were visible in the years immediately following the accession of William and Mary. The period between 1689 and 1713 embraced two wars that began in Europe but ricocheted to America. The colonists failed to see at the time that Europe had thrust these wars upon them. (Tom Paine would be the first to point out that to separate from Britain would also mean separation from her European entanglements.) As far as the colonists were concerned, the French menace at their backs caused the trouble. The apparently American origins of the wars led them to Americanize the names—King William's War, Queen Anne's War, and so forth.

The French Menace

Louis XIV came to the throne of France in 1661 determined, like Charles II of England, to rule, and he brought with him a young man named Jean Baptiste Colbert to help realize that ambition. Louis and Colbert together made France the greatest power in Europe, and at the same time they transformed Canada from a feeble colony into an enemy potentially capable of conquering the English empire in America. (Canada embraced that part of New France that bordered the St. Lawrence River. It contained 3,418 white settlers in 1666, less than the population of Rhode Island.) Colbert assumed that French strength in Europe was related to her resources overseas. Canada played the key role in his precise plan to develop those resources. She would turn out ships, iron, and naval stores for France and produce food for the French West Indies, leaving those islands free to concentrate on tobacco, sugar, and indigo for the home market. The fur trade of New France would be extended to meet the costs of developing the American empire. Colbert's plan differed from England's fuzzy version of mercantilism in that one man was imposing his conception on the empire's development rather than allowing it to mature haphazardly, and the full strength of the French monarchy stood behind this plan, where in England the crown gave only half-hearted direction. Colbert never succeeded in making Canada a profitable enterprise for France—in the 1740's the crown was spending over two million livres to maintain the colony and receiving in import duties and taxes less than a quarter of a million—but when he died in 1683, New France loomed as a threat to the well-being of English America.

Louis XIV and Colbert invigorated New France first by sending competent leaders. Jean Talon was dispatched as intendant. (Two royal officers shared between them all power over the affairs of New France. Military matters and Indian relations were vested in the governor general. The intendant controlled everything else, which meant mainly financial affairs and all local administration. The two officials supposedly checked, as well as helped, one another; but when strong men occupied the posts, the clash of wills often frustrated the sure direction of New France's affairs.) Talon was a man of force, imagination, and boldness.

He centered his attention on the west, where the French advance had stopped after Jean Nicolet's trip to Green Bay in 1634 and where the Jesuits, whom Talon disliked, were the sole authority. In 1670 Talon sent an emissary to take possession of the great inland basin of North America for Louis with all the pomp possible to muster in a wilderness. One of the missionaries who went along returned with a report from Indians of a great river, which he assumed flowed to "the sea of Florida [the Gulf of Mexico] or that of California [the Pacific]." Talon feared that the English, either from the outpost they had erected on Hudson Bay or from Virginia, might reach the great river first, and he persuaded Frontenac, the recently arrived governor general, to send out an exploratory party at once.

Louis de Buade, Count Frontenac, was the second powerful personality Louis XIV sent to the colony. (So powerful, indeed, that Talon left for France not long after Frontenac arrived; he got along no better with Talon's replacement.) He arrived in 1672 at the age of fifty-two, a man of vigor, vision, and strong mind, three virtues that helped to balance but did not cancel out two failings. First, he came to Canada determined to reap profit for himself as much as for New France. (A 2 per cent cut on all beaver pelts exported by the company that monopolized New France's fur trade offered one among several ways that the governor general might line his pockets.) His ego, the size of a mountain, revealed a less tolerable failing. "He could not endure a rival," says a friendly biographer. "Opposition maddened him, and when crossed or thwarted, he forgot everything but his passion." He detested Talon, but instructions from the king reminded him that "after the increase of the colony of Canada, nothing is of greater importance for that country and for the service of his Majesty than the discovery of a passage to the South Sea." And with those words in mind, he backed Talon's suggestion that the Indian rumor of a great river be investigated. The task was given in May 1673 to Louis Jolliet, a onetime priest turned fur trader, and Father Marquette, a Jesuit who had long lived in the western country and knew a number of Indian dialects.

Jolliet and Marquette, with five men, left Green Bay in mid-June, paddled along the Wisconsin River and from there into the Mississippi, where they swept southward into a world unlike anything they had known. The outsize prevailed—prairies that stretched farther than the eye could see, catfish huge enough to upset canoes, cougars the size of tigers. They flushed a band of Indians who rode in dugouts and eyed their birchbark canoes with wonder. They swept past the noisy, muddy, and turbulent Missouri—"I have seen nothing more dreadful," Marquette wrote—and after a talk with Indians decided this was the route to California. Below the Ohio they met Indians who carried English guns, and

Map 24. French Exploration, Before 1740

HUDSON BAY

Albany
English

Albanel, 1672

Ch. 1603

Ft. Maurepas, 1734

Radisson to
Hudson Bay
L. Nipigon

Ft. La Reine, 1738

Ft. Charles, 1732

C A N A D A

Quebec

Voyageurs Route
Rainy R.

Ft. Kaministiquia

L. Superieur

Montreal

Ottawa R.

Champl.
1609

DULHUT

La Pointe 67

Ft. Frontenac

Fr.

Albany

Detroit

Ft. Niagara

York

LE SUEUR

Nicolet's
Radisson '59

Philadelphia
1682

Ft. St. Joseph
1680

Ft. Miami
1704

Ft. St. Louis
Ft. Crevecoeur

BOURGMONT
1724

R. Kansas

Ft. Orleans

Cahokia
1689

This region was known to traders by 1700

Williamsburg

TISNE
1719

Arkansas R.

MALLETS

Ft. Prudhomme

Red R. LA HARPE

Ft. Arkansas Joliet & Marquette 1672

Charlestown

Natchitoches

Ft. Toulouse

L A   F L O R I D A

Ft. St. Louis
1702

Spanish

St. Augustine

La Salle killed, 1687

Ft. Maurepas, 1699

Ft. St. Louis LA SALLE '87

E N G L I S H   C O L O N I E S

Cartier 1534-41	Du Lhut 1678- 81 —DL—	Bourgmont 1724 ··Bo··
Champlain 1604-15 Ch	La Salle 1678- -87 -LS-▲-	Mallet brothers, 1739-40 —M—
Brulé 1608-33 —Br—	Tonty 1690 ·—To-··	
Nicolet '34 —N—Ni—N—	Le Sueur 1700 —L—	The Rio Grande, the lower
Radisson '58-'59—-Ra—	Bienville —Bi—	Missouri, the Ohio and its tribut-
Joliet '69 —J—	St. Denis 1715 —SD—	aries all appear on contemporary
Joliet+Marquette '72-J+M	La Harpe 1719 +'22-LH—maps, and were known to traders
Hennepin 1678-79-He—	Tisné 1719 ı—Ti—ı—	and to the "Coureurs de Bois"

Marquette gave their chief a letter in Latin. (The letter passed to a Virginia trader who gave it to William Byrd, who sent William Penn a copy that eventually ended up in the papers of Robert Harley in England, where it lay hidden for 220 years.) A short while later they met natives who made them understand that the great river emptied into the Gulf of Mexico and that the Indians who lay below were ferocious. In mid-July, though still some seven hundred miles from the mouth, they turned back. The slow, upriver trip lasted until the end of September, when they reached Green Bay after an absence of four months on a trip of some twenty-five hundred miles.

The king's desire to follow Jolliet's and Marquette's explorations was frustrated for nearly a decade, for in 1672 he had launched a series of wars in Europe that left little energy to spare for New France. Fortunately, the exploration had fired the imagination of René-Robert Cavelier, Sieur de La Salle, a man of large dreams who had sailed for Canada in 1666 to make his fortune. La Salle, then twenty-three years old, began as a fur trader and quickly mastered the business. He learned several Indian languages and soon knew more about inland America than any man alive. He set out to revolutionize the fur business by controlling it from a central point, and because the plan had the double virtue of promoting the fortunes of both Frontenac and New France it was put into operation. Fort Frontenac went up on Lake Ontario at a spot designed to check Iroquois forays into the western country and to prevent the drifting of furs from that country southward into the hands of the English. La Salle ran the fort until 1677, when he sailed for France to win royal backing for a larger dream, for he now saw that the fur trade revealed only a small part of the wealth the interior of North America had to offer. Here, he realized, could be created the greatest agricultural and commercial empire in the world. Colbert caught the brilliance of La Salle's vision, and on his urging the king granted a patent to erect all the forts necessary to secure the Mississippi Basin for France.

La Salle returned to Canada late in 1678 accompanied by his able second-in-command, Henri de Tonty, an Italian who had lost an arm fighting in Sicily. First, a fort was built at the mouth of the Niagara River, a spot through which nearly all western trade had to funnel on its way east. Next came a series of forts along the Chicago, St. Joseph, and Illinois Rivers and on Lake Peoria. La Salle used his skill of persuasion with the Indians to bring order among the Western tribes. He taught them to settle close by his forts, where they could bring their furs for trade and come for protection if the Iroquois invaded the country. Once he had secured this territory, he set out in the winter of 1682 to explore the Mississippi to its mouth. On April 9, not far from the present site of New

Orleans, La Salle claimed Louisiana, as he called it, and "all the nations, peoples, provinces, cities, towns, villages, mines, minerals, fisheries, streams, and rivers" that comprised the vast watershed of the Mississippi for King Louis XIV and France.

La Salle fired others with his vision of a great inland empire for France, but in the end the dream came to nothing. The king gave him ships and men to establish a settlement at the mouth of the Mississippi. In 1685 he sailed into Spain's great "lake," the Caribbean, but missed the mouth of the river and landed with four hundred men in Texas at Matagorda Bay. The settlement had dwindled to forty-five by 1687 when La Salle made a desperate overland attempt to reach Fort St. Louis on the Illinois, where Tonty awaited him. On the way, however, he was murdered. He died at forty-three, "one of the greatest men of his age," said Tonty, certainly one of the greatest explorers of any age. His dreams exceeded his grasp, but they "ultimately proved to be so apt and shrewd that history has been right in elevating him to greatness, even though he carried to completion almost nothing of what he essayed."

England and her colonies reacted to French encirclement only as it produced tension in the Iroquois country of upper New York, the one spot France did not dominate. Repeated attempts by Jesuit missionaries and fur traders to alleviate Iroquois antagonism had failed, for the French were allied with the Algonquin-speaking Indians, long the Iroquois' enemy. The furs of the Iroquois country had been exhausted since the early seventeenth century, which meant that to prosper the Iroquois must become middlemen between tribes in the West, mainly Algonquins, and the Dutch merchants of Fort Orange, who supplied them with guns and brandy and other necessities of life purchasable by beaver skins alone. But the French controlled the sources of this trade. The Iroquois, therefore, sought to cut in on it by attacking the Hurons in 1649, then the Hurons' neighbors, the Petuns, and then two years later the Neutrals. The war ended, however, with the furs still flowing into French hands.

The arrival of the English in New York complicated the story after 1664. France dispatched the Marquis de Tracy with one thousand troops into upper New York in 1666. He burned villages, destroyed food caches, and left the Iroquois stunned and quiet. Fort Frontenac on Lake Ontario and La Salle's Fort Niagara strengthened the French hold over Western trade. But the English by this time had introduced a weapon into the trade war that the French could not effectively counter. Bernard De Voto summarizes the situation neatly:

The British could not begin to match the French in wilderness skills or the skill of managing the Indians, but they could always outsell them. British woolens were better than any made in France or any that could be bought elsewhere in the world market. The manufacturing system of Great Britain had developed so far beyond that of France that other goods—hardware, fire-arms, powder, ornaments, the whole miscellany—could be delivered to the cus-tomer so cheaply as to force the French out of competition. A more modern credit system, more efficient government, far freer competition, price flexibil-ity, commercial ethics sufficiently hair-raising but much less sodden with cor-ruption—all these worked to the same end. Beaver would always buy twice as much at Albany as from any French trader, and frequently three or four times as much.

The bargaining power gave the Iroquois a weapon more potent than their skill in battle, and with it they launched an invasion of the West that initiated what came to be known as King William's War.

King William's War

The war came officially in 1689 and was known in Europe as the war of the Rhenish Palatinate, or League of Augsburg. Americans called it King William's War, and as they had changed its name, they should have changed its starting date, for the fighting began in America nearly a decade earlier than in Europe. The opening date could be put at 1680, the year when the Iroquois again invaded the West, this time to massacre the Illinois Indians. But the slaughter failed to detach the Western Indians from the French, and the Iroquois were forced to sit by as furs from the West continued to flow into Canada. Two years later the imperious Frontenac was recalled to France and replaced by the meeker, ineffectual Antoine Lefebvre de la Barre. With Frontenac went the firm hand that had directed the rise of New France for over a decade and allowed a colony of now ten thousand inhabitants—still only a sixth of the number who lived in Massachusetts alone—to hold a continent against twelve vigorous and relatively powerful English colonies.

The loss of Frontenac was made worse by the arrival in 1683 of Thomas Dongan as governor of New York. He inaugurated an aggres-sive policy to sway the Iroquois to the English side. Dongan and Vir-ginia's Lord Howard of Effingham in July 1684 conferred with Iroquois chiefs at Albany to persuade them to cease attacking the back settlements of the Chesapeake area and to acknowledge themselves subjects of Eng-land. The Indians accepted the first request but temporized on the second. ("You say that we are subjects of the King of England and the Duke of York, but we say that we are brothers," they had replied. "We must take care of ourselves.") But English support, English goods, and La Barre's weak rule made them bold. By 1685 English-Iroquois trading parties had penetrated westward to Michilimackinac, Michigan, deep in French terri-

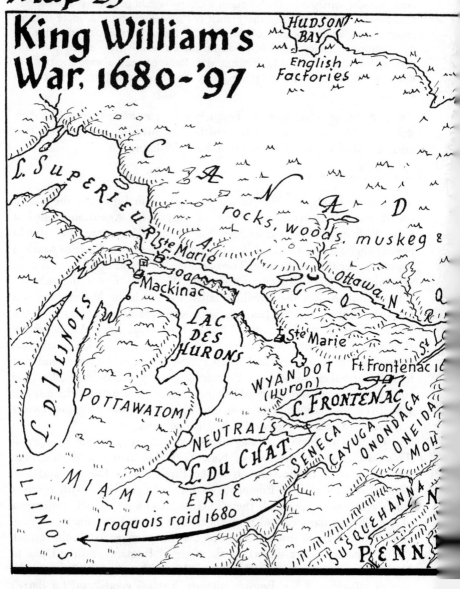

Map 25

King William's War, 1680-'97

HUDSON BAY

English Factories

C A N A D A

rocks, woods, muskeg &

L. SUPERIEUR

Pte Marie

L. SUPERIOR

Ottawa N

Mackinac

LAC DES HURONS

Ste Marie

Ft. Frontenac 16

WYANDOT (Huron)

L. FRONTENAC

L. D'ILLINOIS

POTTAWATOMI

NEUTRALS

SENECA

CAYUGA

ONONDAGA

ONEIDA

MOH

MIAMI

L. DU CHAT

ERIE

ILLINOIS

Iroquois raid 1680

SUSQUEHANNA

PENN

tory, and returned to Albany with a small fortune in beaver fur. Jacques de Denonville, La Barre's replacement, knew these insults must be halted if the French were to keep the Indians' respect. "We may set down Canada as lost," he wrote, "if we do not make war next year; and yet in our present disordered state, war is the most dangerous thing in the world." Forts were needed but to build them would "bring down all the Iroquois upon us before we are in a condition to fight them." His counteroffensive opened with an attack in 1686 against a Hudson Bay Company outpost to the north, where by a circuitous route furs slipped past the French into English hands. The capture of an English-Iroquois flotilla laden with furs in 1687 helped further to restore prestige, and a victory over the Senecas the same year helped even more. Meanwhile, Edmund Andros, as governor of the Dominion of New England, worked to strengthen English defenses, and the Iroquois harried the French steadily. In August 1689, some fifteen hundred warriors attacked the village of La Chine, only six miles from Montreal, and carried out "the most frightful massacre in Canadian history," leaving behind a colony "bewildered and benumbed" at the very moment war had broken out between England and France. Louis XIV lacked money and men to send to Canada; he sent instead Count Frontenac.

Frontenac, now seventy years old, found his colony close to collapse. New England, under Andros' leadership, had attacked and looted the French outpost at Penobscot, Maine (the venture that led to rumors of Andros' pro-French sympathies), the Iroquois waited for a new chance to slaughter, and the Hurons and Ottawas in the West threatened to rebel against French rule. Frontenac's prestige, plus a small reinforcement of troops, sufficed to stop the Western uprising. Next, the old man devised a three-pronged attack against the English to impress the Iroquois with New France's power. The first struck in February 1690 at the village of Schenectady, thirteen miles northwest of Albany. Sixty settlers were slaughtered, nearly a hundred captured, and the village burned to the ground. "You cannot believe, Monseigneur," Frontenac wrote, "the joy that this slight success has caused, and how much it contributes to raise the people from their dejection." The joy increased even more a month later when Salmon Falls, on the Maine–New Hampshire border, was leveled and still more when Fort Loyal, on the site of modern Portland, Maine, was overwhelmed.

Frontenac struck while the colonies were mired in troubles of their own making. Massachusetts had jailed Andros and lived under a provisional government, where "we have no head to command us in case of attack, everyone being Captain." Leisler's Rebellion occupied New York's attention. The French and Indian raids jolted the colonies into action, and in May 1690 Massachusetts, Plymouth, and Connecticut sent delegates to an intercolonial conference at New York. England's European entanglements cut the hope of aid from that source. The colonists in desperation took the initiative and mapped out a two-pronged intercolonial invasion of Canada—by land from Albany and up Lake Champlain, by sea down the St. Lawrence to Quebec. Hope for the success of the grandiose operation rose in late May when news rolled in of a victory Massachusetts had carried off on her own. French cruisers sallying out from Port Royal in Acadia had plagued New England commerce through the year, and to end their attacks Massachusetts determined to capture the base. A task force of seven ships under the leadership of Sir William Phips was collected. Phips sailed from Boston up the Bay of Fundy, landed before Port Royal on May 19, and won a surrender from the French governor with no trouble. Since Port Royal was Acadia's only important town, its capture in effect meant control of the entire peninsula. The easy and also prosperous victory—Phips, though an honorable Puritan soon to be governor of Massachusetts, had allowed his men to loot the town—encouraged Massachusetts to take up the larger task of subduing Quebec.

But the grand campaign failed completely. The overland expedition set out from Albany with the leaders quarreling among themselves, with an inadequate stock of supplies, and with far fewer Iroquois than planned —the Indians had been sufficiently impressed by Frontenac's return to adopt a cautious attitude. The advance collapsed at the lower end of Lake Champlain and everyone returned home. Meanwhile, the largest invasion force ever assembled by Americans had sailed from Boston—some twenty-two hundred "raw fishermen and farmers led by an ignorant civilian," Sir William Phips. Two months later the fleet appeared before Quebec. Phips sent an emissary with a curt demand for surrender. "No," replied Frontenac, "I will answer your general only by the mouths of my cannon, that he may learn that a man like me is not to be summoned after this fashion." Phips lingered before the rock-walled fortress a week; then, after losing two skirmishes that depleted his stock of ammunition, the fleet sailed away, unaware that a shortage of food would have made it hard for Quebec to have held out much longer. A Frenchman said of the New Englanders' effort: "They fought vigorously, though as ill-disciplined as men gathered together at random could be, for they did not lack courage, and if they failed, it was by reason of their entire ignorance of discipline, and because they were exhausted by the fatigues of the voyage."

The war dragged on for seven more years, but intercolonial cooperation, slight as it had been, vanished completely. New York asked Virginia for money or men to build or garrison forts, but Virginia refused. ("Those forts were necessary for New York, to enable that province to engross the trade of the neighbor Indians; which being highly to the disadvantage of Virginia, 'twas unreasonable that country should pay a tribute towards its own ruin.") Worried English authorities sent over Henry Sloughter to urge and persuade the colonies into a united defense, but he died within weeks after his arrival. Governor Benjamin Fletcher, his replacement, came determined to make the war an intercolonial effort. When he asked all colonies to send money and men to the aid of New York, "all of 'em found ways to evade it," said Caleb Heathcote, who went on to give grudging respect to Frontenac's genius: "the French, who were no strangers to our constitution, were always so crafty as not to suffer their Indians to make war on more than one province or colony at a time; and the others were so besotted, as always to sit still." When New York was hit, Connecticut "could patiently bear to see our settlement destroyed and people murdered"; later, when Connecticut felt the Indians' tomahawks, "we as kindly refused to assist them and sat quiet while their towns were cut off and laid in ashes."

Frontenac's troops had meanwhile reoccupied Port Royal, absorbed Newfoundland, destroyed Fort William Henry at Pemaquid, Maine, built in 1692, and driven English traders from posts on Hudson Bay. Frontenac made his last great effort in July 1696 when, at the age of seventy-six, he set out through the wilderness at the head of some two thousand men to attack the villages of the Onondaga and Oneida tribes. Indian bearers carried him to the front to watch as each new village was destroyed. Given a bit more time, Frontenac might have forced the Iroquois permanently to the French side. Diplomats in Europe aborted his strategy. The Peace of Ryswick in 1697 ended the war in Europe and thus in America. Frontenac died soon after receiving the news. Let Francis Parkman's words serve as his epitaph: "Greatness must be denied him, but a more remarkable figure, in its bold and salient individuality and sharply marked light and shadow, is nowhere seen in American history."

The terms of peace must have saddened Frontenac. In eight years he had taken a colony he had found numb with terror to the edge of triumph, only to have the diplomats deny his achievements, for the treaty viewed the war in America a stalemate. All conquests were to be returned within six months. Commissioners were appointed to judge the validity of England's claims to the Hudson Bay area. (They failed to agree and disbanded two years later.) The long, bloody colonial war had solved nothing, despite Frontenac's achievements, but it "so solidified the mutual hatred between the French and British colonies that there could never be a compromise but only a total victory for one or the other." In the breathing space between this war and the next, both England and France gave much thought to their empires in the New World. Five years would elapse before conflict came again, but they were not peaceful years.

Period of Unrest

In 1701 a distressed American said: "We have certain information that the French are now settling upon the mouth of the river Meschasipe [Mississippi]; if so, and some speedy care be not taken, no one can (I think) foretell the fatal consequences that may follow to all the English colonies on the continent." The American's information was correct and his perception of the danger shrewd. The French began with the peace to reinforce their hold on the Mississippi Valley. They made a settlement in 1699 at Cahokia, across the river from St. Louis, and in the same year turned back two English ships loaded with colonists prospecting for a good site near the mouth of the Mississippi. The French established a fort at Biloxi, then three years later another to the east at Mobile, close to the Spanish at Pensacola and in the region where Carolina fur traders operated. They built forts in the north at Michilimackinac, Michigan, in 1700 and Detroit the following year. By the end of these five peaceful years the French had virtually penned in the English behind the Appalachians.

The English had not watched idly. King William's War had opened London's eyes to the stakes involved in America, and even before the peace at Ryswick the crown had set out to protect and increase England's share of the investment. New machinery was created to tighten England's control of the colonies; Lord Bellomont was sent over to reunite the New England colonies and join them again to New York. But the effects of past mistakes, lack of direct control over colonial affairs, and ignorance of political developments in America since the Glorious Revolution hampered English efforts to shore up their American empire. Authorities in London wanted to overhaul the military setup of the colonies, forcing them to pay and provide for their own defense under English supervision. But the authorities still thought it sufficient to instruct the governor to implement these reforms. They failed to see that the example of the Glorious Revolution had helped to strengthen representative government in all the colonies and that what the governor could once do on his own, he must do only with the advice and consent of the assemblies. America had now been revealed as a valuable piece of real estate that France must not monopolize, but to block her expansion required strong military measures. And if the colonial assemblies balked at a joint effort to rebuff the

French, what could the home government do? This, the great problem of
imperial rule in America, first emerged clearly in King William's War;
eventually, the inability to resolve the question of where power lay, in
London or America, would lead to a revolution far less mild than the
glorious one just past.

The colonies' postwar economic difficulties accentuated the English
authorities' problems of inaugurating military reforms in America. The
return of holdings in Newfoundland and Acadia to France nearly ruined
New England's cod fisheries. Competition from England sent down the
price of wheat in the West Indies, which hurt merchants and farmers in
the middle colonies. Assemblies busy coping with these troubles were not
eager to contribute men and money to another war, especially if the seat
of that war should be far from their own homes. Competition among the
colonies for trade and settlers did little to promote mutual affection. Virginia held a grudge against Pennsylvania, which was attracting settlers
who earlier would have streamed into the Chesapeake area. And at the
same time England asked the colonies to sacrifice self-concern for imperial
interests, she oppressed them from other directions. Enforcement of the
Navigation Acts during the half decade between wars further dislocated
the colonial economy. The Royal Navy, meant to protect, became so
feared that when its ships docked in New York, the city became "almost
starved, nobody daring to come to market for fear of being pressed
[into service]." The general quality of governors sent over dimmed colonial enthusiasm for imperial rule. Lord Cornbury, who arrived in New
York during the uneasy period between wars, was accused of "dressing
publicly in woman's clothes every day, and putting a stop to all public
business while he is pleasing himself with that peculiar but detestable
maggot."

The English did a lamentable job in New York at the very time when
their best efforts were required. For one thing, they lost the Iroquois
tribes' allegiance. Frontenac's death had momentarily emboldened the
Indians, but the uncertainty of English support and the impressive activity
of the French during the period of unrest convinced them that their best
interests lay in neutrality, and in 1701, on the eve of Queen Anne's War,
they made peace with their former foes. When James Logan, one of the
shrewdest American politicians of the day, read of the treaty in a London
magazine, he wrote William Penn: "if we lose the Iroquois we are gone
by land." But King William's War had been disastrous for them. The
New York tribes had lost nearly half their warriors; they could field
less than fifteen hundred men. This terrified them; the English, however,
did little to calm their fear that one more war would lead to extinction.
"The slender appearance we make on the frontier in the poorness of our

forts and weakness of our garrisons," wrote one colonist, "makes us contemptible in their eyes, whereas the French allure them by the good figure they make."

The Indians were further encouraged to lay down their arms by the pro-French attitude of New Yorkers themselves. The fur business had shrunk to nearly nothing for Albany traders during King William's War. The traders disliked the London program of erecting a line of forts on the Great Lakes frontier, fearing it would arouse the French again to aggressive action. They undermined English policy by developing an unauthorized but lucrative trade with Montreal, whereby they supplied the French with cheap English goods for the Indian trade in return for furs. The eighteenth century opened with the Iroquois, Albany traders, and Canada tacitly agreeing that it was to their mutual benefit to remain at peace as long as possible. When war between England and France revived in 1702, New York, which might have been expected once again to be the main theater, remained completely out of the war for several years. This time, New England bore the brunt.

Queen Anne's War

It began in Europe as the War of the Spanish Succession. Louis XIV had his grandson, Philip of Anjou, placed on the Spanish throne in 1701, thus giving France indirect control of one of the most powerful monarchies in Europe. In England's eyes this upset the balance of power both in Europe and in the New World. Louis XIV had insinuated himself into Spanish affairs at least in part to strengthen France in America, where France's union with Spain made it possible to press in on England in a concerted movement. Philip V of Spain gave the French Guinea Company a ten-year monopoly on the slave traffic of Spanish America, which up to now English merchants had dominated. With the merchants having promised strong support to any plan to break up the Bourbon alliance, England, carrying the Netherlands and Austria with her, declared war on France in May 1702.

But the colonies felt the war before it began in Europe. Prosperity in the Delaware Valley declined merely on the rumor of trouble early in the year, for merchants began to pull their ships off the seas to avoid capture when hostilities broke forth. French traders' newly acquired monopoly in the Spanish West Indies cut Philadelphia's business in that area, and with the end of that trade, the inflow of Spanish coin, so vital to the colonial economy, also ceased. When Europe finally declared war, it spread almost at once across the ocean, where it came to be called Queen Anne's War.

Canada reversed its previous strategy. This time, Iroquois territory

Map 26. Queen Anne's War, 1702–1713

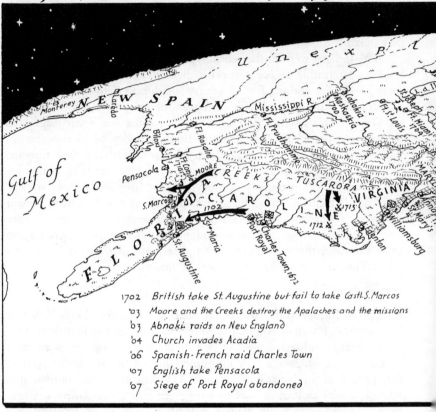

1702   British take St. Augustine but fail to take Castl. S. Marcos
'03   Moore and the Creeks destroy the Apalaches and the missions
'03   Abnaki raids on New England
'04   Church invades Acadia
'06   Spanish-French raid Charles Town
'07   English take Pensacola
'07   Siege of Port Royal abandoned

was avoided. And to prevent the Abnaki Indians of northern New England from allying with the English now that Canada had settled its quarrel with the Iroquois, the Indians were used, as a Frenchman put it, "in such a manner that they would not draw back." Every raiding party sent out consisted mainly of natives, but with a sprinkling of French to direct and spur on the business at hand. Thirty-nine settlers, mostly women and children, were murdered at Wells, Maine, in August 1703, and through the summer and into the autumn bands of Indians sprang from the forest on outlying settlements along a two hundred–mile frontier that stretched from Maine through New Hampshire and into western Massachusetts. The party that raided Deerfield massacred thirty-eight settlers and marched some one hundred captives through the forests to Canada in hope of ransom money. (John Williams, a prisoner for two years, lived to tell his story in *The Redeemed Captive Returning to Zion*, which, like Mary Rowlandson's narrative of captivity, became a best seller.)

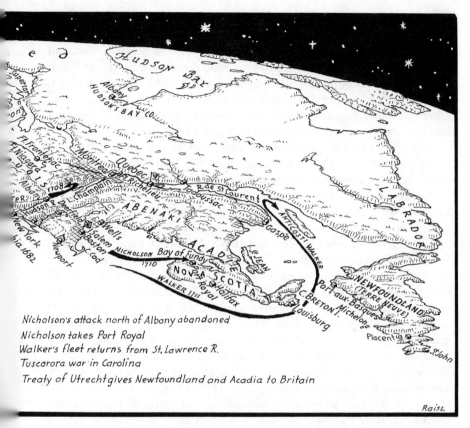

Nicholson's attack north of Albany abandoned
Nicholson takes Port Royal
Walker's fleet returns from St. Lawrence R.
Tuscarora war in Carolina
Treaty of Utrecht gives Newfoundland and Acadia to Britain

New England begged for aid from other colonies. The New York assembly, delighted with the peace on her own frontier and involved in an internal quarrel with Lord Cornbury, refused; the pacific Quakers of Pennsylvania refused; Virginia refused. New England was left to go it alone. In 1704 some five hundred New Englanders set out toward Acadia, once again a wasp's nest of privateers and a trade center for supplying Indians. Benjamin Church, who had won his reputation as an Indian fighter in King Philip's War, led the expedition, though he was now sixty-five and so heavy he had to be pushed up steep spots in the woods. The invaders took two small outposts but failed to get Port Royal. In 1707 another expedition also failed, and the Canadians compounded that defeat the following year by breaking the English hold on Newfoundland.

Meanwhile, the war had come to other colonies. French privateers harassed colonial shipping everywhere. The British took the French half of St. Kitts (St. Christopher), but later failed to capture Guadeloupe. In the fall of 1702 some five hundred Carolinians headed with a small fleet for Saint Augustine; they destroyed the town but could not capture the great stone fort. In 1703 over a dozen Spanish missions scattered through the Gulf Coast country were destroyed and nearly a thousand Indians enslaved in a foray led by James Moore, former governor of South Carolina. Except for abortive raids by the Spanish and French on Charleston in 1706 and by the Americans on Pensacola in 1707, fighting in the South thereafter degenerated into a duel between privateers, with England and her colonies accumulating the better share of prizes.

By 1708 London authorities realized that the colonies lacked the power to crush New France unaided, a view they had been led to take by Samuel Vetch, a Scottish emigrant who had prospered as a Boston merchant. Vetch told Queen Anne that "her Majesty shall be sole empress of the vast North American continent," if she would only help the colonies against the French to the north and the Spanish to the south. The queen gave Vetch all he asked—a fleet and five regiments of royal troops—and thereby converted a provincial fray into an imperial war. The standard two-prong attack would be used to crush New France. The fleet would take the queen's troops and twelve hundred New England volunteers by sea to Quebec; Francis Nicholson would lead men from the middle colonies against Montreal. New York, seeing control of the western fur trade falling her way if the expedition succeeded, dropped her neutral role and raised an army of nearly one thousand. New Jersey, forced to deal with a large minority of Quakers, contributed no men but did advance £3,000. Pennsylvania gave nothing. (James Logan, who had worked to reverse the assembly's stand, decided at this point that politics and Quakerism were incompatible, and he advised Penn to sell his powers of government to the crown before being stripped of them.)

Canada sat waiting "a most bloody war" as Nicholson started northward from Albany with fifteen hundred troops and Indians. When he learned that the task force promised by the queen had been diverted to Portugal, he abandoned the invasion in disgust and New France relaxed. Nicholson, taking five Mohawk chiefs with him, returned to England to revive royal interest in the American enterprise. Addison and Steele wrote essays about the Indians, and the publicity sufficed to win royal approval of another projected invasion. In the fall of 1710 a combined colonial-English expedition led by Nicholson, with Vetch as second-in-command, captured Port Royal on Acadia. (Three times before—Argall in 1616, Sedgwick in 1654, and Phips in 1690—English-American expeditions had taken the fort, only to have it restored to France in peace negotiations. This time the conquest was final.)

A single victory, they believed, would complete the conquest of Canada. In 1711 the classic two-prong attack was tried once more. While Nicholson moved out from Albany, a fleet of nearly seventy ships—among them, nine men-of-war—carrying almost twelve thousand men departed from Boston. Fog, a storm, and mismanagement swept away ten ships and nearly a thousand of the troops near the mouth of the St. Lawrence. The incompetent Admiral Walker hesitated to push up the river without a pilot. The expedition eventually returned to Boston without having fired a shot. ("So discreditable a backing out from a great enterprise," Francis Parkman concludes, "will hardly be found elsewhere in English annals.") News of the retreat led Nicholson to rip off his wig and shout as he jumped upon it, "Roguery! Treachery!" Nicholson withdrew southward and that ended the threat of invasion for Canada during the remainder of Queen Anne's War.

Peace between the belligerents came in 1713 with the Treaty of Utrecht. Those parts of the treaty that concerned the European settlement sought mainly to preserve the balance of power on the Continent; those that dealt with the New World inaugurated a number of important changes, most of which concerned France. The Iroquois, without being consulted in the matter, became English subjects; both England and France agreed not to interfere with the Indians under the other nation's jurisdiction. Newfoundland and Acadia (Nova Scotia) became English possessions—this time for good. France acknowledged English sovereignty over Hudson Bay, she retained Cape Breton Island as well as other islands at the mouth of the St. Lawrence, and her fishermen were allowed to dry their catches on the coast of Newfoundland. In the West Indies England acquired all of St. Kitts and Nevis. Spain suffered most of her losses in Europe—the transference of Gibraltar to England was the most serious— and kept her New World possessions intact. England gained the right annually to ship nearly five thousand Negroes into the Spanish Empire, plus a single shipload of cargo, and that was all.

The old diplomatic view that the peace of Europe did not extend "beyond the line" died with the Treaty of Utrecht. Hereafter, all European settlements would involve the holdings of belligerents in the New World. The treaty settled little else with equal clarity. No one knew whether it gave England all of Acadia or only the seacoast. It ignored the problem of the Abnaki Indians, who accepted French sovereignty but lived in New England. And it did nothing to block French development of the continent's interior. England worried less than it should have about French expansion, for by this time its thoughts centered on another matter—the problem of tightening control over its American colonies.

THE DEVELOPMENT OF IMPERIAL CONTROL

The rise of New France under Louis XIV did much to awaken England to the inadequacy of its own imperial efforts. Between 1660 and 1675,

England constructed a framework to control the trade of the empire that to a large degree reflected respect for Colbert's imperial design. Colbert's success soon prodded England to face other problems that had little to do with trade. Two imperial wars showed that the colonies were unable to cope on their own with New France. England was forced to take on the job of providing an adequate military defense, and that inevitably plunged England deeper than ever into colonial politics. First the crown, then the crown and Parliament together, fumbled with the problem of how to control America without warping the framework of English political traditions. By the end of Queen Anne's War, a set of institutions and techniques had been devised that would remain substantially unchanged down to the American Revolution.

The Crown and the Colonies

The crown controlled colonial affairs, and James I underlined the fact in 1624 when he said that it was "very unfit for the Parliament to trouble themselves with these matters." Even in the eighteenth century, when Parliament asserted its authority in all aspects of home affairs, the king had relinquished little of his power over the colonies. He had the authority, among other things, to make colonial appointments, to issue instructions and commissions, to disallow colonial laws, to hear appeals from colonial courts. The king, of course, delegated much of this power to those who ran the realm for him. First in importance was the secretary of state for the Southern Department, who in addition to handling diplomatic affairs for Southern Europe assumed responsibility for colonial matters. (Not until 1768 was a new secretarial post created solely to deal with the colonies.) The lord treasurer and his department, the Treasury Board, became increasingly involved in colonial affairs as the eighteenth century wore on; until by the eve of the Revolution, the board's views had great weight in shaping imperial policy. The Commissioners of Customs, a bureau within the Treasury Board, became involved after the Navigation Acts; it was their job to enforce the acts and to supervise the collection of duties. The Admiralty, or Navy Department, was supposed to assist the customs collectors and also protect commerce from pirates, privateers, and smugglers. The department's judicial branch, the High Court of Admiralty, would eventually be represented in the colonies by Courts of Vice-admiralty, whose jurisdiction, like the parent body in England, was limited to maritime matters, or so the colonists thought. Also as in England trials were conducted without juries. The military counterpart of the Admiralty, the War Office, began with King William's War to play a part in American affairs that increased steadily up to the Revolution.

The heads of these executive departments, meeting with other advisers, formed the Privy Council, the king's chief advisory body on all matters of state, including colonial affairs. But use of the council, composed of busy men with little time for anything as unimportant as the colonies then were, quickly proved an awkward way to run an empire. James I began the search for a better way, and soon he and his successors, with Parliament briefly stepping into the act, had laid down a thicket of committees and councils and commissions on colonial affairs so confusing that sometimes even the specialist searching for the route through them that ultimately leads to the Board of Trade loses his way.

The trip begins in 1622 when James created a subcommittee of the council to specialize in colonial matters. Charles I replaced this subcommittee in 1634 by a Commission for Regulating Plantations, headed by Archbishop Laud and designed mainly to bring Massachusetts Bay under royal supervision. The outbreak of civil war killed the commission. Control over the colonies soon passed to Parliament, which in 1643 created a Commission for the Plantations, making its chairman, the Earl of Warwick, governor-in-chief and lord high admiral of all the American colonies. The Rump Parliament in 1649 created the Commonwealth and in the process extended its authority over "all the dominions and territories thereunto belonging." A subcommittee of the Council of State, Parliament's executive body, was assigned to oversee imperial trade, the single aspect of the empire that interested Parliament. A separate board was established in 1655, its membership a blend of government officials, merchants, landed gentlemen, and members of Parliament. Charles II in 1660 replaced the Parliamentary committee on trade with two interlocking committees—a Council of Trade and a Council for Foreign Plantations—whose membership consisted of such colonial enthusiasts as Lords Berkeley, Carteret, Colleton, Clarendon, and Shaftesbury. These bodies were replaced in 1672 by the Joint Council for Trade and Plantations, most of whose members were drawn from the earlier groups. Under the vigorous direction of Lord Ashley, Earl of Shaftesbury, who in his spare moments was building up Carolina, more knowledge was accumulated about the American colonies than ever before. Shaftesbury's friend John Locke, who became secretary of the council in 1673, initiated a stream of correspondence with colonial officials. The council was only a fact-finding body and had to defer to the relevant crown officials for decisions, but out of the facts and advice it poured into the king's and his advisers' ears came the basic principles of a colonial policy that lasted well into the eighteenth century.

Early in 1675 the king's new lord treasurer, the Earl of Danby, a talented administrator, dissolved the Joint Council—ostensibly as "a measure of economy," actually in order to replace it with a new group, known officially as the Committee of the Privy Council on Trade and

Plantations, unofficially as the Lords of Trade. This committee differed from its predecessor in that membership was limited to the Privy Council, and it had the power to make and enforce decisions. It was probably the most effective administrative body in the colonies' history, mainly because of its first secretary, William Blathwayt, who, like Edward Randolph, represented the new type of public servant who had come into government with the Restoration. Blathwayt made government his business rather than his hobby. His ethics certainly did not rise above those of the day—Bolingbroke called him the poorest tool "that ever dirtied paper" —but his energy and intelligence combined to make him one of the most important men in English government.

The Lords of Trade concentrated on creating uniform governments subservient to the crown's wishes throughout the American colonies. To that end, it forced colonial governors for the first time to adhere to policies laid down in London. Those policies as far as possible were based on the fullest information of American conditions ever available in England. The committee queried local officials relentlessly; it collected books and maps, to increase its knowledge; it interviewed merchants, ship captains, and colonial agents for information. From the facts assembled, it prepared governors' instructions, issued dispatches, and wrote those of the king's proclamations relevant to the colonies. The committee moved steadily toward its goal of a strong central administration for the empire. It saw to it that the Bay Colony lost control of New Hampshire in 1679 and converted that territory into a royal colony; it won annulments of Massachusetts' and the Bermuda Company's charters in 1684; it failed to prevent the king's grant to Penn but did succeed in limiting the proprietary powers in the charter; and it strengthened royal government in Virginia in 1683 by sending over as governor Lord Howard of Effingham, who ran the colony as it wanted. The Dominion of New England culminated its great effort to dominate the colonies.

The Lords of Trade's authority waned when James II came to the throne and reversed a century's experience. The committee reverted to an advisory body and power over the colonies returned to the whole Privy Council. What had once been the Lords of Trade's business became everybody's business, which meant nobody's business. But the momentum of the committee's activity carried on into the early years of William III's reign. Thus, both Penn and the current Lord Baltimore temporarily lost the power of government in their proprietaries and Andros was absolved of wrongdoing while ruling the dominion and returned to America as governor of Virginia. The Lords of Trade even urged the revival of the dominion; but here they had to compromise. The new charter issued to Massachusetts in 1691 transformed the holy commonwealth into a royal province. A crown-appointed governor received authority to appoint judges and justices of the peace and to veto all acts of the representative assembly. All Protestants were allowed to worship as they pleased. The right to vote was expanded from the Puritans' "freeman" to include all who had freeholds worth 40s. rent a year or other property worth £40 sterling. Settlers gained the right to appeal from local courts to the king whenever the amount in dispute exceeded £300. The harshness of these innovations was softened first by the charter itself (other royal colonies lacked charters that delineated their rights), by the provision that revived its representative assembly (killed under the dominion), by those clauses that called for an elective council (an appointed body in all other royal colonies), and, finally, by the lack of a provision for the governor's salary, which handed the assembly some control over his acts. Also, the crown yielded to New England traditions by confirming all land grants as they stood, without requiring them to be in the king's name or asking for a quitrent, which was a fixed feature of royal colonies. One clause in the charter pleased both the Lords of Trade and Massachusetts: the colony's boundaries were expanded to include Plymouth, Maine, and Nova Scotia, and such off-shore islands as Martha's Vineyard and Nantucket, the point being that while it strengthened the Bay Colony it also reduced the problems of government by consolidating several plantations into one. The crown went a step farther to please the people of Massachusetts by choosing one of their own—Sir William Phips—as the first royal governor. On this genial note did King William inaugurate his tightening-up program for the American colonies.

The end of King William's War found the king surer of himself and also less amiable toward the American colonies, whose wayward ways he had come to know well. Fortunately for him, Parliament, whose role in the government had increased with the Glorious Revolution, shared his view. By 1695 the war with France was having an obviously disastrous effect on the British merchant marine. One estimate said that three thousand English merchantmen had fallen to French privateers before the end of 1692. Coupled with this came a surge in illegal trade out of the colonies, and this was bound to worsen if a Scottish plan to establish a colony at Darien, on the isthmus between North and South America, materialized. For Scotland was still considered outside the British Empire —and would remain so until the union with England in 1707. And a colony at Darien offered a perfect base to pick up American goods illegally and import them duty free into Scotland, where they would drift down into England and undersell those that had paid the heavy duty. Some crown officials thought the best way to meet the Scottish threat was to reorganize all the colonies around the great bays—Chesapeake, Delaware, and New York. The Privy Council and the Customs Commissioners toyed with the idea, agreed that as a long-range plan it had merits, but rejected it as too radical a leap. Instead, crown officials wrote and Parliament passed in 1696 An Act for Preventing Frauds, and Regulating Abuses in the Plantation Trade.

This statute is commonly known as the Navigation Act of 1696. It tightened control over trade by defining English ships as those with crews at least three-quarters Englishmen; by demanding bonds be posted on enumerated articles, even when a duty was paid in a colonial port, to ensure their being kept within the empire; by establishing procedure for the more effective registration of ships; and by defining the duties of naval officers in colonial ports. But it was more than a navigation act. Several of its provisions inaugurated basic changes in the colonies' relations with England. No one shall "at any time hereafter alien, sell, or dispose" land in America owned or claimed by England to any but natural-born Englishmen. All colonial laws that were in "any wise repugnant" to the act were to be "illegal, null, and void." Governors of all colonies, be they royal or not, must have royal approval before assuming office; they must take an oath to enforce the acts of trade; failure to perform could result in removal from office and/or a £1,000 fine. Two of the most significant innovations were, first, the provision to establish Vice-admiralty Courts in America and, second, to give America a full-scale customs organization. The customs officials there were now to have "the same powers and authorities for visiting and searching of ships . . . and also to enter houses or warehouses to search for and seize" illegal goods as were "provided for the officers of the customs in England."

Parliament and the crown joined again in 1699 to put two statutes on the books that at least obliquely were aimed at the colonies. The first, An Act for the More Effectual Suppression of Piracy, let the king erect special courts to try offenders without juries. It was an open secret that American merchants welcomed pirate trade, partly for the nice profit they could turn on the stolen goods, partly for the gold and silver pirates used to pay for what they bought in this land always short of hard money. Good Quakers "wink at Scotch trade and a Dutch one, too," William Penn once told his governor, but "you not only wink at but embrace pirates, ships, and men." The second statute that struck at the colonies was the Woolen Act of 1699, which, in an effort to bolster the sagging cloth industry of England, forbade the exportation of all the wool or woolen cloth produced in America. This restriction permitted wool to be produced for home use, but it legally blocked the growth of a large-scale commercial woolen industry.

From 1696 on, Parliament legislated for the colonies with increasing frequency. But two things should be noted about this legislation: nearly all of it was prompted by the crown, and Parliament took care not to interfere in the administration of the colonies but only with the commerce. After 1696 most of the directives issued by the crown regarding the colonies flowed through the office of the newly created Board of Trade.

The Board of Trade

For the American colonies, 1696 could be called a year of decision. The Treasury enlarged the customs service. The Admiralty created seven Vice-admiralty Courts for checking illicit trade. The Privy Council increased the powers of royal governors and warned them that London would hereafter keep a closer eye on their activities. The secretary of state for the Southern Department concentrated, as he had not before, on colonial business. And the Board of Trade came into being.

The new board was officially known as the Lords Commissioners of Trade and Plantations. William created it hastily to prevent intrusion by Parliament into the crown's control over colonial affairs, which the king considered part of his royal prerogative. He calmed the outraged by handing two seats on the board to members of Commons to balance the two given to members of the Privy Council and by choosing as the board's eight full-time members, who would do most of the work, men Parliament could be assured would protect the realm's mercantile interests. William Blathwayt and John Locke were two selected by the king. They and their colleagues numbered among the most knowledgeable men in England on American affairs.

The board's diverse membership marked the first difference from its predecessor. The Lords of Trade had consisted solely of Privy Council members; all had been aristocrats who held with Sir Francis Bacon that the government of colonies should be in the hands of "noblemen and gentlemen [rather] than merchants; for they look ever to the present gain." Attitudes had changed since Bacon wrote those words in 1625, and King William had been forced to accede to the change. Second, though still only an advisory body, the king's backing gave its advice the effect of royal command. Anything having to do with colonial affairs came within the board's purview. It recommended legislation to Parliament that related to the colonies. It had a strong say in selecting royal governors, though actual control remained with the secretary of state. It wrote governors' instructions. It examined colonial laws and its recommendation whether they should be disallowed or not usually was followed. (Of 8,563 laws submitted to the Board only 469 received the royal veto.) It judged religious matters. (The advice of the Bishop of London, an *ex officio* member, was generally followed here.) It heard and judged all complaints of oppression and maladministration. The board's power over the colonies in fact if not in law exceeded that of any other agency in England.

Soon after the board took form, it initiated a systematic survey of the American colonies. The study convinced the members that before any centralized, uniform control could be developed, all proprietary colonies had to be converted into royal colonies. To that end, the Board of Trade and the Customs Commissioners joined in 1701 to introduce into the House of Lords a bill designed to deprive all proprietors of their right to govern, because' this right had "by experience been prejudicial" to England's trade, to customs revenues, and to the royal colonies. William Penn, whose political skills rarely receive their due, fought the bill. The power to govern, he said, "is as much our property as the soil"; and with that argument as his chief weapon, he proceeded to organize the opposition so effectively that the bill went down to defeat.

Failure to pass the Reunification Bill, as it was called, marked a turning point in American colonial history, for the narrow margin of defeat frightened many proprietors. Those who owned New Jersey surrendered their government in 1702; resistance among the proprietors of Carolina and the Bahama Islands crumbled soon after; even Penn would have sold out in 1703 had he been offered a good price by the crown. The current Lord Baltimore sat tight, and eventually, aided by a timely switch to Protestantism, he retrieved full powers in his province. But despite the proprietors' new amenability, Parliament's refusal to pass the Reunification Bill blocked the crown's long-range plan to make all colonies conform to a single political system. Parliament in effect had refused to do for political administration what it had done through the Navigation Acts for colonial commerce. The compromised crown's confused policies through the eighteenth century, sometimes favoring colonial particularism, sometimes encouraging the centralizing desires of the London bureaucracy, owed something to the Parliamentary rebuff in 1701.

The Board of Trade had its best years during the first decade of its existence; after that, it began to weaken. Its strongest members either died or left for other fields. The ineffectual Queen Anne showed little interest in its work. During the 1720's the secretary of state retrieved full control over colonial patronage and distributed the plums as he pleased, paying no attention to the board's recommendations. From about 1730 to 1748 the board became a shadow of its former self, and it was not until the inception of Lord Halifax as president that it recouped its dominant role in colonial affairs.

Even when the board bloomed full and strong, it never controlled

American affairs as fully as it wished. For one thing, the times worked against it. No direct mail service existed with the colonies before 1755, and before then, it took between two months and two and a half years for a letter to cross the ocean. Mail so often strayed to pirates or wartime enemies that a year could pass before the board heard from a governor. (Once three years slipped by before it heard from North Carolina's governor, though he swore he had written regularly.) Boston lay on the direct route to America, yet Sir William Phips failed to receive orders relevant to his impending invasion of Canada until eight months after they had been issued, and he was already on his way.

For another thing, the board seldom dared to advance a recommendation until all government officials in London concerned in the decision had either approved or been appeased. Threats against a colonial governor could bring the wrath of the secretary of state down upon the board. An accusation against a customs collector might rouse the fury of the Commissioners of Customs. Parliament, the Bishop of London, the Admiralty, the War Office, and, of course, the king all had something to say about colonial affairs, and they usually said it. The division of authority in London was repeated in the colonies, where the imperial machinery seemed to some more a collection of cogs spinnings at their own pace rather than parts of a well-oiled machine operating under a single master.

Imperial Machinery

The Board of Trade had two pipelines to the colonies. One, in England, was the colonial agent. The crown's early difficulties with the Bay Colony led to the insistence that someone be sent to London with the authority to represent Massachusetts' views before crown authorities. By the end of the century, the arrangement had become fixed. Penn's charter called for an agent to represent the colony who resided in or near London, and soon all colonies were forced to be thus represented. The agent could be an Englishman—Edmund Burke, for example, represented New York—or an American—Benjamin Franklin lived comfortably in London on the salaries he collected for representing Pennsylvania and Massachusetts, among other colonies. The agents lobbied for their colonies, kept them informed on matters that affected their welfare, and when called upon, transmitted the crown's views to the colonial governments.

The board's other pipeline was the colonial governor, the king's personal representative in royal colonies and also the key cog in the imperial machinery, the bulk of which was designed to control colonial trade and commerce. In the beginning the governor's primary duties were political, but after 1660 he also had to take an oath to enforce the Navigation Acts. Governors took this duty with varying degrees of seriousness, with royal governors doing the best job. If they tended to be delinquent, it was partly because they, with their close knowledge of a particular colony's affairs, often saw the unfairness of the acts when stringently applied and partly because their authority to enforce them was equally often challenged or flouted by other royal officials.

Second in importance to the governor and first among those he had to contend with was the naval officer. The post originally had been part of the governor's duties, but with the growth of the colonies these duties increased to the point where it seemed wise to turn the office over to another. The governor in the beginning had the power to appoint the naval officer, but collusion between the two became so notorious that after 1700 the crown assumed the assignment. (The shift was convenient, too, in that it opened one more berth for the spoils system in England to fill.) The naval officer kept track of every ship entering and leaving the port, listing its captain and cargo, whence they came and whither they were bound. He was required to make quarterly reports to England. His salary, usually based on fees collected for performing his duties, was slight, which often made him an easy mark for the bribe of a captain with a load of contraband. The naval officer could block the efforts of the diligent governor who sought to keep trade flowing in legal channels. He could also, and often did, thwart the efforts of customs officials.

By the beginning of the eighteenth century, an imposing offshoot of the English customs department had begun to take form in America. A chain of officials spotted at approximately fifty different ports had come into being. Included were ninety surveyors, riding surveyors, comptrollers, collectors, searchers, preventive officers, land waiters, tide waiters, plus watermen, boatmen, and clerks. The annual cost of this establishment prior to 1753 ran between £7,000 and £8,000; the duties collected averaged out to about £1,500 a year.

In time, all customs officials came under the supervision of the surveyor-general of the district. (By the time of the Revolution three surveyor-generals covered the mainland colonies and an additional one the West Indies.) A Surveyor- and Auditor-General Office was set up in England in 1680 to take charge of colonial financial matters. Two men— William Blathwayt and Horatio Walpole—ran the English office for nearly eighty years, giving it continuity, if nothing else. William Dyer pioneered the post in America, then came Patrick Mein, but it was Edward Randolph who made the office one of the most important in the imperial setup. Randolph died in 1703 and was succeeded by Robert Quary, a kindred spirit, equally zealous. The surveyor-general inspected the activities of all customs officers under his direction, examined their books, and searched for illegal goods on his own. He conferred with and advised governors and often quarreled with them; after 1753 he sat as an *ex officio* member of the council of the colony in which he happened to have duties. His zeal or lack of it could set the tone of the entire customs service. Because he spent most of his time on the road traveling from colony to colony, he generally knew more about the operation of the imperial machinery in America than anyone of the day, unless it was the vice-admiralty judge.

The act of 1696 introduced a momentous change in the colonies' regulatory machinery when it authorized the creation of Vice-admiralty Courts. Eventually twelve were erected up and down the coast. Colonial governors, who had the power to appoint the judges, advocates, registrars, and marshals, hunted through their provinces for experienced men to fill vacancies, but the specialized procedures, so different from common-law courts, and the abstruseness of the maritime matters that dominated their agendas made the search difficult. Still, by 1763 Americans filled most of the posts. The colonists found little to complain about the personnel of the courts or, for the most part, the justice they dispensed. The judges dominated the courts, for the cases handled were generally too specialized to depend on juries for decisions. The judges were trained in the intricacies of such matters as prizes, wrecks, insurance, contracts, and the like. The courts were always open for business; ships could await tides and winds, but they could not afford to linger for justice. A sailor with a grievance, a merchant with a perishable lading to dispose of wanted prompt decisions, and they generally got them. Americans castigated the courts steadily in the second half of the eighteenth century, but because their jurisdiction in America, unlike Admiralty Courts in England, had been extended to cover violations of the Navigation Acts. Previously violators of these acts had been tried in the regular common-law courts of the colonies, but, as Governor Shirley remarked at one point, "a trial by jury here is only trying one illicit trader by his fellows, or at least his well-wishers." When the courts moved into this area, colonial merchants complained that their rights as Englishmen were being violated.

GOVERNMENT IN THE COLONIES

It took a century for the mold of colonial government to form and the ingredients to "set." Any variations in the pattern after the first decade of the eighteenth century would be of degree, not kind. The governments divided into two types, royal and chartered, with the royal colony predominating. The crown owned and governed a royal colony and appointed all the chief executive officers. A chartered colony was privately owned, the charter being a gift of royal lands and powers to private persons. A charter granted to a corporate political community created a corporate colony; there were two of these—Rhode Island and Connecticut—and except for being required to abide by the Navigation Acts no restraints were imposed on them. They chose their own governors and public officials; they never worried about disallowed laws, for they did not have to send their legislation to England for approval. (Massachusetts was semicorporate in that it could choose most of its own officials and semiroyal in that it endured a royal governor and had to send its laws to London for approval.) A charter given to individuals created a proprietary colony. By 1720, only Pennsylvania (with contiguous Delaware a part of it) and Maryland remained among the proprietaries. Some individuals continued to hold immense grants within royal colonies, like Lord Fairfax in the northern neck of Virginia and Lord Granville in Carolina, but such holdings were rare.

The chartered colonies considered themselves exceptional, for their charters were to them constitutions that protected their rights. (Connecticut refused to relinquish its charter when the Dominion of New England had been formed and hid it in an oak tree, so tradition has it, until the dominion died.) These "glorious charters," however, were hardly what the colonists made them seem. They could be and had been revoked, and steadily throughout the colonial period they suffered attacks from royal prerogative, courts, and Parliament. But the colonists continued to revere them, and their affection had something to do with the drive for written constitutions in 1776 and thereafter.

The trend toward royalizing colonies at the end of the seventeenth century did not necessarily dishearten Americans, for more often than not the change brought a more liberal government. Massachusetts lost its charter with popular approval, and only a minority resented the royal government that replaced the holy commonwealth. Carolina revolted in 1719 to get a royal government. Maryland for the most part would have welcomed control by the crown. The Pennsylvania legislature got one of its most liberal laws during the brief period of royal control between 1692 and 1694, when the assembly was allowed to initiate legislation. The Quakers wanted royal status after the Penn family turned Anglican, and Benjamin Franklin worked hard for it. Frontier communities in all the colonies preferred being under the crown's wing, for this, they thought, would assure them adequate military protection.

Variety prevailed among the governments of colonial America down to and through the Revolution. Massachusetts had a way of doing things that dismayed a visitor from South Carolina, and New York's politics seemed incomprehensible to a man from Pennsylvania, a judgment the

New Yorker quickly returned to the Pennsylvanian. Yet from the distance of the present, a common pattern can be discerned in the disparate governments. Let us then survey the government of a typical royal colony in eighteenth-century America.

The Governor and Council

The royal governor of an American colony served the interests of the king and Great Britain, as well as the interests of the colony he had been assigned to. His responsibilities often jarred against each other, and sometimes they were impossible to reconcile.

The governor arrived in his colony carrying a commission and instructions, both from the king. The commission authorized the form of the colony's government—a legislature with a crown-appointed council and an elected assembly, which, with the governor, had the power to legislate for "the public welfare, and good government of our said province," as long as such legislation was not "repugnant but as near as may be agreeable" to the laws of Great Britain. The commission was a royal colony's charter, "the known, established constitution," according to Thomas Pownall, a former royal governor of Massachusetts, and it could not "in its essential parts, be altered or destroyed by any royal instructions or proclamation."

The commission was published for the public to read. The governor's instructions, however, were private and except where they specifically authorized it for the governor's eyes alone. There were two sets—one for general matters and one for trade—and by the eighteenth century they numbered slightly over a hundred. They were drawn up primarily by the Board of Trade, approved by the secretary of state and Privy Council, and endorsed finally by the king. The board drew on its own experience and that of former governors in creating the instructions; the Bishop of London inspired those on religion and morals; the Admiralty, the Treasury, and the Customs Commission all had something to insert; and behind the scenes, the British mercantile community exerted its influence. The merchants, assuming that what was good for merchants was good for the country, helped to saddle the governor with instructions often incompatible with a colony's welfare.

The legal character of the instructions was never clarified. The colonists regarded them as rules to guide the governor but dispensable in new situations. The Board of Trade viewed them as royal commands that had the force of law. Not long after a Virginia governor had gone against his instructions in the interest of the colony and been reprimanded by the board for his independent action, Richard Bland, a member of the House of Burgesses, wrote:

To say that a royal instruction to a governor for his own particular conduct is to have the force and validity of a law and must be obeyed without reserve is at once to strip us of all the rights and privileges of British subjects and to put us under the despotic power of a French or Turkish government.

The secrecy of the instructions was an added irritant. The colonists saw them as a constant threat to their rights, all the more dangerous because they lay in hiding waiting until the governor saw the right moment to use them.

Royal governors varied as much as their instructions. Some, like Lewis Morris, Thomas Hutchinson, and Sir William Phips, were native Americans. For all their ability, these men seldom made good governors. Phips, who might be called America's first rags-to-riches hero, is a notable example. He came of a poor family, his mother's twenty-sixth child. He began life as a shepherd, became a ship's carpenter, then had the luck (or intelligence) to marry a rich widow and discover a sunken treasure ship, in that order. Both brought him a fortune; the second, a knighthood. He was chosen to inaugurate the government under Massachusetts' new charter, the hope being that America's first baronet might soften the blow. But Phips was soon quarreling with everybody—"Sir, you must pardon him his dog-days; he cannot help it," a friend remarked after one tantrum—and the crown had to recall him. The home-grown governor was either too familiar an ingredient to win esteem or had acquired too many enemies to be effective as a royal official. The crown more usually chose someone who had influence at court and a dire need for money. (A governor in the West Indies could make a quick fortune from illegal trade and privateering; a post in Jamaica, Barbados, or the Leeward Islands was considered most desirable from this standpoint.) Sometimes, a man began, like William Shirley, eager only to build up his bank account but ended by becoming a distinguished governor. A few men became professional governors. Sir Edmund Andros went from New York to the Dominion of New England to Virginia. Sir Francis Nicholson governed five colonies during his American career. Governor Wentworth ruled New Hampshire for twenty-five years, and Berkeley dominated Virginia even longer. Cadwallader Colden held one post or another in the colonies for nearly a half century. Midway in the eighteenth century a new type of professional appeared, the man with a military background—Sir Jeffrey Amherst in Virginia, Sir Guy Carleton in Canada, Sir Thomas Gage in Massachusetts—but he was a rarity on the American scene.

A governor's tenure averaged five years, about that of a British prime minister or a President of the United States. Slightly more than a hundred governors were appointed to America and the Indies between 1689 and 1775. About seventy-five were the sons of earls; forty-eight had matriculated at some college or university; and over twenty had studied law. Taken as a group they were well-fitted for their job; and considering the spoils system in England, the prevalence of the view that an office is property and, as with real estate, a man deserved to profit from it all he could, they functioned remarkably well. The notorious Lord Culpeper, who reaped a fortune from Virginia, and the perverted Lord Cornbury of New York must be balanced by such able men as Robert Hunter of New York, Henry Grenville of Barbados, Thomas Pownall of Massachusetts, and Alexander Spotswood of Virginia.

The governor was the colony's social leader, and he and his lady took precedence in all gatherings, regardless of what his rank had been at home. (Often, to add prestige to his social standing, he was knighted before assuming his duties in America.) He was also supposed to encourage virtue and goodness, often a difficult duty to enforce for men rarely chosen for their moral uplift. But his primary responsibilities centered on running the colony's political affairs. To that end, the wise governor studied local politics as soon as possible, informing himself of the various factions and their leaders before making any important decisions, particularly patronage appointments. The governor could appoint judges, justices of the peace, and a host of secondary officials; and this power gave him a strong hold over local affairs, for those he appointed tended to back his policies. As the eighteenth century progressed, crown authorities cut back on his control over local patronage and foisted on him more and more appointees from England. These spoilsmen felt little responsibility to the governor and often refused to obey his orders. The governor's authority over local affairs diminished to the point where Lord Dunmore could say in 1774 that if he had had the power of appointments he could have put down the rebellion. (The same could be said for the governor's power to grant land, which could have been one more way of cementing local ties to himself and royal power. Between 1764 and 1767 over five million acres were granted—all of it from England with almost no consultation with the governors concerned.)

The governor was commander-in-chief of the province, but his power was tightly reined by a legislature seldom eager to appropriate money for military ventures unless the colony was sure to prosper thereby. After 1755 his role here was further limited by the presence in America of a British commander-in-chief of all royal troops. The governor's powers in naval affairs were clipped even more: after 1689 he had no jurisdiction over the personnel of British warships stationed in his province; after 1702 he had no control at all over royal ships' activities. As a result, naval commanders tended to flaunt their new powers, to ignore provincial courts, and to constitute a real threat to civil authority.

The governor's council, normally about twelve in number, was essentially an advisory board. Some of the governor's functions had to be performed with its advice and consent—summoning the assembly, issuing paper money, establishing martial law, appointing judges and other officers—but in such matters as the suspension of officers or dissolution of the legislature, he could act on his own. However, he usually sought consent, for council members were men of influence and experience in the colony, and their approval gave the governor some assurance his ruling would be put in effect. The council was chosen with care, technically by the Board of Trade but practically speaking by the governor, who supplied the board with a list of twelve men of good life, without debts, and well-intentioned toward the English government. He starred his three preferences, and the board generally accepted his choices. A councillor served at the crown's pleasure, but most men held the post for life. All were colonials, though often they were, like Nathaniel Bacon and Caleb Heathcote, chosen before they had sunk roots in America. The pay was negligible, but the post carried great prestige and influence; no one was known to have lost money while serving. Members were chosen from all parts of the colony in order to get a cross section of views. Often they were elderly men, and the hazardous traveling conditions of the day sometimes made it difficult to raise a quorum to conduct business.

The council advised the governor but also had executive, legislative, and judicial functions. Its executive duties depended largely on what the governor wished them to be. As a legislative body, it resembled the House of Lords. It had an equal voice in all legislation. The lower house might initiate money bills, but the council reserved the right to amend them. As a judicial body, it also resembled the House of Lords, for it was the highest court in the colony, and in most cases its decision was final. The governor sat with the council on the bench and was president of the court, but his actual voice in rendering a verdict was no greater than theirs.

The council's influence held high through the seventeenth century but waned steadily through the eighteenth. Authorities in England tended to shift executive responsibility to the governor, leaving the council at best with negative control over his actions. It could, through his need for its consent, keep the governor from doing something, but it rarely could force him to do something. The council's judicial functions declined as the number and intricacies of a colony's legal problems increased, for most councillors were legal amateurs at a time when the increasing complexities of the law required professional qualifications. The council's authority in legislation diminished in direct proportion to the assembly's rise. By mid-eighteenth century, the assembly, more representative of provincial opinion, spoke with authority in every colony. The struggle between executive and legislature had narrowed down to a duel between governor and assembly, and the council did little more than sit on the sidelines and watch.

The Assembly

Franchise requirements varied, but in general a voter in provincial elections had to be white, male, twenty-one, Christian, and in most colonies a Protestant, too. Requirements of residence and nationality also entered in, but the most important limitation was the property qualification. A settler usually needed a fifty-acre freehold or £50 of personal property to qualify. Laxer standards prevailed in town and county elections, where it appears that any man in good standing with the community could vote if inclined to, but hardly more than half the men could vote in provincial elections if legal requirements were adhered to. However, the informality of colonial elections makes it hard to judge how rigidly the colonies held to their suffrage qualifications. Men were required to take an oath that they met the property requirements, but sometimes, Tom Paine once complained of an election his side lost, "every man with a chest of tools, a few implements of husbandry, . . . or anything else he could call or even think his own, supposed himself within the pale of an oath, and made no hesitation of taking it." It seems that when interest ran high, the size of the electorate rose proportionally.

A man announced his vote in the open before his neighbors gathered at the county courthouse or town meeting. In New England the town and elsewhere the county formed the basic electoral unit. As in England, the population of the town or county played almost no part in determining the number of representatives sent to the assembly. The older coastal areas dominated the legislatures, and backcountry settlements were notoriously underrepresented. Assembly members were elected by and tended to represent the interests of the town or county where they lived. (Exceptions to this rule persisted. In Virginia a burgess could stand from any county where he owned land. George Washington, for instance, lived in Fairfax County but represented Frederick his first seven years in the House of Burgesses.) This conception of direct representation differed from English practice, where a member of the House of Lords represented a class, the clergy or nobility, and a member of Commons spoke for the interests of the nation and empire and only indirectly or "virtually" represented his constituency. Thus the American could argue that Parliament had no right to tax him because he was not represented there, while the Englishman could insist that the American was as well represented as, say, a man from Bristol.

Americans differed, too, with their English brethren over the status of their assemblies. Governor Francis Bernard of Massachusetts summed up the two views neatly: "In Britain the American governments are considered as corporations empowered to make by-laws, existing only during the pleasure of Parliament. In America they claim to be perfect states, not otherwise dependent upon Great Britain than by having the same king." John Winthrop had stated the American view in the 1640's, and while neither side since then had retreated from its stand, no issue had arisen that led to a showdown or that England or the colonies felt was worth a showdown.

The American belief that their legislatures were analogous to Parliament had been reinforced over the years by the numerous traditions they had borrowed from that source. Assemblies were organized like the House of Commons: the speaker of the house dominated proceedings; standing committees laid the groundwork for discussion on the floor; and informal discussions were carried on by a committee of the whole house. Legislative procedure followed the English pattern. A bill went through three readings—the first to consider the bill on principle, the second to commit it to committee, and the third to discuss and debate it in full. If it passed after the third reading, it went to the council (House of Lords). When assembly and council failed to agree, a conference of three members from each body thrashed out differences. Unless a specific rule called for return to both houses, the bill was then engrossed, that is, put in final form, and sent to the governor. If there was no suspending clause—measures of doubtful legality contained a clause suspending it as law until royal assent had been given—it became law with the governor's signature.

No one knew for certain the powers and privileges of an assembly. Governors queried the Board of Trade, and the board usually returned ambiguous answers. Assemblies solved the problem by coasting along on English precedent. Freedom of discussion and from arrest during sessions became an American as well as English tradition. Assemblies, like the House of Commons, settled contested elections, made their own rules, and reprimanded members. Early in the eighteenth century all assemblies had won the right to initiate legislation and also to initiate money bills, two achievements attained earlier by Commons. Only occasionally did assemblies fail to assume rights garnered by Commons. They could not exclude holders of offices under the crown from their sessions, as Commons could. In some colonies, governor and council continued to dictate the choice of speaker, but the harnessed assemblies evaded this restraint by resorting to the committee of the whole and choosing their own committee chairman, as Commons had done in the sixteenth century.

Colonial assemblies have been heralded as protectors of the people against any arbitrary tendencies in governors and councils. But they could also turn against the people; they tolerated freedom of speech only up to the point where that freedom was used to abuse the assembly. The Zenger case in New York gave the press the right to print the truth only as long as it did not adversely reflect on the assembly; when it did, the paper was suppressed. An irate Pennsylvania assembly in the 1750's jailed a man because he had cast doubt on the members' integrity. More often than not in colonial America it was the legislature rather than the courts that suppressed freedom of speech.

The crown's control over colonial legislation was for a long while confined to the governor's veto. Pennsylvania's charter, with a clause that called for review of legislation in London, inaugurated a new tool; and by 1730 all colonies but Rhode Island and Connecticut were required to submit their statutes to the Board of Trade, which, after a careful study recommended they either be disallowed or approved. Only about 5 per cent of the laws sent over were disallowed, mainly because the crown did not wait passively for the assemblies to pass undesirable legislation. Legislatures and governors alike received instructions on the type of bills that might be voided. All omnibus bills were forbidden: a separate bill for a separate subject was required. No riders were permitted. Temporary laws that might circumvent the crown's rights of review were prohibited. Legislation contrary to an act of Parliament or to the colony's charter risked certain rejection.

Years could pass before an act was disallowed. The lax habits of London officials might account for this delay, but often the Board of Trade preferred to try a doubtful act before passing judgment. The repeal took effect the day the governor received notice of it. Once an act had been approved, only the assembly or Parliament could repeal it. The king could not touch it. This gave the people their greatest protection against the royal prerogative, for their accumulated body of statutes saved them from the crown's arbitrary acts against established political habits and customs.

The Board of Trade came to power too late to curb a good number of American laws it felt should have been disallowed and also too late to cut the legislatures' grips on the purse strings, which allowed them, among other things, to withhold governors' salaries. This control over salaries handed the crown an insolvable dilemma. It expected each colony to bear its own expenses, and yet it did not want the governor dependent on the colonial assembly. Efforts were made to establish a source of revenue beyond control of the legislatures. The crown succeeded in Virginia after Bacon's Rebellion, when the assembly momentarily lost its nerve, in pushing through a 2s. levy on every hogshead of tobacco, and out of this fund came the governor's salary. The situation in Maryland was comparable. In the West Indies, the crown won a similar concession in the 1660's in return for confirmation of disputed land titles. But all these levies were imposed relatively early and before the Board of Trade materialized. Elsewhere, the assemblies kept a tight grip on the disbursement of money raised within the colonies. By 1750 at least five legislatures consistently appropriated governors' salaries for but a year at a time. When the French and Indian War broke forth in 1754, the Board of Trade abandoned further attempts to reform the situation.

Assemblies, like children, could be obstreperous, but they could be cajoled too, into acting reasonably. William Shirley achieved wonders in Massachusetts. Francis Nicholson and Francis Fauquier got along famously with the Virginia legislatures during their stays. Robert Hunter stepped into a seemingly hopeless situation in New York in 1710, where, since Leisler's Rebellion, assembly and governor had bickered steadily and the governor's power had eroded to a shadow of its former self. When Hunter departed nine years later, the assembly eulogized him, even though he had recouped much of the lost power and prestige for the governorship. Hunter had guided his actions by a single rule. Assemblies "must be wrought upon by degrees," he said. "He that thinks he can do everything at once knows little of popular assemblies." William Burnet succeeded to the newly strengthened office, but Burnet, Lawrence Leder has said, "was neither as skillful nor as sagacious as his predecessor, and the unity created by a consummate politician was gradually dissipated by an obstinate administrator."

The Judiciary

The colonial charters required that the laws established should not be contrary to the laws of England, but vagueness surrounded that phrase "laws of England." Those laws included more than the statutes of Parliament and more than the law of the king's courts, generally known as common law. In the days before common law had achieved its later ascendancy, the laws of England embraced the customs of merchants, the local and divergent customs of towns and manors, as well as the laws enforced by ecclesiastical tribunes and by numerous other courts and commissions of specialized jurisdiction. Hence, American law in the early years of settlement drew upon a complex legal heritage that took in everything from national statutes to various local customs, all of which was supplemented by colonial enactments and decisions. During the eighteenth century, a substantial amount of English common law was absorbed into the local product as English lawbooks and reports found their way into colonial libraries and as a number of the colonists went over to the Inns of Court for legal training.

While no uniform "American" law developed throughout the colonies

—"We had much conversation upon the practice of law in our different provinces," John Adams said soon after he arrived in Philadelphia in 1774, adding that Andrew Allen of Pennsylvania "asks me from whence do you derive your laws?"—certain common characteristics emerged from the diversity. English laws on entail and primogeniture, which did so much to preserve the aristocracy there, died quickly in the colonies, where the abundance of land no longer made restrictions on its inheritance necessary. Statutes dealing with punishments of crimes differed from those in England. Since 1620, simple theft, which remained a capital crime in England, had not been punished by death in America. The hundred or more capital offenses listed in English law were cut to twelve in Massachusetts' Body of Liberties in 1641, and that trend continued in all the colonies. These and other divergences between English and colonial practices had become so marked by the end of the seventeenth century that an *Abridgement* was published in 1704 of the laws in the colonies, including those in the West Indies as well as America. By then a recognized body of American law had come into being, which crown authorities accepted as something to live with rather than change.

By then, too, a recognized form of American legal procedure had also come into being, which resembled rather than duplicated English procedure. The county court system of the South and of the Middle Colonies in large measure copied the English pattern. The council served the role of Parliament as the final court of appeal. The king was conceived of as the fountain of justice. His officers acted as prosecutors on the theory that the king's peace had been broken. The king alone had the power to erect courts, but assemblies were urged by the crown to establish their own court systems, which would fit the American rather than the English experience.

The right of appeal depended on the case. Appeals on criminal judgments were virtually unknown in English law until the nineteenth century (and by American standards are still limited), and thus in colonial America there was no judicial review for such cases. The governor was allowed to grant clemency where the fine was £10 or less; where the fine exceeded £200, the case could be appealed to the king. Appeals in civil cases were more general, with the governor and council acting as the court of last resort. Dissatisfied litigants could carry a case to the Privy Council if more than £500 was involved. Few colonists were willing to endure the expense and delay, however, and only sixty-seven cases in the entire colonial period were appealed to England.

Judges were appointed by the governor with the council participating in the selections to a varying degree until 1753, when all governors were ordered to get the advice and consent of their councils. Throughout the seventeenth and well into the eighteenth century the rule had been to appoint judges for life on good behavior. In an effort to keep the judiciary independent, the king instructed governors not to "displace any of the judges . . . without good and sufficient cause to be signified unto us . . ., and to prevent arbitrary removals . . . you shall not express any limitation of time in the commissions. . . ." In the 1750's the Board of Trade demanded that thereafter judicial commissions "be granted during [the king's] pleasure only," and this remained the rule until the Revolution. The board's decision was prompted, at least in part, by the New York assembly's refusal to grant permanent and fixed salaries for the judiciary. Tying a judge's pay to the whim of a legislature made a mockery of the idea of an independent judiciary. The board also felt that the general caliber of the colonial judiciary was low; it wanted a door left open so that when an able man came along, he could, with a minimum of trouble, be substituted for a poor one. Much has been written on the incompetence of colonial judges, but until more work has been done on the subject, the case must rest unproved. And until proved, it should be remembered that the maligned judges were "virtually angels of self-restraint," as Leonard Levy puts it, compared with that bastion of liberty, the assembly, or "with the intolerance of community opinion or the tyranny of the governors, who, acting in a quasi-judicial capacity with their Councils, were a much more dreaded and active instrument of suppression than the common-law courts."

By 1713 the pattern of colonial politics and the institutions of imperial control had been fixed and would change little until the Revolution. The development of an imperial structure, the theory and machinery for administering an empire, and the growth of a body of colonial civil servants all came about quietly and in relative obscurity, always overshadowed by the politics of England. During this "silent revolution," the great political leaders of England gave little of their attention to the burgeoning empire in America. Relatively minor figures on the English scene took control and shaped the empire.

Just at the time when the form of the imperial structure was hardening, the difference between Englishmen and Americans became clearer than ever. The distinctions were still somewhat confused, though, for people on both sides of the ocean insisted, curiously, on reversing the normal way of looking at things. Americans argued they were only Englishmen overseas and demanded the rights of Englishmen, whereas Englishmen said the colonists were Americans with traditions of their own that must be respected. As Englishmen overseas, Americans demanded that all the gains of the Glorious Revolution be extended to America; Englishmen said this not only could not be done but that it would never be done.

No single event in America's colonial history did more to widen the rift between the colonies and England than the Glorious Revolution. Out of that revolution came Parliament's eventual ascendancy in English political affairs and the diminution of royal power. But in the colonies, the king's power remained as strong as, if not stronger than, it had ever been. The colonists were told that the Habeas Corpus Act, a product of the Glorious Revolution, did not extend to them. The Act of Settlement of 1701 said, among other things, that judges should hold office during good behavior, but the Board of Trade declared it inapplicable to America. Some authorities even said that the Bill of Rights dealt with Englishmen's and not Americans' rights. Many achievements of the revolution could not have been extended to America: in England, the interests of the executive and legislative branches of government were welded together; whereas in America, they continued as they had been, in opposition, with the executive representing royal authority and the legislature representing the will of the American electorate. But all those achievements that seemed able to endure an ocean voyage Americans claimed. Indeed, when they came to stage their own revolution, they justified it largely on those rights that Englishmen had obtained in 1689, only by then, Americans were calling them "natural rights."

BIBLIOGRAPHY

Imperial Wars

Two essays on what has been done and still needs to be done in the period 1688–1763 are those by Frederick B. Tolles, "New Approaches to Research in Early American History," *WMQ*, 12 (1955), 456–461; and Clarence L. Ver Steeg, "The North American Colonies in the Eighteenth Century, 1688–1763," in William H. Cartwright and Richard L. Watson, Jr., eds., *Interpreting and Teaching American History* (1961; pb.).

Two recent and reliable introductions to the wars are the early chapters in Edward P. Hamilton, *The French and Indian Wars* (1962), and Howard H. Peckham, *The Colonial Wars, 1689–1762* (1964; pb.). The non-specialist will gain much from both G. M. Wrong's *The Rise and Fall of New France* (1928) and Francis Parkman's *Frontenac and New France Under Louis XIV* (rev. ed., 1885; pb.). For a view that contradicts Parkman's, see W. J. Eccles, *Frontenac: the Courtier Governor* (1959). Bernard De Voto's *Course of Empire* (1952; pb.) relates the highlights of the story in lively fashion, largely from Parkman's point of view. A fuller account of episodes touched on lightly in De Voto can be found in Clarence W. Alvord, *The Illinois Country, 1673–1818* (1920).

G. H. Guttridge's *The Colonial Policy of William III in America and the*

West Indies (1922) is basic. Two other reliable, more detailed, accounts are
Samuel A. Drake, *The Border Wars of New England* (1897), and J. B. Brebner, *New England's Outpost: Acadia Before the Conquest of Canada* (1927).
Also relevant here is Charles B. Judah's *The North American Fisheries and
British Policy to 1713* (1935), which is far more enjoyable reading than the
title suggests. G. M. Waller's *Samuel Vetch: Colonial Enterpriser* (1960)
throws much light on Queen Anne's War and the fumbling way British
policy and action took shape in this period. Lawrence H. Leder has edited
"The Livingston Indian Records, 1666–1723," *Pennsylvania History (PH)*
23 (1956), 5–240. Two valuable articles on the Indians during this period
are William T. Morgan, "The Five Nations and Queen Anne," *MVHR,*
13 (1926), 167–189, and Anthony F. C. Wallace, "Origins of Iroquois
Neutrality: The Grand Settlement of 1701," *PH,* 24 (1957), 223–235. Cadwallader Colden's *History of the Five Indian Nations* (1727; pb.) is still
reliable.

The Development of Imperial Control

Winfred T. Root's "The Lords of Trade and Plantations, 1675–1696," *AHR,*
23 (1917), 20–41 puts more succinctly and perceptively what Ralph P. Bieber
covers in *The Lords of Trade and Plantations, 1675–1696* (1919). The
fullest survey of the reorganization of 1696 is found in Charles M. Andrews,
The Colonial Period of American History, Vol. IV (4 vols., 1936–1938).
Some of Andrew's findings have been amplified and revised in Peter Laslett,
"John Locke, the Great Recoinage, and the Origins of the Board of Trade:
1695–1698," *WMQ,* 14 (1957), 370–402. The standard volumes on the
Board of Trade are Oliver M. Dickerson, *American Colonial Government,
1696–1765—A Study of the British Board of Trade in Its Relation to the
American Colonies, Political, Industrial, Administrative* (1912), and A. H.
Basye, *The Lords Commissioners of Trade and Plantations, 1748–1782*
(1925). Neither of these volumes should cause the interested student to overlook Winfred T. Root's distinguished *Relations of Pennsylvania with the
British Government, 1696–1765* (1912). The board's attempt to unify control
of the colonies as well as its effort to deprive the proprietors of their governments is covered in Louise P. Kellogg, "The American Colonial Charter,"
American Historical Association Annual Report (1903), 187–341, and in
Alison Gilbert Olson, "William Penn, Parliament, and Proprietary Government," *WMQ,* 18 (1961), 176–195.

Various British departments' roles in American affairs are discussed in
Dora M. Clark, *The Rise of the British Treasury* (1960), a recent and important study that traces the department's growing influence in colonial matters;
and Margaret M. Spector, *The American Department of the British Government* (1940), which deals in detail with the secretary of state's relations with
the colonies. Charles M. Andrews' "The Royal Disallowance," in the *American Antiquarian Society's Proceedings,* 24 (1914), 342–362, has been largely
superseded by Joseph Henry Smith's thorough *Appeals to the Privy Council
from the American Plantations* (1950). Among the biographies that cast light

on imperial administration, see Basil Williams, *Carteret and Newcastle* (1963) ; and once again Michael Garibaldi Hall's *Edward Randolph and the American Colonies, 1676–1703* (1960) and Gertrude Ann Jacobsen's *William Blathwayt: A Later Seventeenth-Century English Administrator* (1932), which show how the new breed of public servant coming into being carried out royal policy. Carl Ubbeholde, *The Vice-Admiralty Courts and the American Revolution* (1960), supersedes all previous studies.

Government in the Colonies

The colonial agent is succinctly discussed in the sixth volume of Lawrence H. Gipson's *The British Empire Before the American Revolution* (10 vols., 1958–1961) ; more fully by B. W. Bond, Jr., "The Colonial Agent as a Popular Representative," *Political Science Quarterly (PSQ)*, 35 (1920), 372–392, and E. P. Tanner, "Colonial Agencies in England During the Eighteenth Century," *ibid.*, 16 (1901), 24–49; and most fully in Edward P. Lilly, *The Colonial Agents of New York and New Jersey* (1936), and Ella Lonn, *The Colonial Agents of the Southern Colonies* (1945). A personal account of an agent's life is found in Leonard W. Cowie's *Henry Newman: An American in London, 1708–1743* (1956).

Thomas Pownall's *The Administration of the Colonies* (1764) is a perceptive and dispassionate report by a former royal governor. The basic modern work is Leonard W. Labaree's *Royal Government in America* (1930), which should be used in conjunction with his collection of *Royal Instructions to British Governors, 1670–1776* (2 vols., 1935). Evarts B. Greene's general study of *The Provincial Governor* (1898) should be supplemented by the numerous biographical studies of specific governors. Leonidas Dodson, *Alexander Spotswood* (1932), is superb. John A. Schutz's *Thomas Pownall* (1951) should be read with Pownall's own account; and Schutz's *William Shirley* (1961) can be filled out with Charles H. Lincoln's edition of *The Correspondence of William Shirley* (2 vols., 1912). Those who yearn for more detail on life among New England governors can consult Gertrude S. Kimball, ed., *The Correspondence of the Colonial Governors of Rhode Island* (2 vols., 1902–1903).

The most recent summary of voting qualifications in colonial America, a subject historians are rousing interest in, is Chilton Williamson, *American Suffrage from Property to Democracy* (1960). The bibliography in Williamson's work will lead the student to other recent, more elaborate, and specialized studies. Lawrence H. Leder, "The New York Elections of 1769: An Assault on Privilege," *MVHR*, 49 (1962), 675–682, discusses resident requirements for voting. The best study of the eighteenth-century legislature is Jack P. Greene's distinguished *The Quest for Power: The Lower House of Assembly in the Southern Royal Colonies, 1689–1776* (1963). Percy S. Flippin's first-rate *The Royal Government in Virginia, 1624–1775* (1919) has sound remarks on the relation between the governor and assembly in that colony. Mary P. Clarke, *Parliamentary Privilege in the American Colonies* (1943), discusses with authority the assemblies' attempts to gain and hold rights and privileges. Leonard W. Levy's "Did the Zenger Case Really Matter? Freedom of the Press in Colonial New York," *WMQ,* 17 (1960), 35–50 deals with the legislatures' efforts to repress free speech, a subject Levy treats at length in *Freedom of Speech and Press in Early American History: Legacy of Suppression* (1960; pb.).

For further references see the *Harvard Guide,* Sections 99, "Virginia, New England, and Wars on Northern Frontier, 1689–1713"; 101, "British Colonial Policy and Administration, 1713–1760"; and 102, "Political and Constitutional Development, 1713–1760."

"The Trustees of Georgia," by William Verelst

10. A Half Century of Expansion: 1713–1763

NEW BLOOD AND A NEW COLONY
    Who Came and Where They Went
    What They Found
    Failure in Georgia

THE FRENCH EXPELLED
    The French and Indian War
    The Effect of the War on America

IMPERIAL RELATIONS: 1713–1763
    Parliament and Colonies
    Crown and Colonies
    Ominous Straws in the Wind: 1759–1763

The year 1713 marked a turning point in early American history. The end of Queen Anne's War inaugurated a stretch of good times that lasted down to 1760. Little of importance marred relations between the mother country and the colonies in this period. Great Britain stopped sending over special agents, like Edward Randolph, and obtained its information quietly through governors and other regular officials. The Union of 1707 brought Scotland within the empire, legitimized the heavy but formerly illegal trade with America, and thereby eliminated a cause of tension. Although Parliament broadened its interest in colonial affairs and passed a variety of statutes to restrict or control those affairs, the lack of proper enforcement agencies in America made the new laws easy to evade and thus easy to bear. Prosperity abounded, fed first by a new flood of immigrants—a flood so enormous it made the previous "great migration" seem puny—and also, after 1739, by a new series of imperial wars that brought to the colonies contracts for supplies, along with soldiers and sailors with money to spend.

NEW BLOOD AND A NEW COLONY

A side effect of the wars that had embroiled Europe from William III's accession to 1713 had been to check the flow of new blood to America. The colonial population continued to increase—from around two hundred thousand in 1690 to approximately four hundred thousand in 1710—but with few additions from outside. After the Peace of Utrecht, America encountered a population explosion, an increase of 500 per cent in the number of its citizens in a half century. By 1763 some two million people inhabited America, over a third of whom had been born abroad. More foreigners in proportion to the total population lived in America on the eve of the Revolution than at any other time in the nation's history.

Who Came and Where They Went

A good part of this new blood came from non-English stock, for British authorities throughout the eighteenth century did their best to plug the outflow from England to America of all but one group of citizens. Craftsmen were forbidden by law to emigrate. Orders went out to colonial authorities to send home all sailors who jumped ship, and fishing masters were instructed to return with as many men as they took over. Convicts alone were encouraged—"forced" might be a better word—to emigrate. An act of 1718 commuted jail sentences to seven years' servitude in the colonies. Several colonies passed laws against the use of convict labor, but all such acts were vetoed or disallowed by crown authorities. The large majority of some seventeen thousand convicts sent to America ended up in the Chesapeake area. Maryland in particular welcomed them; for some reason the poor farmers there were delighted to get a man for seven years by paying no more than his transportation. Convicts were cheaper than slaves, and because they spoke English, they were of more help in growing the oronoco, a finicky variety of tobacco Maryland specialized in that required particular handling.

The influx of immigrants after 1713 differed in degree rather than kind from what had come before. America from the beginning had attracted settlers other than English—the Dutch in New York, a sprinkling of Danes, Finns, and Swedes in the Delaware Valley. In the 1680's Penn induced some German Quakers and Pietists to join his holy experiment and also a band of Welsh, who sought to create a New Wales where they "might live together as a civil society to endeavor to decide all controversies and debates amongst ourselves in a Gospel order, and not to entangle ourselves with laws in an unknown tongue." All but the Germans, and even many of them, had by the early eighteenth century intermarried with English stock and largely forgotten their national origins. The Swedes maintained ecclesiastical ties with the Lutheran Church in their homeland, but a Swedish pastor arriving in 1701 found that he had to preach to his flock in English if he was to be understood.

French Huguenots drifted to America after the revocation of the Edict of Nantes in 1685. By 1700 some four thousand were scattered through New England, another one thousand or more in New York (New Rochelle was founded by the Huguenot minister David Bourepos and remained French in tone throughout the colonial period), and an equal number in South Carolina. Most came from the industrious middle class of France; and this, together with their energy, intelligence, and ability to adapt to American life, helped them prosper. Huguenot names that still survive—Bowdoin, Revere, Bernon, and Faneuil in New England; Jay, DeLancey, Bayard, de Forest, Vassar, Gallaudet, and Delano (from de La Noye) in New York; Manigault and Laurens in South Carolina— suggest better than statistics how much their influence exceeded their numbers.

The first Jews had arrived in the mid-seventeenth century, and by the eve of the Revolution, some fifteen hundred were scattered through the colonies. They lived for the most part unmolested; they worshiped as they pleased, and they prospered. Ezra Stiles described his friend Aaron Lopez of Newport as "a merchant of first eminence, for honor and extent of commerce probably surpassed by no merchant in America." A visitor to New York City in 1750 said that the Jews there lived in "large country-seats" and had "several ships, which they load and send out with their own goods." He erred in saying "they enjoy all the privileges common to the other inhabitants of this town and province," for nowhere on the continent were Jews considered first-class citizens, with the right to vote and hold public office.

This sprinkling of non-English immigrants through the seventeenth century turned into a deluge with the onset of peace in 1713. Europe had been enduring a population explosion of its own. Wars, once affairs of mass bloodletting, had become confined to professional armies, leaving the common people largely unaffected. Plagues, possibly because of such advances in medicine as inoculation, no longer hit as often or with the devastating effect they once had had. Improvements in farming techniques increased the food supply, and the popularization of the potato offered year-round sustenance to people whose ancestors had died of malnutrition. The continent's population doubled during the eighteenth century, but the amount of land available remained fixed. The Industrial Revolution, which would eventually absorb much of the new population off the land and into the factories, had yet to take effect. Economic pressure, it would seem, created the basic condition for the mass exodus to America that began after Queen Anne's War.

Actually, the exodus had begun before the war ended. The German Palatinate, bordering the Rhine, was overrun in 1707 by marauding soldiers sent by Louis XIV to destroy the food supply. Two years later some thirteen thousand destitute Palatines arrived in London on invitation from Queen Anne. The city temporarily housed the refugees in tents and empty warehouses, then worked out a relocation program that dispersed them about the empire. Some three thousand were sent to Ireland, with the hope that the stolid Germans might dampen the spirits of the volatile Irish natives. Another group of over six hundred, together with a band of some one hundred German-speaking Swiss led by Baron Christopher de Graffenried, went to North Carolina; about half died on the trip across, and the remainder either perished in the Tuscarora War (1711), when Indians attacked their settlement of New Bern, or were absorbed by English-speaking settlements in the Carolina backcountry. Some three thousand others went to New York, where Governor Robert Hunter planned to set them to work making tar and turpentine from pine trees. His mismanagement compounding one failure with another, he disbanded the tar-turpentine project in 1712 and left the Germans "to shift for themselves." They migrated northward to the valley of the Schoharie River only to learn that the lands they had settled belonged to others who were determined to collect rents. A third move carried them into Pennsylvania, near the present site of Reading. Reports dispatched home of their travails led Palatines forever after to shun New York, an event that caused the colony's development to lag throughout the rest of the colonial period, for by this time the deluge from the Continent had begun.

The Germans came slowly at first, less than a thousand a year until 1727; the rate stepped up to two thousand annually until 1750, a four-year spurt followed and some twenty-five thousand flowed in; thereafter, the stream diminished, and when it dried up with the Revolution, something over one hundred thousand German-speaking people had come to America, nearly all of them settling first in Pennsylvania. They differed ethnically—among them were Alsatians, Bohemians, Moravians, Palatines, Silesians, Swiss, Wurttembergers, and a smattering of French Huguenots who had lived in the Rhine Valley—but all in time would be called Pennsylvania Dutch (from *"Deutsch,"* meaning "German"); and the language they spoke, an Upper Rhine dialect, is today, with many American variants tossed in, "the oldest immigrant language still in daily use in the United States."

They differed religiously, too. First, there were the "plain people"—

drably dressed Mennonites, most of Swiss stock, of whom perhaps five thousand came; Amish, whose women favored brightly colored dresses and whose men dressed in solemn clothes and wore beards; and the smaller sects of Dunkards (officially, the German Baptist Brethren, to which President Eisenhower's ancestors belonged), River Brethren, and Schwenkfelders. Perhaps twenty thousand plain people came in the eighteenth century: all were tied in varying degrees to the Anabaptist sects of the Reformation; they strove to shut themselves off from the world and to live only among themselves; and they were pacifists. The plain people refused to hold public office—that would entail mixing with the world—and from the time of the French and Indian War they appear to have ceased voting. They live today in Lancaster County much as they did two centuries ago. America affected them little, and they influenced America hardly at all. (But the "plain people" have not gone unnoticed by the national government. The Amish, for instance, object to all forms of insurance, holding that it shows a lack of faith in God. The Medicare Act of 1965 exempts from the Social Security system any self-employed person who is a member of a recognized sect conscientiously opposed to public and private insurance, a provision designed to appease the nearly twenty thousand Amish living today in the United States.)

These "Protestant monks and nuns," with their quaint habits, are popularly identified as the Pennsylvania Dutch. But the "church people"—the Lutherans and the Reformed (often called the Dutch or German Presbyterian Church)—comprised the bulk of the German-speaking immigration into Pennsylvania. The church people were of the world's people. They dressed and, outside their homes, spoke as Americans. They entered politics, became merchants, and the numerous skilled craftsmen among them added much to Pennsylvania's prosperity. They rejected pacifism. They centered in Berks County, on Pennsylvania's northern frontier, but could be found anywhere in the backcountry down to Georgia. Like the Scotch-Irish, they settled among their own kind; York and Gettysburg, for example, were their towns, just as Carlisle belonged to the Scotch-Irish. Neither group expressed fondness for the other—the Scotch-Irish probably coined the phrase "dumb Dutch"—but they tolerated one another with only occasional flare-ups.

The Moravians, the third major German-speaking religious group, began, after an exploratory venture in Georgia, to arrive in Pennsylvania in 1740. Their sect, known officially as the Bohemian, or United, Brethren, had been founded in 1457, and after nearly being wiped out in the Thirty Years' War they had been revived in the eighteenth century by Count Nicolaus Zinzendorf, who promoted their emigration to America. Bethlehem became their center in Pennsylvania, Salem (now Winston-

Map 27. Settlement in Early 18th Century

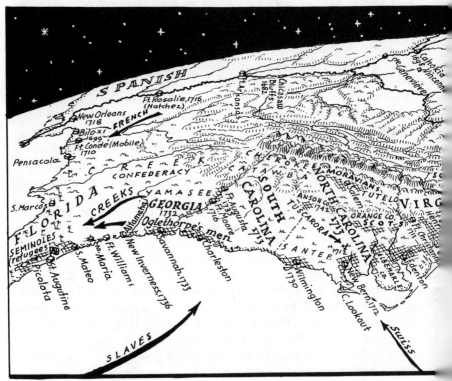

Salem) in the South. They numbered no more than twenty-five hundred at the time of the Revolution. Their missionary effort among the Indians has been called "the most enlightened attempt this country has seen to solve the native race problem." The Moravians were in many ways a blend between plain and church people. They emphasized a life shed of ornaments but did not attempt to live apart from the world. They shunned war and worked to promote peace between Indians and whites, but they would fight when pressed. They were, as they put it, neither *kriegerisch* (war-like) nor *Quäkerisch* (Quaker-like).

The inbound stream of German-speaking people blended at Phila-

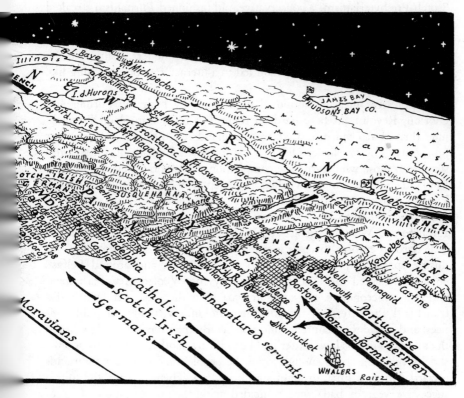

delphia and other ports on Delaware Bay with the even greater stream of Scotch-Irish, who arrived through the eighteenth century in five great waves—1717–1718, 1725–1729, 1740–1741, 1754–1755, and 1771–1775. By the Revolution, over a quarter of a million lived in the backcountry of Pennsylvania and all the Southern colonies.

The name Scotch-Irish is an Americanism. They preferred to be called what they were—Ulster Scots, or Ulstermen. Milton labeled them, these "blockish Presbyterians" from a "barbarous nook of Ireland." They had come originally from the Lowlands of Scotland. In the early seventeenth century, when James I was striving to tame the wild Irish, he en-

couraged the Lowlanders with an offer of good lands to emigrate to the
Ulster "plantation" in northern Ireland. By 1620 some fifty thousand had
settled there, and twenty years later the number had doubled. The flow
continued through the seventeenth century, and near the end of it a smattering of French Huguenots rounded out the resettlement program. The
Lowlanders kept their church and did not intermarry with the Irish, but
they nonetheless ceased to be Scotch. Their Presbyterianism differed from
Scotch Presbyterianism; a conservative, old-fashioned Puritanism streaked
it. The Ulstermen were neither democratic nor tolerant, any more than
seventeenth-century Puritans had been. The church kept tight control over
their personal lives, and the minister, not the parishioners, dominated the
church. Their passion for education led to a literacy rate of something like
95 per cent.

Oppressive measures imposed on Ireland by both the Puritan and
Glorious Revolutions bore hard on them, but these transplanted Scotch-
men thrived—so much, indeed, that England felt the need to curb their
prosperity. The excellence of Ulster cattle caused Parliament, under pressure from those who feared the competition, to prohibit their import into
England. So Ulstermen switched to sheep. But Parliament, to protect
English markets on the Continent, reacted with the Woolen Act of
1699, which allowed Irish wool and woolen cloth to be marketed only in
England and Wales. (The act applied to America, too, but distance made
it as hard to enforce there as it was easy in Ulster.) An infant linen industry, sparked by Huguenots who had settled in and around Belfast,
only partly eased the burden imposed by the Woolen Act. Parliament
added a noneconomic grievance in 1704 with the Test Act, which dis-
franchised Presbyterians, forbade them holding virtually all public offices, and closed their churches and schools. By the time George II relieved
the severities of this law, Ulster had been hit by another series of economic
shocks, this time sharp enough to set the people moving by the thousands
toward America. First, drought struck in 1714. Then, in 1717, the fourth
successive year of bad crops coincided with the inauguration of "rent
racking" by Ulster's absentee landlords. (In 1686, landlords eager for
tenants had granted thirty-one-year leases by the thousands and "set
their lands at very easy rents." When the leases ended, owners racked the
rents up, "in most places double and in many places treble, so that it is
impossible for people to live or subsist on their farms.") So ships were
chartered, possessions sold, and some five thousand Ulstermen headed for
New England, where they assumed fellow-Calvinists would welcome
them. But they were received coldly. Cotton Mather called the influx another of those "formidable attempts of Satan and his Sons to unsettle us."
Though they settled on the frontiers of New England—in Maine, New

Hampshire, and western Massachusetts—towns balked at granting them lands, refused to let them erect their own churches, and forced them in many cases to support the established Congregational meetings. Then the word went out that Pennsylvania rather than New England was the place for Ulstermen to go.

James Logan, who had been reared near Belfast, welcomed his "brave" countrymen to Pennsylvania. "At the time we were apprehensive from the northern Indians," he wrote in 1720. "I therefore thought it might be prudent to plant a settlement of such men as those who formerly had so bravely defended Londonderry and Enniskillen as a frontier in case of any disturbance. . . ." Logan predicted they would be "orderly" if kindly used and "a leading example to others." The prediction proved wrong. "A settlement of five families from the North of Ireland gives me more trouble than fifty of any other people," he soon wrote, adding that "the common fear is, that if they continue to come, they will make themselves proprietors of the province." They continued to come and continued to disregard all rules of settlement. They squatted wherever they found "a spot of vacant ground," and when challenged to show title, they said it was "against the laws of God and nature that so much land should lie idle while so many Christians wanted it to labor on and raise their bread," the identical excuse Puritans had used a century earlier to take Indian lands in the Connecticut Valley.

The Scotch-Irish and Germans pretty much split the backcountry between themselves, except in those few spots where such late arrivals as the Scots made their homes. Scots, both Highlanders and Lowlanders, had come to America throughout the seventeenth and eighteenth centuries, always in small numbers and often as prisoners who were being exiled for an abortive uprising against the crown. However, after 1763 some twenty-five thousand Scots, mostly Highlanders, migrated to America; the stream continued until 1775 when Parliament outlawed further emigration as detrimental to the welfare of Scotland's economy. Poverty provoked their migration, a poverty compounded of crop failures and cattle blights and unemployment among town craftsmen.

The Lowland Scots' life in America resists chronicling, for their numbers were slight and they tended to adapt quickly to the new environment. The Highlanders present another story. They came from parts of Scotland where much of the medieval world still lived. Many were still Roman Catholics and most did not speak English. The clan survived, and its all but absolute chief received unquestioning loyalty from his kinsmen. A good number of the emigrating Highlanders were led by tacksmen—small or intermediate landlords—who hoped to revive the clan system in America with themselves as chiefs (for the old chiefs rarely migrated).

Some three hundred Catholic Scots settled on Sir William Johnson's baronial estate in the upper Mohawk Valley, and while tacksmen continued to favor New York, whose feudal methods of granting land appealed to them, the majority of Highlanders—approximately a quarter of the total migration of twenty-five thousand—gravitated toward the back-country of North Carolina. The Highlanders resisted adjusting to the American environment as stoutly as the plain people. They lived unto themselves, held to their Catholicism, and often resisted learning English. (As late as 1805 Gaelic was still spoken among several families that moved from North Carolina to Mississippi.) Those who settled in the seaport towns as merchants adapted enough to help give Glasgow control of the American tobacco trade. But when the Revolution came, nearly all Scots in America threw in with the English. Highlanders provided the back-bone of loyalist resistance in both New York and North Carolina, largely, it seems, because their leaders, whose word still verged close to law, favored the English cause.

What They Found

Some left home expecting that in America "roasted pigeons are going to fly into their mouths without their having to work for them." The long voyage over helped early to disabuse them of their dream. The trip had changed little in more than a century, except possibly for the worse; one eighteenth-century traveler reported that children under seven rarely survived the voyage. In 1776 a man from New Jersey met a "modest, young Irish widow, who on her passage lost her husband and children at sea," on a crossing where of some six hundred passengers over one hundred died at sea "and many more on landing."

The trip was hardest and longest—it usually lasted six months—for those from the Rhine Valley. Promotion agents called "newlanders" roamed through the valley in the eighteenth century spieling about the glories of the new land. These "thieves of human beings," who received a fee for every person they beguiled aboard an emigrant ship, sought out a village's old people, knowing their authority would "lure other people to go along with them." The trip from one's village down the Rhine passed thirty-six customhouses, each a spot where officials required a bribe for clearance. Once at Rotterdam, the major port of embarkation, travelers who had been fleeced of most of their savings were now at the mercy of a new emigrant virus—the redemption agreement.

The indenture system, for all its faults, had this virtue—before leaving England or northern Ireland, the servant signed a contract, which stated the length and conditions of his servitude in America. The contract held fast no matter who bought the servant's service, and all colonies had laws to protect the rights of indentured servants. Redemption agreements, on the other hand, were vague and unwritten; and the redemptioner never knew the terms of his servitude until after he had reached America, where it was too late to reject them. He and the master of the ship made a verbal agreement that his passage would be paid by whoever purchased his services in America. This bargain left the captain free to sell the emigrant where he wished in America and for whatever the traffic would bear. A redemptioner who had been told his ship was destined for Philadelphia might find himself landing in New York, because the captain had learned servants were bringing a better price there. The time of bondage usually varied from three to six years, depending on a servant's health and age.

The evils of this system did not go unnoticed. Captains normally held all passengers, sick and well alike, on board until the redemptioners had been sold; many invariably died during this dismal period. In 1742 Pennsylvania purchased a site for a pesthouse, where the ill could be nursed back to health; the captain would be reimbursed out of the sick passenger's effects. The colony in 1750 passed An Act for Prohibiting the Importation of Germans or Other Passengers in Too Great Numbers in Any One Vessel. The law sought to force shipowners to provide all passengers with "wholesome meat, drink, room, and other necessaries," but little came of this well-meaning effort. The law was revised in 1766, partly through agitation from the German Society of Pennsylvania, which had been organized two years earlier: passengers were to be limited to two in one berth; ample headroom had to be provided; every emigrant ship had to carry a surgeon and a full assortment of medicine, and during the crossing the ship had to be fumigated twice a week and washed down twice during the voyage with vinegar. But colonial governments were too weak in the eighteenth century to enforce their humanitarian impulses; the statutes had slight effect. An America eager for cheap labor worried little about the privations of those who came.

The deluge of immigrants brought wealth to America and also problems. The influx of non-Britishers raised for the first time the question of citizenship. The view prevailed in the eighteenth century that citizenship was inalienable and that foreigners lacked all civil rights—the right to vote, to hold office, and to own or inherit property. Occasionally a special act of Parliament or a royal decree made it possible for an alien to become a "denizen" of Great Britain with certain limited rights of citizenship. The American colonies, on the other hand, in their eagerness for settlers, made naturalization an easy process, often by a general law and with low resident requirements. (Massachusetts at one time required only a year's residence to become a citizen.) The crown did not interfere with these arrangements, but in 1718 a legal authority for the government re-marked that these colonial laws had local force only and that a naturalized citizen of, say, Pennsylvania or Massachusetts became an alien on moving to another part of the empire. Parliament sought to rectify the confusion with an act in 1740 that systematized the empire's naturalization laws. A foreigner who resided in one colony for seven years, took the oath of supremacy, and was a member of the Church of England could become a naturalized citizen with rights that extended throughout the empire. These relatively stiff requirements—they were to be made stiffer by further restrictive measures in 1760 and 1773—were ignored by the colonies, which held to their old, lenient standards. Pennsylvania continued to ask of a foreigner no more than a two-year wait, the usual resident requirement for all voters, and a two-dollar fee to the lawyer who handled the legal details for naturalization.

Naturalization in the long run proved a trivial issue compared to the political problems raised by the newcomers. Hitherto, the presence of only English stock in the colonies made ethnic appeals unimportant in elections. Factions arose over particular issues, vanished when those issues were settled; new factions arose with new issues. Now, the presence of large groups of self-conscious minorities brought a new element into American politics that would forever after shape the outcome of elections. James Logan saw earlier than most that the man who controlled the German-speaking vote could control Pennsylvania's political affairs. Benjamin Franklin later attempted to sweep an election by centering his appeal on the German vote. The experience Franklin and other Pennsylvania leaders gained in seeking to win elections by attracting various ethnic groups to their side would chart the way for all future American politicians.

Another political problem materialized as immigrants moved farther and farther inland: government of some sort had to order their public lives. The solution here had been decided long ago when the first settlers fanned out from Jamestown. Pennsylvania imported the Virginia system of erecting new counties, which entered the colony with equal status to the old. Lancaster County was created in 1729 to deal with the westward surge of people, then in 1749 came York, Cumberland in 1750, and Bedford in 1771. Virginia erected Frederick and Augusta in 1738 to cope with the growth of her backcountry; and as the waves pushed south, North Carolina created Anson in 1742, Orange in 1752. Care was taken in all the colonies to keep the representation of the backcountry at such a point that control of the legislature remained in the hands of the seaboard counties.

The act of welding the newly settled areas to the older seaboard colonies complicated the affairs of Pennsylvania and of every colony to the south. The westward push carried settlers into hunting grounds and lands the Indians considered their preserves. Clashes between red men and whites were inevitable, and every colony knew that westward expansion eventually would entail the expense of a frontier war. Authorities in England and in the colonies preferred this to what they considered a worse evil—control of the backcountry by the French in the north, the Spanish in the deep south. (The Spanish appear to have had a hand in provoking the Yamasee War, which has been ranked "with the most famous Indian conspiracies of colonial times." In 1715, Yamasee and Creek Indians who had been antagonized by Charleston traders, initiated attacks on the South Carolina frontier that soon flared into a general uprising among southern Indians. The uprising was crushed quickly—if a year of fighting can be considered quickly—by the forehanded action of the "gallant" Governor Charles Craven and the prompt help offered by Virginia's Governor Spotswood, who suspected that the French also had a hand in the uprising and planned to use it to promote a general Indian war in all the colonies. The outburst served, if nothing else, to alert authorities in England to the spread of the French threat to the southern frontier.) The Board of Trade, in noting the encirclement of the American colonies by the French, remarked in 1721 that the "enlarging and extending of the British settlements" westward offered the crown "one of the most effectual means to prevent the growing power and further encroachments of the French in those parts"; and in 1732 that "the well peopling of this province seems a necessary means for the defense and security of all our plantations on the continent of America." The board was speaking of the backcountry of Virginia, but it could as appropriately have been talking of Georgia, whose charter was granted in 1732 largely with the hope that the peopling of that province would check the advance of Spain in that area.

Failure in Georgia

Georgia was the last of the thirteen colonies founded, but the motives that prompted and the techniques that expedited its settlement resembled those used for the first, Virginia, over a century earlier. Spain had been the enemy then, and it remained the enemy still. Only now, the entrenched English had edged down to the northern tip of the Spanish Empire, and it was they who had become Spain's clear and present danger. The Spaniards did their best to block South Carolina's inland expansion. They kept their Indian allies stirred up against the English, and they retaliated with arms against every incursion into the "no man's land" north of Florida that both Spain and England claimed as theirs. South Carolina at one time built an outpost on the Altamaha River to assert its claim in the disputed area, but a fire led to its abandonment in 1727. Three years later the Board of Trade, well aware of the situation, advised that the "debated" land be settled by "the poor persons of London," a suggestion that brought General James Edward Oglethorpe into the picture.

James Oglethorpe came of a distinguished family. He had served honorably in a war against Spain and returned home to enter Parliament as a warm promoter of English over Spanish interests in the Caribbean area. He was more than a routine imperialist: he had what Pope called a "strong benevolence of soul"; Samuel Johnson liked the man and often had him to dinner. General Oglethorpe's Parliamentary duties at one point involved him in a study of English prisons that left him shocked at the inhumane treatment debtors received in a supposedly humane age. Soon the general had blended his antipathy toward Spain and her American empire with his sympathy for ill-treated prisoners; out of the conjunction of the two interests came the conception in 1732 of a buffer colony north of Florida to be peopled by the distressed of England.

There was nothing unique about Oglethorpe's plan, except possibly the humanitarian motive for depopulating debtor prisons. The unique aspect was that the conception for a new colony had emerged out of Parliament, and execution would eventually depend to a large extent on that body. The charter granted Georgia in 1732 gave the land between the Savannah and Altamaha Rivers and from sea to sea to twenty-one "trustees," who were not allowed to own land in or to profit from the colony but could only hold it "in trust" for twenty-one years, at which time, having supposedly been established on a firm footing, it would revert to the crown.

Georgia, much like early Virginia, quickly became all England's project. Collection plates passed in churches around the nation brought in some £18,000 for the colony. The Bank of England contributed, and Parliament, for the first time in British history, appropriated £136,608 to see the colony through the gestation period. All the techniques once used to promote Virginia were revived. Pamphlets announced that Georgia's "air and soil can only be fitly described by a poetical pen because there is little danger of exceeding the truth." Sermons pictured the colony as a new "Macedonia crying for help." The Hakluyt prospectus for Virginia was dusted off, and Georgia became a place where wine grapes and silk and hemp would thrive, a haven that would relieve England of overpopulation, resuscitate the poor, and offer a refuge for the persecuted.

Even the trustees' plan for developing Georgia resembled that for Virginia in 1608. The colony was to be governed as a semi-military frontier outpost and peopled by soldier-settlers who were as handy with a gun as a hoe. Settlements were to be compact and ringed by small farms. Negro slavery was prohibited in order to prevent the development of large plantations, which would disperse the population. The colony would be tightly controlled from above. The trustees would appoint the "President" and "Common Council," and these officials would make all regulations for governing the colony.

Care was taken to seed the colony with able pioneers. The employed were discouraged from applying for fear of depleting England's supply of skilled labor, but the indigent were favored only if "virtuous and industrious." Oppressed Protestants from Europe, such as a band of Lutheran Salzburgers and another of Moravians, were accepted only after they had proved they were no mere "enthusiasts" but sober, hard-working people. Oglethorpe blazed the way in the fall of 1732 with thirty-five families. After an easy crossing and a cordial welcome at Charleston, the party pushed up the Savannah River, where the general chose a spot on a high bluff for his first settlement, the site of modern Savannah.

Oglethorpe played the role of Gates and Dale in early Virginia. He kept the settlers working under martial discipline; they were fed and clothed from a stockpile furnished by the trustees. At the end of a year of communal living the male settlers received land, livestock, and equipment, and thereafter they worked for themselves. A farmer's grant consisted of fifty acres, which could be increased by another fifty acres for every servant up to ten brought to the colony. A limit of five hundred acres on all grants was designed to keep the settlements compact and also protect the farmers from the competition of large plantation owners. No settler received his land outright; the trustees controlled its future disposal. A farmer could pass his grant to his eldest son, but if he had no son it reverted to the trustees. Oglethorpe laid down tight regulations for fur traders, who he feared might disrupt the good relations he had established with Indians in the area. Traders were required to obtain licenses and to renew them annually; the prices of trading goods and furs were fixed; rum was forbidden in all dealings with Indians. (For that matter, "rum, brandies, spirits or strong waters" were prohibited throughout the colony.)

Georgia prospered from this loving supervision no more than Virginia had in the seventeenth century. By 1740 some fifteen hundred settlers had been sent over by the trustees, and probably an equal number had come at their own expense; but a good number of them had left—the Moravians, for example, had made the long trek to Pennsylvania. An agent dispatched by the trustees to investigate conditions in the colony reported that the ground rules for settlement should be changed. In 1738 the restrictions on land holdings were relaxed: women were allowed to inherit, leases were permitted, maximum holdings were stretched to two thousand acres, and quitrents were reduced. General Oglethorpe, who saw Georgia mainly as a defensive military outpost against the Spanish, had opposed this easing of restrictions. He had returned from England with a regiment of soldiers in 1738 to put Georgia on a war footing, for England and Spain verged on the War of Jenkins' Ear, which became official in 1739. After the Creek Indians had assured the general of their neutrality, he invaded Florida, capturing two forts on the St. Johns River. The next summer he attacked and laid siege to Saint Augustine but failed to take it. A vigorous but unsuccessful counterattack by a Spanish army of five thousand was followed by Oglethorpe's own reinvasion of Florida. Again he failed, and soon after he was courtmartialed for maladministration of the army. The court acquitted him of all charges, but by now his feelings for and relations with Georgia had soured.

After the war with Spain, the trustees continued working to make Georgia prosper. They lifted the ban on Negro slavery in 1750 and allowed settlers to buy and sell and otherwise dispose of their land as they wished. By then, too, the restriction on "strong waters" had been repealed. They gave in slightly to the demand for self-government by allowing a provincial assembly but granted it only the right to air grievances, not to make laws. Georgia still refused to thrive, however, and in June 1751 the distraught trustees voted to return the colony to the crown two years before the charter required them to. Once again a well-financed, carefully organized, thoughtfully planned effort to establish a colony had failed.

THE FRENCH EXPELLED

While thousands poured annually into English America, France held to its old emigration policy for Canada: only good Catholics and solid citizens were allowed to go. Otherwise, however, France did not drag her feet. The losses at Utrecht of Newfoundland and Nova Scotia, which flanked the entrance to the Gulf of the St. Lawrence, were somewhat repaired by building Fort Louisbourg on Cape Breton Island. This, the largest fort in the New World, seemed adequately to guard the door to the gulf; it also offered a refuge for French privateers and a base for France's increasingly valuable codfishing fleet, which had once sailed from Newfoundland. French scheming reduced Nova Scotia's value to England by persuading the some five thousand Acadians who lived there to remain so that they might harass their new rulers in time of war. Frenchmen kept the Abnaki Indians stirred up in New England and in 1722 helped spur on their raids against settlements on the Kennebec River. But here French policy failed. New Hampshire and Massachusetts replied with raids of their own that wiped out Jesuit missions on the Kennebec and sent the Abnakis so deep inland that New England ceased to be bothered with a serious Indian problem for the rest of the colonial period.

While the American colonies filled the land east of the Appalachian range, the French further strengthened their hold on the land to the west. They had by 1720 anchored their line of posts on the Mississippi in the south at New Orleans and in the north at Cahokia, across the river from St. Louis. Between these came Fort Chartres (1720), located near the modern Prairie du Rocher, Illinois, and Fort Orleans (1722), on the Missouri. All trade routes in the Great Lakes area received renewed protection. They repaired La Salle's old Fort St. Louis on the Illinois River (near Utica) in 1713; built Fort Michilimackinac (Mackinaw City today) in 1715, and Fort La Baye, at the south end of Green Bay, in 1717; and reestablished Fort La Pointe on Chequamegon Bay in 1718.

The Board of Trade kept tabs on these developments and had sound, informed advice to give the government. It worried little about New Orleans, for it knew that the town lived but did not prosper. (France had granted a monopoly of Louisiana trade to the Mississippi Company; its high prices for goods and low prices for furs let the English traders out of Charleston and the Spanish at Pensacola keep control of the trade in that area.) The board recommended that the Acadians on Nova Scotia be removed and replaced by Protestant settlers and that the peninsula's defenses be strengthened. It urged aggressive action to get control of the fur trade and that forts be built, missionary activity among the Indians be stepped up, and traders be allowed to live among and marry Indians. And, finally, the board sought to convince the government that settlement offered the best check to French advances. In 1721 it suggested that special inducements be offered in the western counties of Virginia in the shape of ten years' exemption from quitrents and a remission of the customary legal fee for taking up land.

But little came of these recommendations. Fort Oswego (1726–1727) materialized on Lake Ontario, and it became an important rendezvous point for Indians and traders; little else, however, was done officially, though unofficially English traders made prosperous sorties deep into French-controlled territory. Peace had reigned for thirty-five years between France and England, and Robert Walpole, who now headed the government, wished to do nothing to disturb the quiet. He was not to have his way.

War Resumed

War came first with Spain, and England provoked it. The Treaty of Utrecht had jarred open the door to the Spanish Indies by allowing England's South Sea Company a thirty-year monopoly of the slave trade and the right annually to bring in one ship with diversified cargo. The company abused its privilege. It stationed the annual ship off Porto Bello, and by surreptitious restocking at night disposed of a fleet's rather than a ship's goods. English ships roamed widely in Spanish waters, and by 1738 an undeclared maritime war was going full tilt, with Spain winning. The excuse to make the war official was furnished in 1739 by Robert Jenkins, a British smuggler, who had lost an ear in a brush with the Spanish off the coast of Florida. Walpole argued against the war, knowing that Spain's alliance with France would inevitably bring that power in and turn a local fray into a world war, but Parliament preferred to see the loss of Jenkins' ear as an insult to British honor and disregarded his warning.

Parliament knew that America was "the only place where Spain is vulnerable" and that it would be the main theater of the war; it knew little more, some members being so ignorant that they "called the colonies the Island," an appalled American visitor to Commons noted. The well-informed Martin Bladen of the Board of Trade endeavored to advance the war effort with a plan to unite the colonies, "since it is generally expected that our colonies should give us some assistance upon this occasion. . . ." Nothing came of Bladen's vision, but the colonies did assist in the war. Massachusetts, led by the able and newly appointed Governor William Shirley, prepared for French entrance into the war by strengthening Bay Colony defenses. Delaware voted £1,000 to supply provisions and transportation for troops recruited within the colony. Pennsylvania, still ruled by Quakers, refused to vote a penny, though French privateers already tormented its commerce and despite James Logan's warning that the western part of the colony "lies exposed to the *French*." When the governor urged all servants to enlist, he was "abridged by the assembly of [his] salary."

While General Oglethorpe plagued the Spanish in Florida, Admiral Edward Vernon captured Porto Bello on the Isthmus of Panama in late 1739. In 1741 the admiral assaulted Cartagena, in modern Colombia, with a large fleet and an army of some ten thousand, perhaps a third of which was drawn from the colonies. Disease, mismanagement, and Spanish resistance forced a retreat; only six hundred Americans survived the catastrophe. (Vernon nonetheless remained a hero to one Virginia volunteer, Lawrence Washington, who named the home he owned on the Potomac, which his brother George eventually inherited, after the admiral.) The War of Jenkins' Ear soon after vanished into a broader conflict—the War of Austrian Succession as Europe called it, King George's War as it was known in America—which, as predicted, brought mighty France officially into action.

France struck first at Nova Scotia. Governor Shirley of Massachusetts dispatched reinforcements to save Annapolis Royal, then used the attack to pry funds from his legislature to build a warship, strengthen Castle

William in Boston harbor, and garrison forts in Maine. The legislature gave all he asked here but rejected as foolhardy his plan to take Fort Louisbourg. So the governor dredged up convincing arguments to support the plan: possession of Louisbourg allowed the French to half ruin "the New England fishery" and to harass "the coasting trade and navigation of the northern colonies as far as Pennsylvania"; Britain after the war would doubtless pay the costs involved in taking the fort; contracts to outfit the expedition and commissions to lead it would go to New Englanders; reliable reports had it that the fort was undermanned and would fall easily. The arguments charmed the legislature, which voted £50,000 for the expedition, an enormous sum for those days. New York contributed cannon, Pennsylvania and New Jersey gave provisions; all the men came from New England.

On March 24, 1745, some ninety vessels, a good number of fishing smacks among them, set out from Boston to take the strongest fort in North America. The venture was the greatest ever attempted by the colonies; it was entirely American in conception and execution, though at the last moment the British supplied a naval covering force. William Pepperrell, a rich merchant of Kittery, Maine, had been chosen to head the expedition, and in less than two months he and his associates had recruited and outfitted over four thousand men. On June 17, a month and a half after a siege had been laid down and some three thousand cannon balls had been poured into the fortress, Louisbourg capitulated. The news delighted all America but displeased British authorities, for it distracted attention from the peace negotiations they wanted to inaugurate. The humiliated French sent two fleets to revenge the defeat; a gale forced the first to return home, and the second bowed to a superior British force in 1747.

The Louisbourg victory overshadowed a less noticeable achievement on the western frontier. Britain's superiority on the sea had cut the flow of supplies to Canada, and the French, for want of trade goods, began to lose out in the competition for furs among the Western Indians, especially those in the Ohio basin. English goods had always been better and cheaper; now they were more plentiful, and England had men on the scene ready to take advantage of the situation—George Croghan in Pennsylvania, for example, and William Johnson in New York. Croghan had arrived in Philadelphia from Dublin in 1741, and soon after he became an Indian trader, the one business that offered a chance for fortune without much investment, for it operated entirely on credit. Croghan would eventually become the greatest trader of his time and would, almost entirely by his own skill, capture the Ohio Valley fur market for American traders during King George's War.

Map 28. King George's War. 1743 - '48

L. Superior

TIMISKAMING

La Pointe
1718

CHIPPEWA

OTTAWA

ALGON

Ft. Mackinac
1712

L. Huron

Ft. La C

Mississippi

Ft. Le Baye
1717

Portage

L. Michigan

PETUN

IROQUOIS

L. Ontario

RENARD
(FOX)

Ft. St. Joseph

Ft. Niagara

IRO

Ft. Detroit

L. Erie

Ft. St. Joseph

Maumee R.

DELAWARE

Ft. St. Louis

Ft. Miami
1704

Logstown

ILLINOIS

Wabash R.

MIAMI

Ft. Quiatenon
1719

Pickawillany

Ohio

Cahokia

SHAWNEE

Ft. Vincennes
1735

Ft. Charles
1720

Ohio R.

Falls

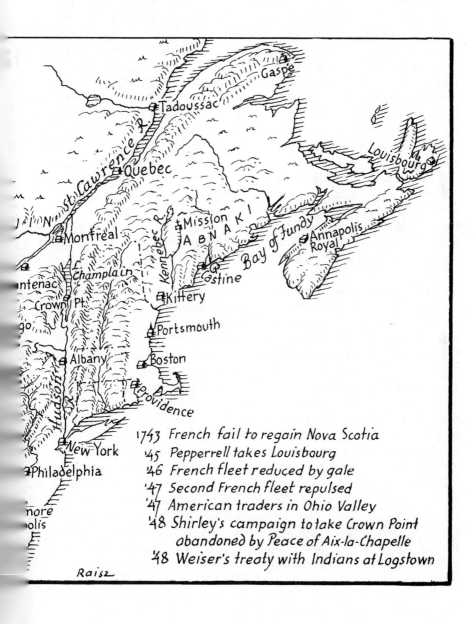

Gaspé
Tadoussac
St. Lawrence R.
Louisbourg
Quebec
Montreal
Mission
ABNAKI
Kennebec R.
Bay of Fundy
Annapolis Royal
ntenac
Champlain
Castine
Crown Pt.
Kittery
go
Portsmouth
Albany
Boston
Hudson R.
Providence
New York
Philadelphia
nore
olis

1743 French fail to regain Nova Scotia
'45 Pepperrell takes Louisbourg
'46 French fleet reduced by gale
'47 Second French fleet repulsed
'47 American traders in Ohio Valley
'48 Shirley's campaign to take Crown Point
     abandoned by Peace of Aix-la-Chapelle
'48 Weiser's treaty with Indians at Logstown

Raisz

Johnson, another Irishman, also began as a trader, with headquarters in the Mohawk Valley. He was that rare Britisher who liked Indians, and they, sensing this, gave him their confidence, the Mohawks going so far as to "adopt" him into their tribe. Johnson might have continued as an Indian trader but for the peculiarities of colonial politics. New York, which had once snapped at every French advance, had lost its bite; the assembly sounded more like its Quaker counterpart in Pennsylvania than its former self. Governor George Clinton, backed by the Board of Trade, wanted to fight the French and court the Iroquois. But the assembly opposed him on both policies, for Albany sent English goods to Montreal, and furs came back. Merchants who profited from this trade and speculators who coveted lands in western New York that the Iroquois nations occupied carried along those who resented spending public money for frontier defense, and this coalition blocked the governor throughout King George's War. Clinton achieved one goal: he put William Johnson in charge of the colony's Indian affairs, and Johnson alone managed to keep the Iroquois on England's side during the war.

New York's distaste for Governor Clinton's belligerency was matched by discontent of another sort in Massachusetts, where soon after the Louisbourg victory the war boom had petered out. Hope bloomed for more war contracts when Shirley announced that his plan to invade Canada had been approved, but the crown soon reversed itself and called the invasion off. An attempt to impress Bostonians into the British Navy raised a mob that gave the governor and the colony's leaders several uneasy days. Something like the unity of the Louisbourg period returned in 1748 with the decision to mount an expedition to take Crown Point on Lake Champlain from the French, but the imminent end of the war caused the project to be abandoned.

The Peace of Aix-la-Chapelle in 1748 judged the war a draw. All conquered territories were returned to their prewar owners, which meant that Louisbourg went back to France. England repaid the colonies for their expenses in the expedition, William Pepperrell was made a baronet, the second American so honored (William Phips had become the first in 1687), but these acts did little to alleviate hard feelings over the decision. If England could so lightly return a conquest like Louisbourg, it was said, "perhaps this goodly land itself . . . may be the purchase of a future peace."

Bitterness over Louisbourg plus a general lack of interest by the seaboard in Western affairs obscured the signing at Logstown, down river from the forks of the Ohio, of another treaty in 1748 more important to Americans than Aix-la-Chapelle. Conrad Weiser, an Indian trader and interpreter, had negotiated the treaty for Pennsylvania. By it, Indians formerly allied with France agreed to welcome Pennsylvania traders into their midst. They had switched sides for a practical reason: they wanted trade goods. The Logstown Treaty was a triumph for the English, for the Ohio Valley had recently become a particularly important Indian trading territory. Some Indians—notably the Delawares and Senecas—had shifted from the East into the area. A large group of Miamis had moved from Illinois, where they had traded with the French, to the site of Piqua, Ohio, where they founded the town of Pickawillany, soon to become the trading center of the Ohio Valley.

The French did not dare ignore the treaty. Captain Pierre Joseph Céloron de Bienville was dispatched into the Ohio Valley with a triple mission: to warn out British traders, to awe the Indians with a show of force, and to post lead plates that stated the Ohio Valley belonged to the king of France.

He left Canada in 1749 with some two hundred soldiers and a band of Indians, traveled down the Allegheny to the forks, thence down the Ohio, planting lead plates at the mouths of streams that emptied into the two great rivers. At the mouth of the Great Miami he turned northward to parley with the Indians at Pickawillany. He urged the Miamis to return to their old lands on the Maumee River, where they would be once again under French protection. Their chief—"La Demoiselle" to the French, "Old Britain" to the English—refused. Céloron soon after cut overland to Fort Miami (Fort Wayne), then up the Maumee to Lake Erie and back home. He returned to Canada having done what he set out to do but knowing his mission had failed.

On the heels of Céloron's departure appeared Christopher Gist, another Indian trader but one who now acted as agent for the Ohio Company. The company had been organized in 1747 by London merchants and Virginia planters. Two years later the king, urged on by a Board of Trade, eager to see the area settled, granted the company two hundred thousand acres of land west of the mountains between the Monongahela and Kanawha Rivers, and he promised three hundred thousand more acres if two hundred families were settled in the area by the company within seven years. Gist crossed the mountains in 1750 to reconnoiter the grant. At the same time, Dr. Thomas Walker was touring through the tramontane region in search of good land sites for another Virginian speculative venture, this one called the Loyal Land Company, which had received a grant of eight hundred thousand acres from the colony's council in 1748.

Pennsylvania's commercial and Virginia's speculative activity was bound eventually to stir the French into action. The moment came in 1752 with the appearance of a new governor for Canada, the Marquis

Duquesne. He arrived with instructions to eliminate the British-Americans from the Ohio, then to erect a new line of forts to seal off the interior from interlopers. The first part of the instructions were carried out in June 1752 when Charles de Langlade led a force of over two hundred Western Indians—mostly Ottawas and a few Chippewas—against Pickawillany: the village was leveled; five English traders and their large store of trading goods were captured; La Demoiselle was boiled and eaten by the attacking Indians. The French had spoken. The fall of Pickawillany reminded Indians of the Ohio Valley what they had forgotten, that west of the mountains the French were mighty. The Miamis returned to Illinois. British trade in the Valley dropped close to zero, and George Croghan, who had been accumulating a fortune, became a bankrupt overnight.

Duquesne set out to fulfill the second part of his instructions in 1753. He sent an army of some two thousand French and Indians to erect a fort at Presque Ile (Erie today). Others were also built at Le Boeuf (Waterford, Pennsylvania), near the head of French Creek, and at Venango (Franklin, Pennsylvania), where French Creek empties into the Allegheny. The new and only recently arrived governor of Virginia, Robert Dinwiddie, had been told to promote the interests of the Ohio Company but to avoid war with France. When the governor heard of the forts going up in Pennsylvania, he sent George Washington, then twenty-one, to tell the French to leave lands claimed by Great Britain. Washington, with Gist and five others, arrived at Fort Le Boeuf on December 11. They were cordially treated, but the French made clear that they would not leave, indeed, that they planned next spring to build their final fort at the forks of the Ohio.

Dinwiddie was an impulsive, stubborn man, and he responded to this news by sending a small work force up to the forks to build an English fort before the French arrived. French troops marched on the scene with the fort only half-completed. The outnumbered Virginians departed, and the French proceeded to erect Fort Duquesne. Washington, meanwhile, had again trekked into the forests, this time with two companies of troops and with orders to protect the work force, not knowing when he set out that it had been expelled by the French. He was camped at Great Meadows (near Uniontown, Pennsylvania) when he learned of a small party of French some miles ahead. He made a night march, and a few hours later "ordered the volley that set the world on fire"; the date was May 28, 1754. Ten Frenchmen were killed, twenty-one were taken prisoners. "A trifling action," Horace Walpole called it, "but remarkable for giving date to the war." William Johnson, when he heard of the affair, thought Washington had lacked "prudence and circumspection."

Washington pushed on after the fight until he learned that the French were about to march against him in force. He retreated to Great Meadows and threw up a stockade, aptly named Fort Necessity. In June his force of one hundred and fifty was reinforced with two hundred more men; on July 3, Washington was attacked by five hundred French soldiers and four hundred Indians. After a nine-hour siege under intensive fire, Washington surrendered. The first round of the French and Indian War had gone to the French.

The French and Indian War

Europeans named it the Seven Years' War once it had widened into a world-wide struggle, but Americans continued to call it the French and Indian War. American historians have labeled it variously: the Fourth Intercolonial War (Osgood); American Revolution: First Phase (Bancroft); the Old French War (Parkman); the Great War (Fiske); and, most recently, by Lawrence H. Gipson, author of the magnificent multivolume study of the British Empire before the American Revolution, The Great War for Empire. Gipson emphasizes that this "was a very great conflict both in scope and in its lasting effects" and also that it was "a war entered into specifically for the defense of the British Empire." Obviously, the struggle cannot be comprehended from the parochial American viewpoint any more than the earlier imperial wars could be, but here, as in those earlier wars, whose titles were Americanized by the colonists into King William's, Queen Anne's, and King George's Wars, the struggle is of interest only as it relates to colonial America. The colonists' title seems as satisfactory for this war as it was for the earlier ones.

Canada and America were born together in the age of absolutism and were created to promote the welfare of the mother country, but all signs of their common background had vanished by the time of the French and Indian War. New France in the eighteenth century resembled what Virginia had been in the seventeenth—a military outpost in the New World comprised of soldier-settlers and ruled by an autocratic government. Old France dictated the way of life of New France: it controlled who came, where they went, and what they did. Government reflected the will of the crown, not of the people. Catholicism was the established and only permitted religion. The colony had no industry, and it had to import much of its food. Its population in the mid-eighteenth century was approximately 55,000 whites, compared to 1,200,000 in the thirteen English colonies.

Numerical weakness did not necessarily assure Canada's defeat in the French and Indian War. The French were winning in 1757, three years after fighting had broken out in the Pennsylvania wilderness. They were winning because they knew the wilderness better than the English, the

Indians favored their side, and their strong central government made it possible to deploy troops swiftly and effectively. America's thirteen self-centered colonies were ripped apart regularly by internal dissension; they suspected the motives of their neighboring colonies and of Great Britain; and to all but Virginia, French activity west of the mountains seemed unrelated to the colonies' welfare. Voting the slightest sum for defense or mobilizing a single militia unit often entailed weeks of debate that ended in stalemate. Britain in the past had resorted to a requisition system, whereby the men, supplies, and matériel required for a war were apportioned among the colonies according to their ability to contribute. Too often, however, this system had collapsed amidst the bickering of the colonial assemblies. Some sort of formal machinery was needed to coordinate the military activities of the thirteen colonies if they wished to avoid being picked off one by one by New France under the able leadership of the Marquis Duquesne.

Joined to the problem of creating adequate defense machinery was the perennial problem of pacifying the Iroquois, who had been filling the air since the end of King George's War with a variety of grievances: the illicit Albany trade with Montreal by-passed them as middlemen; speculators were stealing their lands; Pennsylvanians were trading directly with Indians under Iroquois suzerainty. The British knew that these complaints, whether specious or not, could not be ignored, for the Iroquois had once again maneuvered themselves into a position where the outcome of any war between the French and English in America depended on what the Iroquois did. (Howard Peckham has remarked that no Indians were more skilled at playing the French and English off against one another than the Iroquois. The westward migration rolled past them out to the Pacific, but they alone did not budge, nor did they make a single blunder in their years of negotiating until they decided to side with England during the American Revolution.)

The joint problems of defense and Indians led the Board of Trade in 1753 to send out a call for a conference of colonial leaders to meet at Albany the following June. The Albany Congress assembled as scheduled while Washington waited behind the palisades of Fort Necessity for the French to attack. Seven colonies—New Hampshire, Massachusetts, Connecticut, Rhode Island, Pennsylvania, Maryland, and New York—were represented by twenty-three delegates. The Pennsylvania delegation, led by Franklin, and the New York delegation, led by William Johnson and Governor James DeLancey, were the two strongest and most influential present. The 150 Indians who had gathered for the meeting dealt coolly with the delegates. "Look at the French," one chief said, "they are men, they are fortifying everywhere—but, we are ashamed to say it, you are all like women: bare and open, without fortifications." The Indians gave only evasive replies to requests for an alliance, but when they left for home encumbered with thirty wagonloads of gifts, the delegates had the impression that they had been brought round and would support the English and Americans against the French.

During the Indian negotiations a committee of delegates worked on a plan of union for the colonies—a union that the Congress had already acknowledged "absolutely necessary for their preservation." The plan agreed on was drawn mainly by Franklin. It provided for "one general government" that would manage everything relating to Indian affairs and defense and would have the power to pass laws and raise taxes where these matters were involved. It called for an executive, the president general, to be appointed and supported by the crown. The Grand Council would represent the colonies in proportion to their contributions to the treasury. This continental legislature would have what Franklin called "a concentration of the powers of the several assemblies in certain points for the general welfare." The president general had the power to veto its laws.

By the time the assemblies debated the plan everyone knew of Washington's defeat. The woodcut of the disjointed snake with the caption "Join or Die" had appeared in the *Pennsylvania Gazette,* but it did little to build up a ground swell for Franklin's plan. Hindsight shows it was a perceptive effort to balance the powers of the royal prerogative with "the just liberties of the people," but the crown showed no enthusiasm for it and none of the colonial legislatures except that of Massachusetts even seriously debated its merits. "Everyone cries, a union is necessary," Franklin wrote to Governor Shirley of Massachusetts, "but when they come to the manner and form of the union, their weak noodles are perfectly distracted."

Meanwhile, British authorities had reacted to Washington's defeat in western Pennsylvania. Clearly, the French had to be stopped; equally clearly, a fourth world war had to be avoided. By late 1754, plans had been devised for a limited war—limited in objectives and, it was hoped, to America—to check the French advance. One army, operating from Virginia, would take Fort Duquesne. Others, setting out from New York and New England, would capture Crown Point and Fort Niagara. A French fleet stationed in the St. Lawrence would be attacked. The Acadians would be removed from Nova Scotia. General Edward Braddock, a heavy-set, sixty-year-old professional soldier with an honorable reputation, though he had never led troops in battle, was put in charge of the campaign. But he had doubts about the outcome before he left England, for he was given two undermanned regiments and filled with misinformation. The authorities told him, for instance, that he would have to contend with a mere fifteen miles of mountainous country to reach Fort Duquesne, when in fact over fifty such miles confronted him. "We are sent like lambs to the altar," he said the night before he set sail for America.

Braddock arrived in Virginia early in 1755. He held a conference in April at Annapolis with the governors of Massachusetts, New York, Pennsylvania, Maryland, and Virginia. He named Shirley as second in command and put him in charge of the Niagara expedition, partly because he liked the man and partly because New England had already raised seven thousand men. He appointed William Johnson superintendent of Indian affairs for all New England, New York, and Pennsylvania and delegated the Crown Point expedition to him.

After the conference, Braddock set about recruiting men and supplies for his own expedition, and in the process he learned to hate Americans for their "lies and villainy." He got little official help. The assemblies of Virginia, Pennsylvania, and New York refused to vote more than perfunctory defense funds; the land west of the mountains seemed part of another world, for most Americans still clung to the seaboard. Many also felt that the French threat had been exaggerated by the land companies and traders to serve their own ends. Braddock got much good advice and help from George Washington, whom he had the sense to make his aide. ("His attachments were warm," Washington later said of the general. "His enmities strong, and having no disguise, both appeared in full force. He was generous and disinterested, but plain and blunt in manner, even to rudeness.") When wagons and horses failed to be produced by the colonists, Benjamin Franklin, authorized to use army funds, rented what the general needed from Pennsylvania farmers, who, said Franklin later, suddenly became "good and loyal subjects to his Majesty" at fifteen shillings a day. (Franklin was soon to leave for London, where, as Pennsylvania's agent, he would work to have the Penn family deprived of their province and the colony given over to the crown; a favor to Braddock surely would do no harm to Franklin's cause at court.)

Braddock started over the mountains in June with twenty-five hundred men. The task of cutting a road through a hundred miles of forest, half of it in mountainous terrain, slowed the advance to a mile or two a day. Braddock moved his forces ahead cautiously. On July 8 he had pushed to within ten miles of Fort Duquesne. The end for the French seemed near, for within the fort were only some one hundred French regulars and nearly one hundred fifty Canadian militia; outside were about eight hundred Indians, none of them eager to die for a lost cause. The French, forewarned of Braddock's approach, determined the next day to attempt an ambush, and they persuaded over half their Indians to join the effort. Nine miles from the fort they caught Braddock's vanguard, led

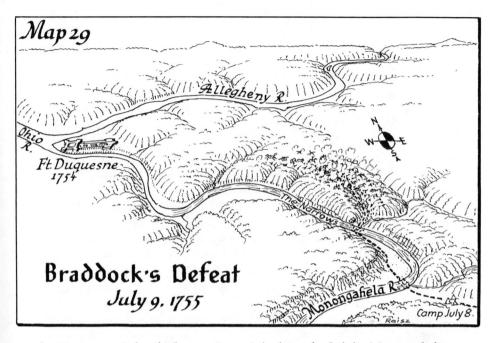

Map 29

Alleghe*ny* R.

Ohio R.

Ft. Duquesne 1754

The Narrows

Monongahela R.

Braddock's Defeat
July 9, 1755

Camp July 8.

Raisz

by Lieutenant Colonel Thomas Gage; it had just forded the Monongahela and was inching up a slope flanked by a hill on one side and a ravine on the other. The French and Indians fired head on, then fanned out into the forest. Gage then made his second mistake—his first had been not to occupy the hill before advancing—by ordering a retreat, instead of holding fast or pushing ahead to open ground. The vanguard careened into nearly a thousand troops double-timing forward to join the action. Chaos reigned by the time Braddock reached the scene. An attempt to move ahead to a clear spot was met by withering fire from the woods. A group attempting to take the hill overlooking the battlefield were cut down by their own men. Washington had two horses shot from under him and his clothes ripped by four bullets; Braddock had five horses shot from beneath him. The troops withstood the onslaught for three hours; then, said Washington, they "broke and ran as sheep pursued by dogs." Over nine hundred men were killed or wounded, among them General Braddock, who died praising the Virginia "blues" and saying of the French and Indians, "We shall better know how to deal with them another time." Something might have been retrieved from the debacle if Thomas Dunbar, in charge of the rear detachment, had moved up, but Dunbar tarried. Braddock's death put him in command, whereupon he spiked his guns, destroyed most of his supplies, and headed eastward. He made for Philadelphia and "went into winter quarters there in the middle of August."

"Our sins, our sins, they are grown up to the very heavens," a young lady said on hearing of the defeat. The news continued to be bad throughout the year. Shirley learned of the disaster and that he had lost a son in it as he was about to leave Albany for the two hundred–mile cross-country trek to Oswego, where boats would take his army the additional two hundred miles to Fort Niagara. Braddock's death made the sixty-one–year–old Shirley, an able man but an amateur general, commander-in-chief of British forces in North America. His failure to move beyond Oswego did little to improve British standing among the Indians, nor did Admiral Boscawen's inability to capture a French fleet, which had brought huge reinforcements to Canada. Robert Monckton alone carried out his assignment; he captured Fort Beauséjour on the northern edge of the Bay of Fundy and carried through the deportation of some five thousand Acadians from Nova Scotia, an event Longfellow let no one forget.

Johnson failed to take Crown Point, yet he ended the year heaped with honors. The French had reinforced the fort after finding the campaign plans among Braddock's papers, then they took the offensive and marched down to meet Johnson, who, with thirty-five hundred Americans and Indians, was camped at the foot of Lake George, as he had renamed what the French called Lac du St. Sacrement. Johnson sent out a detachment to deal with the French, despite a warning from Chief Hendrick, who said: "If they are to fight, they are too few; if they are to die, they are too many." Some two hundred died, among them Chief Hendrick. The French pursued Johnson's forces back to his base, and there the Americans beat off repeated charges. Historians call the battle a draw, but contemporaries, who needed a victory, felt differently. The king knighted Johnson and Parliament voted him a gift of £5,000. New York gave him a hero's welcome, and everywhere in the colonies it was remarked that Braddock, a professional, had with British regulars lost to an inferior French force, where Johnson, an amateur, had with an army of American farmers whipped a superior force of French regulars.

Johnson's "victory" impressed few Indians. Braddock's defeat had cemented every nation north of the Ohio except the Iroquois to the French cause, and none now abandoned it. A few weeks after Braddock's defeat a man from Harrisburg wrote that there had been "upwards of forty of his Majesty's subjects massacred on the frontiers of this and Cumberland C[ount]y, besides a great number carried into captivity." A group of settlers brought their dead to Philadelphia, and the Pennsylvania assembly at last responded with a militia law and a £55,000 appropriation for a series of blockhouses along the frontiers. The string of blockhouses worked no better in Pennsylvania than it had in seventeenth-century Virginia. Indians continued to slip through the lines, spreading havoc everywhere.

Military affairs worsened for the British through 1756. Lord Loudoun became commander-in-chief of British forces and Marquis de Montcalm of those of France. Montcalm, the abler man, kept the French on the offensive. In September 1756, they captured Oswego, deep enough in Iroquois country to impress the Six Nations with English feebleness. The disasters continued into 1757. An expedition against Louisbourg was repulsed. Later in the summer Montcalm marched with eight thousand French and Indians on Fort William Henry on Lake George. It surrendered on August 9 after a six-day siege. Montcalm gave generous terms—he allowed the garrison of twenty-two hundred to return home as long as it agreed to remain out of action a year and a half—but his Indians got out of hand. Over fifty English prisoners were murdered and many others maltreated before Montcalm's pleas—"kill me, but spare the English who are under my protection"—restored order. Loudoun was recalled home shortly after this last defeat.

Few at the time noticed other events that had been obscured by the disasters of 1757. George Croghan, on Johnson's recommendation, had been made superintendent of Indian affairs for the Pennsylvania-Virginia area and through 1757 he had held a series of conferences with the Indians—at Harris' Ferry, Pennsylvania, in March; Winchester, Virginia, in May; Lancaster, Pennsylvania, in July; Easton, Pennsylvania, in August; and with Johnson at Johnson Hall in September. Nothing conclusive emerged from these conferences, but the groundwork had been laid for a shift in allegiance once the English redeemed themselves with a victory or two, which could be used to assure the Indians that the French were not invincible.

In 1758 William Pitt came to power in England. "I believe that I can save this nation and that no one else can," he said. Previously, the strategy had been to hold back the French in America and concentrate on winning the war in Europe. (In 1756 the thus-far limited conflict had escaped its bounds and erupted into the Seven Years' War.) Pitt reversed the pattern. He made America the main theater and called for an aggressive strategy designed to capture Canada. To achieve this, he searched out the ablest military and naval commanders available and gave them the fullest backing. He told the colonies to cease worrying about the cost of the war, that Britain would reimburse all their expenses. (She did; the colonies altogether received nearly one million pounds compensation after the war.) Pitt projected an ambitious plan for 1758: John Forbes would take Fort Duquesne; James Abercromby was assigned Ticonderoga; and Jeffrey Amherst was given Louisbourg.

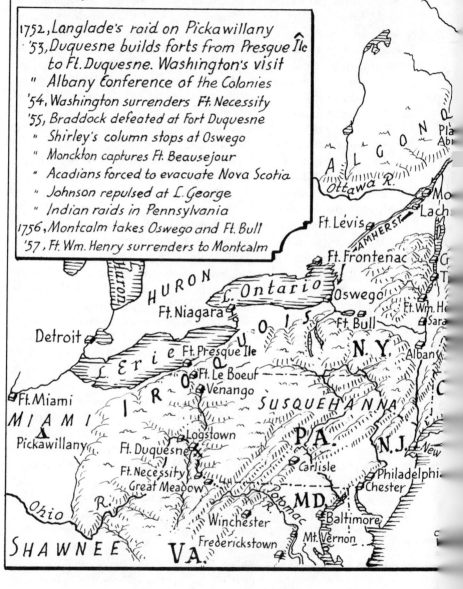

Map 30. French and Indian W:

1752, Langlade's raid on Pickawillany
'53, Duquesne builds forts from Presque Île
    to Ft. Duquesne. Washington's visit
 " Albany Conference of the Colonies
'54, Washington surrenders Ft. Necessity
'55, Braddock defeated at Fort Duquesne
 " Shirley's column stops at Oswego
 " Monckton captures Ft. Beausejour
 " Acadians forced to evacuate Nova Scotia
 " Johnson repulsed at L. George
 " Indian raids in Pennsylvania
1756, Montcalm takes Oswego and Ft. Bull
'57, Ft. Wm. Henry surrenders to Montcalm

ALGONQ Pla
            Abr
Ottawa R.
Ft. Lévis   Mo
AMHERST   Lach
Ft. Frontenac   Gr
                        T
Oswego   Ft. Wm. He
L. Ontario   Sara
Ft. Niagara Ft. Bull
HURON   N.Y. Alban
                    Ft. Presque Ile
Detroit   L Erie   SUSQUEHANNA
            Ft. Le Boeuf
            Venango   PA. N.J. New
Ft. Miami IROQUOIS
MIAMI   Logstown   Carlisle Philadelphi
Pickawillany Ft. Duquesne   Chester
            Ft. Necessity   MD.
            Great Meadow   Baltimore
Ohio   R.   Winchester   Mt. Vernon
SHAWNEE   VA. Frederickstown

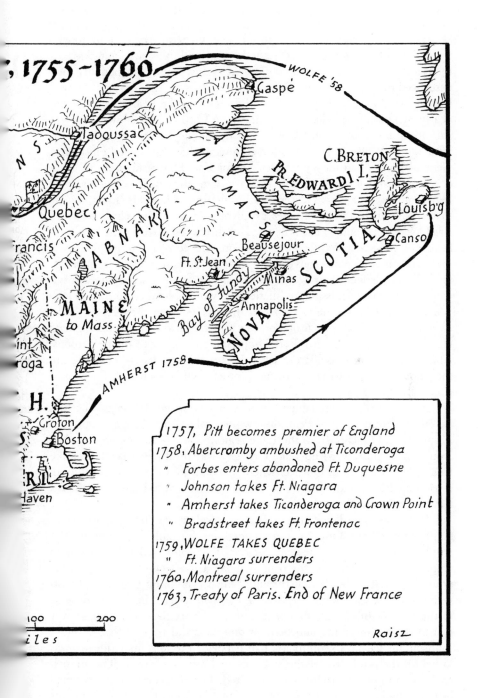

1755-1760.

WOLFE '58

Gaspé

Tadoussac

C. BRETON

MICMACS

Pr. EDWARD I.

Quebec

Louisb'g

ABNAKI

rancis

Beausejour

Ft. St Jean

Canso

NOVA SCOTIA

Minas

MAINE

to Mass.

Bay of Fundy

Annapolis

int

roga

AMHERST 1758

H.

Groton

S

Boston

R.I.

Haven

1757, Pitt becomes premier of England
1758, Abercromby ambushed at Ticonderoga
" Forbes enters abandoned Ft. Duquesne
" Johnson takes Ft. Niagara
" Amherst takes Ticonderoga and Crown Point
" Bradstreet takes Ft. Frontenac
1759, WOLFE TAKES QUEBEC
" Ft. Niagara surrenders
1760, Montreal surrenders
1763, Treaty of Paris. End of New France

100   200

iles

Raisz

The grand scheme began with a defeat. General Abercromby moved up Lake Champlain toward Ticonderoga in June with some fifteen thousand men, nearly half of them Americans. Montcalm had his men ensconced behind a thick wall of fallen trees that let them direct a deadly fire on the attackers. The British withdrew from the field after suffering nearly two thousand casualties, among them Lord George Howe. Pitt was still absorbing this disaster when he learned that late in July, Amherst, with James Wolfe as his second-in-command, had captured Louisbourg. General Forbes had meanwhile set out for Fort Duquesne with an army of six thousand. Forbes, an able military man himself, took with him as regimental commanders George Washington and Henry Bouquet, a German-speaking Swiss and another excellent soldier. Forbes chose to avoid Braddock's road and to cut a new, more direct route west. The road was begun on August 1. While Forbes's troops inched over the mountains, a great Indian conference convened in October at Easton. The Iroquois attended and pledged their wards the Delawares to a peace with Pennsylvania. A Moravian missionary hurried the word westward, and the Delawares on hearing the news detached themselves from the French. This, together with the approach of Forbes's army, caused Captain de Ligneris on November 24 to destroy Fort Duquesne and flee with his few troops. The ruins were still smoldering when Forbes the next day reached the site that the British had struggled so hard for and where soon Fort Pitt would rise. Thus ended the year 1758.

Pitt planned a formidable three-pronged campaign for 1759. The first expedition, under John Prideaux, would take Fort Niagara and cut Montreal and Quebec from the Lake region; the second, under Amherst, would move northward up Lake George, clear the French posts on Lake Champlain, then on to Quebec, where it would join the third expedition, a combined land and sea force under Wolfe that would move up the St. Lawrence toward the rock fortress.

Prideaux moved first. Fort Niagara stood where the Niagara River emptied into Lake Ontario. It remained—as La Salle had conceived it would—the key link in the chain of forts that connected France's inland empire with the Atlantic, for behind it lay a fourteen-mile portage path around the falls, a bottleneck through which everything that moved eastward and westward along the Great Lakes had to pass. Prideaux lay siege to the fort on July 7. He had with him nearly six thousand troops, over half of them Americans, and perhaps one thousand Indians that William Johnson, his second in command, had persuaded to join up. Prideaux was killed on the ninth day of the siege and Johnson took over. The French garrison numbered around five hundred, but the commander worried little, for he knew a relief force of over two thousand French and Indians

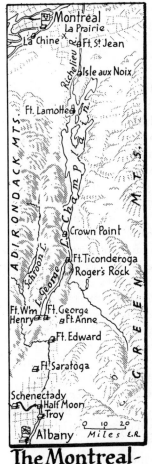

The Montreal-Albany Corridor

was on its way. Johnson trapped the reinforcements on the portage road, and the ensuing battle ended in a rout. The fort surrendered the next day, July 25. It was, as has been said with only slight exaggeration, the surrender of an era, for it opened up the entire West for the first time to the British. Only Wolfe's capture of Quebec rivaled Johnson's achievement.

The second expedition under Amherst took both Ticonderoga and Crown Point, but the onset of winter forced him to halt there on Lake Champlain. Wolfe was compelled to move alone against Quebec, whose high rock cliff that fronted the river made it the greatest natural fortress in the New World. Wolfe, who at thirty-two was considered Britain's best general, arrived opposite the city in June with nine thousand troops. Montcalm remained within, knowing that if Amherst were delayed, as a French rear-guard action was forcing him to be, the siege would be lifted with the arrival of winter. Wolfe tried and failed for two months to entice Montcalm out. Early in September he determined to force the issue. A series of maneuvers followed, whereby Wolfe secretly put men and ships in position to drift down at night to the base of an undefended route up the cliff to the Plains of Abraham above. (Wolfe read to the men in his boat that night from Gray's *Elegy in a Country Churchyard,* which contains the line, "The paths of glory lead but to the grave.") On the morning of September 13 the sun revealed a British army of five thousand lined up in battle array on the Plains of Abraham. Montcalm had no choice but to march out and fight—though he could have delayed the battle until reinforcements, which were close by, had arrived—for from the Plains Wolfe could cut the city's supplies from the interior and up river. Both Montcalm and Wolfe died in the battle that followed, which the French lost. Four days later, on September 17, Quebec surrendered. A year would pass before Montreal fell, and another three years before the Seven Years' War ended; but as far as Americans were concerned, the French and Indian War ended with the fall of Quebec in 1759. The flow of war orders ceased, the troops departed, and the colonies settled back to peacetime routine, only now a routine considerably altered from what it had been five years earlier.

The Effect of the War on America

The French and Indian War hit Pennsylvania first and hardest. Most of the action on American soil centered there, and more of its civilians were killed than in any other colony. Great Britain drew heavily on its craftsmen and its industry for war matériel and on its farmers to feed the troops. The war produced an upheaval in Pennsylvania politics, for it forced the Quakers from a field they had ruled since the colony had been founded. In King George's War, the Quaker-dominated assembly got around its pacifist principles by voting £4,000 for the purchase of "bread, beef, pork, flour, and other grains," knowing the governor would translate "other grains" into gunpowder. In 1755 the assembly approved a militia law that permitted able-bodied men in the counties to "associate" into military companies, and it voted £55,000 "for the king's use," fully aware that the king would use the money to build blockhouses but convincing themselves that this was his business and not theirs. By the fall of 1756, Pennsylvania's frontiers were in flames, and the Quakers saw that they had to abandon either pacifism or politics. They chose to leave politics. Frederick Tolles has pointed out that this decision prompted a reformation in the Society of Friends that made them spiritually and mentally prepared to resist sharing in the violence of the American Revolution.

The war made itself felt in other ways elsewhere in America. It provided the colonies with their first motto—"Join or Die"—and Braddock's defeat coupled with Johnson's "victory" served as the raw material for the first American myth—that a plain, virtuous American farm boy was twice the soldier of a professionally trained British regular. Braddock, thanks somewhat to Franklin, came to exemplify a popular view of the British soldier as arrogant, stupid, and incompetent. "These savages may, indeed, be a formidable enemy to your raw American militia," Franklin quotes the general as saying, "but upon the king's regular and disciplin'd troops, sir, it is impossible they should make any impression." After the defeat, people reminded one another that it was the king's "disciplin'd troops, sir" that broke and ran while the Virginia "blues" held steady. This, together with tales of plundering by the troops, "gave us Americans," Franklin said, "the first suspicion that our exalted ideas of the prowess of British regulars had not been well founded." The defeat, too, gave Americans a new confidence in themselves. By October 1755 young John Adams saw America as the new seat of the British Empire, for once the "turbulent Gallicks" are removed "all Europe will not be able to subdue us," he wrote. "The only way to keep us from setting up for ourselves is to disunite us."

Quebec's capitulation killed America's warborne prosperity but not its confidence or its sense of a new beginning. (So much so that Thomas Hutchinson remarked in 1773, and many historians have echoed him since, that had Canada "remained to the French none of the spirit of opposition to the Mother Country would have yet appeared.") The French, who had "so often interrupted our tranquillity and checked our growth," had been subdued. "What scenes of happiness are we ready to figure to ourselves, from the hope of enjoying, in this good land, all the blessings of an undisturbed and lasting peace!" Dr. Samuel Cooper said in 1759. "From the hope of seeing our towns enlarged; our commerce increased; and our settlements extending with security on every side, and changing a wilderness into a fruitful field." For the first time the West beckoned. Out there, said Nathaniel Ames in his almanac of 1758, lay a region larger than all of France, Germany, and Poland, "and all well provided with rivers, a very fine wholesome air, a rich soil, capable of producing food and physick, and all things necessary for the conveniency and delight of life. In fine, the Garden of the World!" And the war had made the garden accessible. The two roads that had been slashed through the forests to reach the forks of the Ohio would eventually have been cut, but armies subsidized by Great Britain speeded up a process that might have taken decades to complete. Braddock's and Forbes's Roads became the first great trails west, the first "avenues of empire," as they have been called, into the American continent.

These effects of the French and Indian War were observed and commented upon by Americans, but an effect more important than all these went nearly unnoticed by the colonists. The war struck at the moment when Britain had steeled itself to tighten up imperial control over the colonies. Yet when Braddock's defeat made it clear the American war would be no light nor overnight affair, the British government reversed course and went out of its way to conciliate the legislatures it had been about to coerce. It instructed royal governors to avoid disputes over matters of royal prerogative and colonial rights. New York's governor, for instance, had previously been ordered to demand from the assembly a permanent revenue to run the executive wing of the government. In 1756 the Privy Council suggested to the king that "in the present situation of affairs, when peace, unanimity and a good understanding between your Majesty's governor and the people are so absolutely necessary for the good of the province, that the governor should be directed not to press this establishment of a permanent revenue for the present. . . ." In 1758 Governor Pownall of Massachusetts heard from the Board of Trade that while the assembly's incursion into the executive domain must be suppressed, it would be unadvisable to press the point "in the present situation of things." A year later, however, the fall of Quebec had changed the situation. The scene of war now shifted to Europe, which made American aid no longer essential for a British victory. Britain was now free to clamp down on the colonies and to insist that instructions to the royal governors be carried out to the letter. But the colonies were not now what they had been in 1754. A new age was in the making: thirteen American colonies with a new confidence in themselves, with new strength, and new visions of their future were about to lock with a Great Britain more powerful than any nation on earth and soon to be led by a young, vigorous, and stubborn king.

IMPERIAL RELATIONS: 1713–1763

For a good part of the half century after 1713 control of imperial affairs to a large extent lay in the hands of Sir Robert Walpole, the king's chief adviser and administrator between 1721 and 1742, and the Duke of Newcastle, Walpole's secretary of state for the Southern Department and a power in the government until 1763. The decades of their rule have been dubbed the period of "salutary neglect." They reversed the position of the Board of Trade, which urged the tightest possible control over the colonies, by depriving the board of almost all power. They argued that the government should avoid interfering in colonial affairs because a healthy plant thrives best when allowed to develop naturally.

But the label "salutary neglect," like most labels, misleads as much as it informs. First of all, neither man neglected the colonies. Newcastle was especially well-informed about American affairs. He controlled the appointment of a majority of the royal officials in America, and he tended to pick men of ability to strengthen the royal arm in the colonies. It was he, for instance, who chose the able William Shirley for governor of Massachusetts; true, partly because Shirley's family had influence but true also partly because he seemed the best man for a difficult job. Second, the label misleads because it obscures a divisive attitude toward the colonies in the executive wing of the government. The Board of Trade continued through the period of salutary neglect to argue for tighter controls. And after 1748, when Newcastle was still a dominant voice, it began to be heard, for Lord Halifax had become its president, and he recouped much of the power that had drifted from its hands. And, finally, the phrase hides the attitude of Parliament toward the colonies in this half century of so-called neglect. Walpole and Newcastle often thwarted Parliament's concern for the colonies by working to defeat what they considered coercive bills or by refusing to enforce the restrictive measures Parliament actually passed. Parliament may have been ignorant of the American colonies, but it did not neglect them.

Parliament and Colonies

Parliament's interest in the colonies began in the Puritan Revolution and continued into the Restoration, when it passed a revised Navigation Act in 1660. It maintained a desultory and often ill-informed concern for colonial trade during the next three decades. The concern, though no less ill-informed, ceased to be desultory after the accession of William III; by 1753 it had passed over eighty acts relative to colonial trade and a number of others touching on such aspects of colonial life as indentured servitude for minors, the sale of land to aliens, and the naturalization of foreigners. The cumulative effect of these acts worked to undercut the power of royal prerogative in colonial affairs and to make Parliament a partner in the regulation of imperial affairs.

Most of this regulation, of course, sought to control colonial trade in a way that benefited the mother country. The earlier measures centered on the trade of the West Indies and southern continental colonies. A statute in 1705 pieced out that legislation by adding rice and molasses to the enumerated list. The year 1705 saw a shift in Parliament's interest, for it also placed tar, turpentine, hemp, masts, and other naval stores on the enumerated list; copper and furs were tacked on in 1722. These were products mainly of the northern colonies, which in the eighteenth century would receive the attention Parliament had given the southern area in the seventeenth.

Among the first of the legislation aimed at the northern colonies was the White Pines Act of 1711, followed by amplifying acts in 1722 and 1729. The act of 1722 prohibited the felling without license from a crown officer of "any white pine trees, except only such as are the property of private persons" in any part of North America "that now belongs or hereafter shall belong to the crown of Great Britain." The surveyor-general of the king's woods in America, an appointee of the Treasury Board, would enforce the acts. A sound reason motivated the legislation, for Great Britain had been largely denuded of forests, and the needs of a huge navy and merchant marine forced the nation to import timber for masts, spars, and bowsprits from Baltic countries, a highly unsound practice by mercantilistic principles. But the acts unwisely put off limits all white pine, regardless of size or quality, on public land. Now the continent from Pennsylvania to Canada was carpeted mainly with white pine, much of it useless for the British Navy's needs, but most of it reserved for the crown. This, said John Wentworth of New Hampshire, a colony that drew its wealth largely from the forests, "operated so much against the convenience and even necessities of the inhabitants that . . . it became almost a general interest of the country to frustrate laws, which comprehend nearly an unlimited reservation." Enforcement was sporadic, usually ineffectual, and always irritating to the colonists.

The Hat and Felt Act of 1732 was also prompted, according to the principles of the day, by sound reasons. The making of hats from beaver fur had become a large and profitable business in Britain by the end of the seventeenth century, but by 1710 competition from France had pushed the British industry into a slump. Parliament sought first to help the hatter by putting furs on the enumerated list, hoping thereby to block the flow of beaver from Massachusetts, New York, and Pennsylvania to Holland and from there into France. Parliament also tried to make the British market more attractive by cutting import duties from sixteen pence to six pence per beaver skin. The British industry still lagged, for Americans evaded the export restrictions by expanding their own hat industry. They sold their product locally, a market British hatters had once monopolized, and exported the surplus to Spain, Portugal, and the West Indies. British hatters demanded a law that prohibited hat-making in the colonies. Parliament, in an attempt to be fair, passed a compromise bill, which sought only to limit not kill hat-making in the colonies. The Hat and Felt Act required that colonial craftsmen serve an apprenticeship of seven years; that masters limit their employees to two apprentices; and that the sale of hats be confined to the colony in which they were made, which prohibited export anywhere, even to another colony.

The Sugar Act of 1733, more commonly called the Molasses Act, emerged out of much the same situation that produced the Hat Act. British complaints rather than colonial interests prompted it, and like the Hat Act it resulted largely from imperial competition with the French. (New England trade with the Dutch at Surinam and on their island of St. Eustatius was at the moment of only peripheral importance.) By 1730 the bulk of America's sugar and molasses trade, once monopolized by British West Indian planters, had shifted to the French islands of Guadeloupe, Martinique, and St. Domingo (now Haiti). The French sold their molasses at cut-rate prices; it was little more than waste material to them, for France forbade its import, fearing it might be made into rum and thus destroy the lucrative brandy market. On the French, New Englanders unloaded beef and pork, which were blocked from Great Britain in order to protect local markets, oxen and cattle, and, above all, an almost worthless low-grade item called "refuse" fish, which was used to feed slaves and which constituted between one-fourth and one-half the total catch of cod fishermen and a large share of the cargoes brought down from

Newfoundland. The molasses carried back to New England was "consumed amongst us in the brewing of beer, and by the poor sort of people in great quantities in the room [stead] of sugar," and especially in the production of rum. Four-fifths of the rum was drunk in the colonies; the remainder was used in the African trade to barter for slaves, gold dust, and ivory.

As early as 1710, British West Indian planters asked Parliament to outlaw this Franco-American trade. It took Parliament over twenty years, however, to face the issue. The Molasses Act did not outlaw the trade, but by placing a prohibitive duty of six pence per gallon, which was about 100 per cent ad valorem, on all molasses imported from foreign sources—the duties on imported rum and sugar were equally high— it in effect made it possible to stop the trade. The act was to run for only five years, although Parliament continued to extend it down to 1764. Yet despite its long life, the act failed in its purpose, for the government lacked adequate machinery to enforce it. After a brief, ineffectual effort to impose the duties in Massachusetts, no further attempts were made. British planters ceased to complain because the consumption of sugar picked up in England and this allowed them to market their entire crop there.

Complaints at home led Parliament in 1750 again to legislate for—or against, depending on the viewpoint—the American colonies. This time the problem arose over iron. By mid-century every colony north of Virginia was dotted with ironworks. The Chesapeake area had ten blast furnaces producing some five thousand tons of iron annually; seventy-three "iron plantations" were scattered through Pennsylvania by 1755; Massachusetts had fourteen furnaces and forty-one forges in 1758. The number of colonial American iron furnaces did not especially concern Britain, for it had little invested in the production of bar and pig iron, most of which it imported from Sweden. But the colonies did not stop with the production of iron. The influx of new blood had helped to endow America with a large body of skilled craftsmen who were turning the iron into hardware items. Nearly a fourth of Britain's 125 forges were idle and others were running below capacity because of the loss of the American market. The colonies now made their own scythes, axes, pots, kettles, and a variety of other items that had once been made in Britain. One-half of all British iron had formerly been turned into nails, "a trade which had decayed," said one ironmonger, largely because Americans now made their own.

British ironmongers and ironmasters swamped Parliament with requests for relief. It responded in 1721 with an act lifting export duties on British iron to meet colonial competition. But a relief bill in 1738 died with the onset of war, for American aid was needed. With the Peace of Aix-la-Chapelle in 1748, British iron interests at last got a hearing with

Parliament. By this time some two hundred thousand iron workers were unemployed, and Sweden was about to raise the export duty on bar iron. The result was the Iron Act of 1750, an honest and intelligent attempt to deal fairly with a complex situation. The first part of the act encouraged the production of pig and bar iron by allowing it to be imported from the colonies into England duty free. The second part forbade the further erection of steel furnaces; slitting mills, which cut iron into small strip to make nails; and plating forges, which hammered iron into sheets for shaping into utensils. The bill did not prohibit the production of American iron or steel, for it struck Parliament as unfair to deprive colonial manufacturers of their property, even with full compensation. It sought only to limit production and to encourage the export of unwrought iron to Britain.

The Iron Act failed completely. By the eve of the Revolution, the colonies were producing some thirty thousand tons of iron or one-seventh of the world's total production. It failed, it would seem, mainly because Britain leaned heavily on American industry during the French and Indian War. The act's failure showed that Great Britain could not guide the complex economic forces of the empire nor could it balance colonial and British interests in a way that would realize the ideals of an "imperial self-sufficiency and planned economy based on mutual advantage."

The failure did not deter further attempts to legislate for the colonies, for the next year Parliament sought to bring order out of the confusion of New England's financial affairs. Agrarian America in the eighteenth century, Bray Hammond has pointed out, was economically as conservative as England: debt was evil and thrift a virtue. "He that goes a-borrowing goes a-sorrowing," Poor Richard said, and people agreed. But the colonies' economic situation differed from England's. Sound English sterling that flowed in to pay for American raw materials flowed back faster to pay for manufactured goods. The deficit balance of payments left the colonies without an adequate medium of exchange; colonial governments felt the pinch first. The shortage of specie forced Massachusetts in 1690 to print an issue of paper money to finance the expedition against France; this money was in the form of promissory notes or bills of credit. In the beginning these bills were not legal tender; they were security that payment would be made in specie within a fixed time. The interest the government charged on the bills allowed it to underwrite the costs of the expedition. The success of this first venture with paper money popularized it throughout America, and by 1750 nearly all colonies had issued their own form of bills of credit. Maryland, New York, New Jersey, and Delaware managed their issues well, and Pennsylvania's was so wisely administered that Thomas Pownall said of it: "There never was a wiser or better measure, never one better calculated to serve the uses of an increasing country. . . ." Rhode Island put forth eight issues between 1715 and 1750 and lived off the interest of them so successfully that it managed to carry out an internal improvement program that cost the citizens almost nothing in taxes.

Britain regarded these issues with paternal understanding and did not interfere until the colonies insisted that their paper be taken as legal tender. By 1730 Massachusetts' bills of credit had depreciated to two-fifths their face value. Instructions went out to Governor Belcher to call in all outstanding bills promptly when they were due and not to issue more than £30,000 of them thereafter for government expenses; the ruling brought order into the Bay Colony's financial affairs. That pleased the majority of citizens, who believed in thrifty management and freedom from debt; if they objected, it was on the ground that Britain, however well meaning, should not interfere in American affairs. The merchant alone, who could expand only by borrowing and thriving on debt, complained about the restriction. It was his complaints that led to agitation for a private bank that would do what the government had hitherto done. In 1740 a "land bank" was organized in Boston; its bills of credit were secured by real estate but were not redeemable. Then a rival bank was organized that promised to redeem in specie. A third group petitioned against both banks. Governor Belcher warned Parliament that "if some speedy stop be not put to these things, they will be more fatal consequences to the plantations than the South Sea Bubble was, in the year 1720, to Great Britain." Parliament listened, and in 1741 "by express words" extended to America the Bubble Act of 1720, which outlawed corporate enterprises except by special grant from Parliament.

Parliament's action in 1741 killed the formation of private banks in America, but it did nothing to inhibit the issuance of paper money. Governor Shirley was forced soon after to call for a new large issue to finance the expeditions against Louisbourg and Canada. The paper depreciated rapidly during the war, and the clergy moaned that it was "as unstable as water" and as "variable as the wind." When the crown reimbursed Massachusetts for its part in King George's War, it insisted that the bounty be used to retire the paper in circulation. This was done, only the paper was redeemed at the current rate rather than face value in order to frustrate speculators who had accumulated it in hopes of a killing. This arrangement straightened out the Bay Colony's finances but did little to settle the affairs of Rhode Island, the great supplier of paper money to all New England. By 1750 she had over a half million pounds of currency in circulation; it was worth about one-eighth its face value. Rhode Island's indiscretions prompted Parliament to pass the Currency

Act of 1751. This statute forbade the further issuance as legal tender of "any paper bills or bills of credit . . . under any pretense whatsoever," and it ordered all such bills then in circulation be retired punctually. The act permitted colonial governments in New England to issue nonlegal bills for current administrative needs or emergencies. The act left most of New England untouched, but it put the mercantile community in a difficult position. A tight money policy such as Parliament had imposed on New England struck the merchants hardest, and it put them in a sour mood toward Parliamentary interference in American affairs.

Americans, whenever they thought about the matter prior to 1763, resented Parliament, for, as Esmond Wright has said, this curiosity, "which at home appeared as a guarantee of liberty against royal or bureaucratic power, appeared in colonial eyes at best as meddling interference, and in the end as a new species of tyranny." But that resentment took a long time in coming to the surface, mainly because most of Parliament's legislation went unenforced in the colonies. The fault for this lay largely with the crown and the crown's officers both in Britain and in the colonies.

Crown and Colonies

Despite Parliament's steady and broadening concern for American affairs, the colonists in the mid-eighteenth century considered their basic ties with Britain to be with the crown. The king had legalized their existence by granting them charters. All British officials in the colonies were crown-appointed officers. Colonial legislatures battled as much, if not more, against the royal prerogative's incursions on what they considered their rights as against Parliamentary legislation. Ties to the crown were also evident in daily activities: a colonist promised to uphold the king's justice when he took an oath for jury duty; assemblymen stepped beneath the king's arms when they entered their legislative halls; Anglicans prayed for the king's health at every Sunday service.

Loyalty to the king was sincere but always tempered with self-interest. Authorities of the crown learned long before the Revolution that the colonies would balk at every effort to uphold the king's prerogative or to enforce Parliamentary legislation. Nothing better illustrates this than the political troubles of William Shirley during the period of salutary neglect. Shirley did his best to enforce the much flouted White Pines Acts, first as advocate-general of the Vice-admiralty Court, then as governor of Massachusetts, when he told the legislature that those cutting timber for the Royal Navy had been "greatly obstructed in that service by the unreasonable opposition of some people and harassed with vexatious suits upon groundless pretenses. . . ." (The assembly answered not with remedial legislation but with the suggestion that Parliament should clarify the acts.) Shirley also tried to enforce the Navigation Acts. As advocate-general, he ordered careful checks on all ships entering Massachusetts ports, partly because he wished British authority to be respected, partly because he received a third of all confiscated cargoes. The attempt at strict enforcement carried into his governorship and seemed all the more justified because most of the illicit trade was with Britain's current enemy, Spain. Shirley's eagerness won little praise at home, where authorities were perturbed by the merchants' opposition to the seizures. He was urged to tend toward leniency and reminded that with one war at hand and another with France in the offing it was best not to irritate the colonies at a time when their help was needed.

The crown's permissive attitude toward America began to wane in 1748. Assurance that the war with France would soon end had something to do with the change, but the major cause was the appointment of the Earl of Halifax as president of the Board of Trade. The board's power and influence had declined in the early part of the eighteenth century, and the Duke of Newcastle had shifted much of its patronage powers into his office of secretary of state. No one knew for sure what the board's powers were, and any strong personality in the government could, if he worked at it, have usurped or increased its authority and influence. The board itself, other departments of the government, and the colonies all promptly felt the effect of Halifax' personality. He campaigned for a specifically American department, for he resented his inferior position in the government hierarchy and his having to go through the secretary of state to reach the Privy Council. He wanted the board as a full-fledged government office with cabinet rank for its president, and in 1752 he got part of his demands. This Compromise of 1752 did several things: the board got the right to nominate men to colonial offices, a right that hitherto lay with the governors' councils in the colonies; the secretary of state for the Southern Department lost control over colonial affairs; Halifax was to be present at all sessions of the Privy Council that in any way dealt with colonial affairs; and governors were to send their papers directly to the board.

Halifax' dicta radiated to the colonies swiftly. Colonial governors, accustomed to taking orders from the secretary of state, were reminded in 1752 that their correspondence must hereafter be directed to the Board of Trade, that they must abide by their instructions, and that all colonial laws should be brought into conformity with these instructions. The effort to strengthen the royal prerogative throughout America went on apace. Pennsylvania, which had shown a tendency to act like "a pure republic," had its charter studied with an eye to finding ways to tighten control over its affairs. New York's refusal to grant judges permanent salaries prompted instructions in 1754 that stated that all judicial commissions had to be granted at the king's pleasure only. Halifax continued to invigorate colonial administration until 1761, when he resigned his post to become Lord Leftenant of Ireland; but it had been *his* vigor, not the board's. With his departure the board again became a pawn in British politics. It soon lost its nominating power for colonial offices back to the secretary of state, and by 1762 it had been reduced once more to a mere board of report with little direct authority over American affairs. The diminution of the board's power, however, did not mark the end of efforts to tighten control over the American colonies. A perceptive politician in America might have noted that a year before Halifax's departure, William Pitt had made it clear that he, too, would take no nonsense from the colonies. Halifax's departure marked a shift in power rather than a change in attitude toward America's relations and duties to Britain.

Ominous Straws in the Wind: 1759–1763

The year 1760 saw the dawn of a new era for both Great Britian and America. George II died after thirty-four years on the throne. His grandson, who became George III at the age of twenty-two, was regarded as a young man of "quick and just conception, great mildness, great civility"; and even the usually sarcastic Horace Walpole said that he "gives all the indication imaginable of being amiable" and that "his manner is graceful and obliging." The year also marked the beginning of economic troubles for America, particularly the northern colonies, where the shift of hostilities to the West Indies and Europe put an end to the war boom. Hundreds of ships, their sails furled and their holds empty, rocked alongside wharves up and down the coast. "The number of vessels in this harbor, at this time, exceeds any that was known here," a Philadelphian said in 1763. Craftsmen in the cities found it hard to get work, and many drifted out of town to the country in search of employment. The colonies' economic troubles were intensified by their friend at court, William Pitt, who in 1760 cracked down against all illicit trade with the enemy.

America's wartime trade with French colonies appalled Pitt when he realized the magnitude of it. In March 1755, about the time Braddock was having trouble obtaining supplies for his trek over the mountains, at least forty ships from American ports were trading with the French at Louisbourg, which prompted the remark that the French troops who marched "to destroy one English province are actually supported by the bread raised in another." Later, after the capture of Louisbourg, this trade shifted to the West Indies, centering at the neutral Dutch island of St. Eustatius and the Spanish port of Monte Cristi. Ships went there on the pretext of exchanging prisoners of war under flag-of-truce licenses that they could purchase from such men as Governor Denny of Pennsylvania, who sold them for £20 or more. Pitt learned in 1760 that at least a hundred vessels flying the British flag had been observed riding at anchor in the Monte Cristi harbor. Such information convinced him that this illicit trade had "principally, if not alone, enabled, [France] to sustain and protract this long and expensive war." He sent out a circular letter to all colonial governors in 1760 ordering them to "take every step, authorized by law, to bring all such heinous offenders to the most exemplary and condign punishment." He directed that the Molasses Act of 1733 hereafter be enforced to the letter.

Customs officers armed with writs of assistance were soon pulling in illegal cargoes on a large scale; a single shipment from Holland was estimated as worth £10,000. These writs were general warrants that allowed officers to search private property without offering grounds for suspecting the presence of smuggled goods. They had been in use since 1751 without producing complaints, probably because merchants did not wish to make a public issue of their disloyalty to the imperial war effort. Special circumstances led the merchants of Boston to contest the writs' legality in 1760. British law required their renewal within six months after George II's death; the new writs would remain legal throughout the new monarch's reign. (George III died in 1820.) The merchants' case was presented by James Otis, a very able lawyer "of great warmth . . . and much indiscretion" and an "eagle-eyed politician" who detested Thomas Hutchinson, the chief justice of the Massachusetts Superior Court, before whom the case was pleaded. Otis argued that if the writs were justified by Parliamentary legislation, then that legislation must be declared null and void because it was contrary to basic principles embedded in the British constitution. Otis' impassioned defense for the "freedom of one's house" was dismissed, and the writs stood. His plea made little stir at the time; only later, as indignation against the writs spread to other colonies and people looked for arguments to limit Parliament's power to legislate for the colonies, was it resurrected.

No one noticed at the time, and few have since, that a year earlier Otis' argument against British authority had been used by a young Virginia lawyer who was defending the validity of the assembly's Two Penny Act after it had been disallowed by the crown. A severe drought in 1758 had forced "poor times" on Virginia. "There won't be above five thousand hhds. tobacco made this present crop," a Scotch storekeeper wrote; "in a tolerable good crop they have ten times that quantity. . . ." Tobacco served as a form of currency in the Chesapeake area: men bought land, wrote off debts, and paid the clergy with it. (An act of 1748 fixed clerical salaries at 17,280 pounds a year.) Because the short crop of 1758 shot the price up to three times the normal level, the legislature sought to stabilize the situation by fixing its value as currency at two pence a pound. Technically the statute should have included a suspending clause—that is, a clause that suspended the act from being put into effect until the Privy Council approved it—which was required of all acts that amended previous statutes. Governor Francis Fauquier deviated from his instructions because he had not been censured for signing a similar measure three years earlier, "and I conceived it would be a very wrong step for me to take who was an entire stranger to the distresses of the country, to set my face against the whole colony by refusing a bill which I had a precedent for passing."

The act affected all sides of Virginia society, but it was the protests of the clergy, whose salary had been cut from £400 to £140 by legislative fiat, that reached England. The Bishop of London argued their case before the Board of Trade, and the board recommended disallowance of the law, which the king granted in 1759. Several clergymen, among them the Reverend James Maury, at once brought suits to collect the money owed them. The vestry of Fredericksburg hired Patrick Henry to contest Maury's claim. Henry was then twenty-three; he had first tried his hand at storekeeping—Thomas Jefferson first met him just after he had "broken up his store—or, rather, it had broken him up"—then, after six weeks' study, moved into law. Henry's argument, stripped of rhetoric, advanced the proposition, according to Maury's account of the trial, that the disallowance should be ignored because the Two Penny Act "was a law of general utility and could not consistently with what he called the original compact between king and people . . . be annulled." The jury ignored Henry's basic argument and found for Maury, but it revealed its sympathy for the defense by granting the parson damages of only one penny.

Neither Henry nor Otis, strictly speaking, won his case, but their arguments laid the foundations for later resistance to Parliament's and the crown's control over the colonies. A half century after Otis' plea before Judge Hutchinson, John Adams recalled the day and said: "Then and there the child Independence was born." Henry's attack on the king's right to disallow colonial statutes was later expanded into an attack on the royal prerogative in general. Years after the Revolution, the Henry-Otis thesis that statutes or executive acts that violate men's rights are null would be used by Jefferson and Madison in their battle against the Alien and Sedition Acts.

New England's time to quarrel about a religious matter came in that eventful year 1760, when construction began on an Anglican mission church hard by Harvard Yard. This seemingly innocent event produced a turmoil among New England divines, for they were convinced that it was the opening effort of Thomas Secker, Archbishop of Canterbury, to put an Anglican bishop in America. Secker had favored the creation of such a post for years, and in 1760 he told a friend that Lord Halifax, too, was "very earnest for bishops in America." New Englanders objected to such an innovation, for as Horatio Walpole shrewdly saw, they suspected

that this first motion for settling bishops in America to perform certain functions only as ordination and confirmation is laying a foundation for giving them gradually the same authority and powers as the bishops here enjoy and exercise . . . [and] will in a great degree have the effect and be attended with the same consequences of ill humor and discontent as if ecclesiastical government was now to be settled there in its full extent.

The "full extent" of England's ecclesiastical government in 1760 had diminished little since the Puritans had departed over a century earlier. Church courts dealt with wills and marriages and such offenses as adultery and fornication—all of which were handled by secular courts in America.

To help justify the need for an American bishop, Secker had encouraged the activities of the Society for the Propagation of the Gospel in Foreign Parts (commonly known as the S.P.G.)—a group supposedly created to proselytize among the Indians but which New Englanders believed was now designed to bring new members into the Church of England and thus, with its enlarged membership, increase the necessity for a bishop. Why else, they asked, build mission churches in such settled communities as Cambridge, where few if any Indians lived? The Massachusetts legislature sought to frustrate this activity by granting permission for Congregationalists to form their own missionary society. Largely through Secker's efforts, the act was disallowed in May 1763. All this provoked the Reverend Jonathan Mayhew, an able though "turbulent and contentious" man, to publish *Observations on the Charter and Conduct of the Society,* a powerful attack on the S.P.G. as reconstructed by Secker and on the idea of a bishop for America. The pamphlet met with "general approbation and applause." A clergy only recently divided over local issues—Mayhew, for example, had been warmly censured for his liberal political views—now stood united. They, as much as the politicians and merchants, had come to resent interference from England.

Coupled in time with these events were two others that, for those who understood the workings of British politics, hinted at trouble ahead for the colonies. Pitt underscored his objections to the king's prosecution of the Seven Years' War by resigning from the cabinet in October 1761.

He accepted a pension and also a peerage that placed him in the House of Lords and removed him from leadership of Commons. Even more disastrous for the colonies' future, though few of the day realized it then, was the retirement of the Duke of Newcastle in 1762. Bernhard Knollenberg has called the event "calamitous from the standpoint of British relations with the colonies." Newcastle had been a powerful voice in imperial management since 1717, and since 1754 he had held the important post of head of the Treasury Board. Knollenberg contends that had he stayed in office "the provocative colonial measures from 1763 to 1765 would not have been taken," for Newcastle had consistently opposed in the past all "novel or harsh measures likely to dampen colonial good will and thus injure British trade." He and Pitt had often quarreled over colonial policy as over many other issues, but they had nonetheless managed, as Lord Chesterfield put it, "to jog on like man and wife: that is, seldom agreeing, often quarreling; but by mutual interest, upon the whole, not parting." With Newcastle's retirement, both the chancellor of exchequer and the treasury post went to George Grenville, Pitt's brother-in-law. Grenville also took over leadership in Commons now that Pitt had departed. This was the situation in 1763 as Great Britain was about to conclude the negotiations that would bring peace to Europe after seven years of bloody war.

BIBLIOGRAPHY

New Blood and a New Colony

Two introductions to the subject are the early chapters of Marcus L. Hansen, *The Atlantic Migration, 1607–1860* (1940; pb.), and Carl Wittke, *We Who Built America: The Saga of the Immigrant* (1939; pb.). Smith's *Colonists in Bondage* (1947) tells fully the manner in which many of the colonists came. "Report of the Committee on Linguistic and National Stocks in the Population of the United States," *American Historical Association Annual Report*, Vol. I (2 vols., 1932), 105–441, is a work for specialists. Mildred Campbell tells of "English Emigration on the Eve of the American Revolution," in *AHR*, 61 (1955), 1–20.

Walter A. Knittle, *Early Eighteenth-Century Palatine Emigration* (1937), relates the story of those who went to New York. The fullest account of German-speaking people in colonial America is Albert B. Faust's *German Element in the United States* (2 vols., 1909), but by all means read, too, the delightfully written and authoritative *Pennsylvania Dutch* (1950) by Frederic Klees, himself a Pennsylvania Dutchman. Also useful is the collection of essays edited by Ralph Wood, *Pennsylvania Germans* (1942). Among the more specialized studies are Dieter Cunz, *The Maryland Germans* (1948), whose early pages center on the colonial era; Paul A. W. Wallace, *The*

Muhlenbergs of Pennsylvania (1950), an admirable study of a distinguished German Lutheran family; G. D. Bernheim, *History of the German Settlements in . . . North and South Carolina* (1872); Herrmann Schuricht, *History of the German Element in Virginia* (1898); and John W. Wayland, *The German Element in the Shenandoah Valley* (1907). Two articles for specialists are Donald F. Durnbaugh, "Christopher Sauer: Pennsylvania-German Printer," *PMHB*, 82 (1958), 316–340; and Dietmar Rothermund, "The German Problem of Colonial Pennsylvania," *PMHB*, 84 (1960), 3–21. (Anyone interested in exploring the story of either the German-speaking people or Scotch-Irish in America should start his trek by glancing first through the cumulative index of the *PMHB*, which lists a mass of relevant and excellent material on both subjects.)

James G. Leyburn's solid *The Scotch-Irish: A Social History* (1962) reexamines the subject for the first time since H. J. Ford's excellent and still useful *The Scotch-Irish in America* (1915). C. A. Hanna's detailed *The Scotch-Irish* (2 vols., 1902) is more a random chronicle than an organized history. Wayland F. Dunaway overlays solid research in local archives with a pietistic patina in *The Scotch-Irish of Colonial Pennsylvania* (1944).

All the less numerous groups of immigrants have received attention from historians. The Scots have been well treated by Ian C. C. Graham, *Colonists from Scotland: Emigration to North America, 1707–1783* (1956), and Duane Meyer, *The Highland Scots of North Carolina, 1732–1776* (1961). A. H. Hirsch has covered *The Huguenots of Colonial South Carolina* (1928) and Albert B. Faust "The Swiss Emigration to the American Colonies in the Eighteenth Century," *AHR*, 22 (1916), 21–44. The Jews of colonial America have, despite their small numbers, received considerable attention in several excellent volumes. Abram V. Goodman's *American Overture: Jewish Rights in Colonial Times* (1947) and Jacob R. Marcus' *Early American Jewry* (1951) should be supplemented by Hyman B. Grinstein, *The Rise of the Jewish Community in New York, 1654–1860* (1945), and Edwin Wolfe, 2nd, and Maxwell Whiteman, *The History of the Jews of Philadelphia from Colonial Times to the Age of Jackson* (1957).

A surprising amount of the documentary material that has been published about eighteenth-century immigration deals with the German-speaking groups. Their trials are best depicted by Gottlieb Mittelberger, *Journey to Pennsylvania,* most recently edited by Oscar Handlin and John Clive (1960). R. W. Kelsey has edited "An Early Description of Pennsylvania: A Letter of Christopher Sower, Written in 1724, Describing Conditions in Philadelphia and Vicinity, and the Sea Voyage from Europe," *PMHB*, 45 (1921), 243–254. Jacob R. Marcus, ed., *American Jewry: Documents, Eighteenth Century* (1959), is the fullest available source on the subject.

Two counterbalancing essays on the history of early Georgia are Lawrence H. Gipson's chapter in the second volume of his monumental *The British Empire Before the American Revolution* (10 vols., 1956–1961) and Daniel Boorstin's provocative chapter in *The Americans: The Colonial Experience* (1958; pb.). Other fuller accounts are E. Merton Coulter, *Georgia: A*

Short History (1947) ; Trevor Richard Reese, *Colonial Georgia: A Study in British Imperial Policy in the Eighteenth Century* (1963) ; and Albert B. Saye, *New Viewpoints in Georgia History* (1943). See W. E. Dunn, *Spanish and French Rivalry in the Gulf Region of the United States, 1678–1702* (1917), for the story prior to English settlement. Two excellent and complementary views of Oglethorpe are A. A. Ettinger, *James Edward Oglethorpe: Imperial Idealist* (1936), and Leslie F. Church, *Oglethorpe: A Study in Philanthropy in England and America* (1932). The most recent account of another luminary behind the project is Verner W. Crane's "Dr. Thomas Bray and the Colony Project, 1730," *WMQ,* 19 (1962), 49–63. Crane discusses the promotional literature for Georgia in *Southern Frontier, 1670–1732* (1929; pb.).

Georgia's early years, of all the colonies', are the most fully recorded by contemporaries. Two recently issued and well-edited volumes are E. Merton Coulter, ed., *The Journal of William Stephens, 1743–1745* (1958), and Clarence L. Ver Steeg, ed., *A True and Historical Narrative of the Colony of Georgia by Pat. Talifer and Others* (1960). Sarah B. Gober Temple's and Kenneth Coleman's *Georgia Journeys: Being an Account of the Lives of Georgia's Original Settlers and Many Other Settlers from the Founding of the Colony in 1732 Until the Institution of Royal Government in 1754* (1961) blends documents with narrative in order "to show through a picture of life in the infant colony some results of the aims and regulations of the Trustees."

The French Expelled

Two articles that offer suggestive introductions to the subject are Howard H. Peckham, "Speculations on the Colonial Wars," *WMQ,* 17 (1960), 463–472, and Lawrence H. Gipson, "The American Revolution as an Aftermath of the Great War for the Empire," *PSQ,* 55 (1950), 86–104. The relevant volumes of Francis Parkman and Gipson are, of course, indispensable to anyone doing work on the subject.

Walter L. Dorn, *Competition for Empire, 1740–1763* (1940; pb.), is the best brief account for the European background of the Anglo-French rivalry. The War of Jenkins' Ear is covered in John T. Lanning, *The Diplomatic History of Georgia* (1936), and Richard Pares, *War and Trade in the West Indies, 1739–1763* (1936). James T. Adams treats King George's War in *Revolutionary New England, 1691–1776* (1923), an account that should be supplemented by Jack M. Sosin's "Louisbourg and the Peace of Aix-la-Chapelle, 1748," *WMQ,* 14 (1957), 516–535.

The period can be studied through a number of biographies. Paul A. W. Wallace and Arthur D. Graeff have written lives of Conrad Weiser (both volumes were published in 1945) ; Nicholas B. Wainwright's *George Croghan: Wilderness Diplomat* (1959) amplifies A. T. Volwiler's earlier *George Croghan and the Westward Movement, 1741–1782* (1926). Pennsylvania's relations with the Indians are marvelously told in *Teedyuscung: King of the Delawares* (1949) by Anthony F. C. Wallace. The conflict is seen from two royal governors' views in Louis K. Koontz, *Robert Dinwiddie* (1941), and John A. Schutz, *William Shirley: King's Governor of Massachusetts* (1961). Washington's role is briefly recounted in the early pages of Esmond Wright, *George Washington and the American Revolution* (1960; pb.), and Marcus Cunliffe, *George Washington: Man or Monument* (1958; pb.) ; more fully in the early volumes of Douglas S. Freeman, *George Washington* (7 vols., 1948–1957) ; and most fully in Charles H. Ambler, *Washington and the West* (1936) and *George Washington in the Ohio Valley* (1955), the latter buttressed by the documentary record. The two most recent accounts of Washington in this period are Bernhard Knollenberg, *George Washington: The Virginia Period, 1732–1775* (1964), and James T. Flexner, *George Washington: The Forge of Experience (1732–1775)* (1965), the first of a projected three-volume biography. A wonderful account of a French hostage captured at Fort Necessity is Robert C. Alberts, *The Most Extraordinary Adventures of Major Robert Stobo* (1965). Flexner's *Mohawk Baronet* (1960) is a popular and reliable life of Sir William Johnson; the interested student will probably want to pursue the story in *The Papers of Sir William Johnson* (13 vols., 1921–1962).

The fifth (revised) volume in Gipson's *British Empire* is the most reliable account of New France and English North America on the eve of the "Great War for the Empire," as Gipson prefers to call it. Robert C. Newbold's account of *The Albany Congress and Plan of Union* (1955) may be supplemented by Alison G. Olson's "The British Government and Colonial Union, 1754," *WMQ*, 17 (1960), 22–34. Two of the most recent and also most vivid accounts of the French and Indian battles with the English and Americans are Dale Van Every, *Forth to the Wilderness* (1961; pb.), which experts find marred by errors but most of them minor, and Edward P. Hamilton, *The French and Indian Wars* (1962). Hamilton, who is especially knowledgeable on eighteenth-century military matters, drives home the point that the French and Indian War came closer to a "total" war than any of the earlier colonial wars. Lee McCardell honors a maligned man in *Ill-Starred General: Braddock of the Coldstream Guards* (1958). Pitt has been treated briefly but perceptively in Sir Charles G. Robertson, *Chatham and the British Empire* (1946; pb.), and at length in O. A. Sherrard, *Lord Chatham* (3 vols., 1952–1958). Wilbur R. Jacobs, *Diplomacy and Indian Gifts* (1960), is relevant here and also for the Indian uprising of 1763. The bicentennial of Quebec's fall was marked by three volumes in 1959: Christopher Hibbert, *Wolfe at Quebec;* Christopher Lloyd, *The Capture of Quebec;* and C. P. Stacey, *Quebec, 1759: The Siege and the Battle.* All are competent but Stacey's is magnificent. Parkman's version, in *France and England in North America* (8 vols., 1874–1896), however, will remain for many the best. Parkman of recent years has come in for rough handling by young historians. One of the latest articles that censures him for his handling of the Easton conference of 1758 is Francis P. Jennings, "The Vanishing Indian: Francis Parkman and his Sources," *PMHB*, 87 (1963), 306–323.

The source material here is, of course, voluminous. The French and Indian War can be seen from various angles in Gertrude S. Kimball, ed., *Correspondence of William Pitt* (2 vols., 1906) ; Stanley M. Pargellis, ed., *Military Affairs in North America, 1748–1765* (1936) ; and J. C. Webster, ed., *Journal of Jeffrey Amherst* (1931). Edward Hamilton has recently translated and edited one version of the story from the French point of view in *Adventure in the Wilderness: The American Journals of Louis Antoine de Bougainville, 1756–1760* (1964). Three sources on Indian affairs are C. H. McIlwain's edition of Peter Wraxall's *An Abridgement of the Indian Affairs . . . Transacted in the Colony of New York* [1678–1751] (1915) ; Isabel M. Calder, ed., *Colonial Captivities, Marches and Journeys* (1935) ; and Wilbur R. Jacobs, ed., *Indians of the Southern Colonial Frontier* (1954). Indispensable to those concerned with the subject is Lois Mulkearn, ed., *The George Mercer Papers Relating to the Ohio Company of Virginia* (1954). The list of documentary volumes could continue on and on ; the books mentioned here are basic and sufficient to get the interested student on his way.

Imperial Relations: 1713–1763

Several of the studies listed in the previous section and nearly all those in the Bibliography for the third section of Chapter 9 are relevant here. There is still much to gain from George L. Beer, *The Old Colonial System, 1660–1754* (2 vols., 1912), and *British Colonial Policy, 1754–1765* (1907), though Gipson's *British Empire* covers much the same ground and incorporates new material. Much of Oliver M. Dickerson's *The Navigation Acts and the American Revolution* (1951) is relevant here. The role of the Treasury Board in American affairs can be comprehended only in Dora M. Clark, *The Rise of the British Treasury* (1960). Chapter 9, "The Role of Paper Money," in Joseph Dorfman's *The Economic Mind in American Civilization* (3 vols., 1946–1949) is the best brief account on that subject. Dorfman's point that it was the merchants and not the farmers who favored the use of paper money is accepted by Bray Hammond in *Banks and Politics in America from the Revolution to the Civil War* (1957). Carl Bridenbaugh gives a full report of Archbishop Secker's desire for an American bishop in *Mitre and Sceptre: Transatlantic Faiths, Ideas, Personalities, and Politics, 1689–1775* (1962). An excellent account of the trading activity that infuriated Pitt is Victor L. Johnson's "Fair Traders and Smugglers in Philadelphia, 1754–1763," *PMHB*, 83 (1959), 125–149. The early chapters of Bernhard Knollenberg, *Origin of the American Revolution, 1759–1766* (1960; pb.), give the best account of British efforts to tighten control over the American colonies after the fall of Quebec. For a more sympathetic report on the British attitude toward the Two Penny Act and the writs of assistance see Gipson's *Coming of the Revolution* (1954; pb.).

Relevant Orders in Council are found in W. L. Grant, and James Munro, eds., *Acts of the Privy Council of England, Colonial Series* (6 vols., 1908–1912). The orders are arranged chronologically for the period 1613–1783.

Another important collection is Leo F. Stock's edition of the *Proceedings and Debates of the British Parliaments Respecting North America* (5 vols., 1924–1941). Leonard W. Labaree, ed., *Royal Instructions to British Colonial Governors, 1670–1776* (2 vols., 1935), is of great value. Jeremiah Dummer's *A Defence of the New England Charter* [1721] is reprinted in J. Almon, *A Collection of the Most Interesting Tracts . . . on the . . . American Colonies . . .*, Vol. I (2 vols., 1766). Thomas Pownall's *The Administration of the Colonies* (4th ed., 1769) discusses constitutional problems from the point of view of a colonial governor. Two works that give insight into the problems of a colonial governor are Charles H. Lincoln, ed., *Correspondence of William Shirley* (2 vols., 1912), and Gertrude S. Kimball, ed., *The Correspondence of the Colonial Governors of Rhode Island* (2 vols., 1902–1903).

For further references see the *Harvard Guide,* Sections 101, "British Colonial Policy and Administration, 1713–1760"; 102, "Political and Constitutional Development, 1713–1760"; 105, "Georgia and Florida, 1730–1775"; 106, "Louisiana and Spanish Borderlands, 1713–1760"; 107, "King George's War and Nova Scotia, 1745–1755"; and 108, "Politics and War, 1749–1763."

"Watson and the Shark," by John Singleton Copley

11. The American Mind in the Eighteenth Century

THE GREAT AWAKENING
    First Waves
    Floodtide
    Aftermath

THE AMERICAN ENLIGHTENMENT
    Natural Philosophy
    Enlightened Americans
    Town and Country

DAWN OF A NEW ERA
    Education
    Science
    Language and Literature
    The Arts

"The first drudgery of settling new colonies, which confines the attention of people to mere necessaries, is now pretty well over," Benjamin Franklin wrote in 1743; "and there are many in every province in circumstances that set them at ease, and afford leisure to cultivate the finer arts, and improve the common stock of knowledge." Franklin's remarks introduced a proposal "for promoting USEFUL KNOWLEDGE among *British Plantations* in *America*," and out of the proposal eventually came the American Philosophical Society. Franklin and the society he helped to found exemplified one side of the American mind in the eighteenth century, the "enlightened" side, which held that men, by taking thought, could make the world a better place to live. The Great Awakening spoke for another side, that which appealed to men's emotions and held that

417

evil could be exorcized only through a regenerating religious experience. The American Enlightenment and the Great Awakening approached life differently: one appealed to the head; the other flew from "reason" and appealed to the heart. In the nineteenth century, these antipathetic qualities came into the open; American evangelical Protestantism turned against the spirit of the Enlightenment. But during the eighteenth century, goals shared in common by enlightened and awakened men minimized these differences: men of both groups favored religious freedom, fought for separation of church and state, promoted humanitarian reforms, and worked together to improve education. The enlightened encouraged church-going and the evangelists found nothing distressing in natural philosophy, as science was then called. Both relied for guidance upon experience rather than tradition or authority. Awakened and enlightened men worked together to put the seventeenth-century pattern of thought behind and to create the mold for a new one out of which the modern American mind would be born.

THE GREAT AWAKENING

The Great Awakening can be seen as part of a larger awakening that swept through eighteenth-century Britain, where it was known as Methodism; as part of a still larger religious revival that simultaneously struck Protestant Europe, where it was called Pietism; or—as it shall be here— an event that developed mainly out of the American experience. America endured a series of awakenings from 1720 to the Revolution, but *the* Great Awakening struck early in the 1740's. Once the floodtide had passed, men saw the foundations on which American churches had been built washed away and new ones constructed in their place. Perhaps no other event, save the Reformation, wrought greater changes on Protestantism. The Great Awakening would have left an indelible mark regardless of when it had come, but the timing deepened its influence. America, Richard Niebuhr has said, "cannot eradicate, if it would, the marks left upon its social memory, upon its institutions and habits, by an awakening to God that was simultaneous with its awakening to national consciousness."

First Waves

Things were not as they seemed on the religious scene in 1720. A diversity of sects, all antagonistic to one another, marred the landscape, but the divisions were more apparent than real. America remained much as it had been—nearly 99 per cent Protestant. More than that, the Reformed, or Calvinist, version of Protestantism prevailed. Of those within the

Calvinist fold, Congregationalists and Presbyterians accounted for approximately 70 per cent of the churchgoers, Baptists and Anglicans for about 25 per cent. Those without—Lutherans, Mennonites, Dunkers, and Moravians—added up to less than 5 per cent. In 1720 Congregationalists despised Baptists, Anglicans derided Presbyterians, and Quakers kept mainly to themselves. After the Great Awakening highlighted the theology the sects held in common, an eminent Presbyterian could say that Baptists differed from his sect "only in the point of infant baptism," a Congregationalist could become president of Presbyterian Princeton, and Quakers could join with others in humanitarian projects without feeling that they had soiled their consciences.

Outwardly, religious life in America appeared to have changed little from what it had been in Protestant Europe. Established churches persisted in nine of the thirteen colonies—Congregationalism dominated three of the New England colonies and Anglicanism prevailed throughout the South and in parts of New York. The American branch of the Church of England and all the Dutch- and German-speaking sects maintained tight ties with their mother churches across the ocean. A majority of the Presbyterian clergy had been trained in Britain. But here again all was not as it seemed to be. By 1720 Protestantism in America had eroded to a shadow of its old self, as it had existed in Europe since the Reformation. American churches had become voluntary or "gathered" groups that men joined only if they wished. The laity rather than the clergy dominated religious affairs. A minister, whether he was an Anglican, Congregationalist, Baptist, or Presbyterian, was "hired" much as a servant was, and he could be dismissed almost as easily; tenure depended on the congregation. There were no ecclesiastical superiors to please because virtually no ecclesiastical structure existed within the sects. The churches had come first, and by the time each sect got round to contemplating some sort of structure to unite their disparate congregations, local control of religious affairs had become a tradition too fixed to be easily uprooted.

A threat to the welfare of all the sects presented by the Church of England at the turn of the century revealed how deeply the roots of localism went. In 1701 the crown issued a charter to the Society for the Propagation of the Gospel in Foreign Parts. The S.P.G. came to represent for Americans what a historian has called "British imperialism in ecclesiastical guise." Its purpose, according to one bishop, was to propagate Anglicanism "among our *own people*" in America, "then to proceed . . . towards the conversion of the natives." Missionaries, well supplied with funds, came to build churches and do what they could to dampen dissenters' fires. Royal governors like Lord Cornbury in New York and Lewis Morris in New Jersey used their offices to promote the church's welfare. There was talk of sending over a bishop to direct the campaign. All this helped to prod the sects into action: in 1705 the ministers of Massachusetts urged the creation of consociations (rule by councils), which would have the power to implant a degree of order and uniformity on meetings throughout the colony. The legislature's and royal governor's refusal to accept the plan killed it, but self-created ministerial associations with power to license and ordain ministers cropped up in all parts of the colony. The urge to organize touched others, too. The first Baptist Association, consisting of five churches, materialized in Philadelphia in 1707. The next year a synod of Connecticut ministers adopted the Saybrook Platform, whereby a council of ministers and laymen in each county acquired power to discipline and supervise the meetings of their area. The legislature sanctioned the platform and Connecticut became what has been called a halfway house between Congregationalism and Presbyterianism. The Presbyterians, whose numbers grew as the century aged, formed in 1716 the Synod of Philadelphia, which consisted of four presbyteries.

Once the sects organized, arguments over ecclesiastical policies pushed worries about the spreading virus of Anglicanism into the background; rifts appeared among the leadership of every sect. More often than not, the conflicts occurred between two generations, with the older clergy eager to have things as they were and the younger men arguing for change. Dissension developed with special bitterness among the Presbyterians. The older, European-educated ministers fought hard to keep the church much as it had been at home. They believed that doctrinal conformity rather than a regenerating experience offered the best rule for judging a candidate's qualifications for the ministry. They wanted to transfer the power to select and ordain ministers from the presbyteries back to the synod, as it was in Scotland and northern Ireland. They rejected the idea of an American-educated clergy. Most of the Presbyterian ministers failed to grasp the meaning of the American experience; they acted and thought as though they still lived in their homelands. The divisions that had materialized by 1720 among Presbyterians existed in all sects, and they would persist down to the Revolution; the Great Awakening hardened and widened the rifts, but it did not cause them.

In 1720 more unchurched people lived in America than in any country of the Western World. A deadness had settled upon religion the length of the continent. Bright young men like John Adams and Benjamin Rush, who went to college expecting eventually to enter the ministry, ended by becoming lawyers and doctors, and the pulpits were left more and more to second-rate talents who droned out their sermons and scolded rather than inspired their parishioners. Impiety became the fashion. James Franklin's *New-England Courant,* first published in 1721, made a career during its six years of life of attacking the clergy. Old-timers who had known America when it had been a land of the devout said the people now "vomit up their spiritual milk with scoffs." Every year seemed to provide fresh signs of God's displeasure—an epidemic of smallpox or of the "throat distemper," an earthquake, a disastrous fire, "a blast upon the wheat"—but the people went their ways unperturbed. New England had tried to check the decline with the Half-Way Covenant. When that failed, Solomon Stoddard, the "pope" of the Connecticut Valley, flung open the doors to virtually all, allowing even the unregenerate to share in communion. But people still shunned joining the church; perhaps 75 per cent of New England—and probably more elsewhere on the continent—remained outside.

The decline in piety pleased no one. It disturbed an "enlightened" gentleman like Benjamin Franklin, who, though a deist, regularly paid his "annual subscription for the support of the only Presbyterian minister or meeting we had" and urged his daughter to "go constantly to church, whoever preaches." In a land where social controls over a scattered population were few, the church helped to inculcate civilized values. The weak, the ignorant, and the inexperienced, said Franklin, all "have need of the motives of religion to restrain them from vice, to support their virtue, and retain them in practice of it till it become habitual, which is the great point for its security." Somehow the unchurched had to be reached and brought back to the fold. Because churches in America were "gathered," or voluntary, groups, this meant that they had to return of their own accord; new techniques had to be devised to call forth the ungathered. The situation, as Winthrop Hudson has put it, "called for a type of preaching that would prick the conscience, convict men of sin, and lead them through a crisis of individual decision into a personal experience of God's redeeming love." Given the needs of the day, no one should be puzzled as to why the evangelists of the Great Awakening, most of them intelligent and educated men, appealed with all the fervor at their command to the heart rather than to the head.

The first wave of the Great Awakening rolled in with the ship that brought Theodore Frelinghuysen from Holland in 1719. Frelinghuysen was assigned to four Dutch Reformed churches in New Jersey, and he proceeded at once to become a storm center. He had read widely in the works of seventeenth-century English and Dutch Puritans, and his evangelistic sermons emphasized piety over good works, a regenerating experience over an upright life. He discarded Dutch, to the old guard's distress, and preached in English. He argued against the Classis in Holland, which appointed ministers for America, and spoke out for a home-educated clergy. (Queen's College, which is now Rutgers University, was established in 1766 for that purpose.) Slowly Frelinghuysen's congregations began to come alive and by 1726, despite strong opposition from the old-line clergy, the Dutch Reformed of New Jersey were in the midst of a revival. Frelinghuysen's success encouraged Gilbert Tennent, a friend and neighboring Presbyterian minister, and by 1729 Tennent's own congregations had also been awakened. Tennent, like Frelinghuysen, drew on seventeenth-century evangelical Puritanism for his theology. He sought to overcome the "presumptuous security" of his parishioners, who had come to believe that they could ease their way into heaven by leading an upright life.

The techniques that Frelinghuysen and Tennent used to call forth the ungathered fixed the pattern of the Great Awakening. Both, though well-educated men, shunned theological subtleties. They bleached out most of the distinctions and many of the traditions that had divided Protestants for two centuries and exchanged pulpits to emphasize how little value they attached to doctrinal differences among the sects. Both favored an educated clergy, but the current shortage of ministers led them to use lay preachers to keep congregations alive while they visited other pulpits on their circuits. To capture the hearts of their hearers they tossed out stale written sermons and spoke from their own hearts, either extemporaneously or only from notes. Contemporaries called their innovations crude, but judged by later standards they were sedate and mild; they used none of the nineteenth century's revival techniques—the "protracted meeting," which lasted weeks and won converts through exhaustion, or the "anxious bench," on which the sinful sat in public view until they had been humiliated into seeing the light. They worked within the traditional framework, preaching only at Sunday and mid-week service. Neither theirs nor other eighteenth-century revivals burst forth suddenly; they came only after months of awakening sermons and private ministrations among the people.

As the first wave of Frelinghuysen's and Tennent's awakening subsided in the early 1730's, a second wave appeared in New England, prompted by the preaching of Jonathan Edwards, then minister of the meeting in Northampton, Massachusetts. Edwards' later philosophical works reveal him as one of the great intellects of his time, but the people of New England knew him as one of the greatest preachers of the day. "Men no more regard warnings of future punishment because it don't seem real to them," he said, and to that end he saw to it, as Ola Elizabeth Winslow has remarked, that heaven and hell, God's wrath and eternal glory "lost their vague outlines and became visible, imminent realities." In 1735 Edwards' congregations, like those earlier in New Jersey, came alive slowly, but by the following year, a full-scale revival was in progress. The wave of evangelism washed through the Connecticut Valley of Massachusetts and on into Connecticut; in 1736, however, it died out.

The waves of revivalism in the Middle Colonies might have died out, too, but for the presence there of William Tennent, Sr. Tennent, who had been trained for the ministry at the University of Edinburgh, had come to America in 1718. He eventually settled at Neshaminy in Bucks County, Pennsylvania, and there he educated four sons, Gilbert among them, for the ministry. In 1735 he began what opponents within Presbyterianism deprecatingly called the "Log College." Tennent hoped to relieve the shortage of ministers in the then rapidly expanding church, but his seemingly innocuous project raised the hackles of the Scotch-Irish divines who controlled the Philadelphia Synod and who, having tangled already with Tennent, knew the sort of ministers his "college" would turn out—those who would refuse to subscribe to the Westminster Confession, which had been drawn up in Cromwell's time and had ever since determined the doctrines of Presbyterianism. Men like Tennent, who preferred piety to doctrinal purity, were not to be trusted. Still, the Log College prospered in spite of the opposition; and because the presbyteries rather than the synod controlled ordination, Tennent-trained ministers were soon holding down pulpits wherever Presbyterianism had spread. By 1739 old rifts within the church had hardened into two factions—the "Old Side," which wished to keep the church as it had been in Great Britain, and the "New Side," which consisted mainly of native-born divines educated by Tennent. The Old Side controlled the synod and might have continued to do so but for the arrival in Pennsylvania in October 1739 of George Whitefield, the man who would turn the scattered revivals of the 1720's and 1730's into a Great Awakening.

Floodtide

George Whitefield—he pronounced it "Whit-field"—was twenty-four when he arrived in Philadelphia in November 1739 on the second of what were to number seven trips to America, the last of which ended with his death in 1770 at Newburyport, Massachusetts. Whitefield planned to pause in Philadelphia only long enough to collect supplies for an orphanage he was building in Georgia, but William Tennent, Sr., came down from Neshaminy and persuaded him to make a preaching tour of the Middle Colonies. Whitefield had not arrived in Philadelphia an unknown entity; the colonial press for several months had carried accounts of his success as an evangelist throughout England. As a young man at Oxford, where he knew John and Charles Wesley, a long bout

with melancholy suddenly ended with deliverance "from the burden
that had so heavily oppressed me." The regenerate Whitefield became an
Anglican priest, but the fervency of his preaching offended many, and
with few ministers willing to lend him their pulpits he was driven to
preaching in the fields and public halls. Thousands came to hear him, and
by the time Whitefield arrived in Philadelphia, he was one of the most
famous men in England.

Whitefield stayed only nine days in Philadelphia, but that was long
enough to put the sedate city into a frenzy. "It was wonderful to see the
change soon made in the manner of our inhabitants," said Benjamin
Franklin, who had been sufficiently moved by one of Whitefield's sermons to empty his pockets when the collection plate was passed. "From
being thoughtless or indifferent about religion, it seemed as if all the
world were growing religious, so that one could not walk thro' town in
an evening without hearing psalms sung in different families of every
street." A typical Whitefield sermon left his audience exhausted: "Some
were struck pale as Death," goes one report, "others wringing their
hands, others lying on the ground, others sinking into the arms of their
friends, and most lifting up their eyes toward heaven, and crying out to
GOD." Whitefield gave "church-going America its first taste of theater
under the flag of salvation," Ola Elizabeth Winslow has remarked, taking
care to add, however, that theatrics alone did not explain his success:
he arrived in America long after the seeds of the Great Awakening had
been planted and "merely put in his sickle and claimed the harvest."

The harvest proved easy to reap because Whitefield's eloquence was
tied to a faith nicely suited to Americans of the day. He arrived an Anglican tinged with the Arminianism of the Wesleys; Gilbert Tennent
steered him toward Calvinism; but, as Whitefield's latest biographer,
Stuart C. Henry, has observed, his views on predestination and of man's
degeneracy were shot through with an appealing optimism. God, he
hinted, could be encouraged to speed a man on his way to salvation.
Theological inconsistencies did not disturb Whitefield, for he paid little
attention to the doctrines of any church. "Father Abraham," he called
out once during a sermon, "whom have you in heaven? Any Episcopa-
lians?" Whitefield answered his own question "No!" then continued the
question-and-answer dialogue. "Any Presbyterians? No! Any Indepen-
dents or Methodists? No, no, no! Whom have you there? We don't know
those names here. All who are here are Christians. . . . Oh, this is the case?
Then God help us to forget party names and to become Christians in deed
and truth." Whitefield's appeal to end sectarianism hastened a process long
at work in America.

Whitefield left Philadelphia in early November and preached his way

across New Jersey into New York, stirring up the countryside wherever
he went. From New York he headed into New England, and wherever
the word went that Whitefield was coming the dusty roads were crowded
"with men and horses slipping along in the cloud-like shadows," and
"every horse seemed to go with all his might to carry his rider to hear
news from heaven for the saving of souls. . . ." In Boston he preached
to five thousand one afternoon, to eight thousand the next day, to six
thousand the day after that. His farewell sermon was heard by twenty-
three thousand (a newspaper estimate) or thirty thousand (Whitefield's
estimate). Whitefield had a simple explanation for his success: congregations have been dead, he said, "because dead men preach to them." His
tour lasted only a month, but in that time, he jolted New England
out of its religious lethargy.

More than that, he saw to it that the triumph did not wither away.
On the way back from New England, he persuaded Gilbert Tennent—
for Whitefield, that "son of thunder" who "went to the bottom indeed
and did not daub with untempered mortar"—to make a tour of his own.
Tennent liked to roar at his audience that "they were *damned, damned,
damned*," but according to a critic he fascinated them, for "in the most
dreadful winter I ever saw, people wallowed in snow, night and day, for
the benefit of his beastly brayings." On Tennent's heels came James Davenport, whose rash ways so infuriated the sedate of New England that
the courts declared him *non compos mentis* and sent him back to Long
Island. Davenport's rough treatment did nothing to slow the influx of
itinerant preachers into New England and wherever else Whitefield
traveled.

By the end of 1740, Whitefield had toured the South and once again
both the Middle Colonies and New England. Thousands continued to
turn out wherever he spoke, and invariably "the groans and outcries of
the wounded were such that my voice could not be heard." Whitefield left
for England at the start of 1741, but the Great Awakening continued at
fever pitch throughout the land. Anglicans and Quakers and to some
degree the Baptists—"those poor, bigoted, ignorant, prejudiced people,"
the evangelist Eleazar Wheelock called them—watched the frenzy from
a distance, but few others remained calm. Even the pietist sects among
the German-speaking people, though they held aloof from the Whitefield revival, did not escape altogether; their awakening was initiated by
Count Nicolaus Zinzendorf, who sought (and failed) to unite the host
of German sects into a single association. His efforts were somewhat
thwarted by a simultaneous revival among German Lutherans led by
Henry Muhlenberg. Nor did the South escape; New Side Presbyterians
sent Henry Robinson into Virginia in 1742 to follow up Whitefield's

success. Samuel Davies, who in the last year of his life became president of the College of New Jersey, arrived in 1748 and began a decade of preaching so effective that Patrick Henry remembered him as the greatest orator he ever heard. Virginia's revival east of the mountains centered in Hanover County, whose local court—the same court that would later try the Parson's Cause—in 1750 gave the notorious James Davenport a license to preach. That prompted the Anglican governor to issue a proclamation "requiring all magistrates to suppress and prohibit, as far as they lawfully could, all itinerant preachers." The order died on the wind.

Revivals continued to flare up and then sputter out in every colony down to the Revolution, but the Great Awakening itself had ended by 1744. Whitefield continued to attract huge crowds wherever he went during each of his next five trips to America, but never again was he able to spark anything like the Great Awakening of 1740–1741. That awakening had been great, it has been said, because it knew no boundaries, social or geographical, urban or rural. And when the flood tide receded, the perceptive saw that traditional Protestantism, as it had existed since the Reformation, had been shattered. Tests for orthodoxy that had stood for two centuries had vanished in the storm. The religious life of Americans would never again be what it had been.

Aftermath

America listened with only half its heart when Whitefield returned in 1745. "Great talk about Whitefield's preaching," a New Englander remarked, "and the fleet at Cape Breton." But the end of the awakening did not mark the end of its effect. Of the multitudes that had poured into the churches, some, at least, remained within the fold—perhaps as much as 10 per cent of the total population in New England and the Middle Colonies. The newly gathered were not easily absorbed, and as the awakening subsided, meetings everywhere split into factions. Those who favored the revival—they were known as "New Lights" within Congregationalism, the "New Side" within Presbyterianism—sometimes found their reception so cold they departed to build meetinghouses of their own. The decision to separate came hard, for it often challenged loyalties of a lifetime. But the disputes provoked by the awakening cut too deeply to be compromised. The antirevivalists held that the awakening had not been the work of God but only a frenzy that temporarily put the people completely out of their minds. They held, too, and correctly, that the awakening challenged the traditional basis on which Protestantism had been built since the Reformation.

Separatism struck hardest among the Congregationalists of New Eng-

land, but the movement lived only briefly. New Light separatists were
deprived of political offices, particularly in Connecticut, where government stayed in the hands of the orthodox. In many cases marriages by
separatist ministers were disallowed, their sons were expelled from college, and they were taxed to support the established church as well as
their own meetings. The fanatics and cranks, "soreheads and grumble-
tonians," who bulked large in every separatist meeting did little to improve its standing within the community. By the eve of the Revolution,
most of the separatists had either rejoined their old meetings or become
Baptists.

The Baptists made astonishing gains after the Great Awakening.
Their congregations throughout America numbered perhaps a dozen in
1740 but nearly five hundred in 1775. In New England, the Baptists had
endured nearly a century of oppression. Because they favored separation
of church and state and because the regenerative experience had always
been basic to their sect, they offered a natural home to those New Lights
who could not endure the idea of returning to their old meetings. In the
Middle Colonies, where the stronger organization of the Presbyterians
held defections to a minimum, the Baptists made few gains, but their
willingness to tolerate lay exhorters and their indifference to an educated
ministry helped them after 1760 to outdistance Presbyterianism throughout the South and in the backcountry.

The Congregationalists splintered into a multitude of separate
churches, the Presbyterians split into two synods. The Presbyterian break
came in the early summer of 1741, not long after Gilbert Tennent had returned from a tour of New England, where he had preached a contro-
versial sermon on *The Danger of an Unconverted Ministry*. The Philadelphia Synod ejected Tennent and his followers, who thereupon erected
the New York Synod as a home base for the New Side clergy; the
split ended in 1758 when the two sides reunited. By then, New Side Presbyterians had established their own college—the College of New Jersey,
which later became Princeton University—and were turning out American-educated ministers whose outlook was totally American. The predominance of New Side ministers gave them control of the church
machinery.

The schisms that appeared among the Congregationalists and Presbyterians and to a lesser degree among other sects were the debris of an
outworn mold, shattered by the Great Awakening; they cluttered the
landscape only for a short while. By the eve of the Revolution, the debris
had been reassembled into a pattern that gave a new unity to American
Protestantism. Sects vanished in the awakening and denominations
sprouted in their place. A sect by definition sets itself apart and assumes

that it alone manifests the true form and spirit of Christianity. The denomination, less arrogant, less certain of God's mind, considers itself only a denominated group within the Protestant Church. As Winthrop Hudson explains it: "No denomination claims that all other churches are false churches. Each denomination is regarded as constituting a different 'mode' of expressing the outward forms of worship and organization of that larger life of the Church in which they all share." The denominational theory was first fully developed by dissenting sects of seventeenth-century England, who searched for a common ground on which to unite against the establishment. Roger Williams expounded it first in the colonies. It seeped into the American experience through the seventeenth century, but not until the Great Awakening, when Whitefield, an Anglican priest, and the diverse itinerants who followed in his wake chose to preach wherever doors were open to them, did the denominational theory achieve status and become an accepted part of American Protestantism. The transformation of the theory into practice was America's great gift to Protestantism. Religious groups who for over two centuries had bickered and fought one another had at last found a way to live side by side in relative peace.

Denominationalism as it emerged from the Great Awakening eased sectarian antagonisms, but in the process the cleavage between emotion and intellect widened. The seventeenth-century brand of Protestantism brought to the colonies from England appealed both to the head and the heart. But the awakeners, though generally educated men, aware of theological subtleties, willingly discarded the intellectual structure of Protestantism in their eagerness to gather in the unchurched. Charles Chauncy, minister of the First Church in Boston, saw that the awakening's emotional appeal for converts opened the way for a fervent anti-intellectualism within the churches. Chauncy argued warmly with Jonathan Edwards in sermons and pamphlets against the awakening. In their notable debate, Chauncy has been pictured as the embodiment of the Enlightenment's ideals, which he was, and thus the awakening in turn has been pictured as antithetical to the ideals of the Enlightenment, which it was—*ultimately*. Anti-intellectualism did in time come to dominate American Protestantism, but in the eighteenth century, awakeners and enlightened for the most part consciously overlooked or failed to notice their divergent views toward life and worked together toward goals they shared in common.

The Great Awakening, it has been said, "tended to emphasize individualism, to shatter the neat seventeenth-century society into members, but not into classes," and so, too, did the American version of the Enlightenment. Both, reflecting the conditions of eighteenth-century Amer-

ica, appealed to people regardless of their social status, for by the 1740's
the fixed order of society as it was known in Europe had vanished in
the colonies. Such words as "liberty" and "freedom," favored by the
enlightened, turned up in the awakeners' sermons: God left men free to
choose or reject salvation, and they were at liberty to select the church
or minister they wanted. Ironically, the awakeners were among the first
to suffer from their gospel. When Jonathan Edwards reprimanded his
parishioners' children for reading a sex-thriller of the day—*The Midwife Rightly Instructed*—the congregation rose up and turned him out.
"Shall the master of a ship not inquire when he knows the ship is running on rocks?" Edwards had asked, and the congregation had in effect
answered, "No, not when he usurps our rights as parents."

The Great Awakening and the American Enlightenment worked together to promote higher education in the colonies. Four of the colleges
in today's Ivy League—Brown, Princeton, Dartmouth, and the University of Pennsylvania—were direct products of the Great Awakening, as
was Rutgers, too. The schools, though founded to educate ministers, did
not flout the Enlightenment. They showed little antagonism to the new
science, and by the Revolution all had hired professors of natural philosophy. Enlightened and awakened also joined together to promote the
separation of church and state: both groups agreed that in America no
denomination should be singled out for preferment. The clergy saw that
it harmed rather than helped to involve their churches in political affairs,
for favoritism from the government only provoked attacks from the
unfavored. Ministers saw, too, the truth of the argument Roger Williams made over a century earlier, that ties with the state corrupt the
church. "I am a spectator indeed of events, but intermeddle not with politics," Reverend Stiles said in 1773. "We cannot become the dupes of
politicians without alliances, concessions and connections dangerous to
evangelical truth and spiritual liberty."

The quickened effort to cut the churches adrift from the state helped
to direct religious energies into a new channel. Voluntary organizations
came to be the favored way of promoting programs that had once been
carried out for the churches by the state. Such projects as orphanages,
missions for Indians, and the antislavery cause owed as much to Whitefield and other leaders of the awakening as to the enlightened gentlemen
who shared in them.

In the long run the effect of the Great Awakening on America
may have been pernicious; for in giving control of the churches
to the evangelical wing of Protestantism, it drove a wedge between the
plain people and the intellectuals that has remained to the present.
The immediate effects of the awakening, however, were to tighten

rather than break the ties between the two groups. The awakening turned the churches into the mainstream of the Enlightenment, and the alliance between the awakened and enlightened continued down through the Revolution. Indeed, it is not too much to say that the alliance did much not only to promote the Revolution but to make it successful.

THE AMERICAN ENLIGHTENMENT

Throughout the eighteenth century, Americans continued to draw much of their intellectual sustenance from England, but America's Enlightenment did not duplicate England's. The colonists imported enlightened ideas, modified them to suit their own needs, then, to an astonishing degree, put them to use. Fewer, less deeply rooted traditions encrusted society in America, and this made it easier to practice enlightened reforms that in England seldom escaped the bounds of table talk. The Enlightenment in America differed, too, in that the colonists often drew on English thought and theory to justify current practices or Americans' conception of themselves. The truth of a phrase like "all men are created equal" seemed more self-evident to men reared in the open society of the colonies than to Englishmen who still lived surrounded by vestiges of the medieval world.

Natural Philosophy

Men of Western civilization have always searched for laws that governed nature, for a universal scheme of order underlying the universe. The Middle Ages identified those laws of nature with the law of God; men looked at nature mainly to throw light on some theological problem. By the sixteenth century, however, a few had begun to examine nature not necessarily as it illuminated religion but as it provided a sufficiently satisfying study in itself. But more than their attitude toward nature had changed: they now searched for laws governing the universe by asking questions that could be answered by experiments based on observation; they then attempted to express the results of their observations in mathematical abstractions; each of these abstractions became for them a law of nature.

The church did not object to, in fact it encouraged, this new approach to the study of nature. In the seventeenth century Galileo met trouble only when he insisted that Copernicus' theory of the earth revolving about the sun as well as rotating on its axis was true. The church had willingly accepted the theory as a convenient fiction for making calculations, such as those on which the Gregorian calendar was based. The church refused to accept the theory as fact, for this would put fact in conflict with revelation. Did not Psalm 93 say: "The world also is established, that it cannot be moved?" Did not proof that the sun moves appear in Joshua's command on the evening of the battle of Gibeon: "Sun, stand thou still upon Gibeon; and thou, Moon, in the valley of Ajalon; and the sun stood still, and the moon stayed, until the people had avenged themselves upon their enemies"? The church demanded that, unless science absolutely proved the Scriptures wrong, reason must give way to revelation. Galileo eventually endured a humiliating retreat in which he publicly accepted the Copernican theory as "a poetical conceit," to use his own bitter phrase.

Galileo's mortification did not stem the rise of natural philosophy. Johannes Kepler's observations revealed that the planets moved in ellipses, not the perfect circles theologians had assumed, and that they moved at varying rates of speed through their orbits. Kepler said that the universe was "something like a clock work in which a single weight drives all the gears." Isaac Newton found the "single weight." He capped a multitude of seventeenth-century observations with a single postulate—*all* celestial bodies "attract each other by a force of universal strength that diminishes as the square of the distance between them increases." He had used the tools of natural philosophy to find what men had always assumed—complete order in God's universe—and as quickly as his ideas could be popularized, they became accepted.

With Newton's discoveries, in the late seventeenth and early eighteenth centuries, natural philosophy—that is, a philosophy derived from a study of nature—superseded religion in prestige. A new vocabulary began to dominate men's thoughts. The fashionable words—"nature," "natural law," "balance," "machine," "engine," and above all, "reason"—now were drawn from science. Soon men were lifting the new vocabulary out of context and using it to expand the "bounds of moral philosophy," assuming that "our duty towards Him, as well as that towards one another, will appear to us by the light of Nature." If the use of reason could uncover the scheme of the universe, surely it would expose similar laws when applied to the affairs of men. Once the rules of the game had been revealed, what could block man from perfectability? Pope expressed the confidence of the age in a couplet that quickly became *the* cliché of the eighteenth century:

> Nature and Nature's laws lay hid in night.
> God said, *Let Newton be!* and all was light.

Confidence that man verged on solving all God's riddles was the keynote of the age. The eighteenth century came to believe, with the arrogance of the innocent, not only that it was enlightened compared to past epochs, but that it verged on complete enlightenment.

Newtonianism, as it came to be called, "substituted a natural for a supernatural explanation of phenomena." It was natural, then, to subject religion to the rules of reason. John Locke, a young English physician who was a friend of Newton's and had been trained in the methods of experimental science by the chemist Robert Boyle, "proved" that God existed, in his book *The Reasonableness of Christianity*. Locke's work raised hardly a ripple in the contemporary stream of thought, for the slow accretion of scientific findings through the sixteenth and seventeenth centuries had given devout men time to adjust. Moreover, any divergence between the world of Biblical tradition and the world of science was not even dreamed of at the time. Newton himself believed that his findings reinforced rather than destroyed the foundations of Christianity, for "this most beautiful system of the sun, planets, and comets, could only proceed from the counsel and dominion of an intelligent and powerful being." Not only did his findings verify assumptions once taken on faith, but they undermined *none* of the old beliefs. The Scriptures taught that God had created the universe in six days, and nothing Newton discovered destroyed that truth. Indeed, his findings verified the Biblical picture of a static world completely made and not still in the making. Nor did his laws undercut the view of a personal God, for as Newton saw it, God could still step in any time He wished to work a miracle. (A miracle now became something that momentarily defied natural law.) The universe might be a Great Machine, but the operator remained God, a personal God who kept his hand on the throttle.

Locke extended his application of the technique of natural philosophy in *An Essay on Human Understanding,* wherein he "proved" that men's actions are not predetermined by God nor handicapped by the blot of original sin. God, said Locke, had stamped no truths, no innate ideas on men's minds, but had furnished them only with the ability to know. Knowledge itself emerged from experience, and experience was to a large extent determined not by God's will but by man's environment. Locke's great achievement here, in Carl Becker's words, was to make it seem "possible for men, 'barely by the use of their natural faculties,' to bring their ideas and their conduct, and hence the institutions by which they lived, into harmony with the universal natural order."

In another essay, written shortly before the Glorious Revolution, Locke developed a "right of rebellion" theory based on natural law. What, Locke asked, is government's right to authority? Divine right, most contemporaries would have answered: God had given the king the right to rule, and the people had to accept God's dictum. What resources do the people have if the ruler turns out to be bad? God would punish him, went the litany. What would the people do in the meantime? They would suffer, unless someone thought of an acceptable way to dispose of the king. Locke devised a new set of answers to those questions. Men were born free, he said, unhampered by government, and with certain "self-evident" natural rights, among which were the rights to life, liberty, and property. Now, the state of nature is difficult to maintain, for evil exists in the world and there are times when the individual cannot cope with it successfully. To protect their rights, men voluntarily band together and make a compact whereby one of their own is chosen to rule over them. This ruler and the government he creates exist only to protect men's natural rights. If the original compact is broken, the people then have the right to rebel, for they, not God, have chosen their ruler and can depose him.

Locke invited men to test the world around them by the yardstick of reason. For him, traditional Christianity was reasonable, as were such institutions as primogeniture, entail, the established church, and British regulations of trade. Men like Franklin and Jefferson, of a different century and a different country, would find different answers for what met the test of reason. When Locke argued for a minimal state, his seventeenth-century conception of what was the least government failed to jibe with that of eighteenth-century Americans, but it was the generalization rather than its specific application that mattered. America would take from Locke and others who promoted the Enlightenment in England only what it wanted and then adapt and modify it to fit the American environment.

Enlightened Americans

Newton's orderly picture of the universe was open to contradictory interpretations. Read one way, it gave men no more cause to hope for a better world than Calvinism did. Calvinism, as Alfred North Whitehead has pointed out, "exhibited man as helpless to cooperate with Irresistible Grace; the contemporary scheme of science exhibited man as helpless to cooperate with the irresistible mechanism of nature." But men of the eighteenth century preferred for the most part to interpret Newton as leaving the way open to improvement. "The greater our insight into Nature and its laws," Ezra Stiles said, "the greater will be our power over its laws, in altering, suspending, or counteracting them, and the more enlarged will be our sphere of activity."

The second, more optimistic, reading of Newton's picture was also open to various interpretations. Tom Paine immersed himself in Newtonianism and came up a radical in politics and religion. John Adams, about Paine's age, followed a similar intellectual trail, reading the same books, using the same vocabulary; he emerged, as far as labels can be accurately applied, a conservative. Thomas Jefferson, coming along a few years later but exposed to the same books and ideas, came out somewhere between his two friends. Natural philosophy provided the intellectual touchstone for most thinking men in eighteenth-century America, but they absorbed it within the context of beliefs that stemmed from their individual backgrounds. They would use natural philosophy to clarify vague ruminations about the world around them, to justify a mode of action, to explain an intuitive belief—but always in relation to their own experiences, their own "country," be that country Massachusetts, Pennsylvania, or Virginia. What might seem natural and reasonable to an Englishman like Paine, who had known hardship and failure most of his adult life, or to a New Englander like John Adams, would often seem unnatural to Thomas Jefferson.

Yet despite their diverse readings of Newtonianism, enlightened Americans held certain characteristics in common. Few led cloistered lives; they were men of the world. None were estranged from their times, as were such nineteenth-century intellectuals as Emerson, Hawthorne, and Thoreau. Benjamin Franklin was a printer; John Adams a lawyer; Benjamin Rush a doctor; James Logan, an accomplished mathematician and one of the few Americans to read the *Principia Mathematica* in the original rather than in a popularized version, was a skilled politician and a ruthless merchant. Credulity, however, did not vanish with the onset of the Enlightenment. Men continued to believe that a horse could be crossed with a cow, that mermaids existed, that bloodletting hastened a man back to health, and that God refused to allow any species to become extinct within the Great Chain of Being He had created. But they sought constantly to check their credulity by reason and observation: they had a passion for experiments both within and without the laboratory; they were orderly men who loved statistics and believed that if enough facts were collected and correctly ordered a natural law of some sort would emerge. These men believed in progress, but their conception was fixed within the framework of the world as it existed. They did not conceive of drastic alterations in the environment, but hoped only to refine out the grosser evils of the world. They were reformers, not utopians.

Lives, like facts, were ordered as if living were an experiment, too. Here is the way one of these men planned his time:

Tuesday, Sept. 2. By a sparingness in diet and eating as much as may be, what is light and easy of digestion, I shall doubtless be able to think more clearly, and shall gain time; 1. By lengthening out my life; 2. Shall need less time for digestion, after meals; 3. Shall be able to study more closely, without injury to my health; 4. Shall need less time for sleep; 5. Shall more seldom be troubled with the headache.

Franklin, Jefferson, and Adams all constructed similar schedules. (This one happens to be by Jonathan Edwards.) Moderation in all things underscored their lives. They praised common sense because the solutions it suggested were invariably moderate ones. For them, reasonable men were temperate men.

Yet these enlightened Americans were as aware of the evil in man as any Calvinist; experience in daily affairs restrained them from a wildeyed optimism. They sought to change men's environment rather than men, for they saw the limits of free will. (Jefferson prefaced his Bill for Establishing Religious Freedom in Virginia with the remark "that the opinions and beliefs of men depend not on their own will, but follow involuntarily the evidence proposed to their minds.") They steered their barks, as Jefferson put it, toward the end of a long life, "with hope in the head, leaving fear astern." Hopes "indeed sometimes fail," Jefferson added, "but not oftener than the forebodings of the gloomy."

Natural philosophy, pulling the English version of the Enlightenment along in its wake, had swept swiftly across the ocean to America. Cotton Mather had been among the first to welcome it. Mather, who cherished the Puritan tradition of New England's past, offers, it has been said, "a nice illustration of how a man's mind *begins* to make its way from one pole of thought to another." He embraced much of the Enlightenment without discarding the fervent orthodoxy of his ancestors. He called Newton our "perfect dictator," and his fascination with science led, among other things, to a membership in the Royal Society. In *The Christian Philosopher* (1721), he used the latest findings of natural philosophy to strengthen the eroded underpinnings of Puritanism.

The clergy's prompt and wholehearted acceptance of the Enlightenment was striking. Their tolerance of ideas that ultimately would undermine traditional Christianity came about partly because the Enlightenment seemed to buttress rather than attack orthodoxy and partly because they had been so quickly accepted by clerical colleagues in England. These English colleagues were invariably dissenters from the establishment and located on the left in politics.

Ministers, like other men, found what they went fishing for in the new stream of ideas. John Wise told his congregation that the end of government was to "promote the happiness of all" and that "it seems most agreeable with the light of nature that if there be any of the regular government settled in the church of God, it must needs be democracy." Jonathan Edwards, who read Newton and Locke as a youngster at Yale, used enlightened ideas to reinforce his inherited Calvinism. Newton showed him that man cannot master life but must, like the planets, submit to it, accepting the orbit or station that God had predestined him to.

Locke taught Edwards to exalt experience over reason. Man receives God's grace through the senses not through reason; as a man perceives, so he will conduct his life. If he perceives with a corrupt heart, as most men do, he will live corruptly, and only a regenerating religious experience will alter his perception of the world.

The danger Edwards sensed in exalting reason over experience eventually led to an antiseptic version of Christianity known as deism. The deist believed in an impersonal God who, once He had created the universe, left it alone. Doubting the divinity of Jesus Christ, he was skeptical of the Bible as divine revelation; Christianity offered man an excellent set of ethics but little more. The American deist was a milder man than his French counterpart; he privately deprecated organized religion but publicly supported it. Franklin and Jefferson, for instance, regularly attended church because they felt it set a good example. Deism was confined mainly to the educated classes, and they made no effort to propagate their views among the plain people. (An argument can be made that much of the vilification heaped upon Paine for publishing *The Age of Reason* came from the elite who felt that he spread heresy to the people and thus betrayed his class.)

Americans used ideas of the Enlightenment to promote modifications and reforms in society, not revolution. Their temperance to some extent was shaped by the pervading influence of classical thought in eighteenth-century America. (A visiting Spaniard who admired a statue of Pitt in Charleston thought it "a strange idea" he should be dressed in a Roman toga.) Locke gave William Livingston the arguments for an essay in 1753 ". . . on the Origin, Nature, Use and Abuse of Civil Government," but Roman history provided the illustrations on "the sweets of liberty" and "the wretched condition of slaves." Notes the youthful Jefferson made suggest the deep impression the classical authors left on him. He learned from Euripides that "moderation is everywhere beautiful and assures good repute among men." Cicero told him that "it behooves a man . . . to take care that reason shall have the command over that part which is bound to practice obedience." Long acquaintance with the classics taught Jefferson and those of his contemporaries who were to share in leading America through the Revolution that liberty did not give a man a natural right to indulge the acquisitive instinct but must be checked by a man's sense of duty to himself and to society, that happiness came not with the satisfaction of animal or material desires but was the ultimate result of moral virtue.

In the end, however, it was the ideas of the Enlightenment rather than those of the classics that worked with peculiar force on the minds of eighteenth-century Americans. Liberty of conscience, which had come to be a practical necessity in the colonies, was justified on the high ground that it was "right and reasonable." A group of New York Quakers said in 1768 that they were "fully of the mind that Negroes as rational creatures are by Nature born free." Jefferson as a young lawyer argued for a Negro's freedom on the principle that "under the law of nature all men are born free." Within a few years men would argue that the right to vote should be broadened because, as one man put it, Locke had shown "that all power originates from the people." The men who were to lead America into and through the Revolution used the Enlightenment "to complete, formalize, systematize, and symbolize what previously had been only partially realized, confused, and disputed matters of fact," Bernard Bailyn has said. "This completion, this rationalization, this symbolization, this lifting into consciousness and endowing with high moral purpose inchoate, confused elements of social and political change— this was the American Revolution."

Town and Country

The gap between town and country was not then what it is now. Reverend Ezra Stiles of Newport milked his own cow, smoked and salted his own meat, made his own soap, grew most of his own vegetables. Hogs roamed wild through the streets of Boston and New York. Philadelphia in 1776 still sufficiently resembled Penn's dream of a "green country town" that when a resident advertised among the thirty thousand or so inhabitants for his lost red-and-white cow he considered it enough to note that she "had two small hind teats and a star in her forehead."

Despite these bucolic overtones, a new breed of American—the city dweller—had come into being since the seventeenth century. "Don't call me a country girl, Debby Norris," wrote a young lady named Sally Wister from the confinement of a Bucks County farm. "Please observe that I pride myself upon being a Philadelphian, and that a residence of some twenty months has not at all diminished the love I have for that dear place." Miss Wister, who was reared a Quaker, passed her time in the country reading such books as Fielding's *Joseph Andrews* and flirting with soldiers. ("When we were alone our dress and lips were put in order for conquest," she says at one point, and at another, of a handsome army captain, "ain't he pretty, to be sure.") She missed her city friends and, equally, "the rattling of carriages over the streets—harsh music, tho' preferable to croaking frogs and screeching owls."

The eighteenth-century town or city encompassed several sides of America. A stranger could amuse himself "looking at some Indians, who were shooting with bows and arrows before the State House" and the next moment meet "a man with a blue Scotch bonnet on his head, a sight I have not seen a long time and which made me smile." In the space of an hour a visitor to Philadelphia might meet a bearded Amish farmer arguing in German with a shopkeeper, talk to a Jew, visit a Catholic mass, or hear a plainly dressed Quaker asking if "thee is well." The man so inclined might sink himself unobtrusively in sin, mild or otherwise. Every town had its "obscure inn," where patrons "poured down the fiery beverage, and valiant in the novel feeling of intoxication, sallied forth in quest of adventures." And every town had its prostitutes. (New York's prostitutes patrolled the Battery after sunset, and there a visitor might find "a good choice of pretty lasses among them, both English and Dutch.")

Outwardly, cities like Boston, New York, and Philadelphia; coastal towns like Salem, New Haven, and Norfolk; and inland towns like Hartford, Lancaster, and Williamsburg resembled English provincial cities and towns. Furnishings in the homes of the well-to-do either came from England or were Americanized versions of English patterns. Women of style took their cues from the latest in English fashions. The tavern tended to duplicate the English tavern, sometimes even to the name, as in Philadelphia's London Coffee House, where, of course, a brew stronger than coffee was served. Cultural life, too, drew heavily upon England. People read books by English authors and saw mainly English plays, usually performed by a traveling troupe of English actors. Their newspapers were packed with material lifted from English journals, and the news usually carried a European dateline. Yet despite the obviously English influence, any visitor from the mother country knew at once these were American towns and cities. They displayed, as no English provincial town or city did, what Carl Bridenbaugh has called "the unfolding, working out, and institutionalizing of the ideals and aspirations of the Age of Enlightenment."

Take, for example, Philadelphia. No other city in British history had grown more rapidly than Philadelphia—from approximately four thousand at the turn of the century to thirty thousand plus in 1775—and none had coped better with the problems of growth. The streets for the most part were paved and flanked by raised brick sidewalks. Lamps lighted the city at night, except when the moon was full, a provision that pleased the thrifty. The walks were shaded with towering elms and Italian poplars, and every hundred feet or so stood public water pumps—some five hundred in all scattered throughout the city. No other city in the world handled fires more effectively or with more dispatch. Criminals were housed in a "monster of a large strong prison," the poor in the Bettering House, and the sick in the only hospital on the American continent. The city by 1775 had a theater, a college, a medical school, a museum, a public library, a scientific society; it also had an educated public that supported and enjoyed these institutions.

Philadelphia's achievements exemplified what to a lesser extent was going on in towns and cities throughout the land. But often, efforts to improve the quality of urban life failed. (Not too many years after the Pennsylvania Hospital had opened, a visiting doctor found it pervaded by "a strong smell of sores and nastiness [that] rendered it insupportable even to me, who have been pretty much used to such places." Sanitary conditions remained primitive. Flies blackened uncovered food, and bed-bugs, mosquitoes, and roaches were a constant torment. Inoculation, which America had been the first to try on a large scale, had limited the deadliness of smallpox but epidemics of yellow fever, typhus, and diphtheria continued to ravage the population. Prisons did little to cut the rising crime rate.) What distinguished American cities was not that they solved their problems but that they sought to solve them, whereas in England, where cities were encrusted with centuries of tradition and men were "moved only by the wheels of custom," the problems accumulated and increased.

A second distinction was the way Americans sought to solve the problems an urban existence imposed on them. Philadelphia was encumbered with an antiquated charter like that given to English provincial cities. Government was controlled by a closed, self-perpetuating corporation of aldermen and councilmen with a high resistance to all pleas for civic improvements. The corporation could be circumvented by appealing to the assembly—it was the assembly that authorized a board of elected wardens to oversee street lighting, public wells, and the night watch in the city—but when both assembly and corporation balked at needed re-forms, civic leaders invented a new approach: the voluntary society. ("Borrowed" might be a better word, for Americans appear to have taken their cue from dissenters in England who, faced with a belligerently Anglican government and church, had found that through self-created voluntary organizations they could carry out projects that church and state refused either to support or to allow dissenters a hand in.) In 1736 Benjamin Franklin sought to improve fire protection by organizing a group of his neighbors into the Union Fire Company. These volunteers raised money on their own to purchase engines and to build their own firehouse in order to assure adequate protection for at least their part of the city. By 1775 the city had seventeen such fire companies. And by that date, the voluntary organization had become a standard way to deal with any civic problem the government refused to face. The Pennsylvania Hospital had been financed almost entirely by private contributions. The Bettering House—where the poor were put to spinning, sewing, and other forms of gainful employment, and which contained a maternity ward and a school for orphans—was run by a board chosen by the private contributors that supported it. The public library, the College of Philadelphia, the American Philosophical Society—all were organized and financed by private individuals.

The inadequacy of local and provincial government did not alone popularize these voluntary societies. Religious groups turned to them when government fell into alien hands. An Anglican governor and his clique of Anglican appointees caused the Congregationalists of Boston to develop voluntary societies as a means to maintain some control over the city's affairs. Sydney James has shown that the Quakers of Philadelphia, who retired from politics with the French and Indian War, found "in organizations to do good a solution to the problem of retaining the kinds of leadership in society which they wanted and thought it their right to exert." In the beginning these societies were usually tied to a single religious group. Franklin's Union Fire Company, for instance, was composed mainly of Quakers, and other companies that followed were made up of Presbyterians or Anglicans. Each religious group tended to care for its own sick and its own poor. But sectarian exclusiveness tended to relax after the Great Awakening and so, too, did the societies'. The awakening's emphasis on a practical and practicing Christianity also tended to increase the number of societies engaged in humanitarian projects. By the 1770's a civic unity had been created in every city by these voluntary groups, which had come to represent the people rather than a particular denomination or national group.

The voluntary society flourished in the eighteenth-century American city more than in Great Britain, partly because the colonists dared to arouse and use public opinion. This does not mean that American leaders were bolder or more democratic-minded but only that they had less to fear from the people. Englishmen lived in terror of mob violence, for the bulk of their cities were composed of the "poorer sort"—unemployed laborers, vagabonds, beggars—who needed only the slightest prodding to start them on a rampage. Mobs did appear occasionally in America, but more often than not they consisted of "gentlemen rakes" out on a lark. No large laboring class dominated the cities. Except for sailors and those who worked along the wharves, most urban dwellers were of the "better sort"—merchants, lawyers, clergy—and the "middling sort"—self-employed craftsmen, shopkeepers, tradesmen. Probably never before or since was poverty less of an urban problem that it was in eighteenth-century America.

The prosperity that sprang from the expanding towns and cities kept down the number of poor, and it also for the first time gave the colonies a leisure class. In the seventeenth century, when there were "all things to do, as in the beginning of the world," few besides the clergy had the time to read and reflect. But the clergy lost its near monopoly on learning in the eighteenth century. Benjamin Franklin was seventeen when he arrived in Philadelphia, virtually penniless and with only his energy and intelligence to recommend him. At the age of forty-two he retired from business and lived the rest of his life off the income from investments. John Adams, the son of a farmer, left the soil for law and became, among other things, America's profoundest student of political philosophy. Thomas Jefferson, another farmer's son, spent six years in Williamsburg, free of practical concerns, absorbing eighteenth-century thought under the eyes of several sophisticated mentors. These gentlemen, and numerous others less renowned, used the leisure that prosperity had granted them to promote in practical ways the ideals of the Enlightenment as they understood them.

These men of leisure were for the most part city bred. But this is not to say that the Enlightenment was confined to the city. Rather it was, as Daniel Boorstin puts it, "city-filtered," the cities serving as "so many separate funnels through which the bookish culture of Britain poured into the inland areas." It flowed through a variety of funnels. Newspapers carried much of the new thought. Hawkers and peddlers dispersed it in the books that weighed down their carts. The leading lights of country towns picked it up when they went to the city on business. Young city-trained men like James Wilson carried it out. Wilson, who had read deeply in Scottish and English political philosophy, studied law in John Dickinson's Philadelphia office, then traveled westward to settle among the Scotch-Irish of Carlisle. Every inland town of Pennsylvania—of every colony, for that matter—had its version of the well-read James Wilson, whose political and social views had been shaped in the seaboard cities.

Still, for all the funnels into the countryside, the Enlightenment failed to penetrate deeply, even where its findings might have been of use. Experiments in England had led to new ideas about the breeding of cattle to improve their quality, the rotation of crops to reduce soil deterioration, and the plowing of fields to boost yields. Books and newspaper essays spread the results of these experiments throughout the country, but the American farmers continued to treat the land carelessly—because, said a visiting European, "their eyes are fixed upon the present gain, and they are blind to the future"; because, said George Washington, their aim is "not to make the most they can from the land, which is, or has been cheap, but the most of the labour, which is dear. . . ." Country people remained set in their ways. Their minds clung to the seventeenth century long after city dwellers had advanced into a new era. By 1763, Carl Bridenbaugh has said, "the rivalry of the city slicker and the hayseed, so persistent a theme in American life, had made a lasting appearance."

There were, then, two colonial minds: one that tended to cling to the past and eyed change suspiciously, another that accepted the present and was willing to experiment with new methods to solve the problems it raised. The country dweller lived rooted to the soil, and his horizon seldom swept beyond the view that rimmed his farm. The city dweller lived amid change, which he could resist if he wished but could not ignore. His contacts with the world stretched far beyond the boundaries of his towns. The ships that tied up at the wharves brought Europe to his doorstep. The post office, which had been created by an act of Parliament in 1710 but which remained an ineffective organization until Franklin became deputy postmaster in 1753, put New York only thirty-three hours away from Philadelphia; where it had once taken at least three weeks to get a letter from Boston to Philadelphia, it now took only six days. Merchants and craftsmen traveled regularly between cities. Newspapers kept inhabitants posted on developments in other cities. When Boston in 1761 sought to combat a business slump by organizing a Society for Encouraging Trade and Commerce with the Province of Massachusetts Bay, merchants elsewhere heard of the project and had soon created similar organizations. Common interests and problems, Bridenbaugh has observed, "served to forge these communities into an integrated society—the only segment of colonial population so fused."

DAWN OF A NEW ERA

Outwardly, Americans in the eighteenth century lived much as they had in the past. Enemies had diminished but not vanished. ("Dr. John Mitchell is returned from Virginia," Linnaeus reports in 1746, "where he has been closely occupied for six years in collecting plants; but he was plundered in his voyage home by Spanish pirates, to the great misfortune of botany.") No signs of the industrial revolution had appeared to alter the environment. Men sowed seeds and harvested crops as they had always done. Techniques for building a house, making an iron pot, spinning wool into thread and thread into cloth remained as they had been. And the Englishness of the colonies seemed to have increased rather than diminished, for men in all colonies looked to England to set the fashion in education, science, literature, and the arts.

Inwardly, though, Americans had changed a great deal. They vested authority in personalities rather than, as in England, in institutions or traditions. As a people, they lived virtually stripped of traditions. Pomp and ceremony had been washed from their lives and plainness had been elevated into a virtue. The rigid class structure of England had degenerated into a cliché observed in form but not practice. Leadership was open to anyone who had the wit and ability to assert it. The poor no longer dreamed of holding to the station to which they had been born; "The most opulent families, in our memory," said Cadwallader Colden, "have arisen from the lowest rank of the people." The facts of American life no longer fit the European pattern. Together the Great Awakening and the Enlightenment broke apart what remained of the old pattern and laid the mold for the new one, which by the eve of the Revolution had worked its effect on all sides of American culture.

Education

The first of a flock of colleges to emerge from the Great Awakening came in 1746 when the College of New Jersey (Princeton) received a royal charter, the first granted by the crown to a non-Anglican school. The College of Philadelphia (University of Pennsylvania), founded in 1740 and unique for being America's first nondenominational college, was chartered in 1755. Brown, a Baptist school, received a charter in 1764 that called for "free, absolute, and uninterrupted liberty of conscience" to be enjoyed by students and faculty alike forever. Queen's College (Rutgers) came into being in 1766 as part of the Dutch Reformed Church's effort to prepare young men "for the ministry and other good offices." Dartmouth, which grew out of Eleazar Wheelock's Indian School, was chartered in 1769 and shaped to create a reservoir of ministers for New Light Congregationalism. King's College (Columbia), whose charter was granted in 1754, was the single school that did not owe its creation to the awakening. The charter called for an Anglican president but also for a board of governors drawn from diverse faiths.

These colleges resembled those founded in the seventeenth century in that legal responsibility for their affairs rested with a mixed board of ministers and laymen. The quality of the new as well as the old schools, however, was largely determined by its president. Samuel Johnson shaped the early character of King's College, William Smith that of the College of Philadelphia, and Samuel Davies that of the College of New Jersey. These new colleges also, of course, had the power to grant degrees, which in England resided solely with Oxford and Cambridge Universities. And, unlike the English universities, they were, as Daniel Boorstin has noted, "concerned more with the diffusion than with the advancement or perpetuation of learning." But colleges founded during or after the Great Awakening differed from their seventeenth-century predecessors in several ways that gave an entirely new shape to higher education in America. None was controlled by an established church, nor was any supported by a colonial government. Men of diverse faiths sat on the governing boards of all. All but the College of Philadelphia were tied to a particular denomination, but all welcomed students regardless of their religious background.

The Great Awakening's de-emphasis of sectarian issues helped promote religious tolerance among the new colleges. Another, more practical, matter also entered in. The increasing religious diversity of the population made it impossible for any colonial government to join with a single denomination in an educational project, and yet no denomination was either rich enough or had a sufficient reservoir of competent students to keep a college running. The financial problem was solved by widespread appeals for money; fund-raising campaigns were often conducted through the churches associated with a particular school, but equally often they were directed at the public at large, which in effect made the new colleges from the beginning similar to the "gathered" or voluntary churches that had come to typify the religious scene in America. Recruiting campaigns underscored the schools' eagerness for students regardless of their religious affiliation. "Once publicly committed to non-sectarian conduct," Richard Hofstadter has said, "the schools were mortgaged to it as an ideal."

Where American conditions forced changes in the academic structure as it had been inherited from England, changes were made; but tampering was held to a minimum. Reverend James Maury from his Virginia parish ridiculed the emphasis on Latin and Greek. This was a sensible curriculum for a British nobleman whose vast incomes "warrant his indulging himself in the enjoyment of that calm retreat from the bustle of the world," but for the Virginia farmer, Maury advised a sound grounding first in the English language and its literature, then in practical subjects like geography, history, and mathematics. Franklin held similar views and persuaded William Smith, whom he had enticed from New York to become provost of the College of Philadelphia, to put such a program into operation. But the innovations achieved little; the classical curriculum remained inviolate throughout the colonies. Whatever changes occurred "came through accretion rather than rejection of the past tradition," Robert Middlekauff has remarked. "The old was kept; new practical subjects were added on."

The colleges absorbed the Enlightenment at a varying pace. John Locke's *Essay on Human Understanding* appeared in the Harvard curriculum in 1742, in Yale's in 1750. Harvard welcomed the first professor of natural philosophy when John Winthrop (great-grandson of Massachusetts Governor John Winthrop) joined the faculty in 1738, but it was not until 1770 that Yale created a similar professorship, which, said a local paper, would help "dissipate superstitions, chimeras, and old women's fables, which are the natural attendants of ignorance, and the offspring of overheated imaginations." These new professors varied from John Winthrop, who was the most distinguished American astronomer of his day and kept his teaching confined strictly to science, to William Small at

William and Mary, who taught history, ethics, rhetoric, and belles-lettres along with natural philosophy. The arrival of an instructor in science tended to cause concern within a college: he was usually the first layman added to the faculty, for few clerics were sufficiently well grounded in mathematics to teach the field; the novelty and complexity of the subject forced out old methods of rote learning and led to the introduction of the lecture system; finally, these men brought to college education for the first time the idea that "it was the business of the mind to discover things hitherto unknown."

The colleges were contented, however, for the most part, to diffuse the known rather than to experiment with the unknown. They continued to regard themselves as centers for educating men for the church, even though by 1740 less than half those who were graduated entered the ministry; by the time of the Revolution, the number had dropped to around 25 per cent. The fields of medicine and law were attracting more and more young men. John Adams' approach to a career had much that was typical about it. As the eldest son and the family's tithe to God, he entered Harvard expecting to become a minister. Somewhere along the way, as he read Locke and listened to the lectures of Professor Winthrop, he lost interest in the church. Upon graduation he took a teaching post in Worcester, and after a year spent considering his future, he decided to enter law. He read for a time with a Worcester lawyer, then, after further reading on his own, he asked Jeremiah Gridley, one of Boston's most eminent attorneys, "what steps to take for an introduction to the practice of law in this county." Gridley said there was only one—to get sworn in by the courts—and that he would ease the way by serving as Adams' patron. He went on to state what Adams probably already knew—that "the difficulties of the profession are much greater here than in England." There, it was divided among specialists—barristers, who were trained in the Inns of Court and monopolized practice in the High Courts; attorneys, who prepared cases for court but could not plead them; solicitors, who could neither prepare nor plead cases but only handle routine matters like wills, deeds, and the like; and notaries, who authenticated legal documents. "A lawyer in this country," said Gridley, "must study common law, and civil law, natural law, and admiralty law; and must do the duty of a counsellor, a lawyer, an attorney, a solicitor, and even of a scrivener." Prior to 1769, he had achieved these skills much as Adams would, by plugging his way through the turgid prose of Sir Edward Coke's *Coke on Littleton, Coke on Magna Charta,* Coke's *Reports.* After 1769, Blackstone's *Commentaries on the Laws of England,* which has been called "the most ambitious and most successful effort ever made to reduce the disorderly overgrowth of English law to an intelligible and learnable system," became the popular textbook. The wide use of these English works spread common-law doctrine throughout the colonies but not to the point where local distinctions were eliminated. As late as the end of the eighteenth century, Thomas Jefferson, writing as a Virginia lawyer, lumped the law of Bermuda, Barbados, and Massachusetts all under the heading of "foreign law."

Medical education during the first half of the eighteenth century resembled that for the law. Dr. William Douglass, for a time Boston's single formally trained practitioner, said in 1753 that "frequently there is *more danger* from the physician than from the distemper"; occasionally, he added, "nature gets the better of the doctor, and the patient recovers." According to Richard Shryock there were some thirty-five hundred practicing doctors in America on the eve of the Revolution. The large majority of them drew what they knew about medicine from such popular handbooks as *Every Man his Own Doctor; or, the Poor Planter's Physician* (1734). Less than four hundred had been trained in any formal way, such as an apprenticeship in another doctor's office. Less than two hundred held medical degrees, and all these had been obtained abroad, for no American college offered a course of study in medicine. Dr. John Morgan, one of nearly a hundred Americans who had received an M.D. from the University of Edinburgh prior to the Revolution, in 1765 prodded the College of Philadelphia into creating an embryonic medical school. King's College, urged on by another Edinburgh graduate, Dr. Samuel Bard, followed suit in 1768, as did Harvard in 1783.

The college curriculum remained aristocratic in tone and content throughout the eighteenth century. College instruction gave a man the intellectual background to qualify as a gentleman; he must look elsewhere for training that would help him earn a living. The medical school was the colleges' sole concession to practicality. (Even here, if Dr. Morgan had had his way, social distinctions would have been preserved, for he wanted to duplicate the British pattern that divided medicine into specialties—the physician [socially superior, university-trained M.D.], the surgeon [apprentice-trained and called "Mr."], and the apothecary—but the three had too long been blended in America for the innovation to take root.) Courses in "useful" subjects were offered only in private schools on the secondary level. After 1750, when the expanding economy increased the need for skilled people, schools that had once taught only Latin and Greek began to offer courses in surveying, bookkeeping, navigation, and similarly practical subjects.

Secondary education in the eighteenth century did not follow the pattern that had been laid down in New England. Penn's Frame of Government in 1682 assumed that provincial government would "erect and

order all public schools," but nothing came of the provision. State-supported education continued to flourish throughout New England, but in
the Middle Colonies the private or, more often than not, denominational
school dominated the scene. Southern planters depended on tutors to
teach their children the rudiments; some tutors collected youngsters from
the surrounding plantations into an informal school. Jefferson learned the
basics of Latin and Greek in a school run by Reverend Maury. Women
rarely figured in the educational plans of an eighteenth-century American
family; it was a man's world, and the woman's role remained what it had
always been—simply to serve in it.

Science

Men outside more than those within the colleges searched nature for
things unknown in eighteenth-century America. They sought through
their investigations for "useful knowledge," but such knowledge for them
did not have to have an immediate utilitarian value. Franklin expected
nothing practical to come from his studies in electricity. Cadwallader
Colden, with no thought of the immediate usefulness of his efforts, spent
years pondering the cause of gravitation, a question that had baffled Newton (and Colden, too, though he died believing he had found the answer).
James Logan, among the first in America to puzzle out the *Principia
Mathematica,* never sought to produce anything of practical benefit to
mankind. These natural philosophers, like all philosophers, searched only
for truth, which in their terms meant the natural laws underlying the
universe. Although they were not utilitarians, they were confident that
ultimately something of practical benefit to mankind would emerge from
their work; meanwhile, it pleased them to concentrate on what today
would be called pure research.

Newton had ordered the universe. Now the earth, too, had to be
ordered, and to that end men in the eighteenth century began to collect,
describe, and classify all natural things. America, prodded and encouraged by Europe, joined the enterprise with enthusiasm. Peter Collinson,
a London merchant whose ships called regularly at American ports, did
more than anyone to rouse interest in the colonies in natural history.
From his London office he introduced amateur botanists in all parts of
America to one another by mail. More than that, he saw that the specimens his correspondents shipped to him reached the right people—Sir
Hans Sloane, president of the Royal Society; John Frederick Gronovius,
Holland's great botanist; Linnaeus, who from Sweden, "that fag end of
the world," was seeking to create a classificatory system that would cover
the whole range of life—and these men in turn began their own correspondence with Americans.

Natural history was an appropriate field for Americans to explore, for no specialized or academic training was required. John Bartram, for instance, was a "downright plain country man" who knew no Latin and almost nothing about the classification of plants. He was a "wonderful observer" and more "collector than student," as contemporaries put it, yet all agreed that he was the greatest botanist of colonial America. Peter Kalm, a student of Linnaeus' who made a field trip to America, said that Bartram's published journals revealed less than "a thousandth part of the great knowledge which he has acquired." James Logan, whose interest in botany led to experiments with maize that revealed the fertilizing role of pollen, encouraged Bartram first. Peter Collinson soon after helped to cut Bartram free from his farm by subsidizing wide-ranging field trips, which took him from the Great Lakes to Florida. Collinson arranged for the sale of seeds and plants that Bartram sent him either to botanists or to noblemen eager to have American plants growing in their great gardens. (It is said that the number of American plants grown in England doubled during the years of Bartram's travels.) In 1765 through Collinson's doing Bartram was appointed the king's botanist and given £50 a year to continue his work.

Other American naturalists were more sophisticated than Bartram. New York had Cadwallader Colden. Linnaeus called him *Summus Perfectus,* named a plant after him, and published part of his adept description and classification of plants on the Colden estate in New York. John Clayton, who supported himself as a county clerk in Virginia, provided the specimens that Gronovius assembled into *Flora Virginica,* the first systematic compendium of American botany. Dr. John Mitchell, also of Virginia, discovered twenty-one new genera of plants before he returned to London. (Mitchell later achieved renown for his Map of the British and French Dominions of North America [1775], whose accuracy made it the standard map through the rest of the eighteenth century.) Dr. Alexander Garden of South Carolina, after whom Linnaeus named the gardenia, was perhaps the ablest of the lot. His ability to classify plants was notable. Several times he bested even Linnaeus, and one of his classifications, though rejected by Linnaeus, has since been confirmed as correct. (Dr. Garden left America at the time of the Revolution; back in London, he became vice-president of the Royal Society.)

A good number of botanists of early America—Colden, Mitchell, and Garden, for example—were European-trained physicians. In a day when men searched for remedies in the kingdom of plants, botany and medicine went nicely together. Also, the physician and the naturalist shared a similar approach to their specialties. Earlier physicians viewed an illness as a disturbance in the bodily balance of the four fluids, or humors—blood; choler, or yellow bile; phlegm; and melancholy, or black bile. Specific diseases were known—smallpox was one, the great pox (syphilis) was another—but, as a rule, doctors dealt only with such general states of ill health as distemper, biliousness, or fever. During the late seventeenth century, an English physician named Thomas Sydenham suggested that diseases, like plants, could be sorted out and classified, and that once this had been done a specific remedy could be found for a specific disease. Sydenham's views, like other enlightened ideas of the age, did not supplant old attitudes; they were tacked onto the humoral conception of disease and through a good part of the eighteenth century physicians in both Britain and America tried desperately to reconcile the two approaches to medicine.

The latest developments in European medicine came quickly to America through the transactions of the Royal Society and with physicians who had been trained in British universities. The best American practitioners differed from those of Great Britain in only one essential way: Americans often relied on Indian remedies, which by the early eighteenth century had in many instances been found to be effective, though no one could fathom why. Cotton Mather, for instance, recommended the partridge berry for dropsy, "throat-weed" for a sore throat, "bleeding root" for jaundice. It may be that the success of these Indian potions made Mather more receptive to folk cures in general than a sophisticated, Edinburgh-trained gentleman like Dr. William Douglass. When Mather in 1714 read a letter published by the Royal Society describing a practice among the common people in Turkey of inoculation against smallpox, he was reminded of an earlier conversation with his slave Onesimus, whom Mather regarded as "a pretty intelligent fellow." Onesimus had said when asked if he had had smallpox, "Yes and No," adding "that he had undergone an operation which had given him something of the smallpox and would forever preserve him from it." In Mather's time smallpox killed more Americans than any other disease, and it invariably scarred for life those who survived a severe case. Mather resolved to fight the pestilence by inoculation the next time smallpox struck Boston. The day arrived in 1721 when a ship from the West Indies brought several cases into the city. At once from the pulpit and in the press he urged everyone to be inoculated. Dr. Douglass, however, called the idea insane and fought against it. (Inoculation, unlike vaccination, involved the injection of live germs into a person, and the enlightened Douglass assumed that a full-scale case of smallpox would result; reason for once was wrong. No one knew why, but only a mild case, which gave immunity, resulted.) Others railed against the idea on religious grounds: it was wrong to interfere with God's work. If He wished to punish men, then He must be allowed to have His way. But Mather persisted, and his determination persuaded Dr. Zabdiel Boylston to go along with him. Unfortunately, several people who were inoculated only after they had been exposed to smallpox came down with severe cases, which strengthened opposition. A bomb was thrown through Mather's window with a note attached: "Cotton Mather, you Dog; Dam you: I'l enoculate you with this, with a pox to you."

The epidemic lasted out the year 1721. Nearly half of Boston's 12,000 people got the disease; 844, or nearly 15 per cent of those infected, died. Of the 242 persons inoculated by Boylston, only 6, or 2.5 per cent died. The statistics, however, did not convince Douglass nor most of his colleagues; and a venomous war of words ensued for years, with a majority of the conservative clergy, curiously, favoring inoculation and a majority of the doctors opposing it. Eventually, statistics overwhelmed the opposition and by mid-century the proponents of inoculation had won the battle in the cities of the North. Headway in the South, where doctors were fewer, came more slowly. The gains made stemmed from men like Jefferson, who in 1762 traveled up to Philadelphia to be inoculated and in the process learned enough about the technique to perform the "operation" later on his slaves at Monticello and to oversee it on neighboring plantations. The successful outcome of the inoculation controversy, says Richard Shryock, who with Otho Beall was the first to remind historians of Cotton Mather's significance in medicine, marked the beginning of preventive medicine in the Western World, "and the part played therein by Mather and Boylston may be viewed as the chief medical contribution made by Americans prior to the nineteenth century."

Cotton Mather's interest in science went far beyond medicine. His stream of letters to the Royal Society, which admitted him as a member in 1713, discussed rainbows and rattlesnakes and everything else under God's sun that could in any way be related to natural philosophy. Correspondence with European scientists alleviated but did not cure the pains of intellectual isolation Mather and others interested in science endured in America. They yearned for libraries stocked with the latest works on natural philosophy, for scientific journals of their own, and especially, as one man put it, for "the conversations of the learned." Mather sought to fill the gap in part when in 1683 he formed the Philosophical Society, which he hoped would lead to discussions "upon improvements in [natural] philosophy and additions to the stores of natural history." The Junto, a discussion group Franklin later formed in Philadelphia, was patterned on Mather's model. But these were local, rather than intercolonial, societies. Cadwallader Colden in 1728 suggested the creation of "a voluntary society for the advancing of knowledge" that would draw together natural philosophers from all colonies. America was still too young, however, for the idea, and it died on the air.

The Library Company of Philadelphia, a subscription library that developed in 1731 out of Franklin's Junto, was the first well-conceived institution in America to promote scientific interests. It did not cater to an intellectual elite, who Franklin knew were too few at the time to support such an institution; it drew strength and money from everyone in Philadelphia interested in science. Within a decade of its founding, the library's collection of scientific works had become the largest and finest in America, and generous lending privileges made the volumes available to virtually everyone. Along with books, the library welcomed anything that tended to encourage "the improvement of knowledge"—an air pump from John Penn, stuffed snakes, a telescope, an Indian chief's robe. The library's success encouraged others, and by the eve of the Revolution every city and many towns had subscription libraries of their own. Once again in a land where governments were frail and great fortunes few, the voluntary organization had chalked up a notable achievement.

The obviously large audience of those interested in science persuaded Franklin in 1743 to propose the founding of an intercolonial group to be called the American Philosophical Society. This time he moved too swiftly, and it was not until 1769 that the society became organized on an intercolonial footing. Even then, the society's interests tended to center on one aspect of science—natural history—and those interested in physics, astronomy, and other areas of physical science continued to depend on Europe for guidance and inspiration. Few colonial Americans shone in physical science, for few, as Daniel Boorstin has remarked, had the technical foundations or the professional learning required. Cadwallader Colden, for example, distinguished himself in botany without prior training; his attempt to explain the cause of gravity ended as ludicrous, for he knew nothing about theoretical physics nor the recent work of such eminent European scientists as Euler, Huygens, and Leibnitz.

Those attracted to the physical sciences endured another handicap—the continuing belief that lightning and thunder, earthquakes, and other natural events were manifestations of God's wrath. Lightning rods, for instance, were impious, for they wrested "the bolt of vengeance out of His hand." A Boston divine was convinced that those "points of iron" invented by "the sagacious Mr. Franklin" had, by charging the soil with "the electrical substance out of the air," caused the great earthquake that struck New England in 1755. John Winthrop, one of the few distinguished American physical scientists of his day and the single academic from the colonies to be elected to the Royal Society, did his best to counter such ideas. Winthrop's work as a mathematician, astronomer, and physicist was more than competent, and whereas his research cannot be ignored—especially in astronomy, where he was the first to suggest a connection between sunspots and the aurora borealis—it was as a teacher of science that he shone. His extraordinarily clear lectures and essays on comets, earthquakes, and sunspots did much to dispel superstitions about nature among educated laymen.

Esteem for Winthrop prompted Harvard and Massachusetts in 1761 jointly to sponsor America's first scientific expedition—to Newfoundland to observe the transit of Venus across the face of the sun, an event that, when accurately observed (this one was not, either by Winthrop or European scientists), would make it possible to calculate the earth's distance from the sun. Observations for a second transit of Venus in 1769, this time visible throughout most of the northern colonies, were publicized and supervised by David Rittenhouse, America's second luminary among physical scientists. Rittenhouse, a Pennsylvania clock maker by trade, equaled, but did not exceed, Winthrop in talent and learning, yet contemporaries reckoned Rittenhouse among the world's greatest scientists. Jefferson, for one, called him a "mechanical genius." Brooke Hindle, the most knowledgeable historian of science in early America, concludes more quietly that he had a "precision of thought that occasionally led to striking insight." Rittenhouse was the sort of scientist who appealed to Americans —genial, modest, civic-minded, and of great practical ingenuity. He was self-taught, and though, as a visiting Frenchman observed, "not a mathematician of the class of the Eulers and the D'Alemberts," none except Winthrop excelled him in this field. His orreries, accurate and intricate working models of the solar system, charmed students at the College of Philadelphia and the College of New Jersey. During the Revolution he devised imaginative ways to speed the production of cannons and ammunition. His talents and qualities did not, however, make him a great scientist.

That honor belonged alone to Benjamin Franklin, the single scientific genius produced by America during the colonial period. Science for Franklin "was the one mistress to whom he gave himself without reserve." His practical inventions—the Franklin stove, bifocal spectacles, the lightning rod, the grocery store's "long arm," which he devised to pull books from his library shelves—bear little relation to his interest in science. Franklin believed with Bacon that "works themselves are of greater value as pledges of truth than as contributing to the comforts of life." He retired from business to pursue research in electricity. His experiments with the kite flown during a thunderstorm, says I. Bernard Cohen, "constituted the first empirical proof that electrifications occur constantly in nature without the direct intervention of man." Professor Cohen, whose own research has done much to refurbish Franklin's reputation as a "pure" scientist, adds: "To Franklin was reserved the honor of bringing to the scientific world the first demonstration that there are naturally occurring electrical phenomena of significance in the world. From then onwards, no account of physical events could be considered complete if electricity were left out."

No one has bothered to estimate the number of men Franklin inspired to become scientists, but there is at least one on record. In 1771 a New England youngster named Benjamin Thompson nearly killed himself attempting to duplicate Franklin's kite experiment. He survived to become one of the great physicists of the eighteenth century, but America heaped little praise upon him; for after a tour of duty as a British spy during the Revolution, he abandoned America for Europe, where, through marriage, he became Count Rumford.

Language and Literature

By the middle of the eighteenth century, Americans differed from Englishmen in the way they spoke—a Virginian, for instance, preferred American tutors for his children "on account of pronunciation in the English language"—and to some extent in the language they used. Dr. Samuel Johnson, who had little good to say of the colonies, once came across an American book he liked, written he said, "with such elegance as the subject admits, tho' not without some mixture of the American dialect, a trace of corruption to which every language widely diffused must always be exposed."

To some degree the American dialect consisted of words that had dropped out of use in Great Britain. "Burly," "cater-cornered," "deft," "likely," "ornate," and "scant" all survived in America long after they vanished from the vernacular in England. The word "bub" for "boy," which persists today in the United States, died with the seventeenth century among the plain people of England. In the South, Negroes used "den," "dey," and "dat" for "them," "they," and "that" not because they spoke the language slovenly, but because they learned it from indentured servants and convicts fresh from England who talked that way. The dialect the Negroes learned, Edward Eggleston has said, "probably preserved much that was worst in the English of the seventeenth century." Americans preserved platitudes as well. Franklin took the seventeenth-century saying "Three may keep counsel, if two be away" and converted it into "Three may keep a secret, if two of them are dead." "Fresh fish and new come guests smell by they are three days old," printed in 1670, became, in *Poor Richard's Almanack,* "Fish and visitors stink in three days."

A Frenchman complained that Americans had not "notably enriched their native language," and for evidence he noted that they had made the "jay" into a "blue bird," the "cardinal" into a "red bird," and "every water bird is simply a duck." Curiously, he failed to spot the number of French words that had slipped into the language, especially in the North, where "chowder" (from *"chaudière"*) glorified New England's greatest dish, and *"café"* was the popular word for what today would be called a "barroom." ("When darkness came," said a Spanish visitor at the time of the Revolution, "I returned to my lodging, but on entering noticed a large gathering in the so-called 'café,'" a place, he added, where "a cup of this beverage has never been drunk.")

For the most part Americans continued to give direct descriptive names like "popcorn" and "eggplant" to new plants, but a people who dubbed an evil-smelling growth "stinkweed" and had the sense to accept the Algonquin word "skunk" could hardly be accused of failing to enrich the language. Nor did they lack inventiveness. "Branch," "fork," and "run" were created to designate various types of watercourses. The distinctiveness of American weather called for such new terms as "cold snap" and "Indian summer." A small craft that leaped about on the water became a "catboat" and another, more graceful, became a "schooner." ("Oh, how she scoons," a Gloucesterman is supposed to have said when he saw the first one, and the name stuck.)

Franklin remarked in 1752 that every colony had "some peculiar expressions, familiar to its own people, but strange and unintelligible to others." A visitor who asked a man how he felt heard for an answer: "Oh, mighty weak." The word "mighty," the visitor said, "is very much in fashion in this country, and its use is sometimes ridiculous, as in this instance." (He might have mentioned, too, the equally overused word "figure," as in: "I figure I'll make out.") These and similar colloquialisms, along with the slang of the day, rarely if ever turned up in print, for American authors were intent on reproducing the dignified, conventional prose of the mother country. Franklin worked to improve his writing, or so he said, by aping the style of Addison's and Steele's essays. William Livingston took the form and tone of his reforming essays in the *Independent Reflector* from those of Thomas Gordon and John Trenchard in *The Independent Whig* and *Cato's Letters*. The language of literature was that of England rather than that of America in form and style, and in some instances—notably the newspaper and almanac—in content, too.

There were twenty-three newspapers scattered throughout the colonies in 1763; approximately two-thirds of their material dealt with European affairs, and about half was lifted directly from British journals. They were not *news*papers so much as gazettes appealing to the elite. The contents were, for the most part, dull—sedate essays on education, staid reports from the capitals of Europe, listings of ship sailings and arrivals. Only the advertisements livened up the pages. (The healing powers of Maredant's antiscorbutic drops—they cured scurvy, struma, sistules, piles, ulcers, "and by purifying the blood prevent malignant humours of every kind from being thrown upon the lungs"—led to this moving testimonial in a Philadelphia paper:

I was afflicted with a most shocking leprosy, attended with violent rheumatic pains, so that my life was quite miserable; I tried everything that could be thought of for my relief in vain. I am now perfectly cured by the use of Maredant's drops, as my neighbors can testify, who knew the shocking condition I was in.)

The average circulation of a paper was around fifteen hundred prior to the Stamp Act—perhaps a thousand more after that, when news stories began to center on the American scene. Copies were passed from hand to hand and from colony to colony. Although the newspapers may have done much to spread information and ideas about the colonies, they did little to enrich the language.

Nor did the almanacs, except in the rare instances when they were written by such stylists as Benjamin Franklin and Nathaniel Ames. Ames inaugurated the *Astronomical Diary and Almanac* in 1725 and continued it until his death in 1764. He assumed it entered "the solitary dwellings of the poor and illiterate, where the studied ingenuity of the learned writer never comes," and to that end he filled the pages with proverbs ("There are three faithful friends—an old wife, an old dog, and ready cash."), uplifting selections from Addison, Dryden, Milton, and Pope, and such practical matters as tide charts and, of course, weather predictions. (Ames took the business of forecasting lightly. He set the tone for one volume by announcing that "about the beginning of the year expect plenty of rain and snow.") The wit and style of Ames's and Franklin's almanacs were rare; most authors avoided originality and turned out routine productions solely for profit.

Writing of quality, with style and depth to it, continued to come during the first half of the eighteenth century mainly from men of religion. One of the greatest, John Wise of Ipswich, Massachusetts, made his mark defending the congregational ways of worship in *The Churches Quarrel Espoused* (1710) and in *Vindication of the Government of New-England Churches* (1717). Democracy, said Reverend Wise, gave the churches a government "most agreeable with the light of nature," and he added that "the end of all good government is to cultivate humanity, and promote the happiness of all, and the good of every man in all his rights, his life, liberty, estate, honour, etc., without injury or abuse to any." A generation later Reverend Jonathan Mayhew of Boston extended Wise's use of natural law to the political arena in his *Discourse on Unlimited Submission* (1750), wherein he elevated "the everlasting tables of right reason" to a position where they "cannot be repealed, or thrown down and broken like those of Moses." The early use by Wise and Mayhew of natural law to promote democratic values should not obscure their great distinction as men who wrote with force, wit, and even elegance. Of the two, Wise was the greater writer. "Upon the whole," Moses Coit Tyler has said, "no other American author of the colonial time is the equal of John Wise in the union of great breadth of power and thought with great splendor of style; and he stands almost alone among our early writers for the blending of a racy and dainty humor with impassioned earnestness."

Wise and Mayhew turned to Europe for their arguments, but their writing ended by being thoroughly American, an expression of what a contemporary called the "intellectual light within us." That "light" varied, of course—from the garish hue of Gilbert Tennent's *The Danger of an Unconverted Ministry* (1740), one of the most powerful sermons of the day, to the pure intensity found in the Quaker John Woolman's *Journal* (1774) and in such essays of his as *Some Considerations on the Keeping of Negroes* (1754). Unquestionably the greatest of the religious writers was Jonathan Edwards. The thought of Edwards must be left to the philosophers, but a literary historian may be called in to judge the quality of his prose. "He had," says Tyler, "the fundamental virtues of a writer— abundant thought, and the utmost precision, clearness, and simplicity in the utterance of it; his pages, likewise, hold many examples of bold, original, and poetic imagery; and though the nature of his subjects, and the temper of his sect, repressed the exercise of wit, he was possessed of wit in an extraordinary degree, and of the keenest edge."

Clergymen continued, as in the seventeenth century, to concern themselves with the American past, and here again, as before, New England led the field. Cotton Mather's *Magnalia Christi Americana, or the Ecclesiastical History of New England* (1702) saw the past through the lives of New England's great divines, though he did find room for a magnificent sketch of Sir William Phips. Mather's fat volumes were soon followed by another equally prolix work—Thomas Prince's *Chronological History of New England in the Form of Annals* (1736), which meandered through several hundred pages before arriving at the year 1630, where it ended. Prince worked hard for accuracy ("I have done my utmost, first to find out the truth, and then to relate it in the clearest order."), but the virtue vanished in a stream of dull prose only occasionally relieved by a lively sentence. The clergy lost its monopoly over New England's past soon after Prince's work was published, but the quality of historical writing did not improve. Dr. William Douglass' *Summary, His-*

torical and Political of . . . the British Settlements in North America (1748–1753) collected his prejudices (he hated Indians, Frenchmen, Whitefield, medical quacks, paper money, and anyone who favored inoculation), and the work survives as the revelation of a personality rather than as history. The single distinguished work to emerge out of eighteenth-century New England was Thomas Hutchinson's *History of the Colony of Massachusetts Bay,* the first volume of which appeared in 1764 and the second, after an obliging townsman had gathered the manuscript from among the debris of Hutchinson's sacked home, in 1767. The style is plain without being plodding and the narrative as fair and full as the materials then available would allow. Hutchinson may have failed to comprehend the New England experience, but no one of the day came closer than he to succeeding.

Virginia, though its past was less fully recorded, gave almost as much attention to history as Massachusetts. Robert Beverley opened the century with *The History and Present State of Virginia* (1705)—a short, readable volume, remarkable for its sharp, clear style, its reasonably detached attitude toward the past (except for Bacon's Rebellion, in which Beverley's father sided with Governor Berkeley), and its extraordinary friendly and informed account of Indians and their way of life. Reverend Hugh Jones' *Present State of Virginia* (1724) offered, as its title indicates, less a history than an often vivid, sometimes sarcastic, and always perceptive report designed to promote support in England for Virginian enterprises. William Byrd's *History of the Dividing Line Run in the Year 1728* (first published in 1841) was in the main an amusing account by a sophisticated gentleman of life in the backwoods of North Carolina. The first and only work to document in detail the early history of Virginia was that of William Stith, an Anglican clergyman and president of William and Mary. Stith's *History of the First Discovery and Settlement of Virginia* (1747) got no further than 1624, but his accounts of the London Company, of John Smith's role in the settlement of Jamestown ("I take him to have been a very honest man and a strenuous lover of truth"), and of the massacre of 1622 were done with such authority that they became the standard interpretations for Virginians well into the nineteenth century.

The Middle Colonies lacked a Stith or Hutchinson to bring order and meaning out of their pasts. Cadwallader Colden's disjointed *History of the Five Indian Nations* (1727) sought only to educate authorities at home of the Indians' importance in imperial politics. William Smith's desire "rather to inform than please, . . . rather to be honest and dull than agreeable and false . . ." was achieved in his *History of the Province of New-York* (1757), written not really to enlighten New Yorkers of their past but to chastise British authorities for their long train of abuses against the colony.

Pennsylvania's confused and acrimonious past apparently blocked any major effort toward a history of that colony. Under the aegis of Provost William Smith (no relation to his New York namesake), however, a unique literary venture was carried out during the 1740's and 1750's. *The American Magazine and Monthly Chronicle* inaugurated by Smith lasted only a year (1757–1758), but during that time it established itself, according to Frederick Tolles, "as the most brilliant and original literary periodical in colonial America." Those who wrote for the magazine for the first time in America treated literature as an end in itself, devoid of an immediate or practical purpose. Among those encouraged by Smith were Francis Hopkinson, poet, artist, and composer; Thomas Godfrey, whose *Prince of Parthia* (1758) became the first drama by an American to be professionally performed; and Nathanial Evans, a poet who set a tone for future poets by condemning America as a land

> Where few the muse can relish;
> Where all the doctrine now that's told
> Is that a shining heap of gold
> Alone can man embellish.

Belles-lettres failed to take root in pre-Revolutionary America. Literature, especially after 1750, when the clergy faded into the background, became virtually indistinguishable from journalism. Franklin, the best of the lot, nearly always wrote to promote some immediate, practical project —a stove, a hospital, a political maneuver. True, he could venture into other areas—the bawdy (*Old Mistresses Apologue*), the homespun (*The Way to Wealth*), science (*Experiments and Observations on Electricity . . .*), the hoax (*A Witch Trial at Mount Holly*), and, of course, autobiography—for Franklin was easily the most skilled, polished, and prolific writer of his day. Franklin, the printer who had had to scrabble for a living, missed only one side of American life in his writing. It lacked, Leon Howard has remarked, "that peculiar quality sometimes called 'American idealism' and often associated with such of his younger contemporaries as Thomas Jefferson." That "peculiar quality" had been there in American literature during the first half of the eighteenth century; it would return again only after 1765, when, as far as the colonists were concerned, the American way of life seemed endangered.

The Arts

The church spires that began in the eighteenth century to pierce the skyline of American villages and towns offered visible signs of the country's growing wealth, of the increased skill and ingenuity of its craftsmen, and of the continuing influence of English architectural styles. A good number of the spires resembled those designed by Sir Christopher Wren, and those that did not were generally lifted from the work of other English architects, but the American craftsman borrowed rather than made slavish copies. He built with the cheapest material available—wood, stone, or brick. His spires, like the churches they topped, were modest in height, and their simple designs conformed to the capabilities of the workmen. The church spires, like all the architecture in America, differed from the English pattern in a fundamental way—they were the product of amateur architects; no one in colonial America earned his living by designing buildings.

What has been forgotten, John A. Kouwenhoven has said, is that the art tradition of America

is a tradition which was developed by people "who didn't know anything about art" but had to deal with materials of a new and unprecedented environment—a tradition which not only modified and obstructed the traditions carried over from western Europe but which contributed directly . . . to the evolution of new forms of artistic expression.

The colonists, of course, did not see it that way. They believed that their art and architecture, like their politics and government, their society, and their literature duplicated rather than resembled England's. They were convinced, for instance, that the church spires, the homes, and the public buildings they erected during the eighteenth century reproduced the so-called Georgian style of architecture then the fashion in England.

Georgian architecture evolved from the work of Andrea Palladio, an Italian who, out of the classical forms of Greece and Rome, had created colonnaded mansions with a huge central block balanced by adjoining wings, the whole set in a suitably harmonious arrangement of lawns and gardens. Inigo Jones introduced a variation of the Palladian style into seventeenth-century England. The classical overtones and the emphasis on balance and harmony appealed to an age steeped in ancient literature and trained by Newton to appreciate an ordered universe. Christopher Wren, along with William Kent, James Gibbs, and others, added further refinements to Palladio that resulted in what has been loosely called the Georgian style. Americans received the new style in some instances directly from the men who helped create it. Sir Christopher Wren inspired or, as tradition has it, designed the main building of the College of William and Mary in Williamsburg and perhaps, too, Virginia's governor's palace and the capitol, which Reverend Hugh Jones called "the best and most commodious pile of its kind I have seen or heard of." The English architect John Hawks crossed the ocean with North Carolina's Governor Tryon to design the palace at New Bern. The architect for St. Paul's Chapel in New York, Thomas McBean, had worked under James Gibbs in England. More often, however, books rather than men brought English designs to the colonies. The builder for the First Baptist Meeting House in Providence lifted the plan for his steeple from a plate in Gibbs's *Book of Architecture*. Drawings in *Palladio Londiniensis* inspired the designs for a number of Virginia's mansions, Jefferson's among them. Peter Harrison, the ablest American architect of the day, borrowed the façade for his Redwood Library in Newport from Palladio, the doorway from William Kent's *Designs of Inigo Jones,* and the bookcase panels from Batty Langley's *Treasury of Design.*

Borrowings from a common source gave a unity to American architecture it might otherwise have lacked in an age when a man's "country" was his colony. Still, each region managed to impress a shape of its own onto the forms all had borrowed. New England's vernacular, as Oliver Larkin puts it, "was crisp and emphatic." The sharp, clean lines of old did not vanish in the more opulent buildings of the eighteenth century. Wood was still the favored building material; the floor plan was still one where a central hall divided the four rooms on each floor into two balanced wings. The New Englander's taste for fine things went into the details of his house—a beautifully carved pediment over the doorway, an inlaid floor in the parlor, French designed wallpapers, paneling, crimson damask curtains—and, outside the house, into the landscaping. The churches in most towns and villages acquired a steeple, otherwise they changed little. New England's single bold and imaginative creation was Peter Harrison's synagogue of the Congregation Jeshuat Israel in Newport, which, despite a pedestrian exterior, had, says Wayne Andrews, "if not the most beautiful interior of any church in America, at least the only miraculous ecclesiastical interior of colonial times."

A New Englander found the houses of Philadelphia cramped and small. ("I say, give me a wooden one, that I may swing a cat around in. . . .") Outwardly, the houses of the well-to-do there were much alike—long, narrow piles of light red brick two or three stories high—for here again men preferred to lavish their wealth on the interiors. The exterior of Samuel Powel's home differed little from its neighbors, but within were some of the most richly and tastefully furnished rooms on the continent. Philadelphia's collection of public buildings was the most impressive in America, but most visitors found all—the hospital, the prison, the great colonnaded public market, even the statehouse—"greatly lacking in elegance and ornament." Philadelphians leaned as heavily as other American builders upon the work of English architects—Andrew Hamilton appears to have borrowed from at least two plates in James Gibbs's *Book of Architecture* for his design of the statehouse—but the desire to combine "the least expensive" with "the most neat and commodious" tended to promote a Quaker-like plainness in their buildings.

Virginia gentlemen, with a great reservoir of enslaved and often highly skilled labor at their command, worried less about the cost of their homes and public buildings. The designs they drew upon were, of course, like those of New England and the Middle Colonies, inspired by English models. William Byrd's magnificent Westover, for example, with its pedimented doorway, its hipped roof, and its twin chimneys, differed in detail rather than form from, say, James MacPherson's Mount Pleasant outside Philadelphia. But Virginians did not borrow slavishly from England any more than other Americans did. Although Jefferson drew heavily on Palladio and English variations of his work, he then proceeded to refine and modify his design ("They was forty years at work on that house before Mr. Jefferson stopped building," his slave Isaac once said) until Monticello ended by being something entirely his, belonging to no "school," reflective of no single style.

Not all the gentlemen of the Chesapeake region, however, lived in such splendid dwellings as Jefferson and Byrd. George Washington's Mount Vernon was considered by a knowledgeable contemporary to be for the most part "in very indifferent taste," a home "by no means above what could be expected in a plain English country gentleman's house of £500 or £600 a year." A distinctive feature that set both Mount Vernon and Monticello apart from the homes of wealthy northerners was less the style than the setting. The plantation owner's home formed the core of a village. Monticello, for instance, housed nearly the number of people of nearby Charlottesville. Kitchens, stables, storehouses, and sheds spread outward from the main building, and behind these lay the rambling quarters of the slaves.

The country homes of South Carolina's gentlemen did not share this characteristic. A plantation in the Carolina low country consisted of small, usually noncontiguous units of around two hundred acres; slaves lived on the unit they worked rather than at a centrally located spot. The planter's house was invariably more modest than his Virginian counterpart's. Whatever care and money he wished to lavish on a dwelling more often went into his town house in Charleston, where he and his family spent a good deal of their time, especially during the torrid heat of summer. The Charleston gentleman's house was influenced by English styles—Ralph Izard's was said to have been designed by the English architect Thomas Hope, and such public buildings as St. Michael's Church clearly reflect the work of James Gibbs—but climate forced certain refinements. Houses were placed endwise to the street, and the long porches and galleries faced gardens, much as they did in West Indian homes, in order to catch the available breeze; rooms were spacious and ceilings high.

Early in the century, the well-to-do of Charleston, as well as those in the northern cities, imported nearly all the furnishings for their homes from England. After 1750, American craftsmen, many of them fresh from Europe, turned out products so skillfully fashioned that they compared favorably with the best produced in England. Philadelphia became the center for some of the best-made and -designed furniture of the eighteenth century. Its cabinetmakers appear to have "invented" the spidery, but sturdy, Windsor chair, which by the end of the colonial period had become the most widely used piece of furniture in America. When Thomas Chippendale published *The Gentleman and Cabinet-maker's Director* (1754), he gave craftsmen an incomparable handbook, and before long Philadelphia workmen had developed the distinctive and distinguished "Philadelphia Chippendale" style. By the eve of the Revolution, men who had been trained in furniture-making in Philadelphia had fanned out through the colonies, and a lucrative industry, once dominated by English craftsmen, had been nearly completely taken over by Americans.

Something similar occurred in other crafts. In silversmithing, Joseph Richardson of Philadelphia produced work that experts today consider superior to anything turned out in England; and Paul Revere, an outstanding silversmith, engraver, and also maker of false teeth that looked "as well as the natural," was sufficiently eminent to sit for a Copley portrait. Craftsmen in brass, copper, and wood hammered and chiseled out weathervanes, figureheads, and the delicate designs for the pediments over doorways. The art of these folk, most of them anonymous craftsmen, though the work of people who "didn't know anything about art," lives on today in museums scattered across the land.

The formal art of the day, the work of professionals who considered themselves "artists" rather than craftsmen, offered little during the early part of the century to boast about. The anonymous limners of the seventeenth century for the most part vanished, to be replaced by wandering painters from Europe whose ability to imitate the styles of successful artists on the Continent and in Britain appealed to Americans. Charleston supported Jeremiah Theus, a Swiss; Maryland, the German-born Justus Englehardt Kühn; Pennsylvania, Gustavus Hesselius, a Swede. John Smibert, a Scotsman, set the tone for portrait painting in Boston from 1730 until 1748, when his eyes began to fail. Other Britishers—Joseph Blackburn, Charles Bridges, and John Wollaston, to name only the best— toured the South throughout the century. All these men were capable of good work, but their customers did not encourage their best; the elite of America cared little for art. It wanted its features preserved, and more than that, preserved in a way that resembled the style of such successful portrait painters in Britain as the famous Sir Godfrey Kneller. The artists who prospered in the colonies were those who satisfied these desires. Subjects were posed as they might have been in England—a child fondled a doe; a wife, beautifully attired, stood stiffly pointing at a flower from the regal garden that stretched out behind her; a gentleman, suitably bewigged, stood before a looped curtain through which could be seen a ship or the rolling lands of a plantation or another object that gave a quick indication of the source of his wealth. The artist who broke this pattern and sought to experiment risked his livelihood.

Slowly, however, as the century aged, young men who had been reared in America began to paint in a new way. Ralph Earl dared to show Elijah Boardman, a merchant, standing in his office, through whose open door could be seen shelves filled with bolts of cloth. He painted tough, self-made Roger Sherman sitting in an American-made Windsor chair that mirrored the strength of its occupant. Benjamin West dared to paint British soldiers in the boots and uniforms they had worn in battle. Charles Willson Peale made art of a news event when he painted the raising of a mastodon skeleton from its burying place in a marsh. John Singleton Copley had Sam Adams standing with a document clutched in one hand and pointing at another on the desk before him, obviously in the midst of a speech directed against some perfidious act of Governor Hutchinson or his minions. He placed Paul Revere sitting in his work clothes at a table on which lay the tools of his trade and a teapot he had made. Such pictures as this one of Revere, James Flexner has said, "foreshadow the Declaration of Independence. Men so unmoved by tradition and so proud of being themselves that they could glorify manual labor would not long bow the knee to a distant power."

This is not to say that the arts advanced rapidly or far during the colonial period, for they did not. But that, as far as John Adams was concerned, was the way it should be. "I must study politics and war," he once said, "that my sons may have liberty to study mathematics and philosophy, geography, natural history, and naval architecture, navigation, commerce, and agriculture, in order to give their children a right to study painting, poetry, music, architecture, statuary, tapestry, and porcelain." And this, as things worked out, was about what happened. Politics and war became the specialties of John Adams' generation.

BIBLIOGRAPHY

Colonial thought received early attention in Samuel Miller's curious, but still readable, Brief Retrospect of the Eighteenth Century (2 vols., 1803) and then historians turned to other matters. The next important treatment came with

the second volume of Moses Coit Tyler's *History of American Literature,*
1607–1765 (2 vols., 1878; pb.), which was far inferior to his study of the
seventeenth century and to his two volumes on *The Literary History of the*
American Revolution (1897). The first volume of Vernon L. Parrington's
Main Currents in American Thought (1927; pb.) gave eighteenth-century
thought in America its first distinguished and distinctive treatment. Merle
Curti followed in 1943 with *Growth of American Thought* (3rd rev. ed.,
1964), which focused on ideas as they emerged from their social and economic setting. These general accounts have more recently been supplemented
by several works that concentrate on the colonial period. Max Savelle's *Seeds*
of Liberty (1948) was one of the first to explore all sides of colonial
thought, seeking out "every important figure who flourished in the period between 1740 and 1760" in order "to find out what he was thinking, and
where possible, why he thought as he did." Soon after, Michael Kraus chose
to emphasize the cultural and intellectual ties between England and America
in *Atlantic Civilization: Eighteenth-Century Origins* (1949; pb.). Louis B.
Wright surveyed *The Cultural Life of the American Colonies, 1607–1763*
(1957; pb.). Daniel Boorstin's more interpretative, and hence more provocative, *The Americans: The Colonial Experience* (1958; pb.) excels in depict-
ing the interaction between ideas and environment. The bibliographies in
Curti, Wright, and Boorstin are especially good, and the interested student
should consult them.

The Great Awakening

Warren W. Sweett's *Religion in Colonial America* (1942) offers the fullest
account of religion in eighteenth-century America, but perhaps the best spot
for a student to start is Winthrop S. Hudson's brief survey of *American*
Protestantism (1961; pb.), of which only the first chapter and the early pages
of the second are relevant to the colonial period. H. Richard Niebuhr offers
two further general accounts, *The Social Forces of Denominationalism* (1929)
and *The Kingdom of God in America* (1937; pb.). Both Niebuhr and Hudson should be supplemented by two articles by Sidney E. Mead (which
hopefully will someday be collected along with Mead's other essays on colonial
religion in a single volume): "American Protestantism During the Revolutionary Epoch," *Church History,* 22 (1953), 279–297; and "Denominationalism: The Shape of Protestantism in America," *ibid.,* 23 (1954), 291–320.
Carl Bridenbaugh's concern with the establishment of an Anglican bishopric
in America does not prevent him from touching on other aspects of colonial
religion in *Mitre and Sceptre: Transatlantic Faiths, Ideas, Personalities, and*
Politics, 1689–1775 (1962).

Curiously, no single survey of the Great Awakening as it affected all
America has emerged out of the vast literature on the event. Nearly all the
work done discusses it from a sectional viewpoint, with well over half the
literature concentrating on New England's reception and re-creation. The best
of the New England studies is a slight, but tightly written, volume by Edwin
S. Gaustad, *The Great Awakening in New England* (1957; pb.). Gaustad's

bibliography is the latest and fullest on the New England story. C. C. Goen's detailed *Revivalism and Separatism in New England* (1962) sees the Separatist movement mainly as a frontier phenomenon. Of the many works on Jonathan Edwards, the best is Ola Elizabeth Winslow's superbly written *Jonathan Edwards, 1703–1758: A Biography* (1941; pb.). Perry Miller's *Jonathan Edwards* (1949; pb.) concerns itself with Edwards' thought. Miller's view of Edwards as "intellectually the most modern man of his age" has been attacked by Vincent Tomas in "The Modernity of Jonathan Edwards," *NEQ,* 25 (1952), 60–84; and by Thomas A. Schaefer, "Jonathan Edwards and Justification by Faith," *Church History,* 21 (1952), 55–67. The best brief collection of his writings was edited by Clarence H. Faust and Thomas H. Johnson in 1935 and currently available in paperback. A superb biographical sketch of Whitefield as well as of his tour of New England is found in Miss Winslow's volume on Edwards. Stuart C. Henry's *George Whitefield: Wayfaring Witness* (1957) is the fullest modern account of the evangelist's theology.

Charles H. Maxson's *The Great Awakening in the Middle Colonies* (1920) has been the standard work for that section, but it must now be supplemented by Leonard J. Trinterud's *The Forming of an American Tradition* (1958), which virtually eliminates the influence of Pietism, once held to be dominant, on the Great Awakening. Frederick B. Tolles writes of the Quakers and the Great Awakening in *Quakers and Atlantic Culture* (1960), and Dietmar Rothermund of "Political Factions and the Great Awakening," in *PH,* 26 (1959) 317–331. There is only one important volume on the event in the South—Wesley Gewehr's *The Great Awakening in Virginia, 1740–1790* (1930).

The American Enlightenment

It is best for a student to start with Bernard Bailyn's "Political Experience and Enlightenment Ideas in Eighteenth-Century America," *AHR,* 67 (1962), 339–351; then follow this up with Adrienne Koch's *Power, Morals, and the Founding Fathers* (pb. original) and her "Pragmatic Wisdom and the American Enlightenment," *WMQ,* 18 (1961), 313–329. Two excellent biographies are E. N. da C. Andrade's brief *Sir Isaac Newton* (1954; pb.) and Maurice Cranston's full *John Locke: A Biography* (1957). Locke's writings are available in numerous cheap editions; one of the most accessible is Isaiah Berlin, ed., *The Age of Enlightenment* (1956; pb.).

The role of the city is exhaustively explored in Carl Bridenbaugh's *Cities in Revolt: Urban Life in America, 1743–1776* (1955; pb.). S. V. James's *A People Among Peoples: Quaker Benevolence in Eighteenth-Century America* (1963) is, despite its restricted subject matter, a distinguished book on the intellectual history of colonial America. James's tight writing and his refusal to oversimplify call for slow reading, but no students will regret the effort. Herbert Morais has surveyed *Deism in Eighteenth-Century America* (1934) with competence and intelligence. The influence of Greece and Rome on enlightened Americans has been learnedly covered by Richard M. Gummere in *The American Colonial Mind and the Classical Tradition* (1963). Howard Mumford Jones gives a full account of the classical influence in colonial America in Chapter VII, "Roman Virtue," of *O Strange New World* (1964). Nothing has yet supplanted Benjamin F. Wright's standard *American Interpretations of Natural Law: A Study in the Historical Process of Political Thought* (1931). An important work on a hitherto unexplored subject is Caroline Robbins' *The Eighteenth-Century Commonwealthman: Studies in the Transmission, Development, and Circumstance of English Liberal Thought from the Restoration of Charles II Until the War with the Thirteen Colonies* (1959).

Biographical studies offer an awkward but fascinating insight into the way enlightened Americans received, modified, and used ideas from Europe in general and Great Britain in particular. Among the best are the first volume of Page Smith's study of *John Adams* (2 vols., 1963); Carl Van Doren's (1938; pb.) and Verner Crane's (1956; pb.) *Benjamin Franklin;* Albert Jay Nock's *Thomas Jefferson* (1926; pb.) and Dumas Malone's *Thomas Jefferson and the Rights of Man* (1948); Frederick B. Tolles, *James Logan* (1957); Alfred Owen Aldridge, *Man of Reason: The Life of Thomas Paine* (1959); David John Mays, *Edmund Pendleton, 1721–1803* (2 vols., 1952); and Edmund S. Morgan, *The Gentle Puritan: A Life of Ezra Stiles, 1727–1795* (1962). Numerous one-volume editions (several in paperback) are available of the writings of Adams, Franklin, and Jefferson. Milton M. Klein's excellent edition of *The Independent Reflector* (1963), a collection of essays written mainly by William Livingston in the early 1750's, offers a lively introduction to the thought of the times.

Dawn of a New Era

Historians have given little attention to secondary education in the late colonial period. The single recent work is Robert Middlekauff's *Ancients and Axioms: Secondary Education in Eighteenth-Century New England* (1963). Much has been written on the development of higher education. The best work for a student to begin with is Richard Hofstadter's incisive *Academic Freedom in the Age of the College* (1955; pb.), and the best essay is Boorstin's "Educating the Community," in *The Americans: The Colonial Experience* (1958). Boorstin's full bibliographical essay on the subject makes it needless here to do more than mention two first-rate studies that have come out since his own work—Edmund S. Morgan's biography of Ezra Stiles mentioned above and Louis L. Tucker's *Puritan Protagonist: President Thomas Clap of Yale College* (1962).

Boorstin's equally full bibliographies on colonial science and language are recommended. Dirk J. Struik's *Yankee Science in the Making* (1948; rev. in pb.) offers a sound start for the uninitiated. Brooke Hindle's exhaustive study of *The Pursuit of Science in Revolutionary America, 1735–1789* (1956) has been amplified by his biography of *David Rittenhouse* (1964). A detailed and yet to the interested reader an exciting study is I. Bernard Cohen's *Franklin and Newton: An Inquiry into Speculative Newtonian Experimental Science and Franklin's Work in Electricity as an Example Thereof* (1956).

Cohen has also published a well-edited selection of Franklin's writings in one volume (1953). Sanborn C. Brown's brief but illuminating *Count Rumford: Physicist Extraordinary* (pb. original) is a pilot volume for a fuller study. Lester S. King's *The Medical World of the Eighteenth Century* (1958) presents a picture of the quality of European medicine at the time. No similar work has yet been done for the colonies. The closest approach is Richard H. Shryock's *Medicine and Society in America, 1660–1860* (1960). A full, annotated list of *Early American Medical Imprints: A Guide to Works Printed in the United States, 1668–1820* (1961) has been published by the Department of Health, Education, and Welfare and can be purchased from the Government Printing Office for one dollar.

Essays by Louis Wright, Kenneth Murdock, and Frederick Tolles in Robert E. Spiller, *et al.*, eds., *The Literary History of the United States*, Vol. I (3 vols., 1948), discuss the state and quality of literature in eighteenth-century America; the student will find full, annotated bibliographies in Vol. III (rev. ed., 1953). The comments of modern critics and scholars on colonial literature are to be heeded but not to the point where the student shuns the work *(History of American Literature)* of the first and perhaps greatest student of early America's literary life, Moses Coit Tyler. Frank Luther Mott is the most distinguished scholar on the colonial press, and his *American Journalism . . . 1690–1940* (1941) is relevant here. Richard L. Merritt's "The Colonists Discover America: Attention Patterns in the Colonial Press, 1735–1775," *WMQ*, 21 (1964), 270–287 is an excerpt from his forthcoming *The Growth of American Community, 1735–1775.*

The basic book on the arts is Oliver W. Larkin, *Art and Life in America* (1949; rev. ed., 1960). Oskar Hagen's thorough *The Birth of the American Tradition in Art* (1940) should be supplemented with James T. Flexner's excellent *First Flowers of Our Wilderness* (1947) and *The Light of Distant Skies, 1760–1835* (1954), wherein painting is related to the life of the day and the point developed that America's early professional painters were "nurtured in a craftsman's world." Flexner has written a biography of *John Singleton Copley* (1948), and Grose Evans of Benjamin West, in *Benjamin West and the Taste of His Times* (1959).

Those intrigued by colonial architecture should begin with Hugh S. Morrison, *Early American Architecture: From the First Colonial Settlements to the National Period* (1952). The story of *Peter Harrison: First American Architect* (1949) has been well told by Carl Bridenbaugh. Bridenbaugh's comments on *The Colonial Craftsman* (1950; pb.) tie the crafts and the arts neatly together. Two recent general studies that make some perceptive comments on colonial architecture in passing are Alan Gowans' *Images of American Living* (1964) and John Burchard's and Albert Bush-Brown's *Architecture of America: A Social and Cultural History* (1963).

For further references see the *Harvard Guide*, Sections 103, "Social and Economic Development, Northern Colonies, 1713–1760"; 104, "Social and Economic Development, Southern Colonies, 1713–1760"; and 120, "Economic, Social, and Intellectual Movements [during the Revolutionary Era]."

"The Plantation"

12. Life in Eighteenth-Century America

THE NORTH
New England
The Hudson Valley
The Delaware Valley

THE SOUTH
Chesapeake Country
Carolina Country

THE BACKCOUNTRY
Settlement
Customs and Manners
Relations with the East

Distance helps to filter out distinctions and lets twentieth-century Americans see that for all the thirteen colonies' diversity, much bound them together. The colonists, however, saw mainly the differences among themselves; prior to 1763, they seldom thought of themselves as Americans. When they spoke of "my country," they occasionally meant the section they came from, but more often their country was their colony, and when they wandered over the land, they viewed the strange customs and habits much as a visiting foreigner might. A traveling New Englander found Virginia a strange land and the inhabitants' reputation for "hospitality and politeness" exaggerated. Virginians judged the people of Pennsylvania "remarkably grave and reserved; and the women remarkably homely, hard-favoured and sour." Connecticut complained of the "frauds and unfair practices" perpetrated by New York merchants. A New Yorker balked at the thought of his son going to school in Connecticut for fear he might acquire the "low craft and cunning so incident to the people of that country." A traveler in 1760 was convinced that if America ever sought independence, "there would be a civil war from one end of the continent to the other." Certainly, the chance for union among the colonies seemed slight. When the first Continental Congress assembled in 1774, John Adams found "fifty gentlemen meeting together, all strangers, who are not acquainted with each other's language, ideas, views, designs. They are therefore jealous of each other—fearful, timid, skittish." Congress and the country subdued their differences enough to win the war, but at the end, the fears and jealousies among the new states and between the sections persisted much as it had before. It would be a long time before the words "country" and "America" came to be synonymous in the minds of Americans.

THE NORTH

A Virginian who exposed himself to the strangeness of, say, Georgia or South Carolina returned home aware more than ever that he was a Virginian, but a trip above the Mason-Dixon Line broadened his allegiance from colony to section and forced him to realize that he was a Southerner, too. The Southerner saw that the way of life varied within the northern colonies much as it did in the South; he also saw that amid the diversity a unity existed that set the North apart from the South. "I found but little difference in the manner and character of the people in the different provinces I passed thro'," a touring Marylander remarked in 1744, adding that the northern colonies were "in general much better settled than the southern," and that the "air and living to the northward is likewise much preferable, and the people of a more gigantic size and make." The distinctions between North and South of course went deeper than that, and nowhere were they clearer than in New England. George Washington remarked in 1775 that the inhabitants there were "an exceeding dirty and nasty people," and though he later amended that judgment ("I do not believe that any of the states produce better men or persons capable of making better soldiers"), New England to the end remained for him, as for most Southerners, something of a foreign land.

New England

New England in the eighteenth century was still all of a piece—the same "plain, God-fearing, practical society," Henry James later called it. John Winthrop on a trip back from the grave would have found the land more crowded—a half million people inhabited the area by the mid-eighteenth century—and less holy than he had known it, but much that he had helped to shape persisted. The bulk of the people continued to scratch a living from the soil, but still New England could not feed itself; large quantities of flour and pork and other staples had to be imported from the Middle Colonies. No profitable staple crop and no mineral resources had been discovered to bolster the economy. Commerce alone brought prosperity to the region; the "triangular" trade lines laid down in Winthrop's day were essentially unchanged. The four colonies remained religiously and racially homogeneous, for little of the new blood that had poured into America since the turn of the century had been diverted into New England. Towns continued to "warn out" strangers who threatened the *status quo*. Scattered groups of Baptists, Quakers, Presbyterians, and Anglicans adulterated the landscape, but the established church everywhere—except, of course, in Rhode Island—remained Congregational. Winthrop would have been distressed to learn that Old North Church, from whose belfry the lanterns were hung in 1775 to warn Paul Revere and William Dawes of the route the British were taking to Concord and Lexington, was an Anglican church. Old North's spire on the horizon suggested that, for all the past that still persisted, the New England Way had been transmuted into something John Winthrop would have found strange and distasteful.

The economy only resembled seventeenth-century patterns. Old trade lines remained—New England vessels continued to seek out business up and down the American coast and to follow the traditional lanes to the West Indies, southern Europe, and England—but within the old framework a sharp change had occurred. New England prosperity now rested on rum. The fisheries remained important; more than five thousand men drew their living directly from the sea, and perhaps half again as many worked to keep the fleets afloat and helped to dispose of the catch. Connecticut specialized in the export of oxen and horses; Rhode Island prospered from slave trading. Lumbering kept New Hampshire solvent and that in turn fostered New England's shipbuilding industry, which every year sent something like 150 new vessels down the ways. Whaling, encouraged by a British subsidy, kept more than one hundred ships occupied. ("The ships are brigantines of about 160 tons," a traveler observed. "Their crews are in large part Indians, who are the most capable harpoonists and are generally named boat officers.") But the profits from these endeavors were tied directly to a dark, sticky substance called molasses. The rum made from molasses sustained New England's economy as well as its spirits. Rum sent to Africa brought back slaves, gold dust, and ivory. It was the article for barter in the southern coastal trade and a necessity of life for sailors aboard New England's nine hundred or more seagoing vessels.

By 1763 some 150 rum-making distilleries were operating in New

England, and approximately five-sixths of the molasses they used came from the French islands. In the competitive fishing industry, as seen before, the margin of profit often came from the sale of the "refuse" fish, for which the French offered the best market since the decline in the eighteenth century of sugar production in the British islands. (The annual import of molasses into Rhode Island alone exceeded the entire output of the British West Indies.) New England's huge deficit of balance payments for British manufactured goods was covered mainly by profits from the French island trade. Any sudden interference in this trade would have created commercial disaster for New England, yet Parliament in 1733, to please the West Indian landlords, passed a piece of restrictive legislation known as the Molasses Act, which, as seen earlier, imposed a prohibitive import duty on sugar and molasses from non-British sources.

New England in the seventeenth century had for the most part operated comfortably inside the trade and navigation system. Almost none of New England's products appeared on the enumerated list, which allowed merchants to conduct a lucrative and legal commerce in fish and lumber with southern Europe and the islands off Africa's coast. The British islands' then-productive sugar plantations offered the best markets in the Indies. The Molasses Act was the first statute to call for a basic realignment of New England's trade pattern. The merchants' reaction could have been predicted by any informed man of the day; to say they made it "the most flagrantly disregarded act between the Seventh Commandment and the Volstead Act," exaggerates only slightly. British officials were wiser than Parliament and let the law lie unused. Nonetheless, its presence on the books forced merchants into the devious habit of smuggling. Contact with the French in the Indies soon expanded to those at Cape Breton, where English manufactures were exchanged for wine, brandy, silk, and other French products. By 1763 "a settled course of traffic" had developed directly with France and was of such volume that special ships were "purchased for and fixed in this commerce only." Smuggling by the eve of the Revolution had developed into an enterprise so respectable that even the devout engaged in it without feeling uneasy.

Commerce, illegal and otherwise, nourished all New England but particularly Boston. The holdings of the city's seventeenth-century merchants seemed modest alongside the fortunes that had accumulated since then. (Thomas Boylston, for instance, was said to be worth $400,000.) Otherwise, the city had changed little. Visitors still found it "more like an old English town than any in America," and the elite still did their best to ape the English gentry. A merchant rode about in a sedan chair, "as in England," while his wife took the air in a horse-drawn chaise with a Negro at the reins. (Boston had over a thousand slaves, most of whom worked as servants.) Gentlemen wore embroidered waistcoats and ruffled shirts and their hair curled and powdered; their wives favored gowns of rich brocades and sometimes carried silk "umbrilloes" to ward off the sun. A fashion for hooped skirts died quickly when God, seemingly offended by it, visited New England with an earthquake.

A map maker noted in 1722 that Boston had forty-two streets, thirty-six lanes, twenty-two alleys, and "houses near three thousand, one thousand brick, the rest timber." Some forty wharves stretched along the waterfront. The city also had a dozen shipyards, six ropewalks, and upwards of a hundred shops where craftsmen turned out anything from silver bowls or delicate chairs to anchors, spikes, and ships' lanterns. The city appeared to thrive, yet actually, during the half century before the Revolution, Boston all but stagnated. Its population held steady at around sixteen thousand; whereas New York's and Philadelphia's shot upward. Competition from the Middle Colonies for trade that Boston had once monopolized put a crimp in the city's economy, but competition nearer to home hurt even more. Much of the shipbuilding that Boston had once prospered on now centered around Newburyport and Portsmouth, both of which had large stands of good timber within close reach. Newport had usurped the bulk of the Narragansett Bay and Long Island traffic that formerly went in Boston-owned ships, and Newport's lucrative slave trade—nearly half the American vessels engaged in this business were said to be owned by its merchants—gave it an entry into the West Indies. Newport's import of molasses and its rum production nearly equaled Boston's by 1763. By that date, New Haven, too, had become a serious competitor for the business of towns that Boston had served. New Haven had overcome the drawback of a harbor too shallow to take ocean-going vessels by building a pier a third of a mile long out to deep water. By 1775 the former village had become a town of eight thousand inhabitants. It served as a distribution point for villages scattered along the shores of Connecticut and Long Island, and it annually put thirty or more vessels into the West Indian trade, carrying oxen and horses down and mostly molasses back. (These Connecticut traders missed no chance to turn a penny, said a man who had watched their ships arrive in Puerto Rico. "After disembarking their horses, they ran their vessels up to the quay, and converted them into retail shops, where they dealt out their onions, potatoes, salt fish, and *apples,* an article which brought a very high price, in the smallest quantities, for which they received hard dollars. . . .")

Competition from the Middle Colonies and the enterprise of merchants in outlying towns did not fully account for Boston's economic troubles. Boston's stagnation reflected the economic state of health of all New England, which by the mid-eighteenth century had gone about as far as it could go. Hereafter, and until the Industrial Revolution arrived in the nineteenth century, New England would be economically overshadowed by New York and Pennsylvania. Paradoxically, New England's economic decline set in while its political power was on the ascendant. Politics had always figured large in the life of New Englanders. Every town had anywhere from fifty to two hundred elective or appointive offices to be filled—from hog reeve to selectmen—and few who voted could avoid sometime serving without showing that they "were oppressed by such choice" or "that others are unjustly exempted." It was not especially remarkable that in 1758 young John Adams resolved "to aim at an exact knowledge of nature, end, and means of government; compare the different forms of it with each other, and each of them with their effect on public and private happiness."

The average New Englander's political interests centered on local affairs. Prior to 1763, he was no better informed on provincial and imperial matters than other Americans. The complexities of these problems, which seemed irrelevant to his life, he left to those he chose to represent him in the assembly. Those chosen invariably were of the "better sort" —merchants and lawyers and occasionally a prosperous farmer—who made an avocation of politics and could afford the time and expense service in the legislature required. A man who had won office usually held it as long as he wished. Only eleven men occupied the annually elected post of governor and only ninety-seven persons served in the twelve-man House of Assistants in Connecticut during the hundred years that followed the Glorious Revolution.

This apathy toward provincial and imperial affairs would change in every colony after 1763, but New England would move with more dispatch than other parts of America. Religious and racial unity allowed the four outwardly disparate colonies to act with extraordinary single-mindedness once aroused. New England had no large immigrant population to contend with or to absorb. Religious dissidents were too few to split the people apart. No sizable body of disenfranchised adults existed to stir political waters. (Property qualifications similar to those in Britain—a 40s. freehold or £50 of personal property—generally held for provincial elections, but in local elections custom seems to have allowed all adult males "of a quiet and peaceable behaviour and civil conversation," as a Connecticut statute put it, the right to vote.) A long tradition of conflict with crown and Parliament that dated back to John Winthrop's day had forced leaders to clarify what they conceived to be New England's rights and enabled them to react swiftly when those rights seemed about to be trampled under. An equally long tradition of virtual self-government—it was said that king and Parliament had as much influence in Rhode Island and

Connecticut "as in the wilds of Tartary," and Massachusetts' knack for
hamstringing its royal governor gave the remark some relevance there,
too—had accustomed the people to act for themselves. "A whole government of our own choice, managed by persons whom we love, revere, and
can confide in," John Adams wrote on the eve of independence, "has
charms in it for which men will fight." Much of New England's authority in continental affairs from 1763 down to the Revolution stemmed from
its early and united adherence to that view.

New England, however, rarely evoked affection from outsiders. Other
Americans called it the land of the Yankees, and though the origin of the
word was, and is, uncertain, its contemporary meaning as a term of op-
probrium was not. Pennsylvanians were "cordial and inveterate enemies
to the *Yankees*," especially those from Connecticut who had usurped land
to the north of Philadelphia in the Wyoming Valley. Philip Livingston
of New York dreaded them for their "leveling principles," and Edward
Rutledge of South Carolina had distaste for "their low cunning." Some
men during the Revolution argued against a strong central government on
the ground that the Yankees would dominate it. These fears may or may
not have been justified, but by the end of the eighteenth century, the word
"Yankee" had for Europeans became synonymous for American, a development that suggests that if New Englanders did not dominate American society and politics, they had, at least, come to exemplify it in the eyes
of foreigners.

The Hudson Valley

Long before someone coined the word "geopolitics," men of good sense
knew that a region's geography shaped its economy and conditioned its
political boundaries. New York's first governor, Richard Nicolls, heard
with dismay in 1664 that the Duke of York had granted away his holdings west of the Hudson River. Nicolls, being a man of good sense,
pleaded that the gift of New Jersey be retracted, "for if the duke will
improve this place to the utmost," he said, "neither the trade, the river,
nor the adjacent lands must be divided from this colony but remain
entire." The duke refused to repair the amputation, and New York and
New Jersey leaders have since done their best to undo what the duke did
so casually.

Curiously, the later division of the Berkeley-Carteret grant into East
and West Jersey made sense. West Jersey's population resembled the
strange mixture that was Pennsylvania, and its economy fit nicely into
that of the Delaware Valley. East Jersey clearly belonged to the Hudson
Valley: men of Dutch descent peopled both sides of the river; firewood
and food ferried across from East Jersey warmed and fed New York;

Jersey's wheat, pork, and beef left for foreign ports in ships owned by New York merchants; and even its currency was pegged to the New York rate of exchange. These economic ties soon led to political ones. When the Dominion of New England was expanded to include New York, New Jersey came along, too. When the dominion collapsed, New York's governor served also as New Jersey's chief executive, though the colony was allowed its own assembly. When New Jersey acquired its own governor in 1738, a New Yorker, Lewis Morris, got the appointment.

Control of New Jersey assured New York's control of the Hudson Valley, the longest and potentially richest river valley in colonial America and the only one with easy access to the Western lake country. By all rights, New York should have led America in wealth and population. It had a fertile, well-watered hinterland, which, William Smith, the colony's historian, said, "abounds with timber and other materials for naval stores, and is capable . . . to raise annually forty thousand tons of hemp." The long, navigable waterway that drained this country allowed a single boat to "steal into the harbour of New York with a lading of more burden and value than forty wagons, one hundred and sixty horses, and eighty men into Philadelphia." The low cost of transportation made "the profits of farming with us exceed those in Pennsylvania at least by 30 per cent." And yet in 1752, when Smith wrote these words, New York lagged in prosperity and population far behind Massachusetts and Pennsylvania. Moderate expansion in the 1760's pushed New York City ahead of Boston in population, but the province as a whole still had fewer than two hundred thousand people in 1775, hardly equal to Connecticut.

New York's prosperity lagged to a degree because both Pennsylvania and Massachusetts outcompeted New York in markets served by all three colonies. New York in 1768 had seventeen distilleries that produced 540,000 gallons of rum, but the molasses to make that rum came at a high price. Boston merchants, whose home-owned vessels reduced carrying charges, could undercut New Yorkers in the West Indies market. Philadelphia won the major share of the lucrative pork, butter, flour, and grain trade by regulating the quality of its exports. A New York law in 1750 calling for quality controls on flour helped somewhat, but pork and butter out of the Delaware Valley continued to outsell New York's, and Irish cured beef remained preferred to that produced by Hudson Valley farmers.

The explanation for New York's slow growth in population centers on the colony's peculiar land policy. New York landlords preferred to rent, not sell, land to newcomers. And as Governor Bellomont remarked, a man would be a fool to settle as a tenant, "when for crossing the Hudson's River that man can for a song purchase a good freehold in the Jerseys."

The contingent of German-speaking immigrants who came to New York early in the eighteenth century were mistreated and cheated; they eventually migrated on to Pennsylvania and word went back to Europe to avoid New York. A few Scotch-Irish entered the colony but soon followed the German route to Pennsylvania. The great migration of the eighteenth century shunned New York as fully as it did New England.

The uniqueness of New York's land system owed something to the Dutch heritage. The manor erected under the English resembled the feudalistic patroonship of the Dutch, and even where grants did not include such manorial privileges as the right to erect courts or to send a deputy to the assembly, the New York landlord drew from the medieval past to maintain his position and power. He leased his land, exacted payments in kind—a typical rent might call for ten bushels of winter wheat, "four fat hens," and three days' service with a team of horses or oxen on the lord's land—demanded tribute up to a third of the sale if the tenant re-leased his plot to another, and reserved all milling and mineral rights to himself. Though men like Andros and Bellomont tried to limit the size of tracts and to make it possible for the small farmer to own his land, venal governors who followed, like Lord Cornbury, undercut their efforts. (The Hardenbergh Patent handed out by Cornbury exceeded a million acres.) Grants were supposedly limited to two thousand acres, but various tricks were used regularly to enlarge them far beyond the legal limit. Land was bought in the names of servants who released their claim once the grant had cleared the governor's office. Surveys were vaguely worded: a boundary might run from a "burch saplin" to a "hepe of stone," or, if to a clearly fixed point, the happy phrase "be it more or less" might follow. Cadwallader Colden knew of a patent for three hundred acres that had been stretched by this method to over six hundred thousand.

New York's peculiar land policies did not in themselves create a society any more aristocratic than that found elsewhere in America, nor were they responsible for the confused and intricate politics that characterized the colony in the eighteenth century. True, a good deal of political and economic power rested with perhaps twenty families, all connected through intermarriage. (Thus a Schuyler was related to the Van Cortlandts, Bayards, Beekmans, DeLanceys, and DePeysters.) A similar situation, however, prevailed, for example, in Virginia, where Jefferson's Randolph blood allowed him to claim as a relative just about anyone in the colony worth knowing. And in neither colony did kinship play much of a role in shaping political alliances. Although New York's elite, like South Carolina's, for instance, was land-based—a study has shown that of 137 men who held important government posts in New York from around

1750 to the Revolution, 103, or about 75 per cent, owned at least one thousand acres of land—in addition it included a good number of merchants and lawyers, many of whom held large tracts of land for speculative purposes. And New York's aristocracy was no more closed to newcomers than, say, Massachusetts'. Many merchants, Cadwallader Colden said in 1765, "have rose suddenly from the lowest rank of the people to considerable fortunes, and chiefly by illicit trade in the last war." Nor was it an aristocracy that could flout public opinion, for few seats in the assembly were "sure" seats. Robert Livingston could not promise a friend the votes of his tenants, but he suggested that at 40s. a man "they may be had." Candidates enticed votes by holding a day or so before election, a "treat" or "frolic," where beer and brandy flowed freely. Also, easy suffrage requirements gave the vote to almost any adult white male who wanted it. City dwellers could vote if they were "freemen," a privilege obtained for a modest fee; thus between 40 and 55 per cent of all adult white males cast ballots in New York City elections. Statistics are lacking for the country, but a study of Milton Klein's makes clear that "tenant status did not render the smaller farmer politically impotent," for tenants were permitted by law to vote if their leases ran for at least twenty-one years, as most of them did.

The distinguishing feature that set New York apart from New England and the South was its inhabitants' religious and racial diversity and their different economic interests. As a result, New York politics became "a weird mixture of economic rivalries, ethnic-religious factionalism, family feuds, personal enmities, and sectional differences." Settlers of Dutch ancestry, especially around Albany, continued to hold to the language and customs of their forefathers. Presbyterians resisted anything that appeared to favor Anglicans. Immigrants from New England resented New York land policies. Pockets of bitterness left over from the Leisler uprising persisted. The city merchant's interests often put him at odds with the country landlord. Plain people in the city held little sympathy for the tenant farmers' troubles. (When grumblings among tenant farmers finally erupted in 1766 into open revolt and a march on New York City for a redress of grievances, the city-centered Sons of Liberty made it clear they were "great opposers of these rioters.")

Factions, in the sense James Madison used the word (a group of citizens "who are united and actuated by some common impulse of passion, or of interest, adverse to the rights of other citizens, or to the permanent and aggregate interests of the community"), dominated New York politics through the eighteenth century. They traveled under two family banners—Livingston and DeLancey—and though they appeared to be well-organized parties guided by a definite political philosophy, they were really no more than loose coalitions whose membership varied with the issue at hand. "We change sides as serves our interest," Philip Livingston once said. Neither group consistently represented a particular view—the mercantile or the landed interests, the Anglicans or the Presbyterians, town or country. The two factions did unite but only when the self-interests of the elite as a whole seemed threatened. The assembly, for instance, overwhelmingly voted down Cadwallader Colden's proposal in 1764 to annul the eight hundred thousand–acre Kayaderosseras Patent, for which the crown received an annual quitrent of £4 New York currency. The assembly held that royal officials stood to gain if the tract were broken up and resold, which may have been true, but a more convincing argument was that ownership of the grant was shared by "every family of any consideration in the province . . . as well as the principal lawyers of the country . . . ," and to annul the patent would have injured many among the elite.

New York leaders rarely spoke with a united voice, however. The project of a college, which provoked little division in Massachusetts and Virginia, became a major issue in New York, with Anglicans seeking to create King's College in their image and the Presbyterians fighting them at every step. Divisive strands marred the politics of all colonies, but in most some common bond—religion, economic interests, a homogeneous population—bound the people together. Not so in New York, and the division that racked its political affairs through the eighteenth century would widen rather than lessen as America moved toward independence.

Division of another sort and for other reasons prevailed across the Hudson in New Jersey. Governor Lewis Morris, who feuded steadily with the assembly's farmer-politicians (how can a man get wisdom, he asked with some bitterness, who "driveth oxen and is occupied in their labor and whose talk is of bullocks?"), nonetheless considered the settlers of New Jersey "the most easy and happy people of any colony in North America." No foes menaced their borders; they paid no provincial taxes, for the government lived off the interest on the bills of credit it issued; no split existed between town and country, for mainly farmers populated the colony. And yet New Jersey's political affairs were more tempestuous than New York's. Land here, too, caused much of the turmoil. When the crown took control of the colony in 1702, all ungranted tracts remained with the proprietors, who expected to profit from their sale and the collection of quitrents. During the 1740's, Scotch-Irishmen flooded in and squatted where they pleased. When the proprietors sought to collect the sale price and quitrents, the squatters rioted. Animosities emerging out of the land riots, which had centered in East Jersey, carried over into the assembly, and were intensified by divergent views between East and West Jersey representatives. The assembly bickered its way through the eighteenth century, achieving little except when it attacked the power and authority of the governor. The turmoil of New Jersey's politics, Lawrence Gipson has remarked, "illustrates how a people may live in the midst of both economic prosperity and political conditions that border on anarchy, with a government powerless to function in the direction of establishing even the semblance of law and order." It would surprise no one that New Jersey, which had been incapable of action through most of the eighteenth century, would lag when it came to taking a stand on independence.

The Delaware Valley

In 1725, when trade had slumped to a melancholy level, a wealthy Philadelphia Quaker named Francis Rawle published a pamphlet entitled *Ways and Means for the Inhabitants of Delaware to Become Rich,* wherein he argued that regardless of political boundaries the Delaware River tied West Jersey, eastern Pennsylvania, and the Lower Counties, as Delaware was then known, into a single economic unit. Rawle saw boundless prosperity for the region if this fact were kept in mind. During the half century that followed, his wildest hopes came true. By 1775 the Delaware Valley had become the greatest agricultural and manufacturing center in colonial America.

Wheat and rye were the valley's two great cash crops, and the flour made from them rarely had to scramble for markets, for foreign buyers knew Pennsylvania controlled the quality of the product it exported. Hemp and flax were grown in commercial quantities. A large amount of corn was grown but mainly for fodder. A heavy export trade was carried on in pork and beef and also cattle, horses, sheep, and hogs. The navigable Delaware and Schuylkill Rivers and a good highway that cut through the rich farm country of Lancaster County made Philadelphia the hub of this agricultural empire, and by 1763 America's richest and largest city. To the envy of Boston and New York, it continued to grow. In 1765 more vessels cleared Philadelphia "than the city of Bristol, and I believe any other port in Britain except London and Liverpool," an inhabitant said, adding that "we shall begin to be the wonder of the world, and soon rival considerable states in Europe." Between 1764 and 1772 its West Indies trade doubled that of New York's and exceeded Boston's by a third. Her southern European trade was nearly four times greater than New York's and fifteen times that of Boston. For a long while, however, the valley did not, so to speak, own itself, for much of the profits from its trade flowed into the pockets of outsiders. But by 1768, Philadelphia merchants owned about 40 per cent of the vessels that cleared the port and seven years later that figure had jumped to 63 per cent. This shipping was not confined to a small oligarchy but spread among at least 135 merchants.

During the years when the valley came to dominate its commerce, the economy underwent a change. The bulk of the people continued to live off the land, but now, too, "the voice of industry perpetually resounds along the shore." Where once most American-built ships came from New England, a visitor to the Delaware Valley could see being built "as fine ships here as any part of the world and with as great dispatch." Here, too, he could find manufactured "most kinds of hardware, clocks, watches, locks, guns, flints, glass, stoneware, nails, paper, cordage, cloth, etc., etc." (Invariably, any list of items manufactured in the valley ended with a catchall "etc.") The Delaware Valley led the continent in manufacturing to some extent because William Penn's liberal policies had attracted to the area the largest reservoir of skilled craftsmen on the continent. The valley acquired an additional advantage from the abundance of two natural resources—lumber and iron. By 1775 one-seventh of the iron produced in the world came from the American colonies, and though nearly all the colonies shared in this production, by far the bulk of it emerged from the hundred or so iron furnaces scattered through the Delaware Valley.

The Delaware River did more than bind together the economy. It created within the valley a single cultural unit. Presbyterian synods held at Philadelphia brought members from all parts of the valley. The Society of Friends' Yearly Meeting drew from both sides of the river; it met in alternate years in Philadelphia and Burlington, New Jersey. Anglicans saw the whole valley as a spot to be rescued from "Quakerism and heathenism." Philadelphia, peopled with a "strange mixture" that included every race and religion in America, was only a microcosm of the valley's population. The large number of German-speaking settlers centered mainly in Pennsylvania. They cut a broad swath that began at Easton on the northeast, curved through Bethlehem and Lancaster, and ended west of Susquehanna in the vicinity of York. The Scotch-Irish spread along this same belt and also through West Jersey and the Lower Counties. Perhaps three hundred Jews lived in Philadelphia and a scattering of Swedish, Finnish, and Dutch families on farms south of the city. Presbyterians by the eve of the Revolution comprised the single largest religious block. Quakers had become a minority everywhere in the valley except in the counties that bordered both sides of the Delaware. They constituted about one-seventh of Philadelphia's population. (However, twelve of the city's wealthiest inhabitants and over half those who paid taxes of £100 or more were members of the Society of Friends.) "Pockets" of English and Welsh Baptists and Anglicans were scattered through the Quaker country. There were enough Irish, French, and German Catholics to support a church in Philadelphia, and outside the city, small congregations could be found at Reading, Goshenhoppen, Conewago, and Lancaster. (The diversity of people and religions found in the Delaware Valley would one day prompt Crèvecoeur, who had lived in Pennsylvania, to ask: "What then is the American, this new man?" and to answer that he is a mixture of English, Irish, Scotch, French, Dutch, German, and Swedish, melted down into a new race of man, a "promiscuous breed." Crèvecoeur, more intuitive than observant, anticipated a melting-down process still firmly resisted in the Delaware Valley in the eighteenth century; little intermingling occurred among races and religions, and people lived mainly among their own kind. But when the "promiscuous breed" came into being, the Delaware Valley would be the birthplace.)

More than diversity set the valley apart from the rest of the North. Though more wealth had accumulated here than anywhere else in America, the phrase "all men are created equal" seemed an especially self-evident truth. "The poorest labourer upon the shore of the Delaware," an inhabitant said,

thinks himself entitled to deliver his sentiments in matters of religion or politics with as much freedom as the gentleman or scholar. Indeed, there is less distinction among the citizens of Philadelphia, than among those of any civilized city in the world. Riches give none. For every man expects one day or another to be upon a footing with his wealthiest neighbour. . . .

Policies laid down by William Penn had something to do with promoting this idea of equality. He had welcomed all comers, regardless of race or creed. He had made land easy to acquire, and in the eighteenth century a hundred-acre plot still sold for about £5, with a quitrent of a penny an acre attached. The Charter of Privileges he had granted in 1701 gave the assembly extraordinary powers. It met at fixed times each year, adjourned when it wished, and chose its own officers. Sheriffs and coroners, appointive posts in most colonies, were elected in Pennsylvania. Property requirements for voting were about the same as elsewhere in the North— £50 of personal property or a fifty-acre freehold—but they seem to have been observed in the breach. To vote a man needed only to swear or affirm he satisfied the requirements, and few hesitated to do so. Franklin blamed his defeat for an assembly seat in the wild election of 1764 on "the many perjuries procured among the wretched rabble brought to swear themselves entitled to a vote."

Pennsylvania began as a "holy experiment," but by the early years of the eighteenth century, Sydney James has remarked, the colony "ceased to be a demonstration to the world of how different a state could be when conducted by men who were attentive to the light within." The social-minded legislation of Penn's day vanished. "Quakers in the assembly, far

Map 32.

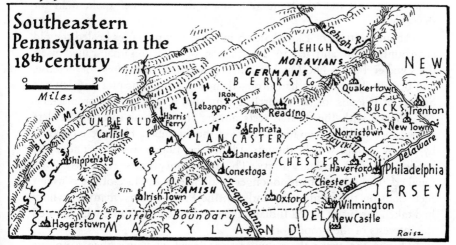

Southeastern Pennsylvania in the 18th century

from distinguishing themselves for benevolence, passed harsh settlement laws and required masters to give sureties of thirty pounds when they freed slaves in order to keep them from becoming a public charge," James says. "The lawmakers tried to put the burden of support for the poor on the users of servile labor, but succeeded in transferring it more and more to private charity."

Thus a prosperous and tolerant society did not, as far as Pennsylvania was concerned, create a harmonious one. The turbulence of Pennsylvania affairs had by the middle of the eighteenth century reached such a point that members of the assembly "dare not disoblige the people thro' fear of losing their seats . . ., and the people, knowing their power, insult the magistrates, contend with the governors, oppose the proprietaries, influence courts of justice, and in short settle lands without the proprietaries' consent, knowing that the sheriffs dare not meddle with them." A saying of the day had it that "Pennsylvania is the heaven of the farmers, the paradise of the mechanics, and the hell of the officials and preachers."

The dissension began as a family affair. A faction of country Quakers, led by the belligerent David Lloyd, fought to widen the powers of the assembly at the expense of the proprietor and to limit the authority of city merchants in politics. Lloyd believed that a plain man of small means "may do more good to the state than a richer or more learned man, who, by his ill temper and aspiring mind becomes an opposer of the constitution by which he should act." His aspersions against the rich and learned no doubt stemmed from a hatred of the able, ruthless, politician-merchant James Logan. Logan's long and close association with Penn put him in the forefront of the fight to preserve the proprietor's powers, and his mercantile interests made him the chief spokesman for that group.

About the time of Lloyd's death in 1731, new pressures healed the old city-country split and led to the creation of a faction that called itself the Quaker Party. The Quaker Party opposed all measures for defense, and because Penn's sons had dropped their pacific principles and left the Society of Friends for the Church of England, it was also antiproprietary. An alliance with the pacifist sects among the German-speaking settlers helped the Quakers keep firm control of the assembly. They were opposed by a new group, which, though still led by Logan, traveled under the banner of the Proprietary Party. The Proprietary Party embraced those Quakers who felt pacifism no longer justifiable in the face of the constant incursions on the frontiers by Indians; the Presbyterians, many of whom had taken the brunt of the Indian raids; and, of course, those who favored the interests of the proprietors.

During the 1750's these two factions faced what was then a unique political problem in America. The influx of German-speaking settlers had by this time reached such proportions that Pennsylvanians feared "that the Dutch, by their numbers and industry, will soon become masters of the province and also a majority in the legislature." Franklin, usually so careful in his public remarks, asked: "Why should the Palatine boors be suffered to swarm into our settlements and, by herding together, establish their language and manners, to the exclusion of ours?" Both factions sought to woo the German voter. Franklin suggested free schools to teach them English, but the Germans rejected the proposal, saying that free education smacked of charity. In addition to their alliance with the German pacifists, the Quaker Party handled the threat of a solid German vote destroying their hold on the assembly by limiting the representation from western counties that held large German-speaking populations and by redrawing the county lines around Reading, an area of heavy German settlement, in a way that would reduce "to a trifle the whole body of the Dutch and consequently forever exclude them from becoming a majority in the assembly." Gerrymandering was at best a short-term resolution but no solution to the "German problem." The Pennsylvania Dutch, like every foreign-speaking immigrant group in American history, solved the "problem" themselves by swinging into the mainstream of Pennsylvania affairs. When it became apparent that Germans were voting on both sides of public issues, apprehension among native Pennsylvanians ended.

Pennsylvania politics entered a new phase in 1756. Most Quakers saw that if the province were to survive, it had to arm and fight the French and Indians raiding the frontiers. That course handed the Friends the choice of abandoning either politics or pacifism. The majority chose to leave politics, and with that act a quiet reformation began within the Society of Friends, during which much of the vigor and strength of an earlier era was retrieved. Twenty years of discipline following the decision of 1756 prepared the Quakers spiritually and mentally to resist the American Revolution. (This, perhaps, puts the story too simply. The abandonment of political life in 1756 was neither complete nor permanent. Once the French and Indian War ended, Quakers slowly drifted back in numbers to public life and remained there through 1774. Only when America abandoned nonintercourse—a policy perfectly adapted to Quaker beliefs and thus one that had their full support—and traded passive resistance for a shooting war did Quakers once again quietly depart from politics.)

The withdrawal of the Quakers altered but did not kill the Quaker Party. Benjamin Franklin, though not a Quaker, took control of the machinery. He reversed the party stand on war measures, and by designing a militia bill that exempted conscientious objectors from service, he held on to the party's old following and gained new strength among the voters. The party continued to oppose proprietary interests and to promote those of the assembly. Skillful manipulation of the issues by Franklin and his associate Joseph Galloway allowed the Quaker Party to dominate Pennsylvania politics down through 1763. In December of that year, twenty Christian Indians were murdered in a drunken riot by the Paxton Boys. The riot soon became a political crusade, and some six hundred or more armed settlers from the Lancaster area marched on Philadelphia. Franklin was among those who dissuaded the army from entering the city by promising its leaders that the assembly would give a full hearing to all grievances. The grievances, however, turned out to be directed against the assembly itself—it had been niggardly in appropriating funds for frontier defense during the Indian uprising; it had refused to increase the representation of the western counties—and after perfunctory discussion that body rejected them all. The Proprietary Party capitalized on this unrest during the election of 1764.

Curiously, in a year when much of America was agitated over the British Army's ineffectual handling of the Indian insurrection and when the crown was in the midst of inaugurating a new revenue policy for the colonies, Franklin and the Quaker Party came out vigorously for making Pennsylvania a royal colony. (Historians still puzzle over Franklin's stand; some think he hoped that after the crown took over, he might become Pennsylvania's first royal governor.) The Proprietary Party answered that royal control would substitute for the colony's treasured Charter of Privileges the ambiguities of the royal prerogative; proprietary rule perhaps had its flaws, but surely the king's rule promised no millennium.

The election was one of the wildest and most scurrilous in Pennsylvania history. Franklin's private life was explored in the press, and German voters were reminded that Franklin had once called them "Palatine boors." When the voting ended, both Franklin and Galloway had lost their assembly seats and the Proprietary Party was at last in control, but by a margin so slight that it was unable during the next decade to give any firmer or stronger direction to Pennsylvania affairs than the Quaker Party had given. Pennsylvania, like New York, approached the Revolution with its politics in a muddle. The weird mixture of its population, which had nourished its economy and its culture, frustrated accomplishments on the political front. When it came time in 1776 for Pennsylvania to make up its mind about independence, it would have as much trouble taking a firm stand as it had during the preceding three-quarters of a century.

THE SOUTH

Shortly after the Revolution, Thomas Jefferson listed for a puzzled foreign friend the distinctions between Northerners and Southerners as he saw them.

In the North they are	In the South they are
cool	fiery
sober	voluptuary
laborious	indolent
independent	unsteady
jealous of their own liberties, and just to those of others	zealous for their own liberties but trampling on those of others
interested	generous
chicaning	candid
superstitious and hypocritical in their religion	without attachment or pretensions to any religion but that of the heart

These characteristics [Jefferson added] become weaker and weaker by gradation from North to South and South to North, insomuch that an observing traveler without the aid of any quadrant may always know his latitude by the character of the people among whom he finds himself. It is in Pennsylvania that the two characters seem to meet and blend and to form a people free from the extremes both of vice and virtue.

Few but Pennsylvanians would have found much to appreciate in Jefferson's analysis. Everyone knew that a good deal set the South apart from the North. The people spoke differently. (Marylanders, it was said, "never pronounce the R at all.") The winters were milder; the growing season longer. Southern economic interests diverged from those of the North. The South had few towns and almost no manufacturing. Its population of seven hundred thousand in 1763 nearly equaled the North's, but over a third of its people were Negro slaves. Men might debate whether these distinctions had created a Southern character; no one, however, doubted that they had created a South whose "honor, interest and sovereignty" must never be "delivered up to the care of the North."

Chesapeake Country

Men from the Chesapeake country found it hard to tolerate New Englanders. Their manners were crude and their "leveling principles" dangerous; they were, "for the most part, a *damned* generation." Perhaps dislike sprang in part from shared similarities. What John Adams said of New England—"The people are purer English blood, less mixed with Scotch, Irish, Dutch, French, Danish, Swedish, etc. than any other; but descended from Englishmen, too, who left Europe in purer times . . ."—could be said for the homogeneous white population of the Chesapeake country. The economies of both regions had been molded in the seventeenth century, had reached their peaks around 1750, and had begun to decline thereafter. And the political power of each region had increased, paradoxically, as its economic strength weakened.

The Chesapeake country included Maryland, Virginia, and the Albemarle section of North Carolina, and extended westward to the piedmont. The great bay dominated the colonies' life without imposing uniformity. Small farms and an economy that wavered only a bit above subsistence level persisted in North Carolina's Albemarle area. The large plantation set the tone of Virginia's life. Maryland had the largest Catholic population and the severest anti-Catholic statutes of any colony in America. She mined and manufactured more iron than any colony except Pennsylvania; Baltimore, with six thousand people in 1775, was the largest port on Chesapeake Bay and the second largest in the South.

These distinctions counted for little against the still overwhelming influence of tobacco on all sides of life in the Chesapeake region. The tobacco farm of a hundred acres or so, worked by the farmer, his family, and a few servants or slaves, still existed; but its importance had faded with the appearance of the plantation, whose size varied from one to six thousand acres and whose lands were worked by anywhere from fifty to a hundred slaves. (Plantations could, of course, go larger. Charles Carroll of Carrollton owned forty thousand acres of land in Maryland and 285 slaves; he was said to be the richest man in America.) The rise of the plantation tightened tobacco's hold on the economy and cemented slavery into the culture. In 1700 there had been only six thousand Negroes in Virginia. In 1775 they had increased by natural means and continually heavy imports to over one hundred and seventy thousand, which was approximately 45 per cent of Virginia's total population.

The growth of the plantation had not altered the pattern of the to-bacco trade. The great fleet continued to arrive in the autumn bringing goods from Britain and returning homeward with the crop. Complaints about Britain's control of the trade had been few until the eighteenth century. A steady downward trend of tobacco prices, due in part to the enormous crops that larger holdings and slave labor made it possible to market, awakened Chesapeake planters to flaws in the system. As much as 75 per cent of the profit from a crop was eaten up by expenses over which the planter had no control—freight and insurance charges, commissions to British merchants, export taxes from the bay region, and customs duties in Britain (these could amount to as much as £400,000 a year). An esti-mate in 1730 put the net profit on a hogshead of tobacco that sold for £27 at 15s. Another estimate had it that planters could have increased their gain by £3 per hogshead if they had been allowed to ship directly to the Continent. This especially vexed the planters, for of the one hundred thousand or so hogsheads of tobacco sent out annually from Chesapeake Bay, approximately 80 per cent were reexported from Britain to European markets.

By the 1750's the price of tobacco had dipped to around a penny a pound and there, except for an occasional spurt, it hovered. By the eve of the Revolution, according to Thomas Jefferson, Virginians alone owed over £2 million sterling to British creditors and had become little more than "a species of property annexed to certain mercantile houses in Lon-don." The planters sought to avoid bankruptcy by all routes but one—reduction of their standard of living. Some chose to embezzle from the government. John Robinson, speaker of the house and Virginia's treasurer, illegally loaned to friends large sums of supposedly retired currency from the treasury. (Patrick Henry broke the scandal in 1766.) Others planted more tobacco, and still others turned to breeding and selling slaves to make up their deficits.

An obvious solution would have been to stop planting tobacco and turn to other cash crops. But Chesapeake planters were set in their ways. ("They are not easily persuaded to the improvement of useful inventions, except a few, such as sawing mills," Reverend Hugh Jones wrote in 1724. "Neither are they great encouragers of manufactures, because of the trouble and certain expense in attempts of this kind, with uncertain prospect of gain; whereas by their staple commodity, tobacco, they are in hopes to get a plentiful provision; nay, often very great estates.") Slowly, however, as the desperateness of the situation increased, a few bold spirits experimented with other crops. By the mid-1740's, Maryland planters were shifting out of tobacco and into wheat, barley, and oats. George Washington eased out of tobacco in the 1760's and put the bulk of his land in wheat, which he ground into flour in his own mill. He put part of his men to fishing the Potomac for whitefish, herring, and shad. Fish and flour went into the West Indian trade, thereby reducing Washington's dependence on British markets and merchants but also placing him at odds with British imperial policy by putting him outside the navigation system.

Despite the experiments of a few like Washington, the Chesapeake economy centered on tobacco down to the Revolution. This primarily set the region apart from the North. The "vast shoals of Negroes" among which the settlers lived also imposed a distinguishing pattern on Chesapeake life. (The Marquis de Chastellux, visiting the area at the end of the Revolution, said that the people "seem grieved at having slaves, and are constantly talking of abolishing slavery and of seeking other means of exploiting their lands." He doubted much would come of this talk, for "it is not only the slave who is beneath his master; it is the Negro who is beneath the white man. No act of enfranchisement can efface this unfortunate distinction.")

Above the Negro on the social scale came the small white farmer, of whom there were considerable numbers still in the eighteenth century. Their "state of poverty" shocked Chastellux. They were the first "poor people" he had seen anywhere in America. Everything about them, their "miserable huts," their "wan looks and ragged garments," bespoke poverty.

At first I found it hard to understand how, in a country where there is still so much land to clear, men who do not refuse to work could remain in misery; but I have since learned that all these useless lands and those immense estates, with which Virginia is still covered, have their proprietors. Nothing is more common than to see some of them possessing five or six thousand acres of land, but exploiting only as much of it as their Negroes can cultivate. Yet they will not give away, or even sell the smallest portion of it, because they are attached to their possessions and always hope to increase eventually the number of their Negroes.

The social hierarchy was clear-cut and fixed in the Chesapeake country. Men strove to obtain social status in the more open society of the Northern colonies; they strove to maintain the *status quo* in the Chesapeake region. The Negro's spot at the bottom was fixed by law. Tradition taught the man who owned only a few acres of land to know his low place. These small farmers were "accustomed to look upon what were called *gentle folks* as being of a superior order," said the son of one of them. They did not hope to rise in the world. "My parents neither sought nor expected any titles, honors, or great things, either for themselves or children." The gentlemen of Chesapeake society, John Adams would find when he dealt with them in Congress, were "accustomed, habituated to higher notions of themselves, and the distinction between them and the common people, than we are. . . ."

The Chesapeake gentleman resembled nothing so much as an English squire of the sort depicted by Fielding in *Tom Jones*. Gambling, hunting, and horse races were his favorite amusements. Cockfights, said one traveler, are "much in fashion in Virginia, where English customs are more in evidence than in the rest of America." His women seldom shared his interests. "Beauty here serves only to find husbands," said Chastellux, adding that "the consequence of this is that they are often coquettish and prudish before marriage, and dull and tiresome afterwards." The gentleman planter worked hard, drank hard; his manner could be crude and his humor ribald, except when on public display. He was "inclined to read men by business and conversation than to dive into books," according to Reverend Hugh Jones, and was "for the most part only desirous of learning what is absolutely necessary in the shortest possible and best method." He traveled the land with the confidence, bearing, and poise of a man accustomed to rule—as he was. Washington directed a larger staff at Mount Vernon than as head of the government in 1789. Shadwell, the early home of Jefferson, housed the population of a small village—among them carpenters, coopers, blacksmiths, tanners, curriers, shoemakers, spinners, weavers, sawyers, and perhaps even a distiller—and Jefferson became responsible for them all at the age of fourteen, when his father died. Chesapeake gentlemen were kings of their plantations and of the countryside, too. Ties with the outside world were thin. When bridges needed to be built, roads improved, rivers deepened, slaves hunted, or the poor cared for, the local gentry handled matters as they saw fit. These gentlemen, an observer remarked, "are haughty and jealous of their liberties, impatient of restraint, and can scarcely bear the thought of being controlled by any superior power."

The political system these gentlemen dominated differed in no striking way from that of other colonies. Elections resembled those in the North. The "treat" and "frolic" were as much a part of Chesapeake politics as of New York's. (James Madison later deplored "the corrupting influence of spirituous liquors and other treats" on elections. He felt it was "inconsistent with the purity of moral and republican principles" and in his first campaign refused to provide refreshment. He lost.) Voting, as in other colonies, was by voice, and when a voter stepped forward from the crowd an exchange similar to this one often occurred:

Sheriff: "Mr. Blair, who do you vote for?"
Blair: "John Marshall."
Marshall: "Your vote is appreciated, Mr. Blair."
Sheriff: "Who do you vote for, Mr. Buchanan?"
Buchanan: "For John Clopton."
Clopton: "Mr. Buchanan, I shall treasure that vote in my memory. It will be regarded as a feather in my cap forever."

Property qualifications, which tended to duplicate those in other colonies, deprived of the vote about "half of those on the roll of the militia, or of the tax-gatherers," according to Jefferson. (Among those excluded were the worthless and floaters, overseers, tenant farmers, craftsmen and merchants and those who worked for them; many were the adult sons of farmers who for various reasons—they lacked the money, the inclination, or the energy—had failed to establish themselves.) Once the voter had delegated his authority, he gave no more attention to the intricacies of provincial or imperial affairs than the average voter of Massachusetts. "You assert that there is a fixed intention to invade our rights and privileges," a group of inhabitants told Benjamin Harrison as he was about to leave for Congress in 1774; "we own that we do not see this clearly, but since you assure us that it is so, we believe the fact. We are about to take a very dangerous step, but we confide in you, and are ready to support you in every measure you shall think proper to adopt."

When Chesapeake politicians came to deal with imperial questions after 1763, only those of Virginia spoke with force and authority. Maryland's voice remained muted almost to the day independence was declared. Divisions inherited from the seventeenth century between Catholic and Protestant, proprietary and antiproprietary factions, continued to plague the colony. North Carolina's political troubles resembled those of New Jersey. The northern part of the colony revolved in Virginia's orbit; the southern part was drawn toward South Carolina. A bitter split between the tidewater and backcountry added to the chaos of North Carolina politics. Only in Virginia did something like stability exist.

Virginia long ago had settled most of the internal political problems that created factions in other colonies. By the end of the seventeenth century, the House of Burgesses had worked out its relationship with the governor, and no deep-rooted problems remained to divide the two wings of government. Within the house itself, an extraordinary stability prevailed. Year after year the same names appeared as chairmen of the powerful standing committees; only death or retirement brought new names forward. John Robinson held the speakership from 1738 to 1766, when he died. Peyton Randolph, after serving for eighteen years as the colony's attorney general, succeeded Robinson to the speakership and held the post until 1775, when he died. The continued stability of this oligarchic system owed much to the old guard's willingness to welcome young talent. Jefferson and Madison were only twenty-five when elected to the house, clearly with the backing of the clique who ran legislative affairs. James Monroe was twenty-four and George Washington twenty-six when they arrived. (Occasionally a maverick slipped in, like Patrick Henry, who assumed a seat when he was twenty-nine. The House, however, tolerated an eccentric if he was able and if he had the interests of the colony at heart. The House chose Henry as a delegate to the first Continental Congress and, later, as the state's first governor.) Sectional tensions, so strong in other colonies, were to an extent relieved in Virginia by a custom that allowed a man to represent any county in which he held land. Washington lived in Fairfax County but first represented Frederick County, some fifty miles to the west. Louisa County first sent Patrick Henry to the house, though he lived in Hanover County.

Virginia gentlemen were neither more nor less responsible than gentlemen elsewhere in America. They ruled in their own interests. Virginia's political voice was strong, however, because the gentlemen's interests coincided with the colony's. Virginia was a land of farmers, distinguished chiefly by the varying size of their operations. This uniformity of interests, backed by a long tradition of self-government, let the House of Burgesses speak forth loud and clear, when the time came, for the rights not only of Virginians but of all Americans.

Carolina Country

North Carolina, that "valley of humility between two mountains of conceit," was linked in name only to the colony on its south. A shoreline ringed by shoals virtually isolated the colony from the world. Travelers could ride through the tideland region "for three hours without seeing anything except pine barrens, that is, white sand grown up in pine trees, which will hardly produce anything else." British subsidies helped make the colony America's largest exporter of naval stores—tar, pitch, and turpentine—but the profits drifted into the pockets of a few. The average settler farmed occasional oases in the pine barrens, raising corn, hogs, and a few acres of tobacco, with the help of a slave or two. (North Carolina had the lowest slave population in the South.) Virginians had only contempt for those who lived in "lubberland," as William Byrd, Jr., called the place. "To speak the truth," said Byrd, " 'tis a thorough aversion to labor that makes people file off to N. Carolina, where plenty and a warm sun confirm them in their disposition to laziness for their whole lives."

No people who stirred up the political storms North Carolina endured through the colonial period could have been as lazy as Byrd suggests. The proprietors abandoned the ghost of a hope for profit and peace from the colony in 1729 and sold out to the crown. An interlude under the ineffectual George Burrington followed, then Gabriel Johnston, a Scotsman, came out as royal governor in 1734. Johnston seems to have been a man of ability with a sense of justice, and given a free hand he might have made this so-called land of lubbers an orderly, prosperous spot. But the odds were against him. Although all ungranted land had reverted to the crown, by the time Johnston arrived, the title to more than half of it belonged to a small group of men. Lord Carteret, later the Earl of Granville, one of the later proprietors, had retained a strip seventy miles wide that stretched the length of the northern boundary; blank patents issued by the previous governor had disposed of another half million acres. Johnston could do nothing about the Granville holdings, but he refused to confirm the other patents. His efforts to protect the settler from the speculator accomplished little, however, for royal officials at home continued to pass out the land to a few influential people—1,200,000 acres to a combine of British merchants headed by Henry McCulloh and 200,000 acres more to a friend of McCulloh's named Arthur Dobbs.

Authorities in England undermined other of Johnston's attempts to bring order into the colony's chaotic affairs. His instructions called for quitrents—out of which would come the governor's salary—to be paid in British currency, though settlers were accustomed to paying in produce or local currency. After some five hundred men gathered to free a settler imprisoned for nonpayment, Johnston had the sense to disregard his instructions. He worked out a compromise plan with the assembly, only to have it eventually disallowed by London officials. Another, more significant, innovation of his was also disallowed. The governor, seeking a fairer distribution of assembly seats, backed a plan that deprived the minority of colonists in the tidewater counties of their hold over the legislature. When it was clear that Johnston meant to push the plan through, the tidewater representatives in 1746 boycotted the assembly; the boycott was still in effect when Johnston died in 1752. He was succeeded, after a gap of two governorless years, by Arthur Dobbs, who brought word that London had disallowed Johnston's redistribution act. This, together with Dobbs's determination to strengthen royal authority in the colony and his prejudice in favor of the large landholders, of whom he was one, did nothing to alleviate the bitterness between inland and coastal counties, which finally erupted in open rebellion in 1771.

Rebellion, too, struck South Carolina about the same time, but the

causes, like the country, differed. Along the strip of low-lying coastland
that stretched southward from Cape Fear, past Charleston, to the plantations on the Savannah River lay a country that was "in the spring a paradise, in the summer a hell, and in the autumn a hospital." (The ague, or
malaria, touched nearly all; and according to one visitor, men "are so
accustomed to the evil that if, in greeting them, one asks: 'How are you?'
they answer, their teeth chattering with the cold of the ague, 'Pretty well,
only the fever!'") This strip of low country extended inland from ten
to sixty miles; a barricade of pine barrens insulated it from the backcountry. The low country held approximately a third of South Carolina's population in 1775, something like 110,000 people, of whom 75 per cent were
Negroes. The little group of whites, living on the edge of a wilderness,
"surrounded by a vast, terrifying population of servile blacks," Carl
Bridenbaugh has remarked, "built its future under unique conditions."
And in the process, it might be added, created a society unique to America. Most of the well-to-planters and their families, perhaps two thousand
all told, lived in Charleston. They comprised the largest, richest group of
leisured people in eighteenth-century America. They lived in elegant
houses, dined with the best wines, dressed in the latest London fashions.
Few went to college. "Cards, dice, the bottle and horses engross prodigious
portions of time and attention," a visiting New Englander observed.

The wealth of the low country came mainly from rice and indigo.
Rice produced immense profits. A man needed no more than £2,500 to
start a plantation in Carolina or, after the land there had been settled, in
Georgia. A 200-acre tract, of which 130 acres were suitable for rice, cost
about £200; the forty slaves needed for cultivation and the harvest cost
approximately £1,800. The planter could expect to harvest some 350 barrels, which in an average year sold for £2 a barrel, giving him around 25
to 30 per cent return on his investment when all incidentals were figured
in. The growing of indigo proved equally profitable. It complemented rice
perfectly, for it thrived on high, dry ground and needed no tending during the months when rice was being planted. Indigo was the source for a
blue dye popular among British clothmakers. Most of the million or so
pounds of indigo that Britain used prior to the 1740's came from the
Spanish and French West Indies. A young lady named Eliza Lucas soon
changed that pattern. Miss Lucas (who eventually became Mrs. Charles
Pinckney) was still in her teens when she took over management of her
father's plantation near Charleston. She searched for ways to increase
profits and after three years of experimentation marketed the first crop of
indigo in 1744. Though the product proved inferior to what Britain had
been using, Parliament encouraged her efforts. In 1748 it authorized a
subsidy of six pence a pound for all indigo produced within the

British Empire. South Carolina's export of the staple shot up from slightly more than thirteen thousand pounds to more than a million by 1754.

A Carolina plantation seldom exceeded three hundred acres or housed more than thirty or forty Negroes. The planters preferred to work a small unit, and they expanded by creating a new plantation rather than adding to the old one. The arrangement seems to have been made to promote an efficient operation. If the purpose was to isolate Negroes into small, relatively harmless groups, it only partly succeeded. "The Negroes have a wonderful art of communicating intelligence among themselves," a Georgian said. "It will run several hundreds of miles in a week or fortnight." Revolt was always a real threat in a land where colored people outnumbered white 3 to 1 and in some spots 50 to 1. After an abortive uprising in 1739, severe codes regulating all sides of Negro life were put into effect. The provincial militia was designed as much to suppress a Negro revolt as to move against Indians or Spanish on the frontiers.

Carolina wealth was rooted in the country but flowered in Charleston. The planter generally lived with his family on one of his plantations during the winter, but in summer he left the management of his holdings in the hands of white overseers and sought the cool sea breezes of Charleston, whose social season then came to its peak. Crèvecoeur found Charleston's inhabitants "the gayest in America," which was a fair description; but beneath the veneer of gaiety, Charleston differed little from other cities on the continent, for whom the main occupation of life was first business, then politics. Charleston merchants dominated the economy of the lower South, and hardly an item imported or exported between Cape Fear and St. Augustine failed at some time to pass through their hands. The backcountry was tied to the city by a rough wagon road over which rumbled tons of lumber and naval stores, wheat, corn, and pork. The barrels of rice and indigo were not picked up, as tobacco was in the Chesapeake Bay, at plantation wharves but were floated down the Savannah, Santee, Edisto, and Pee Dee Rivers into Charleston, where the merchants from there on managed their sale. Charleston continued to dominate the Indian trade even after the rise of such local centers as Savannah, Augusta, St. Augustine, Pensacola, and Mobile. Every year the city exported something close to a million pounds of deerskins. John Adams was told in 1776 that "Carolina very passionately considers this trade as contributory to her grandeur and dignity."

Political as well as economic power centered in Charleston, and again the planter-merchant elite dominated affairs. Since the "revolution" of 1719, when the legislature took power from the proprietors' governor and chose its own, there had been no need to fight for control over internal affairs, over judicial appointments, or over the purse strings. Suffrage

qualifications were reasonable; a man needed only fifty acres to vote.
(Stiffer requirements in 1745 and 1759 that demanded up to three hundred acres of land were disallowed.) Members of the legislature, however,
had to own five hundred acres of land and twenty slaves, a qualification
relatively few could meet. Relations with royal officials were reasonably
good. The popular and able James Glen, who was governor from 1743
to 1756, did much to dampen antagonism between legislature and executive. The removal of rice from the enumerated list in 1730, which allowed
Carolina growers to compete directly in Spanish and Portuguese markets,
and the royal subsidies for indigo and naval stores limited complaints
against Britain's navigation system.

Within the legislature a reasonable harmony prevailed, thanks in
part to a royal order that limited the number of assembly seats at forty-
eight. As new backcountry parishes were erected, slight readjustments in
the distribution of the seats were made, but control of all legislative affairs
remained with the tidewater region. Because no deep divisions split the
tidewater elite, no factions disrupted Carolina politics. When the time
came, South Carolina would speak with force and authority on such
imperial questions as the Stamp Act, even though at the moment it spoke
the colony was racked by a bitter quarrel between the backcountry and
coastal area. The quarrel was unique: the backcountry fought to get government, not against it. South Carolina differed from every colony in
America in that it alone had not developed institutions of local government. Political power centered in Charleston. There were no courts of
justice nor officials of any sort past the pine barrens. The backcountry
had some sarcastic remarks to make during the Stamp Act controversy,
when tidewater people talked warmly about rights and privileges. "Lo! . . .
the men who bounce and make much noise about liberty . . . keep half
their fellow subjects in a state of slavery," said one who lived past the
pine barrens. "All that they set down under the head of *apprehensions*
from the ministry, they now realize and execute over others. What they
pretend for to fear, they make others feel. What they paint in idea, the
people experience in reality." A short while later, the Carolina backcountry staged riots for its own rights. Fortunately for America, the
riots as well as the problems were unique to South Carolina.

THE BACKCOUNTRY

The word "backcountry," a variation of the earlier term "backwoods,"
seems to have been coined near the start of the eighteenth century. Its
meaning varied with time and from person to person. Prior to 1763, it

referred mainly to that block of land between the fall line and the Appalachians that stretched from Pennsylvania to Georgia. The block broadened and merged into the West after 1763, as settlers leaked through the dike of mountains into the Ohio Valley and the eastern parts of what would become Kentucky and Tennessee. People of the day did not know where the backcountry ended, but they could pinpoint where it began. A Philadelphian, an inhabitant of Lancaster or of Carlisle, near the Susquehanna River, knew it lay to *his* west. People spoke the word "backcountry" in a patronizing tone, as if it were an inferior, less civilized place. They had fixed conceptions of what it was like: the backcountry people were crude, their homes filthy, the food dreadful. Travelers into the backcountry stared with disbelief when they came upon "a well-finished parlor, with many pieces of good painting." An evening with a lout who dined on whiskey was to be expected; an evening "in the company of gentlemen where there is no reserve" and where "books and literary improvements were the subject" came as a shock. The stereotyped picture of the backcountry turned out on close inspection to be rooted at best in half-truths.

Settlement

Approximately a quarter of a million people lived in the backcountry in 1776; most of them had been funneled through Pennsylvania. The incoming waves of Scotch-Irish and German-speaking immigrants had rolled through Philadelphia, past Lancaster, up against the Appalachian barrier, then spilled off to the south. By the mid-1730's, settlers were flowing between the Blue Ridge and Appalachians into the Shenandoah Valley. The 1750's saw them moving into the rich lands behind the pine barrens of North Carolina, and by the 1760's the ruts in the land cut by their carts reached all the way to Georgia. The Great Wagon Road, as this seven hundred mile–long backcountry thoroughfare came to be called, soon carried more traffic than any highway in America. Grain in large covered wagons and herds of cattle—"during this month and last more than one thousand head of cattle have been driven by here," a diarist wrote in October 1774—went north to Pennsylvania markets and manufactured goods came back. Hamlets that would in time become villages, then towns—York, Hagerstown, Winchester, Stephensburg, Strasburg, Staunton, Salisbury, Camden—cropped up along the road. Southern colonies did their best to divert goods from the Great Wagon Road to hamlets along the fall line like Bath, Hillsboro, Springhill, Cross Creek, and Cheraw Hill, which could send them on to the tidewater. An east-west road over which something like three thousand wagons a year traveled

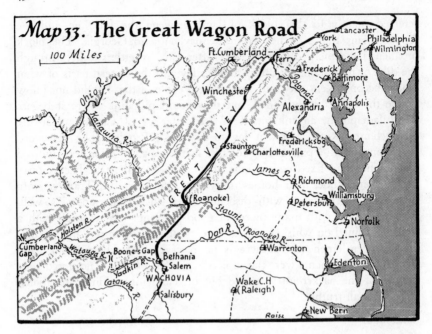

Map 33. The Great Wagon Road

from the backcountry into Charleston allowed South Carolina to cut to nearly nothing its once heavy imports of flour and meat from Pennsylvania.

The people of this country were of the same "strange mixture" that had populated Pennsylvania, and as in that colony, there was little melting-down into a new breed of man. Settlers sorted themselves according to race or religion. German-speaking people founded Frederick Town and Winchester, Salisbury was Scotch-Irish, and Irish Quakers laid out Pine Tree Hill. In South Carolina a group of Welsh Baptists clustered along the Pee Dee River, and a body of French Huguenots lived unto themselves at New Bordeaux. When Virginians, who were usually of English descent, joined the stream, they, too, gathered with their own kind.

The land, as always, drew the people on. Maryland offered its backcountry in lots of two hundred acres to heads of families and one hundred acres to single men, all free of quitrents for three years. Virginia speculators monopolized most of the Shenandoah Valley, but their prices were reasonable—about 15s. an acre in the early years of settlement. The spot especially attracted settlers, for Indians had burned over the area regularly to make hunting game easier, and this made the job of clearing the ground for the first planting relatively simple. As the valley filled up, land prices doubled, and some settlers cashed in on the boom and joined the migrating stream southward. Speculators had snapped up most of the backcountry of North Carolina, but again prices were reasonable, this time partly because of the bait South Carolina dangled before settlers—a headright grant varying from one to two hundred acres.

Backcountry farms resembled those that seventeenth-century settlers had carved from the wilderness. Few exceeded two hundred acres; a farmer and his family could not handle more, for labor was always in short supply. Men at first planted only to feed their families—corn, peas, beans, potatoes, some wheat, barley, or rye. (The Scotch-Irish preferred rye for whiskey; the Germans barley for malt.) As markets opened up, they gave more thought to a cash crop: hemp, flax, and wheat flourished in Maryland; tobacco in the Shenandoah Valley; indigo in South Carolina. Hogs and cattle roamed wild. The hogs were slaughtered in the fall to fill the pork barrel; the cattle were herded into cowpens and from there either driven northward along the Great Wagon Road or eastward to the coast. The heavy traffic on the Great Wagon Road and the lively trade in the hamlets of the backcountry and along the fall line should not mislead. Most backcountry farmers lived close to a subsistence level and cleared next to nothing in cash for a year's work. The scrawny cattle, the few bushels of wheat, the hogshead or two of tobacco the farmer took to market might buy a sickle, a few yards of cloth, some salt, and a saucepan—but not much more. Although few starved in the backcountry, only a few prospered.

Though backcountry society remained through the colonial period in "swaddling clothes," an elite of sorts did emerge. It differed, however, from its counterpart in the East, where culture and family counted for something. Wealth alone, or "driving acquisitiveness," carried a man to the top in the backcountry. Modest wealth was enough to set a man apart, for in a land always short of labor and capital it took a clever, ruthless man to acquire even that. A few slaves and anything from five hundred to a thousand acres of land carried enough prestige to qualify a man for an appointment as justice of the peace or sheriff or a seat in the assembly. These backcountry aristocrats were rarely polished nor were they a close-knit, unified group like the elite in the East—disputes flared constantly among them—but they monopolized the available public offices and ran the backcountry's affairs.

On the rung below the elite stood the mass of backcountry people— the run-of-the-mill farmer and his family, respectable, law-abiding, church-going members of society. They worked hard to improve both themselves and their farms. They reared their children to be God-fearing and, where schools existed, saw that they learned to read and write. Scattered amidst the plain people but below them socially were the riffraff. The back-country, a traveling preacher observed, was filled with men who "were refugees from debt, or had deserted their wives and children, or had fled to escape punishment for evil deeds," and who thought that "no one would find them, and they could go in impunity." Some of these people made a go of their second chance at life. Some failed; their farms reverted to forests, and they turned to gambling or pilfering to survive. These shiftless people went to the backcountry "for the sake of living without trouble," according to one South Carolinian. They grew just enough corn to feed themselves; the woods produced grass for their horses and acorns and chestnuts for their hogs. "They call this kind of life *following the range*. They are very ignorant and hate all men of education. They call them Pen and Ink Men."

The riffraff lived at the edge of society. The outlaws lived outside it, and by the 1760's they were undermining what little order had been achieved in backcountry life. They roamed in bands through the land, plundering and stealing everywhere. South Carolina was hit first and hardest by them shortly after the Cherokee War. The Cherokees had struck the Carolina backcountry in 1760. They used the hit-and-run tactics that had prevailed on the Pennsylvania frontier, and with the same success. By the winter of 1760–1761, some fifteen hundred Carolinians were penned in forts throughout the backcountry; Charleston dispatched troops, who, in the process of driving back the Indians, also plundered "the poor scatter'd inhabitants." Later, the settlers "complain'd that they sustain'd more damage from their protectors than from the enemy, as they stript them of the little the other had left. . . ." Peace came in the last days of 1761. Settlers went back to their farms, free at last of the Indian menace, but now, amid the confusion of the postwar period, confronted with bands of lawless men bent on plundering. And the suppression of the great Indian uprising of 1763, which came on the heels of the treaty that ended the French and Indian War, released through the backcountry hundreds more of "loose fellows who for seven years had been accustomed to murder and pillage" and "choosing a life of idleness . . . form'd themselves into gangs and rang'd over, and laid under contribution the whole Continent."

Although the end of the Indian menace unleashed disorder within the backcountry, freedom from an outside enemy also gave settlers the chance to deal firmly with the one in their midst. By 1772 law and order at least in a rudimentary form prevailed throughout the backcountry. The birth pangs of a new limb of American society had ended. By that time, too, another backcountry had begun to take form, this time across the hitherto virtually impenetrable Appalachian Mountains. Well-intended but vacillating British officials first closed off the tramontane region, then, on second thought, opened up selected parts for settlement. This attempt at controlled settlement succeeded no better than similar attempts in the seventeenth century. Settlers and speculators shoved in where they wished. In 1769 a group staked out claims on the Watauga River in what would one day be Tennessee. The same year a hunter named Daniel Boone pushed over the mountains to explore what would in time become Kentucky; five years later, financed by the Transylvania Company, he headed a group of thirty pioneers who cleared a path over the mountains that soon would be called the Wilderness Trail. By 1776 some twenty-five thousand settlers were scratching a living from the land over the mountains, and the West was about to enter its own period of labor pains.

Customs and Manners

The quality of life in the backcountry varied in time and from place to place. In the early days of settlement, a rough lean-to of logs might suffice for a home; later, a traveler through the same area could come upon a gentleman who "lives elegantly—In the parlor where I am sitting are three windows, each with twenty-four lights of large glass." (One way to measure wealth in a day when the price of glass came high was to count the number of window panes or "lights" in a house.) While one part of the country lived elegantly, another might be enduring its starving time. The month of March was hardest for newly settled areas. It was then that the bottom of the pork barrel that had carried the family through the winter came in sight. "Not a grain of corn for the horse," one traveler wrote during a spring trip. "Nothing but Indian cornmeal to be had. . . . No butter, rice, or milk."

Backcountry pioneers suffered all the perils and hardships of those who made the first plantings in the seventeenth century, and they endured one more—the harsh, patronizing comments of travelers from the East. Visitors judged by standards alien to backcountry life. Customs and manners differed between the settled and backcountry parts of America; what differed, they thought, must be inferior. One man found that "as for tea and coffee, they know it not"; they preferred to "live wholly on butter, milk, clabber, and what in England is given to the hogs and dogs." People in the backcountry shunned tea and coffee because, as they said, it "did not stick by the ribs." "A genuine backwoodsman," said one who had been reared in the region, "would have thought himself disgraced by showing a fondness for these slops."

Much about the backcountry had the flavor of a foreign land. Germans dropped strange words into their talk. ("An old, kind Dutch landlady gave our horses for breakfast a dish of '*spelts*.' ") The Scotch-Irish spoke "in a shrill, acute accent" and filled the air with odd phrases. A lady named Mrs. Ewing provided several for one traveler's journal.

"My son," said Mrs. Ewing, "lately lost his foot in the smallpox." (She meant he could not stand.)

"Will you just take a check?" (She meant a late dinner.)

"Our neighbor McOlahlan since you left us has flitted." (She meant has moved away.)

In the backcountry, past blended to create a present that in many ways seemed out of place in eighteenth-century America, for much of the seventeenth century persisted in the back settlements. People lived on "hog and hominy," ate mostly from wooden bowls and trenchers, and drank from wooden noggins. There were neither physicians nor medicines for the sick, who were cured mainly by waiting "till nature gets the better of the disease or death relieves you." A dipper of whisky before breakfast steadied the man afflicted with the shakes of ague, or malaria. The blood of a black cat cured erysipelas, hence, said a settler, "there was scarcely a black cat whose ears and tail had not been frequently cropped for a contribution of blood." Witches fluttered everywhere about the backcountry. They inoculated children with strange diseases, shot hair balls into cattle, put spells upon guns, changed men into horses. (Here, as handed down by a man reared in the backcountry of Pennsylvania, is one among many cures against witches. "The picture of the supposed witch was drawn on a stump or piece of board and shot at with a bullet containing a little bit of silver. This silver bullet transferred a painful and sometimes mortal spell on that part of the witch corresponding with the part of the portrait struck by the bullet.")

The swift push of people into the backcountry after 1730 outran the institutions of settled society. Ministers and schoolteachers lagged far behind. The inhabitants created a rough form of law to serve until the institutions of government caught up with settlement. A "corn right" gave a man a hundred acres of land for every acre he planted; a dwelling established a man's claim by "cabin right"; a claim bounded by deadened trees was considered established by "tomahawk right." The community stood behind those who acquired land by these "rights," and no one could usurp the claim until he had bought the "rights" from the "owner."

Equality prevailed in the backcountry: everyone in the early years of settlement was equally poor. Women, many of them pretty, came to church service "in their shifts and a short petticoat only, barefooted and bare-legged. . . ." The men's footwear, if any, was "*mockisons* or Indian shoes." Social distinctions vanished in the backcountry. "Every man in all companies, with almost no exception," one traveler observed, "calls his wife, brother, neighbor, or acquaintance by their proper name of Sally, John, James, or Michael, without ever prefixing the customary compliment of 'My Dear,' 'Sir,' 'Mr.,' etc."

Many of the characteristics that have since been called typically American were, though sometimes evident in the settled communities of the East, found full-blown in the backcountry. The people liked practical jokes, for example. Reverend Charles Woodmason tells of the time that Presbyterians, whom this Anglican father considered

the most lowest, vilest crew breathing, . . . hir'd a band of rude fellows to come to service who brought with them fifty-seven dogs (for I counted them), which in time of service they set fighting, and I was obliged to stop. In time of sermon they repeated it, and I was oblig'd to desist and dismiss the people. . . .

(The disturbances ceased thereafter when Reverend Woodmason noised it about that fifty-seven Presbyterians had attended his service that day.) Backcountry humor could also be laced with wit, too, as Philip Vickers Fithian, a roving Presbyterian missionary, found out.

"Peggy," Fithian heard a man called Tom say one night in a backcountry cabin, "bring in some bark to save the fire."

"Indeed, Tom," the girl said, "I am tired [from] pulling flax all day and can't."

"Well, then," said Tom, "run out and call in the neighbors to see it *die.*"

Above all, these were for the most part a restless people. "They acquire no attachment to place," Lord Dunmore once remarked, "but wandering seems engrafted in their nature; and it is a weakness incident to it that they should ever imagine that the lands farther off are still better than those upon which they are already settled." This lack of "attachment to place," so much a characteristic of later Americans, set the man from the backcountry apart from his contemporaries in another way. The particularism found among seaboard colonists either weakened or vanished in the back settlements. Men from all colonies lived there together. Only there was it likely that when a man said "my country," he meant America rather than a particular colony. It was a man reared in the backcountry who rose in 1774 and said to fellow delegates in the first Continental Congress: "The distinctions between Virginians, Pennsylvanians, New Yorkers, and New Englanders, are no more. I am not a Virginian, but an American."

Relations with the East

America reproduced itself in the backcountry. At first, the new settlements floated in a sea of forests moored only by the slimmest lines to the seaboard. But old habits brought from the coast persisted, for when men move into an isolated area they strive to hold on to what little they can salvage from the past; they cling to the old, conventional way of doing things and experiment only when forced to. Once the first plantings took root and the starving times ended, ties between the seaboard and back settlements strengthened. The unique qualities imposed by life in a wilderness deep within the continent, far beyond the sights, sounds, and smells of the sea, should not obscure the bonds that cemented East and West together. Newspapers printed in seaboard towns circulated throughout the back settlements; they carried news of imperial, provincial, and backcountry affairs. Local and provincial officials—surveyors, assemblymen, justices of the peace, king's attorneys, tax collectors, and the like—traveled steadily between the two regions. Seaboard and backcountry merchants communicated constantly. The backcountry from time to time may have felt put upon by the seaboard settlements, but no deep nor inherent antagonism existed between the two sections—at least not prior to the Revolution.

The church was the first seaboard institution to reach the backcountry. But religion at first contributed little order or peace, for the various sects were "eternally jarring among themselves." Presbyterians hounded Anglican services; Baptists railed at Presbyterians. And ministers were always in short supply. Only two of twenty-one Presbyterian congregations in the backcountry of South Carolina in 1768 had clergymen of their own. The few ministers who ventured into the backcountry found God had cut out more than enough work for them. More often than not women were pregnant when they came to be married. A high incidence of venereal disease prevailed throughout the region. Drunkenness was common among men and women alike. Reverend Woodmason, who worked hard to impose civilized standards on his parishioners, had a standard sermon he gave during his circuit of the back settlements: "On Correct Behavior in Church," in which he urged the people not to bring dogs to the service, not to "whisper, talk, gaze about," not to "chew or spit in church," which was an absurd habit, "especially in women in God's house." Reverend Woodmason groused relentlessly about the low state of manners and morals, but he ended with deep affection for what he called "my poor backcountry people." This is the way he summed up his accomplishments in the wilderness:

Thus you have my journal of two years—In which have rode near six thousand miles, almost on one horse. Wore myself to a skeleton and endured all the extremities of hunger, thirst, cold, and heat. Have baptized near twelve hundred children—Given two hundred or more discourses—rais'd almost thirty congregations—Set on foot the building of sundry chapels—Distributed books, medicines, garden seed, turnip, clover, timothy, burnet, and other grass seeds—with fish hooks—Small working tools and variety of implements to set the poor at work, and promote industry to the amount of at least one hundred pounds sterling. Roads are making—boats building—bridges framing, and other useful works begun thro' my means, as will not only be of public utility, but make the countryside wear a new face, and the people become new creatures.

By the time Reverend Woodmason left the backcountry in the late 1760's, the political institutions of every colony from Pennsylvania to Georgia had been extended into the back settlements. All the accouterments of orderly government—county courts, justices of the peace, sheriffs, and the like—together with representation in the provincial assembly, came in most cases—South Carolina excepted—on the heels of settlement. The addition of the new counties did not upset the balance of power, for seaboard counties clung to the bulk of assembly seats in every colony. However, to make certain of responsible government led by moderate men, the seaboard maintained a subtler, though not necessarily obnoxious, form of control over the backcountry's affairs. Justices of the peace and sheriffs in most colonies were appointed by the colonial governor. (Sheriffs were elected in Pennsylvania but had to be approved by the governor.) These appointive offices went only to men whose qualities were known, who could be trusted to govern in a manner of which all right-thinking conservative gentlemen would approve. In Pennsylvania, for instance, Arthur St. Clair, a former British officer, who, with his wealthy wife, circulated in the best Philadelphia society and was a friend of the politically powerful Allen family, guided the affairs of the tramontane county of Bedford. When St. Clair was later transferred to Westmoreland County, where he contended with tact but firmness against the Virginia claim to the land around the forks of the Ohio, Thomas Smith, another backcountry gentleman with Philadelphia connections, was chosen to head Bedford County.

The career of James Wilson, a bright young immigrant from Scotland, exemplifies the neat way in which the seaboard had a hand in determining who got backcountry elective offices. Wilson immigrated to America in 1765, taught Greek briefly at the College of Philadelphia, then read law for a year in the office of John Dickinson. He left to make his fortune in the backcountry, but ties with Philadelphia remained. When Benjamin Franklin's wife wanted a backcountry debt collected, for instance, she was referred to Wilson. Wilson married the daughter of a backcountry patriarch, moved to Carlisle, and there, among the contentious Scotch-Irish, prospered as a lawyer. His practice took him often to Philadelphia. And when Wilson won a seat in the assembly, Philadelphia as much as the backcountry county of Cumberland could claim him as theirs.

Pennsylvania's back counties could truly complain that they were underrepresented in the assembly, that they lacked adequate roads, that they needed help against the Indians. Once, in the Paxton Boys Riots, these grievances led to a short-lived uprising—directed, however, at the assembly rather than at the seaboard settlements in general. Pennsylvania's social, political, and economic affairs were too intertwined for a deep or irremediable split to develop, and the moderate men who ran local and provincial affairs saw to it that it did not.

The story in the Chesapeake colonies duplicates that of Pennsylvania. Both created new counties once settlement justified the need for local government. (Virginia, in fact, created Augusta County partly to speed settlement in the Ohio Valley, where Pennsylvania contested its claim.) Young men from established families filtered into the back parts of both colonies, and when the time came for the governor to appoint local officials they invariably received the posts. Tidewater aristocrats who had speculated heavily in the Shenandoah Valley saw to it that the assembly did not harm their holdings by legislation that prejudiced the welfare of the backcountry. "I have searched fruitlessly for evidence that before 1776 political sectionalism—western resentment of eastern overrepresentation and rule—was an issue, either open or covert, in Maryland or Virginia," Carl Bridenbaugh has written. "Nor were there any undercurrents of economic or social unrest."

The story takes a different tack in the Carolinas, though not one that reveals a fixed and inherent antagonism between the backcountry and the tidewater region. South Carolina's backcountry had by the 1760's accumulated a bundle of grievances. It wanted schools, roads, bridges, all of which the assembly had refused to subsidize. It resented its slim share of assembly seats. The flat, colony-wide tax rate, which treated backcountry holdings as though acre for acre they equaled the lucrative seaboard plantations, seemed unreasonable. The assembly's refusal to provide the back settlements with courts provoked bitterness; all legal business had to be handled in Charleston, and that meant a long, hard, and expensive trip for the backcountry farmer. The government's refusal to send disciplined troops to crush the roving bands of outlaws that had infested the backcountry since the Cherokee War gave the settlers their strongest grievance. In 1767 they created an "association" for "regulating" backcountry affairs. The substantial men of the region, backed by the respectable element among the plain people, were behind this self-created law-enforcement body; their goal was to protect life and property in the back settlements. "The men who constituted the first large-scale vigilante movement in American history," Richard M. Brown, the latest to study the movement, has said, "took the law into their own hands but did so for conservative social purposes."

The government at Charleston, aware of its deficiency, did nothing to crush this extralegal organization. Lieutenant Governor William Bull told London that the Regulators, as they were called, were not "idle vagabonds," and that "tho' poor, they are in general an industrious, hardy race of men." Reverend Woodmason, from his vantage point in the back-country, judged the Regulation movement a success. True, "the people were governed by their militia officers, who decided all disputes over the drumhead in the muster field," but "the country was purged of all villains," he said. "The whores were whipped and drove off. The magistrates and constables associated with the rogues silenc'd and inhibited. Tranquillity reigned. Industry was restor'd." Woodmason simplified matters a bit. Toward the end of 1768, as something like peace and order appeared in the back settlements, resentment broke forth against excesses among certain of the Regulators who had taken it upon themselves to punish immorality as well as lawlessness. A faction of moderates set out to check, the headstrong within the movement, and within a few months they had gathered sufficient support to bring the unruly to heel. A truce between the two factions in March 1769 virtually ended the Regulation movement in South Carolina.

The end of Regulation was hastened to an extent by the assembly's inclination to redress those backcountry grievances it could. However, imperial relations complicated efforts at appeasement. Royal instructions, for instance, forbade enlargement of the assembly, which meant that any increase in backcountry seats would be at the expense of the seaboard; no real readjustment in representation came until the Revolution. A bill establishing circuit courts in 1768 was disallowed. Other efforts to deal with backcountry complaints that year were cut short when the governor dissolved the assembly because it had endorsed the Massachusetts Circular Letter. A bill in 1770 to establish "English Schools" in the backcountry failed to reach the voting stage because the governor prorogued the assembly. Still, one major grievance was resolved. The Circuit Court Act of 1769, framed to meet royal approval, established six court districts for the back settlements. Reverend Woodmason thought the statute inadequate—he said that a man still had to travel the two or three hundred miles to Charleston simply to get a marriage license—but in Richard M. Brown's judgment, "a judicial system appropriate to the state of Back Country society had been established." The act gave the backcountry courts complete jurisdiction in all civil and criminal cases, and provisions called for trials by juries and for speedy and inexpensive justice.

Reverend Woodmason, who had once been a merchant in Charleston, believed the low country "would fetter and chain the back inhabitants, could they get them in their clutches." No doubt this was true, but Woodmason's contemporary judgment does not contradict the modern one of

Brown, who believed the Regulators were neither "a fundamental threat
to the provincial *status quo*" nor engaged in "aggressions against the Low
Country." The movement shows the backcountry coming of age and
"learning to set its house in order in its own way."

The same cannot be said for the Regulation movement in North
Carolina. The backcountry people there did not need to create a government to bring about law and order; they already had one. North Carolina
had been as prompt as any colony to extend the county system into newly
settled areas. No one in the backcountry quarreled with the "form or
mode" of local government nor with "the body of our laws." They were
enraged, though, by "the malpractices of the officers of our county courts,
and abuses that we suffer by those that are empowered to manage our
public affairs." Sheriffs were suspected of pocketing something like half
the taxes they collected. Court officials extorted outrageous fees for routine
procedures. (In one instance, court costs for six cases for amounts totaling
£10 came to £60.) Other grievances—high quitrents, tithes to the established Anglican Church, lack of roads and bridges, underrepresentation
in the assembly—added to the backcountry's anger.

Discontent among the North Carolina back settlements boiled through
the 1760's. Early in the decade, men vented their bitterness in petitions,
and as long as protest was confined to legitimate channels the backcountry
remained united against the governor and assembly that imposed corrupt
officials upon it. Violence was sporadic and unorganized until South
Carolina established a pattern of resistance. (The Regulation, in name
and form, was copied in the northern colony, but that appears to have
been the extent of the connection between the two movements.) However,
organized violence divided rather than unified the backcountry people of
North Carolina. The German-speaking settlers for the most part disas-
sociated themselves from the Regulation. Though a majority of the
Scotch-Irish joined, many of the substantial people among them, including
a number of their Presbyterian ministers, spoke out against the movement.
The Regulators' resistance wilted in 1768 when Governor William Tryon
made a show of force against them. The "reformers" then tried a new
approach: they sought to get rid of the corrupt by filing suits against them,
but the law failed them. A leading Regulator was jailed, according to
even an anti-Regulation newspaper, by a "confederacy of extortionate
officers" who hoped to "cow him from bringing their extortions to light."
The assembly also blocked efforts to reform the government in the back
settlements. When once again the Regulation sought justice through
violence, once again Governor Tryon set out to suppress the rebels.
Two armies, each numbering about one thousand armed men, met in
mid-May 1771 on the field of Alamance, about twenty miles from Hills-

borough. When the two lines had approached to within fifty feet of one another, the governor roared out for his troops to open fire, but everyone was "too busily occupied either in an argument or a fist fight to heed the . . . decree." Eventually, someone began to fire; nine men died on each side. The Regulators fled the field and the government claimed a "glorious and signal victory" over "lawless desperadoes." The Regulation died in North Carolina with the battle of Alamance. The quick collapse of the movement suggests that it developed out of a set of specific grievances rather than any inherent hostility between the seaboard and backcountry. Some reputable historians still propagate the view that the Regulators of both North and South Carolina "were, in their violent but ill-disciplined way, on the Loyalist side" during the Revolution. The research of Richard M. Brown (for South Carolina) and Elmer Douglas Johnson (for North Carolina) has shown this to be false. Brown found only 5 per cent of the Regulators definitely became Tories in his colony and Johnson came up with a similar figure. While loyalism was stronger in the backcountry than along the seaboard, its strength had nothing to do either with tensions between the two regions or with lingering animosities from the Regulation period. One student of loyalism in South Carolina believes "the back settlers in 1775 were not prepared emotionally for the Revolution" and that this, together with their relative isolation and lack of involvement in the provincial government, led them to favor the *status quo* to the uncertainties of independence.

Much obviously divided America in 1763. Divisions persisted in the colonies between town and country, between merchant and farmer, between established and dissenting sects, and the Mason-Dixon Line marked the division for many between North and South. Perceptive men of the day knew, however, that more bound together the disparate colonies and the two regions than divided them, and that nowhere did foundations exist "on which to build a distinct regional culture, no beachhead, even, where such a momentous operation might begin." America's was a single and in many ways mature culture by the eve of the Revolution. Its colleges turned out men of urbanity, well-grounded in the arts and sciences. Its politicians were adept and intelligent. But it was also a provincial culture. It depended on Britain for protection during wartime. British subsidies bolstered the economy. British grants for aid given during the imperial wars allowed virtually every colony to drift along without levying taxes down to the Revolution. Britain provided the bulk of America's manufactured goods. "There can be no room for real apprehension of danger of a revolt of the plantations in future ages" because they "depend entirely upon Great Britain," Reverend Hugh Jones wrote in 1724, and almost no one disputed his logic during the next half century. Though each of the colonies, said Jones, had "views different from one another, and as strenuously pursue their separate interests," they are tied "by blood, religion, language, laws, and customs" to Britain. They "cannot possibly subsist without some trade, correspondence, union, and alliance in Europe, and absolute necessity obliges them to fix these perpetually in Great Britain."

BIBLIOGRAPHY

Most of the books mentioned in the General Section of the Chapter 11 Bibliography are relevant here. Among several others concerned more particularly with the social, political, and economic life of the colonies in the eighteenth century, the most recent and lengthy is Clinton Rossiter's *Seedtime of the Republic* (1953), which has appeared in paperback under the titles *The First American Revolution, The Political Thought of the American Revolution,* and *Six Characters in Search of a Republic.* Rossiter discusses colonial affairs by topics rather than by colonies. Lawrence H. Gipson gives a full, colony by colony survey of America in 1754 in the second and third volumes of *The British Empire Before the American Revolution* (10 vols., 1956–1961). Older, briefer, and still useful accounts are those of Evarts B. Greene, *The Revolutionary Generation, 1763–1790* (1943), and James Truslow Adams, *Provincial Society* (1928). Leonard W. Labaree discusses *Conservatism in Early American History* (1948; pb.) with style and insight. Chilton Williamson has written the most recent survey of *American Suffrage: From Property to Democracy, 1760–1860* (1960), wherein he concludes that colonial America was "pre-democratic in its conscious thought." Percy W. Bidwell and John I. Falconer cover the *History of Agriculture in the Northern United States, 1620–1860* (1925), and Lewis C. Gray the *History of Agriculture in the Southern United States to 1860* (2 vols., 1933). Two contemporary accounts of American agriculture are the anonymous *American Husbandry* (1775), which Harry J. Carman edited in 1939, and Jared Eliot's *Essays upon Field Husbandry in New England, And Other Papers, 1748–1762,* which Carman edited with Rexford G. Tugwell in 1935.

The best, though slowest, way to get at the shape and content of life in eighteenth-century America is through the diaries of men who traveled the land. Newton D. Mereness has collected several firsthand accounts in *Travels in the American Colonies* (1916). Two general accounts are Mark A. De Wolfe, ed., "The Journal of Josiah Quincy, Junior, 1773," *Massachusetts Historical Society Proceedings,* 49 (1915), 424–481, and "Journal of a French Traveller in the Colonies, 1765," *AHR,* 26 (1920), 726–747. Carl Bridenbaugh, ed., *Gentleman's Progress: The Itinerarium of Dr. Alexander Hamilton, 1744* (1948), offers a tour of the northern colonies by a sharp observer. Andrew Burnaby's *Travels Through the Middle Settlements of North America* (1775; pb.) pictures the colonies in 1759, though the author clearly updated some of his views to fit the scene in 1775, the year he published the book in England. A. B. Benson's edition (2 vols., 1937) of Peter Kalm's *Travels into North America* in the 1740's has been enhanced by Martii Kerkkonen's *Peter Kalm's North American Journey: Its Ideological Background and Results* (1959). "Extracts from the Diary of Daniel Fisher, 1755," *PMHB*, 17 (1893), 263–278, excels most descriptions of eighteenth-century Pennsylvania. The observations of the German-speaking inhabitants are found in Gottlieb Mittelberger, *Journey to Pennsylvania*, most recently edited by Oscar Handlin and John Clive (1960), and in Theodore G. Tappert and John W. Doberstein, eds. and trans., *Notebook of a Colonial Clergyman: Condensed from the Journals of Henry Melchoir Muhlenberg* (1959), a one-volume edition of an earlier three-volume work. For the Revolutionary period there is, of course, J. Hector St. John de Crèvecoeur, *Letters from an American Farmer* (1782; pb.). Fewer generalizations and more details about daily life can be found in Philip Padelford, ed., *Colonial Panorama: Dr. Robert Honyman's Journal for March and April, 1775* (1939). Patrick M'Robert's *A Tour Through Part of the North Provinces of America 1774–1775*, can be found, as edited by Carl Bridenbaugh, in *PMHB*, 59 (1935), 134–180. Perhaps the fullest reports on daily life are found in Hunter D. Farish, ed., *Journal and Letters of Philip Vickers Fithian, 1773–1774* (1943), and Robert C. Albion and Leonidas Dodson, eds., *Philip Vickers Fithian: Journal, 1775–1776* (1932). The latter is especially good on the back-country and for some unaccountable reason has been allowed to drop out of print. The lively, earthy *Journal of Nicholas Cresswell, 1774–1776* (1925) ranges from Virginia to the Ohio Valley and back to Philadelphia and New York. Two useful postwar journals are Judson P. Wood, trans., and John S. Ezell, ed., *The New Democracy in America: Travels of Francisco de Miranda in the United States, 1783–1784* (1963), and the Marquis de Chastellux, *Travels in North America in the Years 1780, 1781, and 1782* (2 vols., 1963), recently reedited in a revised translation by Howard C. Rice.

The North

William B. Weeden's *Economic and Social History of New England, 1620–1789* (2 vols., 1890) is still the basic work on the subject. For details of daily life culled from newspaper advertisements see George Francis Dow, *Arts and Crafts in New England 1704–1775: Gleanings from Boston Newspapers* (1927), and *Everyday Life in the Massachusetts Bay Colony* (1935). A selection from Clifford K. Shipton's nine volumes of biographical sketches have been collected in *New England Life in the Eighteenth Century: Representative Biographies from Sibley's Harvard Graduates* (1963). Henry Bamford Parkes tells of "New England in the Seventeenth-Thirties," in *NEQ*, 3 (1930), 397–419. Bernard and Lotte Bailyn have combined their talents and knowledge with a computer to reveal a hitherto hidden story in *Massachusetts Shipping, 1697–1714: A Statistical Study* (1959). Their report may be fleshed out with three detailed accounts of mercantile life: Byron Fairchild,

Messrs. William Pepperrell: Merchants at Piscataqua (1954); James B.
Hedges, *The Browns of Providence Plantations: Colonial Years* (1952); and
Benjamin W. Labaree, *Patriots and Partisans: The Merchants of Newbury-
port, 1764–1815* (1962). Labaree's remarks on democracy in Newburyport
tend to diverge from conclusions reached in Robert E. Brown's *Middle-Class
Democracy and the Revolution in Massachusetts, 1691–1780* (1955), wherein
it is argued that as far as voting went, Massachusetts was much more democratic in the eighteenth century than has hitherto been assumed by historians.
John Cary's criticism of the "Statistical Method and the Brown Thesis on
Colonial Democracy," *WMQ,* 20 (1963), 251–276, is accompanied by a rebuttal from Brown. (It might be mentioned, though the article is really
relevant to the seventeenth century, that Brown's wife, B. Katherine Brown,
has extended her husband's study to an earlier time in her excellent "Puritan
Democracy: A Case Study," *MVHR,* 50 [1963], 377–396.)

The best brief accounts of New York are in the second volume of A. C.
Flick, ed., *History of the State of New York* (10 vols., 1933–1937), and
David Ellis, *et al., A Short History of New York State* (1957). Dixon Ryan
Fox's *Caleb Heathcote, Gentleman Colonist: The Story of a Career in the
Province of New York, 1692–1721* (1926) deserves to be brought back into
print. Alice M. Keys's inadequate biography of *Cadwallader Colden: A
Representative Eighteenth-Century Official* (1906) does little more than intro-
duce one of the most fascinating gentlemen of colonial America. Politics are
well covered, as far as the Livingston faction is concerned, from 1750 to the
Revolution in D. R. Dillon, *The New York Triumvirate: A Study of the
Legal and Political Careers of William Livingston, John Morin Scott, and
William Smith, Jr.* (1949). The role of lawyers in politics from 1760 to
1765 and their skill in making popular issues out of technical points is discussed by Milton M. Klein in "Prelude to Revolution in New York: Jury
Trials and Judicial Tenure," *WMQ,* 17 (1960), 439–462. Nicholas Varga
writes of "Election Procedures and Practices in Colonial New York," *New
York History (NYH),* 41 (1960), 249–277. Klein's "Democracy and Politics in Colonial New York," *NYH,* 40 (1959), 221–246 should not be
missed by any student. Samuel McKee, Jr., gives a good, brief account of
economic affairs in the second volume of Flick's *History of the State of New
York.* Irving Marks's *Agrarian Conflicts in Colonial New York, 1711–1775*
(1940) is by far the best work done on the subject. Material covered generally
in Virginia Harrington's *New York Merchants on the Eve of the Revolution*
(1935) is discussed in detail by Philip L. White in *The Beekmans of New
York in Politics and Commerce, 1647–1877* (1956), and documented in
White's edition of *The Beekman Mercantile Papers, 1746–1790* (1956).
"Interurban Correspondents and the Development of a National Economy
Before the Revolution: New York as a Case Study" by William S. Sacks can
be found in *NYH,* 36 (1955) 320–335. Peter Kalm's *Travels into North
America,* Dr. Hamilton's *Itinerarium,* and Anne Grant's *Memoirs of an
American Lady* (2 vols., 1808) give firsthand accounts of life in the colony.

Two brief, popular accounts by eminent historians of colonial New

Jersey are Wesley Frank Craven's *New Jersey and the English Colonization of North America* (1964) and Richard P. McCormick's *New Jersey from Colony to State, 1609–1789* (1964). McCormick's *History of Voting in New Jersey* [1664–1911] (1953) finds the the roots of modern democracy in the colonial period. Donald L. Kemmerer, *Path to Freedom* (1940), gives the fullest and most reliable account of politics in the colony during the eighteenth century. Remarks on farming are found in Carl R. Woodward, ed., *Ploughs and Politics: Charles Read of New Jersey and His Notes on Agriculture, 1715–1774* (1941).

Theodore Thayer discusses *Pennsylvanian Politics and the Growth of Democracy, 1740–1776* (1954) and "The Quaker Party of Pennsylvania, 1755–1765," *PMHB*, 71 (1947), 19–43. More recent accounts are by John J. Zimmerman, "Benjamin Franklin and the Quaker Party, 1755–1756," *WMQ*, 17 (1960), 291–313; by J. Philip Gleason, "A Scurrilous Colonial Election and Franklin's Reputation," *WMQ*, 18 (1961), 68–84; and by William S. Hanna, *Benjamin Franklin and Pennsylvania Politics* (1964). G. B. Warden tells the opposite faction's story in "The Proprietary Group in Pennsylvania, 1754–1764," *WMQ*, 21 (1964), 367–389. The more recent work on politics should not cause the student to overlook Winifred T. Root's *Relations of Pennsylvania with the British Government, 1696–1765* (1912). Among biographies that illuminate the political scene are Roy N. Locken, *David Lloyd: Colonial Lawmaker* (1959); Theodore Thayer, *Israel Pemberton: King of the Quakers* (1943); and Frederick B. Tolles, *James Logan and the Culture of Provincial America* (1957). Tolles' distinguished *Meeting House and Counting House: The Quaker Merchants of Colonial Philadelphia, 1682–1763* (1948; pb.) offers as much cultural, as it does economic, history. It should be supplemented by his "The Culture of Early Pennsylvania," *PMHB*, 81 (1957), 117–135, which deals with the colony as it was in the 1740's. Whitfield Bell, Jr., carried the story further in time in "Some Aspects of the Social History of Pennsylvania, 1760–1790," *PMHB*, 62 (1938), 281–308; and Carl and Jessica Bridenbaugh amplify it in *Rebels and Gentlemen: Philadelphia in the Age of Franklin* (1942). The economic story has been told in Arthur L. Jensen's *The Maritime Commerce of Colonial Philadelphia* (1963). The detailed picture of the economy given in Anne Bezanson, *Prices and Inflation During the American Revolution: Pennsylvania, 1770–1790* (1951) makes her book pertinent here, though the time span goes beyond that of this chapter.

The South

The best general account of the South's culture in the eighteenth century is found in Carl Bridenbaugh's *Myths and Realities* (1952; pb.). The early pages of John Richard Alden's brief *The First South* (1961) and his fuller *The South in the Revolution, 1763–1789* (1957) fill in the economic and political aspects of the picture. Jack P. Greene's *The Quest for Power: The Lower House of Assembly in the Southern Royal Colonies, 1689–1776* (1963) is an outstanding work.

Out of the flood of books written about Chesapeake society, only those that a student might overlook will be cited. Leonidas Dodson's well-written *Alexander Spotswood: Governor of Colonial Virginia, 1710–1722* (1932) is as much a political-social-economic history for the period covered as it is biography. The same can be said for Aubrey C. Land's *The Dulanys of Maryland: A Biographical Study of Daniel Dulany the Elder (1685–1753) and Daniel Dulany the Younger (1722–1797)* (1955). Politics are covered with skill in Carl Bridenbaugh's *Seat of Empire: The Political Role of Eighteenth-Century Williamsburg* (1950) and with wit by Charles S. Sydnor in *Gentlemen Freeholders: Political Practices in Washington's Virginia* (1952; pb.). The question mark in the title of Robert E. and B. Katherine Brown's *Virginia, 1705–1786: Democracy or Aristocracy?* (1964) is rhetorical; they find democratic political practices well-rooted there long before the Revolution. Among the many volumes of firsthand comments about life in the Chesapeake country, one that has not been mentioned is "The Autobiography of the Reverend Devereux Jarratt, 1732–1763," first printed in 1806, reprinted in *WMQ*, 9 (1952), 346–393, with an introduction by Douglass Adair. Jarratt is one of the few to recall the life of the plain people in eighteenth-century Virginia. The fullest contemporary accounts of life in early eighteenth-century Virginia are found in Louis B. Wright and Marion Tinling, eds., *The Secret Diary of William Byrd of Westover, 1709–1712* (1941), of which a condensed version in paperback is available, and Maude Woodfin and Marion Tinling, eds., *Another Secret Diary of William Byrd of Westover, 1739–1741, with Letters and Literary Exercises, 1696–1726* (1942).

The standard works for North Carolina in the eighteenth century are W. K. Boyd and J. G. deR. Hamilton, *A Syllabus of North Carolina History, 1584–1876* (1913); S. A. Ashe, *History of North Carolina* (2 vols., 1908); and G. G. Johnson, *Ante-Bellum North Carolina: A Social History* (1937). Alonzo Thomas Dill has written competently of *Governor Tryon and His Palace* (1955), and Desmond Clarke of *Arthur Dobbs, Esquire, 1689–1765: Surveyor-General of Ireland, Prospector and Governor of North Carolina* (1957). Harry Roy Merrens, *Colonial North Carolina in the Eighteenth Century: A Study in Historical Geography* (1964), relates the people and their changing economy to historical events in the colony.

David Ramsay's *History of South Carolina: From Its First Settlement in 1670 to the Year 1808* (2 vols., 1809) remains a dependable, useful work. A still standard work on the colonial government is W. Roy Smith, *South Carolina as a Royal Province, 1719–1776* (1903). David D. Wallace's *History of South Carolina* (4 vols., 1934) is excellent; it has been reissued in condensed form under the title *South Carolina: A Short History, 1520–1948* (1951). M. Eugene Sirmans has analyzed "The South Carolina Royal Council, 1720–1763," in *WMQ*, 18 (1961), 373–392. Economic matters are discussed by Lelia Sellers in *Charleston Business on the Eve of the American Revolution* (1934). The first volume of *The Colonial Records of South Carolina: The Journal of the Commons House of Assembly, Septem-*

ber 14, 1742–January 27, 1744 (1954) has appeared under the editorship of J. H. Easterby. Chapman J. Milling has edited *Colonial South Carolina: Two Contemporary Descriptions by Governor James Glen and Doctor George Milligen-Johnson* (1951). "William Logan's Journal of a Journey to Georgia" can be found in *PMHB,* 36 (1912), 1–16, 162–186.

The Backcountry

Many of the books mentioned in the first section of the Chapter 10 Bibliography are relevant here. Carl Bridenbaugh's chapter in *Myths and Realities* (1952; pb.) remains the best essay on the subject. An equally general, but more detailed, treatment is John A. Caruso's *The Appalachian Frontier* (1959). David Hawke discusses the Pennsylvania area with emphasis on its ties with the coastal region in *In the Midst of a Revolution* (1961). *The Valley of Virginia in the American Revolution, 1763–1789* (1942) is handled by Freeman H. Hart; the earlier period is covered by L. K. Koontz in *Virginia Frontier, 1754–1763* (1925). A brief essay worth attention is Thomas P. Abernethy's *Three Virginia Frontiers* (1940). The first chapter of William Wright Abbot, *The Royal Governors of Georgia, 1754–1775* (1959), depicts a colony that at the time was all backcountry. Robert W. Ramsey's *Carolina Cradle: Settlement of the Northwest Carolina Frontier, 1747–1762* (1964) deals competently with an area that has received little attention. John S. Bassett's account of "The Regulators of North Carolina (1765–1771)," *American Historical Association Annual Report for the Year 1894* is still standard. A single aspect of Robert L. Meriwether's definitive *Expansion of South Carolina, 1729–1765* (1940) has been developed with great competence by Richard Maxwell Brown in *The South Carolina Regulators* (1963). The Cherokee War—which Brown makes much of as a cause of the Regulator movement in South Carolina—is treated with usual skill in Lawrence H. Gipson's *The British Empire Before the American Revolution,* Vol. IX, and from the Indians' point of view by David H. Corkran in *Cherokee Frontier: Conflict and Survival, 1740–1762* (1962). Dodson's and Albion's edition of Fithian's *Journal, 1775–1776,* presents the Pennsylvania-Maryland background in unusual detail. The same is done by Richard J. Hooker, ed., *The Carolina Backcountry on the Eve of the Revolution: The Journal and Other Writings of Charles Woodmason, Anglican Itinerant* (1953), an unusually well-edited volume prefaced by a long introduction to the man and the material. Joseph Doddridge's *Notes on the Settlement and Indian Wars* . . . (3rd rev. ed., 1912) gives a fascinating and detailed account of backcountry life in the tramontane region during the latter part of the century.

For further references see the *Harvard Guide,* Sections 102, "Political and Constitutional Development, 1713–1760"; 103, "Social and Economic Development, Northern Colonies, 1713–1760"; 104, "Social and Economic Development, Southern Colonies, 1713–1765"; 105, "Georgia and Florida, 1730–1775"; and 120, "Economic, Social, and Intellectual Movements [During the Revolutionary Era]."

George III, from the Studio of Sir William Beechey

13. Imperial Reorganization: 1763–1770

THE NEW WEST
>   The Proclamation of 1763
>   The Indian Uprising of 1763
>   The Aftermath

THE GRENVILLE-ROCKINGHAM MINISTRY: 1763–1766
>   The Revenue Act of 1764
>   The Stamp Act
>   The Repeal

THE ROAD TO AN UNEASY TRUCE: 1766–1770
>   The Townshend Acts
>   Reception in America
>   A Compromise Accepted

Nothing intrigues colonial historians more than the question of why the American Revolution occurred. Was it a repressible conflict or not? Did Britain's leadership fail, or did the event take place because the machinery for regulating the colonies—both in America and in Britain—was inadequate? The certainty with which some historians answer these questions obscures the fact that the event still remains one of the most mysterious in American history. It is sometimes hard to realize, while browsing through the records, that a cataclysm like the American Revolution ever occurred. The general attitude right up to and often after the shots heard round the world was adherence to things British. People grumbled about various acts of Parliament and certain activities of royal officials, but almost no one talked of independence prior to Lexington and Concord. Franklin, though caustic of British leadership, considered himself an Englishman and as late as 1775 showed so little enthusiasm for independence that rumors in Philadelphia had it he might be a British spy. George Washington may have privately thought otherwise, but when he left for Boston in 1775 as commander-in-chief of the Continental Army he said that the idea of independence repelled him.

The student of this momentous event must, then, approach it with some awareness of the mystery that still surrounds it. Most colonial historians eventually develop or accept a particular explanation for the Revolution, but no single explanation has ever pleased the whole profession. This is not the place to put forth a new theory nor necessarily plump for any of the many available. It is sufficient here to present the story as objectively as possible.

Historians generally begin their accounts of the road to revolution in 1763. Americans had numerous grievances against Great Britain prior to that date, but the signing of the Peace of Paris on February 10, 1763, ending the French and Indian War, cleared the way for a host of new complaints. Overnight the peace transformed the American wing of the empire into something it had never been. Those parts of the treaty relevant to America stated: Canada and all that part of North America east of the Mississippi went to Great Britain; Spain ceded Florida to Britain, and by a secret treaty France was forced to give the Louisiana territory west of the Mississippi to Spain; England left France two islands in the Gulf of the St. Lawrence for fishing stations and allowed her to retain the rich sugar islands of Guadeloupe and Martinique. Pitt thought the treaty a bad one because the islands France kept allowed her "the means of recovering her prodigious losses and of becoming once more formidable to us at sea." The admiration felt for Pitt in America led some there to condemn the treaty; Ezra Stiles calculated that the war had cost Britain £70 million and that she had relinquished the equivalent of £34 million in acquisitions at the peace, leaving "half our conquests given up for nothing." James Otis, on the other hand, said at a meeting in Boston to celebrate the peace that the colonists had reason to be pleased, for the British constitution was admirably fitted for the extension of civil and religious liberty over the whole continent. He also said that jealousies existed between Britain and America but what "God in His Providence has united let no man dare pull asunder."

Otis sensed the enormity of the problems Britain now faced in America. It had taken decades of experience in the seventeenth century for Britain to mold the old colonial system that had governed a strip of land stretching some thousand miles along the Atlantic. Now she must erect a new system to rule a huge inland empire, and there was no certainty she would, as before, be granted the time to experiment and build slowly. Moreover, money, or rather the lack of it, complicated matters.

George Grenville, who believed budgets should be balanced and debts paid as quickly as possible, found himself in the summer of 1763 in charge of a government deep in the red and committed to more responsibilities than the nation had ever carried. Simultaneously, he had to devise new machinery for running the now enormous continental holdings; he had to find ways for underwriting the costs of administering the new possessions; and he had to cut back the debt. All this while the people at home were demanding to be relieved of at least part of their load of wartime taxes. A great man, given the time to experiment, aided by an informed Parliament, and backed by a nation and colonies aware of the complexities of the situation might have solved Britain's postwar troubles. But neither the people of Britain nor of America comprehended the problems; no group well-informed on or sympathetic to American attitudes existed in Parliament; and Grenville was not a great man.

THE NEW WEST

The problem of what to do with the land between the Appalachians and the Mississippi posed questions to which all interested parties—fur traders, merchants, speculators, Indians, Frenchmen, and Englishmen—wanted instant answers. What was to be done with the French who inhabited the land and still maintained strong ties and much influence with the Indians there? The rich fur trade had to be exploited and also controlled but by whom? How was the land to be settled, and what sort of government should be devised for it? Should the land be opened to settlement at all? If so, what happened to the claims of those colonies whose charters gave them rights "from sea to sea"? Were Indian claims to the lands to be ignored? And what about the conflicting claims between such colonies as Pennsylvania and Virginia, both of whom had staked out possession to the area around the forks of the Ohio? The solutions to these problems baffled Britain in 1763, but judgment against her leaders should not be too harsh. The solutions baffled Americans, too, and the problems were eventually resolved only because they vanished.

The Proclamation of 1763

In May 1763 the Board of Trade was asked to suggest answers to the many questions raised by the acquisitions in America. The questions intrigued William Petty, Earl of Shelburne, an intelligent and informed individual, and his search for answers caused him to spend most of his brief tenure as the board's president trying to develop a coherent policy for dealing with the trans-Appalachian region. The past policy had been to place settlers on the soil. For where you had a settler, you had a po-

Map 34. Claims of European

Unexplored

Quebec

Boston

New York

Santa Fe

Charleston

New Orleans

Havana

Mexico

Bogotá

⫽⫽⫽	Spa...
⠂⠂⠂	Fre...
▨▨▨	Eng...
⫽⫽⫽	Rus...

Before 1763

Powers in North America

Unexplored

Russians

Boston

Philadelphia

St. Augustine

Fr.

Vera Cruz

French

After 1763

1000 Miles

Raisz

tential soldier who would fight to protect the soil. Also, a settled land was one where British products could be marketed. But Shelburne decided to reverse this policy. The end of the French menace obviated the need for populating the area with soldier-settlers, and the argument that it developed new markets had lost meaning, for the difficulty of transporting goods to and from the seaboard had caused inland settlements to become close to self-sufficient. There was a strong feeling, too, that settlement of the backcountry drained the coastal areas of their labor supply. A moral obligation buttressed these practical reasons for reversing the old policy; Pennsylvania, at the Treaty of Easton in 1758, had released all its claims to lands west of the mountains in return for the Indians' promise to defect from the French side.

For these reasons Shelburne thought it advisable to keep the Western lands outside the colonies, at least temporarily. He believed that the British Army should patrol the borders, keeping the settlers out and the Indians in; only licensed traders would be permitted past the demarcation line. Shelburne also made it clear that his plan was provisional. He hoped that Britain could obtain cessions from the Indians from time to time, and thus open to settlement one tract after another without the danger of arousing the natives. (He sought to make this hope a reality in 1767, when, after consulting with Benjamin Franklin, he came out with a plan for establishing three new colonies in the West—one centering around Detroit, one in Ohio, and one in Illinois. But nothing came of his plan.)

The government had done nothing about Shelburne's recommendations by the time he departed, and Wills Hill, Earl of Hillsborough, replaced him as president of the Board of Trade. But the outbreak of an Indian uprising, which had been initiated by Pontiac's siege of the British fort at Detroit, prompted the government to act in a way that might reassure the Indians that their land would not be invaded by whites. The king on October 7, 1763, signed the edict that has since been known as the Proclamation of 1763. By it, the three recently acquired territories— Canada and East and West Florida—were created crown colonies with governments similar to those of other crown colonies; their inhabitants were given all the rights of Englishmen at home. A line running from Canada to Florida divided British America into two parts, with the western section reserved for the Indians. The line was clearly located along the crest of the Appalachian system, threading its way between the headwaters of streams that flowed eastward and westward. All colonial claims to territory west of this line were annulled, and title to land west of the line could not henceforth be obtained by any private person. Any intrusion had to be only by permission of the king's agents.

The Proclamation Line has been often represented as a blunder, as something that "has every mark of having been drawn up over a map in the quiet of a Whitehall office. . . ." Such a view overlooks the reception of the proclamation in America. Every colonial assembly—even those of New York, Pennsylvania, and Virginia, which were deeply involved in the tramontane region—gave the edict its approval. Fur traders, the merchants who backed them, and the great land companies supported the Proclamation Line, for they saw that the exclusion of settlers would work in their favor. The major flaw in the edict was that the provisional tone of Shelburne's recommendations had been discarded by Lord Hillsborough, who tended to favor any policy that would keep the colonists hemmed to coastal areas where they could more easily be controlled and of direct benefit to Britain's economy. The tone of the proclamation as issued suggested that the new policy would be permanent. This flaw was soon remedied, for within a few years Britain bowed to the inevitable by moving the demarcation line far enough westward to satisfy the land companies and speculators who had staked out claims in the tramontane region.

The Proclamation of 1763 did not become an issue between Britain and America, but a problem that emerged out of the new Western policy did. Shelburne had included among his early recommendations one for the maintenance of a "considerable military force" in Canada, the Floridas, and along the dividing line for "the security of the settlers, till their numbers enable them to have security by their own internal force." The point was accepted, and plans were drawn up for a standing army of ten thousand troops to be based in America. The Board of Trade was then asked to suggest "in what mode least burthensome and most palatable to the colonies can they contribute towards the support" of this army. The board answered that it was at a loss for ideas on the matter. The problem eventually ended up in the lap of George Grenville, and it was he who not only tried to solve the perplexity but who was forced to take the blame when his attempted solutions failed. Perhaps the problem was insoluble, but the Indians and General Jeffrey Amherst certainly helped to frustrate Grenville's efforts—Amherst by his bungling attempts to control the Indians and the Indians by staging in the summer of 1763 the most massive uprising in American history.

The Indian Uprising of 1763

General Amherst became commander-in-chief of all British forces in North America in 1760. He was an arrogant, vigorous man who ran his army with intelligence and a tight rein. He had done an admirable job in the French and Indian War, but he blundered steadily as a peacetime com-

Map 35. Proclamation Line of 1763

HUDSON'S BAY CO.

NEWF'D LAND

Michelon I.O. St. Pierre (Fr.)

I. of St. John

QUEBEC

INDIAN RESERVE

L. Nipissing

to (MASS.)

NOVA SCOTIA

SPANISH

N.H.

N.Y.

MASS.

CONN.

R.I.

PENN.

N.J.

Ft. Stanwix Line 1768-'69

Ohio R.

Proclamation Line 1763

MD.

DEL.

VA.

N.C.

S.C.

Bermuda (Br.)

GEORGIA

W. FLA.

E. FLORIDA

BAHAMA IS. (Br.)

E. R.

mander, confronted with problems that he knew little about or that required the patience of Job to resolve. He antagonized the Senecas by allowing civilians to erect a settlement at the Niagara portage, though William Johnson told him such action contradicted British treaty agreements with the Indians. He ordered a fort built at Sandusky, though Johnson again warned this would anger the Western Indians who were already uneasy over the English presence in what had always been French territory. And he preferred to coerce rather than court the Indian to the British side by discarding the French practice of favoring him with free ammunition, liquor, clothing, and other gifts. "Services must be rewarded; it has ever been a maxim with me," he said, "But as to the purchasing the good behavior either of Indians or any others, [that] is what I do not understand. When men of whatever race behave ill, they must be punished but not bribed." Amherst's attitude, it should be noted, differed little from that held by Americans since the Indian uprising of 1622, but that does not deny the truth of Howard Peckham's judgment that "Amherst's posture as the stern parent was ridiculous." Croghan and Johnson had told him that Indians required tactful handling; that they could not be judged by white standards, for the French had taught them to expect gifts; and that to deprive them of ammunition took away their means of livelihood. Amherst ignored their advice.

By December 1761 British troops had been spread through the Western forts in the Great Lakes area and southward to Fort Ouiatenon (Lafayette, Indiana). (The high land—*terre haute*—still belonged to the yet unceded part of eastern Louisiana.) The year 1762 passed quietly, though rumblings of discontent were heard among these "rash, inconsistent people" by such traders as Croghan. Frenchmen from forts on the Wabash and Mississippi roamed among them spreading subversion against the English, whom France still fought in Europe, and promising aid if they revolted. Croghan warned that "if the Senecas, Delawares, and Shawnees should break with us, it will end in a general war with all the western nations, though they at present seem jealous of each other." The Delawares and Shawnees were touchy over the number of whites that had moved into their hunting grounds, despite honest efforts by the British to stop the influx. The Senecas actually circulated a warbelt, but the Western Indians refused to join an uprising then. Amherst dismissed all rumors of trouble as "mere *bugbears* . . ." and insisted they would not revolt because "it is their interest to behave peaceably. . . ."

The uprising came in the spring of 1763, mainly because the Western Indians had found a leader in an Ottawa chief named Pontiac, whom Croghan later called "a shrewd, sensible Indian of few words, [who] commands more respect amongst these nations than any Indian I ever saw could do amongst his own tribes." In January, Pontiac and the Western Indians had heard news that "came like a thunderclap to them." They learned of the preliminary treaty at Paris, which ceded all of Canada and eastern Louisiana to Britain. Pontiac did not hate white men, only the patronizing British white men, and he determined at once to free his people from these new masters. He initiated the uprising by first trying to take Fort Detroit by deception, and when that failed, he laid down a siege. But Pontiac did not tarry once the siege had been fixed. He sent out detachments that, augmented by warriors from other Western tribes, struck all other English-occupied forts west of Pittsburgh. Sandusky fell first on May 16, Fort St. Joseph (Niles, Michigan) on May 25, Fort Miami (Fort Wayne, 'Indiana) on May 27, Fort Ouiatenon on June 1. Michilimackinac, the most important fort north of Detroit, put up a bloody resistance against the Chippewas but was finally occupied on June 2. News of its fall led to the abandonment of Fort Edward Augustus (Green Bay, Wisconsin) on June 21, and on that date, Detroit alone, occupied by some 150 soldiers and traders with limited provisions but led by the able and stubborn Major Henry Gladwin, stood out against the Western Indians.

News of Pontiac's action against Detroit stirred up the Delawares, who struck first at a small settlement twenty-five miles south of Fort Pitt (West Newton, Pennsylvania), then besieged Fort Pitt itself. The Senecas attacked Fort Venango (Franklin, Pennsylvania) somewhere around June 16—the lack of survivors makes it hard to fix the date—then Fort Presque Île on June 15, and finally Fort Le Boeuf (Waterford, Pennsylvania) on June 18. By the end of June, only Forts Detroit, Pitt, and Niagara throughout the West still held out against the Indians.

Amherst heard of the uprising in early June. "The post of Fort Pitt, or any of the others commanded by officers, can certainly never be in danger from such a wretched enemy as the Indians are," he said, but perhaps his words were spoken to hide uneasiness, for he dispatched troops at once under Captain James Dalyell to relieve Detroit and under Colonel Henry Bouquet to lift the siege on Fort Pitt. But the uprising was not to be so easily contained. War parties infiltrated the frontiers through the summer, plundering and murdering wherever they found white men. Hundreds of refugees poured into the village of Carlisle, camping on the town's outskirts while they waited for the British Army to crush the savages. (Croghan estimated that during the uprising the Indians "killed or captivated not less than two thousand of his Majesty's subjects and drove some thousands to beggary and the greatest distress.") Virginia raised one thousand militia, and in small platoons they took out after war parties so effectively that the Indians soon became more prudent about

Map 36. Indian Uprising of 1763

1760 Amherst fortifies Sandusky
" '61 British man all western French forts
" '62 Senecas circulate the war belt
" '63 Pontiac attacks Ft. Detroit
" '63 Feb. All western tribes unite under Pon-
    tiac and lay siege to forts
" May. St. Joseph, Sandusky, Ft. Miami fall
" June. Quiatenon, Mackinac and Ft. Edw.
    Augustus fall. Senecas take Venango,
    Le Boeuf and Presque Île.

" July. Raids on the Pennsylvania frontier
" Virginia militia punishes raiders
" Pontiac attacks Detroit
" Bouquet wins at Bushy Run and re-
    lieves Ft. Pitt. Dalyell reaches Detroit
" Sep. Relief party ambushed at Bloody Run
Oct. Delawares raid Wyoming Valley
" Massacre of friendly Indians at Lancas-
    ter
" Pontiac buries the hatchet
" 200 captives returned at Tuscarawa
1766 Great Peace Council at Oswega

raiding that area. Pennsylvania, however, continued to be ravaged. The assembly provided seven hundred militia but said that they were not to be used to reinforce Bouquet; they had to confine themselves to such defensive measures as protecting farmers while they brought in their crops. Bouquet found Pennsylvania's attitude "disgusting to the last degree," for "I find myself utterly abandoned by the very people I am ordered to protect."

Bouquet departed from Carlisle on July 18 with an army of 560 regulars and provincials. (It must have saddened Amherst, who had a low opinion of frontier scouts, to learn that Bouquet had hired thirty of them because his regulars "lose themselves in the woods as soon as they go out of the road . . . and cannot . . . be employed as flankers.") The trip over the mountains was a slow, grim affair, climaxed by a skirmish near Bushy Run. Bouquet lost forty-nine dead and sixty wounded, but by a clever deception that lured the Indians into making a frontal charge he annihilated their forces. He reached Fort Pitt on August 10. Dalyell had meanwhile reached Fort Detroit on July 29 with a relieving force of 260 troops.

While these two posts, plus Fort Niagara, remained secure, the Indians still dominated the tramontane country and the frontiers to the east of the mountains, and they continued to show their power through the early fall. They ambushed a second reinforcement party destined for Detroit in September at the Niagara portage, inflicting heavy losses among the troops and absconding with most of the provisions. In October, bands of Delawares swept down the Susquehanna River into Northampton County and the Wyoming Valley in Pennsylvania, plundering as they went. Amherst wondered in desperation if it could "not be contrived to send the smallpox among the disaffected tribes of Indians." About this time, animosity against *all* Indians had reached such a point that a group of some half hundred men from the Lancaster area vented their fury by massacring a band of innocent Indians who had been converted to Christianity by Moravian missionaries. Governor Penn ordered the Paxton Boys, as they came to be called, arrested and brought to trial, but a sympathetic backcountry refused to aid justice in any way.

By this time, Pontiac's Indian allies sharing in the siege of Detroit had begun to desert. Word arrived in October that the treaty ending the Seven Years' War had been signed and the French told Pontiac he had to make peace with the British, for he and his people could expect no further help from their former protectors. "The word which my father has sent me to make peace I have accepted," Pontiac wrote Major Gladwin; "all my young men have buried their hatchets." Gladwin accepted the surrender but said that Amherst would also have to approve it, not knowing that at that moment the general was on the high seas for England and that Major General Thomas Gage had replaced him as commander-in-chief.

Gage sent word that he would accept Pontiac's surrender if Gladwin, after observation, was convinced his pacific intentions were sincere. At the same time he prepared to attack all those tribes that had not buried the tomahawk. Colonel John Bradstreet was ordered to move westward by the lakes to Detroit punishing all tribes he met along the way. Bouquet would deal with the Indians in the Ohio Valley. Bradstreet failed to follow instructions. He made peace with the Indians without including a single article in the terms, said Gage in a blistering letter, "that might serve to deter them from recommencing their butcheries the next year and cutting our throats the first opportunity. . . ." Bouquet acted more wisely. He moved his army deep into the Ohio country, and at the Indian town of Tuscarawas he demanded the return of all captives. Some two hundred, many of them reluctant to return to civilization, had been handed over by early November, when Bouquet marched back to Fort Pitt. On December 13, Gage wrote to Lord Halifax: "I must flatter myself that the country is restored to its former tranquility and that a general, and, it is hoped, a lasting peace is concluded with all the Indian nations who have taken up arms against his Majesty."

But it was not until July 1766, when Johnson convened a great council of chiefs from Western and Eastern tribes at Oswego, that peace was formally concluded. Here the policy Johnson had tried to impose on Amherst prevailed. The Indians were treated generously—they went unpunished for the recent uprising—and as if they were equals. Pontiac, still proud but no longer bitterly anti-British, spoke for the Western nations at the end of the conference, saying they promised "that since you have been so good as to bury everything that was or might be disagreeable to us, we shall reject everything that tends to evil and strive with each other who shall be of the most service in keeping up that friendship that is so happily established between us." Three years later Pontiac lay dead from a tomahawk wielded by another Indian, but the harmony that had prevailed between British and Indian at Oswego continued down to the Revolution.

The Aftermath

In June 1764, as Bouquet was about to march over the mountains to Fort Pitt, Croghan was in London trying to convince the Board of Trade that the Indian problem could be more effectively handled if management of it was put in the hands of men who understood the natives' ways and were free from interference from military commanders—Croghan had Amherst in mind—and provincial governors. He told the board that Indian uprisings were avoidable if the natives were treated generously, trade goods sold to them at reasonable prices, their land protected from squatters, and their egos flattered with presents. The board agreed and soon announced a Plan for the Future Management of Indian Affairs. It was a good plan. All royal authority on the Indian side of the Line of 1763 would reside with two Indian superintendents and their five deputies. These men would protect Indian interests. The only hitch in the plan was that appropriations to put it in operation would come from the military budget, for Grenville refused further to strain the already heavy burden on his debt-ridden exchequer. In the long run, the uprising of 1763 led to no basic change in policy or attitude toward the Indian. Whatever goodwill prevailed between the Indians and British resulted from Indian respect for such men as Croghan and Johnson rather than from any formal arrangement that might have preserved the good relations once these men were gone.

However, money alone did not deter the creation of a sensible Indian policy. The prejudice of those on the frontier who had been exposed to the ravages of 1763 presented a formidable block to good relations. Their suppressed fury at seeing traders heading over the mountains with gifts for the Indians finally exploded in 1765 in a raid on a trader's train by a band called the Black Boys. That action prompted both Pennsylvania and General Gage to give extensive protection to all traffic bound for the West, and by the summer of 1766 a trade boom of immense proportions was under way in the tramontane region. One Philadelphia firm alone used some six hundred pack horses to transport its goods and at one time sent a shipment of merchandise worth £50,000.

Merchants and traders were not the only ones stirred by the opening of the West. Hunters filtered over the mountains into the rich and all but untapped preserves. Behind them came settlers who squatted upon the best lands they could find. And behind them the great land companies were preparing their own assaults. These companies presented the most serious threat to stability in the Indian country, for they had considerable political influence. Washington, one of many eminent men involved in Western land schemes, said in 1767 that he saw the Proclamation Line only "as a temporary expedient to quiet the minds of the Indians" and that anyone "who neglects the present opportunity of hunting out good lands, and in some measure marking and distinguishing them, will never regain it."

Pennsylvania and Virginia did nothing to slow the influx, which though still slight was sufficient to enrage the Indians. Virginia provided for the improvement of Braddock's Road to speed traffic westward in the hope that by right of settlement she could eliminate Pennsylvania's claim to the land around the forks of the Ohio. Croghan warned that unless something were done, the consequences of this trickle of settlers "may be dreadful and we involved in all the calamities of another general war." The prediction came close to fulfillment in January 1768 when a man named Stump, who lived east of the mountains, murdered ten Indians who slept on his cabin floor. Pennsylvania acted swiftly: Stump was jailed; the assembly passed a law that called for the death sentence against those who squatted on Indian land, and it appropriated £2,500 for gifts to the Indians.

While Croghan circulated in the West soothing Indian tempers, the crown on March 18 adopted a new policy for the American West. Authority to regulate the tramontane trade was taken from the Indian Department and given back to the individual colonies. The Indian Department was reduced to a skeleton staff and deprived of all but advisory power. All posts in the West but those at Niagara, Detroit, and Michilimackinac were ordered abandoned. The expected saving to the government by these retrenchments was estimated at £300,000.

Word kept flowing into London that unless the Proclamation Line was moved farther west, there would soon be another Indian war to deal with. The government bowed to American pressure and ordered its two Indian superintendents to negotiate a new boundary line with the Indians. The Iroquois met with Johnson at Fort Stanwix in September 1768. (The great conference received little attention, for Americans were currently agitated over the Townshend duties.) Twenty boatloads of presents were spread before the Indians, and with that as a backdrop they agreed to renounce their claims to Western lands—those north of the Ohio. John Stuart, the other superintendent, negotiated treaties with the Cherokees at Hard Labor in 1768 and Lochaber in 1770 that extended the new line southward to Florida. Britain by 1770 had done its best to create a stable situation in the American West and to placate American demands before it withdrew its troops and turned all Western problems over to the colonies. It might have done better if the nagging problem of money had not constantly intruded itself into all decisions dealing with the West.

THE GRENVILLE-ROCKINGHAM MINISTRY: 1763–1766

When George Grenville came to power in April 1763, a month after the Peace of Paris had been signed, the national debt had risen from a prewar level of £75 million to £147 million. These figures horrified Grenville, a man so thrifty some said he believed "a national saving of two inches of candle" worth more than all Pitt's victories. Soon after he came to power, Grenville presented an ambitious program to reduce the debt. Britons were loaded with new stamp duties, taxes on the windows in their homes, and excises on malt and cider; even the king was told he must economize on household expenses. The Revenue Act of 1764 was designed to make Americans bear their share of the burden. Americans at this time were, with the curious exception of the Poles, the lowest-taxed people in the Western World. The tax load worked out to twenty-six shillings per head in Britain, one shilling per head in Massachusetts, one of the highest taxed of the colonies. Grenville found that Pitt's energetic enforcement of the trade laws had been at best only briefly effective. The £200,000 collected in customs duties made but a slight dent in the £800,000 Britain spent in America. The requisition system, whereby the colonies themselves raised the sums required to run the imperial machinery in America, had proved completely ineffective. Grenville concluded that Americans would have to be forced to pay by taxes rather than contributions. Parliament had never imposed taxes on the colonies before, but no one in England doubted that it had the power. Chief Justice Mansfield told Grenville that Parliament had an unquestioned right to tax Americans, and that sufficed for Grenville.

The Revenue Act of 1764

A first step in Grenville's program was to push a bill through Parliament that permitted the British Navy to aid the customs service in enforcing the regulation of American trade. Soon, eight warships and twelve armed sloops were patrolling American waters and pulling in smugglers. Grenville next set out to reform rather than reorganize the customs service. During the years of salutary neglect, the chief posts in the service had become sinecures. The appointed collectors gathered in their salaries at home and sent low-paid underlings to do their work in America. These deputies may have arrived "needy wretches," as one colonist put it, but by padding out their fees with bribes they often became men of fortune, according to James Otis. Grenville ended this happy state of affairs by ordering all collectors to take up their offices in America or resign at once. He supplemented this reform with instructions to General Amherst and to all colonial governors that they should use their offices to help eliminate illicit trade.

Grenville knew that reform of the customs service would not balance an American budget that called for the support of ten thousand troops, and not long after news arrived that Amherst had a major Indian uprising on his hands, plans for taxing the colonies began to be developed. The Treasury Board drafted a bill for extending stamp duties to America in September 1763 but then decided to hold that bill back in order to exploit a source of revenue that might cause less disturbance because Americans were more accustomed to it. In March 1764 Grenville asked Parliament to impose new customs duties on the colonies. Pitt and Newcastle, though they opposed a revenue measure against the colonies as inexpedient, did not make an issue over the Revenue Act of 1764 because they believed to do so might split apart their shaky coalition against Grenville's ministry. None of the colonial agents in London objected to it, for though several had informed the colonies whose interests they represented that a revenue bill was being considered, none had been instructed to oppose such a measure on principle. Franklin, when told of the proposed bill, said he was "not much alarm'd about your schemes for raising money on us."

The preamble of the Revenue Act explicitly took note of the necessity "that a revenue be raised in your Majesty's said dominions in America. . . ." The act renewed the molasses duty of 1733, but in an effort to be reasonable, the duty was cut from six to three pence per gallon. New duties were also placed on wines from the Canary and Madeira Islands, silk, French lawns and cambrics, and printed calicoes. Further duties were levied in England on goods being reexported from the Continent to America.

The Revenue, or Sugar, Act, as it is usually called, traveled under false colors, for its provisions embraced much more than those names suggest. It introduced several new trade restrictions. Hides, skins, potash, logwood, and several other colonial products were added to the enumerated list. It forbade further export of iron and lumber directly to Europe and the import from Europe, Ireland, or the East Indies of any merchandise that had not passed first through Great Britain. The act compelled all colonial shippers to post a bond before they loaded their cargoes, rather than after as had previously been the case. This bond applied to all intercolonial trade, even if it traveled no farther than from New Jersey across the Hudson River to New York or across the Delaware River to Pennsylvania. And finally the act bolstered the vice-admiralty system by erecting a new court at Halifax with jurisdictional authority the length of the American coast.

News of the act reached Boston in early May. Instructions from the Boston town meeting to its representatives in the legislature made it clear that Boston objected mainly because it "may be preparatory to new taxations upon us," that is, stamp duties. The legislature did not go on record with a clear-cut objection to the principle that Parliament had a right to levy a revenue measure on the colony. It originally said that the act deprived the people of "the most essential rights of Britons," but the word "rights" was changed to "privileges" before the petition was dispatched to London. In Bernhard Knollenberg's judgment, the petition to

Commons clearly implied that the Massachusetts legislature did not object in principle to "external" taxes, even though for revenue. Connecticut gave explicit approval to such taxes and Rhode Island went on record only against "stamp duties and other internal taxes."

All the colonies filed protests of one sort or another against the Revenue Act, but New York alone took an uncompromising stand against any form of Parliamentary taxation whatsoever. The assembly there said that its exemption from Parliamentary taxation was not "*a Privilege*" but "a Right," a right without which "there can be no Liberty, no Happiness, no Security." New York stated flatly that it objected to "all impositions, whether they be internal taxes, or duties paid, for what we consume," because they "equally diminish the estates upon which they are charged. . . ."

Outside their legislatures the colonists aired other complaints about the act. They objected that the revenue from it would be used to maintain a British army in America that had failed to protect their frontiers, that contained no colonial officers, and, according to John Dickinson, was no more than a force to bleed us "into obedience." Many chafed that the vice-admiralty courts, which no one had hitherto objected to, were now allowed to decide cases that in England were tried under common law and before juries. Merchants complained about the three pence duty on molasses, saying that it was still about two pence more than the traffic could bear. They were especially irritated by the literal manner in which the act was enforced. Prior to the act, a heavy traffic of flatboats and other small craft loaded with "a few staves, or pig iron, or bar iron, or tar, etc." had plied without interruption between the Jersey shore and Philadelphia, but now "those poor fellows," said William Allen, "must go thirty or forty miles or more to give bond, the charge of which and his traveling, make the burden intolerable. It never was the intention of the legislature at home to destroy this little river trade, which is carried on in a kind of general complaint all over the continent."

The more wealthy merchants in New York and Boston, according to Jared Ingersoll, began to urge "the absolute necessity" for America to cut down imports from Britain by turning to manufacturing. "They have actually entered into Associations," he reported, "have advanced monies and set [a] number of hands to spinning, have erected works for the distilling of corn spirits [as a substitute for molasses-based rum], are planning ways and means for the increase of the stock of sheep in this country, and have gone so far as actually to send to Europe for artificers in the several branches of the woolen and linen manufacture."

The Revenue Act itself did not create cause for the strong reaction it evoked. Other festering irritants helped to intensify objections over this particular measure. Royal officers once again were attempting to enforce the White Pines Acts. The country seemed unable to shake the postwar depression, which had begun in 1759 and worsened with the peace of 1763. The Currency Act of 1764, which came forth from Parliament on the heels of the Revenue Act, did little to cheer merchants who favored easy credit, for it forbade the issuance of paper money as legal tender in all colonies not included in the previous restrictive act of 1750. An aroused New England clergy continued to wonder how to deal with Archbishop Secker's plan to transfer the Anglican hierarchy to America. ("The apprehension of Episcopacy," John Adams said years later, "contributed . . . as much as any other cause to arouse the attention not only of the inquiring mind, but of the common people, and urge them to close thinking on the constitutional authority of Parliament over the colonies.") And, finally, an awareness that the new customs duties were only an entering wedge soon to be followed by stamp duties that Grenville had already announced, added strength to objections voiced by every colonial legislature.

The Stamp Act

Grenville had announced at the time the Revenue Act passed Parliament that he also planned to extend stamp duties to America but wished to delay action a year in order to give the colonies time to offer an alternate plan. He said that if they raised an "adequate" or "equivalent" sum themselves, stamp duties would be forgotten. He did not formally submit this offer to the colonies, however, which suggests that he did not take it seriously. But he did at least ask the colonial agents in London for their views. One suggested that the colonies themselves request the duties, for Parliament would then be levying an internal tax with their consent. Franklin wanted a colonial congress to impose the duties; if that failed, he wanted to try again the old system of requisition, which had already proved inadequate. The agents discussed representing the colonies in Parliament but discarded the idea as unworkable. None would assure Grenville that the colonies would voluntarily supply troops or the funds to pay for them. (All the agents knew Grenville's need for American help in running the empire had increased in recent months, for Britons were making it clear that they would take no more taxes. Mobs had attacked excise officers—those "boisterous ruffians" who had the power to invade "the asylum of domestic peace and security; nay, even to rifle the private retreats or *penetralia* of female modesty"—and in 1765 the most onerous of the new taxes, that on cider, was repealed.)

During the year's grace, petitions rolled in from America stating colonial complaints to the Revenue Act but invariably adding even stronger objections to the proposed stamp duties. The government officially ignored them all. Grenville apparently believed these were objections for the record rather than the expression of a deep-seated feeling, and the work of drawing up a stamp act for America continued.

Thomas Whately of the Treasury Department drafted the act. It was expected to raise between £60,000 and £100,000. (The modesty of the expected income led some later to accuse Grenville of seeking to "bring into the Treasury a pepper-corn at the risque of millions to the nation.") Duties varied from a halfpenny (on newspapers) to £2 (on diplomas) and would be levied on all colonial bills of lading, licenses, wills, bonds, deeds, indentures, contracts, leases, newspaper advertisements, almanacs, playing cards, dice—the list seemed endless. Obviously, the act was framed with care. The tax on land sales was proportionate to the amount of acres purchased, the hope being that this would reduce speculation and also hit the rich harder than the poor. Lighter duties than those in England were charged for ordinary documents, but some of the taxes were extremely high. The tax of two shillings sterling on newspaper advertisements was, according to Knollenberg, equal in many instances to a tax of over 200 per cent ad valorem. The £2 stamp required for a college diploma also was steep but was probably justified on the ground that only the well-to-do had their children educated.

A merit in Grenville's eyes of the stamp duty was that it required no enforcement officers. Leases and wills and other documents that lacked their stamps could not be admitted as evidence in court. All infractions were easily spotted. Offenders were to be tried in Vice-admiralty Courts before a crown-appointed judge and without a jury. (This clause of the act particularly irritated the colonists, for it perverted the purpose of the Vice-admiralty Courts, which hitherto had been concerned only with matters connected with the sea and commerce.) Grenville, as if suspecting the act's irritating features, went out of his way to sugar-coat them. All stamp agents were to be Americans, and all revenue from the stamps was to remain in America and to be spent there. Grenville saw that to take the money out of the colonies would "occasion great clamour" and would "give just cause of complaint as being contrary to what was publicly declared upon this subject." The ministry was eager for America to accept the pill because they knew that if it went down, a precedent would have been established. Whately gave the Stamp Act "the appellation of *a great measure* on account of the important point it establishes, the right of Parliament to lay an internal tax upon the colonies."

Grenville presented the proposal for American stamp duties in his budget message on February 6, 1765. Several members of Parliament attacked the proposal, but only one denied that Parliament had any authority to tax the colonies. The others granted the right but argued that it should not be used "until or unless the Americans are allowed to send members to Parliament." Jared Ingersoll, who listened to the debate, said that Isaac Barré gave "a very handsome and moving speech," during which he referred to Americans as "those Sons of Liberty." The speech had little effect, for the vote was five to one (245 to 49) in favor of proceeding with the proposed tax. A week later (February 13), a bill was introduced for a colonial stamp tax "towards further defraying the expenses of defending, protecting and securing" the colonies. According to Ingersoll, the opposition was confined to "the gentlemen interested in the West Indies . . . a few members . . . particularly connected with some of the colonies and a few of the heads of the minority who are sure to thwart and oppose the ministry in every measure of what nature or kind soever. . . ."

Despite the evidence of colonial petitions opposing the proposed measure, no one in England apparently had the slightest idea that the Stamp Act would be resisted. Often before, the colonists had petitioned against a proposed act of Parliament, then either obeyed or, as was more likely, disregarded the act once it had passed. Franklin went out of his way to get collectorships for his friends John Hughes in Philadelphia and Jared Ingersoll in Connecticut. Even some American politicians assumed that it would go into effect with little trouble. Richard Henry Lee, who would later introduce the resolution for independence into Congress, applied for a collectorship, and later found it difficult to explain his conduct.

Virginia reacted first to the Stamp Act. The tone of its reaction was somewhat conditioned by local affairs. A group of young members of the House of Burgesses, among them Patrick Henry, chafed under the control of house affairs by a clique of tidewater planters. The young members had turned up a scandal in the handling of public funds by the former Speaker John Robinson, who had secretly and illegally made large loans, many of them still unpaid, to his friends. Recriminations flew and in the squabble that ensued the house split apart into factions, with the young members mainly on one side and the old guard opposing them. The rebels were still searching for ways to embarrass the old-guard leadership when news of the Stamp Act arrived. Henry—known as "moderate and mild, and in religious matters a saint, but the very devil in politics"—rose toward the end of the May session, when a bare quorum of members was present and most of the old guard had departed for home, and blazed out against the Stamp Act. He said that "in former times Tarquin and Julius had their Brutus, Charles his Cromwell," and was on the way to adding that now George III had his Americans, when the speaker interrupted to say that Mr. Henry's remarks were treasonable. Henry apologized, then went on to conclude his speech by introducing seven far from temperate resolves that made the few old guard present cringe. (Number seven, for example, said that anyone who denied the assembly's right to tax "shall be deemed an enemy of his Majesty's colony.") The house passed the first four, more moderate, of Henry's resolves. All seven, however, were handed to the press and printed throughout the colonies as if they had passed. James Otis called them treasonable when he read them.

Massachusetts at first reacted calmly to the Stamp Act. The legislature on June 8, 1765, ordered an invitation sent out for a congress of delegates from all colonies to meet in New York City in October "to consider of a general and united, dutiful and humble representation of their condition to his Majesty and the Parliament, to implore relief." The next step, which was soon adopted in other colonies, was to force the local stamp collector to resign, for this would leave no one with the authority to distribute the stamped paper. The elite of Boston began this movement but control soon slipped from their hands. Riots broke out in August. The house of Andrew Oliver, the stamp distributor for Massachusetts, and that of Thomas Hutchinson were ransacked. (Hutchinson had opposed the Stamp Act on principle and believed Parliament lacked the right to tax the colonies; he also believed Parliament, right or wrong, must be obeyed and that it alone could correct its wrongdoing by repealing the obnoxious act.) Similar mobs soon arose in Newport and New York City; they all called themselves Sons of Liberty. But their violence probably did more to impair than to improve colonial solidarity against the Stamp Act.

The Stamp Act Congress did its best to put resistance back on a dignified level. The congress met in New York from October 7 to 25; nine colonies were represented—all of New England (except New Hampshire), the Middle Colonies, Maryland, and South Carolina. It was the first such gathering in American history to convene without any prompting from British officials, and the astute Board of Trade regarded the event as a precedent of "dangerous tendency." The twelve resolutions issued by the congress after two and a half weeks of discussion were judicious, restrained, and precise. They accepted Parliament's right to make law for the colonies but rejected its right to tax them. They rejected the idea of representation in Parliament, either "virtually" or actually. And they discarded what has been called the "illogical and risky distinction between internal and external taxes for revenue previously sanctioned by some colonial legislatures. . . ."

By November 1, when the stamps were to go on sale, none were available at any spot in America, for nearly every distributor in the colonies had resigned his post. By that date, too, merchants in New York, Philadelphia, and Boston had agreed to help hasten repeal of the Stamp Act by limiting their imports from Britain to only a few specified items. The merchants' altruism had its limits, and as their cargoes for export piled up on wharves the length of the continent, they put pressure on local customs officials to issue clearances on unstamped paper. Such action was justified, the argument went, because stamped paper was unavailable. The officials, apparently more reasonable men than sometimes pictured, agreed, and by the end of 1765 cargoes were moving out of all large coastal towns. The colonies by an extraordinary show of resourcefulness and, except for the August riots and the outbursts in Newport and New York, of restraint, had for all practical purposes bested Britain's attempt to tax them. How Parliament and the ministry would react to America's resistance remained an unanswered question as the year 1766 opened.

The Repeal

The king removed Grenville from office three months after passage of the Stamp Act and before America's reaction to the act had drifted back to England. The attempt to impose economies on the royal household had irritated the king, but the item that aroused his temper was a bill that Grenville let slip through Parliament that "excluded the king's mother from the government in case the king should become incapacitated by ill health." George was sensitive about his mother, and Grenville's unintended slight ended his career as the king's chief minister.

George III turned to the Marquis of Rockingham to form a new ministry. Rockingham and his followers believed that Parliament had the right to tax the colonies but that the Stamp Act had been inexpedient. American reception of the act convinced Rockingham that it should be repealed, but he knew that this must be done in a way that did not make it appear that Parliament was backing down because of the act's reception in America. Fortunately for Rockingham's purpose, England was in the midst of a depression, which the American boycott of British goods helped to make worse. Merchants, spurred on by Rockingham's ministry, flooded Parliament with petitions detailing their troubles. They reported that there would soon be one hundred thousand unemployed marching on London. As part of the scheme to paint the American view of the act in a softer light, the ministry brought Benjamin Franklin before Commons in mid-February 1766. Franklin, answering prearranged questions, said that Americans objected only to internal taxes, for they were "forced upon the people without their consent, if not laid by their own representatives." They did not object to such external taxes as port duties because "the sea is yours; you maintain, by your fleets, the safety of navigation in it, and keep it clear of pirates," which gives Britain the right to charge duties "towards defraying the expense you are at in ships to maintain the safety of that carriage." Franklin's distinction between internal and external taxes was unfortunate, for the Stamp Act Congress had already made clear that Americans resisted any form of taxation by Parliament. The testimony was, as Edmund Morgan has remarked, "a dangerous piece of deception with unfortunate after-effects." It helped to achieve repeal of the Stamp Act, but it led the British government into a misunderstanding about the American attitude toward Parliamentary taxation.

The ministry's campaign for repeal did little to diminish the warmth of debate on the issue. The government urged repeal solely on the grounds of expediency. The Army and Navy would be needed to enforce the act, and added to the cost of this operation would be the losses to British business interests entailed by American refusal to import goods from the mother country. Grenville rose to warn members that if America succeeded by this show of resistance, the colonies would eventually be lost to the empire; Parliament had to take a firm stand now or expect to be badgered by America on every trivial issue hereafter. Grenville was listened to respectfully, for, as one member noted, anti-American feeling was higher than it had ever been in Parliament. But the argument for expediency won out, and on March 18, 1766, Parliament repealed the Stamp Act. At the same time, it also passed the Declaratory Act, which stated that Parliament had the authority to make laws for the American colonies in "all cases whatsoever."

America rejoiced over the repeal and paid little attention to the Declaratory Act. At the time, few on either side of the water saw the great price that had been paid for a respite in the tension between the mother country and her colonies. Both sides had clarified their views during the fight, and both had taken firm stands on principles that would be hard to back away from. Parliament had flatly come out for its right to tax the colonies, and the colonies, after fumbling about in 1764, had soon after with equal firmness denied Parliament's right to tax. During the crisis Governor Bernard of Massachusetts had told home authorities "that Great Britain and America are got widely different in their notions of their relation to one another, that their connection must be destroyed, if this question is not determined soon." The question had not, of course, been determined, but only postponed.

The crisis had worked a change in the minds of many Britons. Parliament previous to 1765 had been mainly indifferent to and ignorant of American affairs. The ignorance remained, but the indifference had become transformed into a strong anti-American feeling. Worse still, the crisis convinced many that America would be happy only after it had become independent of Great Britain. This conviction was an obsession with many British leaders a decade before Americans gave it serious attention.

The true significance for America of the Stamp Act and its older brother, the Revenue Act of 1764, lay in their effect "upon colonial psychology." Matters that no one had hitherto called into question were now examined with a fresh eye. "Why is the trade of the colonies more circumscribed than the trade of Britain?" a Boston paper asked in 1765. "And why are impositions laid upon the one, which are not laid upon the other?" America began to suspect the motives of every British act, and credence was given to the wildest rumors. One story that arrived on the heels of the Stamp Act had it that London planned to introduce "temporal dignities"—that is, a nobility—into the colonies and that Sir William Johnson and General Gage would be the first honored. Another tale had it that there was "great talk" in London "about the alteration of the governments to be made in the next session of Parliament in the northern districts of America."

The crisis had caused Americans to examine for the first time their relationship between the mother country and the colonies. Ezra Stiles, who had been distressed by the violence in Boston and Newport, believed that the Stamp Act had "diffused a disgust thro' the colonies and laid the basis of an alienation which will never be healed. Henceforth the *European* and *American* interests are separated never more to be joined." Stiles was a clergyman and his sharp reaction points up an aspect of the crisis that Carl Bridenbaugh has recently given new emphasis, namely, that the clergy merged its "long standing religious grievances" with the "fresh civil ones" to give a religious sanction to American protests. Parliament and the king's ministry now came to stand for tyranny in the sermons of Congregational and Presbyterian ministers throughout the land, much as Archbishop Laud and Charles I personified tyranny for seventeenth-century America. Once the ministers had joined the secular movement against Britain, they stayed with it, even after that movement became transformed into a revolution.

Religion's commitment to the cause strengthened American confidence in the rightness of its action. That confidence gained, too, because the colonies had perfected old instruments of protest during the crisis and devised effective new ones in addition. As before, they sent grievances to London, organized protest committees, passed about circular letters, and circulated petitions. But they also refined such new pressure techniques as nonimportation and nonintercourse. The newspapers were used as never before to propagandize their cause. And on their own initiative, the colonists had held the first American-sponsored congress. Nine self-centered colonies that in the past had rarely cooperated on anything had managed after much discussion to show that they shared certain political principles in common. The display of unity that emerged during the Stamp Act crisis bespeaks the appearance for the first time of something akin to an American, a national, feeling. This was the most startling and impressive feature of the agitation of 1765–1766.

Clearly, Great Britain had provoked the crisis, though reasonable men in charge of the government had made no more than reasonable demands on the colonies to share in imperial defense. Could the crisis have been avoided? Over a half century earlier, the Treaty of Union in 1707 between England and Scotland created "one of the most states-manlike and successful arrangements of its kind ever devised," a Scotsman has said. "It destroyed everything that kept the two people apart but nothing that did not threaten unity; it created a political unity but kept alive a healthy nationalism." The ministry of 1763–1766 might have made the same statesmanlike arrangements. It could have sent commissioners to America to explain British needs and work out agreements with the colonial governments. "But to act unilaterally," Bernhard Knollenberg has said with justification, "to change a constitutional relationship established for over a century without prior effort to negotiate a settlement and with-out any offer of compensation or assurance against future exploitation, was high-handed, reckless, and unjust."

THE ROAD TO AN UNEASY TRUCE: 1766–1770

In early June 1766 the Rockingham ministry pushed through another conciliatory measure. The Revenue Act of 1764, which had remained on the books despite the repeal of the Stamp Act, was revised to the extent that the duties on molasses were cut from three pence a gallon to a penny. It would now cost no more, in many cases less, to bring molasses in legally than it had previously to bribe customs officials. This was a palatable tax, and given a period of calm it might have gone down without a grimace. But the people were, in Hutchinson's words, "habituated to wild extrava-gant language and actions," and blood would flow before calm ensued. Massachusetts continued the center of trouble. When the ministry sent a circular letter to the colonies concerned, asking compensation for those who had lost property in the Stamp Act riots, New York paid up promptly but Massachusetts deliberated, then passed a law that compensated the injured but also pardoned all who had participated in the riots. The right to pardon was a sovereign power, and the crown answered Massachusetts' presumption by disallowing the act in May 1767.

The Rockingham ministry's appeasement of America had only complicated Britain's financial problems, and before the end of June, it had been forced to impose a series of new taxes at home. That doomed the ministry. The king asked and Pitt agreed to form a new government. Out of a coalition of diverse factions, the Duke of Grafton became first lord of the Treasury and Shelburne and Henry Seymour Conway became secretaries of state. The king made the Pitt-Grafton ministry, as it was called, more tolerable to himself by making Pitt the Earl of Chatham, which removed his obnoxious talents from Commons. "Champagne Charlie" Townshend, largely by default, became the central character in the new government. It fell to him as chancellor of the Exchequer, whose responsibility was to balance the budget, to solve the problems that had baffled abler men than he.

The Townshend Acts

Parliament reconvened in November 1766 in the midst of "nothing but riots and insurrections over the whole country, on account of the high price of provisions, in particular corn." Commons clearly wanted a tax cut, and yet Townshend appeared before the house in February 1767 and asked to have the land tax of 4s. on the pound continued. The plea was rejected and the tax cut to 3s., which meant a loss to the crown of some £500,000 annually in revenue. It was up to Townshend to piece out the difference. He continued taxes that were about to expire, inaugurated new ones on straw hats, and such cloths as lawn, canvas, and linen, and authorized a lottery. The need for still more income forced the chancellor to face the issue of taxing Americans.

Townshend considered several plans for the colonies. One was to open the Mediterranean trade to American merchants, with the proviso that everything imported from there would be taxed. This suggestion had the virtue of granting a certain freedom of trade to the colonists. Its defects were that it would deprive London merchants of the profits they gained from handling those goods, and it would divert from the Exchequer the duties on merchandise that currently had to pass through Britain en route to the colonies. Townshend then toyed with but finally rejected the idea of levying a tonnage tax on all vessels entering colonial ports. Finally, he hit on a scheme that he believed Americans would not object to and that was ultimately embodied in the Revenue Act of 1767. Customs duties, or, as Franklin had called them, external taxes, would be put on a variety of items that America had to import from Britain—glass, tea, silk, lead, paper, and paints. The duties would be small and thus all the less objectionable, but by spreading them over a number of items, they should bring in a satisfying amount of revenue. The money would remain in America and would be used for "defraying the charge of administration of justice, and the support of civil government, in such provinces where it shall be found necessary; and toward further defraying the expenses of defending, protecting, and securing the said dominions. . . ."

The plan was well-designed, flawed only by being based on the misconception of American views propagated by Franklin. Townshend told Parliament that he thought the distinction between internal and external taxes absurd—"If we have the right to impose one, we have the other," he said—but to please Americans he made this distinction and would "indulge them and chose for that reason to confine himself to regulations of trade, by which a sufficient revenue might be raised in America." The estimated revenue from the duties would be slight—somewhere around £40,000 or less than a tenth of that lost by Parliament's reduction of the land tax—but levying the taxes would help convince the people at home that the Americans were not escaping scot-free while Britons suffered. The scheme had the added merit that, if it worked, it would free governors and judges from the control of colonial legislatures. No one in Parliament opposed the measure as unfair to the colonies. But Grenville spoke against it; he believed it would hurt British merchants more than the Stamp Act, because it would encourage colonial manufacturing, and he warned Townshend that the Americans "will laugh at you for your distinctions about regulations of trade." He urged Commons to face the crisis in Anglo-American affairs now; all who held public office of any sort in America should be forced to take an oath acknowledging the right of Parliament to legislate for the colonies. Commons ignored Grenville, and the Revenue Act of 1767 became law on July 2.

At the same session, Parliament passed another act that reorganized the American customs service. An autonomous Board of Customs Commissioners that did not operate by remote control from Britain was created for the colonies. The reorganization act gave Townshend the chance to toss out officers who had been bought by colonial merchants and to put in new, hand-picked men. Only six seizures of contraband had been made in New England between 1765 and 1767, and of these the crown had won a conviction on only one; perhaps now the statistics would begin to improve in the crown's favor. Townshend, however, had urged the reorganization on Parliament in part to please Americans. Prior to 1767 there had been four surveyor generals in America, but because all acted under orders from the London office, none had authority to make final decisions, which often meant long, costly delays for American merchants. Many colonists had urged the creation of a separate customs commission for America with the same powers as the English board, and Townshend had obliged, thus showing, in John Miller's words, that he "was willing to satisfy Americans' demands for equality with the English, at least to the extent of putting them under the same disabilities as Englishmen."

Three days after these two acts, Parliament passed a third that suspended the New York assembly, for that body still refused to comply with the Mutiny Act—or Quartering Act, as it is often called—that had been passed in 1765. That act required each colony to provide barracks for troops stationed within its borders and to supply them with utensils, vinegar and salt, rum, beer, or cider, and to pay a certain amount of their transportation within the province. As originally written, the act allowed British officers to quarter their men in private houses, but in an effort to please the colonies that section was rewritten to permit only officers the right only to use empty houses and barns where barracks were lacking. No one regarded the Mutiny Act as a grievance until after the ruckus over the Stamp Act. Then, the alert Americans saw that they were being made to give in kind—room and board—what the Stamp Act had tried to force out in cash. People asked what the difference was between a direct tax levied by Parliament and one imposed by a local assembly in order to satisfy the "dictatorial mandates" of Parliament. All the legislatures grumbled about the act, but all except New York soon came round to executing its provisions, though Pennsylvania alone carried it out to the letter and thus formally accepted a law of Parliament as binding. New York objected to the law on principle—the "very essence of the idea of a free representation is totally extinguish'd and destroy'd"—and also because the working of the law was unjust. For New York was the strategic center of America. And because the easiest routes to Canada and to the West lay within its borders, Gage established his headquarters and stationed several regiments of troops there, with the result that the Mutiny Act bore heaviest on that province. New York's refusal to obey the act prompted Parliament's disciplinary action, and that, in turn, provoked the first outcry in the colonies against the Townshend Acts.

Reception in America

News of the Townshend Acts arrived in America in September 1767. There was loud talk that the act against New York made "poor contemptible air castles" of American legislatures, but the roar died to a whimper when New York saw her defiance would not be backed by other assemblies, all of whom had accepted the Mutiny Act in fact if not theory. October 1 was the date the suspending act went into effect, but shortly before the deadline, the New York assembly agreed by a single vote to fulfill its obligations toward the troops within its borders.

Moderation marked the reaction to the other Townshend Acts. The Boston town meeting in late September urged the promotion of American manufactures and called for "the disuse of foreign superfluities" such as sugar, watches, jewelry, anchors, and whatever else might have to be imported from Great Britain, but every effort was made to avoid violence.

Otis set the tone when he said "The Tax! the Tax!" was the "matter of grievance" but added that "redress is to be fought in a legal and constitutional way."

The most cogent attack on the acts came from sedate Philadelphia, where on December 2 the first of twelve *Letters from a Farmer in Pennsylvania to the Inhabitants of the British Colonies* appeared in the press. Their author was John Dickinson, an eminent attorney of the province, who had studied law in England and there acquired a reverential respect for British liberties as they had emerged from the Revolution of 1688. Dickinson used precedents from the past rather than abstract principles to argue against the right of Parliament to tax the colonies in any form. His tone, like that of Otis, was moderate. The cause of liberty, he said, "is a case of too much dignity, to be sullied by turbulence and tumult." He disclaimed the idea that America contemplated independence but also made clear that "we cannot be happy, without being free; that we cannot be free, without being secure in our property; that we cannot be secure in our property, if, without our consent, others may, as by right, take it away; that taxes imposed on us by Parliament, do thus take it away." Dickinson said nothing new, but he said it more effectively than anyone else. The essays were sold as a pamphlet within a month after Dickinson had ended the series, and the Farmer quickly became a man for whom "no mark of honor and respect" was "thought equal to his merit," according to one royal governor.

On February 11, 1768, the day before the last of Dickinson's letters appeared, the Massachusetts legislature approved a circular letter to all the colonies that had protested against the Townshend Acts. Though written by Sam Adams, it was moderate enough to have come from the Farmer's pen. It, too, said nothing that had not been aired before. It rejected the idea of representation in Parliament, criticized the Mutiny Act, attacked the plan to pay royal officials in America out of customs duties as unconstitutional, and ended by urging united action against the acts and denying any intention of seeking independence from Great Britain. The letter presented a firm but respectful view, and few in America judged it improper or harsh.

It was less the circular letter itself than the political changes in the government that caused the letter's sharp reception in England. Townshend had died in September 1767—he was forty-one—and in his place as chancellor of the Exchequer came Lord North, an easy-going politician, who found it possible to compromise on all issues except the authority of Parliament. In January 1768, the king created a third secretary of state, whose job was to concentrate on colonial affairs. He gave the post to Lord Hillsborough, of whom the king later said that he did not know "a man of less judgment. . . ." Hillsborough, who thought the Farmer's *Letters* "extremely wild," reacted strongly to the Massachusetts circular letter. The other advisers of the king wished to reply with a "kind and lenient" circular letter of their own, but Hillsborough would have none of that. After privately consulting the king but not his colleagues in the ministry, who later denounced his action, he instructed Governor Bernard to dissolve the legislature unless it immediately rescinded the letter. He sent out a circular letter of his own, ordering all governors to instruct their legislatures to ignore the Massachusetts letter and to dissolve them if they took notice of it. Governor Bernard carried out his lordship's instructions on June 21. A week later the legislature refused by an overwhelming vote (92 to 17) to rescind the letter. Bernard dissolved the legislature two days later.

Meanwhile, word of further acts of defiance from New England flowed across Hillsborough's desk. A letter dated February 12 from the customs commissioners in Boston said that they had "every reason to expect that we shall find it totally impracticable to enforce the execution of the revenue laws until the hand of government is strengthened." The letter remarked that the nearest troops were 250 miles away in New York City. The government responded with a warship in the summer of 1768 to give a show of force to the commissioners' edicts. On June 10, John Hancock's *Liberty* was seized because Hancock had refused to post his bond before loading, as the law now required. Three days later a mob forced the commissioners to take refuge aboard the warship. News of this event got a quick reaction in London. Two regiments of regulars were dispatched from Great Britain to Boston and two more were ordered down from Halifax. The government's determination to make an example of Boston may have been shaped by an awareness that the resistance to the Townshend Acts lacked the force and unity behind the reaction to the Stamp Act. Boston had found it hard to persuade New York and Philadelphia to join in nonconsumption and nonimportation agreements, and they had come around only after Hillsborough's reaction to the circular letter and after the customs commissioners had begun demanding payment of duties in specie. An essay in a London paper in January 1769 said that Great Britain had, during the preceding year, lost over £7,000,000 in trade from America and collected only £3,500 in customs duties, but the figures are highly suspect, for Benjamin Franklin ghosted the article. The nonconsumption and nonimportation agreements were, in reality, not being rigidly adhered to. All the talk about making America self-sufficient had amounted to little actually being done; Rhode Island, for example, was buying and selling goods at a great rate. The ministry must have felt in September 1769, as the troops made their way toward Boston, that now was the moment for America to back down. Perhaps the turning point in the crisis that had long been building up had come at last.

A Compromise Accepted

Before the troops arrived, Boston's town meeting went on record against a standing army as "an infringement of their natural, constitutional and charter rights," then issued a call for other towns to send delegates to a "convention" on September 22. The convention met; it did not, however, pretend to supplant the prorogued legislature, and the delegates spoke prudently. They praised the assembly's resistance to Parliamentary taxation and agreed that "as Englishmen they have an aversion to an unnecessary standing army, which they look upon as dangerous to their civil liberty," then adjourned on October 1, the day the troops landed. What it had said for the record was less important than that it had met. Conventions, as extralegal bodies meeting to deal with problems formal government could not or would not resolve, had been used as early as 1623 in Virginia, but it was their effectiveness in the Puritan and Glorious Revolutions that had made the deepest impression on Americans. Both times, convention parliaments had carried out changes in government that the established order had resisted. The Massachusetts convention of 1768 was the first to emulate the English pattern, and its meeting would point the way for Americans eager to maintain some form of government as the old form disintegrated.

The troops met no resistance and found no mobs to deal with when they arrived, and as autumn merged into the winter of 1768–1769, Boston remained quiet. Parliament in February handed the defiant in the colonies further fuel for propaganda by resolving that "wicked and designing men" were responsible for the American troubles and reminding the king that those indicted for treason could, under a statute passed in Henry VIII's reign, be brought home to England for trial. (The king never used the act against Americans, but the threat that it could be used sufficed to stir up anti-British feeling in the years ahead.)

The threat to revive the Henry VIII statute belied the true feeling of the king's ministry toward the American disturbance. British-American trade, according to one estimate, had dropped off by some £700,000 during 1768, and though there was no great pressure from business interests to lift the Townshend duties, the ministry was concerned, particularly by rumors that Americans were manufacturing for themselves much that they had once purchased in Britain. On May 1, 1769, the king's cabinet voted to urge Parliament in its next session to rescind the duties. It also agreed, but only by a majority of one vote, that Parliament should be encouraged to leave the tax on tea, an item that could not be produced in America. The tea tax would maintain the principle of Parliament's supremacy over the colonies that had been laid down in the Declaratory Act. On May 13 a subdued Hillsborough informed American governors of the cabinet's plans. Soon after, he told Governor Bernard to permit the Massachusetts legislature to convene again. The legislature reacted to this gesture by unanimously resolving on July 1 "that no man can be taxed, or bound in conscience to obey any law, to which he has not given his consent in person, or by his representative." This extraordinary statement, which carried the argument with Britain to the point where *all* Parliament's legislation was declared not binding on America, was quickly rescinded for a less defiant one that said simply that Massachusetts' legislature alone had power to tax the people of the province. But the damage had been done, for the rejected resolution was published as if it still stood, and General Gage on seeing it put aside plans he had been forming for moving the last two regiments out of the city. (Two of the regiments had already been sent back to Halifax.)

Antagonism between the troops and the town increased during the fall of 1769. The people developed soldier baiting to an art. "Lobsterback" became one of the milder terms used to hound the men that marched guard duty. A mob attacked one detachment of troops in October. The soldiers handled the situation well and no shots were fired. Their commander reported that "Government here is in the hands of the multitude." The tense situation continued through the winter. The troops on hand were "too few to preserve order, yet numerous enough to goad the patriots and remind them of military despotism." The situation exploded on the night of March 5, 1770, when a mob attacked the sentry on duty at the customhouse. Reinforcements were called. Captain Preston, in charge of the detail, tried to reason with the hooting crowd. Someone yelled "fire." When the smoke cleared, five citizens were dead and several more wounded. Newspaper accounts of the "Boston Massacre," as it was instantly labeled, suggested that the affair had been part of a deliberate plot to murder innocent Americans.

At the moment British soldiers were firing into the Boston mob, Parliament was acting in a way that would dampen repercussions from the Boston Massacre, for on March 5 it repealed all the Townshend duties but that on tea. The Pitt-Grafton ministry had collapsed in January, and the king asked Lord North to form a new government. (Lord North would retain power for the next twelve years, an indication that something had changed in British politics, that a stability had arrived that would permit the government to follow a tougher and more consistent policy. A growing bitterness toward America may have contributed toward this stability.) North, following the cabinet decision of the previous May, had asked the tea duty to remain "as a mark of supremacy of Parliament, and an efficient declaration of their right to govern the colonies," and though well over half the members believed the tax would only cause further trouble and should go, North had his way. Two months later Lord North quietly removed another grievance by allowing the Mutiny Act to die without being renewed. His conciliatory gestures had their limits, for the old laws that taxed wine, sugar, molasses, and various other merchandise remained on the books, and none of the elaborate machinery for enforcing trade regulations was abandoned.

North hoped that by allowing the Mutiny Act to lapse, his administration would win sufficient favor in New York to break the united front of the colonies against Britain. His strategy worked. The immediate general reaction to the news that all but the tea duty had been repealed was to "hold out for complete success," but in June, not long after a letter had appeared in a Philadelphia paper alleging that Bostonians had secretly imported some £150,000 worth of British goods, New York merchants ended their boycott. Philadelphia followed New York's lead in September and Boston in October; Virginia held out until July 1771.

On the surface, an era of good feelings seemed in the making. Six years earlier America had a confused idea about its relationship to the mother country. Several colonies at first seemed willing to let Parliament levy "external" taxes, but within a year all agreed that while Parliament might make law for the colonies, it had no right to levy taxes. By 1770 the colonies still admitted "subordination" to Parliament, but as Thomas Hutchinson later remarked, "it was a word without any precise meaning to it." Statesmanship of the highest quality was needed if America and Britain were to work their differences out, and even this might not be enough. In Parliament, no strong pro-American bloc existed to present the colonies' position in a fair light. In America the press was mainly in the hands of men who preferred to increase rather than diminish the tension between Britain and the colonies. The clergy, the merchants, and other colonial leaders did little to promote actively better relations. A cold war had begun in which suspicion reigned on both sides of the water.

BIBLIOGRAPHY

An excellent survey of the various interpretations of the American Revolution since Bancroft's great study in the nineteenth century can be found in the Bibliographical Essay in Esmond Wright's *Fabric of Freedom* (1961). Edmund S. Morgan, "The American Revolution: Revisions in Need of Revision," *WMQ*, 14 (1957), 3–15, should be supplemented by Jack P. Greene, "The Flight from Determinism: A Review of Recent Literature on the Coming of the American Revolution," *South Atlantic Quarterly*, 41 (1962), 235–259.

Page Smith's "David Ramsay and the Causes of the American Revolution," *WMQ*, 17 (1960), 51–77 covers more than its title indicates. Louis M. Hacker argues that the Revolution resulted from the growth of a colonial capitalism eager to be rid of imperial shackles in "The First American Revolution," *Columbia University Quarterly*, 27 (1935), 259–295. Clarence L. Ver Steeg revises this view in "The American Revolution Considered as an Economic Movement," *Huntington Library Quarterly*, 20 (1957) 361–372. Charles H. McIlwain's *The American Revolution: A Constitutional Interpretation* (1923; pb.) is answered by Robert L. Schuyler's *Parliament and the British Empire* (1929). Carl Becker inaugurated an emphasis on the role of internal dissension as a cause of the Revolution in his *History of Political Parties in the Province of New York, 1760–1766* (1909; pb.). Claude H. Van Tyne pointed up the part religion played in promoting revolt in "The Influence of the Clergy, and of Religious and Sectarian Forces in the American Revolution," *AHR*, 19 (1913), 44–64, a view most recently elaborated by Carl Bridenbaugh's *Mitre and Sceptre: Transatlantic Faiths, Ideas, Personalities, and Politics, 1689–1775* (1962). J. C. Wahlke has collected several of these and other views in *The Causes of the American Revolution* (1950). Bernard Bailyn's *Pamphlets of the American Revolution, 1750–1776* (1965), the first of a multivolume edition, is introduced by a distinguished book-length essay on the background and causes of the Revolution.

Several one-volume surveys of the Revolution, each in its own way excellent and all offering individual approaches to the great event, are Charles M. Andrews, *The Colonial Background of the American Revolution* (rev. ed. 1931; pb.), which, along with Lawrence H. Gipson's *The Coming of the Revolution, 1763–1775* (1954; pb.), emphasizes the problems of empire; Carl Becker's *Eve of the Revolution* (1918; pb.) points up the concern that existed over who should rule at home; John C. Miller's *Origins of the American Revolution* (1959; pb.) highlights the conflict emerging from the contrast between the "English Mind" and the "American Mind"; Edmund S. Morgan's *Birth of the Republic, 1763–1789* (1956; pb.) develops the point that America as early as 1764 took a stand on principle that it never abandoned; Eric Robson, an Englishman, discusses *The American Revolution, 1763–1783* (1955) as a problem of British policy. Four studies that approach the Revolution from specialized angles are Philip Davidson, *Propaganda and the American Revolution, 1763–1783* (1941); Oliver M. Dickerson, *The Navigation Acts and the American Revolution* (1951), who makes the point that it was not the acts but the "customs racketeers" who sought to enforce them literally that caused the trouble; Leonard Labaree, *Conservatism in Early American History* (1948; pb.); and Joseph J. Malone, *Pine Trees and Politics: The Naval Stores and Forest Policy in Colonial New England, 1691–1775* (1964), which maintains that "English administrative ignorance of its own colonial policies was a major cause" of the Revolution.

The New West

Much of the material listed in the first section of the Chapter 10 Bibliography is relevant here. Howard H. Peckham's careful study of *Pontiac and the Indian*

Uprising (1947; pb.) supplements and refines Francis Parkman's *Conspiracy of Pontiac* (1851; pb.). The best treatment of the role of the British Army in America at this time is Jack M. Sosin, *Whitehall and the Wilderness* (1961), a picture that can be filled in with J. C. Long, *Lord Jeffrey Amherst* (1933), and John R. Alden, *General Gage in America* (1948). Three sound volumes on British activities in the South are Charles L. Mowat, *East Florida as a British Province, 1763–1784* (1943); Cecil Johnson, *British West Florida, 1763–1783* (1943); and Alden, *John Stuart and the Southern Colonial Frontier* (1944). C. W. Alvord's *The Mississippi Valley in British Politics* (1916), Thomas P. Abernethy's *Western Lands and the American Revolution* (1937), and George I. Lewis' more specialized *Indiana Company, 1763–1798* (1941) should be consulted here. A full account of the crown's administration is found in Lawrence H. Gipson's *Triumphant Empire: New Responsibilities Within the Enlarged Empire, 1763–1766* (1956), the ninth volume of his great study, *The British Empire Before the American Revolution.*

Two useful general collections of documents covering the entire Revolutionary period are Samuel Eliot Morison, ed., *Sources . . . Illustrating the American Revolution, 1764–1788* (1929; pb.), and Max Beloff, ed., *The Debate on the American Revolution, 1761–1783* (1949; pb.). C. W. Alvord and C. E. Carter have edited three volumes on the British in Illinois Country: *The Critical Period, 1763–1765* (1915), *The New Regime, 1765–1767* (1916), and *Trade and Politics, 1767–1769* (1921).

The Grenville-Rockingham Ministry: 1763–1766

Gipson's tenth volume, *Triumphant Empire: Thunder-Clouds Gather in the West, 1763–1766* (1961), offers a sound starting point; the emphasis is on the government's financial troubles. A counterbalance to Gipson are the relevant chapters in Bernhard Knollenberg's *Origin of the American Revolution, 1759–1766* (rev. ed., 1961; pb.). The latest study of *The Reign of George III, 1760–1815* (1962) by J. Steven Watson has, like most recent work on the period, been shaped by the work of Sir Lewis Namier, whose *Structure of Politics at the Accession of George III* (1929) and *England in the Age of the American Revolution* (1930) have forced most historians to use such tags as "Whig" and "Tory" more cautiously and to judge George III with a less opprobrious term than "tyrant." (The best summary of the virtues and flaws of the Namier thesis is in Esmond Wright's Bibliographical Essay for *Fabric of Freedom, 1763–1800* [1961].) Robert R. Palmer disputes Namier's interpretation of the period in *The Age of Democratic Revolution: A Political History of Europe and America, 1760–1800* (1959), and at the same time adds some provocative insights of his own that do much to illuminate the American story, which Namier showed little interest in. C. F. Mullett, "English Imperial Thinking, 1764–1783," *PSQ,* 45 (1930), 548–579, still deserves attention. The best recent discussion of "The Currency Act of 1764 in Imperial-Colonial Relations, 1764–1776" is by Jack P. Greene and Richard M. Jellison, in *WMQ,* 18 (1961), 485–518.

Edmund S. Morgan and Helen M. Morgan, *The Stamp Act: Prologue to Revolution* (1953; pb.), has forced historians to reevaluate American reception to Grenville's acts. But their study should be read in conjunction with Knollenberg's chapters on the subject, and supplemented by Gipson's "The Great Debate in the Committee of the Whole House of Commons on the Stamp Act, 1766, as Reported by Nathaniel Ryder," *PMHB*, 86 (1962), 10–41 and Jack M. Sosin's "A Postscript to the Stamp Act, George Grenville's Revenue Measures: A Drain on Colonial Specie?" *AHR*, 63 (1958), 918–923. Sosin's discussion of "Imperial Regulation of Colonial Paper Money, 1764–1773" can be found in *PMHB*, 88 (1964), 174–198. John C. Miller has detailed the part of *Sam Adams* (1936), and Robert Meade that of *Patrick Henry: Patriot in the Making* (1957). Richard L. Morton's *Colonial Virginia* (1960) and David J. Mays's *Edmund Pendleton, 1721–1803* (1952) give rounded accounts of the Stamp Act's reception in Virginia. Thad W. Tate touches on the Grenville ministry in his more general discussion of "The Coming of the Revolution in Virginia: Britain's Challenge to Virginia's Ruling Class, 1763–1776," *WMQ*, 19 (1962), 323–343. Carl Van Doren's account in *Benjamin Franklin* (1938; pb.) is full but fails to show how his hero misled the ministry. A cleric's contribution to the Stamp Act resistance can be found in Charles W. Akers' excellent biography *Called unto Liberty: A Life of Jonathan Mayhew, 1720–1766* (1965).

The detailed *Colonial Merchants and the American Revolution, 1763–1776* (1918) and *Prelude to Independence: The Newspaper War on Britain, 1764–1776* (1958; pb.) of Arthur M. Schlesinger, can be pieced out with even more detail in any of several specialized works, among the best of which are Oscar Zeichner, *Connecticut's Years of Controversy, 1750–1776* (1949); David S. Lovejoy, *Rhode Island Politics and the American Revolution, 1760–1776* (1959); Carl Becker, *Political Parties in New York;* Charles H. Lincoln, *Revolutionary Movement in Pennsylvania, 1760–1776* (1901); Theodore Thayer, *Pennsylvania Politics and the Growth of Democracy, 1740–1776* (1954); Charles A. Barker, *The Background of the Revolution in Maryland* (1940); Richard Walsh, *Charleston's Sons of Liberty: A Study of the Artisans, 1763–1789* (1959); and Kenneth Coleman, *The American Revolution in Georgia* (1958).

Grenville's correspondence and diary are found in William J. Smith, ed., *The Grenville Papers* (4 vols., 1852–1853). Edward Channing and A. C. Coolidge edited *The Barrington-Bernard Correspondence* (1912). Franklin's role is self-depicted fully in Leonard W. Labaree's new edition of his papers, *Mr. Franklin: A Selection from His Personal Letters* (1956); in Carl Van Doren, ed., *Letters of Benjamin Franklin and Richard Jackson* (1947); and in Verner W. Crane, ed., *Franklin's Letters to the Press, 1758–1775* (1950). Edmund S. Morgan's *Prologue to Revolution: Sources and Documents on the Stamp Act Crisis, 1764–1766* (1959; pb.) gives a student his best introduction to the material. John Dickinson's *Letters of a Pennsylvania Farmer* are available in numerous editions and also in paperback. Paul Leicester Ford's edition of Dickinson's *Writings,* published in 1895, is currently being expanded and reedited by H. Trevor Colburn.

The Road to an Uneasy Truce: 1766–1770

Nearly all the material listed above is useful for this section. John Brooke, a student of Namier's, presents a full account of *The Chatham Administration* (1956). The growth of anti-American feeling is discussed in C. R. Ritcheson, *British Politics and the American Revolution* (1954). H. Trevor Colburn's "John Dickinson: Historical Revolutionary," *PMHB*, 83 (1959), 271–292 amplifies the picture given in Charles Stillé's *Life and Times of John Dickinson* (1891), still the only biography of this important figure. Refinements in the imperial machinery made during this period are discussed generally in Lawrence A. Harper, *The English Navigation Laws* (1939), and Oliver M. Dickerson, *The Navigation Acts and the American Revolution* (1951) ; and specifically in Dora M. Clark, "The American Board of Customs, 1767–1783," *AHR*, 45 (1940), 777–806, Carl Ubbeholde, *Vice-Admiralty Courts and the American Revolution* (1960), and M. M. Spector, *The American Department of the British Government, 1768–1782* (1940). Three articles, all in *WMQ*, 20 (1963) that touch on three specialized aspects of this period are Roger Champagne, "Family Politics Versus Constitutional Principles: The New York Assembly Elections of 1768 and 1769," 57–79; Dorothy Burne Goebel, "The 'New England Trade' and the French West Indies, 1763–1774: A Study in Trade Policies," 331–372; and Pauline Maier, "John Wilkes and American Disillusionment with Britain," 373–395.

For further references see the *Harvard Guide,* Sections 109, "The American Revolution, Introductory and General"; 110, "Renewed Activity in Spanish Borderlands"; 111, "The West in the American Revolution"; 112, "British Policy and Colonial Resistance, 1761–1766"; 113, "From Passive to Active Resistance, 1767–1774."

"Congress Voting Independence," by Robert Pine and Edward Savage

14. The Road to Independence: 1770-1776

IRRITATIONS MOUNT: 1770-1774
    Committees of Correspondence
    Trouble over Tea
    The Intolerable Acts

REBELLION: 1774-1775
    The First Congress
    Lexington and Concord
    Problems of Defense

INDEPENDENCE: 1775-1776
    A House Divided
    Congress Acts
    The Declaration

The fever broke and temperatures returned to normal in 1770—or so it seemed at the time. There began a three-year span of good relations—good relative to what had gone before—between Great Britain and America, with leaders on both sides of the ocean doing their best to prolong the happy mood. Sam Adams was eased from power in Massachusetts, and there, as elsewhere in America, men eager to accept Lord North's friendly overtures at face value stepped into control. Few realized that America verged on independence. Irritations still cropped up between mother country and colonies, but they caused no general dissension; only later did men see how Sam Adams and those who thought like him had "improved" on those irritations to hasten the end of the brief era of good feelings. ("We cannot make events," Adams once said, in explaining his role as a behind-the-scenes manipulator. "Our business is wisely to improve them.")

IRRITATIONS MOUNT: 1770–1774

Quarrels proliferated during the years of calm between Britain and America, but for the most part they centered on internal colonial problems. Connecticut's invasion of the Wyoming Valley and Virginia's claim to the land around the forks of the Ohio agitated Pennsylvanians at this time, while New York squabbled with New Hampshire over the boundary line between them. Massachusetts continued to grumble about the incursions of royal power in its affairs, but the grumbling was subdued compared to what had gone before and might have been forgotten except that out of it came the creation of a piece of political machinery that was to hasten the onset of the Revolution.

Committees of Correspondence

On March 5 of every year after 1770, a Massacre oration was delivered in Boston to mark the horrors of that night. The memorial service inflamed Bostonians briefly but did little real damage to the good relations that had been established between Britain and Massachusetts. A new grievance was needed, and the crown served it up in June 1772 when Thomas Hutchinson, on orders from the home government, announced that hereafter the crown would pay the governor's salary, thus relieving the chief royal officer in Massachusetts of dependence on the legislature. This at once prompted complaints that this "dangerous innovation" infringed on a right embedded in the colony's charter and that it exposed "the province to a despotic administration of government."

Later in the summer came word that the crown had compounded its felony by providing a permanent salary for the judges of the Superior Court, who had previously been paid by the legislature. This was too much. In early November, the Boston town meeting, guided by Sam Adams, voted to create a Committee of Correspondence, something Adams had sought for months. The committee was to be composed of twenty-one members, and its purpose was

to state the rights of the colonists and of this province in particular as men and Christians and as subjects; and to communicate and publish the same to the several towns and to the world as the sense of this town, with the infringements and violations thereof that have been or from time to time may be made.

The eminent in Boston, suspecting that the committee would be used to roil rather than calm the waters, refused to serve on it. James Otis accepted the chairmanship, but his recent bout with insanity did little to enhance the reputation of the committee.

The committee presented its first report toward the end of November. It comprised three papers—one by Sam Adams on the rights of Massachusetts citizens, another by Joseph Warren on their grievances, and the third, by Dr. Benjamin Church, an open letter to all towns in Massachusetts urging them not "to doze or sit supinely indifferent on the brink of destruction" and to create their own Committees of Correspondence. The Boston town meeting approved the report, and Adams immediately dispatched it throughout the Bay Colony and to all assemblies in America. Within three months, eighty additional Committees of Correspondence had been erected in Massachusetts, according to Thomas Hutchinson. "This is the foulest, subtlest, and most venomous serpent ever issued from the egg of sedition," Daniel Leonard wrote, and so far as those eager to strengthen ties with Britain were concerned, he was right.

This development so disturbed Hutchinson that when the legislature convened in January 1773, he sought in a speech he had worked up with great care to point out the dangers in the representatives' new attitude toward the British constitution. "I know of no line that can be drawn between the supreme authority of Parliament and the total independence of the colonies," he said, and then drew at length on precedents from the past to prove his point. The legislature answered with what has been called "one of the most important of all the revolutionary papers." Sam Adams, Dr. Warren, and Joseph Hawley wrote the first draft, which John Adams revised, expunging certain "democratic principles" and furnishing "the law authorities and the legal and constitutional reasonings." The paper renounced all ties with Parliament and drew on precedents cited in Hutchinson's own history of the province to prove such ties had never existed. It insisted that Massachusetts' allegiance was to the king alone, thus advancing a concept of empire that would eventually become embedded in the Declaration of Independence.

Hutchinson had been answered, and now, with help from Benjamin Franklin, he was to be ruined. Franklin, in London as a colonial agent, managed to get hold of letters that Hutchinson and others had written to officials in England. In one of the letters, Hutchinson had said that "there must be a diminution of what are called English liberties" in Massachusetts if the empire was to survive. Franklin sent the letters to friends in the Bay Colony, asking that they be read but not copied. He knew, of course, that he asked the impossible. The letters were read to the legislature in early 1773. It was agreed that the governor's subversive ideas must be exposed to the world, and Sam Adams was chosen to help "edit" the letters for the press. Publication demolished Hutchinson's effectiveness as a crown official, and now it was only a matter of time before he would be replaced. (Franklin won little praise for his role. Men smiled when they now called him "a man of letters," and in Britain the Attorney General subjected him to a humiliating public examination about his part in the affair.)

While Hutchinson was being besmirched, another event—the *Gaspee* affair—came along that Sam Adams managed "wisely to improve" upon. The *Gaspee* was one of the warships that had been loaned to the customs service to help suppress smuggling. In the spring of 1772, its zealous commander was harassing the farmers and fishermen who traded around Narragansett Bay. When in June the ship ran aground a few miles south of Providence while chasing a suspected smuggler, a band of citizens swarmed aboard during the night, forced the crew off, then burned the ship. If the *Gaspee* rioters were not punished, Hutchinson warned, "the friends of government will despond and give up all hopes of being able to withstand the faction." The crown responded by creating a Commission of Inquiry to investigate the affair. A false rumor had it that the commission would force all suspects to stand trial in England. The commission sat for seventeen days in early 1773, and Sam Adams' Committees of Correspondence made the most of every session. The commission eventually reported that it could find no one in all Rhode Island who knew anything about the burning. Despite the seriousness of the affair—attacking and burning one of his majesty's warships must be judged a more serious offense than, say, the destruction of a private company's load of tea—the crown decided to let the matter slide in the hope of promoting harmony between America and Britain. But the damage had been done. The very existence of the commission was taken to be an interference in the internal affairs of a colony, and the Committees of Correspondence made sure all New England got the point.

Concern over the *Gaspee* spread beyond the bounds of New England. The Virginia assembly was in session while the king's investigatory commission sat in Rhode Island. In mid-March, the assembly unanimously agreed to erect a standing Committee of Correspondence of its own and at the same time approved a circular letter that urged all other colonies to do the same. The governor promptly dissolved the assembly for the year, but his action came too late. By the middle of 1773, all New England, plus South Carolina, had received and accepted the Virginia invitation. The foundation for a union of the colonies had been laid.

Few noticed during the disturbance over the *Gaspee* affair that Parliament had continued to legislate for America and in a way designed to promote the best interests of the colonies. In 1773, in "an act to explain and amend" the 1764 Currency Act, Parliament confirmed and enlarged the freedom of American colonies to issue paper money. It did so in consideration of "the want of gold and silver currency" in the colonies, in consideration of "the public advantage," and "in justice to those persons who may have demands upon the public treasuries in the said colonies for services performed." The money might be issued in the form of "certificates, notes, bills, or debentures" and made "a legal tender to the public treasuries" in payment of taxes and other dues. But the concession came too late, for by the time news of it arrived the colonists were wrought up about a matter they considered as serious as the stamp question.

Trouble over Tea

An affair that in the beginning had nothing to do with America led to the worst colonial outburst of all. The giant British East India Company, after a century and three-quarters of great prosperity, verged on bankruptcy. Tea glutted the British market, and the company had some seventeen million pounds of it stored in warehouses along the Thames. Rumor said that the crown might revoke the company's charter and take over management of its affairs. Many in Parliament felt that such an act would be "a direct and dangerous attack upon the liberties of the people," for to deprive one corporation of its chartered rights might prove to be the entering wedge for depriving other corporations—an English borough or a colony like Massachusetts—of its rights. There was a strong feeling that the company's troubles had to be solved in a less drastic way.

Lord North sought to handle the problem in a manner that would please everyone, and to that end he pushed through Parliament the Tea Act of 1773. By the act, the government withdrew all import duties on tea that the company brought into England; it relinquished its right to the considerable annual payment it had received from the company; and it advanced the company a large loan. Further, the company was now permitted to export directly to America the tea it hitherto had been forced to sell in England at public auction to wholesale merchants, who had then sold it to American wholesale merchants, who, in turn, had sold it to American retail merchants.

The Tea Act pleased Lord North in every way. Eliminating English taxes and English middlemen, and leaving only the Townshend duty to be collected in America, should put the East India Company at a competitive advantage in America. Americans should be charmed because the new setup would give them cheaper tea—cheaper, indeed, than in Britain. And the crown would profit in several ways: by undercutting the price of the cheap Dutch tea Americans had been using, a huge hole in colonial smuggling activities would be plugged; the income from the three pence per pound Townshend duty would offset the cost of the crown's loan to the company; and payment of the duty would vindicate Parliament's right to levy taxes on Americans. Lord North was so certain the act would cause no fuss that he did not bother to send instructions to the royal governors in America regarding its enforcement.

The first to complain in America were those merchants who had thrived off the smuggling trade. The smugglers concentrated around Narragansett Bay, the Hudson River, and Delaware Bay, and thus the first loud complaints came from Newport, New York, and Philadelphia. (Boston had too many alert royal ships in its harbor to manage much smuggling.) This early grumbling might have been contained if the East India Company had chosen wisely the agents or "consignees" who would sell the tea to local merchants. Instead of selecting those merchants who had normally handled the London tea trade, it gave the lucrative posts only to those who had opposed the nonimportation agreements.

All the old arguments that had been used since the Revenue Act of 1764 were aired once again, but the offended merchants came up with a new one. They shouted "monopoly," and so effectively did they make their point that the word would remain a battle cry in America down to the present. They argued that the government's concessions to the East India Company were only the first of many to British merchants that would eventually eliminate *all* middlemen in the colonies. In time, so the argument went, all British goods would be sold in America only through specified agents whose loyalty had been carefully checked. A monopoly of the tea market would be followed by a monopoly of wine, spices, silks, hardware, cloth—the list was endless.

The pattern of resistance to the tea act followed that laid down in 1765. New York merchants spoke up first. On October 15 they publicly thanked all ship captains who had refused to load up in London with East India Company tea for the "insidious purpose of levying the duty in America." The next day, the usually discreet Philadelphia merchants said that anyone who helped enforce "this ministerial plan . . . is an enemy to his country." Action soon followed words. A mass meeting held in Philadelphia late in October voted to force the resignation of the company's agents in that city. Boston followed with its own meeting on November 3, New York on December 1, and Charleston on December 2.

Thus far, moderate men had managed to keep resistance from degenerating into mob action. The test of their control over the people came when ships loaded with tea began arriving at the major ports. The tea was landed in Charleston, but authorities locked it in a public warehouse. (The chests remained there unopened until after independence had been declared.) In Philadelphia and New York the tea ships were held out in the harbor far from the people's reach, and no serious trouble developed. In Boston, however, Hutchinson determined to force the issue, for he believed that another retreat would end British sovereignty in America.

He insisted that the tea ships tie up along the wharves and that their cargoes be unloaded. On the night of December 16, somewhere between thirty and sixty men, lightly disguised as Indians, boarded the three ships and dumped forty-five tons of tea overboard. A huge cordon of people watched from the docks. One man swore that John Hancock was there and that he had exchanged the countersign with him—an Indian "ugh" followed by "me know you"—but Hancock never claimed the honor.

John Adams, who had previously been shocked by the mob's role in resisting British measures, now changed his tune. He said: "This destruction of the tea is so bold, so daring, so firm, intrepid, and inflexible, and it must have so important consequences, and so lasting, that I cannot but consider it as an epocha in history." Adams' prediction was right. The Boston Tea Party did become "an epocha in history," but few Americans saw it that way at the time. The act was rebuked throughout America on the ground that it was "calculated to introduce anarchy, confusion and bloodshed among the people."

Lord North was dumbfounded by the news from Boston. He said that he had given the colonists "a relief instead of an oppression" and that of all mankind only "New England fanatics" would have rebelled against it. The dispute was no longer over taxation, he said, but whether Great Britain possessed any authority whatever over the "haughty American republicans." "We must master them or totally leave them to themselves and treat them as aliens," George III said, and for once, few in Parliament disagreed with him. The Boston Tea Party had silenced almost the last appeaser in England.

The Intolerable Acts

Lord North decided to answer the tea party with the Boston Port Bill, which was pushed through Parliament in March 1774. The bill ordered Boston closed to all shipping until the citizens had paid the East India Company for the tea destroyed, compensated the revenue officers for their lost duty on the tea, and otherwise given evidence of their remorse. North was convinced that Boston would stand alone and that the other colonies would be too busy scrambling after her trade to come to her aid. Along with its severity, the Port Bill had the further virtue of being easy to enforce. Four or five frigates stationed in Boston harbor and a few regiments of British regulars in Boston itself to keep order would, North told Commons, "do the business."

The Boston Port Bill passed Commons on March 25, 1774, with voice vote "but after a pretty long debate." News of the Port Act reached Boston on May 11. Even Hutchinson was shocked by its harshness. This had been a riot no worse than many Englishmen had witnessed or participated in.

Was all London so punished when such had occurred there? And why such severity now over the dumping of a private company's tea when only a few months earlier the burning of his majesty's *Gaspee* had been forgotten after a token investigation?

The Boston Committee of Correspondence met soon after news of the act arrived. Paul Revere, who served as express rider for the committee, was handed copies of the act and a circular letter to carry southward. The letter asked all colonies to consider Boston's troubles theirs and to revive the old nonimportation and nonexportation agreements that had been so effective in the past. Word soon came back from Providence, New York, and Philadelphia urging a general congress of the colonies to determine a suitable course of action. This proposal seemed to some in Boston to temporize when fast action was needed; a congress would take time to assemble, and by then tempers might have cooled. Virginia's reaction to the Port Act pleased the radical in Boston more. Prompted by Thomas Jefferson, the House of Burgesses resolved that June 1—the day the act went into effect—should become "a day of fasting, humiliation, and prayer" in order to ask God's help "for averting the heavy calamity which threatens destruction to our civil rights, and the evils of civil war." The governor disliked the tone of the resolution and dissolved the house. The burgesses immediately reassembled into an "association," which then proceeded to declare the attack on Boston an attack on all.

June 1 became the solemn day Jefferson had requested. Throughout the continent, shops closed, flags hung at half mast, muffled church bells gave forth dolorous peals, and parsons spoke movingly of beleaguered Boston. The city that had recently been excoriated by fellow Americans for destroying private property now became "an innocent, a virtuous, a religious and loyal people, ever remarkable for their love of order, peace and good government." Food poured in from all parts of the continent: Charleston sent up rice, Connecticut a flock of sheep, Philadelphia over one thousand barrels of flour. At the moment when they were supposedly being starved into submission, Bostonians dined better than ever.

In the midst of this agitation America learned that Lord North had chosen this moment to begin a full-scale reform movement. The reforms were embodied in three acts passed by Parliament in late May and early June 1774 and known, along with the Port Act, as the Intolerable, or Coercive, Acts. (1) The Quartering Act merely revised the earlier measure. It directed local authorities to find quarters for troops if barracks were not available at the scene of trouble and not, as it had been in 1768, several miles away. (2) The Administration of Justice Act protected soldiers, magistrates, and customs officers who took part in suppressing riots or other disturbances from trial by prejudiced juries by providing that when, in the opinion of the governor, a fair trial could not be had in the province, it might be transferred to England or to another colony. Though the act asked only a change of venue when a fair trial seemed impossible, the time of its passage could not have been worse. It became known in Massachusetts as the Murder Act. Every villain "who ravishes our wives, deflowers our daughters," someone remarked with earthy eloquence, "can evade punishment by being tried in Britain, where no evidence can pursue him."

(3) The Act for Better Regulating the Government of Massachusetts raised the greatest storm. Legally, it only amended the Massachusetts charter of 1691, but actually, it imposed on the colony a new charter meant to be permanent. Its provisions allowed the governor to appoint his council, which had formerly been chosen for him by the General Court. The council could still advise but lost its power to veto the governor's decisions. The governor could forbid all town meetings except the annual one for electing officers. He had the power to appoint "for and during the pleasure of his Majesty" and the right to remove at his own discretion the sheriffs, judges, attorney general, and marshal of the province, and to have fair juries drawn by lot from lists of eligibles assembled by the sheriffs. Lord George Germain made clear during debate over the act in Parliament that the act sought only "to bring the constitution of America as similar to our own as possible." In Britain, the king and the two houses of Parliament checked and balanced one another, but in Massachusetts the "democratic part" of the government dominated the whole. There is something wrong, Lord North told Commons, when a governor cannot "enforce obedience to the laws." The purpose of the new act, he said, was to "take the executive power from the democratic part of the government."

At the end of June, Parliament passed the Quebec Act, which the colonists (but not the historians) lumped with the other Intolerable Acts. The act extended the province of Quebec's borders southward to the Ohio and westward to the Mississippi. It permitted all French-speaking residents to retain the legal code used when France had owned the territory. The Catholic Church became the established church and was to be supported by compulsory taxation. The province would for the time being be ruled much as it had been under the French—by a crown-appointed governor and council and without a representative assembly. The act sought to resolve two problems that had plagued the British government's affairs in America since 1763. It attempted first to deal decently with a people who had their own customs, language, and religion but now suddenly found themselves under British rule. From this point of view, the act can only be judged as a humane and tolerant law. Second, it circumvented the American refusal to pay for administering the territory north of the Ohio and west of the Appalachians by transferring that burden from American to Canadian shoulders.

The colonists noticed none of the act's virtues but saw it only as a further example of the British conspiracy to oppress. Those who were speculating in Western lands believed it ruined their chance for a fortune. Virginia, which claimed the land by the grant in its charter, saw itself deprived of a huge territory by legislative fiat. (At the time the crown transferred the Western lands to Quebec, Lord Dunmore was ranging through the Ohio Valley with Virginia troops seeking to tighten his colony's hold on the area.) Many viewed the establishment of Catholicism in Quebec as the entering wedge for establishing Anglicanism in America. By implication, the act seemed to extend Catholicism into an area where Americans were now pouring. (George Croghan reported in 1773 that no less than sixty thousand were settled between Pittsburgh and the mouth of the Ohio.) Would these settlers have to support the Catholic Church? What would happen now to the "ancient free Protestant colonies" with the anti-Christ on their borders? Sam Adams had once said that "what we have above everything else is to fear popery," and now his prediction, it would seem, had come true. Bitterness reached a point where one newspaper account had the pope inviting Lord North to Rome "to reward his good service done the Catholic faith, by conferring on him some dignified office in the Romish church." In October the first Continental Congress spoke of its "astonishment that a British Parliament should ever consent to establish in that country a religion that has deluged your island in blood, and dispersed impiety, bigotry, persecution, murder and rebellion through every part of the world." (Six months later, the second Continental Congress suppressed that astonishment when it tried to wean Canada from Great Britain. The Canadians would have none of the soft talk and, thanks in large measure to the Quebec Act, they remained loyal to Britain.)

By the time Americans learned of the Quebec Act, they also knew the ministry had capped its reform program for Massachusetts by sending the colony a new governor. Governor Hutchinson was replaced by General Thomas Gage, who was to remain commander-in-chief of the British armed forces in America at the same time he directed Massachusetts' civil affairs. Gage was an amiable, able, and well-intentioned man; his experience in the colonies dated back to 1755; and he was married to an American girl. London believed that if any man could deal firmly, sympathetically, and intelligently with a difficult situation, it was General Gage. The trouble was that the situation had become more than difficult; it had become impossible.

Map 37. The Quebec Act of 1774

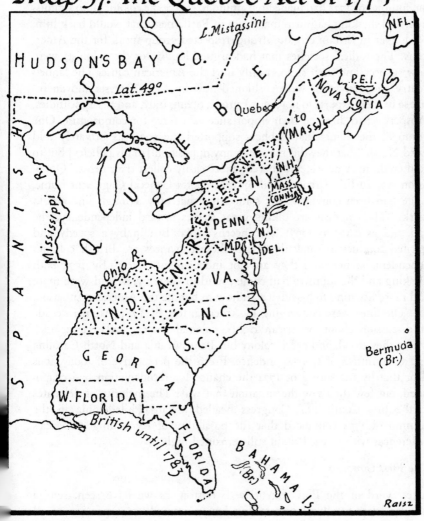

HUDSON'S BAY CO.

L.Mistassini

NFL.

Lat. 49°

Quebec

P.E.I.

NOVA SCOTIA

to (MASS.)

QUEBEC

Mississippi R.

SPANISH

Ohio R.

INDIAN RESERVE

N.Y.

N.H.

MASS.

CONN.

R.I.

PENN.

N.J.

MD.

DEL.

VA.

N.C.

S.C.

GEORGIA

W. FLORIDA

British until 1783

E. FLORIDA

Bermuda (Br.)

BAHAMA Is. (Br.)

Raisz

REBELLION: 1774–1775

By the time of Gage's appointment as governor of Massachusetts in 1774, the guidelines had been laid down and the room for maneuver between America and Britain had become more narrow than ever. England by the summer of 1774 had made up its mind to coerce the colonies into submission, and the king had firm majorities in Parliament that would back him. No longer in Britain did any strong, respected group speak for the Americans. The radical societies that had argued loudly for the colonists were now suspect, and their support only hurt the American cause. The landed gentry and merchants were cushioned now by good harvests and an increase in their exports to northern Europe, Spain, Italy, and the East Indies. Prosperity had dimmed their importance as a force for compromise. One group of merchants that publicly supported the colonists privately told Lord North "that they did not mean any opposition [to his policies] but to gain credit in America, and thereby more easily collect their debts." Opposition was further strengthened by the reports General Gage sent home. Gage had been convinced for some time that only a tough line would work. "The colonists are taking great strides toward independency," he had said as early as 1767; "it concerns Great Britain by a speedy and spirited conduct to show them that these provinces are British colonies dependent on her, and they are not independent states." By 1774 both the king and the ministry had come round to Gage's view and were more and more listening to his advice on how to handle the American situation.

The lines were converging in America, too, by 1774. After a decade of discussion about American rights, colonial leaders had a clear idea where they stood, and every colony but Pennsylvania and North Carolina had Committees of Correspondence. From the perspective of today, it is clear that by the spring of 1774 the chance for reconciliation had evaporated, but few then saw the situation that way. The majority of delegates to the first Continental Congress headed toward Philadelphia in the autumn of 1774 convinced that the possibility of reconciling America's differences with Great Britain still remained high.

The First Congress

After word of the Port Act arrived, Boston, as we have seen, sent a circular letter to all colonies calling for an immediate suspension of all trade between the mother country and the colonies. The suggestion met a lukewarm reception, especially in Philadelphia and New York, both of which urged the calling of a general congress to discuss America's problems. The bolder plan was abandoned, and in mid-June 1774 the Massachusetts legislature sent forth another circular letter, this time requesting a meeting of delegates from colonial Committees of Correspondence. By the end of July, all colonies but Georgia had by one means or another chosen delegates to meet in Philadelphia to discuss American affairs. Pennsylvania alone used its regular legislature to select its delegation. Virginia's "association" of burgesses from the prorogued legislature called a "convention" of the colony's counties, and this extralegal body elected delegates for Congress. The other colonies followed a pattern similar to Virginia's.

The delegates drifted into Philadelphia toward the end of August. Nearly all were experienced politicians and had been involved in their colony's affairs for at least a decade. The majority were lawyers, twelve of whom had studied in Great Britain. All the American colleges were represented by alumni, Harvard leading with five. None were radicals in the true sense of the word, that is, men who wanted to rip the political structure apart and start afresh. John Adams, who was among the first to arrive, sized them up as they came in: James Duane (New York) had "a sly, surveying eye" but was "very sensible, I think, and very artful"; John Dickinson (Pennsylvania) seemed "a very modest man, and very ingenious as well as very agreeable"; Caesar Rodney (Delaware) "is the oddest looking man in the world," with a head "not bigger than a large apple, yet there is sense and fire, spirit, wit, and humor in his countenance"; John Rutledge (South Carolina) had "no keenness in his eye, no depth in his countenance; nothing of the profound, sagacious, brilliant, or sparkling"; Richard Henry Lee (Virginia) was "a masterly man."

Congress assembled for its first meeting on September 5. The Pennsylvania assembly's offer of its spacious hall in the statehouse was rejected for Carpenter's Hall, which had an "excellent library" and "a long entry where gentlemen may walk." Probably, it seemed better at the outset not to associate Congress with a particular colony; moreover, using Carpenter's Hall would be "highly agreeable to the mechanics and citizens in general." Peyton Randolph of Virginia—an affable gentleman of "majestic deportment" who commanded "respect and esteem by his very aspect"— was chosen chairman. It was then agreed to call the assemblage "The Congress" and the chairman "The President." Charles Thomson, known as "the Sam Adams of Philadelphia," was elected secretary, a post he would hold until the Continental Congress died in 1788. Instructions from the home "governments" were read; these made clear that the delegates were empowered to do little more than "consult upon the present state of the colonies." A long discussion followed over voting procedure. The large colonies wanted voting strength related to population, but resistance from the smaller colonies and the lack of population statistics forced the decision—a single vote for each colony, regardless of size. (It was during this debate that Patrick Henry remarked: "Government is dissolved. . . . We are in a state of nature, sir," then added, "The distinctions between Virginians, Pennsylvanians, New Yorkers, and New Englanders, are no more. I am not a Virginian, but an American.")

With the procedural work out of the way, Congress got down to business. Committees were appointed to draw up a statement of American rights, to list infringements of those rights, to study trade and manufacturing regulations that affected the colonies. During these early days, the delegates, many of whom had never traveled beyond their colony's borders, learned something about the diversity of traditions that throve in America. "We' had much conversation," John Adams said, "upon the practice of law in our different provinces. . . . Mr. Allen [of Pennsylvania] asks me, from whence do you derive your laws? How do you entitle yourselves to English privileges? Is it not Lord Mansfield on the side of power?" The delegates turned to philosophers in search of common principles. The city librarian reported that Vattel, Burlamaqui, Locke, and Montesquieu seemed to be "the standard to which they refer when settling the rights of the colonies or when a dispute arises on the justice or propriety of a measure."

The Massachusetts delegation conducted itself discreetly in the beginning, for its past reputation for violence gave it "numberless prejudices to remove here." The delegation's job was to make Massachusetts' cause America's, and to that end, said John Adams, "we have been obliged to keep ourselves out of sight, and to feel pulses, and to sound the depths; to insinuate our sentiments, designs, and desires by means of other persons, sometimes of one province, and sometimes of another." These devious tactics were forced into the open on September 17 when Paul Revere arrived at Carpenter's Hall with a series of resolves from Suffolk County (Boston's county). These resolves declared that no obedience ought to be paid to the Intolerable Acts; that Massachusetts' Provincial Congress should collect all taxes and withhold them from the crown until Massachusetts' government had been "placed upon a constitutional foundation"; that the colony should prepare itself to resist a British attack; and that the jailing of any patriot leader gave citizens the right to imprison "every servant of the present tyrannical and unconstitutional government." The resolves were read to Congress "with great applause," according to Sam Adams, even though, as Joseph Galloway of Pennsylvania noted, they "contained a complete declaration of war against Great Britain." Congress reacted more cautiously the next day, and despite prodding from Adams would only "approve the wisdom and fortitude, with which opposition to these wicked ministerial measures has hitherto been conducted. . . ."

The turning point in the affairs of this first Congress came ten days later when Joseph Galloway introduced his own plan for reorganizing the empire. "We must come upon terms with Great Britain," Galloway said in the speech that introduced his plan. His plan of union called for a separate American legislature or Grand Council, whose members would be elected by the colonial assemblies. The colonies would continue to exercise authority over internal affairs; the Grand Council would regulate all commercial, civil, criminal, and police affairs that concerned the colonies generally. It would have the right to veto all Parliamentary legislation affecting the colonies. Still, the government would be inferior to Parliament, which could initiate legislation relevant to the colonies, and to the crown, which would appoint the President General, who would exercise executive authority and would hold office during the king's pleasure. The great principle behind his plan, Galloway said, "was that no law should bind America without her consent," and its great virtue was that *"the strength of the whole empire may be drawn together on any emergency, the interest of both countries advanced, and the rights and liberties of Americans secured."* Congress debated the plan for several days. When the vote came, the plan was defeated by the slim margin of six colonies to five. The "violent party," as Galloway called it, now controlled Congress. Galloway credited his defeat largely to Sam Adams, who, he said, "eats little, sleeps little, thinks much, and is most decisive and indefatigable in the pursuit of his objects."

After Congress rejected Galloway's plan, the delegates in effect disavowed their instructions, which were to seek ways to reconcile differences with Britain. On October 8, it gave explicit approval to the Suffolk Resolves and went on to say that if Britain attempted to execute the late acts of Parliament by force, then "all America ought to support them in their opposition." Galloway and Duane refused to sanction this threat, but the "violent party" was strong enough to prevent their opposition being noted in the minutes. Six days later Congress approved the most important document to issue from Carpenter's Hall, the Declaration of Rights and Resolves, which the committee assigned to draw it up had labored on for over a month. The difficulty had come about largely because America was following an uncharted path. Never before in Western history had a collection of colonies dared to rebel against the mother country. How was this rebellion without precedent to be justified? Some on the committee wanted to appeal to the colonists' historic rights as Englishmen, their rights under the British constitution; others preferred to stand on the rights of man, on the laws of nature rather than of statutebooks. The committee debated the matter for days, then finally asked John Adams to "produce something that will unite us." He solved the dilemma by appealing in his opening sentence simultaneously to "the immutable laws of nature, the principles of the English constitution, and the several charters and compacts." However, a close reading of the ten resolutions that followed this omnibus appeal makes it clear that Americans at this time were defying Britain on the ground that their rights as Englishmen had been violated. The Declaration of Rights and Resolves was a restrained statement that demanded the right of assembly and petition, the right to be tried "by their peers of the vicinage," the right to be free of a standing army, the right to choose their own councils. It rejected Parliament's right to tax the colonies in any way but accepted its right to regulate "our external commerce."

Once the Congress had approved the statement of American rights, it turned to study the string of "animated addresses" that had been prepared by various members. Richard Henry Lee's feeble Address to the People of Great Britain was rejected for a tougher statement written by John Jay with the same title. John Dickinson's Address to the Inhabitants of the Province of Quebec ("Unhappy people! who are not only injured but insulted") was approved. Open letters were sent to the people of St. John's, Newfoundland, and Nova Scotia as well as to those of East and West Florida. A long letter to the American public warned that if the people failed to accept the "mode of opposition recommended by" Congress, then "you must inevitably be reduced to choose either a more dangerous contest, or a final, ruinous and infamous subjection." And, finally, the Congress accepted John Dickinson's rewrite of an address to the king originally drawn up by Patrick Henry. Dickinson's dignified and restrained draft held to the pattern of blaming Parliament and "the administration" for America's troubles and told the king that "designing and dangerous men" were "daringly interposing themselves between your royal person and your faithful subjects."

These petitions, open letters, and statements of rights served a purpose Congress may have only dimly sensed. The delegates were forced to make clear to themselves, to Americans, and to Great Britain what they believed in and why they acted as they did. They were made to think concretely about objectives, and in the process of composing "animated addresses," they steadily defined, refined, and clarified their thoughts. Objectives might change, but the men of this and of the Congress to follow would always know, as "animated addresses" continued to pour from their sessions, even in the midst of violence, where they stood and what they stood for.

On October 20, Congress implemented words with a weapon. It resolved that every colony should create an "Association," which in effect was a covenant among the people, whereby men agreed not to import nor consume goods from Great Britain nor export goods to the mother country. The association prohibited, in words the early Puritans might have used, "every species of extravagance and dissipation, especially all horse-racing, and all kinds of gaming, cock-fighting, exhibitions of shows, plays, and other expensive diversions and entertainments." Merchants had enforced earlier embargoes against British trade, but failure of the boycott in 1770 led Congress to take control of the association out of the merchants' hands. Throughout the land committees were to be chosen "whose business it shall be attentively to observe the conduct of all persons touching this association ... to the end, that all such foes to the rights of British-America may be publicly known, and universally contemned as the enemies of American liberty." The merchants had clearly been demoted from command. In time, association committees would demand that ledgers and invoices be opened for inspection, and they could maintain a more effective watch upon shipping than had the customhouse officers from whose "tyranny" the merchants had recently freed themselves.

It was agreed that the Nonimportation and Nonconsumption Agreements were to go into effect on December 1, 1774, and to apply against Great Britain, Ireland, and the British West Indies. But here the smooth passage of the program for the association ended. The Nonexportation Agreement provoked a dispute so violent that it nearly broke up the Congress. Virginia pleaded for a two-year postponement to give it time to market its tobacco crops and search out new markets. A compromise granted Virginia a year's delay. South Carolina demanded that rice and indigo, its two chief staple crops, be excepted from the Nonexportation Agreement, and to lend force to the demand walked out of Congress. The delegation returned to the fold when Congress compromised by excepting rice from the ban. These compromises saved the union but weakened the association, and in the North bitterness smoldered against Southern intransigency.

Two days after these compromises had been worked out, Congress agreed that unless all grievances had been redressed, it would meet again in Philadelphia on May 10, 1775. The last session of the first Congress was held on October 26. In a note written that day to Benjamin Franklin, still in London, Charles Thomson said: "Even yet the wound may be healed and peace and love restored. But we are on the brink of a precipice."

Lexington and Concord

About the time news of the Continental Congress filtered into England, elections were being held for a new Parliament. The government had decided to hold the election soon after the Intolerable Acts had passed, though Parliament still had a year to run. (British law required a general election at least once every seven years.) It would weaken the government to halt during a war and engage in an electoral campaign. Four days after the returns were in, the king, with a fat majority in Commons that would give his ministry freedom of action for seven years, pronounced the New England colonies to be "in a state of rebellion" and said that "blows must decide" whether they were to be subject to or independent of Britain.

The government had determined to coerce the colonies, and Parliament sanctioned the decision by endorsing the king's position when it assembled in November 1774. A few still talked compromise, but fewer listened. Chatham's proposals to recall troops from Boston and to impose no taxes for revenue purposes without the consent of the colonial assemblies were defeated in the House of Lords in January 1775, the very month orders went out to all colonial governors to prevent the election of delegates to the second Continental Congress. In February, Parliament, still assuming that the discord centered in Boston and that Massachusetts could be isolated from the other colonies, declared that a rebellion existed in Massachusetts and urged the king "to enforce due obedience to the laws and authority of the supreme legislature." In the same month, both houses agreed that a compromise plan devised by Lord North should be submitted to the colonies. A modern historian has called the plan "not even a halfway measure for peace" but only "a stupid gesture." It "offered freedom from taxation by Parliament to any colony voluntarily making a fair contribution to imperial expenses. It did not exempt the colonies from taxation; it only made the colonies the tax-gatherers." It was designed to show merchants who were again showering Parliament with petitions and others who were pro-American that the government truly sought to appease the colonies. A clearer indication of the government's attitude was an order issued during the month that Parliament was discussing Lord North's peace plan, which dispatched three generals—William Howe, Sir Henry Clinton, and Sir John Burgoyne—to America with reinforcements. Parliament continued to act as the ministry wished. In March came the New England Restraining Act, which denied New England the right to fish off the Grand Banks and confined its trade to Britain, Ireland, and the West Indies. "As Americans had refused to trade with this kingdom, it was but just that we should not suffer them to trade with any other nation," it was said in justification of the act. (During the discussion of this measure, Burke made his memorable plea for conciliation, but to empty benches.) A similar measure was applied to New Jersey, Pennsylvania, and the South in April. Only New York, a center for loyalist sentiment, was exempted.

Map 38. "The shot heard round the world."

--R-- Revere's ride **--BR- British route** Drumlins Salt marsh
--D-- Dawes' ride

Rais2

1773 Dec 16, Boston Tea Party
1774 May, British troops land
  " Ap.18, 700 British march on Concord
  " " " Ride of Dawes and of Revere
  " " " Battles of Lexington and Concord
  " " 22, Mass. is raising 13,000 men

1775 May 10, Continental Congress in Philadelphia
  " " Ethan Allen takes Ticonderoga. Hauls
  " cannons to Dorchester.
  " June 17 Battle of Bunker Hill
  " July 5 Washington takes command.
1776 March 4 Cannon on Dorchester Heights
  " 17 Evacuation of Boston

Back in America, the colonies moved toward a war footing, and the movement accelerated with every piece of news that drifted in from England. By the end of 1774, ten colonies had provincial congresses, all extra-legal bodies and all mainly composed of the same men who had sat in the regular assemblies; these local congresses approved the proceedings of the Continental Congress. All colonies but New York and Georgia adopted the association, and local committees were soon busy with its enforcement; even in the recalcitrant colonies self-created local committees went ahead here and there with the business. It was soon apparent that nonimportation was working: British exports to New York fell from £437,937 in 1774 to £1,228 in 1775; to the Chesapeake area, they dropped from £528,738 in 1774 to £1,921 in 1775.

As war approached, dissension broke forth in America. While New Englanders from December 1774 through April 1775 read a series of essays signed Novanglus (John Adams), which derided all Parliamentary control over the colonies and insisted that their only tie with the mother country was through the king, and Virginians in the spring of 1775 heard Patrick Henry say "I know not what course others may take, but as for me, give me liberty or give me death!" others dared to speak up for conciliation. Daniel Dulany of Maryland, who had argued effectively against the Stamp Act, now said resistance verged on rebellion and he would not have anything to do with this. "If I must be enslaved," Samuel Seabury of New York said, "let it be a KING at least, and not by a parcel of upstart lawless Committee-men. If I must be devoured, let me be devoured by the jaws of a lion, and not gnawed to death by rats and vermin." In Boston, Reverend Mather Byles said: "Which is bet-ter—to be ruled by one tyrant three thousand miles away or three thousand tyrants not a mile away?"

Boston remained the center of discord. General Gage had arrived there with his commission as royal governor and four thousand troops in mid-May 1774. The Boston Committee of Correspondence ordered car-penters not to help the troops construct barracks; it permitted no lumber to be brought into the city; and it made merchants refuse to sell soldiers blankets, tools, or materials of any kind. Gage imported materials and brought in carpenters and bricklayers from Nova Scotia, but the barracks rose slowly. The people burned the straw he got for bedding, split the planks he got for barracks. The harassed soldiers seldom dared move about the town alone.

Gage did his best to be fair. He took care to keep military power subordinate to civil power, and he listened at all times to the complaints of citizens. But his troubles were insoluble: over seven thousand people in Boston were jobless and in no mood to listen to reason; outside the city companies of minutemen were being formed; military supplies were being collected; committees of observation were being appointed to watch the movements of British troops; and everywhere "sedition flowed copiously from the pulpits."

In the midst of this tension, Lord Dartmouth, secretary of war, urged Gage to "arrest and imprison the principal actors and abettors in the provincial Congress. . . ." Dartmouth made clear he did not think "any efforts of the people" would be "very formidable." Gage had his doubts here. He had said all through 1774 that the Americans would fight well, that it would require a large army to subdue them in New England, and that the job would take at least a year or two. He thought Dartmouth's request to pick up the leaders would do little good in itself and so decided to combine that job with another—to send an expedition to Concord to confiscate military stores the patriots had been depositing there since February.

Some seven hundred troops under Major John Pitcairn were ordered to move out of Boston on the night of April 18 "with the utmost expedition and secrecy to Concord, where you will seize and destroy all the artillery and ammunition you can find. . . ." Dr. Joseph Warren saw the embarkation begin; he sent William Dawes and Paul Revere off to warn Hancock and Sam Adams and the people generally. On the march out, the British knew that any hope of surprise had been lost. Church bells clanged in every village they passed through. The troops reached Lexington as the sun rose. They found some seventy Americans armed and gathered on the village green in crude battle formation. Pitcairn demanded they disperse. Captain John Parker, a veteran of the French and Indian War, told his men to withdraw. A musket was fired. Who fired it or which side, no one knows. In the ensuing melee, eight Americans were killed and ten were wounded; one Britisher was slightly hit. The skirmish delayed the British about fifteen minutes.

The British left the Americans to tend their dead and wounded and moved toward Concord, six miles farther on. There, more militia had assembled, but they withdrew across the river and the British entered the town without resistance around eight o'clock. While the redcoats went about destroying what they could find in the way of military supplies, the militia returned to town and tried to take North Bridge. A body of some three or four hundred minutemen attacked the British covering party at the bridge. Here, the British fired first—this was "the shot heard round the world" in Emerson's poem—and killed two Americans. The rebels killed three Britishers and wounded nine. The exchange lasted about five minutes.

The retreat toward Boston began now. During the six miles to Lexington, Americans fired on the troops from behind stone walls, from barns, from the second-story windows of farmhouses. In sight of Lexington, the British broke into a run. They were rescued in mid-afternoon by a relieving force of twelve hundred men sent out from Boston by Gage. The "bloody chute" back to the city saw 70 killed, 165 wounded, and 26 missing, in addition to 13 earlier casualties. The total losses were 273 for the British, 95 for the Americans. Some thirty-five hundred Americans had been involved in the engagements. A British officer, who had previously held New Englanders in contempt, now said: "Whoever looks upon them as an irregular mob, will find himself mistaken."

Reports of the battle swept through the colonies. The continent began to arm for war. Wherever you go, said a citizen, "you see the inhabitants training, making firelocks, casting mortars, shells, and shot, and making saltpetre." The Massachusetts provincial congress met on April 22 and authorized the raising of 13,600 troops, to be led by Artemas Ward. An army of amateur soldiers started a ring of siege works around Boston. In June the New England troops occupied Breed's Hill, which overlooked the city and harbor of Boston. Further moves ceased for the moment, for New England had now turned to the second Continental Congress for leadership.

Problems of Defense

Congress had assembled in Philadelphia on May 10, 1775. Most of the old members turned up again, and, except for Colonel George Washington—who showed up in the buff blue uniform of the Virginia militia—they looked much as they had at the previous session. There were several new faces, however—John Hancock, Boston's richest merchant; Benjamin Franklin, who had arrived back from England only four days earlier, his return announced "by ringing of bells, to the great joy of the city"; James Wilson, a young Scotsman and one of Pennsylvania's ablest lawyers; and Thomas Jefferson, whose pamphlet *A Summary View* had already won him a reputation as a talented writer. New York sent a larger delegation this time, chosen by the provincial congress it had erected after the governor prorogued the assembly. One parish from Georgia sent a delegate; he would soon be followed by a full delegation, which meant that all thirteen colonies were at last represented in Congress.

Thousands of Philadelphians had looked on silently the day New England's delegates rode into town. A company of soldiers led the solemn parade, and the sound of muffled church bells echoed through the city. Congress soon after assembled and accepted the Pennsylvania assembly's offer of their first floor chamber in the statehouse, the city's most impressive building, designed in the clean, plain style that satisfied

Quakers. The king's arms hung over the main entrance, and above the building rose a squat wooden tower that housed a large bell and the works for the two clock dials hanging beneath the eaves of the east and west outer walls. The bell bore a Biblical inscription, which read: "Proclaim liberty throughout all the land unto all the inhabitants thereof." A tavern stood conveniently across the street, and behind the statehouse stretched a large yard, surrounded by a seven-foot brick wall that gave the overworked delegates privacy as they strolled and smoked between their long, tedious sessions.

The delegates to this second Congress were not to be envied. "When fifty or sixty men have a constitution to form for a great empire," John Adams said,

at the same time they have a country of fifteen hundred miles extent to fortify, millions to arm and train, a naval power to begin, an extensive commerce to regulate, numerous tribes of Indians to negotiate with, a standing army of twenty-seven thousand men to raise, pay, victual, and officer, I shall really pity those fifty or sixty men.

The problems Adams delineated, and those he overlooked, were complicated by the slim powers the Congress had to work with. Nothing it did was binding on the new makeshift colonial governments. It could request but not order; it could advise but not demand. It did not legislate; it recommended. And its power and authority over the people depended entirely on the good will and trust the people granted it.

America, said John Adams, was "a great, unwieldy body. It is like a large fleet sailing under convoy. The fleetest sailers must wait for the dullest and slowest." The rub came when someone like Ethan Allen dashed out ahead of the convoy and forced decisions Congress was not prepared to make. Seven days after convening, Congress learned that Allen, accompanied by a brilliant young man from Connecticut named Benedict Arnold, had captured Fort Ticonderoga. Congress had planned to tell the world America was fighting a defensive war against Britain. Allen's and Arnold's offensive move against Ticonderoga—and their later capture of Crown Point and St. John's, which gave the entire Champlain Valley to the Americans—put the delegates in an awkward position. They could justify the action only by claiming that Britain was preparing to invade the colonies from Canada, which at the time was palpably untrue.

Another "fleet sailer"—this time Massachusetts—put a request to Congress in June that led Silas Deane to remark: "Our business has run away with us." The Bay Colony wanted Congress to take over the army then forming about Boston. Congress acceded to the request, knowing that in doing so it was assuming in addition to its legislative responsibilities vast administrative duties. An army needed men and officers, money to pay its bills, supplies to keep it operating, and all this Congress had somehow to produce. Most of June was spent making a start at solving these problems, which, like the plague, would be with Congress at least seven full years. It decided that the Continental Army should be composed of twenty thousand troops, with every colony responsible for a specified quota. On June 15 Congress chose George Washington commander-in-chief. There had never been much doubt about the selection. Everyone considered him the most knowledgeable man in Congress on military affairs. He was an aristocrat, against social upheaval, and obviously a "safe" man to the conservatives in Congress. He was a Southerner, and his appointment would help cement that section to what at the moment was a New England war. The unanimous choice of Washington, it has been said, was the first major decision in American history that men differing among themselves had been able to unite upon. The unanimity vanished when it came to selecting his staff. After much discussion, the delegates settled on Artemas Ward as second in command, and two former British officers, Charles Lee and Horatio Gates. At the end of June, Congress approved sixty-nine articles of war for the "grand army of America." These things done, Washington and his staff headed for Boston. They left in a high mood, for shortly before, news had arrived of the Battle of Bunker Hill. The British had taken the hill—actually Breed's not Bunker Hill—but at such cost that Americans rightfully considered it a victory for their side.

Congress turned next to composing a new round of "animated addresses." On July 5 it approved a second petition to the king, the Olive Branch Petition, so named for its suppliant tone. It begged the king to intercede for the colonies against his designing Parliament. The author was John Dickinson, and soon after Congress accepted it, he told a friend that if the British rejected this humble "application with contempt," they will only "confirm the minds of our countrymen, to endure all the misfortunes that may attend the contest." Pennsylvania's Governor Richard Penn, a loyalist returning home, agreed to present the petition personally to the king. The next day, July 6, the delegates approved a Declaration of Causes of Taking-up Arms, jointly written by Jefferson and Dickinson but with its most powerful phrases coming from Dickinson. ("Our cause is just. Our union is perfect. Our internal resources are great . . . the arms we have been compelled by our enemies to assume, we will, in defiance of every hazard, with unabating firmness and perseverance, employ for the preservation of our liberties; being with one mind resolved to die Freemen rather than live Slaves.") On July 8 the delegates sanctioned a second Address to the Inhabitants of Great Britain, who were warned not to expect an easy victory, for even with their towns destroyed and their coasts ravaged, Americans would still win. "We can retire beyond the reach of your navy, and, without any sensible diminution of the necessities of life, enjoy a luxury, which from that period you will want—the luxury of being free. . . ."

Congress turned now from "spirited manifestoes" back to practical matters. On July 13 it dealt with the Indians, who menaced the colonists on the west as seriously as the British did along the coasts. Three departments, similar to those set up by the British, were created, and their commissioners were empowered to make treaties. Money was appropriated to purchase rum and other gifts to woo the Indians, and an address was drawn up, which explained the war as "a family quarrel between us and Old England" that did not concern the Indians.

On July 18 Congress went a step further in establishing governments by committees by urging the colonies to appoint Committees of Safety, which would direct and superintend all matters necessary for their security and defense. They would be appointed by the provincial congress and would be considered the executive power within a colony, with authority to call up the militia, direct military operations within a colony's borders, hunt down loyalists, and enforce the decrees of Congress.

A notable aspect of the first month and a half of the second session of Congress had been the silence of Benjamin Franklin. He attended meetings regularly but said nothing. Some delegates were beginning

to entertain a great suspicion that Dr. Franklin came rather as a spy than as a friend, and that he means to discover our weak side to make his peace with the ministers by discovering information with regard to affairs at home, but hitherto he has been silent on that head and in every respect behaved more like a spectator than a member.

Franklin ended his silence in July. He told his friend Joseph Galloway and his son William Franklin, governor of New Jersey, that he favored independence, and with that news "the suspicions against Dr. Franklin have died away." On July 21 Franklin placed before Congress his Articles of Confederation and Perpetual Union, in order to let members be "turning the subject in their minds." Those against confederation were strong enough to prevent even mention of Franklin's plan being made in the Congressional journals.

The block of moderates in Congress, who still held out hope for reconciliation, showed their strength a second time on July 21 by defeating a motion to open American ports to the world. John Dickinson led the moderates, and a few days later John Adams relieved his feelings about that gentleman in a letter home, which to his embarrassment the British captured and published. "A certain great fortune and piddling genius, whose fame has been trumpeted so loudly, has given a silly cast to our whole doings," said Adams. Congress, he added, moved too slowly.

We are between the hawk and buzzard. We ought to have had in our hands a month ago the whole legislative, executive and judicial of the whole continent, and have completely modeled a Constitution; to have raised a naval power, and opened all our ports wide; to have arrested every friend to government on the continent and held them as hostages for the poor victims in Boston, and then opened the door as wide as possible for peace and reconciliation. After this they might have petitioned, and negotiated, and addressed etc. if they would.

But Congress could not be moved faster at the moment, and for the next week it only refined its earlier work. On July 25, having already exhausted the $2 million issue of paper money ordered earlier, it authorized the printing of $1 million more. The next day it provided for the erection of a postal system, and chose Benjamin Franklin to head it. On July 27 it approved a plan for a military hospital to be headed by Dr. Benjamin Church, who would later prove to be a traitor. On July 31 Lord North's conciliatory proposal was rejected on the ground, according to Jefferson's report, that his "proposition seems to have been held up to the world, to deceive it into a belief that there was nothing in dispute between us but the *mode* of levying taxes." On August 2, "after the fatigue of many days," Congress adjourned for a month's rest.

INDEPENDENCE: 1775–1776

John Adams had a bag full of similes to describe America's approach to independence. Sometimes he likened the thirteen colonies to a convoy; sometimes to a horse-drawn coach, where "the swiftest horses must be slackened and the slowest quickened, that all may keep an even pace"; sometimes to a house filled with thirteen clocks that must be timed to strike at once. Regardless of the simile, the point came through that independence could not be declared until all thirteen "ships," "horses," or "clocks" were in line. It took ten months from the time Congress reassembled in September to reach the goal. No single group or person could take credit for the achievement. Occasionally Congress had prodded the colonies, but more often it had waited to be prodded; sometimes individuals like Washington and Paine had forced the pace; the king and Parliament had done their share; and once or twice a particular colony brought everyone into line. No trick or conspiracy carried America into independence; it was a decision slowly arrived at and then openly declared before all the world.

A House Divided

The issue of independence intruded itself only occasionally into discussion when Congress reassembled, for through the fall of 1775 those eager for separation found themselves blocked at every turn by the moderates in Congress. Moreover, not a single colony had instructed its delegates to introduce the topic into Congress nor given explicit permission to vote for independence if it came up for decision. A strong grass-roots sentiment had to develop for independence before any faction in Congress dared push the issue.

Though by the autumn of 1775 all colonies but Georgia and Pennsylvania had erected provisional governments of one sort or another, these governments, like all temporary edifices, were rickety affairs. They drew their authority from nowhere, for they were self-created. They professed loyalty to the king, but they resisted the king's men. The case of Dr. Benjamin Church illuminated the confusion in Massachusetts. Dr. Church had been jailed as a traitor after he had been caught spying for the British, but some men wondered how he could be judged disloyal when he only aided the king whose sovereignty Massachusetts still acknowledged. Obviously, a provisional government provided a flimsy platform from which to direct a war against Great Britain. In May the Massachusetts provincial congress had asked Congress for the "most explicit advice" in regard to establishing a permanent civil government. It emphasized the uneasiness felt "at having an army . . . established here without a civil power to provide for and control it." Congress, knowing that to suggest the creation of a new government that drew its authority from the people would, in effect, be an endorsement of independence, phrased its answer with care. It advised a temporary government similar to the one that flourished previously under the charter. Because, at the moment, there was no royal governor, the assembly and council should serve as the executive "until a governor of his majesty's appointment will consent to govern the colony according to its charter."

John Adams wanted Congress to settle this question of government by making "a general recommendation to all the states to call conventions and institute regular governments," but Congress refused to generalize. When New Hampshire, her affairs in a "convuls'd state," asked for advice, Congress replied much as it had to Massachusetts—erect a government for the duration of the emergency. Clearly, if America was to be carried toward independence, leadership had, for the time being at least, to come from somewhere other than Congress.

George Washington provided what Congress could not. "To you they look for decision," Charles Lee had told him; "by your conduct they are to be inspired by decision. In fact, your situation is such that the salvation of the whole depends on your striking, at certain crises, vigorous strokes, without previously communicating your intention." Washington did strike vigorously and his decisions were accepted, as Curtis Nettels has pointed out so clearly, because Congress had full faith in his integrity and moderation. He overthrew the defensive policy Congress favored and, following the offensive tactics of Ethan Allen, initiated an attack upon Canada in September. The exigencies of the military situation led him to disown the king's authority long before Congress dared and to endorse the sovereignty of the American people. When General Gage refused to treat captured American officers with dignity because their rank was "not derived from the king," Washington had answered: "The uncorrupted choice of a brave and free people was the purest source and original fountain of all power." Congress had refused in the spring of 1775 to authorize the creation of an American navy. What Congress refused Washington did. By mid-October he had a fleet of six ships operated by seagoing soldiers picking off British supply ships and transports. A month later Congress approved his action, then drew up rules for the "Navy of the United Colonies."

While forcing decisions upon Congress, Washington was at the same time encouraging the idea of independence throughout New England. A report from General John Sullivan, then in Portsmouth, New Hampshire, detailing the activities of "that infernal crew of Tories," prompted Washington to order the seizure of all officers of the crown who were "acting as enemies of their country." This was the first official definition of Tories and the first directive ordering them to be seized. Washington's order coupled with the presence of Sullivan's troops hamstrung the king's friends in New Hampshire. The militant leaders there now dared to call a constitutional convention, and within a few months New Hampshire became the first colony ruled by a government that drew its authority from the people, not the king.

Connecticut and Rhode Island gave no thought to a new constitution, for their liberal charters, which granted the right to elect their own governors, continued to serve them satisfactorily. Washington promoted the idea of independence in other ways in these colonies. When Governor Trumbull of Connecticut wondered how to deal with Tories in his midst, Washington helped to clarify his thoughts. "Why should persons who are preying upon the vitals of their country be suffered to stalk at large, whilst we know they will do us every mischief in their power?" Connecticut, knowing it would be backed by the Army, became the first colony to produce a series of laws directed against the Tories. In a similar way Washington strengthened the resolve of Rhode Island leaders. The assembly passed acts in November defining treason, and the next month General Lee toured the colony forcing an oath of loyalty on all suspected Tories.

By the end of 1775, each of the four New England colonies had, in effect, committed itself to independence. Events had hastened their actions —the British shelling of Falmouth, a warship's appearance in Newport's harbor, the siege of Boston—but the presence of Washington hastened them even more. He encouraged local leaders by giving them a sense that the whole union stood behind them. The moderates in Congress had little to say about what was going on in New England, partly because they trusted Washington, partly because news from England in November had done much to undermine their position.

On November 9, Congress learned that the king had refused to receive the colonies' Olive Branch Petition and that England was dispatching an army of some twenty thousand troops to crush the colonies. The ship that carried this news also brought a copy of the king's proclamation of August 23, which declared the colonies in "open and avowed rebellion" and called upon all Americans "to disclose and make known all treasons and traitorous conspiracies which they shall know to be against us, our crown and dignity," including "all persons who shall be found carrying on correspondence with, or in any manner or degree aiding or abetting the persons now in open arms and rebellion against our government." The king had, in effect, declared the acts of Congress and all the actions of those who obeyed those acts as treasonable. His proclamation had forced all who had supported the American cause to finish what they had started or otherwise risk hanging.

After a month of discussion, during which confidence was bolstered by news that General Montgomery had taken Montreal and, with Benedict Arnold, now planned to mount an attack on Quebec, Congress on December 6 came forth with an answer to the king's proclamation. "What allegiance is it that we forget?" Congress asked. "Allegiance to Parliament? We never owed—we never owned it. Allegiance to our king? Our words have ever avowed it—our conduct has ever been consistent with it." The paper went on to warn the king "that whatever punishment shall be inflicted upon" anyone for aiding or abetting the American cause "shall be retaliated in kind. . . ." Hardly had this answer been approved when Congress learned of the king's speech of October 26 to Parliament, wherein he leveled the accusation that "the rebellious war now levied . . . is manifestly for the purpose of establishing an independent empire."

The king up to now had been sacrosanct. Not one document issued by Congress had spoken of him in any but submissive and respectful terms. The delegates knew that having dismissed all Parliamentary control over American affairs, the only remaining tie with Great Britain was through the king. To attack that tie was in effect to declare the colonies independent of all ties with the mother country. Congress held its tongue. Tom Paine, who had arrived in Philadelphia from England only two years earlier, did not. On January 9, 1776, his pamphlet *Common Sense* "burst from the press," and "with an effect which has rarely been produced by types and paper in any age or country." Gentlemen who had talked gingerly of independence with friends behind closed doors now found a reckless spirit blustering forth with the idea in print. He assaulted not the tyranny of Parliament but the tyrant. ("O ye that love mankind! Ye that dare oppose not only the tyranny, but also the tyrant, stand forth!") But he struck less at the monarch than at the idea of monarchy. (". . . how a race of men came into the world so exalted above the rest, and distinguished like some new species, is worth inquiring into, and whether they are the means of happiness or of misery to mankind.") He attacked those who believed that the liberties of America stemmed from the British constitution. They were the rights of all mankind, and the British constitution only endangered, it did not nourish, them. British politics and society were corrupt and tended to corrupt America.

Sam Adams, observing the pamphlet's reception in Philadelphia, understated for once when he said, "it has fretted some folks here more than a little." Ten days after the printer had placed it in the bookstalls, copies had reached Alexandria, Virginia, and were already making "a great noise." Edmund Randolph of Virginia later said that "the public sentiment which a few weeks before had shuddered at the tremendous obstacles, with which independence was environed overleaped every barrier." (He added, however, that the pamphlet only "put the torch to combustibles which had been deposited by the different gusts of fury. . . .") An edition in German "works on the minds of those people amazingly," one man said. Another Pennsylvanian, warm for reconciliation, remarked, after watching the pamphlet's arguments "gain ground with the common people," that "this idea of an independence, tho' sometime ago abhorred, may possibly by degrees become so familiar as to be cherished."

Congress Acts

Paine had forced the hand of Congress. The day *Common Sense* appeared, James Wilson, a moderate, moved that "Congress may expressly declare to their constituents and the world their present intentions respecting an independency, observing the king's speech directly charged us with that design." The motion received such equally balanced support and opposition that after long debate it was agreed to postpone a decision for two weeks. Discussion was revived on January 24, and after much had been said "about independency and the mode and propriety of stating our dependence on the king," a committee headed by Wilson was appointed to draft an address. Wilson presented his paper on February 13. But it was ordered to lie on the table and thereafter forgotten, an indication that control of Congress was fast slipping away from the moderates.

The last weeks of February were spent discussing America's trade problems, a discussion that led inevitably to the feasibility of making foreign alliances and opening American ports to the world. Those who still hoped for reconciliation objected vehemently to both propositions, and after two weeks' debate both plans were tabled, and the moderates could rejoice in winning another delaying action.

This was their last such victory, for on February 27 Congress received a copy of the Prohibitory Act, which had passed Parliament on December 22, 1775. The act gave statutory force to the ministry's program and made clear that all branches of the British government were united in coercing the colonies into submission. It embargoed all American trade, called for the seizure of all American ships, and defined American resistance as rebellion and treason. The act left a slight opening for reconciliation by empowering the crown to send commissioners to inquire into American grievances and grant pardons. Moderates were stunned by the measure. "Nothing is left now but to fight it out," said Joseph Hewes of North Carolina. An "Act of Independency," John Adams called it, "for the king, Lords and Commons have united in sundering this country from that I think forever."

What stunned the moderates even more was a rumor that had accompanied the Prohibitory Act to America—that the king had hired German troops to fight his battles for him. During the January debate over Wilson's resolution, several delegates had said "that if a foreign force shall be sent here, they are willing to declare the colonies in a state of independent sovereignty." If the rumor became fact, Great Britain clearly meant to fight the war to the end and not attempt reconciliation. Worse, she no longer meant to prosecute a gentlemanly war in which, once defeated, the obstreperous children would be mildly punished and then welcomed back into the family. For many it meant, too, that America would be indiscriminately ravaged by soldiers who made it their business to profit from war. Homes would be looted and towns plundered and the property of no man, regardless of his political convictions, would be safe, for mercenaries would not distinguish "betwixt friends and foes," and their "avarice and rapacity would not be glutted [even] with the indiscriminate spoils of both." One man said later that "many worthy men" who eventually accepted the idea of independence "would not have wished to go as they have done," but the hiring of mercenaries "cast the die."

Those for independence continued to gain strength through March. Toward the end of the month, Congress learned that the British had evacuated Boston, a victory that more than offset the dismal news received earlier in the year that the assault on Quebec had failed and that in the battle General Montgomery had been killed and Colonel Benedict Arnold had been wounded. Two weeks later, on April 6, the militants persuaded Congress to take its boldest step thus far—the ports of all America were declared open to the world. It was obvious now that a final break with Great Britain was unavoidable. Almost no one in Congress saw hope for a reconciliation, yet a strong block of moderates continued to resist the idea of separation. Some wanted to await the peace commissioners that were supposedly on their way—"a messiah that will never come," said John Adams, ". . . as arrant an illusion as ever was hatched in the brain of an enthusiast, a politician, or a maniac." Some believed that America had to strengthen itself first by erecting a confederation and obtaining the promise of foreign aid before cutting the last tie. And some pointed out that a good number of the delegates were still not permitted by their instructions to vote for independence. Even those warmest for separation were aware that too many ships in the convoy lagged behind. Thought was now given to ways to bring the stragglers swiftly into line.

The South, except for Georgia, was already fairly well in line. Lord Dunmore had helped hurry Virginia toward independence. In early November, after fleeing the governor's palace at Williamsburg, he had told Virginians "to resort to the king's standard or be deemed traitors," and at the same time offered freedom to all slaves who left their "rebel" masters. (It was this attempt to incite the slaves to revolt that most disturbed young James Madison, who believed Virginia might soon "fall like Achilles" if Dunmore managed to carry out his threat.) Congress had responded to Dunmore's proclamation by urging Virginia to call "a full and free representation of the people," which would devise a government for the duration of the "present dispute," and by the late spring a constitutional convention was in the process of assembling.

In March, Congress had ordered General Lee south, and it appears that, as Congress had hoped, his presence helped to nourish the spirit of independence in Virginia and also in the neighboring Carolinas. South Carolina on March 23 instructed its delegates in Congress to "agree to every measure which . . . a majority of the Continental Congress, shall judge necessary for the . . . welfare of this colony . . . and of America," and three days later the colony adopted a new constitution. North Carolina's provincial convention on April 12 became the first to instruct its delegation in Congress "to concur with the delegates of other colonies in declaring independence and forming alliances. . . ."

By the spring of 1776, opposition to independence had come to center in the Middle Colonies. Pennsylvania, New York, New Jersey, and Maryland all objected to the idea, but Pennsylvania's objection was crucial. It was believed that if she could be swung to favor independence, the other colonies would follow her lead. Pennsylvania was the keystone in the arch of colonies that stretched from Florida to Nova Scotia—"what the heart is to the human body in circulating the blood," as a man of the day put it. For a while the militants in Congress hoped that a colonywide election on May 1 for new assembly members would produce an independence-minded assembly, which would, in turn, instruct its delegation in Congress to vote for separation. It was expected that the new members from the western and supposedly proindependence counties, whose representation in the assembly had recently been increased, would swing the balance. Hope died for the militants soon after May 1, for when the election results drifted in from the backcountry, it was clear that the moderates still controlled the assembly. At this point, certain members of Congress, among them John and Sam Adams, decided to take a hand in Pennsylvania affairs.

The strategy was to undermine the power of Pennsylvania's authorized government so that those for independence might take control of provincial affairs. To that end, John Adams on May 10 introduced into Congress a resolution that said that new governments should be erected in those colonies "where no government sufficient to the exigencies of their affairs have been hitherto established." The Pennsylvania delegation said it favored the resolution, and took care to tell Congress that it obviously did not touch their colony, where the government functioned so smoothly that Pennsylvania's contribution to the war effort in men and matériel was exceeded by no other colony. The resolution passed unanimously.

Adams had been only temporarily outflanked. All important resolutions of Congress were, by custom, adorned with a preamble, usually no more than an introductory flourish. Adams' preamble, however, changed the import of the May 10 resolution. It said, in essence, that in the creation of a new government, it was "necessary that the exercise of every kind of authority under the said crown should be totally suppressed. . . ." The preamble was obviously aimed at Pennsylvania, where the official tone of the colony was one that in every way recognized the king's authority. An assembly that had been authorized by the crown dominated provincial affairs; the king's arms hung above the entrance to the statehouse; the king's justice was practiced in the courts, and all legal documents still bore the king's seal. Not surprisingly, the preamble provoked a warm debate. James Wilson said it authorized the wrecking of Pennsylvania's stable government. James Duane argued that Congress had "no right to pass the resolution any more than Parliament has," for it interfered in the internal affairs of a colony. Others made the point that to suppress the king's authority severed the last tie with Britain. But these once weighty arguments had lost their force by mid-May 1776. The majority of Congress was more impressed by the ridiculousness of "continuing to swear allegiance to the power that is cutting our throats" and by the fact that, as Sam Adams remarked, "our petitions have not been heard, yet answered with fleets and armies, and are to be answered with myrmidons from abroad." The preamble passed by a vote of six colonies to four; Georgia was absent, Pennsylvania and Maryland abstained. John Adams exulted over the result: "Great Britain has at last driven America to the last step, a complete separation from her; a total absolute independence, not only of her Parliament, but of her crown, for such is the amount of the resolve of May 15th."

On May 20, the day the Pennsylvania assembly was to convene, a carefully staged mass meeting of Philadelphia citizens in the state house yard voted to oust the assembly and erect a revolutionary government. The assembly nonetheless soon managed to gather for business, and the moderates within it, led by John Dickinson, continued to resist the idea of independence. The effectiveness of their rear-guard action was suddenly undercut by the Virginia convention, which on May 15 had decided to force Congress to face three issues that no other colony had dared present to that body. On the morning of June 7, Richard Henry Lee, following the orders of his home government, rose in Congress to present the following resolution:

That these United Colonies are, and of right ought to be, free and independent States, that they are absolved from all allegiance to the British crown, and that all political connection between them and the state of Great Britain is, and ought to be, totally dissolved.

That it is expedient forthwith to take the most effectual measures for forming foreign alliances.

That a plan of confederation be prepared and transmitted to the respective colonies for their consideration and approbation.

The Declaration

The day-to-day proceedings of the Continental Congress never really fascinated Americans of the day. Even in Philadelphia, the delegates went to and from their meetings in the statehouse almost unnoticed. A single doorkeeper blocked the entrance into their chamber and served to protect the secrecy of the discussions within. No great throngs had ever assembled to pressure a decision out of Congress, and none were on hand on June 8 and 9 when Congress discussed the momentous resolution introduced by Richard Henry Lee. The citizens of Philadelphia went unconcernedly about their business while the delegates in the statehouse debated whether or not the time had come, after a century and three-quarters as colonies, to separate from Great Britain.

Much of the tension and drama that might be expected to be present in the great two-day debate was absent, and it is wrong to inject it into the story. All agreed that a declaration of independence was a foregone conclusion; no one in Congress spoke out flatly against it. Those who objected opposed only the timing, not the propriety, of the measure. They revived all the old arguments for delay once more—the expected peace commissioners, the need for a confederation first to heal "our present disjointed state," the necessity for foreign aid to underwrite the cost of a long war. As the debate wore on, it became apparent that every speaker's remarks revolved around a central question—who should lead the colonies into this fateful decision. Those who resisted independence said, according to Jefferson's notes of the discussion, that it was wrong "to take any capital step till the voice of the people drove us to it," for the people "were our power and without them our declaration could not be carried into effect." The blunt answer to this was: "the people wait for us to lead the way."

By the end of the second day the opponents of an immediate declaration of independence, led by John Dickinson, had made the point that "the people of the Middle Colonies were not yet ripe for bidding adieu to British connection but that they were fast ripening and in a short time would join in the general voice of America." It was agreed that in order to give the Middle Colonies further time to ripen, all discussion of independence should be put off for three weeks, but in the meanwhile a committee should be appointed to draw up a document justifying the act to the world. (Discussion of the other parts of the Lee resolution, which dealt with confederation and a foreign alliance, was also postponed, but committees were created to deal with those matters, too.) The committee chosen to draw up the document was composed of Thomas Jefferson (Virginia), Robert R. Livingston (New York), Roger Sherman (Connecticut), Benjamin Franklin (Pennsylvania), and John Adams (Massachusetts).

Jefferson, having received the most votes, by the custom of Congress automatically became the committee chairman and the man responsible for drawing up the document. It was an honored assignment, but proba-

bly no one regarded it as an especially difficult one. Jefferson did not have
to search far for arguments to explain the American decision, for since the
fall of 1774, Congress had been turning out "animated addresses" justifying American resistance. This would be only one more "animated
address."

Jefferson's paper in neither form nor argument offered anything new.
It began with a statement of purpose—to declare the causes that impelled
the colonies to break from Britain—then proceeded to present a theory of
government to justify separation. Jefferson, like James Wilson, John
Adams, and Tom Paine, argued that all men were created equal and endowed with certain inalienable rights and that when the colonists immigrated to America, they lost none of these rights. Through mutual
compacts among themselves and with the king, governments were created;
the colonists gave their allegiance to the king, who in return became obligated to protect their natural rights. If the king reneged on his obligations,
the compacts with the colonists were abrogated. Jefferson then proceeded
to list the numerous instances where the king had failed in his duty. The
case proved, it became clear that the colonies had now to take their separate but equal station in the world of nations.

After Jefferson's committee had approved his handiwork, he laid the
paper before Congress. But before the delegates dealt with it, they had to
face once again the question of independence itself, and this they proceeded to do the first two days in July. John Dickinson still resisted the
idea; he accepted the inevitability of the act but still objected to performing
it now. He saw little hope for a nation launching into the world in "a
skiff made of paper." The delegates listened respectfully, then in the afternoon of July 2 the vote was taken. Dickinson and two other Pennsylvanians absented themselves from the meeting, leaving the province a
delegation with a majority for independence. New York, pleading a lack
of adequate instructions, abstained. No negative votes were registered
against the resolution, which made it possible to say that the colonies had
unanimously declared themselves independent of Great Britain. "The second day of July, 1776, will be the most memorable epocha in the history
of America," John Adams wrote to his wife, then, after some words
on the manner in which he hoped the day would be celebrated "from
this time forward forevermore," he said:

You will think me transported with enthusiasm, but I am not. I am well aware
of the toil and blood and treasure that it will cost us to maintain this Declaration and support and defend these states. Yet through all the gloom, I can
see the rays of ravishing light and glory. I can see that the end is more than
worth all the means. And that posterity will triumph in that day's transaction,
even although we should rue it, which I trust in God we shall not.

The next two days were spent editing Jefferson's paper. Congress made no basic changes, except to eliminate a long and inappropriate passage that blamed Negro slavery in America on the king. It cut the document by about one-third, and for the most part the editing improved it. On July 4, "The Unanimous Declaration of the Thirteen United States of America" was approved and sent to the printer. Four days later it was read aloud at the statehouse "in the presence of a great concourse of people." The crowd, after the reading, gave three huzzas, shouting with each, "God bless the free states of North America." The king's arms were torn from their perch over the statehouse entrance, and that night amid the sound of clanging bells, they were tossed atop a huge bonfire. With these and "other great demonstrations of joy" the Declaration of Independence was first celebrated in America.

BIBLIOGRAPHY

Irritations Mount: 1770–1774

Many of the books and articles mentioned in the Bibliographies of Chapters 12 and 13 discuss the material covered in this section. Because a period of calm rarely attracts the interest of historians, there are virtually no works that deal exclusively with this period. The soundest surveys are in the third volume of Edward Channing's *The History of the United States* (6 vols., 1905–1925) and John Miller's *Origins of the American Revolution* (1959). (Notice that for Miller's *Origins*, Bernhard Knollenberg has substituted the singular *Origin of the American Revolution, 1759–1766* [rev. ed., 1961; pb.].) James T. Adams' *Revolutionary New England* (1923) carries that section's story up to 1776 and gives full coverage to these years. In addition to John C. Miller's *Sam Adams* (1936), see also John Cary's *Joseph Warren: Physician, Politician, Patriot* (1961)—both of which discuss general conditions in Massachusetts as well as the subjects of their biographies. The picture presented in *The Writings of Samuel Adams* (4 vols., 1904–1908), edited by H. A. Cushing, can be counterbalanced by Douglass Adair and John A. Schutz, eds., *Peter Oliver's Origin & Progress of the American Rebellion, A Tory View* (1961). Benjamin W. Labaree, *The Boston Tea Party* (1964), discusses the drift toward rebellion from the economic point of view.

Rebellion: 1774–1775

Edmund C. Burnett's *Continental Congress* (1941; pb.) gives the best general account. It is based largely on Burnett's careful multivolume edition of the *Letters of the Members of the Continental Congress* (8 vols., 1921–1938), of which the first volume is relevant here. Anyone wishing to study this period in depth must consult not only Burnett's *Letters* but also the massive *Journals of the Continental Congress, 1774–1789* (34 vols., 1904–1937). Lynn Montross,

The Reluctant Rebels (1950), is a lively, reliable account of the Revolutionary Congress that takes advantage of the best scholarship. A specialized study of one aspect of the first Congress is Julian Boyd, *Anglo-American Union: Joseph Galloway's Plans to Preserve the British Empire, 1774–1778* (1941). Weldon A. Brown, *Empire or Independence* (1941), covers the various attempts at reconciliation from 1773 to 1778 with an eye to showing why each effort failed. The authority on the skirmishes at Lexington and Concord is Allen French, *The Day of Lexington and Concord* (1925) and *The First Year of the American Revolution* (1934). A recent popular account based on original research is Arthur B. Tourtelott, *William Diamond's Drum: The Beginnings of the War of the American Revolution* (1959; pb.). The same events told well from the view of one who helped cause them are found in Esther Forbes, *Paul Revere and the World He Lived In* (1942; pb.).

All the important members of the first and second Congress have attracted biographers, though few, curiously, have received anything approaching brilliant treatment. Neither Catherine Drinker Bowen's semifictional *John Adams and the American Revolution* (1950; pb.) nor Page Smith's long and occasionally sentimental *John Adams* (2 vols., 1962) can be called definitive. Gilbert Chinard's *Honest John Adams* (1933; pb.) offers an excellent one-volume study. Zoltán Haraszti, *John Adams and the Prophets of Progress* (1952), still presents the best summary of Adams' ideas. Carl Van Doren's *Benjamin Franklin: A Biography* (1938; pb.) is a full and reliable account, but a student can still gain much from James Parton's *The Life and Times of Benjamin Franklin* (2 vols., 1864). Carl Becker's sketch of Franklin in the *Dictionary of American Biography* (22 vols., 1928–1937) should not be missed. (Nor, for that matter, should those of Jefferson by Dumas Malone and of Paine by Crane Brinton.) The latest volume on Franklin's life is by Alfred Owen Alridge (1965), and the most recent on his political ideas is Paul W. Conner's *Poor Richard's Politics* (1965). John C. Miller's *Sam Adams* (1936) sags when it deals with the Congressional period because Adams left nothing behind on which a biographer can build. Ellen Hart Smith writes of the most eminent Catholic in Congress, *Charles Carroll* (1942); Carroll is fitted into the broad picture in Charles H. Metzger, *Catholics and the American Revolution: A Study in Religious Climate* (1962), which discusses the difficulty many Catholics had in choosing sides in 1776. The best volume on Jefferson during these years is Dumas Malone, *Jefferson the Virginian* (1948). Robert A. Rutland's *George Mason* (1961) is brief and competent. Additional biographies are Richard Barry, *Mr. Rutledge of South Carolina* (1942); R. S. Boardman, *Roger Sherman* (1938); and Charles Page Smith, *James Wilson: Founding Father, 1742–1798* (1956). Don R. Gerlach's *Philip Schuyler and the American Revolution in New York, 1733–1777* (1964) is the first of a planned two-volume study. Because Thomson destroyed all his papers shortly before he died, probably the best that will be done is John Zimmerman's article, "Charles Thomson, 'The Sam Adams of Phildadelphia,' " *MVHR*, 45 (1958), 464–80.

Fortunately, the inadequacy of biographical studies can be remedied somewhat by studying the writings of members of Congress. The new editions of the papers of Jefferson, Franklin, and John Adams, should not lead anyone to overlook the lesser luminaries of the day. J. G. Ballagh has edited *The Letters of Richard Henry Lee* (2 vols., 1911–1914). There is need for a new edition of J. D. Andrews' old, inadequate, and hard to locate *Works of James Wilson* (1896). Among the best of many competently edited one-volume editions of writings are Adrienne Koch and William Peden, eds., *The Selected Writings of John and John Quincy Adams* (1946) and *The Life and Selected Writings of Thomas Jefferson* (1944); Frank Luther Mott and Chester E. Jorgenson, eds., *Benjamin Franklin: Representative Selections* (rev. ed., 1962; pb.); Harry H. Clark, ed., *Thomas Paine: Representative Selections* (1944; pb.)—Clark's long introduction makes up for the absence of certain pieces that the interested student must find in Philip S. Foner, ed., *The Complete Writings of Thomas Paine* (2 vols., 1945); Saxe Commins, ed., *The Basic Writings of George Washington* (1948); and Randolph G. Adams, ed., *Selected Political Writings of James Wilson* (1930).

Independence: 1775–1776

A sound place to begin to understand the ideas behind the Revolution is with Randolph G. Adams, *Political Ideas of the American Revolution* (1922; pb.); though slightly dated in some aspects, his analysis still remains sound. One reason Adams' interpretation has stood so long is that historians of late have concentrated on the affairs of individual colonies on the eve of the Revolution. Among the more recent studies are Lee N. Newcomer, *The Embattled Farmers: The Massachusetts Countryside in the American Revolution* (1953); David S. Lovejoy, *Rhode Island Politics and the American Revolution, 1760–1776;* Theodore Thayer, *Pennsylvania Politics and the Growth of Democracy, 1740–1776* (1953); David Hawke, *In the Midst of a Revolution* (1961), which also deals with Pennsylvania; Leonard Lundin, *Cockpit of the Revolution* (1940), a study of New Jersey; Charles Albro Barker, *The Background of the Revolution in Maryland* (1940); Philip A. Crowl, *Maryland During and After the Revolution* (1943); and Kenneth Coleman, *The American Revolution in Georgia, 1763–1789* (1958). These studies have forced out of fashion many of the ideas introduced by Carl Becker, Charles H. Lincoln, and others at the beginning of the century, and they may soon lead to a new synthesis of American affairs on the eve of the Revolution that will perhaps supplant several of Randolph Adams' generalizations.

Curtis P. Nettels' distinguished *Washington and American Independence* (1951) delineates Washington's role in drawing the colonies toward independence. Alfred Owen Aldridge's *Man of Reason: The Life of Thomas Paine* (1959) is the fullest, most recent biography. The story of the Declaration is fully told in Carl Becker, *The Declaration of Independence* (1922; pb.); Julian P. Boyd, *The Declaration of Independence* (1943); and David Hawke, *A Transaction of Free Men* (1964).

Several frank—often startlingly so—and illuminating travel accounts that depict the state of America at this time are *Journal of Nicholas Cresswell, 1774–1776* (1925) ; Hunter D. Farish, ed., *Journal and Letters of Philip Vickers Fithian, 1773–1774* (1943) ; Robert C. Albion and Leonidas Dodson, eds., *Philip Vickers Fithian: Journal, 1775–1776* (1932) ; Philip Padelford, ed., *Colonial Panorama: Dr. Robert Honyman's Journal for March and April, 1775* (1959) ; Patrick M'Roberts, *A Tour Through Part of the North Provinces of America, 1774–1775,* edited by Carl Bridenbaugh, *PMHB,* 59 (1935), 134–180.

For further references see the *Harvard Guide,* Sections 113, "From Passive to Active Resistance, 1767–1774"; and 114, "From January 1775 Through the Declaration of Independence."

"Surrender of Lord Cornwallis at Yorktown," by John Trumbull

15. War and Peace: 1776–1783

TRYING TIMES: 1775–1777
   Boston and Canada
   Long Island to New Jersey
   The Home Front

THE TURNING POINT: 1777–1778
   Saratoga and Philadelphia
   The Diplomatic Front
   From Valley Forge to a Deadlock

VICTORY: 1778–1783
   The South's Time of Troubles
   The Path to Yorktown
   Peace

By modern standards, it was a quaint and gentlemanly war. The armies on both sides were small, rarely larger than one or two modern divisions, and the generals led their troops in person. Few men died on the battlefield—the British had lost no more than twelve hundred troops in battle after two years of fighting—largely because the weapons of the day conspired to maintain the eighteenth-century ideal of moderation in all things. An alert soldier, for example, could dodge an oncoming cannonball. The smoothbore flintlock musket was not effective much beyond the range of a hundred yards; rain and snow usually silenced it, which contributed for ending combat when the snows fell.

If much of the war fit the pattern of eighteenth-century military experience, much did not. Not many months passed before both sides saw that old concepts had to be altered to fit new situations. The British, for example, faced immense logistic problems. Previously, Americans had contributed men and matériel to the colonial wars; now nearly everything had to be hauled across three thousand miles of ocean. The battlefield stretched from Florida to Canada and from the Atlantic coast to the Mississippi, and nowhere in that vast territory was there a single target to capture, like Quebec, which would signal the war's end. America's strength centered in no city nor even in one colony; it was scattered the length of the continent. Past wars had been fought solely by professional armies; a large part of America's population would share in this one. (Washington's Continental Army never exceeded seventeen thousand, but it has been estimated that during the eight years of war nearly four hundred thousand men, most of them for short-term enlistments, served in the army.) It became a "people's war," partly because Americans were "the greatest weapons-using people" of the time, partly because those who participated fought for something more than personal profit. For all its old-fashioned, eighteenth-century qualities, the American war was, even in the military sense, a revolutionary war.

TRYING TIMES: 1775–1777

Lexington and Concord provoked an outpouring of armed men everywhere on the continent. New England within a few weeks had some fifty thousand men ready for battle. Pennsylvania produced over twenty-five thousand volunteers, and a traveler through the colony found troops drilling in the streets of every town and the men talking bravely of how they would push the lobsterbacks into the sea. Confidence and enthusiasm soared high when news of the capture of Fort Ticonderoga filtered through the colonies in May 1775. It moved up a notch further with news of another victory in late June. The British, penned in Boston, had allowed Americans to occupy Breed's Hill, which overlooked the city. Gage had held off attacking; he awaited reinforcements and hoped, in the lull, to inveigle an armistice from the rebels. In late May reinforcements from England arrived, along with Generals Howe, Clinton, and Burgoyne, all eager for action. On June 17 a full-scale attack was launched against Breed's Hill, where the Americans lay entrenched behind breastworks of hay and wooden rails. Some fifteen hundred British regulars in rigid battle lines marched toward the position at a slow pace. The Americans beat back two assaults. The British rushed in new troops, and the colonists, short of powder, retreated to Bunker Hill, then to the mainland. The Americans suffered some three hundred casualties, the British over one thousand, which comprised nearly half the troops they had thrown into the battle and one-eighth of all the officers they were to lose in the entire war. (Later, a visiting Frenchman heard a story that may have originated at the Battle of Bunker Hill. The tale centered on a British officer "who informed his men that they had nothing to fear, for 'the Americans fired only with powder'; a drummer who was near him and who at that moment received a musket shot, replied, 'Watch out for that powder, Captain.'") Burgoyne remarked that the colonial defense had been "well-conceived and obstinately maintained; the retreat was no flight; it was even covered with bravery and military skill." The disaster led to Gage's recall. Howe replaced him as commander-in-chief not long after George Washington, America's commander-in-chief, arrived outside Boston to take charge of the continental forces.

Boston and Canada

When Washington took over the Continental Army outside Boston on July 3, he assumed his first command since 1754. Then he had directed a small force on the frontier that sought to capture a fort. Now he led an army of twenty thousand whose task was to take a city held by some nine thousand trained and well-entrenched British troops with a fleet at their back to feed them. He knew nothing of strategy, handling large forces, or the placement and use of artillery except what he had gathered from military textbooks. Ignorance was the least of his problems. Two of his Congressionally-appointed staff—Artemas Ward, once uncharitably described as "a fat old gentleman, who . . . had no acquaintance whatever with military affairs," and Israel Putnam, a hard-drinking veteran of the French and Indian War known affectionately by the troops as "Old Put"— were older than he; two others—Horatio Gates and the "great sloven, wretchedly profane" Charles Lee—were former British officers who considered themselves abler than Washington and demanded even more tactful handling.

Washington soon had these gentlemen and others who joined the staff working together trying to form a disciplined army out of a collection of farmers gathered from as far south as Virginia. Eventually, they succeeded, but only after the scene of action shifted from New England; the obstacles to imposing form on chaos were too great to be solved quickly. There were too many shortages—of powder, tents, liquor, clothing, and so forth—and too many men unaccustomed to taking orders. A good part of the army vanished at the end of the year, when short-term enlistments ended, and forced Washington to start rebuilding virtually from nothing.

Fortunately, the cause was saved by British lethargy—and Henry Knox, who arrived in late February with fifty-nine cannon and mortars that had been dragged in the dead of winter over hill and dale all the way from Fort Ticonderoga. Behind a nicely planned maneuver that fooled the British, the cannon were lugged during the night of March 4 up

Dorchester Heights, a high spot that gave command of the city and harbor to whoever occupied it. On March 17 Sir William Howe evacuated the city, after a tacit agreement with Washington that it would be kept intact if the departure went unmolested. More than one thousand loyalists who had herded into Boston left with the British, the first of a new "great migration," this one outward bound, that would eventually amount to around one hundred thousand. Only dismal news from Canada dimmed the joy.

Congress had been persuaded back in June that Canada, the potential fourteenth colony, was a plum ripe for falling. General Guy Carleton's forces were believed to number less than seven hundred and to be thinly scattered over the vast territory. Philip Schuyler and his second-in-command, Richard Montgomery, another former British regular, were ordered to move up the Champlain Valley, taking Forts St. John's and Chambly along the way, then on to Montreal, and finally Quebec. A diversionary force led by Benedict Arnold would push through the forests of Maine and emerge on the St. Lawrence opposite Quebec. Success for the plan depended on beating the onset of winter. Schuyler tarried through the summer to collect an army, gather supplies, build boats, and get assurances of a peaceful passage from the Iroquois. Montgomery, urged on by Washington, moved out on his own, and, when a short while later Schuyler fell ill, he took full command of the expedition. Advance was rapid until he came up against Fort St. John's, where a force of five hundred held out for eight weeks. Cold weather was approaching when they capitulated on November 3. Ten days later, Montreal surrendered without opposition, a victory slightly flawed by the escape of General Carleton, who hurried down river to invigorate the defense of Quebec.

Montgomery allowed two weeks at Montreal for his troops to recuperate, then floated down to join Arnold, who had reached a point opposite Quebec on November 8. Arnold's troops had battled through swamp water up to their necks, endured exhausting portages, and at one point been reduced to living on boiled candles and roasted moccasins. Montgomery and Arnold together could muster only a thousand men fit for duty, though a good number of those on the sick list "acquired health" the day their discharges became official and set off for home "with the greatest alacrity." On December 30, the day before many of the enlistments ran out, a night attack was attempted on the city through drifted snow. Montgomery was killed; Arnold left the field with a shattered leg; and 370 men were captured.

The wrecked army sat out the winter in Canada, tortured first by the frigid weather, then, as the cold waned, by a smallpox epidemic "ten times more terrible than Britons, Canadians and Indians together." Congress sent General John Thomas up with reinforcements in the spring of 1776, but soon after he arrived a British fleet with an army aboard reached Quebec. The Americans retreated to Montreal, where Thomas died of the smallpox that again ravaged the army. Soon after, further "dismals from Canada" reached Congress—Arnold's debilitated army was attacked by the British under Burgoyne and driven back in a "most precipitate and confused retreat." Congress, as it verged on a declaration of independence, temporarily accepted Washington's judgment that the prospects of possessing Canada were now "almost over."

Long Island to New Jersey

With the British evacuation of Boston, military operations virtually ended in New England, and life there returned to normal—or as normal as possible under a British blockade. The scene of action, however, had shifted even before the British left Boston. In January, about the time *Common Sense* came out, Sir Henry Clinton sailed from Boston for the Carolinas, where he thought the presence of a large number of loyalists would make it easy to take control of the colony. About the time of Clinton's departure, Washington dispatched General Lee southward to strengthen the defenses of New York.

Clinton's venture proved a fiasco that helped to spark sentiment for independence in Congress. By the time he had arrived off the Carolina coast, he learned that an army of sixteen hundred loyalists had been routed at the battle of Moores Creek Bridge in late February. Those for the king's cause now kept silent throughout North Carolina, and Clinton realized that any hope of grass-roots support for his invasion had vanished with the defeat. He shifted plans and decided on a surprise attack against Charleston, the single important city south of Philadelphia. Success seemed certain, for in late May his troops had been reinforced by those of General Charles Cornwallis and by the fleet of Admiral Peter Parker. The attack began the first of June and lasted through the month. The fort on Sullivan's Island at the mouth of the harbor proved the stumbling block. Until it was captured no ships could slip past to shell the city. Weeks earlier, Charles Lee had advised abandoning the fort, but its commander, Colonel William Moultrie, had refused. The British wasted four weeks attempting to launch a ground attack against it. Foiled there, Admiral Parker began a naval bombardment. The fort's walls, made of dirt and spongy palmetto, absorbed cannonballs for ten hours, and through it all Moultrie's men kept up a steady cannonade of their own that inflicted heavy damage on several of the admiral's warships and casualties that mounted to 225 wounded and slain. Soon after, the fleet, with the British troops once again on board, departed, leaving Charleston safe for the next four years.

News of the Charleston victory came while Washington dealt with

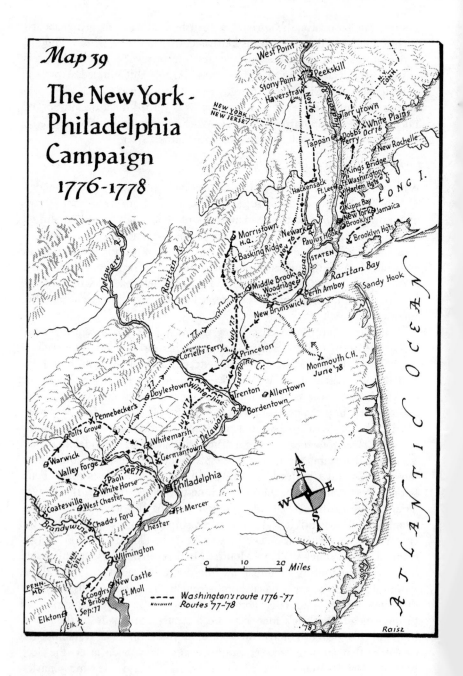

Map 39

The New York -
Philadelphia
Campaign
1776-1778

West Point
Peekskill
Stony Point
Haverstraw
N.Y.
CONT.
NEW YORK
NEW JERSEY
Nov '76
Tappan
Tarrytown
White Plains
Dobb's
Ferry   Oct '76
New Rochelle
Kings Bridge
Ft. Washington
Harlem Hgts.
Hackensack
Ft. Lee
LONG I.
Kipps Bay
New York
Jamaica
Morristown
H.Q.
Newark
Brooklyn
Basking Ridge
Nov '76
Paulus Hook
Brooklyn Hgts.
STATEN
I.
Raritan Bay
Middle Brook
Woodbridge
Perth Amboy
Sandy Hook
New Brunswick
'77
July '77
Coriell's Ferry
Princeton
Ft.
Monmouth C.H.
June '78
'77
Doylestown
Winter line
Trenton
Allentown
Assunpink Cr.
July '77
Bordentown
Pennebecker's
Poll's Grove
Whitemarsh
Delaware
Germantown
Warwick
Valley Forge
Paoli
White Horse
Sep.77
Coatesville
West Chester
Philadelphia
Brandywine Cr.
Chadd's Ford
Ft. Mercer
Chester
PENN.
DEL.
Wilmington
New Castle
Ft. Moll
PENN.
MD.
Coogh's
Bridge   Sep.77
Elkton
Elk R.
0   10   20 Miles

- - - - Washington's route 1776-'77
········· Routes '77-'78

'78

Raisz

ATLANTIC OCEAN

another British invasion—this one directed against New York City. Washington had come down to New York soon after the evacuation of Boston, for it was obvious the British would strike there next. After a quick survey of the city's defenses, he traveled to Philadelphia to confer with Congress on the coming summer campaign. Lee was put in charge of defense preparations in the South. It was agreed to make one more effort to take Canada; Gates would command the expedition this time. General Nathanael Greene, one of Washington's ablest officers, urged burning New York but Congress resisted this plan. Washington concurred in the decision to defend the city and returned there early in June to direct the construction of fortifications. He gave particular attention to Brooklyn Heights, a high spot on the East River that overlooked the city, for he did not wish to be caught as the British had been at Boston.

On July 2, the day Congress voted for independence, Sir William Howe landed on Staten Island, an undefended spot off the lower tip of Manhattan. Ten days later his brother Admiral Richard Howe arrived from England with a battle fleet. When the fleet from Carolina, with Clinton's and Cornwallis' troops aboard, showed up, Britain had assembled the largest invasion force of the eighteenth century—some thirty-four thousand men, plus ten thousand seamen, four hundred transports, and thirty warships, to throw against Washington's twenty-thousand ill-trained and ill-equipped troops. Sir William idled away a month and a half organizing his army and making one more stab at reconciliation by writing to "Mr. Washington." The general refused to accept that letter and another one addressed to "George Washington, Esq. etc., etc.," even though he had been assured the "etc., etc." included his title of general. The failure to open negotiations left the British no choice but to fight.

British strategy was obvious. They would take New York City, then move up the Hudson to join forces with Carleton in Canada, thus isolating New England from the war. Washington sought to meet the attack on New York by splitting his army into five segments—one on northern Manhattan under General Heath, two in the city itself, one on Brooklyn Heights under General Putnam, and the fifth on Long Island under General John Sullivan. Howe surprised him by committing the bulk of his forces to a landing on Long Island on August 26. By swift movements and shrewd tactics, Sullivan's forces were surrounded and fourteen hundred Americans were killed, wounded, or made prisoner in the engagement. Howe could have moved on and overrun Putnam's forces on Brooklyn Heights, but he feared another Bunker Hill. He knew, too, that he had the Americans trapped, for the navy blocked retreat across the East River to Manhattan. But Washington saw the peril. On the night of August 29, a regiment of New England fishermen ferried the troops across the river and into the city. Rain and a stiff northwest wind held the British fleet riding at anchor and, ignorant of the maneuver. Campfires kept burning through the night helped to deceive the enemy. When a heavy morning fog cleared, Howe saw that the entire army had slipped from his grasp.

Washington on Manhattan was still not secure; he still faced entrapment. But the British helped his cause by giving him a two-week respite while they sought once again to negotiate a settlement. General Sullivan, who had been captured, went as an emissary to Congress to hint of a peace proposal in the offing, and Congress sent Franklin, John Adams, and Edward Rutledge to talk. They met on Admiral Howe's flagship in New York harbor, and before they talked they dined, as gentlemen should, on "good claret, good bread, cold ham, tongues and mutton." The admiral said he was empowered "to converse and confer" but could commit his government to nothing. However, he added, "he felt for America as a brother, and, if America should fall, he should feel and lament it like the loss of a brother." "My Lord," Franklin answered, "we will do our utmost endeavors to save your lordship that mortification." The meeting broke up on that note.

The British resumed the war on September 15. They landed at Kipps Bay (farm country then, today where 34th Street meets the East River). Washington blocked their advance long enough for Putnam's troops to escape from the city, then retreated to a safe position on Harlem Heights (in the vicinity of 125th Street). The British refused to give chase but turned to enter the city. They were given a warm welcome by those still there, rested for three weeks, and then, on October 9, began to move again. This time Howe trailed after Washington's army, for while it remained intact, the Americans might still hope for their cause. He landed first at Throg's Neck, met resistance, pulled off, and moved up the bay to land again at New Rochelle. An all-day battle there forced Howe to pause three days to regroup and reinforce his army. Washington backed off toward White Plains, planting his troops on high, secure ground. He left Greene behind with five thousand men to divide between Forts Washington and Lee, which flanked and thus controlled movement on the Hudson. Howe attacked Washington on October 28, but the strength of the American position induced caution. He waited for further reinforcements, but by the time he was ready for an all-out assault, Washington had pulled back to an even more secure position. Howe saw that he could not lure Washington into battle except where the odds overwhelmingly favored the Americans. In disgust he swung round and on November 16 turned his batteries against Fort Washington, which Greene had persuaded his commander-in-chief that his subordinate, Colonel Robert

Magaw, would be able to hold. The fort crumbled after a brutal two-hour battle. The British suffered 452 casualties, but the Americans had to turn over 2,800 men as prisoners, plus large stores of equipment and supplies. It was the most serious defeat thus far in the war. Two days later, Fort Lee, on the Jersey side of the river, fell to Cornwallis. Greene and his troops barely managed to escape.

The British now controlled the lower Hudson, and news from the north made it appear that they would soon have the entire river. Carleton and Burgoyne had pushed down from Canada through the autumn. Arnold contested their advance every foot of the way, slowing their progress considerably. When Carleton decided to move down Lake Champlain in a fleet of galleys, Arnold improvised his own naval force. The two fleets met twice in battle and in the second, off Valcour Island on October 13, the American "navy" was demolished. Washington saw the defeat for the "victory" that it was. Arnold had blocked Carleton's efforts to join up with Howe, and the threat he posed had caused Howe to send men and supplies northward. This weakened Howe's forces and eased the pressure on Washington. But Arnold won no praise for what he had done, except from Washington; Congress ignored the achievement.

Cornwallis' capture of Fort Lee had caught Washington by surprise. A few days earlier, he had crossed to the apparent safety of New Jersey. He had expected Howe to move north to join Carleton, and had left Lee behind with five thousand men and Heath with three thousand to hamper any British move up the Hudson Valley or into New England. Now, with Cornwallis on his heels, he was forced to retreat swiftly across the flatlands of New Jersey, across the Delaware, and into Pennsylvania. The British pursued to Trenton and Bordentown, where they went into winter quarters. Howe offered pardons to all who took an oath of loyalty to the king; three thousand accepted, and more might have if they had not been deterred by the pillaging of British and German troops.

In less than three months, the British had captured New York City and most of New Jersey and controlled both banks of the lower Hudson. "I am wearied to death," Washington wrote on December 18; "I think the game is pretty near up." In Congress, a fellow Virginian, Richard Henry Lee, carped at his generalship and one of his own staff accused Washington in a letter he came upon by accident of being of "an indecisive mind." At this moment, when all seemed lost, the first of Tom Paine's letters on the American crisis appeared in the press. "These are the times that try men's souls," Paine wrote.

The summer soldier and the sunshine patriot will, in this crisis, shrink from the service of his country; but he that stands *now*, deserves the love and thanks of man and woman. Tyranny, like hell, is not easily conquered; yet we have this consolation with us, that the harder the conflict, the more glorious the triumph.

Washington ordered the letter read aloud to every regiment. No one knew it then, but the low point of the Revolution had been passed. The year 1776 drew to an end with Washington planning a bold stroke to revive the spirits of all.

The Home Front

Once the thirteen "clocks" had struck as one for independence, something happened to their timing mechanisms. Each once again moved at a pace that satisfied itself, and made little effort to keep time with its neighbors. The states tended to conduct private wars with Britain rather than unite their resources with the Continental Army and Navy. The various "lines" attached to Washington's army cared for their own alone. Pennsylvania's well-clothed soldiers, for instance, refused to share their abundance with tattered troops from other colonies. "I have labored, ever since I have been in the service," Washington said at one point, "to discourage all kinds of local attachments and distinctions of country, denominating the whole by the greater name of *American*, but I have found it impossible to overcome prejudices. . . ."

Americans found it hard to discard old habits. The states raided each other for manpower to build up their own defenses. All but one had their own navies. Each had its own admiralty board, and each issued letters of marque and reprisal to privateers, a privilege usually accorded sovereign nations. At least three states applied to the French government for aid, and when rejected asked Franklin to intervene on their behalf. The Count de Vergennes, the French foreign minister, declined to deal with separate states, for he wished to strengthen the central government. Nor did any state surrender its financial autonomy to Congress; each printed its own paper money, thus making fourteen currencies circulating in the new nation.

The Continental dollars issued by Congress, however, dominated the financial scene. (Congress chose for its standard unit the Spanish milled dollar, or piece of eight, rather than the British pound; eight bits, to use a phrase of the day, equaled one dollar.) The first issue was a modest $6 million. Congress assumed that the taxes collected by the states would be paid in the new currency, which could then be retired from circulation. But the states refused or were afraid to levy taxes, thus forcing Congress each year to issue more Continentals—$19 million in 1776, $13 million in 1777, $63 million in 1778. And the money depreciated steadily.

Some saw nothing seriously wrong with this. Franklin remarked that it worked as a gradual tax upon each person in whose hands the money lost value and that with it the Americans "supported the war during five years against one of the most powerful nations of Europe." It was a fair tax, he said, because "those people paid most, who, being richest, had most money passing through their hands."

By the end of 1779 Congress had issued nearly $200 million in paper money, most of which remained in circulation. The people suddenly lost faith, and their contempt for the money of Congress gave the new nation its first bit of slang—"not worth a Continental." In 1780 Congress sought to solve the problem of inflation by devaluation; it declared forty Continentals worth one gold dollar and overnight wiped out most of the nation's debt. But inflation continued. Congress created the office of superintendent of finance and gave the job to Robert Morris, who held it from 1781 to 1784. On Morris' urging, the Bank of North America was chartered on the last day of 1781; the notes issued by the bank were backed by specie obtained through foreign loans and subsidies, principally from France, Spain, and Holland. But success evaded Morris' efforts to stabilize the currency. The stream of foreign loans soon dried up; the states continued unwilling or unable to gather taxes. The 5 per cent impost on imports that he asked Congress to levy might have solved the nation's financial problems, but the unanimous approval of the states necessary to effect the change was not forthcoming. (Rhode Island, still the home of the otherwise-minded, refused to agree.) The failure to solve the country's financial troubles, Washington once remarked, was throughout the war "the great impediment to all vigorous measures."

Washington spoke as an Army man, for, curiously, the nation's insolvency at worst worked only minor hardships on the bulk of the people. Few civilians suffered in the Revolution. The farmers, who comprised 90 per cent of the nation, prospered even at the height of the inflation. The Continental Army was their main market, and they forced the Army to pay the prices they asked. But farmers only prospered; those engaged in privateering accumulated fortunes. In 1776 Rhode Island had some twelve hundred men at sea aboard privateers. All told, about twenty thousand men—more than at any one time in Washington's Continental Army— sailed on these freebooting ships during the war. "Had Americans enlisted in the army with the alacrity with which they took to privateering," John Miller has said, "the war might have been won in the span of a few years." (This view, however, should be countered by that of an economic historian. "Britain's total wartime losses of £18,000,000 signify that privateering supplied the states with an immense quantity of goods," Curtis Nettels writes, adding: "The heavy losses inflicted by American raiders on Britain severely crippled its war effort." Great Britain lost two thousand vessels to privateers and some twelve thousand sailors, a good number of whom later served on American ships.) Merchants who marketed the privateers' loot did well, too. Army commissaries and quartermasters, who took their cut from those who sold to the Army, did very well. Indeed, among the civilians only the blue- and white-collar workers—clerks, craftsmen, shopkeepers, the clergy, school teachers, and others who lived on wages—were hit hard by the war. A workingman before the Revolution, especially a skilled one like a blacksmith, mason, carpenter, or surveyor, prospered in an economy where labor was scarce and wages two to three times those in Britain. All that changed when inflation struck the war economy. Wages went up, but they always lagged far behind the price spiral. Price fixing was tried in all the Northern states, but the efforts of the new governments succeeded here no more than British attempts earlier to enforce the Navigation Acts. A people fighting a war in the name of liberty refused to countenance regulation. Robert Morris spoke the mood of the country when he called for an end to "the whole detestable tribe" of economic restraints. "Let the people be put in possession of that freedom for which they are contending . . . ," he said. "Perfect freedom makes the people easy, happy, rich, and able to pay taxes."

Wage earners' economic sufferings were real but also mild compared to what soldiers endured. The greed of profiteers—that "tribe of black-hearted gentry" Washington called them—forced the troops to exist through the war always short of some necessity—food, clothing, guns, or ammunition. Officers, who were required to pay their own living expenses, found the service an especial burden. One from Pennsylvania told his wife that though he lived "as frugally as I possibly can," he had nearly exhausted his supply of money and was "therefore determined to set off next week" for home. Officers and men alike received their pay, when it came, which was usually months late, in Continentals and were thus fleeced three ways—by fixed wages, soaring prices, and a sinking currency. "The long and great suffering of this army is unexampled in history," Washington said.

Only the loyalists suffered more. Figures are vague, but somewhere around one hundred thousand people appear to have departed during the Revolution, a larger number in relation to population than left France during the French Revolution. A majority were of the gentry—lawyers, doctors, clergymen, government officials, and large landowners. Perhaps from half to two-thirds of those who sat on the governors' councils became loyalists. But the Revolution can never be simplified into a struggle between the haves and have-nots. For it split families apart—the Franklins of Pennsylvania, the Randolphs of Virginia, the Morrises of New

York, the Starks of Vermont. And of the thousand or so who left Boston with the British in 1776, 102 had been councilors or provincial officials but nearly 400 were farmers, some 200 more merchants "and others," and slightly over 100 came from country towns. On the question of why they left, Robert Palmer has said: "An obvious explanation . . . is as good as any: that the patriots were those who saw an enlargement of opportunity in the break with Britain, and the loyalists were in large measure those who had benefited from the British connection, or who had organized their careers, and their sense of duty and usefulness, around service to the King and empire."

Most of the loyalists came from the Middle States. New York furnished almost half of the total. It, Pennsylvania, and New Jersey were often called "the enemy country." The largest single block of loyalists in the South turned up among the Highland Scots of North Carolina. About half those who left the United States went to Canada—they settled principally in Nova Scotia, New Brunswick, and Ontario—and the rest divided between the West Indies and Great Britain. Few retrieved the property they left behind or were compensated by the states that confiscated it. (The confiscations mounted well into the millions of acres of land.) Among the acquisitions of Massachusetts was a thirty-mile strip of coastline owned by the Pepperrell family. The lands of fifty-nine loyalists confiscated by New York totaled over two and a half million acres. Pennsylvania paid a nominal sum for the vast tracts of the Penn family but offered nothing for the 490 additional holdings it took from departed loyalists. Great Britain did its best to repay those who left for their loyalty. It created pensions for those who had held official posts in the colonies, spent vast sums relocating people, and eventually awarded nearly £3,300,000 to some four thousand persons for property losses. Few of those who departed ever came back to America. "Had the loyalists returned, received back their property, and resumed the positions of prestige and public influence which many of them had once enjoyed," Palmer has remarked, "it seems unlikely that the subsequent history of the United States would have been like the history that we know."

THE TURNING POINT: 1777–1778

December 1776 overflowed with humiliations for Washington. Congress showed its faith in his ability to protect Philadelphia by abandoning the city for Baltimore. General Lee, through his own negligence, was captured by the British. The troops lacked food, clothing, and pay, and the enlistments of most ended with the year. Washington, who in the leisurely past had enjoyed horse races to the point where he would travel all the way up to Philadelphia for a good meet, now decided on a long-shot gamble. He divided his army into three separate forces; each would take a separate route across the Delaware, converge on Hessian garrisons at Bordentown and Trenton, then join to march on Brunswick, where the British had piled up stores and a treasure chest of £70,000. Washington, with Trenton as his objective—subordinates were assigned other targets in the area—pushed off on the night of December 25 with twenty-four hundred men. The countersign that night was "Victory or Death." Most of the Hessians were caught sleeping-off a night of celebration, and the village of Trenton fell easily after a forty-five–minute battle. Washington had to be satisfied with this victory, for he was in no position either to defend Trenton from a British counterattack or to carry through his plan to attack Brunswick. His other two armies had failed to cross the river, and his troops had sampled the Hessians' liquor supply "too freely to admit of discipline or defense in case of attack." Washington abandoned Trenton and recrossed the Delaware with over nine hundred prisoners.

Four days later, having persuaded over half his men to remain with him six weeks longer by a personal plea and the promise of a $10 bounty, he crossed back to New Jersey with five thousand troops on a daring foray that nearly obliterated the recent triumph. This time, Cornwallis met him with an army of six thousand. "At last we have run down the old fox and we will bag him in the morning," Cornwallis said, knowing Washington's position on Assunpink Creek was indefensible. But once more the old fox's audacity caught the British napping—literally this time, for while Cornwallis and his troops slept, Washington pulled his army out, again behind the screen of burning campfires, and marched *into* enemy territory. Cornwallis awoke to the sound of a battle in progress behind him at Princeton. Washington, having captured Princeton, rested his men while Cornwallis rushed up the road to Brunswick, knowing that if Washington left part of his troops at Princeton and arrived first at Brunswick with the rest, the British would lose the treasure stored there and also be caught between American forces to the north and south. But his exhausted troops forced Washington to forego the seventeen-mile march to Brunswick. He had lost one of the great opportunities of the war. When Washington went into winter quarters in the hills around Morristown, only twenty-five miles from Cornwallis' forces at Brunswick, he had the satisfaction of knowing that in nine days, in the dead of winter, when it was considered ungentlemanly for soldiers to be out and about, he had shoved the British sixty miles back from their objective— Philadelphia. The exploit revived American spirits. "A few days ago they had given up the cause for lost," wrote an Englishman who for the moment lived among Americans. "Their late successes have turned the scale and now they are all liberty mad again. . . . They have recovered their panic and it will not be an easy matter to throw them into that confusion again."

Saratoga and Philadelphia

Howe in New York and Carleton in Canada spent the winter devising an ambitious plan to crush the Americans during the summer of 1777. Carleton would move down the Champlain Valley, take Ticonderoga, then continue down the Hudson to New York City and complete the isolation of New England. Howe, meanwhile, would invade Pennsylvania, where he was sure the loyalists would rally to the British side. He assumed that Philadelphia could be taken quickly; if the Canadian expedition needed reinforcements, Howe would supply them from his Philadelphia garrison. The only alteration Lord Germain, secretary of war, made in the plan was to substitute Burgoyne for Carleton, whom he disliked, as commander of the Canadian force, and to urge Howe, belatedly, to leave a strong detachment in New York to support Burgoyne if the need arose. If the complicated plan worked, it might end the war.

Burgoyne moved first, after, however, he had dispatched Colonel Barry St. Leger with sixteen hundred British and Indians to take Fort Stanwix in western New York, who were then to rejoin the main force at the junction of the Mohawk and Hudson. Burgoyne left in mid-June with an army of seven thousand, nearly half German mercenaries, and over one thousand camp-following women. Two weeks later, he had reached Fort Ticonderoga, whose security was considered impregnable to direct attack but flawed by a nearby hill that Arthur St. Clair, the Fort's commander, lacked the men to fortify. The British saw the flaw at once and roped cannon up to the hill's summit. St. Clair evacuated the fort on the night of July 5, and the British entered the next morning without having to fire a shot.

The easy victory boosted Burgoyne's already high confidence. The army moved southward at a turtle's pace, slowed by nearly half a hundred pieces of artillery, carts that fell apart, tons of superfluous baggage—Burgoyne required thirty carts alone for his—and the subsidiary army of women. Schuyler, still in command of Washington's northern army, slowed the march still more by blocking fording spots with boulders and paths with felled trees. A shortage of supplies had developed by the time in mid-August that the force reached Fort Edward, at the northern tip of the Hudson; Burgoyne paused a month to refurbish the larder and to collect horses to draw the baggage carts. A large foraging party sent into Ver-

Map 40. The Revolutionary War

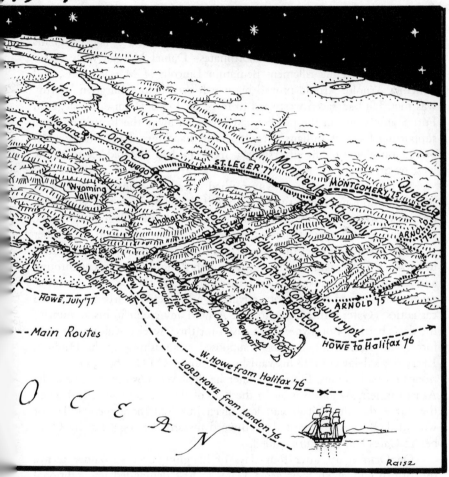

L. Huron

Ft. Niagara

Erie

L. Ontario

Oswego

Wyoming Valley

Cherry V.

Ft Stanwix

Schoharie

ST. LEGER '77

Saratoga

Albany

Bennington

Ft Edward

Ticonderoga

Montreal

Ft Chambly

Valcour

MONTGOMERY '75

Quebec

ARNOLD '75

Newbury pt.

ARNOLD '75

Valley Forge

Morristown

Trenton

Monmouth

Philadelphia

Princeton

New York

West Point

N. Haven

Fairfield

Norwalk

New London

New Bedford

Providence

Concord

Boston

Newport

HOWE, July '77

- - - Main Routes

HOWE to Halifax '76

W. Howe from Halifax '76

LORD HOWE from London '76

O C E A N

Raisz

mont was attacked at Bennington by John Stark, a veteran of Bunker Hill. "We'll beat them before night, or Molly Stark will be a widow," Stark said before he attacked. Molly Stark still had a husband at nightfall, and Burgoyne had lost as prisoners or casualties one thousand men, nearly a seventh of his army.

Burgoyne's troubles now began to accumulate. He learned that Gates had replaced Schuyler as commander of the northern American forces. Gates, though not necessarily a better general, had the confidence of the New England militia, which, after Stark's success, flocked to his colors. Moreover, he had able subordinates—Daniel Morgan with a new company of Virginia riflemen, Benjamin Lincoln of Massachusetts, and Benedict Arnold. Arnold proved his worth even before Burgoyne's army was met. He had raced westward to force St. Leger to raise the siege on Fort Stanwix and in the process had inveigled away the Britisher's large supporting force of Indians. Arnold's swift handling of the situation deprived Burgoyne of the diversionary move he had counted on from the west by St. Leger.

In mid-September, Burgoyne pushed ahead once again. Gates, with seventeen thousand men—twelve thousand militia and five thousand Continentals—waited for him on Bemis Heights, near the village of Saratoga. Burgoyne moved against the entrenched American forces on September 19. Gates wanted to meet the attack from his own lines but was persuaded to let Arnold try a flanking attack. Although Arnold failed to cut through and encircle the British—Gates refused to grant the needed reinforcements—he stopped the redcoats' advance and inflicted nearly six hundred casualties. (Gates refused, too, to give Arnold any credit in his account of the day's battle.) Burgoyne now paused for three weeks, waiting for reinforcements from Clinton, who he supposed was pushing up the Hudson. Every day's delay cut into his vanishing supplies. On October 3 he put the troops on half-rations. Four days later he deployed 1,650 men against the American left. Arnold was again the hero of this second battle, and when the day ended the British had lost seven hundred more men, killed or wounded. Burgoyne retreated northward toward Saratoga, but by October 12 Gates had him surrounded.

On October 17, after four days of haggling over surrender terms, the British laid down their arms. Gates at first demanded unconditional surrender. Burgoyne refused, and Gates, fearful that reinforcements might soon come to Burgoyne's aid, submitted to a convention, as it was called, where only British arms were surrendered and the troops freed to return to England. The flaw in the Convention of Saratoga, as Washington pointed out, was that it would release other troops to serve in America while Burgoyne's army accepted garrison duty elsewhere in the empire.

The surrender terms were never kept, however, and the "convention army" eventually ended up in Virginia. Nevertheless, the agreement at Saratoga transformed the war. It removed a large British army from action; it blocked for good the British threat of controlling the Hudson; and, once news of the battle reached Europe, it made France an open ally of America.

Howe learned of the disaster at Saratoga while comfortably installed in Philadelphia, but having failed in his major objective—to crush Washington's army. The Philadelphia campaign had gone badly at the start for Howe. Washington's control of south Jersey forced him to move his army by sea to the Chesapeake Bay, where he landed a month behind schedule. Washington chose to make his first stand at Brandywine Creek, where the road from Wilmington to Philadelphia crossed at Chadd's Ford. The battle that followed was one Washington always wished to forget. He was outgeneraled and ultimately saved only by a swift movement of Nathanael Greene's. Cornwallis carried out a skillful flanking maneuver he had used on Long Island and with much the same success. Darkness alone saved the Americans from complete defeat. Howe lost some five hundred men, Washington more than one thousand.

Washington retreated northward toward Philadelphia during the following week. He left fifteen hundred men west of the city under Anthony Wayne near Paoli to threaten Howe's rear. Howe moved on toward Philadelphia and was satisfied to send a detachment to deal with Wayne. The British charged with their bayonets while Wayne's men slept and three hundred casualties were inflicted without a shot being fired in what quickly became known as the Paoli Massacre. Howe entered Philadelphia on September 26. He put nine thousand troops in Germantown to the north, twelve miles away, but neglected to have them fortify their position. Washington, still the bold gambler, took advantage of the lapse and on the night of October 3 dispatched four columns to strike the British lines simultaneously at four spots. Fog, a confused guide, a befuddled commander who fired on his own troops, and stout British resistance—all contributed to the lack of success. Cornwallis arrived with reinforcements, and then, though "everything gave the most flattering hopes of victory," Washington said later, "the troops began suddenly to retreat." The Americans lost over a thousand men as casualties and prisoners, the British half that.

Howe did not gloat over the victory, for once again Washington's army had slipped away—now to Valley Forge, where it sat keeping watch over the British. By October, Howe had cleared Delaware Bay and opened it to British shipping. But he was far from happy. He saw no chance to end the war quickly and, with Burgoyne's army gone and Washington's still intact, every chance that it would be a long one. He submitted his resignation, but by the time it was accepted the character of the war had changed. For France had openly declared herself an ally of the Americans.

The Diplomatic Front

Congress told the Indians this was a "family quarrel" and no concern of theirs, but what started as a family quarrel in 1775 had mushroomed by 1778 into another of those world wars that had plagued the Western World through the eighteenth century.

Étienne-François Duc de Choiseul, head of the French Foreign Office in the 1760's, had seen the war coming and done his best to encourage it. He believed that Britain's acquisition of Canada would soon prompt the American colonies to revolt, now that they need not depend on British protection from the French, and that their revolt would start the next world war. He began to prepare for the event as early as 1761 by rebuilding the French Navy. When the revolt came, foreign affairs were in the hands of Comte de Vergennes, a gifted man who held Choiseul's views but pursued them more circumspectly. In the early fall of 1775, he sent a secret agent to America to encourage the rebellion and to learn if America planned to carry through what had been started or to compromise along the way. In November, Congress created the Committee of Secret Correspondence (later known as the Committee for Foreign Affairs), which was instructed to make contacts with "our friends in Great Britain, Ireland, and other parts of the world," but not until the following March was Silas Deane of Connecticut sent as its agent to Paris to buy munitions and determine the extent of French concern for America's welfare. Soon after Deane's arrival, Vergennes convinced the king it would pay France to support the Americans, if only surreptitiously. Aid now would win a friendship that would later allow France to control the lucrative trade Britain had once monopolized. On May 2, 1776, a loan or gift (nobody knows for certain which) of two million livres, half contributed by Spain, was turned over to a dummy organization called Roderigue Hortalez and Company and headed by a most unbusinesslike man, the playwright Caron de Beaumarchais.

This money came unrequested by Congress, for those who hoped for reconciliation still dominated that body. Not until after Richard Henry Lee's resolution of June 7 was a committee appointed "to prepare a plan of treaties to be proposed to foreign powers." Arthur Lee, Silas Deane, and Benjamin Franklin were chosen to represent Congress in Europe. The choice of Franklin to complement the temperamental Lee and the pedestrian Deane was wise, for Franklin was the only American known in Europe at the beginning of the Revolution. He slipped into Paris in the last days of 1776, the unavowed agent of unrecognized revolutionaries; he left nine years later as much a hero of France as of the new United States, having "exploited his own personality, or rather the preconceptions of it that he found in France, with the serene effectiveness of a man free from personal vanity." He dressed simply because the French expected simplicity in Americans and because it made him stand out in court gatherings. He put atrocity stories about the British and Indians into the press. And behind this public activity, he worked steadily to force a treaty from the French.

Twice Vergennes was set to take France into war, only to have his plans undermined by bad news from America—first the battle of Long Island in August 1776 and then the easy capture of Ticonderoga by Burgoyne in July 1777. Unofficial aid, however, continued. In 1777 some eighty ships cleared Bordeaux alone for the United States, and many others set sail for Santo Domingo or other ports in the West Indies, whence their cargoes reached America. When late in the year the British protested this trade, Vergennes pulled back. He imposed an embargo against American privateers and merchantmen using French ports. Franklin reacted by hinting of the possibility that America might settle her difficulties and join with Britain against France. The embargo was soon lifted.

News of Burgoyne's surrender reached France in early December. Two months later, Franklin and Vergennes negotiated two treaties between the United States and France. The first, a Treaty of Amity and Commerce, called for formal recognition by France of the United States as a sovereign nation. France received trading privileges as a favored nation, but America preserved the right to trade with whom it wished. Both nations acceded to the doctrine that free ships make free goods— goods free to be carried and sold where the shippers wished. The second, the Treaty of Alliance, exceeded anything the new nation had any right to hope for. France calculated her generosity, however, for she did not wish to rouse the anger of Europe by seeming to contend "for special privileges for herself in America." This treaty would go into effect only if war should occur between England and France, which it did five months after the signing. The stated purpose was to assure the "liberty, sovereignty, and independence absolute and unlimited of the United States." France renounced claims to the mainland of North America east of the Mississippi or to the Bermuda Islands if captured by America. In return she asked the United States to recognize whatever she might capture in the West Indies. Both sides agreed not to negotiate for peace without the other's consent. There was no time limit on either treaty.

Vergennes had tried to persuade Spain to join in the treaties. Spain shared France's hatred for Britain, but with an empire of its own to discipline, it balked at the thought of dealing with a collection of revolting colonies. Still, with Britain at bay, it was hard to resist the chance to retrieve Gibraltar, and in June 1779 Spain entered the war as an ally of France but not of the United States. Congress sent John Jay to persuade Spain to change her mind, outfitting him with generous instructions. Britain in the treaty of 1763 had acquired from Spain the right of free navigation on the Mississippi, a right now claimed by America but which Congress authorized Jay to sacrifice in return for a Spanish agreement that recognized the independence of the United States. The chance for an alliance was hopeless, and Jay, sensing this and also angered by his patronizing reception, refused even to present the offer Congress had instructed him to make. Congress, too, became disgusted and rescinded the offer in 1782. "Spain has taken four years to consider whether she should treat with us or not," Franklin said. "Give her forty, and let us in the meantime mind our own business."

The French alliance was on the whole well received in America. Some complained that the French were Catholic, that their manners, politics, and society were every bit as corrupt as the British, but for the most part America forgot old hatreds and prejudices and rejoiced. Certain consequences of the alliance became quickly obvious. French engineers and officers, on leave from assignments in their own army, now appeared in droves. The French Navy soon opened up sea lanes recently infested with British men-of-war. Other consequences became obvious only in time. Spain, for instance, had insisted in her agreement with France that the war must last until she retrieved Gibraltar. The United States thus found itself obliged without having consented or been consulted in any way to remain at war until Gibraltar had been won. (The obligation eventually proved one that could be avoided, but the experience nurtured an early and strong feeling against entangling alliances.) Also, it became clear in time that the expanded war now confronting Britain made a side show of the affair in America. After 1778 the real enemy of Britain was her oldest one—France. Affairs in America became peripheral to those in Europe.

The French alliance coincided with Britain's making its most generous peace offer to date. On February 17, 1778, eleven days after the signing of the still secret Franco-American alliance, Lord North handed Parliament a group of Conciliatory Propositions, which called for the repeal of all the acts America had found obnoxious, the virtual granting of home rule to the colonies, and the sending of another peace commission. The commission, headed by Lord Carlisle, was authorized to deal with Congress "as if it were a legal body" and to yield everything that the Americans had officially asked for prior to 1775. The Declaratory Act of 1766 would remain on the books, but Parliament would abandon the right to tax the colonies and confine its regulation to matters of trade and manufacturing. The colonies would raise their own revenues and all would be spent in America. The Continental Congress could continue to legislate for the colonies as long as it acknowledged its authority as derived from Parliament. All who had participated in the rebellion would be forgiven, and the Declaration of Independence would be put aside. The generous but belated offer failed to receive even Lord North's full support. The peace commissioners arrived in America in June to find their bargaining power undercut by news of the French alliance and by Clinton's preparations to evacuate Philadelphia. (Clinton, who had replaced Howe, was acting on orders sent, with Lord North's knowledge, before the commissioners left Britain.) An army on the retreat hardly set the mood for peace negotiations. Congress refused to receive North's commission, and though the peace proposals were published for all to read, no one censured Congress for rejecting them outright.

From Valley Forge to a Deadlock

Howe had wintered comfortably in friendly Philadelphia. Washington hovered only twenty miles away at Valley Forge, "a dreary kind of place, and uncomfortably provided," according to him. He hoped by sticking close to the enemy to hamper efforts to draw supplies from the countryside and by the army's presence to block any stampede among the people of Pennsylvania to the British side. The risks of his location were high, and Washington later said that if Howe had attacked and destroyed his army at Valley Forge, he could have won the war for Britain.

The winter of 1777–1778 was a mild one, but the difference between a temperature of zero and ten below zero means little to men who lack clothing and food. Most of the stories about the winter at Valley Forge are true. "All my men," one officer wrote, "except eighteen are unfit for duty for want of shoes, stockings and shirts, breeches and coats . . . and . . . we are becoming exceedingly lousy." Another reported his officers "so naked they were ashamed to be seen." Farmers sold to the highest bidder, and while barrels of flour and pork and wagons loaded with butter and beef rolled by the hundreds into Philadelphia and New York, the men at Valley Forge drank soup "full of burnt leaves and dirt, enough to make a Hector spew." "Poor food—hard lodging—cold weather—fatigue—nasty clothes—nasty cookery—vomit half my time—smoked out of my senses—the Devil's in't—I can't endure it," wrote an army surgeon. "Why are we sent here to starve and freeze . . . a pox on my bad luck."

At the end of December, enlistments ended again, and over two thousand men went home. But the army endured. Nathanael Greene reluctantly took on the job of quartermaster general. "I hate the place," he said, but assumed the job because Washington asked him to. Greene's energy and administrative skill soon had supplies flowing into camp, and by the end of the winter soldiers wore shoes again, slept beneath blankets, and ate a full ration of reasonably decent food. They needed the strength gained from these comforts, for during the winter Baron von Steuben had joined Washington's staff and inaugurated a new training program. Steuben, who had promoted himself from the captain he had been in Frederick the Great's army to general by the time he arrived in America, was one of the few imports from Europe who injected something of value into the American army. Troops exposed to his barked commands came away with some comprehension of the importance of discipline in fighting a war. Steuben was a martinet but also something of a showman, who knew the troops delighted in his troubles with English. "Viens, Walker," he is supposed to have shouted once to his aide, "mon ami, mon bon ami! sacré! Goddam de gaucheries of dese badauts. Je ne puis plus. I can curse dem no more."

Washington's efforts to hold together the army at Valley Forge were complicated by his relations with Congress that winter. A variety of festering sores came to a head in December 1777 to create what contemporaries called the Conway Cabal. If the dictionary's definition of "cabal" as an "intrigue" is accepted, then no Conway Cabal existed. Washington was censured as never before during the winter of 1777–1778, but to censure is not to conspire. One sore spot that prompted criticism was the adulation developing toward Washington. "The superstitious veneration that is sometimes paid to General Washington" sickened John Adams, and he condemned those in Congress who "were disposed to idolize an image which their own hands have molden." New Englanders tended to be unhappy about the eminence of a Virginian. Others were irritated that Washington had supplanted Congress in the people's affection. "What has been often called a laudable jealousy of military power," a contemporary remarked, "if probed to the bottom, would be found a real rivalship in fame." Washington's strategy by late 1777 had raised another sore spot. "We should on all occasions avoid a general action, nor put anything to the risk unless compelled by a necessity into which we ought never to be drawn," he had once said. Congress had approved then, but in the months since Gates had overwhelmed Burgoyne at Saratoga, some delegates wondered aloud if Washington's approach was the right one. And, finally, many Congressmen feared Washington, though much of this fear was perhaps disguised jealousy.

A trivial incident intensified these various irritants and produced new ones that led to a showdown between Congress and Washington. After the battle of Saratoga, Gates' aide, James Wilkinson—who would one day be involved in the Burr Conspiracy—carried news of the victory southward to Congress. (Gates did not bother to inform his commander-in-chief officially of the victory, an act which contributed to Washington's later judgment of Gates as "a doubtful friend.") En route, Wilkinson remarked to a friend one alcoholic evening that he had seen a letter to Gates from Thomas Conway, an Irishman who had come to America by way of the French Army, wherein it was hinted that Gates would be a good man to replace the "weak general" as head of the army. Washington heard the story about the time Congress, probably ignorant of it, promoted Conway to major-general, on the ground that he was an able officer, which he seems to have been. Nevertheless, the act, occurring against the backdrop of growing criticism from Congressmen, helped to convince Washington that a "malignant faction" was determined to oust him from command, replacing him with Gates. The suspicion increased when Gates, with Thomas Mifflin, whom Washington had little respect for, and Conway as associates, was chosen to head the Board of War, which was now given broad if vague powers over all military affairs. Some people, like Benjamin Rush of Pennsylvania and James Lovell of Massachusetts, may have connived to promote Gates, but the majority in Congress voted him into the board's presidency because he appeared to be the ablest man available. Gates himself did little to advance his candidacy, but he did little also to reduce the suspicions of Washington's friends. As president of the Board of War, he shunned advice from that camp and moved forward with plans to reinvade Canada, a campaign deplored by Washington as hopeless of success.

Tension between Washington and Congress relaxed in the early months of 1778. Officers at Valley Forge made it clear it was either "*Washington* or no army." Tom Paine promoted Washington in the press. Lafayette, who had been assigned to Gates's projected invasion of Canada, refused to accept Conway as his second-in-command, and when Congress agreed to reassign Conway it was clear the wind had shifted. In March, the Canadian venture was abandoned as a badly conceived scheme that lacked a chance to succeed. The spring of 1778 found Washington so firmly seated in his post that to criticize him now verged close to being un-American. Hereafter, it would be impossible to separate the man from the monument. "We derive all the blessings of our present glorious revolution from his arm alone," Benjamin Rush remarked bitterly. "We say in contempt of the very genius of republicanism . . . that no man but our commander-in-chief would have kept our army together, and that his fall would be the extinction of our liberty." (A foreigner visiting America in 1783 was shocked to hear people talk of Washington "as if the Redeemer had entered Jerusalem!" He went on: "It is certainly remarkable that, considering the many illustrious personages in America who through their vigor and talents have accomplished the great and complicated work of this independence, none have either a general approbation or the popularity of this leader.")

The arrival of spring saw the end of dissension between Washington and Congress and also good news from Europe. Clinton replaced Howe as commander of the British forces; Lord North's peace proposals reached Congress; and news of the French alliance followed soon after. With the news of the French treaties, Congress learned, too, that words would be backed by action—in the form of a task force of twelve warships with several regiments of trained and equipped troops aboard—all being dispatched for Delaware Bay. With the French blocking the bay, Philadelphia would become untenable for the British. So Clinton was ordered to evacuate and take the army by sea to New York. But Clinton violated his orders, for the ships lacked room for both the army and the Philadelphia loyalists that wished to accompany him—further, he feared that during the slow sea voyage Washington might rush ahead and take New York before the British arrived. On June 18 a British army of ten thousand set off through the flat Jersey countryside toward New York. Washington pulled out of Valley Forge and trailed close behind with an army nearly as large as Clinton's.

Washington's staff vetoed an all-out battle. Washington therefore compromised for a strike on the slow-moving baggage train at the rear of the British column. General Charles Lee, recently exchanged as a prisoner-of-war, was given charge of the attack. Lee moved ahead with forty-two hundred men and caught the British at Monmouth Courthouse. In the midst of the attack, however, Clinton swung round and confronted Lee with a force of six thousand. The American lines broke, and Lee retreated with them. Washington rode up in a fury and, after berating Lee, took command and beat off two British attacks. Losses for the day were equal—about three hundred casualties on each side—but when Clinton moved on the next day he still had his baggage train intact. (Later, a court-martial that Lee had demanded to clear his reputation found him guilty of disobeying orders and making an unnecessary retreat. He was suspended from command for one year, and died in obscurity in 1782.)

Washington rested his army, then marched to the Hudson and encamped at White Plains. "It is not a little pleasing," he wrote, "nor less wonderful to contemplate, that after two years maneuvering . . . both armies are brought back to the very point they set out from. . . ." What little pleasure Washington took from the stalemate would soon vanish. He had two more winters of discontent ahead before even a hint of victory was to appear.

VICTORY: 1778–1783

Monmouth marked the last major battle in the North but not the end of fighting there. Clinton preferred a war of attrition to risking a battle with Washington, and to that end initiated raids on exposed New England towns. New Bedford, New Haven, and New London were invaded, Norwalk and Fairfield in Connecticut were burned. In May 1779 Clinton threatened West Point, but after capturing Stony Point, a small outpost on the Hudson, he brought his main army back to New York. Washington could not prevent these raids, but he could repay in kind. "Mad Anthony" Wayne stormed the British fort at Stony Point in July 1779, recaptured it, but soon after was forced to abandon the post. "Light-Horse" Harry Lee, Washington's cavalry leader, attacked Paulus Hook in New Jersey in August. None of these raids, for all the terror they inspired in the victims, altered the course of the war in the slightest.

More alarming were the raids carried out by Indian scalping parties from Detroit into the Ohio, Illinois, and Kentucky country. A British offensive using Western Indians began early in 1778 under the leadership of Colonel Henry Hamilton, lieutenant governor of Detroit, and soon known as the "Hair-buyer" because of the price he paid for American scalps. A foray into Kentucky in February 1778 resulted in the capture of Daniel Boone. A few months later, a fierce, red-headed young man of twenty-five named George Rogers Clark retaliated by leading a band of 175 frontiersmen down the Ohio. They took Kaskaskia on July 4, Cahokia a few days later, and Vincennes on July 20, and the Indians of the West began to wonder about the sense of their attachment to the British. Hamilton reoccupied Vincennes in December, which only provoked Clark to make another long march into the wilderness, this time returning with the "Hair-buyer" himself, who spent the rest of the war in a Williamsburg prison. Clark broke the British power in the West but won nothing except ingratitude for the effort; neither he nor his men got a cent of pay either from Virginia, which had sponsored the raids, or Congress, which never fully appreciated their achievements.

The British used the Indians to their advantage throughout the war, particularly the Iroquois, who made the one major mistake of their long history of dealings with the white man by siding with the British. Early in 1778, Colonel Walter Butler, a New York loyalist soon to be known as the "hellhound" of the frontier, was put in command of a band of rangers whose purpose was to divert the attention of Americans from Howe's army in Pennsylvania. Ranger-led Iroquois raided the Wyoming Valley to the north of Philadelphia and carried out a brutal massacre there. They struck next at Cherry Valley on the New York frontier and to the same effect. Washington retaliated by dispatching General Sullivan in 1779 with five thousand troops to wipe out Indian villages throughout northern Pennsylvania and western New York and to capture the British fort at Niagara, the key depot for supplying Indians throughout the northwest. Sullivan failed to get the fort but did level over forty villages. The exploit, for all its immediate success, achieved little in the long run. In 1780 Indians under Sir John Johnson ravaged the Schoharie Valley in New York, destroying wheat the American Army was counting on. Indians still ravaged the Pennsylvania frontier as late as 1782.

The South's Time of Troubles

A misplaced faith in the French Navy contributed much to the South's distress during the next two years. When France entered the war, Congress let the American Navy fade away—from thirty-four ships in 1777 to seven in 1781—on the assumption France would thereafter deal with the war on the sea. Three years passed before that assumption bore fruit. Admiral d'Estaing loitered so long crossing the Atlantic that he missed the British evacuation from Philadelphia. He refused to attack the fleet at Sandy Hook, and his assault on Newport fizzled out. From Newport the admiral took his fleet to the warm winter of the West Indies. The move did force Clinton to detach eight thousand troops to defend British interests in that area, and this weakened his strength in New York. But the French fleet's presence in the Indies also left him free to invade Georgia with little fear that his covering force would be harried.

London had ordered the attack on Georgia, and Clinton responded reluctantly by detaching General Archibald Campbell and thirty-five hundred men for the assignment. Campbell landed near Savannah on December 23, 1778, and the weakly held town of some three thousand citizens fell six days later. Augusta capitulated soon after. General Benjamin Lincoln, whom Washington had sent down to take command of the Southern Department, jousted with the British through the winter and spring of 1779 but could do no more than prevent the capture of Charleston. The British tightened their hold on Georgia and reestablished civil government. Sir James Wright, the last royal governor, returned and governed for the next three years.

The South pleaded for aid from the French fleet. And although Washington wanted the fleet, too, in order to join in an attack on New York, in September 1779 he learned from a Charleston paper that the fleet was hovering off the Georgia coast. There, D'Estaing joined Lincoln in laying down a siege on Savannah and on October 9 an attack was launched against the town. The British defender, General Augustine Prevost, had been alerted by a deserter; his guns slaughtered the Americans as they advanced. The Americans suffered some eight hundred casualties; among the dead was Count Pulaski, among the wounded, D'Estaing. Lincoln retreated to South Carolina and the admiral took his fleet back to France. The slow-moving Clinton saw that the time had now come to stage a full-scale invasion of the South. The arrival of reinforcements from Britain and steady nudging from Lord Germain helped to persuade him to move. The decision to concentrate on the South was one that Washington most feared, for the bulk of the Continental Army would be tied up in the North, dealing with an army that Clinton had left in New York under the command of General Wilhelm von Knyphausen—an army equal in size to Washington's.

Clinton took nearly eight thousand troops to Charleston. By April 1780, after a three-month siege of the city, his artillery was in easy range. On May 9 he opened a bombardment and three days later General Lincoln signed the articles of capitulation. The British got over five thousand prisoners, three generals among them. "It was by all odds the most serious reverse, until Bataan, ever suffered by the United States army," John C. Miller has said. South Carolina fell with Charleston. On May 29 Banastre, or "Bloody," Tarleton as he was hereafter called, annihilated an American regiment under Colonel Abraham Buford at the Waxhaws, near the North Carolina border. Clinton saw victory on the horizon, and on June 8 he departed for New York, where he hoped to finish off Washington's army. Cornwallis now took command in the South, and soon after Clinton's departure he began what has been called "the most serious and sustained effort of the war to defeat the patriot forces, to set up loyalist civil governments, and to regain at least part of America for Britain."

Congress faced the emergency by calling Gates from retirement and ordering him south to deal with Cornwallis. By mid-August, Gates had collected nearly five thousand troops, slightly over one thousand of them experienced Continentals led by Baron de Kalb, the remainder raw militia. He planned a surprise attack on a post near Camden, South Carolina, commanded by Lord Rawdon, unaware that Cornwallis had moved north with reinforcements. On the night of August 15, the two armies each set out on a surprise attack. They met on the road about two in the morning. The battle began at daylight, with the British regulars ripping through the lines of the militia. De Kalb's troops fought to the end, but in vain, for Gates had fled the scene at the first sign of disaster. Gates reported to Congress that he had met "total defeat," as he had.

The British exulted over this second great victory within four months. The defeat at Camden opened the way for a British invasion of North Carolina in much the same fashion that the capture of Fort Washington had exposed New Jersey in 1776. And it saved the ministry of Lord North from a Parliamentary crisis. Two American armies, each as large as the force that had surrendered at Saratoga, had been lost within a year.

To make matters worse, Washington's army lived on short rations through the summer of 1780; he was obliged to dismiss most of the militia lest they starve on his hands. By mid-July, when a summer campaign should have been in full bloom, he had only about one thousand able-bodied men on hand. "I have almost ceased to hope," Washington said. "The country in general is in such a state of insensibility and indifference to its interests that I dare not flatter myself with any change for the better." Worse was to come. On September 25 Benedict Arnold, perhaps the ablest general on the American side and a special favorite of Washington's, defected to the British. He had spent thirteen months negotiating the best deal possible with the enemy and had wangled the command of West Point to make his betrayal more valuable to himself and the British. The act stunned Washington, and with the greatest reluctance he ordered the hanging of the personable young Major André, who had served as a go-between for Arnold and Clinton and whose capture had revealed the plot.

Clinton had troubles, too. He had acquired a good general—it has been said that the best American *and* the best British general during the war was Benedict Arnold—but he was also seeing his victory in the South dissipated away. Cornwallis marched north in early September to take North Carolina, which he expected to fall with the ease of Georgia and South Carolina. He headed for Charlotte, ordering Major Patrick Ferguson to clear the piedmont area on the way. Cornwallis took Charlotte with ease, but Ferguson soon found himself penned atop King's Mountain; and there, nine hundred Tarheels, who recalled Bloody Tarleton's slaughter of Buford's troops, killed, captured, or wounded more than one thousand of Ferguson's men. News of the catastrophe at King's Mountain sent Cornwallis back to the safer country of South Carolina, where he idled away the rest of the year. In January, Clinton sent down twenty-five hundred reinforcements. These, with a diversionary force already in Virginia led by Arnold, were sufficient to impel Cornwallis northward again on what he hoped was the road to victory.

The road led instead to defeat, for Cornwallis was about to come up against the best general he would meet during the war—Nathanael Greene. Congress, at Washington's bidding this time, had appointed Greene commander of the Southern theater. Greene, as Washington's protégé, operated on the principle that the object was not necessarily to win battles but to preserve your army in order to keep harassing the enemy; a pitched battle was never to be risked except on the safest possible ground.

The problem of foraging for food for seventeen hundred men following the same route, forced Greene to adopt a dangerous tactic. He divided his army, directing one part under Daniel Morgan to the southwest and the other, which Greene accompanied, to the southeast. Cornwallis responded by sending Tarleton with one thousand men after Morgan. The two armies met at Hannah's Cowpens, a corral for cattle on the Broad River. Morgan arranged his troops with their backs to the river to cut off retreat; a row of militia, who were asked only to fire two volleys before retreating, was backed by a row of steady Continentals, then by a row of militia, and further back, out of sight, a troop of cavalry. When the smoke cleared, Tarleton's losses numbered nearly nine hundred, or nine-tenths of his force; Morgan's casualties were negligible. Cornwallis called the defeat at Cowpens "a very unexpected and severe blow," but he continued to march into North Carolina after Greene. Greene retreated just swiftly (or slowly) enough to entice Cornwallis northward. When Cornwallis paused to rest and await reinforcements, Greene moved forward to harass, practicing "by finesse that which I dared not attempt by force." By March, Greene's army had swollen to forty-five hundred, a third Continentals. Now he was ready to fight Cornwallis. He chose his ground near Guilford Courthouse on March 14. Technically, Cornwallis won the battle that followed, for at the end of the day Greene withdrew his army. But Cornwallis' casualties were considerably heavier, and Greene's army remained intact. Two days later, Cornwallis turned tail and carried the army southeast to Wilmington, on the coast, where he could get supplies by ship. Within three months, British holdings in the South had been reduced to Charleston, Savannah, and small adjacent areas.

The Path to Yorktown

The year 1781 began badly. On New Year's Day the Pennsylvania Line, fifteen hundred strong, mutinied. For nearly a year now the once well-fed, well-supplied Pennsylvania troops had lived on short rations, and their lack of "clothing beggars all description," said their commander Anthony Wayne. "For God's sake send us our dividend of uniforms, overalls, blankets." Clinton, hearing of the mutiny, tried to woo the men to his side, but they made clear that this was a family quarrel by stringing up his emissaries. Congress belatedly coddled them with provisions and promises; Wayne, though resisting the uprising, worked for "twenty tedious days and nights" negotiating a settlement. No sooner had one been worked out when the New Jersey Line rose up. Washington suppressed this mutiny quickly with troops brought down from West Point, and the two ringleaders were executed. The mutinies of 1781 were the low-water mark of the Revolution. Shortly afterward, a series of events gave a more hopeful aspect to the American cause. Maryland acceded to the Articles of Confederation, at last giving the new nation a constitution; France promised a new loan; Congress reorganized the Departments of Foreign Affairs, Finance, and War; and Robert Morris was appointed superintendent of finance. Morris' job was to find money and supplies for the troops, and whatever might be said about his far from pure business ethics, he did the job well. His energy gave the government a semblance of vigor during the early, trying months of 1781. He started flour, meat, and rum toward the army; he even paid off the troops one month in gold. Washington credited Morris for a large share in the successful campaign of 1781 and said "it will soon be a matter of wonder how Mr. Morris has done so much with so small means."

The campaign of 1781 was to center in Virginia, but through no desire of either Washington or Clinton, both of whom had planned to fight it out in the North that summer. The previous year, Clinton had sent Benedict Arnold to Virginia to serve as a diversionary force to Cornwallis further south. Arnold had ravaged the coastal towns and then settled down for the winter at Portsmouth. Governor Thomas Jefferson followed a policy of passive resistance. He lacked the temperament to rally the people and to impose the forceful measures the emergency demanded. A plea went out to Washington to save his "country" of Virginia. Washington refused to send the army, but he did dispatch a contingent of twelve hundred Continentals commanded by Lafayette. Clinton reinforced Arnold with two thousand men, sufficient, he thought, to deal with a side operation. He failed to consider the wayward Cornwallis, who had remained through the winter at Wilmington and whom Clinton expected to protect British gains south of Virginia. Cornwallis decided on his own that the time had come to invade Virginia, and he joined his army with Arnold's there on May 20. The move perturbed Clinton, for with Greene to the south and Washington to the north the risk was great that Cornwallis' forces might be caught in a pincer movement.

Lafayette, well-trained by Washington, played the master's game while waiting for reinforcements that had been promised him. He held his army just out of Cornwallis' reach, always willing "to skirmish, but not to engage too far," he said, then, with a thought of his twelve hundred men against Cornwallis' seventy-two hundred, added: "I am not strong enough even to get beaten." When Lafayette's forces were supplemented by additions from Wayne, Steuben, and Morgan, bringing his total up to fifty-two hundred, Cornwallis fell back along the coast. En route, he received orders from Clinton to take up a defensive position and send part of his army back to New York, where Clinton was planning a new attack on Philadelphia. Unfortunately, transportation at the moment was lacking, for the admiral assigned to carry the troops from Virginia had suddenly sailed off after a French convoy. He did not return to New York until August 16. Cornwallis, meanwhile, had been ordered to take up a fortified position on the Yorktown peninsula and await the fleet's arrival.

Washington had watched Lafayette's "country dance" with Cornwallis from his post north of New York, where the five thousand Continentals had been joined by an equal number of French troops led by the Comte de Rochambeau. Washington doubted that Cornwallis could be caught on the Yorktown peninsula, but he and Rochambeau urged the new French admiral, the Comte de Grasse, then with the fleet in the West Indies, to sail for Chesapeake Bay, where a combined land and sea operation would be attempted against Cornwallis. If the British evaded the trap, then a similar operation would be undertaken against New York City. On August 14, word arrived at Washington's headquarters that De Grasse was on the way with thirty ships and three thousand French marines. Washington rushed word to Lafayette to slip below Cornwallis in order to prevent his retreat to Carolina. Five days later his own army was on the way south. When British spies reported the movement, Clinton assumed the contemplated assault on New York City would soon begin. But Washington had passed Philadelphia before it dawned that a trap was about to be sprung on Cornwallis. "It would seem that Mr. Washington is moving an army to the southward with an appearance of haste," Clinton wrote Cornwallis—a most discreet suggestion to move to a safer position like Wilmington. Clinton realized the seriousness of the situation, for he knew by now that the French fleet that Admiral Rodney had promised to keep tied to the West Indies had escaped British surveillance. On September 5 Admiral De Grasse, having transported part of Washington's army down Chesapeake Bay, fended off a British sea attack at the mouth of the bay. It was a minor engagement that ended in a draw. (This traditional judgment has been controverted by some historians, most recently by Harold Larrabee, who calls the Battle of the Virginia Capes, to give its official name, one of the most decisive in American history. He writes: "Americans have been understandably reluctant to face up to the fact that their status as a nation was decided by an engagement at which no Americans were present.") The British fleet returned to New York and informed Clinton that it would take a month to restock and repair the ships before sailing to relieve Cornwallis.

Washington's combined forces—fifty-seven hundred Continentals, thirty-one hundred militia, and seven thousand French troops—set up camp at Yorktown and began siege operations on September 28. The siege lasted three weeks. Cornwallis made a few shows of resistance, but though he was outnumbered 2 to 1, at no time attempted the one tactic that might have saved him—a direct assault on the enemy lines to open a path to freedom. He capitulated on October 17, four years to the day after Burgoyne's surrender. He surrendered with a week's provisions still on hand; if he had held out longer, there was a slim chance that the British fleet might have saved him, for it arrived four days after the white flag went up. ". . . All depended on a fleet," Clinton said later. "Sir Henry Clinton was promised one. Washington had one."

Washington demanded and got the total surrender of Cornwallis' army and equipment—7,241 men, 214 cannons, 6,658 muskets, 457 horses, 30 transports, and over £2,000 in cash. Once the terms of capitulation had been signed, the armies of both sides turned out for the formal surrender. Then French and American troops lined up in two columns that stretched for half a mile, the French glittering in their varicolored uniforms, the Americans for the most part arrayed in rough trousers and hunting shirts. The band played several American and French airs, among them *The World Turned Upside Down*. Cornwallis was "indisposed" that day and sent as his deputy General Charles O'Hara. After O'Hara had explained his presence, Washington said the deputy should speak to *his* deputy, General Lincoln. O'Hara turned and handed his sword over to Lincoln, who then requested that the British troops should be ordered to stack their arms. The troops, many of them "much in liquor," marched toward an open field and dropped their arms. Cornwallis ended the day with a letter to Clinton: "I have the mortification to inform your Excellency that I have been forced to . . . surrender the troops under my command by capitulation on the 19th inst. as prisoners of war to the combined forces of America and France." No one knew it then, but the surrender marked the end of the last major battle in the American Revolution.

Peace

Washington did not think that Yorktown would end the war. He urged De Grasse to join in another land-sea operation, this time against Charleston. When the admiral refused, Washington sent his main force back to New York, where sixteen thousand of Clinton's troops were still stationed. Washington, for once, miscalculated. When Lord North learned of the defeat at Yorktown, he said: "Oh, God! It is all over," and from that moment Great Britain searched for the best way to bring about peace in America. In late February, Sir Guy Carleton was chosen to replace Clinton and given orders to avoid a battle unless attacked and to concentrate on evacuating the troops back to Britain. On March 4 Parliament voted to "consider as enemies to his Majesty and the country all those who should advise or by any means attempt to further prosecution of offensive war on the continent of North America." Lord North resigned, to be replaced by the Marquis of Rockingham, then upon Rockingham's death a few months later, by the Earl of Shelburne. Richard Oswald, a lively octogenarian eager to revive good relations with America, went to Paris to open negotiations with Franklin. The absence at the start of the other American peace commissioners—John Adams was in Holland, Jay in Spain, Jefferson in Virginia, and Henry Laurens in London—left the burden of preliminary discussions up to Franklin. He began by disregarding instructions from Congress to carry on no peace talks except in the presence of French officials. Franklin met Oswald in "secret"—Vergennes actually knew of the meetings—because he hoped to persuade Britain to part with Canada, a cession Franklin thought France would never accede to.

Franklin had intentionally overlooked the question of British recognition of American independence in order to discuss Canada, but Jay, when he arrived, insisted that the issue of recognition had to take precedence over all other matters and refused to allow the talks to proceed until it had been settled. Shelburne had hoped a peace could be devised that kept America within the empire. When Jay forced the fact of independence on him, however, Shelburne accepted it, though he immediately balked at giving up Canada, as Franklin knew he would once the issue of independence had been decided.

The British territorial concessions in the treaty were generous. America received all the land westward to the Mississippi, southward to Florida (which, under a secret treaty, was returned by Britain to Spain), and northward to the Great Lakes. (The northern boundary was not finally settled until 1842 by the Webster-Ashburton Treaty. In the 1930's the map used in the 1782 negotiations was found in the archives of Spain; it showed that America in 1842 gave up a large piece of territory originally ceded in the 1782 treaty.) Britain agreed to evacuate its military posts in what became the Northwest Territory—that land west of Pennsylvania, east of the Mississippi, and north of the Ohio.

The fisheries clause was granted in a further effort to create a mood of good will between America and Britain. John Adams, with the interests of New England fishermen in mind, had fought hard for the concession, which gave Americans the right not just to fish off the coast of Newfoundland but also to land on any uninhabited part of the coast to salt, dry, and pack their fish. France had received a variation of this right in 1763, and she was not eager to have American fishermen acquire an equal competitive advantage—one more reason why it was best to negotiate with Britain alone.

The final clauses of the treaty were the most bitterly debated. Shelburne demanded that the United States promise that the private debts of Americans to Britishers be paid and that all loyalists be compensated for property lost in the Revolution. In the end, the Americans pledged that no impediments would be put in the way of the collection of British debts in the United States, and it was agreed that Congress would "recommend" to the states that loyalists be reimbursed for their losses. The Americans, however, reneged on the spirit of both these clauses. Whatever compensation the loyalists eventually received came from Britain. The refusal to repay private debts was answered by the British refusal to evacuate the northwest posts, and not until the Jay Treaty of 1795 were the debts satisfied—the United States government paid them—and the military posts evacuated.

The preliminary treaty was signed by both sides on November 30, 1782, and went into effect two months later, when Britain made peace with Spain and France. Congress ratified the treaty on April 19, 1783, exactly eight years after the shot heard round the world had been fired.

Anyone who attempts to write a history of the American Revolution, Washington said in 1783, runs the risk of having his work called fiction, for who will believe "that such a force as Great Britain has employed for eight years in this country could be baffled in their plan of subjugating it by numbers infinitely less, composed of men sometimes half-starved, always in rags, without pay, and experiencing every species of distress, which human nature is capable of undergoing." The achievement still baffles. All the odds favored Great Britain from the beginning and even after six years of fighting no objective betting man would have wagered much on America's chances. The United States had fourteen new and shaky governments, and none were contributing much to the war effort. The Revolution evoked mass support only where the theater of operations happened at the moment to be; when the fighting shifted elsewhere, enthusiasm waned, and men turned back to private interests. The British Army lived well off supplies sold to them by Americans, only a few of whom would have considered themselves loyalists. The British soldier fought well and bravely, and from the military standpoint, he was well led. American forces were outfought several times, and at least twice—at Long Island and Brandywine—they were outgeneraled.

How, then, did America win against such odds? French aid, of course, helped immensely: most of the American guns at Saratoga came from France; the majority of troops at Yorktown were French; and the French Navy there made the victory possible. France's willingness to turn a British family quarrel into a world war forced Britain to give less than full attention to the American theater, which now became only one of several where the empire was being threatened. Some historians hold that French participation hastened but did not bring about the American victory, that it would have materialized regardless of the stand France took. A large share of the responsibility is pinned on the British generals' indecisiveness, timidity, arrogance, and overconfidence. "The obligation to win the war rested on the British commanders on the spot, and they failed to honour it, failed indeed for five years to show any inclination to do so," Esmond Wright has written. "Germain in London gave full discretion and full support to them. The war was caused by political failures in London, and it was lost by military failures in America." Then there was the role played by the land itself—America's silent ally. At one time or another, every major city in America was occupied by the British, and the outcome of the war was not affected in the slightest. To win, the British would have had to conquer and occupy the continent, and that they lacked the strength to do.

And, finally, there was George Washington. "The sure and staggering truth is that Congress (and America) was luckier than it could reasonably hope to be in choosing Colonel Washington," Marcus Cunliffe writes. "The 'available' man proved to be, despite all his minor defects, the indispensable man." Of all those who shared in winning America's independence, says Wright, "only Washington moves as completely just and completely trustworthy, infinitely patient, inflexibly determined, always seeing the war as a whole and embodying its purposes." He was, as it was said at the time, truly, "the Atlas of America."

BIBLIOGRAPHY

In the past fifteen years a number of general military histories of the Revolution have appeared. All the following, which have full bibliographies, are recommended: John R. Alden, *The American Revolution* (1954; pb.); Douglas S. Freeman, Vols. III–V, *George Washington* (7 vols., 1948–1957); John C. Miller, *Triumph of Freedom, 1775–1783* (1948); Lynn Montross, *Rag, Tag, and Bobtail* (1952); Richard B. Morris' condensation of George O. Trevelyan's four-volume history of *The American Revolution* (1909–1912; 1964); Howard H. Peckham, *The War for Independence* (1958; pb.); Hugh F. Rankin, *The American Revolution* (1964); George F. Scheer and Hugh F. Rankin, *Rebels and Redcoats* (1957; pb.); Willard M. Wallace, *Appeal to Arms* (1951; pb.); and Christopher Ward, edited by J. R. Alden, *War of the Revolution* (2 vols., 1952). A recent and engrossing account from the British viewpoint is Piers Mackesy, *The War for America, 1775–1783* (1964). Paul H. Smith's *Loyalists and Redcoats: A Study in*

THE COLONIAL EXPERIENCE

British Revolutionary Policy (1964) discusses British plans to use loyalists in the war. All these and other military works on the Revolution must apparently be used with a certain amount of caution. Casualty figures vary drastically from book to book and often the simplest fact—for instance, the date the British entered Philadelphia in 1777—will produce a variety of answers: "A path to Philadelphia was thus opened, and the British entered the city on September 25" (Alden, *American Revolution*, p. 124). "It [Congress] adjourned to York, and Howe entered the capital [Philadelphia] on September 26" (Peckham, *War for Independence*, p. 71). "Howe's advance units entered the city on 27th September" (Esmond Wright, *George Washington*, p. 118 of pb. edition).

Once again a mountain of source material confronts the student. The best of it has been mined for popular consumption by Scheer and Rankin for their *Rebels and Redcoats*. A fuller collection is found in Henry S. Commager and Richard B. Morris, eds., *The Spirit of Seventy-Six* (2 vols., 1958). Among the best account by American soldiers are Alexander Graydon, *Memoirs of His Own Time* (1811); Joseph Martin, *A Narrative of Some of the Adventures, Dangers, and Sufferings of a Revolutionary Soldier* (1830); Albigence Waldo, "Valley Forge, 1771–1778 Diary," *PMHB*, 21 (1897), 299–323; and James Collins, *Autobiography of a Revolutionary Soldier* (1889). British soldiers have left an even fuller record: E. H. Tatum, Jr., ed., *The American Journal of Ambrose Serle: Secretary to Lord Howe, 1776–1778* (1940); *The Diary of Frederick Mackenzie* (2 vols., 1930); E. Robson, editor of Sir James Murray's *Letters from America, 1773–1780* (1951); E. A. Benians, ed., *A Journal of Thomas Hughes, 1778–1789* (1947); G. D. Scull, ed., *Memoirs and Letters of William Glanville Evelyn, 4th Foot, 1774–1776* (1897); and *R. Lamb: Memoir of His Own Life* (1811), a fictionalized version of which exists in Robert Graves's *Sargeant Lamb and America* (1941; pb.).

The fullest record left by American commanders is found in J. C. Fitzpatrick's edition of *The Writings of George Washington* (39 vols., 1931–1944), and *The Charles Lee Papers* (4 vols., 1871–1874), published by the New-York Historical Society. George Rogers Clark's papers were edited by James A. James for the Illinois Historical Society (Vol. 8, 1912; Vol. 19, 1926). For Hamilton's journal see J. D. Barnhart, ed., *Henry Hamilton and George Rogers Clark in the American Revolution* (1951). The British leaders' story is given in C. E. Carter, *The Correspondence of General Thomas Gage, 1763–1775* (2 vols., 1931–1933); and William B. Willcox' edition of Sir Henry Clinton's story in *The American Rebellion* (1954), which has recently been supplemented by Willcox' distinguished *Portrait of a General: Sir Henry Clinton in the War of Independence* (1964). Bernard A. Uhlendorf has edited the Baurmeister letters, which give the story from the viewpoint of German mercenaries, in *Revolution in America* (1957). And a graphic report of a Hessian version of the war is printed in Margaret Woelfel's translation of "Memoirs of a Hessian Conscript: J. G. Seume's Reluctant Voyage to America," *WMQ*, 5 (1948), 553–570.

Trying Times: 1775–1777

The early pages of Walter Millis, *Arms and Men: A Study in American Military History* (1956; pb.), presents a lively account of the democratization of war during the Revolution. Edward E. Curtis, *The Organization of the British Army in the American Revolution* (1926), is still basic reading for any understanding of its subject. Alan Valentine's *Lord George Germain* (1962) is the first full biography of the man who was Britain's Secretary of War from 1775 to 1782, but as Ira Gruber remarked in a review, "experts will find little of value" in it and "amateurs should not be allowed near it." Gerald S. Brown's carefully researched *The American Secretary: The Colonial Policy of Lord George Germain, 1775–1778* (1963) offers an excellent antidote to Valentine's work, though it covers only half of Germain's years in office. The New England story is fully told in Allen French, *The Day of Lexington and Concord* (1925), and *The First Year of the American Revolution* (1934); also in John R. Alden's sympathetic study of *General Gage in America* (1948).

The best general accounts of the Canadian campaigns are in George M. Wrong, *Canada and the American Revolution* (1935); and French, *First Year of the American Revolution*. No one has yet replaced Justin H. Smith's *Our Struggle for the Fourteenth Colony* (2 vols., 1907) nor his *Arnold's March from Cambridge to Quebec* (1903). The knowing accept Kenneth Roberts' novel *Rabble in Arms* (1933; pb.) as accurate and immeasurably more trustworthy than his *Northwest Passage* (1937; pb.).

The New York and New Jersey campaigns are recounted in several works, all good history: Alfred H. Bill, *The Campaign of Princeton, 1776–1777* (1940); Bruce Bliven, Jr., *The Battle for Manhattan* (1956; pb.); H. P. Johnston, *The Campaign of 1776 Around New York and Brooklyn* (1878); Leonard H. Lundin, *Cockpit of the Revolution* (1940); and William S. Stryker, *The Battles of Trenton and Princeton* (1898). Troyer S. Anderson's *Command of the Howe Brothers During the American Revolution* (1936) is an able study of these and later campaigns from the British point of view. A distinguished example of local history is Adrian C. Leiby, *The Revolutionary War in the Hackensack Valley: The Jersey Dutch and the Neutral Ground, 1775–1783* (1962).

Robert A. East, *Business Enterprise in the American Revolutionary Era* (1938), is the basic volume on the economic side of life on the home front. The first two chapters of Curtis P. Nettels, *The Emergence of a National Economy, 1775–1815* (1962), discuss the nation's wartime economy. Nettels' footnotes and elaborate bibliography give virtually all the material in print on the subject. The first volume of Joseph Dorfman's *The Economic Mind in American Civilization, 1606–1865* (1946) and Bray Hammond's *Banks and Politics in America* (1957) are important for understanding the financial aspects of the Revolution. Much of what these authors have to say has been amplified by E. James Ferguson, *The Power of the Purse: A History of American Public Finance, 1776–1790* (1961). Two excellent specialized studies, unfortunately not duplicated for other states, are Anne Bezanson, *Prices and Inflation During the American Revolution: Pennsylvania, 1770–1790* (1951), and an article by Oscar and Mary F. Handlin, "Revolutionary Economic Policy in Massachusetts," *WMQ*, 4 (1947), 3–26. See also Richard B. Morris, "Labor and Mercantilism in the Revolutionary Era," in Richard B. Morris, ed., *The Era of the American Revolution: Studies Ascribed to Evarts Boutelle Greene* (1939), 76–139.

The first, and still basic, study of those who opposed the Revolution is Claude H. Van Tyne, *Loyalists in the American Revolution* (1901), which has recently been updated but not replaced by William H. Nelson, *The American Tory* (1961; pb.). R. R. Palmer's *Age of the Democratic Revolution* (1959) should not be overlooked for it has relevant remarks on the loyalists. All those volumes mentioned in the second section of the Chapter 14 Bibliography, dealing with the affairs of particular states during the Revolution, discuss at varying length the loyalist problem. But several other works deal with it in detail, among them: Alexander C. Flick, *Loyalism in New York During the American Revolution* (1901); Ruth M. Keesey, "Loyalism in Bergen County, New Jersey," *WMQ*, 18 (1961), 558–576; Wilbur H. Siebert, *Loyalists in Pennsylvania* (1920); Isaac S. Harrell, *Loyalism in Virginia . . .* (1926); Robert O. DeMond, *Loyalists in North Carolina During the Revolution* (1940); and Robert S. Lambert, "The Confiscation of Loyalist Property in Georgia, 1782–1786," *WMQ*, 20 (1963), 80–94. Leonard W. Labaree's essay, "The Nature of American Loyalism," *Proceedings of the American Antiquarian Society*, 54 (1944), 15–58, and the relevant chapter in his *Conservatism in Early American History* (1948; pb.) must be read by anyone interested in the subject. The dilemmas of various loyalists have been described with sympathy in a number of short sketches: Lewis Einstein, *Divided Loyalties* (1933); Catherine Fennelly, "William Franklin of New Jersey," *WMQ*, 6 (1949), 361–382; Ernest H. Baldwin, "Joseph Galloway: The Loyalist Politician," *PMHB*, 26 (1902), 161–191, 289–321, 417–442; and John E. Alden, "John Mein: Scourge of Patriots," *Colonial Society of Massachusetts Publications*, 34 (1942), 571–599. H. Egerton has edited *The Royal Commission on the Losses and Services of the American Loyalists, 1783–1785* (1915). Jonathan Boucher left an autobiography, published as *Reminiscences of an American Loyalist, 1738–1789* (1925). A more moving account is that of Samuel Curwen in his *Journal and Letters* (1842), most of which deals with his experiences in England

The Turning Point: 1777–1778

Troyer S. Anderson's *Command of the Howe Brothers* is again relevant. Hoffman Nickerson, *The Turning Point of the Revolution* (1928), discusses the events of these years in detail. Samuel D. Patterson, *Horatio Gates* (1941), presents the general in a warm light and in the process gives a full account of the battle of Saratoga. The account of Thomas Anburey, a British lieutenant, has recently been reprinted by Sydney W. Jackman, ed., *With Burgoyne from*

Quebec: An Account of the Life at Quebec and of the Famous Battle at Saratoga (1964). The story of Saratoga from a woman's view is told in lively fashion in Marvin L. Brown, ed., *Baroness von Riedesel and the American Revolution: Journal and Correspondence of a Tour of Duty, 1776–1783* (1965). Alfred H. Bill, *Valley Forge: The Making of an Army* (1952), supersedes all other accounts; the bibliography will lead students to further material. A summary of the Conway Cabal is found in the fourth volume of Freeman's *George Washington,* but the fullest report and the first to explode the "cabal" theory is Bernhard Knollenberg, *Washington and the Revolution* (1940). The details of a pivotal battle, as far as General Lee was concerned, are found in William S. Stryker's and William S. Meyers' *The Battle of Monmouth* (1927) and in John R. Alden's *General Charles Lee: Traitor or Patriot?* (1951).

Samuel Flagg Bemis, *The Diplomacy of the American Revolution* (1935; pb.), remains the basic account of the French alliance and all other diplomatic events of the Revolution. It can be supplemented by Carl Van Doren's *Franklin* (1938; pb.) and Verner W. Crane's *Benjamin Franklin and a Rising People* (1954; pb.). For further details on the French alliance, see E. S. Corwin, *French Policy and the American Alliance of 1778* (1916). A revised view has recently been advanced by Alexander DeConde in *Entangling Alliance* (1958). For source material the student must turn to Francis Wharton, ed., *The Diplomatic Correspondence of the American Revolution* (6 vols., 1889). The Carlisle Commission is fully discussed in Weldon A. Brown's *Empire or Independence* (1941) and more fully still in Alan S. Brown's "The British Peace Offer of 1778," *Papers of the Michigan Academy of Science, Arts, and Letters,* 40 (1955), 249–260 and in William B. Willcox' "British Strategy in America, 1778," *Journal of Modern History,* 19 (1947), 97–121.

Victory: 1778–1783

A sudden interest in military history has recently led to several studies of the men on Washington's staff. Theodore Thayer's *Nathanael Greene: Strategist of the American Revolution* (1960) deals competently with the man many consider the ablest person on the American side—Washington excepted, of course. A fuller study that gives less attention to Greene personally is M. F. Treacy, *Prelude to Yorktown: The Southern Campaign of Nathanael Greene, 1780–1781* (1963). Don Higginbotham's *Daniel Morgan: Revolutionary Rifleman* (1961) centers on the man, with special attention to his post-Revolutionary career; North Callahan's *Daniel Morgan: Ranger of the Revolution* (1961) seeks to put the general in the context of his time and concentrates on his wartime record. The mixed career of *A General of the Revolution: John Sullivan of New Hampshire* (1961) has been covered by Charles P. Whittemore. George Athan Billias, ed., *George Washington's Generals* (1964), is a collection of authoritative essays.

The second British invasion of the South and the second failure of D'Estaing are discussed in Alexander A. Lawrence, *Storm over Savannah*

(1951), and in less detail by Ward in *War of the Revolution*. George Rogers Clark's exploits are covered by Milo M. Quaife in *The Capture of Old Vincennes* (1927), and in John Bakeless, *Background to Glory: The Life of George Rogers Clark* (1957). The New York frontier raids are described with vigor and sometimes questionable detail in Howard Swiggett, *War out of Niagara* (1933).

A naval history of the Revolution remains to be written. Meanwhile, for the casual student, the most satisfactory work is Gardner W. Allen, *A Naval History of the American Revolution* (2 vols., 1913). Edgar S. Maclay, *The History of American Privateers* (1899), is built on a solid foundation of source material. Gerald W. Johnson, *The First Captain* (1947), has been superseded by Samuel Eliot Morison, *John Paul Jones* (1961; pb.), well-written but heavy on nautical lingo. Harold A. Larrabee's account of the most decisive naval engagement in American history, the Battle of the Virginia Capes, can be found in *Decision at the Chesapeake* (1964).

Arnold's treason forms a large part of Carl Van Doren's *Secret History of the American Revolution* (1941) and the bulk of James T. Flexner's *The Traitor and the Spy* (1953) and of Willard M. Wallace's *Traitorous Hero* (1954). The best report of the rebellion within the American Army is Carl Van Doren, *Mutiny in January* (1943). One of the most detailed accounts of the Virginia campaign can be found in Louis Gottschalk, *Lafayette and the Close of the American Revolution* (1942). Thomas J. Fleming's *Beat the Last Drum: The Siege of Yorktown, 1781* (1963) offers a good, popular account. Much of the material in two excellent articles by William B. Willcox—"The British Road to Yorktown: A Study in Divided Command," *AHR*, 52 (1946), 1–35; and "Why Did the British Lose the American Revolution?" *Michigan Alumnus Quarterly Review*, 42 (1956), 317–334—has been incorporated in the author's recent biography of General Clinton.

In addition to Bemis' discussion of the peace negotiations, see also Herbert E. Klingelhofer, "Matthew Ridley's Diary During the Peace Negotiations of 1782," *WMQ*, 20 (1963), 95–133. Richard B. Morris, *The Peacemakers* (1965), is the fullest and most recent account of the history of the 1783 treaty.

For further references see the *Harvard Guide*, Sections 114, "From January 1775 Through the Declaration of Independence"; 115, "The Loyalists"; 116, "The War of Independence, 1776–1781"; 117, "International Aspects of the Revolutionary Era"; and 118, "Naval Warfare and the Yorktown Campaign, 1778–1782."

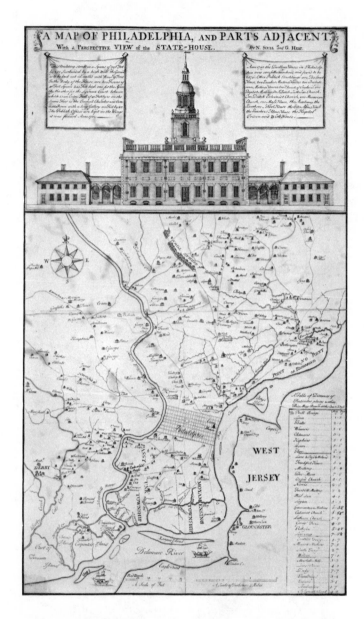

"Map of Philadelphia and Parts Adjacent, with a Perspective
View of the State House," drawn by N. Scull and G. Heap

16. An Age of Experiments: 1775–1788

PROBLEMS OF REVOLUTION
    "Governments of Our Own"
    The Articles of Confederation
    Was It a Real Revolution?

PROBLEMS OF PEACE
    The West
    The Economy
    Political Power

THE CONSTITUTION
    The Convention
    Ratification
    A New Beginning?

A few days after independence had been declared, a Pennsylvanian said, "We shall build *de novo*." For him a new age was about to dawn, one in which the past could be shunted aside; new governments would emerge, and with them a new society erected "upon the most just, rational and equal principles." John Adams dreaded such talk, and even before independence was declared, he sought to make certain the American Revolution did not become a real revolution. Adams agreed with those who previous to independence had said that "the suppression of all authority under the king of Great Britain, *are the only changes desired. . . .*" But the spirit of innovation was afloat. "We are, I think, in the right road of improvement, for we are making experiments," said Benjamin Franklin. "I do not oppose all that seem wrong, for the multitude are more effectually set right by experience, than kept from going wrong by reasoning with them."

PROBLEMS OF REVOLUTION

The great achievement of the American Revolution, Hannah Arendt has remarked, is that it "succeeded where all others were to fail, namely, in founding a new body politic stable enough to survive the onslaught of centuries to come." The achievement owes everything to those who led the colonies to independence. They saw from the start that the central problem of the Revolution was to erect stable governments within each state as well as one for all thirteen states. Effective governments were necessary to win the war. They might also help prevent a war for independence from becoming a real revolution.

"Governments of Our Own"

At a moment when it was obvious that Congress would soon declare America's independence, Jefferson was doing his best to be recalled from Philadelphia. Shortly after Congress had resolved on May 15 that the crown's authority in all colonies "should be totally suppressed," Jefferson told a friend he wished to join the convention then in the process of mapping out a new government for his "country" of Virginia. "In truth," he said, the new government "is the whole object of the present controversy; for should a bad government be instituted for us in the future it had been well to have accepted at first the bad one offered to us from beyond the water without the risk and expense of the contest."

By the end of 1777, ten states had adopted new constitutions or modified old ones—a feat of constitution-making that "remains unparalleled in the history of modern constitutionalism," Benjamin F. Wright has remarked, adding: "It was not an era of destruction; it was one of creativity." The new fundamental laws in theory drew their authority from the people, and most copied from the Virginia constitution the statement that "all power is vested in, and consequently derived from the people; that the magistrates are their trustees and servants, and at all times amenable to them." No one argued with that view. "The only moral foundation of government is the consent of the people," said John Adams. "But to what extent shall we carry this principle?" he asked, and on that question men divided. Jefferson, on the other hand, welcomed that spirit. He wanted to extend "the right of suffrage (or in other words the rights of a citizen) to all who had a permanent intention of living in the country." "Whoever intends to live in a country must wish that country well, and has a natural right of assisting in the preservation of it." To that end, he called for lowering property qualifications for suffrage and for liberal state grants to all who lacked the requisite amount of land.

Men disagreed, too, over the form the new governments should take.

Tom Paine in *Common Sense* had mapped out his views of the ideal government—one with a single legislature, an elected judiciary, and a weak executive. Paine's views had provoked John Adams into setting down his own *Thoughts on Government* (1776), wherein he argued that any new government should be as much like the old as possible—one, that is, similar to the Bay Colony's, with two houses that could check one another's excesses, with the upper house chosen by the lower, a reasonably strong executive, a strong judiciary appointed for good behavior, and the usual property qualifications for voters. Jefferson, on the other hand, wanted power to center in the lower house. The governor would be little more than an administrator, as Jefferson renamed the post, with no power to veto legislation and little control over appointments without the consent of the legislature.

Finally, men differed over who should draw up the new constitutions, and by whose authority they should be put into operation. Paine demanded a constitutional convention, for "a constitution is not the act of a government, but of a people constituting a government." Jefferson wanted the document ratified by all who could vote, otherwise he believed it would lack the consent of the governed. Paine's and Jefferson's views were ignored except in Pennsylvania, the single state in 1776 to call a constitutional convention, and even there the document was not submitted to the voters for ratification. Elsewhere, the revolutionary governments drafted and proclaimed the new fundamental laws, though six, it is true, did so only after receiving specific authority from the people to do so.

The early constitutions were made hastily but not heedlessly. "You know that experimental philosophy was in great repute fifty years ago," a Pennsylvanian told a friend, "and we have a mind to try how the same principle will succeed in politics." But even in Pennsylvania, whose constitution was considered the most radical of the day, experiments were few. It was generally agreed that the old governments had worked well except when the king had tinkered with the machinery, and the new fundamental laws for the most part did little more than codify past practices. None of the first constitutions, for instance, provided for the legislative, judicial, and executive branches to check and balance one another, for everywhere prior to the Revolution the legislature had come to dominate provincial affairs, and it was this fact of political life, rather than a "checks and balances" theory, that found its way into the new fundamental laws. Power of the purse remained with the legislatures in every instance. They retained the right to make their own rules, choose their own officers, and only in New York did the governor have a say in when they should convene. All the governors' major appointments required the legislatures' "advice and consent." They had chipped away at the governors' power throughout the eighteenth century, and the new constitutions in every instance but one (New York) completed the process. The governor lost the absolute veto in all states, and even in New York his veto could be overridden by the legislature. He was elected everywhere but in New York by the legislatures. A long-standing tradition of annual elections for all legislators became part of nine of the new constitutions (South Carolina's called for elections every two years), on the assumption that "the oftener power returns into the hands of the people the better." The "stake in society" concept, which called for a man to own property to vote and even more property to hold office, remained intact in most of the new constitutions. The confident creators of these documents assumed that, like the charters issued by the king, their handiwork would last forever unchanged. No constitution provided for amendment, except Delaware's, which appears to have retrieved the concept from Penn's Frame of Government of 1683.

The striking resemblance to what had gone before should not obscure the few cautious experiments made. Pennsylvania dared to eliminate the office of governor and substitute a twelve-man council in its stead. Pennsylvania sought, as a handbill of the day put it, to "keep the legislative and executive authority forever separate" by having both branches elected by the people. New York followed suit in 1777 by providing for the popular election of its governor. Pennsylvania, North Carolina, and Georgia gave the right to vote for legislators to all white male taxpayers, regardless of the property they owned. Those states whose western counties were underrepresented in the legislature made an effort to redress the wrong. Every state, following a pattern set by Virginia's constitution of 1776, included a bill of rights, which promised among other things protection of life, liberty, and property; freedom of worship, speech, and assembly; and for the accused the right to fair bail, prompt hearings, and trial by jury.

These mild and hesitant experiments underscore the moderate spirit behind the constitutions written in 1776–1777. None made a sharp break with the political traditions of the state for which it was designed. All in various ways, Benjamin Wright has observed, "give evidence of a sceptical view of human nature, of a distrust of popularly elected legislative and executive agents." Forms and procedures that have come to be considered characteristic of American politics—the constitutional convention, popular ratification, separation of powers, popular election of the governor, provision for amendment—crop up somewhere in the ten new constitutions but are concentrated in no single one. Massachusetts' constitution of 1780, which has generally been judged a moderate, if not reactionary, document, was, in fact, the first to make a sharp break with the past.

Massachusetts' first attempt at a constitution offered little more than a revival of the charter of 1691. It was submitted to the people for ratification and rejected by them in 1778. Two years later, the voters chose delegates for a convention whose sole job was to design a new constitution, and with the understanding that it would not go into operation until ratified by the free adult males of the state. John Adams was the major architect of the new document. His skepticism about human nature led him to resist the trend to concentrate power in a single branch of the government. Neither the rich nor the poor, the legislature nor the executive, would dominate. His senate was designed to represent the propertied or aristocratic interests, his house of representatives the people. Both houses as well as the governor were to be elected by the people to assure their independence from one another. The governor received broad powers of appointment of state officials and as a check upon the legislature he had the right to veto bills. Adams wanted to give the governor an absolute veto, such as the king had, but the convention refused to go that far. The convention made a further, more momentous alteration in Adams' draft. Where he had written in the preamble "We, therefore, the delegates . . . ," the delegates substituted "We, therefore, the people of Massachusetts . . . agree, ordain and establish." Previous constitutions had assumed that sovereignty lay with the people, but here the theory was stated for the first time, and much as it would appear in the Constitution of 1787.

John Adams attempted in the constitution of 1780 to reproduce for his state an Americanized version of the British government as he understood it. He favored a system of government somewhat alien to contemporary American beliefs. For those who objected to his effort to create a strong executive and a government whose branches checked and balanced one another, he might have turned for his defense to the one man whose political philosophy he distrusted above all others, Tom Paine. "To object against the present constitution because it is a *novelty,* is to give one of the best indirect reasons for trying it," Paine had said to the people of Pennsylvania in 1778. "We are a people upon experiments and though under one continental government, have the happy opportunity of trying variety in order to discover the best."

The Articles of Confederation

At the time Jefferson's committee was selected to prepare the Declaration of Independence, another committee headed by John Dickinson was chosen to draw up a constitution for the new nation. Congress spent two days editing Jefferson's Declaration; it argued for over a year before approving an emasculated version of Dickinson's constitution on November

15, 1777. Four more years passed before the thirteen states approved a document that in effect gave no more power to Congress than the colonies had been willing to give to Parliament.

No one during this dreary four-year period questioned the need for a union of the states. "Unite or die," Franklin had said, and all Congress had agreed. There was a war to be won, and only a united states could win it. A common heritage helped pull the states together to beat back a common enemy, but once the enemy had vanished, the desperate need for union went, too, and the arguments against it seemed certain to prevail. The land, for one thing, hindered union. Montesquieu held—and those, like Jefferson, who had read *The Spirit of Laws* shared his view—that a large territory could not be successfully organized as a republic, that only a tyrannical government could efficiently administer a vast expanse of land. The colonial experience with Great Britain during the past decade seemed to justify this view. Another block to a union of the thirteen disparate states stemmed from the lack of a strong sense of national feeling among the people. Patrick Henry told Congress he was not a Virginian but an American, then went home to govern his state pretty much as an independent country. Christopher Gadsden in 1765 had said, "there ought to be no New England man, no New Yorker, known on the continent, but all of us Americans," but in 1776 Gadsden made it clear that he wanted no national constitution that whittled away at the sovereignty of his "country" of South Carolina.

Sectional and state rivalries also helped to promote disunion. In the midst of the Revolution, Virginia and Pennsylvania argued warmly over the ownership of land around the forks of the Ohio. Connecticut and Pennsylvania relaxed their effort against Britain to battle it out with each other in the Wyoming Valley. The large states bickered with the small states, who insisted that despite their slight size they should have an equal vote in all decisions made by a national government. Those states whose charters gave them claims to Western lands found themselves at odds with states that lacked such claims. States with large numbers of slaves found themselves defending their "peculiar institution" against the North. Southern ways—the indulgent Sunday, the aristocratic manners— horrified New Englanders, and the "leveling" principles of New England distressed Southerners, who were heard to say that a union of the states might lead to all America being flooded by the democratic tendencies of New England.

Obviously, the barriers to a strong political union were in 1776 too high to surmount. The insuperable odds did not deter John Dickinson, who was convinced that the United States could neither win the war nor survive the peace if they—no one in 1776, not even Dickinson, referred to the United States in the singular—lacked a strong central government. The constitution he drew up for the new nation and pushed through his committee called for a union of the states stronger than the one Great Britain had tried to impose on her colonies. It provided for a national judiciary. Congress could declare war and make peace, establish a national currency, maintain an army and navy, conduct foreign affairs, borrow money, regulate commerce, and control Indian affairs. Its decisions would be the supreme law of the land. States that claimed lands west of the Appalachians would turn those claims over to the national government.

Dickinson's draft of the Articles of Confederation, as the constitution was called, actually did little more than crystallize an informal arrangement that had taken shape since 1774. A close look shows that, like the authors of the state constitutions of 1776–1777, he indulged in few experiments. He gave great power to Congress, but nothing that Congress had not assumed in 1776, and left the crucial power to tax where it was—with the states. He catered to the mood for a weak executive by assigning those duties to Congress itself. Delegates were to be chosen annually, as legislators were in the states. He side-stepped, or thought he did, argument over voting procedure by leaving it as it was; each state's vote would count as one. A requirement of unanimous approval for any change in the fundamental law virtually eliminated the chance for amendments. The risks involved in popular ratification were avoided: only the approval of the thirteen state legislatures was needed to put the constitution into operation.

Dickinson's conciliatory efforts were in vain. "If the plan now proposed should be adopted, nothing less than ruin to some colonies will be the consequence of it," said Edward Rutledge, who represented South Carolina on the drafting committee. "I am resolved to vest the Congress with no more power than what is absolutely necessary, and to use a familiar expression, to keep the staff in our own hands." Congress' reception of the document reflected Rutledge's distaste, for Congress, like Rutledge, was bound to object to any attempt to form a national government. The delegates' thoughts were oriented toward their states. All were experienced politicians on the local level, and except for Franklin none until recently had shared in the problems of administering the American empire. The job of creating a fundamental law for the new nation revived all the old divisive forces that had lain dormant while Congress armed the nation for war. Although the first Congress had been nearly ripped apart by the debate over the procedure for voting, it had been agreed that as a temporary expedient all states, large and small, would have a single vote. The large states had gone along with that decision to preserve harmony, but now that Dickinson sought to formalize forever what had been considered temporary they raised a furor.

The clamor over voting initiated a debate about the Articles that lasted through 1776 and well into 1777. North and South split over the method for assessing a state's contribution to the central government. The South preferred to use population as the basis, as long as its large slave population was not counted; the North objected. The seven states with Western land claims—Massachusetts, Connecticut, Virginia, the Carolinas, and Georgia on the basis of their "sea to sea" charters, and New York on the thin assumption that lordship over the Iroquois gave it a right to the lands claimed by the Indians—split with the six whose borders were limited. Each of the three sections of the nation—New England, the Middle States, and the South—feared that if only a simple majority vote were needed to pass legislation, something might be pushed through to injure its welfare. And there was strong resistance by some individuals to the idea of a national judiciary.

By November 1777, Congress had fought its way through to a series of compromises that resulted in a draft it felt could be sent to the states for ratification. Article 2 in Dickinson's draft had dealt with the specter of civil war by stating that "the said colonies unite themselves so as never to be divided by any act what ever." The new Article 2 read: "Each state retains its sovereignty, freedom, and independence, and every power, jurisdiction, and right, which is not by this Confederation expressly delegated to the United States, in Congress assembled." Article 3 stated that the states (not the people) "hereby severally enter into a firm league of friendship," thus underscoring the fact that a league of nations rather than a single nation was being created by the constitution. All power in the central government would center in Congress, for the judiciary and even a semblance of an executive had been eliminated. All important legislation needed a two-thirds majority to pass, a condition that gave each section the power to veto anything that affected its welfare. No state's Western land claims were disallowed. The Articles gave Congress "the sole and exclusive right and power" to regulate foreign affairs, initiate war and declare peace, fix weights and measures, control Indian affairs, and establish a post office. It had no power to regulate interstate commerce nor to levy taxes of any kind.

Clearly, the success of the Confederation would depend on the good will of the states toward the central government, but given the time and situation, this was understandable. Americans were fighting against a strong central government that regulated their commerce and currency, that imposed upon them officials bound by instructions devised by other officials across the sea, that disallowed laws passed by their own legislatures, that taxed them with imposts, duties, and stamps without their consent. Why, then, while in the midst of eliminating one strong central government, should they be expected to raise up another in its place? The Articles of Confederation, as Merrill Jensen was the first to insist, reflected the colonial experience. This first national constitution, like the state constitutions of 1776–1777, was "a natural outcome of the revolutionary movement within the American colonies."

Congress expected the revised constitution to win quick approval from the states. Instead, it wandered about the nation for four years before the necessary unanimous approval was obtained. Maryland, speaking for the six states with fixed boundaries, refused to sign until the seven landed states renounced their Western-land claims. Maryland argued that because the war was a common effort, all unsettled land west of the mountains should be "considered as common property, subject to be parcelled by Congress into free, convenient, and independent governments." The point was also made that the conflicting state claims in the tramontane territory would only lead to conflict among the states. Speculators throughout the nation who had bought land in the Western territory joined Maryland in urging Congressional control of the area; they felt their claims would fare better at the hands of Congress than with the various state legislatures that would otherwise control the territory. Near the end of 1779, Congress assured the nation that any "unappropriated lands that may be ceded or relinquished to the United States, by any particular state, . . . shall be disposed of for the common benefit of the United States and be settled and formed into distinct Republican states, which shall become members of the federal union. . . ." A short while later, New York, then Virginia, broke the deadlock by relinquishing their Western claims, and with Maryland's acceptance in 1781, the Articles of Confederation officially became the constitution of the new nation.

The Articles had hardly been ratified before men began to talk about the flaws. An author who signed himself "The Continentalist" warned in 1781 that any hope for "a great Federal Republic, closely linked in the pursuit of a common interest," lacked a chance of success unless Congress' powers were greatly increased. Catastrophe for America was certain unless a constitutional convention was called at once to strengthen the central government, said "The Continentalist," whose real name was Alexander Hamilton.

Was It a Real Revolution?

Most of the leaders of 1776 sought to conserve the past rather than change the present. They wanted to restore the old order that the king's reforms had undermined rather than create something new, for they realized that even under British rule Americans had been as "fortunate and satisfied a people as any the world had known." The people seemed to sense this,

Map 41. Cessions of Western Lands

Ceded lands

too, for no internal upheaval occurred in the new nation, either during or after the war. The common man did not take over governments, nor did the backcountry demand a dominant voice in political affairs. The people's ideas about government remained "rather aristocratical than popular," an anonymous citizen of New Jersey remarked. "The rich having been used to govern, seem to think it their right," he added, and the poor, "having hitherto had little or no hand in government, seem to think it does not belong to them to have any."

Tangible evidences of revolutionary changes are not easy to turn up, for it was more the tone of society than society itself that altered. The nation slipped quietly and cautiously into an experimental mood. The divorce rate, for example, increased unobtrusively—in one Connecticut county, from less than one a year prior to 1767 to over five a year in the decade after the Revolution. Reverend Devereux Jarratt, the son of a small-time farmer, had been reared in Virginia when the "difference between *gentle* and *simple*" folk was "universal among all of my rank and age." He grieved "to see a vast alteration in this respect, and the contrary extreme prevail." Old courtesies that had ruled prewar Virginia dropped away; men no longer knew their place. "There is more *leveling* than ought to be," Jarratt remarked, as he observed the shocking tendency to take literally those words in the Declaration of Independence that all men were created equal. The restraints that had once ordered society seemed to be eroding.

The American Revolution may have sought to conserve what already existed, but as Robert R. Palmer has pointed out, no event that led to the migration from America of some one hundred thousand of the "better sort" of people, to use a phrase of the day, can be called a "conservative" movement. In the French Revolution, which no one doubts was a real revolution, there were five *émigrés* per thousand people; in the American Revolution, there were twenty-four *émigrés* per thousand. A majority of the French eventually returned home to revive the aristocratic order; hardly any of those who left America returned after the war. "The sense in which there was no conflict in the American Revolution," says Palmer, "is the sense in which the loyalists are forgotten." The exodus of the contrary-minded, most of whom admired and desired the aristocratic society of England, forever eliminated in America any chance for the establishment of a true hereditary aristocracy.

The absence of any large body dissenting to the ideals behind the American Revolution made it easier to reduce a good part of those abstractions to practice. A Congressional plan to give Revolutionary officers five years' extra pay failed to pass because some said it favored one class against another. The Society of the Cincinnati, whose members were limited to army officers and who were allowed to pass their membership on to their descendants, was censured as an attempt to establish a hereditary aristocracy.

Those who sought to reduce the upper class also worked to raise the status of the deprived, though here the humanitarian instinct of prewar America as much as the leveling instinct was at work. Arguments were aired against the evils of indentured servitude; the practice flourished well into the nineteenth century but on a steadily diminishing scale. A repugnance against slavery spread from the Quakers, who alone up to now had preached against it, into other denominations. Ezra Stiles, a minister in Newport at the outbreak of the Revolution, exemplified the new attitude. Stiles had felt no uneasiness about the slaves he owned until it occurred to him that if it were wrong for the British to enslave Americans, then it must be equally wrong for Americans to enslave Africans. The thought impelled him, as it did others throughout the North and occasionally in the South, to free his Negroes. On the whole, however, the number of manumissions were few. More notable was the changed attitude toward slavery. America at large for the first time revealed feelings of guilt about its "peculiar institution." By the end of the Revolution, all states but Georgia and South Carolina had legislated against the slave trade. The self-created territory of Vermont abolished slavery outright in 1777, and three other Northern states soon after voted for the gradual abolition of the institution.

Several other experimental projects died on the air. The desire for more moderate treatment and punishment of criminals was frustrated in every state until Pennsylvania came up with a revised criminal code in 1794. Imprisonment for debt remained on the law books of all states until well into the nineteenth century. The effort to redistribute the confiscated lands of departed loyalists to the landless was, as far as can be gathered from available statistics, largely ineffectual. Five of the state constitutions called for the government to be responsible for public education, but none of the states at the end of the eighteenth century had done anything to implement that sentiment. The number of town-supported schools diminished steadily throughout New England after the war, largely because the towns considered themselves too burdened with taxes to keep them going. Everywhere in the new nation the private academy, its curriculum a blend of useful and classical subjects, became the central institution for secondary education. The utility of Latin and Greek were ridiculed—a young country needs "the useful, the mechanic arts," John Adams reiterated—but a sound training in the classics continued a requisite for entrance into any college.

During and after the Revolution men sought to cleanse the land of that part of the British heritage that failed to fit the American experience.

Primogeniture and entail, which by custom had fallen into disuse except when a man died intestate, were legally abolished everywhere. Quitrents, which had long ago become almost impossible to enforce—even in Pennsylvania and Maryland, where the proprietors did their best to collect them— were written off the books. Though these relics of feudal Europe had ceased to be a living part of the American tradition, they symbolized a past the new nation wished to disown. The same held true for the established Anglican Church, which by the end of the war had been disestablished throughout the South. The effort to separate church and state, however, made halting progress. The Congregational Church remained established throughout most of New England. Religious liberty—the right to be free *from* religion as well as *to* worship as one pleased—existed nowhere in America. All states required a religious oath of some sort for elected officials, and it was not until 1786, when the Virginia legislature passed Jefferson's bill for religious freedom, that a break with the past came. The slow progress on this front no doubt owed much to the widespread conviction that the war had "unhinged the principles, the morality, and the religion of this country more than could have been done by a peace of forty years," a view that invigorated the devouts' efforts to use the state to revive the godly habits of the past.

"Our nation was the child, not the father, of our revolution," Edmund Morgan has said. The ingredients for a nation had long been present, but it took the Revolution to force them into the open. Soon after the war ended, for example, those religious denominations linked to Europe—the Anglicans, Lutherans, Dutch Reformed, and Methodists—set about cutting their ties and erecting ecclesiastical structures rooted in the American soil. (Those that refused to be Americanized—the Mennonites, Moravians, and other German-speaking denominations—ceased to expand and are today little larger than they were in the eighteenth century.) Noah Webster set out to make America "as independent and illustrious in letters as she is already in arms and civil policy," and to that end he worked to supplant the English with the American language. (It is through Webster's doing that the "u" was dropped from such words as "labour" and "honour" and that such Anglicisms as "gaol" became "jail.") A visiting Frenchman, who was told he spoke "good American," heard that some people wanted Hebrew to replace English as the national language; and though he knew nothing would come of the plan, he said, "we may readily conclude from the mere suggestion that the Americans could not express in a more energetic manner their aversion for the English."

"There is nothing more common, than to confound the term of *American revolution* with those of the late *American war*," Benjamin Rush remarked in 1787. "The American war is over; but this is far from being the case with the *American Revolution*. On the contrary, nothing

but the first act of the great drama is closed. It remains yet to establish
and perfect our new forms of government."

PROBLEMS OF PEACE

College debating societies like to "talk up a storm" over matters of contemporary concern. The topics assigned to the students at Yale suggest
some of the issues agitating the new nation during the Confederation
period. Among them were these:

> *December 26, 1780: whether Vermont is, and of right ought to be a sep-*
> *arate and independent state.*
>
> *April 16, 1782: whether agriculture or commerce needs the most en-*
> *couragement in the United States at present.*
>
> *March 24, 1783: whether a standing army would be dangerous in*
> *America.*
>
> *April 28, 1783: whether it would be best to establish a general amnesty*
> *and restore the refugee Tories to their estates and franchises.*
>
> *June 9, 1783: whether the army at disbanding have any just right to*
> *either half pay for life, or the commutation of five years.*
>
> *December 15, 1783: whether Congress ought to have more power and*
> *authority.*
>
> *April 19, 1784: whether the Institution of Cincinnati will prove detri-*
> *mental to the public.*
>
> *March 20, 1786: whether depreciation ought in justice to be paid on the*
> *public securities.*
>
> *June 8, 1786: whether paper money is a benefit.*
>
> *February 20, 1787: whether the insurrection in the Massachusetts be*
> *justifiable.*
>
> *June 19, 1787: whether the states acted wisely in sending delegates to*
> *the general convention now sitting at Philadelphia.*
>
> *November 26, 1787: whether it is expedient for the states to adopt the*
> *new Constitution.*

Some of the topics—the dangers of a standing army, the virtues of paper
money—were ones Americans had argued about for more than half a century, but the majority posed new problems that required swift resolutions
if the new nation hoped to survive in a world of competing empires, none
of which really wished it well.

The West

Virginia's cession in 1781 of her claim to territory west of the mountains
arrived with so many restrictions tied to it that Congress felt forced to

reject it, and not until March 1784, when the land was turned over without strings attached, was the gift finally accepted. Congress proceeded at once to draw up rules for settlement of the Northwest Territory. Jefferson was the principal architect of the ordinance that Congress approved on April 23, 1784. Jefferson's plan carved the territory into ten approximately equal districts and allowed the settlers within each district immediately to erect their own governments, taking their laws from whatever state they wished. When a district's population reached twenty thousand, it could hold a convention, adopt a constitution, and send a delegate to Congress. When its population matched that of the smallest state, it was to be admitted as an equal into the union. Congress made only two important changes in Jefferson's plan. It dropped his prohibition of slavery in the territory and added a provision that forbade the new government to tax or dispose of federal lands within their jurisdictions.

Congress' gift of self-government was soon followed by the Land Ordinance of 1785, which sought the impossible—to impose a pattern of orderly settlement on the wilderness. The Northwest Territory was to be surveyed into ranges six miles wide. These were to be divided into townships six miles square, and the townships were to be further subdivided into thirty-six sections, each a square mile (640 acres) in size. Four sections within the township were to be reserved for the United States and one for the support of public schools. As the ranges were surveyed, the land would be sold at public auctions held in the East; it had to go in blocks of 640 acres, and bidding would begin at a dollar an acre. This orderly scheme resembled Shelburne's plans for settling the West, for Congress, like Great Britain in 1763, hoped to limit settlement to specific areas and to allow its advance westward only at a controlled pace.

The sale of public lands reversed one of the oldest of American traditions. The colonies in order to attract settlers had given away unclaimed public land, or, at most, charged only nominal prices. It was held that the rigors of opening up new territory—clearing and cultivating the land and fending off Indians, French, and in some cases Spanish intruders—sufficed for payment and that the gains from an increased and productive population more than outweighed any income from land sales. Moreover, settlers who could not afford to pay for their land, as most could not, would simply take or squat on it and dare the ineffective government to eject them. Congress knew all this in 1785, but the exigencies of the moment forced it to ignore the American experience. The new nation lacked the power to tax, and as the debts from the war and the interest on those debts piled up, it had become desperate for funds. The regulated sale of the national domain offered the single hope left for a steady income for the government.

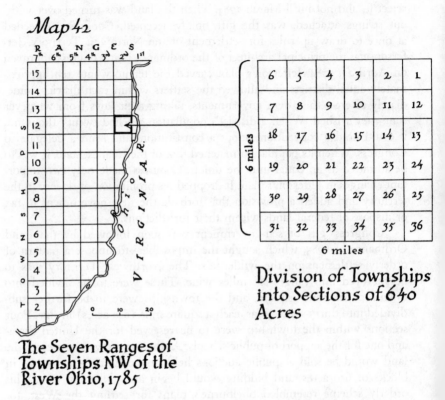

Map 42

R A N G E S
7th 6th 5th 4th 3rd 2nd 1st

6 miles

6	5	4	3	2	1
7	8	9	10	11	12
18	17	16	15	14	13
19	20	21	22	23	24
30	29	28	27	26	25
31	32	33	34	35	36

6 miles

Division of Townships into Sections of 640 Acres

The Seven Ranges of Townships NW of the River Ohio, 1785

Surveys got underway at once, and by 1787 several ranges, the first of which began at Pennsylvania's western border, had been laid out. Before land sales began, a group of New England ex-army officers who had organized themselves into the Ohio Company offered Congress $1 million to disregard the Land Ordinance of 1785 and give their group a large chunk of the national domain. Congress, then waiting to see what would come out of the Constitutional Convention that had just assembled, rejected the offer. The Ohio Company's lobbyist, Reverend Manasseh Cutler, made a deal with William Duer, Congressman from New York, and soon after Congress suspended its conscience and granted away six and a half million acres of land in the Northwest Territory, a million of which went to the Ohio Company and the remainder to Duer and his associates, who had informally organized into the Scioto Company. The official price, minus one-third off for useless land that might come within the grant, was a dollar an acre, which was to be paid in inflated Continental currency, then worth about twelve and a half cents on the dollar. The actual price worked out to about eight cents an acre in hard money. Congress accepted the bargain partly because several of its members had been corrupted, but partly also because squatters had filtered into the Northwest Territory. The Indians complained of their presence. Troops dispatched by Congress failed to eject the illegal settlers. So an arrangement that brought in even eight cents on the dollar was better than nothing, especially if the Ohio Company managed to impose order on the area.

The invasion of Ohio lands by squatters revived the old contempt of easterners toward the backcountry. "The emigrants to the frontier lands are the least worthy subjects in the United States," said one Congressman. "They are little less savage than the Indians, and when possessed of the most fertile spots, for want of industry, live miserably." Congress now decided that because the territory was filling up with "licentious people," as Richard Henry Lee put it, "a strong toned government should exist and the rights of property be clearly defined," and to that end it set about revising Jefferson's plan of 1784. The Northwest Ordinance of 1787, passed on July 13 while the Constitutional Convention sat in Philadelphia, numbered among the last and the greatest of the Continental Congress's statutes. The ordinance drew back the gift of immediate self-government and temporarily treated the territory as a colonial empire. It imposed on the settlers a governor, secretary, and three judges appointed by Congress. These men would control the territory until five thousand adult males had settled there, at which time a general assembly would be allowed to take charge of legislative affairs, though the still Congressionally appointed governor retained his absolute veto over all legislation. Only those who owned fifty acres of land could vote. No more than five and not less than three states could be carved from the region. When a district's population reached sixty thousand, it could write its own constitution and apply for admission to the Union. Congress kept Jefferson's suggestion that the new states be admitted as equals, and it resurrected his previously discarded provision that slavery be prohibited throughout the territory. A bill of rights attached to the ordinance assured settlers of freedoms they were accustomed to in the original thirteen states.

The Northwest Ordinance of 1787 clearly lacked the liberality of Jefferson's earlier plan. It made the West part of a gigantic real-estate operation and saw to it that at the start Congressional appointees protected the promoters' investment. It apparently forbade slavery to please the New England investors in the Ohio Company who hoped to attract settlers from their region. But at the same time the ordinance appealed to special interests, it also created a pattern by which virtually every state since has been admitted to the Union. It became, too, a classic statement of the ideal type of society America wanted—one that protected civil rights, that guaranteed religious liberty, that forbade slavery, that promised equal rather than colonial status within the Union.

Both the 1785 and 1787 statutes did much in the long run to shape the settlement and development of the West. Their immediate effects, however, were slight. The Ohio Company planted a successful settlement at Marietta, Ohio; the Scioto Company enticed into the wilderness a group of Frenchmen, who eventually had to be rescued from their starving time by Congress. That about summed up the achievements of the speculators. The Land Ordinance in effect closed off the West to the individual settler. Few saw the sense of plunking down $640 for a federal tract—fewer still had that much money anyway—when there was still an abundance of open land, much of it free, east of the mountains. Down nearly to the end of the century men preferred to fill in the unsettled parts of the East— Vermont and Maine, inland New York, western Pennsylvania, and the backcountry of the South—rather than buy land over the mountains. (It may be, of course, that this was exactly what Congress wanted; its members represented the interests of their own states, and by virtually closing off the national domain, they in effect helped their own "country.")

Both New York and New Hampshire claimed the land that lay between the Connecticut River and Lake Champlain, but as migrants pushed in during the early 1770's, the claims of both were ignored by the Allen brothers—Ethan, Ira, and Levi—who organized an army of "Green Mountain Boys" to assure the region's independence. They created a government in 1777 and went so far as to promise Britain Vermont's neutrality during the Revolution if its independence was recognized. Some thirty thousand settlers had arrived by the end of the Revolution, but the Allens, who had sought to negotiate a separate peace treaty with Britain and were determined that Congress should not have the chance to parcel out Vermont land "to their avaricious minions," stifled talk of joining the Union. By 1790 population had jumped to eighty-five thousand. Soon after, Yankees and Yorkers settled their long and bitter border dispute, and in 1791 Vermont was admitted as the fourteenth state in the Union.

The division between North and South swung back in balance the following year when Kentucky, with a population of some seventy-five thousand, came in as the fifteenth state. Kentucky throughout the Confederation had been badly split between those for statehood and those for independence. Daniel Boone said in 1775 that the pro-state movement was "intirely against the voce of the people at Large." Some preferred independence in order to negotiate freely with Spain for trading privileges on the Mississippi, which an Eastern-dominated Congress showed little interest in obtaining. The large land speculators, who had watched the deferential treatment given the Ohio Company by Congress, plumped for statehood in 1787, but it was not until Vermont had entered the Union and it became necessary to redress the balance of states that Kentucky was admitted.

Dissension over the question of statehood in the Watauga region, south

of Kentucky, was complicated by the presence of two sets of land speculators—those who had settled the area and those from North Carolina who
had been granted large tracts in the region by the state legislature. The
Watauga Association, which had been organized by local settlers in 1772 to
govern the region, was absorbed into North Carolina as Washington
County in 1776 and remained part of that state until ceded to Congress in
1784. While Congress tarried accepting the gift, the Watauga settlers created the independent state of Franklin. North Carolina thereupon reneged
on its cession to Congress and for the next four years the two governments
contested for control of the region. The issue was settled in 1788 when the
government of Franklin, which had been unable to obtain recognition
anywhere, even from Spain, collapsed. North Carolina reassumed control
for a year, then gave the land again to Congress. By this time virtually no
unclaimed land remained for the federal government either to administer
or sell. After a brief period of tutelage, the region entered the Union in
1796 as the state of Tennessee.

The Congress of the new federal government, not that of the Confederation, brought these three states into the Union. The Continental
Congress' treatment of the West deserves mixed praise at best. It allowed
itself to become to an extent the pawn of speculators. Its desperate need for
funds led it to reverse a long-standing colonial policy toward the disbursement of public land. Its stringent legislation for the sale and settlement of Western land virtually closed off the region for a decade. Still,
Congress should be complimented. Great Britain controlled the West for
over a decade prior to the Revolution and failed to provide a plan for settlement; Congress did so within three years after it had acquired the land.
Moreover, the program it developed has, as Edmund Morgan has said,
"with little alteration carried the United States to its present continental
limits."

The Economy

The war's end forced the United States to face some distressing facts of
life. The new nation came forth into a world of empires, each with its own
version of a mercantilist economy that was not designed to promote the
welfare of thirteen weak states. So the states found themselves on the outside looking in, and for most, the new status particularly hurt what a later
eminent American would call "the pocket-book nerve." Franklin had
worked hard during the peace negotiations to persuade Great Britain to
permit Americans to retain the economic privileges they had once had as
members of the empire, notably the right to trade freely with all its parts.
Some in the British government—notably the Earl of Shelburne and William Pitt, the younger—had been converted to the doctrine of free trade
advanced by Adam Smith in *The Wealth of Nations* in 1776, and they

wanted to grant Franklin's request. But an economic doctrine that had
nurtured the British nation for more than a century was not to be lightly
abandoned, especially when to do so would in effect allow the Americans
to have their cake and eat it too. John Adams, as ambassador to Great
Britain, tried hard to win commercial concessions, but near the end of
1785 he admitted he was at the end of his tether. "No step that I can take,
no language I can hold will do any good, or indeed much harm," he said.

The British predicted—correctly, it turned out—that Americans would
continue to buy British goods because they were accustomed to them and
because they were better and cheaper than anything the French, who had
hoped to take over the American market, could offer. British merchants
advanced full credit to those in the new nation they had dealt with before
the Revolution. American merchants gave the same generous terms to
their dealers, who passed on the easy credit to their customers—soldiers
who expected to receive the back pay owed by the state governments and
the Confederation, farmers who assumed that the wartime prices for their
crops would hold, and civilians who counted on the securities they had
purchased during the war being paid in hard money. Between 1784 and
1786 America imported over £7,500,000 worth of goods from Great Britain.
It sent back during the same period products worth only £2,500,000. The
unfavorable balance of £5,000,000 drained nearly every ounce of gold and
silver in the country back to Britain, wrecked hopes of stabilizing the
currency, depressed prices, caused bankruptcies, and sent the country into
a severe commercial depression.

The immediate hopes for redressing the balance of trade were slight.
Prior to the Revolution, tobacco from the Chesapeake region accounted for
nearly half of Britain's trade with the colonies. During the war, Virginia
alone lost some thirty thousand slaves to the British invaders. A shortage of
labor during the postwar period, coming at a time when every hand was
needed to put long-fallow fields back in production, contributed to the
slump in tobacco exports from the Chesapeake area that averaged around
forty-five million pounds a year after the war. Curtis Nettels, who has
made the most recent study of the postwar economy, holds that this
"drastic decline of tobacco exports to Britain marked the most sweeping
change in American commerce that occurred immediately after the war."

The Chesapeake country did not suffer alone. British bounties that
had once supported the price of naval stores vanished with the peace,
and as a result North Carolina's exports dropped off two thirds from the
prewar level. The value of South Carolina's exports of indigo slipped to a
mere £50,000 during the postwar period, and its exports of rice to nearly
half what they had been before the Revolution. (A labor shortage—the
state lost approximately twenty-five thousand slaves during the war—together with a prohibitive duty levied on rice by Great Britain combined

to create South Carolina's economic troubles.) New England, if anything, took a worse drubbing than the South. Massachusetts shipyards before the war had annually built some 125 vessels, about half of which were sold to merchants in Britain; after the war, fewer than 25 new ships slipped down the ways. Nantucket's fleet of 150 whaling vessels diminished to 24 after the war; the popularization of the tallow candle during the Revolution had killed the home market for whale oil, which had once lighted American homes, and a high import duty eliminated the British market. Exclusion from the West Indies hurt the fishing industry. West Indian prices for horses, pork, beef, and flour dropped sharply after the war, and the economy of the Middle States suffered as a result.

"In every point of view, indeed, the trade of this country is in a deplorable condition," James Madison said in 1785, and the available statistics appear to bear out his gloomy judgment. Prices in the coastal cities during the postwar period dropped an average of 25 per cent. Bankruptcies became common as merchants large and small found it impossible to collect on the goods they had sold on easy terms. (The effect of these failures was felt in Britain, where by August 1784, five large London firms had failed, mainly because they had been unable to collect from American debtors.) America by mid-1784 found itself in the grip of a commercial depression that lasted into 1787. Merrill Jensen perhaps overstates the case when he holds that "there is nothing in the knowable facts to support the ancient myth of idle ships, stagnant commerce, and bankrupt merchants in the new nation," but he is undoubtedly correct in arguing that the American economy after the Revolution was by no means as bad off as many historians have held it to be. The prevailing agrarian aspect of American life limited the hardships it created, for this was a commercial depression whose effects were mainly confined to the mercantile community. Moreover, most merchants knew from experience that the peace that had followed each of Great Britain's previous imperial wars had invariably brought a depression in its wake. (A good argument might be made that the depression that hit the colonies after the capture of Quebec in 1760 exceeded in severity the one that came in 1784.) This one differed from past ones in that American merchants were free, as they had not been in the past, to search out trade and profit where they wished.

France failed after the war to gain an appreciable part of the American market, but the Americans acquired a favorable balance exceeding $1 million in their trade with France almost at once. Trade with Holland and Sweden flourished to a limited extent, with the Dutch trading most heavily with the Middle States. Commercial treaties made with Holland in 1782 and Sweden in 1783 granted concessions that "were well-nigh revolutionary in terms of eighteenth-century policy and practice." Despite steady threats from Barbary pirates, a lucrative Mediterranean trade in fish, wheat, and flour also flourished. United States merchants were bold and imaginative in their search for cargoes. They even sent ships to China in 1784, carrying out ginseng, an aromatic root the Chinese believed would restore virility to the aged, and bringing back tea, silks, tableware, and other exotic products. Soon this trade increased. On the advice of John Ledyard, who had sailed with Captain Cook and knew the Chinese would pay high prices for furs, American vessels began trading with the Indians of the Pacific Northwest for sea-otter skins, which were then carried to China and there exchanged at great profit.

America's postwar depression, while unquestionably hard on the mercantile community, was also short-lived. Jensen is convinced, and until a strong case refutes his view he deserves a hearing, "that independence was a boon to American commerce despite the inevitable dislocations caused by severance from the British Empire." The dislocations prompted gloomy forebodings from the merchants, but "in no case do the records of imports and exports and ship tonnages bear out the cries of havoc." Wherever we have statistics, "they show the same trend: rapid increases of shipping after the war." All authorities agree that by 1786 America was edging its way out of the business slump. In the South, tobacco production had surpassed prewar levels, and there had been a sharp increase in the export of grains and lumber. The three banks in the North (located in Boston, New York, and Philadelphia) were able, through cautious management, to pay dividends that ranged from 2.5 to 14 per cent. The transition from a wartime to a peacetime economy and from a position inside to one outside the British Empire gave everyone something to complain about, but by 1786 it was clear that America's troubles at bottom were political rather than economic.

Political Power

If, as the saying has it, power tends to corrupt, then the Congress of the peacetime Confederation was one of the most virtuous bodies in American history. For although the states gave Congress its power during the war, they retrieved their gift with the peace. The luminaries of the war years—Patrick Henry, Thomas Jefferson, Richard Henry Lee, Benjamin Franklin, John Hancock, the "brace of Adamses"—had long ago either abandoned Congress to serve their states or had been sent to speak for the new nation abroad. And in their places, the states had sent youngsters (James Madison was twenty-nine when he arrived, Alexander Hamilton twenty-six, Charles Pinckney twenty-seven), second-rate men, or no one at all. (During the first four months of 1784 for only three days did Congress have a quorum of nine states, which was needed to make war or peace and to vote appropriations.) The transition from war to peace changed the nature not the number nor seriousness of the problems that confronted the national government, but the states worried only about their own welfare.

Poverty did much to undermine the Confederation's strength. Congress sought to recoup its earlier failure to get a 5 per cent impost on imports with a second try in 1783; this time New York refused to agree. By 1786 less than a third of the states were paying even part of the requisitions needed to run the government; the rest balked at even token contributions. The Confederation owed over $10 million on just the interest of the national debt. (Not everyone, however, saw this as a calamity. "I view the debt of our country with pleasure," Benjamin Rush said in 1782, for he believed it was "a much stronger cement of the States than the labored Articles of Confederation.") Congress appropriated $80,000 to pay for protection from the Barbary pirates, only to learn that this would hardly cover the ransom asked for the crews of two captured ships. John Adams urged borrowing the £200,000 he thought would be needed to buy off the pirates; Jefferson thought a virtuous nation should shun bribery and settle the issue by war. Both proposals were rejected, and Congress used the little money it could round up to buy protection from Morocco in 1787, hoping later to acquire enough to pay off the pirates of other Mediterranean states.

Congressional dealings with Spain revealed the debilitating effect of sectionalism on the national government's power. Spain worried about the American West, whose growth, unless stifled, threatened to overrun the Floridas (acquired by Spain in 1783) and Louisiana (acquired in 1763). Spain closed off the Mississippi in 1784 to American traffic, and then, knowing Congress had expressed interest in a commercial treaty, sent over one of her ablest diplomats, Don Diego de Gardoqui, to negotiate with John Jay, the Confederation's secretary of foreign affairs. Gardoqui offered limited trading privileges with Spain if the United States would abandon use of the Mississippi for twenty-five years. Jay urged Congress to accept the offer. The South, which saw its future tied to a prosperous Southwest, vehemently opposed it. To accept such an agreement, James Madison said, would make the United States "guilty of treason against the very laws under which they obtained and hold their national existence." The North favored it. In the words of Rufus King, it saw "every emigrant to that country from the Atlantic states as forever lost to the Confederacy," if the river were opened to Western traffic. "A treaty disagreeable to one half the nation had better not be made, for it would be violated," John Jay finally said, and settlement of the Mississippi question was left for a later age to solve.

Throughout the Confederation's history, a band of men in and out of Congress—among them George Washington. Alexander Hamilton,

Robert Morris, John Jay, James Madison, and James Wilson, to name only the most prominent—had worked and argued steadily for a stronger union. Wartime duties that had taken them to all parts of the continent and long involvement in Congressional affairs had helped to make these men nationally-minded. They believed that the central government needed an independent source of income to pay its debts, that local industry could be protected only by national tariffs, that local shipping interests could be protected only by a national navigation law. Slowly, as the postwar years wore on, others, originally oriented toward their states, saw that some local problems could be solved only on the national level. New York in 1782 called for a convention to revise the Articles in a way that would strengthen the Union. (Four years later, however, when the state government was in the hands of antinationalists, New York contributed the single vote against the renewed request of "King Cong," as Congress was called, for an impost duty.) Massachusetts' Governor John Hancock in 1783 said that "our very existence as a free nation" required a strengthened central government. Thomas Jefferson admitted in 1785 that "the interests of the States ought to be made joint in every possible instance, in order to cultivate the idea of our being one nation, and to multiply the instances in which the people shall look up to Congress as their head."

Congress in 1784, with the nation in the slough of the depression, warned that unless the United States were "vested with powers competent to the protection of commerce, they can never command reciprocal advantages in trade; and without these, our foreign commerce must decline, and eventually be annihilated." Eleven states agreed that Congress should be allowed to pass a navigation law; North Carolina and once again Rhode Island balked. Meanwhile, Maryland and Virginia set about informally to solve commercial problems that had arisen between the two states over the navigation of Chesapeake Bay and its tributaries. The conference convened early in 1785 at Alexandria, then adjourned to Mount Vernon, where delegates from Delaware and Pennsylvania joined it. James Madison, pleased with the progress made at these meetings and convinced that America's economic troubles required swift remedial action, persuaded the Virginia legislature to invite all thirteen states to a commercial convention at Annapolis "to take into consideration the trade of the United States." The convention met in September 1786. Nine states promised to attend, but only five—New York, Pennsylvania, Delaware, New Jersey, and Virginia—showed up. New England seemed to resent the meeting being held so far from the "marts of trade" and suspected Virginia's concern about commercial problems.

The presence of only a minority of states precluded a successful convention. After a decent interval spent waiting for other delegates to turn up, Madison and Hamilton persuaded those on hand to sanction an address to the states urging another convention, this one to meet the following May in the more centrally located Philadelphia. The states were asked to empower their delegates "to devise such further provisions as shall appear to them necessary to render the constitution of the Federal Government adequate to the exigencies of the Union."

Shortly after the address went out to the states, word spread through the continent that Massachusetts had a rebellion on its hands. Farmers in the western part of the state, angered by the legislature's insistence that taxes, which had recently been increased, should be paid in hard money and by its refusal to issue paper money, had first voiced their protest through county conventions; but matters soon got out of hand, and mobs marched on the courts to block the execution of the hundreds of foreclosures on the dockets. The rebellion was a spontaneous affair created by poor farmers who conceived—quite correctly, it would seem—that they were being oppressed by the eastern-dominated legislature. Daniel Shays, a likable former army captain but no born leader, more by accident than design found himself at the head of the uprising. Turmoil continued through the back parts of Massachusetts from August 1786 into February of the next year, when four thousand Massachusetts troops led by General Benjamin Lincoln crushed it.

Shays's Rebellion, more than any single event since the Revolution, drove home to conservative gentlemen throughout the land the need for remedying the national government. Massachusetts had sent out a plea for help to Congress, only to learn that the Confederation had no troops and no money to raise or supply troops. Hamilton made the fullest use of the rebellion to promote interest in the coming Philadelphia convention. "Who can determine," he asked, "what might have been the issue of her [Massachusetts] later convulsions, if the malcontents had been headed by a Caesar or Cromwell? Who can predict what effect a despotism established in Massachusetts would have upon the liberties of New Hampshire or Rhode Island, of Connecticut or New York?" Ezra Stiles, writing from Connecticut, warned Washington that the rebellion was "doubtless magnified at a distance," but Washington was having none of that. "What, gracious God, is man! that there should be such inconsistency and perfidiousness in his conduct?" he said on hearing of the event.

Unquestionably, Shays's Rebellion put the leaders of America in the proper mood for what would soon issue from the Constitutional Convention, but it should not be forgotten, John Miller has written, that

for seven years or more, Hamilton and his fellow nationalists had been telling the American people that their salvation lay in a strong national government.

Had it not been for these exhortations, it is possible that Americans would have sought some other escape from their predicament—the most likely being a breakup of the union into two or more confederacies.

THE CONSTITUTION

Fifty-five men of the seventy-four invited and twelve of the thirteen states— Rhode Island refused to come—eventually arrived in Philadelphia to take their seats in what would be known as the Constitutional Convention. They met in the statehouse, the same building where a decade before the Articles of Confederation, which they had now come to "amend," had been debated and agreed to. Several of the bright names from the past were absent—John Hancock (governor of Massachusetts), John Adams (ambassador to England), Thomas Jefferson (ambassador to France), Sam Adams, Richard Henry Lee, Patrick Henry. (Henry, though chosen, refused to come. "I smelt a rat," he said.) However, a fair number from the old Congress were once again on hand—George Washington, Roger Sherman, Benjamin Franklin, George Wythe, Elbridge Gerry, James Wilson, John Dickinson, George Mason, William Livingston, and Robert Morris. The average age of the delegates was forty-two. Five were in their twenties, five in their early or mid-thirties; only four were in their sixties. Franklin at eighty-one was by far the oldest man present. All were men of note within their states, and well over half at one time or another had been involved with continental affairs. They had been chosen in the same way delegates to every continental gathering had been selected since the Stamp Act Congress—by their state legislatures. All were practical men of affairs. They came for the most part from the same social and economic backgrounds as the men who had drawn up the Articles of Confederation. They hoped during the long hot summer that lay ahead to devise practical solutions to specific problems that had developed since the Articles had been written. A decade of experience with the first constitution had forced them to revise many of their earlier views on the role of the central government in American affairs, but it would take sixteen weeks of hard, often bitter, discussion to agree on exactly what revisions were needed.

The Convention

The delegates convened on May 25, and except for a pause to celebrate the Fourth of July and one ten-day adjournment, they remained in continuous week-day session until September 17. They agreed at the start that all sessions should be secret in order to promote the freest discussion without fear of pressure or reprisals from the public. Tempers were bound to flare in a group confined day after day to an airless room during the stifling heat of a Philadelphia summer, and especially so when the group consisted of able, successful, strong-minded gentlemen filled with confidence for the rightness of their views. And where personalities failed to inflame debate, other antagonisms—between sections, between large and small states, between agrarian and commercial interests, between nationalists and confederationists—could be counted on to do so.

The differences certain to emerge among these gentlemen should not obscure the much that united them. All agreed that the Articles needed revising (notable among the absentees were the staunch defenders of the old constitution, like Governor George Clinton of New York). They agreed, too, that while the central government had to be made stronger, it had to be republican in form and based on a written constitution. There seems to have been a consensus from the beginning that a single executive, a judiciary, and a two-house legislature were needed; that the government had to have an independent source of income; that some form of proportional representation had to be devised; that control over foreign affairs and commerce belonged to the central government. Finally, they agreed that their chief reason for assembling was somehow to create a central government weak enough to please the states yet strong enough to deal with matters of national concern. "It is when we contrast the debates and the decisions of the Federal Convention with those of comparable bodies in many other countries," Benjamin Wright has said, "that we see how great the area of agreement and how essential it was to the lasting success of the Convention's work."

The convention opened with the delegates listening to Virginia's conception of what they had to do. The Virginia Plan called for scrapping the Articles and substituting "a strong *consolidated* government" with its own executive, judiciary, and bicameral legislature, whose seats in both houses were to be distributed according to a state's population. The legislature would choose the executive and judiciary; it would have power to call out troops against a rebellious state; and it could veto all state laws that contravened the Constitution. Sentiment among Virginia's leaders had come a long way since 1777, when its delegation in Congress led the resistance against Dickinson's draft of the Articles, but not far enough to discard the view that the legislature should dominate the government nor far enough to envision two features that were to be central to the Constitution—the idea of checks and balances and separation of powers among the three branches of government, and the concept of dual sovereignty, which would allow the states and central government to act within their own spheres of power directly upon the people.

Respect for Great Britain's way of running an empire seemed apparent in the Virginia Plan, which allowed the national legislature to coerce the states (as Parliament had with the Coercive Acts of 1774) and to veto their laws (as the crown had, through use of the royal disallowance). Nevertheless, it was out of this plan that the Constitution slowly emerged during the next four months.

The delegates argued all sides of the plan for two weeks and were still arguing when William Paterson of New Jersey on June 15 bluntly reminded the convention that it was authorized only to amend the Articles. To that end, he introduced the so-called New Jersey Plan, which granted additional powers to Congress—the right to levy taxes and to regulate commerce—created a multiple executive, and provided for a limited judiciary, but kept the Articles' unicameral legislature and the customary procedure of voting by states. The convention rejected Paterson's suggestions outright but knew as it did so that unless concessions were made on the issue of representation, the small states would walk out.

Appeasement soon came in the form of the Great Compromise, which provided for a lower house based on proportional representation and an upper house based on equal representation. (A further compromise incorporated within the greater one settled a sectional argument: only three-fifths of the South's Negroes would be counted as the basis for representation *and* for any direct taxes that might be levied by Congress.) The compromise was great because it marked a turning point in the convention. The confederationists, whose strongholds were in the small states, agreed with their acceptance of the compromise, not to bolt the convention and conceded that the Articles would be discarded, not revised. The nationalists, who centered in the large states, abandoned their hope for a consolidated government. They had been willing, up to this point, to break the convention up rather than give the states an equal voice in any part of the new government. The defeat sent Hamilton home in disgust, and he thereafter gave the convention only cursory attention. Madison worked hard during succeeding weeks to overturn the compromise, but it held to the end.

Discussion of the legislature's powers led to another compromise, this one provoked by sectional differences. Both North and South agreed that Congress should regulate foreign and interstate commerce, but the South, knowing that New England and the Middle States could regularly outvote it in the legislature, demanded protection for its interests built into the Constitution. It insisted that a two-thirds majority be required to enact all commercial regulations. This would give the South a veto over any navigation act designed to protect Northern shipping and manufacturing. Also, the South wanted assurance that Congress would never levy an export tax, which would limit the ability of its tobacco, rice, and other staples to compete in the world market. Finally, it demanded protection against a sudden cutting-off of its slave trade by Congress. In the compromise that settled these issues, it was agreed that a majority vote in Congress would suffice to pass acts regulating commerce, a point the North had fought for. The South, in return for this concession, got one clause in the Constitution that prohibited export taxes, another that guaranteed the slave trade for twenty years, a third that required all states to return fugitive slaves, and, finally, a provision requiring a two-thirds majority in the Senate for the ratification of all treaties, a number of which were expected to deal with commercial matters.

The principle of federalism, the greatest of the delegates' compromises—one that cut midway between the desires of the confederationists and of the nationalists—came while they puzzled out the legislature's powers. They found when done that by allowing the legislature to act directly upon the people and not through the states, they had laid the foundation for a federated rather than a confederated republic. The people became the constituent power for both the state and central governments, and sovereignty, hitherto indivisible, now became shared by those governments. The delegates had not yet, however, fully grasped the principle of checks and balances. That concept emerged only as they grappled with the problem of creating an adequate executive for the new government.

The task of devising the office of President provoked the sharpest conflicts of the convention. The delegates groped slowly toward a solution, for they were creating here something unique to the American experience. Except for the monarchy's overruling authority in colonial affairs, the unpleasant recollection of Governor Andros' administration of the Dominion of New England offered the only precedent of an executive whose power spread beyond the boundaries of a single colony. In the early discussions of the office, the delegates could agree only that the executive should be an agent of the legislature with authority "to carry into execution the national laws" and "to appoint to offices in cases not otherwise provided for." Gradually, as the debate wore on, the nationalists won out against those who still longed for a weak executive. The Presidency, as it took shape during the last days of the convention, became the powerful post that Madison and Hamilton conceived it should be. The delegates dared to hand the President extraordinary powers because they had found a way to check his authority. He could veto legislation, but a two-thirds majority of the legislature could override his veto. He needed the advice and consent of the Senate to make appointments. He could negotiate treaties, but they became operative only after two-thirds of the Senate had approved them. He was commander-in-chief of the armed forces, but Congress alone could declare war and appropriate money to fight the war. Something besides these built-in checks allowed the convention to rest easier about the power it had granted the President, for the delegates knew who the first President would be. They undoubtedly would have been less generous, one delegate said, had they not "cast their eyes towards General Washington as President; and shaped their ideas of the powers to be given to a President by their opinion of his virtue."

The method of electing the President was considered by James Wilson "the most difficult of all on which we have had to decide." The Virginia Plan called for him to be chosen by Congress for a single seven-year term. But nationalists like Wilson argued that the people should elect the President. They held that the House of Representatives would reflect local interests and the Senate those of the states; the President alone would represent the nation, and his choice by the people would help cement their attachment to the Union. Most delegates objected to this view: it would be as right to let the people elect the President, said one, "as it would to refer a trial of colours to a blind man"—not necessarily because the people were untrustworthy, but because in this day of slow travel and strong local attachments "the extent of the country renders it impossible that the people can have the requisite capacity to judge of the respective pretensions of the candidates."

The convention escaped its dilemma by creating the electoral college. Each state would choose electors equal to the combined number of their Senators and Representatives. The person who received a *majority* of all votes cast by the electors became the President. If no one received a majority, then the House of Representatives, voting by states, would select the President from the five top candidates with the runner-up becoming vice-president. The electoral college, as the convention conceived it, was a devious device to keep the election of President in the hands of the politicians without seeming to do so. The delegates assumed that except in the case of Washington all succeeding elections would end up in the House. Sectional interests and state loyalties, they thought, would lead to a series of favorite sons being advanced by the electors for the Presidency, with none being able to obtain a majority of the votes cast. (Of course the unexpected development of political parties thwarted the convention's hope on this point.)

"Experience must be our only guide," John Dickinson had remarked at one point during the convention, "Reason may mislead us." The delegates heeded the advice. They avoided innovations and experimented only where past failures demanded a new approach. They drew heavily on the colonial experience. The office of President resembled that of the colonial royal governor; his role of commander-in-chief of the armed forces, for instance, numbered among the duties of the governor. (The duties and powers of the President were lifted almost verbatim from the 1777 constitution of New York, which shaped the governorship on colonial precedents.) The bicameral legislature, standard in all states except Pennsylvania and soon to be introduced even there, came straight from the colonial past, along with such provisions that each house make its own rules, elect its own officers. The provision that no member could be arrested during the legislature's session appears among the earliest statutes of Virginia and Maryland. Money bills continued to originate in the House, as in colonial days, though now, to avoid a concentration of power, the Senate was allowed to amend them. The three-fifths clause, which dealt with the counting of the South's Negroes, did not come out of the blue; it was one among many of the suggested amendments to the Articles that had failed to get unanimous approval. A clause that prohibited any state to pass laws impairing the obligation of contract had been lifted from the Northwest Ordinance of 1787, passed by the Continental Congress while the convention sat. The easier amendment process and the insistence on ratification by the people were refinements taken from the Massachusetts constitution of 1780.

Where experience failed to guide them, the delegates could be ingeniously vague. When they failed to agree whether the President should be allowed to serve more than one term, they settled the issue by avoiding it. A long argument on the status of new states was resolved with a marvelously ambiguous sentence ("New States may be admitted by the Congress into this Union"), which left it up to the future to decide whether or not they should be admitted as equals. Whenever in doubt, the convention purposely worded the Constitution in a way that left posterity free to decide. The delegates knew at every point exactly what they were about. Only once did chance rather than forethought contribute a striking effect. The Preamble, when handed to the Committee on Style, which put the document in its final form, read: "We the People of the States of New Hampshire," and so forth through the thirteen states. Someone remarked that because only nine states were needed to ratify the Constitution and several might reject it—the refusal of George Mason and Edmund Randolph of Virginia, Luther Martin of Maryland, and Elbridge Gerry of Massachusetts to accept the convention's handiwork indicated that there might be trouble in some states—the Preamble should be altered to read: "We the People of the United States. . . ." A slight change for the sake of precision in the opening lines set the tone for all that followed, emphasizing that this was a Constitution by and for the *people,* not the states.

Ratification

On September 17, 1787, the convention sent the Constitution to the Continental Congress for transmittal to the state legislatures. Congress forwarded the document without public comment but not before misgivings had been aired behind closed doors. Richard Henry Lee, who was numbered among those not invited to the convention, spoke the sentiments of many. It struck him as ironical that by sending the Constitution on as requested Congress became a party to its own death. It seemed ludicrous, he said, that the document was directed to the state legislatures, which were excluded from having a say in its approval. He suggested that the Constitution weakened rather than strengthened the Union, for the ratification procedure in effect asked nine states to secede from the old Union in order to form a new one. Finally, he deplored the lack of adequate protection for men's natural rights in the document. (The absence of a bill of rights had been noted by several disgruntled delegates near the end of the convention. Their exhausted colleagues held that individual rights were already well guarded. They pointed out the protections against ex post facto laws and bills of attainder and the clauses that guaranteed habeas corpus and jury trials in all criminal cases. Hamilton and Gouverneur Morris argued that to list some inviolable rights might lead to the conclusion that others were not protected, that the government was, after all, one of limited powers.)

The Constitution aroused even stronger discontent once it reached the states. Local leaders saw a stronger central government undercutting their power at home. George Clinton, for instance, who had governed New York for ten years and found nothing in the Articles to complain about, blended self-interest with principle in his vigorous opposition to the Constitution. He did make a telling point, however, when he remarked that the nation's economy was on the mend and that it therefore made no sense to shift to a new, untried government when the country prospered under the old one. A good number of the opponents talked vaguely, as one man put it, that the Constitution threatened "the liberties of the people" and that it had been made by "men of property and education" rather than by the plain people. But there was also much detailed and specific criticism. Some missed the usual religious oath for office-holders and held that its absence deprived the new government of God's blessing and protection. Others were distressed to see the American custom of annual election for legislators and elected officials dismissed. And many believed too much power centered in the hands of one man, the President. Patrick Henry thought the office "squints toward monarchy" and that it would take but one push for the President to make an "American throne." It saddened him, too, to see taxation substituted for the requisition system. The power to tax gave the power to destroy, and Henry saw the sovereignty of the states withering to a shadow of its former self under this new threat. Might not taxes be used to create a standing army, which could crush the states?

The abuse leveled against the convention's work seemed at first little related to popular feeling about the Constitution. In a month's time, five states—Delaware on December 7, Pennsylvania on December 16, New Jersey on December 18, Georgia on January 2, and Connecticut on January 9—gave either unanimous or overwhelming approval to the document in their popularly chosen conventions. But except for Pennsylvania—there strong-arm tactics had been used by the Federalists, as proponents of the Constitution were now called, to get the state legislature to issue a call for the ratifying convention—these were all small states delighted with the protections the new frame of government gave them. Massachusetts offered the first sign that ratification would have a hard time in the large states. Even after John Hancock and Sam Adams, who had originally opposed the document, had swung to its favor—in the process diverting several Antifederal votes from the opposition—the convention gave its approval on February 6 by the close vote of 187 to 168. The Constitution had little trouble in Maryland, which ratified on April 28, or the following month in South Carolina (May 23). It took two conventions in New Hampshire to win approval, and even then it came by the slimmest of margins on June 21. New Hampshire was the ninth and last state needed to make the Constitution the new supreme law of the land, but it was obvious that a new government could not be formed while two of the largest states—New York and Virginia—remained outside the Union. The Virginia convention's debate on the virtues and defects of the Constitution was the longest and profoundest in the land. George Mason and Patrick Henry led the fight for the Antifederalists, and ratification seemed a lost hope until suddenly Edmund Randolph, who had refused in the convention to sign the Constitution, came to its defense. The moderating influence Washington would undoubtedly exert on the new government and a promise from Madison, who led the Constitution's defense, that a bill of rights would be among the first amendments to the Constitution helped persuade Randolph to change his mind. Virginia ratified the document by a vote of 89 to 79 on June 26.

But New York still tarried. There, Hamilton and Madison, with occasional help from John Jay, sought to move the "mountains of prejudices" with a series of newspaper articles addressed to "the men of intelligence, patriotism, property, and independent circumstances." The essays offered the ablest explication and analysis of the Constitution to come

Map 43. Settlement, 1790

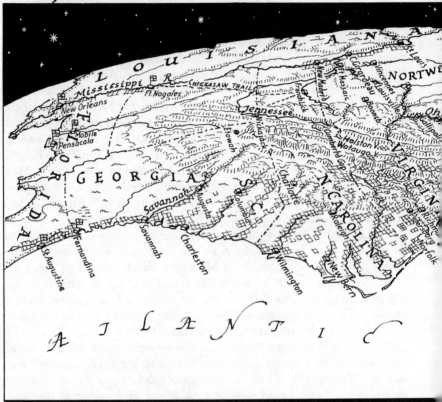

forth during the ratification debate, and collected as *The Federalist* they
are still regarded as a distinguished contribution to political theory. They
did not, however, contribute measurably to the Federalists' victory in
New York. Again, it took the change of heart of a leading Antifederalist
—Melancton Smith—to bring about ratification. Approval came on July
26 by the narrow margin of three votes.

Less than eight months after Delaware began the succession of as-
sents, all but two states had given their approval to the Constitution.
(North Carolina held out until November 21, 1789, and Rhode Island
until May 29, 1790.) The swift success defies a single or simple explanation. The aggressive campaign of the Federalists, whose pressure and
propaganda had helped to initiate the Constitutional Convention, cer-

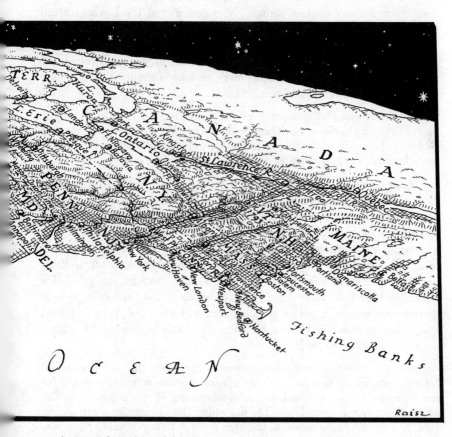

tainly contributed to the outcome. And public apathy no doubt helped their cause. A constitution, even one as well-written as this one, offers something less than lively reading. Nowhere did large numbers of voters turn out to choose delegates to the ratifying conventions; no doubt a people accustomed to elections that centered on personalities found it difficult to work up an interest in the merits and flaws of a constitution. Surely, many voters were swayed by the eminence of those who supported the Constitution, Washington and Franklin especially; if these, America's only two national heroes, were for the document, it must have virtues.

Attractions built into the Constitution to please a diversity of interests made it hard to mount an energetic attack against it. The small states found almost nothing to complain about. The South had been so effectively catered to in the convention—compromises protected its economic interests, an attack on slavery had been avoided, and everyone knew who the first President would be—that the Antifederalists there had to search hard for items to complain about. The arguments of those who revived the specter of concentrated power now had a hollow sound for many who had once feared a strong central government. "I have the same opinion with the Antifederalists of the danger of trusting arbitrary power to any single body of men, but no such power will be committed to our new rulers," Benjamin Rush told a friend.

Neither the House of Representatives, the Senate, or the President can perform a single legislative act by themselves. An hundred principles in man will lead them to watch, to check, and to oppose each other should an attempt be made by either of them upon the liberties of the people.

Rush became an early and enthusiastic supporter of the Constitution. "It contains all the theoretical and practical advantages of the British Constitution without any of its defects or corruptions," he said shortly after the convention had released the document. "While the nations of Europe have waded into order through seas of *blood,* you see we have traveled peaceably into order only through seas of *blunders.*" And when Rush heard that the ninth state had ratified the Constitution, he exulted: " 'Tis done!" For him, the United States had risen above the "influence of local prejudices, opposite interests, popular arts, and even the threats of bold and desperate men" and was about to make a new beginning. "We have become a nation," he said.

America has ceased to be the only power in the world that has derived no benefit from her declaration of independence. We are more than repaid for the distresses of the war and the disappointments of the peace. . . . The reign of violence is over. Justice has descended from heaven to dwell in our land, and ample restitution has at last been made to human nature by our new Constitution for all the injuries she has sustained in the old world from arbitrary government, false religions, and unlawful commerce.

A New Beginning?

A land where a person can pull up stakes and move at will into an unsettled area creates the impression that men can start life afresh. Such cannot be done, by men or nations; the past is always there to shape the present. The government that took shape under the aegis of the Constitution remained tightly tied to the past. Washington culled his bureaucracy from the staff that had run the Confederation. A majority of those elected to the new Congress had served in the old one. The Bill of Rights sent to the states for approval came principally from similar bills enacted by the states. The first tariff law passed by Congress was modeled after that of Pennsylvania. America in 1789 and for many, many years after continued to draw heavily on the past to guide itself through the confusions of the present.

The Constitution provided the means for unity, but not unity itself. It looked for a while as though Washington might be able to pull America out of the localism of its colonial past, to create a national feeling, a sense of oneness within the people, but the task proved too much. With his retirement, the nation lapsed again into old habits. When men mentioned their country, they meant their states rather than the nation. The Presidency became an office inherited rather than fought for, and the country paid little attention to those who occupied it. None who won the office had a strong hold on the people's affection. Not until Andrew Jackson appeared on the scene would the country have a new *national* hero, a man who would use the Presidency to unite the people. Even long after Jackson, the United States remained a plural "they" to the people rather than a singular "it."

America after 1789 was to change a great deal. The door to the West had barely been cracked open. Transportation and communication had progressed little since John Smith had landed on a Virginia beach in 1607. Men of Anglo-Saxon descent and the Protestant religion still dominated the population. And yet as the West filled up, as Irish Catholics and later southern and eastern Europeans flooded in, as the telegraph and the railroad bound the country together, much of the old colonial pattern continued to flourish in a new environment. When Jefferson and Madison early in the nineteenth century, and later still John C. Calhoun, held that a state could declare a law of the national legislature not to their liking null and void, they drew on the colonial past as it had been shaped by English traditions. (One of the arguments used against the Stamp Act had been taken from Lord Coke, who held, according to a contemporary, "that an act of Parliament against the Magna Charta or the peculiar rights of Englishmen is *ipso facto* void.") When still later in the century Americans cried out against the evils of monopoly, they voiced a prejudice that dated back at least to the time when Bostonians dumped a shipload of tea into the harbor, partly because Parliament had given the East India Company a monopoly of the American market. The colonial view that an economic boycott offered an effective, peaceful means to bring an oppressor to heel thrived long enough to be used by President Thomas Jefferson and to remain a fixed part of American foreign policy well into Franklin D. Roosevelt's second adminstration. Those in the twentieth century who made a moral issue of isolationism took their cue from Tom Paine and his contemporaries, who held that America had to cut itself free of decadent Europe if it was to maintain its virtue. If the United States appears to the world as a nation imbued with a sense of mission, something of that spirit must stem from the Puritans, who sought to create a "holy commonwealth" in New England, and the Quakers, who embarked on a "holy experiment" in Pennsylvania.

American greatness owes a deep debt to luck. Its people had the luck to be handed a rich, virgin continent to exploit. They had well over a century of tutelage in self-government under a generous and well-intentioned, if slack and often misinformed, mentor. Their governments, as well as their societies and their economies, had the luck to take form in an age when the world moved more slowly than today; when states were allowed to grow organically rather than to be created artificially; and when men were permitted, as Benjamin Rush put it, to stumble through a sea of blunders rather than blood. Finally, America had the luck to cling to its colonial heritage. The United States, it has been said, was born in the country but moved to the city; fortunately, the move took a long time coming. Abraham Lincoln, born over a half century after Jefferson, was reared in an environment that resembled more than it differed from Jefferson's. He grew to manhood in farm country. The books he read as a law student were those that Jefferson had read. He was as familiar with the language and ideals of those enlightened politicians as Jefferson had been. "Wise statesmen as they were," he said at the time of the Lincoln-Douglas debates in 1858, "they knew the tendency of prosperity to breed tyrants, and so they established these great self-evident truths, that when in the distant future some man, some faction, some interest, should set up the doctrine that none but rich men, or none but white men, were entitled to life, liberty and the pursuit of happiness, their posterity might look up again the Declaration of Independence and take courage to renew the battle which their fathers began." No doubt America's colonial experience offers more to the present than even Lincoln found in it, but if only what he drew from it remains alive, then that experience shall not have been wholly in vain.

BIBLIOGRAPHY

Richard B. Morris presents an introduction to the period in "The Confederation and the American Historian," *WMQ*, 13 (1956), 139–156. Competent general accounts are Andrew C. McLaughlin, *The Confederation and the Constitution, 1783–1789* (1905; pb.), and the survey of Edward Channing in the third volume of *The History of the United States* (6 vols., 1905–1925). The single full and rounded work is Merrill Jensen's *The New Nation: A History of the United States During the Confederation, 1781–1789* (1950; pb.), a modern historian's answer to John Fiske's classic interpretation, *The Critical*

Period in American History (1888). Jensen seeks to show that the years between the Revolution and the Constitution were better in every way than Fiske claimed. Benjamin F. Wright's *Consensus and Continuity, 1776–1787* (1958) is a slim work that should be read by all interested in the period. Wright's quiet statement of the cautious experimenting carried on during the Confederation period offers a pleasant contrast to the polemical literature on the subject that has streamed from historians' pens. Russell B. Nye covers *The Cultural Life of the New Nation, 1776–1830* (1960; pb.) ; a full bibliography is appended. Three excellent journals by travelers through the America of this period are the Marquis de Chastellux' *Travels in North America in the Years 1780, 1781, and 1782,* best read in Howard C. Rice's new edition (2 vols., 1963) ; Judson P. Wood's and John S. Ezell's edition of *The New Democracy in America: Travels of Francisco de Miranda in the United States, 1783–1784* (1963) ; and Alfred J. Morrison, trans. and ed., *Travels in the Confederation, 1783–1784, from the German of Johann David Schoepf* (2 vols., 1911).

Problems of Revolution

The text of all state constitutions and the Articles of Confederation are found in Francis N. Thorpe, *Federal and State Constitutions . . .* (7 vols., 1909). Benjamin F. Wright offers an introduction to the subject in "The Early History of Written Constitutions in America," *Essays in History and Political Theory* (1936), pages 344–371. Allan Nevins' *The American States During and After the Revolution* (1924) gives the fullest account of state politics during the period. Nevins holds to the view that the war prompted an internal revolution, as does Elisha P. Douglass in *Rebels and Democrats: The Struggle for Equal Political Rights and Majority Rule During the American Revolution* (1955; pb.). No one work has yet attempted to revise this traditional interpretation of the period, though several monographs have suggested that as far as particular states are concerned, it does not hold true. See, for example, Robert E. Brown's *Middle-Class Democracy and the Revolution in Massachusetts, 1691–1780* (1955), which should be supplemented by Robert J. Taylor's *Massachusetts, Colony to Commonwealth: Documents on the Formation of Its Constitution, 1775–1780* (1961; pb.) ; David S. Lovejoy's *Rhode Island Politics and the American Revolution, 1760–1776* (1958) ; and David Hawke's *In the Midst of a Revolution* (1961). Thomas C. Cochran's *New York in the Confederation* (1932) was the first to make the point that the weakness of the Confederation owed much to the incapability of the state governments to collect taxes to operate their own organizations—let alone contribute to the support of the central government, a point further developed by Jensen's *New Nation.* Jensen's earlier volume, *The Articles of Confederation* (1940; pb.), drives hard the thesis that the Revolution was "a struggle between those who enjoyed political privileges and those who did not."

Virtually every historian who has written on the early history of the new nation has sought at one time or another to provide his own answer to the question of whether the Revolution was a real one or not. J. Franklin Jameson's *The American Revolution Considered as a Social Movement* (1926; pb.) fixed the interpretative pattern for a generation, until it was reevaluated by Frederick B. Tolles in *AHR*, 60 (1954), 1–12. Tolles' essay, with its consideration of the work that had been done after Jameson's book, provides an excellent starting point for the considerable material that has come forth in the decade since. Howard Mumford Jones explores the question at length in Chapter IX, "Republican Culture," in his *O Strange New World* (1964). Sydney V. James touches on the subject in "The Impact of the American Revolution on Quakers' Ideas About Their Sect," *WMQ*, 19 (1962), 360–382. Richard D. Brown's "The Confiscation and Disposition of Loyalists' Estates in Suffolk County, Massachusetts," *WMQ*, 21 (1964), 534–550 concludes "that the Suffolk sales of loyalist property did not of themselves change the social structure, but merely provided a means for a rising group of men to stabilize their wealth in urban, and to a much lesser extent rural, real estate." Cecelia M. Kenyon's "Republicanism and Radicalism in the American Revolution: An Old-Fashioned Interpretation," *WMQ*, 19 (1962), 153–182 argues that "for all its pluralistic diversity, the American Revolution was still a *revolution*, and it was radical." Robert R. Palmer makes the point in *The Age of the Democratic Revolution: A Political History of Europe and America, 1760–1800* (1959) that the emigration of nearly one hundred thousand loyalists helped to make the Revolution seem more conservative than it was. Louis Hartz, *The Liberal Tradition in America* (1955; pb.), holds that the Revolution conserved traditions and institutions that by European standards were radical to begin with. For a philosopher's interpretation, see the work by Hannah Arendt, *On Revolution* (1963; pb.). R. R. Palmer's short article, "Notes on the Use of the Word 'Democracy,' 1789–1799," *PSQ*, 58 (1953), 203–226, should not be overlooked. The fullest, most recent analysis of *The Social Structure of Revolutionary America* (1965) is by Jackson T. Main.

Problems of Peace

Ray A. Billington offers a sound introductory survey to the general problems of *Westward Expansion* (1949). Benjamin H. Hibbard, *A History of the Public Land Policies* (1924), is detailed and mainly of interest to the specialist. Roy M. Robbins, *Our Landed Heritage: The Public Domain* (1942), seeks "to integrate American land history with the other forces that have shaped our civilization." Thomas P. Abernethy's *Western Lands and the American Revolution* (1937) carries his detailed account of the land companies into the Confederation period. Beverley W. Bond's *The Civilization of the Old Northwest: A Study of Political, Social, and Economic Development, 1788–1812* (1934) is a full and rounded work. The early chapters of Abernethy's *From Frontier to Plantation in Tennessee: A Study in Frontier Democracy* (1932) highlight the activities of the land speculators in that area. Arthur P. Whitaker's *The Spanish-American Frontier, 1783–*

1795 (1927) is a splendid and readable study. Two competent biographies of Western land speculators are W. H. Masterson, *William Blount* (1954), and C. S. Driver, *John Sevier: Pioneer of the Old Southwest* (1932). An account of Congress and the West can be found in Irving Brant's *James Madison* (6 vols., 1941–1961), Vol. II, *The Nationalist, 1780–1787* (1948). Dale Van Every's lively, popular account of the pre-Revolutionary West in *Forth to the Wilderness* (1961) is continued in *A Company of Heroes: The American Frontier, 1775–1783* (1962; pb.) and *Ark of Empire* (1963; pb.).

Historians vary in their judgments of the state of the Confederation's economy. One view is found in Curtis P. Nettels, *The Emergence of a National Economy, 1775–1815* (1962). Nettels finds the nation's economic affairs in a generally dismal state. Merrill Jensen, *The New Nation* (1950), disagrees. The account of the Confederation in the third volume of Edward Channing's *History of the United States* is especially good on the postwar effort to revive commerce. (Nettels, in *National Economy,* disagrees with Channing's findings on at least one point—the effect of the closing of the British West Indies on the American economy.) Robert A. East's *Business Enterprise in the American Revolutionary Era* (1938) carries the story through the Revolution. Bray Hammond makes a complex subject readable and comprehensible in *Banks and Politics in America from the Revolution to the Civil War* (1957). In his discussion of banks and currency during the Confederation, Hammond holds that the farmers' complaint as debtors was "not that their debts were too heavy but that borrowing was not easy enough." The state of the economy as reflected in the career of one man is seen in Robert A. Davidson's *Isaac Hicks: New York Merchant and Quaker, 1767–1820* (1964).

Two studies of the problem of power and politics during the Confederation as told from the viewpoint of two nationalistic Congressmen are Irving Brant's above-mentioned biography of *James Madison* and John C. Miller's *Alexander Hamilton: Portrait in Paradox* (1959; pb.). The view of those who favored a weak central government is most fully told in Jensen's *The New Nation.* The fullest general account of political activity on the national scene is, of course, Edmund C. Burnett, *The Continental Congress* (1941).

The Constitution

A succinct comment on the work done by historians from Charles Beard's *An Economic Interpretation of the Constitution of the United States* (1913) to Forrest McDonald's *We the People: The Economic Origins of the Constitution* (1958) can be found in a pamphlet by Stanley Elkins and Eric McKitrick, *The Founding Fathers: Young Men of the Revolution* (1962), American Historical Association Pamphlet 44. This essay, which in passing advances one more interpretation of how and why the Constitution came into being, should be supplemented by Jackson T. Main's "Charles A. Beard and the Constitution: A Critical Review of Forrest McDonald's *We the*

People," *WMQ*, 17 (1960), 86–110 and Main's own book-length study, *The Antifederalists: Critics of the Constitution, 1781–1788* (1961; pb.), which tends to support the interpretation of the Confederation advanced by Jensen. McDonald has recently added further fuel to the discussion with his *E Pluribus Unum: The Formation of the American Republic, 1776–1790* (1965).

Shays's Rebellion is best described in Robert J. Taylor's *Western Massachusetts in the Revolution* (1954) and in Marion L. Starkey's well-written *A Little Rebellion* (1955), and analyzed in Richard B. Morris' "Insurrection in Massachusetts," in Daniel Aaron, ed., *America in Crisis* (1952). Two brief accounts of the Convention are Max Farrand, *The Framing of the Constitution of the United States* (1913; pb.), and Robert L. Schuyler, *The Constitution of the United States* (1923). Schuyler—as well as Fred Rodell in *Fifty-Five Men* (1936)—holds, for the most part, with Beard's economic interpretation. Charles Warren's *The Making of the Constitution* (1928) dissents from this view. Benjamin F. Wright's brief, judicious *Consensus and Continuity, 1776–1787* (1958) emphasizes the numerous areas of agreement among the framers of the Constitution. The best-written, straight narrative of the Convention and ratification is Carl Van Doren's *The Great Rehearsal* (1948), which is only slightly marred by the suggestion that the experience of the 1780's was a "great rehearsal" for world federation. The nationalist viewpoint among the Founding Fathers is related in the previously mentioned biographies of *Alexander Hamilton* by Miller and of *James Madison* by Brant and in Page Smith's *James Wilson: Founding Father, 1742–1798* (1956). The other side of the story can be found in a splendid essay by Cecelia Kenyon, "Men of Little Faith: The Antifederalists on the Nature of Representative Government," *WMQ*, 12 (1955), 3–43. An excellent collection of documents can be found in Alpheus Thomas Mason, ed., *The States Rights Debate: Antifederalism and the Constitution* (1964; pb.).

The fullest collection of source material is in Max Farrand, ed., *Records of the Federal Convention* (4 vols., 1911–1937). Another useful volume is C. C. Tansill, *Documents Illustrative of the Formation of the Union of the American States* (1927). A. T. Prescott's *Drafting the Federal Constitution* (1941) groups the Convention debates by subjects. The essays of Jay, Hamilton, and Madison on the Constitution, collected as *The Federalist,* are available in numerous editions, several of them in paperback. Jonathan Elliot's edition of *The Debates in the Several State Conventions on the Adoption of the Federal Constitution* (5 vols., 1836–1845) offers the fullest collection of documents on ratification. Finally, there is O. G. Libby's *The Geographical Distribution of the Vote of the Thirteen States on the Federal Constitution, 1787–1788* (1894).

Nearly all the above-mentioned studies on the Constitution have something to say about ratification. Among those that deal with the process within specific states are F. G. Bates, *Rhode Island and the Formation of the Union* (1898); S. B. Harding, *The Contest over Ratification of the Federal Constitution in the State of Massachusetts* (1896); John C. Miller, *Alexander Hamilton;* Broadus Mitchell, *Alexander Hamilton: Youth to Maturity, 1755–*

1788 (1957); C. E. Miner, *Ratification of the Federal Constitution by the State of New York* (1921); J. B. McMaster and F. D. Stone, *Pennsylvania and the Federal Constitution, 1787–1788* (1888); Robert L. Brunhouse, *The Counter-Revolution in Pennsylvania, 1776–1790* (1942); Richard P. McCormick, *Experiment in Independence, 1781–1788* (1953); Philip Crowl, "Antifederalism in Maryland," *WMQ*, 4 (1947), 446–469; Hugh B. Grigsby, *The History of the Virginia Federal Convention of 1788* (2 vols., 1890–1891); Albert J. Beveridge, *The Life of John Marshall*, Vol. I (1916); and Robert Thomas, "Virginia Convention of 1788: A Criticism of Beard's *An Economic Interpretation of the Constitution*," *JSH*, 19 (1953), 63–72.

For further references see the *Harvard Guide*, Sections 119, "Political and Constitutional History of the States, 1775–1788"; 120, "Economic, Social, and Intellectual Movements"; 121, "Confederation, 1777–1778"; and 122, "Federal Convention and Ratification of the Constitution, 1787–1789."

APPENDIX / *The Chief Magistrates*
of the Thirteen
Colonies and States

A chief magistrate's tenure began with the date of his appointment. In the case of a royal governor coming from England, a year or more might elapse between the date of his appointment and his arrival in America. The last chief magistrate listed under each colony was in office at the final ratification of the Constitution. Finally, unless otherwise indicated, the title of the chief magistrate was governor.

Sources

Connecticut: Alexander Johnston, *Connecticut: A Study of a Commonwealth-Democracy* (1887), pp. 401–402.

Georgia: Lawton B. Evans, *A History of Georgia* (1898), p. xii.

Maryland: Matthew Page Andrews, *History of Maryland: Province and State* (1929), pp. 700–701.

Massachusetts: Albert B. Hart, ed., *Commonwealth History of Massachusetts* (5 vols., 1927–1930), Vol. I, pp. 607–608; Vol. II, pp. 591–592; Vol. III, p. 580.

New Hampshire: Jeremy Belknap, *The History of New Hampshire* (2 vols., 1791 ed.), Vol. II, pp. 483–485.

New Jersey: John O. Raum, *The History of New Jersey* (2 vols., 1877), Vol. II, pp. 493–495.

New York: W. Schuyler, *Colonial New York* (2 vols., 1885), Vol. I, pp. 507–509.

North Carolina: Hugh Talmage Lefler and Albert Ray Newsome, *North Carolina: The History of a Southern State* (1954), pp. 595–596.

Pennsylvania and Delaware: Albert S. Bolles, *Pennsylvania, Province and State: A History from 1609 to 1790* (2 vols., 1899), Vol. II, pp. 483–487.

Rhode Island: Samuel G. Arnold, *History of the State of Rhode Island and Providence Plantations* (2 vols., 1859), Vol. II, pp. 565–566.

South Carolina: Edward McCrady, *The History of South Carolina Under the Proprietary Government, 1670–1719* (1897), pp. 719–720; and *South Carolina Under the Royal Government, 1719–1776* (1899), pp. 799–800.

Virginia: Matthew Page Andrews, *Virginia: The Old Dominion* (1937), pp. 593–595.

Connecticut

NEW HAVEN

1639–1657   Theophilus Eaton
1658–1660   Francis Newman
1660–1662   William Leete

New Haven was absorbed into Connecticut by that colony's royal charter of 1662.

CONNECTICUT

1639–1640   John Haynes
1640–1641   Edward Hopkins
1642–1643   George Wyllys
1643–1644   John Haynes
1644–1645   Edward Hopkins
1645–1646   John Haynes
1646–1647   Edward Hopkins
1647–1648   John Haynes
1648–1649   Edward Hopkins
1649–1650   John Haynes
1650–1651   Edward Hopkins
1651–1652   John Haynes
1652–1653   Edward Hopkins
1653–1654   John Haynes
1654–1655   Edward Hopkins
1655–1656   Thomas Welles
1656–1657   John Webster
1657–1658   John Winthrop, Jr.
1658–1659   Thomas Welles
1659–1676   John Winthrop, Jr.
1676–1683   William Leete
1683–1687   Robert Treat
1687–1689   Sir Edmund Andros
1689–1698   Robert Treat

1698–1707   Fitz John Winthrop
1707–1724   Gurdon Saltonstall
1724–1741   Joseph Talcott
1741–1750   Jonathan Law
1750–1754   Roger Wolcott
1754–1766   Thomas Fitch
1766–1769   William Pitkin
1769–1784   Jonathan Trumbull
1784–1786   Matthew Griswold
1786–1796   Samuel Huntington

Georgia

1732–1743   James E. Oglethorpe
1743–1751   Acting Governor William Stephens
1751–1754   Acting Governor Henry Parker
1754–1757   John Reynolds
1758–1760   Henry Ellis
1760–1776   Sir James Wright
1776–1777   President Archibald Bullock
1777   President Button Gwinnett
1777–1778   John A. Treutlen
1778   John Houstoun
1778–1779   John Wereat
1779–1780   George Walton
1780–1781   Richard Howley
1781   Stephen Heard
1781–1782   Nathan Brownson
1782–1783   John Martin
1783–1784   Lyman Hall
1784–1785   John Houstoun
1785–1786   Samuel Elbert
1786–1787   Edward Telfair
1787–1788   George Mathews

Maryland

1634–1647	Leonard Calvert

For brief periods during Leonard Calvert's tenure Richard Ingle and Edward Hill controlled the province.

1647–1649	Thomas Greene
1649–1655	William Stone

Stone was for a time supplanted by the Parliamentary Commissioners. In 1654, he and the commissioners were replaced by a committee consisting largely of Puritans.

1656–1660	Josias Fendall

Fendall was supplanted by others during his nominal term of office.

1660	Philip Calvert
1661–1675	Charles Calvert
1675–1692	Among those having part in the government of Maryland at this time were Jesse Wharton, Thomas Notley, William Joseph, John Coode, Nehemiah Blakiston, and others.
1692–1693	Sir Lionel Copley

Subsequent to Copley's death, those who succeeded him in authority or who claimed succession were Sir Thomas Lawrence, Sir Edmund Andros, and Colonel Nicholas Greenbury.

1693–1698	Sir Francis Nicholson
1698–1702	Nathaniel Blakiston

Thomas Tench, President of the Council, acted as governor during Blakiston's absence in England in 1702.

1704–1709	John Seymour

During interim periods, Francis Jenkins and Edward Lloyd of the Governor's Council served as chief magistrates.

1713–1720	John Hart

Hart was succeeded by Thomas Brooke, President of the Council, in 1720.

1720–1727	Charles Calvert
1727–1731	Benedict Leonard Calvert
1731–1742	Samuel Ogle

Ogle's tenure was broken by a brief period of personal control by the fifth Lord Baltimore in 1733.

1742–1747	Thomas Bladen
1747–1752	Samuel Ogle
1752–1753	Benjamin Tasker
1753–1769	Horatio Sharpe
1769–1776	Robert Eden
1774–1777	Committees, Conventions, and Councils of Safety
1777–1779	Thomas Johnson
1779–1782	Thomas Sim Lee
1782–1785	William Paca
1785–1788	William Smallwood

Massachusetts

PLYMOUTH COLONY

1620–1621	John Carver
1621–1632	William Bradford
1633–1634	Edward Winslow

1634–1635   Thomas Prence
1635–1636   William Bradford
1636–1637   Edward Winslow
1637–1638   William Bradford
1638–1639   Thomas Prence
1639–1644   William Bradford
1644–1645   Edward Winslow
1645–1657   William Bradford
1657–1673   Thomas Prence
1673–1680   Josiah Winslow
1680–1692   Thomas Hinckley

Plymouth was absorbed into Massachusetts Bay by the new charter issued to the Bay Colony in 1691.

MASSACHUSETTS BAY

1629–1630   John Endecott
1630–1633   John Winthrop
1634–1635   Thomas Dudley
1635–1636   John Haynes
1636–1637   Sir Henry Vane
1637–1640   John Winthrop
1640–1641   Thomas Dudley
1641–1642   Richard Bellingham
1642–1644   John Winthrop
1644–1645   John Endecott
1645–1646   Thomas Dudley
1646–1649   John Winthrop
1649–1650   John Endecott
1650–1651   Thomas Dudley
1651–1654   John Endecott
1654–1655   Richard Bellingham
1655–1665   John Endecott
1665–1672   Richard Bellingham
1672–1679   John Leverett
1679–1685   Simon Bradstreet
1686   Joseph Dudley
1687–1689   Sir Edmund Andros
1689–1691   Simon Bradstreet
1691–1694   Sir William Phips
1694–1699   Lieutenant Governor
            William Stoughton
1699–1700   Richard Coote, Earl of
            Bellomont
1700–1701   Lieutenant Governor
            William Stoughton

1701–1702   The Council
1702–1714   Joseph Dudley
1715–1716   Lieutenant Governor
            William Tailer
1716–1722   Samuel Shute
1722–1727   Lieutenant Governor
            William Dummer
1727–1729   William Burnet
1729–1730   Lieutenant Governor
            William Dummer
1730–1741   Jonathan Belcher
1741–1757   William Shirley
1757–1760   Thomas Pownall
1760   Lieutenant Governor
            Thomas Hutchinson
1760–1769   Sir Francis Bernard
1769–1774   Thomas Hutchinson
            (Acting Governor
            1769–1770)
1774–1775   General Thomas Gage
1775–1780   Massachusetts was governed by committees
            during the Revolution
            and acquired a chief
            magistrate only with
            the state's new constitution in 1780.

MASSACHUSETTS

1780–1785   John Hancock
1785–1787   James Bowdoin
1787–1793   John Hancock

New Hampshire

The governor of Massachusetts served as the chief magistrate of New Hampshire from 1641, when the Bay Colony first claimed the region, until 1679, when it became a royal province. Between 1680 and 1741, when the royal governor resided in Massachusetts, the lieutenant governor acted as chief magistrate.

1680–1681   John Cutt (President of
            the Council)

1681–1682   Richard Waldron (President of the Council)

1682–1685   Lieutenant Governor Edward Cranfield

1685–1686   Deputy Governor Walter Barefoote

1686–1687   Joseph Dudley

1687–1689   Sir Edmund Andros

1689–1692   Simon Bradstreet

1692–1697   Lieutenant Governor John Usher

1697–1698   Lieutenant Governor William Partridge

1698–1699   Samuel Allen

1699–1702   Lieutenant Governor William Partridge

1702–1715   Lieutenant Governor John Usher

1715–1716   Lieutenant Governor George Vaughan

1717–1730   Lieutenant Governor John Wentworth

1731–1741   Lieutenant Governor Daniel Dunbar

1741–1766   Benning Wentworth

1767–1775   John Wentworth

1776–1785   Meshech Ware

1785–1786   John Langdon

1786–1788   John Sullivan

1788–1789   John Langdon

New Jersey

EAST JERSEY

1677–1682   Philip Carteret

1682–1690   Robert Barclay (Proprietary Governor in England)

1682–1683   Deputy Governor Thomas Rudyard

1683–1686   Deputy Governor Gawen Lawrie

1686–1687   Deputy Governor Lord Neil Campbell

1687–1688   Deputy Governor Andrew Hamilton

1688–1689   Sir Edmund Andros

1690   John Tatham (Proprietary Governor, rejected by province)

1691   Joseph Dudley (Proprietary Governor, rejected by province)

WEST JERSEY

1676–1679   Board of Commissioners

1679–1687   Edward Byllinge

1679–1684   Deputy Governor Samuel Jennings

1684–1685   Thomas Ollive

1685–1687   John Skene

1687–1690   Daniel Coxe

1690   Deputy Governor Edward Hunloke

1691   West Jersey Society of Proprietors

NEW JERSEY

1692–1697   Andrew Hamilton

1697–1699   Jeremiah Basse

1699–1702   Andrew Hamilton

From 1702–1736, the governor of New Jersey was also the governor of New York.

1702–1708   Edward Hyde, Viscount Cornbury

1708–1709   John Lovelace, Baron Lovelace of Hurley

1709–1710   Lieutenant Governor Richard Ingoldesby

1710–1720   Robert Hunter

1720–1728   William Burnet

1728–1731   John Montgomerie

1731–1732   Lewis Morris (President of the Council)

1732–1736   William Cosby

1736   John Anderson (President of the Council)

1736–1738   John Hamilton (President of the Council)
1738–1746   Lewis Morris
1746   John Hamilton (President of the Council)
1746–1747   John Reading (President of the Council)
1747–1757   Jonathan Belcher
1757–1758.   John Reading (President of the Council)
1758–1760   Sir Francis Bernard
1760–1761   Thomas Boone
1761–1763   Josiah Hardy
1763–1776   William Franklin
1776–1790   William Livingston

New York

NEW NETHERLAND

The chief magistrate was called Director-General.
1623   Adriaen Joris
1624–1625   Cornelis Jacobsen May
1625–1626   Willem Verhulst
1626–1632   Peter Minuit
1632–1633   The Council
1633–1638   Wouter van Twiller
1638–1647   Willem Kieft
1647–1664   Peter Stuyvesant
New Netherland was captured by the English in 1664.

NEW SWEDEN

1638–1640   Peter Minuit
1640   Acting Governor Jost van Bogardt
1640–1643˙   Peter Hollander
1643–1653   Johan Printz
1653–1654   Acting Governor John Papegoga
1654–1655   Johan Rising
New Sweden was captured by the Dutch in 1655 and thereafter became part of New Netherland; and in 1664 part of the Duke of York's grant.

NEW YORK

1664–1667   Richard Nicolls
1667–1673   Francis Lovelace
The Dutch recaptured the colony in 1673 and Anthony Colve held the post of Director-General until the province once again came under English rule in 1674.
1674–1682   Edmund Andros
1682–1687   Thomas Dongan
1687–1689   Sir Edmund Andros
1688–1689   Lieutenant Governor Francis Nicholson
1689–1691   Jacob Leisler
1691   Henry Sloughter
1691–1692   Acting Governor Richard Ingoldesby
1692–1698   Benjamin Fletcher
1698–1699   Richard Coote, Earl of Bellomont
1699–1700   Lieutenant Governor John Nanfan
1700–1701   Richard Coote, Earl of Bellomont
1701   The Council
1701–1702   Lieutenant Governor John Nanfan
1702–1708   Edward Hyde, Viscount Cornbury
1708–1709   John Lovelace, Baron Lovelace of Hurley
1709–1710   During a period of transition until a new royal governor was appointed, the office of chief magistrate shifted between the council's presidents— Peter Schuyler, who was succeeded by Gerardus Beekman— and Lieutenant Governor Richard Ingoldesby.
1710–1719   Robert Hunter

1719–1720   Peter Schuyler (President of the Council)
1720–1728   William Burnet
1728–1731   John Montgomerie
1731–1732   Rip Van Dam (President of the Council)
1732–1736   William Cosby
1736–1743   Lieutenant Governor George Clarke
            Lord De La Warr was appointed governor in June 1737, but resigned the following September.
1743–1753   George Clinton
1753   Sir Danvers Osborne
1753–1755   Lieutenant Governor James DeLancey
1755–1757   Sir Charles Hardy
1757–1760   Lieutenant Governor James DeLancey
1760–1761   Lieutenant Governor Cadwallader Colden
1761   Robert Monckton
1761–1762   Lieutenant Governor Cadwallader Colden
1762–1763   Robert Monckton
1763–1765   Lieutenant Governor Cadwallader Colden
1765–1769   Sir Henry Moore
1769–1770   Lieutenant Governor Cadwallader Colden
1770–1771   John Murray, Earl of Dunmore
1771–1774   William Tryon
1774–1775   Lieutenant Governor Cadwallader Colden
1775   William Tryon
1776–1795   George Clinton

North Carolina

GOVERNORS OF "ALBEMARLE COUNTY"
UNDER THE LORDS PROPRIETORS

1663–1667   William Drummond
1667–1669   Samuel Stephens

1670–1673   Peter Carteret
1673–1676   John Jenkins (President of the Council)
1676–1678   Thomas Eastchurch
1677   Deputy Governor Thomas Miller
1677–1678   John Culpeper (elected by "the rebels")
1678   Seth Sothel
1679   Deputy Governor John Harvey
1679–1681   John Jenkins (President of the Council)
1682–1689   Seth Sothel

GOVERNORS OF "THAT PART OF THE PROVINCE OF CAROLINA THAT LIES NORTH AND EAST OF CAPE FEAR" UNDER THE LORDS PROPRIETORS

1689–1691   Deputy Governor Philip Ludwell
1691–1694   Deputy Governor Thomas Jarvis
1694–1699   Deputy Governor Thomas Harvey
1699–1704   Henderson Walker (President of the Council)
1704–1705   Deputy Governor Robert Daniel
1705–1706   Deputy Governor Thomas Cary
1706–1708   William Glover (President of the Council)
1708–1710   Thomas Cary (President of the Council)
1710–1712   Edward Hyde

GOVERNORS OF "NORTH CAROLINA" UNDER THE LORDS PROPRIETORS

1712   Edward Hyde
1712–1714   Thomas Pollock (President of the Council)
1714–1722   Charles Eden

1722	Thomas Pollock (President of the Council)
1722–1724	William Reed (President of the Council)
1724–1725	George Burrington
1725–1729	Richard Everard

ROYAL GOVERNORS

1729–1731	Richard Everard
	Everard held office until George Burrington, the royal governor, arrived from England.
1731–1734	George Burrington
1734–1752	Gabriel Johnston
1752–1753	Nathaniel Rice (President of the Council)
1753–1754	Matthew Rowan (President of the Council)
1754–1765	Arthur Dobbs
1765–1771	William Tryon
1771	James Hasell (President of the Council)
1771–1775	Josiah Martin

PRESIDENTS OF THE COUNCIL UNDER THE REVOLUTIONARY GOVERNMENT

1775–1776	Cornelius Harnett
1776	Samuel Ashe
1776	Willie Jones

GOVERNORS OF THE STATE

1776–1780	Richard Caswell
1780–1781	Abner Nash
1781–1782	Thomas Burke
1782–1784	Alexander Martin
1784–1787	Richard Caswell
1787–1789	Samuel Johnston

Pennsylvania and Delaware

PENNSYLVANIA

1681–1682	Deputy Governor William Markham
1682–1684	William Penn
1684–1688	The Council (Thomas Lloyd, President)
1688–1690	Deputy Governor John Blackwell
1690–1691	The Council (Thomas Lloyd, President)
1691–1693	Deputy Governor Thomas Lloyd
1693–1694	Royal Governor Benjamin Fletcher
1693–1694	Lieutenant Governor William Markham
1694–1699	Lieutenant Governor William Markham
1699–1701	William Penn
1701–1703	Deputy Governor Andrew Hamilton
1703–1704	The Council (Edward Shippen, President)
1704–1709	Deputy Governor John Evans
1709–1717	Deputy Governor Charles Gookin
1717–1718	Deputy Governor Sir William Keith
1718–1726	Deputy Governor Sir William Keith
1726–1736	Deputy Governor Patrick Gordon
1736–1738	The Council (James Logan, President)
1738–1746	Deputy Governor George Thomas
1746–1747	Deputy Governor George Thomas
1747–1748	The Council (Anthony Palmer, President)
1748–1754	Deputy Governor James Hamilton
1754–1756	Deputy Governor Robert Hunter Morris
1756–1759	Deputy Governor William Denny

1759–1763	Deputy Governor James Hamilton
1763–1771	Deputy Governor John Penn
1771	The Council (James Hamilton, President)
1771–1773	Lieutenant Governor Richard Penn
1773	The Council (James Hamilton, President)
1773–1776	John Penn

PRESIDENTS OF THE SUPREME
EXECUTIVE COUNCIL

1777–1778	Thomas Wharton, Jr.
1778	George Bryan (Vice-President, Acting President after Thomas Wharton's death)
1778–1781	Joseph Reed
1781–1782	William Moore
1782–1785	John Dickinson
1785–1788	Benjamin Franklin

DELAWARE

1777	President John Mc-Kinly
1777	President George Read
1777–1778	Thomas McKean
1778–1781	Caesar Rodney
1781–1783	John Dickinson
1782–1783	John Cook (Speaker of the Council)
1783–1786	Nicholas Van Dyke
1786–1789	Thomas Collins

Rhode Island

1663–1666	Benedict Arnold
1666–1669	William Brenton
1669–1672	Benedict Arnold
1672–1674	Nicholas Easton
1674–1676	William Coddington
1676–1677	Walter Clarke
1677–1678	Benedict Arnold

1678	William Coddington
1678–1680	John Cranston
1680–1683	Peleg Stanford
1683–1685	William Coddington, Jr.
1685–1686	Henry Bull
1686	Walter Clarke
1687–1689	Sir Edmund Andros
1689–1690	Deputy Governor John Coggeshall
1690	Henry Bull
1690–1695	John Easton
1695	Caleb Carr
1696–1698	Walter Clarke
1698–1727	Samuel Cranston
1727–1732	Joseph Jenckes
1732–1733	William Wanton
1734–1740	John Wanton
1740–1743	Richard Ward
1743–1745	William Greene
1745–1746	Gideon Wanton
1746–1747	William Greene
1747–1748	Gideon Wanton
1748–1755	William Greene
1755–1757	Stephen Hopkins
1757–1758	William Greene
1758–1762	Stephen Hopkins
1762–1763	Samuel Ward
1763–1765	Stephen Hopkins
1765–1767	Samuel Ward
1767–1768	Stephen Hopkins
1768–1769	Josias Lyndon
1769–1775	Joseph Wanton
1775–1778	Nicholas Cooke
1778–1786	William Greene, Jr.
1786–1790	John Collins

South Carolina

1669–1670	William Sayle (first governor of the colony established on the Ashley River)
1670–1672	Joseph West (chosen by the council)
1672–1674	Sir John Yeamans
1674–1682	Joseph West

1682–1684	Joseph Morton
1684	Richard Kyrle
1684–1685	Robert Quary (chosen by the council)
1684–1685	Joseph West
1685–1686	Joseph Morton
1686–1690	John Colleton
1690–1691	Seth Sothel
1691–1693	Philip Ludwell
1693–1694	Thomas Smith
1694	Joseph Blake (chosen by the council)
1694–1696	John Archdale
1696–1700	Deputy Governor Joseph Blake
1700–1702	James Moore (chosen by the council)
1702–1708	Sir Nathaniel Johnson
1708–1709	Colonel Edward Tynte
1709–1712	Robert Gibbes
1712–1716	Charles Craven
1716–1717	Deputy Governor Robert Daniel
1717–1719	Robert Johnson

ROYAL GOVERNORS

1719–1721	James Moore (revolutionary governor)
1721–1729	Sir Francis Nicholson Nicholson administered the government from 1721 to 1724, when he returned to England.
1724–1729	Arthur Middleton (President of the Council)
1729–1735	Robert Johnson
1735–1737	Lieutenant Governor Thomas Broughton
1738–1743	Lieutenant Governor William Bull Bull administered the government as President of the Council

	from 1737 to 1738; he was Lieutenant Governor from 1738 to his death in 1755 and, as such, administered the government from 1738 to 1743.
1738	Samuel Horsey Horsey died soon after his appointment and did not come to America.
1738–1756	James Glen Glen was appointed governor in 1738 but did not arrive until 1743, from which time he ran the government until he was superseded in 1756.
1756–1760	William Henry Lyttleton
1760–1761	Lieutenant Governor William Bull, 2nd Bull held office from 1759 to 1775.
1760	Thomas Pownall Pownall never assumed his post.
1761–1764	Thomas Boone
1764–1766	Lieutenant Governor William Bull, 2nd
1766–1773	Lord Charles Greville Montagu Montagu administered the government from 1766 to 1768 and 1769 to 1773; during his absence, Lieutenant Governor William Bull, 2nd ran the colony's affairs.
1773–1775	Lieutenant Governor William Bull, 2nd

1775–1776   Lord William Campbell

GOVERNORS OF THE STATE

1776–1778   President John Rutledge
1778–1779   President Rawlins
            Lowndes
1779–1782   John Randolph
1782–1783   John Mathews
1783–1785   Benjamin Guerard
1785–1787   William Moultrie
1787–1789   Thomas Pinckney

Virginia

1607   Edward Maria Wing-
            field (President of
            the Council)
1607–1608   Captain John Ratcliffe
            (President of the
            Council)
1608–1609   Captain John Smith
            (President of the
            Council)
1609–1610   Captain George Percy
            (President of the
            Council)
1610   Lieutenant and Deputy
            Governor Sir Thomas
            Gates
1610–1611   Governor and Captain
            General Thomas,
            Lord De La Warr
1611   Deputy Governor Cap-
            tain George Percy
1611   Sir Thomas Dale (High
            Marshal)
1611–1614   Acting Governor   Sir
            Thomas Gates
1614–1616   Acting Governor   Sir
            Thomas Dale
1616–1617   Lieutenant Governor
            Captain George
            Yeardley
1617–1619   Lieutenant Governor
            Captain Samuel Ar-
            gall

1619   Captain Nathaniel Pow-
            ell (President of the
            Council)
1619–1621   Governor and Captain
            General Sir George
            Yeardley
1621–1626   Governor and Captain
            General Sir Francis
            Wyatt
1626–1627   Governor and Captain
            General Sir George
            Yeardley
1627–1629   Captain Francis West
            (President of the
            Council)
1629–1630   Dr. John Pott (Presi-
            dent of the Council)
1630–1635   Governor and Captain
            General Sir John
            Harvey
1635–1637   Deputy Governor Cap-
            tain John West
1637–1639   Governor and Captain
            General Sir John
            Harvey
1639–1642   Governor and Captain
            General Sir Francis
            Wyatt
1642–1644   Governor and Captain
            General Sir William
            Berkeley
1644–1645   Deputy Governor Rich-
            ard Kemp
1645–1652   Governor and Captain
            General Sir William
            Berkeley
1652–1655   Acting Governor Rich-
            ard Bennett
1655–1658   Edward Digges (Presi-
            dent of the Council)
1658–1660   Captain Samuel Math-
            ews (President of the
            Council)
1661–1662   Lieutenant Governor
            Colonel Francis Mo-
            ryson

1662–1677 Governor and Captain General Sir William Berkeley

1677–1678 Lieutenant Governor Sir Herbert Jeffreys

1678–1680 Deputy Governor Sir Henry Chicheley

1680 Governor and Captain General Thomas Culpeper, Baron Culpeper of Thoresway

1680–1682 Deputy Governor Sir Henry Chicheley

1682–1683 Governor and Captain General Thomas Culpeper, Baron Culpeper of Thoresway

1683–1684 Colonel Nicholas Spencer (President of the Council)

1684–1688 Lieutenant Governor Francis Howard, Baron Howard of Effingham

1688–1690 Colonel Nathaniel Bacon, Sr. (President of the Council)

1690–1692 Lieutenant Governor Colonel Francis Nicholson

1692–1698 Governor and Captain General Sir Edmund Andros

1697–1737 Governor - in - Chief George Hamilton, Earl of Orkney

1698–1705 Lieutenant Governor Colonel Francis Nicholson

1705–1706 Chief Governor Colonel Edward Nott

1706–1710 Colonel Edmund Jennings (President of the Council

1710–1722 Lieutenant Governor Colonel Alexander Spotswood

1722–1726 Lieutenant Governor Colonel Hugh Drysdale

1726–1727 Colonel Robert Carter (President of the Council)

1727–1740 Lieutenant Governor Colonel William Gooch

1737–1754 Governor-in-Chief William Anne Keppel, Earl of Albemarle

1740–1741 Commissary James Blair (President of the Council)

1741–1749 Lieutenant Governor Colonel William Gooch

1749 Colonel John Robinson (President of the Council)

1749–1751 Colonel Thomas Lee (President of the Council)

1751 Colonel Lewis Burwell (President of the Council)

1751–1758 Lieutenant Governor Robert Dinwiddie

1756–1763 Governor-in-Chief and Captain General John Campbell, Earl of Loudoun

1758 Colonel John Blair (President of the Council)

1758–1768 Lieutenant Governor Colonel Francis Fauquier

1763–1768 Governor-in-Chief and Captain General Sir Jeffrey Amherst

1768	Colonel John Blair (President of the Council)	1775–1776	Edmund Pendleton (Chairman of the Committee of Safety)
1768–1770	Governor in-Chief Norborne Berkeley, Baron de Botetourt	1776–1779	Patrick Henry
		1779–1781	Thomas Jefferson
1770–1771	Colonel William Nelson (President of the Council)	1781	William Fleming (President of the Council)
		1781	Thomas Nelson
1771–1775	Governor-in-Chief John Murray, Earl of Dunmore	1781–1784	Benjamin Harrison
		1784–1786	Patrick Henry
		1786–1788	Edmund Randolph

Index

Under each main entry, subentries indicating chronological periods come first; titles of books and articles come last. All volumes mentioned in the Bibliographical Essays have been indexed by author the first time they are referred to. Books touched on in the text have been listed under title.

Aaron, Daniel: *America in Crisis*, 684

Abbott, W. W.: *Royal Governors of Georgia*, 515

Abercromby, James (1706–1781): and French and Indian War, 391, 394

Abernethy, T. P.: *Frontier to Plantation*, 682; *Three Virginia Frontiers*, 515; *Western Lands and the American Revolution*, 552

Abnaki Indians: and French, 330, 376

Acadia; *see* Nova Scotia

Act Concerning Religion (1649), 182

Act for Preventing Frauds; *see* Navigation Act of 1696

Act for Prohibiting the Importation of Germans (1750), 371

Act for . . . Suppression of Piracy (1699), 338

Act of Settlement (1701), 355

Act of Toleration (1689), 301

Act of Union (1682): Delaware and Pennsylvania united by, 236

Adair, Douglass: Jarratt "Autobiography," 514; *Peter Oliver*, 593

Adams, C. F.: *Three Episodes*, 162

Adams, Henry: study of John Smith, 119

Adams, John (1735–1826), 441, 664, 668; on America as "unwieldy body," 579; on American law's diversity, 353; on Anglican hierarchy and fear of, 535; and Barbary Pirates, 665; biographies of, 466, 594; on Boston Tea Party, 563; as British ambassador, 662; on British Empire's future seat, 396; on Charleston fur trade, 495; on Congress's burdens, 579; on Congress's diversity, 470; Con-

Adams, John (*cont.*)
gress sized up by, 569; and constitution of 1780, 647; and Declaration of Rights, 571–72; on Dickinson, 582; on government, 475, 644, 645; with Howe, 606; Hutchinson answered by, 559; and independence, 583, 589–90, 591, 592; law chosen as profession by, 420, 445; law talk with Allen, 570; on Massachusetts role in Congress, 570; on mechanic arts, 654; on New England, 487; and New-tonianism, 433; Novanglus essays, 576; on Otis and writs of assistance, 408; as peace commissioner, 633; on peace commissioners, 588; on Prohibitory Act, 587; resolves to study governments, 474; similes for colonies approaching independence, 582; on social revolution, 643; on Southern gentry, 490; on study of politics and war, 463; on Washington cult, 623

Adams, J. T.: *Founding of New England*, 82; *Provincial Society*, 510; *Revolutionary New England*, 593

Adams, R. G.: *Political Ideas*, 595; Wilson writings, selected, 595

Adams, Samuel (1722–1803), 664; biography of, 553; British search for, 577; on Catholics, 566; and Committee of Correspondence, 558; on *Common Sense*, 586; on Congress and Suffolk Reserves, 570; and Constitution, 668, 675; Copley paints, 463; Galloway on, 571; and *Gaspee* incident, 560; and Hutchinson, 559; and independence, 589, 590; and Massachusetts circular letter, 546; seeks to "improve" events, 557; *Writings* of, 593

Addison, Joseph (1672–1719): in almanacs, 455; Franklin apes style of, 454;
writes on Indians, 332
Address to the Inhabitants of Great Britain (1775), 581
Address to the Inhabitants of . . . Quebec
(1774), 572
Address to the People of Great Britain
(1774), 572
Administration of Justice Act (1774),
564–65
admiralty: courts of, in America, 334, 339;
and governor's instructions, 345; jurisdiction of courts, 343; and protection
against pirates, 279; see also vice-admiralty courts
Africa: and Navigation Act (1651), 190;
Portuguese explore coast of, 8–9, 12–13
agent, colonial: duties of, 341; and Massachusetts, 256, 258; Penn's charter requires, 233; and Revenue Act (1764),
533; and Stamp Act, 535; studies of,
357
Age of Reason (Paine, 1794), 436
agriculture: in backcountry, 499; and careless land treatment, 44; as debate topic,
656; and Carolina country, 484–95; and
Carolina experimental program, 211,
213; in Chesapeake region (seventeenth
century), 115–17, 181; in Chesapeake
region (eighteenth century), 487-89; in
Delaware Valley, 480–81; in Hudson
Valley, 476; and La Salle's dreams for
New France, 319; in medieval world, 3;
in New England, 153; in Spanish
America, 24; studies of, 310, 510;
and Virginia experimental program, 91,
102–3; and Washington's experiments,
489
Ailly, Pierre d' (1350–1420): influence on
Columbus, 14
Aix-la-Chapelle, Peace of (1748), 401;
provisions, 382
Akagi, R. A.: Town Proprietors, 163
Alamance, Battle of, 508–9
Albany Congress (1754), 386–87; studies
on, 413
Albany (Fort Orange), 217, 221, 324; and
Canadian invasion (1690), 325; as
Dutch stronghold, 170, 478; as Dutch
village, 222; Hudson passes site of, 216;
Indian conference at (1684), 321; and
Iroquois, 324; and King William's War,
328; and Leisler, 268; Montreal's trade
with, 386; and Van Rensselaer patroon-
ship, 218

Albemarle County (North Carolina), 212;
and Culpeper's rebellion, 250–51; econ-
omy of, 487; settlement of, 211
Albemarle, George Monck, 1st Duke of
(1608–1670): proprietor of Carolina,
209
Albemarle Sound: Amadas visits, 34; Vir-
ginians in, 208; Carolina charter in-
cludes, 209; population of, 215
Albemarle, William Anne Keppel, Earl of
(1732–1754): as governor-in-chief of
Virginia, 697
Alberts, R. C.: Major Robert Stobo, 413
Albion, R. C.: Fithian Journal, 511
Alcaçovas, Treaty of (1479), 12, 17
Alden, J. E.: "John Mein," 639
Alden, John (c. 1599–1687), 125
Alden, J. R.: American Revolution, 636;
Charles Lee, 640; First South, 513; Gen-
eral Gage, 552; John Stuart, 552; South
in Revolution, 513
Alderfer, E. G.: Witness of Penn, 273
Aldridge, A, O.: Paine, 466; Franklin,
594
Alembert, Jean le Rond d' (1717–1783);
Rittenhouse compared to, 452
Alexander VI (1431–1503): papal bulls
of, 17
Alexander, Sir William; see Stirling,
Earl of
Alexandria (Virginia): Common Sense
read in, 586; conference site, 666
Algonquin Indians: as French allies, 320;
locations, 79; westward retreat blocked,
251
Allen, Andrew (1740–1825): talks law
with John Adams, 353, 370
Allen, Ethan (1783–1789), 584; takes Ti-
conderoga, 579; and Vermont, 660
Allen, G. W.: Naval History of Revolu-
tion, 641
Allen, Ira (1751–1814): and Vermont,
660
Allen, Levi: and Vermont, 660
Allen, Samuel: as New Hampshire gover-
nor, 690
Allen, William (1704–1780): on Revenue
Act enforcement, 534
Allen family: St. Clair friend of, 505
almanacs, 297; in seventeenth century,
298; in eighteenth century, 455
Almon, John: Tract on American Colo-
nies, 415
Alsatians: as immigrants, 364
Alsop, George (b. 1638): on immigrants,
71–72

Alvord, C. W.: *First Explorations*, 239; *Mississippi Valley*, 552; works on Illinois country, 355, 552

Amadas, Philip (fl. 1584): voyage to Virginia, 34

Amazon River: Columbus discovers, 18

Ambler, C. H.: *Washington*, 413

American History and Life, 37

American Act of 1764; *see* Revenue Act of 1764

American Historical Association Guide, 37

American Husbandry (1775), 510

American Magazine (1757–1758), 458

American Philosophical Society, 440; founding of, 451; and Franklin, 417

American Revolution: economic aspects of, 608–11; foreign affairs during, 618–21, 633–35; and loyalists, 610–11; military aspects of, 599–635; political background of, 532–50, 557–93; as social movement, 651–56; studies of economic aspects, 637–38; studies of foreign affairs, 639; studies of loyalists, 638; studies of military aspects, 635–40; studies of political background, 550–51, 552–54, 593–96; studies of social aspects, 682

Ames, Nathaniel (1708–1764): almanacs of, 455; on the West, 397

Amherst, Sir Jeffrey (1717–1797): biography of, 552; and French and Indian War, 391; and Indian uprising of 1763, 523–25, 529; journal of, 414; ordered to war on smugglers, 532; as Virginia governor, 346, 697

Amish, beliefs of, 47; and Medicare, 365

Amsterdam, 190; Pilgrims in, 124

Anabaptism: history of, 46–49; and Massachusetts, 178; New Netherland dreads, 220; sects immigrate to colonies, 365; and Virginia, 302

Anburey, Thomas: journal of, 638

Anderson, John: as New Jersey governor, 690

Anderson, T. S.: *Howe Brothers*, 637

Andover (Massachusetts): and witches, 304

Andrade, E. N. da C.: *Sir Isaac Newton*, 465

André, John (1751–1780): as spy, 628

Andrews, C. M.: on Culpeper's Rebellion, 251; on Plantation duty (1673), 194; *Background of American Revolution*, 551; *Beginnings of Connecticut*, 163; *Colonial Period*, 119; *Narratives of In-*

Andrews, C. M. (*cont.*) *surrections*, 273; *New Haven*, 163; "Royal Disallowance," 356

Andrews, M. P.: *Founding of Maryland*, 120; *History of Maryland*, 120

Andrews, Wayne: on Harrison synagogue, 460

Andros, Sir Edmund (1637–1714): crown absolves, 336; deposed, 266; and Dominion of New England, 261–65, 291, 687, 688, 689, 690, 691, 694; establishes political precedent, 671; and King Phillip's War, 255; and New England defenses, 324; and New Jersey, 228; as New York governor, 223–25, 447, 691; as professional governor, 346; searches for lawyers, 293; as Virginia governor, 271, 697

Andros Tracts, 274

Anglicans: in backcountry, 504; in Delaware Valley, 481; in New York, 478; *see also* Church of England

Anglo-Dutch Wars: (1652–1654)— 190–91; and Admiral Penn, 230; and Confederation of New England, 174; and New Netherland, 219; (1664–1667)—200, 220; English goal in, 193–94; and royal commission, 199; (1672–1674)—194; New York recaptured, 223

Annapolis (Maryland), 185; Braddock conference at, 388; convention at (1786), 666–67

Annapolis Royal (Nova Scotia): in King George's War, 378

Anne, Queen (1665–1714): and Board of Trade, 340; invites Palatines to England, 364; supports Vetch scheme, 332

Anson County (North Carolina): created, 372

Antifederalism: and ratification of Constitution, 675, 676

Antigua: ceded to England, 194; Parliament restricts trade of, 190

Antilla, 18

Antilles, 191; Spanish tighten hold on, 21

Antinomians: and Anne Hutchinson, 145–46; judgment on name, 182; protection of urged, 178; and St. Stephens congregation, 150; studies of, 162

apprenticeship: in Boston, 283; in England, 60; and Hat Act, 400; *see also* indentured servitude

Arbella, 133, 134; crossing of, 73

Arber, Edward: *First Three English Books on America*, 39; Smith *Works*, 119

Archdale, John (c. 1642–c. 1717); as South Carolina governor, 695

Archibald, W. S.: *Hooker*, 163

architecture, in seventeenth–century America, 285–86; in eighteenth–century America, 458–61 and Dutch heritage, 221; studies of, 309, 467

Archives of the State of New Jersey, 240

Arendt, Hannah: on the American Revolution, 644; *On Revolution*, 682

Argall, Sir Samuel (fl. 1609–1624), 100; captures Pocahontas, 280; captures Port Royal, 332; as Virginia governor, 99, 696

Arizona: Coronado explores, 26

Ark: brings settlers to Maryland, 112

Arlington, Lord: and Virginia grant, 244, 270

Arminianism: and Laud, 140; and Puritans, 70; and Whitefield, 424

Arminius, Jacobus (1560–1609), 140

Arnold, Benedict (fl. 1670): as Rhode Island governor, 694

Arnold, Benedict (1741–1801): and Canadian invasion, 602, 603; and Fort Ticonderoga, 579; and Fort Stanwix siege, 616; and Quebec, 585; at Saratoga, 616; slows British advance down Lake Champlain, 607; in the South, 628, 630; studies of, 640; treason of, 628; wounded, 588, 602

art: in seventeenth-century America, 285–88; in eighteenth-century America, 462–63; studies of, 309–10, 467

Art of Physic (Galen), 300

Articles of Capitulation (1664), 220–21

Articles of Confederation: Clinton favors, 674; drafting and adoption of, 647–51; Franklin draft of, 581; Maryland accedes to, 631; revision of called for, 666

Ashe, S. A.: *History of North Carolina*, 239

Ashe, Samuel (1725–1813): as North Carolina governor, 693

Association, the: Congress creates, 572–73; colonies adopt, 576

assemblies: backcountry representation in, 372, 506, 507, 508; described, 349–52; English and American views of, 349–50; first in colonies, 101; and freedom of speech, 350–51; and the French menace, 327–28; and Glorious Revolution, 327; and judiciary, 354; and royal governor, 347; and royal governor's instructions regarding, 106; study of, in South, 357

Astronomical Diary and Almanac (1725–1764), 455

Atlantis: and Gilbert, 31

attorney: duties of, 445

audiencias: role in the empire, 22

Augsburg, Peace of (1555), 49

Augsburg, War of the League of; *see* King William's War

Augusta County (Virginia): created, 372, 506

Augusta (Georgia), 495

Aulnay de Charnisé, Charles de Menou, Sieur d': seizes Penobscot, 154

Austrian Succession, War of; *see* King George's War

Avalon Peninsula, 108–9

Avignon: as home of popes, 5

ax: seventeenth-century version described, 286

Azores: as New England market, 176; and papal bulls, 17; and Portugal, 8, 12, 17; and Staple Act, 193

Aztecs: fall to Cortez, 21

Azurara, Gomes Eannes de: on Portuguese explorations, 12

"Babylonian captivity" (1305–1378), 6

backcountry: attitude toward crown, 344; and Board of Trade, 377; customs and manners in, 501–3; described, 496–509; Eastern attitude toward, 497, 501, 659; Eastern relations, 503–6; and fall line, 78; government in, 372, 505; humor in, 503; land prices in, 498–99; and legislatures, 349; loyalism in, 509; and Paxton riots, 528–29, 530; and Pennsylvania politics, 589; people in, 498; settlement of, 497–501; and South Carolina, 216, 495, 496; studies of, 514; and Virginia, 245, 246, 247; *see also* West

Bacon family: in Virginia, 291

Bacon, Sir Francis (1561–1626): on colonial governments, 339; on science, 452

Bacon, Nathaniel, Sr.: befriends cousin, 246; as acting governor, 246

Bacon, Nathaniel (1647–1676): characterized, 246; as councilor, 348; Craven on, 249; death of, 248

Bacon's Laws (1676): described, 247; revoked, 249

Bacon's Rebellion, 267, 291; Beverley on, 457; described, 244–49; influence outside Virginia, 250, 251; influence on governor's salary, 351; Randolph's proposal for troops used in, 257; studies of, 273

Baer, Elizabeth: *Seventeenth-Century Maryland,* 120

Bahama Islands: Columbus discovers, 16; Ponce de León explores, 21; proprietors sell out to crown, 340

Bailyn, Bernard: on American Enlightenment, 437; on New England trade, 176; on New England merchants, 198; *Education in the Forming of American Society,* 310; *Massachusetts Shipping,* 511; *New England Merchants,* 163; *Pamphlets of American Revolution,* 551; "Political Experience and Enlightenment Ideas," 465; "Politics and Social Structure in Virginia," 273

Bailyn, Lotte: *Massachusetts Shipping,* 511

Bainton, R. H.: *Here I Stand,* 81; "Interpretations of Reformation," 83; *Reformation,* 81

Baker, J. N. L.: *History of Geographical Discovery,* 39

Bakeless, John: *George Rogers Clark,* 640

Balboa, Vasco Núñez de (1475–1517), 21

Baldwin, E. H.: "Galloway, Loyalist," 639

Balkans: and John Smith, 91

Ballagh, J. G.: Lee *Letters,* 595

Baltimore, Lords; see Calverts

Baltimore (Maryland), 115; Congress meets in, 611

Bangor (Maine): as Plymouth Company boundary, 87

Bank of England: and Georgia, 374

Bank of North America: created, 609

Baptist Association, 420

Baptists, 419; in backcountry, 504; and Brown University, 443; and Great Awakening, 425, 427; in New England, 471; in Newport, 284; in Pennsylvania, 481

Barbados: and Carolina settlement, 211, 212–13; Colleton immigrates to, 209; economy of, 212; Fox visits, 232; and laws of, 446; as lucrative post for governor, 346; and New England trade, 176; Parliament restricts trade of, 190; Penn-Venable expedition pauses at, 191; and Pennsylvania trade, 237; population compared to Virginia, 167; and South Carolina trade, 215

Barbary pirates: Virginia ships captured by, 278; and United States trade, 663, 665

Barbour, P. L.: *John Smith,* 119

Barclay, Robert (1648–1690): as East Jersey governor, 690

Bard, Samuel (1742–1821); founds medical school, 446

Barefoote, Walter: as New Hampshire governor, 690

Bark, W. C.: on medieval heritage, 4; *Origins of Medieval World,* 38

Barker, C. A.: *Revolution in Maryland,* 553

Barlow, Arthur (fl. 1584): voyages to Virginia, 34

Barnes, V. F.: *Dominion of New England,* 273

Barnhart, J. D.: *Hamilton and Clark,* 636

Barony: in Carolina, 213

Barré, Isaac (1726–1802): and Sons of Liberty, 537

Barrough, Philip (fl. 1583), 300

Barry, Richard: *Mr. Rutledge,* 594

Bartram, John (1699–1777): as botanist, 448

Basse, Jeremiah (d. 1725): as New Jersey governor, 690

Bassett, J. S.: "Regulators of North Carolina," 515

Basye, A. H.: *Lords Commissioners of Trade,* 356

Bates, F. G.: *Rhode Island and the Union,* 684

Battis, Emery: *Saints and Sectaries,* 162

Bayard family, 267, 363, 477

"Bay Psalm Book" (1640), 297

Beall, Otho: on Mather, 450; *Cotton Mather,* 311; "Landmark in Medicine," 311

Beard, C. A.: critiques of 683, 685; *Economic Interpretation of Constitution,* 683

Beaumarchais, Pierre Austin Caron de (1732–1799), 618

beaver: Parliamentary interest in, 400

Beazley, C. R.: *Dawn of Modern Geography,* 38

Becker, C. L.: on Locke, 432; *Declaration of Independence,* 595; *Eve of Revolution,* 551; *Political Parties in New York,* 551

Bedford County (Pennsylvania): created, 372; Smith and St. Clair in, 505

Beech-Brown, Albert: *Architecture of America,* 467

Beekman family: biography and papers of, 512

Beekman, Gerardus: as New York governor, 691

Beer, G. L.: colonial histories of, 414

Belcher, Jonathan (1681–1757): as Massachusetts governor, 689; as New Jersey governor, 691; and paper money, 403

Belfast: Huguenots in, 368; as Logan's home, 369
Belknap, W. P., Jr.: *American Colonial Painting*, 310
Bell, W. J., Jr.: *Early American Science*, 311; "Social History of Pennsylvania," 513
Bellingham, Richard (c. 1592–1672): as Massachusetts governor, 689
Bellomont, Earl of; *see* Coote, Richard
Bemis Heights: and Battle of Saratoga, 616
Bemis, S. F.: *Diplomacy of American Revolution*, 639
Benét, Stephen Vincent: on immigrants' resolve, 277
Benians, E. A.: *Hughes Journal*, 636
Bennett, Richard: as Virginia governor, 184, 696
Bennington: battle at, 613–16
Benson, A. B.: Kalm's *Travels*, 511
Berkeley, Sir John (John, Lord Berkeley), 209; on royal council, 335; receives New Jersey, 222, 226; sells share of New Jersey, 227
Berkeley, Sir William (1606–1677), 106; agricultural experiments of, 181; and Bacon, 246–47, 291; biographies of, 273; and "church people," 365; and Carolina, 209, 211; Craven on, 248; death of, 249; on Dutch traders, 189; on free schools, 297; goes to England, 200, 249; as governor, 180, 346, 696, 697; governorship resumed by, 200; grievances against, 244; and Maryland, 181; on Negro population of Virginia, 290; on New England Indian policy, 251; and Opechancanough, 184; resists Parliamentary force, 184; Stuyvesant bluster likened to, 220
Berlin, Isaiah: *Age of Enlightenment*, 465
Bermuda, 102; and 1612 charter, 96; English "discover," 94; and French treaty, 619; Jamestown depends on, 95; law of, 446; prosperity of, 99, 108; Parliament restricts trade of, 190; and tobacco contract, 105
Bermuda Company, 96; charter annulled, 336
Bernard, Sir Francis (1712–1779): on confusion of colonies' constitutional position, 540; contrasts English and American views on legislatures, 350; correspondence of, 553; and Massachusetts legislature, 547, 549; as Massachusetts governor, 689; as New Jersey governor, 691

Bernheim, G. D.: *German Settlements*, 411
Bernon family, 363
Bethlehem (Pennsylvania): Germans in, 481
Bettering House (Philadelphia), 438, 439
Beverley (Massachusetts): and witches, 304
Beverley, Robert (c. 1673–1722): attitude toward Indians, 80; on Chesapeake society, 114, 117; on Cohabitation Act, 283; as historian, 457; History of Virginia, 310; on lost Roanoke colony, 36; on Opechancanough's death, 184; on physicians, 292
Beveridge, A. J.: *Marshall*, 685
Bezanson, Anne: *Prices and Inflation in Pennsylvania*, 513
Bible: and Anabaptists, 47; and Body of Liberties, 177; and civil institutions, 136; and deism, 436; and education, 295; and eighteenth-century science, 432; and "liberty bell" inscription, 579; and Luther, 44, 45; and New England courts, 262; and New England merchants, 198; proves God created all with purpose, 300; Puritans use to restrict power of church and state, 138; Puritans' view of, 145; and Quakers, 230; Randolph's view of role in legal system, 257; on saints, 134; as a source for first names, 60; Williams' view of, 144; on witches, 304; and word "church," 152
Bidgood, Lee: *First Explorations*, 239
Bidwell, P. W.: *Agriculture in Northern United States*, 310
Bieber, R. P.: *Lords of Trade and Plantations*, 356
Bill, A. H.: *Princeton Campaign*, 637; *Valley Forge*, 639
Bill for Establishing Religious Freedom in Virginia, 435
bill of attainder: and Constitution, 674; and Maryland, 114; and Virginia, 249
bill of rights: and Constitution, 674, 678; and Northwest Ordinance, 659
Billias, G. A.: *Washington's Generals*, 639
Billington, R. A.: *Westward Expansion*, 682
Biloxi: French fort at, 327
Bishop, Bridget: and Salem trial, 304, 305
Bishop of Durham clause: and Carolina charter, 209; and Maryland charter, 110–11; and Penn's charter, 233; and Plowden charter, 111

Bishop of London, 341; and Board of Trade, 339–40; and governor's instructions, 345; and Two Penny Act, 408; and Virginia, 271, 302

Black Boys: raid of, 530

Blackburn, Joseph (fl. 1753–1763): painter, 463

Blackstone, Sir William (1723–1780): textbook of, 445

Blackwell, John: as Pennsylvania governor, 238, 693

Bladen, Martin: and plan to unify colonies, 378

Bladen, Thomas: as Maryland governor, 688

Blair, James (1655–1743): as Commissary, 302; as Virginia's acting governor, 697; and William and Mary College, 271

Blair, John: as Virginia's acting governor, 697, 698

Blair, Mr., 491

Blake, Joseph: as South Carolina governor, 695

Blakston, Nathanial: as Maryland governor, 688

Blakston, Nehemiah: as Maryland governor, 688; and Protestant Association, 271

Bland, Edward: on Carolina, 208

Bland, Richard (1710–1776): on governor's instructions, 345–46

Blathwayt, William: and Auditor General Office, 342; biography of, 274; on Board of Trade, 339; as secretary of Lords of Trade, 336

Bliven, Bruce, Jr.: Battle for Manhattan, 637

Block, Adrien: tours of Long Island, 217; sails up the Connecticut River, 86

Blommaert, Samuel: patroon, 218

bloodletting: in eighteenth century, 300

Blount, William (1749–1800): biography of, 683

Board of Customs Commissioners: created for colonies, 544

Board of Trade: Acadians' deportation asked by, 377; and Act of Settlement (1701), 355; Albany conference called by, 386; on assemblies' powers, 350; backcountry settlement favored by, 373, 377; backcountry settlement opposed by, 519–22; and disallowance, 351; duties and powers of, 339–40; and governor's council, 348; and governor's instructions, 345; Halifax as president of,

Board of Trade (cont.)
405–6; instructions on relations with assemblies during French and Indian War, 397; and judiciary, 354; and Plan for Management of Indian Affairs, 530; and plan to unite colonies, 378; during "salutary neglect" period, 398; and Stamp Act Congress, 538; on standing army in America, 525; studies of, 356; and Two Penny Act, 408

Board of War: Gates heads, 623

Boardman, Elijah: painting of, 463

Boardman, R. S.: Roger Sherman, 594

Boas, Louise: Cotton Mather, 312

Body of Liberties (1641), 138; Cambridge press prints, 297; on capital punishment, 353; contents of, 177

Bohemia: and Calvanism, 51; emigrants from, 364; and John Huss, 5

Bohemian Brethren; see Moravians

Bojador, Cape, 12

Bolingbroke, Henry St. John, first Viscount (1678–1751): on Blathwayt, 336

Bolton, H. E.: Rim of Christendom, 39

Bond, B. W., Jr.: "Colonial Agent," 357; Old Northwest, 682

Book of Architecture (Gibbs, 1728), 460

Boone, Daniel (1734–1820), 501; British capture, 625; on Kentucky statehood, 629

Boone, Thomas: as New Jersey governor, 691; as South Carolina governor, 695

Boorstin, Daniel: on colleges, 443; on colonial science, 451; on Enlightenment, 441; on Puritans, 161–62; on sermons, 307; Americans: Colonial Experience, 441

Bordentown (New Jersey): British in, 608; attempt to take, 612

boroughs: in colonies, 283; and Roanoke government, 36; in Virginia, 100

Boscawen, Edward (1711–1761): and French fleet, 390

Boston: in seventeenth century, 283–84; in eighteenth century, 437, 472–73; and Anne Hutchinson, 145, 146; British evacuate, 588, 602; British occupy, 547, 548, 549, 576–77, 601; and Committee of Correspondence, 558; and first newspaper, 297; founded, 133; fur trade of, 154; and Glorious Revolution, 265–66; Gorton departs, 147; and King Philip's War, 253; and merchants, 155–56; molasses trade of, 476; and Philadelphia, 237, 480; press established in, 297–98; and Revenue Act (1764), 533, 534;

Boston (*cont.*)
   silversmiths in, 287; smallpox in, 449–
   50; taxes New England imports, 174;
   and Tea Act, 562; Whitefield in, 525;
   Williams offered post in, 143; and
   witches, 304; and writs of assistance,
   407
Boston Massacre, 549; oration commemo-
   rates, 558
Boston News-Letter: founded, 297
Boston Port Act (1774): provisions,
   563–64
Boston Tea Party, 563; study of, 593
botany: in seventeenth-century America,
   300–1; in eighteenth-century America,
   447–48
Botetourt, Norborne Berkeley, Baron de
   (c. 1718–1770): as Virginia governor,
   698
Boucher, Jonathan (1738–1789): *Remi-
   niscences,* 638
Boungainville, Louis Antoine de: *Journals,*
   414
Bouquet, Henry (1719–1765): accompa-
   nies Forbes, 394; and Ohio Valley In-
   dians, 529; and Fort Pitt, 526; on Penn-
   sylvanian indifference, 528
Bourepos, David: Huguenot minister, 363
Bourne, E. G.: *Spain in America,* 39
Bowdoin family, 363
Bowdoin, James (1726–1790): as Massa-
   chusetts governor, 689
Bowen, C. D.: *John Adams,* 594
Boyd, J. P.: *Anglo-American Union,* 594;
   Declaration of Independence, 595; *New
   Jersey,* 241
Boyd, W. K.: *North Carolina History,* 514
Boyle, Robert (1627–1691): credulity of,
   300
Boylston, Thomas: wealth of, 472
Boylston, Zabdiel (1679–1766): and inoc-
   ulation, 450
Braddock, Edward (1695–1755): biogra-
   phy of, 413; characterized, 387; death
   of, 389; expedition of, 388–90; reaction
   to defeat of, 390, 396
Braddock's Road: Virginia improves, 530;
   and Western Settlement, 397
Bradford, William (1590–1657), 124;
   abandons communal plan, 127; biography of, 160; on Confederation of New
   England, 170; on dispersal of his people, 282; on loss of life at sea, 72; on
   "muskeeto," 78; on Pequots, 156; on
   Pilgrims' achievements, 129; on Pilgrims' distaste for city life, 124; on

Bradford, William (*cont.*)
   Pilgrims' lack of provisions, 126; as
   Plymouth governor, 127, 688, 689; *Of
   Plymouth Plantation,* 160; works for
   royal charter, 127–9; as writer, 306
Bradstreet, Anne (c. 1612–1672), 308
Bradstreet, Howard: *Pequot War,* 163
Bradstreet, John (c. 1711–1774): and In-
   dians, 529
Bradstreet, Simon (1603–1697): and
   Council of Safety, 266; as Massachu-
   setts governor, 689; as New Hampshire
   governor, 690
Braintree (Massachusetts): iron deposits
   near, 174
Brandywine Creek, Battle of, 618
Branford (Connecticut): founded, 151
Brant, Irving: *Madison,* 683
Brathwaite, Richard (1588–1673): on
   gentlemen, 293
Brattle Street Church: founded, 303
Brattle, Thomas (1658–1713): on Salem
   trials, 305; as scientist, 298–99
Brauer, J. C.: "English Puritanism," 81
Bray, Thomas (1656–1730): article on,
   412
Brazil, 79; Cabral discovers, 18–20; Cabot
   searches for island of, 25; and Dutch,
   189, 217; and Huguenots, 27; and papal
   bulls, 17
Brebner, J. B.: *Explorers of North Amer-
   ica,* 39; *New England's Outpost,* 356
Breda, Treaty of (1667), 194
Breed's Hill: attacked, 600–1; British take,
   580; Americans occupy, 578; *see also*
   Bunker Hill
Brewster, William (1567–1644): and Pil-
   grims, 124–25
Bridenbaugh, Carl: on Carolina society,
   494; on cities and Enlightenment, 438,
   442; on clergy and Stamp Act, 541; on
   East-West tension, 506; on town-coun-
   try tension, 441; *Cities in Revolt,* 465;
   Colonial Craftsmen, 467; Hamilton's
   Itinerarium, 510; M'Roberts' *Tour,* 511;
   Mitre and Sceptre, 414; *Myths and Re-
   alities,* 513; "New England Town,"
   163; *Peter Harrison,* 467; *Rebels and
   Gentlemen,* 513; *Seat of Empire,* 514
Bridenbaugh, Jessica: *Rebels and Gentle-
   men,* 513
Bridges, Charles: painter, 463
Brief . . . Report . . . of Virginia (Hariot,
   1588), 35
Brigham, A. P.: *Geographic Influences,* 83

Bristol, 292; Cabot departs from, 25; and colonization, 86–87; and fishing industry, 25, 57, 175–76; Philadelphia outdistances, 480: and Popham, 87; and tobacco trade, 180

Brockholls, Anthony; receives Penn, 236

Brockunier, S. H.: *Irrepressible Democrat*, 162

Bronner, E. B.: *Penn's "Holy Experiment,"* 241

Brooke, John: *Chatham Administration*, 554

Brooke, Lord; see Grenville, Robert

Brooke, Thomas: as Maryland governor, 688

Brookhaven (New York): founded, 169

Brooklyn Heights: defended, 605; evacuated, 606

Broughton, Thomas: as South Carolina governor, 695

Brown, Alexander: *Genesis of United States*, 119

Brown, A. S.: "British Peace Offer, 1778," 639

Brown, B. K.: *"Puritan Democracy,"* 163; *Virginia*, 514

Brown, G. S.: *Policy of Germain*, 637

Brown, L. A.: *Story of Maps*, 38

Brown, M. L.: *Riedesel Journal*, 639

Brown, R. D.: "Loyalists Estates," 682

Brown, R. E.: *Democracy in Massachusetts*, 512; *Virginia*, 514

Brown, R. H.: *Historical Geography*, 83

Brown, R. M.: on Circuit Court Act, 507; on South Carolina Regulators, 506, 508, 509; *South Carolina Regulators*, 515

Brown, S. C.: *Count Rumford*, 467

Brownson, Nathan: as Georgia governor, 687

Brown University: founded, 429, 443

Brown, W. A.: *Empire or Independence*, 594

Bruce, P. A.: *Economic History of Virginia*, 203; *Institutional History of Virginia*, 310

Brunhouse, R. L.: *Counter-Revolution in Pennsylvania*, 685

Brunswick (New Jersey): attempt to capture, 612

Bryan, George (1731–1791): as Pennsylvania chief magistrate, 694

Bubble Act (1720): extended to colonies, 403

Buchanan, Mr., 491

Buck, P.: *Mercantilism*, 82

Bucks County (Pennsylvania): Log College in, 423

Buford, Abraham (1749–1833): Tarleton defeats, 627

Bull, Henry: as Rhode Island governor, 694

bullionism, 66; see also mercantilism

Bullock, Archibald (1730–1777); as Georgia governor, 687

Bull, William (1638–1755): as South Carolina governor, 695

Bull, William (1710–1791): as South Carolina governor, 695; on Regulators, 507

Bunker Hill, Battle of, 580; casualties, 600–1

Burchard, John: *Architecture of America*, 467

Burgoyne, Sir John (1723–1792); sent to America, 574; on Americans at Bunker Hill, 601; in Boston, 600; attacks Arnold, 603; Saratoga campaign, 613

Burke, Edmund (1729–1797): as colonial agent, 341; plea for conciliation, 574

Burke, Thomas (c. 1747–1783): as North Carolina governor, 693

Burlamaqui, Jean Jacques: Congress refers to, 570

Burlington (New Jersey): Quaker Yearly Meeting in, 481

Burnaby, Andrew: *Travels*, 510–11

Burnet, William (1688–1729): as Massachusetts governor, 689; and New Jersey governor, 690; as New York governor, 352, 692

Burnett, E. C.: *Continental Congress*, 683; *Letters of Congress*, 593

Burr Conspiracy, 623

Burrington, George (c. 1680–1759): as North Carolina governor, 493, 693

Burroughs, Alan: *Limners*, 309

Burwell, Lewis: as Virginia governor, 697

Bushel, Edward: and Penn-Mead trial, 231

Bushy Run (Pennsylvania): battle at, 528

Butler, Walter N. (d. 1781): loyalist, 625

Butterfield, L. H.: *American Indian and White Relations*, 309

Byles, Mather (1707–1788): opposes Revolution, 576

Byllinge, Edward (d. 1687): purchases share of New Jersey, 227; as West Jersey governor, 690

Byrd, William (1652–1704): and Bacon's Rebellion, 244; furnishes home, 287; on reasons for emigration, 71; receives letter from Marquette, 319; on religious

Byrd, William (*cont.*)
  indifference in New York, 302; on unsettled times, 265; and Westover, 461
Byrd, William (1674–1744): *Diaries*, 514; as historian, 457; on North Carolina, 492–93; as Royal Society member, 299; sea imagery in letter of, 73–77

cabin right: in backcountry, 502
Cabot, John (1425–c. 1500): Cipangu goal of, 18; Polo's influence on, 5; second voyage of, 25–26
Cabral, Alvarez (c. 1467–c. 1520): discovers Brazil, 18–20
"caciques": in Carolina, 213
Cady, Edwin: *Gentleman in America*, 310
Cahokia: Clark captures, 625; French fort at, 327, 377
Calder, I. M., Jr., *Colonial Captivities*, 414
Calhoun, A. W.: *Social History of American Family*, 310
Calhoun, John C. (1782–1850): and nullification, 679
calico: and English reexport trade, 195
California: Missouri River supposed route to, 317; as Spanish name, 24
Callahan, North: *Daniel Morgan*, 640
"calling": and Calvin, 50
Calvert, Benedict, fourth Lord Baltimore: retrieves Maryland, 272, 340
Calvert, Benedict Leonard (d. 1732): as Maryland governor, 688
Calvert, Cecilius, second Lord Baltimore (c. 1605–1675): and assembly, 113; inherits colony, 111, orders oath of loyalty to, 185; retrieves colony, 185, 201; and religious toleration, 181–82; seeks absolute control, 202, 250; seeks governorship of Virginia, 114; seeks to make Maryland attractive, 112
Calvert, Charles, third Lord Baltimore (1637–1715): loses control of Maryland, 272, 336; orders William and Mary proclaimed, 271
Calvert, Charles (fl. 1720): as Maryland governor, 688
Calvert, Charles, fifth Lord Baltimore: as Maryland governor, 688
Calvert, George, first Lord Baltimore (c. 1580–1632): characterized, 108–9; death of, 111; grant to, 110; seeks Carolina, 208; and Roger Williams, 147; and Virginia, 109
Calvert, Leonard (1606–1647): and assembly, 113; captures Kent Island, 114;

Calvert, Leonard (*cont.*)
  instructions regarding Protestants, 112; flees Maryland, 181, 184; as Maryland governor, 688
Calvert, Philip: as Maryland governor, 202, 688
Calvin, John (1509–1564), 301; biographies of, 81; biographical sketch of, 49; and covenant theology, 55; and Luther, 45; views on marriage, 56; and Zwingli, 46
Calvinism, 49–51; attitude toward state, 55–56; in colonies, 418–19; and Congregationalism, 135; and Edwards, 436; in England, 51–52; and Enlightenment, 435; studies of, 81; and Whitefield, 424; Whitehead on, 433
Cambridge Agreement (1629), 132
Cambridge (Massachusetts): Anglican mission in, 409; and Hooker's congregation, 148; land for Harvard in, 293; printing in, 287, 297; *see also* Newtown (Massachusetts)
Cambridge Platform of Church Discipline: contents, 179
Cambridge University, 60; and American colleges, 293, 443; Bacon graduate of, 246; Brewster graduate of, 124; graduates of in Massachusetts, 295; Williams attends, 143; Winthrop attends, 132
Cambuluc (Peking): Polos visit, 5
Camden (South Carolina): on Great Wagon Road, 497
Campbell, Archibald: invades Georgia, 626
Campbell, John; *see* Loudoun, fourth Earl of
Campbell, Mildred: "English Emigration," 410; *English Yeoman*, 82; "Social Origins of Some Early Americans," 83
Campbell, Lord Neil: as East Jersey governor, 690
Campbell, Lord William (d. 1778): as South Carolina governor, 696
Canada: boundaries after Quebec Act, 565; British acquire, 518; and Cartier, 26; Champlain and, 86; Colbert's vision of, 316; colonies compared to, 485–86; effect on colonies, 397; Franklin seeks for United States, 633; invasion by Americans, 584, 602; invasion projected (1690), 325; invasion projected by Gates, 623; loyalists immigrate to, 611; population of, 316, 321, 385; in Queen Anne's War, 329–33; as royal colony, 522; size of, 316; studies of, 356

Canary Islands: and Columbus, 16; on English route to America, 34, 72; English trade with, 30; as New England market, 176; rediscovered by Portuguese, 8; Spain keeps, 12; and wine duties, 533

Cão, Diego (fl. 1485), 12

Cape Ann: and Dorchester Company, 129

Cape Breton, 426; Louisbourg on, 376; New England trade with, 472

Cape Cod: Pilgrims sight, 126

Cape Fear: early settlements on, 208, 212

Cape Verde Islands: and Staple Act, 193

caravel: design of, 9

Carleton, Guy, first Baron Dorchester (1724–1808): as governor of Canada, 346, 602; replaces Clinton, 632

Carlisle Commission, 620–21; studies on, 639

Carlisle (Pennsylvania): Bouquet departs from, 528; flooded with refugees, 526; as Scotch-Irish town, 365; Wilson in, 441, 505

Carman, H. J.: American Husbandry, 510; Eliot essays, 510

Carolina, 33, 108, 208–16; attitude toward crown, 344; Baltimore eyes, 109; charter of, 111, 209–11; charter and Spanish influence, 24; and Glorious Revolution, 269; Granville grant in, 344; made two colonies, 493; proprietors sell out, 340; in Queen Anne's War, 331; settlement, 208–16; settlements within Spanish Florida, 279; and Shaftesbury, 209–15, 335; uprising in, 250–51; and Virginia's social pattern, 291; see also North Carolina, South Carolina

Carpenter's Hall: Congress meets in, 569

Carr, Caleb: as Rhode Island governor, 694

Carr, Sir Robert: on royal commission, 199

Carroll, Charles (1737–1832), 594; wealth of, 487

Carrollton Manor, 487

Cartagena: and Penn-Venable expedition, 191; Vernon attacks, 378

Carter, C. E.: Gage correspondence, 636; works on Illinois country, 552

Carter family, 184, 291

Carter, Robert (1663–1732): as Virginia governor, 697

Carteret, Sir George: death of, 229; Carolina proprietor, 209; New Jersey proprietor, 222, 226, 227, 228; on royal council, 335

Carteret, John, first Earl of Granville (1690–1763): holdings in North Carolina, 344, 493; study of, 357

Carteret, Peter: as Carolina governor, 692

Carteret, Philip (1639–1682): and Andros, 228; as New Jersey governor, 226, 690

Cartier, Jacques (1491–1557), 86; in Canada, 26

cartography: Boston described, 473; map of America by Verrazano's brother, 26; map of Chesapeake Bay by Smith, 91–92; map of Virginia by Mitchell, 448; map of New World by Waldseemüller, 20; Ptolemaic influence on, 9

Cartwright, George: member of royal commission, 199

Cartwright, W. H.: Teaching American History, 355

Caruso, J. A.: Appalachian Frontier, 515

Carver, John (c. 1576–1621): as Plymouth governor, 126–27, 688

Cary, John: "Brown Thesis on Colonial Democracy," 512; Joseph Warren, 593

Cary, Thomas: as Carolina governor, 692

Casa de contratación (House of Trade), 23

Catharine of Aragon (1485–1536): and Henry VIII, 51

Castillo de San Marcos: at St. Augustine, 27

Castle William: strengthened, 378–79

Caswell, Richard (1729–1789): as North Carolina governor, 693

Catawba Indians, 80, 216

Cathay: Cartier searches for, 26; and Columbus, 17; Gilbert seeks, 31; medieval view of, 4–5; Polos visit, 4–5; see also China

Catholic Church: and Anglicanism, 51–52; Calvert joins, 109; and Calvinism, 50; established in Canada, 385; and Galileo, 430–31; and Henry VIII, 51; and Luther, 44–46; in medieval world, 2–3; and new monarchs, 5; Puritans reject traditions of, 134; and Quebec Act, 565; in Spanish Empire, 22, 25

Catholic Counter-Reformation, 30

Catholics: in Andros company, 265–66; in Maryland, 111–12, 181–82, 184–85, 250; in New York, 267; in Newport, 284; and parochial school, 222; in Pennsylvania, 481–82; Pilgrims' attitude toward, 126; propaganda against, 112, 113–14; and Scots, 369–70; studies of, 594; Virginia and Lord Baltimore, 109; in Virginia, 270, 302; William III on, 265

Cato's Letters, 454

cattle: and Plymouth economy, 154; price falls, 168

Cavaliers: in Virginia, 184

Cayuga Indians, 79

Cecil, Robert, first Earl of Salisbury (c. 1563–1612): friend of Calvert, 108

Céloron de Bienville, Pierre Joseph de (1693–1759): tours Ohio Valley, 383

Central America: Spanish explore, 21

Chadd's Ford (Pennsylvania), 617

Chadwick, Owen: *Reformation*, 81

Champagne, Roger: "New York Elections 1768–69," 554

Champlain, Samuel de (1567–1635): sketch of, 86

Chancellor, Richard (d. 1556): and Russia, 30

Channing, Edward: on Van Twiller, 218; Barrington-Bernard correspondence, 553, *History of United States*, 239

Charles I (1600–1649), 61, 541; and Calvert grant, 110; Commons rebuffs, 62; creates Laud Commission, 141, 335; dissolves Parliament, 70, 131; execution of, 168; favors proprietory grants, 108; and Laud, 140; orders Virginia assembly convened, 106; Patrick Henry refers to, 537; personal rule ends, 180; returns Acadia to France, 170; Virginia made royal colony by, 106, 107; Williams informs Massachusetts charter worthless, 143

Charles II (1630–1685): accession of, 168, 192; Berkeley visits, 200, 201, 249; and Carolina grant, 209; creates committees to supervise colonies, 335; and customs officers, 258; death of, 259; Iroquois reject as sovereign, 321; and Lovelace, 223; and New York charter, 222; and Penn, 230, 232–33; proprietary grant favored by, 207–8; and Rhode Island and Connecticut, 195; sends fleet to Virginia, 248; and Virginia, 201

Charles V (1500–1558): and Reformation, 51

Charles VIII (1470–1498): and Columbus, 14

Charleston (South Carolina): in seventeenth century, 215, 284; in eighteenth century, 494, 495; architecture in, 461; and backcountry, 216, 497–98, 506; painter in, 462; Pitt statue in, 436; in Queen Anne's War, 332; in Revolution, 603, 626, 627, 632; and Tea Act, 562, 564; welcomes Oglethorpe, 375; and Yamasee War, 373

Charlestown (Massachusetts): Cheever teaches in, 296; and witches, 304

Charlotte (North Carolina): Cornwallis takes, 628

Charlottesville (Virginia), 461, 490

chartered colony: defined, 343

Charter of Freedoms and Exemptions (1629), 217

Charter of Liberties and Privileges (1683), 225; study on, 240

Charter of Privileges (1701): provisions, 482; threatened loss of, 485

charters (granted by colonies): Bank of North America (1781), 609; Harvard (1650), 294; Yale (1701), 294

charters (royal): Avalon (1620), 108–9, 111; Bermuda Company annulled (1684), 336; Carolina (1663), 209–11; to colleges, 443; Connecticut (1662), 195–97; Council for New England (1620), 89, 108; East India Company (1599), 67; Georgia (1732), 374; to Gilbert (1578), 31–32; and governor's commission, 345; Maryland (1632), 110–11; Massachusetts Bay Company, 130–32; Massachusetts Bay annulled (1684), 259, 336; Massachusetts Bay (1691), 336–37; Massachusetts Bay revised (1774), 565; New York (1664), 222; Pennsylvania (1681), 232–33; to Plowden, 111; to Raleigh (1584), 34; Rhode Island (1663), 197; to Society for the Propagation of the Gospel (1701), 419; Spanish influence on, 24; studies of, 119, 274; Virginia (1606), 86; Virginia (1609), 93; Virginia (1612), 96; Virginia annulled (1624), 105

Chastellux, Marquis de: on poverty in Chesapeake country, 489; on Southern attitude toward Negro, 489; on Southern women, 490; *Travels*, 511

Chatham, William Pitt, first Earl of (1708–1778): biographies of, 413; conciliatory efforts vetoed, 574; correspondence of, 414; elevated to peerage, 410, 543; and free trade, 661; and French and Indian War, 391, 413; on illicit trade, 406, 407; and Newcastle, 410; on Peace of Paris, 518; resigns from cabinet, 409; and Revenue Act (1764), 533; statue of, 436; study of, 554

Chaucer, Geoffrey (c. 1345–1400), 62

Chauncy, Charles (1705–1787): on Great Awakening, 428

Cheever, Ezekiel (1615–1708): schoolmaster, 296

Chemistry (Glauber), 300

Chequamegon Bay: French fort on, 377

Cherokee Indians, 79, 216; treaty with, 531

Cherokee War: and backcountry, 500, 506; studies on, 515

Cheraw Hill: fall-line town, 497

Cherry Valley (New York): raided, 626

Chesapeake Bay: Claiborne explores, 113–14; encourages dispersion, 151–52; lack of towns on, 282–84; reconnoitered (1585), 35; and Roanoke party, 36; size of, 114; Smith explores, 91–92; society formed around, 114–19; and Verrazano, 26

Cheseldyne, Kenelm: and Protestant Association, 271

Chester (Upland): Penn lands at, 236

Chesterfield, Philip Dormer Stanhope, fourth Earl of (1694–1773): on Pitt and Newcastle, 410

Cheyney, E. P.: Dawn of New Era, 38; European Background, 38

Chicago River: La Salle fort on, 319

Chicheley, Sir Henry: as Virginia governor, 249, 697

Chickasaw Indians, 80, 126

Children of the Light; see Quakers

Child, Robert (c. 1613–1654): and church membership, 178–79

China: silks from, 57; United States trade with, 664

Chinard, Gilbert: John Adams, 594

Chippendale, Thomas (1718–1779): influence in colonies, 462

Chippewa Indians: and Pickawillany, 384; take Michilimackinac, 526

Choctaw Indians, 80, 216

Choiseul-Amboise, Étienne-François, Duc de (1719–1785): foresees Revolution, 618

Christian Philosopher (Mather, 1721), 435

Chronological History of New England (Prince, 1736), 456

Church, Benjamin (1639–1718): and Nova Scotia, 331; as writer, 307

Church, Benjamin (1734–c. 1778): chosen to head hospitals, 582; letter to Massachusetts towns, 559; as spy, 583

Church, L. F.: Oglethorpe, 412

Church of England: and American bishop, 535; and backcountry, 504, 508; Brewster's distaste for, 124; in Dominion, 260, 261; in England, 51–53; and English Puritans, 52–55; and English village life, 64; and Glorious Revolution,

Church of England (cont.)
272; and governor's instructions, 345; and Great Awakening, 425; hierarchy in, 59; and King's College, 443, 479; and Laud, 140–41; and Lutheran, 52; and naturalization, 372; and New England, 198, 200, 257, 260, 261, 408–9; and Penn family, 484; and Quebec Act, 556; and Society for the Propagation of the Gospel mission, 408–9; in United States, 655; in Virginia, 118, 181, 200–1, 302; and Whitefield, 424

"Church people": in Pennsylvania, 365

Churches Quarrel Espoused (Wise, 1710), 455

Churchill, E. S.: Geographic Conditions, 83

churchwarden: in England, 64

Cicero: and Jefferson, 436

Cipangu: Cabot sails for, 18, 25; and Columbus, 14, 16, 17; Polo on, 5; see also Japan

citizenship: questions about, 371–72

city; see town

City Madam (Massinger, 1632), 68–69

Claiborne, William (c. 1587–c. 1677): biographical sketch of, 113–14; and Maryland during Commonwealth, 184–85

clapboard: method of making, 286

Clap, Thomas (1703–1767): biography of, 466

Clarendon County (South Carolina), 212

Clarendon, Edward Hyde, first Earl of (1608–1674): and Carolina, 209; on Charles II's goals, 192, 209–11; falls from power, 200; Penn's disgust with, 231; on royal council, 335

Clark, D. M.: British Treasury, 356; "American Board of Customs, 554

Clark, George Rogers (1752–1818): papers of, 636; and the Revolution, 625; studies of, 640

Clark, G. K.: English Inheritance, 82

Clark, H. H.: Paine's writings, 595

Clarke, Desmond: Arthur Dobbs, 514

Clarke, George (1676–1760): as New York governor, 692

Clarke, John (1609–1676): and Rhode Island charter, 197

Clarke, M. P.: Parliamentary Privilege in the Colonies, 357

Clarke, Walter (c. 1638–1714): as Rhode Island governor, 694

class structure: in seventeenth-century America, 288–93; in eighteenth-century

class structure (*cont.*)
America, 442–43, 489–90; in back-country, 499–500; in cities, 440–41; in England, 58–59
Classis: and Dutch Reformed ministers in America, 421
Clayton, John (c. 1685–1773): as botanist, 448
Clement VII (c. 1478–1534): and Henry VIII, 51
clergy: and American bishop, 535; American role of, 419; authority in New England, 135–36, 138, 291–92; in back-country, 502, 504; and college faculties, 445; divisions within, 420; and education, 293–94, 296; in England, 59, 140–41; and Enlightenment, 435–36; and government by laws, 138; James Franklin attacks, 421; and inoculation, 450; during King Philip's War, 254; and Laud's efforts to improve, 140–44; as leisure class, 440; and Maryland politics, 113; and medicine, 292; in the Revolution, 610; and salary in Virginia, 407–8; and Salem trials, 305; and science, 301; and Stamp Act, 541; as writers, 456; *see also* ministers
Cleveland, John (1613–1658): on Newcastle as Peru, 65
Clinton, George (c. 1686–1761): and assembly, 382; as New York governor, 692
Clinton, George (1739–1812): and Constitution, 669, 674; as New York governor, 692
Clinton, Sir Henry (c. 1738–1795): to America, 574; *American Rebellion,* 636; biography of, 636; in Boston, 600; and Burgoyne, 616; and Carolina invasion, 603; favors war of attrition, 625; and Monmouth Court House battle, 624; in New York, 605; and Pennsylvania Line mutiny, 629; Philadelphia evacuated by, 624; replaces Howe, 621, 624; Southern invasion by, 627; and Yorktown campaign, 631, 632
Clive, John: *Journey to Pennsylvania,* 411
Clopton, John, 491
Cochran, T. C.: *New York in the Confederation,* 681
Coddington, William (1601–1678): characterized, 147–48; as Rhode Island governor, 694
Coercive Acts; *see* Intolerable Acts
Coggeshall, John: as Rhode Island governor, 694

Cohabitation Act (1680): 283
Cohasset (Massachusetts): banishes Doughty, 169
Cohen, I. B.: *Franklin and Newton,* 466; on Franklin as scientist, 452–53
Coke, Sir Edward (1552–1634): on voiding acts of Parliament, 679; and Williams, 143; works of, used by Americans, 445
Colbert, Jean Baptiste (1619–1683): achievements of, 316; on Dutch merchant marine, 189; influence on English imperialism, 334; and La Salle, 319; mercantilistic vision of, 187
Colbourn, H. T.: Dickinson's works, 553; "John Dickinson," 274
Colden, Cadwallader (1688–1776): on America's open society, 443, 478; and assembly, 479; biography of, 512; as botanist, 448, 451; as historian of Indians, 457; *History of Five Nations,* 356; as New York governor, 692; on New York land grants, 477; as royal official, 346; and scientific society, 450; as scientist, 447
Coleman, Kenneth: *Georgia Journeys,* 412; *Revolution in Georgia,* 553
Coligny, Gaspard de (1519–1572): and New World settlement, 27, 31
College of New Jersey: Davies as president, 426; founded, 427, 429, 443; Rittenhouse orrery at, 452
College of Philadelphia, 439; founded, 429, 443; medical school founded, 446; and Provost Smith, 444; Rittenhouse orrery at, 452; Wilson as instructor at, 505
College of William and Mary: and English universities, 293, 294; established, 271; Sith as president, 457; Small at, 444–45; Wren works in, 459
colleges: in seventeenth-century America, 293–94; in eighteenth-century America, 443–45; representation in Congress, 569
Colleton, Sir John (d. 1666): and Carolina, 209; on royal council, 335
Colleton, John (fl. 1686): as Carolina governor, 269, 695
Collins, James: *Autobiography of a Revolutionary Soldier,* 636
Collins, John (1717–1795): as Rhode Island governor, 694
Collins, Thomas: as Delaware governor, 694
Collinson, Peter: promotes botany in America, 447, 448
Colonial Records of North Carolina, 239

"Colony": in Carolina, 213
Colorado: as Spanish name, 24
Columbia University; *see* King's College
Columbus, Bartholomew (d. 1514): brother joins in Lisbon, 13; on Hispaniola, 18
Columbus, Christopher (1451–1506): biographical sketch of, 13; contract with crown, 14–16; death of, 20, 44; English and route to America, 34, 72; influence of D'Ailly on, 14; influence of Polo on, 5; letter on New World, 17; and Prester John, 4; and Viking sagas, 13; voyage's goal, 7; voyage one, 16; voyage two, 18; voyage three, 18; voyage four, 20
Columbus, Diego (fl. 1495): on Hispaniola, 18
Columbus, Ferdinand (1488–1539): on why father traveled westward, 13–14
Comfort, W. W.: biography of Penn, 241
Commager, H. S.: *Spirit of Seventy-Six*, 637
Commentaries on the Laws of England (Blackstone, 1765–1769), 445
Commins, Saxe: Washington writings, 595
Commission for Regulating Plantations (1634–1643), 141, 335
Commission for the Plantations (1643–1648), 335
commission of royal governor, 345
Committee for Foreign Affairs, 618
Committees of Correspondence: Boston creates, 558–59; and Boston Port Act, 564; and Gage, 576; and *Gaspee* incident, 560; number in 1774, 568–69; in Virginia, 560
Committee of Public Safety (1689): Leisler sets up, 268
Committee of Safety (1775): duties and power of, 581
Committee of Secret Correspondence, 618
Committee of the Privy Council on Trade and Plantations; *see* Lords of Trade and Plantations
Common Sense (Paine, 1776), 603; effect of, 586; on government, 645
Commonwealth of Oceana (Harrington, 1656), 213–14
communal plan: in Georgia, 375; Massachusetts Bay avoids, 133; in Plymouth, 125, 127; in Virginia, 92–93, 98–99
Compromise of 1752, 405
Conant, Roger (c. 1592–1679): and Dorchester Company, 130
Concessions and Agreements: Carolina, 212; New Jersey, 212, 226

Conciliatory Propositions (1778): provisions, 620–21
Concord (Massachusetts), 471; Battle of, 577; reaction to battle, 600
Conewago (Pennsylvania): Catholic congregation in, 482
Coney Island: fleet anchors off, 220
Confederation of New England, 170–74; death of, 255; distribution of power in, 171, 262; and foreign affairs, 179
Confederation of the United States: and American economy, 661–64; and Articles, 647–51; financial troubles of, 665; impost sought, 610; opposition to, 664–68; related to independence, 590, 591; and Shays's Rebellion, 667; and the West, 656–61
Congregational Church: in seventeenth-century New England, 134–36, 179, 198; in eighteenth-century New England, 471; English antecedents of, 54; and Great Awakening, 426–27; and Half-Way Covenant, 198–99; historical importance of, 158; Hooker on membership qualifications, 148; organization of, 135; and Scotch-Irish, 369; in the United States, 655; and voluntary societies, 440
Congregation Jeshuat Israel, 460
Congress, Continental (First): and Harrison's constituents, 491; Henry speaks in, 503; meets, 568–73; and Quebec Act, 566; suggested, 564; voting procedure debate, 569–70
Congress, Continental (Second): on Americans' allegiance, 585; and Articles, 647–51; and the Confederation, 664–66; and Constitution, 674; and Continental Army, 579–80; and Conway Cabal, 624; and Declaration of Causes, 580; and Declaration of Independence, 587–93; delegates arrive, 578; North's peace plan, 582; Olive Branch Petition of, 580; and opening of ports to world, 581, 588; and paper money, 608–9; powers of, 579; powers of, as debate topic, 656; and Shays's Rebellion, 667; and state governments, 583, 589–90, 664; and the states, 608; studies of, 593–94; voting procedure debate, 649; and the West, 651, 657–60
Connecticut: and Albany Congress, 386; Boston aided by, 564; Boston taxes imports from, 174; and boundary of, 199, 223; charter, 195–97; charter and Spanish influence, 24; and Confederation of New England, 171; as corporate colony,

Connecticut (*cont.*)
344; and disallowance, 344, 351; divorce in, 653; in Dominion of New England, 259, 262, 263, 344; Dutch in, 218, 219; exports of, 471; founded, 148–50; and Glorious Revolution, 226; and King Philip's War, 253; legal code and Duke's Laws, 223; and Leisler's Rebellion, 268; and New Lights, 427; and New York conference (1690), 325; and New York merchants, 469; and Pennsylvania's Wyoming Valley, 475, 558, 648; and Pequot War, 156–57, 171; ratifies Constitution, 675; and Revenue Act (1764), 534; revival of 1735, 423; and Saybrook Platform, 420; as smuggling center, 260; stamp collector in, 537; studies of, 163; Washington promotes independence in, 584; and West Indian trade, 473; and Western land claims of, 650; see also New Haven

Conner, P. W.: *Poor Richard's Politics,* 594

Connor, R. D.: *History of North Carolina,* 239

conquistador: and relation to crown, 21–22

consociations: promoted, 420

constable: in Chesapeake society, 118; in England, 64

Constantinople: depot for Eastern goods, 4; Harborne visits, 30; and Levant Company, 86

Constitution of the United States: Convention, 668–73; as debate topic, 656; and Maryland charter, 110; ratification of, 674–78; studies of, 681, 683–85; translated into Dutch, 222

constitutions: for Carolina (1665), 213–14; and charters, 197, 344; of Dominion of New England, 260–61; and governor's commission, 345; states devise, 644–47; for West Jersey (1677), 288

Continental dollar: values of, 608

"Continentalist" (Hamilton), 651

Convention of Saratoga, 616–17

conventions: in Boston (1689), 266; Leisler calls, 268; in Massachusetts (1768), 548; in New Netherland, 219; for ratification of Constitution, 675; and ratification of state constitutions, 645; in Virginia (1774), 569; Wyatt calls (1625), 106

convicts: as immigrants, 69, 362

Conway Cabal, 622–23; studies on, 639

Conway, Henry Seymour (1721–1795): as secretary of state, 543

Conway, Thomas (1735–c. 1800): and Conway Cabal, 623

Coode, John (d. 1709): charged with sedition, 250; as Maryland governor, 688; and Protestant Association, 271

Cook, James (1728–1779): Ledyard sails with, 664

Cook, John: as Delaware governor, 694

Cooke, Nicholas: as Rhode Island governor, 694

Coolidge, A. C.: Barrington-Bernard correspondence, 553

Coolidge, Calvin (1872–1933), 49

Cooper, Sir Anthony Ashley (Lord Ashley; first Earl of Shaftesbury) (1621–1683): and Carolina, 209–15; and Culpeper acquittal, 251; rivers named after, 214; on royal council, 335

Cooper, Samuel (1725–1783): on Western settlement, 397

Coote, Richard, Earl of Bellomont: as Massachusetts governor, 689; as New York governor, 327, 477, 691; on New York land policy, 476; on pirates, 279

Copernicus, Nicolas (1473–1543): almanacs and ideas of, 298; and Galileo, 430–31; and Puritans, 160; reception of ideas, 299

Copley, John Singleton (c. 1738–1815): biography of, 467; paints Sam Adams, 463; paints Revere, 462

Copley, Sir Lionel (d. 1693): as Maryland governor, 272, 688

copper: on enumerated list, 399

Corey, Giles: death as witch, 304

Corkran, D. H.: *Cherokee Frontier,* 515

corn: Carolina export, 215; in Delaware Valley, 480

Cornbury, Edward Hyde, Viscount (1661–1723), 347; and assembly, 331; as New Jersey governor, 690; as New York governor, 328, 477, 691; promotes Anglicanism, 419

corn right: in backcountry, 502

coroner: in Pennsylvania, 482

Cornwallis, Charles, first Marquis Cornwallis (1738–1805): arrives New York, 605; attacks Charleston, 603; and Battle of Brandywine, 617; and Battle of Germantown, 617; captures Fort Lee, 607; in the South, 627; and Washington, 607, 612; and Yorktown campaign, 631–32

Cornwallis, Thomas: quarrels with proprietary, 113

Coronado, Francisco (c. 1510–1554): explores West, 26

corporate colony: defined, 344

Cortez, Hernando (1485–1547): invades Mexico, 21

Corwin, E. S.: *French Policy, 1778,* 639

Cosby, William (c. 1690–1736): as New Jersey governor, 690; as New York governor, 692

cotton: on enumerated list, 192

Cotton, Joel, *History of Modern World,* 38

Cotton, John (1584–1652): and Anne Hutchinson, 145; biography of, 162; on congregationalism, 134, 138; death of, 179; and English Puritans, 135; erudition of, 135–36; on fashioning the commonwealth, 134; and Hooker, 148; and Laud, 141; on political power, 138, 140; role in altering Puritanism, 135; and Synod of 1637, 141

Coulter, E. M.: *Georgia,* 411–12; *Journal of Stephens,* 412

council (governor's): Bacon's Laws on, 247–48; in Dominion of New England, 261–62; duties of, 348; in early Virginia, 106–7; judiciary role of, 353; in Massachusetts charter (1691), 337; as Penn conceived, 235

Council for New England, 89; and Dorchester Company, 129; and grants to Mason and Gorges, 108; and Massachusetts, 141; and New England Company, 130; and New Hampshire, 257; and Pilgrims, 126, 127; Warwick as president of, 148

Council of Safety: in Massachusetts (1689), 266

Council of the Indies (Spain), 23

county: and backcountry, 485, 505, 506; in Carolina, 213; in Chesapeake colonies, 117–18, 185; as electoral unit, 349; in England, 62–63; in Pennsylvania, 372

county court: Bacon's Laws on, 247; in Chesapeake colonies, 185; in England, 62; in North Carolina, 508; retain power in Virginia, 200

Court of Assistants: powers of, 136–37

Court of Chancery, 259

Court of Common Pleas (England), 63

covenant: and congregationalism, 134, 152; and Zwingli, 46

Cowie, L. W.: *Henry Newman,* 357

Coxe, Daniel (c. 1640–1730): West Jersey controlled by, 229; as West Jersey governor, 690

craftsmen: in seventeenth-century America, 287; in cities, 440; in Delaware Valley, 481; effect of Hat Act on, 400; effect of inflation on, 611; forbidden to emigrate, 362; and French and Indian War, 396; in furniture, 462; as immigrants, 69; and iron industry, 401; unemployment of, 406; Virginia encourages, 181

Crane, V. W.: "Dr. Thomas Bray," 412; *Franklin,* 466; Franklin *Letters,* 553; *Southern Frontier,* 239

Cranfield, Edward: as New Hampshire governor, 690

Cranston, John (1625–1680): as Rhode Island governor, 694

Cranston, Maurice: *John Locke,* 465

Cranston, Samuel (1659–1727): as Rhode Island governor, 694

Craven, Charles: as South Carolina governor, 695; and Yamasee War, 373

Craven County (South Carolina), 212

Craven, W. F.: on Bacon, 249; on Berkeley, 248; on Chesapeake region, 119; on county court, 185; on Maryland Act Concerning Religion, 182; on self-government as local right, 200; *Dissolution of Virginia Company,* 120; *Legend of Founding Fathers,* 161; *New Jersey,* 241; *Southern Colonies,* 82; *Virginia Company,* 119

Craven, William Craven, Earl of (1608–1697): as Carolina proprietor, 209

Creek Indians, 80, 216, 373

Cresswell, Nicholas: *Journal,* 511

Crèvecoeur, Michel-Guillaume Jean (J. Hector St. John) de (1735–1813): on Americans, 482; on Charlestonians, 495; *Letters,* 511

crime: Body of Liberties on, 353; Pennsylvania reforms code on, 654

Croatoan Indians, 36

Croghan, George (d. 1782): advises Amherst, 525; advises Board of Trade, 529–30; bankrupt, 384; biographies of, 412; on casualties in 1763 uprising, 526; in King George's War, 379; on Pontiac, 525–26; on population of Ohio Valley, 566; as superintendent of Indian affairs, 391; on Western settlement, 531

Cromwell, Oliver (1599–1658), 209; and Admiral Penn, 229; attitudes toward Dutch and Spanish, 190; Hamilton refers to, 667; Henry refers to, 537; imperial version of, 187; Masham's friend, 143; and Penn-Venable expedition, 191;

Cromwell, Oliver (*cont.*)
and Quakers, 230–31; victories of, 168; and Williams, 170
Crone, G. R.: *Maps,* 38
Cross Creek: fall-line town, 497
Crowl, P. A.: "Antifederalism in Maryland," 685; *Maryland and the Revolution,* 595
crown: and the colonies: 106, 107, 140–42, 258–59, 260–61, 334–41, 563, 585; and Parliament, 52–53, 61–62, 65, 337, 339, 574; and proprietaries, 31–32, 33, 34–35, 108, 207–8, 340; *see also* Board of Trade, Lords of Trade, and Parliament
Crown Point: in French and Indian War, 387, 390, 395; in King George's War, 382; in Revolution, 579
Cuba: and Columbus, 16, 18
Culpeper-Arlington grant, 244, 270
Culpeper, John: as North Carolina governor, 692; and rebellion of, 251
Culpeper Rebellion, 251
Culpeper, Thomas, Baron of Thoresway (1635–1689): on printing in Virginia, 298; as Virginia governor, 249, 269–70, 347, 697
Cumberland County (Pennsylvania): created, 372; Indians raid, 390; Wilson in, 505
Cunliffe, Marcus: on Washington, 637; *Literature of United States,* 311; *Washington,* 413
Cunningham, William: *Growth of English Industry and Commerce,* 20
Cunz, Dieter: *Maryland Germans,* 410
Curaçao: importance to Dutch, 191; and Stuyvesant, 219
currency: Andros recommends mint, 263; and North Carolina quitrents, 493; Pine Tree Shilling, 179; during Revolution, 582, 608–9; shortage of, 260, 402–4; and Spanish coin, 181, 257, 329; studies of, 414, 553; tobacco as, 407; Virginia plans mint, 181; *see also* paper money
Currency Act (1751): provisions, 403–4
Currency Act (1764), 535; revised (1773), 560–61; study of, 552
Curti, Merle: *Growth of American Thought,* 309
Curtis, E. E.: *British Army in the Revolution,* 637
Curwen, Samuel: *Journal,* 638
Cushing, H. A.: *Writings of Samuel Adams,* 593
customs agents: and admiralty, 334; authority of, 258; and deputies, 532; and

customs agents (*cont.*)
the naval officer, 342; and Navigation Act of 1696, 338; and Plantation Duty Act, 194
Customs, Commissioners of: attitude toward proprietary colonies, 334; board created for colonies, 544; and governor's instructions, 345; and New England's illicit trade, 256; and plan to reorganize colonies (1695), 338
customs duties: Carolina exemption, 209; in England, 61, 65; and enumerated items, 192; Franklin on, 543; and London Company, 96, 102; in New York, 223–25; and Plantation Duty, 194; and Revenue Act (1764), 532–39; and Revenue Act (1767), 543–44, 549–50; Stuyvesant levies, 219; and tobacco, 488; on wine, 533
customs service (in America), 339, 342; and Boston troubles, 547; reformed, 532; reorganized, 544; and surveyor-general, 342–43
Cutler, Manasseh (1742–1823): and Ohio Company, 658
Cutt, John: as New Hampshire governor, 689

Dakar: explorers reach, 12
Dale, Sir Thomas (d. 1619): and Bradford, 127; and church service, 116; and Oglethorpe, 375; returns to England, 99; and Rolfe, 103; sails for Jamestown, 96; as Virginia governor, 97–99, 696; and Winthrop, 132
Dale's Laws, 97; abandoned, 100
Dayell, James: and Fort Detroit, 526, 528
Danby, Earl of (Thomas Osborne, Duke of Leeds) (1632–1712): creates royal committee, 335
Danger of an Unconverted Ministry (Tennent, 1740), 427, 456
Daniel, Robert: as South Carolina governor, 692, 695
Danish: in Delaware Valley, 362
Dare, Virginia (b. 1587), 36
Darien: and Scotland, 337
Dartmouth, Lord (William Legge, second Earl of), 577
Dartmouth College: chartered, 443; founded, 429
Davenport, James (1716–1767) and Great Awakening, 425; in Virginia, 426
Davenport, John (1597–1670), 142; characterized, 150; on church and state, 138; as rival of Cotton, 148

Davidson, Philip: *Propaganda and American Revolution,* 551
Davidson, R. A.: *Isaac Hicks,* 683
Davies, Samuel (1723–1761), 426; and College of New Jersey, 443
Davies, R. T.: *Golden Century of Spain,* 39
Davyes, William: and Maryland uprising, 250
Dawes, William (1745–1799): and midnight ride, 471, 577
Day of Doom (Wigglesworth, 1662), 308
deacon: in Congregational Church, 135
Deane, Silas (1737–1789): as agent in France, 618; on Congress, 579
Decades of the New World (Eden, 1555), 28
Declaration and Proposals to All That Will Plant in Carolina (1663), 211, 212
Declaration and Remonstrance (1676), 246
Declaration of Causes of Taking-up Arms (1775), 580
Declaration of Rights and Resolves (1774), 571–72
Declaration of Independence, 590–93, 647; and eighteenth-century painting, 463; studies of, 595; words taken literally, 653
Declaration . . . for Appearing in Arms (1689), 272
Declaratory Act (1766), 540, 549, 622
DeConde, Alexander: *Entangling Alliance,* 639
Deerfield (Massachusetts): raided, 330
"Defender of the Faith," 51
Defense of the Seven Sacraments (1521), 51
Defoe, Daniel (1660–1731): on London fire, 200
deism: in colonies, 436; and Franklin, 421
De Kalb, Baron; see Kalb, Johann
Dekker, Thomas (c. 1570–c. 1641): on Elizabeth I, 56
DeLancey family, 363, 477; backs Leisler, 268; and New York politics, 478–79
DeLancey, James (1703–1760): at Albany Congress, 386; as New York governor, 692
Delano family, 363
Delaware, 344; at Annapolis Convention, 666; constitution of, 646; at Mt. Vernon conference, 666; and paper money, 402; and Penn, 222, 234, 236; ratifies Constitution, 675; Scotch-Irish in, 481; and War of Jenkins' Ear, 378

Delaware Bay, 218; and Dutch, 170, 189, 227, 228; Howe opens, 617; Hudson investigates, 216; May travels up, 217; as patroonship, 218; and Swedes, 220, 228; and Verrazano, 26
Delaware Indians: in Ohio Valley, 383; and Penn, 237; pledged to peace, 394; and 1763 uprising, 525, 526, 528
Delaware Valley: in eighteenth-century, 480–86; economic slump, 329
De La Warr, Lord (fl. 1740): as New York governor, 692
De La Warr, Thomas West, Baron (1577–1618): as Virginia governor, 93–94, 95–96, 696
Delmarva Peninsula, 110
demarcation line: Francis I ignores, 26; Henry VII ignores, 25; "no peace beyond the line" policy, 85–86, 279, 333; Pope draws, 17
Deming, Dorothy: *Connecticut Towns,* 163
DeMond, R. O.: *Loyalism in North Carolina,* 638
"denizen," 371
Denny, William: as Pennsylvania governor, 693; sells flags of truce, 407
denominationalism: defined, 428
Denonville, Jacques de: replaces La Barre, 324
De Orbe Novo (Martyr, 1516), 28
De Peyster, family, 477; backs Leisler, 268
Description of New England (Smith, 1616), 124
Description of the World (Polo, 1299), 5
Designs of Inigo Jones (Kent, 1727), 460
De Soto, Hernando: see Soto, Hernando de
Detroit: center for proposed colony, 522; fort built at, 327; see also Fort Detroit
De Voto, Bernard: on British advantage in fur trade, 320–21; on Indians' resistance to decadence, 80; on pre-Columbian explorers, 13; *Course of Empire,* 83
Dexter, E. A.: *Colonial Women,* 310
Diaz, Bartholomew (c. 1450–1500): rounds Cape, 12–13, 14
Dickerson, O. M.: *American Colonial Government,* 356; *Navigation Acts,* 414
Dickinson, John (1732–1808): Adams on, 569, 582; and Articles, 647–49; and Congress (1774), 572; and Congress (1775–1776), 580; and Constitution, 668; as Delaware governor, 694; and independence, 590; as Pennsylvania farmer, 272, 546; as Pennsylvania governor, 694; on Revenue Act (1767), 546; on

Dickinson, John (*cont.*)
  standing army, 534; studies of, 274, 553, 554; Wilson studies with, 441, 505
Dictionary of American History, 82
Diffie, B. W.: *Latin America,* 39
Digges, Edward: as Virginia governor, 696
Digges family, 291
Dill, A. T.: *Governor Tryon,* 514
Dillon, D. R.: *New York Triumvirate,* 512
Dinwiddie, Robert (1693–1770): biography of, 413; as Virginia governor, 697; and Washington, 384
disallowance, royal, 334, 670; and Board of Trade, 339; and corporate colonies, 344; discussion of, 351; and Massachusetts, 344, 409, 542; and North Carolina, 493; number of statutes involved, 339; and Penn's charter, 233; and South Carolina, 507; studies of, 356; and Virginia, 408; Virginia assembly and London Company, 101
Discourse of a Discovery for a New Passage to Catia (Gilbert, 1566), 31
Discourse of Western Planting (Hakluyt, 1584), 34
Discourse on Unlimited Submission (Mayhew, 1750), 456
Discovery, 89
Discovery of New Britain (Bland, 1650), 208
distilleries: in New England, 471–72; in New York, 476
Divers Voyages . . . (Hakluyt, 1582), 33
divorce: in Connecticut, 653
Dobbs, Arthur (1689–1765): biography of, 514; holdings in North Carolina, 493; as North Carolina governor, 493, 693
Doberstein, J. W.: *Muhlenberg Journals,* 511
Dobrée, Bonamy: *William Penn,* 241
Doddridge, Joseph: *Notes* (on backcountry), 515
Dodson, Leonidas: *Fithian Journal,* 511; *Spotswood,* 357
Doeg Indians, 245
Dominica: Columbus discovers, 18
Dominion of New England, 671, 259–265; and Charter of Liberties, 225; and Connecticut, 344; and defenses against French, 324; and Lords of Trade, 336; New Jersey and New York, 229, 476; and representative assembly, 337; study of, 273
Dongan, Thomas (1634–1715): Indian policy of, 321; as New York governor,

Dongan, Thomas (*cont.*)
  225, 259, 691; as New York resident, 267
Donne, John (1573–1631), 278; and Virginia, 71, 103
Dorchester Company, 129–30
Dorchester Heights: occupied, 601–2
Dorchester (Massachusetts): citizens found Windsor, 154; and lack of land, 149
Dorfman, Joseph: *Economic Mind in American Civilization,* 163; "Paper Money," 414
Dorn, W. L.: *Competition for Empire,* 412
Dorsetshire: and colonization, 86–87
Doughty, Francis: immigrates to New Netherland, 169
Dove, 112
Douglass, E. P.: *Rebels and Democrats,* 681
Douglass, William (c. 1691–1752): and inoculation, 449, 450; as writer, 456–57
Dow, G. F.: *Arts and Crafts in New England,* 511; *Everyday Life in Massachusetts,* 310
Downing, Sir George (c. 1623–1684): and Navigation Act of 1660, 193
Drake, Sir Francis (c. 1540–1596): attacks galleons, 31; escapes from Spanish, 30; joint stock company finances, 67; visits Roanoke, 35
Drake, S. A.: *Border Wars of New England,* 356
Dress, Louisa: *Seventeenth-Century Painting,* 309
Driver, C. S.: *John Sevier,* 683
Drummond, William: in Bacon's Rebellion, 244–45; death of, 248–49; as North Carolina governor, 692
Dryden, John (1631–1700): in almanacs, 455
Drysdale, Hugh: as Virginia governor, 697
Duane, James (1733–1797): Adams on, 569; in Congress (1774), 571; opposes May 15 preamble, 590
Dudley, Joseph (1647–1720): biography of, 274; on Dominion of New England council, 262; as East Jersey governor, 690; and land patents, 263; as New Hampshire governor, 690; and provisional government, 259
Dudley, Thomas (1576–1653): as Massachusetts governor, 689; resists Winthrop, 137

Duer, William (1747–1799): and Northwest Territory, 658
Duke of York; *see* James II
Duke's Laws (1665), 223; study of, 240
Dulany, Daniel (1722–1797): on rebellion, 576
Dulany family: biography of, 514
Dummer, Jeremiah: *Defence of New England Charter*, 415
Dummer, William: as Massachusetts governor, 689
Dunaway, W. F.: *Pennsylvania*, 24; Scotch-Irish, 411
Dunbar, David: as New Hampshire governor, 690
Dunbar, Thomas: and Braddock expedition, 389–90
Dunkards: 47, 365, 419
Dunlap, A. R.: *Dutch Explorers*, 240
Dunmore, John Murray, Earl of (1732–1809): on backcountry people, 503; calls on slaves to revolt, 588; as New York governor, 692; on spoils system, 347; as Virginia governor, 698
Dunmore's War, 566
Dunn, Richard: on Massachusetts, 142; *Puritans and Yankees*, 162
Dunn, W. E.: *Spanish and French Rivalry*, 412
Dunster, Henry (1609–c. 1659): and Harvard, 294
Duquesne, Marquis: as governor of Canada, 384, 386
Durant, George: and North Carolina uprising, 250–51
Durant, Will: *Age of Faith*, 38
Durham, Bishop of; *see* Bishop of Durham clause
Durie, John, 296
Durnbaugh, D. F.: "Christopher Sauer," 411
Dutch: and Confederation of New England, 171–74; in Connecticut Valley, 148, 218; and Curaçao, 219; in Delaware Valley, 226, 227, 236, 481; as England's competitor, 109, 187; and explorations, 217; heritage from, 221–22, 225, 284, 487; and illegal colonial trade, 180, 189, 338, 407, 561; and Iroquois, 320; lands on, 189; and Leisler, 268; and Navigation Acts, 190, 192–93, 194; and New England, 170; and parochial schools, 297; and Pennsylvania trade, 338; and Pilgrims, 124–25; recapture New York, 223; studies on, 240; study on Anglo-Dutch rivalry, 203; and tea

Dutch (*cont.*)
smuggling, 561; and tobacco trade, 180; and Virginia, 189; and William III, 267; *see also* Holland and Anglo-Dutch Wars
Dutch East India Company, 189
Dutch language: contribution to English, 221; Frelinghuysen discards for preaching, 421; Penn tracts translated into, 234; persists in Albany area, 478
Dutch Reformed Church, 51; and Queen's College, 443; and Frelinghuysen revival, 421–22; in New Netherland, 220; in Pennsylvania, 365; after the Revolution, 655
Dutch West India Company: attacks Spanish vessels, 187; and Brazil, 217; and Hudson, 216; and James II, 222; Leisler employee of, 268; and New Amsterdam, 217; and Stuyvesant, 220; and surrender of New Netherland, 220–21
Dyer, William: as surveyor-general, 342
dyewoods: on enumerated list, 192

Eannes, Gil: rounds Cape Bojador, 12
Earl, Ralph (1751–1801): painter, 463
Earle, A. M.: *Child Life in Colonial Days*, 310; *Home Life in Colonial Days*, 310
Early American Medical Imprints, 467
East Anglia, 131
East Florida: as royal colony, 522; study on, 552
East India Company, 679; chartered, 67; and London merchants, 86; and Smith, 68; and tea, 562; troubles of, 561
East Jersey, 226–27; in eighteenth century, 479; and New York, 228–29, 475; *see also* New Jersey
East, R. A.: *Business in the Revolution*, 637
Eastchurch, Thomas: as North Carolina governor, 251, 692
Easterby, J. H.: *Colonial Records of South Carolina*, 514
Easton, Nicholas: as Rhode Island governor, 694
Easton (Pennsylvania): Germans in, 481; Indian conference at (1757), 391; Indian conference at (1758), 394, 522; studies of Indian conferences at, 413
Eaton, Theophilus (1590–1658): immigrates to New England, 150; as New Haven governor, 687
Eccles, W. J.: *Frontenac*, 355
ecclesiastical structure: in America, 419–20; in England, 59

economy: of backcountry, 497–99; of Barbados, 212; of Chesapeake colonies, 115–17, 180–81, 487–89; and colonial ties with Spanish Empire, 24; in Confederation, 661; of Delaware Valley, 480–81; of England, 64–68, 337, 568; after fall of Quebec, 406, 534–35; of Hudson Valley, 476; after King William's War, 328; of New England, 154–56, 174–77, 471–72; and New England merchants, 145–46, 291–92; and Plymouth, 154; in the Revolution, 609–10; of South Carolina, 494–95; studies on, in United States, 683; in United States, 661–64

economic regulation: in Boston, 283; in England, 66; in Massachusetts, 155; in New York, 476; in Philadelphia, 284; Robert Morris on, 611

Eden, Charles (1673–1722): as North Carolina governor, 692

Eden, Richard, 39; translates Martyr work, 28

Eden, Robert (1741–1784): as Maryland governor, 688

Edinburgh University: Bard trained at, 446; Morgan trained at, 446; Tennent graduate of, 423

Edmundson, George: Anglo-Dutch Rivalry, 203

education: in seventeenth-century America, 293–97; in eighteenth-century America, 443–47; in Chesapeake region, 283; in England, 60, 296; Enlightenment–Great Awakening influence on, 429; free schools for Germans, 484; and Log College, 423; in New Netherland, 219; and Scotch-Irish, 368; in the South, 447; in South Carolina backcountry, 507; and stamp duty, 536; and state constitutions, 654; studies of, 311, 466; Virginia seeks college, 103, 200; William and Mary founded, 270–71

Edward IV (1442–1483): mercantilistic ideas of, 66

Edward VI (1537–1553), 51

Edwards, Jonathan (1703–1758): biographies of, 465; and Chauncy, 428; congregation dismisses, 429; and the Enlightenment, 435–36; and revival of 1735, 422–23; and self-improvement, 434; as writer, 456

Effingham, Lord Howard of; see Howard of Effingham, Francis, fifth Baron

Egerton, H. E.: Losses of Loyalists, 638

Eggleston, Edward: on Cotton, 148; on Negro dialect, 453; on rattlesnake oil, 300; Transit of Civilization, 309

Einstein, Lewis: Dividend Loyalists, 638

Eisenhower, D. D.: Dunkard background of, 365

Elbert, Samuel (1740–1788): as Georgia governor, 687

elder: role in Congregational Church, 135

elections: Berkeley avoids, 244; in Chesapeake colonies, 490–91; to Congress (1774), 569; Constitution on, 674; to Constitutional Convention, 668; Dickinson draft of Articles on, 649; in New York, 478; Parliament (1774), 574; in Pennsylvania, 372, 482, 485–86, 589; in Plymouth, 127; and Presidency, 672; in state constitutions, 646; see also suffrage requirements

electoral college: devised, 672

electricity: Franklin on, 458

Elegy in a Country Churchyard (Gray, 1751), 395

Eliot, Jared (1685–1763), 510

Eliot, John (1604–1690), 143; and Indians, 80, 252, 253

Elizabeth I (1533–1603): attitude toward New World, 28–29, 30; charters granted by, 30, 31–32, 34; and Drake's forays, 67; financial troubles of, 61, 65; and mercantilism, 66; and Puritans, 52–53; and Raleigh, 34; and Reformation, 52–53; sketch of, 56

Elkins, Stanley: Founding Fathers, 683

Elliot, Jonathan: Debates in State Conventions, 684

Ellis, D. M.: Short History of New York, 240

Ellis, G. W.: King Philip's War, 273

Ellis, Henry (1721–1806): as Georgia governor, 687

embargo: by British, 587; and colonial heritage, 679; and Congress, 572–73; and Port Act, 568

Emerson, Ralph Waldo (1803–1882), 434; on North Bridge skirmish, 577; on Puritans, 124, 160

Encyclopedia of Social Sciences, 82

Endecott, John (c. 1589–1665): adapts wigwam, 285; biography of, 162; as Massachusetts governor, 689; and Pequot War, 156; at Salem, 130, 131, 132

England: and American language, 305; attitude toward Indian, 80; Church of, 51–53; class structure in, 59; economy of, 64–68; government of, 61–64; influ-

England (*cont.*)
ence on American life and thought, 277, 285–86, 292, 296, 438, 439, 446, 490; influence on local government, 118; medieval pattern in, 6–7; and mercantilism, 187; and Palatines, 364; people of, 57–61; Pilgrims' emotional ties to, 124–25; and Puritanism, 52–55, 70; and Scottish union, 361; studies of, 82; studies on religion in, 81; and Treaty of Utrecht, 333; *see also* crown, imperial structure, Parliament
England's Treasure by Foreign Trade (Mun, 1630), 187
English Gentleman (1630), 293
English, Philip (Philip L'Anglois): and illicit trade, 256
engraving: in seventeenth-century America, 287
Engrossing: defined, 180
Enlightenment, 430–53; and anti-intellectualism, 428–29; characteristics of, in America, 435; and cities, 437–42; credulity in, 434; and education, 444–45; Great Awakening compared to, 417–18, 428–29; and natural philosophy, 430–33; and science, 447–53; studies of, 465–66
Enniskillon, 369
entail, 433; defined, 58; fades in America, 292, 353; after the Revolution, 655
enumerated list: additions to, 399, 533; and Navigation Act of 1660, 192–93; and Navigation Act of 1696, 338; and New England, 472; rice removed from, 496
equality: and Anabaptists, 47; in back-country, 502; in Delaware Valley, 482; in Chesapeake region, 117; Quaker views on, 230; after the Revolution, 653; at the top, 292
Erasmus, Desiderius (1466–1536), 44
Ericson, Leif (fl. 1000): and America, 13
Erie (Pennsylvania): French fort at, 384
Eskimo, 13; and Columbus, 31; and Frobisher, 31
Essay for the Recording of Illustrious Providences (Mather, 1684), 304
Essay on Human Understanding (Locke, 1690), 432, 444
Estaing, Charles Hector Théodat, Comte d' (1729–1794): and the Revolution, 626–27
Ettinger, A. A.: *Oglethorpe,* 412
Euler, Leonhard (1707–1783), 451; Rittenhouse compared to, 452

Euripides: and Jefferson, 436
Europe: American physicians trained in, 448; and Columbus's voyage, 17; inflation in, 64–65; and medieval world, 2–6; New England trade with, 176; and new monarchs, 6–7; Penn's agents in, 234; Philadelphia trade with, 480; and Reformation, 43–56; tobacco imports from Britain, 488
Euseden, J. D.: *Puritans,* 81
Evans, Grose: *Benjamin West,* 467
Evans, John (fl. 1703–1731): as Pennsylvania governor, 693
Evans, Nathaniel (1742–1767): and *American Magazine,* 458
Evelyn, Robert, 72
Evelyn, W. G.: *Memoirs,* 636
Everard, Richard: as North Carolina governor, 693
Every Man His Own Doctor (1734), 446
Ewing, Mrs., 502
Exeter (New Hampshire): founded, 146
Experiments . . . on Electricity (Franklin), 458
ex post facto law: and Constitution, 674
Ezell, J. S.: *Miranda Travels,* 511

Fagg, J. E.: *Latin America,* 39
Fairchild, Byron: *Messrs. Pepperrell,* 511–12
Fairfax County (Virginia): Washington resides in, 349, 492
Fairfax grant, 270, 344
Fairfield (Connecticut): British burn, 625; founded, 151
"fair price": in medieval Europe, 2, 3; and new merchants, 6–7; Philadelphia enforcement of, 284; Winthrop's view on, 155
Falconer, J. I.: *History of Agriculture in Northern United States,* 310
fall line: defined, 78
Falmouth (Maine): British shell, 585
Familists, 47
family: in America, 288–89, 292; and education, 293, 295; in England, 60; Protestantism's influence on, 56; study of, 310
Faneuil family, 363
Farish, H. D.: *Fithian Journal,* 511
farm: in Chesapeake region, 115–17, 487; in New England, 153, 282
Farrand, Max: *Framing the Constitution,* 684; *Records of the Federal Convention,* 684

Fauquier, Francis (c. 1704–1768): as Virginia governor, 352, 697; and Two Penny Act, 408

Faust, A. B.: *German Element*, 410; "Swiss Emigration," 411

Faust, C. H.: Edwards writings, selected, 465

Federalism: principle of, 671

Federalists: and ratification of Constitution, 675, 676

Fendall, Josias (c. 1620–c. 1687): charged with sedition, 250; as Maryland governor, 201, 688

Fennelly, Catharine: "Franklin of New Jersey," 638

Fenton, W. N.: *American Indian and White Relations*, 309

Fenwick, John (1618–1683): and New Jersey, 227, 228, 229

Ferdinand, King of Aragon (1452–1516): and Columbus, 7, 17, 20; as new monarch, 6

Ferguson, E. J.: *Power of Purse*, 637

Ferguson, Patrick: defeated at King's Mountain, 628

Ferguson, W. K.: *Renaissance*, 38

Fernandez, Simon: voyages to America, 34, 36

Fernow, Berthold: *Documents of Colonial New York*, 240

feudalism: and Carolina, 213; and Coddington, 147; and Delaware ceremony, 236; in England, 6–7, 61, 65; in medieval world, 2; in New York, 477; and patroonship, 217–18; and proprietary grants, 108, 207–8; and Scottish immigrants, 370

Fielding, Henry, 437, 490

Fiennes, William, Viscount Say and Seal: and America, 130, 148, 187

Finche, Lady, 72

Finns: in Delaware Valley, 228, 362, 481; naturalized, 236

fire companies: in Philadelphia, 439

First Baptist Meeting House (Providence), 460

First Church (Boston), 428

Fisher, Daniel: diary of, 511

Fisher, S. G.: *Making of Pennsylvania*, 241; *Quaker Colonies*, 241

fishing industry: and enumerated list, 192; early English interest in, 29; and French fleets, 376; and New England economy, 471–72; New England ventures into, 175; and Peace of Paris (1783), 634;

fishing industry (*cont.*)
and Washington, 489; and West Indies trade, 400–1, 663

Fiske, John: *Critical Period*, 680–81

Fitch, Thomas (c. 1700–1774): as Connecticut governor, 687

Fithian, Philip V.: and backcountry humor, 503; journals and letters of, 511

Fitzgerald, J. C.: *Washington Writings*, 636

Fitzhugh, William (1651–1701): on England, 277; and Negroes, 290

Flatbush (Midwout), 221

flax: grown in backcountry, 499

Fleming, E. McC.: "Early American Decorative Arts," 310

Fleming, Miss Kitty, 73

Fleming, T. J.: *Yorktown*, 641

Fleming, William (1729–1795): as Virginia governor, 698

Fletcher, Benjamin (1640–1703): as New York governor, 326, 691; as Pennsylvania governor, 693

Flexner, J. T.: on American painting, 463; *American Painting*, 309; *Copley*, 467; *First Flowers*, 467; *Light of Distant Skies*, 467; *Mohawk Baronet*, 413; *Traitor and Spy*, 641; *Washington*, 413

Flick, A. C.: *History of New York*, 239–40; *Loyalism in New York*, 638

Flippen, P. S.: *Royal Government in Virginia*, 357

Flora Virginica (1739), 448

Florida: Bartram visits, 448; ceded to Britain, 518; Oglethorpe invades, 376; Ponce de León discovers, 21; Spain retrieves, 633; as Spanish name, 24; studies of, 552

flour: in Delaware Valley economy, 480; and Mt. Vernon, 489; and South Carolina, 498

Folestone (Oyster Bay), 221

Folger, Peter (1617–1690): on King Philip's War, 254

Foner, Philip: *Paine's Writings*, 595

fool's gold: and Cartier, 26

Forbes, Esther, *Paul Revere*, 594

Forbes, John (1710–1759): and French and Indian War, 391, 394

Forbes Road: cut, 394; and Western settlement, 397

Force, Peter, *Tracts*, 119

Fordham, Robert: founds Hempstead, 169

Ford, H. J.: *Scotch-Irish*, 411

Ford, P. L.: *Dickinson Writings*, 553

Foreman, C. T.: *Indians Abroad*, 309

Forman, H. C.: *Architecture of the Old South,* 309
Forrest family, 363
Fort Beauséjour: English capture, 390
Fort Christina: and Swedes, 220
Fort Caroline: French build, 27; Hawkins visits, 30; Spanish level, 27
Fort Chartres: French build, 377
Fort Detroit: abandoned, 531; French build, 327; Pontiac besieges, 522, 526
Fort Duquesne: and Braddock expedition, 387, 388; destroyed, 394; French build, 384
Fort Edward: Burgoyne reaches, 613
Fort Edward Augustus: abandoned, 526
Fort Frontenac: La Salle builds, 319, 320
Fort James: and Leisler's Rebellion, 267, 268, 269
Fort La Baye: French build, 377
Fort La Point: and French, 377
Fort Le Boeuf: captured, 526; Washington visits, 384
Fort Lee: captured, 608
Fort Louisbourg: built, 376; expedition against (1745), 379; expedition against (1757), 391; returned to France, 382; *see also* Louisbourg
Fort Loyal: French raze, 324
Fort Miami, 383; captured, 526
Fort Michilimackinac: abandoned, 531; built, 377; captured, 526
Fort Nassau: Dutch build, 227
Fort Necessity: and Washington, 385, 387
Fort Niagara: abandoned, 531; built, 320; in French and Indian War, 387; holds out (1763), 526; and Johnson, 394–95; and Sullivan, 627
Fort Orange, 320; and May, 217; *see also* Albany
Fort Orleans: built, 377
Fort Oswego: built, 377; captured, 391; Indian conference at, 529
Fort Ouiatenon, 525; captured, 526
Fort Pitt, 394; besieged, 526
Fort Presque Île: captured, 526
Fort St. George (Sagadahoc), 88, 91
Fort St. John's: Allen and Arnold take, 579; Montgomery takes, 602
Fort St. Joseph: captured, 526
Fort St. Louis: built, 320; repaired, 377
Fort Sandusky: built, 525; captured, 526
Fort Stanwix: Indian conference at, 531; in Revolution, 613, 616
Fort Sullivan: saves Charleston, 603
Fort Ticonderoga: Abercromby fails to take, 394; Allen and Arnold take, 579;

Fort Ticonderoga (*cont.*)
  Amherst takes, 395; Burgoyne takes, 613; cannons from, in Boston, 601; reaction to capture by Congress, 600, 619
Fort Venango: captured, 526
Fort Washington: captured, 606–7
Fort Wayne (Indiana): and Fort Miami, 526; site of French fort, 383
Fort William Henry: (Lake George) captured, 391; (Pemaquid) destroyed, 326
Foster, John (1648–1681): engraver, 287
Fourth Intercolonial War; *see* French and Indian War
Fox, D. R.: on greatness of Holland, 189; *Caleb Heathcote,* 512; *Yankees and Yorkers,* 239
Fox, George (1624–1691): beliefs of, 230; tours colonies, 227, 232
Frame of Government (1682), 235; on education, 446–47; expanded, 236; influence on Delaware constitution, 646
France: and the American Revolution, 620, 633, 634; Calvinism carried to, 51; church lands in, 3; and Dominion of New England, 264; and English hat industry, 400; and English sugar industry, 400; Huguenots leave, 27, 363; and King George's War, 378–82; and James II, 260; under Louis XIV, 316; and mercantilism, 187; and Navigation Acts, 190; New England trade with, 256, 257, 472; and New France, 385–86; and Peace of Paris (1763), 518; and Peace of Paris (1783), 633, 634; studies on United States alliance, 639; studies on wars in America, 355; and Treaty of Utrecht, 333; and United States alliance, 617, 619, 620; United States loans, 609, 618; and United States trade, 663
Francis I: subsidizes explorations, 26
Francis, W. N.: "Hakluyt's *Voyages,*" 40
Franklin: as independent state, 661
Franklin, Benjamin (1706–1790), 301, 433, 434, 435; on age of experiments, 643; apes Addison and Steele style, 454; and Articles of Confederation, 581; biographies and studies of, 466, 513, 553, 594, 639; and Braddock, 388, 396; on church-going, 421; as colonial agent, 341; and Congress, 578, 664; considers self Englishman, 517; and Constitution, 668, 677; as deist, 436; on debt (as Poor Richard), 402; educational ideas of, 444; and election of 1764, 482, 485–86; and fire company, 439; in France, 618; on German immigrants, 372, 484;

Franklin, Benjamin (*cont.*)
and Howe peace feelers, 606; and
Hutchinson, 559–60; and independence,
581, 591; on inflated paper money, 609;
as journalist, 458; and Junto, 450; and
lightning rod, 451; and Parliamentary
testimony, 539–40; and Paxton Boys,
485; and Peace of Paris (1783), 633,
661; and Pennsylvania as royal colony,
344; as Pennsylvania governor, 694;
and Plan of Union, 387; plants newspaper article on American embargo,
547; and post office, 442; proposes society to promote useful knowledge, 417,
451; proverbs of, 453; and Quaker
Party, 485; retires from business, 441;
on Revenue Act (1764), 533; and Revenue Act (1767), 539–40, 544; as scientist, 447, 452; as scientist, study of, 466;
Shelburne consults, 522; on Spanish
coyness, 620; and Stamp Act, 535, 537;
Thomson sends note to, 573; on unity,
648; and Vergennes, 608, 633; on
Whitefield sermon, 424; writings of, selected, 595
Franklin, Mrs. Benjamin (Deborah Read),
505
Franklin family: Revolution splits, 610
Franklin, James (1697–1735): attacks
clergy, 421
Franklin, William (1731–1813): and independence, 581; as New Jersey governor, 591; study of, 638
Franklin (Pennsylvania): site of French
fort, 384, 526
Frederick County (Virginia): created,
372; Washington represents, 349, 492
Fredericksburg (Virginia), 115; vestry
hires Henry, 408
Frederick Town: as German settlement,
498
Freeman, D. S.: *Washington*, 413
Free Society of Traders (Pennsylvania),
234–35
Frelinghuysen, Theodore Jacob (1691–c.
1748): and revival of, 421–22
French: attitude toward Indians, 525; and
Calvert in Newfoundland, 109; and explorations of Canada, 26; incursions into
colonial fishing grounds, 260; and influence of immigrants in America, 363;
and Iroquois, 319, 320, 324, 328, 329,
381; and King Philip's War, 254; in
Maine, 154; as menace to colonies, 170,
259, 279, 316–21, 327; and Pontiac,
528; traveler's journal, 510; and *May-*

French (*cont.*)
flower, 127; in Virginia, 102; and Yamasee War, 373; and Yorktown campaign, 631-32
French, Allen: *First Year of Revolution,*
594; *Lexington and Concord,* 594
French and Indian War, 385–96; begins,
384; and British dependence on colonial
iron, 402; effect on America, 396–98;
effect on Board of Trade's attitude
toward colonies, 352; and plain people,
365; studies of, 412
French Creek: site of French fort, 384
French Guinea Company: and slave trade,
329
French language: Penn's tracts translated
into, 234; words in American, 454
French Revolution: and *émigrés,* 653
Freund, Virginia: *History of Travel into
Virginia,* 119
Frobisher, Sir Martin (c. 1535–1594):
seeks Northwest Passage, 31
Frontenac, Louis de Buade, Comte de
(1620–1698): arrives in Canada, 317;
biographies of, 355; on burning of Schenectady, 324; death of, 326; Heathcote
praises, 326; and Phips, 325; recalled,
321; returns to Canada, 324, 325
Fuller, William: as Maryland governor, 185
Fundamental Articles of New Haven
(1639), 151
Fundamental Constitutions for Carolina
(1669), 213–14; on lawyers, 292; objected to, 269
Fundamental Orders of Connecticut
(1639), 150; on governor's tenure, 197
funding: as debate topic, 656
Fugger (banking house), 31
fur trade: and Canada, 316, 317; English
involvement in, 29; and enumerated list,
399, 400; French advantage in, 320–21;
La Salle revolutionizes, 319; and New
England, 174; and New Haven, 227;
and New York, 225, 329; and Pilgrims,
148, 154; and Proclamation of 1763,
523; and Senecas, 245; and South Carolina, 216, 495; and Yamasee War, 373
furniture: in America, 286–87, 462

Gadsden, Christopher (1724–1805): on colonial union, 648
Gaelic: in colonies, 370
Gage, Thomas (fl. 1648): and Cromwell,
191
Gage, Thomas (1721–1787): and American prisoners, 584; biography of, 552;

Gage, Thomas (*cont.*)
in Boston, 576–77, 578; and Braddock's expedition, 389; and Breed's Hill, 600; correspondence of, 536; as Massachusetts governor, 689; New York as headquarters of, 545; and plan to remove troops from Boston, 549; recalled, 601; replaces Amherst, 628; replaces Hutchinson, 566; reprimands Bradstreet, 529; as royal governor, 346; seen as first of an American nobility, 541; urges tough line toward colonies, 568; and Western fur trade, 530
Gaillard, T. L.: *County Palatine of Durham,* 120
Galen, 300
Galileo (1564–1642), 298; and the church, 430–31; reception of ideas, 299; and satellites of Jupiter, 299
Gallaudet family, 363
Galloway, Joseph (c. 1731–1803): and independence, 581; loses assembly seat, 486; studies of, 594, 639; Plan of Union of, 571; and Quaker Party, 485; on Suffolk Resolves, 570
Gama, Vasco da (c. 1469–1525): and voyage to India, 18
Garden, Alexander (c. 1730–1791): as botanist, 448
Gardoqui, Don Diego de: negotiates for Spain, 665
Garnett, David: on Indians, 280
Garvan, Anthony: on colonial architecture, 285; *Architecture and Town Planning,* 309
Gaspee, 564; burned, 560
Gates, Horatio (1729–1806): and Battle of Camden, 627; biography of, 638; and Conway Cabal, 624; and Saratoga, 616; and Washington, 580, 601, 623
Gates, Sir Thomas (d. 1621): and Jamestown, 94, 95, 96, 97; and Oglethorpe, 375; returns to England, 95; as Virginia governor, 97–98, 696; wrecked on Bermuda, 94
Gaustad, E. S.: *Great Awakening in New England,* 464
General Court (Massachusetts): becomes bicameral, 178; and Connecticut, 150; censors printing, 297; and education, 295; on English law in Massachusetts, 257; first session, 136; and Harvard, 293, 294; and local government, 153; and Massachusetts economy, 155, 174–75; and meetinghouse placement, 152; and provisional government, 260; and

General Court (*cont.*)
religious persecution, 178; and royal commission, 200; and Salem trials, 305; and towns' size, 152–53; and Williams, 143
Geneva, 135; Calvin tests ideas in, 51; Marian Exiles in, 52
Genoa; Columbus' birthplace, 13; Polo prisoner in, 5
Gentleman and Cabinet-maker's Director (Chippendale, 1754), 462
gentry: in seventeenth-century America, 288, 291–93; in eighteenth-century America, 440–41; in Boston, 472; in Chesapeake region, 117, 490; effect of inflation on, 65; in England, 58; as immigrants, 69; as justices of peace, 63; and Massachusetts merchants, 155; planned role in Carolina, 213; in South Carolina, 494; and Stuarts, 70; studies of, 82; in Virginia, 107, 291
geography: influence on colonies, 151–52
George I (1660–1727): and Maryland, 272
George II (1683–1760), 407; death of, 406; and Test Act, 368
George III (1738–1820): accession, 406; biography of, 552; death of, 407; declares colonies rebellious, 585; and Grenville, 539; and Patrick Henry, 537; reaction to Boston tea party, 563
George, C. H.: *English Reformation,* 81
Georgia: British invade, 626; and Congress, 578; government of (1775), 583; and independence, 588; Moravians in, 365; orphanage in, 423; ratifies Constitution, 675; rejects Association, 576; settlement of, 373–76; and slave trade, 654; studies of, 411; Western land claims of, 650
Georgian architecture, 459
Gerlach, D. R.: *Philip Schuyler,* 594
Germain, Lord George; *see* Sackville, Lord George
German Baptist Brethren; *see* Dunkards
German language: *Common Sense* translated into, 586; Penn's tracts translated into, 234
German Lutherans: revival among, 425
German mercenaries; *see* Hessians
German Palatinate: and colonial immigration, 364
German Quakers: attack slavery, 289; in Pennsylvania, 237, 362
German Reformed Presbyterian Church; *see* Dutch Reformed Church

German Society of Pennsylvania, 371
Germans: in backcountry, 497; in England, 364; as immigrants, 364–66; in Ireland, 364; legislation to protect, 371; and Pennsylvania politics, 372, 484; and Regulators of North Carolina, 508; studies of, 410–11; in Virginia, 92, 102
Germantown: Battle of, 617; founded, 237
Germany: Calvinism carried to, 51; church lands in, 3; and emigrants from, 237; influence on meetinghouse, 286; and Luther, 44–46; peasants' revolt, 46–47
Gerry, Elbridge (1744–1814): and Constitution, 688, 673
Gettysburg (Pennsylvania) as German town, 365
Gewehr, W. M.: *Great Awakening in Virginia*, 465
Gibbes, Robert: as South Carolina governor, 695
Gibbs children (fl. 1670): painting of, 288
Gibbs, James (1682–1754): as architect, 459, 460, 461
Gibraltar, 8; Spain loses, 333; Spain seeks to retrieve, 620
Gilbert, Sir Humphrey (1537–1583), 88; biographical sketch of, 31–32; dream of, 107; dream of and Carolina proprietors, 211; Irish experience of, 32; study of, 41; voyages of, 33
Gilbert, Raleigh: and Council for New England, 89; and Sagadahoc, 88
Gillespie, J. E.: *History of Geographical Discovery*, 39
ginger: on enumerated list, 192
Ginseng: and China trade, 664
Gipson, L. H.: on name for French and Indian War, 385; on New Jersey politics, 480; "Aftermath of the Great War for Empire," 412; *British Empire*, 411; *Coming of the Revolution*, 551; "Debate on Stamp Act," 553
Gist, Christopher (c. 1706–1759): accompanies Washington, 384; and Ohio Company, 383
Gladwin, Henry (1729–1791): and Fort Detroit, 526, 528
Glasgow: and tobacco trade, 370
Glauber, Johan (c. 1603–1668), 300
Gleason, J. P.: "A Scurrilous Election," 513
Glen, James: as South Carolina governor, 496, 695; essay of, 514
Glorious Revolution: in America, 265–73; and Dickinson, 272, 546; documents on, 274; effect on relations with England,

Glorious Revolution (*cont.*)
327, 354–55; effect on Ulster, 368; in Maryland, 250; and Parliament, 337; significance for colonies, 272–73, 548
Gloucester (England): as wool trade center, 57
Gloucester (Massachusetts): and witches, 304
Glover, William: as Carolina governor, 692
Godfrey, Thomas (1736–1763): and *American Magazine*, 458
Godspeed, 89
Godyn, Samuel: patroon, 218
Goebel, D. B.: "Trade Politics," 554
Goen, C. C.: *Revivalism and Separatism in New England*, 465
Gómez, Estevan: and Northwest Passage, 21
Gooch, Sir William (1681–1751): as Virginia governor, 697
Good News from Virginia (Whitaker, 1613), 118
Goode, John: warns Bacon, 248
Goodman, A. V.: *Jewish Rights*, 411
Goodrick, A. T. S.: *Edward Randolph*, 274
Goodwin, M. W.: *Dutch and English on the Hudson*, 240
Godkin, Charles: as Pennsylvania governor, 693
Gordon, Patrick: as Pennsylvania governor, 693
Gordon, Thomas, 454
Gorges, Sir Ferdinando (c. 1566–1647): and Council for New England, 89; and Maine, 108, 151; and Massachusetts, 141–42; and Plymouth Company, 108; and Sagadahoc, 88–89
Gorton, Samuel (c. 1592–1677): characterized, 147; and Massachusetts, 169
Goshenhoppen (Pennsylvania): Catholics in, 482
Gosnold, Bartholomew (c. 1572–1607): voyages to New England, 86
Gottschalk, Louis: *Lafayette*, 640
government: Hooker's views on, 149–50; Locke on source of authority, 432–33; Penn's views on, 230, 232, 235; Williams' views on, 144; Wise on end of, 435
government (local): and backcountry, 502, 505; in Chesapeake colonies, 101, 115, 117–18, 185; and Dominion of New England, 264; and Duke's Laws, 223; and Dutch, 222; and education, 447; in England, 62–64; in New England, 151–

government (local) (*cont.*)
54, 155; and royal governor, 347; and Virginia code (1664), 200–1; Virginia rebels seek to strengthen, 249
government (provincial): in 1775, 583; and backcountry, 505–6; and city, 439; in Chesapeake colonies, 115, 117–18; and Chesapeake economy, 180; Chesapeake voters apathy toward, 491; Congress calls for new ones, 589; in Connecticut River towns, 149–50; and education, 443; Lords of Trade seek to royalize, 255–56; in Massachusetts, 132, 136–40; and New England economy, 155; New Englanders' apathy toward, 474; and Pennsylvania, 235; survey of a royal colony, 343–55; Virginia creates, 100; Virginia rebels seek to weaken, 249
government (state), 644–47
government (territorial), 657, 659
governor: Adams' conception of post, 645; Bacon's Laws on, 248, 249; and Board of Trade, 405; and communication with England, 341; in Connecticut River towns, 150; and corporate colony, 344; correspondence of, 415; and disallowance, 351; duties of, 345–47; and French and Indian War, 397; and Glorious Revolution, 327; and instructions of, 345–46; Jefferson's conception of post, 645; in joint-stock company, 67; and judiciary, 353–54; and local offices, 505; and Lords of Trade, 336; in Maryland, 113, 117–18; and Massachusetts charter (1691), 337; and Navigation Acts, 192, 258, 338; number in colonial period, 346; and office of President, 671; Paine's conception of post, 645; powers of, 339, 341–42; quality of, 346; in a regulated company, 67; salary of, 337, 351–52; selection of, 339; and smuggling, 532; in state constitutions, 646; studies of, 357; in Virginia, 93–104, 107, 117–18
governor general (Canada): duties of, 316
Gowans, Alan: *Images of American Living,* 309
Graeff, A. D.: *Weiser,* 412
Graffenried, Christopher, Baron de (1661–1743): and New Bern, 364
Grafton, Augustus Henry Fitzroy, third Duke of (1735–1811): and Treasury, 543
Graham, I. C. C.: *Colonists from Scotland,* 411
grammar schools: in England, 297; in New England, 295, 296

Grand Khan; see Kublai Khan
Grant, Anne: *Memoirs,* 513
Grant, W. L.: *Acts of Privy Council,* 414
Granville, Earl of; see Carteret, John, first Earl of Granville
Grasse, Comte de: and Charleston, 632; and Yorktown, 631
Gravesend (New York): founded, 169
Graves, Robert: *Sargeant Lamb,* 636
Gray, L. C.: *Agriculture in Southern United States,* 310
Gray's Inn: Bacon studies at, 246; Winthrop studies at, 132
Gray, Thomas (1716–1771): Wolfe reads from, 395
Graydon, Alexander: *Memoirs,* 636
Great Awakening, 417–430; and colleges, 294, 443–44; and Enlightenment, 428–29; opponents of, 426–27, 428; studies of, 464; and voluntary societies, 440
"great chain of being," 2
"Great Charter" (Virginia), 100–1
Great Meadows: Washington at, 384–85
Great Schism (1378–1415), 6
Great Wagon Road: towns along, 497; traffic on, 497, 499
Great War for Empire; see French and Indian War
Greek: attitude toward, after Revolution, 654; in New England education, 296; in English curriculum, 60; and Jefferson, 447; Maury derides for Americans, 444; as practical subject, 295; Wilson teaches, 505
Green, C. McL.: essay on Confederation of New England, 203
Green, V. H. H.: *Renaissance and Reformation,* 38
Green Bay: Jolliet and Marquette at, 317, 319; site of Fort Edward Augustus, 526; site of French fort, 377
Green Mountain Boys, 660
Greenbury, Nicholas: as Maryland governor, 688
Greene, E. B.: *Provincial Governor,* 357; *Revolutionary Generation,* 510
Greene, J. P.: "Currency Act of 1764," 522; "Flight from Determinism," 550; *Quest for Power,* 357
Greene, Nathanael (1742–1786): at Battle of Brandywine, 617; at Battle of Guilford Courthouse, 629; biography of, 639; protects forts Washington and Lee, 606; as quartermaster general, 622; Southern campaign of, 628–29; urges New York burned, 605

Greene, Thomas: as Maryland governor, 688

Greene, William (1696–1758): as Rhode Island governor, 694

Greene, William (1731–1809): as Rhode Island governor, 694

Greenwich (Connecticut): founded, 151

Gregorian calendar, 430

Grenville, George (1712–1770), 523; and Board of Trade Indian plan, 530; as House leader, 410; papers of, 553; program of, 531–39; problems of, 519; and Stamp Act, 535–37; and Stamp Act repeal, 540; and Townshend duties, 544

Grenville, Henry: as royal governor, 347

Grenville, Sir Richard (c. 1541–1591): voyages to Virginia, 35

Grenville, Robert, Lord Brooke: obtains patent for American settlement, 148

Gridley, Jeremiah (1702–1767): on American lawyers, 445

Grigsby, H. B.: Virginia Convention of 1788, 685

Grimm, H. J.: Reformation, 81

Grinstein, H. B.: Jewish Community in New York, 411

Griswold, Matthew (1714–1799): as Connecticut governor, 687

Gronovius, Johan Frederick (1690–1760): and American botanists, 447–48

Groton Manor, 132

Grotius, Hugo (1583–1645), 189

Gruber, Ira: on German biography, 637

Guadeloupe, 400; Columbus discovers, 18; France keeps, 518; in Queen Anne's War, 331

Guerard, Benjamin: as South Carolina governor, 696

Guide to Study of United States of America, 37

guilds: in medieval world, 2; in New England, 155; and new merchants, 6–7; and regulated company, 67; studies of, 82

Guilford (Connecticut): founded, 151

Guilford Courthouse, Battle of, 629

Gummere, R. M.: American Colonial Mind and Classical Tradition, 465–66

Guttridge, G. H.: Colonial Policy of William III, 355–56

Gwinnett, Button (c. 1735–1777): as Georgia governor, 687

habeas corpus: in Constitution, 674

Habeas Corpus Act (1679): and colonies, 355

Hacker, L. M.: "First American Revolution," 551

Hadley, John (1682–1744): quadrant of, 72

Hadley (Massachusetts): and King Philip's War, 254

Haffenden, P. S.: "Anglican Church in Restoration Policy," 204; "Crown and Colonial Charters," 274

Hagen, Oskar: Birth of American Tradition in Art, 309

Hagerstown (Maryland): on Great Wagon Road, 497

Hakluyt, Richard, the elder (c. 1535–1591), 31; advice followed, 35; and Gilbert, 102; "Notes" of, 32; as Protestant, 43; on value of colonies, 66

Hakluyt, Richard, the younger (c. 1552–1616), 31, 211; biography of, 40; and Gilbert, 33, 34; Principal Navigations, 40; as Protestant, 43; and Raleigh, 34, 35; sketch of, 33; and Spanish Empire, 89; on value of colonies, 66; and Virginia, 92

Hale, John: and Salem trials, 305

Half Moon, 216

Half-Way Covenant (1657), 198–99, 303, 421

Halifax, Earl of: favors Anglican bishop in colonies, 409; letter from Gage, 529; as president of Board of Trade, 340, 398, 405–6

Halifax (Nova Scotia): troops from, 547, 549

Hall, C. C.: Narratives of Early Maryland, 120

Hall, Bishop Joseph (1574–1656): on Anglicanism, 53

Hall, Lyman: as Georgia governor (1724–1790), 687

Hall, M. G.: on Randolph, 256; Edward Randolph, 274; Glorious Revolution, 274

Haller, William: Rise of Puritanism, 81

Hamilton, Dr. Alexander: Itinerarium of, 510

Hamilton, Alexander (1755–1804): at Annapolis Convention, 666–67; and bill of rights, 674; biographies of, 683, 684; on the Confederation, 651; in Congress, 664; and Constitution, 670; continental outlook of, 665; and Federalist, 675; and Shays's Rebellion, 667

Hamilton, Andrew (d. 1703): as New Jersey governor, 690; as Pennsylvania governor, 693

Hamilton, Andrew (d. 1741): and Pennsylvania statehouse, 460

Hamilton, E. P.: *Bougainville Journals*, 414; *French and Indian Wars*, 355

Hamilton, George, Earl of Orkney: as Virginia governor-in-chief, 697

Hamilton, Henry, 636; in the Revolution, 625

Hamilton, James (c. 1710–1783): as Pennsylvania governor, 693, 694

Hamilton, J. G. deR.: *North Carolina History*, 514

Hamilton, John: as New Jersey governor, 691

Hammond, Bray: on agrarian America, 402; *Banks and Politics*, 414

Hamor, Ralph (fl. 1616): on Dale's Laws, 97

Hampton Court Conference (1604), 53

Hancock, John (1737–1793): and Congress, 578, 664; and Constitution, 668, 675; as Massachusetts governor, 689; on revision of Articles of Confederation, 666; ship of, seized, 547; and tea party, 563; warned British coming, 577

Handlin, Mary F., "Economic Policy in Massachusetts," 638

Handlin, Oscar: "Economic Policy in Massachusetts," 638; *Journey to Pennsylvania*, 411

Hanna, C. A.: *Scotch-Irish*, 411

Hanna, W. S.: *Franklin and Pennsylvania Politics*, 513

Hannah's Cowpens: Morgan victory at, 629

Hannary, David: *Great Chartered Companies*, 82

Hansen, M. L.: *Atlantic Migration*, 83

Hanover County (Virginia): and Great Awakening, 426; Henry lives in, 492

Haraszti, Zoltán: *John Adams*, 594

Harbison, E. H.: *Reformation*, 81

Harborne, William: visits Constantinople, 30

Hard Labor: Indian conference at, 531

Hardenbergh Patent, 447

Harding, S. B.: *Ratification of Constitution in Massachusetts*, 684

Hardy, Josiah: as New Jersey governor, 691

Haring, C. H.: *Spanish America*, 39

Hariot, Thomas: voyages to Virginia, 35

Harkness, Georgia: Luther biography by, 81

Harlem Heights: Washington ensconced on, 607

Harley, Robert, first Earl of Oxford (1661–1724): and Marquette letter, 319

Harnett, Cornelius (c. 1723–1781): as North Carolina governor, 693

Harper, L. A.: *English Navigation Laws*, 203

Harrell, I. S.: *Loyalism in Virginia*, 638

Harrington, James (1611–1677): and Penn, 235; and plan for Carolina, 213–14

Harrington, Virginia: *New York Merchants*, 512

Harris's Ferry (Pennsylvania): Indian conference at, 391

Harrison, Benjamin (1726–1791): constituents put trust in, 491; as Virginia governor, 698

Harrison, Peter (1716–1775): as architect, 460; biography of, 467

Harrison, William (1534–1593): on England's "laboring poor," 59

Harris, William (fl. 1635): and Williams, 147

Harrower, John: *Journal* of, 310

Hart, A. B.: *Commonwealth History of Massachusetts*, 203

Hart, F. H.: *Valley of Virginia in Revolution*, 515

Hartford (Connecticut), 438; and Block, 217; as Dutch stronghold, 170; General Court held at, 149; settled, 148, 149; treaty of (1650), 171–74

Hart, John: as Maryland governor, 688

Hartlib, Samuel (c. 1600–1670), 296

Hartz, Louis: *Liberal Tradition*, 682

Harvard College, 23, 158; Anglican mission near, 409; Cheever students at, 296; and English universities, 294; founded, 293–94; and Indian fund, 171; John Adams at, 445; and Locke, 444; medical school founded, 446; and science, 299, 444, 452

Harvard Guide, 37

Harvard, John (1607–1638), 293

Harvey, Sir John (d. 1646), 106; council rebukes, 106–7; opposes Claiborne, 114; as Virginia governor, 107, 243, 696; welcomes Calvert, 109; welcomes Maryland settlers, 112

Harvey, John (fl. 1679): as North Carolina governor, 692

Harvey, Thomas: as Carolina governor, 692

Harvey, William (1578–1657), 298; credulity of, 300; reception of ideas, 299

Hasell, James: as North Carolina acting governor, 693

Haskins, G. L.: on Laws and Liberties, 178; *Law and Authority,* 162

Hat and Felt Act (1732), 400

Hatteras Island: Amadas-Barlowe land on, 34

Havana: Gage reports defenseless, 191

Hawke, David: *Midst of a Revolution,* 515; *Transaction,* 595

Hawkins, Sir John (1532–1595): visits Fort Caroline, 27, 30; and West Indies, 30

Hawks, John (1731–1790): builds governor's palace, 459–60

Hawley, Joseph (1723–1788), 559

Hawthorne, Nathaniel, 434

Haynes, John (ca. 1594–1654): as Connecticut governor, 687; as Massachusetts governor, 689

headright system, 116; backcountry variations of, 499; in Carolina, 214; Dutch variation of, 217–18; in Georgia, 375; London Company introduces, 100; Penn's variation of, 234; Virginia and suffrage regulations, 244; Virginia extends to Indians, 184

Heard, Stephen: as Georgia governor, 687

Heath, D. B.: *Journal of Pilgrims,* 160

Heath, Sir Robert: Carolina grant to (1629), 109, 208, 209

Heath, William (1737–1814): commands army on Manhattan, 605, 607

Heathcote, Caleb (1666–1721): biography of, 512; on council, 291, 348; emigrates, 71; on French menace, 326

Heaton, Herbert: *Economic History of Europe,* 82

Hebrew: as national language, 655

Hecksher, Eli: *Mercantilism,* 82

Hedges, J. B.: *Browns of Providence,* 512

hemp: grown in backcountry, 499

Hempstead (New York): founded, 169

Hendrick, Chief (c. 1680–1755): death of, 390

Henrico (Virginia), 103; as borough, 100; founded, 97

Henrietta Maria (1609–1669): Queen of Charles I, 70; and Maryland, 110

Henrique, Infante Dom (Prince Henry the Navigator) (1394–1460), 7; goal of, 8; ridiculed, 9

Henry VII (1457–1509): and Cabot, 18, 25; and Columbus, 14; and doctrine of effective occupation, 25; as new monarch, 6

Henry VIII (1491–1547): death of, 51; and monastery lands, 65, 140; and Reformation, 51; and statute on trials, 548

Henry, Patrick (1736–1799): on being an American, 503, 570; biography of, 553; and Congress, 572, 664; and Constitution, 668, 674–75; on Davies, 426; in House of Burgesses, 492; on liberty and death, 576; and Robinson scandal, 488; and Stamp Act, 537–38; and Two Penny Act, 407–8; as Virginia governor, 648, 698

Henry, S. C.: on Whitefield, 424; *George Whitefield,* 465

Hesselius, Gustavus (1682–1755): painter, 462

Hessians: in Burgoyne's army, 613; Congressional reaction to hiring of, 587–88; pillaging in New Jersey, 607; Samuel Adams on, 590; studies on, 637; at Trenton, 612

Hewes, Joseph (1730–1779): and Prohibitory Act, 587

Hibbard, B. H.: *Public Land Policies,* 682

Hibbert, Christopher: *Wolfe at Quebec,* 413

Hicks, Isaac: biography of, 683

hides: on enumerated list, 533

Higginbotham, Don: *Daniel Morgan,* 639

Higginson, Francis (1586–1630): on ocean storm, 73

Highland Scots; *see* Scots

Hill, Christopher: on Cromwell's "Western Design," 192; on effect of navigation system, 194–95; *Century of Revolution,* 82; *England in the Seventeenth Century,* 204

Hill, Edward: as Maryland governor, 688

Hillsboro: fall line town, 497

Hillsborough (North Carolina), 508–9

Hillsborough, Wills Hill, first Earl of, 522; and Proclamation of 1763, 523; and Townshend duties, 549; as secretary of state, 546–47

Hilton, William: explores Cape Fear, 212

Hinckley, Thomas: as Plymouth governor, 689

Hindle, Brooke: on Rittenhouse, 452; *Pursuit of Science,* 466; *Rittenhouse,* 466

Hirsch, A. H.: *Huguenots of South Carolina,* 411

Hispaniola: and Columbus, 16, 18; and Penn-Venable expedition, 191

Hexter, J. H.: "Storm over the Gentry," 82

History and Present State of Virginia (Beverly, 1705), 457

History of . . . New-York (Smith, 1757), 457
History of the Colony of Massachusetts Bay (Hutchinson, 1764), 457
History of the Dividing Line (Byrd, 1841), 457
History of the Five Nations (Colden, 1727), 457
History of the World (Raleigh, 1614), 37
History of . . . Virginia (Stith, 1747), 457
Hofstadter, Richard: on non-sectarianism of colleges, 444; on Yale's break with past, 294; *Academic Freedom,* 311
Holland: Anabaptists in, 49; Davenport in, 150; Frelinghuysen from, 421; influence on meeting houses, 286; loans from, 609; loses American holdings, 194; and Pennsylvania immigration, 237; Pilgrims in, 124–25; and Spain's control over, 124–25; and trade with United States, 663; and Treaty of Hartford, 174; in War of Spanish Succession, 329; as world trader, 189
Hollander, Peter: as new Sweden governor, 691
Holmes, V. B.: *History of Americas,* 39
"holy commonwealth"; *see* Massachusetts Bay
"holy experiment"; *see* Pennsylvania
Honyman, Robert: Journal of, 511
Hooker, R. J.: Woodmason's *Journal,* 515
Hooker, Thomas (c. 1586–1647), 142, 154; acquaintance of Masham, 143; biography of, 163; characterized, 136; and Cotton, 148; death of, 179; and immigration to Connecticut, 148–49; and Laud, 141; on religion in England, 70; on sermons, 307; views on government, 149–50
Hope, Thomas (1769–1831): and Izard's house, 461
Hopkins, Edward (1600–1657): as Connecticut governor, 687; immigrates to colonies, 150
Hopkinson, Francis (1737–1791): and *American Magazine,* 458
Hopkins, Stephen (1707–1785): as Rhode Island governor, 694
Hornberger, Theodore: *Scientific Thought in American Colleges,* 311
Horrocks, J. W.: *Mercantilism,* 82
Horsey, Samuel: as South Carolina governor, 695
Hosmer, J. K.: Winthrop *Journal,* 161
House of Commons: and American assemblies, 62, 202, 238, 350; composition of,

House of Commons (*cont.*)
58; king's power in (1774), 574; members on Board of Trade, 339; Popham on, 87; rights and privileges of, 62; *see also* Parliament
House of Lords: constituents, 349; described, 62; and governor's council, 202, 348, 350; wealth of members, 58; *see also* Parliament
House of Trade (*Casa de contratación*), 23
Houstoun, John (1744–1796): as Georgia governor, 687
Howard of Effingham, Francis, fifth Baron: confers with Iroquois, 321; instructions on printing, 298; as Virginia governor, 270, 697
Howard, Leon: on Franklin, 458
Howe, George Augustus (c. 1724–1758): killed, 394
Howe, Richard, first Earl (1726–1799): arrives with fleet, 605; seeks reconciliation, 606; study of, 637
Howe, Sir William, fifth Viscount Howe (1729–1814): in Boston, 600, 601, 602; offers pardons, 607; and Philadelphia campaign, 617; seeks reconciliation, 605; sent to America, 574; study of, 637
Howley, Richard (1740–1784): as Georgia governor, 687
Hubbard, William (c. 1621–1704): *Narrative* of, 287; as writer, 307
Hudson Bay: English outpost attacked, 324, 326; English outpost on, 317; English sovereignty over, 333
Hudson, Henry (d. 1611): Dutch hire, 86; voyages to America, 216
Hudson River: Dutch holdings on, 189; Hudson explores, 216; and Pilgrims, 126
Hudson, W. S.: on churches as voluntary societies, 421; on denominations, 428; *American Protestantism,* 464
Hudson Valley: in eighteenth century, 475–80
Huguenots: off Brazil, 27; as Calvinists, 51; immigrate to America, 363, 364; influence on English explorers, 27–28, 31; influence on Gilbert, 32; influence on meetinghouse, 286; in South Carolina, 27, 215, 498; in Ulster, 368
Hughes, John: as stamp collector, 537
Hughes, Thomas: *Journal,* 636
Huizinga, Johan: on medieval life, 3; *Waning of Middle Ages,* 38
Hull, John (1624–1683): investments of, 177; on the law, 292

Hull, W. I.: biography of Penn, 241
Hulton, Paul: *White Drawings,* 41
humoral conception of disease, 449
Hungary: Calvinism carried to, 51
Hunloke, Edward: as West Jersey governor, 690
Hunter, Robert (d. 1734): on assemblies, 352; as New Jersey governor, 690; as New York governor, 352, 691; and Palatine immigrants, 364; as royal governor, 347
Huntington (New York): founded, 169
Huntington, Samuel (1731–1796): as Connecticut governor, 687
Huron Indians: Iroquois attack, 320; threaten to leave French, 324
Huss, John (c. 1369–1415), 5
Hutchinson, Anne (1591–1643), 142, 293; biographical sketch of, 145–46; biography of, 162; in New Netherland, 169; in Rhode Island, 147
Hutchinson, Thomas (1711–1780), 346, 558; and Boston tea party, 562–63; on committees of correspondence, 559; and Franklin, 559–60; and *Gaspee* incident, 560; as historian, 457; house ransacked, 538; as Massachusetts governor, 689; on meaning of "subordination," 550; and Otis, 407; on people's extravagances, 542; and Port Act, 563; on removal of French menace, 396; on Stamp Act, 538; on supremacy of Parliament, 559; *History of Massachusetts Bay,* 161
Huygens, Christian (1629–1693), 451
Hyde, Edward (fl. 1710): as Carolina governor, 692
Hyde, Edward; *see* Cornbury, Edward Hyde, Viscount

Illinois country: center for proposed colony, 522; Miamis leave, 383; works on, 355, 552
Illinois Indians: Iroquois attack, 321
Imago Mundi (D'Ailly, c. 1410), 14
immigration: in seventeenth century, 68–72; in eighteenth century, 362–70; to Carolina, 211; and Cavaliers, 184; into Connecticut, 148; Connecticut outlaws, 254; and the crossing, 72–77, 126, 370–72; French policy for Canada, 376; lack of during English civil war, 180; and Georgia, 375; into Maryland, 202; into Massachusetts, 131, 133, 142; New England shunned, 477; New York shunned, 477; in Northwest Territory, 658; into Pennsylvania, 236, 237, 364–72; politi-

immigration (*cont.*)
cal problems raised by, 372, 484; reasons for, 68–72, 363–64; into Virginia, 102, 184; Virginia shunned, 290
Imitation of Christ (Kempis, 1471): Massachusetts authorities on, 297
imperial structure: and Charles I, 105–7, 110–11, 140–42, 355; and Charles II, 192–95, 207–8, 209–11, 222–23, 232–33, 256–59, 335–36; and Cromwell, 187–92, 335; and Georges I and II, 398–406; and George III, 406–10, 519–50; and James II, 259–65, 336–37; and machinery in colonies, 343–55; and machinery in England, 341–43; studies of, 203, 356–57, 414–15, 551–54; and William III, 337–41; *see also* Board of Trade, crown, Lords of Trade, Parliament
impressment: resented in Massachusetts, 382; resented in New York, 328
Incas: fall to Pizarro, 21
indentured servitude: in seventeenth-century America, 69, 289, 290; attacked after Revolution, 654; journal on, 310; and James II, 259–65, 336–37; and machinery in colonies, 343–55; and machinery in England, 341–43; studies of,
independence: Bacon talks of, 248; and *Common Sense,* 586; Congressional debate on, 590–92; and Franklin, 581; Gage on sentiment for, 568; Hessians influence on, 587–88; South's attitude toward, 588; Washington promotes, 584–85
Independent Reflector: English influence on, 54
Independent Whig, 454
Indiana Company: study of, 552
Indians: and American diet, 116; and American language, 306; Americans seek to remold, 130, 184, 279–81; Americans' patronizing attitude toward, 80, 252–53, 300–1; and Beverley, 457; and Board of Trade, 280, 530; and Braddock expedition, 388; and captive tales, 307, 330; and Cherokee War, 500; and Claiborne, 113–14; and Columbus, 16–17, 18; and Confederation of New England, 171; and Congress, 581, 649; and Dutch, 217, 219, 222; and French and Indian War, 390, 522; and French attitude toward, 525; and Georgia, 375; and Jamestown, 91, 92, 95; Jesuits among, 170; and Jolliet and Marquette, 317; and King George's War, 379, 382–83; and King

Indians (*cont.*)
Philip's War, 251–55; and King William's War, 268; and La Salle, 319; and lost Israeli tribes, 130; and Maryland, 112, 182–83, 271; medical remedies of, 449; and Merry Mount, 129; and Moravian missionaries, 366; and New England, 133, 170, 266, 376; as "noble savages," 80; nomenclature resisted, 78; and Paxton Boys riot, 485; and Penn, 236–37; and Pequot War, 149 and Pilgrims, 127; and pre-Columbian explorers, 13; Puritan attitude toward, 130, 156; in Queen Anne's War, 329–30; and reports on to Royal Society, 299; in the Revolution, 625; and Roanoke, 34, 35; and Sagadahoc, 88; and Spanish, 21, 23, 25, 373; and the Society for the Propagation of the Gospel, 409; studies of, 83, 309, 356, 414, 552; tribes east of Mississippi, 79–80; and Tuscarora War, 364; and uprising of 1763, 500, 525–29; and Virginia, 101, 103, 104, 182–83, 184, 243, 245, 249; as whalers, 471; and Williams, 143, 147, 169; and Yamasee War, 373
indigo: in backcountry, 499; and British subsidy, 662; on enumerated list, 192; and South Carolina, 494
indulgences: Luther attacks, 44
Ingersoll, Jared (1722–1781): on Associations, 534; on Stamp Act debate, 536; as stamp collector, 537
Ingle, Richard (1609–c. 1653): arrested, 184; as Maryland governor, 688
Ingoldesby, Richard: as New Jersey governor, 690; and New York governor, 269, 691
Innes, J. H.: *New Amsterdam,* 240
Inns of Court, 352, 445
inoculation, 439; and Mather, 449–50; and Douglass, 449, 457
Institutes of the Christian Religion (Calvin, 1536), 49
instructions (to royal governor): Bland on, 345–46; and Board of trade, 339; compilation of, 415; and Lords of Trade, 336; and South Carolina assembly, 507; study of, 357; and Virginia assembly, 106
intendant: duties of, 316
intercolonial cooperation: and Braddock's expedition, 388; lack of, 326, 327–28, 330–31; and King George's War, 379; in Revolution, 609
Intolerable Acts, 563–65, 670

Introduction to Cosmography (Waldsee-müller, 1507), 20
Ipswich (Massachusetts), 296, 455
Ireland: colonization of, 61; and colonization of America, 32; and Congress, 573, 618; and Gilbert, 32; and Jamestown, 96; and Maryland charter, 111; and navigation system, 190, 533; and New England town pattern, 153; Palatines sent to, 364; and Penn, 230, 231, 234; Pennsylvania settlers from, 237; poor whisked off to, 59; and Restraining Act, 574; Scots immigration to, 367–68; and Staple Act, 193; Tories from sent to America, 69; and Virginia, 106
iron: in Delaware Valley, 481; and export duties, 401; manufacturing of, in colonies, 401; and Massachusetts manufacturing of, 174–75; and Revenue Act of 1764, 533
Iron Act (1750): provisions, 402
Iroquois Indians: advantage in fur trade, 320–21; at Albany Congress, 386–87; Colden's history of, 457; and Delawares, 237, 394; and Dutch, 222, 320; and English sovereignty, 321, 328, 333; and Frontenac, 319; and French, 319, 320, 324, 328, 381; grievances of, 386; and Johnson, 531; in King George's War, 382; in Leisler's Rebellion, 268; locations of, 79–80; and New York lordship over, 650; in Queen Anne's War, 329–30; in the Revolution, 625–26; studies of, 356; at war (1643), 170–71; and Western Indians, 319, 320, 321
Irving, Washington (1783–1859): on Van Twiller, 218
Irwin, Margaret: *Great Lucifer,* 40
Isabela (Hispaniola), 18
Isabella, Queen of Castile (1451–1504): and Columbus, 7, 14, 17; as new monarch, 6
Isaac: Jefferson's slave, 461
Italians: in Virginia, 102
Ivan IV (1530–1584): and Chancellor, 30
Izard, Ralph (1742–1804): house of, 461

Jackman, S. W.: Anburey journal, 638–39
Jackson, Andrew (1767–1845), 679
Jacobs, W. R.: *Diplomacy and Indian Gifts,* 413; *Indians on the Southern Frontier,* 414
Jacobsen, G. A.: *William Blathwayt,* 273–74
James I (1566-1625): creates colonial committee, 335; financial troubles of,

James I (*cont.*)
  61; on king's authority, 60–61; and proprietary grants, 108; and Puritans, 53;
  and tobacco, 104; and Ulster, 367–68;
  and Virginia charter, 93
James II (1633–1701): 266, 270; accession, 259; authoritarian views of, 222;
  deposed, 265; and Dominion of New England, 260–61; Iroquois reject as sovereign, 321; and Lords of Trade, 336;
  Lovelace friend of, 223; Millbourne on,
  268; and New Jersey, 226, 227, 228,
  229, 475; and New York, 220, 222, 225;
  on Parliament and colonies, 334; and
  Penn, 230, 232, 234, 237
James, Henry: on New England, 470
James, James A.: Clark papers, 636
James, S. V.: on the "holy experiment,"
  482–83; on Quakers and voluntary societies, 440; "Impact of the Revolution
  on Quakers," 682; *People Among Peoples,* 465; *Three Visitors to Early Plymouth,* 161
Jameson, J. F.: *American Revolution as Social Movement,* 682; *Narratives of New
  Netherland,* 240
Jamestown, 115, 117; and Bacon's Rebellion, 246–47, 248; Calvert in, 109; first
  assembly in, 101; and Indians, 95; and
  Plymouth compared, 125; and Pocahontas, 103; settlement of, 89–94; and Sir
  Thomas Smith, 68; "starving time" of,
  95; studies of, 119
Jamestown Booklets, 119
Jamaica: Columbus discovers, 18; Columbus marooned on, 20; George Fox visits,
  232; importance to English, 191–92;
  and Penn-Venable expedition, 191, 195;
  as profitable post for royal governor, 346
Japan; *see* Cipangu
Jarratt, Devereux (1733–1801): on leveling after Revolution, 653
Jarvis, Thomas: as Carolina governor, 692
Jay family, 363
Jay, John (1745–1829): in Congress, 572;
  continental outlook of, 666; and *Federalist,* 675; as peace commissioner, 633;
  and Spain, 665; as Spanish envoy, 620
Jay Treaty (1795), 633
Jefferson, Thomas (1743–1826), 447,
  458; and Barbary pirates, 665; biographies of, 594, 466; cautious optimism of,
  435; and classics, 436; and Congress,
  578, 664; and Constitution, 668; defines
  "foreign" law, 446; and Declaration of
  Causes, 580; and Declaration of Inde-

Jefferson, Thomas (*cont.*)
  pendence, 591–92; as deist, 436; education of, 433; and embargo, 680; and
  House of Burgesses, 492; and inoculation, 450; on independence debate, 591;
  as intellectual, 441; and Lincoln compared, 680; and Monticello, 461; on
  Negro rights, 437; and Newtonianism,
  433; on North and South characteristics,
  486; and Northwest Ordinance (1784),
  657; and nullification, 679; on Patrick
  Henry, 408; as peace commissioner, 633;
  as plantation executive, 490; and Port
  Act, 564; Randolph blood of, 477; religious freedom bill, 435, 655; and separation between church and state, 144; on
  stronger central government, 666; on
  state governments, 644, 645; on suffrage
  requirements, 644; on Virginia electorate, 491; as Virginia governor, 630, 698;
  on Virginia planters' debts, 488
Jeffreys, Sir Herbert: as Virginia governor,
  697
Jellison, R. M.: "Currency Act of 1764,"
  552
Jenckes, Joseph (1656–1740): as Rhode
  Island governor, 694
Jenkins' Ear, War of: and the colonies,
  376, 378; studies of, 412
Jenkins, Francis: as Maryland governor,
  688
Jenkins, John: as Carolina governor, 692
Jenkins, Robert: promotes war with Spain,
  378
Jenkinson, Anthony (fl. 1550): visits East,
  30
Jennings, Edmund: as Virginia governor,
  697
Jennings, F. P.: "Parkman and his
  Sources," 413
Jennings, Samuel (d. 1708): as West Jer-
  sey governor
Jensen, A. L.: *Commerce of Philadelphia,*
  513
Jensen, Merrill: on Articles of Confedera-
  tion, 651; on United States economy,
  663–64; *Articles of Confederation,* 681;
  New Nation, 680
Jernegan, M. W.: *Laboring and Dependent Classes,* 120
Jesuits: Marquette explores Mississippi,
  317–19; as Indian missionaries, 170,
  320; as Maryland immigrants, 112; missions on Kennebec, 376
Jews: in the colonies, 363; in Newport,
  284; in Philadelphia, 481; studies on, 411

John II (reigned 1481–1495): and Columbus, 14, 17; promotes route to India, 12–13

Johnson, Amandus: *Swedish Settlements,* 240

Johnson, Ben (1572–1637): 72

Johnson, Cecil: *British West Florida,* 552

Johnson, E. A. J.: *American Economic Thought in Seventeenth Century,* 120

Johnson, E. D.: and North Carolina Regulators, 509

Johnson, Edward (1598–1672): on first Salem winter, 285; on merchants, 178; on popery in England, 70

Johnson, G. G.: *North Carolina,* 514

Johnson, G. W.: *First Captain,* 640

Johnson, Sir John (1742–1830): ravages Schoharie Valley, 626

Johnson, Sir Nathaniel (c. 1645–1713): as South Carolina governor, 695

Johnson, Robert (fl. 1609): promotes Virginia, 92

Johnson, Robert (c. 1676–1735): as South Carolina governor, 695

Johnson, Samuel (1696–1722): and King's College, 443

Johnson, Samuel (1709–1784): on American dialect, 453; and Oglethorpe, 374

Johnson, T. H.: Edwards' writings, selections of, 465; *Puritans,* 161

Johnson, Thomas (1732–1819): as Maryland governor, 688

Johnson, V. L.: "Fair Traders and Smugglers in Philadelphia," 414

Johnson, Sir William (1715–1774): at Albany Congress, 386; biography and papers of, 413; and Crown Point expedition, 388, 390; and French and Indian War, 394–95; and Indian conference (1757), 391; and Indian conference (1766), 529; and Indian conference (1768), 531; and Indian uprising, 525; and King George's War, 379, 382; knighted, 390; opposes Niagara settlement, 525; and Scots, 370; seen as first of an American nobility, 541; on Washington, 384

Johnston, Gabriel (1699–1752): death of, 493; as North Carolina governor, 493, 693

Johnston, H. P.: *Campaign of 1776,* 637

Johnston, Samuel (1733–1816): as North Carolina governor, 693

"Join or Die," 387, 396

joint-stock company: organization of, 67

Jolliet, Louis (1645–1700): explores Mississippi, 317–19

Jones, H. M.: on medieval world and America, 3; "European Background," 38; *Ideas in America,* 311–12; *Strange New World,* 38

Jones, Hugh (c. 1670–1760): on colonial ties to Britain, 509–10; on governor's palace, 459; as historian, 457; on Southern attitude toward manufacturing, 488–89; on Southern gentleman, 490

Jones, Inigo (1573–1652): architect, 459, 460

Jones, John Paul: biographies of, 640

Jones, R. M.: *Quakers in the American Colonies,* 241

Jones, Willie (c. 1741–1801): as North Carolina governor, 693

Jordan, W. K.: on education during Commonwealth, 296

Jorgenson, C. E.: Franklin writings, 595

Joris, Adriaen: as New Netherland governor, 691

Joseph Andrews (Fielding, 1742), 437

Joseph, William: as Maryland governor, 271, 688

Josselyn, John (fl. 1638–1675): on medicinal plants, 300–1

Journal (Woolman, 1774), 456

"Journal of a French Traveler in the Colonies, 1765," 510

Jowles, Henry: and Protestant Association, 271

Judah, C. B.: *North American Fisheries,* 356

judiciary: Adams conception of, 645; and appointments to, 406; and Constitution, 669; and county court, 185; and courts of vice-admiralty, 343; in Dominion of New England, 262–63; in Dickinson's draft of Articles, 649; in England, 63; and governor, 347; and governor's council, 348, 353; and Leislerian courts, 268; in Massachusetts, 136–37, 337, 558; and North Carolina backcountry, 508; Paine's conception of, 645; in South Carolina, 496, 507; in Virginia, 117–18, 270

Junto: Franklin founds, 450

"just price"; *see* "fair price"

justices of peace: Bacon's laws on, 247; in Dominion of New England, 262; and Duke's Laws, 223; in England, 63; and Massachusetts governor, 337; in New England, 153; and provincial control of office, 505; Virginia gives title to, 200

Kalb, Johann (1721–1780): and Battle of Camden, 628

Kalm, Peter (1716–1779): and Bartram, 448; *Travels,* 511

Kammen, M. G.: *Glorious Revolution,* 274

Karraker, C. H.: *Seventeenth Century Sheriff,* 203

Kaskaskia: Clark captures, 625

Kayaderosseras Patent, 479

Keayne, Robert: and sow dispute, 178

Kecoughtan: as borough, 100

Keesey, R. M.: "Loyalism in New Jersey," 638

Keith, George (fl. 1617): on religion in Virginia, 118

Keith, George (c. 1638–1716): converted to Anglicanism, 272

Keith, Sir William (1680–1749): as Pennsylvania governor, 693

Kellogg, L. P.: "American Colonial Charters," 119

Kemmerer, D. L.: *Path to Freedom,* 513

Kemp, Richard: as Virginia governor, 696

Kempis, Thomas (1380–1471), 297

Kennebec River: boundary in Duke of York grant, 222; Jesuit missions on, 376; Sagadahoc on, 88; settlements on, raided, 376

Kent, William (1684–1748): architect, 459, 460

Kent Island: and Clairborne, 113–14, 184

Kentucky, 497; Boone explores, 501; in Revolution, 626; settled, 660

Kenyon, C. M.: "Republicanism and Radicalism in the Revolution," 682; "Men of Little Faith," 684

Kepler, Johan (1571–1630): laws of, 298, 431

Keppel, William Anne; *see* Albemarle, Earl of

Kerkkonen, Martii, *Peter Kalm,* 511

Kessler, Henry: *Stuyvesant,* 240

Key into the Language of America (Williams, 1643), 169

Keynes, John Maynard: on seventeenth-century entrepreneurs, 65

Keys, A. M.: *Cadwallader Colden,* 512

kidney bean: medicinal use of, 300

Kieft, Willem (1597–1647): as director-general, 219, 691

Kimball, Everett: *Joseph Dudley,* 274

Kimball, G. S. *Correspondence of Rhode Island Governors,* 357; *Pitt Correspondence,* 414

Kimball, S. F.: *Domestic Architecture,* 309

"King Cong," 666

King George's War, 378–82; Massachusetts reimbursed for part in, 403; studies of, 412

King Philip's War, 157, 251–55, 256, 265, 302, 331; debt from, 260; effect on education, 297; memoirs of, 307; memory of, in Salem, 303; studies of, 273

King, L. S.: *Medical World of Eighteenth Century,* 467

King, Rufus (1755–1827): on closing of Mississippi, 665

King William's War, 321–27, 337; and Albany fur trade, 329; and Leisler, 268; and Massachusetts financing of, 402; and problem of imperial rule, 327–28; studies on, 355; and War Office, 334

King's Bench, 63

King's College; founded, 443; medical school founded, 446; as political issue, 479

King's Mountain, Battle of, 628

Kipps Bay: landing at, 607

Klees, Frederic: *Pennsylvania Dutch,* 410

Klein, M. M.: on tenants and New York elections, 478; "Democracy in New York," 512; *Independent Reflector,* 466; "Prelude to Revolution in New York," 512

Klingelhofer, H. E.: "Diary of Peace Negotiations," 640

Knappen, M. M.: *Puritanism,* 81

Kneller, Sir Godfrey (1646–1723): influence on American painting, 463

Knickerbocker History (Irving, 1809), 218

Knight, Sarah Kemble (1666–1737): journal of, 307

Knittle, W. A.: *Palatine Emigration,* 410

Knollenberg, Bernhard: censures British ministry, 542; on Massachusetts and Revenue Act of 1764, 533–34; on Newcastle's retirement, 410; on stamp duties, 536; *Origin of Revolution,* 414; *Washington,* 413; *Washington and the Revolution,* 639

Knox, Henry (1750–1806): brings cannons to Boston, 601

Knox, John (c. 1513–1572): and Calvinism, 51

Knyphausen, Wilhelm von: commands troops in New York, 627

Koch, Adrienne: Adams writings, selected, 595; Jefferson's writings, selected, 595; *Power, Morals, and Founding Fathers,* 465; "Pragmatic Wisdom and the American Enlightenment," 465

Koontz, L. K.: *Dinwiddle*, 413; *Virginia Frontier*, 515

Kouwenhoven, J. A.: on vernacular tradition in art, 459

Kramer, S.: *English Craft Gilds*, 82

Kraus, Michael: *Atlantic Civilization*, 464

Kublai Khan (c. 1216–1294): Cabot anchors off coast of kingdom, 25; eludes Columbus, 17; and English dreams, 29–30; Gómez searches for kingdom of, 21; and Polos, 4–5

Kuhn, Justus Englehardt (fl. 1712): painter, 462

Kyrle, Richard: as South Carolina governor, 695

L'Anglois, Phillipe (Philip English): and illicit trade, 256

La Barre, Antoine Lefebvre de: replaces Frontenac, 321

La Chine (Canada): Iroquois burn, 324

La Demoiselle (Old Britain), 383, 384

La Salle, René-Robert Cavalier, Sieur de (1643–1687): death of, 320; explorations of, 319; and Fort Niagara, 394

Labaree, B. W.: *Boston Tea Party*, 593; *Merchants of Newburyport*, 512

Labaree, L. W.: *Conservatism*, 510; "Nature of American Loyalism," 638; *Mr. Franklin*, 553; *Royal Government*, 357; *Royal Instructions*, 357

Lafarge, Oliver, *American Indian*, 83

Lafayette (Indiana): site of French fort, 525

Lafayette, Marie Joseph Paul Yves Roch Gilbert du Motier, Marquis de (1757–1834): and Conway, 623; study of, 640; and Yorktown campaign, 630–31

Lambert, R. S.: "Confiscation of Loyalist Property in Georgia," 638

Lancaster County (Pennsylvania): created, 372; Indian conference at, 391; and "plain people," 365; richness of, 480

Lancaster (Pennsylvania), 438; Catholic congregation in, 482; Germans in, 481; and Paxton Boys riots, 485, 528

land: and governor's control over grants, 347; grants by England, 347; grants in New York, 217–18, 222, 476–77, 479; grants in North Carolina, 493; Maryland uses to attract settlers, 112; in New England, 152, 263; and New England merchant, 176–77; and New England titles, 257; and Scotch-Irish as squatters on, 369; and status in England, 108; and taxes in Dominion of New England,

land (*cont.*)
262; and tenure in Georgia, 375; treatment of, by colonists, 441; and Virginia's "Great Charter," 100; and Williams, 143, 147; *see also* headright system

Land, A. C.: *Dulanys of Maryland*, 514

Land Ordinance (1785), 657, 658, 660; and Fundamental Constitutions, 213

landgrave: and Andros, 223; in Carolina, 213

Lane, Sir Ralph (c. 1530–1603): at Roanoke, 35

Langdon, John (1741–1819): as New Hampshire governor, 690

Langlade, Charles Michel de (1729–c. 1801): and Pickawillany, 384

Langley, Batty: borrowings from, 460

language: in seventeenth-century America, 305–6; in eighteenth-century America, 453–54; and backcountry settlers, 501–2; and Dutch heritage, 221; and Indian contributions, 78; and science, 431

Lanning, J. T.: *Diplomatic History of Georgia*, 412

Larkin, Oliver: on New England architecture, 460; on seventeenth-century painting, 287, 288; *Art and Life in America*, 309

Larrabee, H. A.: on Battle of Virginia Capes, 632; *Decision at Chesapeake*, 641

Laslett, Peter: "Locke and Board of Trade," 356

Latané, J. H.: *Relations between Maryland and Virginia*, 120

Latin: attitude toward after Revolution, 654; and Bartram, 448; Calvin writes in, 51; and Church of England, 52; in English education, 60, 295; and Jefferson, 447; and Luther, 46; Marquette uses, 319; Maury derides for Americans, 444; in New England education, 296

Latourette, K. S.: "Religion of Colonial Period and Life in United States," 311

Laud, William (1573–1645), 168, 541; characterized, 140; and Davenport, 150; and English Puritans, 131; and Massachusetts, 140–42; and royal commission, 141, 335; and Williams, 71, 143

Laurens, Henry (1724–1792): as peace commissioner, 633

Laurens family, 363

Laudonnière, René de: in Florida, 27

law: ambiguity of laws of England, 352; American attitude toward, 292–93; in England, 63; governors trained in, 347;

law *(cont.)*
  Hooker agitates for government by, 148;
  and indentured servant, 289; and Indians, 279–80; and John Adams, 353,
  420, 445, 570; and judiciary, 352–54;
  legal character of governor's instructions,
  345; and marriage, 185; Massachusetts'
  Body of Liberties, 138, 177; Massachusetts' Laws and Liberties, 177–78; and
  new monarchs, 6; and New York's
  Duke's Laws, 223; Penn studies, 231;
  and Penn-Mead trial, 231; Randolph's
  view of New England's, 257; Virginia
  codifies (1664), 200–1; Virginia's Bacon's Laws, 247; Virginia's Dale's Laws,
  97; Winthrop's view of, 137–38
lawyers: and classics, 295; in Congress,
  569; English and American distinctions,
  445; Gridley on, 445; and naturalization
  procedure, 372; status in America, 292–
  93; studies on in New York, 512
Lawrence, A. A.: *Storm over Savannah,*
  639–40
Lawrence, Richard: and Bacon's Rebellion,
  245
Lawrence, Sir Thomas: as Maryland governor, 688
Lawrie, Gawen: as East Jersey governor,
  690
Laws and Liberties (1648), 177–78
Laws, Concessions, and Agreements
  (1677): for West Jersey, 228
Laws Divine, Moral and Martial (Strachey,
  1612), 97
Law, Jonathan (1674–1750): as Connecti-
  cut governor, 687
Leach, D. E.: on King Philip's War, 255;
  Flintlock and Tomahawk, 273; *Rhode
  Islander on King Philip's War,* 273
Leder, Lawrence: on Burnet, 352; *Glorious
  Revolution,* 274; "Livingston Records,"
  356; "New York Elections of 1769,"
  357; *Robert Livingston,* 274
Ledyard, John (1751–1789): promotes fur
  trade, 664
Lee, Arthur (1740–1792): United States
  representative to France, 618
Lee, Charles (1731–1782), 580, 607; and
  Battle of Monmouth Court House, 624;
  biography of, 639; captured, 611; court-
  martial and death of, 624; described,
  601; and Fort Sullivan, 603; papers of,
  636; in Rhode Island, 585; in South,
  588, 603; on Washington, 584
Lee family, 184

Lee, Henry (1756–1818): attacks Paulus
  Hook, 624
Lee, Richard Henry (1732–1794): and
  Congress, 572; and Constitution, 668,
  674; and independence, 590, 618; John
  Adams on, 569; letters of, 595; and
  stamp collectorship, 537; on settlers in
  Northwest Territory, 659; on Washing-
  ton, 607
Lee, Thomas: as Virginia governor, 697
Lee, Thomas Sim (1745–1819): as Mary-
  land governor, 688
Leete, William (c. 1613–1683): as New
  Haven governor, 687
Leeuwenhoek, Anton van (1632–1723),
  189
Lefler, H. T.: *North Carolina History,* 239
Leibnitz, Gottfried Wilhelm von (1646–
  1716), 451
Leiby, A. C.: *Early Settlers of New Jersey,*
  241; *Revolution in Hackensack Valley,*
  637
Leisler, Jacob (1640–1691), 267–69;
  death of, 269; as New York governor,
  691; studies of, 274
Leisler's Rebellion, 267–69; and King Wil-
  liam's War, 324–25, 325–26; and New
  York politics, 352, 478; studies of, 274
Leo X (1475–1521): Luther attacks, 44–
  45
Leonard, Daniel (1740–1829): on com-
  mittees of correspondence, 559
Letters from a Farmer in Pennsylvania
  (Dickinson, 1768), 272, 546; Hillsbor-
  ough's reaction to, 547
Levant Company: charter, 30; and London
  merchants, 86
Leverett, John (1616–1679): as Massachu-
  setts governor, 689; and Randolph, 256–
  57
Levy, Leonard: on assemblies, 354; "Did
  the Zenger Case Really Matter?" 357;
  Freedom of Speech and Press, 357
Lewis, G. I.: *Indiana Company,* 552
Lexington (Massachusetts), 471; Battle of,
  577; reaction to battle, 600; study of
  battle, 594, 637
Leyburn, J. G.: *Scotch-Irish,* 411
Leyden Agreement, 125
Libby, O. G.: *Geographical Distribution of
  Vote on Constitution,* 684
Liberty: seized, 547
Library Company of Philadelphia, 451
lightning rod: reception of, 451
Lilly, E. P.: *Colonial Agents of New York
  and New Jersey,* 357

limners: in seventeenth-century America, 287–88; vanish, 462

Lincoln, Abraham (1809–1865): and colonial heritage, 680

Lincoln, Benjamin (1733–1810): at Saratoga, 616; and Shays's Rebellion, 667; in the South, 626; surrenders Charleston, 627; at Yorktown, 632

Lincoln, C. H.: *Narratives of Indian Wars*, 273; *Revolutionary Pennsylvania*, 553; *Shirley Correspondence*, 357

Linnaeus, Carolus (1708–1778): and American botanists, 447, 448; on plundered collection, 442

Lipson, Ephraim: *Economic History of England*, 82

Lisbon: and Columbus, 13

literacy: in seventeenth-century America, 294–95

literature: in seventeenth-century America, 306–8; in eighteenth-century America, 455–58; studies of, 164, 311, 467

Livermore, H. V.: *History of Portugal*, 39

Liverpool, 480

"livings": defined, 140

Livingston family, 267; and New York politics, 478–79

Livingston, Philip (1716–1778): on New Englanders, 475; on New York factions, 479

Livingston, Robert (1654–1728): biography of, 274; on how to win an assembly seat, 478; and Leisler's Rebellion, 268; papers of, 356

Livingston, Robert R. (1745–1813): and Declaration of Independence, 591

Livingston, William (1723–1790): biography of, 512; and classical influence on, 436; and Constitution, 668; English influence on, 454; as New Jersey governor, 691; writings of, 466

Lloyd, Christopher: *Capture of Quebec*, 413

Lloyd, David (c. 1656–1731): biography of, 513; and country Quakers, 483

Lloyd, Edward: as Maryland governor, 688

Lloyd, Thomas (1640–1694): as Pennsylvania governor, 693

Lochaber: Indian conference at, 531

Locken, R. N.: *David Lloyd*, 513

Locke, John (1632–1704), 278, 444; biography of, 465; and Board of Trade, 339; and Carolina, 213; Congress refers to, 570; and Edwards, 436; and the Enlightenment, 437; ideas of, 432; John Adams reads, 445; and Livingston, 436; on

Locke, John (*cont.*)
Penn's Frame of Government, 235–36; and royal council, 335; study of, 356; writings of, 465

Lodwyck family: backs Leisler, 268

Logan, James (1674–1751): advises Penn to sell colony, 332; biography of, 513; on French menace, 378; and German vote, 372; and Lloyd, 483; on Iroquois, 328; as man of his times, 434; as Pennsylvania governor, 693; and science, 447, 448; and Scotch-Irish, 369

Logan, William; journal of, 515

log cabin: and Swedes, 285

Log College, 423

Logstown (Pennsylvania): Indian treaty at, 382–83

logwood: on enumerated list, 533

London: and Chesapeake tobacco crop, 180; importance to England, 57; influence of great fire on America, 234, 283, 284, 286; influence on American life and thought, 285, 292, 438; finances iron furnace, 174–75; and merchants of, 86; and New England economy, 175–76

London, 73

London Coffee House (Philadelphia), 438

London Company: and Bermuda Company, 96; charter lost by, 105; and charters, 87, 93, 96; dissolution of, 109; and East India Company, 68; on emigrants, 70–71; influence on royal government, 107; instructions from, 89–91; and Jamestown, 89–94; and Massachusetts Bay Company, 131; mercantile support of, 93; and Pilgrims, 125; reasons for failure, 105–6; and Sandys, 100–4; in Stith's *History*, 457; and subsidiary company technique, 217

Londonderry, 369

Long, J. C,: *Amherst*, 552

Long Island: Battle of, 605–6; Battle of, and France, 619; Block tours, 217; and Duke of York grant, 222; George Fox visits, 232; Puritans and New York government, 267; Puritans and Dutch, 219; Puritans on, 169, 223, 225, 226; in Revolution, 605–6; and royal commission, 199; Verrazano visits, 26

Long Parliament, 179–80; and House of Burgesses in Berkeley's regime, 244; and king, 168

Longfellow, Henry W., 390

Lonn, Ella: *Colonial Agents of Southern Colonies*, 357

Lopez, Aaron (1731–1782), 363

Lorant, Stephen: *New World,* 41
Lords Commissioners of Trade and Planta-
    tions; *see* Board of Trade
Lords of Trade: and Board of Trade, 339;
    and Dominion of New England, 261–
    65; on proprietary grants, 238; history
    of, 335–37; Massachusetts rebuffs, 257,
    258; and Massachusetts' provisional gov-
    ernment, 259–60; purpose of, 255–56;
    studies of, 274, 356; and Virginia, 270
lottery: and Virginia, 103
Loudoun, John Campbell, fourth Earl of
    (1705–1782): and French and Indian
    War, 391; as Virginia governor, 697
Louis XI (1423–1483): as new monarch,
    6
Louis XIV (1638–1715), 316, 317; and
    Frontenac, 324; La Salle claims Louisi-
    ana for, 320; and Palatinate, 364; and
    War of Spanish Succession, 329; wars
    of, deter exploration, 319
Louisa County (Virginia): Henry repre-
    sents, 492
Louisbourg: Amherst and Wolfe capture,
    394; and illicit trade, 406; and New
    England financing of expedition to, 403;
    study on, 412; *see also* Fort Louisbourg
Louisiana: ceded to Spain, 518; La Salle
    claims for France, 320; trade monopoly
    granted in, 327
Lovejoy, D. S.: "New York Charter of Lib-
    erties," 240; *Rhode Island Politics,* 553
Lovelace, Francis (c. 1621–1675): as New
    York governor, 223, 691
Lovelace, John, Baron Lovelace of Hurley:
    as New Jersey governor, 690; as New
    York governor, 691
Lovell, James (1737–1814): favors Gates,
    623
Lowery, Woodbury: *Spanish Settlements,*
    39
Lowland Scots; *see* Scots
Lowndes, Rawlins (1721–1800): as South
    Carolina governor, 696
Loyal Land Company, 383
loyalists: arguments of, against rebellion,
    576; depart Boston, 602; defeated at
    Moores Creek Bridge, 603; effect of de-
    parture on nation, 653; lands of, 654;
    lands of as debate topic, 656; laws
    against, 584; number and composition
    of, 610–11; and Regulators, 509; and
    Scots, 370, and Treaty of 1783, 633;
    studies of, 638, 682; Washington de-
    fines, 584

Lucas, H. S.: *Renaissance and Reformation,*
    38
Ludwell family, 291
Ludwell, Philip (fl. 1660–1704): as South
    Carolina governor, 692, 695
lumber: as Carolina export, 215; in Dela-
    ware Valley, 481; in New Hampshire,
    471; and Revenue Act of 1764, 533; and
    White Pines Acts, 399, 404, 535
Lundin, L. H.: *Cockpit of Revolution,* 637
Lurie, N. O.: "Indian Cultural Adjust-
    ment," 83
Luther, Martin (1483–1546), 301; and
    Anabaptists, 47; biographical sketch of,
    44–45; biographies of, 81; and Calvin's
    views, 50–51; death of, 49; and family
    life, 56; and peasants' revolt, 46–47
Lutheranism: doctrines of, 45–46; in En-
    gland, 51–52; and individualism, 47–49;
    spread of, 45–46, 49
Lutherans, 419; in Georgia, 375; in New
    Netherland, 219–20; in Pennsylvania,
    365; and ties with Europe, 363, 655
Lyndon, Josias: as Rhode Island governor,
    694
Lynn (Massachusetts), 169
Lyttleton, William Henry (1724–1808):
    as South Carolina governor, 695

McBean, Thomas: architect, 460
McCaffrey, W. T.: *Exeter,* 82
McCann, F. T.: *English Discovery,* 40
McCardell, Lee: *Braddock,* 413
McCormick, R. P.: *Experiment in Inde-
    pendence,* 685; *New Jersey,* 513; *Voting
    in New Jersey,* 513
McCrady, Edward: *South Carolina,* 239
McCulloh, Henry: North Carolina hold-
    ings of, 493
McDonald, Forrest: critique of, 684; *We
    the People,* 683
Machiavelli, Niccolo (1469–1527): and
    medieval pattern, 7
McIlwain, C. H.: *American Revolution,*
    551; Wraxall's *Indian Affairs,* 414
McIntyre, R. A.: *Financing the Plymouth
    Colony,* 161
McKean, Thomas (1734–1817): as Dela-
    ware governor, 694
McKee, Samuel, Jr.: on New York econ-
    omy, 512
Mackenzie, Frederick: *Diary,* 636
Mackesy, Piers: *War for America,* 635
Mackinaw City (Michigan): site of French
    fort, 377

McKinley, A. E.: "English and Dutch Towns," 240

McKinly, John (1721–1796): as Delaware governor, 694

MacKinnon, James: biography of Luther by, 81

McKitrick, Eric: *Founding Fathers*, 683

McLaughlin, A. C.: *Confederation and Constitution*, 680

Maclay, E. S.: *American Privateers*, 640

McMaster, J. B.: *Pennsylvania and the Constitution*, 685

McNeill, J. T.: *Calvinism*, 81

MacNutt, F. A.: editor of Richard Eden, 39

MacPherson, James: and Mount Pleasant, 461

M'Roberts, Patrick: *Tour*, 511

Madeira Islands: as New England market, 12; Portugal acquires, 12; rediscovered, 8; and Revenue Act of 1764, 533

Madison, James (1751–1836): at Annapolis Convention, 666–67; biography of, 683; on closing of Mississippi, 665; in Congress, 664; and Constitutional Convention, 670; elected to House, 492; on factions, 478; fears slave revolt, 588; and *Federalist*, 675; and Henry argument, 408; on liquor and elections, 490; and nullification, 679; promises bill of rights, 675; on United States economy, 663

Madrid, Treaty of (1670), 279

Magaw, Robert: loses Fort Washington, 607

Magellan, Ferdinand (c. 1480–1521): rounds world, 21

Magnalia Christi Americana (Mather, 1702), 456

Maier, Pauline: "Wilkes and American Disillusionment with Britain," 554

Maine, J. T.: *Antifederalists*, 684; "Beard and the Constitution," 683; *Social Structure of Revolutionary America*, 484

Maine, 108; in Dominion of New England, 262; and Duke of York grant, 222; excluded from Confederation of New England, 171; French incursions in, 254, 255, 324; and Gorges, 108, 151; in King George's War, 379; in King Philip's War, 254, 255; and Massachusetts, 151, 169, 179, 200, 257, 337; in provisional government, 259; in Queen Anne's War, 330; royal commission visits, 200; Scotch-Irish in, 368; unsettled land in, 660; Verrazano visits, 26

malaria: in Jamestown, 91; in South Carolina, 494

Malbon, Richard, 150

Malone, Dumas: *Jefferson*, 466

Malone, J. J.: *Pine Trees and Politics*, 551

Manhate Indians: sell Manhattan, 217

Manhattan: battle for, 606; study of, 637

Manigault family, 363

Mansfield, William Murray, first Earl of (1705–1793): John Adams queries position of, 570; on Parliament's power to tax the colonies, 532

manufacturing: Boston seeks to promote, 545; in Delaware Valley, 480, 481; in England, 65; Grenville fears Townshend duties will encourage, 544; in New England, 174–75, 176; and Revenue Act of 1764, 534; Southern attitude toward, 488–89; and Staple Act, 193; and Woolen Act, 338

Map of the British and French Dominions of North America (Mitchell, 1755), 448

Marcus, J. R.: *American Jewry: Documents*, 411; *Early American Jewry*, 411

Maredant's antiscorbutic drops: testimonial for, 455

Marian Exiles, 52

Marietta (Ohio): and Ohio Company, 659

Markham, William (c. 1635–1704): as Pennsylvania governor, 693

Marks, Irving: *Agrarian Conflicts in New York*, 512

Marquette, Jacques (1637–1675): explores Mississippi, 317–19

Marshall, John (1755–1835): biography of, 685

Marshall, John, 491

Marston Moor (1644): battle of, 168

Martha's Vineyard: in Duke of York grant, 222; incorporated into Massachusetts, 337

Martin, Alexander (1740–1807): as North Carolina governor, 693

Martinique, 400; France keeps, 518

Martin, John: as Georgia governor, 687

Martin, Joseph: *Narrative*, 636

Martin, Josiah (1737–1786): as North Carolina governor, 693

Martin, Luther (c. 1748–1826): opposes Constitution, 673

Martyr, Peter; *see* Peter Martyr Anglerius

Mary, Queen of Scots (1542–1587): Spain befriends, 30

Mary I (1516–1558): and Reformation, 52

Mary II (1662–1694): accession of, 265

Maryland: in the seventeenth century, 107–114; accent of people, 487; agriculture in, 489; at Albany Congress, 386; and Articles of Confederation, 630, 651; charter, 110–11; and backcountry, 498; boundaries, 110; and boundary dispute with Pennsylvania, 110, 236, 237; civil war in, 184–85; and convict labor, 362; George Fox visits, 232; governor's salary, 351; and Glorious Revolution, 271–72; homes for first settlers, 285; and independence, 590; issues paper money, 402; opens ports to world (1649), 187; painter in, 462; and commission of Parliament, 184–85; and quitrents, 655; ratifies Constitution, 675; religious tension in, 181–82; during Restoration, 201–2; as royal colony, 272; settlement of, 107–14; at Stamp Act Congress, 538; studies of, 120, 685; and Susquehannocks, 245; uprising in, 250; urge to be royalized, 344; and Virginia, 94, 112, 114, 117–18, 180

Masham, Sir William, 143

Mason family, 184, 291

Mason, George (fl. 1685), 259

Mason, George (1725–1792): biography of, 594; and Constitution, 668, 673, 675

Mason, John (c. 1600–1672): and Pequot War, 157, 163; and New Hampshire, 151

Mason-Dixon Line (1769), 237

Massachusetts: in the seventeenth century, 134–42, 168–78, 195–200, 255–66; at Albany Congress, 386; at Braddock conference, 308; and charters, 130–33, 137, 143, 200, 259, 336–37, 565; church and half-way covenant, 198–99; church and state, 138–40; church in, 134–36; circular letter of, 507, 546; and colonial agents, 256, 258, 341; and Confederation of New England, 171; and Congress, 568–69, 570, 579, 583; and constitution (1780), 646, 673; convention in (1768), 548; and Dominion of New England, 262; and Duke's Laws, 223; and education, 293–95; Gage as governor, 566; and Glorious Revolution, 265–66; government in, 36–40; and governor and disputes with, 397–98; and Great Awakening, 426–27, 428; iron manufacturing in, 174–75, 401; in King George's War, 382, 403; and King Philip's War, 254; and King William's War, 324, 325; and Laud, 141–42, 335; and Louisbourg expedition, 379; and loyalists,

Massachusetts (cont.)
612; and mint, 179; naturalization requirements, 371; and New Hampshire, 238, 256–57; and New York conference (1690), 325; opens ports to world (1645), 187; and paper money, 403; Parliament declares rebellious, 574; Penn-Venable fleet provisioned by, 195; and provisional government, 260; and Randolph, 256–57; ratifies Constitution, 675; and Revenue Act of 1764, 533; revival in 1735, 422–23; and royal commission, 199–200; royalized, 344; and science, 452; Scotch-Irish in, 369; sense of mission, 132–34; and Shays's Rebellion, 667; and Stamp Act, 538, 542; studies on, 161, 512, 681, 682, 684; tax rate in, 532; and White Pines Acts, 404–5; and War of Jenkins' Ear, 378; and Western land claims of, 650; witches in, 303–5

Massachusetts Bay Company: antecedents of, 129–30; backing of, 132; charter of, 131

Massacre of 1622, 103, 116; in Indian memory, 183; and Maryland charter, 111; and plans for a college, 293; in Stith's history, 457

Massacre of 1644, 183–84; and aftermath, 245

Massasoit (d. 1661): father of King Philip, 253

Massinger, Philip (1583–1640), 68–69

Masterson, W. H.: William Blount, 683

Matagorda Bay (Texas): La Salle at, 320

Mather, Cotton (1663–1728): and Barbary pirate captives, 278–79; biographies of, 274, 311, 312; on Cotton, 135–36; and Indian remedies, 449; and Indians, 252, 279–80; and inoculation, 301, 449–50; literary style of, 308–9; on meetinghouse, 152; and microscope, 301; on Negroes, 289–90; on Newton, 435; as physician, 292; and Royal Society, 299–300; and Salem trials, 300, 303–4, 305; on Scotch-Irish, 368; on sermons, 307; as transitional figure, 308–9, 435; as writer, 456

Mather, Increase (1639–1723): on Andros' friends, 261; on hivings-out, 282; on Puritan immigration, 272; and William III's circular, 265

Mather, Richard (1596–1669): woodcut of, 287

Mathews, John (1744–1802): as South Carolina governor, 696

Mathews, Samuel (c. 1600–1660): as Virginia governor, 696
Matthews, George (1739–1812): as Georgia governor, 687
Matthiesen, Peter: *Wildlife in America*, 83
Mattingly, Garrett: "Navigator to the Modern Age," 39
Maumee River: and Miami Indians, 383
Maury, James: educational ideas of, 444; and Jefferson, 447; and Two Penny Act, 408
Maverick, Samuel (c. 1602–c. 1676): on royal commission, 199
Maxson, C. H.: *Great Awakening*, 465
May, Cornelis: explores Delaware River, 217; as New Netherland governor, 691
Mayflower: crossing, 125–26; departs with first cargo, 127; loss of life on, 72
Mayflower Compact, 126, 129
Mayhew, Jonathan (1720–1766): attacks Society for the Propagation of the Gospel, 409; on natural law, 455–56
Mayhew, Thomas (1593–1682): and Indians, 252
Mayo, L. S.: *Endecott*, 162; Hutchinson *History of Massachusetts Bay*, 161
Mays, D. J.: *Pendleton*, 466
Mead, S. E.: "American Protestantism," 464; "Denominationalism," 464; "Religion in English America," 311
Mead, William: and Penn-Meal trial, 231
Meade, Robert: *Patrick Henry*, 553
Medford (Connecticut): founded, 151
Medicare Act (1965): and Amish, 365
medicine: in seventeenth-century America, 300–1; in eighteenth-century America, 446, 448–49; quack's advertisement, 455; and Rush, 420; studies of, 311, 467
medieval world, 2–6; and seventeenth-century America, 278; and apprentice system, 69; and Bishop of Durham clause, 111; and Calvin's debt to, 50–51; and Coddington, 147; and Luther, 50–51; and natural law, 430; and New England gentry, 155–56; and New England town, 153–54; persists in Scotland, 369; and regulatory attitude in England, 66; and Williams, 147
Mediterranean: Townshend contemplates opening to American trade, 543; and United States trade, 663
meetinghouse: architecture of, 286; and New England town, 153
Mein, John: biography of, 639
Mein, Patrick: as surveyor general, 342

Memorable Providences Relating to Witchcraft (Mather, 1689), 304
Menéndez de Avilés, Pedro: and Fort Caroline, 27
Mennonites, 365, 419; beliefs of, 47; after Revolution, 655
mercantilism: described, 66, 187; French version of, 316; studies on, 82, 203
Mercer, George: papers of, 414
merchants: and Anne Hutchinson, 145–46; and Board of Trade, 339; and Brattle Street Church, 303; Carolina discourages, 213; and Chesapeake tobacco, 180; during the Confederation, 662, 663–64; and Congress's Association, 573; in Delaware Valley, 234, 329; and Dominion of New England, 262, 264; and enumeration list, 192–93; in England, 66–68; in Gilbert and Raleigh ventures, 37, 107; and governor's instructions on trade, 345; and Half-Way Covenant, 198–99; and Hudson Valley farmers, 267; and London's overseas enterprises, 57, 86, 107; and medieval world, 6–7; and Navigation Act of 1660, 192, 194; in New England, 145–46, 155–56, 168, 176–77, 178, 192, 199, 291–92; and New Haven, 150; and paper money, 403; and pirates, 338; and the Revolution, 610; and the Stuarts, 108; studies of, 163, 511–12; and writs of assistance, 407
Mereness, N. D.: *Maryland as Proprietary Province*, 120; *Travels in American Colonies*, 510
Meriwether, R. L.: *Expansion of South Carolina*, 239
Merrens, H. R.: *Colonial North Carolina*, 514
Merritt, R. L.: "Colonial Press," 467
Merry Mount: and Morton, 129
Meschasipe River; *see* Mississippi River
Metacomet; *see* Philip, King
Methodists, 418; after the Revolution, 655
Metzger, C. H.: *Catholics and the Revolution*, 594
Mexico City: Cortez captures, 21; Gage reports defenseless, 191
Meyer, Duane: *Highland Scots of North Carolina*, 411
Meyers, W. S.: *Battle of Monmouth*, 639
Miami Indians: in Ohio Valley, 383, 384
Michilimackinac: French fort at, 327; Iroquois come to, 321–24
microscope: Mather views through, 301
Midwife Rightly Instructed, 429

Middlekauff, Robert: *Ancients and Axioms*, 311
Middleton, A. P.: *Tobacco Coast*, 83
Middleton, Arthur (1681–1737): as South Carolina governor, 695
Middletown (New Jersey): and Monmouth Patent, 226
Midwout (Flatbush), 221
Mifflin, Thomas (1744–1800): and Gates, 623
Milford (Connecticut): founded, 151
militia: under Andros, 264; and Gates, 616; and King Philip's War, 254; and Negroes in South Carolina, 495; and Pennsylvania, 390, 396, 528; of Virginia in 1763, 526; Washington dismisses, 628
Millborne, Jacob: at Albany, 268; death of, 269
Miller, J. C.: on loss of Charleston, 627; on nationalists, 667–68; on privateers, 609; on Townshend, 544; *Hamilton*, 683; *Origins of American Revolution*, 551; *Sam Adams*, 553; *Triumph of Freedom*, 635
Miller, Perry: *American Puritans*, 161; *Errand into Wilderness*, 81; *Jonathan Edwards*, 465; *New England Mind: From Colony to Province*, 274; *New England Mind: Seventeenth Century*, 161; *Orthodoxy in Massachusetts*, 161; *Puritans*, 161; *Williams' Writings*, selected, 162
Miller, Samuel: *Brief Retrospect of Eighteenth Century*, 463
Miller, Thomas: and Culpeper Rebellion, 251; as North Carolina governor, 692
Milligen-Johnson, George: essay of, 514
Milling, C. J.: *Colonial South Carolina*, 515
Millis, Walter: *Arms and Men*, 637
Milton, John (1608–1674), 278; in almanacs, 455; on Scotch-Irish, 367
Miner, C. E.: *Ratification of Constitution in New York*, 685
ministers: and Brattle Street Church, 303; in Congregational Church, 135; on decay in New England education, 297; and education, 293–94; as "hired" persons, 302, 419; during King Philip's War, 254; and Latin and Greek, 295; and Log College, 423; Luther's conception of role, 45; in New England during Restoration, 198; Randolph's view of New England's, 257; and sermon, 307; in Virginia during Interregnum, 181; Vir-

ministers (*cont.*)
ginia requests more of, 200; Virginia's, and quality of, 302; *see also* clergy
mint: Andros favors, 263, 264; in New England, 179, 260; Virginia plans, 181
Minuit, Peter (1580–1638): as New Netherland director-general, 217, 691; as New Sweden governor, 220, 227, 691
Miranda, Francisco de: *Travels*, 511
missionaries: and Confederation of New England, 171; and Indians, 252, 280–81; Jesuit, 170, 317, 320; Moravian, 366, 394, 528; of Society for the Propagation of the Gospel, 409, 419
Mississippi Company (French), 377
Mississippi River: and Carolina fur traders, 216; French strengthen hold on, 327; Jay negotiates with Spain on, 620; Joliet and Marquette explore, 317; La Salle explores, 319; Spain closes to United States, 665
Missouri River: French fort on, 377; Jolliet and Marquette pass mouth of, 317
Mitchell, Broadus: *Hamilton*, 684
Mitchell, John (d. 1768): botanist, 442, 448
Mittelberger, Gottlieb: *Journey to Pennsylvania*, 411
Mobile (Alabama), 327, 495
mobs: American attitude toward, 440; in Boston, 547, 549; in Britain, 535; and Shays's Rebellion, 667; and Stamp Act, 538
Modest Inquiry into . . . Witchcraft (Hale, 1697), 305
Mohawk Indians, 79; adopt Johnson, 382; and Andros, 255; visit England, 332
Mohegan Indians: Williams confers with, 157
Molasses: duty in 1764, 534; duty lowered, 542; on enumerated list, 399; high cost to New York, 476; and New England economy, 471–72; in West Indies trade, 400–1
Molasses Act (1733), 400–1, 472; Pitt orders enforced, 407
Monck, George; *see* Albemarle, Duke of
Monckton, Robert (1726–1782): captures Fort Beauséjour, 390; as New York governor, 692
Monmouth Court House: battle at, 624
Monmouth Patent, 226
monopoly: and colonial heritage, 679; crown dispenses, 61, 66; and French company, 329, 377; and Free Society of Traders, 234–35; and furs in Canada, 317; Leislerian assembly abolishes, 269;

monopoly *(cont.)*
and New York flour merchants, 267; and South Seas Company, 377–78; and Staple Act, 193; and Tea Act, 562; and trading companies, 67; of Virginia trade by London, 99, 105
Monroe, James (1758–1831): elected to House of Burgesses, 492
Montague, Lord Charles Greville: as South Carolina governor, 695
Montcalm, Louis Joseph, Marquis de (1712–1759): and French and Indian War, 391, 395
Monte Cristi: illicit trade with, 407
Montesquieu, Baron de (1689–1755): Congress refers to, 570; on size of republics, 648
Montgomerie, John: as New Jersey governor, 690; as New York governor, 692
Montgomery, Richard (1738–1775): death of, 588, 602; and Montreal, 585, 602
Monticello: architecture of, 461
Montreal: Cartier at, 26; nearby La Chine burned, 324; Montgomery takes, 585, 602; in Queen Anne's War, 332; as trade center for New York, 382, 386
Montross, Lynn: *Rag, Tag, Bobtail,* 635; *Reluctant Rebels,* 594
Montserrat: ceded to England, 194
Moody, Lady Deborah: founds Gravesend, 169
Moore, Sir Henry (1713–1769): as New York governor, 692
Moore, James (d. 1706): and Queen Anne's War, 332; as South Carolina governor, 695
Moore, William (c. 1735–1793): as Pennsylvania governor, 694
Moore's Creek Bridge: battle at, 603
Morais, Herbert: *Deism,* 465
Moravians, 419; described, 365–66; in Georgia, 375; as immigrants, 364; missionaries, 394, 528; after the Revolution, 655
More, Sir Thomas (1478–1535): Gilbert quotes, 33; on sheep, 65
Morgan, Daniel (1736–1802): biographies on, 639; at Saratoga, 616; victory at Hannah's Cowpens, 629
Morgan, E. S.: on Congressional program for West, 661; on creation of American nation, 655; on Franklin and taxes, 540; on Half-Way Covenant, 198; on New England innovations in Puritanism, 134–35; "American Revolution: Revisions in Need of Revisions," 550; *Birth of Re-*

Morgan, E. S. *(cont.)*
public, 551; *Ezra Stiles,* 466; "New England Puritanism," 162; *Prologue to Revolution,* 553; *Puritan Dilemma,* 162; *Puritan Family,* 310; *Stamp Act,* 553; *Visible Saints,* 162
Morgan, H. M.: *Stamp Act,* 553
Morgan, John (1735–1789): favors distinctions among medical practitioners, 446; founds medical school, 446
Morgan, W. T.: "Five Nations and Queen Anne," 356
Morison, S. E.: on Elizabethan English, 306; on Puritan's literary skill, 308; on Winthrop yarn, 72–73; *Admiral of the Ocean,* 39; *Builders of the Bay Colony,* 40; *Columbus,* 39; *Harvard College in Seventeenth Century,* 203; *John Paul Jones,* 640; *Journals of Columbus,* 39; "New Light Wanted on the Old Colony," 161; *Of Plymouth Plantation,* 160; "Pilgrim Fathers' Significance," 161; *Puritan Pronaos,* 311; *Sources American Revolution,* 552
Mormonism, 130
Morocco: United States buys protection from, 665
Morris family, 610
Morris, Gouverneur (1752–1816): and bill of rights, 674
Morris, J. E.: *King Philip's War,* 273
Morris, Lewis (1671–1746): as native born governor, 346; as New Jersey governor, 476, 479, 690, 691; on New Jersey settlers, 479; promotes Anglicanism, 419
Morrison, A. J.: Schoepf *Travels,* 681
Morrison, H. S.: *Early American Architecture,* 309
Morris, R. B.: *American Law,* 120; "Confederation and American Historians," 680; *Era of American Revolution,* 638; *Government and Labor,* 310; "Insurrection in Massachusetts," 684; "Labor and Mercantilism in Revolutionary Era," 638; *Peacemakers,* 640; *Spirit of Seventy-Six,* 636; Trevelyan's *American Revolution,* 635
Morris, Robert (1734–1806): and Constitution, 668; continental outlook of, 666; on economic restraints, 610; as financier of the Revolution, 609, 630
Morris, Robert Hunter (c. 1700–1764): as Pennsylvania governor, 693
Morristown (New Jersey): and Washington, 612

Morton, George: *Mourt's Relation,* 160

Morton, Joseph: as South Carolina governor, 695

Morton, R. L.: *Colonial Virginia,* 119

Morton, Thomas (fl. 1622–1647): and Merry Mount, 129; *New English Canaan,* 160

Moryson, Francis: as Virginia governor, 696

Moslems: and caravel design, 9; and Portugal, 8; and Spain, 14

Mosse, G. L.: *Reformation,* 81

Mott, F. L.: *American Journalism,* 467; *Franklin Selections,* 595

Moultrie, William (1730–1805): and Fort Sullivan, 603; as South Carolina governor, 696

Mount Pleasant (Philadelphia), 461

Mount Vernon: Admiral Edward Vernon, 378; conference at, 666; judgments on, 461

Mourt's Relation (1622), 160

Mowat, C. L.: *East Florida,* 552

Muhlenberg, Henry Melchior (1711–1787): *Journals,* 511; and revival among German Lutherans, 425

Mulkearn, Lois: *Mercer Papers,* 414

Müller, Johann (1436–1476): devises ephemerides, 9

Mullett, C. F.: "English Imperial Thinking," 552

Mumford, Lewis: on American settlement, 3; on Americans and the wilderness, 282

Mun, Thomas: and mercantilism, 187; *England's Treasure by Foreign Trade,* 203

Munro, James: *Acts of Privy Council,* 414

Murder Act; *see* Administration of Justice Act

Murdock, Kenneth: on *Day of Doom,* 308; *Increase Mather,* 274; *Literature and Theology in Colonial New England,* 164

Murray, Sir James: *Letters,* 636

Murray, John; *see* Dunmore, Earl of

Muscovy Company: created, 30; and London merchants, 86; underwrites Hudson voyage, 216

Muskogean Indians: location of, 80

Mutiny Act (1705): censured by Massachusetts, 546; dies, 550; provisions, 545

Myers, A. C.: *Narratives of Early Pennsylvania,* 240

Nahum Keike, 130

Namier, Sir Lewis: works of, 552

Nanfan, John: as New York governor, 691

Nantes, Edict of (1685), 363

Nantucket Island: incorporated into Massachusetts, 337; part of Duke of York grant, 222; whaling of declines, 663

Narragansett Bay: and *Gaspee,* 560; Verrazano visits, 26; Williams heads for, 144–45

Narragansett Indians: and Confederation of New England, 170; in King Philip's War, 253; and Pequots, 156–57

Narragansett Territory: and Dominion of New England, 262; in provisional government, 259

Narratives of the Troubles with the Indians (Hubbard, 1677), 287, 307

Naseby (1645): battle of, 168

Nash, Abner (c. 1740–1786): as North Carolina governor, 693

naturalization: in colonies, 236, 371–72

natural law, 430; Jefferson's use of, 437; John Adams refers to, 572; Locke's use of, 432; Wise and Mayhew on, 455–56

Natural Philosophy; *see* Science

Naumkeag (Salem), 130

naval officer: duties of, 258, 338, 342, 358

naval stores: on enumerated list, 399; in New York, 364, 476; and North Carolina, 492; subsidy for ends, 662

navigation: and Prince Henry, 8–9; in seventeenth century, 72

Navigation Acts: of 1650, 190; of 1651, 190; of 1660, 190, 192, 199, 220, 221, 258; of 1662, 193; Staple Act of 1663, 193, 258; Plantation Duty of 1673, 194, 244, 251, 258; of 1696, 338, 343

navigation system: attitudes toward at Constitutional Convention, 670; Berkeley derides, 201; Congress favors, 666; and courts of vice-admiralty, 343; and customs officers, 258, 334; and Dominion of New England, 263, 264; Dudley seeks to enforce, 260; and economy of colonies, 328; effect on America, 195; effect on England, 194–95; and the governor, 258, 341–42; and New England, 199. 405, 472; and Penn's charter, 233; and Pitt, 532; Shirley seeks to enforce, 405; studies of, 203, 414; and Virginia, 244

Nef, J. U.: *Industry and Government,* 82

Negroes: in Barbados, 212; Chastellux on Southern attitude toward, 489; and Constitution, 670, 673; and Dunmore's call to revolt, 588; early attitudes toward, 289–90; England gains right to ship into Spanish Empire, 333; Hawkins carries to West Indies, 30; and inoculation, 449; Jefferson on rights of, 437; language of,

Negroes (*cont.*)
453; in Newport, 284; number in the South, 487; number in Virginia, 116, 488, 662; Quakers on, 437; and the Revolution, 662; in South Carolina, 494, 495; in Spanish Empire, 23, 24; West Indian and Salem trials, 304; Woolman essay on, 456; *see also* slavery

Nelson, John (1654–1734): proposed for expedition against French, 292

Nelson, Thomas (1738–1789): as Virginia governor, 698

Nelson, W. H.: *American Tory*, 638

Nelson, William (1711–1782): as Virginia governor, 698

Neshaminy (Pennsylvania), 423

Nettels, Curtis: on privateers in Revolution, 609–10; on tobacco exports in Confederation, 662; on Washington and independence, 584; *Emergence of a National Economy*, 683; *Washington and Independence*, 595

Neutral Indians: Iroquois attack, 320

Nevada: as Spanish name, 24

Nevins, Allan: *American States During and After the Revolution*, 681

Nevis: English acquire, 333

New Amsterdam, 220; and Anglo-Dutch wars, 193–94; founded, 217; Leisler immigrates to, 267; studies of, 240; Williams sails from, 169

New Bedford (Massachusetts): British raid, 626

New Bern (North Carolina): founded, 364; and governor's palace, 459–60

New Bordeau: Huguenot settlement, 498

New Brunswick (Canada): loyalists immigrate to, 611

New Castle (Delaware): Penn lands at, 236

New England: in the seventeenth century, 151–60, 255–66; in eighteenth century, 470–75; almanacs issued from, 298; Annapolis Convention absentee, 666; architecture in, 286, 460, and Baptists, 427; and Carolina, 208, 211; contemporary histories of, 456; divisions within (1640), 151; early voyages to, 86; economy of, 174–75, 328, 663; and education, 295, 654; emotional ties to England, 124; and enumerated list, 192; family life in, 289; fear of Anglican establishment, 535; flora and fauna studied, 300–1; gentry in, 288; hivings-out, 142–51, 168–69; and Great Awakening, 422–23, 425; Huguenots in, 363; and inocula-

New England (*cont.*)
tion, 450; Indian problem ends, 376; John Adams on, 487; and John Smith, 123–24; judgments on, 77, 79, 470, 487; and King Philip's War, 253–55; and King William's War, 324–26; literacy in, 294–95; and Louisbourg expedition, 379, 382; and New Amsterdam, 189, 219, 220; and paper money, 402–4; and Queen Anne's War, 329–31; and Randolph, 256–57; and Restraining Act (1775), 574; in the Revolution, 600–3, 608–9; Scotch-Irish in, 368–69; at Stamp Act Congress, 538; studies of, 81, 163, 203, 273, 309, 465; and Surinam trade, 400; topography of, 77; unchurched in, 421; and village life, 282; and Virginia, 77, 118–19, 180, 251, 302, 487; Washington on, 470; Washington promotes independence in, 584; witches in, 304

New England Company, 130

New England Way: heritage of, 157–60; transmuted, 471

New-England Courant: attacks clergy, 421

New England Restraining Act (1775), 574

New France; *see* Canada

New Hampshire: absent from Stamp Act Congress, 538; attends Albany Congress, 386; Congress advises on government, 583; in Dominion of New England, 262; and Jesuit settlements, 376; and King Philip's War, 255; lumbering in, 471; and Massachusetts, 151, 169, 177, 179, 256–57; and New York boundary, 558; as proprietary grant, 108; in provisional government, 259; and Queen Anne's War, 330; ratifies Constitution, 675; royal commission visits, 200; royalized, 238, 257, 336; Scotch-Irish in, 369; Washington promotes independence in, 584; Wentworth as governor, 346; Wheelwright immigrates to, 146

New Haven (Connecticut), 438; Boston taxes imports from, 174; British raid, 625; checkerboard pattern of town, 215; Cheever teaches in, 296; and Confederation of New England, 171; and Dutch on the Delaware, 170, 218, 227; economy of, 473; founded, 150–51; immigration to East Jersey, 226; incorporated into Connecticut, 197; study of, 163

New Jersey: in seventeenth century, 225–29; in eighteenth century, 479–80; attends Annapolis Convention, 666; in Dominion of New England, 229, 259,

New Jersey (*cont.*)
  262; and Frelinghuysen revival, 421–22;
  George Fox visits, 232; and Glorious
  Revolution, 266; line of, mutinies, 631;
  and Louisbourg expedition, 379; and
  loyalism, 611; natural division within,
  475–76; and paper money, 402; and
  Penn, 227; politics of, 479; proprietors
  sell out to crown, 340; and Queen
  Anne's War, 332; ratifies Constitution,
  675; Restraining Act imposed against,
  574; in the Revolution, 612–13; studies
  of, 240, 241, 357, 513, 638; topography
  of, 77
"New Lights": in Congregationalism,
  426–27
New London: British raid, 626
New Mexico: Coronado explores, 26
new monarchs: and Calvinism, 50; and the
  Church, 6; and Columbus, 14
New Netherland, 217–21; and Confederation of New England, 171–74; and New
  England, 255; Puritans immigrate to,
  169; and royal commission, 199; studies
  on, 239
New Orleans: French fort at, 377; La Salle
  reaches site of, 319–20
New Rochelle (New York), 363; Howe
  at, 606
"New Side," 426; defined, 423
New Spain: viceroyalty of, 22
New Wales: Penn's name for colony, 233;
  in Pennsylvania, 362
New York: in seventeenth century, 216–
  25; in eighteenth century, 476–79; and
  access to West, 216; at Albany Congress,
  386; at Annapolis Convention, 666; and
  Articles' revision, 665, 666; Association
  rejected by, 576; and Braddock, 388;
  Burke as agent for, 341; and Congress,
  564, 568, 578; and Connecticut boundary, 199; and constitution (1777), 646,
  672; Cornbury as governor, 328; and
  Dominion of New England, 259, 261,
  262, 264; Dongan as governor, 321; education in, 297; and embargo of British
  goods, 547, 550, 576; French attack Iroquois in (1666), 320; gentry in, 291;
  and governor's salary, 397; immigrants
  avoid, 364; and independence, 592; and
  judiciary, 354, 406; in King George's
  War, 382; and King William's War,
  324–25, 325–26, 328–29; and Leisler's
  Rebellion, 266–69; and Louisbourg expedition, 379; and loyalists, 611; mammoth bones found in, 300; and Mutiny

New York (*cont.*)
  Act, 545; and paper money, 402; and
  New Hampshire boundary, 558; Parliament exempts from Restraining Act
  (1775), 574; politics in, 478–79; and
  Proclamation of 1763, 523; and Queen
  Anne's War, 329–30, 330–31, 332; ratifies Constitution, 675; and Revenue Act
  of 1764, 534; in Revolution, 606–7;
  Scots attracted to, 370; Smith's history
  of, 457; studies of, 239, 240, 357, 512,
  554, 631, 681, 685; unsettled land in,
  660; and Vermont, 660; Western land
  claims of, 650; Whitefield in, 425
New York City: in seventeenth century,
  284; in eighteenth century, 476; and almanacs, 298; attitude toward Connecticut, 469–70; and Dutch heritage, 221;
  and East Jersey, 226; elections in, 478;
  fears of impressment, 328; and Hudson
  Valley farmers, 267; and Indian purchase, 217; intercolonial conference at
  (1690), 325; Jews and Huguenots in,
  363; Johnson honored by, 390; lawyers
  in, 292–93; and Leisler's Rebellion, 267–
  68; Negroes (free) in, 290; Penn visits,
  236; prostitution in, 438; religious indifference of citizens, 302; and Stamp
  Act riots, 538, 542; and Tea Act, 562;
  Verrazano visits harbor of, 26
Newark (New Jersey): founded, 226
Newbold, R. C.: *Albany Congress*, 413
Newburyport (Massachusetts): shipbuilding in, 473; study of, 512; Whitefield
  dies in, 423
Newcastle (England): and coals from, 57,
  65
Newcastle, Thomas Pelham-Holles, first
  Duke of (1693–1768): and patronage,
  405; retires, 410; and Revenue Act of
  1764, 533; as secretary of state, 398;
  study of, 357
Newcomer, L. N.: *Embattled Farmers*, 595
Newfoundland: Cabot reaches, 25; and
  Calvert's reaction to, 108–9, 111; Con-
  gress sends letter to, 572; as English
  colony, 333; and fishing rights (1783),
  634; French occupy, 326, 331; Gilbert
  visits, 33; Hudson pauses at, 216; and
  New England economy, 260, 328; transit
  of Venus observed from, 452; and West
  Country fishermen, 29, 86
Newfoundland Island: and Vikings, 13
Newgate Prison: and Penn, 232; and Penn-
  Mead trial, 231

"Newlanders," 370

Newman, Francis: as New Haven governor, 687

Newman, Henry: biography of, 357

Newport, Christopher (d. 1617): captures Pocahontas, 103; and Jamestown, 89, 91, 92, 94, 95

Newport (Rhode Island): in seventeenth century, 284; in eighteenth century, 473; architecture of, 460; D'Estaing assaults, 626; founded, 147; Jews in, 363; and Stamp Act mobs, 538; and Tea Act, 562

Newsome, A. R.: North Carolina, 239

Newspapers: in seventeenth century, 284; in eighteenth century, 454–55; in backcountry, 504; and Enlightenment, 441; English influence on, 438; as propaganda sheets, 541; and stamp duties, 536; studies of, 357, 467

Newton, A. P.: on Virginia charter of 1606, 88; Great Age of Discovery, 39; "Great Migration," 82

Newton, Sir Isaac (1642–1727), 278, 298; achievement of, 431; biography of, 465; Colden seeks to elaborate findings of, 447; credulity of, 300; and Edwards, 435; religious views of, 432; study of, 466

Newtonianism: and the Bible, 432; influence on architecture, 459; interpretations of, 433–34

Newtown (Cambridge, Massachusetts): and Hooker's congregation, 148, 149; and Shepard's congregation, 154

Newtown (New York): founded, 169

Niagara portage: Amherst allows settlement at, 525; Indians stage ambush at, 528; see also Fort Niagara

Nicholson, Sir Francis (1655–1728): and Dominion of New England, 262; and Leisler's Rebellion, 267–68; on immigration to Virginia, 290; as Maryland governor, 688; as New York governor, 691; as professional royal governor, 346; in Queen Anne's War, 332, 333; as South Carolina governor, 695; as Virginia governor, 270–71, 352, 697

Nickerson, Hoffman: Turning Point of Revolution, 638

Nicolet, Jean (1598–1642): reaches Green Bay, 317

Nicolls, Richard (1624–1672): characterized, 223; on Duke's gift of New Jersey, 475; and New Jersey settlement, 226; as New York governor, 199, 221, 691;

Nicolls, Richard (cont.)
takes Dutch holdings in Delaware Valley, 228; takes New Amsterdam, 220

Niebuhr, Reinhold: on Pilgrims, 129

Niebuhr, Richard: on Great Awakening, 418; Kingdom of God, 464; Social Forces of Denominationalism, 464

Niles (Michigan): site of French fort, 526

Niña, 16; design of, 9

Nipmuck Indians: and King Philip's War, 253

No Cross, No Crown (Penn, 1669), 231

Nock, A. J.: Jefferson, 466

nonconsumption, 547; and Congress, 573

nonexportation: and Congress, 573

nonimportation, 547; and Congress, 573; effect of, 576; Quakers attitude toward, 485; and Revenue Act of 1764, 534; and Stamp Act, 538–39

Norfolk (Virginia), 438

Norfolk, Thomas Howard, fifth Duke of: Heath's rights to Carolina assigned to, 208

Norris, Deborah, 437

North: in eighteenth century, 470–86; attitude on closing of Mississippi, 665; Jefferson on characteristics of, 486; a Marylander on, 470; views of in Constitutional Convention, 670

North Bridge: skirmish at, 577

North Carolina: in the eighteenth century, 491, 492–93; and backcountry, 497, 499, 508–9; British invade, 628; Byrd as historian of, 457; creates new counties, 372; economy of, 487; Gaelic spoken in, 370; governor's communication with England, 341; and governor's palace, 459–60; and independence, 589; lacks committee of correspondence, 568; loyalists in, 603, 611; objects to navigation law during Confederation, 666; ratifies Constitution, 676; and Regulators, 508–9; Scots attracted to, 370; studies of, 239, 514; Swiss and Palatine emigrants, 364; and Watauga region, 660–61; and Western land claims, 650

North Carolina Charters and Constitutions, 239

North, Frederick, eighth Lord North and second Earl of Guilford (1732–1792): Americans accuse as pro-Catholic, 566; and Boston Tea Party, 563; Camden victory saves ministry of, 628; and Carlisle Commission, 620–21, 624; as chancellor of exchequer, 546–47; and East India Company's troubles, 561–62; forms gov-

North, Frederick (*cont.*)
  ernment, 550; and Intolerable Acts, 564;
  on Massachusetts governor, 565; mer-
  chants support, 568; and peace plan
  (1774), 574, 582; resigns, 633; on
  Yorktown defeat, 632
North River; *see* Hudson River
North Virginia; *see* New England
Northampton (Massachusetts): Edwards'
  home, 422
Northampton County (Pennsylvania): at-
  tacked, 528
Northeast Passage: English search for, 30
Northern Neck grant, 270
Northfield (Massachusetts): raided, 265
Northwest Ordinance (1784), 657
Northwest Ordinance (1787), 659; and
  Constitution, 673
Northwest Passage: and Cartier, 26; and
  Frobisher, 31; and Frontenac, 317; and
  Gilbert, 31; and Gómez, 21; and Hud-
  son, 216–17; and London Company, 91
Northwest Territory: and Congress, 657–60
Norumbega; *see* New England
notary: duties of, 445
Notestein, Wallace: *England on the Eve,*
  81–82
Notley, Thomas: as Maryland governor,
  688
Nott, Edward: as Virginia governor, 697
Nova Caesaria; *see* New Jersey
Nova Scotia (Acadia), 108, 576; and Acadians, 376, 377, 387, 390; ceded to
  France (1632), 170; ceded to France
  (1667), 194; Congress sends letter to,
  572; as English colony, 333; granted to
  William Alexander (1621), 108; incorporated into Massachusetts, 337; in
  King George's War, 378; loyalists immigrate to, 611; Massachusetts aids French
  expedition against, 174; and New England economy, 328; New England fails
  to capture (1704, 1707), 331; Nicholson captures (1710), 332; Phips captures (1690), 325; and Pilgrims, 126;
  study of, 356
Novanglus (John Adams): essays of, 576
Norwalk (Connecticut): British burn, 625
Nye, R. B.: *Cultural Life,* 681

Observations on . . . the Society (Mayhew,
  1763), 409
O'Callaghan, E. B.: *Documents of Colonial
  New York,* 240
Of Plymouth Plantation (Bradford), 160

Ogle, Samuel (c. 1702–1752): as Mary-
  land governor, 688
Oglethorpe, James (1696–1785): biogra-
  phies of, 412; and Georgia, 374–76; as
  Georgia governor, 687
O'Hara, Charles: at Yorktown, 632
Ohio Company of Associates, 666; and
  Northwest Territory, 659, 660
Ohio Company of Virginia: and Dinwid-
  die, 384; grant to, 383; study of, 414
Ohio Valley: Céloron tours, 383; drop-off
  in British trade, 384; Indians of in King
  George's War, 379; as part of backcoun-
  try, 497; population (1774), 566
Old French War; *see* French and Indian
  War
Oldham, John (c. 1600–1636): Pequots
  kill, 156
"Old Lights": and Congregationalism,
  426–27
Old Mistress Apologue (Franklin), 458
Old North Church (Anglican), 471
Old Point Comfort: and Virginia charter,
  93
Old Side, 426; defined, 423
Olive, Thomas: as West Jersey governor,
  690
Olive Branch Petition (1775): king re-
  fuses, 585; sent to king, 580
Oliver, Andrew (1706–1774): house ran-
  sacked, 538
Oliver, Peter; memoir of, 593
Olson, A. G.: "Colonial Union, 1754,"
  413; "William Penn," 356
Oneida Indians: Frontenac attacks villages
  of, 326; location of, 79
Onesimus: Mather slave, 449
Onondaga Indians: Frontenac attacks vil-
  lages of, 326; location of, 79
Ontario: loyalists immigrate to, 611
Opechancanough: and Massacre of 1622,
  104; and Massacre of 1644, 182–83
opossum: report on, to Royal Society, 299
Orange County (North Carolina), 372
Osborne, Sir Danvers: as New York gover-
  nor, 692
Oswald, Richard: and Treaty of Paris
  (1783), 633
Otis, James (1725–1783): and Boston
  committee of correspondence, 558; on
  bribery by customs collectors, 532; on
  Peace of Paris (1763), 518; on Revenue
  Act of 1767, 546; on Virginia's Stamp
  Act resolutions, 538; and writs of as-
  sistance, 407, 408

Ottawa Indians: and Pickawillany, 384; and Pontiac, 525; threaten to leave French, 324

Ovando, Nicholas de: heads expedition to Indies, 20

Oxford University, 60; and American colleges, 293, 294, 443; Berkeley graduate of, 180; Calvert and Cecil graduates of, 108; Davenport graduate of, 150; Eaton graduate of, 150; and graduates of grammar school, 295; graduates of, in Massachusetts, 295; and Lawrence graduate of, 245; Nicolls graduate of, 223; Penn attends, 230, 231; Sandys graduate of, 101; Whitefield graduate of, 423

Oyster Bay (Foleston), 221

Paca, William (1740–1799): as Maryland governor, 688

Pacific Northwest: and fur trade, 664

Packard, L. B.: Commercial Revolution, 82

Padelford, Philip: Honyman Journal, 511

Page family, 184

Paine, Thomas (1737–1809): biography of, 466, 595; and Common Sense, 586; and deism, 436; and European entanglements, 316; first Crisis letter, 607–8; on government, 645; and Newtonianism, 433; and novelty in constitutions, 647; on suffrage requirements, 349; and Washington, 623; writings of, 595

Painter, Sidney: Medieval Life, 38

painting: in seventeenth-century America, 287–88; in eighteenth-century America, 462–63; studies of, 309–10, 467

Palfrey, J. G.: History of New England, 274

Palladio, Andrea (1518–1580): influence in America, 459, 460, 461

Palladio Londiniensis, 460

Palmer, Anthony: as Pennsylvania governor, 693

Palmer, R, R.: on loyalists, 611, 653; Age of Democratic Revolution, 552; History of Modern World, 38; "Notes on Word 'Democracy,' " 682

Paltsits, V. H.: "Founding of New Amsterdam," 240

Pamlico Sound: and Verrazano, 26

Paoli Massacre, 617

Papegoga, John: as New Sweden governor, 691

paper money, 402–4; and currency acts, 403–4, 535, 560–61; as debate topic, 656; and Dr. Douglass, 457; in Revolu-

paper money (cont.) tion, 582, 608–9; and Shays's Rebellion, 667; studies on, 552, 553

Pares, Richard: War and Trade in West Indies, 412

Pargellis, S. M.: Military Affairs, 414

Paris: Treaty of 1763, 518, 526, 528; Treaty of 1783, 633–34

parish: in Virginia, 302

Parker, Henry: as Georgia governor, 687

Parker, John (1729–1775): and battle of Lexington, 577

Parker, Peter: in attack on Charleston, 603

Parkes, H. B.: on emigration, 71; on sense of sin in Massachusetts, 303; American Experience, 83; "Cotton and Williams Debate Toleration," 162; "New England in 1730's," 511

Parkman, Francis: criticized, 413; on Frontenac, 326; on Walker expedition, 333; Conspiracy of Pontiac, 552; France and England in North America, 40; Frontenac, 355

Parks, G. B.: Richard Hakluyt, 40

Parliament: and American representation in, 349; anti-American feeling in, 540; British taxes cut by, 543; and the colonies, 187–95, 335, 338–41, 361, 378, 399–404; Congress's attitude toward, 572; and the crown, 52–53, 61–62, 65, 337, 339, 574; Dickinson on power to tax, 546; election (1774), 574; and Georgia, 374; and Glorious Revolution, 273, 337; Hutchinson on powers of, 538; influence on colonial legislatures, 113, 177, 202, 236, 350, 357; James II on relationship to colonies, 334; Massachusetts on powers of, in colonies, 257; and North peace plan, 574; Otis on limitation of power over colonies, 407; and Penn, 232, 340; and Popham, 87; power to tax colonies according to chief justice, 532; power to tax according to colonies, 534; Proceedings of, 415; and proprietary grants, 208; under Puritan leadership, 168, 180, 184, 187–92; Sandys and king's prerogative, 101; and Scottish emigration, 369; and Stamp Act, 537, 539; Stamp Act Congress on powers of, 538; and Ulster cattle, 368; and William III, 337, 339; Winthrop's attitude toward, 168

Parliament, statutes of, relevant to America: Administration of Justice Act (1774), 564–65; Boston Port Bill (1774), 563–64; Bubble Act (1741),

Parliament, statutes of (*cont.*)
403; convicts encouraged to emigrate
(1718), 362; Currency Act (1751),
403-4; Currency Act (1764), 535; Currency Act revised (1773), 560-61; and
customs service in America (1767),
544; Declaratory Act (1766), 540;
Frauds, and Regulating Abuses in the
Plantation Trade, an Act for Preventing
(Navigation Act of 1696), 338; Habeas
Corpus Act (1679), 335; Hat and Felt
Act (1732), 400; Iron Act (1750), 402;
Massachusetts, Act for Better Regulating
the Government of (1774), 565; Mutiny Act (1705), 545; naturalization
acts (1740, 1760, 1763), 372; Navigation Act (1650), 190; Navigation Act
(1651), 190; Navigation Act (1660),
192; Navigation Act (1662), 193; New
England Restraining Act (1775), 574;
New York assembly suspended (1767),
545; Piracy, Act for the More Effectual
Suppression of (1699), 338; Prohibitory
Act (1775), 587; Quartering Act
(1774), 564; Quebec Act (1774), 565-
66; Reunification Bill (1701), 340;
Revenue Act (1764), 532-33; Revenue
Act (1767), 543-44; Settlement, Act of
(1701), 355; Scotland, Act of Union
with (1707), 361; Stamp Act (1765),
535-37; Staple Act (1663), 193; Sugar
Act (1733), 400; Tea Act (1773), 561;
Test Act (1704), 368; Toleration, Act
of (1689), 301; White Pines Acts
(1711, 1722, 1729), 339; Woolen Act
(1699), 338, 368
parochial school: and Dutch, 222
Parrington, V. L.: *Main Currents*, 162
Parry, J. H.: *Age of Reconnaissance*, 38;
European Hegemony, 38; *Spanish The-
ory of Empire*, 39
Parson's Cause, 426
Parton, James, *Franklin*, 594
Partridge, William: as New Hampshire
governor, 690
Pastoral Letter to English Captives in Af-
rica (Mather), 278-79
Pastorius, Francis Daniel (1651-1720),
237
Pate, John: and Maryland uprising, 250
Paterson, William (1745-1806): and New
Jersey Plan, 670
patroon, 217-18
patroonship: and New York, 222, 477
Patterson, S. D.: *Horatio Gates*, 639
Paulus Hook: Lee attacks, 626

Pauw, Michael: patroon of Staten Island,
218
Paxton Boys riots, 485, 528; grievances of,
506
Peale, Charles Willson (1741-1827):
painter, 463
Pearce, R. H.: *Savages of America*, 83
Peare, C. O.: *William Penn*, 241
Peckham, H. H.: on Amherst, 525; *Colonial Wars*, 355; *Pontiac*, 551-52; "Speculations on Colonial Wars," 412; *War
for Independence*, 635
Peden, William: *Jefferson Selections*, 595;
John and John Quincy Adams Selections,
595
Peking (Cambuluc), 5
Pemaquid (Maine) French destroy fort at,
326
Pemberton, Israel (1715-1779): biogra-
phy of, 513
Pendleton, Edmund (1721-1803): biogra-
phy of, 466; as Virginia governor, 698
Penn family: and Church of England, 344;
drops pacifism, 484; Franklin seeks to
deprive of proprietary, 388; and Pennsylvania lands of, after Revolution,
611
Penn, John (son of Founder): gives air
pump to Library Company, 451
Penn, John (1729-1795; grandson of
founder): and Paxton Boys, 528; as
Pennsylvania governor, 694
Penn, Lady Margaret Jasper: and son William, 231
Penn-Mead trial, 231-32
Penn, Richard (1735-1811): as Pennsylvania governor, 694
Penn, Sir William (1621-1670): biographical sketch of, 229-30; and Cromwell's "Western Design," 191; loan to
king, 232
Penn, William (1644-1718): and assembly, 238; biographical sketch of, 229-
30; biographies of, 241; and charter,
232-33, 336, 341; and Delaware, 110,
222; and dream of green country town,
437; on education, 446-47; equality
promoted by, 482; on government, 235,
340; government of colony temporarily
lost by, 336; and Logan, 328, 332; and
Marquette letter, 319; and New Jersey,
227, 228, 229; and Parliament, 340; in
Pennsylvania, 236-37; as Pennsylvania
governor, 693; on Pennsylvania's illicit
trade, 338; on Randolph, 256; study of,
as proprietary, 356

Pennsylvania, 34, 108; in seventeenth century, 229–38; in eighteenth century, 480–86; at Albany Congress, 386; and Anabaptists, 49; at Annapolis Convention, 666; architecture in, 286; and assembly, 351, 569; and backcountry, 497, 505–6; and Braddock, 388; charter of, 232–33; charter and Board of Trade view of, 405; charter and Lords of Trade view of, 256; *Common Sense* in, 586; constitution (1776), 645; counties created by, 372; criminal code of, reformed (1794), 654; Delawares at peace with, 394; education in, 296, 297; Fisher's diary on (1755), 511; Frame of Government and, 235, 236; Franklin as colonial agent for, 341; and French and Indian War, 390–91, 396; and Glorious Revolution, 266; and Great Wagon Road, 497; illegal trade of, 338; and immigration, 237, 364–72; and independence, 589–90, 592; Indian treaty with (1784), 382–83; iron plantations in, 401; Jefferson on character of, 486; lacks committee of correspondence, 568; and Line in Revolution, 608, 629; and Louisbourg expedition, 379; and loyalism, 612; and Maryland boundary, 110, 236, 237; and Mount Vernon conference, 666; and Mutiny Act, 545; and naturalization, 372; painters in, 462; and paper money, 402; and Paxton Boys riots, 485, 506, 528; politics in, 372, 482–86, 583; and Proclamation of 1763, 523; and Queen Anne's War, 331, 332; and quitrents, 655; ratifies Constitution, 675; and Restraining Act (1775), 574; settlement, 236–38; settlement, plans for, 234–36; stamp collector in, 537; studies of, 241, 513, 681, 685; topography of, 77; and United States tariff, 679; unsettled land in, 660; and uprising of 1763, 528; and Virginia and Forks of Ohio, 328, 505, 506, 558, 648; and War of Jenkins' Ear, 378; and Wyoming Valley, 475, 558, 648; and Yankees, 475

Pennsylvania Dutch: diverse backgrounds of, 364; locations of, 481; and Pennsylvania politics, 484; *see also* Germans

Pennsylvania Gazette: and "Join or Die" motto, 387

Pennsylvania Hospital: sanitary condition of, 439

Pennsylvania Line: and the Revolution, 608, 629

Pennypacker, Morton: *Duke's Laws,* 240

Penobscot Bay: and Andros, 324; and French, 154; Hudson visits, 216; Indians raid, 265

Penrose, Boies: on Prince Henry, 8; *Travel and Discovery in the Renaissance,* 39

Pensacola (Florida), 495; French fort at, 327; and Queen Anne's War, 332; Spanish trade of, 377

People's Ancient and Just Liberties Asserted (1670), 232

Pepperrell family: land confiscated, 611

Pepperrell, Sir William (1696–1759): biography of, 512; knighted, 382; and Louisbourg expedition, 379

Pequot War (1637), 149, 156–57, 171, 252, 293; studies of, 163

Percy, George (1580–1632): as Virginia governor, 696

Perry, T. W.: "New Plymouth and Old England," 161

Peru: Pizarro invades, 21; silver of and English economy, 64–65; university of, 23; as viceroyalty, 22

Peter, Hugh (1598–1660): acquaintance of Masham, 143; rival of Cotton, 148

Peter Martyr Anglerius (1459–1525): *De Orbe Novo,* 39; on gold, 21

Petty, Sir William (1623–1687), 296

Petun Indians: Iroquois attack, 320

pewter, 287

Philadelphia: in seventeenth century, 284; in eighteenth century, 437, 438, 476, 480; aids Boston, 564; almanac printed in, 298; architecture in, 460–61; and backcountry, 505; Catholic congregation in, 482; checkboard pattern for, 215; and *Common Sense,* 586; and Congress, 564, 568, 578, 611; and Constitutional Convention, 669; and embargo of British goods, 547, 550; evacuated, 624; as furniture-making center, 462; and independence, 590; Jefferson visits, 450; literary efforts in, 458; located with care, 234; as occupied city, 617; Quakers' power in, 481; regulates exports, 476; and science, 451; studies of, 414; and Tea Act, 562; and West Indies trade, 329; and West Jersey, 226; Whitefield in, 423–24

Philip, King (Metacomet) (d. 1676): biographical sketch of, 253; death of, 254

Philip II (1527–1598): seeks chart of Frobisher voyage, 31; and Spanish Florida, 27

Philip V (1683–1746): gives French Company trading monopoly, 329

Philosophical Society (Boston): Mather founds, 450

Phips, Lady: accused as witch, 305

Phips, Sir William (1651–1695), 341; biographical sketch of, 346; knighted, 382; as Massachusetts governor, 337, 689; Mather sketch on, 456; and Port Royal expedition, 292, 325, 332; and Quebec, 325; and Salem trials, 305

physicians: in seventeenth-century America, 292; in eighteenth-century America, 448–49, 451; in backcountry, 502; in England, 60; need to know classics, 295

Pickawillany: Indian trading town, 383, 384

Pierce, John (fl. 1620): and Pilgrims, 102, 125

Pierce Patent (1620), 102, 125

Pietists, 418; and Georgia, 425; immigrate to Pennsylvania, 362

pigeons: Mather on home of, 299

Pilgrims: in Connecticut Valley, 148, 149; economy of, 154–56; historical importance of, 129; and London Company, 100; and Massasoit, 253; and Pierce Patent, 102, 125; and Puritans as market, 133

Pinckney, Charles: husband of Elizabeth, 494

Pinckney, Charles (1757–1824): in Congress, 664

Pinckney, Elizabeth Lucas (c. 1722–1793): and indigo, 494

Pinckney, Thomas (1750–1828): as South Carolina governor, 696

pine cones: medicinal use of, 300

Pine Tree Hill: Irish Quaker settlement, 498

Pine Tree Shilling, 179

Pinta: design of, 9; lookout spots land, 16

Piqua (Ohio), 383

pirates: and mail service, 341; Parliamentary statute on, 338; plunder botanical collection, 442; and Virginia, 270; welcomed in colonies, 278

Pirenne, Henri: *Economic and Social History,* 38; *History of Europe,* 38

Piscataqua River: Massachusetts absorbs settlements on, 169

Pitcairn, John (1722–1775): and Lexington and Concord, 577

Pitkin, William (1694–1769): as Connecticut governor, 687

Pitt, William; see Chatham, first Earl of

Pitt-Grafton ministry, 543; collapses, 549

Pittsburgh, 566

Pizarro, Francisco (c. 1478–1541): invades Peru, 21

"Plain people," 364–65

plain style: of Puritans, 160, 308

Plains of Abraham, 395

Plan for the Future Management of Indian Affairs (1764), 530

plantation: private version as conceived by Sandys, 100–1, 102; in South Carolina, 494–95; in Virginia, 487–88

Plantation Duty (1673); *see* Navigation Acts

Planter's Plea (White, 1630), 71

Plowden, Sir Edmund: charter issued to, 111

Plymouth Company: charter of, 87; and Gorges, 108; and Sagadahoc, 88–89

Plymouth (England): emigrants from, 94; fishing fleets of, 57; and colonization, 86–87

Plymouth (Massachusetts): Boston taxes imports from, 174; and Confederation of New England, 171; and crown, 127–29; and Dominion of New England, 262, 263; economy of, 133, 154–56; Gorton expelled from, 147; government of, 129; incorporated into Massachusetts, 337; and King Philip's War, 253; lack of plows in, 153; at New York conference (1690), 325; political problems, 127–29; and royal commission, 199; settlement of, 124–29; studies of, 160–61; Williams in, 143

Pocahontas (c. 1595–1617): captured, 103; marries, 103; visits England, 99

Poland: Calvinism carried to, 51; glass experts from in Virginia, 92; tax rate in, 532

Pollard, Ann (c. 1620–c. 1721): painting of, 288

Pollock, Thomas: as North Carolina governor, 692, 693

Polo, Maffeo: in Asia, 4–5

Polo, Marco (c. 1254–c. 1324): in Asia, 5; and Columbus, 17

Polo, Nicolo: in Asia, 4–5

Pomfret, J. E.: *East New Jersey,* 240; *New Jersey Proprietors,* 241; *West New Jersey,* 240

Ponce de León, Juan: and Columbus, 18; and Haiti, 21

Pontiac (d. 1769): biographies of, 552; death of, 529; and Indian uprising of 1763, 525–29

poor laws: in England, 7

Poor Richard's Almanack: on debt, 402; sayings from, 453

Pope, Alexander (1688–1744): and almanacs, 455; on Newton, 431; on Oglethorpe, 374

Popham, Sir Francis: and Council for New England, 89

Popham, George (d. 1608): and Sagadahoc, 88

Popham, Sir John (c. 1531–1607): biographical sketch of, 87; death of, 88

population (estimated): of the colonies in seventeenth century, 167, 278, 362; of backcountry, 497, 501; of Boston, 283, 473; of Canada, 316, 385; of Carolina, 215; of Kentucky, 660; of New England, 251; of New York, 225, 476; of Ohio Valley, 566; of Pennsylvania, 236, 237; of Philadelphia, 438; of South, 487; of South Carolina, 494; of Virginia, 184; of Vermont, 660

pork: as Carolina export, 215

Port Royal; *see* Nova Scotia

Port Royal (South Carolina): in 1670, 214; Barbadians settle, 212; Huguenots settle, 27; as Spanish-English boundary, 279

Portland (Maine): fort on site of, 324

Portland Point (New Jersey): and Monmouth Patent, 226

Porto Bello, 377, 378

Portsmouth (New Hampshire): shipbuilding in, 473

Portsmouth (Rhode Island): founded, 147

Portsmouth (Virginia): Arnold in, 630

Portugal: Cabral sails for, 18–20; and Columbus, 13, 17; and expedition for India, 18; explorations of, 8–13; and Queen Anne, 332; reasons for rise of, 8

Pory, John (1572–1635): and Virginia assembly, 101

postal system: Congress creates, 582; Parliament creates, 442

potash: on enumerated list, 533

Pott, John: as Virginia governor, 696

Powel, Samuel: house of, 460

Powell, Nathaniel: as Virginia governor, 696

Powell, S. C.: *Puritan Village,* 163

Power, Eileen: on Polo, 5; *Medieval People,* 38

Powhatan (d. 1618): and Jamestown, 91, 103

Powicke, Maurice: *Reformation in England,* 81

Pownall, Thomas (1722–1805): biogra-

Pownall, Thomas (*cont.*)
phy of, 357; and disputes with Assembly, 397–98; as Massachusetts governor, 689; on Pennsylvania's paper money, 402–3; as professional royal governor, 347; as South Carolina governor, 695; *Administration of the Colonies,* 415

Prairie du Rocher (Illinois), 377

"Praying Indians," 252, 254

"precinct": in Carolina, 213

predestination: Calvin on, 50; and Edwards, 436; and Locke, 432; Luther on, 50; and Whitefield, 424

Prence, Thomas: as Plymouth governor, 688, 689

prerogative, royal: and colonies, 404; disallowance leads to attack on, 408; effort to strengthen, 405–6; and governor's instructions, 345–46; Sandys fights, 101; and William III, 339

Presbyterian Church: in backcountry, 503, 504; in Delaware Valley, 481, 484; and Great Awakening, 423, 426, 427; and King's College, 479; in New England, 471; in New York, 478; and Puritanism, 53–54; and Regulators, 508; in Scotland, 51; and Synod of Philadelphia, 420, 423; and Test Act, 368; in Ulster, 368; in Virginia, 118, 425–26; and Westminster Confession, 423

Presbyterianism: and Calvin, 51; importance in America, 420

Prescott, A. T.: *Drafting the Constitution,* 684

Present State of Virginia (Jones, 1724), 457

President: Constitutional Convention's creation of office, 671–72, 673–74

Presque Île: French fort at, 384

Prestage, Edgar: *Portuguese Pioneers,* 39

Prester (Priest) John, 4: Polo on, 5; and Prince Henry, 8

Preston, Thomas: and Boston Massacre, 549

Prideaux, John: and French and Indian War, 394

Priestley, H. I.: *Coming of White Man,* 39

primogeniture: defined, 58; fades in America, 292, 353, 433; after Revolution, 655

Prince, Thomas (1687–1758): as historian, 456

Prince of Parthia (Godfrey, 1758), 458

Princeton: battle of 612; studies of battle, 637

Princeton University; *see* College of New Jersey

Principia Mathematica (Newton, 1687), 298; and Logan, 434, 447

Pring, Martin (c. 1580–1626): voyages to New England, 86

printing: in seventeenth-century America, 287, 297–98; Berkeley on dangers from, 297

Printz, Johan Björnsson (1592–1663): as New Sweden governor, 227, 691

privateers: and French, 337, 619; Louisbourg as base for, 331, 376; in Queen Anne's War, 332; during Revolution, 608, 609–10; off Virginia coast, 270; welcomed in colonies, 278

Privy Council: and Board of Trade, 339; Calvert clerk of, 108; and colonial supervision, 255–56, 335–36, 338, 339; duties and powers of, 61–62; and governor of New York, 397; and governor's instructions 345; and governor's powers, 339; and judicial review, 353; and Lords of Trade, 255–56, 339; and Massachusetts charter, 141; members of, 335; and Parliament, 62; and Penn grant, 232; study of Acts of, relevant to America, 414; and Virginia, 105–6

Proclamation Line of 1763, 522–23; pushed westward, 531; Washington on, 530

Professors of the Light; *see* Quakers

Prohibitory Act (1775): provisions, 587

proprietary colony: defined, 344

proprietary grants: Board of Trade objects to, 340; and Gilbert's vision, 33–34; Lords of Trade object to, 238, 256; Puritans in New Jersey balk over, 226–27; and Stuarts, 108, 207–8; *see also individual grants and colonies*

proprietary party: and election of 1764, 485–86; platform of, 484

prostitution: in New York, 438

protectionism, 66; *see also* mercantilism

Protestant Association: in Maryland, 271

Protestants: and Calvert's instructions, 112; and Calvin, 49–51; and denominationalism, 428; in England, 51–53; and Great Awakening, 422; in Holland, 124; influence on America, 43–44, 55–56; influence on American colleges, 293–94; and Luther, 44–46; and Zwingli, 45, 46

proverbs: in Franklin almanacs, 454; in Ames almanacs, 455

Providence Island (Nicaragua): seized, 191

Providence (Maryland): Puritans settle, 185

Providence (Rhode Island): founded, 147; suggests a continental congress, 564

Prevost, Augustine: holds Savannah for British, 627

provost marshal: post in early Virginia, 118

Ptolemy (fl. A.D. 127–151): D'Ailly contradicts, 14; influence on cartography, 9

Public Occurrences (1690), 297

Puerto Rico: and Columbus, 16, 18; Connecticut vessel at, 473; and Penn-Venable expedition, 191; Ponce de León visits, 21

Pulaski, Casimir (c, 1748–1779): killed, 627

Puritanism (in America): and Anne Hutchinson, 145–46; and Cambridge University, 124–25; and Congregational Church, 134–36; in East Jersey, 226; and Great Awakening, 421–22; heritage of, 157–60; and Laud, 140–42; on Long Island, 219, 223, 225; in Maryland, 181, 185; and the merchant, 176–77, 178–79; and New England society, 157–60; Newark founded by, 226; in Newport, 284; Quaker debt to, 230; and regeneration, 50, 55, 135; and Sandys, 101; and Scotch-Irish, 368; sense of mission, 133, 133–34, 160; and Separatism, 142; and the state, 136–40, 158; studies of, 161, 162, 310; and Virginia, 118, 181, 302; and Williams, 143–44

Puritans (in England): and Anglican Church, 59, 141; and Charles I, 70; and Congregational Church, 135; history of, 52–55; and Laud, 131, 140–41; and religious toleration, 178; in Restoration, 199; studies of, 81; and Zwingli, 46

Putnam, Israel (1718–1790): and battle of Manhattan, 605, 606; characterized, 601

quadrant: use of, 72

Quaife, M. M.: *Capture of Old Vincennes*, 640

Quaker Party: platform of, 484; realignment, 485

Quakers: and Anabaptism, 49; and Anglicans, 272, 481; beliefs of, 230; and Confederation of New England, 171; and education, 296–97; in England, 23–32, 237; and French and Indian War, 396; and Great Awakening, 425; Logan opposes pacifism of, 332; on Negroes, 289, 437; in New England, 257, 471; and New Jersey, 227, 228, 229, 332; New Netherland dreads, 220; in Newport,

Quakers (*cont.*)
284; in Philadelphia, 284, 481; and politics, 396, 440, 485; in Queen Anne's War, 331, 332; reformation among, 485; and royalizing of Pennsylvania, 344; and smuggling, 338; studies on, 241, 682; town and country rift among, 483; and Virginia, 181, 302; and voluntary societies, 440; and War of Jenkins' Ear, 378; and Williams, 144
Quarter Sessions Court (England), 63
Quartering Act (1774), 564
Quary, Robert: as surveyor general, 342; as South Carolina governor, 695
Quebec: attacked (1690), 325; attacked (1711), 332; attacked (1775), 588, 602; captured (1759), 395; Champlain founds, 86; Charles I returns to France, 170; studies of, 413
Quebec Act (1774): provisions, 565–66
Quebec (Province of): Congress sends letter to, 572; enlarged, 565
Queen Anne's War, 329–33, 361; immigration during and after, 364; and Iroquois, 328; studies on, 355
Queen's College: founded, 422, 429, 443
Quincy, Josiah, Jr.: journal of, 510
Quinn, D. B.: *Raleigh,* 40; *Roanoke Voyages,* 40; *Voyages of Gilbert,* 40–41; *White Drawings,* 41
Quinnipiac River: site of New Haven, 150
quitrents: in Carolina, 269; in Dominion of New England, 261; in Georgia, 375; in Maryland, 112, 202, 250, 271, 498; in New England, 263, 337; in New Jersey, 226, 479; in New York, 479; in North Carolina, 211, 250, 493, 508; in Pennsylvania, 234, 237, 482; in Virginia, 112, 211, 270, 377; in the United States, 655

Raleigh, Sir Walter (1552–1618), 31, 43, 107, 211; abandons right to colonize Virginia, 37, 86; biographies of, 40; charter of, 34; on colonization, 37; on controlling sea lanes, 187; on gentry, 58; and Gilbert, 33; and Hakluyt, 34; Popham presides at trial of, 87; and Virginia voyages, 34, 35; on why men emigrate, 71
Ramsay, David: essay on his *History of Revolution,* 551; *History of South Carolina,* 514
Ramsey, R. W.: *Carolina Cradle,* 515
Randolph, Edmund (1753–1813): on *Common Sense,* 586; and Constitution, 673, 675; as Virginia governor, 698

Randolph, Edward (c. 1632–1703), 361; American career, 256–58; biography and papers of, 274; and Dominion of New England, 262, 266; and provisional government, 259, 260; as surveyor general, 342
Randolph family, 184, 477, 610
Randolph, John: as South Carolina governor, 696
Randolph, Peyton (c. 1721–1775): in Congress, 569; as Virginia politician, 492
Rankin, H. F.: *Rebels and Redcoats,,* 635
Raper, C. L.: *North Carolina,* 239
Ratcliffe, John: as Virginia governor, 696
rattlesnake: medicinal uses of, 300; power of venom, 299
Rawdon, Lord: and Battle of Camden, 627
Rawle, Francis (c. 1662–1727): on Delaware Valley as economic unit, 480
Read, Charles: *Notes on Agriculture,* 513
Read, George (1733–1798): as Delaware governor, 694
Reading, John: as New Jersey governor, 691
Reading (Massachusetts): and witches, 304
Reading (Pennsylvania): Catholic congregation in, 482; founded, 364; gerrymandered, 484
Reasonableness of Christianity (Locke, 1695), 432
Redeemed Captive Returning to Zion (Williams, 1707), 330
redemption system: evils of, 371
Redwood Library, 460
Reed, Joseph (1741–1785): as Pennsylvania governor, 694
Reed, William: as North Carolina governor, 693
Reese, T. R.: *Colonial Georgia,* 412
Reformation: and Anabaptists, 46–49; and Calvin, 49–51; effect on America, 43, 55–56; in England, 51–53; and Luther, 44–46; studies of, 81; and Zwingli, 45, 46
Regeneration: and American Puritanism, 50, 55, 135; and Baptists, 427; and Calvin, 50; and Great Awakening, 420
regulated company: organization of, 67
Regulation movement: studies of, 515
Regulators: of North Carolina, 508–9; of South Carolina, 506–8
Reich, J R.: *Leisler's Rebellion,* 274
religion: and backcountry, 504; and Board of Trade, 339–40; changes in seventeenth-century America, 301–5; and governor's instructions, 345; as impulse to

religion (*cont.*)
    colonization, 130; prestige lost to science, 431; and Stamp Act, 541; and voluntary societies, 440; *see also* Protestantism, *individual colonies and specific denominations*
religious toleration: at Brown College, 443; in Carolina, 209–11; and Constitution, 674; in Dominion of New England, 260; in Duke's Laws, 223; justification for, 436–37; in Maryland, 181–82; and Massachusetts charter of 1691, 337; in New Jersey, 226, 228; and New Netherland, 219–20; reasons for growth of, 444; in Rhode Island charter, 197; in the United States, 655; and Williams, 144
Rembrandt Harmenszoon van Rijn (1606–1669), 189
"Remonstrance and Petition" (1646): to General Court, 178–79
"Report on Linguistic and National Stocks," 410
requisition system: during Confederation, 665; and Constitution, 675; ineffectiveness of, 386, 532
Restoration, 176; in the colonies, 192–202; influence on education, 297; influence on literary style, 308; studies on, 204
Restraining Act; *see* New England Restraining Act
Reunification Bill (1701): fails to pass, 340
Revenue Act of 1764: objections to, 534, 535–36; purpose and provisions, 532–35; revised (1766), 542; significance, 540
Revenue Act of 1767: provisions, 543–44; repeal urged, 548–49; repealed, 549
Revere, Paul (1735–1818): biography of, 594; Copley paints, 463; as craftsman, 462; as post rider for Boston Committee of Correspondence, 471, 564, 570, 577
Revere family, 363
Reynolds, John (1713–1788): as Georgia governor, 687
Rhine Valley: trip down for immigrants, 370
Rhineland States: Anabaptists in, 49; emigrants from, 237, 364; Marian Exiles in, 52, 55
Rhode Island: at Albany Congress, 386; charter, (1644), 170; charter (1663), 197, 211, 259; and Confederation of New England, 170, 171; as corporate colony, 344; and disallowance, 351; and

Rhode Island (*cont.*)
    Dominion of New England, 262; and education, 296; and embargo, 547; and *Gaspee* incident, 560; and Glorious Revolution, 266; governors' correspondence, 415; as "home of the otherwise minded," 147–48; and molasses, 472; objects to navigation law during Confederation, 666; and paper money, 403; and Quakers, 231; ratifies Constitution, 676; rejects impost, 609; and religious freedom in, 211; and Revenue Act of 1764, 534; royal commission visits, 199; as smuggling center, 260; studies of, 681, 684; Washington promotes independence in, 585
Ribaut, Jean: and Hakluyt, 33; and Port Royal, 27
rice: and Constitutional Convention, 670; on enumerated list, 399; exempted from Nonexportation Agreement, 573; and South Carolina, 215, 494
Rice, H. C.: *Chastellux Travels,* 511
Rice, Nathaniel: as North Carolina governor, 693
Rich, Robert, Earl of Warwick: and Baltimore's colony, 182; grants patent, 148; and Massachusetts, 130; tolerant attitude toward colonies, 187
Richard II (1367–1400): mercantilistic ideas of, 66
Richardson, Joseph (1711–1784): silversmith, 462
Ridley, Matthew: "Diary," 640
Riedesel, Baroness von: *Journal,* 639
Riley, E. M.: *Harrower Journal,* 310
Rippy, J. F.: *Latin America,* 39
Rising, Johan (1617–1672): as New Sweden governor, 228, 691
Ritcheson, C. R.: *British Politics,* 554
Rittenhouse, David (1732–1796): biographical sketch of, 452; biography of, 466
River Brethren, 365
River Indians: attack New Netherland, 219
Roanoke: Amadas at, 34; government for, 36; Grenville at, 35; and London Company, 89; and "lost" colony, 36; and Plymouth Company, 88
Robbins, Caroline: *Eighteenth-Century Commonwealthman,* 466
Robbins: R. M.: *Our Landed Heritage,* 682
Roberts, Kenneth: historical novels of, 637
Robertson, Sir C. G.: *Chatham,* 413
Robinson, Henry: and Virginia revival, 425

Robinson, John (d. 1525): Pilgrims' pastor, 124, 125

Robinson, John (1683–1749): as Virginia governor, 697

Robinson, John (1704–1766): in scandal, 488, 537; as speaker of the House, 492

Robson, Eric, *American Revolution,* 551; Murray's *Letters,* 637

Rochambeau, Jean Baptiste Donatien de Vimeur, Comte de (1725–1807): and Yorktown campaign, 631

Rockingham, Charles Watson-Wentworth, second Marquis of (1730–1782): ministry falls, 542–43; ministry of, 539; replaces North, 633

Rodell, Fred: *Fifty-Five Men,* 684

Roderigue Hortalez and Company, 618

Rodney, Caesar (1728–1784): as Delaware governor, 694; John Adams on, 569

Rodney, George Brydges Rodney, first Baron (1719–1792): allows De Grasse to escape, 631

Rolfe, John (1585–1622): death of, 104; and Pocahontas, 103; and tobacco, 99

Roosevelt, F. D. (1884–1945), 679

Roosevelt family, 221

Root, W. T.: "Lords of Trade and Plantations," 274; *Relations of Pennsylvania,* 513

Rose, J. H.: *Cambridge History,* 39

Rossiter, Clinton: *Seedtime,* 510

Rothermund, Dietmar: "German Problem of Pennsylvania," 411; "Political Factions and Great Awakening," 465

Rotterdam: Byrd gets bedstead from, 287; Germans at, 370

Rowan, Matthew: as North Carolina governor, 693

Rowlandson, Mary White (c. 1635–c. 1678): Indian captive, 307, 330

Rowse, A. L.: *Elizabethans and America,* 40; *Expansion and Elizabethan England,* 40

Roxbury (Massachusetts): lacks land, 149

royal colony: colonial desire to be, 344; defined, 343; survey of government in, 344–54

royal commission: to New England (1664–1665), 199–200; to Virginia (1623), 105; to Virginia (1676), 248–49

Royal Society: and Dr. Garden, 448; and Mather, 435, 450; and transactions of, 449; and John Winthrop, Jr., 197, 299; and Professor John Winthrop, 451

Rudyard, Thomas (d. 1692): as East Jersey governor, 690

rum: and New England economy, 401, 471–72; and New York economy, 476

Rumford, Count; *see* Thompson, Benjamin

Rush, Benjamin (1746–1813), 420, 434, 680; on American nation, 678; on American Revolution, 655–56; on Constitution, 678; favors Gates, 623; on national debt, 665; on Washington, 623

Rutgers University; *see* Queen's College

Rutland, R. A.: *George Mason,* 594

Rutledge, Edward (1749–1800): biography of, 594; in Congress, 606; on Dickinson draft of Articles of Confederation, 649; on New Englanders, 475

Rutledge, John (1739–1800): John Adams on, 569; as South Carolina governor, 696

Rutman, D. B.: "God's Bridge Falling Down," 162; "Pilgrims and Their Harbor," 161; *Winthrop's Boston,* 162; "Winthrop's Garden Crop," 163

Ryder, Nathaniel, 553

rye: in Delaware Valley economy, 480; Scotch-Irish prefer, 499

Ryswick, Peace of (1697): and New England economy, 328; provisions, 326

Sacks, W. S.: "Development of a National Economy," 512

Sackville, Lord George (George Sackville Germain, first Viscount Sackville) (1716–1785): biographies of, 637; and Clinton, 627; and Howe, 613; on Massachusetts Government Act, 565; Esmond Wright on, 635

Sagadahoc, 91, 93; and Gorges, 108; settlement of, 88–89; study of, 119

Sagres: site of Prince Henry's school, 8, 9

St. Augustine (Florida), 214, 495; founded, 27; Drake levels, 35; Oglethorpe attacks, 376; in Queen Anne's War, 332; stone fortress at, 24–25, 279

St. Bartholomew's Massacre (1572), 27

St. Christopher; *see* St. Kitts

St. Clair, Arthur (1736–1818): and backcountry, 505; surrenders Fort Ticonderoga, 613

St. Croix: Columbus discovers, 18

St. Eustatius: illicit trade with, 406

St. John's: Congress sends letter to, 572

St. Kitts: conquered half ceded to England (1667), 194; English acquire (1713),

St. Kitts (*cont.*)
333; population compared to Massachusetts, 167; in Queen Anne's War, 331
St. Leger, Barry (1737–1789): and Fort Stanwix, 613, 616
St. Louis, 327, 377
St. Mary's (Maryland), 112, 115, 118
St. Michael's (Charleston), 461
St. Nicholas: and Dutch, 221
St. Paul's Chapel (New York), 460
St. Peter's (Rome), 44
St. Stephen's (London), 150
saints: and Calvinism, 50–51; changing definition among Puritans, 134–35
Salem (Massachusetts), 438; citizens covenant, 134; and Conant, 130; Philip English lives in, 256; settled, 130, 131, 133; wigwam adapted by settlers, 285; and Williams, 143, 145, 146; witchcraft in, 303–5
Salisbury (North Carolina): on Great Wagon Road, 497; as Scotch-Irish settlement, 498
Salley, A. B.: *Narratives of Early Carolina,* 239
Salmon, E. D.: *Imperial Spain,* 39
Salmon Falls: French level, 324
Saltonstall, Gurdon (1666–1724): as Connecticut governor, 687
"Salutary neglect": customs service during, 532; period of, 398; Shirley during, 404
Salzburgers: in Georgia, 375
San Juan de Ulúa: Hawkins attacked at, 30
San Salvador: Columbus reaches, 16
Sanceau, Elaine: *Henry the Navigator,* 39
Sandy Hook, 626
Sandys, Sir Edwin (1578–1644): biographical sketch of, 101–2; befriends Pilgrims, 125; on dangers of dispersed settlement, 115; leadership attacked, 105; program for Virginia, 102–4; program revived, 181; on tobacco, 104–5
Santa Claus: and Dutch, 221
Santa Maria: wreck, 16
Santo Domingo, 400, 619; founded, 18
Saratoga: battle of, 613–17; battle of and France, 619, 634; study of, 638–39
Sargasso Sea, 16
Sauer, Christopher: essay on, 411
Saugus (Massachusetts): and iron manufacturing, 174, 175
Savage, James: *Winthrop Journal,* 161
Savannah (Georgia), 495; British take, 626; founded, 375
Savannah Town (Augusta), 216

Savelle, Max: *Colonial Period* (translator of), 39; *Seeds of Liberty,* 464
Say and Seal, Lord; *see* Fiennes, William
Saybrook (Connecticut): founded, 148; Pequots sack, 156
Saybrook Platform (1708): provisions, 420
Saye, A. B.: *New Viewpoints in Georgia History,* 412
Sayle, William: as South Carolina governor, 694
Schafer, T. A.: "Jonathan Edwards and Justification by Faith," 465
Scheer, G. F.: *Rebels and Redcoats,* 635
Schenectady (New York): burned, 268, 324
Schlesinger, A. M.: *Colonial Merchants,* 553; *Prelude to Independence,* 553
Schoepf, J. D.: *Travels,* 681
Schoharie Valley: Johnson ravages, 626
Schuricht, Hermann: *German Element in Virginia,* 411
Schutz, J. A.: *Peter Oliver,* 593; *Thomas Pownall,* 357; *William Shirley,* 357
Schuyler, Peter (1657–1724): as New York governor, 691, 692
Schuyler, Philip (1733–1804): biography of, 594; in Revolution, 602, 613, 616
Schuyler, R. L.: *Constitution of United States,* 684; *Parliament and British Empire,* 551
Schuyler family, 267, 477
Schwenkfelders, 47, 365
science: in seventeenth-century America, 294, 298–301; in eighteenth-century America, 447–53; and Catholic Church, 430–31; and colleges, 429, 444–45; studies of, 311, 466–67; Whitehead on, 433
Scioto Company: and Northwest Territory, 658, 660
Scotch-Irish: in backcountry, 497; and German settlers, 365; immigration of, 367–68; locations of, 481; in New Jersey, 479; in New York, 477; preference for whisky, 499; and Regulators, 508; studies of, 411
Scotland: Calvinism carried to, 51; illegal trade with Pennsylvania, 338; Penn's agents in, 234; relation to England, 337; and Staple Act, 193; union with England, 361, 542
Scots: found Stuart Town, 215; as immigrants, 69, 369–70; as loyalists, 370, 611; studies on, 411
Scott, Austin: *Proprietors in Founding of New Jersey,* 240

Scott, John Morin: biography of, 512
Scrooby (England): and Pilgrims, 124
Scull, G. D.: Evelyn *Memoirs,* 636
Sea of Darkness, 12
Sea of Verrazano, 26
Seabury, Samuel (1729–1796): opposes Revolution, 576
Secker, Thomas: Bridenbaugh on, 414; and plans for American bishop, 409, 535
secretary of state, 341; and patronage, 340, 406; and Compromise of 1752, 405; duties, 334; and selection of governors, 339; separate post created for colonies, 546; study of, 356
sectarianism: defined, 427; and voluntary societies, 440; and Whitefield, 424
Sedgwick, Robert (1613–1656): takes Port Royal, 332
seigniory: in Carolina, 213
Seiler, W. H.: "Anglican Parish in Virginia," 311; "Church of England in Seventeenth Century Virginia," 311
Sellers, Leila: *Charleston Business,* 514
Selling of Joseph (Sewall, 1700), 289
Seminole Indians: location of, 80
Seneca Indians: Amherst antagonizes, 525; attack English forts, 526; and French, 245; location of, 79; in Ohio Valley, 383
Separatism: defined, 54; and Great Awakening, 426–27; and Pilgrims, 124–29; and Winthrop, 142
Serle, Ambrose: *Journal,* 636
sermon: in America, 289, 306, 307; and Georgia settlement, 374; Luther's use of, 45, 46; and Whitefield, 424; Zwingli's use of, 46
Seume, J. G.: "Memoirs," 636
Seven Years' War, 395, 409; Indians learn of end, 528; *see also* French and Indian War
Severn River: Battle of (1655), 185
Sevier, John: biography of, 683
Sewall, Samuel (1652–1730): attacks slavery, 289; and Salem trials, 305
Seymour, John: as Maryland governor, 688
Shadwell, 490
Shaftesbury, Earl of; *see* Cooper, Sir Anthony Ashley
Sharpe, Horatio (1718–1790): as Maryland governor, 688
Shawnee Indians: grievances against Amherst, 525
Shays, Daniel (c. 1747–1825): and Massachusetts uprising, 667

Shays's Rebellion, 667; as debate topic, 656; studies of, 684
Shelburne, William Petty, second Earl of (1737–1805): and Board of Trade's Western policy, 519–522; and free trade, 661; and Land Ordinance of 1785, 657; and peace negotiations, 633; and Proclamation of 1763, 523; as secretary of state, 543
Shenandoah Valley: settlement of, 497, 499; and speculators, 498, 506
Shepard, Thomas (1605–1649): characterized, 136; congregation of, purchases Newtown, 154; on decay of education, 297; and Laud, 141; reasons for emigration, 71
Shepherd, W. R.: *New Amsterdam,* 240
sheriff: Bacon's laws on, 247; in Chesapeake colonies, 185–86; in England, 62–63; and governor, 505; in North Carolina backcountry, 508; in Pennsylvania, 482; study on, 203; in Virginia, 118, 200
Sherman, Mrs. Richard: and sow dispute, 178
Sherman, Roger (1721–1793): biography of, 594; at Constitutional Convention, 668; and Declaration of Independence, 591; painting of, 463
Sherrard, O. A.: *Lord Chatham,* 413
shingles: in America, 286
shipbuilding: in Delaware Valley, 481; in Massachusetts after the Revolution, 663; in New England, 471, 473; Virginia encourages, 181
Shippen, Edward (1639–1712): as Pennsylvania governor, 693
ships: defined as English in navigation acts, 190, 192, 338; Dutch improvements in, 189; number owned by Philadelphia merchants, 480; registration of, 193, 338; revolution in design by Prince Henry's men, 9
Shipton, C. K.: *New England Life,* 511; "Plea for Puritanism," 161
shire, 62
Shirley, William (1694–1771): biography of, 357; commands British forces, 390; correspondence of, 357; Franklin to on plan of union, 387; as governor, 346–52, 404–5, 689; on jury trials, 343; and Louisbourg expedition, 378–79; and Newcastle, 398; and Niagara expedition, 388; and paper money, 403
Shrewsbury (New Jersey): and Monmouth Patent, 226

Shryock, Richard: on credulity of seventeenth century, 300; on Mather's significance to medicine, 450; on physicians in eighteenth-century America, 446; *Cotton Mather,* 311; *Medicine and Society,* 311

Shute, Samuel (1662–1742): as Massachusetts governor, 689

Sidney, Algernon (c. 1622–1683): Penn consults, 235

Siebert, W. H.: *Loyalists in Pennsylvania,* 638

Silesians: as immigrants, 364

Silversmiths: in eighteenth-century America, 462; in Boston, 287

Simmons, R. C.: "Freemanship in Early Massachusetts," 163

Simple Cobbler of Agawam (Ward, 1647), 136, 308

Simpson, Alan: on Puritans, 158; "How Democratic was Roger Williams?", 162; *Puritanism,* 81

Singer, Charles: *History of Technology,* 38

Sinnot, E. W.: *Meeting House and Church in Early New England,* 309

Sioux Indians: location of, 80

Sirmans, M. E.: "South Carolina Royal Council," 514

Six Nations; *see* Iroquois Indians

Sixtus V (1521–1590): on Elizabeth I, 56

Skene, John (d. 1690): as West Jersey governor, 690

skins: on enumerated list, 533

slavery: in seventeenth-century America, 116, 289–90; in eighteenth-century South, 461, 487–89, 494–95, 499, 662; attacked, 289, 654; in Boston, 472–73; and Constitutional Convention, 671; and Declaration of Independence, 592; and Fundamental Constitutions, 214; Georgia forbids, 374–75; Georgia permits, 376; and Indians, 216, 255, 331; in North Carolina, 492; and Northwest Ordinance (1784), 657; and Northwest Ordinance (1787), 659; and South Sea Company, 372–78; in Spanish Empire, 23; studies of, 310; *see also* Negroes

slave trade: and Hawkins, 30; and Jamaica, 191; and New England, 176; Rhode Island prospers on, 471; and rum, 471; and South Carolina, 654

Sloane, Sir Hans (1660–1753): and American botanists, 447

Sloughter, Henry: as New York governor, 269, 326, 691

Sly, J. F.: *Town Government in Massachusetts,* 163

Small, William: at William and Mary, 444–45

smallpox, 439; and American army in Canada, 602; Amherst considers sending among Indians, 528; cure for, 300; and Indians, 127, 148, 156; and inoculation, 301, 449–50; on Penn's ship, 236

Smallwood, William (1732–1792): as Maryland governor, 688

Smibert, John (1688–1751): painter, 462

Smith, A. E.: *Colonists in Bondage,* 120

Smith, Adam (1723–1790): and free trade, 661; coins word "mercantilism," 66

Smith, Bradford: *Bradford of Plymouth,* 160; *Captain John Smith,* 119

Smith, E. H.: *Charles Carroll,* 594

Smith, H. M.: *Reformation,* 81

Smith, J. H.: *Appeals to Privy Council,* 356; *Arnold's March,* 637; *Struggle for Fourteenth Colony,* 637

Smith, J. M.: *Seventeenth Century,* 83

Smith, John (1580–1631): biographies of, 119; on gold fever in Jamestown, 92; Hudson's friend, 216; in irons, 89; and Jamestown, 91, 92, 93, 94; and New England, 71, 123–24; and Pilgrims, 125; praised, 94–95; Stith on, 457; on "starving time," 95; on Virginia as land of death, 69; as Virginia governor, 696; on Virginia's value, 66; on the wilderness, 282; *Works,* 119; as writer, 306

Smith, Joseph (1805–1844), 130

Smith, Melancton (1744–1798): votes for Constitution, 676

Smith, Page: "David Ramsay," 511; *James Wilson,* 594; *John Adams,* 466

Smith, P. H.: *Loyalists and Redcoats,* 635–36; "Politics and Sainthood," 312

Smith, Preserved: *Reformation,* 81

Smith, Samuel: *History of New Jersey,* 240

Smith, Sir Thomas (1514–1577): on gentlemen, 293

Smith, Sir Thomas (1558–1625), 99, 103; characterized, 68; and London Company, 93, 96, 101–2

Smith, Thomas (fl. 1679): self-portrait of, 288

Smith, Thomas (fl. 1693): as South Carolina governor, 695

Smith, Thomas (1745–1809): and backcountry, 505

Smith, William (1728–1793): biography of, 512; as historian of New York, 457; on New York resources, 476

Smith, William (1727–1803): and College of Philadelphia, 443, 444; literary achievements of, 458

Smith, William J.: *Grenville Papers,* 553

Smith, W. R.: *South Carolina,* 514

smuggling: Grenville makes war on, 532; and New England, 472; seizures for, 544; study on, 414; and tea, 561

Social Security: and Amish, 365

Society for Encouraging Trade and Commerce with . . . Massachusetts, 442

society for propagating the Gospel in New England, 171

Society for the Propagation of the Gospel in Foreign Parts: charter issued (1701), 419; Mayhew attacks, 409; purpose, 272

Society of Friends; *see* Quakers

Society of Particular Adventurers for Traffique with Virginia, 99

Society of the Cincinnati, 653–54: as debate topic, 656

solicitor: defined, 445

Some Considerations on the Keeping of Negroes (Woolman, 1754), 456

Somers, Sir George (1554–1610), 94

Somers Island; *see* Bermuda

Sons of Liberty: and Barré, 537; of New York, 478; and Stamp Act riots, 538

Sosin, J. M.: "Louisbourg," 412; "Postscript on Stamp Act," 553; "Regulation of Paper Money," 553; *Whitehall and the Wilderness,* 552

Sothel, Seth (d. 1694): as North Carolina governor, 692; as South Carolina governor, 695

Soto, Hernando de (c. 1496–1542), 92

South: in the eighteenth-century, 486–96; and closing of Mississippi, 665; education in, 295, 447; family life in, 289; and Great Awakening, 425–26; Jefferson on characteristics of, 486; loyalists in 611; path to power in, 291; studies on, 513; study of legislature, 357; study on colonial agents of, 357; study on Great Awakening in, 465; unsettled land in, 660; views in Constitutional Convention, 670

South America, 79; Columbus discovers, 18; and papal bulls, 17; and Spanish explorers, 21; *see also* Spanish Empire

South Carolina: adopts state constitution, 589; architecture in, 461; and backcountry, 500, 506; botanist in, 448; and committee of correspondence, 560; economy of, 494–95; elections in, 646; Huguenots in, 363, 498; and independence,

South Carolina (*cont.*)
588; and Nonexportation Agreement, 573; politics in, 495–96; population (1700), 215; ratifies Constitution, 675; and Regulators, 506–8; and Restraining Act (1775), 574; Revolution in, 603, 626, 627, 632; and slave trade, 654; slaves lost in Revolution, 662; society of, and Fundamental Constitutions, 214; at Stamp Act Congress, 538; studies on, 239, 514; topography of, 77–78; Welsh Baptists in, 498; and Western land claims of, 650; and Yamasee War, 373

South Sea: Balboa sights, 21; Louis XIV seeks passage to, 317; Verrazano supposedly sights, 26

South Sea Bubble Act (1720): and the colonies, 403

South Sea Company: and West Indies, 377

Southampton (New York): founded, 169

Spain: and Bermuda, 94; and Columbus, 14–20; and Cromwell, 190, 191; the crown and colonies relationship, 21–22; Florida ceded to Britain, 518; and Canada, 26; and England, 35, 36, 43, 85, 93; and Holland, 124, 187, 189; and Jamestown, 89; and Navigation Act (1651), 190; as New England market, 176; Oglethorpe's attitude toward, 374; Pope allots New World to, 17; and Portugal, 12; and the Revolution, 609–618, 620, 634; and slave trade, 329; and Treaty of Utrecht, 333; and the United States, 620, 661, 665; and War of Jenkins' Ear, 378

Spanish Armada, 30; and relief for Roanoke, 36

Spanish Empire: born, 18–24; and Carolina, 208, 214; and Cromwell, 190, 191; Dutch attack vessels from, 189; and Georgia, 373; heritage from, 21–25, 608; and Huguenots, 27; and Indians, 21, 23, 25, 79, 373; influence on British Empire, 23–24; influence on English colonization, 28, 31, 33, 34; influence of silver from on England's economy, 64–65; as menace to colonies, 112, 279, 373; organization of, 21–22; and Queen Anne's War, 331–32; study of, 683; and War of Jenkins' Ear, 378

Spanish Succession, War of; *see* Queen Anne's War

Spector, M. M.: *American Department of British Government,* 356

spectral evidence, 304, 305

speculators: attitude toward Articles of Confederation, 651; attitude toward Quebec Act, 566; attitude toward statehood for Kentucky, 660; and Northwest Territory, 659, 661; and settlement of backcountry, 498–99

Speedwell, 125–26

Spencer, Nicholas: as Virginia governor, 697

Spencer, Robert, second Earl of Sunderland (1641–1702): and Penn, 233

S.P.G.; *see* Society for the Propagation of the Gospel in Foreign Parts

spice trade: and Dutch, 189

Spiller, Robert: *Literary History of the United States*, 311

Spotswood, Alexander (1676–1740), 347; biography of, 357; as Virginia governor, 697; and Yamasee War, 373

Springfield (Massachusetts): burned, 254; and Connecticut's power to tax, 174; founded, 149

Springhill: on fall line, 497

Squanto (d. 1622): and Pilgrims, 127

Stacey, C. P.: *Quebec, 1759*, 413

Stamford (Connecticut): founded, 151

Stamp Act: background of, 533, 535–36; and Coke, 679; Dulany attacks, 576; and newspapers, 455; provisions, 535–37; reaction to, 537–39; and reaction to Mutiny Act, 545; repeal of, 539–40; significance for America, 540–41; and South Carolina, 496; studies on, 553

Stamp Act Congress, 668; deliberations of, 538; on Parliament's power to tax, 540

Stamp Act Resolves (Virginia), 538

Standish, Miles (c. 1584–1656), 125; and Merry Mount, 129

Stanford, Peleg: as Rhode Island governor, 694

Staple Act, 1663; *see* Navigation Acts

Star Chamber, 70

Stark family, 611

Stark, John (1728–1822): and battle of Bennington, 613–16

Stark, Molly, 613–16

Starkey, M. L.: *Devil in Massachusetts*, 311; *Little Rebellion*, 684

"starving time": Maryland avoids, 112; in Plymouth, 127; in Virginia, 95

statehouse (Philadelphia), 437; architecture of, 460–61; Congress uses, 578; Constitutional Convention, 668

Staten Island: Howe lands on, 605; as patroonship, 218

Staunton (Virginia): on Great Wagon Road, 497

Stearns, R. E.: "Great Migration," 82

Steele, Sir Richard (1672–1729): Franklin apes style of, 454; and Indians, 332

Steiner, B. C.: *Beginnings of Maryland*, 120; *Maryland During the English Civil War*, 203; *Maryland Under the Commonwealth*, 203

Stephensburg: on Great Wagon Road, 497

Stephens, Samuel: as North Carolina governor, 692

Stephens, William: as Georgia governor, 687

Steuben, Friedrich Wilhelm Ludolf Gerhard Augustin, Baron von (1730–1794): joins Lafayette forces, 630; at Valley Forge, 622

Stevenson, Elizabeth: *Henry Adams Reader*, 119

Stiles, Ezra (1727–1795): biography of, 466; on colonial reaction to Stamp Act, 541; on friend Lopez, 363; on laws of nature, 433; on separation of church and state, 429; on Shays's Rebellion, 667; on slavery, 654; on surviving Pequots, 157; and town life, 437; on Treaty of Paris (1763), 518

Stillé, C. J.: *Dickinson*, 553

Stirling, first Earl of (William Alexander) (c. 1567–1640): Nova Scotia granted to, 108

Stith, William (1707–1755): as historian, 457

Stobo, Robert: biography of, 413

Stock, L. F.: *Proceedings of Parliament*, 415

Stoddard, Solomon (1643–1729): and church membership, 421

Stone, F. D.: *Pennsylvania and the Constitution*, 685

Stone, John: provokes Pequot War, 156

Stone, William (c. 1603–c. 1660): as Maryland governor, 182, 184, 688

Stony Point, 625

Stoughton, William (1631–1701): on Dominion of New England council, 262; as Massachusetts governor, 689

Strachey, William (fl. 1606–1618): on Pocahontas, 103; publishes Dale's Laws, 97; *History* of, 119

Strasburg: on Great Wagon Road, 497

Struik, D. J.: *Yankee Science*, 466

Stryker, W. S.: *Battle of Monmouth*, 639; *Battles of Trenton and Princeton*, 637

Stuart, John (c. 1700–1779): negotiates Indian treaties, 531
Stuart Town: founded, 215
Stump, a man named: murders Indians, 531
Stuyvesant, Peter (c. 1595–1672): biography of, 240; and Navigation Act of 1651, 190; as New Netherland director-general, 219–21, 691; subdues Swedes on Delaware, 228
subsidies: ended, 662; for indigo, 494–95, 496; for naval stores, 492, 496; for whales, 471
Sudbury (Massachusetts) in King Philip's War, 254
Suffolk County (New York): and Leislerian assembly, 268
Suffolk Resolves: contents of, 570
suffrage requirements: in America, 349; in Connecticut, 150, 197; in England, 62; Jefferson on, 644; Jews excluded, 363; John Adams on, 645; in Maryland, 250, 491; in Massachusetts, 137, 153, 337; in New England, 179, 474; in New York, 478; in Northwest Territory, 659; in Pennsylvania, 482; in Plymouth, 129; in South Carolina, 496; studies of, 357, 510, 512, 513, 514; in Virginia, 201, 244, 246, 247, 491
sugar: and Barbados, 176, 212; and England's economy, 193, 194, 195; on enumerated list, 192
Sugar Act (1733); see Molasses Act
Sugar Act (1764); see Revenue Act (1764)
Sullivan, John (1740–1795): and Battle of Long Island, 605; biography of, 639; destroys Indian villages, 626; emissary to Congress, 606; in New Hampshire, 584; as New Hampshire governor, 690
Sullivan's Island: fort on, 603
Sumatra: Dutch holding, 189
Summary . . . of . . . British Settlements (Douglass, 1748–1753), 456–57
Summary View of the Rights of British America (Jefferson, 1774), 578
Sunderland, Lord; see Spencer, Robert
Surinam: New England trade with, 400
surveyor-general (of customs): duties, 342–43; lack of authority, 544
surveyor-general (of king's woods), 399
Susan Constant, 89
Susquehanna River: and Claiborne, 113; as proposed site for Quaker settlement, 227
Susquehannock Indians: Senecas invade territory of, 245

Swansea: family in, murdered, 253
Sweden: commercial treaty with, 663; English and iron of, 401
Swedes: in Delaware Valley, 218, 219, 220, 226, 227, 228, 481; and log cabin, 285; naturalized by Pennsylvania, 236; studies of, 240; and ties to Lutheran Church, 363
Swedish West India Company, 220
Sweet, W. W.: Religion in Colonial America, 331
Swem, E. G.: Jamestown Booklets, 119
Swiggett, Howard, War out of Niagara, 640
Swiss: in America, 364, 365; Anabaptists among, 49; studies of, 411
Sydenham, Thomas (1624–1689): on diseases, 449
Sydnor, C. S.: Gentleman Freeholders, 514
Sylvania: proposed for Penn's colony, 233
synod of New York: on New Side clergy, 427
synod of Philadelphia, 423; ejects Tennent, 427; formed, 420
synod of 1637, 146
synod of 1647, 179
synod of 1657: and Half-Way Covenant, 198
synod of 1798 (Connecticut), 420

Tacksman: leads Scots to America, 369
Tailer, William: as Massachusetts governor, 689
Talcott, Joseph (1669–1741): as Connecticut governor, 687
Talifer, Patrick: Narrative of Georgia, 412
Talon, Jean: as intendant, 316–17
Tanner, E. P.: "Colonial Agencies," 357; New Jersey, 240
Tansill, C. C.: Documents of the Formation of the Union, 684
Tappert, T. G.: Muhlenberg's Journals, 511
tariff: United States' first, 679
Tarleton, Sir Banastre (1754–1833): defeated at Hannah's Cowpens, 629; ravages South, 627
Tasker, Benjamin: as Maryland governor, 688
Tate, T. W.: "Coming of the Revolution in Virginia," 553
Tatham, John: as East Jersey governor, 690
Tatum, E. H., Jr.: Serle's Journal, 636
Tawney, R. H.: Agrarian Problem, 82; Religion and Rise of Capitalism, 81; "Rise of the Gentry," 82

taxation: American views on, 536; Congress on, 571; Franklin on, 544; Massachusetts on, 549; Parliament's views on, 536; Townshend on, 544

Taylor, Edward (c. 1645–1729), 308

Taylor, E. G. R.: *Haven-Finding Art*, 38

Taylor, R. J.: *Massachusetts, Colony to Commonwealth*, 681; *Western Massachusetts in the Revolution*, 684

tea: duty left on, 549; and East India Company, 561; and Townshend duties, 543

Tea Act (1773): provisions, 561; reaction to, 562

teacher: in Congregational Church, 135

Teedyuscung (c. 1700–1763): biography of, 412

telescope: and Mather, 301; and Winthrop, Jr., 299

Telfair, Edward (c. 1735–1807): as Georgia governor, 687

Temple, S. B. G.: *Georgia Journeys*, 412

tenant farmers: in New York, 478

Tench, Thomas: as Maryland governor, 688

Tennent, Gilbert (1703–1764): and Great Awakening, 422, 425; sermon of, 456; synod ejects, 427

Tennent, William (1673–1746): and Great Awakening, 423–24

Tennessee: enters Union, 661; as part of backcountry, 497; and Watauga River settlement, 501

Test Act (1704), 368

Texas: La Salle lands in, 320

Thacker, Thomas (d. 1679): painting of, 298

Thanksgiving: and Pilgrims, 127

Thayer, Theodore: *Israel Pemberton*, 513; *Nathanael Greene*, 639; *Pennsylvania Politics*, 513; "Quaker Party," 513

Theus, Jeremiah (c. 1719–1774): painter, 462

Thirty-Nine Articles (1571), 52

Thirty Years' War: and Dutch and Swedes, 227; and immigration, 68, 70; and Moravians, 365

Thomas a Kempis (1380–1471), 297

Thomas, George (c. 1695–1774): as Pennsylvania governor, 693

Thomas, John (1724–1776): death of, 602–3

Thomas, Robert: "Virginia Convention of 1788," 685

Thompson, Benjamin (Count Rumford) (1753–1814): biography of, 467; and kite experiment, 453

Thomson, Charles (1729–1824): and Congress, 569; essay on, 594; note to Franklin, 573

Thoreau, Henry David (1817–1862), 434; admires Puritan style, 160

Thorpe, F. N.: *Federal and State Constitutions*, 681

Thoughts on Government (Adams, 1776), 645

Throgmorton, John: hives out, 169

Throg's Neck: Howe lands at, 606; settled, 169

Tinling, Marion: *Byrd Diaries*, 514

tobacco: and Chesapeake society, 103, 116, 487; and Columbus, 17; in Confederation period, 662; and Constitutional Convention, 670; and county commissioners, 185; and Dutch, 109; on enumerated list, 192; and English trade, 102, 195; James I's views on, 104; Maryland undermines market, 114; in Massachusetts, 141; and ministers' salaries, 302; and Nonexportation Agreement, 573; in North Carolina, 215; and the plantation, 487–88; price fluctuations, 194, 244, 250, 270, 271, 407, 488; production after the Revolution, 662, 664; quality of early product, 99; and Rolfe, 99; and Scots merchants, 370; statutory efforts to promote quality and price of, 112, 180; in Shenandoah Valley, 499; Virginia seed purloined from Spanish, 24; Virginia taxes, 101, 112; and water transportation, 115

tobacco contract, 104–5

Tolles, F. B.: on *American Magazine*, 458; on Quaker educational ideals, 296–97; "Culture in Early Pennsylvania," 513; *James Logan*, 466; *Meeting House and Counting House*, 241; "New Approaches to Early American History," 355; *Quakers and the Atlantic Culture*, 241; re-evaluation of social aspects of the Revolution, 682; *Witness of Penn*, 273

Tom Jones (Fielding, 1749), 490

"tomahawk right": in backcountry, 502

Tomas, Vincent: "Modernity of Jonathan Edwards," 465

Tonty, Henri de (1650–1704): and La Salle, 319, 320

Toppan, R. N.: *Edward Randolph*, 274

Tordesillas, Treaty of (1494), 17–18

Tortuga: Spanish seize, 191

Tourtelott, A. B.: *Beginnings of the Revolution*, 594

town: in the eighteenth century, 437–42; Carolina encourages, 214, 215; in Chesapeake region, 115, 117, 282–83; in England, 64; Duke's Laws undercut authority of, 223; and education, 295; and Enlightenment, 437–42; and Indians, 252; in medieval Europe, 2; in New England, 151–54, 471, 474; as New England electoral unit, 349; and the new merchants, 6–7; Penn encourages, 234; studies of, 163

town meeting: under Dominion of New England, 262; in New England, 283

Towner, L. W.: "Sewall-Saffin Dialogue," 310

Townshend, Charles (1725–1767): as chancellor of exchequer, 543; death of, 546; on taxation, 544

Townshend duties, 531, 543–44; reception in America, 545–48

Tracy, Marquis de: attacks Iroquois, 320

trade: Congress discusses, 587, 588; and governor's instructions, 345; Penn encourages, 234; and Restraining Act, 574; after the Revolution, 663–64; see also economy, Navigation Acts, Parliament

Transylvania Company: and Boone, 501

Travels in the New World (Gage, 1648), 191

Travels of Marco Polo (1299), 5

Treacy, M. F.: Prelude to Yorktown, 639

Treasury Board: and the colonies, 334; and governor's instructions, 345; and Newcastle, 410; and Stamp Act, 532–33, 536; study of, 356, 414; and surveyor-general of king's woods, 399

Treasury of Design (Langley), 460

Treat, Robert (c. 1622–1710): as Connecticut governor, 687

Treaty of Alliance (1778), 619

Treaty of Amity and Commerce (1778), 619

Trenchard, John, 454

Trenton: British in, 607; Washington takes, 612

Treutlen, John A.: as Georgia governor, 687

Trevelyan, G. M.: England Under the Stuarts, 204; American Revolution, 635

triangular trade: in eighteenth century, 471; established, 176; of South Carolina, 215

Trinidad: Columbus discovers, 18

Trinterud, L. J.: "Origins of Puritanism," 81; Forming of an American Tradition, 465

True Relation (Smith, 1608), 71

Trumbull, Jonathan (1710–1785): as Connecticut governor, 687; and Washington, 584

Tryon, William (1729–1788): biography of, 514; as New York governor, 692; as North Carolina governor, 693; palace of, 459–60; and Regulators, 508–9

Tucker, L. L.: Thomas Clap, 466

Tugwell, R. G.: Eliot's Essays, 510

Turkey: and inoculation, 499; Smith in, 91

turkey egg: medicinal use of, 300

Tuscarawas (Indian town): Bouquet at, 529

Tuscarora Indians: location of, 79

Tuscarora War (1717): immigrants die in, 364

Two Acres Act (1624), 112

Two Penny Act (1758), 407; study of, 414

Tyler, L. G.: Narratives of Early Virginia, 119

Tyler, M. C.: on seventeenth-century American writers, 306–7; on Edwards as writer, 456; on influence of Restoration on literary style, 308; on role of sermon, 307; on Wise as writer, 456; History of American Literature, 311; Literary History of the American Revolution, 464

Tynte, Edward: as South Carolina governor, 695

Ubbeholde, Carl: Vice-Admiralty Courts, 357

Uhlendorf, B. A.: Baurmeister Letters, 636

Ulster: emigrants from, 367–68; and New England town pattern, 153

Ulster County (New York): and Leislerian assembly, 268

Ulster Scots; see Scotch-Irish

Underhill, John (c. 1597–1672): and Pequots, 157, 163

Underhill, R. M.: Red Man's America, 83

Union Fire Company, 439, 440

Uniontown (Pennsylvania), 384

United Brethren; see Moravians

United States: in an age of experiments, 644–85; coastline of, compared to Chesapeake Bay, 114; as experiment in Protestantism, 44; and Spain, 620; Spanish influence on currency of, 24; treaties with France, 620

University of Pennsylvania; see College of Philadelphia

Unlearned Chemist (Galen), 300

Unwin, George: *Gilds and Companies of London,* 82

Upland (Chester, Pennsylvania): Penn lands at, 236

Usher, John: on Dominion of New England council, 262; as New Hampshire governor, 690

usury: in medieval world, 3

Utica (Illinois): French fort near site of, 377

Utopia (More, 1516): Gilbert quotes from, 33; on sheep, 65

Utrecht, Treaty of (1713), 362; France repairs losses from, 376; provisions, 333; result of, 377

vaccination: distinguished from inoculation, 449

Valcour Island: battle off, 607

Valentine, Alan: *Lord Germain,* 637

Valley Forge: studies on, 639; Washington at, 617; winter of 1777–78, 621–22

Van Bogardt, Jost: as New Sweden governor, 691

Van Buren family, 221

Van Cortlandt family, 477

Van Dam, Rip (c. 1660–1749): as New York governor, 692

Van Doren, Carl: *Franklin,* 466; Franklin *Letters,* selected, 553; *Great Rehearsal,* 684; *Mutiny in January,* 640; *Secret History of Revolution,* 640

Van Dyke, Nicholas (1738–1789): as Delaware governor, 694

Vane, Sir Henry (1613–1662): and Anne Hutchinson, 146; as Massachusetts governor, 689

Van Every, Dale: *Ark of Empire,* 683; *Company of Heroes,* 683; *Forth to the Wilderness,* 413

Van Rensselaer family, 221, 267

Van Rensselaer, Kiliaen: and New Netherland, 217, 218

Van Twiller, Wouter (c. 1580–c. 1656): as New Netherland director-general, 218–19, 691

Van Tyne, C. H.: *Loyalists,* 638; "Religious Forces in Revolution," 551

Varga, Nicholas: "Election Procedures in New York," 512

Vassar family, 363

Vattel, Emmerich von (1714–1767): Congress refers to, 570

Vaughan, A. T.: "Pequots and Puritans," 163

Vaughan, George: as New Hampshire governor, 690

Vaughan, Sir John: and Penn-Mead trial, 231

Venable, Robert: in West Indies, 191

Venango: French fort at, 384

Venice: Polos return to, 5

Venus: transit studied, 452

Vergennes, Charles Gravier (1717–1787): and United States, 608, 618, 633

Verhulst, Willem: as New Netherland director-general, 691

Vermont: abolishes slavery, 654; Burgoyne foraging party in, 613; history of, 660; and New York, 223; statehood of as debate topic, 656; unsettled land in, 660

Vernon, Edward (1684–1757): and War of Jenkins' Ear, 378

Verrazano, Giovanni da (c. 1480–c. 1572): and Hakluyt, 33; voyage of, 26

Ver Steeg, C. L.: "American Revolution as Economic Movement," 551; "The Colonies in the Eighteenth Century," 355; *Narrative of Georgia,* 412

Vespucci, Amerigo (1451–1512), 20

vestry: in Virginia, 118, 200–1, 247, 302

Vetch, Samuel (1668–1732): biography of, 356; and Queen Anne's War, 332

vice-admiralty courts: under Andros, 263, 264; Dudley creates, 260; duties of, 334, 343; at Halifax, 533; Leisler creates, 269; and Navigation Act of 1696, 338, 339; objections to, 534; perversion of intent, 536; and Shirley, 404; and Stamp Act, 536; study of, 357

Viking: and America, 13

Vincennes: in the Revolution, 625

Vindication of the Government of New-England Churches (Wise, 1717), 455

Virgin Islands: Columbus discovers, 18

Virginia: Andros as governor, 336; at Annapolis Convention, 666; architecture in, 285, 460, 461; and backcountry, 506; and Bacon's Rebellion, 244–49; and Boston Port Act, 564; botanists in, 448; boundaries of, 86; and Braddock, 388; and Carolina, 208, 211; charters of, 24, 86, 93, 96, 105; and Church of England, 302; and Claiborne 113–14; and Committee of Correspondence, 560; *Common Sense's* effect on, 586; and the Commonwealth, 184–85, 186, 190; and Congress, 588; and Constitution, 669–70, 675; and

Virginia (*cont.*)
"convention army," 617; creates new counties, 372; under Dale's Laws, 97; and Delaware settlements, 218, 228; early historians of, 457; economy of, 105, 115–17, 180–81, 488; education in, 293; Effingham as governor, 270; and embargo, 550; and Fairfax grant, 344; George Fox visits, 232; and Glorious Revolution, 269–70; government of (local), 117–18; government of (provincial), 101, 117–18; and governor's salary, 351; and Great Awakening, 425–26; Harvey as governor, 107; and independence, 590; Jamestown settlement, 89–94; laws codified, 200–1; literacy in, 294; and Loyal Land Company, 383; and Maryland, 112, 114, 117–18, 250; and New England, 302–3; and New York, 326; and Nonexportation Agreement, 573; opens ports to world (1643), 187; and Pennsylvania, 328, 505, 506, 558, 648; politics in, 491–92; population, 184; and Proclamation of 1763, 523; Puritans in, 118; and Quebec Act, 566; and Queen Anne's War, 331; and quitrents, 112, 211, 270, 377; Raleigh names, 34; religion in, 118, 655; in Restoration, 200–1; in Revolution, 630–32; and royal commissions, 105, 248–49; "starving time," 95; and Georgia settlement, 374–75; and slavery, 116, 489, 662; and Spanish, 37, 93; and Stamp Act, 537–38; and state constitution, 644; studies of, 119, 203, 311, 514, 685; and uprising of 1763, 526; and Western land claims, 650, 657; and Western settlement, 530–31; Wyatt as governor, 106; and Yeardley as governor, 100

Virginia Capes, Battle of, 631

Virginia Company of Plymouth; see Plymouth Company

Virginia Company of Virginia; see London Company

Virginia richly valued . . . (Hakluyt, 1609), 92

Volstead Act, 472

voluntary societies, 284, 451; and churches, 419–20, 421, 429; Colden suggests, for science, 450; and colleges, 444; English borrowings, 439–40

Volwiler, A. T.: *Croghan,* 412

voting: method of, 349; "plain people" cease to vote, 365; studies of, 357; *see also* suffrage requirements

Wahlke, J. C.: *Causes of American Revolution,* 551

Wainwright, N. B.: *Croghan,* 412

Waldo, Albigence: "Valley Forge Diary," 636

Waldron (Walderne), Richard (c. 1615–1689): as New Hampshire governor, 690

Waldseemüller, Martin (c. 1480–c. 1521): names America, 20

Wales: immigrants to Pennsylvania from, 237; Penn's agents in, 234

Walker, Henderson: as Carolina governor, 692

Walker, Hovenden: and Quebec expedition, 332–33

Walker, Thomas (1715–1794): in backcountry, 383

Walker, W.: biography of Luther by, 81

Wallace, A. F. C.: "Origins of Iroquois Neutrality," 356; *Teedyuscung,* 412–13

Wallace, D. D.: *South Carolina,* 239

Wallace, P. A. W.: *Muhlenbergs of Pennsylvania,* 410–11; *Pennsylvania,* 241; *Weiser,* 412

Wallace, W. M.: *Appeal to Arms,* 635; *Raleigh,* 40; *Traitorous Hero,* 640

Waller, G. M.: *Samuel Vetch,* 356

Walloons: settle at Fort Orange, 217

Walpole, Horace, fourth Earl of Orford (1717–1797), 384; on George III, 406

Walpole, Horatio: on Anglican bishop in America, 409; and auditor-general's office, 342

Walpole, Sir Robert, first Earl of Orford (1676–1745): as king's chief adviser, 398; opposes war with France, 377; opposes war with Spain, 378

Walsh, Richard: *Charleston's Sons of Liberty,* 553

Walter the Doubter; *see* Van Twiller, Wouter

Walton, George (1741–1804): as Georgia governor, 687

Wampanoag Indians: and King Philip's War, 253

Wanton, Gideon: as Rhode Island governor, 694

Wanton, John: as Rhode Island governor, 694

Wanton, Joseph (1705–1780): as Rhode Island governor, 694

Wanton, William: as Rhode Island governor, 694

War Office: and colonies, 334, 341

Ward, Artemas (1727–1800): character-
ized, 601; commands Massachusetts
troops, 578; on Washington's staff, 580
Ward, Christopher: *Dutch and Swedes on
the Delaware,* 240; *New Sweden on the
Delaware,* 240; *War of Revolution,* 635
Ward, Nathaniel (c. 1578–1652), 307,
308; and Body of Liberties, 138; charac-
terized, 136; on England, 217
Ward, Richard (1689–1763): as Rhode Is-
land governor, 694
Ward, Samuel (1725–1776): as Rhode Is-
land governor, 694
Warden, G. B.: "Proprietary Group in
Pennsylvania," 513
Warren, Charles: *Making the Constitution,*
684
Warren, Joseph (1741–1775): answers
Hutchinson, 559; biography of, 593;
paper on Massachusetts grievances, 559;
sees troops leave for Lexington, 577
Warwick, Earl of; *see* Rich, Robert
Warwick (Rhode Island): founded, 147
Washburn, W. E.: "Dispossessing the Indians," 83; *Governor and Rebel,* 273;
Indian and White Man, 309
Washington, George (1732–1799): adulation of, 622–23, 624; on American affairs (1778), 624–25; on Americans'
careless treatment of land, 441; on army
suffering, 610; and Arnold, 607, 628;
biographies of, 413, 595, 639; at Boston,
601; and Braddock, 388; chosen commander-in-chief, 580; in Congress, 578;
and Constitution, 668, 671, 675, 677;
continental outlook of, 665; criticized,
607, 622, 623; despondent, 607, 628; as
farmer, 489; on financial affairs in Revolution, 609; and French and Indian War,
384, 387, 394; in House of Burgesses,
492; and Howe, 605; and independence,
518, 584–85; on local attachments, 608;
and Manhattan, Battle of, 606; and Mt.
Vernon, 378, 461, 490; on New Englanders, 470; and New Jersey campaigns, 607, 612; and Philadelphia
campaign, 618; as President, 678; on
Proclamation Line, 530; on profiteers,
610; on Robert Morris, 631; role in victory assessed, 635; on Shays's Rebellion,
667; writings of, 595, 636; and Yorktown campaign, 631–32
Washington, Lawrence: names home after
Vernon, 378
Washington County (North Carolina),
661

Watauga region: settlement of, 501,
660–61
Water, D. W.: *Art of Navigation,* 40
Waterford (Pennsylvania): site of French
fort, 384, 526
Watertown (Massachusetts): and lack of
land, 149; and Winthrop, 137
Watson, J. S.: *Reign of George III,* 552
Watson, R. L.: *Teaching American His-
tory,* 355
Waxhaws: battle at, 627
Way to Wealth (Franklin), 458
Wayland, J. W.: *German Element in Shen-
andoah Valley,* 411
Wayne, Anthony (1745–1796): joins La-
fayette's force, 630; and Paoli Massacre,
617; and Pennsylvania mutiny, 629;
takes Stony Point, 625
*Ways and Means for the Inhabitants of
Delaware to Become Rich* (Rawle,
1725), 480
Wealth of Nations (Smith, 1776), 661
Weare, Meshech (1713–1786): as New
Hampshire governor, 690
Webster, J. C.: *Amherst Journal,* 414
Webster, John: as Connecticut governor,
687
Webster, Noah (1758–1843): and Ameri-
can language, 655
Webster-Ashburton Treaty (1842), 633
Wedgwood, C. V.: *King's Peace,* 82
Weeden, W. B.: *Economic and Social His-
tory of New England,* 163
Weiser, Johann Conrad (1696–1760),
382; biographies of, 412
Welles, Thomas: as Connecticut governor,
687
Wells (Maine): attacked, 330
Welsh: come to Pennsylvania, 362
Welsh Baptists: in Pennsylvania, 481; in
South Carolina, 498
Welsh Tract: in Pennsylvania, 237
Wendal, François: *Calvin,* 81
Wendell, Barrett: *Cotton Mather,* 312
Wentworth, Benning (1696–1770), 346;
as New Hampshire governor, 690
Wentworth, John (d. 1730): as New
Hampshire governor, 690
Wentworth, John (1737–1820): as New
Hampshire governor, 690; on White
Pines Acts, 399–400
Wereat, John: as Georgia governor, 687
Wertenbaker, T. J.: *Bacon's Rebellion,*
273; *Patrician and Plebeian in Virginia,*
120; *Middle Colonies,* 239; *Old South,*
239; *Puritan Oligarchy,* 161; *Torch-*

Wertenbaker, T. J. (*cont.*)
bearer of the Revolution, 273; *Virginia Under the Stuarts,* 170

Weslager, C. A.: *Dutch Explorers,* 240

Wesley, Charles (1707): and Whitefield, 423

Wesley, John (1703–1791): and Whitefield, 423

West: after the French and Indian War, 397, 519–31; in Revolution, 625; after the Revolution, 656–61; and Spain during Confederation, 665; studies of, 355, 552, 682

West, Benjamin (1738–1820): biography of, 467; as painter, 463

West Country: and London Merchants, 86; and New England fishing, 175–76

West Florida: becomes royal colony, 522; study on, 552

West, Francis (1568–1634): as Virginia governor, 696

West India Company, 220

West Indies: and Charleston, 215, 461; clapboards and trade with, 286; Columbus in, 16–17, 18, 20; French captures in, to be recognized by United States, 619; Negroes from, 116; and New England trade, 176; and Newport trade, 473; and Parliamentary interest in, 399; and Philadelphia trade, 480; smallpox imported from, 449; as stopping off spot, 35, 72, 89, 251; tobacco from, 57; and Treaty of Utrecht, 333; and Virginia, 102

West Indies, British: American exclusion from after Revolution, 663; American trade with declines, 400; and Congress embargoes trade of, 573; and enumerated list, 192; and governors' incomes from, 346, 351–52; Indian prisoners sent to, 157, 255; loyalists immigrate to, 611; population of, 167; Puritans immigrate to, 169; and Restraining Act, 574; and Stamp Act, 537

West Indies, Dutch: illicit trade with, 406

West Indies, French: in Colbert's dream, 316; as depot during Revolution, 619; D'Estaing takes fleet to, 626; and molasses trade, 400; and New England economy, 472; source of indigo, 494

West Indies, Spanish: and Cromwell, 191; Drake ravages, 35; English eager to trade with, 30; English open trade door to, 377–78; Negroes from, 24; as source of indigo, 494

West Jersey: in the seventeenth century, 227–29; in eighteenth century, 475–76, 479–80, 481; *see also* New Jersey

West, John: as Virginia governor, 107, 696

West, Joseph (d. c. 1692): as South Carolina governor, 694

West Newton (Pennsylvania): and Indian attack, 526

West Point: Arnold at, 628; threatened, 625; troops from, and New Jersey mutiny, 630

"Western Design," 191

Westminster Confession of Faith (1648), 423

Westmoreland County (Pennsylvania): St. Clair in, 505

Weston, Thomas (c. 1575–c. 1644): exploits Pilgrims, 125, 126, 127

Westover, 461

Wethersfield (Connecticut), 149; sacked, 156

Weymouth, George: voyages to New England, 86

whales: John Smith seeks, 123–24; report on, to Royal Society, 299

whaling: decline of, after Revolution, 663; in New England, 471

Wharton, Francis: *Diplomatic Correspondence,* 639

Wharton, Jesse: as Maryland governor, 688

Wharton, Thomas (1735–1778): as Pennsylvania governor, 694

Whately, Thomas: and Stamp Act, 536

wheat: in backcountry, 499; in Delaware Valley economy, 480; price declines, 328; Washington plants, 489

Wheelock, Eleazar (1711–1779), 443; on Baptists, 425

Wheelwright, John (c. 1592–1679): and Antinomians, 146

Whitaker, A. P.: *Spanish-American Frontier,* 682

Whitaker, Alexander (1585–1617): on clergy in Virginia, 118

White, John (1575–1648): and Dorchester Company, 129–30; on unemployment, 70; on why men emigrate, 71

White, John (fl. 1585–1593): drawings of, 36, 41; as governor of Roanoke, 36; voyages to Virginia, 35

White, P. L.: *Beekman Papers,* 512; *Beekmans of New York,* 512

White Pines Acts (1711, 1722, and 1729), 399; enforcement of, 535; Shirley seeks to enforce, 404; study of, 551

White Plains (New York): Washington at, 606, 624

Whitefield, George (1714–1770): biographies of, 465; and denominationalism, 428; Douglass hates, 457; and Great Awakening, 423–26

Whitehead, A. N.: on seventeenth century, 298; on Calvinism and science, 433

Whiteman, Maxwell: *Jews of Philadelphia,* 411

Whittmore, C. P.: *John Sullivan,* 639

Wigglesworth, Michael (1631–1705): poetry of, 308; on the wilderness, 282

Wilderness Trail: and Boone, 501

Wilkes, John: essay on, 554

Wilkinson, James (1757–1825): and Conway Cabal, 623

Willard, Samuel (1640–1707): and Salem trials, 304

Willcox, W. B.: "British Road to Yorktown," 640; "British Strategy," 639; Clinton's *American Rebellion,* 636; *Sir Henry Clinton,* 636; "Why did British Lose?", 640

William of Rubruck (fl. 1250), 4

William III (1650–1702): accession of, 265; and administration of colonies, 273; creates Board of Trade, 339; and New York, 268, 269; and Parliament's view toward colonies, 399; study of imperial policy of, 355–56; supervision of colonies during reign of, 336–39

William and Mary College; *see* College of William and Mary

Williams, Basil: *Carteret and Newcastle,* 357

Williams, John (1664–1729): captured by Indians, 330

Williams, Roger (c. 1603–1683), 142, 243, 307; biographies of, 162; and charter (1644), 170; on Cotton, 136; Cotton as rival of, 148; and denominationalism, 428; and George Fox, 232; and Indians, 80, 156–57, 169, 252; *A Key,* 169–70; and Laud, 71, 141; and Quakers 231; religious views of, 144, 178; sea imagery in writing of, 73; and separation of church and state, 143–44, 429; views on property, 147; *Writings,* 162

Williamsburg (Virginia), 438, 441; study of, 514; Wren works in, 459

Williamson, Chilton: *American Suffrage,* 357

Williamson, J. A.: *Age of Drake,* 40; "Beginnings of an Imperial Policy," 203;

Williamson, J. A. (*cont.*)
Cabot Voyages, 40; *Drake,* 40; "England and Opening of Atlantic," 39–40; *English Discovery of America,* 40; *Ocean in English History,* 40

Willison, G. F.: *Saints and Strangers,* 160

Willoughby, Sir Hugh (d. 1554): and Northeast Passage, 30

Wilmington (Delaware), 220

Wilmington (North Carolina): Cornwallis at, 629, 630, 631

Wilson, Charles: "Mercantilism," 203; *Profit and Power,* 203

Wilson, James (1742–1798): biographical sketch of, 441, 505; biography of, 684; in Congress, 578; and Constitution, 668, 672; continental outlook of, 666; and independence, 586–87, 590; writings of, 595

Wilson, John (c. 1591–1667): and Anne Hutchinson, 145

Winchester (Virginia): on Great Wagon Road, 497; Indian conference at, 391; as Scotch-Irish settlement, 498

window panes: as indication of wealth, 501

Windsor (Connecticut): founded, 148; immigration to, 149, 154

Windsor chair, 462

Wine Islands, 176, 177; and Columbus, 13; *see also* Azore Islands, Canary Islands, Madeira Islands

Wingfield, Edward (fl. 1586–1613): as Virginia's president of the council, 89, 696

Winslow, Edward (1595–1655): and *Mourt's Relation,* 160; as Plymouth's governor, 688, 689

Winslow, Josiah (c. 1629–1680): as Plymouth governor, 689

Winslow, O. E.: on Edwards, 422; on Whitefield, 424; *Jonathan Edwards,* 465; *Master Roger Williams,* 162; *Meetinghouse Hill,* 163

Winston-Salem (North Carolina), 365–66

Winthrop, Adam (1620–1652), 59

Winthrop, Fitz John (1638–1707): as Connecticut governor, 687

Winthrop, John (1588–1649): attitude toward crown, 141–42; attitude toward Parliament (Puritan), 168; biographical sketch of, 131, 132; biographies of, 162; on the crossing, 72–73; death of, 179; death of, and Massachusetts aggressiveness, 198; dissatisfaction with rule of, 148, 150; economic ideas of, 155; on

Winthrop, John (*cont.*)
England, 70; of the gentry, 58; as governor, 136–40, 689; and hivings-out, 142; and Hooker, 148–49; and Hutchinson, 146; *Journal* of, 161; on Lady Moody, 169; as Masham's neighbor, 143; on Massachusetts' depression, 168–69; on Massachusetts' purpose, 132–33, 133–34; and New England in eighteenth century, 471; on Pilgrims and fur trade, 154; political views of, 136–38, 177, 178, 350; on servants' prosperity, 155; on status and society, 58; and Wheelwright, 146; and Williams, 142–43, 144–45; as writer, 306

Winthrop, John, Jr. (1606–1676): and Connecticut charter (1663), 197; as Connecticut governor, 197, 687; and iron manufacturing, 174–75; and Navigation Act of 1651, 190; and New Amsterdam surrender, 220; as physician, 300; Saybrook founded by, 148; and science, 299

Winthrop, Professor John (1714–1779): biographical sketch of, 451–52; as Harvard professor, 444, 445

Wise, John (1652–1725): Andros jails, 262; on democracy, 455; on end of government, 435

Wissler, Clark: *American Indian,* 83

Wister, Sally: distaste for country, 437

Witch Trial (Franklin), 458

witches: aboard ship, 73; in backcountry, 502; in England, 60; in Salem, 300, 303–5

witchcraft: study of, 311

Wittenberg: and Luther, 44

Wittke, Carl: *We Who Built America,* 410

Woefel, Margaert: Hessian "Memoir," 636

Wolcott, Roger (1679–1767): as Connecticut governor, 687

wolf fangs: use for, 300

Wolfe, Edwin, 2nd: *Jews of Philadelphia,* 411

Wolfe, James (1727–1759): and French and Indian War, 394, 395

Wolfe, Mark A. De: *Quincy Journal,* 510

Wollaston, John: painter, 463

women: in seventeenth-century America, 289; in backcountry, 502, 503; in Burgoyne's army, 613; in Chesapeake colonies, 490; and education, 447; in Georgia, 375; study of, 310

Wood, Abraham: study of, 239

Wood, J. P.: *Miranda's Travels,* 511

Wood, Ralph: *Pennsylvania Germans,* 410

Woodfin, Maude: *Byrd Diaries,* 514

Woodmason, Charles: on his achievements in backcountry, 504–5; on backcountry Presbyterians, 503; on church behavior, 504; *Journal* of, 515; on Regulators, 507–8

Woodward, C. R.: *Charles Read Notes on Agriculture,* 513

Woolen Act (1699): provisions, 338; and Ulster, 368

Woolman, John (1720–1772): as writer, 456

Worcester, Battle of (1651), 69

Worcester (Massachusetts): Adams in, 445

World Turned Upside Down, 632

Wraxall, Peter: *Indian Affairs,* 414

Wren, Sir Christopher (1632–1723): and American architecture, 459

Wright, B. F.: on age of creativity, 644; on consensus at Constitutional Convention, 669; on state constitutions, 646; *Consensus and Continuity,* 681; *American Interpretation of Natural Law,* 466; "Early History of Written Constitutions in America," 681

Wright, Esmond: on British defeat, 635; on colonial attitude toward Parliament, 404; *Fabric of Freedom,* 550; *Washington,* 413

Wright, Sir James: as Georgia governor, 687; as Georgia war governor, 626

Wright, L. B.: Beverly's *History of Virginia,* 310; *Byrd Diaries,* 514; *Cultural Life of the Colonies,* 464; *Religion and Empire,* 82; Strachey's *History,* 119

Wright, T. G.: *Literary Culture in Early New England,* 312

writ of quo warranto: and London Company, 105

writs of assistance, 407; study on, 414

Wrong, G. M.: *Canada and the Revolution,* 637; *Rise and Fall of New France,* 40

Wurttembergers: as emigrants, 364

Wyatt, Sir Francis (1588–1644): on management of an overseas colony, 131; as Virginia governor, 106, 696

Wycliffe, John (c. 1320–1384), 5

Wyllys, George: as Connecticut governor, 687

Wyoming Valley: attacked by Delawares, 528; British-led Indians attack, 626; Pennsylvania-Connecticut quarrel over, 475, 558, 648

Wythe, George (1726–1806): at Constitutional Convention, 668

Yale College: breaks with past, 294; debating topics at, 656; Edwards at, 435; and Locke, 444; and natural philosophy, 444

Yale, David: emigrates, 150

Yamasee War, 373

Yankee: contemporary meaning, 475

Yeamans, Sir John (1611–1674): as South Carolina governor, 694

Yeardley, Francis: purchases tracts in Carolina, 208

Yeardley, Sir George (c. 1587–1627), 100; as Virginia governor, 99, 696; and company instructions, 100–1

yeoman: in America, 116; as constable, 64; in England, 58–59; house of, in America, 285–86; study of, 82

York County (Pennsylvania): created, 372

York (England), 57, 292

York (Pennsylvania): as Dutch town, 365, 481; on Great Wagon Road, 497

Yorkshire (England), 124

Yorkshire (Long Island), 221

Yorktown: campaign, 631–32; French part in victory at, 634–35; studies of, 640

Young, Alexander: *Chronicles of Massachusetts Bay,* 161; *Chronicles of Plymouth,* 160

Zacuto, Abraham (fl. 1478): devises ephemerides, 9

Zagorim, Perez: "English History, 1558–1640," 83

Zaiton: as spice port, 5

Zavala, Silvio: *Colonial Period,* 39

Zeichner, Oscar: *Connecticut, 1750–1776,* 553

Zenger, John Peter (1697–1746): case of, 351; study of, 357

Ziff, Larzer: *John Cotton,* 162

Zimmerman, J. J.: "Charles Thomson," 594; "Franklin and the Quaker Party," 513

Zinzendorf, Nicolaus Ludwig, Count von (1700–1760): brings Moravians to America, 365; seeks to unite German sects, 425

Zwingli, Huldreich (1484–1531): and Anabaptists, 47; beliefs of, 46; ideas in England, 52; and Luther, 45; and Puritans, 55

DATE DUE

L. des Hurons
Unexplore
SUSQUEHANNA
MARYLAND
DELAWARE
VIRGINIA
POWHATAN
USCARORA
PAMUNKEY
ECOTAN
PAMLICO
Edenton 1658
Norfolk
Hampton
Jamestown
Williamsburg
St Mary's
Mattapony
Kent I.
Providence 1640
Calvert Town
Zwaanendael 1631
Ft. Casimir
Ft. Christina
Ft. Nas
C. Hatteras